Dear West Customer:

West Academic Publishing has changed the look of its American Casebook Series®.

In keeping with our efforts to promote sustainability, we have replaced our former covers with book covers that are more environmentally friendly. Our casebooks will now be covered in a 100% renewable natural fiber. In addition, we have migrated to an ink supplier that favors vegetable-based materials, such as soy.

Using soy inks and natural fibers to print our textbooks reduces VOC emissions. Moreover, our primary paper supplier is certified by the Forest Stewardship Council, which is testament to our commitment to conservation and responsible business management.

The new cover design has migrated from the long-standing brown cover to a contemporary charcoal fabric cover with silver-stamped lettering and black accents. Please know that inside the cover, our books continue to provide the same trusted content that you've come to expect from West.

We've retained the ample margins that you have told us you appreciate in our texts while moving to a new, larger font, improving readability. We hope that you will find these books a pleasing addition to your bookshelf.

Another visible change is that you will no longer see the brand name Thomson West on our print products. With the recent merger of Thomson and Reuters, I am pleased to announce that books published under the West Academic Publishing imprint will once again display the West brand.

It will likely be several years before all of our casebooks are published with the new cover and interior design. We ask for your patience as the new covers are rolled out on new and revised books knowing that behind both the new and old covers, you will find the finest in legal education materials for teaching and learning.

Thank you for your continued patronage of the West brand, which is both rooted in history and forward looking towards future innovations in legal education. We invite you to be a part of our next evolution.

Best regards,

Louis H. Higgins
Editor in Chief, West Academic Publishing

STATE AND LOCAL TAXATION
CASES AND MATERIALS

Ninth Edition

■ ■ ■

By

Walter Hellerstein
Francis Shackelford Professor of Taxation,
University of Georgia School of Law

Kirk J. Stark
Professor of Law
University of California, Los Angeles

John A. Swain
Professor of Law
University of Arizona

Joan M. Youngman
Senior Fellow, Lincoln Institute of Land Policy

AMERICAN CASEBOOK SERIES®

WEST®
A Thomson Reuters business

Mat #40659005

COPYRIGHT © 1961, 1969, 1978, 1988 WEST PUBLISHING CO.
© West, a Thomson business, 1997, 2001, 2005
© 2009 Thomson Reuters
    610 Opperman Drive
    St. Paul, MN 55123
    1–800–313–9378
Printed in the United States of America

ISBN: 978–0–314–18506–8

PREFACE

The first edition of this casebook was published over half a century ago in 1952. Since that time, the field of state and local taxation has undergone dramatic changes. Tax revenues collected by state and local governments have increased more than sixty-fold, rising from some $21 billion in 1952 to $1.3 trillion in 2008. These astronomical tax increases, which reflect comparable increases in state and local government expenditures, are attributable in part to inflation. But a substantial portion of the increase is also attributable to the broadening of the nature and scope of state and local government services. Beyond augmenting their tax collections to meet the increased costs of traditional services such as education, welfare, and police protection, states have been required to raise revenues to fund additional services such as Medicaid and environmental protection. In so doing, state and local governments have been compelled not only to raise tax rates under existing levies, but also to enact new taxes.

In 1952, state sales taxes were in force in 34 states, were confined largely to sales of tangible personal property, and their rates averaged between two and three percent. Today state sales taxes are in force in 45 states, they apply to an increasing number of services, and their rates average between five and six percent. In 1952, 33 states imposed general personal income taxes and 35 states imposed general corporate net income taxes. Today, 41 states impose general personal income taxes and 43 states impose general corporate net income taxes, with four other states imposing broad-based taxes on corporate gross receipts. Moreover, during the past 50 years, states have enacted a variety of new taxes on admissions, occupancy, unincorporated businesses, and other activities. There has also been a proliferation of local tax levies—including income, sales, and business license taxes—as local governments have reached out for new sources of revenues to meet recurring fiscal crises. As a consequence, taxpayers in many states pay not only state income, sales, and selected excise taxes, but also similar levies to literally thousands of cities and other local government subdivisions.

The increasing significance of state and local taxation has generated considerable conflict between taxpayers and taxing authorities and with it a substantial body of case law. The U.S. Supreme Court has handed down an extraordinary number of significant decisions delineating the scope of state taxing authority under the Commerce, Due Process, Equal Protection, Import–Export, and Supremacy Clauses. There has likewise been an outpouring of important state court decisions construing state statutory provisions addressed to state taxation.

The growth of state and local taxation in fiscal terms, coupled with the legal controversies that such growth has spawned, has created a strong demand for lawyers with expertise in state and local taxation. As more and more business taxpayers discover that their state and local tax issues and liabilities equal or exceed their federal tax issues and liabilities in dollar terms, they are increasingly looking for legal advice and assistance in state and local tax planning and controversy work. Law firms across the country have responded to this demand by forming state and local tax groups (along with their traditional federal tax groups), and accounting firms (often staffed with lawyers) have rapidly expanded their state and local tax consulting practices. Furthermore, lawyers are often involved not only in the day-to-day problems of state and local taxpayers, but also in the formulation of tax policies, the enactment of legislation, the drafting of statutes and regulations, and the administration of levies.

Beyond the usual update to take account of the key developments in the law of state and local taxation over the past several years, the current edition of the casebook reflects a fundamental restructuring and "facelift" of the materials, attributable in part to the addition of two new co-authors. Specifically, we have reorganized the materials to focus first on the constitutional underpinnings of state and local taxes (jurisdictional limitations, interstate and foreign commerce limitations, and uniformity and equality limitations) before exploring, in the second part of the book, the major state and local taxes (personal and corporate income taxes, sales taxes, and property taxes). We are hopeful that both students and professors will find the revised organization more logical and user-friendly.

As in prior editions, but even more assiduously in the current edition, we have made a concerted effort to design the casebook as a teaching tool rather than a comprehensive description of the law of state and local taxation. Accordingly, we have emphasized the principal cases and have raised a large number of structured questions designed to induce the student (and the teacher) to focus on the critical issues raised by the cases and materials. We have also ruthlessly trimmed the notes and the less significant cases, with the result that the current edition is nearly 200 pages shorter than the previous edition. For a more expository examination of many of the subjects covered in the casebook, we would refer readers to JEROME R. HELLERSTEIN & WALTER HELLERSTEIN, STATE TAXATION (3d ed. 1998–2009), which is supplemented triannually along with frequent chapter revisions. This two-volume treatise contains an extensive treatment of the law of state taxation for tax practitioners, courts, and scholars. The treatise does not, however, cover the important subject of property taxation, to which Chapter 9 of the casebook is devoted.

Although we have been generous in retaining citations to cases and statutes in the opinions that we have reprinted or quoted, where we have omitted such citations we have done so without so specifying. All omissions of text are indicated by asterisks. The courts' own omissions of quoted text are indicated by the more traditional ellipses. We have eliminated footnotes from cases and secondary materials without so specifying. Where we have reproduced such footnotes, we have retained their original number. Our own footnotes are indicated by letters.

WALTER HELLERSTEIN
KIRK J. STARK
JOHN A. SWAIN
JOAN M. YOUNGMAN

October 2009

*

SUMMARY OF CONTENTS

*

TABLE OF CONTENTS

PART 2.   MAJOR STATE AND LOCAL TAXES

*

TABLE OF CASES

The principal cases are in bold type. Cases cited or discussed in the text are in roman type. References are to pages. Cases cited in principal cases and within other quoted materials are not included.

STATE AND LOCAL TAXATION
CASES AND MATERIALS

Ninth Edition

*

CHAPTER 1

INTRODUCTION

■ ■ ■

STATE AND LOCAL TAXATION:
AN INTRODUCTION TO THE FIELD

Most students who enroll in a course on state and local taxation have already taken a law school course on federal income taxation and possibly one or more other advanced tax courses on topics such as corporate taxation, partnership taxation, or estate and gift taxation. Because these courses are focused on substantive areas of federal law, it is natural to assume that a course on "state and local taxation" will cover the substantive tax law of state and local jurisdictions. If that were the task at hand, it would indeed be a daunting undertaking. According to the most recent Census of Governments published by the U.S. Census Bureau, there were 89,526 governmental units in the United States (other than the Federal Government) as of February 2008. While not all of these governmental units have independent taxing authority, mastering the tax laws of even a small fraction of them (e.g., the 50 states) would require far more time and effort than one could possibly marshal in a single semester. What then is the target of a course or book on "state and local taxation" if not the tax laws of state and local governments?

In this brief introductory chapter, we would like to take an opportunity to answer this question and also to provide a more general introduction to the field of state and local taxation. Among the four of us, we have well over a century of experience working in this field—advising clients, teaching students, testifying before legislatures, arguing cases, and authoring treatises, reports, and academic articles. Perhaps not surprisingly, our views on the field are not unbiased. In fact, we find it difficult to imagine how, after getting a taste of state and local tax, one could not be drawn into this dynamic and fascinating field as a possible career. Our chief objective in this chapter, as well as the book as a whole, is to substantiate our enthusiasm for the study of state and local taxation and to give you some idea of what's in store for the next several hundred pages. We begin with a brief discussion of what state and local tax lawyers do.

A. THE ECLECTIC EXPERTISE OF STATE AND LOCAL TAX LAWYERS

Perhaps more than lawyers working in any other field, the state and local tax lawyer is truly a jack of all trades, although, we must also stress from the outset, a master of at least some. If you happen to know someone who works in this field, pick up the phone and ask her how she spends her day. More likely than not, here's what you'll learn. She is at once a business planner, a litigator, a constitutional lawyer, a political consultant, and a public finance expert. She follows legal developments in a far broader range of jurisdictions than most of her co-workers or law school classmates. She is just as likely to opine on the latest budget battles in Sacramento, Springfield, or Tallahassee as she is to comment on the likely consequences of a newly announced Supreme Court decision. More so than most of her colleagues practicing in other areas, the state and local tax lawyer stands at the intersection of public law and private law, with an expertise that reaches across a broad range of legal subfields. In addition, unlike her federal tax counterparts, she is likely to be familiar not only with income taxes, but also with sales, property, and other excise taxes imposed by states and localities, but not by the Federal Government.

What accounts for the "eclectic expertise" of state and local tax lawyers? At the root of the state and local tax field is the federalist structure of American government. In a unitary government, with no public responsibilities assigned to lower levels of government, allocating the cost of government through taxation is much more straightforward. The central lawmaking body can simply decide how the burden of financing government should be shared and craft tax legislation accordingly. In a federation, by contrast, lawmaking is decentralized among numerous subunits, which are typically defined by reference to certain geographic areas. Matters are complicated further still when those subunits assign taxing authority to their own sub-subunits. Once the decision to structure government as a federation is made, legal questions abound:

- What is the scope of the taxing authority of subnational governments?

- Must there be some connection or relationship between a taxing jurisdiction and a person or entity before a tax can be imposed? If so, what is the relevant threshold?

- How should a tax base that spans multiple jurisdictions be allocated among those jurisdictions?

- If a subnational government asserts broader taxing authority than the putative taxpayer believes is allowed, what recourse is there for challenging that authority?

- Who makes the rules (if any) that govern or limit a subnational jurisdiction's power to tax?

- How do those rules evolve over time (if at all) in response to the revenue demands of subnational governments or changes in the nature of economic activity?

In the foregoing paragraph we have intentionally used abstract wording (federation, subunit, taxing jurisdiction, etc.) in order to emphasize that the basic problem of "state and local taxation" is inherent in the federalist structure of government. The focus of this book is, of course, state and local taxation in the United States, but it bears emphasizing that many of the same issues discussed in the next several chapters have arisen in federations throughout the world, including Australia, Brazil, Canada, the European Union, and numerous others. In addition, it deserves mention that the basic problem of state and local taxation can be recast more generally as one of "multijurisdictional taxation." Thus, the concepts and doctrines discussed throughout this book have potential relevance not only for taxation within federations, but also taxation among sovereign nations. The question is fundamentally one of how to structure the rights and responsibilities of taxpayers and governments in a multijurisdictional setting. Indeed, as discussed later in the book, scholars working in international taxation have begun to look to the U.S. state and local tax context for potential solutions to the problem of how best to coordinate the global taxation of multinational corporations.

It should come as no surprise then that the state and local tax lawyer is a jack of all trades (and a master of some) with an eclectic expertise. Her specialty is the regulation of public finance in a multijurisdictional setting. Her sources of legal authority are broad-ranging, including not just state and local tax statutes, but also federal statutory and constitutional law, as well as international norms of cross-border taxation. Her clients, whether taxpayers or state and local governments, will expect her to understand the operation of a variety of different tax instruments, as well as questions such as how a business operating in several states might use (or attempt to use) alternative legal structures to minimize its overall tax liability. These are the questions we hope to address throughout the book. To lay the groundwork for that discussion, we turn now to a basic overview of the tax policies of U.S. state and local governments.

B. A BRIEF OVERVIEW OF U.S. SUBNATIONAL PUBLIC FINANCE

State and local governments play a significant role in the American economy, spending approximately $2.5 trillion per year on education, health, welfare, police and fire protection, and various other public programs. About half of that sum is paid by user fees and other charges (e.g., college tuition) or by transfers from the Federal Government. The rest is financed by state and local taxes. According to the U.S. Census Bureau, state and local tax collections totaled nearly $1.3 trillion for 2008, an amount representing approximately 9 percent of total gross domestic product. In absolute terms, this amount represents a dramatic growth in economic resources devoted to state and local governments, though the percentage of GDP consumed by state and local taxes has remained relatively steady over the past several decades. Some sense of the growth in state and local government taxes can be gleaned from historical data. In 1930, state and local governments collected roughly $6.8 billion in tax revenue (an amount equivalent to $87.2 billion in 2008 dollars), or just under 7.5 percent of gross domestic product. Thus, in constant 2008 dollars, state and local tax collections have increased fifteen-fold since 1930. Table 1 below shows the trend from 1930 to 2008.

TABLE 1 State and Local Tax Collections, 1930–2008 (dollar amounts in billions)			
Year	**Tax Collections**	**Tax Collections, in 08$**	**Percentage of GDP**
1930	$ 6.8	$ 87.2	7.5
1940	$ 7.9	$ 119.7	7.8
1950	$ 15.9	$ 140.7	5.4
1960	$ 36.1	$ 259.7	6.9
1970	$ 86.8	$ 476.9	8.4
1980	$ 230.0	$ 594.3	8.3
1990	$ 505.0	$ 823.8	8.7
2000	$ 914.0	$1,131.0	9.3
2008	$1,298.0	$1,298.0	9.1

One of the defining characteristics of U.S. state and local public finance is the diversity of the tax base. The Federal Government collects nearly all of its revenue from income taxes. In fact, of the $2.7 trillion expected to be collected by the Federal Government in 2009, roughly 60 percent comes from the individual and corporate income taxes, while an additional 35 percent comes from social insurance taxes, which are imposed on individual wages.[a] Thus, approximately 95 percent of all federal revenue comes from a combination of income and wage taxes. By contrast, state and local governments rely on a substantially more diverse array of revenue sources. One recent study, in attempting to describe a "representative revenue system" for all 50 states, identified 23 separate revenue sources employed by state and local governments, ranging from tobacco taxes to taxes on distilled spirits to lotteries and other nontax revenues.[b] Still, for most of the past century, state and local governments have relied upon three principal sources of tax revenue: property taxes, sales taxes, and income taxes.

a. The Budget for Fiscal Year 2009, Historical Tables, available at www.gpoaccess.gpo.gov/usbudget.

b. Yesim Yilmaz, Sonya Hoo, Matthew Najowski, Kim Rueben & Robert Tannenwald, Measuring Fiscal Disparities across the U.S. States: A Representative Revenue System/Representative Expenditure System Approach, Fiscal Year 2002 (November 2006), available at http://www.urban.org/UploadedPDF/311384_fiscal_disparities.pdf.

Figure 1 below shows the composition of state and local tax bases for 2008. Note that the "Big 3" state and local taxes—property, sales, and income—account for 82.9 percent of the total. At several points throughout the book we will make reference to other types of taxes, and indeed some key U.S. Supreme Court decisions concern different levies.[c] It bears noting, however, that at some fundamental level to talk about U.S. state and local taxes is to talk about the combination of property, sales, and income taxes.

FIGURE 1: Sources of State and Local Tax Revenue for 2008

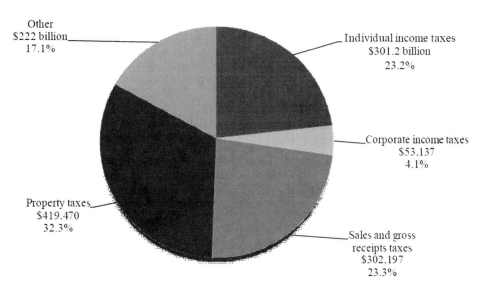

Other
$222 billion
17.1%

Individual income taxes
$301.2 billion
23.2%

Corporate income taxes
$53.137
4.1%

Property taxes
$419.470
32.3%

Sales and gross
receipts taxes
$302.197
23.3%

Each of the major revenue sources described above has its own peculiar history. Until the twentieth century, the most important source of revenue for state and local governments was the property tax. Indeed, as Richard Ely noted in his classic study of early American state and local public finances, "the distinguishing feature of the system of state and local taxation in America may be described in one sentence. It is the taxation of all property, movable or immovable, visible or invisible, real or personal * * * at one uniform rate."[d] Over the past century, state governments have significantly reduced their reliance on the property tax and turned to other revenue sources. Whereas in 1902 the property tax accounted for 50 percent of total state tax revenues, that figured had dropped to 7.8 percent by 1940. The decline continued, so that by 2008 the property tax accounted for only 1.6 percent of state tax revenue. However, property taxes continue to bring in most of *local governments'* tax revenue, approximately 72 percent in 2005–2006.

---

c. See, e.g., Commonwealth Edison Co. v. Montana, 453 U.S. 609, 101 S.Ct. 2946 (1981) (concerning state severance tax).

d. Richard T. Ely, Taxation in American States and Cities 131 (1888).

During the twentieth century, state governments found new sources of revenues in non-property taxes including income taxes, beginning with Wisconsin in 1911; motor vehicle taxes, starting in New York in 1901; gasoline taxes, which were first introduced in 1919; tobacco and liquor taxes and general sales taxes, which became widespread in the 1930s; and corporate franchise and other types of business taxes. Over time, as state and local government spending expanded and revenue sources diversified, the mix of taxes available to states and their political subdivisions also began to shift. Thus, another theme to keep in mind while reading this book is that state governments often rely on a very different mix of taxes than do local governments.

1. STATE TAX REVENUES: INCOME AND SALES TAXES

Recall the $1.3 trillion figure above—i.e., the amount of total state and local tax collections for 2008. Of this figure, $782 billion, or 60 percent, consists of state taxes, while the remaining 40 percent, or $518 billion, consists of local taxes. Individual income taxes and general sales taxes are the two leading sources of state tax revenue, each accounting for roughly one-third of state tax revenues over the past decade. In 1932, the individual income tax produced only $74 million—or 3.9 percent of state tax revenue. By 2008, these figures had risen to $280.7 billion and 36.5 percent of state tax revenue. Corporate income taxes produced $79 million of revenue in 1932 and represented 4.2 percent of the state tax base. In 2008, state corporate income taxes yielded $52 billion and generated 6.1 percent of state tax collections. The general sales tax vies with the personal income tax as the leading source of state tax revenue. It was the leading source of state tax revenue during the mid–1990s, fell to second place during the booming economy of the late 1990s, and was in a virtual dead heat with the personal income tax in 2008. This tax produced only $7 million in 1932 or 0.4 of 1 percent of total state tax revenues. In 2008, by contrast it yielded $240.6 billion, or 30.9 percent of the total. Table 2 shows the changes in the composition of state tax collections from 1902 to 2008.

TABLE 2: Percentage Distribution of State Tax Collections by Source, Selected Fiscal Years 1902-2008

Year	Total tax collections[a]	General sales, use, or gross receipts	Motor vehicle fuels sales	Tobacco products sales	Alcoholic beverage sales and licenses	Motor vehicle and operator's licenses	Income Total	Income Individual	Income Corporation	Property	Death and gift	Severance	Other
1902	100	—	—	—	b	1.7	—	—	—	52.6			47.4
1913	100	—	—	—	0.7[c]	1.6	—	—	—	46.5			51.2
1922	100	—	1.4	—	—	16	10.7	4.5	6.1	36.7	7.0	—	28.2
1927	100	—	16.1	—	—	18.7	10.1	4.4	5.7	23	6.6	—	25.5
1932	100	0.4	27.9	1.0	0.1	17.7	8.1	3.9	4.2	17.4	7.8	1.0	18.7
1936	100	13.9	26.2	1.7	6.3	13.8	10.2	5.8	4.3	8.7	4.5	1.3	13.5
1940	100	15.1	25.3	2.9	7.7	11.7	10.9	6.2	4.7	7.8	3.4	1.6	13.6
1945	100	17.8	16	3.3	8.5	9.5	18.6	8.2	10.4	6.3	3.1	1.9	14.8
1950	100	21.1	19.5	5.2	6.3	9.5	16.5	9.1	7.4	3.9	2.1	2.7	13.3
1955	100	22.7	20.3	4	4.7	10.2	15.8	9.4	6.4	3.6	2.1	2.6	13.9
1960	100	23.8	18.5	5.1	4.1	8.7	18.8	12.2	6.5	3.4	2.3	2.3	12.9
1965	100	25.7	16.5	4.9	4.0	7.7	21.4	14	7.4	2.9	2.8	1.9	12.1
1970	100	29.5	13.1	4.8	3.2	6.2	27	19.2	7.8	2.3	2.1	1.4	10.4
1975	100	30.9	10.3	4.1	2.6	5.2	31.8	23.5	8.3	1.8	1.8	2.2	9.3
1980	100	31.5	7.1	1.9	2.7	3.9	36.8	27.1	9.7	2.1	1.5	3.0	9.3
1985	100	32.2	6.2	1.5	2.0	3.5	37.8	29.6	8.2	1.8	1.1	3.3	10.4
1990	100	33.5	6.5	1.9	1.1	3.5	38.7	31.9	6.8	2.0			12.8
1995	100	33.6	6.5	1.8	0.9	3.6	39	31.7	7.3	2.0			12.6
2000	100	32.3	5.4	1.5	0.7	3	42.9	36.8	6.1	1.8			12.3
2004	100	33.4	5.8	2.1	0.8	3.3	38.5	33.2	5.3	1.9			14.3
2008	100	30.9	4.8	2.2	0.7	2.8	42.6	36.5	6.1	1.6			14.4

Source: U.S. Census Bureau, National Totals of State Tax Revenue by Type of Tax, available at http://www.census.gov/govs/qtax/table2.txt, and compilations by Tax Foundation, Inc. (used with the consent of Tax Foundation, Inc.). Figures reported for 2008 are for the twelve-month period ending December 31, 2008.
a Total does not include unemployment taxes.
b Unallocable, included in Other.
c License taxes included in Other.

2. LOCAL TAX REVENUES: PROPERTY TAXES

As noted above, for 2008 local governments collected $518 billion in tax revenue. The most significant source of tax revenues for local governments has long been—and continues to be—the property tax. Of the $518 billion total for 2008, about $407 billion, or just under 80 percent, comes from property taxes. It bears noting that these figures can sometimes be misleading. Many states have adopted constitutional limitations on local property taxes, circumscribing the ability of local governments to control this particular revenue source. In California, for example, the state constitution generally limits the property tax rate to 1 percent of the property's acquisition value and confers upon the state legislature the power to allocate property tax revenues among local governments. These state-level controls on the tax have left some commentators wondering whether California's property tax still deserves to be labeled a "local" tax at all. In part because of such constitutional limitations on the property tax, many states have begun to allow their local governments to tap other sources of tax revenue. Indeed, since 1940, one of the most significant trends in state-local fiscal relations has been the grant to localities of authority to enact non-property taxes. From 1940 to 2008, the percentage of local tax revenues attributable to property taxes declined from 92.8 percent to 78.6 percent.

Non-property taxes are sometimes referred to as "permissive" or "local option" taxes and include levies on incomes, sales, hotel room occupancy, restaurant meals, taxi rides, amusements, occupations, realty transfers, trailers, utility bills, cigarettes, cigars, gasoline, gross receipts of business, licenses, fees, and the like imposed by local authorities such as cities, counties, townships, school districts, and special districts. Some of these taxes are as old as the localities themselves; many of them, however, are new levies for local governments. They have become relatively important because of their revenue yields, their diversity, their economic impact, and their place in the state-local tax structure. Prior to 1940 only a few localities made practical use of such measures and the revenues from them were quite insignificant. Factors such as the public demand for new and improved local governmental services, the preemption of tax sources by the state and federal governments, and the crisis in property tax revenues during the Great Depression caused local governmental officials to look for new and more productive sources of revenue. In the immediate postwar years, fiscal problems created by rising expenditures and the tendency of assessed values to lag behind price changes plagued localities. Proposals for expanding local taxing powers became increasingly frequent, and, in the space of a few years, the status of non-property taxes in municipal finance changed from virtual nonexistence to an important source of revenue.

Local Sales Taxes. Although many cities had attempted to adopt sales taxes, at the beginning of World War II there were only two municipal sales taxes in the United States—in New York City (1934) and in New Orleans (1941). Toward the end of the war, demands for increased local spending were made upon local governments with resulting increased pressure to find new sources of revenue. The number of local governments imposing sales taxes during the next several years burgeoned. This development was attributable in part to the adoption by California, Illinois, Mississippi, and Utah of systems for state collection of locally imposed taxes. By 1949 more than 100 cities in California had adopted retail sales taxes.[e] Compared with the mere handful of states that had local sales taxes 60 years ago, today there are more than 7,500 local sales tax jurisdictions in the United States. These include municipalities, counties, school districts, transit districts, and other special taxing districts.

Local Income Taxes. A similar story applies to local income taxes. Prior to World War II, municipal income taxation was exceedingly rare. After the war, selected cities across the nation began to adopt income taxes to supplement their revenue. Beginning in 1946, Ohio and Pennsylvania localities made greater use of net income taxes. In 1947, New York and Pennsylvania made broad grants of taxing powers to local governments, and Philadelphia's enactment of an income-payroll tax was an innovation in local finance. Today, Baltimore, Cincinnati, Cleveland, Columbus, Detroit, Indianapolis, Kansas City (Missouri), New York City, Philadelphia, Pittsburgh, St. Louis, Toledo, and Washington, D.C., among others, impose local income taxes. In addition, various other states—including California—have considered legislation that would authorize local governments to impose income taxes.

3. DIVERSITY IN THE TAX MIX AMONG THE STATES

Before moving on, we would like to make one further point about the general landscape of U.S. subnational public finance. As you probably already knew, perhaps even long before you picked up this book, there is substantial diversity among the 50 states in terms of the composition of their state and local tax bases. Much of what we have said in the previous two subsections was phrased in terms of aggregate national data, but of course a more finely grained analysis reveals substantial state-by-state variation. This "local color" is part of what makes state and local tax so interesting, and, from the standpoint of a lawyer whose clients are seeking "straightforward" answers, challenging. Once you start examining the differences in state revenue structures, you may be left feeling like a fiscal anthropologist trying to get a handle on local peculiarities.

Some of the most obvious differences relate to states that have not adopted one or more of the "Big 3" revenue sources. For example, there are nine states (Alaska, Florida, Nevada, New Hampshire, South Dakota, Tennessee, Texas, Washington, and Wyoming) that have not adopted a broad-based individual income tax. New Hampshire and Tennessee do impose a tax on some income (principally interest and dividends), but do not tax wages and other sources of income. In addition, there are five states (Alaska, Delaware, Montana, New Hampshire, and Oregon) that have not adopted a general retail sales tax. Most likely you have heard stories about residents of states with sales taxes (e.g., Massachusetts and

---

e. Again, however, one might question whether these taxes are truly "local" in character. For example, the California "Bradley–Burns" sales tax is administered by the state Board of Equalization and the tax rate is determined by state law. Is it a "local" tax? Or is it a "state" tax coupled with a system of state grants to local governments?

California) crossing the border to their neighboring no-sales-tax states (e.g., New Hampshire and Oregon) to make various retail purchases. You may have noticed that two states, Alaska and New Hampshire, appear on both the no-income-tax and no-sales-tax lists. Alaska derives the vast majority of its government revenue—89 percent for fiscal year 2008—from energy taxes.[f] In New Hampshire, where residents are encouraged to *Live Free or Die*, lawmakers have eschewed reliance on income and sales taxes in favor of a system in which nearly two-thirds of all tax revenue comes from property taxes. Meanwhile, some of the most obvious tourist destinations—most notably Hawaii and Nevada—generate substantial revenue from hotel room taxes. Finally, state and local taxes almost always loom large in the news reports that surface periodically about America's "wackiest" taxes, such as the West Virginia "sparklers and novelties" tax and the Alabama tax on decks of playing cards that have "no more than 54 cards."[g] We won't belabor the point. The bottom line is that, while state and local governments derive the bulk of their revenue from income, sales, and property taxes, sometimes lawmakers can't resist the urge to reveal their fiscal idiosyncrasies.

C. THE LEGAL FRAMEWORK OF U.S. STATE AND LOCAL TAXATION

What is state and local tax law? To be sure, the most logical starting point in answering this question is the state statute or local ordinance imposing the tax. For example, consider section 422.5 of the Iowa Code, which provides that a "tax is imposed upon every resident and nonresident of the state which tax shall be levied, collected, and paid annually upon and with respect to the entire taxable income as defined in this division* * *" Alternatively, take a look at section 1811 of the Maine Taxation Code, which provides that a "tax is imposed on the value of all tangible personal property and taxable services sold at retail in this State." Like section 1 of the Internal Revenue Code, these provisions stand out as the most relevant starting point in learning about "state and local tax law." And indeed, we will devote considerable attention to state tax statutes in the second half of the book when examining the key features of income, sales, and property taxes. Yet as noted at the outset of this chapter, the object of this book is *not* to provide a comprehensive examination of the substantive tax law of any particular state or locality. Beyond providing you with a familiarity with the broad contours of the principal state and local tax bases, the book's equally important goal is to provide you with an understanding of the numerous and diverse limitations on state and local taxes arising from state and federal law. The limitations we will examine, which encompass roughly the first half of the

---

f. See Alaska Department of Revenue—Tax Division, Revenue Sources Book (Fall 2007).

g. Jeanne Sahadi & Les Christie, "America's Wackiest Taxes: You Might Pay Taxes on Illegal Drugs, Pepsi, Playing Cards, and Being a Star, and That's Not All," CNN Money.com, February 22, 2005. The West Virginia sparklers tax is set forth in section W. Va. Code § 11–12–86 (Westlaw 2009). The Alabama playing card tax is set forth in Ala. Code § 40–12–144 (Westlaw 2009).

ensuing materials, have three principal sources: the U.S. Constitution, federal legislation, and state constitutions.

1. FEDERAL CONSTITUTIONAL LIMITATIONS ON STATE AND LOCAL TAXES

Like all other forms of legislation, state and local tax laws must comply with the requirements of the Federal Constitution. In the state and local tax arena, the principal sources of federal constitutional limits are the Commerce and Import–Export Clauses of Article I, the Privileges and Immunities Clause of Article IV, the Due Process and Equal Protection Clauses of the Fourteenth Amendment, and the Supremacy Clause of Article VI. These six clauses are not the only federal constitutional provisions that are potentially relevant to state and local tax laws, but they are by far the most common source of constitutional challenges in the courts. As you may have already noticed by perusing the table of contents, a considerable portion of the casebook is devoted to these provisions, so there will be ample opportunity to familiarize yourself with the basic law in these areas. Still, we encourage you to crack open your own personal copy of the U.S. Constitution, highlight the text of these provisions, dog-ear the relevant pages, write in the margins, etc. Better yet, pull out your notes and your casebook from your constitutional law class and try to connect what you learned in that course with what you will be studying here. In other words, use this opportunity to "take ownership" of the topic. As mentioned at the outset of this chapter, the state and local tax lawyer is a practitioner of U.S. constitutional law. She must know the text, structure, and history of the key constitutional provisions, trace the origins of relevant Supreme Court doctrine, and follow ongoing developments in the courts.

2. FEDERAL STATUTORY LIMITATIONS ON STATE AND LOCAL TAXES

A second major pillar of the legal framework for state and local taxation is federal legislation dealing with state and local taxes. As you will quickly learn, congressional action in this area is relatively rare. Indeed, a recent book on the topic of federal legislation regarding state and local taxation is entitled *The Silence of Congress*.[h] Still, Congress has occasionally entered the state and local tax fray and enacted federal legislation regulating the ability of state and local governments to impose taxes. Of course, Congress does not have unlimited power to legislate in this area. It is clear, for example, that Congress cannot enact legislation authorizing states to violate the Federal Constitution by, say, imposing racially discriminatory taxes inconsistent with the Equal Protection Clause of the Fourteenth Amendment. However, Congress does have the

---

h. Joseph F. Zimmerman, The Silence of Congress: State Taxation of Interstate Commerce (2007).

power, by virtue of Article I, Section 8, Clause 3 of the U.S. Constitution, to "regulate commerce with foreign Nations, and among the several States * * * " It is well established that Congress may exercise its Commerce Clause authority by regulating state and local taxes substantially affecting interstate and foreign commerce. Thus, in September 1959, Congress enacted, and President Eisenhower signed into law, Public Law 86–272, which imposes certain limitations on the ability of states to tax the net income of businesses engaged in interstate commerce. More recently, several states have advocated federal legislation that would allow them to impose use tax collection obligations on out-of-state vendors without a physical presence in the state, which is something states are not currently permitted to do by virtue of a 1992 U.S. Supreme Court decision.[i] We will be examining these topics in more detail than you can probably imagine later in the book.

3. STATE CONSTITUTIONAL LIMITATIONS ON STATE AND LOCAL TAXES

Finally, in addition to federal constitutional and statutory limitations on state and local taxes, there are also various *state* constitutional limitations that must be considered. Some of these provisions simply parallel similar federal constitutional provisions. For example, most state constitutions contain an equal protection clause similar to that provision in the Fourteenth Amendment of the Federal Constitution.[j] There are also, however, several tax-specific state constitutional provisions that commonly form the basis of constitutional challenge in the courts. Foremost among these is the standard "uniformity clause" that is found in most state constitutions, which typically requires local property taxes (and sometimes other taxes as well) to be "uniform and equal" throughout the state. State constitutions contain numerous other provisions dealing with taxation, such as California's "Proposition 13," which prescribes various limitations on the property tax. Where relevant, we will discuss these and other state constitutional limits on state and local taxing power.

D. KEY INSTITUTIONS IN U.S. STATE AND LOCAL TAXATION

Most likely you are reading this book in connection with a law school course on state and local taxation. This does not mean, however, that your exclusive focus should be a mastery of the U.S. *law* of state and local taxation. To fully understand this practice area, you must also familiarize yourself with the basic *institutions* of the field as well. By "institutions" we mean the key organizations, entities, websites, publications, etc. relating to state and local taxation. Some of this we will discuss in a subse-

---

i. Quill Corp. v. North Dakota, 504 U.S. 298, 112 S.Ct. 1904 (1992).

j. Stanley Friedelbaum, "State Equal Protection: Its Diverse Guises and Effects," 66 Albany Law Review 599 (2003).

quent section (see "Additional Resources for Learning About U.S. State and Local Taxation" below). Here we would like to offer a brief listing—not meant to be exhaustive—of some of the key institutions anyone working in this field should know about.

State Departments of Revenue. Obviously the various state tax collection agencies are central players in the administration of state and local tax systems. The design and organization of these departments vary from state to state. In most states, there is a single "Department of Revenue" or "Tax Commission" that administers the state's various taxes. In some states, however, responsibility is divided between multiple departments. In California, for example, the Franchise Tax Board administers the state's individual and corporate income taxes, while the Board of Equalization administers the sales and use tax, certain elements of the property tax, and various other special levies. In most states, property taxes are administered locally, typically by a county tax assessor's office, although the important responsibility for the complex valuation issues that often arise with regard to public utility property is usually carried out by a central state assessment authority. Additional information on state tax collection agencies can be found on the website of the Federation of Tax Administrators, an organization established in 1937 to provide services to state tax authorities and administrators. You may wish to take a moment to browse the FTA website (http://www.taxadmin.org), which features a great deal of useful information about state and local taxes.

The Structure of State Tax Adjudication. One of things you will immediately notice while reading through this book is that there are almost no decisions from federal courts other than the U.S. Supreme Court. Almost all state and local tax controversies are adjudicated in the state court system, going as far (sometimes) as the state supreme court and then (only rarely) to the U.S. Supreme Court. With only a few exceptions, you will not find state and local tax cases being decided by U.S. District Courts or the U.S. Courts of Appeals. The reason for this state of affairs can be found at 28 U.S.C § 1341, which provides that "the district courts shall not enjoin, suspend or restrain the assessment, levy or collection of any tax under State law where a plain, speedy and efficient remedy may be had in the courts of such State." We discuss the Tax Injunction Act in further detail in Chapter 11.

State Tax Courts. You may recall from the basic federal income tax course that the United States Tax Court, an Article I court established by Congress in 1924 (originally named the U.S. Board of Tax Appeals), is the principal trial court for the resolution of tax disputes between taxpayers and the Internal Revenue Service. Similarly, some states have established their own tax tribunals with jurisdiction to decide tax controversies between taxpayers and the state tax collection agency. Thus, for example, in 1986 Indiana established the Indiana Tax Court,[k] which has "exclusive jurisdiction over any case that arises under the Indiana tax laws and that

---

k. Ind. Code Ann. § 33–26–1–1 (Westlaw 2009).

is an initial appeal of a final determination made by the Indiana Department of State Revenue or the Indiana Board of Tax Review."[l] Similar tax tribunals have been established in several other states.[m]

The Multistate Tax Commission. The Multistate Tax Commission (MTC) was established in August 1967 after seven states adopted the Multistate Tax Compact. Originally created to head off federal legislation designed to limit the taxing authority of the states, the MTC has become a central player in the formulation of laws, regulations and administrative practices in the area of state and local taxation. The MTC's website (at http://www.mtc.gov) lists the organization's various member states and gives an overview of its activities in several areas.

The Streamlined Sales Tax Governing Board. The Streamlined Sales Tax Governing Board (Governing Board) was established in October 2007 after 14 states brought their sales and use tax codes into full compliance with the Streamlined Sales and Use Tax Agreement (SSUTA). As its name suggests, the general purpose of SSUTA is to streamline state and local sales and use tax compliance and administration. The Governing Board's website (at http://www.streamlinedsalestax.org) lists the organization's various member states, provides an updated version of SSUTA and related documents, and gives an overview of the Governing Board's activities.

State Tax Politics Inside the Beltway. State and local tax issues sometimes surface in Washington politics, typically with regard to some proposed legislation that would expand or contract the taxing authority of state and local governments. These issues are a perennial source of interest to concerned parties in the field, including taxpayers, lawyers, economists, state tax administrators, and political representatives of state and local constituencies. Over the years, several organizations have emerged to represent the interests of these various parties in Washington. As you familiarize yourself with the field of state and local tax, you will no doubt begin to notice the influence of several key Washington players, including the Council on State Taxation (COST), the Federation of Tax Administrators ("FTA"), the National Conference of State Legislatures (NCSL), the U.S. Conference of Mayors, and the National Governors Association (NGA). This is by no means an exhaustive list of parties interested in federal legislation concerning state and local taxes, but chances are the next time a bill is introduced that would impact the state and local tax field, these organizations will be prepared to offer their views to the relevant lawmakers.

E. THE ANATOMY OF A STATE TAX CASE

This book is filled with cases—principal cases, note cases, cases discussed in other cases, and cases cited without explanation. That, of

---

l. See http://www.in.gov/judiciary/tax/statutes.html.

m. For a listing, see the website of the National Center for State Courts (NCSC) at http://www.ncsconline.org/.

course, is why it is called a casebook. While there are good pedagogical reasons for using cases as a vehicle for exploring a body of law, it is sometimes easy to forget that cases, especially the appellate cases that dominate casebooks, are the culmination of a long process, often involving many hundreds of hours of lawyers' and clients' time, thousands of pages of documents (including tax returns and supporting memoranda), and countless emails, phone calls, meetings, and other communications.

We therefore felt that it would be useful at the outset to give you some sense of what typically has preceded the issuance of a written state tax decision like those set forth in the ensuing materials. Although the opinions generally summarize the facts and proceedings below, they do not normally give you the full flavor of what has transpired prior to the final decision of the appellate tribunal. We try to do that briefly through the lens of a case that was ultimately resolved by the U.S. Supreme Court, Allied–Signal, Inc. v. Director, Division of Taxation, 504 U.S. 768, 112 S.Ct. 2251 (1992), set out in Chapter 7 (pp. 420–33 infra).[n] We are not concerned here with the substantive issues involved—you will get to those soon enough—but rather with how state tax controversies ordinarily unfold.

1. FILING THE TAX RETURN: THE "RETURN POSITION"

The seeds of most state tax controversies are sown in the return. To be sure, the underlying transactions reflected in the return may have been structured with an eye towards the tax collector, but the first formal "defining moment" for tax controversy purposes is normally the position that the taxpayer takes in filing its return. In *Allied–Signal*, the taxpayer was the Bendix Corporation, a Michigan-based company doing business in many states including New Jersey, where the tax controversy arose. Bendix was engaged in activities in four core areas: automotive, aerospace/electronics, industrial/energy, and forest products. In 1978, Bendix purchased a 20.6 percent interest in another company, ASARCO, formerly the American Smelting and Refining Company, which was engaged largely in mining. Three years later, in 1981, Bendix sold its ASARCO stock and realized a capital gain of $211 million for federal income tax purposes.

If the lawyers and accountants responsible for Bendix's tax function had simply followed the New Jersey tax law and return instructions as written, they would have included the $211 million gain in the New Jersey return, because New Jersey law generally required that the starting point for determining the New Jersey tax base be all of the taxpayer's federal taxable income. From this starting point, New Jersey provided for the taxpayer's federal income to be attributed or "apportioned" to the various

---

n. In the interest of full disclosure, it should be noted that our familiarity with this case is due in part to the fact that the senior author argued the case before the U.S. Supreme Court on behalf of the taxpayer. We have done our best, however, to shed the advocate's role in describing the case.

states in which the taxpayer did business according to what, for present purposes, you may assume was a fair method of apportionment.

Bendix's tax professionals, however, believed that they had a federal constitutional basis for not following New Jersey law. Specifically, they believed that Bendix's investment in (and subsequent disposition of) its ASARCO stock had nothing to do with New Jersey and that the U.S. Constitution's Commerce and Due Process Clauses[o] therefore precluded New Jersey from even considering the ASARCO gain in the initial amount used as the starting point for determining the appropriate New Jersey tax base. Accordingly, after extensive internal deliberations that considered such questions as:

- whether it was more appropriate to pay the tax according to New Jersey law and sue for a refund or to exclude the gain and expect to be assessed a deficiency;

- whether failure to comply with the statute would result in penalties;

- whether taking an uncertain tax position would require management to create a "reserve" on Bendix's income statement filed with the Securities and Exchange Commission for a contingent future liability (an issue that has become increasingly sensitive in recent years because of changes in accounting rules); and

- whether costs associated with litigation of the issue were justified by the probability of success (an issue that normally calls for consultation with outside counsel, who will be largely responsible for the litigation),

Bendix filed a tax return in July 1982 for fiscal year 1981 that excluded altogether the $211 million gain it had realized from the sale of its ASARCO stock.

2. STATE ADMINISTRATIVE PROCEEDINGS

Most of the time between the filing of a return and the ultimate judicial resolution of a state tax controversy is usually consumed by state administrative proceedings (including proceedings before state administrative law tribunals, which normally function as administrative agencies outside the traditional "independent" court system). New Jersey was a little unusual in this regard, because it has an independent tax court (analogous to the Indiana Tax Court described above), which functions as an integral part of the judicial system, although its jurisdiction is limited to tax cases.

In November 1983, approximately one year after it filed its tax return excluding the ASARCO gain, Bendix received an Initial Notice from the

---

o. The U.S. Constitution contains two Due Process Clauses, U.S. Const. amend.V. and U.S. Const. amend. XIV, § 1. Here and throughout these materials references to the "Due Process Clause" are to the latter, which explicitly restrains state power.

New Jersey Division of Taxation based on the Division's audit of Bendix's return. Among other things, the notice added the gain to the amount that served as the starting point for determining Bendix's New Jersey taxable income. Such notices normally mark the beginning of a period of negotiation between the taxpayer and the state tax administration, conducted with varying degrees of formality, and often accompanied by extensive correspondence or memoranda setting out the parties' respective legal positions. Typically, these negotiations entail meetings with the responsible auditor as well as one or more conferences with supervisory personnel in the tax administration. After the negotiations have run their course, and after any internal administrative adjudication that may be provided by the tax administration, the taxing authority will normally issue a final administrative determination that may be appealed to the court system. In *Allied–Signal*, after a conference in April 1984 and various written submissions, the Division of Taxation issued its Final Determination that included the $211 million ASARCO gain in the New Jersey tax calculation and assessed a deficiency against the taxpayer for failing to do so.

3. STATE JUDICIAL PROCEEDINGS

Approximately two years after filing its tax return, in August 1984, Bendix filed a complaint in the New Jersey Tax Court challenging the final administrative determination on constitutional grounds. As we observed earlier, New Jersey is somewhat unusual in having a specialized, independent tax tribunal as part of its judicial system. In most other states, the challenge to the final determination of the state tax administration would occur in a trial court of general jurisdiction (e.g., the district court, the circuit court, or the superior court).

Litigation of state tax cases in state trial courts proceeds much like other litigation, with interrogatories, depositions, and other discovery (frequently including experts' reports) and a formal trial (almost always before a judge sitting without a jury) at which the key fact witnesses and the experts testify. In many cases, the facts are stipulated, the expert reports are submitted for the record, and the court hearing is limited largely to argument of counsel. In *Allied–Signal*, for example, nearly three years of extensive discovery (including depositions of key company personal and the submission of expert reports) culminated in the filing of a lengthy stipulation of facts (and even lengthier exhibits) that constituted the voluminous record in the case. The case was heard by the New Jersey Tax Court in January 1988.

Following briefing by lawyers for Bendix and the New Jersey Division of Taxation, the Tax Court issued its decision in July 1988, affirming the deficiency the Division had assessed based on Bendix's failure to include the ASARCO gain in its New Jersey tax calculation. Bendix filed an appeal to the Superior Court, Appellate Division, the intermediate appellate court in New Jersey, and, after another round of briefing and oral argument, that court issued its decision affirming the Tax Court in October 1989.

Bendix again appealed, this time to the New Jersey Supreme Court, and, after another round of briefing and oral argument, nearly two years later the New Jersey Supreme Court affirmed the Appellate Division in July 1991.

4. U.S. SUPREME COURT PROCEEDINGS

In October 1991, Allied–Signal, which by then had acquired Bendix and was now its successor-in-interest, filed a petition for certiorari in U.S. Supreme Court seeking review of the New Jersey Supreme Court's decision. After the filing of two more briefs—New Jersey's brief in opposition to the petition and the petitioner's reply brief, the U.S. Supreme Court granted certiorari in November 1991. Prior to oral argument, the parties filed the usual round of briefs (the petitioner's brief, the respondent's brief, and the petitioner's reply), but, after hearing oral argument, the U.S. Supreme Court set the case for reargument and ordered another round of briefs to be filed simultaneously, and each side filed both a principal brief and a reply. In addition, the Court invited the filing of briefs by amici curiae and fourteen briefs were filed in response to this invitation.

Finally, in June 1992, nearly 10 years after Bendix first took its return position excluding the ASARCO gain from its New Jersey tax calculation, the U.S. Supreme Court resolved the controversy sustaining the taxpayer's position. The opinion—one of the most important you will read in this course—is essential to understanding the law in this area but only dimly reflects the decade of legal work that preceded it. That back and forth occupies the lion's share of the professional life of many state and local tax lawyers, and you should not to lose sight of that fact as you read through the many appellate opinions that will provide your basis for understanding the "law" of state and local taxation.

F. ADDITIONAL RESOURCES FOR LEARNING ABOUT U.S. STATE AND LOCAL TAXATION

The details of the current state and local tax structures (including the statutes, the regulations, recent judicial and administrative rulings, and editorial commentary) may be found in the Research Institute of America and Commerce Clearing House state and local tax services, which are available on line, on CD–ROMs, and, for the moment at least, in print for the Commerce Clearing House service. In addition, Tax Analysts, the publisher of Tax Notes and other tax-related publications, produces a state tax data base that contains all of the current state statutes and regulations, as well as other state and local tax material. Tax Analysts also publishes State Tax Notes, a weekly periodical that is far and away the most useful source of current information and commentary regarding state taxes. Other periodicals devoted to state and local taxation include the Journal of Multistate Taxation and Incentives, published bi-monthly by Warren Gorham & Lamont, the Journal of State Taxation, published bimonthly by Commerce Clearing House, and The State and Local Tax Lawyer, published annually by the State and Local Tax Committee of the Tax Section of the American Bar Association. The Tax Law Review, published by the graduate tax faculty of the New York University Law School, occasionally publishes scholarly articles devoted to state taxation, as, of course, do the general law reviews. The Bureau of National Affairs publishes a series of Multistate Tax Portfolios addressed to specific topics in the field of state taxation.

One of the authors of your casebook has written a treatise on state taxation, a two-volume work, published by Warren Gorham & Lamont of Research Institute of America. Jerome R. Hellerstein & Walter Hellerstein, State Taxation (3d ed.), originally published in 1998 but substantially revised through replacement chapters and tri-annual supplements. Many of the issues covered in the casebook are treated in considerably more detail in the treatise as are topics that the casebook does not touch at all. The treatise does not, however, cover property taxation.

In addition to acquiring a working knowledge of the standard legal materials in the state and local tax field, you will be well served by developing some familiarity with the publications of economists, tax administrators, and other public finance specialists that bear on state and local taxation. The National Tax Journal and the annual proceedings of the National Tax Association are probably the most useful distinctly "nonlegal" publications for the lawyer. The extensive studies made by state tax and legislative commissions, research reports prepared in universities, and publications and proceedings of organizations, such as the Multistate Tax Commission, the Federation of Tax Administrators, the International Association of Assessing Officers, and the National Conference of State Legislatures are useful in providing history, data, and analyses in many branches of the field. Periodic compilations of fiscal statistical data of states, cities, and other local governments are published by the U.S. Census Bureau, U.S. Department of Commerce. For students interested in the historical development of state and local taxation, the contributions of Professor Edwin R.A. Seligman, Essays in Taxation (10th ed. 1931) and The Income Tax (2d ed. 1914), are classics.

G. A NOTE ON THE STRUCTURE OF THE BOOK

One final note deserves mention. As with any casebook concerning a large and complicated field of law, we have made certain decisions regarding how to organize the materials in this book in order to convey the substance of the law most effectively. One of the challenges of undertaking a broad survey introduction to the field of state and local tax is that that there is no obvious roadmap for how to lay out the material. In an ideal world, students would have a core understanding of the most important state and local taxes before embarking on a study of constitutional limitations on those taxes. At the same time, however, it would be helpful to have some basic knowledge of the constitutional framework before examining the application of that framework to specific taxes. In short, there is an inescapable chicken-and-egg problem in deciding how to present the material. We have done our best to minimize any adverse pedagogical consequences arising from this dilemma by offering introductory comments, cross-references to other materials that may be helpful, etc. Perhaps the most important thing, however, is simply for you to be aware of the issue. Feel free to peek ahead (or back, if your instructor assigns the reading in some other order) and skim through other parts of the book. The ultimate objective, of course, is to master the material, not to master it in some particular order.

As you will see from the table of contents, we have divided the book into two parts—Part I on Constitutional Foundations of State and Local Taxation and Part II on Major State and Local Taxes. Part I provides a general overview of the most important state and federal constitutional limitations on state and local taxation, as well as a brief discussion of federal statutory limits. Part II then goes into greater depth with respect to the most important state and local taxes. Hopefully once you reach the end of the book, we will have convinced you that the time you have devoted to learning about this dynamic and important field was well worth the effort.

Part 1

Constitutional Foundations of State and Local Tax

■ ■ ■

CHAPTER 2

JURISDICTION TO TAX

■ ■ ■

A threshold question in analyzing any state or local tax is whether the government imposing the tax has the jurisdiction to do so. In many instances, of course, jurisdiction is self-evident. For example, consider Nora, the general counsel of a corporation headquartered in Los Angeles, California. A lifelong resident of the Golden State, Nora earns a salary for services provided entirely in Los Angeles, owns a home in nearby Santa Monica, and makes all of her purchases in the greater L.A. metropolitan area. Few would disagree that California has the requisite jurisdiction to impose income, sales, and property taxes on Nora—but what about Maine, Indiana, or Arizona? May those states also require Nora to pay income, sales, or property taxes? Here the answer is equally self-evident. Without any connection or relationship to the taxpayer, her property, or her activities, these states plainly lack the jurisdiction to tax. Between these two extremes—obvious jurisdiction and obvious lack of jurisdiction—there are many points of legal controversy. What level of activity is required before a state can successfully assert jurisdiction over a taxpayer's income, consumption, or property? Is physical presence in the state a necessary precondition of jurisdiction to tax? Under what circumstances may a state enlist the assistance of nonresidents in the collection of its taxes? The materials that follow offer a basic introduction to the law of state tax jurisdiction. We begin with a brief discussion of the two major sources of constitutional limitations on state taxing jurisdiction—the Due Process Clause and the Commerce Clause.

A. CONSTITUTIONAL LIMITS ON STATE TAXING JURISDICTION

During the first year of law school, typically in a course on civil procedure, most law students learn that a state may not, consistent with the Due Process Clause of the Fourteenth Amendment, assert personal jurisdiction over a defendant unless that person has certain "minimum contacts" with the state. You may recall that this standard has its origins in a U.S. Supreme Court decision, International Shoe Co. v. Washington, 326 U.S. 310, 66 S.Ct. 154 (1945), concerning the State of Washington's attempt to collect unemployment taxes on commissions paid by an out-of-state corporation to its salespersons in the state. In his opinion for the Court, Chief Justice Stone wrote that the company's activities in the state, which "were systematic and continuous throughout the years in question" and "resulted in a large volume of interstate business," made it "reasonable and just, according to our traditional conception of fair play and substantial justice, to permit the state to enforce the obligations" that the company had incurred in the state. Id., 326 U.S. at 320. Stone's opinion has been credited with "freeing [state court jurisdiction] from rigid and artificial territorial constraints" and focusing instead on "the nature of the defendant's activities and on their effect within the forum without regard to physical presence or other strictly territorial connecting factors."[a] As we will see, however, state tax jurisdiction has developed along a somewhat different path.

In the tax context, the Court has indicated that "due process requires some definite link, some minimum connection, between a state and the person, property, or transaction it seeks to tax." Miller Bros. Co. v. Maryland, 347 U.S. 340, 345, 74 S.Ct. 535 (1954). This language, from a case decided less than a decade after *International Shoe*, bears a striking similarity to the controlling passages of Stone's famous opinion. Yet unlike the question of personal jurisdiction, state tax jurisdiction generally implicates not only due process concerns but also Commerce Clause concerns.[b] The Commerce Clause, set forth in clause 3, section 8 of Article I of the U.S. Constitution, provides that Congress shall have the power "to regulate Commerce with foreign Nations, and among the several States, and with the Indian Tribes." Chapter 3 will explore in some detail the Supreme Court's Commerce Clause jurisprudence as it relates to state and local taxation. For now, our focus is on the threshold question of jurisdiction and the manner in which Commerce Clause concerns have led the Court to develop a tax-specific set of jurisdictional rules.

Our first case, *Quill Corporation v. North Dakota*, is the centerpiece of the Supreme Court's modern jurisprudence on state tax jurisdiction. Before reading the opinion below, you may wish to review the materials in the introduction relating to the design of state retail sales and use taxes. Chapter 8 contains even more detailed information. For present purposes, the most important thing to note is that all states with a general retail sales tax also impose a companion "use tax" that is designed to apply to

---

a. Peter Hay, "Refining Personal Jurisdiction in the United States," 35 Int'l & Comp. L. Q. 32 (1986).

b. When jurisdictional tax issues do not implicate the Commerce Clause (e.g., jurisdiction to tax income earned by nonresident trusts and estates) or when Congress has removed a matter from dormant Commerce Clause scrutiny (e.g., in connection with the business of insurance (see Chapter 4, pp. 261–75 infra)), taxpayers must rely entirely on the Due Process Clause as a constitutional restraint on state taxing jurisdiction. Moreover, questions of personal jurisdiction, at least in the context of jurisdiction to tax a nonresident business, can implicate the Commerce Clause as well as the Due Process Clause. See, e.g., Scanapico v. Richmond, F. & P. RR, 439 F.2d 17 (2d Cir. 1970) (addressing claim that Commerce Clause barred assertion of personal jurisdiction over nonresident railroad company with respect to out-of-state injury suffered by in-state resident).

the consumption or "use" within the state of goods purchased outside the state, in the sense that "title" to the goods has passed at origin or before the goods enter the state of the purchaser. Thus, in most states the sales tax applies to in-state purchases and is both collected and remitted by retail vendors, while the use tax applies to out-of-state purchases. The question presented in *Quill*—and at the heart of ongoing tax policy debates in the 45 states with retail sales taxes—is whether a state may impose a use tax collection obligation on out-of-state vendors.

QUILL CORPORATION v. NORTH DAKOTA

Supreme Court of the United States, 1992.
504 U.S. 298, 112 S.Ct. 1904.

JUSTICE STEVENS delivered the opinion of the Court.

This case, like National Bellas Hess, Inc. v. Department of Revenue of Ill., 386 U.S. 753, 87 S.Ct. 1389 (1967), involves a State's attempt to require an out-of-state mail-order house that has neither outlets nor sales representatives in the State to collect and pay a use tax on goods purchased for use within the State. In *Bellas Hess* we held that a similar Illinois statute violated the Due Process Clause of the Fourteenth Amendment and created an unconstitutional burden on interstate commerce. In particular, we ruled that a "seller whose only connection with customers in the State is by common carrier or the United States mail" lacked the requisite minimum contacts with the State. Id., at 758, 87 S.Ct., at 1392.

In this case the Supreme Court of North Dakota declined to follow *Bellas Hess* because "the tremendous social, economic, commercial, and legal innovations" of the past quarter-century have rendered its holding "obsole[te]." 470 N.W.2d 203, 208 (1991). Having granted certiorari, we must either reverse the State Supreme Court or overrule *Bellas Hess*. While we agree with much of the state court's reasoning, we take the former course.

I

Quill is a Delaware corporation with offices and warehouses in Illinois, California, and Georgia. None of its employees work or reside in North Dakota and its ownership of tangible property in that State is either insignificant or nonexistent.[1] Quill sells office equipment and supplies; it solicits business through catalogs and flyers, advertisements in national periodicals, and telephone calls. Its annual national sales exceed

---

1. In the trial court, the State argued that because Quill gave its customers an unconditional 90–day guarantee, it retained title to the merchandise during the 90–day period after delivery. The trial court held, however, that title passed to the purchaser when the merchandise was received. See App. to Pet. for Cert. A40–A41. The State Supreme Court assumed for the purposes of its decision that that ruling was correct. 470 N.W.2d 203, 217, n. 13. The State Supreme Court also noted that Quill licensed a computer software program to some of its North Dakota customers that enabled them to check Quill's current inventories and prices and to place orders directly. Id., at 216–217. As we shall explain, Quill's interests in the licensed software does [*sic*] not affect our analysis of the due process issue and does [*sic*] not comprise the "substantial nexus" required by the Commerce Clause. See n.8, infra.

$200,000,000, of which almost $1,000,000 are made to about 3,000 customers in North Dakota. It is the sixth largest vendor of office supplies in the State. It delivers all of its merchandise to its North Dakota customers by mail or common carrier from out-of-state locations.

As a corollary to its sales tax, North Dakota imposes a use tax upon property purchased for storage, use or consumption within the State. North Dakota requires every "retailer maintaining a place of business in" the State to collect the tax from the consumer and remit it to the State. N.D.Cent.Code § 57–40.2–07 (Supp.1991). In 1987 North Dakota amended the statutory definition of the term "retailer" to include "every person who engages in regular or systematic solicitation of a consumer market in th[e] state." § 57–40.2–01(6). State regulations in turn define "regular or systematic solicitation" to mean three or more advertisements within a 12–month period. N.D. Admin. Code § 81–04.1–01–03.1 (1988). Thus, since 1987, mail-order companies that engage in such solicitation have been subject to the tax even if they maintain no property or personnel in North Dakota.

Quill has taken the position that North Dakota does not have the power to compel it to collect a use tax from its North Dakota customers. Consequently, the State, through its Tax Commissioner, filed this action to require Quill to pay taxes (as well as interest and penalties) on all such sales made after July 1, 1987. The trial court ruled in Quill's favor, finding the case indistinguishable from *Bellas Hess;* specifically, it found that because the State had not shown that it had spent tax revenues for the benefit of the mail-order business, there was no "nexus to allow the state to define retailer in the manner it chose." App. to Pet. for Cert. A41.

The North Dakota Supreme Court reversed, concluding that "wholesale changes" in both the economy and the law made it inappropriate to follow *Bellas Hess* today. 470 N.W.2d, at 213. The principal economic change noted by the court was the remarkable growth of the mail-order business "from a relatively inconsequential market niche" in 1967 to a "goliath" with annual sales that reached "the staggering figure of $183.3 billion in 1989." Id., at 208, 209. Moreover, the court observed, advances in computer technology greatly eased the burden of compliance with a " 'welter of complicated obligations' " imposed by state and local taxing authorities. Id., at 215 (quoting Bellas Hess, 386 U.S., at 759–760, 87 S.Ct., at 1393).

Equally important, in the court's view, were the changes in the "legal landscape." With respect to the Commerce Clause, the court emphasized that Complete Auto Transit, Inc. v. Brady, 430 U.S. 274, 97 S.Ct. 1076 (1977), rejected the line of cases holding that the direct taxation of interstate commerce was impermissible and adopted instead a "consistent and rational method of inquiry [that focused on] the practical effect of [the] challenged tax." Mobil Oil Corp. v. Commissioner of Taxes of Vt., 445 U.S. 425, 443, 100 S.Ct. 1223, 1234 (1980). This and subsequent rulings, the court maintained, indicated that the Commerce Clause no longer mandated the sort of physical-presence nexus suggested in *Bellas Hess*.

Similarly, with respect to the Due Process Clause, the North Dakota court observed that cases following *Bellas Hess* had not construed "minimum contacts" to require physical presence within a State as a prerequisite to the legitimate exercise of state power. The State Court then concluded that "the Due Process requirement of a 'minimal connection' to establish nexus is encompassed within the *Complete Auto* test" and that the relevant inquiry under the latter test was whether "the state has provided some protection, opportunities, or benefit for which it can expect a return." 470 N.W.2d, at 216.

Turning to the case at hand, the state court emphasized that North Dakota had created "an economic climate that fosters demand for" Quill's products, maintained a legal infrastructure that protected that market, and disposed of 24 tons of catalogs and flyers mailed by Quill into the State every year. Id., at 218–219. Based on these facts, the court concluded that Quill's "economic presence" in North Dakota depended on services and benefits provided by the State and therefore generated "a constitutionally sufficient nexus to justify imposition of the purely administrative duty of collecting and remitting the use tax." Id., at 219.[2]

II

As in a number of other cases involving the application of state taxing statutes to out-of-state sellers, our holding in *Bellas Hess* relied on both the Due Process Clause and the Commerce Clause. Although the "two claims are closely related," Bellas Hess, 386 U.S., at 756, 87 S.Ct., at 1391, the clauses pose distinct limits on the taxing powers of the States. Accordingly, while a State may, consistent with the Due Process Clause, have the authority to tax a particular taxpayer, imposition of the tax may nonetheless violate the Commerce Clause. See, e.g., Tyler Pipe Industries, Inc. v. Washington State Dept. of Revenue, 483 U.S. 232, 107 S.Ct. 2810 (1987).

The two constitutional requirements differ fundamentally, in several ways. As discussed at greater length below, see infra, at Part IV, the Due Process Clause and the Commerce Clause reflect different constitutional concerns. Moreover, while Congress has plenary power to regulate commerce among the States and thus may authorize state actions that burden interstate commerce, see International Shoe Co. v. Washington, 326 U.S. 310, 315, 66 S.Ct. 154, 157 (1945), it does not similarly have the power to authorize violations of the Due Process Clause.

---

2. The court also suggested that, in view of the fact that the "touchstone of Due Process is fundamental fairness" and that the "very object" of the Commerce Clause is protection of interstate business against discriminatory local practices, it would be ironic to exempt Quill from this burden and thereby allow it to enjoy a significant competitive advantage over local retailers. 470 N.W.2d, at 214–215.

Thus, although we have not always been precise in distinguishing between the two, the Due Process Clause and the Commerce Clause are analytically distinct.

> " 'Due process' and 'commerce clause' conceptions are not always sharply separable in dealing with these problems. . . . To some extent they overlap. If there is a want of due process to sustain the tax, by that fact alone any burden the tax imposes on the commerce among the states becomes 'undue.' But, though overlapping, the two conceptions are not identical. There may be more than sufficient factual connections, with economic and legal effects, between the transaction and the taxing state to sustain the tax as against due process objections. Yet it may fall because of its burdening effect upon the commerce. And, although the two notions cannot always be separated, clarity of consideration and of decision would be promoted if the two issues are approached, where they are presented, at least tentatively as if they were separate and distinct, not intermingled ones." International Harvester Co. v. Department of Treasury, 322 U.S. 340, 353, 64 S.Ct. 1019, 1032–1033 (1944) (Rutledge, J., concurring in part and dissenting in part).

Heeding Justice Rutledge's counsel, we consider each constitutional limit in turn.

III

The Due Process Clause "requires some definite link, some minimum connection, between a state and the person, property or transaction it seeks to tax," Miller Bros. Co. v. Maryland, 347 U.S. 340, 344–345, 74 S.Ct. 535, 539 (1954), and that the "income attributed to the State for tax purposes must be rationally related to 'values connected with the taxing State.' " Moorman Mfg. Co. v. Bair, 437 U.S. 267, 273, 98 S.Ct. 2340, 2344 (1978) (citation omitted). Here, we are concerned primarily with the first of these requirements. Prior to Bellas Hess, we had held that that requirement was satisfied in a variety of circumstances involving use taxes. For example, the presence of sales personnel in the State,[3] or the maintenance of local retail stores in the State,[4] justified the exercise of that power because the seller's local activities were "plainly accorded the protection and services of the taxing State." Bellas Hess, 386 U.S., at 757, 87 S.Ct., at 1391. The furthest extension of that power was recognized in Scripto, Inc. v. Carson, 362 U.S. 207, 80 S.Ct. 619 (1960), in which the Court upheld a use tax despite the fact that all of the seller's in-state solicitation was performed by independent contractors. These cases all involved some sort of physical presence within the State, and in *Bellas Hess* the Court suggested that such presence was not only sufficient for jurisdiction under the Due Process Clause, but also necessary. We expressly declined to obliterate the "sharp distinction . . . between mail order

---

3. Felt & Tarrant Mfg. Co. v. Gallagher, 306 U.S. 62, 59 S.Ct. 376 (1939).

4. Nelson v. Sears, Roebuck & Co., 312 U.S. 359, 61 S.Ct. 586 (1941).

sellers with retail outlets, solicitors, or property within a State, and those who do no more than communicate with customers in the State by mail or common carrier as a part of a general interstate business." 386 U.S., at 758, 87 S.Ct., at 1392.

Our due process jurisprudence has evolved substantially in the 25 years since *Bellas Hess*, particularly in the area of judicial jurisdiction. Building on the seminal case of International Shoe Co. v. Washington, 326 U.S. 310, 66 S.Ct. 154 (1945), we have framed the relevant inquiry as whether a defendant had minimum contacts with the jurisdiction "such that the maintenance of the suit does not offend 'traditional notions of fair play and substantial justice.'" Id., at 316, 66 S.Ct., at 158 (quoting Milliken v. Meyer, 311 U.S. 457, 463, 61 S.Ct. 339, 343 (1940)). In that spirit, we have abandoned more formalistic tests that focused on a defendant's "presence" within a State in favor of a more flexible inquiry into whether a defendant's contacts with the forum made it reasonable, in the context of our federal system of government, to require it to defend the suit in that State. In Shaffer v. Heitner, 433 U.S. 186, 212, 97 S.Ct. 2569, 2584 (1977), the Court extended the flexible approach that *International Shoe* had prescribed for purposes of *in personam* jurisdiction to *in rem* jurisdiction, concluding that "all assertions of state-court jurisdiction must be evaluated according to the standards set forth in *International Shoe* and its progeny."

Applying these principles, we have held that if a foreign corporation purposefully avails itself of the benefits of an economic market in the forum State, it may subject itself to the State's *in personam* jurisdiction even if it has no physical presence in the State. As we explained in Burger King Corp. v. Rudzewicz, 471 U.S. 462, 105 S.Ct. 2174 (1985):

> "Jurisdiction in these circumstances may not be avoided merely because the defendant did not *physically* enter the forum State. Although territorial presence frequently will enhance a potential defendant's affiliation with a State and reinforce the reasonable foreseeability of suit there, it is an inescapable fact of modern commercial life that a substantial amount of business is transacted solely by mail and wire communications across state lines, thus obviating the need for physical presence within a State in which business is conducted. So long as a commercial actor's efforts are 'purposefully directed' toward residents of another State, we have consistently rejected the notion that an absence of physical contacts can defeat personal jurisdiction there." Id., at 476, 105 S.Ct. at 2184 (emphasis in original).

Comparable reasoning justifies the imposition of the collection duty on a mail-order house that is engaged in continuous and widespread solicitation of business within a State. Such a corporation clearly has "fair warning that [its] activity may subject [it] to the jurisdiction of a foreign sovereign." Shaffer v. Heitner, 433 U.S., at 218, 97 S.Ct., at 2587 (STEVENS, J., concurring in judgment). In "modern commercial life" it matters little that such solicitation is accomplished by a deluge of catalogs rather than a phalanx of drummers: the requirements of due process are met irrespective of a corporation's lack of physical presence in the taxing State. Thus, to the extent that our decisions have indicated that the Due Process Clause requires physical presence in a State for the imposition of duty to collect a use tax, we overrule those holdings as superseded by developments in the law of due process.

In this case, there is no question that Quill has purposefully directed its activities at North Dakota residents, that the magnitude of those contacts are more than sufficient for due process purposes, and that the use tax is related to the benefits Quill receives from access to the State. We therefore agree with the North Dakota Supreme Court's conclusion that the Due Process Clause does not bar enforcement of that State's use tax against Quill.

IV

Article I, § 8, cl. 3 of the Constitution expressly authorizes Congress to "regulate Commerce with foreign Nations, and among the several States." It says nothing about the protection of interstate commerce in the absence of any action by Congress. Nevertheless, as Justice Johnson suggested in his concurring opinion in Gibbons v. Ogden, 9 Wheat. 1, 231–232, 239 (1824), the Commerce Clause is more than an affirmative grant of power; it has a negative sweep as well. The clause, in Justice Stone's phrasing, "by its own force" prohibits certain state actions that interfere with interstate commerce. South Carolina State Highway Dept. v. Barnwell Bros., Inc., 303 U.S. 177, 185, 58 S.Ct. 510, 514 (1938).

Our interpretation of the "negative" or "dormant" Commerce Clause has evolved substantially over the years, particularly as that clause concerns limitations on state taxation powers. See generally, P. Hartman, Federal Limitations on State and Local Taxation §§ 2:9–2:17 (1981).

[Justice Stevens briefly traced the history from Brown v. Maryland, 25 U.S. (12 Wheat.) 419 (1827) to Complete Auto Transit, Inc. v. Brady, 430 U.S. 274, 97 S.Ct. 1076 (1977).]

Bellas Hess was decided in 1967, in the middle of this latest rally between formalism and pragmatism. Contrary to the suggestion of the North Dakota Supreme Court, this timing does not mean that *Complete Auto* rendered *Bellas Hess* "obsolete." *Complete Auto* rejected *Freeman* and *Spector's* formal distinction between "direct" and "indirect" taxes on interstate commerce because that formalism allowed the validity of statutes to hinge on "legal terminology," "draftsmanship and phraseology." 430 U.S., at 281, 97 S.Ct., at 1080. *Bellas Hess* did not rely on any such labeling of taxes and therefore did not automatically fall with *Freeman* and its progeny.

While contemporary Commerce Clause jurisprudence might not dictate the same result were the issue to arise for the first time today, *Bellas Hess* is not inconsistent with *Complete Auto* and our recent cases. Under

Complete Auto's four-part test, we will sustain a tax against a Commerce Clause challenge so long as the "tax [1] is applied to an activity with a substantial nexus with the taxing State, [2] is fairly apportioned, [3] does not discriminate against interstate commerce, and [4] is fairly related to the services provided by the State." 430 U.S., at 279, 97 S.Ct., at 1079. *Bellas Hess* concerns the first of these tests and stands for the proposition that a vendor whose only contacts with the taxing State are by mail or common carrier lacks the "substantial nexus" required by the Commerce Clause.

Thus, three weeks after *Complete Auto* was handed down, we cited *Bellas Hess'* for this proposition and discussed the case at some length. In National Geographic Society v. California Bd. of Equalization, 430 U.S. 551, 559, 97 S.Ct. 1386, 1392 (1977), we affirmed the continuing vitality of *Bellas Hess'* "sharp distinction ... between mail-order sellers with [a physical presence in the taxing] State and those ... who do no more than communicate with customers in the State by mail or common carrier as part of a general interstate business." We have continued to cite *Bellas Hess* with approval ever since. For example, in Goldberg v. Sweet, 488 U.S. 252, 263, 109 S.Ct. 582, 589 (1989), we expressed "doubt that termination of an interstate telephone call, by itself, provides a substantial enough nexus for a State to tax a call. See National Bellas Hess ... (receipt of mail provides insufficient nexus)." * * * For these reasons, we disagree with the State Supreme Court's conclusion that our decision in *Complete Auto* undercut the *Bellas Hess* rule.

The State of North Dakota relies less on *Complete Auto* and more on the evolution of our due process jurisprudence. The State contends that the nexus requirements imposed by the Due Process and Commerce Clauses are equivalent and that if, as we concluded above, a mail-order house that lacks a physical presence in the taxing State nonetheless satisfies the due process "minimum contacts" test, then that corporation also meets the Commerce Clause "substantial nexus" test. We disagree. Despite the similarity in phrasing, the nexus requirements of the Due Process and Commerce Clauses are not identical. The two standards are animated by different constitutional concerns and policies.

Due process centrally concerns the fundamental fairness of governmental activity. Thus, at the most general level, the due process nexus analysis requires that we ask whether an individual's connections with a State are substantial enough to legitimate the State's exercise of power over him. We have, therefore, often identified "notice" or "fair warning" as the analytic touchstone of due process nexus analysis. In contrast, the Commerce Clause, and its nexus requirement, are informed not so much by concerns about fairness for the individual defendant as by structural concerns about the effects of state regulation on the national economy. Under the Articles of Confederation, state taxes and duties hindered and suppressed interstate commerce; the Framers intended the Commerce Clause as a cure for these structural ills. See generally The Federalist Nos. 7, 11 (A. Hamilton). It is in this light that we have interpreted the negative implication of the Commerce Clause. Accordingly, we have ruled that that Clause prohibits discrimination against interstate commerce, and bars state regulations that unduly burden interstate commerce.

The *Complete Auto* analysis reflects these concerns about the national economy. The second and third parts of that analysis, which require fair apportionment and non-discrimination, prohibit taxes that pass an unfair share of the tax burden onto interstate commerce. The first and fourth prongs, which require a substantial nexus and a relationship between the tax and state-provided services, limit the reach of state taxing authority so as to ensure that state taxation does not unduly burden interstate commerce.[6] Thus, the "substantial-nexus" requirement is not, like due process' "minimum-contacts" requirement, a proxy for notice, but rather a means for limiting state burdens on interstate commerce. Accordingly, contrary to the State's suggestion, a corporation may have the "minimum contacts" with a taxing State as required by the Due Process Clause, and yet lack the "substantial nexus" with that State as required by the Commerce Clause.[7]

The State Supreme Court reviewed our recent Commerce Clause decisions and concluded that those rulings signalled a "retreat from the formalistic constrictions of a stringent physical presence test in favor of a more flexible substantive approach" and thus supported its decision not to apply *Bellas Hess*. 470 N.W.2d, at 214. Although we agree with the State Court's assessment of the evolution of our cases, we do not share its conclusion that this evolution indicates that the Commerce Clause ruling of *Bellas Hess* is no longer good law.

First, as the state court itself noted, all of these cases involved taxpayers who had a physical presence in the taxing State and therefore do not directly conflict with the rule of *Bellas Hess* or compel that it be overruled. Second, and more importantly, although our Commerce Clause jurisprudence now favors more flexible balancing analyses, we have never intimated a desire to reject all established "bright-line" tests. Although we have not, in our review of other types of taxes, articulated the same

---

6. North Dakota's use tax illustrates well how a state tax might unduly burden interstate commerce. On its face, North Dakota law imposes a collection duty on every vendor who advertises in the State three times in a single year. Thus, absent the *Bellas Hess* rule, a publisher who included a subscription card in three issues of its magazine, a vendor whose radio advertisements were heard in North Dakota on three occasions, and a corporation whose telephone sales force made three calls into the State, all would be subject to the collection duty. What is more significant, similar obligations might be imposed by the Nation's 6,000–plus taxing jurisdictions. See National Bellas Hess, Inc. v. Department of Revenue of Ill., 386 U.S. 753, 759–760, 87 S.Ct. 1389, 1393 (1967) (noting that the "many variations in rates of tax, in allowable exemptions, and in administrative and record-keeping requirements could entangle [a mail-order house] in a virtual welter of complicated obligations") (footnotes omitted); see also Shaviro, An Economic and Political Look at Federalism in Taxation, 90 Mich.L.Rev. 895, 925–926 (1992).

7. We have sometimes stated that the "*Complete Auto* test, while responsive to Commerce Clause dictates, encompasses as well ... Due Process requirement[s]." Trinova Corp. v. Michigan Dept. of Treasury, 498 U.S. 358, 373, 111 S.Ct. 818, 828 (1991). Although such comments might suggest that every tax that passes contemporary Commerce Clause analysis is also valid under the Due Process Clause, it does not follow that the converse is as well true: a tax may be consistent with Due Process and yet unduly burden interstate commerce. See, e.g., Tyler Pipe Industries, Inc. v. Washington State Dept. of Revenue, 483 U.S. 232, 107 S.Ct. 2810 (1987).

physical-presence requirement that *Bellas Hess* established for sales and use taxes, that silence does not imply repudiation of the *Bellas Hess* rule.

Complete Auto, it is true, renounced *Freeman* and its progeny as "formalistic." But not all formalism is alike. *Spector's* formal distinction between taxes on the "privilege of doing business" and all other taxes served no purpose within our Commerce Clause jurisprudence, but stood "only as a trap for the unwary draftsman." Complete Auto, 430 U.S., at 279, 97 S.Ct. at 1079. In contrast, the bright-line rule of *Bellas Hess* furthers the ends of the dormant Commerce Clause. Undue burdens on interstate commerce may be avoided not only by a case-by-case evaluation of the actual burdens imposed by particular regulations or taxes, but also, in some situations, by the demarcation of a discrete realm of commercial activity that is free from interstate taxation. *Bellas Hess* followed the latter approach and created a safe harbor for vendors "whose only connection with customers in the [taxing] State is by common carrier or the United States mail." Under *Bellas Hess*, such vendors are free from state-imposed duties to collect sales and use taxes.[8]

Like other bright-line tests, the *Bellas Hess* rule appears artificial at its edges: whether or not a State may compel a vendor to collect a sales or use tax may turn on the presence in the taxing State of a small sales force, plant, or office. Cf. National Geographic Society v. California Bd. of Equalization, 430 U.S. 551, 97 S.Ct. 1386 (1977); Scripto, Inc. v. Carson, 362 U.S. 207, 80 S.Ct. 619 (1960). This artificiality, however, is more than offset by the benefits of a clear rule. Such a rule firmly establishes the boundaries of legitimate state authority to impose a duty to collect sales and use taxes and reduces litigation concerning those taxes. This benefit is important, for as we have so frequently noted, our law in this area is something of a "quagmire" and the "application of constitutional principles to specific state statutes leaves much room for controversy and confusion and little in the way of precise guides to the States in the exercise of their indispensable power of taxation." Northwestern States Portland Cement Co. v. Minnesota, 358 U.S. 450, 457–458, 79 S.Ct. 357, 362 (1959).

Moreover, a bright-line rule in the area of sales and use taxes also encourages settled expectations and, in doing so, fosters investment by businesses and individuals. Indeed, it is not unlikely that the mail-order industry's dramatic growth over the last quarter-century is due in part to the bright-line exemption from state taxation created in *Bellas Hess*.

---

8. In addition to its common-carrier contacts with the State, Quill also licensed software to some of its North Dakota clients. See n.1, supra. The State "concedes that the existence in North Dakota of a few floppy diskettes to which Quill holds title seems a slender thread upon which to base nexus." Brief for Respondent 46. We agree. Although title to "a few floppy diskettes" present in a State might constitute some minimal nexus, in National Geographic Society v. California Bd. of Equalization, 430 U.S. 551, 556, 97 S.Ct. 1386, 1390 (1977), we expressly rejected a " 'slightest presence' standard of constitutional nexus." We therefore conclude that Quill's licensing of software in this case does not meet the "substantial nexus" requirement of the Commerce Clause.

Notwithstanding the benefits of bright-line tests, we have, in some situations, decided to replace such tests with more contextual balancing inquiries. For example, in Arkansas Electric Cooperative Corp. v. Arkansas Pub. Serv. Comm'n, 461 U.S. 375, 103 S.Ct. 1905 (1983), we reconsidered a bright-line test set forth in Public Utilities Comm'n of R.I. v. Attleboro Steam & Electric Co., 273 U.S. 83, 47 S.Ct. 294 (1927). *Attleboro* distinguished between state regulation of *wholesale* sales of electricity, which was constitutional as an "indirect" regulation of interstate commerce, and state regulation of *retail* sales of electricity, which was unconstitutional as a "direct regulation" of commerce. In *Arkansas Electric*, we considered whether to "follow the mechanical test set out in *Attleboro*, or the balance-of-interests test applied in our Commerce Clause cases." Arkansas Electric Cooperative Corp., 461 U.S., at 390–391, 103 S.Ct., at 1916. We first observed that "the principle of *stare decisis* counsels us, here as elsewhere, not lightly to set aside specific guidance of the sort we find in *Attleboro*." Id., at 391, 103 S.Ct., at 1916. In deciding to reject the *Attleboro* analysis, we were influenced by the fact that the "mechanical test" was "anachronistic," that the Court had rarely relied on the test, and that we could "see no strong reliance interests" that would be upset by the rejection of that test. Id., at 391–392, 103 S.Ct., at 1916. None of those factors obtains in this case. First, the *Attleboro* rule was "anachronistic" because it relied on formal distinctions between "direct" and "indirect" regulation (and on the regulatory counterparts of our *Freeman* line of cases); as discussed above, *Bellas Hess* turned on a different logic and thus remained sound after the Court repudiated an analogous distinction in *Complete Auto*. Second, unlike the *Attleboro* rule, we have, in our decisions, frequently relied on the *Bellas Hess* rule in the last 25 years, see supra, at 1912, and we have never intimated in our review of sales or use taxes that *Bellas Hess* was unsound. Finally, again unlike the *Attleboro* rule, the *Bellas Hess* rule has engendered substantial reliance and has become part of the basic framework of a sizeable industry. The "interest in stability and orderly development of the law" that undergirds the doctrine of *stare decisis*, see Runyon v. McCrary, 427 U.S. 160, 190–191, 96 S.Ct. 2586, 2604–2605 (1976) (STEVENS, J., concurring), therefore counsels adherence to settled precedent.

In sum, although in our cases subsequent to *Bellas Hess* and concerning other types of taxes we have not adopted a similar bright-line, physical-presence requirement, our reasoning in those cases does not compel that we now reject the rule that *Bellas Hess* established in the area of sales and use taxes. To the contrary, the continuing value of a bright-line rule in this area and the doctrine and principles of *stare decisis* indicate that the *Bellas Hess* rule remains good law. For these reasons, we disagree with the North Dakota Supreme Court's conclusion that the time has come to renounce the bright-line test of *Bellas Hess*.

This aspect of our decision is made easier by the fact that the underlying issue is not only one that Congress may be better qualified to resolve,[10] but also one that Congress has the ultimate power to resolve. No matter how we evaluate the burdens that use taxes impose on interstate commerce, Congress remains free to disagree with our conclusions. See Prudential Insurance Co. v. Benjamin, 328 U.S. 408, 66 S.Ct. 1142 (1946). Indeed, in recent years Congress has considered legislation that would "overrule" the *Bellas Hess* rule. Its decision not to take action in this direction may, of course, have been dictated by respect for our holding in *Bellas Hess* that the Due Process Clause prohibits States from imposing such taxes, but today we have put that problem to rest. Accordingly, Congress is now free to decide whether, when, and to what extent the States may burden interstate mail-order concerns with a duty to collect use taxes.

Indeed, even if we were convinced that *Bellas Hess* was inconsistent with our Commerce Clause jurisprudence, "this very fact [might] giv[e us] pause and counse[l] withholding our hand, at least for now. Congress has the power to protect interstate commerce from intolerable or even undesirable burdens." Commonwealth Edison Co. v. Montana, 453 U.S. 609, 637, 101 S.Ct. 2946, 2964 (1981) (WHITE, J., concurring). In this situation, it may be that "the better part of both wisdom and valor is to respect the judgment of the other branches of the Government." Id., at 638, 101 S.Ct., at 2964.

The judgment of the Supreme Court of North Dakota is reversed and the case is remanded for further proceedings not inconsistent with this opinion.

It is so ordered.

JUSTICE SCALIA, with whom JUSTICE KENNEDY and JUSTICE THOMAS join, concurring in part and concurring in the judgment.

* * * I agree with the Court that the Due Process Clause holding of *Bellas Hess* should be overruled. Even before *Bellas Hess*, we had held, correctly I think, that state regulatory jurisdiction could be asserted on the basis of contacts with the State through the United States mail. See Travelers Health Assn. v. Virginia ex rel. State Corp. Comm'n, 339 U.S. 643, 646–650, 70 S.Ct. 927, 928–931 (1950) (Blue Sky laws). It is difficult to discern any principled basis for distinguishing between jurisdiction to regulate and jurisdiction to tax. As an original matter, it might have been possible to distinguish between jurisdiction to tax and jurisdiction to compel collection of taxes as agent for the State, but we have rejected that. National Geographic Soc. v. California Bd. of Equalization, 430 U.S. 551, 558, 97 S.Ct. 1386, 1391 (1977); Scripto, Inc. v. Carson, 362 U.S. 207, 211, 80 S.Ct. 619, 621 (1960). I agree with the Court, moreover, that abandonment of *Bellas Hess's* due process holding is compelled by reasoning "[c]omparable" to that contained in our post–1967 cases dealing with

---

10. Many States have enacted use taxes. See App. 3 to Brief for Direct Marketing Association as *Amicus Curiae*. An overruling of *Bellas Hess* might raise thorny questions concerning the retroactive application of those taxes and might trigger substantial unanticipated liability for mail-order houses. The precise allocation of such burdens is better resolved by Congress rather than this Court.

state jurisdiction to adjudicate. Ante, at 1911. I do not understand this to mean that the due process standards for adjudicative jurisdiction and those for legislative (or prescriptive) jurisdiction are necessarily identical; and on that basis I join Parts I, II, and III of the Court's opinion.

I also agree that the Commerce Clause holding of *Bellas Hess* should not be overruled. Unlike the Court, however, I would not revisit the merits of that holding, but would adhere to it on the basis of *stare decisis*. American Trucking Assns., Inc. v. Smith, 496 U.S. 167, 204, 110 S.Ct. 2323, 2345 (1990) (SCALIA, J., concurring in judgment). Congress has the final say over regulation of interstate commerce, and it can change the rule of *Bellas Hess* by simply saying so. We have long recognized that the doctrine of *stare decisis* has "special force" where "Congress remains free to alter what we have done." Patterson v. McLean Credit Union, 491 U.S. 164, 172–173, 109 S.Ct. 2363, 2370 (1989). Moreover, the demands of the doctrine are "at their acme ... where reliance interests are involved," Payne v. Tennessee, 501 U.S. 808, 828, 111 S.Ct. 2597, 2610 (1991). As the Court notes, "the *Bellas Hess* rule has engendered substantial reliance and has become part of the basic framework of a sizeable industry," ante, at 1916.

JUSTICE WHITE, concurring in part and dissenting in part.

Today the Court repudiates that aspect of our decision in National Bellas Hess, Inc. v. Department of Revenue of Ill., 386 U.S. 753, 87 S.Ct. 1389 (1967), which restricts, under the Due Process Clause of the Fourteenth Amendment, the power of the States to impose use tax collection responsibilities on out-of-state mail order businesses that do not have a "physical presence" in the State. The Court stops short, however, of giving *Bellas Hess* the complete burial it justly deserves. In my view, the Court should also overrule that part of *Bellas Hess* which justifies its holding under the Commerce Clause. I, therefore, respectfully dissent from Part IV.

I

In Part IV of its opinion, the majority goes to some lengths to justify the *Bellas Hess* physical presence requirement under our Commerce Clause jurisprudence. I am unpersuaded by its interpretation of our cases. In *Bellas Hess*, the majority placed great weight on the interstate quality of the mail order sales, stating that "it is difficult to conceive of commercial transactions more exclusively interstate in character than the mail order transactions here involved." Bellas Hess, supra, at 759, 87 S.Ct., at 1392. As the majority correctly observes, the idea of prohibiting States from taxing "exclusively interstate" transactions had been an important part of our jurisprudence for many decades, ranging intermittently from such cases as Case of State Freight Tax, 15 Wall. 232, 279 (1873), through Freeman v. Hewit, 329 U.S. 249, 256, 67 S.Ct. 274, 278 (1946), and Spector Motor Service, Inc. v. O'Connor, 340 U.S. 602, 71 S.Ct. 508 (1951). But though it recognizes that *Bellas Hess* was decided amidst an upheaval in our Commerce Clause jurisprudence, in which we began to hold that "a

State, with proper drafting, may tax exclusively interstate commerce so long as the tax does not create any effect forbidden by the Commerce Clause," Complete Auto Transit, Inc. v. Brady, 430 U.S. 274, 285, 97 S.Ct. 1076, 1082 (1977), the majority draws entirely the wrong conclusion from this period of ferment.

The Court attempts to paint *Bellas Hess* in a different hue from *Freeman* and *Spector* because the former "did not rely" on labeling taxes that had "direct" and "indirect" effects on interstate commerce. See ante, at 1912. Thus, the Court concludes, *Bellas Hess* "did not automatically fall with *Freeman* and its progeny" in our decision in *Complete Auto*. See id., at 11. I am unpersuaded by this attempt to distinguish *Bellas Hess* from *Freeman* and *Spector*, both of which were repudiated by this Court. See Complete Auto, supra, at 288–289, and n. 15, 97 S.Ct., at 1084, and n. 15. What we disavowed in *Complete Auto* was not just the "formal distinction between 'direct' and 'indirect' taxes on interstate commerce," ante, at 1912, but also the whole notion underlying the *Bellas Hess* physical presence rule—that "interstate commerce is immune from state taxation." Complete Auto, supra, at 288, 97 S.Ct., at 1083.

* * *

II

The Court next launches into an uncharted and treacherous foray into differentiating between the "nexus" requirements under the Due Process and Commerce Clauses. * * *

The majority's attempt to disavow language in our opinions acknowledging the presence of due process requirements in the *Complete Auto* test is also unpersuasive. See ante, at 1913–1914, n. 7 (citing Trinova Corp. v. Michigan Dept. of Treasury, 498 U.S. 358, 373, 111 S.Ct. 818, 828 (1991)). Instead of explaining the doctrinal origins of the Commerce Clause nexus requirement, the majority breezily announces the rule and moves on to other matters. See ante, at 1913–1914. In my view, before resting on the assertion that the Constitution mandates inquiry into two readily distinct "nexus" requirements, it would seem prudent to discern the origins of the "nexus" requirement in order better to understand whether the Court's concern traditionally has been with the fairness of a State's tax or some other value.

The cases from which the *Complete Auto* Court derived the nexus requirement in its four-part test convince me that the issue of "nexus" is really a due process fairness inquiry. In explaining the sources of the four-part inquiry in *Complete Auto*, the Court relied heavily on Justice Rutledge's separate concurring opinion in Freeman v. Hewit, 329 U.S. 249, 67 S.Ct. 274 (1946). * * * In conducting his inquiry, Justice Rutledge used language that by now should be familiar, arguing that a tax was unconstitutional if the activity lacked a sufficient connection to the State to give "jurisdiction to tax," Freeman, supra, at 271, 67 S.Ct., at 286; or if the tax discriminated against interstate commerce; or if the activity was subjected to multiple tax burdens. 329 U.S., at 276–277, 67 S.Ct., at 289–290. Justice Rutledge later refined these principles in Memphis Natural Gas Co. v. Stone, 335 U.S. 80, 68 S.Ct. 1475 (1948), in which he described the principles that the *Complete Auto* Court would later substantially adopt: "[I]t is enough for me to sustain the tax imposed in this case that it is one clearly within the state's power to lay insofar as any limitation of due process or 'jurisdiction to tax' in that sense is concerned; it is nondiscriminatory . . .; [it] is duly apportioned . . .; and cannot be repeated by any other state." 335 U.S., at 96–97, 68 S.Ct., at 1483–1484 (concurring opinion) (footnotes omitted).

By the time the Court decided Northwestern States Portland Cement Co. v. Minnesota, 358 U.S. 450, 79 S.Ct. 357 (1959), Justice Rutledge was no longer on the Court, but his view of the nexus requirement as grounded in the Due Process Clause was decisively adopted. In rejecting challenges to a state tax based on the Due Process and Commerce Clauses, the Court stated that "[t]he taxes imposed are levied only on that portion of the taxpayer's net income which arises from its activities within the taxing State. These activities form a sufficient 'nexus between such a tax and transactions within a state for which the tax is an exaction.'" Id., at 464, 79 S.Ct., at 366 (citation omitted). The Court went on to observe that "[i]t strains reality to say, in terms of our decisions, that each of the corporations here was not sufficiently involved in local events to forge 'some definite link, some minimum connection' sufficient to satisfy due process requirements." Id., at 464–465, 79 S.Ct., at 366 (quoting Miller Bros. v. Maryland, 347 U.S. 340, 344–345, 74 S.Ct. 535, 538–539 (1954)). When the Court announced its four-part synthesis in *Complete Auto*, the nexus requirement was definitely traceable to concerns grounded in the Due Process Clause, and not the Commerce Clause, as the Court's discussion of the doctrinal antecedents for its rule made clear. See Complete Auto, supra, at 281–282, 285, 97 S.Ct., at 1080–1081, 1082. For the Court now to assert that our Commerce Clause jurisprudence supports a separate notion of nexus is without precedent or explanation.

Even were there to be such an independent requirement under the Commerce Clause, there is no relationship between the physical presence/nexus rule the Court retains and Commerce Clause considerations that allegedly justify it. Perhaps long ago a seller's "physical presence" was a sufficient part of a trade to condition imposition of a tax on such presence. But in today's economy, physical presence frequently has very little to do with a transaction a State might seek to tax. Wire transfers of money involving billions of dollars occur every day; purchasers place orders with sellers by fax, phone, and computer linkup; sellers ship goods by air, road, and sea through sundry delivery services without leaving their place of business. It is certainly true that the days of the door-to-door salesperson are not gone. Nevertheless, an out-of-state direct marketer derives numerous commercial benefits from the State in which it does business. These advantages include laws establishing sound local banking institutions to support credit transactions; courts to insure collection of the purchase price from the seller's customers; means of waste disposal from garbage generated by mail order solicitations; and creation and enforcement of consumer protection laws, which protect buyers and sellers alike, the former by ensuring that they will have a ready means of protecting against fraud, and the latter by creating a climate of consumer confidence that inures to the benefit of reputable dealers in mail order transactions. To create, for the first time, a nexus requirement under the Commerce Clause independent of that established for due process purposes is one thing; to attempt to justify an anachronistic notion of physical presence in economic terms is quite another.

III

The illogic of retaining the physical presence requirement in these circumstances is palpable. Under the majority's analysis, and our decision in *National Geographic*, an out-of-state seller with one salesperson in a State would be subject to use tax collection burdens on its entire mail order sales even if those sales were unrelated to the salesperson's solicitation efforts. By contrast, an out-of-state seller in a neighboring State could be the dominant business in the putative taxing State, creating the greatest infrastructure burdens and undercutting the State's home companies by its comparative price advantage in selling products free of use taxes, and yet not have to collect such taxes if it lacks a physical presence in the taxing State. The majority clings to the physical presence rule not because of any logical relation to fairness or any economic rationale related to principles underlying the Commerce Clause, but simply out of the supposed convenience of having a bright-line rule. I am less impressed by the convenience of such adherence than the unfairness it produces. Here, convenience should give way. Cf. Complete Auto, supra, at 289, n. 15, 97 S.Ct., at 1084 n. 15 ("We believe, however, that administrative convenience ... is insufficient justification for abandoning the principle that 'interstate commerce may be made to pay its way' ").

Also very questionable is the rationality of perpetuating a rule that creates an interstate tax shelter for one form of business—mail order sellers—but no countervailing advantage for its competitors. If the Commerce Clause was intended to put businesses on an even playing field, the majority's rule is hardly a way to achieve that goal. Indeed, arguably even under the majority's explanation for its "Commerce Clause nexus" requirement, the unfairness of its rule on retailers other than direct marketers should be taken into account. See ante, at 1913 (stating that the Commerce Clause nexus requirement addresses the "structural concerns about the effects of state regulation on the national economy"). I would think that protectionist rules favoring a $180 billion-a-year industry might come within the scope of such "structural concerns."

NOTES AND QUESTIONS

A. *Due Process Clause Nexus and Commerce Clause Nexus.* Prior to *Quill*, the Court had considered the nexus requirement as an element of both its Due Process and Commerce Clause doctrines, and it had never indicated that there was any distinction in the meaning of the nexus requirement under either clause. Indeed, it had suggested precisely the opposite, noting in *Bellas Hess* the close affinity between the nexus inquiry under both clauses and in *Trinova* that the Commerce Clause nexus requirement "encompasses as well the Due Process requirement that there be 'a "minimal connection" between the interstate activities and the taxing State.'" Trinova Corp. v. Michigan Department of Treasury, 498 U.S. 358, 373, 111 S.Ct. 818 (1991). "The Court's discovery that '[d]espite the similarity in phrasing, the nexus requirements of the Due Process and Commerce Clauses are not identical' is more accurately viewed as a doctrinal epiphany than a logical inference to be drawn from a careful reading of its precedents." Walter Hellerstein, "Supreme Court Says No State Use Tax Imposed on Mail Order Sellers ... for Now," 77 J. Tax'n 120 (1992).

What motivated the Court to bifurcate the nexus analysis in *Quill?* Does footnote 10 and the accompanying text of the Court's opinion provide a partial answer to this question? What is the distinction, as a practical matter, between Due Process Clause "nexus" and Commerce Clause "substantial nexus"? Does the Commerce Clause "substantial nexus" requirement always require physical presence? If so, why did the Court declare that "we have not, in our review of other types of taxes, articulated the same physical-presence requirement that *Bellas Hess* established for sales and use taxes"? If not, does that mean that the Commerce Clause envisions one nexus requirement for mail-order sales tax collection responsibility, a second for income tax liability, a third for gross receipts tax liability, and so on? Can that possibility be squared with the Chief Justice Marshall's observation that "it is *constitution* we are expounding"? McCulloch v. Maryland, 17 U.S. (4 Wheat.) 316, 407 (1819) (emphasis in original). Suppose, moreover, that *Bellas Hess* had never been decided? What, then, would the result have been in *Quill?*

B. *The Commerce Clause "Substantial Nexus" Requirement in Light of* Quill. Wholly apart from the important question whether *Quill's* "bright-line, physical-presence" standard of Commerce Clause nexus applies to levies other than sales and use taxes, see Note A supra and pp. 51–81 infra, what precisely is the "substantial nexus" Commerce Clause standard that the Court articulated in *Quill?* If Quill had retained title to the merchandise it sold until during the 90–day money-back guarantee period, would the result have been different? See footnote 1 of the Court's opinion. If a "few floppy diskettes" do not meet the Commerce Clause " 'substantial nexus' requirement," how many floppy diskettes does it take? And does the requirement of "substantial nexus" equate to a requirement of "substantial physical presence"?

The lingering ambiguity in the *Quill* opinion has prompted extensive litigation in state courts over the two decades since *Quill* was decided. For example, the New York Court of Appeals answered the last question in the negative in the companion cases of Orvis v. Tax Appeals Tribunal and Vermont Information Processing, Inc. v. Tax Appeals Tribunal, 86 N.Y.2d 165, 654 N.E.2d 954, 630 N.Y.S.2d 680, cert. denied (in *Vermont Information Processing*), 516 U.S. 989, 116 S.Ct. 518 (1995). The court concluded that "any measurable amount" of physical presence rather than "substantial physical presence" was the governing Commerce Clause standard. Id., 654 N.E.2d at 959. Under that standard, the decision in *Orvis* and *Vermont Information Processing* followed easily because the taxpayers' employees were physically present in New York in both cases. The Court of Appeals' ruling, however, has by no means been established as the definitive reading of *Quill*. In Florida Dep't of Revenue v. Share Int'l, 676 So.2d 1362 (Fla. 1996), aff'g 667 So.2d 226 (Fla. Dist. Ct. App. 1995), cert. denied, 519 U.S. 1056, 117 S.Ct. 685 (1997), for example, the Florida Supreme Court relied on the Florida Court of Appeals' opinion in affirming a determination that the temporary presence in the state of the president and the vice-president of an out-of-state seller of chiropractic equipment, through attendance at Florida seminars, was insufficient to establish "substantial nexus" for purposes of collecting use tax on mail-order or telephone-order sales. The court so held despite the fact that the taxpayer displayed and sold its products during the seminars, collected sales tax on items sold in Florida during the seminars, and approximately 4.6 percent of the taxpayer's annual sales resulted from products sold directly to chiropractors at seminars held in Florida. If you were in charge of tax policy for a state department of revenue, would you recommend pursuing cases like *Share*? Suppose you were in charge of state economic development policy, would your answer be the same?

How many in-state visits by an out-of-state corporation's employees does it take to establish "substantial nexus" for use tax collection purposes? In Kansas, the answer is more than 11 over a four-year period. From 1992–96, technicians from Intercard, a manufacturer of electronic data cards and card readers, made 11 visits to Kinko's to install card readers that Kinko's purchased from Intercard. The Kansas Supreme Court concluded that "Intercard's 11 incursions to install cardreaders in Kansas were isolated, sporadic, and insufficient to establish a substantial nexus in Kansas." In re Appeal of Intercard, Inc., 270 Kan. 346, 14 P.3d 1111, 1122 (2000). In Arizona, the answer to the same question is 80 within a similar time-frame. The Arizona Court of Appeals concluded that 80 visits over approximately a four-year period was sufficient to establish nexus over an out-of-state vendor of computer hardware and software to nursing homes. Arizona Department of Revenue v. Care Computer Systems, Inc., 197 Ariz. 414, 4 P.3d 469 (Ct. App. 2000). In Illinois, 30 in-state deliveries by an out-of-state furniture dealer over a 26–month period (along with installation of window dressings on five occasions) was enough. Town Crier, Inc. v. Department of Revenue, 315 Ill.App.3d 286, 248 Ill.Dec. 105, 733 N.E.2d 780 (1st Dist. 2000). How about 40 visits over a four-year period? Or 20 visits? Suppose the visits are spread unevenly over the audit period, say, one visit in 2007, 40 visits in 2008, 35 visits in 2009, and one visit in 2010. Should nexus rules be determined on an average basis over the audit period? On an annual basis? Or on some other basis?

C. *Nexus and Independent Contractors.* In Tyler Pipe Industries, Inc. v. Washington State Dep't of Revenue, 483 U.S. 232, 107 S.Ct. 2810 (1987), set out in chapter 3, pp. 120–22 infra, the Court reiterated the proposition it had articulated earlier in Scripto, Inc. v. Carson, 362 U.S. 207, 80 S.Ct. 619 (1960), that the presence of an out-of-state taxpayer's representative in the state could provide a constitutional basis for nexus and that it was not constitutionally significant whether such a representative was denominated an "employee" or an "independent contractor." On the other hand, it would stretch the concept of nexus beyond all recognition to suggest that any time one deals with an independent contractor in a state that "contact" satisfies constitutional nexus requirements. The difficulty is to determine under what circumstances the in-state activities of a third party with whom the taxpayer has contractual relations will be attributed to the taxpayer for nexus purposes.

A series of cases dealing with the sale of books and related materials to elementary school children, with the assistance of their teachers, reveals that the resolution of this issue will not come easily. In each of the cases, the facts were essentially the same. The taxpayer sent its promotional literature to teachers and school librarians from locations outside the state. The teachers passed out the order forms to students, collected the students' orders and payments, and remitted the orders with a single check to the taxpayer. The teachers were neither the employees of the taxpayer nor under any contractual obligation to the taxpayer. They were rewarded by "points" from the taxpayer for obtaining orders, for which they received additional books or teaching aids. Query: In light of *Quill*, *Tyler Pipe*, and *Scripto*, can the out-of-state vendor be required to collect use tax on the books and related materials sold to students, assuming that the vendor has no physical presence in the state other than that arguably attributable to the teachers? For different answers to this question, compare In the Appeal of Scholastic Book Clubs, Inc., 260 Kan. 528, 920 P.2d 947 (1996) (yes) and Scholastic Book Clubs, Inc. v. State Bd. of Equalization, 207 Cal.App.3d 734, 255 Cal.Rptr. 77 (1st Dist. 1989) (yes, pre-*Quill*) with Pledger v. Troll Book Clubs, Inc., 316 Ark. 195, 871 S.W.2d 389 (1994) (no) and Scholastic Book Clubs, Inc. v. Michigan, 223 Mich.App. 576, 567 N.W.2d 692 (1997) (no).

D. *Nexus through Related Corporations.* Does the presence of a subsidiary in the state establish nexus over the out-of-state parent for tax purposes and vice versa? With respect to personal jurisdiction, the Restatement provides:

> Judicial jurisdiction over a subsidiary corporation does not of itself give a state judicial jurisdiction over the parent corporation. This is true even though the parent owns all of the subsidiary's stock. So a state does not have judicial jurisdiction over a parent corporation merely because a subsidiary of the parent does business in the territory.

> Judicial jurisdiction over a subsidiary corporation will * * * give the state judicial jurisdiction over the parent corporation if the parent so controls and dominates the subsidiary so as in effect to disregard the latter's independent corporate existence.

> Judicial jurisdiction over the parent corporation will give the state judicial jurisdiction over the subsidiary corporation if the parent so controls and dominates the subsidiary so as in effect to disregard the latter's independent corporate existence.

Restatement (Second) Conflict of Laws § 52, comment b at 180–81 (1971).

Courts have generally followed the same rule with respect to tax jurisdiction. See, e.g., SFA Folio Collections, Inc. v. Tracy, 73 Ohio St.3d 119, 652 N.E.2d 693 (1995) (Saks Fifth Avenue's retail store in Ohio does not establish nexus for use tax collection purposes over Saks Fifth Avenue's out-of-state mail-order subsidiary); Bloomingdale's By Mail, Ltd. v. Commonwealth Dep't of Revenue, 130 Pa.Cmwlth. 190, 567 A.2d 773 (1989), aff'd per curiam, 527 Pa. 347, 591 A.2d 1047 (1991), cert. denied, 504 U.S. 955, 112 S.Ct. 2299 (1992) (Bloomingdale's retail store in Pennsylvania does not establish nexus for use tax collection purposes over Bloomingdale's out-of-state mail-order subsidiary). But see Reader's Digest Ass'n v. Mahin, 44 Ill.2d 354, 255 N.E.2d 458, cert. denied, 399 U.S. 919, 90 S.Ct. 2237 (1970) (out-of-state mail-order seller of books and albums required to collect use tax on sales into state due to presence of in-state subsidiaries that solicited advertising and orders for the taxpayer's magazine). As discussed below, this issue has gained new currency in the context of online retailers.

B. THE "PHYSICAL PRESENCE" STANDARD AND THE RISE OF E–COMMERCE

The "physical presence" standard of the Supreme Court's *Quill* decision has been particularly important in the context of electronic commerce. To the extent that online retailers can avoid establishing physical presence in the states where their products are consumed, *Quill* would seem to prohibit those states from imposing a use tax collection obligation on such vendors. Although consumers are nonetheless legally obligated to pay use taxes on items purchased online, as a practical matter enforcement of this obligation is not possible without the assistance of the retailer. The explosive growth of online sales over the past decade has brought this issue to the forefront of state and local tax policy. One recent study indicates that e-commerce sales increased from $995 billion in 1999 to $2.4 trillion in 2006.[c] Not all of these sales would otherwise be taxable under state sales tax rules. Even so, lower bound estimates put the revenue loss to states at roughly $52 billion over the six-year period from 2007–2012.[d]

States have not sat idly by as their sales tax bases have escaped taxation. One strategy has been to assert "attributional nexus" based on the in-state activities of affiliated entities.[e] In California, for example, a state Court of Appeal ruled in 2005 that the state could require bookseller Borders Online LLC ("Online") to collect and remit use taxes for items purchased online by its California consumers. See Borders Online LLC v. State Board of Equalization, 129 Cal.App.4th 1179, 29 Cal.Rptr.3d 176

---

c. Donald Bruce, William F. Fox & LeAnn Luna, "State and Local Government Sales Tax Revenue Losses from Electronic Commerce," State Tax Notes, May 18, 2009, p. 537.

d. Id.

e. For an argument that corporate affiliation should be the predicate for establishing nexus, see John Swain, "Cybertaxation and the Commerce Clause: Entity Isolation or Affiliate Nexus," 75 S. Cal. L. Rev. 419 (2002).

(2005). While Online was technically a separate entity from Borders, Inc. (i.e., the Borders Group, Inc. subsidiary that owns the physical stores located throughout the state), the two entities engaged in a sufficient degree of cross-marketing and other joint activities that the court concluded Borders, Inc. was acting as Online's agent. Whether these legal strategies will actually result in increased sales/use tax revenues remains an open question. To the extent that consumers have tax-free options available to them, one would expect them simply to shift their purchases to a retailer that has avoided use tax collection obligations. Until recently, one such retailer has been Amazon.com. As of May 1, 2009, the Amazon.com website indicated that sales tax would be charged only for items shipped to destinations in 5 states (Kansas, Kentucky, New York, North Dakota, and Washington). The inclusion of New York in this list is attributable to the litigation that led to the trial court decision reproduced below.

AMAZON.COM LLC v. NEW YORK STATE DEPARTMENT OF TAXATION AND FINANCE

Supreme Court, New York County, New York, 2009.
23 Misc.3d 418, 877 N.Y.S.2d 842.

EILEEN BRANSTON, J.

Pursuant to [New York's Civil Practice Law and Rules], defendants New York State Department of Taxation and Finance, Robert Megna, in his Official Capacity as Commissioner of the New York State Department of Taxation and Finance, The State of New York, and David A. Paterson, in his Official Capacity as the Governor of the State of New York (collectively "the State") move to dismiss the complaint. Plaintiffs Amazon.com LLC and Amazon Services, LLC (collectively "Amazon") oppose dismissal and cross-move for summary judgment.

Background

Since 1995, Amazon has been operating a retail internet business. Its goods are sold online and shipped to buyers worldwide, including to New York. Amazon does not own property in New York or maintain any New York offices.[1] None of its employees work or reside in New York.

Amazon's Associates Program

Amazon created an "Associates Program," which allows participants ("Associates") to maintain links to Amazon.com on their own websites and compensates them by paying "a percentage of the proceeds of the sale." Amazon also offers incentives to Associates that "directly refer" customers to its Amazon Prime program through website links, paying them a "$12 bounty" for each new enrollee.

---

1. Facts taken from the Verified Complaint are deemed true solely for purposes of this motion to dismiss. [References to the verified complaint, which is the source of the quotations in the ensuing paragraphs of the court's opinion, have been omitted. Eds.]

Prospective Associates must apply to join the program. Assuming that Amazon accepts the application, the parties enter into an Operating Agreement, which makes clear that the "Relationship of [the] Parties" is that of "independent contractors." Associates are granted "a revocable, non-exclusive, worldwide, royalty-free license ... solely for purposes of facilitating referrals from [their sites] to the Amazon Site."

Amazon authorizes Associates to place different types of links from their websites to its own. For example, Associates can set up a "product link," generally allowing them to "select one or more Products [on Amazon's site] to list on [their own] site," a "search box link," which permits visitors to the Associate's site to view Amazon merchandise related to their queries, or a "cart link," which "when clicked will allow visitors [of the Associate's site] to add products to their shopping cart and/or purchase products via [Amazon's] 1–Click feature."

As a condition of participation, Associates acknowledge that Amazon "may receive information from or about visitors to [their sites]" and that Amazon "may from time to time send [them] email updates about the Program."

The Operating Agreement further sets forth that Associates will be paid through a "referral fee" and can elect between the "Classic Fee Structure" (generally 4% of qualifying revenues from sales of products sold through special links) or the "Performance Fee Structure" (a percentage of qualifying revenues set forth in a table that varies with the number of total items shipped).

Amazon has hundreds of thousands of Associates. Thousands "of them have provided Amazon with addresses in New York." Sales to New York customers originating from New York-based Associate referrals constitute less than 1.5% of Amazon's New York sales. Without disclosing the dollar amount of those sales, Amazon simply acknowledges that its "Associates Program generates more than $10,000 per year in sales to customers located in New York."

2008 Amendment of New York's Tax Law

In New York, "every vendor of tangible personal property" is required to collect sales tax (see NY Tax Law §§ 1131[1], 1105). Included in the definition of "vendor" is:

"A person who solicits business either:

(I) by employees, independent contractors, agents or other representatives ...

and by reason thereof makes sales to persons within the state of tangible personal property or services, the use of which is taxed by this article" (NY Tax Law § 1101[b][8][i][C]).

On April 23, 2008, Governor Paterson signed into law N.Y. Tax Law § 1101(b)(8)(vi) ("Commission–Agreement Provision"), which provides that for purposes of the above-quoted section of the Tax Law:

"a person making sales of tangible personal property or services taxable under this article ('seller') shall be presumed to be soliciting business through an independent contractor or other representative if the seller enters into an agreement with a resident of this state under which the resident, for a commission or other consideration, directly or indirectly refers potential customers, whether by a link on an internet website or otherwise, to the seller, if the cumulative gross receipts from sales by the seller to customers in the state who are referred to the seller by all residents with this type of an agreement with the seller is in excess of ten thousand dollars during the preceding four quarterly periods ... This presumption may be rebutted by proof that the resident with whom the seller has an agreement did not engage in any solicitation in the state on behalf of the seller that would satisfy the nexus requirement of the United States constitution during the four quarterly periods in question."

The Commission–Agreement Provision thus requires collection of New York taxes from New Yorkers by out-of-state sellers that contractually agree to pay commissions to New York residents for referring potential customers to them, provided that more than $10,000 was generated from such New York referrals during the preceding four quarterly periods.

An out-of-state seller that could establish its commissioned New York residents did not engage in any solicitation that would satisfy the United States Constitution's "nexus requirement," would be exempt from tax collection. The State has clarified that an out-of-state seller that includes in its agreement a condition that in-state commissioned representatives are prohibited from engaging in solicitation activities in New York on its behalf and ensures compliance through a certification, may rebut the presumption that the seller is a vendor so long as the State does not subsequently determine that in-state solicitation actually took place.

Once the Commission–Agreement Provision was enacted, Amazon began collecting taxes from its New York customers under protest.

This Action

On April 25, 2008, Amazon commenced this action, alleging that the Commission–Agreement Provision "violates the Commerce Clause of the United States Constitution, both facially and as applied to Amazon, because it imposes tax collection obligations on out-of-state entities who have no substantial nexus with New York." * * *

Analysis

Amazon's complaint must be dismissed in its entirety for failure to state a cause of action. Even accepting all the facts alleged to be true, there is no basis upon which Amazon can prevail.

Commerce Clause

A State may require an entity engaged in interstate commerce to collect taxes on its behalf provided the "tax is applied to an activity with a substantial nexus with the taxing State, is fairly apportioned, does not discriminate against interstate commerce, and is fairly related to the services provided by the State" (Complete Auto Transit, Inc. v. Brady, 430 US 274, 279 [1977]).

To establish a "substantial nexus" with the taxing State, "physical presence of the vendor is required [however] it need not be substantial. Rather, it must be demonstrably more than a 'slightest presence.' And it may be manifested by ... economic activities in the taxing State performed by the vendor's personnel or on its behalf" (Matter of Orvis Co. v. Tax Appeals Tribunal, 86 NY2d 165, 178 [1995] [citations omitted], cert denied sub nom. Vermont Information Processing v. Commissioner, N.Y State Dept. of Taxation & Fin., 516 US 989). As Amazon acknowledges, physical presence "can be actual or imputed based on the in-state solicitation of sales by an employee, agent, or independent contractor of the retailer on its behalf."

In Scripto v. Carson, 362 US 207, 209 (1960), for example, the United States Supreme Court held that a State could require tax collection by an out-of-state company that had contracts with 10 in-state residents—deemed "independent contractors"—who solicited orders for products on its behalf. The agreement with the contractors provided that they were to be paid by commission and salespeople sent orders out of state for fulfillment (id.; see also Standard Pressed Steel Co. v. Washington Dept. of Revenue, 419 US 560, 561 [1975] [sufficient nexus based on single employee who resided in-state and consulted with customer therein]); Felt & Tarrant Mfg. Co. v. Gallagher, 306 US 62, 64 [1939] [collection mandated based on presence of two general agents contractually granted the right to solicit in-state orders who were to be paid by commission]; Matter of Orvis Co., 86 NY2d at 165 [in-state activity sufficient based on employee visits to solicit business]).

In contrast, if the *only* connection with the State is solicitation from out of State—through catalogs, flyers, advertisements in national periodicals or telephone calls—and delivery of merchandise to customers by common carrier or use of mail, there is an insufficient nexus for taxation purposes (see Quill Corp v. North Dakota, 504 US 298 [1992]; National Bellas Hess, Inc. v. Department of Revenue, 386 US 753 [1967]).

So long as there is a "substantial nexus" with the taxing State, the taxes that must be collected need not derive from the seller's in-state activity (National Geographic Society v. California Board of Equalization, 430 US 551, 560 [1977] [nonprofit society required to collect taxes from California mail-order customers based on maintenance of two offices in California from which advertising was solicited for its monthly magazine]).

Facial Challenge

"A party mounting a facial constitutional challenge bears the substantial burden of demonstrating that 'in any degree and in every conceivable application' the law suffers wholesale constitutional impairment" (Matter of Moran Towing Corp. v. Urbach, 99 NY2d 443, 448 [2003] [citations omitted]). The statute's "challenger must establish that no set of circumstances exists under which the Act would be valid" (id. [citation omitted]).

Amazon argues that the statute is facially invalid because "it imposes tax collection obligations based on activities that are insufficient to create a substantial nexus under the dormant Commerce Clause." Amazon is wrong.

The Commission–Agreement Provision is carefully crafted to ensure that there is a sufficient basis for requiring collection of New York taxes and, if such a basis does not exist, it gives the seller an out. The statute first requires that a seller enter into a contract with a New York resident before any obligation will be imposed. Next, before tax-collection is required, it mandates that the New York resident refer potential customers to the seller. The measure further necessitates an arrangement whereby the seller pays the New York resident a commission or provides other consideration for the referral. Finally, New York's Tax Law requires that the seller receive in excess of $10,000 from New York customers referred to it through its business arrangement.

All of these requirements make clear that a tax-collection obligation will only be imposed based on an out-of-state seller's conscious decision to contract with in-state residents who collectively refer more than $10,000 of New York based business. The statute is targeted at requiring tax collection when an out-of-state seller avails itself of the benefit of in-state contractors compensated for referrals. As an added safeguard the Commission–Agreement Provision makes plain that a seller does not have to collect taxes so long as its New York actors "did not engage in any solicitation in the state [on its behalf] that would satisfy the nexus requirement of the United States Constitution." Thus, a seller is afforded the opportunity to prove that none of its contractors actively sought sales on its behalf in New York.

There is nothing infirm about the Commission–Agreement Provision, which contemplates a substantial nexus with New York. Significantly, New York residents, with whom out-of-state sellers entered into agreements, must refer more than $10,000 of business—and New York business no less—before there is any collection obligation. The statute thus requires " 'demonstrably more than a 'slightest presence' and obligates collection of taxes based on economic activities in New York performed by the vendor's personnel or on its behalf' " (Matter of Orvis Co., 86 NY2d at 178 [citations omitted]).

Amazon urges that the statute would bring within its ambit "simple advertising by in-state advertisers." The Commission–Agreement Provision, however, does no such thing. It imposes a tax-collection obligation on sellers who contractually agree to compensate New York residents for business that they generate and not simply for publicity. Amazon has not come close to refuting the Tax Law's presumed constitutionality and the statute must be upheld.

As–Applied Challenge

Amazon maintains that it lacks a substantial nexus with New York and that its Associates' activities are insufficient to justify imposition of New York tax-collection obligations. It argues that it has no physical presence in New York and that its Associates have no role in its sales transactions, which are completed out-of-state. Amazon emphasizes that its Associates "are mere advertisers who do not solicit sales at Amazon's behest" and that they are not "traveling salesmen"—they do not necessarily personally solicit sales from New York residents. It asserts that all its Operating Agreements provide for is placement of links on Associates' websites.

Amazon further states that Associates' referrals to New York customers are not significantly associated with its ability to establish and maintain a market for sales in New York because they account for less than 1.5% of its New York sales. Amazon complains that "it is practically impossible" for it to determine with certainty which of its Associates are New York residents and then to disprove solicitation.

None of these allegations, however, sufficiently state a claim for violation of the Commerce Clause.

Amazon contracts with thousands of Associates that provided it with a New York address. Certainly, if Amazon were to have a dispute with any of them, it could easily ascertain New York residency for purposes of a lawsuit. All of the information is publicly available. Indeed, there is no reason that the Associates application, which Amazon may accept or reject, cannot inquire about New York resident status.

It does not matter, moreover, that Associates do not solicit New York business at Amazon's direct behest or that Amazon contractually prohibits them from engaging in certain limited specified conduct such as offering its customers money back for Amazon purchases made through Associate links.[2] Amazon chooses to benefit from New York Associates that are free to target New Yorkers and encourage Amazon sales, all the while earning money for Amazon in return for which Amazon pays them commissions. Amazon does not discourage its Associates from reaching out to customers or contributors and pressing Amazon sales.

Amazon has not contested that it contracts with thousands of New Yorkers and that as a result of New York referrals to New York residents it obtains the benefit of more than $10,000 annually. Amazon should not be permitted to escape tax collection indirectly, through use of an incentivized New York sales force to generate revenue, when it would not be able to achieve tax avoidance directly through use of New York employees engaged in the very same activities.

In its complaint, Amazon fails to allege that its New York Associates do not solicit business for it from New York customers. None of Amazon's claims, even if all true, would justify a conclusion that the Commission-

---

2. Amazon does not contractually prohibit in-state solicitation of business on its behalf.

Agreement Provision cannot legally be applied to Amazon. Amazon's first cause of action for declaratory relief based on violation of the Commerce Clause is therefore dismissed.

* * *

[The court rejected two additional claims advanced by Amazon.com LLC.]

In the end, the Commission–Agreement Provision does not broadly tax any and all internet sales to New York consumers. It requires a substantial nexus between an out-of-state seller and New York through a contract to pay commissions for referrals with a New York resident along with realization of more than $10,000 of revenue from New York sales earned through the arrangement. The neutral statute simply obligates out-of-state sellers to shoulder their fair-share of the tax-collection burden when using New Yorkers to earn profit from other New Yorkers.

Accordingly, it is ORDERED that the State's motion to dismiss the complaint * * * is GRANTED and Amazon's cross-motion for summary judgment is denied as moot.

NOTES AND QUESTIONS

A. *The Scope of the New York Statute.* Recall that the New York statute presumes nexus "if the seller enters into an agreement with a resident of this state under which the resident, for a commission *or other consideration*, directly or indirectly refers potential customers, whether by a link on an internet website *or otherwise*, to the seller* * *" (emphasis added). Does the statute establish nexus in cases where an online retailer hires a New York resident to advertise on its behalf? In a memorandum issued in May 2008, the state's Taxpayer Guidance Division ruled that "an agreement to place an advertisement does not give rise to the presumption" of nexus. See, New Presumption Applicable to Definition of Sales Tax Vendor, May 8, 2008, TSB–M–8(3)S. Is this interpretation consistent with the plain language of the statute? Note also that the statute presumes nexus where the online retailer "enters into an agreement with a *resident* of this state* * *" (emphasis added). The statutory language seems to assume that the resident's activities on behalf of the retailer are taking place in New York. Is it possible for a New York resident to engage in the direct or indirect referral of customers to the online retailer outside of New York? If so, would the presumption of nexus be consistent with *Quill*? In other words, is it the residency of Amazon's Associates that matters or the location of that person's activities on behalf of Amazon?

B. *The Prospect of Congressional Intervention.* For the past several years, as part of the "Streamlined Sales Tax Project" (SSTP), several states have undertaken to simplify and coordinate their sales and use tax rules in an effort to persuade Congress to enact legislation granting them the authority to require remote sellers (i.e., those without a physical presence in the state) to collect and remit taxes to the participating states. Although numerous bills have been introduced over the years, Congress has not yet (as of late 2009) approved the legislation. Chapter 8, infra, provides further detail regarding the SSTP.

C. *Reconsidering Nexus Criteria in an Age of Electronic Commerce.* The advent of the Internet and the explosion of electronic commerce have caused many observers to question the appropriateness of existing nexus standards. Traditional nexus principles, after all, are rooted in concepts of territoriality and the physical presence of the taxpayer in the state. But the emphasis on territoriality and physical presence makes little sense in cyberspace. The signal characteristic of cyberspace is the irrelevance of geographic borders. As the co-directors of the Cyberspace Law Institute have declared, "[g]lobal computer-based communications cut across territorial borders, creating a new realm of human activity and undermining the feasibility—and legitimacy—of laws based on geographic boundaries." David R. Johnson & David Post, "Law and Borders—The Rise of Law in Cyberspace," 48 Stan. L. Rev. 1367 (1996). This thought has not been lost on those grappling with the problems raised by state taxation of electronic commerce. They recognize that traditional concepts of nexus may not be entirely appropriate for electronic commerce and Internet-related services, and that we need to "rethink nexus standards as they apply to the Internet and Internet-based transactions." Interactive Services Association, "Logging On to Cyberspace Tax Policy: An Interactive Services Association Task Force White Paper" (December 1996), reprinted in State Tax Notes, Jan. 20, 1997, pp. 209, 221. The U.S. Treasury has made the same point in the context of U.S. income taxation of international transactions:

> The concept of a U.S. trade or business was developed in the context of conventional types of commerce, which generally are conducted through identifiable physical locations. Electronic commerce, on the other hand, may be conducted without regard to national boundaries and may dissolve the link between an income producing activity and a specific location. From a certain perspective, electronic commerce doesn't seem to occur in any physical location but instead takes place in the nebulous world of "cyberspace." Persons engaged in electronic commerce could be located anywhere in the world and their customers will be ignorant of, or indifferent to, their location.

Department of the Treasury, Office of Tax Policy, Selected Tax Policy Implications of Global Electronic Commerce 26 (1996).

These developments raise the question whether jurisdictional principles based on physical presence will remain viable or whether they will gradually be regarded, at least in some sectors of the economy, as relics of a bygone era when physical—rather than digital—contact was the norm and when productive activity was defined largely in terms of transfers of tangible personal property rather than in terms of the exchange of services, information, and other intangibles. See generally Walter Hellerstein, "Jurisdiction to Tax Income and Consumption in the New Economy: A Theoretical and Comparative Perspective," 38 Ga. L. Rev. 1 (2003); Walter Hellerstein, "Deconstructing the Debate Over State Taxation of Electronic Commerce," 13 Harv. J.L. & Tech. 549 (2000); Walter Hellerstein, "State and Local Taxation of Electronic Commerce: Reflections on the Emerging Issues," 52 Miami L. Rev. 691

(1998); John A. Swain, "State Income Taxation: A Jurisprudential and Policy Perspective," 45 Wm. & Mary L. Rev. 319 (2003); John A. Swain, "State Sales and Use Tax Jurisdiction: An Economic Nexus Standard for the Twenty–First Century," 38 Ga. L. Rev. 343 (2003). The fall 2003 issue of the *Georgia Law Review*, in which two of the articles cited above appear, contains a valuable symposium entitled "Jurisdiction to Tax in the New Economy: International, National, and Subnational Perspectives," 38 Ga. L. Rev. 1 et seq. (2003).

C. CONSTITUTIONAL PARAMETERS OF STATE INCOME TAX JURISDICTION

The Court in *Quill* embraced a bright-line test of physical presence for sales and use tax collection nexus. Recall, however, that in so doing the Court declared that "we have not, in our review of other types of taxes, articulated the same physical-presence requirement that *Bellas Hess* established for sales and use taxes" and that "our Commerce Clause jurisprudence now favors more flexible balancing analyses." This naturally raises the question whether *Quill*'s "physical presence" requirement extends to income taxes, which are addressed by the cases in this section.

As you work your way through these nexus or jurisdiction-to-tax questions, you should keep in mind that they often involve two separate inquiries, even though these inquiries may not be separately explicated. First, there is the question whether there is jurisdiction over the taxpayer. Second, there is the question whether there is jurisdiction over the transaction, activity, or event (in the case of an excise tax) or the income (in the case of an income tax) or the property (in the case of a property tax). For example, a state could have jurisdiction over a taxpayer, but not over a sale that the taxpayer makes in another state. Alternatively, the state could have jurisdiction over a sale, but not over the taxpayer who makes it. Similarly, a state could have jurisdiction over a taxpayer, but not over income the taxpayer earns, or, alternatively, jurisdiction over income, but not over the taxpayer who earns it. In considering the materials below on income tax jurisdiction, you should be especially careful to keep both nexus questions in mind and to ask yourself which nexus question is at issue. In Chapter 7, we will consider in greater detail the matter of jurisdiction over the income tax base in the context of state corporate franchise and income taxes.

TAX COMMISSIONER OF THE STATE OF WEST VIRGINIA v. MBNA AMERICA BANK, N.A.

Supreme Court of Appeals of West Virginia, 2006.
220 W.Va. 163, 640 S.E.2d 226, cert. denied, 551 U.S. 1141, 127 S.Ct. 2997 (2007).

MAYNARD, JUSTICE:

Appellant MBNA America Bank appeals the June 27, 2005, order of the Circuit Court of Kanawha County that ruled that imposition of West

Virginia's business franchise tax and corporation net income tax on
MBNA, a Delaware Corporation, for tax years 1998 and 1999, does not
violate the Commerce Clause. For the reasons that follow, we affirm the
circuit court.

I.

FACTS

Appellant MBNA America Bank is a foreign corporation which has its
principal place of business and commercial domicile in Wilmington, Delaware. During the two years in question, 1998 and 1999, MBNA had no
real or tangible personal property and no employees located in West
Virginia. The principal business of MBNA at the relevant times in this
case was issuing and servicing VISA and MasterCard credit cards. This
business included the extension of unsecured credit to customers who use
these credit cards. MBNA promoted its business in West Virginia via mail
and telephone solicitation.

* * * In 1998, MBNA's gross receipts attributable to West Virginia
customers amounted to $8,419,431.00, and in 1999, its gross receipts
amounted to $10,163,788.00. For tax year 1998, MBNA paid a West
Virginia Business Franchise Tax[1] of $32,010.00 and a West Virginia
Corporation Net Income tax of $168,034.00. For tax year 1999, MBNA
paid a Business Franchise Tax in the amount of $42,339.00 and a
Corporation Net Income Tax in the amount of $220,897.00.

Thereafter, MBNA filed refund claims with the State Tax Commissioner * * * on the basis that the Tax Commissioner lacked jurisdiction
over MBNA. The Commissioner denied the refunds based on its finding
that MBNA regularly engaged in business in West Virginia under the
applicable statutes.[3]

MBNA subsequently filed an appeal from the Tax Commissioner's
decision with the Office of Tax Appeals (hereafter "OTA"). By decision
dated October 22, 2004, the Chief Administrative Law Judge (hereafter
"ALJ") of the OTA ruled in favor of MBNA * * *. The ALJ reasoned that
under the Commerce Clause, a state may not subject an activity to a tax
unless that activity has a "substantial nexus" with the taxing state. The
ALJ further reasoned that a substantial nexus requires a finding that the
putative taxpayer has a physical presence in the taxing state, and mere
economic exploitation of the market is not sufficient. Because it was
agreed that MBNA does not have a physical presence in West Virginia, the

---

1. The West Virginia Business Franchise Tax is * * * imposed on corporations and partnerships for the privilege of doing business in this state.

3. The statutory nexus required for the business franchise tax is found in W.Va.Code § 11–
23–5a(d) (1996), which states in part:

A financial organization that has its commercial domicile in another state is presumed to be
regularly engaging in business in this state if during any year it obtains or solicits business
with twenty or more persons within this state, or if the sum of the value of its gross receipts
attributable to sources in this state equals or exceeds one hundred thousand dollars.

[An identical standard applies to the corporation net income tax. Eds.].

ALJ concluded that the State's business franchise and corporation net income taxes could not be imposed on MBNA's activity within the State.

The Tax Commissioner appealed the ALJ's decision to the Circuit Court of Kanawha County. The circuit court reversed the decision of the ALJ. According to the circuit court, physical presence is not necessary in order to show a substantial nexus for purposes of state taxation of foreign corporations. Rather, the circuit court found that MBNA's significant business in the state is sufficient to meet the substantial nexus standard. Therefore, concluded the circuit court, MBNA had a substantial nexus with West Virginia during the tax years in question so that imposition of the State's business franchise and corporate net income taxes on MBNA did not violate the Commerce Clause. MBNA now appeals the circuit court's order.

II.

STANDARD OF REVIEW

The Court has previously recognized that a lower court's determination of whether a state tax violates the Commerce Clause is reviewed de novo.

III.

DISCUSSION

The single issue raised in this appeal is whether application of West Virginia's business franchise and corporation net income taxes to MBNA, a business with no physical presence in this state, violates the Commerce Clause of the United States Constitution. * * *

The Supreme Court's interpretation of the dormant Commerce Clause "has evolved substantially over the years, particularly as that Clause concerns limitations on state taxation powers." Quill Corp. v. North Dakota, 504 U.S. 298, 309, 112 S.Ct. 1904, 1911 (1992) (citation omitted). * * * In Complete Auto Transit, Inc. v. Brady, 430 U.S. 274, 97 S.Ct. 1076 (1977), the Court set forth the current test for determining whether a state tax violated the Commerce Clause. * * * A state tax on interstate commerce will not be sustained unless it: "(1) has a substantial nexus with the State; (2) is fairly apportioned; (3) does not discriminate; and (4) is fairly related to the services provided by the State."[7]

The current issue deals solely with the "substantial nexus" prong of the *Complete Auto* test. Specifically, we are asked to decide whether the substantial nexus standard can only be met by showing that the putative taxpayer has an actual physical presence in the taxing state. In answering this question, we must consider the Supreme Court's decisions in National Bellas Hess, Inc. v. Department of Revenue, 386 U.S. 753, 87 S.Ct. 1389

---

7. This test is referred to * * * as the *Complete Auto* test and is generally known by that name. Therefore, we refer to it as the *Complete Auto* test in this opinion.

(1967), overruled, in part, Quill supra, and *Quill*, the Court's most recent pronouncement on state tax jurisdiction.

* * *

[The court proceeds to summarize the facts and holdings of *Bellas Hess* and *Quill*.]

The major question left open by the Supreme Court's opinion in *Quill* is the one that now confronts us: Does the physical presence requirement applicable to determining the constitutionality of requiring out-of-state mail-order houses to collect use taxes on in-state sales under the Commerce Clause extend to other types of state taxes? MBNA's position is that *Quill* extends to the business franchise and corporation net income taxes at issue. The Tax Commissioner posits, on the other hand, that physical presence is not a requirement of the substantial nexus standard in regards to the taxes at issue.[11]

After careful consideration of the parties' arguments, the relevant legal authority, and the Court's reasoning in *Quill*, we conclude that *Quill*'s physical-presence requirement for showing a substantial Commerce Clause nexus applies only to use and sales taxes and not to business franchise and corporation net income taxes. There are several reasons for our conclusion. First, we agree with the Tax Commissioner that a close reading of *Quill* indicates that its reaffirmation of the *Bellas Hess* physical-presence test for use and sales taxes under the Commerce Clause is grounded primarily on *stare decisis*. For example, the Court in *Quill* notes that "[w]hile contemporary Commerce Clause jurisprudence might not dictate the same result were the issue to arise for the first time today, *Bellas Hess* is not inconsistent with *Complete Auto* and our recent cases." Quill, 504 U.S. at 311, 112 S.Ct. at 1912. The Court further indicated that "the *Bellas Hess* rule has engendered substantial reliance and has become part of the basic framework of a sizable industry. The interest in stability and orderly development of the law that undergirds the doctrine of *stare decisis* therefore counsels adherence to settled precedent." Id., 504 U.S. at 317, 112 S.Ct. at 1916 (internal quotations and citation omitted). Finally, the Court concluded that "the continuing value of a bright-line rule in this area and the doctrine and principles of *stare decisis* indicate that the *Bellas Hess* rule remains good law." Id.

---

11. The Tax Commissioner cites several cases to this Court in support of its position that *Quill*'s physical-presence requirement applies only to sales and use taxes including Lanco, Inc. v. Director of Taxation, 379 N.J.Super. 562, 879 A.2d 1234 (2005); A & F Trademark, Inc. v. Tolson, 167 N.C.App. 150, 605 S.E.2d 187 (2004), cert. denied, 546 U.S. 821, 126 S.Ct. 353 (2005); Secretary, Dep't of Revenue, State of La. v. Gap (Apparel), Inc., 886 So.2d 459 (La.App. 2004); and Geoffrey, Inc. v. S.C. Tax Com'n, 313 S.C. 15, 437 S.E.2d 13 (1993). We find the persuasiveness of these cases to be limited, however, because the primary issue in each case is whether a state has jurisdiction to impose a state income tax on foreign corporations with no physical presence in the taxing state but whose intangibles, such as a trademark, are used in the state by a licensee. These courts reason, in part, that the intangibles located in the state provide a sufficient nexus for income tax purposes. In the instant case, there is no claim that MBNA has intangibles in West Virginia that provide a sufficient nexus for tax purposes.

This reasoning is supported by several legal commentators. See John A. Swain, State Income Tax Jurisdiction: A Jurisprudential and Policy Perspective, 45 Wm. & Mary L. Rev. 319 (October 2003) (arguing that the *Quill* Court relied on *stare decisis* rather than defending the physical presence test on the merits); Richard D. Pomp & Michael J. McIntyre, State Taxation of Mail–Order Sales of Computers After *Quill*: An Evaluation of MTC Bulletin 95–1, 11 State Tax Notes 177, 179–80 (July 15, 1996) (maintaining that *Quill* is essentially a political decision responding to concerns about retroactivity and the practical consequences of overruling *Bellas Hess*); Michael T. Fatale, State Tax Jurisdiction and the Mythical "Physical Presence" Constitutional Standard, 54 Tax Lawyer 105, 113 (Fall, 2000) (opining that "[a] primary basis for the [*Quill*] holding was the Court's conclusion that the mail order industry had grown in large part in reliance on *Bellas Hess*[,] [and] [b]ecause the *Bellas Hess* rule had become the 'basic framework' of a sizable industry") (footnotes omitted). Thus, because *Quill*'s physical-presence test for sales and use taxes was based in large part on the mail order industry's reliance on *Bellas Hess*, we are not compelled to apply *Quill*'s physical presence standard to the present circumstances.

Second, the Supreme Court appears to have expressly limited *Quill*'s scope to sales and use taxes. First, the *Quill* Court noted that "[a]lthough we have not, in our review of other types of taxes, articulated the same physical-presence requirement that *Bellas Hess* established for sales and use taxes, that silence does not imply repudiation of the *Bellas Hess* rule." Quill, 504 U.S. at 314, 112 S.Ct. at 1914. Also, the Court commented that "although in our cases subsequent to *Bellas Hess* and concerning other types of taxes we have not adopted a similar bright-line, physical-presence requirement, our reasoning in those cases does not compel that we now reject the rule that *Bellas Hess* established in the area of sales and use taxes." Id., 504 U.S. at 317, 112 S.Ct. at 1916. We believe that a reasonable construction of this language clearly implies that *Quill* applies only to sales and use taxes and not to other types of state taxes.

Third, the *Bellas Hess* and *Quill* Courts based their decisions in part on the fact that compliance with administrative regulations in the collection of sales and use taxes places an undue burden on interstate commerce. Specifically, the *Bellas Hess* Court explained:

* * *

... For if Illinois can impose such burdens, so can every other State, and so, indeed, can every municipality, every school district, and every other political subdivision throughout the Nation with power to impose sales and use taxes. The many variations in rates of tax, in allowable exemptions, and in administrative and record-keeping requirements could entangle National's interstate business in a virtual welter of complicated obligations to local jurisdictions with no legitimate claim to impose a fair share of the cost of the local government.

The very purpose of the Commerce Clause was to ensure a national economy free from such unjustifiable local entanglements. Under the Constitution, this is a domain where Congress alone has the power of regulation and control.

Bellas Hess, 386 U.S. at 758–760, 87 S.Ct. at 1392–1393 (internal quotation marks and footnotes omitted). * * *

The *Quill* Court likewise recognized the potential burden on interstate commerce posed by North Dakota's sales and use taxes.

North Dakota's use tax illustrates well how a state tax might unduly burden interstate commerce. On its face, North Dakota law imposes a collection duty on every vendor who advertises in the State three times in a single year. Thus, absent the *Bellas Hess* rule, a publisher who included a subscription card in three issues of its magazine, a vendor whose radio advertisements were heard in North Dakota on three occasions, and a corporation whose telephone sales force made three calls into the State, all would be subject to the collection duty. What is more significant, similar obligations might be imposed by the Nation's 6,000–plus taxing jurisdictions.

Quill, 504 U.S. at 313 fn. 6, 112 S.Ct. at 1913 fn. 6, citing Bellas Hess, 386 U.S. at 759–760, 87 S.Ct. at 1393 * * *.

In contrast to the sales and use taxes described in *Bellas Hess* and *Quill*, the franchise and income taxes at issue in this case do not appear to cause the same degree of compliance burdens. As noted above, the task of collecting taxes and remitting them to the government demands knowledge of a multitude of administrative regulations, including various deductions and tax rates, as well as record-keeping requirements. Also, as a general matter, sales and use taxes must be remitted to the government on a more frequent basis than income and franchise taxes. For example, in West Virginia vendors are charged with the duty of collecting from purchasers the consumer sales and service tax and paying the tax to the Tax Commissioner on a monthly basis. This entails making out and mailing to the Commissioner a return for the preceding month on a prescribed form showing the total gross proceeds of the vendor's business during that time, the gross proceeds of the vendor's business upon which the tax is based, the amount of the tax for which the vendor is liable, and any further information necessary in the computation and collection of the tax which the Commissioner may require. In contrast, income and franchise taxes are paid by the business entity itself so that no collection duties are involved. Also, income and franchise taxes are generally paid annually.

Finally, we believe that the *Bellas Hess* physical-presence test, articulated in 1967, makes little sense in today's world. In the previous almost forty years, business practices have changed dramatically. When *Bellas Hess* was decided, it was generally necessary that an entity have a physical presence of some sort, such as a warehouse, office, or salesperson, in a state in order to generate substantial business in that state. This is no longer true. The development and proliferation of communication technology exhibited, for example, by the growth of electronic commerce now makes it possible for an entity to have a significant economic presence in a state absent any physical presence there. For this reason, we believe that the mechanical application of a physical-presence standard to franchise and income taxes is a poor measuring stick of an entity's true nexus with a state.

Accordingly, we now hold that the United States Supreme Court's determination in Quill Corp. v. North Dakota, 504 U.S. 298, 112 S.Ct. 1904 (1992), that an entity's physical presence in a state is required to meet the "substantial nexus" prong of Complete Auto Transit, Inc. v. Brady, 430 U.S. 274, 97 S.Ct. 1076, 51 L.Ed.2d 326 (1977), applies only to state sales and use taxes and not to state business franchise and corporation net income taxes.

Rather than a physical presence standard, this Court believes that a significant economic presence test is a better indicator of whether substantial nexus exists for Commerce Clause purposes. At least one legal commentator has suggested such a test and to some degree defined its parameters. See [Christina R.] Edson, [*Quill's* Constitutional Jurisprudence and Tax Nexus Standards in and Age of Electronic Commerce,] 49 Tax Lawyer [893,] at 943 (1996).] According to this commentator, a substantial economic presence standard "incorporates due process 'purposeful direction' towards a state while examining the degree to which a company has exploited a local market." Id. Further, "[a] substantial economic presence analysis involves an examination of both the quality and quantity of the company's economic presence." Id., 49 Tax Law. at 944. Finally, under this test, "[p]urposeful direction towards a state is analyzed as it is for Due Process Clause purposes," and the Commerce Clause analysis requires the additional examination of "the frequency, quantity and systematic nature of a taxpayer's economic contacts with a state." Id., 49 Tax Law. at 945. We find this rationale persuasive and will apply it in determining the constitutionality of the taxes at issue.

First, however, we must address several objections proffered by MBNA to the application of any standard other than physical presence. Initially, MBNA contends that a greater nexus requirement should be applied to the imposition of direct taxes such as those at issue because such taxes are actually more burdensome. This is because sales and use taxes merely require an entity to collect the tax from consumers and remit the tax money to the government, thus suffering the administrative complications and inconvenience but not the cost of the tax. In sharp contrast, says MBNA, franchise and income taxes not only have compliance burdens but also must be paid from the entity's own pocket. For support, MBNA cites National Geographic Society v. California Bd. of Equalization, 430 U.S. 551, 97 S.Ct. 1386 (1977), in which the Supreme Court distinguished between a use tax and a direct tax and implied that a higher Commerce Clause standard would be required to support the imposition of a direct tax.[16]

We do not agree with MBNA's argument on this issue. Notably, the Supreme Court's comment in *National Geographic Society* was dicta in that it was not necessary to the decision in that case. In contrast, the *Bellas Hess* and *Quill* Courts placed significant weight on the fact that there are substantial compliance burdens attached to the collection of sales and use taxes. Therefore, we reject MBNA's claim that the imposition of direct taxes is a greater burden than the duty to collect taxes so that the *Bellas Hess/Quill* physical-presence test should also apply to the imposition of the direct taxes at issue.

MBNA also argues that adoption of any substantial nexus requirement short of showing actual physical presence is in fact simply applying a Due Process minimum contacts standard in violation of *Quill* which expressly held that the Due Process and Commerce Clause analyses are separate. We disagree. The Due Process Clause requires merely some minimum connection between a state and the person, property or transaction it seeks to tax. In contrast, a substantial nexus under the Commerce Clause requires that an entity's contacts with the taxing state be more frequent and systematic in nature. Additionally, an entity's exploitation of the market must be greater in degree than under the Due Process standard so that its economic presence can be characterized as significant or substantial. In sum, although a substantial economic presence standard is by nature more elastic than the bright-line physical presence test, we are convinced that when properly applied, a greater nexus is required under the substantial economic presence standard that under the minimum contacts analysis.

Finally, MBNA avers that the only case from a foreign jurisdiction that is factually on point with the instant case is J.C. Penney Nat'l Bank v. Johnson, 19 S.W.3d 831 (Tenn.Ct.App.1999), in which the Tennessee appellate court applied the physical-presence test to Tennessee's attempted imposition of income taxes on an out-of-state credit card company. While we acknowledge that *J.C. Penney* is factually on point and addresses the same issue as the one before us, for the reasons set forth above we reject the reasoning in *J.C. Penney*, and decline to apply it to the instant case.[18]

---

16. Specifically, the Court in *National Geographic Society* reasoned that,

The case for the validity of the imposition upon the out-of-state seller enjoying such services of a duty to collect a use tax is even stronger. The out-of-state seller runs no risk of double taxation. The consumer's identification as a resident of the taxing State is self-evident. The out-of-state seller becomes liable for the tax only by failing or refusing to collect the tax from that resident consumer. Thus, the sole burden imposed upon the out-of-state seller by statutes [imposing a use tax] is the administrative one of collecting it.

430 U.S. at 558, 97 S.Ct. at 1391 (citations omitted).

18. MBNA also argues that physical presence has been a base-line fact in every tax nexus case decided by the Supreme Court since *Complete Auto*. In other words, says MBNA, the Supreme Court has never upheld a finding of nexus in any case involving a state tax where the putative taxpayer had no in-state presence. It is equally true, however, as noted by the Commissioner, that

We now turn our attention to the facts of the instant case to determine whether MBNA had a substantial nexus with this State during the time period in question. The record shows that MBNA continuously and systematically engaged in direct mail and telephone solicitation and promotion in West Virginia. Further, in tax year 1998, MBNA had significant gross receipts attributable to West Virginia customers in the amount of $8,419,431.00, and in tax year 1999, MBNA had significant gross receipts attributable to its West Virginia customers in the amount of $10,163,788.00. In light of these facts, this Court has no trouble concluding that MBNA's systematic and continuous business activity in this State produced significant gross receipts attributable to its West Virginia customers which indicate a significant economic presence sufficient to meet the substantial nexus prong of *Complete Auto*.

Finally, prior to concluding, we simply wish to acknowledge the great challenge in applying the Commerce Clause to the ever-evolving practices of the marketplace. James Madison, Benjamin Franklin, and the other Framers at the Constitutional Convention who adopted the Commerce Clause lived in a world that is impossible for people living today to imagine. The Framers' concept of commerce consisted of goods transported in horse-drawn, wooden-wheeled wagons or ships with sails. They lived in a world with no electricity, no indoor plumbing, no automobiles, no paved roads, no airplanes, no telephones, no televisions, no computers, no plastic credit cards, no recorded music, and no iPods. Likewise, it would have been impossible for the Framers to imagine our world. When they fashioned the Commerce Clause, they could not possibly have foreseen the complex and varied ways that commerce is conducted today, especially via the internet and electronic commerce. It would be nonsense to suggest that they could foresee or fathom a time in which a person's telephone call to his or her local credit card company would be routinely answered by a person in Bombay, India, or that a consumer could purchase virtually any product on a computer with the click of a mouse without leaving home. This recognition of the staggering evolution in commerce from the Framers' time up through today suggests to this Court that in applying the Commerce Clause we must eschew rigid and mechanical legal formulas in favor of a fresh application of Commerce Clause principles tempered with healthy doses of fairness and common sense. This is what we have attempted to do herein.

* * *

Affirmed.

BENJAMIN, JUSTICE, dissenting:

In its opinion finding tax liability for an out-of-state corporation with no presence, tangible or intangible, in West Virginia on income realized out-of-state by that corporation from accounts kept out-of-state, the majority, in its opinion, boldly goes where no court has gone before. In doing

---

no Supreme Court decision has applied the *Bellas Hess* physical presence requirement to a state income tax. Thus, we are not persuaded by MBNA's argument.

so, the majority relies not on bedrock constitutional principles or on established legal precedent, but rather on legal commentaries with thinly veiled state-favoring taxing agendas, a strained and inaccurate reading of the United States Supreme Court's decision in Quill Corp. v. North Dakota, 504 U.S. 298, 112 S.Ct. 1904 (1992), and a unilateral restatement of the important policy considerations which led to the inclusion of the Commerce Clause within the United States Constitution because, according to the majority opinion, the framers could not possibly have foreseen the future. The majority opinion gives legal sanction to a state taxing scheme which impermissibly burdens the interstate commerce of the nation. I therefore dissent.

There is no precedential support whatsoever for the conclusions reached by the majority decision. None. None at the state level. None at the federal level. Ignoring that our consideration here should be the effect of the tax in question on interstate commerce, rather than the type of tax it is, none of the rhetoric raised by the majority opinion explains why a state's imposition of a tax on an out-of-state corporation with no presence, tangible or intangible, on income realized from an out-of-state account does not adversely affect the nation's interstate commerce, an analysis identified by the United States Supreme Court as the cornerstone of constitutional jurisprudence. The only state court decision on point with the specific credit card issues raised herein determined that the State of Tennessee exceeded its taxing jurisdiction in attempting to collect taxes from an out-of-state corporation on income generated by out-of-state credit accounts. J.C. Penney National Bank v. Johnson, 19 S.W.3d 831 (Tenn.Ct.App. 1999), cert. denied, 531 U.S. 927, 121 S.Ct. 305 (2000).

* * *

Among the most fundamental precepts of state taxation from a Commerce Clause perspective is that there must be a "substantial nexus" between the interstate activity sought to be taxed and the taxing State. Complete Auto Transit, Inc. v. Brady, 430 U.S. 274 97 S.Ct. 1076 (1977). Under *Complete Auto* a state tax is permitted under the Commerce Clause if it (1) is applied to an activity with a substantial nexus with the taxing state, (2) is fairly apportioned, (3) does not discriminate against interstate commerce, and (4) is fairly related to the services provided by the state. While I agree with my colleagues that the "substantial nexus" prong of this test is ripe for clarification by the United States Supreme Court, I disagree with them to the extent that the majority opinion finds insufficient guidance in the existing jurisprudence of the United States Supreme Court to conclude that the State's present attempt to levy a tax on income realized outside the State by an out-of-state corporation with no presence, tangible or intangible, in the State violates the Commerce Clause.

* * *

We must assume that the United States Supreme Court chose its words carefully in setting forth the first prong of the *Complete Auto* test, that the tax in question is sought by the taxing state to be applied "to an activity" with a substantial nexus with the taxing state. Even if the majority opinion was correct, which I believe it was not, that MBNA's interstate activities constitute a sufficiently high showing of presence to permit taxing jurisdiction under the "substantial" nexus test of the Commerce Clause, the majority opinion simply reaches the question of whether the State of West Virginia may seek to tax MBNA as an out-of-state corporation. The majority opinion completely fails to consider the effect of the tax on interstate commerce. On this second question of whether a state can impose tax on income generated out-of-state, the majority opinion likewise fails. Here, there is no question but that the credit card accounts which give rise to MBNA's income are located outside West Virginia.

I must admit to being intrigued by the majority opinion's description of its nexus requirement as a "significant economic presence test" as much for its vagueness as for its embodiment as the antithesis of the "bright line" standards set forth by the United States Supreme Court in *Quill* and National Bellas Hess v. Department of Revenue of Illinois, 386 U.S. 753, 87 S.Ct. 1389 (1967), overruled, in part, by *Quill*. The reality is that by endorsing a nexus standard which permits West Virginia to assess a tax on an out-of-state corporation with no property, tangible or intangible, in this state on income realized from credit accounts maintained and serviced in another state, the majority merges the nexus requirements of the Due Process Clause and the Commerce Clause and effectively returns to the merged nexus jurisprudence of 1967, in *Bellas Hess*, albeit with the minimal due process requirements now carrying the day for nexus determination rather that the physical presence requirement of *Bellas Hess*. While MBNA may meet the minimal nexus requirement for it to be on notice from a due process basis that it may be subject to taxation, the majority opinion fails to show how the out-of-state credit account, which is the basis for the income sought to be taxed, meets the substantial nexus requirements of *Complete Auto* and *Quill*. * * *

The majority opinion attempts mightily to distinguish between forms of taxes, such as sales and use taxes on the one hand, and income and franchise taxes on the other hand, in attempting to defend its disregard for the substantial nexus standards required in *Quill*. The majority's argument appears to be that because the instant case concerns the taxation of income realized by an out-of-state corporation from accounts in Delaware and because *Quill* instead involved use and sales taxes from purchases made by purchasers within the taxing state with delivery of goods to occur also within the taxing state, this Court is at liberty to disregard those parts of *Quill* with which it disagrees. This argument is not persuasive. In so disregarding the substantial nexus requirements of *Quill* because *Quill* involved use and sales taxes, it is interesting that the majority opinion nevertheless fully embraces the precedent of the United

States Supreme Court in *Complete Auto*, a case which also involved use and sales taxes—not income taxes. * * *

* * *

The jurisprudential reality is that the United States Supreme Court has never held in any state tax case that the nexus requirements of the Commerce Clause can be satisfied in the absence of a taxpayer's physical presence in the taxing state. The principles of *stare decisis* are no less relevant to state taxes in general, than they are to sales and use taxes * * * It would be a strange constitutional doctrine that would countenance one nexus standard for sales and use taxes under the Commerce Clause, and a more relaxed nexus standard for corporate net income and other state taxes.

In the first place, it does not appear that the differences between the use tax collection obligation and liability for income taxation are so significant as to justify different rules under the Commerce Clause. It is certainly difficult to see distinctions that give effect to physical presence as a necessary element for "substantial nexus" for some taxes and not for others. Arguably, the collection of use and sales taxes involves no more complexity than the determination of individual state income tax liability for a multistate corporation involved in interstate commerce where each taxing state has separate laws and seeks to maximize the definition of that which each such state contends may be taxed from out-of-state. * * * Absent precedential support for differentiating "substantial nexus" standards based upon tax types, this Court should resist the State's invitation for us to speculate based on semantics and, instead, focus on the effect which the state tax has on interstate commerce—here, attempting to levy an income tax on an out-of-state corporation with no property, tangible or intangible, in West Virginia where the income in question was generated from credit accounts held outside of this state.

The majority opinion also claims that a variety of changes—changes which it claims were not of a type which could be foreseen by the framers of the United States Constitution—support their extension of state tax jurisdiction into a realm considered by all others to be unconstitutional. * * * [T]he rationale for the majority's "economic exploitation" nexus approach, which might more accurately be termed a "tax it if you can follow it, even if it is earned in another state" nexus approach, rings remarkably like the arguments set forth in Justice Fortas' dissent in *Bellas Hess*. In his dissent to the 1967 case, Justice Fortas advocated for an "economic exploitation nexus" test for state taxing jurisdiction. Bellas Hess, 386 U.S. at 761–62, 87 S.Ct. 1389. Justice Fortas argued that Bellas Hess should be subject to the taxing jurisdiction of Illinois because of its "large-scale, systematic, continuous solicitation and exploitation of the Illinois consumer market." Id., at 761, 87 S.Ct. 1389. Furthermore, Justice Fortas argued that Bellas Hess enjoyed " . . . the benefits of, and profits from the facilities nurtured by, the State of Illinois as fully as if it were a retail store or maintained salesmen therein." Id., at 762, 87 S.Ct. 1389. I find it remarkable that our Court now endorses this same position—a position which the United States Supreme Court has rejected.

Yet our Court has not been the only court to embrace Justice Fortas' arguments. So too did the North Dakota Supreme Court, in its decision in *Quill*. Therein, that state supreme court, also claiming changes in society and economy, stated that "... within the context of contemporary society and commercial practice, we conclude that the concept of nexus encompasses more than mere physical presence within the state, and that the determination of nexus should take into consideration all connections between the out-of-state seller and the state, all benefits and opportunities provided by the State, and should stress economic realities rather than artificial benchmarks." State By and Through Heitkamp v. Quill Corp., 470 N.W.2d 203, 215 (N.D. 1991), rev'd, 504 U.S. 298, 112 S.Ct. 1904 (1992). As *Quill* demonstrates, when given the chance to again consider the "economic exploitation" nexus argument, the United States Supreme Court once again declined.

* * * I believe the sage reminder of Justice Scalia (joined in by Justices Kennedy and Thomas) should serve as a reminder of our duty in considering this case:

> We have recently told lower courts that "[i]f a precedent of this Court has direct application in a case, yet appears to rest on reasons rejected in some other line of decisions, [they] should follow the case which directly controls, leaving to this Court the prerogative of overruling its own decisions.".

Quill, 504 U.S. at 321, 112 S.Ct. 1904. We would do well to follow the precedent that is applicable herein and not attempt to anticipate an overruling by the United Supreme Court of its prior jurisprudence. The taxes in question are unconstitutional.

DAVIS, CHIEF JUSTICE, concurring:

* * * I fully concur in the majority decision and its analysis. I have chosen to write separately to emphasize the correctness of the legal analysis articulated in the majority decision and, further, to respond to several misconceptions contained in the dissenting opinion.

In the lone dissenting opinion, my colleague chastises the majority and states that "[t]here is no precedential support whatsoever for the conclusions reached by the majority decision. None. None at the state level. None at the federal level." The critical point that the dissent fails to acknowledge is that there is no established precedent, either way, from the United States Supreme Court. The sole decision on this topic is from the Tennessee Court of Appeals. See generally J.C. Penney Nat'l Bank v. Johnson, 19 S.W.3d 831 (Tenn.Ct.App. 1999). * * *

* * *

The final point I wish to address is the dissent's unexplained and rigid adherence to a physical presence requirement for all types of taxes. The dissenting opinion argues that the taxing scheme at issue impermissibly burdens interstate commerce, yet it fails to explain how such an impermissible scheme occurs. When a company, whether out-of-state or in-state, earns millions of dollars directly as a result of its dealings with West Virginia customers, should it not be compelled to pay taxes? If not, then all companies would only deal with out-of-state customers so as to avoid all business franchise and corporation net income taxes. Such a result is perverse, especially when considering the climate of today's business world where new technology has made it possible for businesses to span the globe. I see no reason why a small "mom and pop" store in the State of West Virginia, with gross receipts in the thousands, should be compelled to pay business franchise and corporation net income taxes due to its physical presence in the State, while a large corporation, like MBNA, who makes millions of dollars from West Virginia's economy, would be exempt from such taxes simply because it has no physical presence here. As the majority shrewdly points out, in today's world, a business does not necessarily need a physical presence anywhere. MBNA's significant economic presence in this State meets the substantial nexus standard; thus, it should not be exempt from state taxation.

* * *

NOTES AND QUESTIONS

A. As the *MBNA* case suggests, there is considerable controversy over the question whether *Quill*'s physical-presence test of "substantial nexus" for sales and use taxes extends to income taxes. Indeed, the *MBNA* court acknowledged an explicit conflict between its decision and the decision of the Tennessee Court of Appeals in *J.C. Penney*. In a case with facts quite similar to those of *MBNA*, the Supreme Judicial Court of Massachussetts, relying on *MBNA*, reached a similar conclusion. Capital One Bank v. Commissioner of Revenue, 453 Mass. 1, 899 N.E.2d 76, cert. denied, ___ U.S. ___, 129 S.Ct. 2827 (2009). See also MBNA America Bank, N.A. v. Indiana Department of State Revenue, 895 N.E.2d 140 (Ind. Tax 2008) (following West Virginia *MBNA* case).

As a matter of principle, should the jurisdictional rules governing use tax collection obligations be different from the jurisdictional rules regarding liability for income taxation? If so, in which context should the jurisdictional threshold be higher? Does the answer to this question turn on the relative complexity of the taxing regimes at issue? What were the views of the majority and the dissent in *MBNA* on these questions? For a general analysis of these issues in both the international and U.S. subnational contexts, see Walter Hellerstein, "Jurisdiction to Tax Income and Consumption in the New Economy: A Theoretical and Comparative Perspective," 38 Ga. L. Rev. 1 (2003).

The dissent in *MBNA* takes the majority to task for purportedly failing to resolve properly both of the discrete jurisdictional issues we identified at the outset of this section: jurisdiction over the taxpayer and jurisdiction over the income. Most of the dissent's fire was directed at the majority's alleged failure to require "a sufficiently high showing of presence to permit taxing jurisdiction under the 'substantial' nexus test of the Commerce Clause." But the dissent also complained that the "majority opinion completely fails" to consider the "second question of whether a state can impose tax on income generated out-of-state," and "[h]ere, there is no question but that the credit card accounts which give rise to MBNA's income are located outside West Virginia." What is the premise of the dissent's assertion that taxpayer's income is generated outside the state? Is that premise sound? What is the source of a lender's interest income? See I.R.C. §§ 861(a)(1), 862(a)(2) (defining source of interest income for purposes of U.S. international income taxation).

What are the implications of the dissent's position (and the holding of the *J.C. Penney* case on which the dissent relies) for an economy that is becoming increasingly digitized and in which "virtual corporations" can operate effectively with only minimal physical manifestations? Consider the following description of Contentville, an on-line business designed by Steven Brill, who founded *The American Lawyer*:

> The site aims at being a cross between the world's greatest newsstand and your corner bookstore, and will eventually sell books, screenplays, magazine subscriptions, dissertations, journal articles, legal documents, speeches, and more.* * *

> Contentville is what's called a virtual corporation. Ingram Book Group will handle the back end—picking, packing, and shipping—for books and magazines. EBSCO will provide the archive of downloadable articles from periodicals. Bell & Howell, which owns the rights to nearly every dissertation published in America since 1861, will get you that copy of Newt Gingrich's Ph.D. thesis, "Belgian Education Policy in the Congo, 1945–1960." Customer service is provided by a company called Ivus, situated in Oakland's inner city. The Web site itself is maintained by a team of IT Web Solutions. And Contentville will be able to draw on writers from *Brill's Content*, the print magazine.

James Surowiecki, "The Financial Page: Can Contentville Compete?," The New Yorker, July 24, 2000, p. 29. Assuming that Contentville earns millions of dollars from its on-line venture, which states would have jurisdiction to tax that income under a physical-presence test of "substantial nexus"? Only New York, where Brill and his handful of employees work? Every state in which the "independent contractors" that constitute the "substance" of Contentville maintain a physical presence? Or some subset of those states, depending perhaps on the precise function served by those independent contractors?

B. *Residence and Source as a Basis for Taxing Income.* There are two fundamental, but alternative, foundations for state power to tax income: residence and source. American Law Institute, Federal Income Tax Project, International Aspects of United States Income Taxation 6 (1987). With regard to residence, the Supreme Court has observed: "That the receipt of income by a resident of the territory of a taxing sovereignty is a taxable event is universally recognized. Domicil itself affords a basis for such taxation." New York ex rel. Cohn v. Graves, 300 U.S. 308, 312, 57 S.Ct. 466 (1937).

Accordingly, "[a]s to residents [a State] may, and does, exert its taxing power over their income from all sources, whether within or without the State." Shaffer v. Carter, 252 U.S. 37, 57, 40 S.Ct. 221 (1920). See also Oklahoma Tax Commission v. Chickasaw Nation, 515 U.S. 450, 462–63, 115 S.Ct. 2214 (1995) (applying "well-established principle of interstate and international taxation—namely, that a jurisdiction * * * may tax *all* of the income of its residents, even income earned outside the taxing jurisdiction") (emphasis in original). The rationale for allowing states to tax residents upon their income without regard to source is "founded upon the protection afforded to the recipient of the income by the state, in his person, on his right to receive the income, and in his enjoyment of it when received," Lawrence v. State Tax Commission, 286 U.S. 276, 281, 52 S.Ct. 556 (1932), as well as his "[e]njoyment of privileges of residence in the state and the attendant right to invoke the protection of its laws." Cohn, 300 U.S. at 313. Indeed, it is the residence principle of taxation that underlies the United States' undisputed power to tax its resident individuals and corporations (i.e., domestic corporations) on all of their income regardless of source. 3 Boris I. Bittker & Lawrence Lokken, Federal Taxation of Income, Estates and Gifts ¶ 65.1 (3d ed. 1999); American Law Institute, supra, at 6.

The states' power to tax on the basis of source is as well recognized as their power to tax on the basis of residence. Shaffer v. Carter, supra, 252 U.S. at 57; Curry v. McCanless, 307 U.S. 357, 368, 59 S.Ct. 900 (1939) ("income may be taxed both by the state where it is earned and by the state of the recipient's domicile. Protection, benefit, and power over the subject matter are not confined to either state"). Because such power derives only from the protection that the states provide to "persons, property, and business transactions *within their borders*," Shaffer, 252 U.S. at 57 (emphasis supplied), however, it is necessarily more circumscribed than the power to tax that flows from "[d]omicil itself." Cohn, 300 U.S. at 312. Consequently, when states seek to tax nonresident individuals and corporations, for which source is the sole jurisdictional basis, their power extends only to the nonresident's "property owned within the State and their business, trade, or profession carried on therein, and the tax is only on such income as is derived from those sources." Shaffer, 252 U.S. at 57. Again, the analogy to federal income taxation of nonresident individuals and corporations (i.e., nonresident aliens and foreign corporations) is apt; tax is generally imposed only on income from sources within the United States. See I.R.C. §§ 871, 881, 882; Bittker & Lokken, supra, at ¶ 65.1.3.

Although the source principle is more circumscribed than the residence principle in a geographical sense, it is the dominant principle in cases of conflict between residence and source principles. In other words, when both the state of domicile and the state of source have a legitimate claim to tax income, the state of domicile ordinarily yields to the state of source to avoid double taxation. This is true both as a matter of national and international practice, see American Law Institute, supra, at 6; 2 Jerome R. Hellerstein & Walter Hellerstein, State Taxation ¶ 20.10 (3d ed. 2003), and as a matter of federal constitutional law. See Walter Hellerstein, "State Taxation of Corporate Income From Intangibles: *Allied–Signal* and Beyond," 48 Tax L. Rev.

739, 804–05 (1993). This is not to suggest, however, that the Constitution always forbids double taxation of income. In fact, it does not. See Guaranty Trust Co. v. Virginia, 305 U.S. 19, 22–23, 59 S.Ct. 1 (1938) (Due Process Clause does not bar multiple taxation of income from trust); Moorman Mfg. Co. v. Bair, 437 U.S. 267, 98 S.Ct. 2340 (1978), pp. 457–69 infra (Commerce Clause does not bar all multiple taxation of income). Rather, insofar as the Constitution does forbid double taxation of income when there is a conflict between the state of residence and the state of source, it permits the latter rather than the former to tax the income. Hellerstein, supra, at 744 n.11, 804–05.

C. *Alternative Justifications for the Jurisdiction to Tax?* Although the traditional jurisdictional bases for attributing income to a state are residence and source, it bears noting that the Supreme Court has occasionally taken a much broader view of the states' taxing jurisdiction. In Wisconsin v. J.C. Penney Co., 311 U.S. 435, 61 S.Ct. 246 (1940), for example, the Court sustained a state's power to impose a tax on a foreign corporation for the privilege of declaring dividends on income earned within the state, declaring that a "State is free to pursue its own fiscal policies, unembarrassed by the Constitution, if by the practical operation of a tax the State has exerted its power in relation to opportunities which it has given, to protection which it has afforded, to benefits which it has conferred by the fact of being an orderly, civilized society." Id., 311 U.S. at 444. In an even more sweeping oversimplification of the matter, the Court continued that "[t]he simple but controlling question is whether the State has given anything for which it can ask return." Id. In yet another decision, the Court declared that a corporation's income could be attributed to a state on the basis of "the distribution of *either* a corporation's sources of income *or* the social costs which it generates." General Motors Corp. v. District of Columbia, 380 U.S. 553, 561, 85 S.Ct. 1156 (1965) (emphasis supplied).

D. *Income from Intangibles Licensed for Use in the State: The* Geoffrey *Case and Its Progeny.* In *MBNA*, the court observed (in footnote 11) that the "Tax Commissioner cites several cases to this Court in support of its position that *Quill*'s physical-presence requirement applies only to sales and use taxes including * * * Geoffrey, Inc. v. S.C. Tax Com'n, 313 S.C. 15, 437 S.E.2d 13 (1993)." However, the MBNA court found "the persuasiveness of these cases to be limited * * * because the primary issue in each case is whether a state has jurisdiction to impose a state income tax on foreign corporations with no physical presence in the taxing state but whose intangibles, such as a trademark, are used in the state by a licensee." The *Geoffrey* line of cases, however, and issues they raise have been a major battleground in the ongoing war over the appropriate constitutional standard for income tax jurisdiction. Indeed, the South Carolina decision in *Geoffrey*, which was handed down barely a year after *Quill*, was the first state supreme court case to hold that *Quill*'s physical-presence test of Commerce Clause nexus did not apply to income taxes.

GEOFFREY, INC. v. SOUTH CAROLINA TAX COMMISSION

Supreme Court of South Carolina, 1993.
313 S.C. 15, 437 S.E.2d 13, cert. denied, 510 U.S. 992, 114 S.Ct. 550 (1993).

HARWELL, CHIEF JUSTICE:

Geoffrey, Inc. (Geoffrey), a foreign corporation, appeals from a ruling that requires it to pay South Carolina income tax and business license fees. We affirm.

I. FACTS

Geoffrey is a wholly-owned, second-tier subsidiary of Toys R Us, Inc. (Toys R Us) incorporated in Delaware with its principal offices in that state. It has no employees or offices in South Carolina and owns no tangible property here.

In 1984, Geoffrey became the owner of several valuable trademarks and trade names, including "Toys R Us." Later that year, Geoffrey executed a License Agreement (Agreement) that allows Toys R Us to use the "Toys R Us" trade name, as well as other trademarks and trade names, in all states except New York, Texas, Pennsylvania, Massachusetts, and New Jersey. The Agreement further grants Toys R Us a right to use Geoffrey's merchandising skills, techniques, and "know-how" in connection with marketing, promotion, advertising, and sale of products covered by the Agreement.

As consideration for the licenses granted by the Agreement, Geoffrey receives a royalty of one percent "of the net sales by [Toys R Us], or any of its affiliated, associated, or subsidiary companies, of the Licensed Products sold or the Licensed Services rendered under the Licensed Mark." Toys R Us reports the aggregate sales of all stores to Geoffrey in a single figure on a monthly basis. The royalty payment is made annually via wire transfer from a Toys R Us account in Pennsylvania to a Geoffrey account in New York.[1]

Toys R Us began doing business in South Carolina in 1985 and has since then made royalty payments to Geoffrey based on South Carolina sales. In 1986 and 1987, Toys R Us deducted the royalty payments made to Geoffrey from its South Carolina taxable income. The South Carolina Tax Commission (Commission) initially disallowed the deduction, but later took the position that Toys R Us was entitled to the deduction and that Geoffrey was required to pay South Carolina income tax on the royalty

---

1. The net effect of this corporate structure has been the production of "nowhere" income that escapes all state income taxation. One commentator has recognized such income as the "product of a divide and conquer strategy that some members of the corporate world have exercised effectively for decades." Corrigan, Interstate Corporate Income Taxation—Recent Revolutions and a Modern Response, 29 Vand.L.Rev. 423, 429 (1976). The strategy's effectiveness is unquestionable. In 1990, Geoffrey, without any full-time employees, had an income of approximately $55 million and paid no income taxes to any state.

income. The Commission also held that Geoffrey was required to pay the South Carolina corporate license fee.

Geoffrey paid the taxes under protest and filed this action for a refund, claiming, among other things, that it did not do business in South Carolina and that it did not have a sufficient nexus with South Carolina for its royalty income to be taxable here. The trial judge upheld the Commission's assessment of taxes against Geoffrey. Geoffrey appealed.

II. DISCUSSION

S.C.Code Ann. § 12–7–230 (Supp.1992), pursuant to which both foreign and domestic corporations are taxed, provides:

> [E]xcept as otherwise provided, every foreign corporation transacting, conducting, doing business, or having an income within the jurisdiction of this State, whether or not the corporation is engaged in or the income derived from intrastate, interstate, or foreign commerce, shall make a return and shall pay annually an income tax equivalent to five percent of a proportion of its entire net income, to be determined as provided in this chapter. The term "transacting", "conducting", or "doing business", as used in this section, includes the engaging in or the transacting of any activity in this State for the purpose of financial profit or gain.

Section 12–7–230 levies a tax on the income of foreign corporations "transacting, conducting, doing business, or having an income *within the jurisdiction of this State,*" which "includes," but is not limited to, "the engaging in or the transacting of any activity in this State for the purpose of financial profit or gain." We construe this language as extending to the limits of the constitution South Carolina's authority to tax foreign corporations. Here, Geoffrey contends that the Due Process Clause, U.S. Const. amend. XIV, § 1, and the Commerce Clause, U.S. Const. art. I, § 8, cl. 3, prohibit the taxation of its royalty income by South Carolina. We disagree.

A. Due Process

The Due Process Clause requires "some definite link, some minimum connection, between a state and the person, property or transaction it seeks to tax," and that the "income attributed to the state for tax purposes must be rationally related to values connected with the taxing State." Quill Corp. v. North Dakota, 112 S.Ct. 1904, 1909–10 (1992). Geoffrey argues that the Commission has failed to satisfy both of these requirements. We disagree.

The nexus requirement of the Due Process Clause can be satisfied even where the corporation has no physical presence in the taxing state if the corporation has purposefully directed its activity at the state's economic forum. Quill, 504 U.S. at 306–07, 112 S.Ct. at 1909–10. Geoffrey asserts that it has not purposefully directed its activities toward South Carolina. To support its position, Geoffrey points out that Toys R Us had no South Carolina stores when it entered into the Agreement and urges, therefore, that Toys R Us's subsequent expansion into South Carolina was unilateral activity that cannot create the minimum connection between Geoffrey and South Carolina required by due process.

In our view, Geoffrey has not been unwillingly brought into contact with South Carolina through the unilateral activity of an independent party. Geoffrey's business is the ownership, licensing, and management of trademarks, trade names, and franchises. By electing to license its trademarks and trade names for use by Toys R Us in many states, Geoffrey contemplated and purposefully sought the benefit of economic contact with those states. Geoffrey has been aware of, consented to, and benefitted from Toys R Us's use of Geoffrey's intangibles in South Carolina. Moreover, Geoffrey had the ability to control its contact with South Carolina by prohibiting the use of its intangibles here as it did with other states. We reject Geoffrey's claim that it has not purposefully directed its activities toward South Carolina's economic forum and hold that by licensing intangibles for use in South Carolina and receiving income in exchange for their use, Geoffrey has the "minimum connection" with this State that is required by due process. See American Dairy Queen Corp. v. Taxation and Revenue Dep't, 93 N.M. 743, 605 P.2d 251 (1979); AAMCO Transmissions, Inc. v. Taxation and Revenue Dep't, 93 N.M. 389, 600 P.2d 841, cert. denied, 93 N.M. 205, 598 P.2d 1165 (1979).

In addition to our finding that Geoffrey purposefully directed its activities toward South Carolina, we find that the "minimum connection" required by due process also is satisfied by the presence of Geoffrey's intangible property in this State. Geoffrey's Secretary, a certified public accountant, agreed during cross examination that sales by Toys R Us in South Carolina create an account receivable for Geoffrey. In addition, the trial judge found that Geoffrey had a franchise in South Carolina.[2] That the presence of these intangibles is sufficient to sustain a tax is settled law. In Virginia v. Imperial Coal Sales Co., Inc., 293 U.S. 15, 20, 55 S.Ct. 12, 14 (1934), the United States Supreme Court stated:

> It is not the character of the property that makes it subject to such a tax, but the fact that the property has a situs within the state and that the owner should give appropriate support to the government that protects it. That duty is not less when the property is intangible than when it is tangible. Nor are we able to perceive any sound reason for holding that the owner must have real estate or tangible property within the state in order to subject its intangible property within the state to taxation.[3]

---

2. "In its simplest terms, a franchise is a license from the owner of a trademark or trade name permitting another to sell a product or service under that name or mark. More broadly stated, a 'franchise' has evolved into an elaborate agreement under which the franchisee undertakes to conduct a business or sell a product or service in accordance with methods and procedures prescribed by the franchisor, and the franchisor undertakes to assist the franchisee through advertising, promotion, and other advisory services." Black's Law Dictionary 592 (5th ed. 1979). Geoffrey has not challenged the trial judge's finding that the Agreement created a franchise.

3. Although the tax at issue in *Imperial Coal* was an *ad valorem* property tax imposed upon the accounts receivable of a Virginia corporation, we do not find that fact distinguishing.

Geoffrey asserts that under the doctrine of *mobilia sequuntur personam*, the situs of its intangibles is its corporate headquarters in Delaware, not South Carolina. However, in Mobil Oil Corp. v. Comm'r of Taxes of Vermont, 445 U.S. 425, 100 S.Ct. 1223 (1980), the United States Supreme Court rejected the view that the constitution requires taxation of intangibles by allocation to a *single* situs, finding no adequate justification for preferring that rule over taxation by apportionment. The High Court concluded that:

> [a]lthough a fictionalized situs of intangible property sometimes has been invoked to avoid multiple taxation of ownership, there is nothing talismanic about the concepts of "business situs" or "commercial domicile" that automatically renders those concepts applicable when taxation of income from intangibles is at issue. The Court has observed that the maxim *mobilia sequuntur personam*, upon which these fictions of situs are based, "states a rule without disclosing the reasons for it." ... The Court has also recognized that "the reason for a single place of taxation no longer obtains" when the taxpayer's activities with respect to the intangible property involve relations with more than one jurisdiction.... Even for property or franchise taxes, apportionment of intangible values is not unknown.... Moreover, cases upholding allocation to a single situs for property tax purposes have distinguished income tax situations where the apportionment principle prevails. (Citations omitted).

Id. at 445, 100 S.Ct. at 1235. See also Wheeling Steel Corp. v. Fox, 298 U.S. 193, 56 S.Ct. 773 (1936) (intangibles may acquire a situs for taxation other than at the domicile of the owner if they have become integral parts of some local business); Southern Express Co. v. Spigener, 118 S.C. 413, 110 S.E. 403 (1920) (the situs of intangible property is within this State if the right afforded by it is exercised here); Dexter, Taxation of Income from Intangibles of Multistate–Multinational Corporations, 29 Vand. L.Rev. 401 (1976); J. Hellerstein & W. Hellerstein, State Taxation, Para. 9.08–.09 (2d ed. 1992). We reject Geoffrey's claim that its intangible assets are located exclusively in Delaware. Accordingly, we find that Geoffrey's purposeful direction of activity toward South Carolina as well as its possessing intangible property here provide a definite link between South Carolina and the income derived by Geoffrey from the use of its trademarks and trade names in this State.

We also find that the second prong of *Quill* test has been met. Contrary to Geoffrey's assertion, South Carolina has conferred benefits upon Geoffrey to which the challenged tax is rationally related. As the United States Supreme Court recognized in Curry v. McCanless, 307 U.S. 357, 365–66, 59 S.Ct. 900, 905 (1939):

Authority to tax the property extends to income produced by the property. "That [a state] may tax the land but not the crop, the tree but not the fruit, the mine or well but not the product, the business but not the profit derived from it is wholly inadmissible." Shaffer v. Carter, 252 U.S. 37, 49–50, 40 S.Ct. 221, 225 (1920).

Very different considerations, both theoretical and practical, apply to the taxation of intangibles, that is, rights which are not related to physical things. Such rights are but relationships between persons, natural or corporate, which the law recognizes by attaching to them certain sanctions enforceable in courts. The power of government over them and the protection which it gives them cannot be exerted through control of a physical thing. *They can be made effective only through control over and protection afforded to those persons whose relationships are the origin of the rights....* Obviously, as sources of actual or potential wealth—which is an appropriate measure of any tax imposed on ownership or its exercise—*they cannot be dissociated from the persons from whose relationships they are derived.* (Citations omitted). (Emphasis added).

The real source of Geoffrey's income is not a paper agreement, but South Carolina's Toys R Us customers. Cf. Avco Financial Services Consumer Discount Co. v. Director, Division of Taxation, 100 N.J. 27, 494 A.2d 788 (1985). By providing an orderly society in which Toys R Us conducts business, South Carolina has made it possible for Geoffrey to earn income pursuant to the royalty agreement. See, e.g., Allied–Signal v. Comm'r of Finance, 79 N.Y.2d 73, 580 N.Y.S.2d 696, 588 N.E.2d 731 (1991) (benefits afforded to an in-state corporation inure to non-resident shareholders). That Geoffrey has received protection, benefits, and opportunities from South Carolina is manifested by the fact that it earns income in this state. Accord AAMCO, 93 N.M. at 393, 600 P.2d at 845 (quoting Besser Co. v. Bureau of Revenue, 74 N.M. 377, 394 P.2d 141 (1964)). That the tax is rationally related to these protections, benefits, and opportunities is evidenced by the fact that the State seeks to tax only that portion of Geoffrey's income generated within its borders. Based on the foregoing reasons, we hold that the Due Process Clause does not prohibit South Carolina's taxation of Geoffrey's royalty income.

B. Commerce Clause

A tax will survive challenge under the Commerce Clause so long as it 1) is applied to an activity with a substantial nexus with the taxing state, 2) is fairly apportioned, 3) does not discriminate against interstate commerce, and 4) is fairly related to the services provided by the State. Complete Auto Transit, Inc. v. Brady, 430 U.S. 274, 279, 97 S.Ct. 1076, 1079 (1977). Relying on Nat'l Bellas Hess, Inc. v. Dep't of Revenue of Ill., 386 U.S. 753, 87 S.Ct. 1389 (1967), Geoffrey contends that it does not have a substantial nexus with South Carolina because it is not physically present in this state. In our view, Geoffrey's reliance on the physical presence requirement of *Bellas Hess* is misplaced.[4]

---

4. The U.S. Supreme Court recently revisited the physical presence requirement of *Bellas Hess* and, while reaffirming its vitality as to *sales and use taxes*, noted that the physical presence requirement had not been extended to other types of taxes. Quill, 504 U.S. at 314, 112 S.Ct. at 1914.

It is well settled that the taxpayer need not have a tangible, physical presence in a state for income to be taxable there. The presence of intangible property alone is sufficient to establish nexus. American Dairy Queen, 93 N.M. at 747, 605 P.2d at 255. See also Int'l Harvester Co. v. Wisconsin Dep't of Taxation, 322 U.S. 435, 441–442, 64 S.Ct. 1060, 1063–64 (1944) (a state may tax such part of the income of a non-resident as is fairly attributable either to property located in the state or to events or transactions which, occurring there, are within the protection of the state and entitled to the numerous other benefits which its confers); J. Hellerstein & W. Hellerstein, supra, at 6.08 (any corporation that regularly exploits the markets of a state should be subject to its jurisdiction to impose an income tax even though not physically present). A taxpayer who is domiciled in one state but carries on business in another is subject to taxation measured by the value of the intangibles used in his business. Curry, 307 U.S. at 368, 59 S.Ct. at 906. We hold that by licensing intangibles for use in this State and deriving income from their use here, Geoffrey has a "substantial nexus" with South Carolina.[5]

* * *

In conclusion, we hold that the taxation of Geoffrey's royalty income pursuant to section 12–7–230 is not prohibited by the Due Process Clause or the Commerce Clause of the United States Constitution. Our finding that Geoffrey may be taxed pursuant to section 12–7–230 settles the question whether Geoffrey must pay the corporate license fee. All corporations subject to section 12–7–230 are required to do so. See S.C.Code Ann. §§ 12–19–20, 12–19–70 (1977 & Supp.1992). The order of the trial judge is

AFFIRMED.

CHANDLER, FINNEY, TOAL and MOORE, JJ., concur.

NOTES AND QUESTIONS

A. In its unsuccessful petition for certiorari to the U.S. Supreme Court, Geoffrey asserted that the South Carolina Supreme Court's *Geoffrey* decision would have "staggering implications for taxpayers doing business across state lines, particularly the ever increasing number of taxpayers who deal with intangible property." In urging the Supreme Court to hear the case, the taxpayer characterized the decision as follows:

In substance, the court has held that, regardless of a taxpayer's tangible contacts with a state, the taxpayer is subject to the state's constitutional taxing jurisdiction so long as the taxpayer derives some economic benefit from the state's market. Under the court's holding, an author paid royalties by a publisher from the sale of a book would be subject to tax in every state in which the book was sold. A television producer paid

---

5. Further discussion of the remaining requirements of the Commerce Clause is unnecessary. Our Due Process analysis of the benefits conferred upon Geoffrey applies with equal force here and need not be repeated. Moreover, Geoffrey raised no constitutional claim that the challenged tax is not fairly apportioned or discriminates against interstate commerce.

royalties by a network for the use of a program would be subject to tax in every state in which the program was televised. An electronic data bank receiving payments for the use of its services would be subject to tax in every state in which its logo flashed across the computer screen.

* * *

The practical implications of the South Carolina Supreme Court's sweeping conception of state tax jurisdiction are simply astonishing. Under the court's ruling, whenever a person's intangible property is used by others, the person will be subject to tax wherever such property is used. A small, start-up company in Silicon Valley will be subject to tax in every state in which its software licensees operate, even if, like Geoffrey, it has no office, employees, or tangible property in the state and has never solicited business there. A bank purchasing a security representing a bundle of loans will be subject to tax in every state in which the underlying borrowers reside because, just as "[t]he real source of Geoffrey's income is not a paper agreement, but South Carolina's Toys R Us customers" (App. A at 8a) so the "real source" of the bank's income is not the security but the underlying borrowers spread across the nation. An athlete receiving royalties from his or her endorsement of a product will be subject to tax in every state in which the product is sold, regardless of any other connection the athlete may have had with the state, because the athlete, like Geoffrey, failed to prohibit the use of the endorsement in those states, and thus "consented to, and benefitted from" (App. A at 5a) the licensee's use of intangible property in the state. A company receiving payment for a covenant not to compete will be taxable in every state in which it has agreed *not* to do business because that is where the covenantee is enjoying the intangible rights that are the "source" of the covenantor's income. The list goes on and on.

Petition for Certiorari at 9, 20, Geoffrey, Inc. v. South Carolina Dep't of Revenue and Taxation, No. 93–520 (Oct. 1, 1993). Did the petitioner accurately characterize the implications of *Geoffrey*? If you had been representing the State of South Carolina, how would you responded to Geoffrey's petition in an effort to dissuade the U.S. Supreme Court from taking the case?

B.   Geoffrey *and* Quill. Is *Geoffrey* faithful to the teachings of *Quill*? How does the *Geoffrey* court's Due Process Clause nexus analysis differ from its Commerce Clause nexus analysis? Does *Geoffrey* satisfactorily distinguish *Quill's* "bright-line, physical presence" rule? See footnote 4 of the *Geoffrey* opinion. What is the significance of the U.S. Supreme Court's denial of certiorari in *Geoffrey*? If you were a Supreme Court Justice would you have voted to consider the case? One of the critical criteria for the Court's grant of certiorari is whether "a state court * * * has decided an important question of federal law that has not been, but should be, settled by this Court." U.S. Supreme Court Rule 10(c). Does *Geoffrey* satisfy that criterion? Does *Geoffrey* present a stronger or a weaker case than *MBNA* for assertion of jurisdiction over a non-physically present taxpayer?

C.   Geoffrey's *Progeny*. In seven other states, there have been decisions of courts and administrative tribunals addressing essentially the same question raised by *Geoffrey* on essentially the same facts—indeed, many of the cases involved Geoffrey itself—and in every state the most recent determination is in accord with the South Carolina court's conclusion. KFC Corp. v. Iowa Dep't of Revenue, No. 07DORFC016, Iowa Dep't of Inspections and Appeals, Admin. Hearings Div., Aug. 8, 2008, available at www.checkpoint.riag.com; Bridges v. Geoffrey, Inc., 984 So.2d 115 (La. App.), rev. denied, 978 So. 2d 370 (La. 2008); Geoffrey, Inc. v. Commissioner of Revenue, 453 Mass. 17, 899 N.E.2d 87, cert. denied ___ U.S. ___, 129 S.Ct. 2853 (2009); Acme Royalty Co. v. Director of Revenue, No. 99–2839 RI, 2002 WL 31969411 (Mo. Admin. Hearing Comm'n Jan. 3, 2002), rev'd on statutory grounds, 96 S.W.3d 72 (Mo. banc 2002); Gore Enterprise Holdings, Inc. v. Director of Revenue, No. 99–2856 RI, 2002 WL 31969419 (Mo. Admin. Hearing Comm'n Jan. 3, 2002), rev'd on statutory grounds, 96 S.W.3d 72 (Mo. banc 2002); Lanco, Inc. v. Director, Division of Taxation, 188 N.J. 380, 908 A.2d 176 (2006), cert. denied, 551 U.S. 1131, 127 S.Ct. 2974 (2007); Kmart Properties, Inc. v. Taxation and Revenue Department, 139 N.M. 177, 131 P.3d 27 (App. 2001); A & F Trademark, Inc. v. Tolson, 167 N.C.App. 150, 605 S.E.2d 187 (2004). *Geoffrey* has inspired an enormous outpouring of commentary, some of which the *MBNA* court cited in its opinion. See, e.g., Paul Comeau, et al., "Intangible Holding Companies: There Is Life After *Geoffrey*," 10 J. Multistate Tax'n 6 (2001); Michael T. Fatale, "*Geoffrey* Sidesteps *Quill*: Constitutional Nexus, Intangible Property, and the State Taxation of Income," 23 Hofstra L. Rev. 407 (1994); John Swain, "State Income Tax Jurisdiction: A Jurisprudential and Policy Perspective," 45 Wm. & Mary L. Rev. 319 (2003); Note, "State Income Taxation of Out-of-State Trademark Holding Companies," 70 U. Chi. L. Rev. 1533 (2003).

D. *Intangible Holding Companies, Tax Planning, and the State Legislative Response.* The fact pattern in *Geoffrey* illustrates one of the most common structures that corporations have employed to reduce state income tax liability. Corporations owning valuable intellectual property, such as trademarks, trade names, and patents, transfer these intangibles to subsidiaries that they create to hold and manage such property. The transfer itself is tax free under established principles. See I.R.C. § 351. The subsidiaries are typically incorporated in a state like Delaware that does not tax income from intangible holding companies (IHCs). The IHC licenses the intangibles back to its parent or to another operating subsidiary, and the operating company deducts the royalty, with the aim of reducing its income in those "separate company reporting" states[f] in which its operations occur.

In addition to the question of whether the IHC has nexus in the state in which the IHC's licensee uses the intangible—the question raised by *Geoffrey*, there is the question of whether these structures, and the tax consequences to which they purportedly give rise, may nevertheless be disregarded because they are "sham" transactions or because they are lacking in economic substance or business purpose. Compare, e.g., Syms Corp. v. Commissioner of Revenue, 436 Mass. 505, 765 N.E.2d 758 (2002) (denying deduction of royalty payments by Massachusetts operating company to affiliated IHC because transfer and license back of trademarks, trade names, and service marks had

---

f. In a state requiring combined reporting of unitary affiliates, this planning structure would have no impact, because the companies would be combined and the intercompany payment would be eliminated. See Chapter 7, Section B(2), p. 495 infra.

no practical economic effect other than the creation of tax benefits) with Sherwin–Williams Co. v. Commissioner of Revenue, 438 Mass. 71, 778 N.E.2d 504 (2002) (sustaining deduction of royalty and interest payments by Massachusetts operating company to affiliated IHCs because there was no evidence that transfer of the marks to the IHC was specifically devised as a tax avoidance scheme and the IHCs were viable businesses engaged in substantive economic activity apart from the creation of tax benefits). For a detailed discussion of these and similar cases and the issues they raise, see 1 Jerome R. Hellerstein & Walter Hellerstein, State Taxation ¶ 7.17 (3d ed. 2007 & Cum. Supp. 2009).

In response to the creation of tax-motivated corporate structures employing related-company transactions to reduce corporate income tax liabilities, a growing number of states have enacted expense-disallowance provisions that require the add-back of certain intercompany expenses. See, e.g., See Ala. Code § 40–18–35(b)(1) (Westlaw 2009); Mass. Gen. Laws Ann. ch. 63, §§ 31I, 31J (Westlaw 2009); N.J. Stat. Ann. §§ 54:10A–4.4(b), 54:10A–4(k)(2)(I) (Westlaw 2009). The common thread running throughout these measures is the disallowance of related-company expense deductions for the use of intangible assets, such as trademarks and trade names, and the disallowance of deductions for related-company interest expense. Despite these common features, there are significant variations from state to state in the types of deductions disallowed and in the numerous exceptions to the required add-back of disallowed expenses. These provisions are considered in detail in 1 Hellerstein & Hellerstein, supra, ¶ 7.17[3].

CORPORATE EXCISE DOR DIRECTIVE 96–2

Massachusetts Department of Revenue.
July 3, 1996.

CREATION OF NEXUS THROUGH THE IN-STATE OWNERSHIP AND USE OF INTANGIBLE PROPERTY

Issue

Under what circumstances will the in-state ownership and use of intangible property subject a foreign corporation to the corporate excise?

Directive

A foreign corporation's intangible property used within Massachusetts will subject that corporation to the corporate excise when:

1. The intangible property generates, or is otherwise a source of, gross receipts within the state for the corporation, including through a license or franchise; and

2. The activity through which the corporation obtains such gross receipts from its intangible property is purposeful (e.g., a contract with an in-state company); and

3. The corporation's presence within the state, as indicated by its intangible property and its activities with respect to that property, is more than de minimis.

Explanation

Under G.L. c. 63, § 39, a foreign corporation is subject to the corporate excise when, inter alia, it does business in Massachusetts, or owns or uses any part or all of its capital, plant, or any other property in the state. The Commissioner construes this provision to the full extent permitted by the Constitution and laws of the United States.

The definition of intangible property generally includes, but is not limited to, copyrights, patents, trademarks, trade names, trade secrets, service marks, and know-how. However, for purposes of this directive, the Commissioner will treat a license of canned software, transferred on a tangible medium to be used for any purpose other than commercial reproduction, as the sale of tangible personal property, not the license of intangible property.

A foreign corporation whose in-state activity is described in G.L. c. 63, § 39 is not subject to the Massachusetts corporate excise if such in-state activity is within the confines of Public Law 86–272 (15 U.S.C. § 381 et seq.). Public Law 86–272 precludes the imposition of a corporate tax measured by net income when a foreign corporation's sole activity in Massachusetts is solicitation of sales of tangible personal property, provided certain conditions are met. For example, Public Law 86–272 could potentially apply to a foreign corporation's solicitation of sales in Massachusetts of tangible personal property which contains intangible property (such as books, recordings, or canned software). In contrast, the focus of this directive is transactions in which a foreign corporation derives gross receipts from intangible property that is licensed or otherwise transferred for continuing commercial exploitation in the state. These latter transactions are not protected by Public Law 86–272.

EXAMPLES

The following examples illustrate the application of this directive. In Examples 1–3, it is presumed that the foreign corporation's presence in Massachusetts, as indicated by its intangible property and its activities with respect to that property, is more than de minimis. Moreover, in Example 1–3 it is presumed that the foreign corporation does not otherwise transact business or own property in the state.

Example 1

Dress Shop, a Delaware corporation located in Wisconsin, manufactures and sells girls' clothing under the name Tinker Bell. In Year 1, Dress Shop licenses the name Tinker Bell to Girl Towne, a Massachusetts company, for use in connection with the sale of clothing produced by Girl Towne in Massachusetts. Pursuant to the contract entered into between Dress Shop and Girl Towne, Girl Towne is to pay Dress Shop a royalty of 2% on the sale of every item of clothing sold under the Tinker Bell name. Girl Towne makes sales under the Tinker Bell name in Massachusetts during Year 1 and makes the corresponding royalty payments to Dress Shop, as required. Dress Shop has nexus with Massachusetts in Year 1.

Example 2

Motor Way, a Delaware corporation located in Alabama, develops the technology for a new low-weight motor scooter and patents this technology. In Year 2, Motor Way licenses its patented technology to Speed Rider, a Massachusetts company, for use in connection with the manufacture and sale of scooters in Massachusetts. Pursuant to the contract entered into between Motor Way and Speed Rider, Speed Rider is to pay Motor Way an upfront fee for the right to make use of Motor Way's patented technology, and a royalty of 4% on the sale of every scooter that Speed Rider manufactures and sells using this technology. Speed Rider manufacturers scooters using the Motor Way technology in Year 2, and sells these scooters in Massachusetts during that same year. In addition, Speed Rider makes the corresponding royalty payments to Motor Way for Year 2, as required. Motor Way has nexus with Massachusetts in Year 2.

Example 3

Ginzu Ltd. is a fast-food franchiser, incorporated in Delaware and located in New Jersey. In Year 3, Ginzu Ltd. franchises the rights to one of its "Ginzu Gardens" fast-food restaurants to a franchisee, John Cook, a New Hampshire resident, for a location in Massachusetts. The terms of the franchise agreement both permit and require Mr. Cook to use the various items of intangible property owned by Ginzu Ltd. (e.g., the name "Ginzu Gardens," certain service marks, a patented food process, trade secrets, and know-how). In addition, the terms of the franchise agreement require Mr. Cook to pay Ginzu Ltd. a monthly franchise fee, as well as a royalty charge of 6% of the sales proceeds received by the Massachusetts' restaurant, Ginzu Gardens. Mr. Cook makes such payments to Ginzu Ltd. during Year 3, as required. Ginzu Ltd. has nexus with Massachusetts in Year 3.

Example 4

Golf Time is a corporation, incorporated in South Carolina and located there. Golf Time is the creator of "cold day" golf clubs. "Cold day" golf clubs have grips that emit warmth when squeezed since they are specially treated with Golf Time's "heat-grip" technology. Golf Time has patented its "heat grip" technology, and obtained registered trademarks for each of the terms "cold day" and "heat-grip." Golf Time solicits sales of its "cold day" golf clubs in Massachusetts, touting the merits of its "heat grip" technology. Golf Time's activities result in significant sales of "cold day" golf clubs in Massachusetts. Golf Time engages in no other business activity with respect to Massachusetts. Assuming Golf Time's Massachusetts activities are protected by Public Law 86–272, Golf Time will not be subject to the corporate excise for the years in question.

Effective Date

The principles set forth in this directive will apply to taxable years beginning on or after January 1, 1996.

NOTES AND QUESTIONS

A. *Variations on* DOR Directive 96–2. What would be the result under *DOR Directive 96–2*, and under the Due Process and Commerce Clauses, if the facts of the examples in *DOR Directive 96–2* were altered in the following manner:

(1) Same facts as Example 1 in the Directive except that the rights to the Tinker Bell name are held by Nameco, a wholly-owned subsidiary of Dress Shop which qualifies as a Delaware holding company.

(2) Same facts as Example 1 in the Directive except that Girl Towne produces the dresses sold under the Tinker Bell name at a plant located in New Hampshire and sells 98 percent of its dress production annually in states other than Massachusetts.

(3) Same facts as (2) above except that Girl Towne has no contacts with Massachusetts but sells 98 percent of its New Hampshire production of Tinker Bell dresses to Massachusetts purchasers.

(4) Same facts as Example 2 in the Directive except that Motor Way is a Dutch licensing company which is not "engaged in business in the United States" for federal income tax purposes.

These examples, as well as the hypotheticals in Note B infra, are taken from Massachusetts Taxpayers Foundation, "*Geoffrey* Case and Corporate Nexus—Beyond Directive 96–2" (July 26, 1996).

B. Geoffrey *and Beyond.* In the following hypotheticals, consider whether Massachusetts would have jurisdiction to tax Source Code, Webco, Duller Image, and Ace Products on the income earned from their activities described below. Your analysis should take into account *Geoffrey, DOR Directive 96–2,* and federal constitutional constraints.

(1) Source Code, Inc. is a California-based software company that licenses custom-designed or specialized database management systems to customers throughout the United States, including Massachusetts. The licenses typically provide for a perpetual license fee of $500,000 payable initially. The licenses also provide for an optional annual maintenance fee of 15 percent of the perpetual license fee amount which, if paid, entitles the licensee to system upgrades.

(2) Webco is a California corporation engaged in business as an Internet service provider. Webco's main server is located in Alabama. Webco stores Internet web sites for third parties on its main server which may be accessed by customers located throughout the United States, including Massachusetts. Customers of Webco access the system through their domestic telephone lines to small local computer-based communication units. Upon receipt of customer calls, these local units automatically establish communications links between the customer and the main

server. Webco derives income from its customers, including customers in Massachusetts, from usage fees, connection charges, sign-up fees, storage fees (web site), and data processing service fees.

(3) Duller Image, Inc. produces a mail-order catalog of useless home appliances. The company mails out millions of catalogs from its Fargo, North Dakota headquarters, 100,000 of which are addressed to unsuspecting homeowners in Massachusetts. Duller Image has no sales people and relies totally on its catalog mailings to generate its sales revenues. For totally unknown reasons, Duller Image realized $1 million in sales from its Massachusetts customers in 2009.

(4) Duller Image over a number of years manages to sells thousands of Duller Image "Dullards," 3–foot high, house-cleaning robots which are covered with Duller Image decals (including an 800 telephone number), to Massachusetts residents. As the population of Dullards in Massachusetts grows, Duller Image catalog sales in Massachusetts soar dramatically.

(5) Ace Products is a Delaware corporation based in Illinois engaged in the manufacture and sale of copper tubing. Ace delivers all goods which it sells outside Illinois through the use of third-party commercial vendors and is not physically present in any state other than Illinois. Ace solicits sales in Massachusetts in 2009 by direct mail, telephone and telecopier from its Illinois offices. Ace effects substantial sales in Massachusetts in 2009, such that, at the conclusion of that year, Ace is due millions of dollars in accounts receivable from various Massachusetts companies.

C. *Jurisdiction to Tax Income Based on the Presence of Mobile Property in the State.* The ownership of property in a state has generally been regarded as an appropriate basis for jurisdiction to tax the income of the owner of such property (but see *Quill* where ownership of a "few floppy diskettes" did not establish nexus). Thus the ownership of an office, a warehouse, or a stock of goods in a state would ordinarily provide a constitutionally sufficient foundation for a state to tax the property's owner on the income it derives from the state. There has, however, been a division of authority over the question whether the presence of mobile property in the state provides a sufficient nexus to subject the owner to income taxation in the state. In American Refrigerator Transit Co. v. State Tax Comm'n, 238 Or. 340, 395 P.2d 127 (1964), the taxpayer (ART) owned refrigerator cars, which it leased to operating railroads for use by them in rendering transportation service. ART had no rental agreement with any railroad operating in Oregon, but under railroad interchange practice some of ART's cars were interchanged with railroads that operated in the state. The railroads provided servicing and light repairs on ART's cars, but ART handled all major repairs outside of Oregon. ART delivered the cars to the railroads outside of Oregon, and ART had no control over their routing, movement, interchange or route. The court sustained a tax on the income that ART derived from its lease of the cars in Oregon, despite the taxpayer's lack of control over the leased property. In so holding, the court declared:

> We do not regard it as essential to the existence of a nexus that the taxpayer, through its agents, *directly* engage in some form of physical

activity within the state in furtherance of a business purpose. The connection between the taxing state and the out-of-state taxpayer necessary to establish nexus is essentially an economic rather than a physical relationship. * * *

The nexus exists whenever the corporation takes advantage of the economic milieu within the state to realize a profit. The state is entitled to tax if the benefits it provides are a substantial economic factor in the production of the taxpayer's income. The benefits are found in the maintenance of conditions essential to the production or marketing of goods. They may be realized simply in the protection of the taxpayer's property used in the production of income.

Id., 395 P.2d at 130 (emphasis in original).

Can this position be squared with *Quill*? While the presence of the taxpayer's property in the state would certainly appear to meet the "bright-line, physical-presence" requirement, does it meet the due process standards the Court articulated in *Quill*? On facts essentially identical to those at issue in the Oregon case, the Supreme Court of Arkansas and Oklahoma reached similar results, Commissioner of Revenues v. Pacific Fruit Express Co., 227 Ark. 8, 296 S.W.2d 676 (1956); Oklahoma Tax Comm'n v. American Refrigerator Transit Co., 349 P.2d 746 (Okl. 1959), but the Supreme Court of Kentucky held no nexus existed. Kentucky Tax Commission v. American Refrigerator Transit Co., 294 S.W.2d 554 (Ky. 1956); cf. TTX Co. v. Idaho State Tax Comm'n, 128 Idaho 483, 915 P.2d 713 (1996) (railroad carline's income from leased rolling stock in state not taxable under statute because carline "conducts no business transactions or activities" in state and income from rolling stock rentals is therefore "nonbusiness" income allocable to other states).

D. FEDERAL STATUTORY LIMITATIONS ON STATE TAX JURISDICTION: PUBLIC LAW 86–272

The materials presented in this chapter so far have been concerned with federal *constitutional* limitations on state tax jurisdiction. It is also possible, however, for Congress to impose limitations on states' jurisdiction to tax. In fact, legislation enacted in 1959—Public Law 86–272 (commonly known as "P.L. 86–272")—did precisely this. P.L. 86–272 was crafted in response to a U.S. Supreme Court decision, Northwestern States Portland Cement Co. v. Minnesota, 358 U.S. 450, 79 S.Ct. 357 (1959). We will examine that decision in greater detail in Chapter 3. For now, we are interested in gauging the effect of P.L. 86–272 on state tax jurisdiction.[g]

---

g. P.L. 86–272 has been codified at 15 U.S.C. §§ 381–384.

PUBLIC LAW 86–272

73 Stat. 555, 15 U.S.C. §§ 381–84.
Title I—Imposition of Minimum Standard.**h**

Sec. 101. (a) No State, or political subdivision thereof, shall have power to impose, for any taxable year ending after the date of the enactment of this Act, a net income tax on the income derived within such State by any person from interstate commerce if the only business activities within such State by or on behalf of such person during such taxable year are either, or both, of the following:

(1) the solicitation of orders by such person, or his representative, in such State for sales of tangible personal property, which orders are sent outside the State for approval or rejection, and, if approved, are filled by shipment or delivery from a point outside the State; and

(2) the solicitation of orders by such person, or his representative, in such State in the name of or for the benefit of a prospective customer of such person, if orders by such customer to such person to enable such customer to fill orders resulting from such solicitation are orders described in paragraph (1).

(b) The provisions of subsection (a) shall not apply to the imposition of a net income tax by any State, or political subdivision thereof, with respect to—

(1) any corporation which is incorporated under the laws of such State; or

(2) any individual who, under the laws of such State, is domiciled in, or a resident of, such State.

(c) For purposes of subsection (a), a person shall not be considered to have engaged in business activities within a State during any taxable year merely by reason of sales in such State, or the solicitation of orders for sales in such State, of tangible personal property on behalf of such person by one or more independent contractors, or by reason of the maintenance of an office in such State by one or more independent contractors whose activities on behalf of such person in such State consist solely of making sales, or soliciting orders for sales, of tangible personal property.

(d) For purposes of this section—

(1) the term "independent contractor" means a commission agent, broker, or other independent contractor who is engaged in selling, or soliciting orders for the sale of, tangible personal property for more

---

h. As noted, the excerpted text is from Title I of P.L. 86–272. Title II provided for the making by the House Judiciary Committee and the Senate Finance Committee of "full and complete studies of all matters pertaining to the taxation by the States of income derived within the States from the conduct of business activities which are exclusively in furtherance of interstate commerce or which are a part of interstate commerce, for the purpose of recommending to the Congress proposed legislation providing uniform standards to be observed by the States in imposing income taxes on income so derived." The result of this directive was an extensive and invaluable four-volume study. Special Subcomm. on State Taxation of Interstate Commerce of the House Comm. on the Judiciary, State Taxation of Interstate Commerce, H.R. Rep. No. 1480, 88th Cong., 2d Sess. (1964); H.R. Rep. Nos. 565 and 982, 89th Cong., 1st Sess. (1965) (the "Willis Committee Report"). We will hereafter cite this report as ___ Willis Comm. Rep. ___, with the volume number preceding and the page number succeeding the citations.

than one principal and who holds himself out as such in the regular course of his business activities; and

(2) the term "representative" does not include an independent contractor.

Sec. 102. (a) No State, or political subdivision thereof, shall have power to assess, after the date of the enactment of this Act, any net income tax which was imposed by such State or political subdivision, as the case may be, for any taxable year ending on or before such date, on the income derived within such State by any person from interstate commerce, if the imposition of such tax for a taxable year ending after such date is prohibited by section 101.

* * *

Sec. 103. For purposes of this title, the term "net income tax" means any tax imposed on, or measured by, net income.

* * *

NOTES AND QUESTIONS

A. *Analysis of Public Law 86–272.* The principal effect of P.L. 86–272 is to deny the states the power to impose taxes on or measured by net income derived within the state from interstate commerce if the "only business activities carried on within the State" are the solicitation of orders for sales of tangible personal property, where the orders are sent outside the state for approval or rejection and are filled by shipment or delivery from a point outside the state.

The legislation is carefully circumscribed and is limited to:

(1) *Selling tangible personal property.* The statute excludes from its scope airlines, railroads, pipelines, telecommunications, trucking, bus, other companies involved in the transportation industry as well as those involved in the broadcast industry. Many questions arise in the penumbral area between sales of tangible personal property and sales of services. Is the sale of machines that the vendor installs in the state a sale of tangible personal property or a sale of tangible personal property along with the sale of an installation service? And does the installation activity, whether or not a service, take the case outside the minimum standards of immunity? Or should minor services "incidental" to the sale of tangible personal property be ignored? If so, fine lines may be drawn between "incidental installation" and extensive installation, such as the erection of the steel framework of a building out of girders fabricated outside the state.

(2) *Solicitation and related activities.* (A) Solicitation of orders is an immune activity under the statute. The statute does not, however, grant explicit immunity to collecting any part of the purchase price from the customer. Controversy as to the scope of solicitation has produced extensive litigation. Suppose the door-to-door canvasser, as is often the case, collects a deposit from the customer. Does this mean the immunity will be

lost? Furthermore, what about other activities that could be seen as incidental to solicitation such as the handling of consumer complaints or checking of a customer's credit. The U.S. Supreme Court addressed these questions in Wisconsin Department of Revenue v. William Wrigley, Jr., Co., 505 U.S. 214, 112 S.Ct. 2447 (1992), set forth following this introductory discussion at pp. 85–98 infra.

(B) It is important to remember that there are two categories of solicitation that are protected by Public Law 86–272. Direct solicitation of orders from prospective purchasers by the seller or its representative (under the first paragraph of Section 101(a)) and indirect solicitation "in the name of or for the benefit of a prospective customer" by the seller or its representative (under the second paragraph of Section 101(a)). The typical fact pattern toward which the second paragraph is directed involves the out-of-state manufacturer/seller who makes sales to a local distributor who in turn sells the products to the manufacturer/seller's ultimate customer. This pattern is particularly prevalent in the alcoholic beverages and pharmaceutical industries, where the out-of-state manufacturer is often precluded by law from selling directly to the ultimate consumer.

(3) *Local warehousing.* Local warehousing and delivery of goods out of a local warehouse clearly lie beyond the pale of the minimum standards established for immunity. Instead, shipment must be made from a point outside the state. Presumably, the protected area includes not only delivery by common carrier or the post office, but also by the vendor's trucks, for the test appears to be the point of origin of the shipment. Some states, however, have taken the position that delivery by the vendor's trucks deprives the vendor of the statute's protection. What about delivery by the vendor to the local salesperson for such person to make delivery to the customer. Does this constitute a continuous shipment from outside the state to the customer, or is it a local delivery not protected by the statute?

(4) *Sales office.* The legislative history of the statute leaves little doubt that the maintenance of a sales office within the state designed to serve local solicitors takes the taxpayer outside the area of immunity from taxation. This restriction raises some perplexing questions. Any kind of office—if the taxpayer more or less permanently maintains an employment office, a purchasing office, a repair shop, a garage or terminal—would appear to deprive the taxpayer of the statutory immunity. Suppose the out-of-state vendor rents a hotel suite, which the salesman uses for a few days or few weeks on her periodic trips to the state. Does this constitute the maintenance of an office or other activities beyond the immunity granted for "solicitation of orders"? What if a local salesman makes his home in effect the business and display office of his out-of-state employer and is in one way or another reimbursed for it? See Wisconsin Department of Revenue v. William Wrigley, Jr., Co., supra, set forth following this introductory discussion at pp. 85–98 infra.

(5) *Domestic corporations.* The law does not seek to restrict the state's powers to tax either domestic corporations or individuals domiciled in the state.

(6) *Net Income Taxes.* The law applies only to net income taxes, which include "any tax imposed on, or measured by, net income." Consequently, the law does not apply to the general business taxes of states that do not employ a net income measure, such as Ohio's Commercial Activity Tax or Washington's Business and Occupation Tax, which are measured by gross receipts. In those states, the only federal limitations on the states' jurisdiction to tax are those attributable to constitutional restraints.

(7) *Independent sales representatives.* The immunity statute extends to the use of sales representatives, that is, persons who are not employees but are independent contractors soliciting orders or making sales of tangible property for the out-of-state vendor. To qualify, these brokers or independent sales representatives must represent more than one principal and hold themselves out as such sales representatives. Unlike the employee sales representative, the independent broker *may complete sales in the state,* that is, at least accept orders; and the maintenance by the independent sales representative of his or her own sales office will not affect immunity. The difference in treatment between the independent broker-solicitor and the employee-solicitor can give rise to tax motivated efforts to transform employee-sales representatives into independent contractors.

WISCONSIN DEPARTMENT OF REVENUE
v. WILLIAM WRIGLEY, JR., CO.

Supreme Court of the United States, 1992.
505 U.S. 214, 112 S.Ct. 2447.

Jᴜsᴛɪᴄᴇ Sᴄᴀʟɪᴀ delivered the opinion of the Court.

Section 101(a) of Public Law 86–272, 73 Stat. 555 (1959), 15 U.S.C. § 381, prohibits a State from taxing the income of a corporation whose only business activities within the State consist of "solicitation of orders" for tangible goods, provided that the orders are sent outside the State for approval and the goods are delivered from out-of-state. The issue in this case is whether respondent's activities in Wisconsin fell outside the protection of this provision.

I

Respondent William Wrigley, Jr., Co. is the world's largest manufacturer of chewing gum. Based in Chicago, it sells gum nationwide through a marketing system that divides the country into districts, regions, and territories. During the relevant period (1973–1978), the Midwestern district included a Milwaukee region, covering most of Wisconsin and parts of other States, which was subdivided into several geographic territories.

The district manager for the Midwestern district had his residence and company office in Illinois, and visited Wisconsin only six to nine days each year, usually for a sales meeting or to call on a particularly important account. The regional manager of the Milwaukee region resided in Wisconsin, but Wrigley did not provide him with a company office. He had general responsibility for sales activities in the region, and would typically spend 80–95% of his time working with the sales representatives in the field or contacting certain "key" accounts. The remainder of his time was devoted to administrative activities, including writing and reviewing company reports, recruiting new sales representatives, making recommendations to the district manager concerning the hiring, firing, and compensation of sales representatives, and evaluating their performance. He would preside at full-day sales strategy meetings for all regional sales representatives once or twice a year. The manager from 1973 to 1976, John Kroyer, generally held these meetings in the "office" he maintained in the basement of his home, whereas his successor, Gary Hecht, usually held them at a hotel or motel. (Kroyer claimed income tax deductions for this office, but Wrigley did not reimburse him for it, though it provided a filing cabinet.) Mr. Kroyer also intervened two or three times a year to help arrange a solution to credit disputes between the Chicago office and important local accounts. Mr. Hecht testified that he never engaged in such activities, although Wrigley's formal position description for regional sales manager continued to list as one of the assigned duties "[r]epresent[ing] the company on credit problems as necessary."

The sales or "field" representatives in the Milwaukee region, each of whom was assigned his own territory, resided in Wisconsin. They were provided with company cars, but not with offices. They were also furnished a stock of gum (with an average wholesale value of about $1000), a supply of display racks, and promotional literature. These materials were kept at home, except that one salesman, whose apartment was too small, rented storage space at about $25 per month, for which he was reimbursed by Wrigley.

On a typical day, the sales representative would load up the company car with a supply of display racks and several cases of gum, and would visit accounts within his territory. In addition to handing out promotional materials and free samples, and directly requesting orders of Wrigley products, he would engage in a number of other activities which Wrigley asserts were designed to promote sales of its products. He would, for example, provide free display racks to retailers (perhaps several on any given day), and would seek to have these new racks, as well as pre-existing ones, prominently located. The new racks were usually filled from the retailer's existing stock of Wrigley gum, but it would sometimes happen—perhaps once a month—that the retailer had no Wrigley products on hand and did not want to wait until they could be ordered from the wholesaler. In that event, the rack would be filled from the stock of gum in the salesman's car. This gum, which would have a retail value of $15 to $20, was not provided without charge. The representative would issue an "agency stock check" to the retailer, indicating the quantity supplied; he would send a copy of this to the Chicago office or to the wholesaler, and the retailer would ultimately be billed (by the wholesaler) in the proper amount.

When visiting a retail account, Wrigley's sales representative would also check the retailer's stock of gum for freshness, and would replace stale gum at no cost to the retailer. This was a regular part of a representative's duties, and at any given time up to 40% of the stock of gum in his possession would be stale gum that had been removed from retail stores. After accumulating a sufficient amount of stale product, the representative either would ship it back to Wrigley's Chicago office or would dispose of it at a local Wisconsin landfill.

Wrigley did not own or lease real property in Wisconsin, did not operate any manufacturing, training, or warehouse facility, and did not have a telephone listing or bank account. All Wisconsin orders were sent to Chicago for acceptance, and were filled by shipment through common carrier from outside the State. Credit and collection activities were similarly handled by the Chicago office. Although Wrigley engaged in print, radio, and television advertising in Wisconsin, the purchase and placement of that advertising was managed by an independent advertising agency located in Chicago.

Wrigley had never filed tax returns or paid taxes in Wisconsin; indeed, it was not licensed to do business in that State. In 1980, petitioner Wisconsin Department of Revenue concluded that the company's instate business activities during the years 1973–1978 had been sufficient to support imposition of a franchise tax, and issued a tax assessment on a percentage of the company's apportionable income for those years. Wrigley objected to the assessment, maintaining that its Wisconsin activities were limited to "solicitation of orders" within the meaning of 15 U.S.C. § 381, and that it was therefore immune from Wisconsin franchise taxes. After an evidentiary hearing, the Wisconsin Tax Appeals Commission unanimously upheld the imposition of the tax. * * * The County Circuit Court then reversed on the merits, but that decision was in turn reversed by the Wisconsin Court of Appeals, with one judge dissenting. The Wisconsin Supreme Court, in a unanimous opinion, reversed yet once again, thus finally disallowing the Wisconsin tax. We granted the State's petition for certiorari.

II

In Northwestern States Portland Cement Co. v. Minnesota, 358 U.S. 450, 454, 79 S.Ct. 357, 360 (1959), we considered Minnesota's imposition of a properly apportioned tax on the net income of an Iowa cement corporation whose "activities in Minnesota consisted of a regular and systematic course of solicitation of orders for the sale of its products, each order being subject to acceptance, filling and delivery by it from its plant [in Iowa]." The company's salesmen, operating out of a three-room office in Minneapolis rented by their employer, solicited purchases by cement dealers and by customers of cement dealers. They also received complaints about goods that had been lost or damaged in shipment, and forwarded these back to Iowa for further instructions. The cement company's contacts with Minnesota were otherwise very limited; it had no bank account, real property, or warehoused merchandise in the State. We nonetheless rejected Commerce Clause and due process challenges to the tax:

> "We conclude that net income from the interstate operations of a foreign corporation may be subjected to state taxation provided the levy is not discriminatory and is properly apportioned to local activities within the taxing State forming sufficient nexus to support the same." Id., at 452, 79 S.Ct., at 359.

The opinion in *Northwestern States* was handed down in February 1959. Less than a week later, we granted a motion to dismiss (apparently on mootness grounds) the appeal of a Louisiana Supreme Court decision that had rejected due process and Commerce Clause challenges to the imposition of state net-income taxes based on local solicitation of orders that were sent out-of-state for approval and shipping. Brown–Forman Distillers Corp. v. Collector of Revenue, 234 La. 651, 101 So.2d 70 (1958), appeal dism'd, 359 U.S. 28, 79 S.Ct. 602 (1959). That decision was particularly significant because, unlike the Iowa cement company in *Northwestern States,* the Kentucky liquor company in *Brown–Forman* did *not* lease (or own) any real estate in the taxing state. Rather, its activities were limited to

> "the presence of 'missionary men' who call upon wholesale dealers [in Louisiana] and who, on occasion, accompany the salesmen of these wholesalers to assist them in obtaining a suitable display of appellant's merchandise at the business establishments of said retailers...." 234 La., at 653–654, 101 So.2d, at 70.

Two months later, we denied certiorari in another Louisiana case upholding the imposition of state tax on the income of an out-of-state corporation that neither leased nor owned real property in Louisiana and whose only activities in that State "consist[ed] of the regular and systematic solicitation of orders for its product by fifteen salesmen." International Shoe Co. v. Fontenot, 236 La. 279, 280, 107 So.2d 640, 640 (1958), cert. denied, 359 U.S. 984, 79 S.Ct. 943 (1959).

Although our refusals to disturb the Louisiana Supreme Court's decisions in *Brown–Forman* and *International Shoe* did not themselves have any legal significance, our actions in those cases raised concerns that the broad language of *Northwestern States* might ultimately be read to suggest that a company whose only contacts with a State consisted of sending "drummers" or salesmen into that State could lawfully be subjected to (properly apportioned) income taxation based on the interstate sales those representatives generated. In Heublein, Inc. v. South Carolina Tax Comm'n, 409 U.S. 275, 93 S.Ct. 483 (1972), we reviewed the history of § 381 and noted that the complaints of the business community over the uncertainty created by these cases were the driving force behind the enactment of § 381:

> " 'Persons engaged in interstate commerce are in doubt as to the amount of local activities within a State that will be regarded as forming a sufficient ... connectio[n] with the State to support the

imposition of a tax on net income from interstate operations and "properly apportioned" to the State.'" Id., at 280, 93 S.Ct., at 487 (quoting S.Rep. No. 658, 86th Cong., 1st Sess., pp. 2–3 (1959)),[1] U.S.Code Cong. & Admin.News 1959, pp. 2548, 2549.

Within months after our actions in these three cases, Congress responded to the concerns that had been expressed by enacting Public Law 86–272, which established what the relevant section heading referred to as a "minimum standard" for imposition of a state net-income tax based on solicitation of interstate sales:

> "No State ... shall have power to impose, for any taxable year ..., a net income tax on the income derived within such State by any person from interstate commerce if the only business activities within such State by or on behalf of such person during such taxable year are either, or both, of the following:

> "(1) the solicitation of orders by such person, or his representative, in such State for sales of tangible personal property, which orders are sent outside the State for approval or rejection, and, if approved, are filled by shipment or delivery from a point outside the State; and

> "(2) the solicitation of orders by such person, or his representative, in such State in the name of or for the benefit of a prospective customer of such person, if orders by such customer to such person to enable such customer to fill orders resulting from such solicitation are orders described in paragraph (1)." 73 Stat. 555, 15 U.S.C. § 381(a).

Although we have stated that § 381 was "designed to define clearly a lower limit" for the exercise of state taxing power, and that "Congress' primary goal" was to provide "[c]larity that would remove [the] uncertainty" created by *Northwestern States,* see Heublein, supra, at 280, 93 S.Ct., at 487, experience has proved § 381's "minimum standard" to be somewhat less than entirely clear. The primary sources of confusion, in this case as in others, have been two questions: (1) what is the scope of the crucial term "solicitation of orders"; and (2) whether there is a *de minimis* exception to the activity (beyond "solicitation of orders") that forfeits § 381 immunity. We address these issues in turn.

A

Section 381(a)(1) confers immunity from state income taxes on any company whose "only business activities" in that State consist of "solicitation of orders" for interstate sales. "Solicitation," commonly understood, means "[a]sking" for, or "enticing" to, something, see Black's Law Dictionary 1393 (6th ed. 1990); Webster's Third New International Dictionary 2169 (1981) ("solicit" means "to approach with a request or plea (as

---

1. See also H.R.Rep. No. 936, 86th Cong., 1st Sess., p. 2 (1959) ("While it is true that the denial of certiorari is not a decision on the merits, and although grounds other than the preceden[t] of the *Northwestern [States]* cas[e] were advanced as a basis for sustaining the *Brown–Forman* and *International Shoe* decisions, the fact that a tax was successfully imposed in those cases has given strength to the apprehensions which had already been generated among small and moderate size businesses").

in selling or begging)''). We think it evident that in this statute the term includes, not just explicit verbal requests for orders, but also any speech or conduct that implicitly invites an order. Thus, for example, a salesman who extols the virtues of his company's product to the retailer of a competitive brand is engaged in "solicitation" even if he does not come right out and ask the retailer to buy some. The key question in this case is whether, and to what extent, "solicitation of orders" covers activities that neither explicitly nor implicitly propose a sale.

In seeking the answer to that question, we reject the proposition put forward by Wisconsin and its *amici* that we must construe § 381 narrowly because we said in *Heublein* that " 'unless Congress conveys its purpose clearly, it will not be deemed to have significantly changed the Federal–State balance,' " 409 U.S., at 281–282, 93 S.Ct., at 487–488 (citation omitted). That principle—which we applied in *Heublein* to reject a suggested inference from § 381 that States cannot regulate solicitation in a manner that might cause an out-of-state company to forfeit its tax immunity—has no application in the present case. Because § 381 unquestionably *does* limit the power of States to tax companies whose only in-state activity is "the solicitation of orders," our task is simply to ascertain the fair meaning of that term.

Wisconsin views some courts as having adopted the position that an out-of-state company forfeits its § 381 immunity if it engages in "any activity other than requesting the customer to purchase the product." Brief for Petitioner 21; see also id., at 19, n. 8 (citing Hervey v. AMF Beaird, Inc., 250 Ark. 147, 464 S.W.2d 557 (1971); Clairol, Inc. v. Kingsley, 109 N.J.Super. 22, 262 A.2d 213, aff'd, 57 N.J. 199, 270 A.2d 702 (1970), appeal dism'd, 402 U.S. 902, 91 S.Ct. 1377 (1971)). Arguably supporting this interpretation is subsection (c) of § 381, which expands the immunity of subsection (a) when the out-of-state seller does its marketing through independent contractors, to include not only solicitation of orders for sales, but also actual sales, and *in addition* "the maintenance ... of an office ... by one or more independent contractors whose activities ... consist solely of making sales, or soliciting orders for sales...."[3] The plain implication of this is that without that separate indulgence the maintenance of an office for the exclusive purpose of conducting the exempted solicitation and sales would have provided a basis for taxation—i.e., that the phrase "solicitation of orders" does not embrace the maintenance of an office for the exclusive purpose of soliciting orders. Of course the phrase "solicitation of orders" ought to be accorded a consistent meaning within the section, and if it does not embrace maintaining an office for

---

3.   15 U.S.C. § 381(c) reads in its entirety as follows:

"For purposes of subsection (a) of this section, a person shall not be considered to have engaged in business activities within a State during any taxable year merely by reason of sales in such State, or the solicitation of orders for sales in such State, of tangible personal property on behalf of such person by one or more independent contractors, or by reason of the maintenance, of an office in such State by one or more independent contractors whose activities on behalf of such person in such State consist solely of making sales, or soliciting orders for sales, or [*sic*] tangible personal property."

soliciting in subsection (c), it does not do so in subsection (a) either. One might argue that the necessity of special permission for an office establishes that the phrase "solicitation of orders" covers only the actual requests for purchases or, at most, the actions absolutely essential to making those requests.

We think, however, that would be an unreasonable reading of the text. That the statutory phrase uses the term "solicitation" in a more general sense that includes not merely the ultimate act of inviting an order but the entire process associated with the invitation, is suggested by the fact that § 381 describes "the solicitation of orders" as a subcategory, not of in-state *acts,* but rather of in-state *"business activities"*—a term that more naturally connotes courses by conduct. See Webster's Third New International Dictionary 22 (1981) (defining "activity" as "an occupation, pursuit, or recreation in which a person is active—often used in pl. <business *activities*>"). Moreover, limiting "solicitation of orders" to actual requests for purchases would reduce § 381(a)(1) to a nullity. (It is obviously impossible to make a request without some accompanying action, such as placing a phone call or driving a car to the customer's location.) And limiting it to acts "essential" for making requests would engender endless uncertainty, contrary to the whole purpose of the statute. (Is it "essential" to use a company car, or to take a taxi, in order to conduct in-person solicitation? For that matter, is it "essential" to solicit in person?) It seems to us evident that "solicitation of orders" embraces request-related activity that is not even, strictly speaking, essential, or else it would not cover salesmen's driving on the State's roads, spending the night in the State's hotels, or displaying within the State samples of their product. We hardly think the statute had in mind only day-trips into the taxing jurisdiction by empty-handed drummers on foot. See United States Tobacco Co. v. Commonwealth, 478 Pa. 125, 140, 386 A.2d 471, 478 ("Congress could hardly have intended to exempt only walking solicitors"), cert. denied, 439 U.S. 880, 99 S.Ct. 217 (1978). And finally, this extremely narrow interpretation of "solicitation" would cause § 381 to leave virtually unchanged the law that existed before its enactment. Both *Brown–Forman* (where the salesman assisted wholesalers in obtaining suitable displays for whiskey at retail stores) and *International Shoe* (where hotel rooms were used to display shoes) would be decided as they were before, upholding the taxation.

At the other extreme, Wrigley urges that we adopt a broad interpretation of "solicitation" which it describes as having been adopted by the Wisconsin Supreme Court based on that court's reading of cases in Pennsylvania and New York, see 160 Wis.2d, at 82, 465 N.W.2d, at 811–812 (citing United States Tobacco Co. v. Commonwealth, supra; Gillette Co. v. State Tax Comm'n, 56 App.Div.2d 475, 393 N.Y.S.2d 186 (1977), aff'd, 45 N.Y.2d 846, 410 N.Y.S.2d 65, 382 N.E.2d 764 (1978)). See also Indiana Dept. of Revenue v. Kimberly–Clark Corp., 275 Ind. 378, 384, 416 N.E.2d 1264, 1268 (1981). According to Wrigley, this would treat as "solicitation of orders" any activities that are "ordinary and necessary 'business activities' accompanying the solicitation process" or are "routinely associated with deploying a sales force to conduct the solicitation, so long as there is no office, plant, warehouse or inventory in the State." Brief for Respondent 9, 19–20; see also J. Hellerstein, State Taxation ¶ 6.11[2], p. 245 (1983) ("solicitation ought to be held to embrace other normal incidents of activities of salesmen" or the "customary functions of sales representatives of out-of-state merchants"). We reject this "routinely-associated-with-solicitation" or "customarily-performed-by-salesmen" approach, since it converts a standard embracing only a particular activity ("solicitation") into a standard embracing all activities routinely conducted by those who engage in that particular activity ("salesmen"). If, moreover, the approach were to be applied (as respondent apparently intends) on an industry-by-industry basis, it would render the limitations of § 381(a) toothless, permitting "solicitation of orders" to be whatever a particular industry wants its salesmen to do.[4]

In any case, we do not regard respondent's proposed approach to be an accurate characterization of the Wisconsin Supreme Court's opinion. The Wisconsin court construed "solicitation of orders" to reach only those activities that are "closely associated" with solicitation, industry practice being only one factor to be considered in judging the "close[ness]" of the connection between the challenged activity and the actual requests for orders. 160 Wis.2d, at 82, 465 N.W.2d, at 811–812. The problem with that standard, it seems to us, is that it merely reformulates rather than answers the crucial question. "What constitutes the 'solicitation of orders'?" becomes "What is 'closely related' to a solicitation request?" This fails to provide the "[c]larity that would remove uncertainty" which we identified as the primary goal of § 381. Heublein, 409 U.S., at 280, 93 S.Ct., at 487.

We proceed, therefore, to describe what we think the proper standard to be. Once it is acknowledged, as we have concluded it must be, that "solicitation of orders" covers more than what is strictly *essential* to making requests for purchases, the next (and perhaps the only other) clear line is the one between those activities that are *entirely ancillary* to

---

4. The dissent explicitly agrees with our rejection of the "ordinary and necessary" standard advocated by Wrigley. Post, at 236. It then proceeds, however, to adopt that very standard. It states that the test should be whether a given activity is one that "reasonable buyers would consider . . . to be a part of the solicitation itself and not a significant and independent service or component of value." Post, at 237. It is obvious that those activities that a reasonable buyer would consider "part of the solicitation itself" rather than an "independent service" are those that are *customarily* performed in connection with solicitation. Any doubt that this is what the dissent intends is removed by its later elaboration of its test in the context of the facts of this case. The dissent repeatedly inquires whether an activity is a "*normal* ac[t] of courtesy from seller to buyer," post, at 242 (emphasis added); whether it is a "*common* solicitation practic[e]," post, at 244 (emphasis added); and whether Wrigley "exceed[ed] the *normal* scope of solicitation," post, at 242 (emphasis added). Of course, given Wrigley's significant share of the Wisconsin chewing gum market, *most* activities it chooses to "conduc[t] in the course of solicitation," post, at 246 will be viewed as a normal part of the solicitation process itself. Had Wrigley's sales representatives routinely approved orders on the spot; or accepted payments on past-due accounts; or even made outright sales of gum, it is difficult to see how a reasonable buyer would have thought that was *not* "part of the solicitation itself"—it certainly has no "independent value" to *him*. Nothing in the text of the statute suggests that it was intended to confer tax immunity on whatever activities are engaged in by sales agents in a particular industry.

requests for purchases—those that serve no independent business function apart from their connection to the soliciting of orders—and those
activities that the company would have reason to engage in anyway but
chooses to allocate to its in-state sales force.[5] Cf. National Tires, Inc. v.
Lindley, 68 Ohio App.2d 71, 78–79, 22 O.O.3d 69, 73–74, 426 N.E.2d 793,
798 (1980) (company's activities went beyond solicitation to "functions
more commonly related to maintaining an on-going business"). Providing
a car and a stock of free samples to salesmen is part of the "solicitation of
orders," because the only reason to do it is to facilitate requests for
purchases. Contrariwise, employing salesmen to repair or service the
company's products is not part of the "solicitation of orders," since there
is good reason to get that done whether or not the company has a sales
force. Repair and servicing may help to *increase* purchases; but it is not
ancillary to *requesting purchases,* and cannot be converted into "solicitation" by merely being assigned to salesmen. See, e.g., Herff Jones Co. v.
State Tax Comm'n, 247 Or. 404, 412, 430 P.2d 998, 1001–1002 (1967) (no
§ 381 immunity for sales representatives' collection activities).[6]

As we have discussed earlier, the text of the statute (the "office"
exception in subsection (c)) requires one exception to this principle: Even
if engaged in exclusively to facilitate requests for purchases, the maintenance of an office within the State, by the company or on its behalf, would
go beyond the "solicitation of orders." We would not make any more
generalized exception to our immunity standard on the basis of the
"office" provision. It seemingly represents a judgment that a company
office within a State is such a significant manifestation of company
"presence" that, absent a specific exemption, income taxation should
always be allowed. Jantzen, Inc. v. District of Columbia, 395 A.2d 29, 32
(D.C.1978); see generally Hellerstein, supra, ¶ 6.4.

Wisconsin urges us to hold that no *post-sale* activities can be included
within the scope of covered "solicitation." We decline to do so. Activities
that take place after a sale will ordinarily not be entirely ancillary in the
sense we have described, see, e.g., Miles Laboratories v. Department of

---

5. The dissent states that ancillarity should be judged, not from the perspective of the seller,
but from the perspective of the *buyer.* Post, at 237 (test is whether "reasonable *buyers* would
consider [the activities] to be a part of the solicitation itself") (emphasis added); post, at 243
("The test I propose . . . requires an objective assessment from the vantage point of a reasonable
buyer") (emphasis added); post, at 246 (question is whether the activities "possess independent
value to the *customer*") (emphasis added). As explained earlier, see n. 4, supra, this rule
inevitably results in a whatever-the-industry-wants standard, despite the dissent's unequivocal
disavowal of such a test. The dissent also suggests that ancillarity should be judged by asking
whether a particular challenged activity is "*related to a particular* sales call or to a particular
sales solicitation," post, at 244 (emphasis added). This standard, besides being amorphous, cannot
be correct. Those activities that are most clearly *not* immunized by the statute—*e.g.,* actual sales,
collection of funds—would seem to be the ones *most* closely "related" to particular acts of actual
solicitation. And activities the dissent finds immunized in the present case—maintenance of a
storage facility, and use of a home office—are extremely remote.

6. Contrary to the dissent's suggestion, post, at 242, 246, both *Brown–Forman* and *International Shoe* would have been decided differently under these principles. The various activities at
issue in those cases (renting a room for temporary display of sample products; assisting
wholesalers in obtaining suitable product display in retail shops) would be considered merely
ancillary to either wholesale solicitation or downstream (consumer or retailer) solicitation.

Revenue, 274 Or. 395, 400, 546 P.2d 1081, 1083 (1976) (replacing damaged goods), but we are not prepared to say that will invariably be true. Moreover, the pre-sale/post-sale distinction is hopelessly unworkable. Even if one disregards the confusion that may exist concerning when a sale takes place, cf. Uniform Commercial Code § 2–401, 1A U.L.A. 675 (1989), manufacturers and distributors ordinarily have ongoing relationships that involve continuous sales, making it often impossible to determine whether a particular incidental activity was related to the sale that preceded it or the sale that followed it.

B

The Wisconsin Supreme Court also held that a company does not necessarily forfeit its tax immunity under § 381 by performing *some* in-state business activities that go beyond "solicitation of orders"; rather, it said, "[c]ourts should also analyze" whether these additional activities were " 'deviations from the norm' " or *"de minimis* activities." 160 Wis.2d, at 82, 465 N.W.2d, at 811 (citation omitted). Wisconsin asserts that the plain language of the statute bars this recognition of a *de minimis* exception, because the immunity is limited to situations where "the *only* business activities within [the] State" are those described, 15 U.S.C. § 381 (emphasis added). This ignores the fact that the venerable maxim *de minimis non curat lex* ("the law cares not for trifles") is part of the established background of legal principles against which all enactments are adopted, and which all enactments (absent contrary indication) are deemed to accept. See, e.g., Republic of Argentina v. Weltover, Inc., 112 S.Ct. 2160, 2168 (1992); * * * It would be especially unreasonable to abandon normal application of the *de minimis* principle in construing § 381, which operates in such stark, all-or-nothing fashion: A company either has complete net-income tax immunity or it has none at all, even for its solicitation activities. Wisconsin's reading of the statute renders a company liable for hundreds of thousands of dollars in taxes if one of its salesmen sells a 10–cent item in-state. Finally, Wisconsin is wrong in asserting that application of the *de minimis* principle "excise[s] the word 'only' from the statute." Brief for Petitioner 27. The word "only" places a strict limit upon the *categories* of activities that are covered by § 381, not upon their *substantiality*. See, e.g., Drackett Prods. Co. v. Conrad, 370 N.W.2d 723, 726 (N.D.1985); Kimberly–Clark, 275 Ind., at 383–384, 416 N.E.2d, at 1268.

Whether a particular activity is a *de minimis* deviation from a prescribed standard must, of course, be determined with reference to the purpose of the standard. Section 381 was designed to increase—beyond what *Northwestern States* suggested was required by the Constitution— the connection that a company could have with a State before subjecting itself to tax. Accordingly, whether in-state activity other than "solicitation of orders" is sufficiently *de minimis* to avoid loss of the tax immunity conferred by § 381 depends upon whether that activity establishes a nontrivial additional connection with the taxing State.

III

Wisconsin asserts that at least six activities performed by Wrigley within its borders went beyond the "solicitation of orders": the replacement of stale gum by sales representatives; the supplying of gum through "agency stock checks"; the storage of gum, racks, and promotional materials; the rental of space for storage; the regional manager's recruitment, training, and evaluation of employees; and the regional manager's intervention in credit disputes.[7] Since none of these activities can reasonably be viewed as requests for orders covered by § 381, Wrigley was subject to tax unless they were either ancillary to requesting orders or *de minimis*.

We conclude that the replacement of stale gum, the supplying of gum through "agency stock checks," and the storage of gum were not ancillary. As to the first: Wrigley would wish to attend to the replacement of spoiled product whether or not it employed a sales force. Because that activity serves an independent business function quite separate from requesting orders, it does not qualify for § 381 immunity. Miles Laboratories, 274 Or., at 400, 546 P.2d, at 1083. Although Wrigley argues that gum replacement was a "promotional necessity" designed to ensure continued sales, Brief for Respondent 31, it is not enough that the activity facilitate *sales;* it must facilitate the *requesting of sales,* which this did not.[8]

The provision of gum through "agency stock checks" presents a somewhat more complicated question. It appears from the record that this activity occurred only in connection with the furnishing of display racks to retailers, so that it was arguably ancillary to a form of *consumer* solicitation. Section 381(a)(2) shields a manufacturer's "missionary" request that an indirect customer (such as a consumer) place an order, if a successful request would ultimately result in an order's being filled by a § 381 *"customer"* of the manufacturer, i.e., by the wholesaler who fills the orders of the retailer with goods shipped to the wholesaler from out-of-state. Cf. Gillette, 56 App.Div.2d, at 482, 393 N.Y.S.2d, at 191 ("Advice to retailers on the art of displaying goods to the public can hardly be more thoroughly solicitation ..."). It might seem, therefore, that setting up gum-filled display racks, like Wrigley's general advertising in Wisconsin,

---

7. Wisconsin has also argued that the scope of the regional managers' activities caused their residences to be, "[in] economic reality," Wrigley offices in the State. Brief for Petitioner 32. If this means that having resident salesmen without offices can sometimes be as commercially effective as having nonresident salesmen with offices, perhaps it is true. But it does not establish that Wrigley "maintained an office" in the sense necessary to come within the exception to the "entirely ancillary" standard we have announced. See supra, at 230. Nor does the regional managers' occasional use of their homes for meetings with salesmen, or Kroyer's uncompensated dedication of a portion of his home basement to his own office. The maintenance of an office necessary to trigger the exception must be more formally attributed to the out-of-state company itself, or to the agents of that company in their agency capacity—as was, for example, the rented office in *Northwestern States.*

8. The dissent argues that this activity must be considered part of "solicitation" because, inter alia, it was "minimal," and not "significant." Post, at 243. We disagree. It was not, as the dissent suggests, a practice that involved simple "acts of courtesy" that occurred only because a salesman happened to be on the scene and did not wish to "harm the company." Post, at 242, 244. Wrigley deliberately chose to use its sales force to engage in regular and systematic replacement of stale product on a level that amounted to several thousand dollars per year, which is a lot of chewing gum.

would be immunized by § 381(a)(2). What destroys this analysis, however, is the fact that Wrigley *made the retailers pay for the gum,* thereby providing a business purpose for supplying the gum quite independent from the purpose of soliciting consumers. Since providing the gum was not entirely ancillary to requesting purchases, it was not within the scope of "solicitation of orders."[9] And because the vast majority of the gum stored by Wrigley in Wisconsin was used in connection with stale gum swaps and agency stock checks, that storage (and the indirect rental of space for that storage) was in no sense ancillary to "solicitation."

By contrast, Wrigley's in-state recruitment, training, and evaluation of sales representatives and its use of hotels and homes for sales-related meetings served no purpose apart from their role in facilitating solicitation. The same must be said of the instances in which Wrigley's regional sales manager contacted the Chicago office about "rather nasty" credit disputes involving important accounts in order to "get the account and [Wrigley's] credit department communicating," App. 71, 72. It hardly appears likely that this mediating function between the customer and the central office would have been performed by some other employee—some company ombudsman, so to speak—if the on-location sales staff did not exist. The purpose of the activity, in other words, was to ingratiate the salesman with the customer, thereby facilitating requests for purchases.

Finally, Wrigley argues that the various nonimmune activities, considered singly or together, are *de minimis.* In particular, Wrigley emphasizes that the gum sales through "agency stock checks" accounted for only 0.00007% of Wrigley's annual Wisconsin sales, and in absolute terms amounted to only several hundred dollars a year. We need not decide whether any of the nonimmune activities was *de minimis* in isolation; taken together, they clearly are not. Wrigley's sales representatives exchanged stale gum, as a matter of regular company policy, on a continuing basis, and Wrigley maintained a stock of gum worth several thousand dollars in the State for this purpose as well as for the less frequently pursued (but equally unprotected) purpose of selling gum through "agency stock checks." Although the relative magnitude of these activities was not large compared to Wrigley's other operations in Wisconsin, we have little difficulty concluding that they constituted a nontrivial additional connection with the State. Because Wrigley's business activities within Wisconsin were not limited to those specified in § 381, the prohibition on net-income taxation contained in that provision was inapplicable.

* * *

9. The dissent speculates, without any basis in the record, that Wrigley might have chosen to charge for the gum, not for the profit, but because giving it away would "lower the per unit cost of all goods purchased," which "could create either the fact or the perception that retailers were not receiving the same price." Post, at 245. Though Wrigley's *motive* for choosing to make a profit on these items seems to us irrelevant in any event, we cannot avoid observing how unlikely it is that this was the reason Wrigley did not include free gum in its (per-unit-cost-distorting) free racks, although it did, as the record shows, regularly give away *other* (presumably per-unit-cost-distorting) free gum. Wrigley itself did not have the temerity to make this argument.

Accordingly, the judgment of the Supreme Court of Wisconsin is reversed, and the case is remanded for further proceedings not inconsistent with this opinion.

It is so ordered. *end of court case - following is other opinion*

JUSTICE O'CONNOR, concurring in Parts I and II, and concurring in the judgment.

I join sections I and II of the Court's opinion. I do not agree, however, that the replacement of stale gum served an independent business function. The replacement of stale gum by the sales representatives was part of ensuring the product was available to the public in a form that may be purchased. Making sure that one's product is available and properly displayed serves no independent business function apart from requesting purchases; one cannot offer a product for sale if it is not available. I agree, however, that the storage of gum in the State and the use of agency stock checks were not ancillary to solicitation and were not *de minimis*. On that basis, I would hold that Wrigley's income is subject to taxation by Wisconsin.

JUSTICE KENNEDY, with whom THE CHIEF JUSTICE and JUSTICE BLACKMUN join, dissenting.

[Justice Kennedy first reviewed the history and background of Section 381(a), including International Shoe Co. v. Fontenot, 236 La. 279, 107 So.2d 640 (1958), cert. denied 359 U.S. 984, 79 S.Ct. 943 (1959), and Brown–Forman Distillers Corp. v. Collector of Revenue, 234 La. 651, 101 So.2d 70 (1958), appeal dismissed and cert. denied 359 U.S. 28, 79 S.Ct. 602 (1959).]

* * * [T]he history of enactment makes clear that § 381(a) exempts from state income taxation at least those business activities at issue in *International Shoe* and *Brown–Forman*. These cases must inform any attempt to give meaning to § 381(a).

* * *

The activities in *International Shoe* and *Brown–Forman* extended beyond specific acts of entreaty; they included merchandising and display, as well as other simple acts of courtesy from buyer to seller, such as arranging product displays and calling on the customer of a customer. The activities considered in *International Shoe* and *Brown–Forman* are by no means exceptional. Checking inventories, displaying products, replacing stale product, and verifying credit are all normal acts of courtesy from seller to buyer. J. Hellerstein, 1 State Taxation: Corporate Income and Franchise Taxes ¶ 6.11[2], p. 245 (1983). A salesperson cannot solicit orders with any degree of effectiveness if he is constrained from performing small acts of courtesy. Note, State Taxation of Interstate Commerce: Public Law 86–272, 46 Va.L.Rev. 297, 315 (1960).

* * *

The Court pursues a laudable effort to state a workable rule, but in the attempt condemns business activities that are bound to solicitation and do not possess independent value to the customer apart from what often accompanies a successful solicitation. The business activities of Wrigley in Wisconsin, just as those considered in *International Shoe* and *Brown–Forman,* are the solicitation of orders. The swapping of stale gum and the infrequent stocking of fresh gum into new displays are not services that Wrigley was under contract to perform; they are not activities that can be said to have provided their own component of significant value; rather they are activities conducted in the course of solicitation and whose legal effect should be the same. My examination of the language of the statute, considered in the context of its enactment, demonstrates that the concerns to which § 381(a) was directed, and for which its language was drafted, are misapprehended by the Court's decision today.

I would affirm the judgment of the Wisconsin Supreme Court.

NOTES AND QUESTIONS

A. *The Scope of "Solicitation of Orders" in Light of* Wrigley. The Supreme Court interpreted Public Law 86–272 to define "solicitation of orders" as not just explicit verbal requests for orders, but also any speech or conduct that implicitly invites an order. Thus, a salesperson who extols the virtues of her product is engaged in "solicitation," even if she does not come right out and ask the purchaser to buy her product. But to what extent does a taxpayer's immunity extend to activities that neither explicitly nor implicitly propose a sale? The Court interpreted "solicitation of orders" as "not merely the ultimate activity of inviting an order but the entire process associated with the invitation." Thus, those activities that are "entirely ancillary to requests for purchases," in other words, those that serve no independent business function apart from their connection to the soliciting of orders, are permissible and therefore nontaxable. The Court then went on to find as unprotected (because they fell outside the definition of "solicitation of orders") those activities that the company would have had reason to engage in anyway but chose to allocate to its in-state sales force. See, e.g., Alcoa Building Products, Inc. v. Commissioner of Revenue, 440 Mass. 224, 797 N.E.2d 357 (2003) (warranty claims-related activity of taxpayer's salesmen were not "entirely ancillary" to "solicitation of orders" because they served a purpose independent of solicitation, even though they led to increased sales of the taxpayer's products).

B. *De Minimis Activities That Go Beyond the Scope of Mere Solicitation.* The *Wrigley* Court carved out an exception to the language of Public Law 86–272 for those de minimis activities that, despite being beyond the scope of "solicitation of orders," constitute trivial additional connections with the taxing state. The Court did not, however, provide much guidance as to its understanding of "de minimis activities." In Kelly–Springfield Tire Co. v. Bajorski, 228 Conn. 137, 635 A.2d 771 (1993), the Connecticut Supreme Court noted the difficulty of applying the de minimis test where the taxpayer sent a credit manager into the state for an annual visit with each of its dealers.

Pointing to the sparsity of the record on such facts as the length of the annual visits, the number of dealers visited, and the extent to which credit information gleaned from the annual visits was made available to the in-state sales representatives to facilitate their solicitation of sales on behalf of the taxpayer, the court found that the activities were de minimis since the commissioner failed to prove otherwise. Query: why did the commissioner have the burden of proof on the de minimis issue? *maybe the two company*

proved they were de minimis the com. couldn't counterprove

C. *MTC Guidelines on Protected and Unprotected Activities.* In light of *Wrigley,* the Multistate Tax Commission (MTC) (described at pp. 535–36 infra), issued a revised Statement of Information Concerning Practices of Multistate Tax Commission and Signatory States Under Public Law 86–272, available at www.mtc.gov. Provided that they are not de minimis, the MTC guidelines (as amended through July 27, 2001) characterize the following activities, among others, as "unprotected" because they exceed "solicitation of orders": making repairs or providing maintenance or service to the property sold or to be sold; collecting current or delinquent accounts, whether directly or by third parties, through assignment or otherwise; investigating credit worthiness; conducting training courses, seminars, or lectures for personnel other than personnel involved only in solicitation; providing any kind of technical assistance or service including, but not limited to, engineering assistance or design service, when one of the purposes thereof is other than the facilitation of the solicitation of orders; investigating, handling, or otherwise assisting in resolving customer complaints, other than mediating direct customer complaints when the sole purpose of such mediation is to ingratiate the sales personnel with the customer; approving or accepting orders; repossessing property; securing deposits on sale; picking up or replacing damaged or returned property; hiring, training, or supervising personnel, other than personnel involved only in solicitation; using agency stock checks or any other instrument or process by which sales are made within the state by sales personnel; maintaining a sample or display room in excess of two weeks (14 days) at any one location within the state during the tax year; carrying samples for sale, exchange, or distribution in any manner for consideration or other value.

The MTC guidelines characterize the following activities, among others, as protected by Public Law 86–272: soliciting orders for sales by any type of advertising; soliciting of orders by an in-state resident employee or representative of the company, so long as such person does not maintain or use any office or other place of business in the state other than an "in-home" office; carrying samples and promotional materials only for display or distribution without charge or other consideration; furnishing and setting up display racks and advising customers on the display of the company's products without charge or other consideration; providing automobiles to sales personnel for their use in conducting protected activities; passing orders, inquiries, and complaints on to the home office; missionary sales activities; i.e., the solicitation of indirect customers for the company's goods; coordinating shipment or delivery without payment or other consideration and providing information relating thereto either prior or subsequent to the placement of an order; checking of customers' inventories without a charge therefor (for re-order, but not for other purposes such as quality control); maintaining a sample or display room for two weeks (14 days) or less at any one location within the state during the tax year.

Do you believe that the MTC's guidelines fairly reflect the Supreme Court's opinion in *Wrigley*? If you were counsel to a taxpayer, which of the MTC's listing of "unprotected" activities would you tell your client are most vulnerable to challenge? If you were counsel to a state revenue department, which of the MTC's listing of "protected" activities would you advise your client are not required by *Wrigley*?

D. *Income Tax Immunity of In–State Representatives Soliciting Orders Falling Within Scope of Public Law 86–272 for Out-of-State Sellers.* It is clear that an out-of-state seller that directly, or through an in-state representative, does no more than solicit orders described in Public Law 86–272 enjoys immunity from state income taxation in the state of solicitation. It is less clear, however, whether a legally separate in-state representative, whose sole activity is the solicitation of orders described in Public Law 86–272 on behalf of the out-of-state seller, enjoys such immunity. Several states have taken the position that a manufacturer's representative who solicits orders for an out-of-state company is subject to tax on its income, because it derives income from the sale of marketing services rather than from the sale of tangible personal property. For example, the Iowa regulations provide:

> Public Law 86–272 does not extend to those corporations which sell services, real estate, or intangibles in more than one state or to domestic corporations. For example, Public Law 86–272 does not extend to brokers or manufacturers' representatives or other persons or entities selling products for another person or entity.

Iowa Admin. Code § 701–52.1(2)(422) (Westlaw 2009). See also North Carolina Dep't of Revenue, Directive No. CD–98–2, April 7, 1998.

In Schering–Plough Healthcare Product Sales Corp. v. Commonwealth, 805 A.2d 1284 (Pa. Cmwlth. 2002), Schering–Plough Healthcare Products Sales Corp. (S–P Sales), a wholly owned subsidiary of Schering–Plough Healthcare Products, Inc. (S–P Products), manufactured and sold over-the-counter healthcare products. S–P Sales was engaged in the business of soliciting orders for S–P Products in Pennsylvania and in other states. All of the orders that S–P Sales solicited in Pennsylvania fell squarely within the definition of activities protected by Public Law 86–272, i.e., they were sent outside the state for approval or rejection and, if approved, were filled by a shipment or delivery from a point outside the state. S–P Products paid S–P Sales a commission based on a fixed percentage of the net final sales consummated by S–P Products.

The Department of Revenue contended that S–P Sales was taxable on its commission income, notwithstanding Public Law 86–272, because it was not the seller of tangible personal property (title to the property was transferred by S–P Products directly to the purchaser). According to the Department, S–P Sales "was merely providing marketing services" to its parent. Id at 1286. Relying on the language of the statute, the court rejected the proposition that obtaining title to the goods is necessary to qualify for exemption under Public Law 86–272. The statute immunizes a person from a state's income tax if the only business activities within such State * * * are * * *the solicitation of orders by such person * * * in such State for sales of tangible personal property, which orders are sent outside the State for approval or rejection, and, if approved, are filled by shipment or delivery from a point outside the State.

Public Law 86–272, § 101(a)(1). Referring to this language, the court observed that "the plain language of the statute is devoid of any suggestion that ownership of the goods is significant." Schering–Plough, 805 A.2d at 1289. The court further remarked that it could see "no logical basis" for the Department's construction of the statute:

> It cannot be seriously argued that a company which limits its activity in a State to solicitation of orders for goods to which it will never take title has a greater nexus to that State than a company taking similar orders for goods it owns somewhere else.

Id. Finally, the court pointed to the extensive legislative history of the statute indicating that Congress's intent was to "set a clearly lower limit of activity below which no business can be taxed." Id. Requiring that a business that did not exceed this activity but lacked title to the property was nevertheless subject to tax would be inconsistent with this intent. Is the Pennsylvania court's decision sound? Would or should the result have been any different if the taxpayer were providing a similar sales solicitation service for one or more unrelated out-of-state vendors?

E. *Independent Contractors and Public Law 86–272.* Public Law 86–272 immunizes a person from state income taxation if the actions of the person do not exceed "solicitation of orders" in the state or activities that are "entirely ancillary" to such solicitation. However, consummating a sale in the state (i.e., accepting the solicited orders) and maintaining an office in the state generally exceed protected "solicitation of orders," with one important exception. The exception occurs when these otherwise nexus-creating activities are carried on by independent contractors. See Public Law 86–272, § 101(c) (p. 82 supra). Accordingly, the vendor itself, acting in a state through its own employees or "representatives," may neither make sales in the state nor maintain an office in the state without losing its statutory immunity. However, when an "independent contractor" makes sales of tangible personal property within the state on behalf of the out-of-state vendor, the vendor will not thereby lose its statutory immunity. Similarly, when an "independent contractor" maintains an office in the state and its in-state activities on behalf of the out-of-state vendor consist solely of making (or soliciting orders for) sales of tangible personal property, the vendor will not thereby lose its statutory immunity.

Public Law 86–272 defines an "independent contractor" as

> a commission agent, broker, or other independent contractor who is engaged in selling, or soliciting orders for the sale of, tangible personal property for more than one principal and who holds himself out as such in the regular course of his business activities.

Public Law 86–272, § 101(d)(1). Although the definition has been criticized as being circular because it uses the term to be defined as part of the definition,

Walter Beaman, Paying Taxes to Other States 6–23 (1963), and "somewhat valueless in practice," Note, "State Taxation of Interstate Commerce: Public Law 86–272," 46 Va. L. Rev. 297, 318 (1960), it does establish two criteria that differentiate "independent contractors" from "dependent" agents, employees, or representatives: (1) the independent contractor must be engaged in selling or soliciting orders for more than one principal; (2) the independent contractor must "hold himself out" as an independent contractor. The first of these criteria is a simple question of fact that generally is (or ought to be) amenable to objective determination, namely, does the contractor work for more than one principal? The second criterion—whether one "holds oneself out" as an independent contractor engaged in selling or soliciting for more than one principal—is more subjective in nature. There has been relatively little litigation over the meaning of the term "independent contractor" in Public Law 86–272, and what little case law we have has been quite fact-sensitive. See, e.g., Reader's Digest Association, Inc. v. Franchise Tax Bd., 94 Cal.App.4th 1240, 115 Cal.Rptr.2d 53 (3d Dist. 2001) (out-of-state magazine vendor's in-state subsidiary that solicited advertising sales for parent and unrelated foreign publishers of the same magazine was not "independent contractor" within the meaning of Public Law 86–272); Tonka Corp. v. Commissioner of Taxation, 284 Minn. 185, 169 N.W.2d 589 (1969) (in-state sales representative was not an "independent contractor" within the meaning of Public Law 86–272 because detailed examination of the facts revealed that the representative "was more like an employee").

E. NEXUS DECISION TREE

On the following page, we have created a nexus "decision tree" designed to assist you in thinking through the analysis you need to undertake when confronting the nexus issues that you have studied in this chapter. By its very nature, the "decision tree" is an oversimplified framework for addressing these questions. Nevertheless, it should provide you with a starting point for structuring your approach to these issues, and it identifies some of the key cases and statutes you should consider in undertaking your analysis.

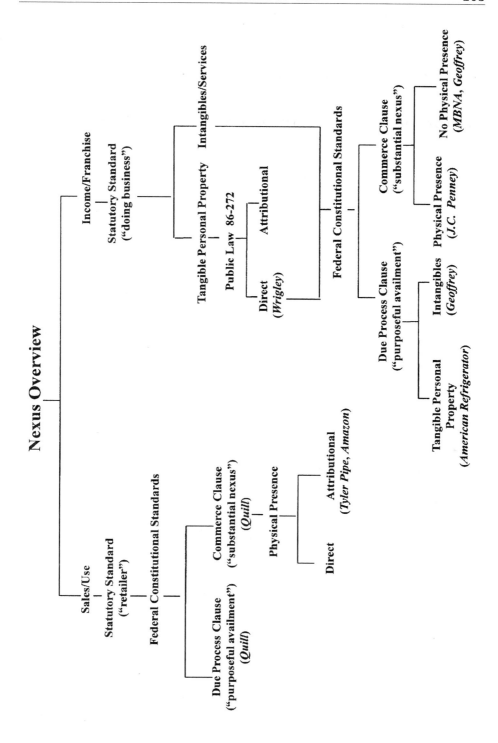

CHAPTER 3

STATE TAXES AS REGULATION OF INTERSTATE AND FOREIGN COMMERCE

■ ■ ■

The previous chapter considered the law of state tax jurisdiction, tracing the Due Process and Commerce Clause limitations on state authority to impose a tax or require a party to collect and remit taxes the state is owed. Of course, jurisdiction alone will not establish the constitutionality of a tax. Like all legislation, state and local taxes are also potentially subject to challenge under various other provisions of the Federal Constitution, such as the Privileges and Immunities Clause of Article IV and the Equal Protection Clause of the Fourteenth Amendment. In Chapter 4, we will examine various state tax controversies arising under those and other constitutional provisions. In this chapter, we offer a closer look at the Commerce Clause, emphasizing limitations on state taxing power beyond those relating to jurisdiction. Once again, we begin with the language of the clause itself, which provides simply that Congress shall have the power "[t]o regulate Commerce with foreign Nations, and among the several States, and with the Indian Tribes."[a] As we will see, despite its concise text, the Commerce Clause has spawned a thicket of doctrinal complexity beyond the nexus requirement. To set the stage, we begin with some brief historical background.

A. HISTORICAL BACKGROUND OF THE COMMERCE CLAUSE

Although the Commerce Clause has been described as "the Framers' response to the central problem that gave rise to the Constitution itself,"[b] the basis for its adoption has long been the subject of dispute among historians. According to the standard account, the clause was inserted in response to the conflict among the states during the years of the Articles

---

a. U.S. Const. art I, § 8, cl. 3.

b. E.E.O.C. v. Wyoming, 460 U.S. 226, 244, 103 S.Ct. 1054 (1983) (Stevens, J., concurring). See also Robert L. Stern, "That Commerce Which Concerns More States Than One," 47 Harv. L. Rev. 1335, 1340–41 (1934) (asserting that "the need for centralized commercial regulation was universally recognized as the primary reason for preparing a new constitution").

of Confederation.[c] Lacking the power to regulate interstate commerce, the Confederation Congress was helpless in the face of beggar-thy-neighbor state legislation that sought to exploit the residents of other states.[d] For example, as one historian of the era recently noted, "States that were blessed with thriving ports—including Massachusetts, New York, Pennsylvania, South Carolina—happily taxed any shipment on the way to or from bordering states."[e] The situation left residents of those bordering states at the mercy of their well-positioned neighbors. James Madison later described New Jersey, positioned between Philadelphia and New York, as "a cask tapped at both ends" and North Carolina, between Virginia and South Carolina, like "a patient bleeding at both arms."[f] The resulting conflict, Madison explained, "never ceased to be a source of dissatisfaction & discord, until the new Constitution, superseded the old."[g]

More recently, historians have begun to question the extent of actual "interstate commercial warfare" among the states in the 1780s.[h] These scholars have cast doubt on the supposed drift toward anarchy, noting that "by the time of the Constitutional Convention the states were deescalating rather than escalating the exactions on each others' goods and shipping."[i] Support for this view can be found in the most comprehensive study of state tariff and tonnage policies during the Confederation period, which concludes that, by 1787, all states "had established tariff systems that allowed U.S.-made and U.S.-grown goods to enter duty free."[j] As for the problem of state imposts on foreign products destined for consumers in other states, that issue was addressed by the Tax Clause (U.S. Const. art. I, § 8, cl. 1), which grants Congress the power to "lay and collect Taxes, Duties, Imposts and Excises," and the Import–Export Clause (U.S. Const. art. I, § 10, cl. 2), which prohibits states from laying "any Imposts or Duties on Imports or Exports" without the consent of Congress. Given the effect of these provisions, it is not clear what independent work the Commerce Clause was designed to do. Indeed, under this view, the Commerce Clause approaches mere surplusage, a "modest little power"[k] with an intended scope comparable, perhaps, to the bankruptcy clause that follows it.[l]

---

c. See, e.g., John Fiske, The Critical Period of American History: 1783–1789 (1888).

d. Id. at 146.

e. David O. Stewart, The Summer of 1787 21 (2007).

f. Id.

g. Notes of Debate in the Federal Convention of 1787, Reported by James Madison 7 (1787).

h. See, e.g., Roger H. Brown, Redeeming the Republic: Federalists, Taxation, and the Origins of the Constitution 146–148 (1993). See also Calvin H. Johnson, Righteous Anger at the Wicked States: The Meaning of the Founders' Constitution 198–200 (2005).

i. Brown, supra note h, at 146.

j. Id. at 147 (citing studies undertaken by William F. Zornow—See, e.g., William F. Zornow, "The Tariff Policies of Virginia," 62 The Virginia Magazine of History and Biography 306 (1954)).

k. Albert S. Abel, "The Commerce Clause in the Constitutional Convention and in Contemporary Comment," 25 Minn. L. Rev. 432, 481 (1941).

l. U.S. Const. art. I, § 8, cl. 4 (Congress shall have the power "[t]o establish * * * uniform Laws on the subject of Bankruptcies throughout the United States."). See Calvin H. Johnson,

Whatever the basis for its inclusion in Article I, the belief that the Commerce Clause was meant to quell commercial animosities among the states has exerted a powerful influence on the development of the Supreme Court's jurisprudence in this area. In the early part of the nineteenth century, Chief Justice John Marshall took the first critical step of reading into the Commerce Clause a negative implication for state legislation. In his 1824 opinion for the Court in *Gibbons v. Ogden*,[m] Marshall struck down as unconstitutional New York legislation granting a steamboat monopoly to Robert Fulton, inventor of the first commercially viable steamboat, and his business partner, Robert Livingston.[n] Marshall concluded that New York, by attempting to regulate navigation between its shores and those of other states, was encroaching upon a power that the Constitution had granted to Congress. The holding proved consequential. From *Gibbons* onward, the Commerce Clause would be understood as imposing an implicit restriction on the ability of states to regulate interstate commerce. Indeed, as Felix Frankfurter would write more than a century later, this "negative" or "dormant" Commerce Clause, "became central to our whole constitutional scheme: the doctrine that the commerce clause, by its own force and without national legislation, puts it into the power of the Court to place limits upon state authority."[o]

During the tenures of Chief Justices Marshall and Taney (1801–1864), the Supreme Court had few opportunities to consider the implications of the "dormant" Commerce Clause for state taxing authority.[p] Most Commerce Clause cases arising during this period dealt with aspects of state regulation other than taxes. Even so, the decisions laid the groundwork for the Court's consideration of state tax controversies in later years. Perhaps the most significant Commerce Clause decision during the Taney years was the *Cooley* case,[q] in which the Court established a doctrine dividing potential subjects of regulation into two classes: "(a) those *national in character* and requiring uniform rules of regulation, as to which the power of Congress was said to be *exclusive*; and (b) those *local in character* permitting or adapted to diversity of regulation, as to which the power of the states was said to be *concurrent* with that of Congress."[r] This approach represented a compromise between the views of Marshall, who had favored exclusive federal power over interstate commerce, and

---

"The Panda's Thumb: The Modest and Mercantilist Original Meaning of the Commerce Clause," 13 Wm. & Mary Bill of Rights J. 1, 55 (2004).

m. 22 U.S. (9 Wheat.) 1 (1824).

n. Daniel Walker Howe, What Hath God Wrought: The Transformation of America, 1815–1848 235 (2007).

o. Felix Frankfurter, The Commerce Clause Under Marshall, Taney and Waite 18–19 (Quadrangle Paperback ed. 1964)

p. See, e.g., The Passenger Cases, 48 U.S. (7 How.) 283 (1849) (declaring unconstitutional New York and Massachusetts taxes imposed on alien passengers arriving in ports of those states).

q. Cooley v. Board of Wardens, 53 U.S. (12 How.) 299 (1851).

r. Paul J. Hartman, "State Taxation of Interstate Commerce: A Survey and an Appraisal," 46 Va. L. Rev. 1051, 1067 (1960) (emphasis in original).

Taney, who "flatly denied that the mere grant of the commerce power operated to limit state power."[s]

In the years following the Civil War, the Supreme Court decided a spate of state tax controversies whose resolution turned on the application of the *Cooley* doctrine. Central among these was the celebrated *Case of the State Freight Tax*[t] involving Pennsylvania's tonnage tax on all freight transported in the state, including freight originating in or destined for other states. Aptly described "one of the most important [decisions] ever made under the Commerce Clause,"[u] the *Case of the State Freight Tax* marked the inauguration of what came to be known as the "free trade" approach to deciding controversies over state taxation. In a series of decisions from the late nineteenth century, the Supreme Court sharply curtailed the states' taxing power, striking down as unconstitutional a broad range of levies. While some taxes were upheld as "indirect" levies on interstate commerce, many of the Court's opinions from this era contain sweeping admonitions, such as the Court's 1887 pronouncement that "interstate commerce cannot be taxed *at all*, even though the same amount of tax should be laid on domestic commerce, or that which is carried on solely within the state."[v] A year later, the Court asserted that "no state has the right to lay a tax on interstate commerce *in any form*," reasoning that "such taxation is a burden on that commerce, and amounts to a regulation of it, which belongs solely to Congress."[w] Over the next few decades, the Court set aside license, franchise, and privilege taxes on foreign corporations or individuals doing an exclusively interstate business within a state.[x] The states, it was said, have no power to tax the "privilege of doing interstate commerce" because it is a privilege granted by the Federal Government.

While these decisions established an area of trade for the interstate business that was free of state and local license, franchise, and privilege taxes, the Court did not strike down all state taxes affecting interstate commerce. In seeking to draw a line between the prohibited and permissible exercise of state taxation of interstate business and transactions and property employed in interstate commerce, the Court developed a distinction between "direct" and "indirect" taxes. Only the former constituted an "undue burden" on or "regulations" of commerce and therefore ran afoul of the unexercised power of Congress to regulate interstate commerce. Thus, while striking down various levies thought to impose a

---

s. See Frankfurter, supra note o, at 50.

t. 82 U.S. (15 Wall.) 232 (1872).

u. John B. Sholley, "The Negative Implications of the Commerce Clause," 3 U. Chi. L. Rev. 556 (1936).

v. Robbins v. Taxing District of Shelby County, 120 U.S. 489, 497, 7 S.Ct. 592 (1887) (emphasis supplied).

w. Leloup v. Port of Mobile, 127 U.S. 640, 648, 8 S.Ct. 1380 (1888) (emphasis supplied).

x. Robbins v. Taxing District of Shelby County, supra; Leloup v. Port of Mobile, supra; Atlantic & Pacific Telegraph Co. v. Philadelphia, 190 U.S. 160, 23 S.Ct. 817 (1903); Western Union Telegraph Co. v. Kansas, 216 U.S. 1, 30 S.Ct. 190 (1910).

"direct" burden on interstate commerce,[y] the Court nonetheless upheld certain taxes on the theory that they imposed only "indirect" burdens on interstate.[z]

Perhaps not surprisingly, the Court's direct-indirect distinction did not stand the test of time. The adjudication of state tax controversies increasingly became an exercise in semantics, as litigants sought to fit challenged levies into the desired category. More importantly, changes in the economy and the role of government from the Great Depression onward prompted a new attitude toward state taxation among certain members of the Supreme Court. Gradually, the Court began to embrace a more expansive view of the states' power to tax interstate business, perhaps out of a reluctance to thwart the states' response to modern economic conditions.

The chief architect of the Court's new approach was Justice Harlan Fiske Stone. In a handful of decisions, Justice Stone assailed the Court's earlier "free trade" approach, with its emphasis on the unworkable distinction between "direct" and "indirect" burdens, and instead urged consideration of the practical effects of state taxes on interstate commerce. Stone articulated a "multiple taxation" doctrine, which focused on whether state taxes subjected interstate commerce to a greater burden than that borne by purely intrastate commerce. In the key decision, *Western Live Stock v. Bureau of Revenue*,[aa] Stone rejected the formal analysis of the "free trade" approach, emphasizing instead "the practical needs of a taxing system which, under constitutional limitations, must accommodate itself to the double demand that interstate commerce shall pay its way, and that at the same time it shall not be burdened with cumulative exactions which are not similarly laid on local business."[bb]

Despite Stone's efforts, the Court's "free trade" approach did not die off completely. Within eight years after the Court's enunciation of the multiple taxation doctrine in *Western Live Stock*, a new majority led by Justice Frankfurter repudiated the doctrine. In *Freeman v. Hewit*,[cc] the

---

y. These included taxes on gross receipts from interstate commerce, Crew Levick Co. v. Pennsylvania, 245 U.S. 292, 38 S.Ct. 126 (1917); Sonneborn Bros. v. Cureton, 262 U.S. 506, 43 S.Ct. 643 (1923), levies on transportation and communication companies and other instrumentalities of interstate commerce, Fargo v. Stevens, 121 U.S. 230, 7 S.Ct. 857 (1887); Philadelphia & Southern Steamship Co. v. Pennsylvania, 122 U.S. 326, 7 S.Ct. 1118 (1887); Western Union Telegraph Co. v. Pennsylvania, 128 U.S. 39, 9 S.Ct. 6 (1888); Galveston, H. & S.A. Ry. Co. v. Texas, 210 U.S. 217, 28 S.Ct. 638 (1908); Fisher's Blend Station, Inc. v. State Tax Commission, 297 U.S. 650, 56 S.Ct. 608 (1936), and levies that discriminated against interstate commerce. Welton v. Missouri, 91 U.S. (1 Otto) 275 (1875); Robbins v. Shelby County Taxing District, 120 U.S. 489, 7 S.Ct. 592 (1887); Caldwell v. North Carolina, 187 U.S. 622, 23 S.Ct. 229 (1903); Rearick v. Pennsylvania, 203 U.S. 507, 27 S.Ct. 159 (1906); Real Silk Hosiery Mills v. Portland, 268 U.S. 325, 45 S.Ct. 525 (1925); Nippert v. City of Richmond, 327 U.S. 416, 66 S.Ct. 586 (1946).

z. Pullmans Palace Car Co. v. Pennsylvania, 141 U.S. 18, 11 S.Ct. 876 (1891); Cleveland, Cincinnati, Chicago & St. Louis Railway Co. v. Backus, 154 U.S. 439, 14 S.Ct. 1122 (1894); Postal Telegraph Cable Co. v. Adams, 155 U.S. 688, 15 S.Ct. 268 (1895); Sanford v. Poe, 165 U.S. 194, 17 S.Ct. 305 (1897).

aa. 303 U.S. 250, 58 S.Ct. 546 (1938).

bb. Id., 303 U.S. at 258, 260.

cc. 329 U.S. 249, 67 S.Ct. 274 (1946).

Court held that Indiana's gross income tax could not be applied to the proceeds of a sale of securities made by a resident of Indiana through a local broker on the New York Stock Exchange. In so holding the Court went out of its way to repudiate the multiple taxation doctrine and to reassert the direct-indirect test of taxation of interstate commerce. Speaking for the Court, Justice Frankfurter declared that the Commerce Clause by its own force created an area of trade free from interference by the states. Declaring that a state cannot "justify what amounts to a levy on the very process of commerce across state lines by pointing to a similar hobble on its local trade," the Court struck down the tax as "direct imposition on that very freedom of commercial flow which for more than a hundred and fifty years has been the ward of the Commerce Clause."[dd]

The partial restoration of the *ancien régime* reached its high water mark in *Spector Motor Service, Inc. v. O'Connor*.[ee] In *Spector*, Connecticut levied a tax on the privilege of doing business measured by net income apportioned to the state. The taxpayer, a foreign corporation, operated an interstate trucking business with terminals and pick-up trucks and over-the-road trucks operated in Connecticut. A strong opinion by the Court of Appeals for the Second Circuit took the position that the states have the power to impose a tax on the privilege of doing business measured by net income, where the measure of the tax is properly apportioned.[ff] In an opinion authored by Justice Harold Burton, the Supreme Court held otherwise, determining that the states are precluded from taxing the privilege of doing an exclusively interstate business even when the tax is measured by net income fairly apportioned to the state.

Notwithstanding cases like *Freeman* and *Spector*, the revival of the Court's "free trade" approach to deciding Commerce Clause cases was short-lived. With changes in the composition of the Court, including the death of Robert Jackson (1954) and the retirement of Harold Burton (1958), Frankfurter's ability to sustain a coalition in favor of the "free trade" approach began to wane. In 1959, the Supreme Court for the first time explicitly held, in *Northwestern States Portland Cement Co. v. Minnesota*,[gg] that there is no Commerce Clause barrier to the imposition of a nondiscriminatory, fairly apportioned direct net income tax on a foreign corporation carrying on an exclusively interstate business within the taxing state. While the *Northwestern States* decision did not expressly overrule *Freeman* or *Spector*, subsequent decisions suggested a greater willingness to defer to state tax powers in the face of Commerce Clause challenges.[hh] In 1977, the Court took the final step in its retreat from the position that the privilege of doing interstate business is immune from

dd.   Id., 329 U.S. at 254, 256.

ee.   340 U.S. 602, 71 S.Ct. 508 (1951).

ff.   Spector Motor Service, Inc. v. O'Connor, 181 F.2d 150 (2d Cir. 1950).

gg.   358 U.S. 450, 79 S.Ct. 357 (1959).

hh.   See General Motors Corp. v. Washington, 377 U.S. 436, 84 S.Ct. 1564 (1964), and Standard Pressed Steel Co. v. Washington Department of Revenue, 419 U.S. 560, 95 S.Ct. 706 (1975).

state taxation: it repudiated the doctrine altogether, along with the philosophy underlying it. Its decision in *Complete Auto Transit, Inc. v. Brady*, authored by former tax lawyer Harry Blackmun, created the analytical framework governing all subsequent Commerce Clause challenges to state taxes.

B. THE *COMPLETE AUTO* FRAMEWORK FOR COMMERCE CLAUSE CHALLENGES

COMPLETE AUTO TRANSIT, INC. v. BRADY

Supreme Court of the United States, 1977.
430 U.S. 274, 97 S.Ct. 1076.

MR. JUSTICE BLACKMUN delivered the opinion of the Court.

Once again we are presented with " 'the perennial problem of the validity of a state tax for the privilege of carrying on within a state, certain activities' relating to a corporation's operation of an interstate business." Colonial Pipeline Co. v. Traigle, 421 U.S. 100, 101, 95 S.Ct. 1538, 1539 (1975), quoting Memphis Natural Gas Co. v. Stone, 335 U.S. 80, 85, 68 S.Ct. 1475, 1477 (1948). The issue in this case is whether Mississippi runs afoul of the Commerce Clause, U.S. Const., Art. I, § 8, cl. 3, when it applies the tax it imposes on "the privilege of ... doing business" within the State to appellant's activity in interstate commerce. The Supreme Court of Mississippi unanimously sustained the tax against appellant's constitutional challenge. We noted probable jurisdiction in order to consider anew the applicable principles in this troublesome area.

I

The taxes in question are sales taxes assessed by the Mississippi State Tax Commission against the appellant, Complete Auto Transit, Inc., for the period from August 1, 1968, through July 31, 1972. The assessments were made pursuant to the following Mississippi statutes:

"There is hereby levied and assessed and shall be collected privilege taxes for the privilege of engaging or continuing in business or doing business within this state to be determined by the application of rates against gross proceeds of sales or gross income or values, as the case may be, as provided in the following sections." Miss.Code Ann., 1942, § 10105 (1972 Supp.), as amended.[1]

"Upon every person operating a pipeline, railroad, airplane, bus, truck, or any other transportation business for the transportation of persons or property for compensation or hire between points within this State, there is hereby levied, assessed, and shall be collected, a tax equal to five per cent of the gross income of such business...." § 10109(2), as amended.[2]

---

1. The statute is now § 27–65–13 of the State's 1972 Code.

2. This statute is now § 27–65–19(2) of the 1972 Code. It was amended, effective August 1, 1972, to exclude the transportation of property. Laws 1972, c. 506, § 2.

Any person liable for the tax is required to add it to the gross sales price and, "insofar as practicable," to collect it at the time the sale price is collected. § 10117, as amended.[3]

Appellant is a Michigan corporation engaged in the business of transporting motor vehicles by motor carrier for General Motors Corporation. General Motors assembles outside Mississippi vehicles that are destined for dealers within the State. The vehicles are then shipped by rail to Jackson, Miss., where, usually within 48 hours, they are loaded onto appellant's trucks and transported by appellant to the Mississippi dealers. Appellant is paid on a contract basis for the transportation from the railhead to the dealers.[4]

By letter dated October 5, 1971, the Mississippi Tax Commission informed appellant that it was being assessed taxes and interest totalling $122,160.59 for the sales of transportation services during the three-year period from August 1, 1968, through July 31, 1971.[5] Remittance within 10 days was requested. By similar letter dated December 28, 1972, the Commission advised appellant of an assessment of $42,990.89 for the period from August 1, 1971, through July 31, 1972. Appellant paid the assessments under protest and, in April 1973, pursuant to § 10121.1, as amended, of the 1942 Code (now § 27–65–47 of the 1972 Code), instituted the present refund action in the Chancery Court of the First Judicial District of Hinds County.

Appellant claimed that its transportation was but one part of an interstate movement, and that the taxes assessed and paid were unconstitutional as applied to operations in interstate commerce. The Chancery Court, in an unreported opinion, sustained the assessments.

The Mississippi Supreme Court affirmed. It concluded:

"It will be noted that Taxpayer has a large operation in this State. It is dependent upon the State for police protection and other State services the same as other citizens. It should pay its fair share of taxes so long, but only so long, as the tax does not discriminate against interstate commerce, and there is no danger of interstate commerce being smothered by cumulative taxes of several states. There is no possibility of any other state duplicating the tax involved in this case." 330 So.2d, at 272.

---

3. This statute is now § 27–65–31 of the 1972 Code. Violation of the requirements of the section is a misdemeanor. Ibid.

4. The parties understandably go to great pains to describe the details of the bills of lading, and the responsibility of various entities for the vehicles as they travel from the assembly plant to the dealers. Appellant seeks to demonstrate that the transportation it provides from the railhead to the dealers is part of a movement in interstate commerce. Appellee argues that appellant's transportation is intrastate business, but further argues that even if the activity is part of interstate commerce, the tax is not unconstitutional. Brief for Appellant 11–14; Brief for Appellee 12–24; Reply Brief for Appellant 14–16. The Mississippi courts, in upholding the tax, assumed that the transportation is in interstate commerce. For present purposes, we make the same assumption.

5. Although appellant had been operating in Mississippi since 1960, the state audit and assessment covered only the period beginning August 1, 1968. No effort had been made to apply the tax to appellant for any period prior to that date.

Appellant, in its complaint in Chancery Court did not allege that its activity which Mississippi taxes does not have a sufficient nexus with the State; or that the tax discriminates against interstate commerce; or that the tax is unfairly apportioned; or that it is unrelated to services provided by the State.[6] No such claims were made before the Mississippi Supreme Court, and although appellant argues here that a tax on "the privilege of doing interstate commerce" creates an unacceptable risk of discrimination and undue burdens, Brief for Appellant 20–27, it does not claim that discrimination or undue burdens exist in fact.

Appellant's attack is based solely on decisions of this Court holding that a tax on the "privilege" of engaging in an activity in the State may not be applied to an activity that is part of interstate commerce. See, e.g., Spector Motor Service v. O'Connor, 340 U.S. 602, 71 S.Ct. 508 (1951); Freeman v. Hewit, 329 U.S. 249, 67 S.Ct. 274 (1946). This rule looks only to the fact that the incidence of the tax is the "privilege of doing business"; it deems irrelevant any consideration of the practical effect of the tax. The rule reflects an underlying philosophy that interstate commerce should enjoy a sort of "free trade" immunity from state taxation.[7]

Appellee, in its turn, relies on decisions of this Court stating that "[i]t was not the purpose of the commerce clause to relieve those engaged in interstate commerce from their just share of state tax burden even though it increases the cost of doing the business," Western Live Stock v. Bureau of Revenue, 303 U.S. 250, 254, 58 S.Ct. 546, 548 (1938). These decisions[8] have considered not the formal language of the tax statute, but rather its practical effect, and have sustained a tax against Commerce Clause challenge when the tax is applied to an activity with a substantial nexus with the taxing State, is fairly apportioned, does not discriminate against interstate commerce, and is fairly related to the services provided by the State.

Over the years, the Court has applied this practical analysis in approving many types of tax that avoided running afoul of the prohibition against taxing the "privilege of doing business," but in each instance it

---

6. See Boston Stock Exchange v. State Tax Comm'n, 429 U.S. 318, 97 S.Ct. 599 (1977); General Motors Corp. v. Washington, 377 U.S. 436, 84 S.Ct. 1564 (1964); Illinois Cent. R. Co. v. Minnesota, 309 U.S. 157, 60 S.Ct. 419 (1940); Ingels v. Morf, 300 U.S. 290, 57 S.Ct. 439 (1937). See also Standard Pressed Steel Co. v. Department of Revenue, 419 U.S. 560, 95 S.Ct. 706 (1975), and Clark v. Paul Gray, Inc., 306 U.S. 583, 59 S.Ct. 744 (1939).

7. The Court summarized the "free trade" view in Freeman v. Hewit, 329 U.S., at 252, 67 S.Ct. at 276:

"[T]he Commerce Clause was not merely an authorization to Congress to enact laws for the protection and encouragement of commerce among the States, but by its own force created an area of trade free from interference by the States. In short, the Commerce Clause even without implementing legislation by Congress is a limitation upon the power of the States. ... This limitation on State power ... does not merely forbid a State to single out interstate commerce for hostile action. A State is also precluded from taking any action which may fairly be deemed to have the effect of impeding the free flow of trade between States. It is immaterial that local commerce is subjected to a similar encumbrance."

8. See, e.g., General Motors Corp. v. Washington, supra; Northwestern States Portland Cement Co. v. Minnesota, 358 U.S. 450, 79 S.Ct. 357 (1959); Memphis Natural Gas Co. v. Stone, 335 U.S. 80, 68 S.Ct. 1475 (1948); Wisconsin v. J.C. Penney Co., 311 U.S. 435, 444, 61 S.Ct. 246, 249 (1940).

has refused to overrule the prohibition. Under the present state of the law, the *Spector* rule, as it has come to be known, has no relationship to economic realities. Rather it stands only as a trap for the unwary draftsman.

II

The modern origin of the *Spector* rule may be found in Freeman v. Hewit, supra.[9] At issue in *Freeman* was the application of an Indiana tax upon "the receipt of the entire gross income" of residents and domiciliaries. 329 U.S., at 250, 67 S.Ct., at 275. Indiana sought to impose this tax on income generated when a trustee of an Indiana estate instructed his local stockbroker to sell certain securities. The broker arranged with correspondents in New York to sell the securities on the New York Stock Exchange. The securities were sold, and the New York brokers, after deducting expense and commission, transmitted the proceeds to the Indiana broker who in turn delivered them, less his commission, to the trustee. The Indiana Supreme Court sustained the tax, but this Court reversed.

Mr. Justice Frankfurter, speaking for five Members of the Court, announced a blanket prohibition against any state taxation imposed directly on an interstate transaction. He explicitly deemed unnecessary to the decision of the case any showing of discrimination against interstate commerce or error in apportionment of the tax. Id., at 254, 256–257, 67 S.Ct., at 277, 278–79. He recognized that a State could constitutionally tax local manufacture, impose license taxes on corporations doing business in the State, tax property within the State, and tax the privilege of residence in the State and measure the privilege by net income, including that derived from interstate commerce. Id., at 255, 67 S.Ct., at 278. Nevertheless, a direct tax on interstate sales, even if fairly apportioned and nondiscriminatory, was held to be unconstitutional *per se*.

Mr. Justice Rutledge, in a lengthy concurring opinion, argued that the tax should be judged by its economic effects rather than by its formal phrasing. After reviewing the Court's prior decisions, he concluded: "The fact is that 'direct incidence' of a state tax or regulation ... has long since been discarded as being itself sufficient to outlaw state legislation." Id., at 265–266, 67 S.Ct., at 283–284. In his view, a state tax is unconstitutional only if the activity lacks the necessary connection with the taxing State to give "jurisdiction to tax," id., at 271, 67 S.Ct., at 286, or if the tax

---

9. Although we mention *Freeman* as the starting point, elements of the views expressed therein, and the positions that underlie that debate, were evident in prior opinions. Compare State Tax on Railway Gross Receipts, 15 Wall. (82 U.S.) 284 (1872), with Fargo v. Stevens, 121 U.S. 230, 7 S.Ct. 857 (1887); and compare Di Santo v. Pennsylvania, 273 U.S. 34, 47 S.Ct. 267 (1927), and Cooney v. Mountain States Tel. Co., 294 U.S. 384, 55 S.Ct. 477 (1935), with Western Live Stock v. Bureau of Revenue, 303 U.S. 250, 58 S.Ct. 546 (1938). See generally, P. Hartman, State Taxation of Interstate Commerce (1953); Barrett, "State Taxation of Interstate Commerce—'Direct Burdens,' 'Multiple Burdens,' or What Have You?," 4 Vand.L.Rev. 496 (1951), and writings cited therein at 496 n. 1; Dunham, "Gross Receipts Taxes on Interstate Transactions," 47 Col.L.Rev. 211 (1947).

discriminates against interstate commerce, or if the activity is subject to multiple taxation. Id., at 276–277, 67 S.Ct., at 289.[10]

The rule announced in *Freeman* was viewed in the commentary as a triumph of formalism over substance, providing little guidance even as to formal requirements. See P. Hartman, State Taxation of Interstate Commerce 200–204 (1953); Dunham, "Gross Receipts Taxes on Interstate Transactions," 47 Col.L.Rev. 211 (1947). Although the rule might have been utilized as the keystone of a movement toward absolute immunity of interstate commerce from state taxation,[11] the Court consistently has indicated that "interstate commerce may be made to pay its way," and has moved toward a standard of permissibility of state taxation based upon its actual effect rather than its legal terminology.

The narrowing of the rule to one of draftsmanship and phraseology began with another Mississippi case, Memphis Gas Co. v. Stone, 335 U.S. 80, 68 S.Ct. 1475 (1948). Memphis Natural Gas Company owned and operated a pipeline running from Louisiana to Memphis. Approximately 135 miles of the line were in Mississippi. Mississippi imposed a "franchise or excise" tax measured by "the value of the capital used, invested or employed in the exercise of any power, privilege or right enjoyed by [a corporation] within this state." Miss.Code Ann. § 9313 (1942). The Mississippi Supreme Court upheld the tax, and this Court affirmed.

In an opinion for himself and two others, Mr. Justice Reed noted that the tax was not discriminatory, that there was no possibility of multiple taxation, that the amount of the tax was reasonable, and that the tax was properly apportioned to the investment in Mississippi. 335 U.S., at 87–88, 68 S.Ct., at 1478–79. He then went on to consider whether the tax was "upon the privilege of doing interstate business within the state." Id., at 88, 68 S.Ct., at 1479. He drew a distinction between a tax on "the privilege of doing business" and a tax on "the privilege of exercising corporate functions within the State," and held that while the former is unconstitutional, the latter is not barred by the Commerce Clause. Id., at 88–93, 68 S.Ct., at 1481. He then approved the tax there at issue because

> "there is no attempt to tax the privilege of doing an interstate business or to secure anything from the corporation by this statute except compensation for the protection of the enumerated local activities of 'maintaining, keeping in repair, and otherwise in manning the facilities.'" Id., at 93, 68 S.Ct., at 1482.

Mr. Justice Black concurred in the judgment without opinion. Id., at 96, 68 S.Ct., at 1483. Mr. Justice Rutledge provided the fifth vote, stating in his concurrence:

---

10. Mr. Justice Rutledge agreed with the result the Court reached in *Freeman* because of his belief that the apportionment problem was best solved if States other than the market State were forbidden to impose unapportioned gross receipts taxes of the kind Indiana sought to exact.

11. A consistent application of the doctrine of immunity for interstate commerce, of course, would have necessitated overruling the cases approved by the *Freeman* Court that upheld taxes whose burden, although indirect, fell on interstate commerce.

"[I]t is enough for me to sustain the tax imposed in this case that it is one clearly within the state's power to lay insofar as any limitation of due process or 'jurisdiction to tax' in that sense is concerned; it is nondiscriminatory, that is, places no greater burden upon interstate commerce than the state places upon competing intrastate commerce of like character; is duly apportioned, that is, does not undertake to tax any interstate activities carried on outside the state's borders; and cannot be repeated by any other state." Id., at 96–97, 68 S.Ct., at 1483–1484 (footnotes omitted).

Four Justices dissented, id., at 99, 68 S.Ct., at 1485, on the grounds that it had not been shown that the State afforded any protection in return for the tax,[12] and that, therefore, the tax must be viewed as one on the "privilege" of engaging in interstate commerce. The dissenters recognized that an identical effect could be achieved by an increase in the ad valorem property tax, id., at 104, 68 S.Ct., at 1487 but would have held, notwithstanding, that a tax on the "privilege" is unconstitutional.

The prohibition against state taxation of the "privilege" of engaging in commerce that is interstate was reaffirmed in Spector Motor Service v. O'Connor, 340 U.S. 602, 71 S.Ct. 508 (1951), a case similar on its facts to the instant case. The taxpayer there was a Missouri corporation engaged exclusively in interstate trucking. Some of its shipments originated or terminated in Connecticut. Connecticut imposed on a corporation a "tax or excise upon its franchise for the privilege of carrying on or doing business within the state," measured by apportioned net income. 340 U.S., at 603–604, n. 1, 71 S.Ct. at 509. Spector brought suit in federal court to enjoin collection of the tax as applied to its activities. The District Court issued the injunction. The Second Circuit reversed. This Court, with three Justices in dissent, in turn reversed the Court of Appeals and held the tax unconstitutional as applied.

The Court recognized that "where a taxpayer is engaged both in intrastate and interstate commerce, a state may tax the privilege of carrying on intrastate business and, within reasonable limits, may compute the amount of the charge by applying the tax rate to a fair proportion of the taxpayer's business done within the state, including both interstate and intrastate." Id., at 609–610, 71 S.Ct., at 512 (footnote omitted). It held, nevertheless, that a tax on the "privilege" of doing business is unconstitutional if applied against what is exclusively interstate commerce. The dissenters argued, on the other hand, id., at 610, 71 S.Ct., at 512, that there is no constitutional difference between an "exclusively interstate" business and a "mixed" business, and that a fairly apportioned

---

12. In arriving at this conclusion, the dissent relied upon a construction of a stipulation entered into by the parties, 335 U.S. at 100–101, 68 S.Ct., at 1485–86, and upon an independent review of the record. The plurality rejected the dissent's reading of the stipulation and noted, in addition, that the question presented in the petition for certiorari did not raise a claim that the State was providing no service for which it could ask recompense. Id., at 83–84, 68 S.Ct., at 1476–77. The plurality then relied on the Supreme Court of Mississippi's holding that the State did provide protection that could properly be the subject of a tax.

and nondiscriminatory tax on either type is not prohibited by the Commerce Clause.

The *Spector* rule was applied in Railway Express Agency v. Virginia, 347 U.S. 359, 74 S.Ct. 558 (1954) (*Railway Express I*), to declare unconstitutional a State's "annual license tax" levied on gross receipts for the "privilege of doing business in this State." The Court, by a 5 to 4 vote, held that the tax on gross receipts was a tax on the privilege of doing business rather than a tax on property in the State, as Virginia contended.

Virginia thereupon revised the wording of its statute to impose a "franchise tax" on "intangible property" in the form of "going concern" value as measured by gross receipts. The tax was again asserted against the Agency which in Virginia was engaged exclusively in interstate commerce. This Court's opinion, buttressed by two concurring opinions and one concurrence in the result, upheld the reworded statute as not violative of the *Spector* rule. Railway Express Agency v. Virginia, 358 U.S. 434, 79 S.Ct. 411 (1959) (*Railway Express II*). In upholding the statute, the Court's opinion recognized that the rule against taxing the "privilege" of doing interstate business had created a situation where "the use of magic words or labels" could "disable an otherwise constitutional levy." Id., at 441, 79 S.Ct., at 416.

There was no real economic difference between the statutes in *Railway Express I* and *Railway Express II*. The Court long since had recognized that interstate commerce may be made to pay its way. Yet under the *Spector* rule, the economic realities in *Railway Express I* became irrelevant. The *Spector* rule had come to operate only as a rule of draftsmanship, and served only to distract the courts and parties from their inquiry into whether the challenged tax produced results forbidden by the Commerce Clause.

On the day it announced *Railway Express II*, the Court further confirmed that a State, with proper drafting, may tax exclusively interstate commerce so long as the tax does not create any effect forbidden by the Commerce Clause. In Northwestern States Portland Cement Co. v. Minnesota, 358 U.S. 450, 79 S.Ct. 357 (1959), the Court held that net income from the interstate operations of a foreign corporation may be subjected to state taxation, provided the levy is not discriminatory and is properly apportioned to local activities within the taxing State forming sufficient nexus to support the tax. Limited in that way, the tax could be levied even though the income was generated exclusively by interstate sales. *Spector* was distinguished, briefly and in passing, as a case in which "the incidence" of the tax "was the privilege of doing business." Id., 358 U.S. at 464, 79 S.Ct., at 365.

Thus, applying the rule of *Northwestern Cement* to the facts of *Spector*, it is clear that Connecticut could have taxed the apportioned net income derived from the exclusively interstate commerce. It could not, however, tax the "privilege" of doing business as measured by the apportioned net income. The reason for attaching constitutional significance to a semantic difference is difficult to discern.

The unsatisfactory operation of the *Spector* rule is well demonstrated by our recent case of Colonial Pipeline Co. v. Traigle, 421 U.S. 100, 95 S.Ct. 1538 (1975). Colonial was a Delaware corporation with an interstate pipeline running through Louisiana for approximately 258 miles. It maintained a work force and pumping stations in Louisiana to keep the pipeline flowing, but it did no intrastate business in that State. Id., at 101–102, 95 S.Ct., at 1539–40. In 1962, Louisiana imposed on Colonial a franchise tax for "the privilege of carrying on or doing business" in the State. The Louisiana Court of Appeal invalidated the tax as violative of the rule of *Spector*. 228 So.2d 718 (La.App.1969). The Supreme Court of Louisiana refused review. 255 La. 474, 231 So.2d 393 (1970). The Louisiana Legislature, perhaps recognizing that it had run afoul of a rule of words rather than a rule of substance, then redrafted the statute to levy the tax, as an alternative incident, on the "qualification to carry on or do business in this state or the actual doing of business within this state in a corporate form." Again, the Court of Appeal held the tax unconstitutional as applied to the appellant. 275 So.2d 834 (La.App.1973). But this time the Louisiana Supreme Court upheld the new tax. 289 So.2d 93 (La.1974).

By a 7 to 1 vote, this Court affirmed. No question had been raised as to the propriety of the apportionment of the tax, and no claim was made that the tax was discriminatory. 421 U.S., at 101, 95 S.Ct., at 1539. The Court noted that the tax was imposed on that aspect of interstate commerce to which the State bore a special relation, and that the State bestowed powers, privileges, and benefits sufficient to support a tax on doing business in the corporate form in Louisiana. Id., at 109, 95 S.Ct., at 1543. Accordingly, on the authority of *Memphis Gas*, the tax was held to be constitutional. The Court distinguished *Spector* on the familiar ground that it involved a tax on the privilege of carrying on interstate commerce, while the Louisiana Legislature, in contrast, had worded the statute at issue "narrowly to confine the impost to one related to appellant's activities within the State in the corporate form." Id., at 113–114, 95 S.Ct., at 1546.[13]

While refraining from overruling *Spector,* the Court noted:

"[D]ecisions of this Court, particularly during recent decades, have sustained nondiscriminatory, properly apportioned state corporate taxes upon foreign corporations doing an exclusively interstate business when the tax is related to a corporation's local activities and the State has provided benefits and protections for those activities for which it is justified in asking a fair and reasonable return." Id., at 108, 95 S.Ct., at 1543.

13. Five Members of the Court joined in the opinion distinguishing *Spector*. Two concurred in the judgment, but viewed *Spector* as indistinguishable and would have overruled it. 421 U.S., at 114–116, 95 S.Ct., at 1546–47. One also viewed *Spector* as indistinguishable, but felt that it was an established precedent until forthrightly overruled. Id., at 116, 95 S.Ct., at 1547. Mr. Justice Douglas took no part.

One commentator concluded: "After reading *Colonial,* only the most sanguine taxpayer would conclude that the Court maintains a serious belief in the doctrine that the privilege of doing interstate business is immune from state taxation." W. Hellerstein, "State Taxation of Interstate Business and the Supreme Court, 1974 Term: Standard Pressed Steel and Colonial Pipeline," 62 Va.L.Rev. 149, 188 (1976).[14]

III

In this case, of course, we are confronted with a situation like that presented in *Spector.* The tax is labeled a privilege tax "for the privilege of ... doing business" in Mississippi, § 10105 of the State's 1942 Code, as amended, and the activity taxed is, or has been assumed to be, interstate commerce. We note again that no claim is made that the activity is not sufficiently connected to the State to justify a tax, or that the tax is not fairly related to benefits provided the taxpayer, or that the tax discriminates against interstate commerce, or that the tax is not fairly apportioned.

The view of the Commerce Clause that gave rise to the rule of *Spector* perhaps was not without some substance. Nonetheless, the possibility of defending it in the abstract does not alter the fact that the Court has rejected the proposition that interstate commerce is immune from state taxation:

> "It is a truism that the mere act of carrying on business in interstate commerce does not exempt a corporation from state taxation. 'It was not the purpose of the commerce clause to relieve those engaged in interstate commerce from their just share of state tax burden even though it increases the cost of doing business.' Western Live Stock v. Bureau of Revenue, 303 U.S. 250, 254, 58 S.Ct. 546, 548 (1938)." Colonial Pipeline Co. v. Traigle, 421 U.S., at 108, 95 S.Ct., at 1543.

Not only has the philosophy underlying the rule been rejected, but the rule itself has been stripped of any practical significance. If Mississippi had called its tax one on "net income" or on the "going concern value" of appellant's business, the *Spector* rule could not invalidate it. There is no economic consequence that follows necessarily from the use of the particular words, "privilege of doing business," and a focus on that formalism merely obscures the question whether the tax produces a forbidden effect. Simply put, the *Spector* rule does not address the problems with which the Commerce Clause is concerned.[15] Accordingly, we now reject the rule of

---

14. Less charitably put: "In light of the expanding scope of the state taxing power over interstate commerce, *Spector* is an anachronism. ... Continued adherence to *Spector,* especially after *Northwestern States Portland Cement,* cannot be justified." Comment, "Pipelines, Privileges and Labels: Colonial Pipeline Co. v. Traigle," 70 Nw.U.L.Rev. 835, 854 (1975).

15. It might be argued that "privilege" taxes, by focusing on the doing of business, are easily tailored to single out interstate businesses and subject them to effects forbidden by the Commerce Clause, and that, therefore, "privilege" taxes should be subjected to a *per se* rule against their imposition on interstate business. Yet property taxes also may be tailored to differentiate between property used in transportation and other types of property, see *Railway Express II,* supra; an

Spector Motor Service, Inc. v. O'Connor, supra, that a state tax on the "privilege of doing business" is *per se* unconstitutional when it is applied to interstate commerce, and that case is overruled.

There being no objection to Mississippi's tax on appellant except that it was imposed on nothing other than the "privilege of doing business" that is interstate, the judgment of the Supreme Court of Mississippi is affirmed.

It is so ordered.

NOTES AND QUESTIONS

A. *The Significance of* Complete Auto. In *Complete Auto*, the Court not only discarded *Spector,* it also embraced a view of the states' taxing powers that makes irrelevant the classification of a tax as a direct, as distinguished from an indirect, levy on interstate commerce. The Court repudiated the philosophy that interstate commerce enjoyed an immunity from taxation, and instead articulated the guiding principles in the following terms: "[Our] decisions * * * have sustained a tax against Commerce Clause challenge when the tax is applied to an activity with a substantial nexus with the taxing State, is fairly apportioned, does not discriminate against interstate commerce, and is fairly related to the services provided by the State." The Court has reiterated this four-part test in virtually every subsequent state tax case involving Commerce Clause challenges to state taxation. The "four-prong" test of *Complete Auto*, as it is commonly labeled, has thus emerged as the starting point for modern Commerce Clause analysis of state taxes.

Although *Complete Auto* may properly be regarded as a watershed in the Supreme Court's Commerce Clause jurisprudence, it is critical to recognize that much of the doctrine it articulated—the requirement of nexus and apportionment and the bar against discrimination—is deeply embedded in the Court's decisions decided over the past century. One of the key challenges for you (as it is for practitioners who must deal with these issues every day) is to evaluate properly the viability of earlier cases in light of the Court's current views. In some instances, the cases may no longer be good law; in others they may state a proper result, but for the wrong reason; in still others, they may be as sound today as they were 100 years ago. The trick, of course, is to figure out which cases fall into which category. Given the large number of decisions the Court has handed down in this area, the task is not an easy one. But it is

---

income tax could use different rates for different types of business; and a tax on the "privilege of doing business in corporate form" could be made to change with the nature of the corporate activity involved. Any tailored tax of this sort creates an increased danger of error in apportionment, of discrimination against interstate commerce, and of a lack of relationship to the services provided by the State. See Freeman v. Hewit, 329 U.S., at 265–266, n. 13, 67 S.Ct., at 283 (concurring opinion). A tailored tax, however accomplished, must receive the careful scrutiny of the courts to determine whether it produces a forbidden effect on interstate commerce. We perceive no reason, however, why a tax on the "privilege of doing business" should be viewed as creating a qualitatively different danger so as to require a *per se* rule of unconstitutionality. It might also be argued that adoption of a rule of absolute immunity for interstate commerce (a rule that would, of course, go beyond *Spector*) would relieve this Court of difficult judgments that on occasion will have to be made. We believe, however, that administrative convenience, in this instance, is insufficient justification for abandoning the principle that "interstate commerce may be made to pay its way."

nevertheless one you must undertake if you are to master the material in this field.

B. Although the tax at issue in *Complete Auto* is designated a "sales tax," the statutory provisions involved are not those imposing a retail sales tax. Instead, the Mississippi levy is imposed for "the privilege of doing business in the state," and it applies to transportation, manufacturing, wholesaling, and various other types of businesses. The tax is measured by "the gross proceeds of sales or gross income or values." Miss. Code Ann. § 27–65–13 (Westlaw 2009), quoted at note 1 of the Court's opinion. The same statute also imposes a retail sales and use tax which is patterned after sales and use taxes in force in most states and which is required to be collected as such by the vendor from the purchaser. Miss. Code Ann. §§ 27–65–17, 27–65–31 (Westlaw 2009).

There was no apportionment controversy in *Complete Auto*, even though the tax was imposed on the full amounts paid by General Motors to the taxpayer, because the entire transportation service was rendered between points in Mississippi. Under the usual methods of dividing the measures of taxes on transportation companies, receipts or income are apportioned or allocated to the state to the extent the transportation takes place within its borders.

In the next four subsections, we explore each "prong" of *Complete Auto*'s "four-prong" test in more detail, and, in the succeeding subsection, revisit all four prongs in a "reprise."

1. FIRST PRONG: SUBSTANTIAL NEXUS (REVISITED)

You will recall that Chapter 2 dealt with the Commerce Clause requirement of substantial nexus and the Supreme Court's decision in the *Quill* case. We return to that analysis here by focusing on one of the Court's "substantial nexus" decisions in the context of a state gross receipts tax. If you have already read Chapter 2, the analysis should be familiar.

TYLER PIPE INDUSTRIES, INC. v. WASHINGTON STATE DEPARTMENT OF REVENUE

Supreme Court of the United States, 1987.
483 U.S. 232, 107 S.Ct. 2810.

JUSTICE STEVENS delivered the opinion of the Court.

* * *

I

For over half a century Washington has imposed a business and occupation (B & O) tax on "the act or privilege of engaging in business activities" in the State. Wash.Rev.Code § 82.04.220 (1985). The tax applies to the activities of extracting raw materials in the State, manufacturing in the State, making wholesale sales in the State, and making retail sales in the State. The State has typically applied the same tax rates to these different activities. The measure of the selling tax is the "gross proceeds of sales," and the measure of the manufacturing tax is the value of the manufactured products. §§ 82.04.220, 82.04.240.

* * *

IV

* * *

Tyler seeks a refund of wholesale taxes it paid on sales to customers in Washington for the period from January 1, 1976, through September 30, 1980. These products were manufactured outside of Washington. Tyler argues that its business does not have a sufficient nexus with the State of Washington to justify the collection of a gross receipts tax on its sales. Tyler sells a large volume of cast iron, pressure and plastic pipe and fittings, and drainage products in Washington, but all of those products are manufactured in other States. Tyler maintains no office, owns no property, and has no employees residing in the State of Washington. Its solicitation of business in Washington is directed by executives who maintain their offices out-of-state and by an independent contractor located in Seattle.

The trial court found that the in-state sales representative engaged in substantial activities that helped Tyler to establish and maintain its market in Washington. The State Supreme Court concluded that those findings were supported by the evidence, and summarized them as follows:

> "The sales representatives acted daily on behalf of Tyler Pipe in calling on its customers and soliciting orders. They have long-established and valuable relationships with Tyler Pipe's customers. Through sales contacts, the representatives maintain and improve the name recognition, market share, goodwill, and individual customer relations of Tyler Pipe.

> "Tyler Pipe sells in a very competitive market in Washington. The sales representatives provide Tyler Pipe with virtually all their information regarding the Washington market, including: product performance; competing products; pricing, market conditions and trends; existing and upcoming construction products; customer financial liability; and other critical information of a local nature concerning Tyler Pipe's Washington market. The sales representatives in Washington have helped Tyler Pipe and have a special relationship to that corporation. The activities of Tyler Pipe's agents in Washington have been substantial." 105 Wash.2d, at 325, 715 P.2d, at 127.

As a matter of law, the Washington Supreme Court concluded that this showing of a sufficient nexus could not be defeated by the argument that the taxpayer's representative was properly characterized as an independent contractor instead of as an agent. We agree with this analysis. In Scripto, Inc. v. Carson, 362 U.S. 207, 80 S.Ct. 619 (1960), Scripto, a Georgia corporation, had no office or regular employees in Florida, but it employed wholesalers or jobbers to solicit sales of its products in Florida. We held that Florida may require these solicitors to collect a use tax from Florida customers. Although the "salesmen" were not employees of Scripto, we determined that "such a fine distinction is without constitutional significance." Id., at 211, 80 S.Ct., at 621. This conclusion is consistent with our more recent cases. See National Geographic Society v. California Equalization Board, 430 U.S. 551, 556–558, 97 S.Ct. 1386, 1390–1391 (1977).

As the Washington Supreme Court determined, "the crucial factor governing nexus is whether the activities performed in this state on behalf of the taxpayer are significantly associated with the taxpayer's ability to establish and maintain a market in this state for the sales." 105 Wash.2d, at 323, 715 P.2d, at 126. The court found this standard was satisfied because Tyler's "sales representatives perform any local activities necessary for maintenance of Tyler Pipe's market and protection of its interests. . . ." Id., at 321, 715 P.2d, at 125. We agree that the activities of Tyler's sales representatives adequately support the State's jurisdiction to impose its wholesale tax on Tyler.

* * *

VI

* * * We reject appellant Tyler's nexus * * * challenge * * * to the State's wholesale tax. * * *

[JUSTICE O'CONNOR's concurring opinion and JUSTICE SCALIA's opinion, concurring in part and dissenting in part, have been omitted.]

NOTES AND QUESTIONS

A. *Broad-based Gross Receipts Taxes.* Washington is one of the few states that impose a gross receipts tax (rather than a net income tax) as its general tax on business activity in the state. For many years, no other state imposed such a tax, but Michigan, Ohio, and Texas have recently enacted levies that in whole or in part are based on gross receipts. See Mich. Comp. Laws § 208.1101 et seq. (Westlaw 2009) (Michigan Business Tax); Ohio Rev. Code Ann. § 5751.01 et seq. (Westlaw 2009) (Ohio Commercial Activity Tax); Tex. Tax Code Ann. § 171.001 et seq. (Westlaw 2009) (Texas Margins Tax). Hawaii and New Mexico also employ broad-based taxes measured by gross receipts, although these levies in many respects resemble retail sales taxes more than they do a general tax on business activity. Moreover, both Hawaii and New Mexico impose corporate net income taxes. Many municipalities, however, impose general business activity taxes measured by gross receipts that resemble the Washington tax at issue in *Tyler Pipe*. These municipal gross receipts taxes raise issues identical to those raised by Washington's gross receipts tax when they apply to activities carried on across state lines.

See, e.g., M & Associates, Inc. v. City of Irondale, 723 So.2d 592 (Ala. 1998) (Commerce Clause bars city from imposing business license tax on the total gross receipts from taxpayer's sales from its facilities both within and without the city); Philadelphia Eagles Football Club, Inc. v. City of Philadelphia, 573 Pa. 189, 823 A.2d 108 (2003) (Commerce Clause prohibits city from imposing unapportioned gross receipts tax on 100 percent of local professional football team's media receipts generated in part from out-of-state activities).

B. *Nexus.* In *Tyler Pipe*, the Court reaffirmed the view, first articulated in Scripto, Inc. v. Carson, 362 U.S. 207, 80 S.Ct. 619 (1960), that whether the taxpayer's representatives in a state were characterized as "employees" or "independent contractors" was "without constitutional significance." Id., 362 U.S. at 211. It also approved the Washington Supreme Court's statement that "the crucial factor governing nexus is whether the activities performed in this state on behalf of the taxpayer are significantly associated with the taxpayer's ability to establish and maintain a market in this state for the sales." How far can the Court's statements be taken? Can they be read to suggest that any time an out-of-state taxpayer hires an independent contractor to provide it with goods or services in a state it has sufficient nexus with the state to withstand constitutional scrutiny? For example, suppose a magazine publisher in State A hires a printer in State B to produce its magazines. If the publisher does not otherwise have nexus with State B, would the contractual relationship with the printer in State B establish nexus over the magazine publisher so that State B could impose a gross receipts tax upon the publisher's magazine sales to State B residents? What about an out-of-state mail-order computer company that arranges for in-state warranty service by unrelated third parties? These are questions to which you should already have given some thought when you considered the materials in Chapter 2.

2. SECOND PRONG: FAIR APPORTIONMENT

One of the most perplexing components of the *Complete Auto* analysis is the second prong—i.e., the requirement that state taxes be "fairly apportioned" to the taxpayer's activities carried on in the taxing state. The following case, *Norfolk & Western*, provides you with your initial opportunity to explore the meaning of this requirement. In this connection, you should keep two things in mind. First, the question of fair apportionment—how fairly to divide the tax base among two or more jurisdictions that have a legitimate claim to a portion of that base—is a central problem of state taxation in our federal system and one that you will consider in much more detail in Chapter 7. Second, *Norfolk & Western* was decided in 1968, nine years before *Complete Auto*. It therefore illustrates an essential feature of *Complete Auto*'s four-part test that we have alluded to above and that bears repeating. *Complete Auto*'s four-part test was in substantial part a distillation of a century of preexisting case law establishing settled restraints on state tax power. Although the case discarded the formalism that had informed some of the Court's earlier Commerce Clause doctrine, it left much of that doctrine intact. Indeed, the foundations of the fair apportionment requirement, as the *Norfolk &*

Western case reveals, lay in cases decided during the late nineteenth and early twentieth centuries.

NORFOLK AND WESTERN RAILWAY COMPANY v. MISSOURI STATE TAX COMMISSION

Supreme Court of the United States, 1968.
390 U.S. 317, 88 S.Ct. 995.

MR. JUSTICE FORTAS delivered the opinion of the Court.

This case brings before us, once again, troublesome problems arising from state taxation of an interstate commercial enterprise. At issue is a tax assessment pursuant to a Missouri statute specifying the manner in which railroad rolling stock is to be assessed for the State's ad valorem tax on that property.[1]

In 1964 the Norfolk & Western Railway Co. (N & W), a Virginia corporation with interstate rail operations, leased all of the property of appellant Wabash Railroad Company. The Wabash owned substantial fixed property and rolling stock, and did substantial business in Missouri as well as in other States. Prior to the lease, N & W owned no fixed property and only a minimal amount of rolling stock in Missouri. N & W is primarily a coal-carrying railroad. Much of its equipment and all of its specialized coal-carrying equipment are generally located in the coal regions of Virginia, West Virginia, and Kentucky, and along the coal-ferrying routes from those regions to the eastern seaboard and the Great Lakes. Scarcely any of the specialized equipment ever enters Missouri. According to appellants, the Wabash property in Missouri was leased by N & W in order to diversify its business, not to provide the opportunity for an integrated through movement of traffic.

By the terms of the lease, the N & W became obligated to pay the 1965 taxes on the property of the Wabash in Missouri and elsewhere.[2] Upon receiving notice of the 1965 assessment from the appellee Missouri Tax Commission, the N & W filed a request for an adjustment and hearing before the Commission. The hearing was held, and the Commission sustained its assessment against the taxpayer's challenge. On judicial review, the Commission's decision was affirmed without opinion by the Circuit Court of Cole County, and then by the Supreme Court of Missouri. Appellants filed an appeal in this Court, contending that the assessment in effect reached property not located in Missouri and thus violated the Due Process Clause and the Interstate Commerce Clause of the United States Constitution. We noted probable jurisdiction.

---

1. The tax in question applies to "all real property ... [and] tangible personal property ... owned, hired or leased by any railroad company ... in this state." Intangible personal property is explicitly exempted from this tax. Mo.V.A.S. § 151.010.

2. As of January 1, 1966, the N & W purchased the Wabash rolling stock that it had previously leased, while continuing to lease Wabash fixed property. This change in the relationship between N & W and the Wabash has no effect on the issues presented to us. Our analysis would apply both before and after the purchase of the Wabash rolling stock.

I.

The Missouri property taxable to the N & W was assessed by the State Tax Commission at $31,298,939. Of this sum, $12,177,597 relates to fixed property within the State, an assessment that is not challenged by appellants. Their attack is aimed only at that portion of the assessment relating to rolling stock, $19,981,757.[3]

With respect to the assessment of rolling stock, the Commission used the familiar mileage formula authorized by the Missouri statute. In relevant part, this provides (§ 151.060(3)):

"... when any railroad shall extend beyond the limits of this state and into another state in which a tax is levied and paid on the rolling stock of such road, then the said commission shall assess, equalize and adjust only such proportion of the total value of all the rolling stock of such railroad company as the number of miles of such road in this state bears to the total length of the road as owned or controlled by such company."

The Commission arrived at the assessment of rolling stock by first determining the value of all rolling stock, regardless of where located, owned or leased by the N & W as of the tax day, January 1, 1965. Value was ascertained by totaling the original cost, less accrued depreciation at 5% a year up to 75% of cost, of each locomotive, car, and other piece of mobile equipment. To the total value, $513,309,877, was applied an "equalizing factor" of 47%, employed in assessing all railroad property in an attempt to bring such assessments down to the level of other property assessments in Missouri. The Commission next found that 8.2824% of all the main and branch line road (excluding secondary and side tracks) owned, leased, or controlled by the N & W was situated in Missouri. This percentage was applied to the equalized value of all N & W rolling stock, and the resulting figure was $19,981,757.

There is no suggestion in this case that the Commission failed to follow the literal command of the statute. The problem arises because of appellants' contention that, in mechanically applying the statutory formula, the Commission here arrived at an unconscionable and unconstitutional result. It is their submission that the assessment was so far out of line with the actual facts of record with respect to the value of taxable rolling stock in the State as to amount to an unconstitutional attempt to exercise state taxing power on out-of-state property.

Appellants submitted evidence based upon an inventory of all N & W rolling stock that was actually in Missouri on tax day. The equalized value of this rolling stock, calculated on the same cost-less-depreciation basis employed by the Commission, was approximately $7,600,000, as compared with the assessed value of $19,981,000. Appellants also submitted evidence to show that the tax-day inventory was not unusual. The evidence showed

---

3. The Commission deducted from the sum of these two figures $860,415, representing an "economic factor" which is allowed to all railroads in varying amounts. Exactly the same deduction had been allowed the Wabash in each of the three preceding years.

that, both before and in the months immediately after the Wabash lease, the equalized value of the N & W rolling stock actually in Missouri never ranged far above the $7,600,000 figure. In the preceding year, 1964, the rolling stock assessment against the Wabash was only $9,177,683, and appellants demonstrated that neither the amount of rolling stock in Missouri nor the Missouri operations of the N & W and Wabash had materially increased in the intervening period.[4] The assessment of the fixed properties (for which no mileage formula was applied) hardly increased between 1964 and 1965. In 1964, prior to the lease, the fixed properties in Missouri were assessed at $12,092,594; in 1965, after the lease, the assessment was $12,177,597.

The Supreme Court of Missouri concluded that the result reached by the Commission was justifiable. It pointed out that the statutory method used by the Commission proceeds on the assumption that "rolling stock is substantially evenly divided throughout the railroad's system, and the percentage of all units which are located in Missouri at any given time, or for any given period of time, will be substantially the same as the percentage of all the miles of road of the railroad located in Missouri." It then held that the valuation found by the Commission could be justified on the theory of "enhancement," although the Commission had not referred to that principle. The court described the theory as follows:

> "The theory underlying such method of assessment is that rolling stock regularly employed in one state has an enhanced or augmented value when it is connected to, and because of its connection with, an integrated operational whole and may, therefore, be taxed according to its value as part of the system, although the other parts be outside the state;—in other words, the tax may be made to cover the enhanced value which comes to the property in the state through its organic relation to the system. Pullman Co. v. Richardson, 261 U.S. 330, 338, 43 S.Ct. 366."

The court correctly noted, however, that "even if the validity of such methods be conceded, the results, to be valid must be free of excessiveness and discrimination." It concluded that in the present case, the result reached by the Commission was justifiable. We disagree. In our opinion, the assessment violates the Due Process and Commerce Clauses of the Constitution.

II.

Established principles are not lacking in this much discussed area of the law. It is of course settled that a State may impose a property tax upon its fair share of an interstate transportation enterprise. That fair share may be regarded as the value, appropriately ascertained, of tangible assets permanently or habitually employed in the taxing State, including a

---

4. Appellants further argue that the arbitrariness of the result reached here is shown by the fact that if the rolling stock in Missouri had been taxable to the Wabash in 1965, rather than to N & W, the application of the formula to the same rolling stock would have resulted in an assessment of little more than half of that which was actually levied ($10,103,340).

portion of the intangible, or "going-concern," value of the enterprise. The value may be ascertained by reference to the total system of which the intrastate assets are a part. As the Court has stated the rule, "the tax may be made to cover the enhanced value which comes to the [tangible] property in the state through its organic relation to the [interstate] system." Pullman Co. v. Richardson, 261 U.S. 330, 338, 43 S.Ct. 366, 368 (1923). Going-concern value, of course, is an elusive concept not susceptible of exact measurement. As a consequence, the States have been permitted considerable latitude in devising formulas to measure the value of tangible property located within their borders. Such formulas usually involve a determination of the percentage of the taxpayer's tangible assets situated in the taxing State and the application of this percentage to a figure representing the total going-concern value of the enterprise. A number of such formulas have been sustained by the Court, even though it could not be demonstrated that the results they yielded were precise evaluations of assets located within the taxing State. See, e.g., Nashville, C. & St. L.R. Co. v. Browning, 310 U.S. 362, 365–366, 60 S.Ct. 968, 970 (1940).

On the other hand, the Court has insisted for many years that a State is not entitled to tax tangible or intangible property that is unconnected with the State. Delaware R. Tax, 18 Wall. 206, 229 (1873); Fargo v. Hart, 193 U.S. 490, 499, 24 S.Ct. 498, 500 (1904). In some cases the Court has concluded that States have, in fact, cast their tax burden upon property located beyond their borders. Fargo v. Hart, 193 U.S. 490, 499–503, 24 S.Ct. 498, 500, 501 (1904); Wallace v. Hines, 253 U.S. 66, 69–70, 40 S.Ct. 435, 436 (1920). The taxation of property not located in the taxing State is constitutionally invalid, both because it imposes an illegitimate restraint on interstate commerce and because it denies to the taxpayer the process that is his due.[5] A State will not be permitted, under the shelter of an imprecise allocation formula or by ignoring the peculiarities of a given enterprise, to "project the taxing power of the state plainly beyond its borders." Nashville, Chattanooga & St. Louis R. Co. v. Browning, 310 U.S. 362, 365, 60 S.Ct. 968, 970 (1940). Any formula used must bear a rational relationship, both on its face and in its application, to property values connected with the taxing State. Fargo v. Hart, 193 U.S. 490, 499–500, 24 S.Ct. 498, 500 (1904).[6]

---

5. We have said: "The problem under the Commerce Clause is to determine 'what portion of an interstate organism may appropriately be attributed to each of the various states in which it functions.' Nashville, Chattanooga & St. Louis R. Co. v. Browning, 310 U.S. 362, 365, 60 S.Ct. 968, 970. So far as due process is concerned, the only question is whether the tax in practical operation has relation to opportunities, benefits, or protection conferred or afforded by the taxing State. See State of Wisconsin v. J.C. Penney Co., 311 U.S. 435, 444, 61 S.Ct. 246, 249, 130 A.L.R. 1229. Those requirements are satisfied if the tax is fairly apportioned to the commerce carried on within the State." Ott v. Mississippi Barge Line, 336 U.S. 169, 174, 69 S.Ct. 432, 434 (1949). Neither appellants nor appellee contend that these two analyses bear different implications insofar as our present case is concerned.

6. As the Court stated in Wallace v. Hines, 253 U.S. 66, at 69, 40 S.Ct. 435, at 436: "The only reason for allowing a state to look beyond its borders when it taxes the property of foreign corporations is that it may get the true value of the things within it, when they are part of an organic system of wide extent, that gives them a value above what they otherwise would possess."

III.

Applying these principles to the facts of the case now before us, we conclude that Missouri's assessment of N & W's rolling stock cannot be sustained. This Court has, in various contexts, permitted mileage formulas as a basis for taxation. A railroad challenging the result reached by the application of such a formula has a heavy burden. It is confronted by the vastness of the State's taxing power and the latitude that the exercise of that power must be given before it encounters constitutional restraints. Its task is to show that application of the mileage method in its case has resulted in such gross overreaching, beyond the values represented by the intrastate assets purported to be taxed, as to violate the Due Process and Commerce Clauses of the Constitution. But here the appellants have borne that burden, and the State has made no effort to offset the convincing case that they have made.

Here, the record shows that rigid application of the mileage formula led to a grossly distorted result. The rolling stock in Missouri was assessed to N & W at $19,981,757. It was practically the same property that had been assessed the preceding year at $9,177,683 to the Wabash. Appellants introduced evidence of the results of an actual count of the rolling stock in Missouri. On the basis of this actual count, the equalized assessment would have been less than half of the value assessed by the State Commission. The commission's mileage formula resulted in postulating that N & W's rolling stock in Missouri constituted 8.2824% of its rolling stock. But appellants showed that the rolling stock usually employed in the State comprised only about 2.71% by number of units (and only 3.16% by cost-less-depreciation value) of the total N & W fleet.

Our decisions recognize the practical difficulties involved and do not require any close correspondence between the result of computations using the mileage formula and the value of property actually located in the State, but our cases certainly forbid an unexplained discrepancy as gross as that in this case.[7] Such discrepancy certainly means that the impact of the state tax is not confined to intrastate property even within the broad tolerance permitted. The facts of life do not neatly lend themselves to the niceties of constitutionalism; but neither does the Constitution tolerate any result, however distorted, just because it is the product of a convenient mathematical formula which, in most situations, may produce a tolerable product.

The basic difficulty here is that the record is totally barren of any evidence relating to enhancement or to going-concern or intangible value,

---

The purpose is not ... to open to taxation what is not within the State. Therefore no property of ... an interstate road situated elsewhere can be taken into account unless it can be seen in some plain and fairly intelligible way that it adds to the value of the road and the rights exercised in the State."

7. "If the ratio of the value of the property in [the State] to the value of the whole property of the company be less than that which the length of the road in [the State] bears to its entire length ... a tax imposed upon the property in [the State] according to the ratio of the length of the whole road must necessarily fall upon property out of the State." Delaware Railroad Tax, 18 Wall. 206, 230–231 (1873).

or to any other factor which might offset the devastating effect of the demonstrated discrepancy. The Missouri Supreme Court attempted to justify the result by verbal reference to "enhanced" value, but the Missouri Commission made no effort to show such value or to measure the extent to which it might be attributed to the rolling stock in the State. In fact, N & W showed that it is chiefly a coal-carrying railroad, 70% of whose 1964 revenue was derived from coal traffic. It demonstrated that its coal operations require a great deal of specialized equipment, scarcely any of which ever enters Missouri. It showed that traffic density on its Missouri tracks was only 54% of traffic density on the N & W system as a whole. Finally, it proved that the overwhelming majority of its rolling stock regularly present in Missouri was rolling stock it had leased from the Wabash. As long ago as Pittsburgh, Cincinnati, Chicago & St. Louis R. Co. v. Backus, 154 U.S. 421, 14 S.Ct. 1114 (1894), we indicated that an otherwise valid mileage formula might not be validly applied to ascertain the value of tangible assets within the taxing State in exceptional situations, for example, "where, in certain localities, the company is engaged in a particular kind of business, requiring for sole use in such localities an extra amount of rolling stock." Id., at 431, 14 S.Ct. at 1119.

The Missouri Supreme Court did not challenge the factual data submitted by the N & W. Its decision that this data did not place this case within the realm of "exceptional situations" recognized by this Court was apparently based on the conclusion that the lease transaction between Wabash and the N & W had increased the value of tangible assets formerly belonging to the two separate lines. This may be true, but it does not follow that the Constitution permits us, without evidence as to the amount of enhancement that may be assumed, to bridge the chasm between the formula and the facts of record. The difference between the assessed value and the actual value as shown by the evidence to which we have referred is too great to be explained by the mere assertion, without more, that it is due to an assumed and nonparticularized increase in intangible value. See Wallace v. Hines, 253 U.S. 66, 69, 40 S.Ct. 435, 436 (1920).

As the Court recognized in Fargo v. Hart, 193 U.S. 490, 499, 24 S.Ct. 498, 500 (1904), care must be exercised lest the mileage formula "be made a means of unlawfully taxing the privilege, or property outside the state, under the name of enhanced value or goodwill, if it is not closely confined to its true meaning. So long as it fairly may be assumed that the different parts of a line are about equal in value a division by mileage is justifiable. But it is recognized in the cases that if for instance a railroad company had terminals in one state equal in value to all the rest of the line through another, the latter state could not make use of the unity of the road to equalize the value of every mile. That would be taxing property outside of the state under a pretense." We repeat that it is not necessary that a State demonstrate that its use of the mileage formula has resulted in an exact measure of value. But when a taxpayer comes forward with strong evidence tending to prove that the mileage formula will yield a grossly distorted result in its particular case, the State is obliged to counter that evidence or to make the accommodations necessary to assure that its taxing power is confined to its constitutional limits. If it fails to do so and if the record shows that the taxpayer has sustained the burden of proof to show that the tax is so excessive as to burden interstate commerce, the taxpayer must prevail.

IV.

Accordingly, we conclude that, on the present record, Missouri has in this case exceeded the limits of her constitutional power to tax, as defined by the Due Process and Commerce Clauses. It will be open to the Missouri Supreme Court, so far as our action today is concerned, to remand the case to the appropriate tribunal to reopen the record for additional evidence to support the assessment. We vacate the judgment of the Supreme Court of Missouri and remand the cause to it for further proceedings not inconsistent with our decision.

Vacated and remanded.

[The dissenting opinion of JUSTICE BLACK has been omitted.]

NOTES AND QUESTIONS

A. *The Meaning of the Fair Apportionment Requirement.* The *Norfolk & Western* case presents an application of *Complete Auto*'s fair apportionment requirement that is relatively easy to understand. The essential question was whether the state's formula for determining its "slice" of the taxable "pie" (in this case, personal property) produced a "fair" result, in light of evidence suggesting that the true size of that "slice" was smaller than the amount attributed by formula. As we already noted, much of Chapter 7 is devoted to the study of this problem, though largely in the context of an income tax "pie" or base rather than the property tax base at issue in *Norfolk & Western*. But *Complete Auto*'s fair apportionment requirement is not limited to property and income taxes, where the slice/pie metaphor seems to capture the fair apportionment issue. How does this requirement apply, say, to a sales tax, which is imposed on a transaction with a seller in State A and buyer in State B, where the "pie" is the sales price, and the formula or other mechanism for the determining the "slice" may not readily come to mind ? Do not try to answer that question at this juncture, but keep it in mind. You will in fact read two cases that squarely confront this problem, one later in this chapter (*Goldberg v. Sweet*, pp. 176–85 infra) and the other in Chapter 8 dealing with sales taxes (*Oklahoma Tax Commission v. Jefferson Lines, Inc.*, pp. 743–58 infra).

3. THIRD PRONG: NONDISCRIMINATION

Long before *Complete Auto*, the Supreme Court regularly invalidated state taxes that discriminated against interstate commerce. In some of the earliest cases, decided in the years following the Civil War, the Court struck down drummers' and merchants' license taxes imposed on vendors of goods from other states. The taxes were enacted chiefly by the southern and western states and were aimed at an army of northern drummers descending upon rural sections with order blanks for the products of industrial centers.[ii] Some of the taxes invalidated were unmistakably discriminatory against interstate business since they were expressly limited to the merchants or products of other states.[jj] In others, the discrimination was less clear. They involved taxes limited either to persons not having an established place of business in the taxing jurisdiction or to selected articles not produced in the state.[kk] Later cases involved more flagrant instances of discrimination, such as levies that subjected nonresident businesses to higher tax rates than those applied to local businesses.[ll]

The following materials address the development of the law in this area in more recent years. Our first case, *Camps Newfound/Owatonna*, addresses the question of discrimination against interstate commerce in the latter half of the opinion; however, it begins with a discussion of an issue that is important but often taken for granted—should the Commerce Clause even apply?

CAMPS NEWFOUND/OWATONNA, INC. v. TOWN OF HARRISON

Supreme Court of the United States, 1997.
520 U.S. 564, 117 S.Ct. 1590.

JUSTICE STEVENS delivered the opinion of the Court.

The question presented is whether an otherwise generally applicable state property tax violates the Commerce Clause of the United States Constitution, Art. I, § 8, cl. 3, because its exemption for property owned by charitable institutions excludes organizations operated principally for the benefit of nonresidents.

I

Petitioner is a Maine nonprofit corporation that operates a summer camp for the benefit of children of the Christian Science faith. The regimen at the camp includes supervised prayer, meditation, and church services designed to help the children grow spiritually and physically in accordance with the tenets of their religion. * * * About 95 percent of the campers are not residents of Maine.

* * *

---

ii. See, e.g., Welton v. Missouri, 91 U.S. 275 (1875); Robbins v. Taxing District of Shelby County, 120 U.S. 489, 7 S.Ct. 592 (1887).

jj. Cook v. Pennsylvania, 97 U.S. (7 Otto) 566 (1878); Webber v. Virginia, 103 U.S. (13 Otto) 344 (1880); Walling v. Michigan, 116 U.S. 446, 6 S.Ct. 454 (1886).

kk. Caldwell v. North Carolina, 187 U.S. 622, 23 S.Ct. 229 (1903); Norfolk & Western Ry. v. Sims, 191 U.S. 441, 24 S.Ct. 151 (1903); Dozier v. Alabama, 218 U.S. 124, 30 S.Ct. 649 (1910); Stewart v. Michigan, 232 U.S. 665, 34 S.Ct. 476 (1914); cf. West Point Wholesale Grocery Co. v. City of Opelika, 354 U.S. 390, 77 S.Ct. 1096 (1957)

ll. See, e.g., Memphis Steam Laundry Cleaner v. Stone, 342 U.S. 389, 72 S.Ct. 424 (1952) ("privilege tax" struck down under the Commerce Clause as discriminating against interstate commerce).

The Maine statute at issue provides a general exemption from real estate and personal property taxes for "benevolent and charitable institutions incorporated" in the State. With respect to institutions that are "in fact conducted or operated principally for the benefit of persons who are not residents of Maine," however, a charity may only qualify for a more limited tax benefit, and then only if the weekly charge for services provided does not exceed $30 per person. Because most of the campers come from out of State, petitioner could not qualify for a complete exemption. And, since the weekly tuition was roughly $400, petitioner was ineligible for any charitable tax exemption at all.

In 1992 petitioner made a formal request to the Town for a refund of taxes paid from 1989 through 1991, and a continuing exemption from future property taxes, based principally on a claim that the tax exemption statute violated the Commerce Clause of the Federal Constitution. * * *

* * *

II

During the first years of our history as an independent confederation, the National Government lacked the power to regulate commerce among the States. Because each State was free to adopt measures fostering its own local interests without regard to possible prejudice to nonresidents, what Justice Johnson characterized as a "conflict of commercial regulations, destructive to the harmony of the States", ensued. See Gibbons v. Ogden, 9 Wheat. 1, 224, 6 L.Ed. 23 (1824) (opinion concurring in judgment). In his view, this "was the immediate cause that led to the forming of a [constitutional] convention." Ibid. "If there was any one object riding over every other in the adoption of the constitution, it was to keep the commercial intercourse among the States free from all invidious and partial restraints." Id., at 231.[7]

We have subsequently endorsed Justice Johnson's appraisal of the central importance of federal control over interstate and foreign commerce and, more narrowly, his conclusion that the Commerce Clause had not only granted Congress express authority to override restrictive and conflicting commercial regulations adopted by the States, but that it also had immediately effected a curtailment of state power. "In short, the Commerce Clause even without implementing legislation by Congress is a limitation upon the power of the States. Southern Pacific Co. v. Arizona ex rel. Sullivan, 325 U.S. 761, 65 S.Ct. 1515 [(1945)].; Morgan v. Virginia, 328 U.S. 373, 66 S.Ct. 1050 [(1946)]." Freeman v. Hewit, 329 U.S. 249, 252, 67 S.Ct. 274, 276 (1946). Our decisions on this point reflect, "upon fullest consideration, the course of adjudication unbroken through the Nation's

---

7. See also West Lynn Creamery, Inc. v. Healy, 512 U.S. 186, 193, n. 9, 114 S.Ct. 2205, 2211, n. 9 (1994) (noting that "[t]he 'negative' aspect of the Commerce Clause was considered the more important by the 'father of the Constitution,' James Madison"); Hughes v. Oklahoma, 441 U.S. 322, 325–326, 99 S.Ct. 1727, 1730–1732 (1979); Hughes v. Alexandria Scrap Corp., 426 U.S. 794, 807, n. 16, 96 S.Ct. 2488, 2496, n. 16 (1976) (quoting W. Rutledge, A Declaration of Legal Faith 25–26 (1947)).

history." Ibid. Although Congress unquestionably has the power to repudiate or substantially modify that course of adjudication,[8] it has not done so.

This case involves an issue that we have not previously addressed—the disparate real estate tax treatment of a nonprofit service provider based on the residence of the consumers that it serves. The Town argues that our dormant Commerce Clause jurisprudence is wholly inapplicable to this case, because interstate commerce is not implicated here and Congress has no power to enact a tax on real estate. We first reject these arguments, and then explain why we think our prior cases make it clear that if profit-making enterprises were at issue, Maine could not tax petitioner more heavily than other camp operators simply because its campers come principally from other States. We next address the novel question whether a different rule should apply to a discriminatory tax exemption for charitable and benevolent institutions. Finally, we reject the Town's argument that the exemption should either be viewed as a permissible subsidy or as a purchase of services by the State acting as a "market participant."

III

We are unpersuaded by the Town's argument that the dormant Commerce Clause is inapplicable here, either because campers are not "articles of commerce," or more generally because the camp's "product is delivered and 'consumed' entirely within Maine." Brief for Respondents. Even though petitioner's camp does not make a profit, it is unquestionably engaged in commerce, not only as a purchaser, see Katzenbach v. McClung, 379 U.S. 294, 300–301, 85 S.Ct. 377, 382 (1964); United States v. Lopez, 514 U.S. 549, 558, 115 S.Ct. 1624, 1629–1630 (1995), but also as a provider of goods and services. It markets those services, together with an opportunity to enjoy the natural beauty of an inland lake in Maine, to campers who are attracted to its facility from all parts of the Nation. The record reflects that petitioner "advertises for campers in [out-of-state] periodicals ... and sends its Executive Director annually on camper recruiting trips across the country." App. 49–50. Petitioner's efforts are quite successful; 95 percent of its campers come from out of State. The attendance of these campers necessarily generates the transportation of persons across state lines that has long been recognized as a form of "commerce." Edwards v. California, 314 U.S. 160, 172, 62 S.Ct. 164, 166 (1941).

Summer camps are comparable to hotels that offer their guests goods and services that are consumed locally. In Heart of Atlanta Motel, Inc. v. United States, 379 U.S. 241, 85 S.Ct. 348 (1964), we recognized that interstate commerce is substantially affected by the activities of a hotel that "solicits patronage from outside the State of Georgia through various national advertising media, including magazines of national circulation."

---

8. See New York v. United States, 505 U.S. 144, 171, 112 S.Ct. 2408, 2425–2426 (1992); Quill Corp. v. North Dakota, 504 U.S. 298, 318, 112 S.Ct. 1904, 1916 (1992); Prudential Ins. Co. v. Benjamin, 328 U.S. 408, 429–430, 434–435, 66 S.Ct. 1142, 1154–1155, 1157–1158 (1946).

Id., at 243, 85 S.Ct., at 350. In that case, we held that commerce was substantially affected by private race discrimination that limited access to the hotel and thereby impeded interstate commerce in the form of travel. Official discrimination that limits the access of nonresidents to summer camps creates a similar impediment. Even when business activities are purely local, if " 'it is interstate commerce that feels the pinch, it does not matter how local the operation which applies the squeeze.' " Heart of Atlanta, 379 U.S., at 258, 85 S.Ct., at 358 (quoting United States v. Women's Sportswear Mfrs. Assn., 336 U.S. 460, 464, 69 S.Ct. 714, 716 (1949)).

Although *Heart of Atlanta* involved Congress' affirmative Commerce Clause powers, its reasoning is applicable here. As we stated in Hughes v. Oklahoma, 441 U.S. 322, 99 S.Ct. 1727 (1979): "The definition of 'commerce' is the same when relied on to strike down or restrict state legislation as when relied on to support some exertion of federal control or regulation." Id., at 326, n. 2, 99 S.Ct., at 1731, n. 2. * * *

The Town's arguments that the dormant Commerce Clause is inapplicable to petitioner because the campers are not "articles of commerce," or more generally that interstate commerce is not at issue here, are therefore unpersuasive. The services that petitioner provides to its principally out-of-state campers clearly have a substantial effect on commerce, as do state restrictions on making those services available to nonresidents.

The Town also argues that the dormant Commerce Clause is inapplicable because a real estate tax is at issue. We disagree. A tax on real estate, like any other tax, may impermissibly burden interstate commerce. We may assume as the Town argues (though the question is not before us) that Congress could not impose a national real estate tax. It does not follow that the States may impose real estate taxes in a manner that discriminates against interstate commerce. A State's "power to lay and collect taxes, comprehensive and necessary as that power is, cannot be exerted in a way which involves a discrimination against [interstate] commerce." Pennsylvania v. West Virginia, 262 U.S. 553, 596, 43 S.Ct. 658, 665 (1923).

To allow a State to avoid the strictures of the dormant Commerce Clause by the simple device of labeling its discriminatory tax a levy on real estate would destroy the barrier against protectionism that the Constitution provides. We noted in West Lynn Creamery, Inc. v. Healy, 512 U.S. 186, 114 S.Ct. 2205 (1994), that "[t]he paradigmatic ... law discriminating against interstate commerce is the protective [import] tariff or customs duty, which taxes goods imported from other States, but does not tax similar products produced in State." Id., at 193, 114 S.Ct., at 2211. Such tariffs are "so patently unconstitutional that our cases reveal not a single attempt by a State to enact one." Ibid. Yet, were the Town's theory adopted, a State could create just such a tariff with ease. The State would need only to pass a statute imposing a special real estate tax on property used to store, process, or sell imported goods. By gearing the increased tax to the value of the imported goods at issue, the State could create the functional equivalent of an import tariff. As this example demonstrates, to accept the Town's theory would have radical and unacceptable results.

We therefore turn to the question whether our prior cases preclude a State from imposing a higher tax on a camp that serves principally nonresidents than on one that limits its services primarily to residents.

IV

There is no question that were this statute targeted at profit-making entities, it would violate the dormant Commerce Clause. "State laws discriminating against interstate commerce on their face are 'virtually *per se* invalid.'" Fulton Corp. v. Faulkner, 516 U.S. 325, 331, 116 S.Ct. 848, 854 (1996) (quoting Oregon Waste Systems, Inc. v. Department of Environmental Quality of Ore., 511 U.S. 93, 99, 114 S.Ct. 1345, 1350 (1994)). It is not necessary to look beyond the text of this statute to determine that it discriminates against interstate commerce. The Maine law expressly distinguishes between entities that serve a principally interstate clientele and those that primarily serve an intrastate market, singling out camps that serve mostly in-staters for beneficial tax treatment, and penalizing those camps that do a principally interstate business. As a practical matter, the statute encourages affected entities to limit their out-of-state clientele, and penalizes the principally nonresident customers of businesses catering to a primarily interstate market.

If such a policy were implemented by a statutory prohibition against providing camp services to nonresidents, the statute would almost certainly be invalid. We have "consistently ... held that the Commerce Clause ... precludes a state from mandating that its residents be given a preferred right of access, over out-of-state consumers, to natural resources located within its borders or to the products derived therefrom." New England Power Co. v. New Hampshire, 455 U.S. 331, 338, 102 S.Ct. 1096, 1100 (1982). * * * Petitioner's "product" is in part the natural beauty of Maine itself and, in addition, the special services that the camp provides. In this way, the Maine statute is like a law that burdens out-of-state access to domestically generated hydroelectric power, New England Power, or to local landfills, Philadelphia v. New Jersey, 437 U.S. 617, 98 S.Ct. 2531 (1978). In those cases, as in this case, the burden fell on out-of-state access both to a natural resource, and to related services provided by state residents.

Avoiding this sort of "economic Balkanization," Hughes v. Oklahoma, 441 U.S., at 325, 99 S.Ct., at 1731, and the retaliatory acts of other States that may follow, is one of the central purposes of our negative Commerce Clause jurisprudence. See ibid.; West v. Kansas Natural Gas Co., 221 U.S. 229, 255, 31 S.Ct. 564, 571 (1911) (expressing concern that "embargo may be retaliated by embargo, and commerce will be halted at state lines"). And, as we noted in Brown–Forman Distillers Corp. v. New York State Liquor Authority, 476 U.S. 573, 580, 106 S.Ct. 2080, 2085 (1986): "Economic protectionism is not limited to attempts to convey advantages on local merchants; it may include attempts to give local consumers an advantage over consumers in other States."[11] By encouraging economic isolationism, prohibitions on out-of-state access to in-state resources serve the very evil that the dormant Commerce Clause was designed to prevent.

Of course, this case does not involve a total prohibition. Rather, the statute provides a strong incentive for affected entities not to do business with nonresidents if they are able to so avoid the discriminatory tax. In this way, the statute is similar to the North Carolina "intangibles tax" that we struck down in Fulton Corp. v. Faulkner, 516 U.S., at 327, 116 S.Ct., at 852. That case involved the constitutionality under the Commerce Clause of a state "regime that taxe[d] stock [held by in-state shareholders] only to the degree that its issuing corporation participates in interstate commerce." Id., at 333, 116 S.Ct., at 855. We held the statute facially discriminatory, in part because it tended "to discourage domestic corporations from plying their trades in interstate commerce." Ibid. Maine's statute has a like effect.

To the extent that affected Maine organizations are not deterred by the statute from doing a principally interstate business, it is clear that discriminatory burdens on interstate commerce imposed by regulation or taxation may also violate the Commerce Clause. We have held that special fees assessed on nonresidents directly by the State when they attempt to use local services impose an impermissible burden on interstate commerce. See, e.g., Chemical Waste Management, Inc. v. Hunt, 504 U.S. 334, 342, 112 S.Ct. 2009, 2013–2014 (1992) (discriminatory tax imposed on disposal of out-of-state hazardous waste). That the tax discrimination comes in the form of a deprivation of a generally available tax benefit, rather than a specific penalty on the activity itself, is of no moment. Thus, in New Energy Co. of Ind. v. Limbach, 486 U.S. 269, 274, 108 S.Ct. 1803, 1808 (1988), the Court invalidated an Ohio statute that provided a tax credit for sales of ethanol produced in State, but not ethanol produced in certain other States; the law "deprive[d] certain products of generally available beneficial tax treatment because they are made in certain other States, and thus on its face appear[ed] to violate the cardinal requirement of nondiscrimination."[12] Given the fact that the burden of Maine's facially discriminatory tax scheme falls by design in a predictably disproportionate way on out-of-staters, [footnote omitted] the pernicious effect on interstate commerce is the same as in our cases involving taxes targeting out-of-staters alone.

---

11. The Town argues that "the Commerce Clause protects out-of-state competitors but does not protect out-of-state consumers." Brief for Respondents 16. As the discussion above indicates, our cases have rejected this view.

12. See Bacchus Imports, Ltd. v. Dias, 468 U.S. 263, 268, 104 S.Ct. 3049, 3053–3054 (1984) (discriminatory excise tax exemption); Maryland v. Louisiana, 451 U.S. 725, 756, 101 S.Ct. 2114, 2134 (1981) (tax scheme "unquestionably discriminates against interstate commerce . . . as the necessary result of various tax credits and exclusions"); Westinghouse Elec. Corp. v. Tully, 466 U.S. 388, 399–400, and n. 9, 104 S.Ct. 1856, 1863–1865, and n. 9 (1984) (per curiam);; see also West Lynn Creamery, Inc. v. Healy, 512 U.S., at 210, 114 S.Ct., at 2220 (SCALIA, J., concurring in judgment).

Unlike in *Chemical Waste,* we recognize that here the discriminatory burden is imposed on the out-of-state customer indirectly by means of a tax on the entity transacting business with the non-Maine customer. This distinction makes no analytic difference. As we noted in *West Lynn Creamery* discussing the general phenomenon of import tariffs: "For over 150 years, our cases have rightly concluded that the imposition of a differential burden on any part of the stream of commerce-from wholesaler to retailer to consumer-is invalid, because a burden placed at any point will result in a disadvantage to the out-of-state producer." 512 U.S., at 202, 114 S.Ct., at 2216 (citing cases). So too here, it matters little that it is the camp that is taxed rather than the campers. The record demonstrates that the economic incidence of the tax falls at least in part on the campers, the Town has not contested the point, and the courts below based their decision on this presumption.

With respect to those businesses—like petitioner's—that continue to engage in a primarily interstate trade, the Maine statute therefore functionally serves as an export tariff that targets out-of-state consumers by taxing the businesses that principally serve them. As our cases make clear, this sort of discrimination is at the very core of activities forbidden by the dormant Commerce Clause. * * *

Ninety-five percent of petitioner's campers come from out of State. Insofar as Maine's discriminatory tax has increased tuition, that burden is felt almost entirely by out-of-staters, deterring them from enjoying the benefits of camping in Maine.[15] In sum, the Maine statute facially discriminates against interstate commerce, and is all but *per se* invalid. See, e.g., Oregon Waste, 511 U.S., at 100–101, 114 S.Ct., at 1350–1351.

We recognize that the Town might have attempted to defend the Maine law under the *per se* rule by demonstrating that it " 'advances a legitimate local purpose that cannot be adequately served by reasonable nondiscriminatory alternatives.' " Id., at 101, 114 S.Ct., at 1351 (quoting New Energy Co., 486 U.S., at 278, 108 S.Ct., at 1810). In assessing respondents' arguments, we would have applied our "strictest scrutiny." Hughes v. Oklahoma, 441 U.S., at 337, 99 S.Ct., at 1737. This is an extremely difficult burden, "so heavy that 'facial discrimination by itself may be a fatal defect.' " Oregon Waste, 511 U.S., at 101, 114 S.Ct., at 1351 (quoting Hughes, 441 U.S., at 337, 99 S.Ct., at 1737); see Chemical Waste Management, Inc. v. Hunt, 504 U.S., at 342, 112 S.Ct., at 2014 ("Once a

---

15. The Town argues that these effects are entirely speculative, because the record does not reflect any decision by a potential camper not to attend petitioner's camp as a result of the burden imposed. Brief for Respondents 16. The Supreme Judicial Court appears to have adopted similar reasoning. 655 A.2d, at 879. This misconstrues the proper analysis. As we made clear most recently in Fulton Corp. v. Faulkner, 516 U.S., at 333, n. 3, 116 S.Ct., at 855, n. 3, there is no " '*de minimis*' defense to a charge of discriminatory taxation under the Commerce Clause." A particularized showing of the sort respondent seeks is not required. See Associated Industries of Mo. v. Lohman, 511 U.S. 641, 650, 114 S.Ct. 1815, 1822 (1994) ("[A]ctual discrimination, wherever it is found, is impermissible, and the magnitude and scope of the discrimination have no bearing on the determinative question whether discrimination has occurred"); Maryland v. Louisiana, 451 U.S., at 756, 101 S.Ct., at 2134; see also Boston Stock Exchange v. State Tax Comm'n, 429 U.S.,at 334, n. 13, 97 S.Ct., at 609, n. 13.

state tax is found to discriminate against out-of-state commerce, it is typically struck down without further inquiry"). Perhaps realizing the weight of its burden, the Town has made no effort to defend the statute under the *per se* rule, and so we do not address this question. We have no doubt that if petitioner's camp were a profit-making entity, the discriminatory tax exemption would be impermissible.

V

The unresolved question presented by this case is whether a different rule should apply to tax exemptions for charitable and benevolent institutions. Though we have never had cause to address the issue directly, the applicability of the dormant Commerce Clause to the nonprofit sector of the economy follows from our prior decisions.

Our cases have frequently applied laws regulating commerce to not-for-profit institutions. In Associated Press v. NLRB, 301 U.S. 103, 57 S.Ct. 650 (1937), for example, we held the National Labor Relations Act as applied to the Associated Press' (A.P.'s) news gathering activities to be an enactment entirely within Congress' Commerce Clause power, despite the fact that the A.P. "does not sell news and does not operate for a profit." Id., at 129, 57 S.Ct., at 654. * * *

We have similarly held that federal antitrust laws are applicable to the anticompetitive activities of nonprofit organizations. See National Collegiate Athletic Assn. v. Board of Regents of Univ. of Okla., 468 U.S. 85, 100, n. 22, 104 S.Ct. 2948, 2960, n. 22 (1984) * * * The nonprofit character of an enterprise does not place it beyond the purview of federal laws regulating commerce. See also NLRB v. Yeshiva Univ., 444 U.S. 672, 681, n. 11, 100 S.Ct. 856, 862, n. 11 (1980) (noting that in context of amendments to National Labor Relations Act "Congress appears to have agreed that nonprofit institutions 'affect commerce' under modern economic conditions").

We have already held that the dormant Commerce Clause is applicable to activities undertaken without the intention of earning a profit. In Edwards v. California, 314 U.S. 160, 62 S.Ct. 164 (1941), we addressed the constitutionality of a California statute prohibiting the transport into that State of indigent persons. We struck the statute down as a violation of the dormant Commerce Clause, reasoning that "the transportation of persons is 'commerce,' " and that the California statute was an "unconstitutional barrier to [that] interstate commerce." Id., at 172–173, 62 S.Ct., at 166. In determining whether the transportation of persons is "commerce," we noted that "[i]t is immaterial whether or not the transportation is commercial in character." Id., at 172, n. 1, 62 S.Ct., at 166, n. 1.

We see no reason why the nonprofit character of an enterprise should exclude it from the coverage of either the affirmative or the negative aspect of the Commerce Clause. There are a number of lines of commerce in which both for-profit and nonprofit entities participate. Some educational institutions, some hospitals, some child care facilities, some research organizations, and some museums generate significant earnings; and some are operated by not-for-profit corporations.

* * *

For purposes of Commerce Clause analysis, any categorical distinction between the activities of profit-making enterprises and not-for-profit entities is therefore wholly illusory. Entities in both categories are major participants in interstate markets. And, although the summer camp involved in this case may have a relatively insignificant impact on the commerce of the entire Nation, the interstate commercial activities of nonprofit entities as a class are unquestionably significant.

From the State's standpoint it may well be reasonable to use tax exemptions as a means of encouraging nonprofit institutions to favor local citizens, notwithstanding any possible adverse impact on the larger markets in which those institutions participate. Indeed, if we view the issue solely from the State's perspective, it is equally reasonable to use discriminatory tax exemptions as a means of encouraging the growth of local trade. But as our cases clearly hold, such exemptions are impermissible. See, e.g., Bacchus Imports Ltd. v. Dias, 468 U.S. 263, 273, 104 S.Ct. 3049, 3056 (1984). Protectionism, whether targeted at for-profit entities or serving, as here, to encourage nonprofits to keep their efforts close to home, is forbidden under the dormant Commerce Clause. If there is need for a special exception for nonprofits, Congress not only has the power to create it, but is also in a far better position than we to determine its dimensions.

VI

* * * [T]he Town argues that Maine's exemption statute should be viewed as an expenditure of government money designed to lessen its social service burden and to foster the societal benefits provided by charitable organizations. So characterized, the Town submits that its tax exemption scheme is either a legitimate discriminatory subsidy of only those charities that choose to focus their activities on local concerns, or alternatively a governmental "purchase" of charitable services falling within the narrow exception to the dormant Commerce Clause for States in their role as "market participants," see, e.g., Hughes v. Alexandria Scrap Corp., 426 U.S. 794, 96 S.Ct. 2488 (1976); Reeves, Inc. v. Stake, 447 U.S. 429, 100 S.Ct. 2271 (1980). We find these arguments unpersuasive. Although tax exemptions and subsidies serve similar ends, they differ in important and relevant respects, and our cases have recognized these distinctions. As for the "market participant" argument, we have already rejected the Town's position in a prior case, and in any event respondents' open-ended exemption for charitable and benevolent institutions is not analogous to the industry-specific state actions that we reviewed in *Alexandria Scrap* and *Reeves*.

The Town argues that its discriminatory tax exemption is, in economic reality, no different from a discriminatory subsidy of those charities that cater principally to local needs. Noting our statement in *West Lynn*

Creamery that "[a] pure subsidy funded out of general revenue ordinarily imposes no burden on interstate commerce, but merely assists local business," 512 U.S., at 199, 114 S.Ct., at 2214, the Town submits that since a discriminatory subsidy may be permissible, a discriminatory exemption must be, too. We have "never squarely confronted the constitutionality of subsidies," id., at 199, n. 15, 114 S.Ct., at 2214, n. 15, and we need not address these questions today. Assuming, *arguendo,* that the Town is correct that a direct subsidy benefiting only those nonprofits serving principally Maine residents would be permissible, our cases do not sanction a tax exemption serving similar ends.[22]

In Walz v. Tax Comm'n of City of New York, 397 U.S. 664, 90 S.Ct. 1409 (1970), notwithstanding our assumption that a direct subsidy of religious activity would be invalid,[23] we held that New York's tax exemption for church property did not violate the Establishment Clause of the First Amendment.[24] That holding rested, in part, on the premise that there is a constitutionally significant difference between subsidies and tax exemptions.[25] We have expressly recognized that this distinction is also applicable to claims that certain state action designed to give residents an advantage in the market-place is prohibited by the Commerce Clause.

In New Energy Co. of Ind. v. Limbach, 486 U.S. 269, 108 S.Ct. 1803 (1988), we found unconstitutional under the Commerce Clause an Ohio tax scheme that provided a sales tax credit for ethanol produced in State, or manufactured in another State to the extent that State gave similar tax advantages to ethanol produced in Ohio. We recognized that the party challenging the Ohio scheme was "eligible to receive a cash subsidy" from its home State, and was therefore "the potential beneficiary of a scheme no less discriminatory than the one that it attacks, and no less effective in conferring a commercial advantage over out-of-state competitors." Id., at 278, 108 S.Ct., at 1810. That was of no importance. We noted: "The Commerce Clause does not prohibit all state action designed to give its residents an advantage in the marketplace, but only action of that

---

22. As the Supreme Judicial Court made clear, 655 A.2d, at 878, under Maine law an exemption is categorized as a "tax expenditure." Me.Rev.Stat. Ann., Tit. 36, § 196 (1990). The Town's effort to argue that this state statutory categorization allows it to elide the federal constitutional distinction between tax exemptions and subsidies is unavailing. We recognized long ago that a tax exemption can be viewed as a form of government spending. See Regan v. Taxation with Representation of Wash., 461 U.S. 540, 544, 103 S.Ct. 1997, 2000 (1983). The distinction we have drawn for dormant Commerce Clause purposes does not turn on this point.

23. We noted: "Obviously a direct money subsidy would be a relationship pregnant with involvement and, as with most governmental grant programs, could encompass sustained and detailed administrative relationships for enforcement of statutory or administrative standards, but that is not this case." Walz, 397 U.S., at 675, 90 S.Ct., at 1414.

24. We reasoned that "New York's statute [cannot be read] as attempting to establish religion; it ... simply spar[es] the exercise of religion from the burden of property taxation levied on private profit institutions." Id., at 673, 90 S.Ct., at 1414.

25. "The grant of a tax exemption is not sponsorship since the government does not transfer part of its revenue to churches but simply abstains from demanding that the church support the state. No one has ever suggested that tax exemption has converted libraries, art galleries, or hospitals into arms of the state or put employees 'on the public payroll.' " Id., at 675, 90 S.Ct., at 1415. As Justice Brennan noted: "Tax exemptions and general subsidies ... are qualitatively different." Id., at 690, 90 S.Ct., at 1422 (concurring opinion).

description *in connection with the State's regulation of interstate commerce.* Direct subsidization of domestic industry does not ordinarily run afoul of that prohibition; discriminatory taxation ... does." Ibid. (emphasis in original). See also West Lynn, 512 U.S., at 210, 114 S.Ct., at 2220 (SCALIA, J., concurring in judgment) (drawing similar distinction between forbidden generally applicable tax with discriminatory "exemption" and permissible "subsidy ... funded from the State's general revenues"). This distinction is supported by scholarly commentary as well as precedent, and we see no reason to depart from it. See Enrich, Saving the States from Themselves: Commerce Clause Constraints on State Tax Incentives for Business, 110 Harv. L. Rev. 377, 442–443 (1996); Hellerstein & Coenen, Commerce Clause Restraints on State Business Development Incentives, 81 Cornell L. Rev. 789, 846–848 (1996).[26] The Town's claim that its discriminatory tax scheme should be viewed as a permissible subsidy is therefore unpersuasive.

Finally, the Town argues that its discriminatory tax exemption scheme falls within the "market-participant" exception. As we explained in *New Energy Co.*: "That doctrine differentiates between a State's acting in its distinctive governmental capacity, and a State's acting in the more general capacity of a market participant; only the former is subject to the limitations of the negative Commerce Clause." 486 U.S., at 277, 108 S.Ct., at 1809.

In *Alexandria Scrap* we concluded that the State of Maryland had, in effect, entered the market for abandoned automobile hulks as a purchaser because it was using state funds to provide bounties for their removal from Maryland streets and junkyards. Id., at 809–810, 96 S.Ct., at 2497–2498. In *Reeves*, the State of South Dakota similarly participated in the market for cement as a seller of the output of the cement plant that it had owned and operated for many years. 447 U.S., at 431–432, 100 S.Ct., at 2274–2275. And in *White*, the city of Boston had participated in the construction industry by funding certain projects. 460 U.S., at 205–206, 103 S.Ct., at 1043–1044. These three cases stand for the proposition that, for purposes of analysis under the dormant Commerce Clause, a State acting in its proprietary capacity as a purchaser or seller may "favor its own citizens over others." Alexandria Scrap, 426 U.S., at 810, 96 S.Ct., at 2498.

Maine's tax exemption statute cannot be characterized as a proprietary activity falling within the market-participant exception. In *New Energy Co.*, Ohio argued similarly that a discriminatory tax credit program fell within the exception. We noted that the tax program had "the purpose and effect of subsidizing a particular industry, as do many dispositions of the tax laws." 486 U.S., at 277, 108 S.Ct., at 1809. "That," we explained, "does not transform it into a form of state participation in the free market." Ibid. "The Ohio action ultimately at issue is neither its

---

26. The distinction provides a sufficient response to the Town's argument that our ruling today would invalidate a State's subsidization of all or part of its residents' tuition at state-owned universities.

purchase nor its sale of ethanol, but its assessment and computation of taxes-a primeval governmental activity." Ibid. As we indicated in *White:* "[I]n this kind of case there is 'a single inquiry: whether the challenged "program constituted direct state participation in the market."' " 460 U.S., at 208, 103 S.Ct., at 1044–1045 (quoting Reeves, 447 U.S., at 436, n. 7). A tax exemption is not the sort of direct state involvement in the market that falls within the market-participation doctrine.

Even if we were prepared to expand the exception in the manner suggested by the Town, the Maine tax statute at issue here would be a poor candidate. Like the tax exemption upheld in *Walz*—which applied to libraries, art galleries, and hospitals as well as churches[28]—the exemption that has been denied to petitioner is available to a broad category of charitable and benevolent institutions.[29] For that reason, nothing short of a dramatic expansion of the "market-participant" exception would support its application to this case. *Alexandria Scrap* involved Maryland's entry into the market for automobile hulks, a discrete activity focused on a single industry. Similarly, South Dakota's participation in the market for cement was-in part because of its narrow scope-readily conceived as a proprietary action of the State. In contrast, Maine's tax exemption—which sweeps to cover broad swathes of the nonprofit sector—must be viewed as action taken in the State's sovereign capacity rather than a proprietary decision to make an entry into all of the markets in which the exempted charities function. See White, 460 U.S., at 211, n. 7, 103 S.Ct., at 1046, n. 7 (noting that "there are some limits on a state or local government's ability to impose restrictions that reach beyond the immediate parties with which the government transacts business"). The Town's version of the "market-participant" exception would swallow the rule against discriminatory tax schemes. Contrary to the Town's submission, the notion that whenever a State provides a discriminatory tax abatement it is "purchasing" some service in its proprietary capacity is not readily confined to the charitable context. A special tax concession for liquors indigenous to Hawaii, for example, might be conceived as a "purchase" of the jobs produced by local industry, or an investment in the unique local cultural value provided by these beverages. Cf. Bacchus, 468 U.S., at 270–271, 104 S.Ct., at 3054–3055. Discriminatory schemes favoring local farmers might be seen as the "purchase" of agricultural services in order to ensure that the State's citizens will have a steady local supply of the product. Cf. West Lynn, 512 U.S., at 190, 114 S.Ct., at 2209–2210 (striking down statute protecting in-state milk producers designed to "preserve ... local industry," "thereby ensur[ing] a continuous and adequate supply of fresh milk for our market" (internal quotation marks omitted)). Our cases provide no support for the Town's radical effort to expand the market-participant doctrine.

---

28. See Walz, 397 U.S., at 666–667, and n. 1, 90 S.Ct., at 1410 and n. 1.

29. See Me.Rev.Stat. Ann., Tit. 36, § 652(1)(A) (Supp. 1996) ("For the purposes of this paragraph, 'benevolent and charitable institutions' *include, but are not limited to,* nonprofit nursing homes and nonprofit boarding homes and boarding care facilities ..., nonprofit community mental health service facilities ... [,] and nonprofit child care centers") (emphasis added).

VII

As was true in *Bacchus Imports, Ltd. v. Dias*, the facts of this particular case, viewed in isolation, do not appear to pose any threat to the health of the national economy. Nevertheless, history, including the history of commercial conflict that preceded the Constitutional Convention as well as the uniform course of Commerce Clause jurisprudence animated and enlightened by that early history, provides the context in which each individual controversy must be judged. The history of our Commerce Clause jurisprudence has shown that even the smallest scale discrimination can interfere with the project of our Federal Union. As Justice Cardozo recognized, to countenance discrimination of the sort that Maine's statute represents would invite significant inroads on our "national solidarity":

> "The Constitution was framed under the dominion of a political philosophy less parochial in range. It was framed upon the theory that the peoples of the several states must sink or swim together, and that in the long run prosperity and salvation are in union and not division." Baldwin v. G.A.F. Seelig, Inc., 294 U.S. 511, 523, 55 S.Ct. 497, 500 (1935).

The judgment of the Maine Supreme Judicial Court is reversed.

It is so ordered.

[The dissenting opinion of JUSTICE SCALIA, joined by CHIEF JUSTICE REHNQUIST and JUSTICE GINSBURG, and the dissenting opinion of JUSTICE THOMAS, joined by JUSTICE SCALIA and in part by CHIEF JUSTICE REHNQUIST, have been omitted.]

NOTES AND QUESTIONS

A. *The Scope of the Commerce Clause.* Given the Court's broad view of the scope of the dormant Commerce Clause as reflected in *Camps Newfound* and in other opinions, it will be the rare case in which any serious claim can be made that a tax is immune from scrutiny under substantive Commerce Clause standards on the ground that the tax does not substantially affect interstate commerce. The Court's position, reiterated in *Camps Newfound*, that "the definition of 'commerce' is the same when relied on to strike down or restrict state legislation as when relied on to support some exertion of federal control or regulation," Hughes v. Oklahoma, 441 U.S. 322, 326 n. 2, 99 S.Ct. 1727 (1979), reinforces this conclusion. After all, the Court has sustained as a legitimate exercise of Congress' power to regulate interstate commerce such activities as (1) the amount of wheat a farmer can grow for his own consumption, Wickard v. Filburn, 317 U.S. 111, 63 S.Ct. 82 (1942), (2) discriminatory practices in local hotels and restaurants, Heart of Atlanta Motel v. United States, 379 U.S. 241, 85 S.Ct. 348 (1964) (discussed in *Camps Newfound*); and (3) local criminal activity, Perez v. United States, 402 U.S. 146, 91 S.Ct. 1357 (1971). To be sure, there may be some instances in which a tax is imposed on an activity so attenuated from the common understanding of "commerce" that it will not be subjected to Commerce Clause review. Cf.

United States v. Morrison, 529 U.S. 598, 120 S.Ct. 1740 (2000) (Congress lacks the power under the Commerce Clause to provide a civil remedy for victims of gender-motivated violence because gender-motivated crimes do not substantially affect interstate commerce); United States v. Lopez, 514 U.S. 549, 115 S.Ct. 1624 (1995) (Congress lacks the power under the Commerce Clause to prohibit possession of firearms in school zones because possession of a gun in a local school zone does not substantially affect interstate commerce). In recent years, however, the threshold question of the application of the Commerce Clause to a state tax alleged to burden commerce generally has been more theoretical than real.

B. *The Outer Limits of Dormant Commerce Clause Scrutiny of State and Local Taxation.* The scope of the dormant Commerce Clause continues to generate controversy in connection with federalism-based claims arising under state personal income taxes and state death taxes. Interstate commuters, for example, have claimed that the Commerce Clause shields them from the risk of multiple taxation resulting from the fact that both the state in which they work and the state in which they are domiciled treats them as residents taxable on all of their income. Yet the New York Court of Appeals refused to consider the substance of these contentions on the ground that the personal income "tax does not fall on any interstate activity, but rather on a purely local occurrence—the taxpayer's status as a resident of New York State." Tamagni v. Tax Appeals Tribunal, 91 N.Y.2d 530, 695 N.E.2d 1125, 673 N.Y.S.2d 44, 52, cert. denied, 525 U.S. 931, 119 S.Ct. 340 (1998). See also Luther v. Commissioner of Revenue, 588 N.W.2d 502 (Minn. 1999), cert. denied, 528 U.S. 821, 120 S.Ct. 66 (1999) (nondomiciliary taxpayer's claim that Minnesota's definition of "resident" exposes her to double taxation in violation of the Commerce Clause does not involve interstate commerce and therefore is not cognizable under the Commerce Clause). Can these decisions be squared with *Camps Newfound*? Is it relevant that commuting expenses are not deductible for federal income tax purposes? See Treas. Reg. § 1.262–1(b)(5); Commissioner v. Flowers, 326 U.S. 465, 66 S.Ct. 250 (1946). If so, why? If not, why not? Do inconsistent definitions of resident trusts and estates that expose such trusts or estates to claims of multiple taxation implicate the Commerce Clause? Can one distinguish this question from the analogous question raised by the personal income tax cases cited above by the fact that these inconsistent assertions of state taxing power affect not only the taxable trust or estate but also interstate financial institutions that manage the trusts and estates and have a fiduciary obligation not to overpay or underpay the trust's or estate's taxes? See Chase Manhattan Bank v. Gavin, 249 Conn. 172, 733 A.2d 782, cert. denied, 528 U.S. 965, 120 S.Ct. 401 (1999), discussed in Chapter 6, pp. 390–96 infra.

C. *Tax Exemption Favoring Local Alcoholic Beverages.* In Bacchus Imports, Ltd. v. Dias, 468 U.S. 263, 104 S.Ct. 3049 (1984), the Supreme Court struck down an exemption from Hawaii's excise tax on wholesale liquor sales for certain locally produced alcoholic beverages. The beverages at issue were pineapple wine and okolehao, a brandy distilled from the root of the indigenous Hawaiian ti shrub. The state sought to avoid the force of the Court's precedents prohibiting such local favoritism by arguing that the locally produced beverages did not compete with other products sold by the wholesalers and that this in substance mooted the Commerce Clause issue. The Court rejected this argument on the ground that some competition existed between the exempted and the nonexempted liquors and that the extent of the competition was irrelevant under Commerce Clause analysis. The state also claimed the exemption was designed to promote a struggling industry, but the Court found that fact unacceptable as a justification for the discriminatory tax under the Commerce Clause.

D. *Discriminatory "Multiple Activities" Exemption in Business and Occupation Tax and the "Internal Consistency" Requirement.* In Armco Inc. v. Hardesty, 467 U.S. 638, 104 S.Ct. 2620 (1984), the Court considered a claim of state tax discrimination under West Virginia's former broad-based gross receipts tax (repealed in 1987), which was denominated a Business and Occupation (B & O) tax. The tax was levied upon both manufacturers and wholesalers, but it exempted manufacturers who were subject to the manufacturing tax from liability for the wholesaling tax. The manufacturing tax was imposed at a higher rate than the wholesaling tax.

The Supreme Court agreed that the tax discriminated on its face against interstate commerce. The existence of a higher B & O tax on in-state manufacturers did not cure the discrimination because the manufacturing tax could not be viewed as substantially equivalent to the wholesaling tax. Furthermore, the Court did not saddle the taxpayer with the burden of demonstrating actual discrimination, i.e., that it was disadvantaged in comparison to an intrastate West Virginia manufacturer-wholesaler because it was required to pay both a wholesaling tax to West Virginia as well as a manufacturing tax elsewhere. The Court instead held that the tax would violate the Commerce Clause's bar against state tax discrimination so long as it lacked "internal consistency." As the Court declared in *Armco*:

> In Container Corporation of America v. Franchise Tax Board, 463 U.S. 159, 103 S.Ct. 2933 (1983), the Court noted that a tax must have "what might be called internal consistency—that is the [tax] must be such that, if applied by every jurisdiction," there would be no impermissible interference with free trade. In that case, the Court was discussing the requirement that a tax be fairly apportioned to reflect the business conducted in the State. A similar rule applies where the allegation is that a tax on its face discriminates against interstate commerce. A tax that unfairly apportions income from other States is a form of discrimination against interstate commerce. * * * Any other rule would mean that the constitutionality of West Virginia's tax laws would depend on the shifting complexities of the tax codes of 49 other States, and that the validity of the taxes imposed on each taxpayer would depend on the particular other States in which it operated.

Id., 467 U.S. at 644–45.

In Tyler Pipe Industries, Inc. v. Washington Department of Revenue, 483 U.S. 232, 107 S.Ct. 2810 (1987), set out in part in Section B(1), pp. 120–22 supra, the Court applied the internal consistency doctrine to invalidate a provision of Washington's B & O tax, which closely resembles West Virginia's former B & O tax. Washington's B & O tax applied to the gross receipts from various business activities carried on in the state, including manufacturing and wholesaling. Like West Virginia in the *Armco* case, Washington had a "multiple activities" exemption that limited to one tax the levy on taxpayers engaged in both manufacturing and wholesaling in the state. However, instead of exempting local manufacturer-wholesalers from the wholesaling tax, as West Virginia had done, Washington exempted local manufacturer-wholesalers from the manufacturing tax. Consequently, the Washington tax no longer discriminated on its face against out–of–state manufacturers. Out-of-state manufacturers that made wholesale sales in Washington would pay the same tax on their wholesaling activities as would their Washington-based competitors who manufactured and wholesaled their products in the state.

Nevertheless, the Court struck down the tax as discriminatory against out-of-state wholesalers under the internal consistency doctrine. It observed that if every state adopted Washington's taxing scheme, the interstate manufacturer-wholesaler would be put at a competitive disadvantage in relation to the intrastate manufacturer-wholesaler. The interstate manufacturer-wholesaler would pay both a manufacturing tax to the state of manufacture and a wholesaling tax to the state of sale, whereas the intrastate manufacturer would pay but one tax—a manufacturing tax. For a detailed consideration of *Tyler Pipe* and the internal consistency doctrine, see Walter Hellerstein, "Is 'Internal Consistency' Foolish?: Reflections on an Emerging Commerce Clause Restraint on State Taxation," 87 Mich. L. Rev. 138 (1988).

E. *Flat Highway Taxes, Discrimination Against Interstate Commerce, and the "Internal Consistency" Requirement.* In American Trucking Ass'ns, Inc. v. Scheiner, 483 U.S. 266, 107 S.Ct. 2829 (1987) (*American Trucking I*), the Court considered the question whether Pennsylvania's lump sum annual taxes on the operation of trucks in the state discriminated against interstate commerce. The taxes at issue were an axle tax ranging from $72 to $180 per truck and a $25 identification marker fee. The truckers attacked these levies under the Commerce Clause on the ground, among others, that if Pennsylvania had the right to impose a flat tax on their operations, so could every other state, and the cumulative consequences of such a regime would impose a crippling financial burden on the interstate motor carriers. Relying on the internal consistency test, see Note D supra, the Court concluded that the taxes were discriminatory. The "inevitable effect" of the "unapportioned flat taxes" is

> to threaten the free movement of commerce by placing a financial barrier around the State of Pennsylvania. To pass the internal consistency test, a state tax must be of a kind that, "if applied by every jurisdiction, there would be no impermissible interference with free trade." Armco Inc. v. Hardesty, 467 U.S., at 644, 104 S.Ct., at 2623 (1984). If each State imposed flat taxes for the privilege of making commercial entrances into its territory, there is no conceivable doubt that commerce among the States would be deterred.

Id., 483 U.S. at 284.

In American Trucking Ass'ns, Inc. v. Michigan Public Service Commission (*American Trucking II*), 545 U.S. 429, 125 S.Ct. 2419 (2005), the Court revisited the internal consistency question it had addressed in *American Trucking I*, in the context of Michigan's $100 flat fee on trucks. The fee applied only to vehicles that engaged in intrastate commercial operations, i.e., to trucks that made point-to-point hauls within Michigan. The taxpayers challenged the fee as applied to trucks engaged in interstate commerce on the ground that it bore more heavily on trucks engaged in interstate commerce that made point-to-point hauls in Michigan than on trucks engaged only in intrastate commerce, i.e. on trucks that made *only* point-to-point hauls within Michigan. Based on the Court's analysis in *American Trucking I*, the flat tax in *American Trucking II* appeared to fail the internal consistency test, a point the Court recognized: "We must concede that here, as petitioners argue, if all States did the same, an interstate truck would have to pay fees totaling several hundred dollars, or even several thousand dollars, were it to 'top off' its business by carrying local loads in many (or even all) other States." Id., 545 U.S. at 438. Nevertheless, the Court did not strike the tax down. Instead, it sustained the levy over internal consistency objections, observing that an interstate truck would have to pay fees exceeding those imposed on an intrastate truck

> only because it engages in *local* business in all those States. An interstate firm with local outlets normally expects to pay local fees that are uniformly assessed upon all those who engage in local business, interstate and domestic firms alike. A motor carrier is not special in this respect.

Id. at 438 (citations omitted, emphasis in original).

The Court's disposition of the internal consistency claim in *American Trucking II* marks a clear retreat from the internal consistency doctrine as explicated in earlier cases. The Court candidly conceded as much it its opinion. In effect, the Court looked the implications of the internal consistency doctrine squarely in the eye and it blinked. Those implications were that "the imposition of *any* unapportioned flat state or local tax on a multistate business would appear to be vulnerable to attack under the 'internal consistency' doctrine, unless administrative considerations make 'more finely calibrated' levies 'impracticable.' " Hellerstein, supra Note D, 87 Mich. L. Rev. at 153–54 (emphasis in original). The Court was obviously uncomfortable with those implications, having noted earlier in its opinion that "States impose numerous flat fees upon local businesses and service providers, including, for example, upon insurers, auctioneers, ambulance operators, and hosts of others." American Trucking II, 545 U.S. at 434. Accordingly, the Court simply refused to extend the doctrine to a flat tax on "local" business.

Although the Court may get high marks for candor, its analysis leaves the scope of the internal consistency doctrine in a state of considerable uncertainty. *American Trucking II* appears to exclude "local fees that are uniformly assessed upon all those who engage in local business, interstate and domestic firms alike" (American Trucking II, 545 U.S. at 438) from the scope of the internal consistency doctrine. However, virtually all local fees satisfy this criterion. Indeed, if they did not, they would be vulnerable to attack under the long-standing Commerce Clause doctrine barring local levies discriminating against interstate commerce. Indeed, one may legitimately inquire whether *American Trucking II* requires reconsideration of the defensibility of the taxes that the Court struck down in earlier cases as violating the internal consistency doctrine. For an extended inquiry into this question, see Walter Hellerstein, "Is 'Internal Consistency' Dead?: Reflections on an Evolving Commerce Clause Restraint on State Taxation," 61 Tax L. Rev. 1 (2007).

F. *Complementary Taxes as a Defense to State Tax Discrimination Under the Commerce Clause.* The Court has sometimes held that a state tax that appears to discriminate against interstate commerce is nevertheless constitutionally permissible because a complementary exaction offsets the apparent discrimination. See, e.g., Henneford v. Silas Mason Co., 300 U.S. 577, 57 S.Ct. 524 (1937) (use tax imposed on goods purchased outside the state complemented by sales tax on in-state purchases); Hinson v. Lott, 75 U.S. (8 Wall.) 148 (1868) (tax on importation of liquor into state complemented by tax on in-state distillers). In later cases, however, the Court has rejected the states' attempts to cure the apparent discrimination in their taxing statutes by reference to allegedly complementary taxes. See Maryland v. Louisiana, 451 U.S. 725, 101 S.Ct. 2114 (1981) (first-use tax on natural gas not complemented by local severance tax); Armco, Inc. v. Hardesty, Note D supra (tax on wholesaling not complemented by tax on manufacturing).

The Court's most recent encounters with the "complementary" or "compensatory" tax doctrine continue its modern trend of evaluating states' "complementary tax" arguments with considerable skepticism. In particular, the Court's decisions in Oregon Waste Systems, Inc. v. Department of Environmental Quality, 511 U.S. 93, 114 S.Ct. 1345 (1994), Associated Industries of Missouri v. Lohman, 511 U.S. 641, 114 S.Ct. 1815 (1994), Fulton Corp. v. Faulkner, 516 U.S. 325, 116 S.Ct. 848 (1996), and South Central Bell Telephone Co. v. Alabama, 526 U.S. 160, 119 S.Ct. 1180 (1999), reveal the Court's hostility to a defense that relies on the "overall" tax burden borne by local interests as an acceptable antidote to a facially discriminatory levy on interstate commerce. Unless the state can identify a specific tax on local activities that complements the allegedly offensive tax on interstate commerce, the state's defense is likely to be given short shrift.

In *Oregon Waste Systems*, for example, Oregon imposed a fee for the in-state disposal of waste that was generated outside the state at the rate of $2.25 per ton while imposing a fee of only $0.85 per ton for the disposal of waste generated within Oregon. Oregon's principal defense of the facially discriminatory tax on out-of-state waste was that it was "a 'compensatory tax' necessary to make shippers of such waste pay their 'fair share' of the costs on Oregon by the disposal of their waste in the State." Oregon Waste, 511 U.S. at 102. In rejecting this argument, the Court carefully delineated its current understanding of the scope of the complementary tax doctrine.

The Court first noted that the complementary tax doctrine was not a "doctrine unto itself" but "merely a specific way of justifying a facially discriminatory tax as achieving a legitimate local purpose that cannot be achieved through nondiscriminatory means." Id. Under the doctrine, the Court observed, "a facially discriminatory tax that imposes on interstate commerce the rough equivalent of an identifiable and 'substantially similar' tax on intrastate commerce does not offend the negative Commerce Clause." Id. at 102–03 Significantly, the Court insisted that the complementary exaction must be both *identifiable* and *substantially similar*. Broad allegations that intrastate commerce is subject to tax burdens equivalent to that imposed by a specific tax on interstate commerce will not suffice.

Extracting from its earlier cases, the Court articulated a three-prong inquiry for determining whether the complementary tax doctrine applies:

(1) The state must identify the intrastate tax burden for which the state is attempting to compensate.

(2) The tax on interstate commerce must be shown to roughly approximate—but not exceed—the amount of the tax on intrastate commerce.

(3) The events on which the interstate and intrastate taxes are imposed must be "substantially equivalent," i.e., they must be sufficiently similar in substance to serve as mutually exclusive proxies for each other.

Id. at 103.

Applying these criteria to Oregon's taxing scheme, the Court had little difficulty concluding that the complementary tax doctrine could not be invoked to salvage Oregon's discriminatory levy on out-of-state waste. First, the state had failed to identify a specific charge on intrastate commerce equal to or exceeding the charge on interstate commerce. This failure by itself was "fatal" to the state's claim. Id. at 104. Second, in response to the state's contention that intrastate commerce "through general taxation" bore taxes equivalent to the levy on interstate commerce, the Court declared that, even assuming the burdens were equivalent, the argument "fails because the in-state and out-of-state levies are not imposed on substantially equivalent events." Id.

Finally, and perhaps most significantly, the Court indicated its own disenchantment with an expansive view of the complementary tax doctrine. It explicitly acknowledged its "recent reluctance to recognize new categories of compensatory taxes." Id. at 105. Moreover, it unequivocally rejected the state's effort to expand the scope of the complementary tax doctrine by comparing the specific tax on out-of-state waste with general taxes imposed on intrastate commerce. The consequence of such an approach "would allow a state to tax interstate commerce more heavily than in-state commerce anytime the entities involved in interstate commerce happened to use facilities supported by general state tax funds." Id. at 105 n.8. The Court declined the state's "invitation to open such an expansive loophole in our carefully confined compensatory tax jurisprudence." Id.

The *Associated Industries, Fulton,* and *South Central Bell* cases, each of which closely tracks the analysis the Court articulated in *Oregon Waste,* similarly reject "complementary tax" defenses. The complementary tax doctrine is explored in detail in Walter Hellerstein, "Complementary Taxes as a Defense to Unconstitutional State Tax Discrimination," 39 Tax Law. 405 (1986).

G. *Nondiscriminatory Tax on In–State and Out-of-State Milk Dealers Coupled With a Tax Rebate Limited to In–State Milk Producers.* In West Lynn Creamery, Inc. v. Healy, 512 U.S. 186, 114 S.Ct. 2205 (1994), which the Court discusses in *Camps Newfound,* the Court considered the constitutionality of a "milk pricing order." The order in essence placed a tax on milk dealers for every local sale of milk, whether the milk was produced inside or outside the state. In addition, the order stipulated that all proceeds of the tax would go into a segregated fund from which they would be distributed to dairy farmers. The issue in the case was one of characterization: Did the pricing order, as Massachusetts argued, impose a permissible nondiscriminatory tax coupled with a permissible subsidy for local industry? Cf. New Energy Co. v. Limbach, 486 U.S. 269, 278, 108 S.Ct. 1803 (1988) ("[d]irect subsidization of domestic industry does not ordinarily run afoul" of the Commerce Clause). Or did it embody a tax, coupled with relief for local industry, in violation of the Court's well settled anti-discrimination rule? The Court adopted the latter characterization, and condemned the pricing order. It observed:

> It is the entire program—not just the contributions to the fund or the distributions from that fund—that simultaneously burdens interstate commerce and discriminates in favor of local producers. The choice of constitutional means—nondiscriminatory tax and local subsidy—cannot guaranty the constitutionality of the program as a whole.

West Lynn, 512 U.S. at 201.

How far does the reasoning of *West Lynn* extend? If a state imposes a nondiscriminatory tax on in-state and out-of-state business can it ever provide a subsidy to in-state business without being subject to the charge that "in substance" it has imposed a discriminatory tax on out-of-state businesses? How closely must the taxpayers and the beneficiary of the subsidy be linked before the Court will treat the two together for purposes of the constitutional analysis? Does it make a difference whether the subsidy is paid out of a segregated fund derived from the "nondiscriminatory" tax payments as in *West Lynn*, i.e., would the result have been different in *West Lynn* if the subsidies to milk producers had been made from the general fund? These and other questions relating to the "linkage" question are explored in Dan T. Coenen & Walter Hellerstein, "Suspect Linkage: The Interplay of State Taxing and Spending Measures in the Application of Constitutional Antidiscrimination Rules," 95 Mich. L. Rev. 2167 (1997); the *West Lynn* case and its implications are also considered in detail in Dan T. Coenen, "Business Subsidies and the Dormant Commerce Clause," 107 Yale L.J. 965 (1998); Walter Hellerstein & Dan T. Coenen, "Commerce Clause Restraints on State Business Development Incentives," 81 Cornell L. Rev. 789 (1996).

H. *Differential Treatment of Transactions in Different Markets.* In General Motors Corp. v. Tracy, 519 U.S. 278, 117 S.Ct. 811 (1997), the Court confronted the question whether a sales and use tax scheme that exempted certain in-state sales of natural gas while taxing out-of-state sales of natural gas discriminated against interstate commerce in violation of the Commerce Clause. Like most states, Ohio imposes a sales tax on tangible personal property purchased in the state and a complementary use tax on tangible personal property purchased outside the state but used within the state. The sale or use of natural gas in Ohio is generally subject to sales or use tax under this taxing regime. However, when natural gas is purchased from a "natural gas company," it is exempt from Ohio sales and use tax.

The Ohio statute defines a "natural gas company" as "[a]ny person * * * engaged in the business of supplying natural gas for lighting, power or heating purposes to consumers within this state." Ohio Rev. Code Ann.

§ 5727.01(D)(4) (Westlaw 2009). The Ohio Supreme Court has construed this definition as limited to companies that own or operate the transportation and distribution equipment and deliver natural gas to consumers in Ohio. Accordingly, only purchases of natural gas from local distribution companies (i.e., public utilities) are exempt from Ohio sales and use tax.

Public utilities, however, are not the only sellers of natural gas to ultimate consumers in today's natural gas market. Although natural gas was traditionally sold to interstate pipeline companies, who transported gas to public utilities for sale to the end user, federal law now requires interstate pipeline companies to serve as common carriers (rather than merchants) of natural gas. As a consequence, natural gas producers and independent gas marketers may now arrange for interstate pipelines to transport natural gas and may thus compete directly with local public utilities for sales of natural gas to burner-tip consumers.

General Motors Corporation ("GM") purchased natural gas from independent natural gas marketers to heat its manufacturing plants. These marketers obtained natural gas from producers outside the state and arranged for transportation to the initial receiving pipeline outside the state. These marketers did not own the facilities used to transport the gas. Instead, they paid a fee to the pipelines to transport the gas to the out-of-state delivery point, where GM took title to the gas. GM then arranged to have the gas transported into Ohio and delivered to its various plants in the state. Because GM purchased the gas outside the state for use in Ohio, and did not purchase the gas from a "natural gas company," the Ohio Tax Commissioner assessed a use tax against GM on the natural gas that it used in the state.

Despite the apparent discrimination in favor of local over out-of-state purchases, the U.S. Supreme Court sustained the tax. The Court found that the market for exempt natural gas purchases from local public utilities was discrete from the market for taxable natural gas purchases from interstate gas marketers. The Court declared:

> [I]n the absence of actual or prospective competition between the supposedly favored and disfavored entities in a single market there can be no local preference, whether by express discrimination against interstate commerce or undue burden upon it, to which the dormant Commerce Clause may apply. The dormant Commerce Clause protects markets and participants in markets, not taxpayers as such.

Id., 519 U.S. at 300.

The critical predicate underlying the Court's determination was the absence of demonstrated competition between sales of natural gas by regulated local public utilities and sales of natural gas by unregulated gas marketers. Thus in an important footnote the Court observed:

> [P]etitioner contended at oral argument that during the tax period in question here, Ohio permitted some natural gas sales by public utilities at unregulated, negotiated rates, and that those sales were not subject to sales tax. The record provides no support for this contention, and the constitutionality of Ohio exempting from state sales tax utility sales that are not price-regulated is therefore not before the Court in this case.

Id. at 296–97 n.11. If the petitioner's assertion had been reinforced by record support, would the *General Motors* case have been decided differently? Why?

What are the implications of *General Motors* as a defense to claims of unconstitutional discrimination outside of the regulated industry context? In Smith v. New Hampshire Department of Revenue Administration, 141 N.H. 681, 692 A.2d 486 (1997), the state conceded that the New Hampshire income and dividends tax, which exempted from tax any interest and dividends received from New Hampshire financial institutions, violated the Commerce Clause. In determining whether taxpayers who had received interest and dividends from out-of-state corporate entities were entitled to relief, however, the court invoked *General Motors* to suggest that taxpayers would not be entitled to relief unless they could demonstrate that the out-of-state corporate entities in which they invested competed in the same market with New Hampshire banks. On remand, the trial court held that the taxpayers had produced no evidence that the exemptions affected the behavior of any out-of-state nonbank entity or that it ever induced any investor to choose a New Hampshire bank investment or product over an out-of-state nonbank investment. Consequently, it limited the taxpayers' refunds to taxes paid on income from interest and dividends in out-of-state banks. The New Hampshire Supreme Court affirmed. Smith v. New Hampshire Department of Revenue Administration, 148 N.H. 536, 813 A.2d 372 (2002). In Jordan v. California Department of Motor Vehicles, 75 Cal.App.4th 449, 89 Cal.Rptr.2d 333 (3d Dist. 1999), on the other hand, the court dismissed for want of evidence the state's suggestion that California's discriminatory smog impact fee, which applied only to vehicles previously registered outside the state, could be defended under *General Motors* on the theory that such vehicles did not compete in the same market as vehicles first registered in California.

I. *Discrimination Against Other States' Municipal Bonds.* The Court's dormant Commerce Clause doctrine forbidding discriminatory taxation would appear to cast doubt on the constitutionality of the widespread practice among states of exempting from income tax the interest from federally tax-exempt bonds issued by the state or its political subdivisions while taxing the interest from tax-exempt bonds issued by other states or their political subdivisions. Indeed, if ever one needed proof that such discriminatory state taxes Balkanize our national capital markets, one need look no further than the state-specific municipal bond funds that have arisen directly as a result of these discriminatory state taxes. Nevertheless, when the Supreme Court finally considered the issue in Department of Revenue v. Davis, 553 U.S. ___, 128 S.Ct. 1801 (2008), it sustained Kentucky's differential treatment of in-state and out-of-state municipal bond income over Commerce Clause objections. It did so, however, on grounds narrowly confined to a state's right to favor itself against all competitors—private or public—in pursuit of traditional governmental functions. Accordingly, the decision does not disturb, or in any significant way affect, dormant Commerce Clause doctrine prohibiting discrimination in favor of in-state private interests over out-of-state private interests.

In sustaining the discrimination against out-of-state municipal bonds, the Court relied heavily on its decision a year earlier in United Haulers Association, Inc. v. Oneida–Herkimer Solid Waste Management Authority, 550 U.S.

330, 127 S.Ct. 1786 (2007). *United Haulers* held that a municipal trash-flow control ordinance did not violate the Commerce Clause even though it granted a monopoly to a local trash-processing facility, thereby preventing out-of-state trash-processing facilities from competing for trash-processing business in the locality. In the Court's eyes, its decision in *Davis* was foreordained by *United Haulers*:

> Just like the ordinances upheld there, Kentucky's tax exemption favors a traditional government function without any differential treatment favoring local entities over substantially similar out-of-state interests. This type of law does "not 'discriminate against interstate commerce' for purposes of the dormant Commerce Clause."

Id., 128 S.Ct. at 1811 (quoting *United Haulers*).

CUNO v. DAIMLERCHRYSLER, INC.

United States Court of Appeals for the Sixth Circuit, 2004.
386 F.3d 738, rev'd in part on other grounds, 547 U.S. 332, 126 S.Ct. 1854
(2006), cert. denied in part, 547 U.S. 1147, 126 S.Ct. 2286 (2006).

DAUGHTREY, CIRCUIT JUDGE.

The plaintiffs initiated this litigation in state court, challenging the validity of certain state tax credits and local property tax abatements that were granted to DaimlerChrysler Corporation as an inducement to the company to expand its business operations in Toledo, Ohio. They contend that the tax scheme discriminates against interstate commerce by granting preferential treatment to in-state investment and activity, in violation of the Commerce Clause of the United States Constitution and the Equal Protection Clause of the Ohio Constitution. After the defendants removed the action to federal court, the district court entered an order dismissing the complaint under Federal Rules of Civil Procedure 12(b)(1) and 12(b)(6) for failure to state a claim. Because we conclude that the investment tax credit runs afoul of the Commerce Clause, we can affirm only part of the district court's judgment.

I. FACTUAL AND PROCEDURAL BACKGROUND

In 1998, DaimlerChrysler entered into an agreement with the City of Toledo to construct a new vehicle-assembly plant near the company's existing facility in exchange for various tax incentives. DaimlerChrysler estimated that it would invest approximately $1.2 billion in this project, which would provide the region with several thousand new jobs. In return, the City and two local school districts agreed to give DaimlerChrysler a ten-year 100 percent property tax exemption, as well as an investment tax credit of 13.5 percent against the state corporate franchise tax for certain qualifying investments. The total value of the tax incentives was estimated to be $280 million.

Ohio's investment tax credit grants a taxpayer a non-refundable credit against the state's corporate franchise tax if the taxpayer "purchases new manufacturing machinery and equipment during the qualifying period, provided that the new manufacturing machinery and equipment are installed in [Ohio]." Ohio Rev. Code Ann. § 5733.33(B)(1). The investment tax credit is generally 7.5 percent "of the excess of the cost of the new manufacturing machinery and equipment purchased during the calendar year for use in a county over the county average new manufacturing machinery and equipment investment for that county." See Ohio Rev. Code Ann. § 5733.33(C)(1). The rate increases to 13.5 percent of the cost of the new investment if it is purchased for use in specific economically depressed areas. The credit may not exceed $1 million unless the taxpayer has increased its overall ownership of manufacturing equipment in the state during the year for which the credit is claimed. To the extent that the credit exceeds the corporation's total Ohio franchise tax liability in a particular year, the balance of the credit is carried forward and can be used to reduce its liability in any of the three following years.

The personal property tax exemption is authorized under §§ 5709.62 and 5709.631; it permits municipalities to offer specified incentives to an enterprise that "agrees to establish, expand, renovate, or occupy a facility and hire new employees, or preserve employment opportunities for existing employees" in economically depressed areas. Ohio Rev.Code Ann. § 5709.62(C)(1). An exemption may be granted "for a specified number of years, not to exceed ten, of a specified portion, up to seventy-five per cent, of the assessed value of tangible personal property first used in business at the project site as a result of the agreement." Ohio Rev. Code Ann. § 5709.62(C)(1)(a). The exemption may exceed 75 percent with consent of the affected school districts.

The district court held that the investment tax credit and the property tax exemption do not violate the Commerce Clause because, although "an increase in activity in Ohio could increase the credit and exemption amount" under the two statutes, an increase in activity *outside* the state would not *decrease* the amount of the tax credit or exemption and therefore would not run afoul of the United States Supreme Court's ruling in Westinghouse Electric Corp. v. Tully, 466 U.S. 388, 400–01, 104 S.Ct. 1856, 80 L.Ed.2d 388 (1984). From that decision, the plaintiffs now appeal.

II. ANALYSIS

We review *de novo* a district court's order granting a motion to dismiss for failure to state a claim upon which relief may be granted. In considering a motion to dismiss pursuant to Rule 12(b)(6), all well-pleaded factual allegations of the complaint must be accepted as true and the complaint construed in the light most favorable to the plaintiffs. It is well-settled that dismissal of a complaint is proper "only if it is clear that no relief could be granted under any set of facts that could be proved consistent with the allegations." Hishon v. King & Spalding, 467 U.S. 69, 73, 104 S.Ct. 2229 (1984). On appeal, the plaintiffs' primary contention is that the Ohio statutes authorizing the investment tax credit and personal property tax exemption violate the Commerce Clause of the United States Constitution. * * *

A. Commerce Clause Claim

The United States Constitution expressly authorizes Congress to "regulate Commerce with foreign Nations, and among the several States," U.S. Const. art. I, § 8, cl. 3, and the "negative" or "dormant" aspect of the Commerce Clause implicitly limits the State's right to tax interstate commerce. A tax provision satisfies the requirements of the Commerce Clause if (1) the activity taxed has a substantial nexus with the taxing State; (2) the tax is fairly apportioned to reflect the degree of activity that occurs within the State; (3) the tax does not discriminate against interstate commerce; and (4) the tax is fairly related to benefits provided by the state. See Complete Auto Transit, Inc. v. Brady, 430 U.S. 274, 279, 97 S.Ct. 1076 (1977).

The parties do not dispute that the tax provisions at issue have a sufficient nexus with the state, are fairly apportioned, and are related to benefits provided by the state. Nor do the parties dispute that it is legitimate for Ohio to structure its tax system to encourage new intrastate economic activity. Indeed, the United States Supreme Court has indicated that the Commerce Clause "does not prevent the States from structuring their tax systems to encourage the growth and development of intrastate commerce and industry," nor does it prevent a state from "compet[ing] with other States for a share of interstate commerce" so long as "no State [ ] discriminatorily tax[es] the products manufactured or the business operations performed in any other State." Boston Stock Exch. v. State Tax Comm'n, 429 U.S. 318, 336–37, 97 S.Ct. 599 (1977); see also Bacchus Imports, Ltd. v. Dias, 468 U.S. 263, 272, 104 S.Ct. 3049 (1984) (the federal Commerce Clause "limits the manner in which States may legitimately compete for interstate trade"). Rather, the parties dispute whether Ohio's method for encouraging new economic investment—conferring investment tax incentives and property tax exemptions—discriminates against interstate commerce.

The United States Supreme Court has never precisely delineated the scope of the doctrine that bars discriminatory taxes. The Court has made clear, however, that a tax statute's "constitutionality does not depend upon whether one focuses upon the benefited or the burdened party." Bacchus Imports, 468 U.S. at 273, 104 S.Ct. 3049. The fact that a statute "discriminates against business carried on outside the State by disallowing a tax credit rather than by imposing a higher tax" is therefore legally irrelevant. Westinghouse Elec. Corp. v. Tully, 466 U.S. 388, 404, 104 S.Ct. 1856 (1984).

In general, a challenged credit or exemption will fail Commerce Clause scrutiny if it discriminates on its face or if, on the basis of "a sensitive, case-by-case analysis of purposes and effects," the provision "will in its practical operation work discrimination against interstate commerce," West Lynn Creamery v. Healy, 512 U.S. 186, 201, 114 S.Ct. 2205 (1994) (citations omitted), by "providing a direct commercial advantage to local business." Bacchus Imports, 468 U.S. at 268, 104 S.Ct. 3049 (citations omitted). " '[D]iscrimination' simply means differential treatment of in-state and out-of-state economic interests that benefits the former and burdens the latter." Oregon Waste Sys., Inc. v. Dep't. of Envtl. Quality, 511 U.S. 93, 99, 114 S.Ct. 1345 (1994). A state tax provision that discriminates against interstate commerce is invalid unless "it advances a legitimate local purpose that cannot be adequately served by reasonable nondiscriminatory alternatives." Id. at 101, 114 S.Ct. 1345 (quoting New Energy Co. of Ind. v. Limbach, 486 U.S. 269, 278, 108 S.Ct. 1803 (1988)).

1. Investment Tax Credit

Although the investment tax credit at issue here is equally available to in-state and out-of-state businesses, the plaintiffs nevertheless maintain that it discriminates against interstate economic activity by coercing businesses already subject to the Ohio franchise tax to expand locally rather than out-of-state. Specifically, any corporation currently doing business in Ohio, and therefore paying the state's corporate franchise tax in Ohio, can reduce its existing tax liability by locating significant new machinery and equipment within the state, but it will receive no such reduction in tax liability if it locates a comparable plant and equipment elsewhere. Moreover, as between two businesses, otherwise similarly situated and each subject to Ohio taxation, the business that chooses to expand its local presence will enjoy a reduced tax burden, based directly on its new in-state investment, while a competitor that invests out-of-state will face a comparatively higher tax burden because it will be ineligible for any credit against its Ohio tax.

The plaintiffs' argument principally relies on the Supreme Court's own explanation of its Commerce Clause jurisprudence in cases invalidating tax schemes that encourage the development of local industry by imposing greater burdens on economic activity taking place outside the state. In *Boston Stock Exchange,* for example, the Supreme Court held unconstitutional amendments to New York's securities transfer tax that aimed to offset the competitive advantage that the transfer tax otherwise created for out-of-state exchanges that did not tax transfers. Prior to the amendment, New York uniformly taxed in-state transfers of securities without regard to the place of sale. The amendment created a 50 percent reduction in the tax rate on transfers by nonresidents and limited liability on transfers of large blocks of shares as long as the sales were made in New York. As a result, the amendment caused transactions involving out-of-state sales to be taxed more heavily than transactions involving in-state sales. The Court held that the reduction offended the Commerce Clause's anti-discrimination principle by converting a tax that was previously "neutral as to in-state and out-of-state sales" into one that which would induce a seller to trade through a New York broker in order to reduce its tax liability. Boston Stock Exchange, 429 U.S. at 330–32, 97 S.Ct. 599. In doing so, New York effectively "foreclose[d] tax-neutral decisions" and "creat[ed] both an advantage for the exchanges in New York and a discriminatory burden on commerce to its sister States." Id. at 331, 97

S.Ct. 599. The diversion of interstate commerce from the most economically efficient channels that resulted from New York's use of "its power to tax an in-state operation as a means of 'requiring [other] business operations to be performed in the home state,'" id. at 336, 97 S.Ct. 599 (quoting Pike v. Bruce Church, Inc., 397 U.S. 137, 145, 90 S.Ct. 844 (1970)), was seen by the Court as "wholly inconsistent with the free trade purpose of the Commerce Clause."

Shortly thereafter, in Maryland v. Louisiana, 451 U.S. 725, 101 S.Ct. 2114, 68 L.Ed.2d 576 (1981), the Supreme Court reviewed a Louisiana statute that imposed a first-use tax on natural gas extracted from the continental shelf in an amount equivalent to the severance tax imposed on natural gas extracted in Louisiana. Taxpayers subject to the first-use tax were entitled to a direct tax credit on any Louisiana Severance Tax owed in connection with the extraction of natural resources within the state. Most Louisiana consumers of offshore gas were eligible for tax credits and exemptions, but the tax applied in full to offshore gas moving through and out of state. Noting that the state severance tax credit "favor[ed] those who both own [offshore] gas and engage in Louisiana production" and that the "obvious economic effect of this Severance Tax Credit [was] to encourage natural gas owners involved in the production of [offshore] gas to invest in mineral exploration and development within Louisiana rather than to invest in further [offshore] development or in production in other States," the Court held that the statute "unquestionably discriminate[d] against interstate commerce in favor of local interests." Id. at 756–57, 101 S.Ct. 2114.

In Westinghouse Electric Corp. v. Tully, 466 U.S. 388, 104 S.Ct. 1856 (1984), the Supreme Court invalidated a New York franchise tax that gave corporations an income tax credit based on the portion of their exports shipped from New York. Under the law, income from a subsidiary engaged exclusively in exports was to be combined with the income of its parent company for state tax purposes. In an effort to provide an incentive to increase export activity in New York, the parent company was given a partially offsetting credit against income tax attributable to the subsidiary's income generated from New York exports. Because the credit was based on the ratio of the subsidiary's New York exports to its income from all export shipments, a company's overall New York tax liability would decrease as exports from New York increased relative to exports from other states. Conversely, a company's New York tax liability increased when exports from New York decreased relative to exports from other states. The Court found that the tax scheme "penalize[d] increases in the [export] shipping activities in other states," id. at 401, 104 S.Ct. 1856, and that it was therefore a discriminatory tax that advantaged New York firms "by placing 'a discriminatory burden on commerce to its sister States.'" Id. at 406, 104 S.Ct. 1856 (quoting Boston Stock Exchange, 429 U.S. at 331, 97 S.Ct. 599).

Analogizing to the provisions considered in *Boston Stock Exchange*, *Maryland v. Louisiana*, and *Westinghouse*, the plaintiffs argue that the investment tax credit at issue here encourages the development of local business through the use of Ohio's "power to tax an in-state operation as a means of 'requiring [other] business operations to be performed in the home State.' " Boston Stock Exch., 429 U.S. at 336, 97 S.Ct. 599 (quoting Bruce Church, 397 U.S. at 145, 90 S.Ct. 844). Thus, they contend that like the tax credit in *Maryland v. Louisiana*, the economic effect of the Ohio investment tax credit is to encourage further investment in-state at the expense of development in other states and that the result is to hinder free trade among the states.

The defendants maintain that the Supreme Court's opinions should be read narrowly to hold that tax incentives, like the Ohio tax credit, are permissible as long as they do not penalize out-of-state economic activity, citing Philip M. Tatarowicz & Rebecca F. Mims–Velarde, An Analytical Approach to State Tax Discrimination Under the Commerce Clause, 39 Vand. L. Rev. 879, 929 (1986) (elaborating upon and applying this distinction to the Court's precedents). In their view, the Commerce Clause is primarily concerned with preventing economic protectionism—that is, regulatory measures designed to benefit local interests by burdening out-of-state commerce. According to their theory, the only tax credits and exemptions that would run afoul of the Commerce Clause fall into two categories: those that function like a tariff by placing a higher tax upon out-of-state business or products and those that penalize out-of-state economic activity by relying on both the taxpayer's in-state and out-of-state activities to determine the taxpayer's effective tax rate.

Although it is arguably possible to fit certain of the Supreme Court's cases into this framework, it is clear that the Court itself has not adopted this approach in analyzing dormant Commerce Clause cases, undoubtedly because it rests on the distinction between laws that benefit in-state activity and laws that burden out-of-state activity. Such a distinction is tenuous in light of the Court's acknowledgment that "[v]irtually every discriminatory statute allocates benefits or burdens unequally; each can be viewed as conferring a benefit on one party and a detriment on the other, in either an absolute or relative sense." Bacchus Imports, 468 U.S. at 273, 104 S.Ct. 3049. Indeed, economically speaking, the effect of a tax benefit or burden is the same. Moreover, the Court's command to examine the practical effect of challenged tax schemes suggests that "constitutionality [should] not depend upon whether one focuses upon the benefited or the burdened party." Id.

Although the defendants liken the investment tax credit to a direct subsidy, which would no doubt have the same economic effect, the Court has intimated that attempts to create location incentives through the state's power to tax are to be treated differently from direct subsidies despite their similarity in terms of end-result economic impact. The majority in *New Energy* noted in dicta that subsidies do not "ordinarily run afoul of [the Commerce Clause]" because they are not generally "connect[ed] with the State's regulation of interstate commerce." New Energy Co., 486 U.S. at 278, 108 S.Ct. 1803; see also West Lynn Creamery, 512 U.S. at 199 n. 15, 114 S.Ct. 2205 ("We have never squarely confronted the constitutionality of subsidies, and we need not do so now. We have, however, noted that '[d]irect subsidization of domestic industry does not ordinarily run afoul' of the negative Commerce Clause." (quoting New Energy Co., 486 U.S. at 278, 108 S.Ct. 1803)). Thus, the distinction between a subsidy and a tax credit, in the constitutional sense, results from the fact that the tax credit involves state regulation of interstate commerce through its power to tax.[1]

In short, while we may be sympathetic to efforts by the City of Toledo to attract industry into its economically depressed areas, we conclude that Ohio's investment tax credit cannot be upheld under the Commerce Clause of the United States Constitution.

2. Personal Property Tax Exemption

The plaintiffs maintain that the discriminatory characteristic of the City's personal property tax exemption rests not on the fact that only in-state property is eligible for exemption, but rather on the conditions that Ohio places on eligibility—conditions that require beneficiaries of the exemptions to agree to maintain a specified level of employment and investment in the state. The effect, they argue, is to subject two similarly situated owners of Ohio personal property to differential tax rates. A taxpayer who agrees to focus his employment or investment in Ohio receives preferential treatment in the form of a tax break, while a taxpayer who prefers to preserve the freedom to hire or invest elsewhere does not.

Although conditions imposed on property tax exemptions may independently violate the Commerce Clause, conditional exemptions raise no constitutional issues when the conditions for obtaining the favorable tax treatment are related to the use or location of the property itself. Stated differently, an exemption may be discriminatory if it requires the beneficiary to engage in another form of business in order to receive the benefit or is limited to businesses with a specified economic presence. However, if the conditions imposed on the exemption do not discriminate based on an independent form of commerce, they are permissible.

Contrary to the plaintiffs' assertions, the conditions imposed on the receipt of the Ohio property tax exemption are minor collateral requirements and are directly linked to the use of the exempted personal property. The authorizing statute requires only an investment in new or existing property within an enterprise zone and maintenance of employees. The statute does not impose specific monetary requirements, require the creation of new jobs, or encourage a beneficiary to engage in an additional form of commerce independent of the newly acquired property.[2]

---

1. For further discussion of the constitutionality of coercive and non-coercive state regulation of interstate commerce through the state power to tax, see Walter Hellerstein and Dan T. Coenen, Commerce Clause Restraints on State Business Development Incentives, 81 Cornell L. Rev. 789, 806–09 (1996) (explaining the non-coercive nature of a similar tax exemption.)

2. Plaintiffs' assertion that the exemption, once received, coerces business into continual reinvestment in Ohio in order to preserve the tax exemption is not persuasive. The exemption is

As a consequence, the conditions placed on eligibility for the exemption do not independently burden interstate commerce.

The cases on which the plaintiffs rely are inapplicable here, because they fail to address the question of whether conditions attached to the receipt of an exemption violate the anti-discrimination principle where the conditions themselves do not impose independent burdens upon commerce. In Camps Newfound/Owatonna, Inc. v. Town of Harrison, 520 U.S. 564, 117 S.Ct. 1590 (1997), the Supreme Court reviewed a property tax exemption for charitable organizations that excluded organizations operated principally for the benefit of nonresidents and found the exemption unconstitutionally discriminatory because the effect of the statute was to "distinguish[ ] between entities that serve a principally interstate clientele and those that primarily serve an intrastate market, singling out [entities] that serve mostly in-staters for beneficial tax treatment, and penalizing those camps that do a principally interstate business." Id. at 576, 117 S.Ct. 1590. Similarly, the Fifth Circuit in Pelican Chapter, Associated Builders & Contractors, Inc. v. Edwards, 128 F.3d 910 (5th Cir.1997), invalidated a tax exemption because it required beneficiaries to give a preference to in-state manufacturers, suppliers, and laborers. The Ohio provision at issue contains no restriction on the individuals employed or served. Therefore, the conditional character of the Ohio property tax exemption does not resemble characteristics of property tax exemptions found unconstitutional by previous courts.

Finally, the plaintiffs' argument regarding the effect of the exemption overlooks fundamental differences between tax credits and exemptions. Unlike an investment tax credit that reduces pre-existing income tax liability, the personal property exemption does not reduce any existing property tax liability. The exemption merely allows a taxpayer to avoid tax liability for new personal property put into first use in conjunction with a qualified new investment. Thus, a taxpayer's failure to locate new investments within Ohio simply means that the taxpayer is not subject to the state's property tax at all, and any discriminatory treatment between a company that invests in Ohio and one that invests out-of-state cannot be attributed the Ohio tax regime or its failure to reduce current property taxes. See Walter Hellerstein and Dan T. Coenen, Commerce Clause Restraints on State Business Development Incentives, 81 Cornell L.Rev. 789, 806–09 (1996) (explaining the non-coercive nature of a similar tax exemption.) Additionally, the personal property tax exemption is internally consistent because, if universally applied, the new property would escape tax liability irrespective of location. Every new investment, no matter where undertaken, would be exempt from a tax. Thus, businesses that desire to expand are neither discriminated against nor pressured into investing in Ohio. Accordingly, we hold that the Ohio personal property tax exemption does not violate the dormant Commerce Clause.

---

project-specific and, therefore, a business does not lose its existing exemption by deciding to make its next investment elsewhere.

III. CONCLUSION

For the reasons set out above, we REVERSE that portion of the district court's judgment upholding as constitutional the investment tax credit provision of Ohio Rev. Code Ann. § 5733.33, and we enjoin its enforcement. We AFFIRM the remaining portions of the district court's judgment.

NOTES AND QUESTIONS

A. Cuno *in the U.S. Supreme Court.* All parties sought review in the U.S. Supreme Court of the portion of the Court of Appeals' decision that was adverse to them—the defendants from the invalidation of the income tax credit and the plaintiffs from the sustaining of the property tax exemption. The U.S. Supreme Court granted review only of the defendants' petition, denying certiorari with respect to the portion of the decision sustaining the constitutionality of the property tax exemption and thereby leaving that portion of the decision intact. Cuno v. DaimlerChrysler, Inc., 386 F.3d 738, 746 (6th Cir. 2004), cert. denied, 547 U.S. 1147, 126 S.Ct. 2286 (2006). In DaimlerChrysler Corp. v. Cuno, 547 U.S. 332, 126 S.Ct. 1854 (2006), the U.S. Supreme Court never reached the merits of the validity of the Ohio investment tax credit under the Commerce Clause. Instead, the Court held that the plaintiffs, who were state taxpayers unhappy with the "corporate welfare" that Ohio was bestowing upon DaimlerChrysler, lacked standing in federal court to challenge the tax incentive. See Chapter 11, p. ___ infra for further consideration of the standing issue. The Court therefore vacated the judgment of the Sixth Circuit on the investment tax credit issue and remanded for dismissal of plaintiffs' challenge to the credit.

B. *Analysis of the* Cuno *Opinion.* Can the line the *Cuno* court drew between unconstitutional "coercive" tax incentives like Ohio's investment tax credit and "noncoercive" tax incentives like Ohio's property tax exemption withstand critical analysis? In *Cuno,* the court observed that "[u]nlike an investment tax credit that reduces pre-existing income tax liability, the personal property exemption does not reduce any existing property tax liability." The exemption "merely allows a taxpayer to avoid tax liability for new personal property put into first use in conjunction with a qualified new investment." Is this distinction sound? Suppose a taxpayer with no prior investment (and, consequently, no "pre-existing income tax liability") builds a new facility in Ohio. Would the credit be constitutional under the coercive/noncoercive distinction the court articulated?

Was the court's distinction between constitutional and unconstitutional exemptions persuasive? The court suggested that "conditions imposed on property tax exemptions may independently violate the Commerce Clause," e.g, if they require "the beneficiary to engage in another form of business in order to receive the benefit or is limited to businesses with a specified economic presence." But why did not the requirement that the taxpayer invest in new equipment in Ohio and maintain employees in the state violate that principle? Can you draw the line between "minor collateral require-

ments" that pass constitutional muster and other more substantial requirements associated with a property tax exemption that do not?

Is the court to be "blamed" for the weaknesses in its constitutional
analysis or is it just playing the hand it was dealt by the U.S. Supreme Court?
Do these weaknesses suggest that Justices Scalia and Thomas are correct in
criticizing the entire body of the Court's dormant Commerce Clause doctrine
as little more than unprincipled ad hoc judgments that courts have no
business making because such judgments are essentially political and should
be left to the institution to which the Constitution explicitly assigned them,
namely, Congress? Finally, how did this case get into federal court? Doesn't
the Tax Injunction Act, 28 U.S.C. § 1341 (discussed in Chapter 11, pp. 964–72
infra) generally keep challenges to state taxes out of federal court? Moreover,
who were the plaintiffs in this case and how did they get standing to challenge
the tax credits and exemptions?

For a detailed discussion of the issues raised by the *Cuno* case, see Peter
D. Enrich, "Saving the States From Themselves: Commerce Clause Con-
straints on State Tax Incentives for Business," 110 Harv. L. Rev. 377 (1996);
Walter Hellerstein & Dan T. Coenen, "Commerce Clause Restraints on State
Business Development Incentives," 81 Cornell L. Rev. 789, 806–09 (1996)
(cited by the *Cuno* court).

C. *The Reaction to the* Cuno *Decision.* The Court of Appeals decision in
Cuno sent shock waves throughout the business community because it put a
constitutional cloud over billions of dollars of tax incentives that virtually
every state has enacted in one form or another. Indeed, shortly after the
decision was handed down, legislation was introduced in Congress to overturn
the result in *Cuno*. See "Jobs Investment Act of 2004," H.R. 5427, 108th
Cong., 2d Sess. (2004); see also "The Economic Development Act of 2005," S.
1066, 109th Cong. 1st Sess. (2005). Although the U.S. Supreme Court's
vacation of the portion Court of Appeals decision striking down the investment tax credit seems to have reduced the immediate pressure for legislation
addressing the question of the constitutionality of state tax incentives, the
question remains one of enormous legal and economic significance. See, e.g.,
Symposium: *DaimlerChrysler v. Cuno* and the Constitutionality of State Tax
Incentives for Economic Development, 5 Geo. J.L. & Pub. Pol'y 15 (2006), to
which two of your casebook authors contributed (Walter Hellerstein, "*Cuno*
and Congress: An Analysis of Proposed Federal Legislation Authorizing State
Economic Development Incentives," 5 Geo. J.L. & Pub. Pol'y 73 (2006); Kirk
J. Stark & Daniel J. Wilson, "What Do We Know About the Interstate
Economic Effects of State Tax Incentives?," 5 Geo. J.L. & Pub. Pol'y 133
(2006)).

4. FOURTH PRONG: FAIR RELATION TO SERVICES PROVIDED BY THE STATE

We come finally to *Complete Auto*'s fourth prong, the requirement
that to pass muster under the Commerce Clause a tax must be "fairly
related to services provided by the State." While the other three parts of

Complete Auto's four-part test—substantial nexus, fair apportionment, and nondiscrimination—reflected familiar Commerce Clause doctrine, the precise meaning of the fourth part was less apparent prior to *Commonwealth Edison*.

COMMONWEALTH EDISON CO. v. MONTANA

Supreme Court of the United States, 1981.
453 U.S. 609, 101 S.Ct. 2946.

JUSTICE MARSHALL delivered the opinion of the Court.

Montana, like many other States, imposes a severance tax on mineral production in the State. In this appeal, we consider whether the tax Montana levies on each ton of coal mined in the State violates the Commerce and Supremacy Clauses of the United States Constitution.

I

Buried beneath Montana are large deposits of low sulfur coal, most of it on federal land. Since 1921, Montana has imposed a severance tax on the output of Montana coal mines, including coal mined on federal land. After commissioning a study of coal production taxes in 1974, the Montana Legislature enacted the tax schedule at issue in this case. The tax is levied at varying rates depending on the value, energy content, and method of extraction of the coal, and may equal at a maximum, 30% of the "contract sales price."[1] Under the terms of a 1976 amendment to the Montana Constitution, after Dec. 31, 1979, at least 50% of the revenues generated by the tax must be paid into a permanent trust fund, the principal of which may be appropriated only by a vote of three-fourths of the members of each house of the legislature.

Appellants, 4 Montana coal producers and 11 of their out-of-state utility company customers, filed these suits in Montana state court in 1978. They sought refunds of over $5.4 million in severance taxes paid under protest, a declaration that the tax is invalid under the Supremacy and Commerce Clauses, and an injunction against further collection of the tax. Without receiving any evidence the court upheld the tax and dismissed the complaints.

On appeal, the Montana Supreme Court affirmed the judgment of the trial court. Mont., 615 P.2d 847 (1980). The supreme court held that the tax is not subject to scrutiny under the Commerce Clause because it is imposed on the severance of coal, which the court characterized as an intrastate activity preceding entry of the coal into interstate commerce. In this regard, the Montana court relied on this Court's decisions in Heisler v. Thomas Colliery Co., 260 U.S. 245, 43 S.Ct. 83 (1922), Oliver Iron

---

1. Under Mont.Code § 15–35–103 (1979), the value of the coal is determined by the "contract sales price" which is defined as "the price of coal extracted and prepared for shipment f.o.b. mine, excluding the amount charged by the seller to pay taxes paid on production...." § 15–35–102(1) (1979). Taxes paid on production are defined in § 15–35–102(6) (1979). Because production taxes are excluded from the computation of the value of the coal, the effective rate of the tax is lower than the statutory rate.

Mining Co. v. Lord, 262 U.S. 172, 43 S.Ct. 526 (1923), and Hope Natural Gas Co. v. Hall, 274 U.S. 284, 47 S.Ct. 639 (1927), which employed similar reasoning in upholding state severance taxes against Commerce Clause challenges. As an alternative basis for its resolution of the Commerce Clause issue, the Montana court held, as a matter of law, that the tax survives scrutiny under the four-part test articulated by this Court in Complete Auto Transit, Inc. v. Brady, 430 U.S. 274, 97 S.Ct. 1076 (1977). The Montana court also rejected appellants' Supremacy Clause challenge, concluding that appellants had failed to show that the Montana tax conflicts with any federal statute.

We noted probable jurisdiction to consider the important issues raised. We now affirm.

II

A

As an initial matter, appellants assert that the Montana Supreme Court erred in concluding that the Montana tax is not subject to the strictures of the Commerce Clause. In appellants' view, *Heisler's* "mechanical" approach, which looks to whether a state tax is levied on goods prior to their entry into interstate commerce, no longer accurately reflects the law. Appellants contend that the correct analysis focuses on whether the challenged tax substantially affects interstate commerce, in which case it must be scrutinized under the *Complete Auto Transit* test.

We agree that *Heisler's* reasoning has been undermined by more recent cases. The *Heisler* analysis evolved at a time when the Commerce Clause was thought to prohibit the States from imposing any direct taxes on interstate commerce. Consequently, the distinction between intrastate activities and interstate commerce was crucial to protecting the States' taxing power.

The Court has, however, long since rejected any suggestion that a state tax or regulation affecting interstate commerce is immune from Commerce Clause scrutiny because it attaches only to a "local" or intrastate activity. See Hunt v. Washington Apple Advertising Comm'n, 432 U.S. 333, 350, 97 S.Ct. 2434, 2445 (1977); Pike v. Bruce Church, Inc., 397 U.S. 137, 141–142, 90 S.Ct. 844, 847 (1970); Nippert v. City of Richmond, 327 U.S. 416, 423–424, 66 S.Ct. 586, 589–90 (1946). Correspondingly, the Court has rejected the notion that state taxes levied on interstate commerce are *per se* invalid. See, e.g., Washington Revenue Dept. v. Association of Wash. Stevedoring Cos., 435 U.S. 734, 98 S.Ct. 1388 (1978); Complete Auto Transit, Inc. v. Brady, supra. In reviewing Commerce Clause challenges to state taxes, our goal has instead been to "establish a consistent and rational method of inquiry" focusing on "the practical effect of a challenged tax." We conclude that the same "practical" analysis should apply in reviewing Commerce Clause challenges to state severance taxes.

In the first place, there is no real distinction—in terms of economic effects—between severance taxes and other types of state taxes that have been subjected to Commerce Clause scrutiny. State taxes levied on a "local" activity preceding entry of the goods into interstate commerce may substantially affect interstate commerce, and this effect is the proper focus of Commerce Clause inquiry. Second, this Court has acknowledged that "a State has a significant interest in exacting from interstate commerce its fair share of the cost of state government," Washington Revenue Dept. v. Association of Wash. Stevedoring Cos., supra, 435 U.S., at 748, 98 S.Ct., at 1398. As the Court has stated, " '[e]ven interstate business must pay its way.' " Consequently, the *Heisler* Court's concern that a loss of state taxing authority would be an inevitable result of subjecting taxes on "local" activities to Commerce Clause scrutiny is no longer tenable.

We therefore hold that a state severance tax is not immunized from Commerce Clause scrutiny by a claim that the tax is imposed on goods prior to their entry into the stream of interstate commerce. Any contrary statements in *Heisler* and its progeny are disapproved. We agree with appellants that the Montana tax must be evaluated under *Complete Auto Transit's* four-part test. Under that test, a state tax does not offend the Commerce Clause if it "is applied to an activity with a substantial nexus with the taxing State, is fairly apportioned, does not discriminate against interstate commerce, and is fairly related to services provided by the State." 430 U.S., at 279, 97 S.Ct. at 1079.

B

* * * Appellants do contend * * * that the Montana tax is invalid under the third and fourth prongs of the *Complete Auto Transit* test.

Appellants assert that the Montana tax "discriminate[s] against interstate commerce" because 90% of Montana coal is shipped to other States under contracts that shift the tax burden primarily to non-Montana utility companies and thus to citizens of other States. But the Montana tax is computed at the same rate regardless of the final destination of the coal, and there is no suggestion here that the tax is administered in a manner that departs from this evenhanded formula. We are not, therefore, confronted here with the type of differential tax treatment of interstate and intrastate commerce that the Court has found in other "discrimination" cases. See, e.g., Boston Stock Exchange v. State Tax Comm'n, 429 U.S. 318, 97 S.Ct. 599 (1977). * * *

Instead, the gravamen of appellants' claim is that a state tax must be considered discriminatory for purposes of the Commerce Clause if the tax burden is borne primarily by out-of-state consumers. Appellants do not suggest that this assertion is based on any of this Court's prior discriminatory tax cases. In fact, a similar claim was considered and rejected in *Heisler*. There, it was argued that Pennsylvania had a virtual monopoly of anthracite coal and that, because 80% of the coal was shipped out of State, the tax discriminated against and impermissibly burdened interstate commerce. 260 U.S. 251–253, 43 S.Ct., at 84. The Court, however, dismissed these factors as "adventitious considerations." 260 U.S., at 259, 43 S.Ct., at 86. We share the *Heisler* Court's misgivings about judging the validity of a state tax by assessing the State's "monopoly" position or its "exportation" of the tax burden out of State.

The premise of our discrimination cases is that "[t]he very purpose of the Commerce Clause was to create an area of free trade among the several States." McLeod v. J.E. Dilworth Co., 322 U.S. 327, 330, 64 S.Ct. 1023, 1025 (1944). * * * Under such a regime, the borders between the States are essentially irrelevant. As the Court stated in West v. Kansas Natural Gas Co., 221 U.S. 229, 255, 31 S.Ct. 564, 571 (1911), "in matters of foreign and interstate commerce there are no state lines." See Boston Stock Exchange v. State Tax Comm'n, supra, 429 U.S., at 331–332, 97 S.Ct., at 607–08. Consequently, to accept appellants' theory and invalidate the Montana tax solely because most of Montana's coal is shipped across the very state borders that ordinarily are to be considered irrelevant would require a significant and, in our view, unwarranted departure from the rationale of our prior discrimination cases.

Furthermore, appellants' assertion that Montana may not "exploit" its "monopoly" position by exporting tax burdens to other States, cannot rest on a claim that there is need to protect the out-of-state consumers of Montana coal from discriminatory tax treatment. As previously noted, there is no real discrimination in this case; the tax burden is borne according to the amount of coal consumed and not according to any distinction between in-state and out-of-state consumers. Rather, appellants assume that the Commerce Clause gives residents of one State a right of access at "reasonable" prices to resources located in another State that is richly endowed with such resources, without regard to whether and on what terms residents of the resource-rich State have access to the resources. We are not convinced that the Commerce Clause, of its own force, gives the residents of one State the right to control in this fashion the terms of resource development and depletion in a sister State. Cf. Philadelphia v. New Jersey, supra, 437 U.S., at 626, 98 S.Ct., at 2536.

In any event, appellants' discrimination theory ultimately collapses into their claim that the Montana tax is invalid under the fourth prong of the *Complete Auto Transit* test: that the tax is not "fairly related to the services provided by the State." 430 U.S., at 279, 97 S.Ct., at 1079. Because appellants concede that Montana may impose *some* severance tax on coal mined in the State, the only remaining foundation for their discrimination theory is a claim that the tax burden borne by the out-of-state consumers of Montana coal is excessive. This is, of course, merely a variant of appellants' assertion that the Montana tax does not satisfy the "fairly related" prong of the *Complete Auto Transit* test, and it is to this contention that we now turn.

Appellants argue that they are entitled to an opportunity to prove that the amount collected under the Montana tax is not fairly related to the additional costs the State incurs because of coal mining. Thus, appellants' objection is to the *rate* of the Montana tax, and even then, their only complaint is that the *amount* the State receives in taxes far exceeds the *value* of the services provided to the coal mining industry. In objecting to the tax on this ground, appellants may be assuming that the Montana tax is, in fact, intended to reimburse the State for the cost of specific services furnished to the coal mining industry. Alternatively, appellants could be arguing that a State's power to tax an activity connected to interstate commerce cannot exceed the value of the services specifically provided to the activity. Either way, the premise of appellants' argument is invalid. Furthermore, appellants have completely misunderstood the nature of the inquiry under the fourth prong of the *Complete Auto Transit* test.

The Montana Supreme Court held that the coal severance tax is "imposed for the general support of the government." Mont., 615 P.2d, at 856, and we have no reason to question this characterization of the Montana tax as a general revenue tax. Consequently, in reviewing appellant's contentions, we put to one side those cases in which the Court reviewed challenges to "user" fees or "taxes" that were designed and defended as a specific charge imposed by the State for the use of state-owned or state-provided transportation or other facilities and services.
* * *

This Court has indicated that States have considerable latitude in imposing general revenue taxes. The Court has, for example, consistently rejected claims that the Due Process Clause of the Fourteenth Amendment stands as a barrier against taxes that are "unreasonable" or "unduly burdensome." * * * Moreover, there is no requirement under the Due Process Clause that the amount of general revenue taxes collected from a particular activity must be reasonably related to the value of the services provided to the activity. Instead, our consistent rule has been:

> "Nothing is more familiar in taxation than the imposition of a tax upon a class or upon individuals who enjoy no direct benefit from its expenditure, and who are not responsible for the condition to be remedied.

> "A tax is not an assessment of benefits. It is, as we have said, a means of distributing the burden of the cost of government. The only benefit to which the taxpayer is constitutionally entitled is that derived from his enjoyment of the privileges of living in an organized society, established and safeguarded by the devotion of taxes to public purposes. Any other view would preclude the levying of taxes except as they are used to compensate for the burden on those who pay them, and would involve abandonment of the most fundamental principle of government—that it exists primarily to provide for the common good." Carmichael v. Southern Coal & Coke Co., 301 U.S. 495, 521–522, 57 S.Ct. 868, 878–79 (1937) (citations omitted).

* * *

There is no reason to suppose that this latitude afforded the States under the Due Process Clause is somehow divested by the Commerce Clause merely because the taxed activity has some connection to interstate commerce; particularly when the tax is levied on an activity conducted within the State. "The exploitation by foreign corporations [or consumers] of intrastate opportunities under the protection and encouragement of local government offers a basis for taxation as unrestricted as that for domestic corporations." Ford Motor Co. v. Beauchamp, 308 U.S. 331, 334–335, 60 S.Ct. 273, 275 (1939). To accept appellants' apparent suggestion that the Commerce Clause prohibits the States from requiring an activity connected to interstate commerce to contribute to the general cost of providing governmental services, as distinct from those costs attributable to the taxed activity, would place such commerce in a privileged position. But as we recently reiterated, " '[i]t was not the purpose of the commerce clause to relieve those engaged in interstate commerce from their just share of state tax burden even though it increases the cost of doing business.' " * * * The "just share of state tax burden" includes sharing in the cost of providing "police and fire protection, the benefit of a trained work force, and 'the advantages of a civilized society.' " Exxon Corp. v. Wisconsin Dept. of Revenue, 447 U.S. 207, 228, 100 S.Ct. 2109, 2123, quoting Japan Line, Ltd. v. County of Los Angeles, 441 U.S., at 445, 99 S.Ct. 1813, 1819–20. * * *

Furthermore, there can be no question that Montana may constitutionally raise general revenue by imposing a severance tax on coal mined in the State. The entire value of the coal, before transportation, originates in the State, and mining of the coal depletes the resource base and wealth of the State, thereby diminishing a future source of taxes and economic activity.[13] In many respects, a severance tax is like a real property tax, which has never been doubted as a legitimate means of raising revenue by the situs State (quite apart from the right of that or any other State to tax income derived from use of the property). When, as here, a general revenue tax does not discriminate against interstate commerce and is apportioned to activities occurring within the State, the State "is free to pursue its own fiscal policies, unembarrassed by the Constitution, if by the practical operation of a tax the state has exerted its power in relation to opportunities which it has given, to protection which it has afforded, to benefits which it has conferred by the fact of being an orderly civilized society." Wisconsin v. J.C. Penney Co., 311 U.S. 435, 444, 61 S.Ct. 246, 249 (1940). * * *

The relevant inquiry under the fourth prong of the *Complete Auto Transit* test is not as appellants suggest, the *amount* of the tax or the *value* of the benefits allegedly bestowed as measured by the costs the State incurs on account of the taxpayer's activities. Rather, the test is closely

13. Most of the States raise revenue by levying a severance tax on mineral production. The first such tax was imposed by Michigan in 1846. See United States Department of Agriculture, State Taxation of Mineral Deposits and Production (1978). By 1979, 33 States had adopted some type of severance tax. See Bureau of Census, State Government Tax Collections in 1979, Table 3 (1980).

connected to the first prong of the *Complete Auto Transit* test. Under this threshold test, the interstate business must have a substantial nexus with the State before *any* tax may be levied on it. See National Bellas Hess, Inc. v. Illinois Revenue Dept., 386 U.S. 753, 87 S.Ct. 1389 (1967). Beyond that threshold requirement, the fourth prong of the *Complete Auto Transit* test imposes the additional limitation that the *measure* of the tax must be reasonably related to the extent of the contact, since it is the activities or presence of the taxpayer in the State that may properly be made to bear a "just share of state tax burden," Western Live Stock Bureau v. Bureau of Revenue, 303 U.S., at 254, 58 S.Ct., at 548. As the Court explained in Wisconsin v. J.C. Penney Co., supra, 311 U.S., at 446, 61 S.Ct., at 250 (emphasis added), "the incidence of the tax *as well as its measure* [must be] tied to the earnings which the State ... has made possible, insofar as government is the prerequisite for the fruits of civilization for which, as Mr. Justice Holmes was fond of saying, we pay taxes."

Against this background, we have little difficulty concluding that the Montana tax satisfies the fourth prong of the *Complete Auto Transit* test. The "operating incidence" of the tax, see General Motors Corp. v. Washington, supra, 377 U.S., at 440–441, 84 S.Ct., at 1567–68, is on the mining of coal within Montana. Because it is measured as a percentage of the value of the coal taken, the Montana tax is in "proper proportion" to appellants' activities within the State and, therefore, to their "consequent enjoyment of the opportunities and protections which the State has afforded" in connection to those activities. Id., at 441, 84 S.Ct., at 1568. When a tax is assessed in proportion to a taxpayer's activities or presence in a State, the taxpayer is shouldering its fair share of supporting the State's provision of "police and fire protection, the benefit of a trained work force, and 'the advantages of a civilized society.' " Exxon Corp. v. Wisconsin Dept. of Revenue, 447 U.S., at 228, 100 S.Ct., at 2123, quoting Japan Line, Ltd. v. County of Los Angeles, 441 U.S., at 445, 99 S.Ct., at 1819–20.

Appellants argue, however, that the fourth prong of the *Complete Auto Transit* test must be construed as requiring a factual inquiry into the relationship between the revenues generated by a tax and costs incurred on account of the taxed activity, in order to provide a mechanism for judicial disapproval under the Commerce Clause of state taxes that are excessive. This assertion reveals that appellants labor under a misconception about a court's role in cases such as this. The simple fact is that the appropriate level or rate of taxation is essentially a matter for legislative, and not judicial, resolution. See Helson & Randolph v. Kentucky, 279 U.S. 245, 252, 49 S.Ct. 279, 281 (1929). In essence, appellants ask this Court to prescribe a test for the validity of state taxes that would require state and federal courts, as a matter of federal constitutional law, to calculate acceptable rates or levels of taxation of activities that are conceded to be legitimate subjects of taxation. This we decline to do.

In the first place, it is doubtful whether any legal test could adequately reflect the numerous and competing economic, geographic, demographic, social, and political considerations that must inform a decision about an acceptable rate or level of state taxation, and yet be reasonably capable of application in a wide variety of individual cases. But even apart from the difficulty of the judicial undertaking, the nature of the factfinding and judgment that would be required of the courts merely reinforces the conclusion that questions about the appropriate level of state taxes must be resolved through the political process. Under our federal system, the determination is to be made by state legislatures in the first instance and, if necessary, by Congress, when particular state taxes are thought to be contrary to federal interests.

Furthermore, the reference in the cases to police and fire protection and other advantages of civilized society is not, as appellants suggest, a disingenuous incantation designed to avoid a more searching inquiry into the relationship between the *value* of the benefits conferred on the taxpayer and the *amount* of taxes it pays. Rather, when the measure of a tax is reasonably related to the taxpayer's activities or presence in the State—from which it derives some benefit such as the substantial privilege of mining coal—the taxpayer will realize, in proper proportion to the taxes it pays, "[t]he only benefit to which it is constitutionally entitled ...[:] that derived from his enjoyment of the privileges of living in an organized society, established and safeguarded by the devotion of taxes to public purposes." Carmichael v. Southern Coal & Coke Co., 301 U.S., at 522, 57 S.Ct., at 878. Correspondingly, when the measure of a tax bears no relationship to the taxpayer's presence or activities in a State, a court may properly conclude under the fourth prong of the *Complete Auto Transit* test that the State is imposing an undue burden on interstate commerce. We are satisfied that the Montana tax, assessed under a formula that relates the tax liability to the value of appellant coal producers' activities within the State, comports with the requirements of the *Complete Auto Transit* test. We therefore turn to appellants' contention that the tax is invalid under the Supremacy Clause.

* * *

[The Court rejected the taxpayer's contention that the Montana tax, as applied to mining of federally owned coal, is invalid under the Supremacy Clause, because it substantially frustrates the purposes of the Mineral Land Leasing Act of 1920, as amended by the Federal Coal Leasing Amendments Act of 1975. Similarly, the Court found no merit in the taxpayer's claim that the Montana tax substantially frustrates national energy policies as embodied in several statutes encouraging the production and use of coal, particularly low-sulphur coal, such as that found in Montana.]

IV

In sum, we conclude that appellants have failed to demonstrate either that the Montana tax suffers from any of the constitutional defects alleged in their complaints, or that a trial is necessary to resolve the issue of the constitutionality of the tax. Consequently, the judgment of the Supreme Court of Montana is affirmed.

So ordered.

JUSTICE WHITE, concurring.

This is a very troublesome case for me, and I join the Court's opinion with considerable doubt and with the realization that Montana's levy on consumers in other States may in the long run prove to be an intolerable and unacceptable burden on commerce. Indeed, there is particular force in the argument that the tax is here and now unconstitutional. Montana collects most of its tax from coal lands owned by the Federal Government and hence by all of the people of this country, while at the same time sharing equally and directly with the Federal Government all of the royalties reserved under the leases the United States has negotiated on its land in the State of Montana. This share is intended to compensate the State for the burdens that coal mining may impose upon it. Also, as Justice Blackmun cogently points out * * * another 40% of the federal revenue from mineral leases is indirectly returned to the States through a reclamation fund. In addition, there is statutory provision for federal grants to areas affected by increased coal production.

But this very fact gives me pause and counsels withholding our hand, at least for now. Congress has the power to protect interstate commerce from intolerable or even undesirable burdens. It is also very much aware of the Nation's energy needs, of the Montana tax and of the trend in the energy-rich States to aggrandize their position and perhaps lessen the tax burdens on their own citizens by imposing unusually high taxes on mineral extraction. Yet, Congress is so far content to let the matter rest, and we are counseled by the Executive Branch through the Solicitor General not to overturn the Montana tax as inconsistent with either the Commerce Clause or federal statutory policy in the field of energy or otherwise. The constitutional authority and the machinery to thwart efforts such as those of Montana, if thought unacceptable, are available to Congress, and surely Montana and other similarly situated States do not have the political power to impose their will on the rest of the country. As I presently see it, therefore, the better part of both wisdom and valor is to respect the judgment of the other branches of the Government. I join the opinion and the judgment of the Court.

JUSTICE BLACKMUN, with whom JUSTICE POWELL and JUSTICE STEVENS join, dissenting.

In Complete Auto Transit, Inc. v. Brady, 430 U.S. 274, 97 S.Ct. 1076 (1977), a unanimous Court observed: "A tailored tax, however, accomplished, must receive the careful scrutiny of the courts to determine whether it produces a forbidden effect upon interstate commerce." Id., at 288–289, n. 15, 97 S.Ct., at 1084, n. 15. In this case, appellants have alleged that Montana's severance tax on coal is tailored to single out interstate commerce, and that it produces a forbidden effect on that commerce because the tax bears no "relationship to the services provided by the State." Ibid. The Court today concludes that appellants are not entitled to a *trial* on this claim. Because I believe that the "careful scrutiny" due a tailored tax makes a trial here necessary, I respectfully dissent.

* * *

II

This Court's Commerce Clause cases have been marked by tension between two competing concepts: the view that interstate commerce should enjoy a "free trade" immunity from state taxation, see, e.g., Freeman v. Hewit, 329 U.S. 249, 252, 67 S.Ct. 274, 276 (1946), and the view that interstate commerce may be required to " 'pay its way,' " see, e.g., Western Live Stock v. Bureau of Revenue, 303 U.S. 250, 254, 58 S.Ct. 546, 548 (1938). See generally Complete Auto Transit, Inc. v. Brady, 430 U.S., at 278–281, 288–289, n. 15, 97 S.Ct., at 1078–80, 1083–1084, n. 15. In *Complete Auto Transit,* the Court resolved that tension by unanimously reaffirming that interstate commerce is not immune from state taxation. But at the same time the Court made clear that not all state taxation of interstate commerce is valid; a state tax will be sustained against Commerce Clause challenge *only* if "the tax is applied to an activity with a substantial nexus with the taxing State, is fairly apportioned, does not discriminate against interstate commerce, and is fairly related to the services provided by the State." Id., at 279, 97 S.Ct., at 1079.

* * * The Court also correctly observes that Montana's severance tax is facially neutral. It does not automatically follow, however, that the Montana severance tax does not unduly burden or interfere with interstate commerce. The gravamen of appellants' complaint is that the severance tax does not satisfy the fourth prong of the *Complete Auto Transit* test because it is tailored to, and does, force interstate commerce to pay *more* than its way. Under our established precedents, appellants are entitled to a trial on this claim.

The Court's conclusion to the contrary rests on the premise that the relevant inquiry under the fourth prong of the *Complete Auto Transit* test is simply whether the *measure* of the tax is fixed as a percentage of the value of the coal taken. This interpretation emasculates the fourth prong. No trial will ever be necessary on the issue of fair relationship so long as a State is careful to impose a proportional rather than a flat tax rate; thus, the Court's rule is no less "mechanical" than the approach entertained in Heisler v. Thomas Colliery Co., 260 U.S. 245, 43 S.Ct. 83 (1922), disapproved today. Under the Court's reasoning any ad valorem tax will satisfy the fourth prong; indeed, the Court implicitly ratifies Montana's contention that it is free to tax this coal at 100% or even 1000% of value should it choose to do so. Likewise, the Court's analysis indicates that Montana's severance tax would not run afoul of the Commerce Clause even if it raised sufficient revenue to allow Montana to eliminate all other taxes upon its citizens.

The Court's prior cases neither require nor support such a startling result. * * *

[T]he Court has been particularly vigilant to review taxes that "single out interstate business," since "[a]ny tailored tax of this sort creates an increased danger of error in apportionment, of discrimination against interstate commerce, and of a lack of relationship to the services provided by the State." Complete Auto Transit, 430 U.S., at 288–289, n. 15, 97 S.Ct., at 1084, n. 15. Moreover, the Court's vigilance has not been limited to taxes that discriminate upon their face: "Not the tax in a vacuum of words, but its practical consequences for the doing of interstate commerce in applications to concrete facts are our concern." Nippert, 327 U.S., at 431, 66 S.Ct., at 593. This is particularly true when the challenged tax, while facially neutral, falls so heavily upon interstate commerce that its burden "is not likely to be alleviated by those political restraints which are normally exerted on legislation where it affects adversely interests within the state." McGoldrick v. Berwind–White Co., 309 U.S. 33, 46, n. 2, 60 S.Ct. 388, 392, n. 2 (1940). In sum, then, when a tax has been "tailored" to reach interstate commerce, the Court's cases suggest that we require a closer "fit" under the fourth prong of the *Complete Auto Transit* test than when interstate commerce has not been singled out by the challenged tax.

As a number of commentators have noted, state severance taxes upon minerals are particularly susceptible to "tailoring." "Like a tollgate lying athwart a trade route, a severance or processing tax conditions access to natural resources." Developments in the Law, Federal Limitations on State Taxation of Interstate Business, 75 Harv.L.Rev. 953, 970 (1962) (Harvard Developments). Thus, to the extent that the taxing jurisdiction approaches a monopoly position in the mineral, and consumption is largely outside the State, such taxes are "[e]conomically and politically analogous to transportation taxes exploiting geographical position." Brown, The Open Economy: Justice Frankfurter and the Position of the Judiciary, 67 Yale L.J. 219, 232 (1957). See also Hellerstein, Constitutional Constraints on State and Local Taxation of Energy Resources, 31 Nat.Tax J. 245, 249–250 (1978); R. Posner, Economic Analysis of Law 510–514 (2d ed. 1977). But just as a port State may require that imports pay their own way even though the tax levied increases the cost of goods purchased by inland customers, see Michelin Tire Corp. v. Wages, 423 U.S. 276, 288, 96 S.Ct. 535, 542 (1976), so also may a mineral-rich State require that those who consume its sources pay a fair share of the general costs of government, as well as the specific costs attributable to the commerce itself. Thus, the mere fact that the burden of a severance tax is largely shifted forward to out-of-state consumers does not, standing alone, make out a Commerce Clause violation. See Hellerstein, supra, at 249. But the Clause *is* violated when, as appellants allege is the case here, the State effectively selects "a class of out-of-state taxpayers to shoulder a tax burden grossly in excess of any costs imposed directly or indirectly by such taxpayers on the State." Ibid.

III

It is true that a trial in this case would require "complex factual inquiries" into whether economic conditions are such that Montana is in fact able to export the burden of its severance tax. I do not believe, however, that this threshold inquiry is beyond judicial competence. If the trial court were to determine that the tax is exported, it would then have to determine whether the tax is "fairly related," within the meaning of *Complete Auto Transit.* The Court to the contrary, this would not require the trial court "to second-guess legislative decisions about the amount or disposition of tax revenues." If the tax is in fact a legitimate general revenue measure identical or roughly comparable to taxes imposed upon similar industries, a court's inquiry is at an end; on the other hand, if the tax singles out this particular interstate activity and charges it with a grossly disproportionate share of the general costs of government, the court must determine whether there is some reasonable basis for the legislative judgment that the tax is necessary to compensate the State for the particular costs imposed by the activity.

To be sure, the task is likely to prove to be a formidable one; but its difficulty does not excuse our failure to undertake it. This case poses extremely grave issues that threaten both to "polarize the Nation," see H.R.Rep. No. 96–1527, pt. 1, p. 2 (1980), and to reawaken "the tendencies toward economic Balkanization" that the Commerce Clause was designed to remedy. See Hughes v. Oklahoma, 441 U.S. 322, 325–326, 99 S.Ct. 1727, 1731 (1979). It is no answer to say that the matter is better left to Congress[.] * * *

I would not lightly abandon that role. Because I believe that appellants are entitled to an opportunity to prove that, in Holmes' words, Montana's severance tax "embodies what the Commerce Clause was meant to end," I dissent.

Notes and Questions

A. In light of *Commonwealth Edison,* are there any limits that the Commerce Clause imposes on states in exploiting their natural advantages through their taxing schemes? Suppose Florida were to impose a selectively high tax on oranges produced in the state, while Washington imposed a selectively high tax on apples produced in the state, and Texas imposed a selectively high tax on oil produced in the state? Any Commerce Clause problem? Indeed, during the conflict over Montana's severance tax, a Kansas legislator threatened to retaliate by imposing a severance tax on corn grown in the state. Do any of these proposals make economic, as opposed to political, sense? What do you suppose would happen to the price of corn if Kansas imposed a 30 percent severance tax on all corn produced in Kansas? Does this suggest that Montana was being short-sighted in imposing its 30 percent severance tax on coal? Or do other facts in the case suggest that Montana might have been insulated from the effects of its high severance tax? The *Commonwealth Edison* case is analyzed in Walter Hellerstein, "Constitutional

Limitations on State Tax Exportation," 1982 A.B.F. Res. J. 1; Note, "The Supreme Court, 1980 Term," 95 Harv. L. Rev. 93, 102 (1981).

B.   Complete Auto's *Fourth Prong After* Commonwealth Edison. What is the significance of *Complete Auto*'s fourth prong—that a tax must be fairly related to services provided by the state—in light of the reading the Court gave it in *Commonwealth Edison*? Was Justice Blackmun overstating the case when he said that the Court had emasculated the fourth prong? If so, what independent role does the fourth prong continue to play? Specifically, can you posit a case in which a tax would violate *Complete Auto*'s fourth prong without violating one of the other three prongs? In fact, the Court has found that a tax violates *Complete Auto*'s fourth prong in only one case, involving flat highway taxes on trucks engaged in interstate commerce. See American Trucking Associations, Inc. v. Scheiner, 483 U.S. 266, 107 S.Ct. 2829 (1987), discussed in Section B(3), Note E, pp. 146–47 supra. In that case, the Court also found that the taxes at issue violated *Complete Auto*'s fair apportionment and nondiscrimination strictures. But see American River Transportation Co. v. Bower, 351 Ill.App.3d 208, 286 Ill.Dec. 397, 813 N.E.2d 1090 (2004) (invalidating use tax imposed on fuel and supplies purchased for use on tugboats that spent at least 50 percent of their time within Illinois waters on the ground that the tax was not fairly related to services provided by Illinois, even though it satisfied *Complete Auto*'s other three prongs). Was *American River Transportation* correctly decided?

5. REPRISE: *COMPLETE AUTO*'S COMMERCE CLAUSE TEST REEXAMINED

In the preceding materials, we have explored *Complete Auto*'s four-part test through cases that focused on, or were edited to emphasize, a particular prong of the test, namely, substantial nexus, fair apportionment, nondiscrimination, and fair relation between a tax and the services provided by the state. Commerce Clause cases, however, do not come in hermetically sealed packages labeled "nexus," or "apportionment" or "discrimination" or "fair relation." Thus, in the case you just read, *Commonwealth Edison*, the Court devoted considerable attention both to *Complete Auto*'s nondiscrimination requirement and to its "fairly related" criterion, and the Court adverted to the nexus and fair apportionment issues as well. In fact, Commerce Clause challenges to state taxes typically involve serious disputes over several of *Complete Auto*'s standards. The next case, *Goldberg v. Sweet*, illustrates this point and provides you with an opportunity to reexamine the Court's Commerce Clause doctrine in a case not only touching on all of *Complete Auto's* requirements, but also arising in a context of considerable contemporary significance—interstate telecommunications.

GOLDBERG v. SWEET

Supreme Court of the United States, 1989.
488 U.S. 252, 109 S.Ct. 582.

JUSTICE MARSHALL delivered the opinion of the Court.

In this appeal, we must decide whether a tax on interstate telecommunications imposed by the State of Illinois violates the Commerce Clause. We hold that it does not.

I

A

This case comes to us against a backdrop of massive technological and legal changes in the telecommunications industry. Years ago, all interstate telephone calls were relayed through electric wires and transferred by human operators working switchboards. Those days are past. Today, a computerized network of electronic paths transmits thousands of electronic signals per minute through a complex system of microwave radios, fiber optics, satellites and cables. When fully connected, this network offers billions of paths from one point to another. When a direct path is full or not working efficiently, the computer system instantly activates another path. Signals may even change paths in the middle of a telephone call without perceptible interruption. Thus, the path taken by the electronic signals is often indirect and typically bears no relation to state boundaries.[2] The number of possible paths, the nature of the electronic signals, and the system of computerized switching make it virtually impossible to trace and record the actual paths taken by the electronic signals which create an individual telephone call.

The explosion in new telecommunications technologies and the breakup of the AT & T monopoly has led a number of States to revise the taxes they impose on the telecommunications industry. In 1985, Illinois passed the Illinois Telecommunications Excise Tax Act, Ill.Rev.Stat., ch. 120, ¶¶ 2001–2021 (1987) (Tax Act). The Tax Act imposes a 5% tax on the gross charge of interstate telecommunications (1) originated or terminated in Illinois, ¶ 2004, § 4 (Section 4)[5] and (2) charged to an Illinois service

---

2. A signal traveling from one microwave tower to another may pass through a State but never touch anything in it. A satellite transmission may leave a caller's building, travel to outer space and remain there until it is received by a satellite dish at the building housing the receiving party.

5. Section 4 states in part:

"A tax is imposed upon the act or privilege of originating in this State or receiving in this State interstate telecommunications by a person in this State at the rate of 5% of the gross charge for such telecommunications purchased at retail from a retailer by such person." Ill.Rev.Stat., ch. 120, ¶ 2004, § 4 (1987).

"Gross charge" is defined as the amount paid for the telephone call, ¶ 2002, §§ 2(a) and (b), less charges for certain types of special equipment not at issue here. ¶ 2002, §§ 2(a)(1)–(5).

The Tax Act defines telecommunications broadly to include:

address, regardless where the telephone call is billed or paid. ¶ 2002, §§ 2(a) and (b).[6] The Tax Act imposes an identical 5% tax on interstate telecommunications. ¶ 2003, § 3. In order to prevent "actual multi-state taxation," the Tax Act provides a credit to any taxpayer upon proof that the taxpayer has paid a tax in another State on the same telephone call which triggered the Illinois tax. ¶ 2004, § 4. To facilitate collection, the Tax Act requires telecommunications retailers, like appellant GTE Sprint Communications Corporation (Sprint), to collect the tax from the consumer who charged the call to his service address. ¶ 2005, § 5.

B

Eight months after the Tax Act was passed, Jerome Goldberg and Robert McTigue, Illinois residents who are subject to and have paid telecommunications taxes through their retailers, filed a class action complaint in the Circuit Court of Cook County, Illinois. They named as defendants J. Thomas Johnson, Director of the Department of Revenue for the State of Illinois, (Director),[7] and various long-distance telephone carriers, including Sprint. The complaint alleged that Section 4 of the Tax Act violates the Commerce Clause of the United States Constitution. Sprint cross-claimed against the Director, seeking a declaration that the Tax Act is unconstitutional under the Commerce Clause. The Director then filed a motion for summary judgment against Sprint and the other long-distance carriers. Sprint responded with a motion for summary judgment against the Director; Goldberg and McTigue, in turn, filed their own motion for summary judgment against both the Director and Sprint.

After briefing and a hearing, the trial court declared Section 4 unconstitutional. It found that Complete Auto Transit, Inc. v. Brady, 430 U.S. 274, 97 S.Ct. 1076 (1977), and its progeny, control this case. Under the four-prong test originated in *Complete Auto,* a state tax will withstand scrutiny under the Commerce Clause if "the tax is applied to an activity with a substantial nexus with the taxing State, is fairly apportioned, does not discriminate against interstate commerce, and is fairly related to the services provided by the State." Id., at 279, 97 S.Ct., at 1079.[9] In the view

---

"[I]n addition to the meaning ordinarily and popularly ascribed to it, ... without limitation, messages or information transmitted through use of local, toll and wide area telephone service; private line services; channel services; telegraph services; teletypewriter; computer exchange services; cellular mobile telecommunications service; specialized mobile radio; stationary two way radio; paging service; or any other form of mobile and portable one-way or two-way communications; or any other transmission of messages or information by electronic or similar means, between or among points by wire, cable, fiber-optics, laser, microwave, radio, satellite or similar facilities." ¶ 2002, § 2(b).

For the sake of simplicity, we use the terms "call" and "telephone call" to refer to these multifarious forms of telecommunications.

6. Although not defined in the Tax Act, we understand the term "service address" to mean the address where the telephone equipment is located and to which the telephone number is assigned. See ¶ 2002, §§ 2(b) and (h).

7. Roger Sweet has since replaced J. Thomas Johnson as Director of the Department of Revenue.

9. All parties conceded before the trial court, as they do here, that Illinois has a substantial nexus with the interstate telecommunications reached by the Tax Act.

of the trial court, the Tax Act did not satisfy the last three prongs of the *Complete Auto* test because:

> "Illinois is attempting to tax the entire cost of an interstate act which takes place only partially in Illinois. This tax by its own terms is not fairly apportioned. It discriminates against interstate commerce and it is not related to services provided in Illinois. For all of these reasons the Act must fail." Goldberg v. Johnson, No. 85 CH 8081 (Cook County, Oct. 21, 1986), App. to Juris. Statement in No. 87–826, p. 24a.

The Illinois Supreme Court reversed, Goldberg v. Johnson, 117 Ill.2d 493, 111 Ill.Dec. 625, 512 N.E.2d 1262 (1987) (per curiam) despite its finding that the tax is "not an apportioned tax" because it "applies to the entirety of each and every interstate telecommunication." Id., at 501, 111 Ill.Dec., at 629, 512 N.E.2d, at 1266. The court reasoned that an unapportioned tax is "constitutionally suspect" because of the risk of multiple taxation, ibid., but decided that the Tax Act adequately avoided this danger. With respect to interstate calls originating in Illinois, the court noted that no other State could levy a tax on such calls. Id., at 502, 111 Ill.Dec., at 629, 512 N.E.2d, at 1266. As for calls terminating in Illinois and charged to an Illinois service address, the court found that even though the tax created "a real risk of multiple taxation," id., at 502, 111 Ill.Dec., at 630, 512 N.E.2d, at 1267,[10] that risk was eliminated by Section 4's credit provision. Id., at 503, 111 Ill.Dec., at 630, 512 N.E.2d, at 1267.

As for discrimination, the third prong of the *Complete Auto* test, the court held that the Tax Act is constitutionally valid since a 5% tax is imposed on intrastate as well as interstate telecommunications. Turning to the fourth prong, the court held that the tax is fairly related to services provided by Illinois. The court explained that Illinois provided services and other benefits with respect to that portion of an interstate call occurring within the State, and that "the benefits afforded by other States in facilitating the same interstate telecommunication are too speculative to override the substantial benefits extended by Illinois." Id., at 504, 111 Ill.Dec., at 630, 512 N.E.2d, at 1267.

Having found that the Tax Act satisfied the requirements of *Complete Auto,* the Illinois Supreme Court concluded that it did not violate the Commerce Clause. Sprint, Goldberg and McTigue appealed to this Court. We noted probable jurisdiction and now affirm.

II

A

This Court has frequently had occasion to consider whether state taxes violate the Commerce Clause. The wavering doctrinal lines of our pre-*Complete Auto* cases reflect the tension between two competing concepts: the view that interstate commerce enjoys a "free trade" immunity

---

10. A collect call is one example of a telephone call which originates in another State but terminates in Illinois and is charged to an Illinois service address.

from state taxation; and the view that businesses engaged in interstate commerce may be required to pay their own way. Complete Auto, supra, 430 U.S., at 278–279, 97 S.Ct., at 1078–1079; see also American Trucking Assns., Inc. v. Scheiner, 483 U.S. 266, nn. 12, 13, 107 S.Ct. 2829, nn. 12, 13 (1987). *Complete Auto* sought to resolve this tension by specifically rejecting the view that the States cannot tax interstate commerce, while at the same time placing limits on state taxation of interstate commerce. 430 U.S., at 288, 97 S.Ct., at 1083. Since the *Complete Auto* decision we have applied its four-prong test on numerous occasions. We now apply it to the Illinois tax.

B

As all parties agree that Illinois has a substantial nexus with the interstate telecommunications reached by the Tax Act, we begin our inquiry with apportionment, the second prong of the *Complete Auto* test. Appellants argue that the telecommunications tax is not fairly apportioned because Illinois taxes the gross charge of each telephone call. They interpret our prior cases, specifically Michigan–Wisconsin Pipe Line Co. v. Calvert, 347 U.S. 157, 74 S.Ct. 396 (1954), Central Greyhound Lines, Inc. v. Mealey, 334 U.S. 653, 68 S.Ct. 1260 (1948), and Western Live Stock v. Bureau of Revenue, 303 U.S. 250, 58 S.Ct. 546 (1938), to require Illinois to tax only a fraction of the gross charge of each telephone call based on the miles which the electronic signals traveled within Illinois as a portion of the total miles traveled. The Director, in turn, argues that Illinois apportions its telecommunications tax by carefully limiting the type of interstate telephone calls which it reaches.

In analyzing these contentions, we are mindful that the central purpose behind the apportionment requirement is to ensure that each State taxes only its fair share of an interstate transaction. See, e.g., Container Corp. of America v. Franchise Tax Bd., 463 U.S. 159, 169, 103 S.Ct. 2933, 2942 (1983). But "we have long held that the Constitution imposes no single [apportionment] formula on the States," id., at 164, 103 S.Ct., at 2939, and therefore have declined to undertake the essentially legislative task of establishing a "single constitutionally mandated method of taxation." Id., at 171, 103 S.Ct., at 2943; see also Moorman Mfg. Co. v. Bair, 437 U.S. 267, 278–280, 98 S.Ct. 2340, 2347–2348 (1978). Instead, we determine whether a tax is fairly apportioned by examining whether it is internally and externally consistent. Armco Inc. v. Hardesty, 467 U.S. 638, 644, 104 S.Ct. 2620, 2623 (1984); Container Corp., supra, 463 U.S., at 169–170, 103 S.Ct., at 2942–2943.

To be internally consistent, a tax must be structured so that if every State were to impose an identical tax, no multiple taxation would result. Thus, the internal consistency test focuses on the text of the challenged statute and hypothesizes a situation where other States have passed an identical statute. We conclude that the Tax Act is internally consistent, for if every State taxed only those interstate phone calls which are charged to an in-state service address, only one State would tax each interstate telephone call.

Appellant Sprint argues that our decision in *Armco* dictates a different standard. It contends that, under *Armco,* a court evaluating the internal consistency of a challenged tax must also compare the tax to the similar, but not identical, taxes imposed by other States. Sprint misreads *Armco.* If we were to determine the internal consistency of one State's tax by comparing it with slightly different taxes imposed by other States, the validity of state taxes would turn solely on "the shifting complexities of the tax codes of 49 other States." Armco, supra, 467 U.S., at 645, 104 S.Ct., at 2624; see also Moorman, supra, 437 U.S., at 277, n. 12, 98 S.Ct., at 2346, n. 12. In any event, to the extent that other States have passed tax statutes which create a risk of multiple taxation, we reach that issue under the external consistency test, to which we now turn.

The external consistency test asks whether the State has taxed only that portion of the revenues from the interstate activity which reasonably reflects the in-state component of the activity being taxed. Container Corp., supra, 463 U.S., at 169–170, 103 S.Ct., at 2942–2943. We thus examine the in-state business activity which triggers the taxable event and the practical or economic effect of the tax on that interstate activity. Appellants first contend that any tax assessed on the gross charge of an interstate activity cannot reasonably reflect in-state business activity and therefore must be unapportioned. The Director argues that, because the Tax Act has the same economic effect as a sales tax, it can be based on the gross charge of the telephone call. See, e.g., McGoldrick v. Berwind–White Coal Mining Co., 309 U.S. 33, 58, 60 S.Ct. 388, 398 (1940) (sales tax); cf. D.H. Holmes Co. v. McNamara, 486 U.S. 24, 31–32, 108 S.Ct. 1619, 1623–1624 (1988) (use tax); Tyler Pipe Industries, Inc. v. Washington Dept. of Revenue, 483 U.S. 232, 251, 107 S.Ct. 2810, 2822 (1987) (gross receipts).

We believe that the Director has the better of this argument. The tax at issue has many of the characteristics of a sales tax. It is assessed on the individual consumer, collected by the retailer, and accompanies the retail purchase of an interstate telephone call. Even though such a retail purchase is not a purely local event since it triggers simultaneous activity in several States, the Tax Act reasonably reflects the way that consumers purchase interstate telephone calls.

The Director further contends that the Illinois telecommunications tax is fairly apportioned because the Tax Act reaches only those interstate calls which are (1) originated or terminated in Illinois and (2) charged to an Illinois service address. Appellants Goldberg and McTigue, by contrast, raise the spectre of many States assessing a tax on the gross charge of an interstate telephone call. Appellants have exaggerated the extent to which the Tax Act creates a risk of multiple taxation. We doubt that States through which the telephone call's electronic signals merely pass have a sufficient nexus to tax that call. See United Air Lines, Inc. v. Mahin, 410 U.S. 623, 631, 93 S.Ct. 1186, 1191 (1973) (State has no nexus to tax an airplane based solely on its flight over the State); Northwest Airlines, Inc. v. Minnesota, 322 U.S. 292, 302–304, 64 S.Ct. 950, 955–956 (1944) (Jackson, J., concurring) (same). We also doubt that termination of an interstate telephone call, by itself, provides a substantial enough nexus for a State to tax a call. See National Bellas Hess, Inc. v. Department of Revenue of Illinois, 386 U.S. 753, 87 S.Ct. 1389 (1967) (receipt of mail provides insufficient nexus).

We believe that only two States have a nexus substantial enough to tax a consumer's purchase of an interstate telephone call. The first is a State like Illinois which taxes the origination or termination of an interstate telephone call charged to a service address within that State. The second is a State which taxes the origination or termination of an interstate telephone call billed or paid within that State. See, e.g., Ark. Code Ann. § 26–52–301(3) (Supp.1987); Wash.Rev.Code § 82.04.065(2) (1987).

We recognize that, if the service address and billing location of a taxpayer are in different States, some interstate telephone calls could be subject to multiple taxation.[13] This limited possibility of multiple taxation, however, is not sufficient to invalidate the Illinois statutory scheme. See Container Corp., 463 U.S., at 171, 103 S.Ct., at 2943; Moorman, 437 U.S., at 272–273, 98 S.Ct., at 2343–2344. To the extent that other States' telecommunications taxes pose a risk of multiple taxation, the credit provision contained in the Tax Act operates to avoid actual multiple taxation. D.H. Holmes, supra, at 31, 108 S.Ct., at 1623 ("[t]he ... taxing scheme is fairly apportioned, for it provides a credit against its use tax for sales taxes that have been paid in other States"); see also Tyler Pipe, supra, at 245, n. 13, 107 S.Ct. at 2819, n. 13.

It should not be overlooked, moreover, that the external consistency test is essentially a practical inquiry. In previous cases we have endorsed apportionment formulas based upon the miles a bus, train, or truck traveled within the taxing State. But those cases all dealt with the movement of large physical objects over identifiable routes, where it was practicable to keep track of the distance actually traveled within the taxing State. See, e.g., Central Greyhound, 334 U.S., at 663, 68 S.Ct., at 1266 ("[t]here is no dispute as to feasibility in apportioning this tax"); see also Western Live Stock, 303 U.S., at 257, 58 S.Ct., at 549. This case, by contrast, involves the more intangible movement of electronic impulses

---

13. Those taxpayers who split their billing and service addresses between two different States face a risk of multiple taxation on a limited number of their interstate telephone calls. For example, if a company's Arkansas headquarters paid the telephone bills of its Illinois subsidiary, two state taxes would be paid on telephone calls made by the Illinois subsidiary to the head office or any other Arkansas location. Such calls would terminate and be billed or paid in Arkansas, and they would also originate and be charged to an Illinois service address. Likewise, a collect call from the Arkansas headquarters to the Illinois subsidiary could be taxed in both States. The collect call would originate and be billed or paid in Arkansas, and it would also terminate and be charged to an Illinois service address. Non-collect calls from the Arkansas headquarters to the Illinois subsidiary would not, however, be captured by the Illinois Tax Act. Likewise, the Arkansas statute would not tax interstate calls made by the Illinois subsidiary to States other than Arkansas.

through computerized networks. An apportionment formula based on mileage or some other geographic division of individual telephone calls would produce insurmountable administrative and technological barriers. See Scheiner, 483 U.S., at 296, 107 S.Ct., at 2847 (apportionment does not require State to adopt a tax which would "pose genuine administrative burdens").[15] We thus find it significant that Illinois' method of taxation is a realistic legislative solution to the technology of the present-day telecommunications industry.[16]

In sum, we hold that the Tax Act is fairly apportioned. Its economic effect is like a sales tax, the risk of multiple taxation is low, and actual multiple taxation is precluded by the credit provision. Moreover, we conclude that mileage or some other geographic division of individual telephone calls would be infeasible.

C

We turn next to the third prong of the *Complete Auto* test, which prohibits a State from imposing a discriminatory tax on interstate commerce. Appellants argue that irrespective of the identical 5% tax on the gross charge of intrastate telephone calls, the Tax Act discriminates against interstate commerce by allocating a larger share of the tax burden to interstate telephone calls. They rely on *Scheiner,* where we stated that, "[i]n its guarantee of a free trade area among the States, ... the Commerce Clause has a deeper meaning that may be implicated even though state provisions, ... do not allocate tax burdens between insiders and outsiders in a manner that is facially discriminatory." Scheiner, supra, at 281, 107 S.Ct., at 2839.

In *Scheiner,* we held that Pennsylvania's flat taxes on the operation of all trucks on Pennsylvania highways imposed a disproportionate burden on interstate trucks, as compared with intrastate trucks, because the interstate trucks traveled fewer miles per year on Pennsylvania highways. Id., at 286, 107 S.Ct., at 2841. The Illinois tax differs from the flat taxes found discriminatory in *Scheiner* in two important ways. First, whereas Pennsylvania's flat taxes burdened out-of-state truckers who would have difficulty effecting legislative change, the economic burden of the Illinois telecommunications tax falls on the Illinois telecommunications consumer, the insider who presumably is able to complain about and change the tax

---

15. Sprint alleges that it is "capable, administratively, of billing more than one state's tax on a single interstate communication." Brief for Appellant GTE Sprint Communications Corp. 4. This statement, however, tells us no more than that Sprint's computerized billing system is capable of adding another line to consumers' bills. Sprint does not explain, however, how it would keep track of and record the exact paths and in-state mileage of thousands of electronic impulses per minute.

16. Years ago, we considered and rejected certain state taxes on interstate telecommunications. See, e.g., Cooney v. Mountain States Tel. & Tel. Co., 294 U.S. 384, 55 S.Ct. 477 (1935); Western Union Tel. Co. v. Pennsylvania, 128 U.S. 39, 9 S.Ct. 6 (1888); cf. Pensacola Tel. Co. v. Western Union Tel. Co., 96 U.S. 1 (1878) (because the telegraph industry is interstate commerce, Act of Congress pre-empts state regulation). These cases considered a telecommunications technology only distantly related to modern telecommunications technology and were decided in a pre-*Complete Auto* era when this Court held the view that interstate commerce itself could not be taxed.

through the Illinois political process. It is not a purpose of the Commerce Clause to protect state residents from their own state taxes.

Second, whereas with Pennsylvania's flat taxes it was possible to measure the activities within the State because truck mileage on state highways could be tallied, reported, and apportioned, the exact path of thousands of electronic signals can neither be traced nor recorded. We therefore conclude that the Tax Act does not discriminate in favor of intrastate commerce at the expense of interstate commerce.

D

Finally, we reach the fourth prong of the *Complete Auto* test, namely, whether the Illinois tax is fairly related to the presence and activities of the taxpayer within the State. See D.H. Holmes, 486 U.S., at 32–34, 108 S.Ct., at 1624–1625. The purpose of this test is to ensure that a State's tax burden is not placed upon persons who do not benefit from services provided by the State. Commonwealth Edison, 453 U.S., at 627, 101 S.Ct., at 2958.

Appellants would severely limit this test by focusing solely on those services which Illinois provides to telecommunications equipment located within the State. We cannot accept this view. The tax which may be imposed on a particular interstate transaction need not be limited to the cost of the services incurred by the State on account of that particular activity. Id., at 627, n. 16, 101 S.Ct., at 2958, n. 16. On the contrary, "interstate commerce may be required to contribute to the cost of providing *all* governmental services, including those services from which it arguably receives no direct 'benefit.'" Ibid. (emphasis in original). The fourth prong of the *Complete Auto* test thus focuses on the wide range of benefits provided to the taxpayer, not just the precise activity connected to the interstate activity at issue. Indeed, last Term, in D.H. Holmes, supra, at 32, 108 S.Ct., at 1624, we noted that a taxpayer's receipt of police and fire protection, the use of public roads and mass transit, and the other advantages of civilized society satisfied the requirement that the tax be fairly related to benefits provided by the State to the taxpayer.

In light of the foregoing, we have little difficulty concluding that the Tax Act is fairly related to the benefits received by Illinois telephone consumers. The benefits that Illinois provides cannot be limited to those exact services provided to the equipment used during each interstate telephone call. Illinois telephone consumers also subscribe to telephone service in Illinois, own or rent telephone equipment at an Illinois service address, and they receive police and fire protection as well as the other general services provided by the State of Illinois.

III

For the reasons stated above, we hold that the telecommunications tax imposed by the Tax Act is consistent with the Commerce Clause. It is fairly apportioned, does not discriminate against interstate commerce, and is fairly related to services which the State of Illinois provides to the taxpayer. The judgment of the Illinois Supreme Court is hereby

Affirmed.

JUSTICE STEVENS, concurring in part and concurring in the judgment.

My reasons for concluding that the Illinois tax does not discriminate against interstate commerce are different from those expressed in Part II(C) of the Court's opinion. Unlike the Court, I do not believe Illinois may discriminate among its own residents by placing a heavier tax on those who engage in interstate commerce than on those who merely engage in local commerce. See ante, at 591 ("It is not a purpose of the Commerce Clause to protect state residents from their own state taxes."). In fact, such a holding is a clear departure from our precedents. See, e.g., Tyler Pipe Industries, Inc. v. Washington State Dept. of Revenue, 483 U.S. 232, 107 S.Ct. 2810, 2816–2820 (1987) (invalidating manufacturing tax that discriminated between in-state manufacturers that sold at wholesale out-of-state); Bacchus Imports, Ltd. v. Dias, 468 U.S. 263, 104 S.Ct. 3049 (1984) (invalidating tax exemption for locally produced alcoholic beverages in case brought by local wholesalers); Boston Stock Exchange v. State Tax Commission, 429 U.S. 318, 333–334, 97 S.Ct. 599, 608–609 (1977) (invalidating securities transfer tax that discriminated against those state residents who sold out-of-state rather than in-state). Surely a state tax of 3% on the shipment of goods intrastate and of 5% on the shipment of goods interstate would violate the Commerce Clause.

Appellants' discrimination claim can best be illustrated by example: A call originating and terminating in Illinois that costs $10 is taxed at full value at 5%. A second call, originating in Illinois but terminating in Indiana, costs the same $10 and is taxed at the same full value at the same 5% rate. But while Illinois may properly tax the entire $10 of the first call, it (technically) may tax only that portion of the second call over which it has jurisdiction, namely, the intrastate portion of the call (say, for example, $5). By imposing an identical 50 cents tax on the two calls, Illinois has imposed a disproportionate economic burden on the interstate call. See American Trucking Associations, Inc. v. Scheiner, 483 U.S. 266, 107 S.Ct. 2829 (1987) (invalidating flat tax that imposed disproportionate economic burden on interstate commerce).

This argument, however, overlooks the true overall incidence of the Illinois tax. Although Illinois taxes the entirety of every call charged to an Illinois number, it does not tax any part of the calls that are received at an Illinois number but charged elsewhere. Thus, although Illinois taxes the entire Illinois–Indiana $10 call, it taxes no part of the reciprocal Indiana–Illinois $10 call. At the 5% rate, Illinois receives 50 cents from the two calls combined, precisely the amount it receives from one $10 purely intrastate call. By taxing half of the relevant universe of interstate calls at full value, Illinois achieves the same economic result as taxing all of those calls at half value would achieve. As a result, interstate phone calls are taxed at a lower effective rate than intrastate calls,[2] and accordingly bear a proportional tax burden.[3]

With the exception of Part II(C), I join the Court's opinion.

[The concurring opinions of Justices O'Connor and Scalia have been omitted.]

NOTES AND QUESTIONS

A. Goldberg *and Nexus*. Although the case did not raise a nexus issue (see the first sentence of Part II(B) of the Court's opinion), the Court adverted to the nexus question in the context of its discussion of fair apportionment. While doubting that "States through which the telephone call's electronic signals merely pass have a sufficient nexus to tax that call," the Court did identify two states that do have sufficient nexus to tax a consumer's purchase of an interstate telephone call: a state like Illinois that taxes the origination or termination of an interstate call charged to a service address within that state, and a state that taxes the origination or termination of an interstate telephone call billed or paid for within that state.

In light of the foregoing, is it fair to say that the Court has indicated that while neither the receipt of a telephone call nor the receipt of mail by itself creates a taxable nexus under the Commerce Clause, the two events in common do create such nexus? If not, how could the Court have declared that a state that taxes the termination of an interstate telephone call billed within the state would have nexus to tax such call? And, if so, does this mean that if a customer receives a telephone call from an out-of-state bank soliciting her to use its credit card and she agrees to do so, receiving the credit card in the mail, the state then has sufficient nexus with the bank to require it to pay a tax on the interest income it earns on the card? Or is there a difference between nexus with respect to a transaction tax, like the tax at issue in *Goldberg*, and nexus for purposes of an income tax? If you absorbed the materials in the preceding chapter, you should be able to articulate an answer to this question.

More fundamentally, you should reconsider a question we raised in Chapter 2, namely, whether the nexus question involves one or two inquiries: Can there be nexus with the taxpayer—in the sense that there is jurisdiction to tax the taxpayer—without there being nexus with the taxable transaction in which the taxpayer has engaged? Alternatively, can there be nexus with the transaction in which the taxpayer has engaged, without there being nexus with the taxpayer? The Court in *Goldberg* referred only to "nexus with the

2. That is, half of the interstate calls are taxed at 5%, but the other half are taxed at 0%; the effective rate is 2½%. On the other hand, all intrastate calls are taxed at 5%.

3. This analysis is not obviated by the Court's statement, with which I agree, that "We doubt that termination of an interstate telephone call, by itself, provides a substantial enough nexus for a State to tax a call." Supra, at 589. That one State through which interstate commerce flows may not constitutionally tax such commerce does not mean that another State may make up for the gap, as it were, by taxing its share as well as the first State's share. Thus, even if Indiana could not constitutionally tax the mere termination of an Illinois–Indiana call, Illinois still may tax only the portion of the call over which it has jurisdiction.

interstate telecommunications." Why did it not refer to the question of nexus with the taxpayer?

B.   Goldberg, *Fair Apportionment, and the "Internal" and "External Consistency" Tests.* In addressing the fair apportionment question, the Court declared that "we determine whether a tax is fairly apportioned by examining whether it is internally and externally consistent." See Section B(3), Notes D and E, pp. 145–48 supra (discussing "internal consistency" test). What made the tax in *Goldberg* "internally consistent"? The billed-to-an-Illinois-service address limitation? The credit for taxes paid to other states? Or both? What made the tax in *Goldberg* "externally consistent"? Will a tax be found to be "fairly apportioned" so long as it does not create a risk of multiple taxation? If so, could a state constitutionally impose a tax on all of the gross receipts earned by an interstate telephone company, while providing a credit for any gross receipts taxes that the company paid to other states, and defend the levy on the ground that the taxpayer was not subject to the risk of multiple taxation? Cf. D.H. Holmes Co. v. McNamara, 486 U.S. 24, 31, 108 S.Ct. 1619 (1988) ("The Louisiana taxing scheme is fairly apportioned, for it provides a credit against its use tax for sales taxes that have been paid to other States").

C.   Goldberg *and Discrimination.* Was Justice Stevens correct in taking the Court to task for suggesting that "[i]t is not the purpose of the Commerce Clause to protect state residents from their own state taxes." If Illinois had imposed a tax on state residents' purchases of out-of-state but not in-state goods, would the tax would have been sustained on the ground that "[i]t is not the purpose of the Commerce Clause to protect state residents from their own state taxes"?

D.   Goldberg *and Wireless Telecommunications.* What are the implications of the *Goldberg* case for the wireless telecommunications industry? Consider a business traveler who lives in State A, where she receives her monthly phone bill, and, while in State B on business, makes a call to State C. Under *Goldberg*, which state can tax the charges for the phone call? Suppose the customer is billed not on a transaction-by-transaction basis, but instead pays, say, $50 per month for 500 minutes of calls regardless of where the calls originate or terminate. Does this make it easier or harder to respond to the preceding query? The difficulties in answering these questions led Congress, with the joint support of the telecommunications industry and the states, to enact legislation permitting the states to tax *all* mobile telecommunications charges (for services provided by the customer's home service provider) at the customer's "place of primary use." Mobile Telecommunications Sourcing Act, 114 Stat. 626 (July 28, 2000), codified at 4 U.S.C. § 116 et seq. The Act defines the "place of primary use" as the residential street address or the primary business street address of the customer. Assuming that in many instances the Court's reasoning in *Goldberg* would have limited the power of the state of a customer's "place of primary use" to tax the charges for a wireless phone call, is it clear that Congress has the constitutional authority to change the rule of *Goldberg*?

C. RESTRICTIONS ON STATE TAXATION OF FOREIGN COMMERCE

JAPAN LINE, LTD. v. COUNTY OF LOS ANGELES

Supreme Court of the United States, 1979.
441 U.S. 434, 99 S.Ct. 1813.

MR. JUSTICE BLACKMUN delivered the opinion of the Court.

This case presents the question whether a State, consistently with the Commerce Clause of the Constitution, may impose a nondiscriminatory ad valorem property tax on foreign-owned instrumentalities (cargo containers) of international commerce.

I

The facts were "stipulated on appeal," App. 29, and were found by the trial court as follows:

Appellants are six Japanese shipping companies; they are incorporated under the laws of Japan, and they have their principal places of business and commercial domiciles in that country. Appellants operate vessels used exclusively in foreign commerce; these vessels are registered in Japan and have their home ports there. The vessels are specifically designed and constructed to accommodate large cargo shipping containers. The containers, like the ships, are owned by appellants, have their home ports in Japan, and are used exclusively for hire in the transportation of cargo in foreign commerce. Each container is in constant transit save for time spent undergoing repair or awaiting loading and unloading of cargo. All appellants' containers are subject to property tax in Japan and, in fact, are taxed there.

Appellees are political subdivisions of the State of California. Appellants' containers, in the course of their international journeys, pass through appellees' jurisdictions intermittently. Although none of appellants' containers stays permanently in California, some are there at any given time; a container's average stay in the State is less than three weeks. The containers engage in no intrastate or interstate transportation of cargo except as continuations of international voyages. Any movements or periods of nonmovement of containers in appellees' jurisdictions are essential to, and inseparable from, the containers' efficient use as instrumentalities of foreign commerce.

Property present in California on March 1 (the "lien date" under California law) of any year is subject to ad valorem property tax. Cal.Rev. & Tax.Code Ann. §§ 117, 405, 2192 (West 1970 & Supp.1978). A number of appellants' containers were physically present in appellees' jurisdictions on the lien dates in 1970, 1971, and 1972; this number was fairly representative of the containers' "average presence" during each year. Appellees levied property taxes in excess of $550,000 on the assessed value of the containers present on March 1 of the three years in question. During the same period, similar containers owned or controlled by steamship companies domiciled in the United States, that appeared from time to time in Japan during the course of international commerce, were not subject to property taxation in Japan, and therefore were not, in fact, taxed in that country.

Appellants paid the taxes, so levied, under protest and sued for their refund in the Superior Court for the County of Los Angeles. * * * [The California Supreme Court rejected the "home port" doctrine, under which the trial court had held that the vessels were taxable only in Japan, and it sustained the Los Angeles tax. 20 Cal.3d 180, 141 Cal.Rptr. 905, 571 P.2d 254 (1977).]

The California Supreme Court * * * concluded that "the threat of double taxation from foreign taxing authorities has no role in commerce clause considerations of multiple burdens, since burdens in international commerce are not attributable to discrimination by the taxing state and are matters for international agreement." Id., at 185, 141 Cal.Rptr., at 908, 571 P.2d, at 257. Deeming the containers' foreign ownership and use irrelevant for purposes of constitutional analysis, the court rejected appellants' Commerce Clause challenge and sustained the validity of the tax as applied.

* * *

III

A

[The U.S. Supreme Court first considered the challenge to the tax under the home port doctrine. It reviewed the cases and concluded that the home port doctrine "has fallen into desuetude, and * * * has yielded to a rule" that "various instrumentalities of commerce may be taxed, on a properly apportioned basis, by the nondomiciliary States through which they travel." The Court nevertheless recognized that "[i]n discarding the 'home port' theory for the theory of apportionment * * * the Court consistently has distinguished the case of ocean-going vessels," but it found even that exception "anachronistic," and stated that "it may indeed be said to have been 'abandoned.'" Accordingly, the Court declined to rest its decision on the home port doctrine, and it continued:] The question here is a * * * narrow one, that is, whether instrumentalities of commerce that are owned, based, and registered abroad and that are used exclusively in international commerce, may be subjected to apportioned ad valorem property taxation by a State.[7]

---

7. Accordingly, we do not reach questions as to the taxability of foreign-owned instrumentalities engaged in interstate commerce, or of domestically-owned instrumentalities engaged in foreign commerce. Cf. Sea–Land Service, Inc. v. County of Alameda, 12 Cal.3d 772, 117 Cal.Rptr. 448, 528 P.2d 56 (1974) (domestically-owned containers used in intercoastal and foreign commerce held subject to apportioned property tax); Flying Tiger Line, Inc. v. County of Los Angeles, 51 Cal.2d 314, 333 P.2d 323 (1958) (domestically-owned aircraft used in foreign commerce held subject to apportioned property tax).

B

The Constitution provides that "Congress shall have Power ... To regulate Commerce with foreign Nations, and among the several States, and with the Indian Tribes." Art. I, § 8, cl. 3. In construing Congress' power to "regulate Commerce ... among the several States," the Court recently has affirmed that the Constitution confers no immunity from state taxation, and that "interstate commerce must bear its fair share of the state tax burden." Washington Revenue Dept. v. Association of Wash. Stevedoring Cos., 435 U.S. 734, 750, 98 S.Ct. 1388, 1399 (1978). Instrumentalities of interstate commerce are no exception to this rule, and the Court regularly has sustained property taxes as applied to various forms of transportation equipment. See Pullmans Palace, supra (railroad rolling stock); Ott, supra (barges on inland waterways); Braniff, supra (domestic aircraft). Cf. Central Greyhound Lines v. Mealey, 334 U.S. 653, 663, 68 S.Ct. 1260, 1266 (1948) (motor vehicles). If the state tax "is applied to an activity with a substantial nexus with the taxing State, is fairly apportioned, does not discriminate against interstate commerce, and is fairly related to the services provided by the State," no impermissible burden on interstate commerce will be found. Complete Auto Transit, Inc. v. Brady, 430 U.S. 274, 279, 97 S.Ct. 1076, 1079 (1977); Washington Revenue Dept., 435 U.S., at 750, 98 S.Ct. at 1399.

Appellees contend that cargo shipping containers, like other vehicles of commercial transport, are subject to property taxation, and that the taxes imposed here meet *Complete Auto's* four-fold requirements. The containers, they argue, have a "substantial nexus" with California because some of them are present in that State at all times; jurisdiction to tax is based on "the habitual employment of the property within the State," Braniff, 347 U.S., at 601, 74 S.Ct. at 764, and appellants' containers habitually are so employed. The tax, moreover, is "fairly apportioned," since it is levied only on the containers' "average presence" in California.[8] The tax "does not discriminate," thirdly, since it falls evenhandedly on all personal property in the State; indeed, as an ad valorem tax of general application, it is of necessity nondiscriminatory. The tax, finally, is "fairly related to the services provided by" California, services that include not only police and fire protection, but the benefits of a trained work force and the advantages of a civilized society.

These observations are not without force. We may assume that, if the containers at issue here were instrumentalities of purely interstate commerce, *Complete Auto* would apply and be satisfied, and our Commerce Clause inquiry would be at an end. Appellants' containers, however, are instrumentalities of foreign commerce, both as a matter of fact and as a

---

8. By taxing property present on the "lien date," California roughly apportions its property tax for mobile goods like containers. For example, if each of appellants' containers is in California for three weeks a year, the number present on any arbitrarily selected date would be roughly $\frac{3}{52}$ of the total entering the State that year. Taxing $\frac{3}{52}$ of the containers at full value, however, is the same as taxing all the containers at $\frac{3}{52}$ value. Thus, California effectively apportions its tax to reflect the containers' "average presence," i.e., the time each container spends in the State per year.

matter of law.[10] The premise of appellees' argument is that the Commerce Clause analysis is identical, regardless of whether interstate or foreign commerce is involved. This premise, we have concluded, must be rejected. When construing Congress' power to "regulate Commerce with foreign Nations," a more extensive constitutional inquiry is required.

When a State seeks to tax the instrumentalities of foreign commerce, two additional considerations, beyond those articulated in *Complete Auto*, come into play. The first is the enhanced risk of multiple taxation. It is a commonplace of constitutional jurisprudence that multiple taxation may well be offensive to the Commerce Clause. . . . In order to prevent multiple taxation of interstate commerce, this Court has required that taxes be apportioned among taxing jurisdictions, so that no instrumentality of commerce is subjected to more than one tax on its full value. The corollary of the apportionment principle, of course, is that no jurisdiction may tax the instrumentality in full. "The rule which permits taxation by two or more states on an apportionment basis precludes taxation of all of the property by the state of the domicile. . . . Otherwise there would be multiple taxation of interstate operations." Standard Oil Co. v. Peck, 342 U.S., at 384–385, 72 S.Ct. at 310; Braniff, 347 U.S., at 601, 74 S.Ct. at 764. The basis for this Court's approval of apportioned property taxation, in other words, has been its ability to enforce full apportionment by all potential taxing bodies.

Yet neither this Court nor this Nation can ensure full apportionment when one of the taxing entities is a foreign sovereign. If an instrumentality of commerce is domiciled abroad, the country of domicile may have the right, consistently with the custom of nations, to impose a tax on its full value.[11] If a State should seek to tax the same instrumentality on an apportioned basis, multiple taxation inevitably results. Hence, whereas the fact of apportionment in interstate commerce means that "multiple burdens logically cannot occur," Washington Revenue Dept., 435 U.S., at 746–747, 98 S.Ct. at 1397–98, the same conclusion, as to foreign commerce, logically cannot be drawn. Due to the absence of an authoritative tribunal

---

10. Appellants' containers entered the United States pursuant to the Customs Convention on Containers, which grants containers "temporary admission free of import duties and import taxes and free of import prohibitions and restrictions," provided they are used solely in foreign commerce and are subject to re-exportation. 20 U.S.T., at 304. Similarly, 19 CFR § 10.41a(a)(3) (1978) designates containers "instruments of international traffic," with the result that they "may be released without entry or the payment of duty" under 19 U.S.C. § 1322(a). See 19 CFR § 10.41a(a)(1) (1978). A bilateral tax Convention between Japan and the United States associates containers with the vehicles that carry them, and provides that income "derived by a resident of a Contracting State . . . from the use, maintenance, and lease of containers and related equipment . . . in connection with the operation in international traffic of ships or aircraft . . . is exempt from tax in the other Contracting State." Convention Between the United States of America and Japan for the Avoidance of Double Taxation, Mar. 8, 1971, [1972] 23 U.S.T. 967, 1084–1085, T.I.A.S. No. 7365.

11. Ocean-going vessels, for example, are generally taxed only in their nation of registry; this fact in part explains the phenomenon of "flags of convenience" (a term deemed derogatory in some quarters), whereby vessels are registered under the flags of countries that permit the operation of ships "at a nominal level of taxation." See B. Boczek, Flags of Convenience 5, 56–57 (1962). Aircraft engaged in international traffic, apparently, are likewise "subject to taxation on an unapportioned basis by their country of origin." Note, 11 Stan.L.Rev., at 519, and n. 11. See, e.g., SAS, 56 Cal.3d, at 17, and n. 3, 14 Cal.Rptr., at 28, 363 P.2d, at 28, and n. 3.

capable of ensuring that the aggregation of taxes is computed on no more than one full value, a state tax, even though "fairly apportioned" to reflect an instrumentality's presence within the State, may subject foreign commerce " 'to the risk of a double tax burden to which [domestic] commerce is not exposed, and which the commerce clause forbids.' " Evco v. Jones, 409 U.S., at 94, 93 S.Ct. at 351, quoting J.D. Adams Mfg. Co., 304 U.S., at 311, 58 S.Ct. at 915.

Second, a state tax on the instrumentalities of foreign commerce may impair federal uniformity in an area where federal uniformity is essential. Foreign commerce is pre-eminently a matter of national concern. "In international relations and with respect to foreign intercourse and trade the people of the United States act through a single government with unified and adequate national power." Board of Trustees v. United States, 289 U.S. 48, 59, 53 S.Ct. 509, 510 (1933). Although the Constitution, Art. I, § 8, cl. 3, grants Congress power to regulate commerce "with foreign Nations" and "among the several States" in parallel phrases, there is evidence that the Founders intended the scope of the foreign commerce power to be the greater. Cases of this Court, stressing the need for uniformity in treating with other nations, echo this distinction. In approving state taxes on the instrumentalities of interstate commerce, the Court consistently has distinguished ocean-going traffic * * * [T]hese cases reflect an awareness that the taxation of foreign commerce may necessitate a uniform national rule. Indeed, in Pullmans Palace, supra, the Court wrote that the " 'vehicles of commerce by water being instruments of intercommunication with other nations, the regulation of them is assumed by the national legislature.' " 141 U.S., at 24, 11 S.Ct. at 878, quoting Railroad Co. v. Maryland, 21 Wall. 456, 470 (1874). Finally, in discussing the Import–Export Clause, this Court, in Michelin Tire Corp. v. Wages, 423 U.S. 276, 285, 96 S.Ct. 535, 540 (1976), spoke of the Framers' overriding concern that "the Federal Government must speak with one voice when regulating commercial relations with foreign governments." The need for federal uniformity is no less paramount in ascertaining the negative implications of Congress' power to "regulate Commerce with foreign Nations" under the Commerce Clause.

A state tax on instrumentalities of foreign commerce may frustrate the achievement of federal uniformity in several ways. If the State imposes an apportioned tax, international disputes over reconciling apportionment formulae may arise. If a novel state tax creates an asymmetry in the international tax structure, foreign nations disadvantaged by the levy may retaliate against American-owned instrumentalities present in their jurisdictions. Such retaliation of necessity would be directed at American transportation equipment in general, not just that of the taxing State, so that the Nation as a whole would suffer. If other States followed the taxing State's example, various instrumentalities of commerce could be subjected to varying degrees of multiple taxation, a result that would plainly prevent this Nation from "speaking with one voice" in regulating foreign commerce.

For these reasons, we believe that an inquiry more elaborate than that mandated by *Complete Auto* is necessary when a State seeks to tax the instrumentalities of foreign, rather than of interstate, commerce. In addition to answering the nexus, apportionment, and nondiscrimination questions posed in *Complete Auto,* a court must also inquire, first, whether the tax, notwithstanding apportionment, creates a substantial risk of international multiple taxation, and, second, whether the tax prevents the Federal Government from "speaking with one voice when regulating commercial relations with foreign governments." If a state tax contravenes either of these precepts, it is unconstitutional under the Commerce Clause.

C

Analysis of California's tax under these principles dictates that the tax, as applied to appellants' containers, is impermissible. Assuming, *arguendo,* that the tax passes muster under *Complete Auto,* it cannot withstand scrutiny under either of the additional tests that a tax on foreign commerce must satisfy.

First, California's tax results in multiple taxation of the instrumentalities of foreign commerce. By stipulation, appellants' containers are owned, based, and registered in Japan; they are used exclusively in international commerce; and they remain outside Japan only so long as needed to complete their international missions. Under these circumstances, Japan has the right and the power to tax the containers in full. California's tax, however, creates more than the *risk* of multiple taxation; it produces multiple taxation in fact. Appellants' containers not only "are subject to property tax ... in Japan," App. 32, but, as the trial court found, they "are, in fact, taxed in Japan." Id., at 35. Thus, if appellees' levies were sustained, appellants "would be paying a double tax." Id., at 23.[17]

Second, California's tax prevents this Nation from "speaking with one voice" in regulating foreign trade. The desirability of uniform treatment

---

17. The stipulation of facts, App. 32, like the trial court's finding, id., at 35, states that "[a]ll containers of [appellants] are subject to property tax and are, in fact, taxed in Japan." The record does not further elaborate on the nature of Japan's property tax. Appellants have uniformly insisted, Brief 9, Tr. of Oral Arg. 3, that Japan's property tax is unapportioned, i.e., that it is imposed on the containers' full value, and we so understand the trial court's finding. Although appellees do not seriously challenge this understanding, Brief 10–11, and n. 2, amicus curiae Multistate Tax Commission suggests that the record is inadequate to establish double taxation in fact: Japan, amicus says, may offer "credits ... for taxes paid elsewhere." Brief 8. Amicus provides no evidence to support this theory. Both the Solicitor General, Brief for United States as Amicus Curiae 19 n. 9, and the Department of State, id., at 17a, assure us that Japan taxes appellants' containers at their "full value," and we accept this interpretation of the trial court's factual finding.

Because California's tax in this case creates multiple taxation in fact, we have no occasion here to decide under what circumstances the mere *risk* of multiple taxation would invalidate a state tax, or whether this risk would be evaluated differently in foreign, as opposed to interstate, commerce. Compare Moorman Mfg. Co. v. Bair, 437 U.S. 267, 276–277, 98 S.Ct. 2340, 2346 (1978), and Washington Revenue Dept., 435 U.S., at 746, 98 S.Ct. at 1397, with e.g., Central R. Co., 370 U.S., at 615, 82 S.Ct. at 1303; Ott, 336 U.S., at 175, 69 S.Ct., at 435; and Northwest Airlines, 322 U.S., at 326, 64 S.Ct. at 967 (Stone, C.J., dissenting).

of containers used exclusively in foreign commerce is evidenced by the Customs Convention on Containers, which the United States and Japan have signed. See n. 10, supra. Under this Convention, containers temporarily imported are admitted free of "all duties and taxes whatsoever chargeable by reason of importation," 20 U.S.T., at 304. The Convention reflects a national policy to remove impediments to the use of containers as "instruments of international traffic." 19 U.S.C. § 1322(a). California's tax, however, will frustrate attainment of federal uniformity. It is stipulated that American-owned containers are not taxed in Japan. App. 35. California's tax thus creates an asymmetry in international maritime taxation operating to Japan's disadvantage. The risk of retaliation by Japan, under these circumstances, is acute, and such retaliation of necessity would be felt by the Nation as a whole.[18] If other States follow California's example (Oregon already has done so), foreign-owned containers will be subjected to various degrees of multiple taxation, depending on which American ports they enter. This result, obviously, would make "speaking with one voice" impossible. California, by its unilateral act, cannot be permitted to place these impediments before this Nation's conduct of its foreign relations and its foreign trade.

Because California's ad valorem tax, as applied to appellants' containers, results in multiple taxation of the instrumentalities of foreign commerce, and because it prevents the Federal Government from "speaking with one voice" in international trade, the tax is inconsistent with Congress' power to "regulate Commerce with foreign Nations." We hold the tax, as applied, unconstitutional under the Commerce Clause.

D

Appellees proffer several objections to this holding. They contend, first, that any multiple taxation in this case is attributable, not to California, but to Japan. California, they say, is just trying to take its share; it should not be foreclosed by Japan's election to tax the containers in full. California's tax, however, must be evaluated in the realistic framework of the custom of nations. Japan has the right and the power to tax appellants' containers at their full value; nothing could prevent it from doing so. Appellees' argument may have force in the interstate commerce context. Cf. Moorman Mfg. Co. v. Bair, 437 U.S. 267, 277, and n. 12, 98 S.Ct. 2340, 2346 (1978). In interstate commerce, if the domiciliary State is "to blame" for exacting an excessive tax, this Court is able to insist upon rationalization of the apportionment. As noted above, however, this Court is powerless to correct malapportionment of taxes imposed from abroad in foreign commerce.

---

18. Retaliation by some nations could be automatic. West Germany's wealth tax statute, for example, provides an exemption for foreign-owned instrumentalities of commerce, but only if the owner's country grants a reciprocal exemption for German-owned instrumentalities. Vermögensteuergesetz (VStG) § 2, ¶ 3, reprinted in I Bundesgesetzblatt (BGBl) 949 (Apr. 23, 1974). The European Economic Community (EEC), when apprised of California's tax on foreign-owned containers, apparently determined to consider "suitable counter-measures." Press Release, 521st Council Meeting—Transport (Luxembourg, June 12, 1978), p. 21.

Appellees contend, secondly, that any multiple taxation created by California's tax can be cured by congressional action or by international agreement. We find no merit in this contention. The premise of appellees' argument is that a State is free to impose demonstrable burdens on commerce, so long as Congress has not preempted the field by affirmative regulation. But it long has been "accepted constitutional doctrine that the commerce clause, without the aid of Congressional legislation ... affords some protection from state legislation inimical to the national commerce, and that in such cases, where Congress has not acted, this Court, and not the state legislature, is under the commerce clause the final arbiter of the competing demands of state and national interests." Southern Pacific Co. v. Arizona, 325 U.S. 761, 769, 65 S.Ct. 1515, 1520 (1945). Appellees' argument, moreover, defeats, rather than supports, the cause it aims to promote. For to say that California has created a problem susceptible only of congressional—indeed, only of international—solution is to concede that the taxation of foreign-owned containers is an area where a uniform federal rule is essential. California may not tell this Nation or Japan how to run their foreign policies.

Third, appellees argue that, even if California's tax results in multiple taxation, that fact, after *Moorman* is insufficient to condemn a state tax under the Commerce Clause. In *Moorman,* the Court refused to invalidate Iowa's single-factor income tax apportionment formula, even though it posed a credible threat of overlapping taxation because of the use of three-factor formulae by other States. See also the several opinions in *Moorman* in dissent. 437 U.S., at 281, 282, and 283, 98 S.Ct. at 2348–2349. That case, however, is quite different from this one. In *Moorman,* the existence of multiple taxation, on the record then before the Court, was "speculative," id., at 276, 98 S.Ct. at 2346; on the record of the present case, multiple taxation is a fact. In *Moorman,* the problem arose, not from lack of apportionment, but from mathematical imprecision in apportionment formulae. Yet, this Court consistently had held that the Commerce Clause "does not call for mathematical exactness nor for the rigid application of a particular formula; only if the resulting valuation is palpably excessive will it be set aside." Northwest Airlines v. Minnesota, 322 U.S., at 325, 64 S.Ct. at 967 (Stone, C.J., dissenting). Accord, Moorman, 437 U.S., at 274, 98 S.Ct. at 2345 (citing cases). This case, by contrast, involves no mere mathematical imprecision in apportionment; it involves a situation where true apportionment does not exist and cannot be policed by this Court at all. *Moorman,* finally, concerned interstate commerce. This case concerns foreign commerce. Even a slight overlapping of tax—a problem that might be deemed *de minimis* in a domestic context—assumes importance when sensitive matters of foreign relations and national sovereignty are concerned.

Finally, appellees present policy arguments. If California cannot tax appellants' containers, they complain, the State will lose revenue, even though the containers plainly have a nexus with California; the State will go uncompensated for the services it undeniably renders the containers;

and, by exempting appellants' containers from tax, the State in effect will be forced to discriminate against domestic, in favor of foreign, commerce. These arguments are not without weight, and, to the extent appellees cannot recoup the value of their services through user fees, they may indeed be disadvantaged by our decision today. These arguments, however, are directed to the wrong forum. "Whatever subjects of this [the commercial] power are in their nature national, or admit only of one uniform system, or plan of regulation, may justly be said to be of such a nature as to require exclusive legislation by Congress." Cooley v. Board of Wardens, 12 How. 299, 319, 53 U.S. 299 (1851). The problems to which appellees refer are problems that admit only of a federal remedy. They do not admit of a unilateral solution by a State.

The judgment of the Supreme Court of California is reversed.

It is so ordered.

Substantially for the reasons set forth by JUSTICE MANUEL in his opinion for the unanimous Supreme Court of California, MR. JUSTICE REHNQUIST is of the opinion that the judgment of that court should be affirmed.

NOTES AND QUESTIONS

A. What are the implications of *Japan Line* for other taxes affecting foreign commerce? In Itel Containers International Corp. v. Huddleston, 507 U.S. 60, 113 S.Ct. 1095 (1993), the Court sustained a sales tax on the proceeds from a domestic company's lease of cargo containers for use exclusively in international commerce. The Court found that the tax was not preempted by federal law and did not violate either the Foreign Commerce Clause or the Import–Export Clause. The tax satisfied the standard four-prong inquiry under *Complete Auto,* because it was a nondiscriminatory sales tax applied to transactions occurring within Tennessee. It likewise satisfied the two additional prongs of the Court's Foreign Commerce Clause standard articulated in *Japan Line.* The tax did not create a substantial risk of multiple taxation implicating foreign commerce concerns because Tennessee was taxing a discrete transaction occurring within the state. Moreover, Tennessee granted a credit for taxes paid to other jurisdictions. Nor did the tax prevent the Federal Government from "speaking with one voice," since it did not offend federal policy regarding taxation of cargo containers.

The Court distinguished *Japan Line* on two grounds. First, in contrast to *Japan Line,* other nations had chosen not to tax leases of cargo containers, so there was no actual multiple taxation. Second, the Court declared that

> the foreign commerce clause cannot be interpreted to demand that a state refrain from taxing any business transaction that is also potentially subject to taxation by a foreign sovereign. "*Japan Line* does not require forbearance so extreme or so one-sided."

Id., 507 U.S. at 74 (quoting Container Corp. of America v. Franchise Tax Bd., 463 U.S. 159, 193, 103 S.Ct. 2933 (1983)).

In the context of state taxation of income from foreign commerce, the Court has limited the force of *Japan Line.* See Barclays Bank PLC v. Franchise Tax Bd., 512 U.S. 298, 114 S.Ct. 2268 (1994), discussed at pp. 518–20 infra, and Container Corp. of America v. Franchise Tax Bd., supra, set out at pp. 496–517 infra, in which the Court upheld worldwide combined apportionment of corporate income despite evidence of multiple taxation; see also Mobil Oil Corp. v. Commissioner of Taxes, 445 U.S. 425, 100 S.Ct. 1223 (1980), set out at pp. 473–89 infra, in which the Court upheld state taxation of foreign source dividends. In the *Container* case, the Court distinguished *Japan Line* on the grounds, inter alia, that it involved a property tax, instrumentalities of foreign commerce, and actual—not merely potential—multiple taxation that it found could be remedied only by an apportionment approach. In both *Container* and *Mobil Oil,* the taxpayers also challenged the assessments as frustrating federal income tax policy, but the Court found no such conflict. In other cases that potentially raised the question whether the state tax at issue was barred by the negative implications of the Foreign Commerce Clause, the Court found either that Congress had consented to the tax at issue, see Wardair Canada, Inc. v. Florida Department of Revenue, 477 U.S. 1, 106 S.Ct. 2369 (1986), or that Congress had preempted it. See Xerox Corp. v. County of Harris, 459 U.S. 145, 103 S.Ct. 523 (1982).

B.   *The Theoretical Underpinning of* Japan Line's *Multiple Taxation Argument.* Was the Court on sound ground in suggesting that the problem of overlapping taxes by Japan and California constituted a constitutionally cognizable case of international "multiple taxation"? If the United States imposed property taxes (which it does not by virtue of U.S. Const. art. I, § 9, cl. 4, forbidding the imposition of "direct" taxes unless laid in proportion to the population), would the imposition of a tax by the United States and California be regarded as "multiple taxation"? Or might it more properly be characterized as "concurrent taxation," i.e. simultaneous taxation by two different sovereigns with jurisdiction over the same property? If so, why does such taxation become "multiple taxation" when one of the sovereigns happens to be foreign rather than domestic?

C.   *Discrimination in Favor of Domestic Over Foreign Dividends.* In Kraft General Foods, Inc. v. Iowa Department of Revenue, 505 U.S. 71, 112 S.Ct. 2365 (1992), the U.S. Supreme Court held that Iowa's corporate income tax unconstitutionally discriminated against foreign commerce because it included dividends from foreign subsidiaries, but not from domestic (U.S.) subsidiaries, in a taxpayer's apportionable tax base. Although there was a rational legislative purpose behind Iowa's discrimination,[mm] which was based on Iowa's conformity to the federal corporate income tax scheme, the Court held that "[t]he Iowa statute cannot withstand * * * scrutiny, for it facially

---

mm. Under the federal corporate income tax, there is a deduction for dividends received from domestic subsidiaries but generally not for dividends received from foreign subsidiaries. I.R.C. §§ 243–45. The purpose of the former deduction is to avoid a second tax on the earnings of domestic corporations, all of which are subject to federal taxation. To avoid double taxation of the earnings of foreign corporations, which are not generally subject to federal taxation, the Internal Revenue Code provides for a credit against foreign taxes paid on such earnings that are also subject to federal taxation, including taxes paid on earnings that are repatriated in the form of dividends. I.R.C. §§ 901, 902.

discriminates against foreign commerce and therefore violates the Foreign Commerce Clause." Id., 505 U.S. at 82.

In so concluding, the Court made it clear that discrimination against foreign, as compared to interstate, commerce is no more tolerable under the Commerce Clause than is discrimination against interstate commerce in favor of local commerce. Iowa sought to defend the discrimination on the ground, among others, that its tax did not favor Iowa commerce over interstate commerce. While agreeing with Iowa that there was no preference for local commerce, the Court found that the state's discrimination against foreign commerce in favor of domestic (U.S.) commerce, could not pass muster:

> We think that a State's preference for domestic commerce over foreign commerce is inconsistent with the Commerce Clause even if the State's own economy is not a beneficiary of the discrimination. As the absence of local benefit does not eliminate the international implications of the discrimination, it cannot exempt such discrimination from Commerce Clause prohibitions.

Id. at 79.

D. *Preferential Treatment of Foreign Vis-a-Vis Interstate Commerce.* Do the states discriminate against interstate commerce in violation of the Commerce Clause by providing preferential treatment to foreign as compared to interstate commerce? The California Court of Appeal held that the grant of a property tax exemption for goods imported from abroad but not for goods shipped from other states violated the Commerce Clause because it gave goods of foreign origin a competitive advantage over goods manufactured in other states. Sears Roebuck & Co. v. County of Los Angeles and Zee Toys, Inc. v. County of Los Angeles (consolidated cases), 85 Cal.App.3d 763, 149 Cal.Rptr. 750 (2d Dist.1978). The court declared that the levy violated the Commerce Clause because "state taxes which discriminate between classes of interstate and foreign goods on the basis of their origin are not permitted." Id., 149 Cal.Rptr. at 758. The U.S. Supreme Court affirmed the California court's decision without opinion by an equally divided Court. Sears, Roebuck & Co. v. County of Los Angeles, 449 U.S. 1119, 101 S.Ct. 933 (1981). The U.S. Solicitor General had filed an amicus brief supporting the constitutionality of the exemption. The California Supreme Court has subsequently reaffirmed the view that the exemption for foreign but not for interstate imports is unconstitutional. Star–Kist Foods, Inc. v. County of Los Angeles, 42 Cal.3d 1, 719 P.2d 987, 227 Cal.Rptr. 391 (1986), cert. denied, 480 U.S. 930, 107 S.Ct. 1565 (1987).

D. THE ROLE OF CONGRESS IN REGULATING INTERSTATE/FOREIGN COMMERCE

In 1959 Congress for the first time in our history enacted legislation restricting the powers of the states to tax interstate businesses. For more than 100 years the great Commerce Clause controversies had been fought out largely in the courts, with little aid from Congress. Although Congress possessed the constitutional power and legislative resources adequate to cope with the major conflicts, it failed to take the required action. The role that Congress neglected to perform was assumed by the Supreme Court, employing as its principal instruments the Commerce Clause and the Due Process Clause.

The Inadequacy of Judicial Solutions to the Interstate Commerce Tax Problem. Because the Court has only the restricted function of invalidating state action by fixing the "outside limits of decency" (Thomas R. Powell, "Indirect Encroachment on Federal Authority by the Taxing Powers of the States," 32 Harv.L.Rev. 634, 670 (1919)), some observers (including a number of Justices) have maintained that the Court is incapable of reconciling the competing interests involved in a satisfactory manner. They argue that more refined and flexible methods are required. Thus, in McCarroll v. Dixie Greyhound Lines, 309 U.S. 176, 60 S.Ct. 504 (1940), Justices Black, Frankfurter, and Douglas wrote a dissenting opinion in which they said:

> Judicial control of national commerce—unlike legislative regulations—must from inherent limitations of the judicial process treat the subject by the hit-and-miss method of deciding single local controversies upon evidence and information limited by the narrow rules of litigation. Spasmodic and unrelated instances of litigation cannot afford an adequate basis for the creation of integrated national rules which alone can afford that full protection for interstate commerce intended by the Constitution. We would, therefore, leave the questions raised by the Arkansas tax for consideration of Congress in a nationwide survey of the constantly increasing barriers to trade among the States. Unconfined by "the narrow scope of judicial proceedings" Congress alone can, in the exercise of its plenary constitutional control over interstate commerce, not only consider whether such a tax as now under scrutiny is consistent with the best interests of our national economy, but can also on the basis of full exploration of the many aspects of a complicated problem devise a national policy fair alike to the States and our Union.

Id., 309 U.S. at 188–89.

In Northwestern States Portland Cement Co. v. Minnesota, 358 U.S. 450, 79 S.Ct. 357 (1959), Justice Frankfurter declared in a dissenting opinion:

> Congress alone can provide for a full and thorough canvassing of the multitudinous and intricate factors which compose the problem of the taxing freedom of the States and the needed limits on such state taxing power.

Id., 358 U.S. at 476. The Court expressed similar sentiments in Commonwealth Edison Co. v. Montana, 453 U.S. 609, 101 S.Ct. 2946 (1981), pp. 163–74 supra, and in Moorman Manufacturing Co. v. Bair, 437 U.S. 267, 98 S.Ct. 2340 (1978), pp. 457–69 infra.

Cooperation Among the States. Cooperative action among the states affords another means of alleviating some of the problems in the field of taxation of national businesses. Through the work of the Federation of Tax Administrators, the Multistate Tax Commission, the National Tax Association, the National Conference of Commissioners on Uniform State Laws (NCCUSL), and, most recently, the Streamlined Sales Tax Project, some progress has been made in addressing the problems created by state taxation of interstate commerce. We will consider the most significant piece of uniform state legislation in the state tax field—the Uniform of Division of Income for Tax Purposes Act—in Chapter 7, which addresses questions of apportionment.

1. THE POWER OF CONGRESS TO REGULATE STATE TAXING AUTHORITY

NOTES AND QUESTIONS

A. *The Power of Congress to Broaden and Restrict State Taxing Authority Under the Commerce Clause.* If Congress were to legislate broadly with respect to state taxation of interstate business in an effort to reconcile the competing interests, many believe that Congress would need both to *restrict* and to *broaden* state taxing powers. Congress might in effect give the following mandate to the states, regarding taxes on or measured by net income, gross receipts, capital stock, or any other base:

> You may tax all interstate businesses that touch your borders or that derive income from your state, whether or not the Commerce Clause up to now prevented such taxation, provided you tax local businesses on the same basis and utilize congressionally approved uniform apportionment and allocation formulas or methods. Likewise, you are prohibited from taxing any business that engages in interstate commerce to any extent, even though it is now clearly subject to your taxing power, unless you apply the congressionally approved uniform formulas or methods.

Similarly, Congress might say to the states:

> You may require an Internet or mail-order seller to collect use taxes on products sold to in-state consumers, even though you may not currently impose such a requirement on an out-of-state vendor without physical presence in your state, but only if you radically simplify your sales and use tax system, in accordance with federally prescribed criteria, to permit the out-of-state vendor to comply with your laws at reasonable administrative costs.

Cf. Mobile Telecommunications Sourcing Act, 4 U.S.C. § 116 et seq. (authorizing states to tax charges for mobile telecommunications services), discussed in Section B(5), Note D, p. 186 supra.

Decisions of the U.S. Supreme Court firmly establish not only Congress's authority to restrict state taxing powers under the Commerce Clause, but also its authority to lift the barriers that the dormant Commerce Clause imposes on state tax powers in the absence of congressional legislation. In Prudential

Insurance Co. v. Benjamin, 328 U.S. 408, 66 S.Ct. 1142 (1946), for example, the Court declared:

> The power of Congress over commerce exercised entirely without reference to coordinated actions of the states is not restricted, except as the Constitution expressly provides, by any limitation which forbids it to discriminate against interstate commerce and in favor of local trade. Its plenary scope enables Congress not only to promote but also to prohibit interstate commerce, as it has done frequently and for a great variety of reasons. That power does not run down a one-way street or one of narrowly fixed dimensions. Congress may keep the way open, confine it broadly or closely, or close it entirely, subject only to the restrictions placed upon its authority by other constitutional provisions and the requirement that it shall not invade the domains of action reserved exclusively for the states.

Id., 328 U.S. at 434. In *Prudential*, the Court sustained a South Carolina insurance premiums tax imposed solely on foreign insurance companies—a levy that clearly would have been struck down under the Commerce Clause if Congress had not consented to such legislation in the McCarran–Ferguson Act. See also Western & Southern Life Ins. Co. v. State Bd. of Equalization, 451 U.S. 648, 101 S.Ct. 2070 (1981) ("McCarran–Ferguson Act removes entirely any Commerce Clause restriction upon California's power to tax the insurance business"); Chapter 4, pp. 261–75 infra. Does Congress possess the power under the Commerce Clause to remove the restraints that the Due Process Clause imposes on the exercise of state taxing authority? See William Cohen, "Congressional Power to Validate Unconstitutional State Laws: A Forgotten Solution to an Old Enigma," 35 Stan. L. Rev. 387 (1983).

B. *Possible Limitations on the Congressional Power to Restrict State Taxation of Interstate Commerce.* As the Court's statement in *Prudential* suggests, Congress' power to regulate interstate commerce—including state taxation of interstate commerce—appeared for many years to be "plenary." In National League of Cities v. Usery, 426 U.S. 833, 96 S.Ct. 2465 (1976), however, the Court held that Congress had exceeded its power under the Commerce Clause by amending the Fair Labor Standards Act to extend its minimum wage and maximum hours requirements to almost all state and local government employees. The Court held that "there are limits upon the power of Congress to override state sovereignty, even when exercising its otherwise plenary powers to tax or regulate commerce * * *." Id., 426 U.S. at 833. The Court rested its decision on the Tenth Amendment, which, in the Court's eyes, "expressly declares the constitutional policy that Congress may not exercise power in a fashion that impairs the State's integrity or their ability to function effectively in a federal system." Id.

The reign of *National League of Cities* was short-lived. In 1985, the Court overruled the decision in Garcia v. San Antonio Metropolitan Transit Authority, 469 U.S. 528, 105 S.Ct. 1005 (1985). Justice Blackmun, speaking for the Court's five-to-four majority, repudiated the earlier case on both doctrinal and practical grounds, and sustained the application of the Fair Labor Standards Act to employees of San Antonio's public transportation system. Largely adopting the views of the dissenters in *National League of Cities*, the Court concluded that the states' continued role in the federal system is primarily guaranteed not by any externally imposed limits on the commerce power, but by "the structure of the Federal Government itself." Id., 469 U.S. at 556. It is through their control over and representation in the Federal Government that the states are protected from overreaching by Congress. Moreover, the Court found it "difficult, if not impossible" to draw the boundaries of state immunity by reference to "integral operations of areas of traditional governmental functions" described by *National League of Cities.* Id. at 539. The Court therefore rejected "as unsound in principle and unworkable in practice, a rule of state immunity from federal regulation that turns on a judicial appraisal of whether a particular governmental function is 'integral' or 'traditional.' " Id. at 546–47.

Despite the overruling of *National League of Cities,* some of the Court's more recent decisions have taken a narrower view of Congress's power under the Commerce Clause than the view reflected in its earlier decisions. Compare, e.g., Perez v. United States, 402 U.S. 146, 91 S.Ct. 1357 (1971) (Congress possesses power under the Commerce Clause to regulate local criminal activity); Heart of Atlanta Motel v. United States, 379 U.S. 241, 85 S.Ct. 348 (1964) (Congress possesses power under the Commerce Clause to regulate discriminatory practices in local restaurants); Wickard v. Filburn, 317 U.S. 111, 63 S.Ct. 82 (1942) (Congress possesses power under the Commerce Clause to regulate the amount of wheat a farmer grows for his own consumption) with United States v. Morrison, 529 U.S. 598, 120 S.Ct. 1740 (2000) (Congress lacks the power under the Commerce Clause to provide a civil remedy for victims of gender-motivated violence); Printz v. United States, 521 U.S. 898, 117 S.Ct. 2365 (1997) (Congress lacks the power under the Commerce Clause to require state officials to conduct background checks on prospective gun purchasers under the Brady Handgun Violence Prevention Act); United States v. Lopez, 514 U.S. 549, 115 S.Ct. 1624 (1995) (Congress lacks the power under the Commerce Clause to prohibit possession of firearms in school zones because possess of a gun in a local school zone does not affect interstate commerce). But these decisions do not seriously inhibit the broad power that Congress plainly possesses to deal with virtually any of the significant contemporary problems raised by state taxation of interstate commerce. These include such matters as prescribing uniform division of income tax rules, Moorman Manufacturing Co. v. Bair, 437 U.S. 267, 280, 98 S.Ct. 2340 (1978) ("It is clear that the legislative power granted by the Commerce Clause of the Constitution to Congress would amply justify the enactment of legislation requiring all States to adhere to uniform rules for the division of income"); empowering the states to collect use taxes on mail-order sales, Quill Corp. v. North Dakota, 504 U.S. 298, 318, 112 S.Ct. 1904 (1992) ("Congress is * * * free to decide whether, when, and to what extent the States may burden interstate mail-order concerns with a duty to collect use taxes"); and limiting the states' power to tax transactions over the Internet. Internet Tax Freedom Act, Pub. L. No. 105–277, Div. C, Title XI, § 1104(3), 112 Stat. 2681 (1998). See generally Walter Hellerstein, "Federal Constitutional Limitations on State Taxation to Legislate Regarding State Taxation of Electronic Commerce," 53 Nat'l Tax J. 1307 (2000).

2. STATE TAXES THAT CONFLICT WITH OR FRUSTRATE FEDERAL POLICY

Under the Supremacy Clause of the Constitution, a valid exercise of congressional power preempts any conflicting state legislation. U.S. Const. art. VI. Consequently, state taxes affecting interstate or foreign commerce that conflict with federal legislation, enacted pursuant to Congress' power to regulate commerce, are invalid. In Aloha Airlines, Inc. v. Director of Taxation, 464 U.S. 7, 104 S.Ct. 291 (1983), for example, the Supreme Court struck down a Hawaii tax on the gross income of airlines because it conflicted with congressional legislation prohibiting any state taxes on "the gross receipts from * * * air commerce or transportation." 49 U.S.C. § 40116(b). See also Exxon Corp. v. Hunt, 475 U.S. 355, 106 S.Ct. 1103 (1986) (express language of federal "Superfund" legislation designed to provide relief for specified environmental costs partially preempts a New Jersey tax designed to fund the state's Spill Compensation and Control Act).

The Supremacy Clause extends beyond taxes that Congress expressly prohibits or that directly conflict with congressional legislation. State taxes that frustrate the purposes and objectives of federal legislation likewise violate the Supremacy Clause. In McGoldrick v. Gulf Oil Corp., 309 U.S. 414, 60 S.Ct. 664 (1940), the taxpayer attacked a New York City sales tax imposed on sales of fuel oil made by the company to the owners of vessels engaged in foreign commerce. Gulf imported crude oil from Venezuela and entered it with the U.S. Customs Service under bond. The federal statute authorized the importation of crude oil duty free, if the oil was placed under bond in the importer's warehouse for export or for manufacture by the importer for sale as ships' stores to vessels engaged in foreign commerce. Gulf fell within the federal exemption from import duty because it manufactured the fuel oil for sale as ships' stores to foreign oceangoing vessels. Gulf challenged the New York City tax on those sales as conflicting with federal policy. The Court agreed, and invalidated the tax, saying:

> As we have seen, the exemption and drawback provisions were designed, among other purposes, to relieve the importer of the import tax so that he might meet foreign competition in the sale of fuel as ships' stores. * * * It is evident that the purpose of the Congressional regulation of the commerce would fail if the state were free at any stage of the transaction to impose a tax which would lessen the competitive advantage conferred on the importer by Congress, and which might equal or exceed the remitted import duty. * * * The Congressional regulation, read in the light of its purpose, is tantamount to a declaration that in order to accomplish constitutionally permissible ends, the imported merchandise shall not become a part of the common mass of taxable property within the state, pending its disposition as ships' stores and shall not become subject to the state

taxing power. * * * The state tax in the circumstances must fail as an infringement of the Congressional regulation of the commerce.

Id., 309 U.S. at 428–29. See also Xerox Corp. v. County of Harris, 459 U.S. 145, 103 S.Ct. 523 (1982) (applying *Gulf Oil* case to invalidate a property tax on copying machines held in a bonded warehouse in Texas).

The Court has also held that congressional legislation preempted state taxes that sought to control the manner in which the economic burden of a tax on natural gas was distributed. In Maryland v. Louisiana, 451 U.S. 725, 101 S.Ct. 2114 (1981), the Louisiana legislature had sought to ensure that the economic burden of the state's first-use tax on natural gas would fall on the owners of natural gas, or their customers, by providing that the "tax shall be deemed a cost associated with uses made by the owner in preparation of marketing of the natural gas." Former La. Rev. Stat. Ann. § 47:1303(C). Agreements to the contrary were declared to be against public policy. In substance, the legislation prohibited the statutory "owners" of natural gas, who were generally pipeline companies, from passing back the burden of the first-use tax to producers, and compelled the pipelines either to absorb the burden of the tax themselves or to pass it on to their customers, who would ordinarily be out-of-state consumers.

The Supreme Court held that these provisions of the Louisiana statute were preempted by the Federal Natural Gas Act. That act was designed "to assure that consumers of natural gas receive a fair price and also to protect against the economic power of the interstate pipelines." Maryland v. Louisiana, 451 U.S. at 747–48. The Court concluded:

> The effect of [these provisions] is to interfere with the FERC's authority to regulate the determination of the proper allocation of costs associated with the sale of natural gas to consumers. * * * By specifying that the First–Use Tax is a processing cost to be either borne by the pipeline or other owner without compensation, an unlikely event in light of the large sums involved, or passed on to purchasers, Louisiana has attempted a substantial usurpation of the authority of the FERC by dictating to the pipelines the allocation of processing costs for the interstate shipment of natural gas.

Id. at 749–50. See also Exxon Corp. v. Eagerton, 462 U.S. 176, 103 S.Ct. 2296 (1983) (relying on Maryland v. Louisiana to strike down a provision of Alabama's oil and gas severance tax that forbade producers from passing the tax on to consumers).

Notwithstanding the foregoing decisions, the cases in which the Court has invalidated state taxes that Congress has not explicitly prohibited or that do not directly conflict with congressional action are relatively rare. The Court has generally rebuffed arguments by taxpayers that taxes are preempted because they frustrate the policy or objectives of congressional legislation. See, e.g., Barclays Bank PLC v. Franchise Tax Bd., 512 U.S. 298, 114 S.Ct. 2268 (1994) (rejecting claim that federal income tax policy favoring separate accounting for foreign subsidiaries preempts state's use of worldwide combined reporting); Wardair Canada, Inc. v. Florida Department of Revenue, 477 U.S. 1, 106 S.Ct. 2369 (1986) (rejecting claim that Congress had occupied the field of international aviation and preempted a Florida tax on the sale of airline fuel to foreign carriers); Mobil Oil Corp. v. Commissioner of Taxes, 445 U.S. 425, 100 S.Ct. 1223 (1980), set out at pp. 473–89 infra (rejecting claim that federal policy not to tax foreign source dividends preempts state taxation of such dividends); Commonwealth Edison Co. v. Montana, 453 U.S. 609, 101 S.Ct. 2946 (1981), set out at pp. 163–74 supra (rejecting claim that federal policy intended to encourage the use of low sulphur coal preempts state severance tax on such coal).

3. FEDERAL LEGISLATION RESTRICTING STATE POWER TO TAX

Although Public Law 86–272, enacted in 1959, is the most significant piece of federal legislation restricting state taxing powers under the Commerce Clause, see Chapter 2, Section D, p. 81 supra, congressional limitations affecting particular industries have also been enacted in recent years. In adopting the Railroad Revitalization and Regulatory Reform Act of 1976, 49 U.S.C. § 11501, Congress prohibited the states from taxing railroad property more heavily than other commercial and industrial property. Congress subsequently extended similar protection to motor carriers, 49 U.S.C. § 14502, and to air carriers. 49 U.S.C. § 40116. In amending the securities acts in 1975, Congress imposed limitations on the power of states to levy stock transfer taxes. See 15 U.S.C. § 78bb(d). Federal legislation also prohibits the states from imposing user charges in connection with the carriage of persons in air commerce, 49 U.S.C. § 40116; it "supersede[s] any and all State taxes insofar as they now or hereafter relate to any employee benefit plan" instituted pursuant to the Employee Retirement Income Security Act (ERISA), 29 U.S.C. § 1144(a); it prohibits the states from imposing electrical energy taxes discriminating against out-of-state purchasers, 15 U.S.C. § 391; it prohibits state and local governments from taxing flights of commercial aircraft or any activity or service aboard such aircraft unless the aircraft takes off or lands in the taxing jurisdiction, 49 U.S.C. § 40116(c); it prohibits localities from taxing providers of direct-to-home satellite services, 47 U.S.C. § 251; it limits state and local franchise fees, 47 U.S.C. § 542; it prohibits states from taxing interstate passenger transportation by motor carriers, 49 U.S.C. § 14505; it imposes specified restraints on state taxation of transactions over the Internet, Internet Tax Freedom Act, Pub. L. No. 105–277, Div. C, Title XI, § 1104(3), 112 Stat. 2681 (1998) (as amended); and it authorizes, under specified conditions, state taxation of charges for mobile telecommunications services. Mobile Telecommunications Sourcing Act, 4 U.S.C. § 116.

E.   THE IMPORT–EXPORT CLAUSE

The Import–Export Clause of the U.S. Constitution provides:

No State shall, without the Consent of the Congress, lay any Imposts or Duties on Imports or Exports, except what may be absolutely necessary for executing it's Inspection Laws: and the net Produce of all Duties and Imposts, laid by any State on Imports or Exports, shall be for the Use of the Treasury of the United States; and all such Laws shall be subject to the Revision and Controul of the Congress.

U.S. Const. art. I, § 10, cl. 2.

1.   STATE TAXATION OF IMPORTS

MICHELIN TIRE CORP. v. WAGES

Supreme Court of the United States, 1976.
423 U.S. 276, 96 S.Ct. 535.

MR. JUSTICE BRENNAN delivered the opinion of the Court.

Respondents, the Tax Commissioner and Tax Assessors of Gwinnett County, Ga., assessed ad valorem property taxes against tires and tubes imported by petitioner from France and Nova Scotia that were included on the assessment dates in an inventory maintained at its wholesale distribution warehouse in the county. Petitioner brought this action for declaratory and injunctive relief in the Superior Court of Gwinnett County, alleging that with the exception of certain passenger tubes that had been removed from the original shipping cartons,[1] the ad valorem property taxes assessed against its inventory of imported tires and tubes were prohibited by Art. I, § 10, cl. 2, of the Constitution, which provides in pertinent part that "No State shall, without the Consent of the Congress, lay any Imposts or Duties on Imports or Exports, except what may be absolutely necessary for executing its Inspection Laws. . . ." After trial, the Superior Court granted the requested declaratory and injunctive relief. On Appeal, the Supreme Court of Georgia affirmed in part and reversed in part, agreeing that the tubes in the corrugated shipping cartons were immune from ad valorem taxation, but holding that the tires had lost their status as imports and become subject to such taxation because they had been mingled with other tires imported in bulk, sorted, and arranged for sale. Wages v. Michelin Tire Corp., 233 Ga. 712, 214 S.E.2d 349 (1975). We granted petitioner's petition for certiorari, 422 U.S. 1040, 95 S.Ct. 2652 (1975). The only question presented is whether the Georgia Supreme Court was correct in holding that the tires were subject to the ad valorem

---

1. Petitioner's complaint conceded the taxability of certain passenger tubes that had been removed from the original shipping cartons. These had a value of $633.92 on the assessment date January 1, 1972, and of $664.22 on the assessment date January 1, 1973. The tax for 1972 on the tubes was $8.03 and for 1973 was $8.73.

property tax.[2] We affirm without addressing the question whether the Georgia Supreme Court was correct in holding that the tires had lost their status as imports. We hold that, in any event, Georgia's assessment of a nondiscriminatory ad valorem property tax against the imported tires is not within the constitutional prohibition against laying "any Imposts or Duties on Imports ..." and that insofar as Low v. Austin, 13 Wall. 29 (1871) is to the contrary, that decision is overruled.

I

Petitioner, a New York corporation qualified to do business in Georgia, operates as an importer and wholesale distributor in the United States of automobile and truck tires and tubes manufactured in France and Nova Scotia by Michelin Tires Ltd. The business is operated from distribution warehouses in various parts of the country. Distribution and sale of tires and tubes from the Gwinnett County warehouse is limited to the 250–300 franchised dealers with whom petitioner does all of its business in six southeastern States. Some 25% of the tires and tubes are manufactured in and imported from Nova Scotia and are brought to the United States in tractor-driven over-the-road trailers packed and sealed at the Nova Scotia factory. The remaining 75% of the imported tires and tubes are brought to the United States by sea from France and Nova Scotia in sea vans packed and sealed at the foreign factories. Sea vans are essentially over-the-road trailers from which the wheels are removed before being loaded aboard ship. Upon arrival of the ship at the United States port of entry, the vans are unloaded, the wheels are replaced, and the vans are tractor-hauled to petitioner's distribution warehouse after clearing customs upon payment of a 4% import duty.

The imported tires, each of which has its own serial number, are packed in bulk into the trailers and vans, without otherwise being packaged or bundled. They lose their identity as a unit, however, when unloaded from the trailers and vans at the distribution warehouse. When unloaded they are sorted by size and style, without segregation by place of manufacture, stacked on wooden pallets each bearing four stacks of five tires of the same size and style, and stored in pallet stacks of three pallets each. This is the only processing required or performed to ready the tires for sale and delivery to the franchised dealers.

Sales of tires and tubes from the Gwinnett County distribution warehouse to the franchised dealers average 4,000–5,000 pounds per sale. Orders are filled without regard to the shipments in which the tires and tubes arrived in the United States or the place of their manufacture. Delivery to the franchised dealers is by common carrier or customer pickup.

---

2. The respondents did not cross-petition from the affirmance of the holding of the Superior Court that the tubes in the corrugated shipping cartons were immune from the tax, and that holding is therefore not before us for review.

II

Both Georgia courts addressed the question whether, without regard to whether the imported tires had lost their character as imports, Georgia's nondiscriminatory ad valorem tax fell within the constitutional prohibition against the laying by States of "any Imposts or Duties on Imports. . . ." The Superior Court expressed strong doubts that the ad valorem tax fell within the prohibition but concluded that it was bound by this Court's decisions to the contrary. * * * [The Georgia Supreme Court likewise rested the decision on the cases.]

Low v. Austin, supra [80 U.S. (13 Wall.) 29 (1872)], is the leading decision of this Court holding that the States are prohibited by the Import–Export Clause from imposing a nondiscriminatory ad valorem property tax on imported goods until they lose their character as imports and become incorporated into the mass of property in the State. The Court there reviewed a decision of the California Supreme Court that had sustained the constitutionality of California's nondiscriminatory ad valorem tax on the ground that the Import–Export Clause only prohibited taxes upon the character of the goods as imports and therefore did not prohibit nondiscriminatory taxes upon the goods as property. See 13 Wall., at 30–31. This Court reversed on its reading of the seminal opinion construing the Import–Export Clause, Brown v. Maryland, 12 Wheat. 419 (1827), as holding that "Whilst retaining their character as imports, a tax upon them, in any shape, is within the constitutional prohibition." 13 Wall., at 34.

Scholarly analysis has been uniformly critical of Low v. Austin. It is true that Chief Justice Marshall, speaking for the Court in Brown v. Maryland, 12 Wheat., at 442, said that ". . . while [the thing imported remains] the property of the importer, in his warehouse, in the original form or package in which it was imported, a tax upon it is too plainly a duty on imports to escape the prohibition in the constitution." Commentators have uniformly agreed that Low v. Austin misread this dictum in holding that the Court in *Brown* included nondiscriminatory ad valorem property taxes among prohibited "imposts" or "duties," for the contrary conclusion is plainly to be inferred from consideration of the specific abuses which led the Framers to include the Import–Export Clause in the Constitution. See, e.g., Powell, State Taxation of Imports—When Does an Import Cease to Be an Import?, 58 Harv.L.Rev. 858 (1945); The Supreme Court, 1958 Term, 73 Harv.L.Rev. 126, 176 (1959); Early & Weitzman, A Century of Dissent: The Immunity of Goods Imported for Resale From Nondiscriminatory State Personal Property Taxes, 7 S.W.U.L.Rev. 247 (1975); Dakin, The Protective Cloak of the Export–Import Clause: Immunity for the Goods or Immunity for the Process?, 19 La.L.Rev. 747 (1959).

Our independent study persuades us that a nondiscriminatory ad valorem property tax is not the type of state exaction which the Framers of the Constitution or the Court in *Brown* had in mind as being an "impost" or "duty" and that *Low v. Austin's* reliance upon the *Brown* dictum to reach the contrary conclusion was misplaced.

III

One of the major defects of the Articles of Confederation, and a compelling reason for the calling of the Constitutional Convention of 1787, was the fact that the Articles essentially left the individual States free to burden commerce both among themselves and with foreign countries very much as they pleased. Before 1787 it was commonplace for seaboard States to derive revenue to defray the costs of state and local governments by imposing taxes on imported goods destined for customers in inland States. At the same time, there was no secure source of revenue for the central government. James Madison, in his Preface to Debates in the Convention of 1787, 3 M. Farrand, The Records of the Federal Convention of 1787, at 542 (1911), provides a graphic description of the situation:

> "The other source of dissatisfaction was the peculiar situation of some of the States, which having no convenient ports for foreign commerce, were subject to be taxed by their neighbors, thro whose ports, their commerce was carried on. New Jersey, placed between Phila. & N. York, was likened to a Cask tapped at both ends: and N. Carolina between Virga. & S. Carolina to a patient bleeding at both Arms. The Articles of Confederation provided no remedy for the complaint: which produced a strong protest on the part of N. Jersey; and never ceased to be a source of dissatisfaction & discord, until the new Constitution, superseded the old."

And further, id., at 546–547:

> "Rh. I. was the only exception to a compliance with the recommendation from Annapolis (to have a Const. Convention), well known to have been swayed by an obdurate adherence to an advantage which her position gave her of taxing her neighbors thro' their consumption of imported supplies, an advantage which it was foreseen would be taken from her by a revisal of the Articles of Confederation.

. . .

> "The same want of a general power over Commerce led to an exercise of this power separately, by the States, which not only proved abortive, but engendered rival, conflicting and angry regulations. Besides the vain attempts to supply their respective treasuries by imposts, which turned their commerce into the neighbouring ports, and to co-erce a relaxation of the British monopoly of the W. Indn. navigation, which was attempted by Virga. . . . the States having ports for foreign commerce, taxed & irritated the adjoining States, trading thro' them, as N.Y. Pena. Virga. & S–Carolina."

The Framers of the Constitution thus sought to alleviate three main concerns by committing sole power to lay imposts and duties on imports in the Federal Government, with no concurrent state power: the Federal Government must speak with one voice when regulating commercial relations with foreign governments, and tariffs, which might affect foreign relations, could not be implemented by the States consistently with that exclusive power;[4] import revenues were to be the major source of revenue of the Federal Government and should not be diverted to the States;[5] and harmony among the States might be disturbed unless seaboard States, with their crucial ports of entry, were prohibited from levying taxes on citizens of other States by taxing goods merely flowing through their ports to the inland States not situated as favorably geographically.[6]

Nothing in the history of the Import–Export Clause even remotely suggests that a nondiscriminatory ad valorem property tax which is also imposed on imported goods that are no longer in import transit was the type of exaction that was regarded as objectionable by the Framers of the Constitution. For such an exaction, unlike discriminatory state taxation against imported goods as imports, was not regarded as an impediment that severely hampered commerce or constituted a form of tribute by seaboard States to the disadvantage of the interior States.

It is obvious that such nondiscriminatory property taxation can have no impact whatsoever on the Federal Government's exclusive regulation of foreign commerce, probably the most important purpose of the clause's prohibition. By definition, such a tax does not fall on imports as such because of their place of origin. It cannot be used to create special protective tariffs or particular preferences for certain domestic goods, and it cannot be applied selectively to encourage or discourage any importation in a manner inconsistent with federal regulation.

Nor will such taxation deprive the Federal Government of the exclusive right to all revenues from imposts and duties on imports and exports, since that right by definition only extends to revenues from exactions of a particular category; if nondiscriminatory ad valorem taxation is not in that category, it deprives the Federal Government of nothing to which it is entitled. Unlike imposts and duties, which are essentially taxes on the commercial privilege of bringing goods into a country, such property taxes are taxes by which a State apportions the cost of such services as police and fire protection among the beneficiaries according to their respective wealth; there is no reason why an importer should not bear his share of these costs along with his competitors handling only domestic goods. The Import–Export Clause clearly prohibits state taxation based on the foreign origin of the imported goods, but it cannot be read to accord imported

---

4. See, e.g., Brown v. Maryland, 12 Wheat. 419, 439 (1827); Cook v. Pennsylvania, 7 Otto 566, 574 (1878); Youngstown Sheet & Tube Co. v. Bowers, 358 U.S. 534, 555–556, 79 S.Ct. 383 (1959) (Frankfurter, J., dissenting); Federalist Nos. 11 (Hamilton), 12 (Hamilton), 42 (Madison), 44 (Madison); 2 M. Farrand, The Records of the Constitutional Convention of 1787, at 135, 157–158, 169 (1911) (notes of Committee of Detail); id., at 441; 3 id., at 520–521 (letter of James Madison to Professor Davis); 3 id., at 547–548.

5. See, e.g., Brown v. Maryland, 12 Wheat. 419, 439 (1827); Youngstown Sheet & Tube Co. v. Bowers, 358 U.S. 534, 556, 79 S.Ct. 383 (1959) (Frankfurter, J., dissenting); Federalist No. 12.

6. See, e.g., Brown v. Maryland, 12 Wheat. 419, 440 (1827); Cook v. Pennsylvania, 7 Otto 566, 574 (1878); Youngstown Sheet & Tube Co. v. Bowers, 358 U.S. 534, 545, 79 S.Ct. 383 (1959); id., at 556–557, 79 S.Ct. 383 (Frankfurter, J., dissenting); 2 M. Farrand, The Records of the Constitutional Convention of 1787, at 441–442, 589 (1911); 3 id., at 519 (letter of James Madison to Professor Davis).

goods preferential treatment that permits escape from uniform taxes imposed without regard to foreign origin for services which the State supplies. See, e.g., May v. New Orleans, 178 U.S. 496, 20 S.Ct. 976 (1900). It may be that such taxation could diminish federal impost revenues to the extent its economic burden may discourage purchase or importation of foreign goods. The prevention or avoidance of this incidental effect was not, however, even remotely an objective of the Framers in enacting the prohibition. Certainly the Court in *Brown* did not think so. See 12 Wheat., at 443–444. Taxes imposed after an initial sale, after the breakup of the shipping packages, or the moment goods imported for use are committed to current operational needs are also all likely to have an incidental effect on the volume of goods imported; yet all are permissible. See, e.g., Waring v. The Mayor, 8 Wall. 110 (1868) (taxation after initial sale); May v. New Orleans, 178 U.S. 496, 20 S.Ct. 976 (1900) (taxation after breakup of shipping packages); Youngstown Sheet & Tube Co. v. Bowers, 358 U.S. 534, 79 S.Ct. 383 (1959) (taxation of goods committed to current operational needs by manufacturer). What those taxes and nondiscriminatory ad valorem property taxes share, it should be emphasized, is the characteristic that they cannot be selectively imposed and increased so as substantially to impair or prohibit importation.[7]

Finally, nondiscriminatory ad valorem property taxes do not interfere with the free flow of imported goods among the States, as did the exactions by States under the Articles of Confederation directed solely at imported goods. Indeed, importers of goods destined for inland States can easily avoid even those taxes in today's world. Modern transportation methods such as air freight and containerized packaging, and the development of railroads and the Nation's internal waterways, enable importation directly into the inland States. Petitioner, for example, operates other distribution centers from wholesale warehouses in inland States. Actually, a quarter of the tires distributed from petitioner's Georgia warehouse are imported interstate directly from Canada. To be sure, allowance of nondiscriminatory ad valorem property taxation may increase the cost of goods purchased by "inland" consumers.[8] But as already noted, such taxation is the *quid pro quo* for benefits actually conferred by the taxing State. There is no reason why local taxpayers should subsidize the services used by the importer; ultimate consumers should pay for such services as police and

---

7. Of course, discriminatory taxation in such circumstances is not inconceivable. For example, a State could pass a law which only taxed the retail sale of imported goods, while the retail sale of domestic goods was not taxed. Such a tax, even though operating after an "initial sale" of the imports would, of course, be invalidated as a discriminatory imposition that was, in practical effect, an impost. Nothing in the opinion in *Brown v. Maryland* should suggest otherwise. The Court in *Brown* merely presumed that at these later stages of commercial activity, state impositions would not be discriminatory. But merely because *Brown* would have authorized a nondiscriminatory charge on even an importer's use of the services of a public auctioneer, see 12 Wheat., at 443, does not mean that it would have disapproved the holding of Cook v. Pennsylvania, 7 Otto 566 (1878), which invalidated a tax on the sale of goods by auction that discriminated against foreign goods.

8. Of course, depending on the relevant competition from domestic goods, an importer may be forced to absorb some of these ad valorem property assessments rather than passing them on to consumers.

fire protection accorded the goods just as much as they should pay transportation costs associated with those goods. An evil to be prevented by the Import–Export Clause was the levying of taxes which could only be imposed because of the peculiar geographical situation of certain States that enabled them to single out goods destined for other States. In effect, the clause was fashioned to prevent the imposition of exactions which were no more than transit fees on the privilege of moving through a State. A nondiscriminatory ad valorem property tax obviously stands on a different footing, and to the extent there is any conflict whatsoever with this purpose of the clause, it may be secured merely by prohibiting the assessment of even nondiscriminatory property taxes on goods which are merely in transit through the State when the tax is assessed.[11]

Admittedly, the wording of the prohibition of the Import–Export Clause does not in terms except nondiscriminatory taxes with some impact on imports or exports. But just as clearly, the clause is not written in terms of a broad prohibition of every "tax." The prohibition is only against States laying "imposts or duties" on "imports." By contrast, Congress is empowered to "lay and collect Taxes, Duties, Imposts, and Excises" which plainly lends support to a reading of the Import–Export Clause as not prohibiting every exaction or "tax" which falls in some measure on imported goods. Indeed, Professor Crosskey makes a persuasive demonstration that the words "imposts" and "duties" as used in 1787 had meanings well understood to be exactions upon imported goods as imports. "Imposts" were like customs duties, that is charges levied on imports at the time and place of importation. "Duties" was a broader term embracing excises as well as customs duties, and probably only capitation, land, and general property exactions were known by the term "tax" rather than the term "duty." 1 W. Crosskey, Politics and the Constitution in the History of the United States, at 296–297 (1953). The characteristic common to both "imposts" and "duties" was that they were exactions directed at imports or commercial activity as such and, as imposed by the seaboard States under the Articles of Confederation, were purposefully employed to regulate interstate and foreign commerce and tax States situated less favorably geographically.

In any event, since prohibition of nondiscriminatory ad valorem property taxation would not further the objectives of the Import–Export Clause, only the clearest constitutional mandate should lead us to condemn such taxation. The terminology employed in the clause—"Imposts or Duties"—is sufficiently ambiguous that we decline to presume it was intended to embrace taxation that does not create the evils the clause was specifically intended to eliminate.

IV

The Court in *Low v. Austin* nevertheless expanded the prohibition of the clause to include nondiscriminatory ad valorem property taxes, and

---

11. Such an assessment would also be invalid under traditional Commerce Clause analysis.

did so with no analysis, but with only the statement that Brown v. Maryland had marked the line "where the power of Congress over the goods imported ends, and that of the State begins, with as much precision as the subject admits." 13 Wall., at 32. But the opinion in Brown v. Maryland cannot properly be read to propose such a broad definition of "imposts" or "duties." The tax there held to be prohibited by the Import–Export Clause was imposed under a Maryland statute that required importers of foreign goods, and wholesalers selling the same by bale or package, to obtain a license and pay a $50 fee therefor, subject to certain forfeitures and penalties for noncompliance. The importers contested the validity of the statute, arguing that the license was a "palpable invasion" of the Import–Export Clause because it was essentially equivalent to a duty on imports. They contended that asserted differences between the license fee and a tax directly imposed on imports were more formal than substantial: the privilege of bringing the goods into the country could not realistically be divorced from the privilege of selling the goods, since the power to prohibit sale would be the power to prohibit importation, 12 Wheat., at 422; the payment of the tax at the time of sale rather than at the time of importation would be irrelevant since it would still be a tax on the same privilege at either time, id., at 423; and the fact that a license operates on the person of the importer while the duty operates on the goods themselves is irrelevant in that either levy would directly increase the cost of the goods, ibid. Since the power to impose a license on importers would also entail a power to price them out of the market or prohibit them entirely, the importers concluded that such a power must be repugnant to the exclusive federal power to regulate foreign commerce, id., at 423–425.

The Attorney General of Maryland, Roger Taney, later Chief Justice Taney, defended the constitutionality of Maryland's law. He argued that the fee was not a prohibited "impost" or "duty" because the license fee was not a tax upon the imported goods, but on the importers, a tax upon the occupation and nothing more, and the Import–Export Clause prohibited only exactions on the right of importation and not an exaction upon the occupation of importers. He contended that, in any event, the clause, if not read as prohibiting only exactions on the right of importation, but more broadly as also prohibiting exactions on goods imported, would necessarily immunize imports from all state taxation at any time. Moreover, if the privilege of selling is a concomitant of the privilege of importing, the argument proved too much; the importer could sell free of regulation by the States in any place and in any manner, even importing free of regulations concerning the bringing of noxious goods into the city, or auctioning the goods in public warehouses, or selling at retail or as a traveling peddler, activities that had traditionally been subject to state regulation and taxation.

The Court in *Brown* refused to define "imposts" or "duties" comprehensively, since the Maryland statute presented only the question "whether the legislature of a State can constitutionally require the importer of foreign articles to take out a license from the State, before he shall be permitted to sell a bale or package so imported." 12 Wheat., at 436. However, in holding that the Maryland license fee was within prohibited "imposts, or duties on imports ..." the Court significantly characterized an impost or duty as "a custom or a tax levied on articles brought into a country," id., at 437, although also holding that, while normally levied before the articles are permitted to enter, the exactions are no less within the prohibition if levied upon the goods as imports after entry; since "imports" are the goods imported, the prohibition of imposts or duties on "imports" was more than a prohibition of a tax on the act of importation; it "extends to a duty levied after [the thing imported] has entered the country," id., at 438. And since the power to prohibit sale of an article is the power to prohibit its introduction into the country, the privilege of sale must be a concomitant of the privilege of importation, and licenses on the right to sell must therefore also fall within the constitutional prohibition. Id., at 439.

Taney's argument was persuasive, however, to the extent that the Court was prompted to declare that "... the words of the prohibition ought not to be pressed to their utmost extent; ... in our complex system, the object of the powers conferred on the government of the Union, and the nature of the often conflicting powers which remain in the States, must always be taken into view...." Id., at 441. "... [T]here must be a point of time when the prohibition ceases, and the power of the State to tax commences...." Ibid.

The Court stated that there were two situations in which the prohibition would not apply. One was the case of a state tax levied after the imported goods had lost their status as imports. The Court devised an evidentiary tool, the "original package" test, for use in making that determination. The formula was: "It is sufficient for the present to say, generally, that when the importer has so acted upon the thing imported, that it has become incorporated and mixed up with the mass of property in the country, it has, perhaps, lost its distinctive character as an import, and has become subject to the taxing power of the State; but while remaining the property of the importer, in his warehouse, in the original form or package in which it was imported, a tax upon it is too plainly a duty on imports to escape the prohibition in the constitution." 12 Wheat., at 441–442. "It is a matter of hornbook knowledge that the original package statement of Justice Marshall was an illustration, rather than a formula, and that its application is evidentiary, and not substantive...." Galveston v. Mexican Petroleum Corp., 15 F.2d 208 (S.D.Tex.1926).

The other was the situation of particular significance to our decision of this case, that is, when the particular state exaction is not a prohibited "impost" or "duty." The Court first stated its view of the characteristics of prohibited state levies. It said that the obvious clue was the express exception of the Import–Export Clause authorizing "imposts or duties" that "may be absolutely necessary for executing [the state's] Inspection Laws." "[T]his exception," said the Court, "in favour of duties for the support of inspection laws, goes far in proving that the framers of the constitution classed taxes of a *similar character* with those imposed for the purposes of inspection, with duties on imports and exports, and supposed them to be prohibited." Id., at 438 (emphasis supplied). The characteristic of the prohibited levy, the Court said later in the opinion— illustrated by the Maryland license tax—was that "... the tax intercepts the import, *as an import,* in its way to become incorporated with the general mass of property, and denies it the privilege of becoming so incorporated until it shall have contributed to the revenue of the State." Id., at 443 (emphasis supplied). The Court illustrated the kinds of state exactions that in its view fell without the prohibition as examples of neutral and nondiscriminatory taxation: a tax on itinerant peddlers, a service charge for the use of a public auctioneer, a property tax on plate or furniture personally used by the importer. These could not be considered within the constitutional prohibition because they were imposed without regard to the origin of the goods taxed. Id., at 443, 444. In contrast, the Maryland exaction in question was a license fee which singled out imports, and therefore was prohibited because "the tax intercepts the import, *as an import,* in its way to become incorporated with the general mass of property." Id., at 443. (Emphasis supplied.)

Thus, it is clear that the Court's view in *Brown* was that merely because certain actions taken by the importer on his imported goods would so mingle them with the common property within the State so as to "lose their distinctive character as imports" and render them subject to the taxing power of the State, did not mean that in the absence of such action, no exaction could be imposed on the goods. Rather, the Court clearly implied that the prohibition would not apply to a state tax that treated imported goods in their original packages no differently from the "common mass of property in the country"; that is, treated it in a manner that did not depend on the foreign origins of the goods.

Despite the language and objectives of the Import–Export Clause, and despite the limited nature of the holding in *Brown v. Maryland*, the Court in *Low v. Austin*, ignored the warning that the boundary between the power of States to tax persons and property within their jurisdictions and the limitations on the power of the States to impose imposts or duties with respect to "imports" was a subtle and difficult line which must be drawn as the cases arise. *Low v. Austin* also ignored the cautionary remark that, for those reasons, it "might be premature to state any rule as being universal in its application." 12 Wheat., at 441. Although it was "sufficient" in the context of Maryland's license tax on the right to sell imported goods to note that a tax imposed directly on imported goods which have not been acted upon in any way would clearly fall within the constitutional prohibition, that observation did not apply, as the foregoing analysis indicates, to a state tax which treated those same goods without regard to the fact of their foreign origin.

* * *

It follows from the foregoing that *Low v. Austin* was wrongly decided. That decision therefore must be, and is, overruled.[13]

V

Petitioner's tires in this case were no longer in transit. They were stored in a distribution warehouse from which petitioner operated a wholesale operation, taking orders from franchised dealers and filling them from a constantly replenished inventory. The warehouse was operated no differently than would be a distribution warehouse utilized by a wholesaler dealing solely in domestic goods, and we therefore hold that the nondiscriminatory property tax levied on petitioner's inventory of imported tires was not interdicted by the Import–Export Clause of the Constitution. The judgment of the Supreme Court of Georgia is accordingly

Affirmed.

MR. JUSTICE STEVENS took no part in the consideration or decision of this case.

MR. JUSTICE WHITE, concurring in the judgment.

Being of the view that the goods involved here had lost their character as imports and that subjecting them to ad valorem taxation was consistent with the Constitution as interpreted by prior cases, including Low v. Austin, 13 Wall. 29 (1871), I would affirm the judgment. There is little reason and no necessity at this time to overrule *Low v. Austin*. None of the parties has challenged that case here, and the issue of its overruling has not been briefed or argued.

NOTES AND QUESTIONS

A.   Michelin *and the "Original Package" Doctrine.* The Supreme Court's opinion in *Michelin* marks a fundamental reexamination of the purpose and scope of the Import–Export Clause's prohibition against state taxation of

---

13.   In another context, this Court said that "[i]n view of the fact that the Constitution gives Congress authority to consent to state taxation of imports and hence to lay down its own test for determining when the immunity ends, we see no convincing practical reason for abandoning the test which has been applied for more than a century...." Hooven & Allison Co. v. Evatt, 324 U.S. 652, 668, 65 S.Ct. 870, 878 (1945). However, this overlooked the fact that the Import–Export Clause contains a provision that "the Net Produce of all Duties and Imposts, laid by any State on Imports or Exports, shall be for the Use of the Treasury of the United States...." Although the Constitutional Convention had refused to make the Import–Export Clause's prohibition of state exactions absolute, it immediately added this proviso, which Mr. Madison supported "as preventing all State imposts." 2 M. Farrand, at 441–442. See also, e.g., 3 id., at 215–216 (Luther Martin's "General Information"). Of course, Congress presumably could enact other legislation transferring the funds back to the States after they were put to "the Use of the Treasury of the United States." But may Congress consent to state exactions if they are not uniform throughout the United States, since any congressional taxation must conform to the mandate of Art. I, § 8, cl. 1, that "all Duties, Imposts and Excises shall be uniform throughout the United States?" If Congress may authorize, under the Import–Export Clause, an exaction that it could not directly impose under the Tax Clause, would that not permit Congress to undermine the policies which both clauses were fashioned to secure? Since, however, we hold that *Low v. Austin* was not properly decided, there is no occasion to address the question whether Congress could have constitutionally consented to state nondiscriminatory ad valorem property taxes if they had been within the prohibition of the Import–Export Clause.

imports. The Court's prior opinions in this area were often characterized by a mechanistic application of the "original package" doctrine to determine whether the goods under consideration had ceased to be imports. Thus, French champagne stored by the importer in a San Francisco warehouse, "whilst remaining in the original cases, unbroken and unsold," enjoyed immunity from state taxation. Low v. Austin, 80 U.S. (13 Wall.) 29 (1872) (ad valorem property tax). European dry goods packed in separate parcels or bundles but exposed or offered for sale in opened shipping boxes did not. May v. New Orleans, 178 U.S. 496, 20 S.Ct. 976 (1900) (ad valorem property tax). An importer of hundred-pound bags of Chilean nitrate stored in an Alabama warehouse and kept in the original packages until sold enjoyed immunity from state taxation. Anglo–Chilean Nitrate Sales Corp. v. Alabama, 288 U.S. 218, 53 S.Ct. 373 (1933) (franchise tax). A wholesaler of fish caught in the Gulf of Mexico who is assessed by their weight after washing and re-icing did not. Gulf Fisheries Co. v. MacInerney, 276 U.S. 124, 48 S.Ct. 227 (1928) (license tax). Bales of Philippine hemp stored in an Ohio warehouse awaiting use in the manufacture of cordage and similar products enjoyed immunity from state taxation. Hooven & Allison Co. v. Evatt, 324 U.S. 652, 65 S.Ct. 870 (1945) (ad valorem property tax). Piles of foreign ore and plywood awaiting use in manufacturing processes did not. Youngstown Sheet and Tube Co. v. Bowers and United States Plywood Corp. v. City of Algoma, 358 U.S. 534, 79 S.Ct. 383 (1959) (ad valorem property taxes).

Moreover, the application of the original package doctrine often raised a host of theoretical questions. Are sea vans and trailers considered to be the "original packages"? Compare Volkswagen Pacific, Inc. v. City of Los Angeles, 7 Cal.3d 48, 496 P.2d 1237, 101 Cal.Rptr. 869 (1972) (sea van constitutes "original package") with Michigan State Tax Commission v. Garment Corp. of America, 32 Mich.App. 715, 189 N.W.2d 72 (1971) (sea van does not constitute "original package"). Do unpackaged imports enjoy an immunity different in scope from packaged imports, and, in any event, how does one apply the doctrine to an unpackaged import that never changes its "original form"? And is there a distinction between the application of the doctrine to goods imported for use and goods imported for sale? See, e.g., E.J. Stanton & Sons v. Los Angeles County, 78 Cal.App.2d 181, 177 P.2d 804 (1947).

In contrast to the factual and theoretical inquiries that lay at the heart of the opinions applying the original package doctrine, the Court's opinion in *Michelin* focused on the nature of the exaction at issue to ascertain whether it constituted a forbidden "impost" or "duty." Although the determination whether an exaction is an "impost" or "duty" will not necessarily render academic the question whether it has been imposed upon an "import," the Court's approach to the former issue appears substantially to reduce the need for inquiring into that question. See generally Walter Hellerstein, "*Michelin Tire Corp. v. Wages*: Enhanced State Power to Tax Imports," 1976 Sup. Ct. Rev. 99.

B. *State Taxation of Imports After* Michelin. In the wake of *Michelin,* the two most critical questions confronting courts faced with a contention that a state tax constitutes an "impost" or "duty" on "imports" will be (1) whether the levy in question is an "impost" or "duty" and (2) if not, whether the goods are still "in transit." The Court's opinion gives adequate guidance on how to approach the first question. With respect to the second, although the Court does not deal with it in detail, there is abundant case law on essentially the same question as it arises under the Commerce Clause. See, e.g., Minnesota v. Blasius, 290 U.S. 1, 54 S.Ct. 34 (1933). See Section E(2), Note B, p. 226 infra for a discussion of state taxation of goods "in transit" after *Michelin.*

C. *The Overruling of* Hooven & Allison Co. v. Evatt. In Hooven & Allison Co. v. Evatt, 324 U.S. 652, 65 S.Ct. 870 (1945) (*Hooven I*), cited in Note A supra, the Court held that the Import–Export Clause barred a state ad valorem property tax on bales of Philippine hemp stored in an Ohio warehouse awaiting use in the manufacture of cordage and similar products. In Limbach v. Hooven & Allison Co., 466 U.S. 353, 104 S.Ct. 1837 (1984) (*Hooven II*), involving the same parties and the same issues as *Hooven I,* the Court overruled *Hooven I* on the ground that, under the analytical framework established in *Michelin,* the Ohio tax was not an "Impost or Duty." The Court also rejected the claim that Ohio was collaterally estopped from relitigating the issue that had been decided in *Hooven I.* The doctrine was held inapplicable in cases in which intervening decisions make manifest the error of the earlier decision. See Commissioner v. Sunnen, 333 U.S. 591, 68 S.Ct. 715 (1948).

D. *The Duty of Tonnage Prohibition.* The only constitutional constraint other than the Import–Export Clause directed expressly to state tax powers is the highly specific provision that "[n]o State shall, without the consent of Congress, lay any Duty of Tonnage." U.S. Const. art. I, § 10, cl. 3. In Clyde Mallory Lines v. Alabama ex rel. State Docks Commission, 296 U.S. 261, 56 S.Ct. 194 (1935), the Court declared:

> It seems clear that the prohibition against the imposition of any duty of tonnage was due to the desire of the Framers to supplement Art. I, § 10, Clause 2, denying to the states power to lay duties on imports or exports * * * by forbidding a corresponding tax on the privilege of access by vessels to the ports of a state, and to their doubts whether the commerce clause would accomplish the purpose.

Id., 296 U.S. at 264–65.

A "Duty of Tonnage" includes "all taxes and duties regardless of their manner or form, and even though not measured by the tonnage of the vessel, which operate to impose a charge for the privilege of entering, trading in, or lying in a port." Id. at 265–66. It does not, however, extend to charges made by state authority, even if graduated according to tonnage, for services rendered to the vessel, such as pilotage, towage, wharfage, or storage. See, e.g., Ouachita & M.R. Packet Co. v. Aiken, 121 U.S. 444, 7 S.Ct. 907 (1887); Parkersburg & O.R. Transportation Co. v. Parkersburg, 107 U.S. 691, 2 S.Ct. 732 (1883); Cincinnati, P., B.S. & P. Packet Co. v. Catlettsburg, 105 U.S. 559 (1882). While the tonnage duty prohibition has been the basis of judicial decisions invalidating state taxes on interstate activities, Peete v. Morgan, 86 U.S. (19 Wall.) 581 (1874); cf. State Tonnage Tax Cases, 79 U.S. (12 Wall.) 204 (1871), its narrow reach has confined its impact to a small class of cases; it has therefore not imposed a significant restraint on state tax power. In one of the rare modern cases invoking the Duty of Tonnage prohibition, the Rhode Island Supreme Court invalidated a registration fee, based on the length of the vessel, for any vessel that spent more than 90 days in the state. Rhode Island v. Turnbaugh, 705 A.2d 530 (R.I. 1997). The court concluded that the levy was not a tax on ownership but rather a fee on a vessel for the mere entry into (or lying in the water of) the state and therefore a prohibited Duty of Tonnage.

In the most recent U.S. Supreme Court case involving the Tonnage Clause, Polar Tankers, Inc. v. City of Valdez, 557 U.S. ___, 129 S.Ct. 2277 (2009), a badly splintered Supreme Court held that a municipal property tax that fell exclusively on large vessels using the municipality's harbor violated the clause. Seven Justices agreed with the following proposition, which was sufficient to condemn the levy:

> This case lies at the heart of what the Tonnage Clause forbids. The ordinance applies almost exclusively to oil tankers. And a tax on the value of such vessels is closely correlated with cargo capacity. Because the imposition of the tax depends on a factor related to tonnage and that tonnage-based tax is not for services provided to the vessel, it is unconstitutional.

Id., 129 S.Ct. at 2284. Four Justices (Breyer, Scalia, Kennedy, and Ginsburg) went on to consider the City's contention that the levy, though concededly "operat[ing] much like a duty applied exclusively to ships," id., was in substance simply one piece of the state's overall and purportedly nondiscriminatory personal property tax regime. The plurality nevertheless rejected this contention on the facts because "it is clear that the vessels subject to the City's ordinance are not taxed in the same manner as other personal property." Id. at 2287.

Two other Justices (Chief Justice Roberts and Justices Thomas) found this additional inquiry irrelevant. In their view, "the Tonnage Clause says nothing about discrimination," id. at 2288, and, once it has been determined that the levy is one that relates to tonnage, that is the end of the inquiry. Justice Alito, while unwilling to go as far as the Chief Justice and Justice Thomas in rejecting the relevance of the nondiscrimination argument, was also unwilling to pursue that argument in *Polar Tankers*: "It is sufficient for present purposes," he said in a separate concurrence," that the Valdez tax is not such a personal property tax and even if the Tonnage Clause permits a true, evenhanded property tax to be applied to vessels, the Valdez tax is an unconstitutional duty of tonnage." Id. at 2289.

Finally, Justice Stevens (joined by Justice Souter) dissented on the ground that (a) property taxes based on a ship's value were not barred by the Tonnage Clause and (b) even if such taxes were permitted on the condition that other property in the jurisdiction was also taxed, that condition was satisfied by Valdez because, according to Justice Stevens, "Valdez also taxes mobile homes, trailers, and a wide variety of property used in producing oil." Id. at 2294. In light of the opinions in *Polar Tankers*, and the current membership of the U.S. Supreme Court, what is the Court's position as to whether a property tax on a ship's value, imposed as part of a broad-based tax on other personal property in the state, violates the Tonnage Clause?

2. STATE TAXATION OF EXPORTS

DEPARTMENT OF REVENUE OF THE STATE OF WASHINGTON v. ASSOCIATION OF WASHINGTON STEVEDORING COMPANIES

Supreme Court of the United States, 1978.
435 U.S. 734, 98 S.Ct. 1388.

MR. JUSTICE BLACKMUN delivered the opinion of the Court.

For the second time in this century, the State of Washington would apply its business and occupation tax to stevedoring. The State's first application of the tax to stevedoring was unsuccessful, for it was held to be unconstitutional as violative of the Commerce Clause of the United States Constitution. Puget Sound Stevedoring Co. v. State Tax Comm'n, 302 U.S. 90, 58 S.Ct. 72 (1937). The Court now faces the question whether Washington's second attempt violates either the Commerce Clause or the Import–Export Clause.

I

Stevedoring is the business of loading and unloading cargo from ships. Private stevedoring companies constitute respondent Association of Washington Stevedoring Companies; respondent Washington Public Ports Association is a nonprofit corporation consisting of port authorities that engage in stevedoring activities. App. 3. In 1974 petitioner Department of Revenue of the State of Washington adopted Revised Rule 193, pt. D, Wash.Admin.Code 458–20–193–D, to implement the State's 1% business and occupation tax on services, set forth in Wash.Rev.Code §§ 82.04.220 and 82.04.290 (1976). The Rule applies the tax to stevedoring. * * *

Seeking to retain their theretofore-enjoyed exemption from the tax, respondents in January 1975 sought from the Superior Court of Thurston County, Wash., a declaratory judgment to the effect that Revised Rule 193D violated both the Commerce Clause and the Import–Export Clause. They urged that the case was controlled by *Puget Sound,* which this Court had reaffirmed in Joseph v. Carter & Weekes Stevedoring Co., 330 U.S. 422, 433, 67 S.Ct. 815, 821 (1947) (together, the *Stevedoring Cases*). * * *

[The Washington Supreme Court invalidated the tax on the basis of the *Stevedoring Cases.*]

II

The Commerce Clause

A

[The Court held the tax did not violate the Commerce Clause in light of *Complete Auto.*]

III

The Import–Export Clause

Having decided that the Commerce Clause does not *per se* invalidate the application of the Washington tax to stevedoring, we must face the question whether the tax contravenes the Import–Export Clause.* * *

A

* * *

Michelin initiated a different approach to Import–Export Clause cases. It ignored the simple question whether the tires and tubes were imports. Instead, it analyzed the nature of the tax to determine whether it was an "Impost or Duty." 423 U.S., at 279, 290–294, 96 S.Ct., at 537, 543–544. Specifically, the analysis examined whether the exaction offended any of the three policy considerations leading to the presence of the Clause. * * *

A similar approach demonstrates that the application of the Washington business and occupation tax to stevedoring threatens no Import–Export Clause policy. First, the tax does not restrain the ability of the Federal Government to conduct foreign policy. As a general business tax that applies to virtually all businesses in the State, it has not created any special protective tariff. The assessments in this case are only upon business conducted entirely within Washington. No foreign business or vessel is taxed. Respondents, therefore, have demonstrated no impediment posed by the tax upon the regulation of foreign trade by the United States.

Second, the effect of the Washington tax on federal import revenues is identical to the effect in *Michelin*. The tax merely compensates the State for services and protection extended by Washington to the stevedoring business. Any indirect effect on the demand for imported goods because of the tax on the value of loading and unloading them from their ships is even less substantial than the effect of the direct ad valorem property tax on the imported goods themselves.

Third, the desire to prevent interstate rivalry and friction does not vary significantly from the primary purpose of the Commerce Clause. See P. Hartman, State Taxation of Interstate Commerce 2–3 (1953). The third Import–Export Clause policy, therefore, is vindicated if the tax falls upon a taxpayer with reasonable nexus to the State, is properly apportioned, does not discriminate, and relates reasonably to services provided by the State. As has been explained in Part II–C, supra, the record in this case, as presently developed, reveals the presence of all these factors.

Under the analysis of *Michelin*, then, the application of the Washington business and occupation tax to stevedoring violates no Import–Export Clause policy and therefore should not qualify as an "Impost or Duty" subject to the absolute ban of the Clause.

B

The Court in *Michelin* qualified its holding with the observation that Georgia had applied the property tax to goods "no longer in transit." 423 U.S., at 302, 96 S.Ct., at 548.[20] Because the goods were no longer in transit, however, the Court did not have to face the question whether a tax relating to goods in transit would be an "Impost or Duty" even if it offended none of the policies behind the Clause. Inasmuch as we now face this inquiry, we note two distinctions between this case and *Michelin*. First, the activity taxed here occurs while imports and exports are in transit. Second, however, the tax does not fall on the goods themselves. The levy reaches only the business of loading and unloading ships or, in other words, the business of transporting cargo within the State of Washington. Despite the existence of the first distinction, the presence of the second leads to the conclusion that the Washington tax is not a prohibited "Impost or Duty" when it violates none of the policies.

In Canton R. Co. v. Rogan, 340 U.S. 511, 71 S.Ct. 447 (1951), the Court upheld a gross-receipts tax on a steam railroad operating exclusively within the Port of Baltimore. The railroad operated a marine terminal and owned rail lines connecting the docks to the trunk lines of major railroads. It switched and pulled cars, stored imports and exports pending transport, supplied wharfage, weighed imports and exports, and rented a stevedoring crane. Somewhat less than half of the company's 1946 gross receipts were derived from the transport of imports or exports. The company contended that this income was immune, under the Import–Export Clause, from the state tax. The Court rejected that argument primarily on the ground that immunity of services incidental to importing and exporting was not so broad as the immunity of the goods themselves:[21]

> "The difference is that in the present case the tax is not on the *goods*, but on the *handling* of them at the port. An article may be an export and immune from a tax long before or long after it reaches the port. But when the tax is on activities connected with the export or import the range of immunity cannot be so wide.

---

20. Commentators have noted the qualification but have questioned its significance. See W. Hellerstein, *Michelin Tire Corp. v. Wages*: Enhanced State Power to Tax Imports, 1976 S.Ct.Rev. 99, 122–126; Comment, 30 Rutgers L.Rev. 193, 203 (1976); Note, 12 Wake Forest L.Rev. 1055, 1062 (1976).

21. The Court distinguished the Maryland tax from others struck down by the Court. 340 U.S., at 513–514, 71 S.Ct., at 448, distinguishing Richfield Oil Corp. v. State Board, 329 U.S. 69, 67 S.Ct. 156 (1946); Thames & Mersey Marine Ins. Co. v. United States, 237 U.S. 19, 35 S.Ct. 496 (1915); and Fairbank v. United States, 181 U.S. 283, 21 S.Ct. 648 (1901). In these cases the State had taxed either the goods or activity so connected with the goods that the levy amounted to a tax on the goods themselves. In *Richfield*, the tax fell upon the sale of goods and was overturned because the Court had always considered a tax on the sale of goods to be a tax on the goods themselves. See Brown v. Maryland, 12 Wheat. 419, 439 (1827). The sale had no value or significance apart from the goods. Similarly, the stamp tax on bills of lading in *Fairbank* effectively taxed the goods because the bills represented the goods. The basis for distinguishing *Thames & Mersey* is less clear because there the tax fell upon marine insurance policies. Arguably, the policies had a value apart from the value of the goods. In distinguishing that case from the taxation of stevedoring activities, however, one might note that the value of goods bears a much closer relation to the value of insurance policies on them than to the value of loading and unloading ships.

"... The broader definition which appellant tenders distorts the ordinary meaning of the terms. It would lead back to every forest, mine, and factory in the land and create a zone of tax immunity never before imagined." Id., at 514–515, 71 S.Ct., at 449. (emphasis in original).

In *Canton R. Co.* the Court did not have to reach the question about taxation of stevedoring because the company did not load or unload ships.[22] As implied in the opinion, however, id., at 515, 71 S.Ct., at 449, the only distinction between stevedoring and the railroad services was that the loading and unloading of ships crossed the waterline. This is a distinction without economic significance in the present context. The transportation services in both settings are necessary to the import-export process. Taxation in neither setting relates to the value of the goods, and therefore in neither can it be considered taxation upon the goods themselves. The force of *Canton R. Co.* therefore prompts the conclusion that the *Michelin* policy analysis should not be discarded merely because the goods are in transit, at least where the taxation falls upon a service distinct from the goods and their value.[23]

C

Another factual distinction between this case and *Michelin* is that here the stevedores load and unload imports and exports whereas in *Michelin* the Georgia tax touched only imports. As noted in Part III–A, supra, the analysis in the export cases has differed from that in the import cases. In the former, the question was when did the export enter the export stream; in the latter, the question was when did the goods escape their original package. The questions differed, for example, because an export could enter its export package and not secure tax immunity until later when it began its journey out of the country. Until *Michelin*, an import retained its immunity so long as it remained in its original package.

Despite these formal differences, the *Michelin* approach should apply to taxation involving exports as well as imports. The prohibition on the taxation of exports is contained in the same Clause as that regarding imports. The export-tax ban vindicates two of the three policies identified in *Michelin*. It precludes state disruption of the United States foreign policy. It does not serve to protect federal revenues, however, because the Constitution forbids federal taxation of exports. U.S.Const., Art. I, § 9, cl. 5;[25] see United States v. Hvoslef, 237 U.S. 1, 35 S.Ct. 459 (1915). But it

---

22. The Court expressly noted that it did not need to reach the stevedoring issue. 340 U.S., at 515, 71 S.Ct., at 449. It was also reserved in the companion case of Western Maryland R. Co. v. Rogan, 340 U.S. 520, 522, 71 S.Ct. 450, 451 (1951).

23. We do not reach the question of the applicability of the *Michelin* approach when a State directly taxes imports or exports in transit. Our Brother Powell, as his concurring opinion indicates, obviously would prefer to reach the issue today, even though the facts of the present case, as he agrees, do not present a case of a tax on goods in transit. As in *Michelin*, decided less than three years ago, we prefer to defer decision until a case with pertinent facts is presented. At that time, with full argument, the issue with all its ramifications may be decided.

25. "No Tax or Duty shall be laid on Articles exported from any State."

does avoid friction and trade barriers among the States. As a result, any tax relating to exports can be tested for its conformance with the first and third policies. If the constitutional interests are not disturbed, the tax should not be considered an "Impost or Duty" any more than should a tax related to imports. This approach is consistent with *Canton R. Co.*, which permitted taxation of income from services connected to both imports and exports. The respondents' gross receipts from loading exports, therefore, are as subject to the Washington business and occupation tax as are the receipts from unloading imports.

* * *

E

The Washington business and occupation tax, as applied to stevedoring, reaches services provided wholly within the State of Washington to imports, exports, and other goods. The application violates none of the constitutional policies identified in *Michelin*. It is, therefore, not among the "Imposts or Duties" within the prohibition of the Import–Export Clause.

IV

The judgment of the Supreme Court of Washington is reversed, and the case is remanded for further proceedings not inconsistent with this opinion.[27]

It is so ordered.

MR. JUSTICE BRENNAN took no part in the consideration or decision of this case.

MR. JUSTICE POWELL, concurring in part and concurring in the result.

I join the opinion of the Court with the exception of Part III–B. As that section of the Court's opinion appears to resurrect the discarded "direct-indirect" test, I cannot join it.

* * *

The question the Court addresses today in Part III–B is whether the business tax at issue here is such a tax upon goods in transit. The Court gives a negative answer, apparently for two reasons. The first is that Canton R. Co. v. Rogan, 340 U.S. 511, 71 S.Ct. 447 (1951), indicates that this is a tax "not on the goods, but on the handling of them at the port." Id., at 514, 71 S.Ct., at 449. (emphasis in original). While *Canton R. Co.* provides precedential support for the proposition that a tax of this kind is not invalid under the Import–Export Clause, its rather artificial distinction between taxes on the handling of the goods and taxes on the goods themselves harks back to the arid "direct-indirect" distinction that we

---

27. See generally Hellerstein, State Taxation and the Supreme Court: Toward a More Unified Approach to Constitutional Adjudication?, 75 Mich.L.Rev. 1426 (1977).

rejected in Complete Auto Transit, Inc. v. Brady, 430 U.S. 274, 97 S.Ct. 1076 (1977), in favor of analysis framed in light of economic reality.

The Court's second reason for holding that the instant tax is not one on goods in transit has the surface appearance of economic-reality analysis, but turns out to be the "direct-indirect" test in another guise. The Court likens this tax to the one at issue in *Canton R. Co.* and declares that since "[t]axation in neither setting relates to the value of the goods, ... in neither can it be considered taxation upon the goods themselves." Ante, at 1403. That this distinction has no economic significance is apparent from the fact that it is possible to design transit fees that are imposed "directly" upon the goods, even though the amount of the exaction bears no relation to the value of the goods. For example, a State could levy a transit fee of $5 per ton or $10 per cubic yard. These taxes would bear no more relation to the value of the goods than does the tax at issue here, which is based on the volume of the stevedoring companies' business, and, in turn, on the volume of goods passing through the port. Thus, the Court does not explain satisfactorily its pronouncement that Washington's business tax upon stevedoring—in economic terms—is not the type of transit fee that the *Michelin* Court questioned.

In my view, this issue can be resolved only with reference to the analysis adopted in *Michelin*. The Court's initial mention of the validity of transit fees in that decision is found in a discussion concerning the right of the taxing state to seek a *quid pro quo* for benefits conferred by the State:

> "There is no reason why local taxpayers should subsidize the services used by the importer; ultimate consumers should pay for such services as police and fire protection accorded the goods just as much as they should pay transportation costs associated with those goods. An evil to be prevented by the Import–Export Clause was the levying of taxes which could only be imposed because of the peculiar geographical situation of certain States that enabled them to single out goods destined for other States. In effect, the Clause was fashioned to prevent the imposition of exactions which were no more than transit fees on the privilege of moving through a State. [The tax at issue] obviously stands on a different footing, and to the extent there is any conflict whatsoever with this purpose of the Clause, it may be secured merely by prohibiting the assessment of even nondiscriminatory property taxes on goods which are merely in transit through the State when the tax is assessed." 423 U.S., at 289–290, 96 S.Ct., at 542. (Footnotes omitted.)

In questioning the validity of "transit fees," the *Michelin* Court was concerned with exactions that bore no relation to services and benefits conferred by the State. Thus, the transit-fee inquiry cannot be answered by determining whether or not the tax relates to the value of the goods; instead, it must be answered by inquiring whether the State is simply making the imported goods pay their own way, as opposed to exacting a fee merely for "the privilege of moving through a State." Ibid.

The Court already has answered that question in this case. In Part II–C, the Court observes that "nothing in the record suggests that the tax is not fairly related to services and protection provided by the State." Ante, at 1399. Since the stevedoring companies undoubtedly avail themselves of police and fire protection, as well as other benefits Washington offers its local businesses, this statement cannot be questioned. For that reason, I agree with the Court's conclusion that the business tax at issue here is not a "transit fee" within the prohibition of the Import–Export Clause.

NOTES AND QUESTIONS

A. *State Taxation of Exports Prior to* Washington Stevedoring. Just as the limitations of the Import–Export Clause on the power of the states to tax imports were delineated during most of our constitutional history by reference to the status of the goods as an "import," so the parallel limitations on the taxation of goods as exports have been delineated during most of our constitutional history by reference to the status of goods as an "export." Whether goods were an "export" depended on whether exportation had commenced. Thus in Richfield Oil Corp. v. State Board of Equalization, 329 U.S. 69, 67 S.Ct. 156 (1946), the taxpayer sold oil to the New Zealand government f.o.b. Los Angeles. The taxpayer transported the oil by pipeline from its California refinery to storage tanks at the harbor where the oil was pumped into a New Zealand navy vessel. California sought to impose a sales tax on the transaction, but the Court held the levy was an invalid exaction on exports, because when the tax was imposed "the oil had started upon its export journey." Id., 329 U.S. at 83.

In Kosydar v. National Cash Register Co., 417 U.S. 62, 94 S.Ct. 2108 (1974), on the other hand, the Court upheld an ad valorem personal property tax on the taxpayer's "international inventory" of business machines which were stored in a warehouse awaiting shipment abroad. In support of its contention that the inventory in question was made up of exports, the taxpayer offered evidence to show that because of their unique construction and special adaptation for foreign use, the machines in question were not salable domestically; that none of the machines built for its international division had ever gone anywhere but into that division; that there was no recorded instance of a machine sold to a foreign purchaser being returned; and that no exported item ever found its way back into the United States market. In sustaining the tax, the Court reaffirmed the "settled doctrine" that the "essential question" in such cases is the "narrow one: is the property upon which a tax has been sought to be imposed an 'export'"; that it therefore had to "decide whether a sufficient commencement of the process of exportation has occurred so as to immunize the article at issue from state taxation"; and that this depends on the factual inquiry whether the article has begun "its physical entry into the stream of exportation." Id., 417 U.S. at 66–71. See also Empresa Siderurgica, S.A. v. County of Merced, 337 U.S. 154, 69 S.Ct. 995 (1949) (tax on portion of manufacturing plant committed for export, 12 percent of which had already been shipped abroad, sustained because portion of plant still in country had not yet entered the "export stream" by delivery to common carrier). See generally Leslie W. Abramson,

"State Taxation of Exports: The Stream of Constitutionality," 54 N.C.L. Rev. 59 (1975).

B. *State Taxation of Goods in Import or Export Transit.* Perhaps the most significant question left open by the *Michelin* and *Washington Stevedoring* cases is the scope of the exemption for imports or exports "in transit." Was Justice Powell on sound ground in taking the Court to task for reverting to a "direct-indirect" test for resolving the "in transit" question? In particular, is the distinction drawn by Justice Powell in the *Washington Stevedoring* case between "making the imported goods pay their own way," as opposed to exacting a fee for the "privilege of moving through a state," as simple as the Justice assumes? To be sure, Justice Powell's statement that "the stevedores undoubtedly avail themselves of police and fire protection, as well as other benefits Washington offers its local businesses" was correct. But cannot the same thing also be said of the police, fire, and other benefits and protection the imports and exports themselves receive from the state as they are being loaded or unloaded onto or from the vessels? In short, does Justice Powell's proffered distinction do anything to advance the analysis as to whether a tax is a prohibited "transit fee"?

The uncertainty over the meaning of the "in transit" exemption is reflected in the Court's own pronouncements. In Itel Containers Int'l Corp. v. Huddleston, 507 U.S. 60, 113 S.Ct. 1095 (1993), the Court rejected an Import–Export Clause challenge to a sales tax on the transfer of possession in Tennessee of domestically owned cargo containers used exclusively in international commerce. In so holding, the Court cast doubt on the continuing force of the *Richfield Oil* case (considered in Note A supra), and "the rule we followed in *Richfield Oil*"—that the Import–Export Clause prohibited the "direct taxation of imports and exports 'in transit.' " Id., 507 U.S. at 77. The Court found the rule inapplicable because the Tennessee tax, like the tax at issue in *Washington Stevedoring*, was not a "direct" tax on the containers or goods being imported in the containers, but so found "*even assuming* that rule has not been altered by the approach we adopted in *Michelin*." Id. (emphasis supplied). On the other hand, in United States v. International Business Machines Corp., 517 U.S. 843, 116 S.Ct. 1793 (1996), the Court suggested that a "direct" tax on goods in import or export transit might still be invalid under its contemporary Import–Export Clause doctrine. The Court there rejected the United States' contention, in a case striking down the application of a federal excise tax under the Export Clause, U.S. Const. art. I, § 1, cl. 5, that "our Import–Export Clause jurisprudence now permits a State to impose a nondiscriminatory tax directly on goods in import or export transit." Id., 517 U.S. at 861–62.

State courts have likewise struggled over the application of the "in transit" exemption. In an extensive opinion reviewing the Import–Export Clause policies and precedents, the Supreme Court of Texas held that the Clause barred a nondiscriminatory ad valorem property tax on exports because they remained in the export stream of commerce. Virginia Indonesia Co. v. Harris County Appraisal District, 910 S.W.2d 905 (Tex. 1995), cert. denied, 518 U.S. 1004, 116 S.Ct. 2523 (1996). The court recognized that *Michelin* and *Washington Stevedoring* had altered the focus of the constitutional analysis from the nature of the goods at issue to the nature of the tax at issue. "Nonetheless," the court declared:

> the rejection of the original package doctrine does not compel the conclusion that the *Michelin* court abandoned the rule of immunity for in-transit goods. To the contrary, by explicitly articulating an exception for in-transit goods, *Michelin* appears to preserve the bright-line immunity for goods in the stream of export.

Id. at 911. The court acknowledged that there is some uncertainty over this point in light of the fact that none of the U.S. Supreme Court's post-*Michelin* cases has involved a direct tax on goods in transit and that the Court has declined to "reach the question of the applicability of the *Michelin* approach when a State directly taxes imports or exports in transit." Id. at 909 (citing *Washington Stevedoring*, 435 U.S. at 757 n.23). Faced with the decision whether to abandon the "stream of commerce" rule or apply it, the court chose the latter course, in light of the fact that the U.S. Supreme Court had not overruled the stream of commerce cases.

An extensive dissenting opinion argued that the tax should be sustained because it did not offend the policies underlying the Import–Export Clause. It declared:

> The Supreme Court does not suggest that taxes directly on goods in transit may be absolutely prohibited; to the contrary, the Supreme Court states that "nondiscriminatory ad valorem property taxation . . . is the *quid pro quo* for benefits actually conferred by the taxing State." The Import–Export Clause was intended to prohibit exaction of fees for nothing more than the privilege of moving through the State's ports. The Clause was not intended to exempt imports and exports from their fair share of the cost of police and fire protection and other such services rendered by the state through which the goods pass.

Virginia Indonesia, 910 S.W.2d at 919. In U.S. Steel Mining Co. v. Helton, 219 W.Va. 1, 631 S.E.2d 559 (2005), cert. denied, 547 U.S. 1179, 126 S.Ct. 2355 (2006), however, the positions of the majority and the dissent were reversed by comparison to *Virginia Indonesia*. The majority confined its consideration to the "*Michelin* policy-based analysis" and found it unnecessary to analyze the Export Clause question under the "mechanistic 'in export transit' approach of cases like *Richfield Oil*." Id., 631 S.E.2d at 564. The dissent declared that "*Richfield Oil*'s 'stream of export' rule rather than * * * the policy rule set forth in *Michelin* * * * and *Washington Stevedoring* * * * should control." Id. at 581 (Benjamin, J., dissenting).

Does the majority or dissent in *Virginia Indonesia* and *U.S. Steel Mining* cases have the better of the argument? Regardless of who has the better argument on the merits, which position more accurately reflects that of the U.S. Supreme Court? In answering the latter question, what weight should be given to the fact that the U.S. Supreme Court in the *IBM* case cited the *Virginia Indonesia* case in rejecting the proposition that "our Import–Export Clause jurisprudence now permits a State to impose a nondiscriminatory tax directly on goods in import or export transit" (517 U.S. at 862)?

CHAPTER 4

THE CONSTITUTIONAL REQUIREMENTS OF EQUALITY AND UNIFORMITY

■ ■ ■

The proper role of equality in taxation is one of the great philosophical questions of the ages. Political theorists from Adam Smith to John Rawls have long debated whether and how tax burdens should vary from person to person. Who should pay more and who should pay less? On what basis should we determine whether two taxpayers should be taxed the same or differently? If you've ever discussed these questions with family or friends, you will no doubt appreciate that these are hot-button issues about which everyone has an opinion. While a broad consensus may be elusive, the fact is that state and local governments regularly provide their own "answers" when enacting or amending their revenue codes. For the most part, taxpayers must simply live with these legislative decisions. The usual remedy for those who feel they are being taxed unfairly is at the ballot box. Yet this does not mean that governments are unconstrained in their ability to impose differential tax burdens. Like all legislation, tax statutes must comply with basic principles of equality expressed in state and federal constitutions. Where tax laws exceed the bounds of what is constitutionally permissible, the taxpayer will have a cause of action to challenge the validity of the tax.

In this chapter, we will examine three major constitutional provisions expressing principles of uniformity or equality that have served as the basis for legal challenges to state and local tax laws. Our first topic will be the so-called "uniformity clauses" that appear in many state constitutions and typically require that taxes (or a subset of taxes, usually property taxes) be uniform throughout the taxing jurisdiction, i.e., the state or one of its political subdivisions. We then turn to the Federal Constitution, examining the Equal Protection Clause of the Fourteenth Amendment and the Privileges and Immunities Clause of Article IV.

A. STATE CONSTITUTIONAL UNIFORMITY AND EQUALITY CLAUSES

1. INTRODUCTION

Almost all the state constitutions contain some provision for uniform or equal taxes, though most of these provisions are limited to property taxes.[a] The Georgia and Maine uniformity provisions are typical. In Georgia, the state constitution specifies that "all taxation shall be uniform upon the same class of subjects within the territorial limits of the authority levying the tax."[b] Similarly, in Maine, all property taxes must "be apportioned and assessed equally, according to the just value thereof."[c] In some states, the constitution expressly requires the *rate* of taxation or assessment to be equal and uniform. In Indiana, for example, the General Assembly is required to provide for "a uniform and equal rate of property assessment and taxation."[d] Still other states specify broader "rules of taxation," such as New Jersey's requirement that property shall be assessed "under general laws and by uniform rules * * * according to the same standard of value * * * at the general tax rate of the taxing district in which the property is situated * * *."[e] Several state constitutions require taxes to be both "equal" and "uniform," while others require only "uniformity." An even more common approach is for the constitution to require "uniformity" only within the classes of persons or property taxed. Thus, the Delaware Constitution requires that taxes "be uniform upon the same class of subjects within the territorial limits of the authority levying the tax,"[f] while the West Virginia Constitution provides that "taxation shall be * * * uniform throughout the State."[g] As this sampling of provisions suggests, the key norm underlying uniformity clauses is one of equal treatment. Where a uniformity provision applies, lawmakers are constrained in their ability to impose differential tax burdens.

Recent historical research has shed new light on the political origins of state tax uniformity clauses. The conventional view pointed to the adoption of uniformity clauses in the frontier states of the Old Northwest (e.g., Illinois, Indiana, Ohio) and explained the development as a sign of the increased acceptance of " 'liberal" or 'democratic' public finance doctrines" that sought to "tax all property at the same rate, based on

---

a. The Connecticut and New York constitutions contain no guarantees of equality or uniformity in taxation. Professor Wade J. Newhouse's Constitutional Uniformity in State Taxation (2d ed. 1984) contains a state-by-state discussion of the uniformity and equality provisions and their judicial interpretation.

b. Ga. Const. art. VII, § 1.

c. Me. Const. art. IX, § 8.

d. Ind. Const. art. X, § 1.

e. N.J. Const. art. VIII, § 1.

f. Del. Const. art. VIII,

g. W.Va. Const. art. X, § 1.

objective, market-value assessments."[h] In his comprehensive history of the American property tax, for example, Glenn Fisher writes that "[u]niform taxation of all property appealed to the spirit of equality, which was a strong influence long after Jackson's Democratic Party lost the presidency."[i] Under this view, uniformity clauses satisfied a populist instinct for transparent government and against legislative favoritism in the formulation of tax laws. Ensuring equal treatment of all types of property was especially important with the rise of commercial wealth in the nineteenth century. Long subject to property taxes on their land, farmers wanted assurances that wealthy merchants would bear a fair share of the tax burden. Subject to a properly crafted uniformity rule, "[l]egislatures could not hide taxes or impose taxes disproportionately on politically weak groups."[j]

More recent historical research has begun to cast doubt on this conventional view on the political origins of state tax uniformity clauses. In a 2006 study of the early development of U.S. state and local taxation, historian Robin Einhorn shows that, contrary to received wisdom, the first uniformity provisions appeared not in the Old Northwest as prior scholarship had suggested, but rather in the South in response to demands from the region's slaveholding elite.[k] The story Einhorn tells is not one that evokes images of equality or liberal democratic government. Rather, her evidence shows that plantation owners urged the adoption of uniformity clauses in order to prevent the overtaxation of slaves. In the early nineteenth century, as nonslaveholding yeoman majorities agitated for greater political power through legislative reapportionment, the planter class urged tax uniformity clauses as a type of "security against the apprehension that the whole weight [of taxation] would be thrown upon slave property."[l] Thus, Einhorn concludes, the "first uniformity clauses emerged not "from the egalitarian demands of frontier farmers" but rather "from the explicitly antidemocratic demands of slaveholders in the South."[m]

Whatever their original rationale, tax uniformity clauses are now a common fixture in state constitutions throughout the country, providing legal ammunition to taxpayers who feel that they are being taxed inequitably. Most of the litigation in this area concerns property taxes and requires more detailed understanding of property tax assessment methodologies. Therefore, we will leave discussion of these issues for Chapter 9 on property taxes. The materials below discuss more general aspects of state uniformity clauses.

---

h. Dennis Hale, "The Evolution of the Property Tax: A Study of the Relation between Public Finance and Political Theory," 47 J. Politics 382, 394 (1985).

i. Glenn W. Fisher, The Worst Tax? A History of the Property Tax in America 62 (1996).

j. Id. at 60.

k. Robin Einhorn, American Taxation, American Slavery (2006).

l. Proceedings and Debates of the Virginia State Convention of 1829–30, 170 (1830), quoted in id. at 239.

m. See Robin Einhorn, "Species of Property: The American Property–Tax Uniformity Clauses Reconsidered," 61 J. Econ. Hist. 974, 995 (2001).

2. THE SCOPE OF STATE UNIFORMITY AND EQUALITY PROVISIONS

Because uniformity provisions often apply only to property taxes, the question arises whether a particular exaction should be characterized as a property tax. During the first half of the twentieth century, there was a considerable amount of litigation over whether the income tax was in fact a type of property tax and thus subject to state constitutional uniformity requirements. Featherstone v. Norman, 170 Ga. 370, 153 S.E. 58 (1930), is a leading authority for the proposition that an income tax is not a property tax within the meaning of state uniformity provisions. In holding that Georgia's income tax was not limited by the constitutional provision that "all taxation shall be * * * ad valorem on all property subject to be taxed," the court relied upon the frequently quoted passage from Cooley on Taxation § 1751 (4th ed.):

> Constitutional prohibitions and limitations applicable to property taxes are generally held not applicable to an income tax, unless the income tax is held to be a property tax. And even where an income tax is held to be a tax on property, the courts sometimes have failed to apply such constitutional limitations to them. The better rule seems to be that an income tax is not a tax on property within a constitutional requirement that taxation on property shall be in proportion to value.

Featherstone, 153 S.E. at 65 (quoting Cooley). Accord: Thorpe v. Mahin, 43 Ill.2d 36, 250 N.E.2d 633 (1969).

Many of the cases holding that an income tax is subject to a state's uniformity and equality provisions have their roots in Pollock v. Farmers' Loan & Trust Co., 157 U.S. 429, 15 S.Ct. 673 (1895). These cases have read *Pollock* as holding that an income tax should be classified as a property tax. See, e.g., Eliasberg Bros. Mercantile Co. v. Grimes, 204 Ala. 492, 86 So. 56 (1920). Other courts, however, have rejected this interpretation of *Pollock* and have sustained graduated income taxes. See, e.g., Miles v. Department of Treasury, 193 N.E. 855 (Ind. 1935), aff'd, 209 Ind. 172, 199 N.E. 372, appeal dismissed, 298 U.S. 640, 56 S.Ct. 750 (1936). The history of this controversy is explored in detail in Wade J. Newhouse, Constitutional Uniformity and Equality in State Taxation (2d ed. 1984). The author identifies the 1915 Advisory Opinion of the Massachusetts Supreme Court as an early landmark decision in this area. Relying on the *Pollock* case, the court held that a tax on income from property would constitute a property tax; that it would be subject to the uniformity and equality clause; and, if graduated, it would be unconstitutional. In re Opinion of the Justices, 220 Mass. 613, 108 N.E. 570 (1915).[n] Three years

[n] As a result of this decision Massachusetts does not have a graduated income tax. The state adopted a constitutional amendment in 1915 to limit the impact of the court's decision, but the court held that the new provision merely permits specific and varying rates on differing types of income but does not permit a general graduated income tax. In re Opinion of the Justices, 266

later the Supreme Court of Missouri rejected this holding and concluded that an income tax is not a property tax and fell outside the scope of the state's uniformity and equality clause. Ludlow–Saylor Wire Co. v. Wollbrinck, 275 Mo. 339, 205 S.W. 196 (1918). These two decisions spearheaded the struggle in the courts over the constitutionality of state income taxes, a struggle that swept the country as more and more states enacted income taxes. Holdings that a graduated income tax violated the state constitutional restrictions have had their repercussions to this day and have thwarted the efforts of legislators in Illinois, Massachusetts, New Hampshire, Pennsylvania, Washington, and other states to adopt this modern, progressive levy.[o] Some states (including Alabama, Kentucky, and Wisconsin) dealt with the problem by adopting constitutional amendments explicitly authorizing the enactment of graduated net income taxes.

In addition, the question sometimes arises whether a particular levy is a "tax" within the meaning of state uniformity and equality provisions. In Holmes v. Cheney, 234 Ark. 503, 352 S.W.2d 943 (1962), the court held that a charge for a motor vehicle certificate of title was a "fee" rather than a "tax" and therefore was not subject to the state's constitutional uniformity and equality requirements. Similarly, special assessments for local improvements accruing to the benefit of particular property generally are not considered to be "taxes" for the purposes of such provisions. Newman v. City of Indianola, 232 N.W.2d 568 (Iowa 1975); Heavens v. King County Rural Library Dist., 66 Wash.2d 558, 404 P.2d 453 (1965). On the other hand, in a case out of Washington, it was determined that a residential street utility charge was a "tax" rather than a "special assessment" because the charge was not levied for any specific improvements. Covell v. City of Seattle, 127 Wash.2d 874, 905 P.2d 324 (1995).

Finally, consider the uniformity implication of a legislature's decision to grant some class of taxpayers a tax credit for some activity or expenditure. For example, a credit against property taxes for low-income property owners may result in two identical parcels of property bearing different effective tax rates merely because one of the parcels is owned by a low-income taxpayer. Some courts have nevertheless sustained such provisions on the ground that state uniformity and equality provisions apply only to *taxing* measures, as distinguished from *spending* measures, and that credits fall into the latter category. In Westvaco Corp. v. South Carolina Dep't of Revenue, 321 S.C. 59, 467 S.E.2d 739 (1995), for example, the

---

Mass. 583, 165 N.E. 900 (1929). In 1981, the court reaffirmed that a graduated state income tax would be unconstitutional. Opinion of the Justices, 383 Mass. 940, 423 N.E.2d 751 (1981). In 1986, the court struck down legislation providing a graduated series of personal exemptions from the personal income tax because it violated the state's uniformity requirement. Massachusetts Taxpayers Foundation, Inc. v. Secretary of Administration, 398 Mass. 40, 494 N.E.2d 1311 (1986). In Peterson v. Commissioner of Revenue, 441 Mass. 420, 806 N.E.2d 78 (2004), the court reiterated its view that "the only permissible differences in tax rates under [the uniformity clause] are those that flow from the differences in classes of property," id., 806 N.E.2d at 85 (2004), in holding that the legislature could not change the tax rate on gains from the sale or exchange of capital assets in the middle of the year.

o. Bachrach v. Nelson, 349 Ill. 579, 182 N.E. 909 (1932), overruled by Thorpe v. Mahin, 43 Ill.2d 36, 250 N.E.2d 633 (1969); Opinion of the Justices, 99 N.H. 525, 113 A.2d 547 (1955); Kelley v. Kalodner, 320 Pa. 180, 181 A. 598 (1935); Culliton v. Chase, 174 Wash. 363, 25 P.2d 81 (1933).

court sustained a local option sales tax, whose proceeds were used to provide a property tax credit, because the state's uniformity and equality provision "does not impose uniformity on the *distribution* of taxes." Id., 467 S.E.2d at 741 (emphasis in original). Other courts, however, have reasoned that "[i]t is the effect of the statute, not the form, which determines whether it is a tax statute subject to the uniformity clause." State ex rel. La Follette v. Torphy, 85 Wis.2d 94, 270 N.W.2d 187, 192 (1978).

3. THE OPERATION OF STATE UNIFORMITY AND EQUALITY PROVISIONS

IN RE OPINION OF THE JUSTICES

Supreme Court of New Hampshire, 1989.
131 N.H. 640, 557 A.2d 273.

The following resolution, House of Representatives Resolution No. 24, requesting an opinion of the justices, was adopted on April 13, 1989, and filed with the Supreme Court on April 14, 1989:

"Whereas, there is pending in the House, House Bill 412–FN–A, as amended, 'An Act relative to a maximum deduction for compensation for business organizations under the business profits tax'; and

"Whereas, an amendment has been proposed to HB 412–FN–A; and

"Whereas, RSA 77–A:4, XIV(a) as proposed in HB 412–FN–A as amended would limit the amount of compensation which may be paid or deducted as reasonable compensation for the purposes of the business profits tax to $100,000, the excess being subject to the business profits tax; and

"Whereas, RSA 77–A:4, XIV(b) as proposed in HB 412–FN–A as amended would require that compensation received by one individual from all business organizations subject to the business profits tax be aggregated for the purpose of determining compensation paid or deducted under RSA 77–A:4, XIV(a);

"Whereas, a question has arisen as to the constitutionality of the provisions of said bill as amended; and

"Whereas, it is important that the question of the constitutionality of said provisions should be settled in advance of its enactment; now, therefore, be it

"Resolved by the House:

"That the Justices of the Supreme Court be respectfully requested to give their opinion on the following questions of law:

1. Would the enactment of RSA 77–A:4, XIV(a) or (b) offend the requirements mandated by Part I, Article 12 and Part II, Articles 5 and 6 of the New Hampshire Constitution in any of the following ways or in any other way:

(a) Would either provision offend the constitutional requirements for equality, proportionality, and reasonableness?

(b) Would either provision have the effect of impermissibly classifying taxpayers?

(c) Would either provision impermissibly classify property for the purposes of taxation?

2. Would the enactment of RSA 77–A:4, XIV(a) or (b) be contrary to any other provision of the New Hampshire Constitution or the United States Constitution?

"That the clerk of the house of representatives transmit copies of this resolution and HB 412–FN–A and the amendment to the Justices of the New Hampshire Supreme Court."

The following answers are returned to the Honorable House of Representatives:

The undersigned justices of the Supreme Court submit the following reply to the questions presented in your resolution adopted April 13, 1989, and filed with this court on April 14, 1989. Interested parties were permitted to file memoranda with the court until May 1, 1989.

The New Hampshire "business profits tax," codified at RSA chapter 77–A, is imposed on the "taxable business profits" of business organizations. These profits are "gross business profits" adjusted by certain additions and deductions, and then further adjusted by a method of apportionment. Under the current tax scheme, reasonable compensation is deductible in full. House Bill 412–FN–A proposes an amendment to RSA 77–A:4 which would limit the compensation deduction to no more than $100,000 for "any individual employee, proprietor, partner, or trustee of the business organization," regardless of the compensation actually or reasonably paid. The individual's compensation which exceeds $100,000 would thus be included in the "taxable business profits," which are essentially the "net" taxable business income of the organization. The bill also proposes an amendment to RSA 77–A:4 which would provide that "[i]n determining the compensation paid or deducted ... for instances where an employee, proprietor, partner, or trustee is employed by, or performs services for more than one business organization, compensation shall be the aggregate of all compensation received from such business organizations."

Question (1) inquires whether proposed RSA 77–A:4, XIV(a) or (b) violate part I, article 12 and part II, articles 5 and 6 of the State Constitution. It asks specifically whether either of these provisions offends the constitutional requirements for equality, proportionality, and reasonableness, or whether they have the effect of impermissibly classifying taxpayers or impermissibly classifying property. For the following reasons, we answer in the affirmative.

Part II, article 5 of our Constitution requires that "all taxes be proportionate and reasonable, ... equal in valuation and uniform in rate, and just." Part I, article 12 of the State Constitution also requires uniform and equal treatment in the taxation of business entities. Although we do not concern ourselves with the wisdom and practicality of proposed legislation, and we recognize that the legislature has broad power to create exemptions, such as deductions, adjustments and credits, these exemptions must be reasonable and uniform.

It is our opinion that the proposed amendments to RSA 77–A:4 (Supp.1988) do not meet these constitutional mandates. In a previous opinion of the justices, we advised that the legislature may not create systems of taxation which would result in "two classes of taxpayers paying differing rates of tax on essentially the same class of property, business income." Such is the constitutional infirmity here. The proposed amendment would have the effect of impermissibly classifying taxpayers in violation of part I, article 12 and part II, article 5 of the State Constitution. House Bill 412–FN–A creates two classifications of taxpayers: business organizations which compensate individual employees in excess of $100,000 and those which do not. The effect of this bill would be to impose differing tax burdens and differing tax rates on business organizations which have identical gross income and aggregate reasonable compensation expenses. A simple illustration of this would be the situation where two business organizations have the same amount of gross business profits and reasonable compensation expenses totalling $200,000, but one organization has only one employee, whose salary is $200,000, and the other organization has two employees, each with a salary of $100,000. It is clear that an unequal and unreasonable tax burden would result because the organization with two employees could fully deduct $200,000 while the organization with one employee could only deduct $100,000 of compensation.

We have stated that a deduction for compensation under the "business profits tax" is not constitutionally required; however, to the extent that it is allowed, "it must be available to *all* business organizations." The proposed $100,000 cap on reasonable compensation deductions would result in disproportionate taxation and would violate the constitutional principle that the legislature "must substantially treat *all* business entities uniformly and equally. It follows, therefore, that proposed RSA 77–A:4, XIV(b) would also be unconstitutional, since it requires the aggregation of an individual's compensation from all organizations subject to the "business profits tax" for the purpose of determining compensation paid or deducted under proposed RSA 77–A:4, XIV(a).

Finally, we fail to see any just or valid distinction between these two classes of taxpayers which would permit the discrimination inherent in the proposed amendment. Our Constitution cannot support the apparently arbitrary limitation on the amount of compensation which may be deducted as reasonable. See Felder v. Portsmouth, 114 N.H. 573, 578, 324 A.2d 708, 710 (1974) (classification must reasonably promote proper object of public welfare and must not be arbitrary). As discussed earlier, the net result of this limitation on the deduction, without reference to the reasonableness of the compensation paid, would be preferential tax treatment for organizations paying individual employees less than $100,000. In sum, the provision would offend the constitutional requirements for equality, proportionality, and reasonableness and would impermissibly classify taxpayers in violation of our State Constitution.

In light of the foregoing discussion we need not determine whether the proposed amendment would also impermissibly classify property. For the same reason, there is no need to answer question (2), which asks whether HB 412–FN–A violates any other provision of the New Hampshire or United States Constitutions, a question which we would in any event respectfully decline to answer because of its generality.

NOTES AND QUESTIONS

A. *Tax Uniformity in the Granite State.* The New Hampshire Supreme Court has rendered a number of decisions and advisory opinions to the state legislature interpreting the provision, which was the focus of the principal case, that "all taxes be proportionate and reasonable, * * * equal in valuation and uniform in rate, and just." N.H. Const. pt. II, art. 5. Construing this provision, the court has ruled that a tax on corporations would be invalid if individuals engaged in like businesses were not taxed. Opinion of the Justices, 106 N.H. 202, 208 A.2d 458 (1965). In an opinion written by former U.S. Supreme Court Justice David Souter, when he was sitting on the New Hampshire Supreme Court, the court invalidated a tax on sales of prepackaged snacks from vending machines, because sales of such snacks by supermarkets were not taxed. Cagan's, Inc. v. New Hampshire Dep't of Revenue, 126 N.H. 239, 490 A.2d 1354 (1985). The court also has held that a property tax on electric power plants with a kilowatt capacity of 500,000 kilowatts would violate the constitutional provision because "no valid reason has been presented to us which would justify classifying electric power plants by size for the purpose of imposing an ad valorem property tax." Opinion of the Justices, 118 N.H. 343, 386 A.2d 1273, 1274 (1978).

B. *Uniformity Challenges to Tax Rate Structures.* In addition to the issues discussed above, the New Hampshire Supreme Court has considered the restraints that the state's uniformity and equality provisions impose on tax rate structures. New Hampshire imposed its business profits tax at the rate of 9.08 percent (8 percent plus a 13.5 percent surcharge) on taxable business profits. In addition, it imposed a minimum tax of $250 on all businesses with gross income in excess of $12,000 but with business profits of less than $2,753. (At the latter amount, the regular business profits tax applied, because it exceeded the minimum). The court held that the minimum tax violated the state's uniformity requirement because it imposed a regressive tax, i.e., the effective tax rate on business profits was higher when the profits were less than $2,753 than it was when the profits exceeded $2,753, assuming that gross income exceeded $12,000 in both instances. Such a tax, in the court's eyes, was neither uniform nor proportional. Johnson & Porter Realty Co., Inc. v. Commissioner of Revenue Administration, 122 N.H. 696, 448 A.2d 435 (1982).

The Georgia Supreme Court considered an analogous question in Pharr Road Inv. Co. v. City of Atlanta, 224 Ga. 403, 162 S.E.2d 333 (1968). In *Pharr*, the court invalidated a city ordinance imposing varying license fees on occupations, measured by gross revenues, on the ground that it conflicted with the uniformity provision of the Georgia Constitution. The court found "palpable * * * discrimination" in the provisions that (a) exempted from the license fees businesses with gross revenues of $8,000 or less and (b) levied differing rates depending on the number of employees. Under the Atlanta taxing scheme, businesses with given gross revenues but fewer than 1,600 employees were subject to a fee of $12,000, whereas those with the same gross revenues but having more than 1,600 employees were subject to a fee of $18,000. Conceding that the classification and graduation schedule "manifest a desire to gear the amounts to ability to pay and the expenses to protect and serve," the court nevertheless was "convinced that uniformity as demanded by the Constitution is lacking." Id., 162 S.E.2d at 335. Accord: Saulsbury v. Bethlehem Steel Co., 413 Pa. 316, 196 A.2d 664 (1964).

Both the *Johnson & Porter* and *Pharr* cases present essentially the same problem, namely, the constitutionality of applying different effective tax rates under business excise taxes to taxpayers whose businesses have differing characteristics. The critical question in the cases is whether the differing characteristics—the amount of gross revenues, the number of employees, or the amount of net profits, and the like—justify the separate classification for purposes of the levies' effective tax rate. In both the *Johnson & Porter* and *Pharr* cases the courts applied a standard of strict scrutiny in invalidating the nonuniform rate under the state's uniformity and equality provision. Would the courts in these cases have evinced the same hostility to rate differentials found in most personal income taxes? If not, why not?

C. *Differentiation in Taxation Based on Geography or Population.* The Georgia legislature granted counties that imposed sales taxes the option of reducing county property taxes in unincorporated areas outside municipalities, but not in incorporated areas within municipalities. The Georgia Supreme Court struck down this geographical differentiation under the state's uniformity and equality provision. Martin v. Ellis, 242 Ga. 340, 249 S.E.2d 23 (1978). The Ohio Supreme Court likewise has held that a state law authorizing additional sales taxes on islands in Ohio violated the state's constitutional requirement that "[a]ll laws of a general nature shall have a uniform operation throughout the state." Put–In–Bay Island Taxing Dist. v. Colonial, Inc., 65 Ohio St.3d 449, 605 N.E.2d 21, 22 (1992), cert. denied, 508 U.S. 930, 113 S.Ct. 2396 (1993). Legislatures often draw geographical lines in state taxing statutes under the pretext that they are drawing lines based on population. For example, legislation in Illinois provides rules for "counties with more than 3,000,000 inhabitants"—an unmistakable reference to Cook County, where Chicago is located. These population-based distinctions have generally withstood constitutional scrutiny under the state uniformity and equality provisions. See Annot., 98 A.L.R.3d 1083.

B. EQUAL PROTECTION OF THE LAWS

The Fourteenth Amendment to the U.S. Constitution provides in part: "[N]or shall any State * * * deny to any person within its jurisdiction the equal protection of the laws."[p] Although aimed at the Black Codes adopted in Southern states following the Civil War, the Equal Protection Clause reaches well beyond racial classifications, targeting a broad range of discriminatory legislation. Thus, in addition to providing the basis for some of the most famous Supreme Court opinions in U.S. history, such as the historic *Brown* decision,[q] the Equal Protection Clause has also figured prominently in challenges to state and local taxes. Early on, the Supreme Court expanded the pool of potential litigants capable of asserting equal protection challenges by holding that the term "person" as used in the Equal Protection Clause (as well as in the Due Process Clause) includes corporations.[r] Our first case features a challenge by firms operating racetracks to a state tax on their slot machine revenues. The issue may seem narrow, but the case is illustrative of the Court's approach to equal protection challenges to state tax statutes.

1. CLASSIFICATION OF PROPERTY AND TAXPAYERS

FITZGERALD v. RACING ASSOCIATION OF CENTRAL IOWA

Supreme Court of the United States, 2003.
539 U.S. 103, 123 S.Ct. 2156.

MR. JUSTICE BREYER delivered the opinion of the Court.

Iowa taxes adjusted revenues from slot machines on excursion riverboats at a maximum rate of 20 percent. Iowa law provides for a maximum tax rate of 36 percent on adjusted revenues from slot machines at racetracks. The Iowa Supreme Court held that this 20 percent/36 percent difference in tax rates violates the Federal Constitution's Equal Protection Clause, Amdt. 14, § 1. We disagree and reverse the Iowa Supreme Court's determination.

I

Before 1989, Iowa permitted only one form of gambling—parimutuel betting at racetracks—the proceeds of which it taxed at a six percent rate. In 1989, it authorized other forms of gambling, including slot machines and other gambling games on riverboats, though it limited bets to $5 and

---

p. U.S. Const. amend. XIV, § 1.

q. Brown v. Board of Education of Topeka, 347 U.S. 483, 74 S.Ct. 686 (1954).

r. Santa Clara County v. Southern Pacific R.R. Co., 118 U.S. 394, 6 S.Ct. 1132 (1886). It is, however, well settled that corporations are not "citizens" and therefore are not protected by the Privileges and Immunities Clause of the Fourteenth Amendment. See Western Turf Ass'n v. Greenberg, 204 U.S. 359, 27 S.Ct. 384 (1907).

losses to $200 per excursion. Iowa taxed adjusted revenues from slot machine gambling at graduated rates, with a top rate of 20 percent.

In 1994, Iowa enacted a law that, among other things, removed the riverboat gambling $5/$200 bet/loss limits, authorized racetracks to operate slot machines, and imposed a graduated tax upon racetrack slot machine adjusted revenues with a top rate that started at 20 percent and would automatically rise over time to 36 percent. The Act did not alter the tax rate on riverboat slot machine adjusted revenues, thereby leaving the existing 20 percent rate in place.

Respondents, a group of racetracks and an association of dog owners, brought this lawsuit in state court challenging the 1994 legislation on the ground that the 20 percent/36 percent tax rate difference that it created violated the Federal Constitution's Equal Protection Clause, Amdt. 14, § 1. The State District Court upheld the statute. The Iowa Supreme Court disagreed and, by a 4-to-3 vote, reversed the District Court. The majority wrote that the "differential tax completely defeats the alleged purpose" of the statute, namely, "to help the racetracks recover from economic distress," that there could "be no rational reason for this differential tax," and that the Equal Protection Clause consequently forbids its imposition. We granted certiorari to review this determination.

II

Respondents initially claim that the Iowa Supreme Court's decision rests independently upon state law. And they argue that this state-law holding bars review of the federal issue. We disagree. The Iowa Supreme Court's opinion, after setting forth the language of both State and Federal Equal Protection Clauses, says that "Iowa courts are to 'apply the same analysis in considering the state equal protection claims as . . . in considering the federal equal protection claim.'" We have previously held that, in such circumstances, we shall consider a state-court decision as resting upon federal grounds sufficient to support this Court's jurisdiction. We therefore find that this Court has jurisdiction to review the Iowa Supreme Court's determination.

III

We here consider whether a difference in state tax rates violates the Fourteenth Amendment's mandate that "[n]o State shall . . . deny to any person . . . the equal protection of the laws." The law in question does not distinguish on the basis of, for example, race or gender. See, e.g., Loving v. Virginia, 388 U.S. 1, 87 S.Ct. 1817 (1967); United States v. Virginia, 518 U.S. 515, 116 S.Ct. 2264 (1996). It does not distinguish between in-state and out-of-state businesses. See, e.g., Metropolitan Life Ins. Co. v. Ward, 470 U.S. 869, 105 S.Ct. 1676 (1985). Neither does it favor a State's long-time residents at the expense of residents who have more recently arrived from other States. Cf. Hooper v. Bernalillo County Assessor, 472 U.S. 612, 105 S.Ct. 2862 (1985). Rather, the law distinguishes for tax purposes among revenues obtained within the State of Iowa by two enterprises, each of which does business in the State. Where that is so, the law is subject to rational-basis review:

> "[T]he Equal Protection Clause is satisfied so long as there is a plausible policy reason for the classification, the legislative facts on which the classification is apparently based rationally may have been considered to be true by the governmental decisionmaker, and the relationship of the classification to its goal is not so attenuated as to render the distinction arbitrary or irrational." Nordlinger v. Hahn, 505 U.S. 1, 11–12, 112 S.Ct. 2326 (1992) (citations omitted).

See also id., at 11, 112 S.Ct. 2326 (rational-basis review "is especially deferential in the context of classifications made by complex tax laws"); Allied Stores of Ohio, Inc. v. Bowers, 358 U.S. 522, 527, 79 S.Ct. 437 (1959) (the Equal Protection Clause requires States, when enacting tax laws, to "proceed upon a rational basis" and not to "resort to a classification that is palpably arbitrary").

The Iowa Supreme Court found that the 20 percent/36 percent tax rate differential failed to meet this standard because, in its view, that difference "frustrated" what it saw as the law's basic objective, namely, rescuing the racetracks from economic distress. And no rational person, it believed, could claim the contrary. The Iowa Supreme Court could not deny, however, that the Iowa law, like most laws, might predominately serve one general objective, say, helping the racetracks, while containing subsidiary provisions that seek to achieve other desirable (perhaps even contrary) ends as well, thereby producing a law that balances objectives but still serves the general objective when seen as a whole. See Railroad Retirement Bd. v. Fritz, 449 U.S. 166, 181, 101 S.Ct. 453 (1980) (STEVENS, J., concurring in judgment) (legislation is often the "product of multiple and somewhat inconsistent purposes that led to certain compromises"). After all, if *every* subsidiary provision in a law designed to help racetracks had to help those racetracks and nothing more, then (since any tax rate hurts the racetracks when compared with a lower rate) there could be no taxation of the racetracks at all.

Neither could the Iowa Supreme Court deny that the 1994 legislation, *seen as a whole,* can rationally be understood to do what that court says it seeks to do, namely, advance the racetracks' economic interests. Its grant to the racetracks of authority to operate slot machines should help the racetracks economically to some degree—even if its simultaneous imposition of a tax on slot machine adjusted revenue means that the law provides less help than respondents might like. At least a rational legislator might so believe. And the Constitution grants legislators, not courts, broad authority (within the bounds of rationality) to decide whom they wish to help with their tax laws and how much help those laws ought to provide. "The 'task of classifying persons for ... benefits ... inevitably requires that some persons who have an almost equally strong claim to favored treatment be placed on different sides of the line,' and the fact the line might have been drawn differently at some points is a matter for legislative, rather than judicial, consideration." Id., at 179, 101 S.Ct. 453 (citation omitted). See also ibid. (judicial review is "at an end" once the court identifies a plausible basis on which the legislature may have relied).

Once one realizes that not every provision in a law must share a single objective, one has no difficulty finding the necessary rational support for the 20 percent/36 percent differential here at issue. That difference, harmful to the racetracks, is helpful to the riverboats, which, as respondents concede, were also facing financial peril. These two characterizations are but opposite sides of the same coin. Each reflects a rational way for a legislator to view the matter. And aside from simply aiding the financial position of the riverboats, the legislators may have wanted to encourage the economic development of river communities or to promote riverboat history, say, by providing incentives for riverboats to remain in the State, rather than relocate to other States. See Gaming Study Committee Report (Sept. 3, 1993), reprinted in App. 76–84, 86. Alternatively, they may have wanted to protect the reliance interests of riverboat operators, whose adjusted slot machine revenue had previously been taxed at the 20 percent rate. All these objectives are rational ones, which lower riverboat tax rates could further and which suffice to uphold the different tax rates. See * * * Madden v. Kentucky, 309 U.S. 83, 88, 60 S.Ct. 406 (1940) (imposing burden on respondents to "negative every conceivable basis" that might support different treatment).

* * *

IV

We conclude that there is "a plausible policy reason for the classification," that the legislature "rationally may have ... considered ... true" the related justifying "legislative facts," and that the "relationship of the classification to its goal is not so attenuated as to render the distinction arbitrary or irrational." [Nordlinger, 505 U.S,] at 11, 112 S.Ct. 2326. Consequently the State's differential tax rate does not violate the Federal Equal Protection Clause. The Iowa Supreme Court's judgment to the contrary is reversed, and the case is remanded for further proceedings not inconsistent with this opinion.

NOTES AND QUESTIONS

A. *The Supreme Court's General Approach to the Equal Protection Clause. Fitzgerald* is the latest in a long string of Supreme Court decisions rejecting equal protection challenges to state tax classifications under "rational basis" review. As the Court observed in Lehnhausen v. Lake Shore Auto Parts Co., 410 U.S. 356, 93 S.Ct. 1001 (1973), which dismissed equal protection objections to an Illinois personal property tax that applied to corporations but not to individuals: "Where taxation is concerned and no specific federal right, apart from equal protection, is imperiled, the States have large leeway in making classifications and drawing lines which in their judgment produce reasonable systems of taxation." Id., 410 U.S. at 359. In General Motors Corp.

v. Tracy, 519 U.S. 278, 117 S.Ct. 811 (1997), the Court rejected General Motors' (GMC's) equal protection attack on the state's differential tax treatment of public utilities and non-public utility marketers of natural gas. It observed that "the hurdle facing GMC is a high one, since state tax classifications require only a rational basis to satisfy the Equal Protection Clause." Id., 519 U.S. at 311. " '[I]n taxation,' " the Court noted, " 'even more than in other fields, legislatures possess the greatest freedom in classification.' " Id. (quoting Madden v. Kentucky, 309 U.S. 83, 88, 60 S.Ct. 406 (1940)).

B. *Classification by Gender.* In Kahn v. Shevin, 416 U.S. 351, 94 S.Ct. 1734 (1974), the Supreme Court held that a Florida statute that provided an annual $500 property tax exemption for widows without providing any comparable exemption for widowers did not offend the Equal Protection Clause. The Court found that the gender-based classification had a rational basis and thus lay well within permissible limits as established by its equal protection precedents. The dissenters would have struck down the exemption on the ground that a gender-based classification, like classifications based on race and national origin, cannot be sustained simply because it rationally promotes legitimate governmental interests. In the dissent's view, the state had failed to show that its interest could not be achieved by a more precisely tailored statute or by the use of less drastic means. Do the Court's more recent decisions involving gender-based classification, which declare that "[p]arties who seek to defend gender-based government action must demonstrate an 'exceedingly persuasive justification' for that action," United States v. Virginia, 518 U.S. 515, 531, 116 S.Ct. 2264 (1996), cast doubt on the continuing validity of Kahn v. Shevin? Does the Court's opinion in *Fitzgerald* shed any light on this question?

2. THE EQUAL PROTECTION CLAUSE AND PROPERTY TAX DISPARITIES

Disparities in real property tax assessments do not ordinarily imperil any protected federal interests (other than freedom from arbitrary classification) and therefore would appear to fall into the class of equal protection cases in which the Court would tend to grant the states broad latitude. The Court's decision in Allegheny Pittsburgh Coal Co. v. County Commission, 488 U.S. 336, 109 S.Ct. 633 (1989), however, suggests that the Equal Protection Clause may nevertheless have a significant role to play in challenges to discriminatory property tax assessments. *Allegheny Pittsburgh* concerned a challenge to gross disparities in ad valorem property tax assessments resulting from the practice of assessing property based on its recent sales price. Like many taxing jurisdictions across the country, Webster County, West Virginia relied on sales prices of recently conveyed property in determining its value for ad valorem tax purposes and did not systematically adjust the assessment of unsold comparable properties to reflect current value. So long as property was unsold, it remained on the tax rolls with the same assessment it bore in prior years, with only minor and infrequent adjustments. As a consequence, the county often assessed recently conveyed property at a much higher percentage of its fair market value than comparable property that had not recently been sold. Indeed, the record in *Allegheny Pittsburgh* revealed that the county assessed the taxpayers' property—consisting of coal-bearing lands—at approximately eight to 35 times more than comparable neighboring properties.

In a brief opinion, the Court sustained the taxpayers' claim that the county's assessment practice violated the Equal Protection Clause. While reiterating the well-entrenched principle that the states have broad powers under the clause to impose different types of taxes upon different types of taxpayers and property, the Court observed that the county assessor made no attempt to justify the disparities in assessment on the ground that recently sold and unsold property constituted two different classes of property that were to be taxed differently according to deliberate state policy. In fact, the opposite was true: West Virginia's constitution and implementing statutes provided that all the property in question was to be taxed at a uniform rate throughout the state according to its value. Given the state's own professed adherence to a standard of uniformity and equality of property assessments based on market value, the county assessor's reliance on actual sales prices as the basis for achieving such equality could not be justified as state-sanctioned classification scheme.

The Court's decision in *Allegheny Pittsburgh* appeared to raise serious questions about the constitutionality of California's Proposition 13. Proposition 13 amended the state constitution to limit property taxes to one percent of 1975–76 valuations and to prohibit annual increases in valuations of more than two percent, *unless the property is sold*. The Court in *Allegheny Pittsburgh* was well aware of the potential implications of its decision for California's taxing system, and observed in a footnote:

> We need not and do not decide today whether the Webster County assessment method would stand on a different footing if it were the law of a State, generally applied, instead of the aberrational enforcement policy it appears to be. The State of California has adopted a similar policy * * * popularly known as "Proposition 13." * * * The system is grounded on the belief that taxes should based on the original cost of property and should not tax unrealized paper gains in the value of property.

Allegheny, 488 U.S. at 344–45 n.4. This footnote set in motion litigation in California that eventually led to the decision reproduced below.

NORDLINGER v. HAHN

Supreme Court of the United States, 1992.
505 U.S. 1, 112 S.Ct. 2326.

JUSTICE BLACKMUN delivered the opinion of the Court.

In 1978, California voters staged what has been described as a property tax revolt by approving a statewide ballot initiative known as Proposition 13. The adoption of Proposition 13 served to amend the California Constitution to impose strict limits on the rate at which real property is taxed and on the rate at which real property assessments are increased from year to year. In this litigation, we consider a challenge under the Equal Protection Clause of the Fourteenth Amendment to the manner in which real property now is assessed under the California Constitution.

I

A

Proposition 13 followed many years of rapidly rising real property taxes in California. From fiscal years 1967–1968 to 1971–1972, revenues from these taxes increased on an average of 11.5 percent per year. In response, the California Legislature enacted several property tax relief measures, including a cap on tax rates in 1972. The boom in the State's real estate market persevered, however, and the median price of an existing home doubled from $31,530 in 1973 to $62,430 in 1977. As a result, tax levies continued to rise because of sharply increasing assessment values. Some homeowners saw their tax bills double or triple during this period, well outpacing any growth in their income and ability to pay.

By 1978, property tax relief had emerged as a major political issue in California. In only one month's time, tax relief advocates collected over 1.2 million signatures to qualify Proposition 13 for the June 1978 ballot. On election day, Proposition 13 received a favorable vote of 64.8 percent and carried 55 of the State's 58 counties. California Secretary of State, Statement of Vote and Supplement, Primary Election, June 6, 1978, p. 39. California thus had a novel constitutional amendment that led to a property tax cut of approximately $7 billion in the first year. A California homeowner with a $50,000 home enjoyed an immediate reduction of about $750 per year in property taxes.

As enacted by Proposition 13, Article XIIIA of the California Constitution caps real property taxes at 1% of a property's "full cash value." § 1(a). "Full cash value" is defined as the assessed valuation as of the 1975–1976 tax year or, "thereafter, the appraised value of real property when purchased, newly constructed, or a change in ownership has occurred after the 1975 assessment." § 2(a). The assessment "may reflect from year to year the inflationary rate not to exceed 2 percent for any given year." § 2(b).

Article XIIIA also contains several exemptions from this reassessment provision. One exemption authorizes the legislature to allow homeowners over the age of 55 who sell their principal residences to carry their previous base-year assessments with them to replacement residences of equal or lesser value. § 2(a). A second exemption applies to transfers of a principal residence (and up to $1 million of other real property) between parents and children. § 2(h).

In short, Article XIIIA combines a 1% ceiling on the property tax rate with a 2% cap on annual increases in assessed valuations. The assessment limitation, however, is subject to the exception that new construction or a change of ownership triggers a reassessment up to current appraised value. Thus, the assessment provisions of Article XIIIA essentially embody an "acquisition value" system of taxation rather than the more commonplace "current value" taxation. Real property is assessed at values related to the value of the property at the time it is acquired by the taxpayer rather than to the value it has in the current real estate market.

Over time, this acquisition-value system has created dramatic disparities in the taxes paid by persons owning similar pieces of property. Property values in California have inflated far in excess of the allowed 2% cap on increases in assessments for property that is not newly constructed or that has not changed hands. As a result, longer-term property owners pay lower property taxes reflecting historic property values, while newer owners pay higher property taxes reflecting more recent values. For that reason, Proposition 13 has been labeled by some as a "welcome stranger" system—the newcomer to an established community is "welcome" in anticipation that he will contribute a larger percentage of support for local government than his settled neighbor who owns a comparable home. Indeed, in dollar terms, the differences in tax burdens are staggering. By 1989, the 44% of California homeowners who have owned their homes since enactment of Proposition 13 in 1978 shouldered only 25% of the more than $4 billion in residential property taxes paid by homeowners statewide. If property values continue to rise more than the annual 2% inflationary cap, this disparity will continue to grow.

B

According to her amended complaint, petitioner Stephanie Nordlinger in November 1988 purchased a house in the Baldwin Hills neighborhood of Los Angeles County for $170,000. The prior owners bought the home just two years before for $121,500. Before her purchase, petitioner had lived in a rented apartment in Los Angeles and had not owned any real property in California. In early 1989, petitioner received a notice from the Los Angeles County Tax Assessor, who is a respondent here, informing her that her home had been reassessed upward to $170,100 on account of its change in ownership. She learned that the reassessment resulted in a property tax increase of $453.60, up 36% to $1,701, for the 1988–1989 fiscal year.

Petitioner later discovered she was paying about five times more in taxes than some of her neighbors who owned comparable homes since 1975 within the same residential development. For example, one block away, a house of identical size on a lot slightly larger than petitioner's was subject to a general tax levy of only $358.20 (based on an assessed valuation of $35,820, which reflected the home's value in 1975 plus the up-to–2% per year inflation factor). According to petitioner, her total property taxes over the first 10 years in her home will approach $19,000, while any neighbor who bought a comparable home in 1975 stands to pay just $4,100. The general tax levied against her modest home is only a few dollars short of that paid by a pre–1976 owner of a $2.1 million Malibu beachfront home.

After exhausting administrative remedies, petitioner brought suit against respondents in Los Angeles County Superior Court. She sought a tax refund and a declaration that her tax was unconstitutional. In her amended complaint, she alleged: "Article XIIIA has created an arbitrary system which assigns disparate real property tax burdens on owners of generally comparable and similarly situated properties without regard to the use of the real property taxed, the burden the property places on government, the actual value of the property or the financial capability of the property owner."

* * *

II

The Equal Protection Clause of the Fourteenth Amendment, § 1, commands that no State shall "deny to any person within its jurisdiction the equal protection of the laws." Of course, most laws differentiate in some fashion between classes of persons. The Equal Protection Clause does not forbid classifications. It simply keeps governmental decision makers from treating differently persons who are in all relevant respects alike. F.S. Royster Guano Co. v. Virginia, 253 U.S. 412, 415, 40 S.Ct. 560, 561 (1920). As a general rule, "legislatures are presumed to have acted within their constitutional power despite the fact that, in practice, their laws result in some inequality." McGowan v. Maryland, 366 U.S. 420, 425–426, 81 S.Ct. 1101, 1105 (1961). Accordingly, this Court's cases are clear that, unless a classification warrants some form of heightened review because it jeopardizes exercise of a fundamental right or categorizes on the basis of an inherently suspect characteristic, the Equal Protection Clause requires only that the classification rationally further a legitimate state interest.

A

At the outset, petitioner suggests that her challenge to Article XIIIA qualifies for heightened scrutiny because it infringes upon the constitutional right to travel. See, e.g., Zobel v. Williams, 457 U.S. 55, 60, n. 6, 102 S.Ct. 2309, 2312, n.6 (1982); Memorial Hospital v. Maricopa County, 415 U.S. 250, 254–256, 94 S.Ct. 1076, 1080–1081 (1974). In particular, petitioner alleges that the exemptions to reassessment for transfers by owners over 55 and for transfers between parents and children run afoul of the right to travel, because they classify directly on the basis of California residency. But the complaint does not allege that petitioner herself has been impeded from traveling or from settling in California because, as has been noted, prior to purchasing her home, petitioner lived in an apartment in Los Angeles. This Court's prudential standing principles impose a "general prohibition on a litigant's raising another person's legal rights." Allen v. Wright, 468 U. S. 737, 751, 104 S.Ct. 3315, 3324 (1984). Petitioner has not identified any obstacle preventing others who wish to travel or settle in California from asserting claims on their own behalf, nor has she shown any special relationship with those whose rights she seeks to assert, such that we might overlook this prudential limitation. Accordingly, petitioner may not assert the constitutional right to travel as a basis for heightened review.

B

The appropriate standard of review is whether the difference in treatment between newer and older owners rationally furthers a legitimate state interest. In general, the Equal Protection Clause is satisfied so long as there is a plausible policy reason for the classification, see United States Railroad Retirement Bd. v. Fritz, 449 U.S. 166, 174, 179, 101 S.Ct. 453, 459, 461 (1980), the legislative facts on which the classification is apparently based rationally may have been considered to be true by the governmental decision maker, see Minnesota v. Clover Leaf Creamery Co., 449 U.S. 456, 464, 101 S.Ct. 715, 724 (1981), and the relationship of the classification to its goal is not so attenuated as to render the distinction arbitrary or irrational, see Cleburne v. Cleburne Living Center, Inc., 473 U.S., at 446, 105 S.Ct., at 3257. This standard is especially deferential in the context of classifications made by complex tax laws.* * *

As between newer and older owners, Article XIIIA does not discriminate with respect to either the tax rate or the annual rate of adjustment in assessments. Newer and older owners alike benefit in both the short and long run from the protections of a 1% tax rate ceiling and no more than a 2% increase in assessment value per year. New owners and old owners are treated differently with respect to one factor only—the basis on which their property is initially assessed. Petitioner's true complaint is that the State has denied her—a new owner—the benefit of the same assessment value that her neighbors—older owners—enjoy.

We have no difficulty in ascertaining at least two rational or reasonable considerations of difference or policy that justify denying petitioner the benefits of her neighbors' lower assessments. First, the State has a legitimate interest in local neighborhood preservation, continuity, and stability. Euclid v. Ambler Realty Co., 272 U.S. 365, 47 S.Ct. 114 (1926). The State therefore legitimately can decide to structure its tax system to discourage rapid turnover in ownership of homes and businesses, for example, in order to inhibit displacement of lower income families by the forces of gentrification or of established, "mom-and-pop" businesses by newer chain operations. By permitting older owners to pay progressively less in taxes than new owners of comparable property, the Article XIIIA assessment scheme rationally furthers this interest.

Second, the State legitimately can conclude that a new owner at the time of acquiring his property does not have the same reliance interest warranting protection against higher taxes as does an existing owner. The State may deny a new owner at the point of purchase the right to "lock in" to the same assessed value as is enjoyed by an existing owner of comparable property, because an existing owner rationally may be thought to have vested expectations in his property or home that are more deserving of protection than the anticipatory expectations of a new owner at the point of purchase. A new owner has full information about the scope of future tax liability before acquiring the property, and if he thinks the future tax burden is too demanding, he can decide not to complete the purchase at all. By contrast, the existing owner, already saddled with his purchase, does not have the option of deciding not to buy his home if taxes become prohibitively high. To meet his tax obligations, he might be forced to sell his home or to divert his income away from the purchase of food, clothing, and other necessities. In short, the State may decide that it is worse to have owned and lost, than never to have owned at all.

This Court previously has acknowledged that classifications serving to protect legitimate expectation and reliance interests do not deny equal protection of the laws. "The protection of reasonable reliance interests is not only a legitimate governmental objective: it provides an exceedingly persuasive justification...." Heckler v. Mathews, 465 U.S. 728, 746, 104 S.Ct. 1387, 1399 (1984) (internal quotation marks omitted). For example, in Kadrmas v. Dickinson Public Schools, 487 U.S. 450., 108 S.Ct. 2481 (1988), the Court determined that a prohibition on user fees for bus service in "reorganized" school districts but not in "nonreorganized" school districts does not violate the Equal Protection Clause, because "the legislature could conceivably have believed that such a policy would serve the legitimate purpose of fulfilling the reasonable expectations of those residing in districts with free busing arrangements imposed by reorganization plans." Id., at 465, 108 S.Ct., at 2491. Similarly, in United States Railroad Retirement Bd. v. Fritz, supra, the Court determined that a denial of dual "windfall" retirement benefits to some railroad workers but not others did not violate the Equal Protection Clause, because "Congress could properly conclude that persons who had actually acquired statutory entitlement to windfall benefits while still employed in the railroad industry had a greater equitable claim to those benefits than the members of appellee's class who were no longer in railroad employment when they became eligible for dual benefits." 449 U.S., at 178, 101 S.Ct., at 461. Finally, in New Orleans v. Dukes, 427 U.S. 297, 96 S.Ct. 2513 (1976), the Court determined that an ordinance banning certain street-vendor operations, but grandfathering existing vendors who had been in operation for more than eight years, did not violate the Equal Protection Clause because the "city could reasonably decide that newer businesses were less likely to have built up substantial reliance interests in continued operation." Id., at 305, 96 S.Ct., at 2518.

Petitioner argues that Article XIIIA cannot be distinguished from the tax assessment practice found to violate the Equal Protection Clause in *Allegheny Pittsburgh*. Like Article XIIIA, the practice at issue in *Allegheny Pittsburgh* resulted in dramatic disparities in taxation of properties of comparable value. But an obvious and critical factual difference between this case and *Allegheny Pittsburgh* is the absence of any indication in

Allegheny Pittsburgh that the policies underlying an acquisition-value taxation scheme could conceivably have been the purpose for the Webster County tax assessor's unequal assessment scheme. In the first place, Webster County argued that "its assessment scheme is rationally related to its purpose of assessing properties *at true current value*" (emphasis added). 488 U.S., at 343, 109 S.Ct., at 637. Moreover, the West Virginia "Constitution and laws provide that all property of the kind held by petitioners shall be taxed at a rate uniform throughout the State according to its estimated market value," and the Court found "no suggestion" that "the State may have adopted a different system in practice from that specified by statute." Id., at 345, 109 S.Ct., at 638–639.

To be sure, the Equal Protection Clause does not demand for purposes of rational-basis review that a legislature or governing decisionmaker actually articulate at any time the purpose or rationale supporting its classification. United States Railroad Retirement Bd. v. Fritz, 449 U.S., at 179, 101 S.Ct., at 461 See also McDonald v. Board of Election Comm'rs of Chicago, 394 U.S. 802, 809, 89 S.Ct. 1404, 1408 (1969) (legitimate state purpose may be ascertained even when the legislative or administrative history is silent). Nevertheless, this Court's review does require that a purpose may conceivably or "may reasonably have been the purpose and policy" of the relevant governmental decisionmaker. Allied Stores of Ohio, Inc. v. Bowers, 358 U.S. 522, 528–529, 79 S.Ct.437, 442 (1959). See also Schweiker v. Wilson, 450 U.S. 221, 235, 101 S.Ct. 1074, 1083 (1981) (classificatory scheme must "rationally advanc[e] a reasonable and *identifiable* governmental objective" (emphasis added)). *Allegheny Pittsburgh* was the rare case where the facts precluded any plausible inference that the reason for the unequal assessment practice was to achieve the benefits of an acquisition-value tax scheme. By contrast, Article XIIIA was enacted precisely to achieve the benefits of an acquisition-value system. Allegheny Pittsburgh is not controlling here.

Finally, petitioner contends that the unfairness of Article XIIIA is made worse by its exemptions from reassessment for two special classes of new owners: persons aged 55 and older, who exchange principal residences, and children who acquire property from their parents. This Court previously has declined to hold that narrow exemptions from a general scheme of taxation necessarily render the overall scheme invidiously discriminatory. See, e.g., Regan v. Taxation with Representation of Washington, 461 U.S. at 550–551, 103 S.Ct., at 2003 (denial of tax exemption to nonprofit lobbying organizations, but with an exception for veterans' groups, does not violate equal protection). For purposes of rational-basis review, the "latitude of discretion is notably wide in ... the granting of partial or total exemptions upon grounds of policy." F.S. Royster Guano Co. v. Virginia, 253 U.S., at 415, 40 S.Ct., at 562.

The two exemptions at issue here rationally further legitimate purposes. The people of California reasonably could have concluded that older persons in general should not be discouraged from moving to a residence more suitable to their changing family size or income. Similarly, the people of California reasonably could have concluded that the interests of family and neighborhood continuity and stability are furthered by and warrant an exemption for transfers between parents and children. Petitioner has not demonstrated that no rational bases lie for either of these exemptions.

III

Petitioner and *amici* argue with some appeal that Article XIIIA frustrates the "American dream" of home ownership for many younger and poorer California families. They argue that Article XIIIA places start-up businesses that depend on ownership of property at a severe disadvantage in competing with established businesses. They argue that Article XIIIA dampens demand for and construction of new housing and buildings. And they argue that Article XIIIA constricts local tax revenues at the expense of public education and vital services.

Time and again, however, this Court has made clear in the rational-basis context that the "Constitution presumes that, absent some reason to infer antipathy, even improvident decisions will eventually be rectified by the democratic process and that judicial intervention is generally unwarranted no matter how unwisely we may think a political branch has acted" (footnote omitted). Vance v. Bradley, 440 U.S. 93, 97, 99 S.Ct. 939, 942–943 (1979). Certainly, California's grand experiment appears to vest benefits in a broad, powerful, and entrenched segment of society, and, as the Court of Appeal surmised, ordinary democratic processes may be unlikely to prompt its reconsideration or repeal. Yet many wise and well-intentioned laws suffer from the same malady. Article XIIIA is not palpably arbitrary, and we must decline petitioner's request to upset the will of the people of California.

The judgment of the Court of Appeal is affirmed.

It is so ordered.

[The opinion of JUSTICE THOMAS, concurring in part and concurring in the judgment, has been omitted.]

JUSTICE STEVENS, dissenting.

During the two past decades, California property owners have enjoyed extraordinary prosperity. As the State's population has mushroomed, so has the value of its real estate. Between 1976 and 1986 alone, the total assessed value of California property subject to property taxation increased tenfold. Simply put, those who invested in California real estate in the 1970s are among the most fortunate capitalists in the world.

Proposition 13 has provided these successful investors with a tremendous windfall and, in doing so, has created severe inequities in California's property tax scheme. These property owners (hereinafter "the Squires") are guaranteed that, so long as they retain their property and do not improve it, their taxes will not increase more than 2% in any given year.

As a direct result of this windfall for the Squires, later purchasers must pay far more than their fair share of property taxes.

The specific disparity that prompted petitioner to challenge the constitutionality of Proposition 13 is the fact that her annual property tax bill is almost 5 times as large as that of her neighbors who own comparable homes: While her neighbors' 1989 taxes averaged less than $400, petitioner was taxed $1,700. This disparity is not unusual under Proposition 13. Indeed, some homeowners pay 17 times as much in taxes as their neighbors with comparable property. For vacant land, the disparities may be as great as 500 to 1. Moreover, as Proposition 13 controls the taxation of commercial property as well as residential property, the regime greatly favors the commercial enterprises of the Squires, placing new businesses at a substantial disadvantage.

As a result of Proposition 13, the Squires, who own 44% of the owner occupied residences, paid only 25% of the total taxes collected from homeowners in 1989. These disparities are aggravated by § 2 of Proposition 13, which exempts from reappraisal a property owner's home and up to $1 million of other real property when that property is transferred to a child of the owner. This exemption can be invoked repeatedly and indefinitely, allowing the Proposition 13 windfall to be passed from generation to generation. As the California Senate Commission on Property Tax Equity and Revenue observed:

> "The inequity is clear. One young family buys a new home and is assessed at full market value. Another young family inherits its home, but pays taxes based on their parents' date of acquisition even though both homes are of identical value. Not only does this constitutional provision offend a policy of equal tax treatment for taxpayers in similar situations, it appears to favor the housing needs of children with homeowner parents over children with non homeowner parents. With the repeal of the state's gift and inheritance tax in 1982, the rationale for this exemption is negligible." Commission Report, at 9–10.

The Commission was too generous. To my mind, the rationale for such disparity is not merely "negligible," it is nonexistent. Such a law establishes a privilege of a medieval character: Two families with equal needs and equal resources are treated differently solely because of their different heritage.

In my opinion, such disparate treatment of similarly situated taxpayers is arbitrary and unreasonable. Although the Court today recognizes these gross inequities, its analysis of the justification for those inequities consists largely of a restatement of the benefits that accrue to long time property owners. That a law benefits those it benefits cannot be an adequate justification for severe inequalities such as those created by Proposition 13.

I

The standard by which we review equal protection challenges to state tax regimes is well established and properly deferential. "Where taxation is concerned and no specific federal right, apart from equal protection, is imperiled, the States have large leeway in making classifications and drawing lines which in their judgment produce reasonable systems of taxation." Lehnhausen v. Lake Shore Auto Parts Co., 410 U.S. 356, 359, 93 S.Ct. 1001, 1003 (1973). Thus, as the Court today notes, the issue in this case is "whether the difference in treatment between newer and older owners rationally furthers a legitimate state interest."

But deference is not abdication and "rational basis scrutiny" is still scrutiny. Thus we have, on several recent occasions, invalidated tax schemes under such a standard of review. See, e.g., Allegheny Pittsburgh Coal Co. v. County Comm'n of Webster County, 488 U.S. 336, 109 S.Ct. 633 (1989).

Just three Terms ago, this Court unanimously invalidated Webster County, West Virginia's assessment scheme under rational basis scrutiny. Webster County employed a *de facto* Proposition 13 assessment system: The County assessed recently purchased property on the basis of its purchase price but made only occasional adjustments (averaging 3–4% per year) to the assessments of other properties. Just as in this case, "[t]his approach systematically produced dramatic differences in valuation between ... recently transferred property and otherwise comparable surrounding land." Allegheny Pittsburgh, 488 U. S., at 341, 109 S.Ct., at 637.

The " '[i]ntentional systematic undervaluation,' " *id.*, at 345, 109 S.Ct., at 638, found constitutionally infirm in *Allegheny Pittsburgh* has been codified in California by Proposition 13. That the discrimination in *Allegheny Pittsburgh* was *de facto* and the discrimination in this case *de jure* makes little difference. "The purpose of the equal protection clause of the Fourteenth Amendment is to secure every person within the State's jurisdiction against intentional and arbitrary discrimination, *whether occasioned by express terms of a statute or by its improper execution through duly constituted agents*." Sunday Lake Iron Co. v. Wakefield, 247 U.S. 350, 352–353, 38 S.Ct. 495, 495 (1918) (emphasis added). If anything, the inequality created by Proposition 13 is constitutionally more problematic because it is the product of a state wide policy rather than the result of an individual assessor's maladministration.

Nor can *Allegheny Pittsburgh* be distinguished because West Virginia law established a market value assessment regime. Webster County's scheme was constitutionally invalid not because it was a departure from *state law*, but because it involved the relative " 'systematic undervaluation ... [of] property *in the same class*' " (as that class was defined by state law). Allegheny Pittsburgh, 488 U.S., at 345, 109 S.Ct., at 639 (emphasis added). Our decisions have established that the Equal Protection Clause is offended as much by the arbitrary delineation of classes of property (as in this case) as by the arbitrary treatment of properties within the same class (as in *Allegheny Pittsburgh*). Thus, if our unanimous holding in *Allegheny Pittsburgh* was sound—and I remain convinced that it was—it follows inexorably that Proposition 13, like Webster County's assessment scheme, violates the Equal Protection Clause. Indeed, in my opinion, state wide discrimination is far more invidious than a local aberration that creates a tax disparity.

The States, of course, have broad power to classify property in their taxing schemes and if the "classification is neither capricious nor arbitrary, and rests upon some reasonable consideration of difference or policy, there is no denial of the equal protection of the law." Brown Forman Co. v. Kentucky, 217 U.S., at 573, 30 S.Ct., at 580. As we stated in *Allegheny Pittsburgh,* a "State may divide different kinds of property into classes and assign to each class a different tax burden so long as those divisions and burdens are reasonable." 488 U.S., at 344, 109 S.Ct., at 588.

Consistent with this standard, the Court has long upheld tax classes based on the taxpayer's ability to pay, see, e. g., Fox v. Standard Oil Co. of New Jersey, 294 U.S. 87, 101, 55 S.Ct. 333, 339 (1935); the nature (tangible or intangible) of the property, see, e.g., Klein v. Jefferson County Board of Tax Supervisors, 282 U.S. 19, 23–24, 51 S.Ct. 15, 16 (1930); the use of the property, see, e.g., Clark v. Kansas City, 176 U.S. 114, 20 S.Ct. 284 (1900); and the status (corporate or individual) of the property owner, see, e.g., Lehnhausen v. Lake Shore Auto Parts Co., 410 U.S. 356, 93 S.Ct. 1001 (1973). Proposition 13 employs none of these familiar classifications. Instead it classifies property based on its nominal purchase price: All property purchased for the same price is taxed the same amount (leaving aside the 2% annual adjustment). That this scheme can be named (an "acquisition value" system) does not render it any less arbitrary or unreasonable. Under Proposition 13, a majestic estate purchased for $150,000 in 1975 (and now worth more than $2 million) is placed in the same tax class as a humble cottage purchased today for $150,000. The only feature those two properties have in common is that somewhere, sometime a sale contract for each was executed that contained the price "$150,000." Particularly in an environment of phenomenal real property appreciation, to classify property based on its purchase price is "palpably arbitrary." Allied Stores of Ohio, Inc. v. Bowers, 358 U.S. 522, 530, 79 S.Ct. 437, 442 (1959).

II

Under contemporary equal protection doctrine, the test of whether a classification is arbitrary is "whether the difference in treatment between [earlier and later purchasers] rationally furthers a legitimate state interest." Ante, at 8. The adjectives and adverbs in this standard are more important than the nouns and verbs.

A *legitimate* state interest must encompass the interests of members of the disadvantaged class and the community at large as well as the direct interests of the members of the favored class. It must have a purpose or goal independent of the direct effect of the legislation and one

" 'that we may reasonably presume to have motivated an impartial legislature.' " Cleburne v. Cleburne Living Center, Inc., 473 U.S. 432, 452, n. 4, 105 S.Ct. 3249, 3261, n. 4 (1985) (Stevens, J., concurring) (quoting United States Railroad Retirement Board v. Fritz, 449 U.S. 166, 180–181, 101 S.Ct. 453, 462 (1980) (Stevens, J., concurring in judgment)). That a classification must find justification outside itself saves judicial review of such classifications from becoming an exercise in tautological reasoning.

"A State cannot deflect an equal protection challenge by observing that in light of the statutory classification all those within the burdened class are similarly situated. The classification must reflect pre-existing differences; it cannot create new ones that are supported by only their own bootstraps. 'The Equal Protection Clause requires more of a state law than nondiscriminatory application within the class it establishes.' Rinaldi v. Yeager, 384 U.S. 305, 308 [86 S.Ct. 1497, 1499] (1966)." Williams v. Vermont, 472 U.S., at 27, 105 S.Ct., at 2474.

If the goal of the discriminatory classification is not independent from the policy itself, "each choice [of classification] will import its own goal, each goal will count as acceptable, and the requirement of a 'rational' choice goal relation will be satisfied by the very making of the choice." Ely, Legislative and Administrative Motivation in Constitutional Law, 79 Yale L. J. 1205, 1247 (1970).

A classification *rationally* furthers a state interest when there is some fit between the disparate treatment and the legislative purpose. As noted above, in the review of tax statutes we have allowed such fit to be generous and approximate, recognizing that "rational distinctions may be made with substantially less than mathematical exactitude." New Orleans v. Dukes, 427 U.S. 297, 303, 96 S.Ct. 2513, 2516 (1976). Nonetheless, in some cases the underinclusiveness or the overinclusiveness of a classification will be so severe that it cannot be said that the legislative distinction "rationally furthers" the posited state interest. See, e. g., Jimenez v. Weinberger, 417 U.S. 628, 636–638, 94 S.Ct. 2496, 2501–2502 (1974).

The Court's cursory analysis of Proposition 13 pays little attention to either of these aspects of the controlling standard of review. The first state interest identified by the Court is California's "interest in local neighborhood preservation, continuity, and stability." *Ante,* at 9 (citing Euclid v. Ambler Realty Co., 272 U.S. 365, 47 S.Ct. 114 (1926)). It is beyond question that "inhibit[ing the] displacement of lower income families by the forces of gentrification," ante, at 9–10, is a legitimate state interest; the central issue is whether the disparate treatment of earlier and later purchasers *rationally furthers* this goal. Here the Court offers not an analysis, but only a conclusion: "By permitting older owners to pay progressively less in taxes than new owners of comparable property, [Proposition 13] rationally furthers this interest." Ante, at 10.

I disagree. In my opinion, Proposition 13 sweeps too broadly and operates too indiscriminately to "rationally further" the State's interest in neighborhood preservation. No doubt there are some early purchasers living on fixed or limited incomes who could not afford to pay higher taxes and still maintain their homes. California has enacted special legislation to respond to their plight. Those concerns cannot provide an adequate justification for Proposition 13. A state wide, across the board tax windfall for *all* property owners and their descendants is no more a "rational" means for protecting this small subgroup than a blanket tax exemption for all taxpayers named Smith would be a rational means to protect a particular taxpayer named Smith who demonstrated difficulty paying her tax bill.

Even within densely populated Los Angeles County, residential property comprises less than half of the market value of the property tax roll. It cannot be said that the legitimate state interest in preserving neighborhood character is "rationally furthered" by tax benefits for owners of commercial, industrial, vacant, and other nonresidential properties. It is just short of absurd to conclude that the legitimate state interest in protecting a relatively small number of economically vulnerable families is "rationally furthered" by a tax windfall for all 9,787,887 property owners in California.

The Court's conclusion is unsound not only because of the lack of numerical fit between the posited state interest and Proposition 13's inequities but also because of the lack of logical fit between ends and means. Although the State may have a valid interest in preserving some neighborhoods, Proposition 13 not only "inhibit[s the] displacement" of settled families, it also inhibits the transfer of unimproved land, abandoned buildings, and substandard uses. Thus, contrary to the Court's suggestion, Proposition 13 is not like a zoning system. A zoning system functions by recognizing different uses of property and treating those different uses differently. See Euclid v. Ambler Realty Co., 272 U. S., at 388–390, 47 S.Ct., at 118–119. Proposition 13 treats all property alike, giving *all* owners tax breaks, and discouraging the transfer or improvement of *all* property—the developed and the dilapidated, the neighborly and the nuisance.

In short, although I agree with the Court that "neighborhood preservation" is a legitimate state interest, I cannot agree that a tax windfall for all persons who purchased property before 1978 *rationally* furthers that interest. To my mind, Proposition 13 is too blunt a tool to accomplish such a specialized goal. The severe inequalities created by Proposition 13 cannot be justified by such an interest.

The second state interest identified by the Court is the "reliance interests" of the earlier purchasers. Here I find the Court's reasoning difficult to follow. Although the protection of reasonable reliance interests is a legitimate governmental purpose, see Heckler v. Mathews, 465 U.S. 728, 746, 104 S.Ct. 1387, 1399 (1984), this case does not implicate such interests. A reliance interest is created when an individual justifiably acts under the assumption that an existing legal condition will persist; thus reliance interests are most often implicated when the government provides some benefit and then acts to eliminate the benefit. See, e.g., New Orleans v. Dukes, 427 U.S. 297, 96 S.Ct. 2513 (1976). In this case, those who purchased property before Proposition 13 was enacted received no assurances that assessments would only increase at a limited rate; indeed, to the contrary, many purchased property in the hope that property values (and assessments) would appreciate substantially and quickly. It cannot be said, therefore, that the earlier purchasers of property somehow have a reliance interest in limited tax increases.

Perhaps what the Court means is that post-Proposition 13 purchasers have less reliance interests than pre-Proposition 13 purchasers. The Court reasons that the State may tax earlier and later purchasers differently because

"an existing owner rationally may be thought to have vested expectations in his property or home that are more deserving of protection than the anticipatory expectations of a new owner at the point of purchase. A new owner has full information about the scope of future tax liability before acquiring the property, and if he thinks the future tax burden is too demanding, he can decide not to complete the purchase at all. By contrast, the existing owner, already saddled with his purchase, does not have the option of deciding not to buy his home if taxes become prohibitively high." Ante, at 10.

This simply restates the effects of Proposition 13. A pre-Proposition 13 owner has "vested expectations" in reduced taxes *only* because Proposition 13 gave her such expectations; a later purchaser has no such expectations because Proposition 13 does not provide her such expectations. But the same can be said of any arbitrary protection for an existing class of taxpayers. Consider a law that establishes that homes with even street numbers would be taxed at twice the rate of homes with odd street numbers. It is certainly true that the even numbered homeowners could not decide to "unpurchase" their homes and that those considering buying an even numbered home would know that it came with an extra tax burden, but certainly that would not justify the arbitrary imposition of disparate tax burdens based on house numbers. So it is in this case. Proposition 13 provides a benefit for earlier purchasers and imposes a burden on later purchasers. To say that the later purchasers know what they are getting into does not answer the critical question: Is it reasonable and constitutional to tax early purchasers less than late purchasers when at the time of taxation their properties are comparable? This question the Court does not answer.

Distilled to its essence, the Court seems to be saying that earlier purchasers can benefit under Proposition 13 because earlier purchasers benefit under Proposition 13. If, however, a law creates a disparity, the State's interest preserving that disparity cannot be a "*legitimate* state interest" justifying that inequity. As noted above, a statute's disparate treatment must be justified by a purpose *distinct* from the very effects created by that statute. Thus, I disagree with the Court that the severe inequities wrought by Proposition 13 can be justified by what the Court calls the "reliance interests" of those who benefit from that scheme.

In my opinion, it is irrational to treat similarly situated persons differently on the basis of the date they joined the class of property owners. Until today, I would have thought this proposition far from controversial. In Zobel v. Williams, 457 U.S. 55, 102 S.Ct. 2309 (1982), we ruled that Alaska's program of distributing cash dividends on the basis of the recipient's years of residency in the State violated the Equal Protection Clause. The Court wrote:

> "If the states can make the amount of a cash dividend depend on length of residence, what would preclude varying university tuition on a sliding scale based on years of residence—or even limiting access offinite public facilities, eligibility for student loans, for civil service jobs, or for government contracts by length of domicile? *Could states impose different taxes based on length of residence?* Alaska's reasoning could open the door to state apportionment of other rights, benefits, and services according to length of residency. It would permit the states to divide citizens into expanding numbers of permanent classes. Such a result would be clearly impermissible." Id., at 64, 102 S.Ct., at 2315 (emphasis added) (footnotes omitted).

Similarly, the Court invalidated on equal protection grounds New Mexico's policy of providing a permanent tax exemption for Vietnam veterans who had been state residents before May 8, 1976, but not to more recent arrivals. Hooper v. Bernalillo County Assessor, 472 U.S. 612, 105 S.Ct. 2862 (1985). The Court expressly rejected the State's claim that it had a legitimate interest in providing special rewards to veterans who lived in the State before 1976 and concluded that "[n]either the Equal Protection Clause, nor this Court's precedents, permit the State to prefer established resident veterans over newcomers in the retroactive apportionment of an economic benefit." Id., at 623, 105 S.Ct., at 2868.

As these decisions demonstrate, the selective provision of benefits based on the timing of one's membership in a class (whether that class be the class of residents or the class of property owners) is rarely a "legitimate state interest." Similarly situated neighbors have an equal right to share in the benefits of local government. It would obviously be unconstitutional to provide one with more or better fire or police protection than the other; it is just as plainly unconstitutional to require one to pay five times as much in property taxes as the other for the same government services. In my opinion, the severe inequalities created by Proposition 13 are arbitrary and unreasonable and do not rationally further a legitimate state interest.

Accordingly, I respectfully dissent.

Nᴏᴛᴇꜱ ᴀɴᴅ Qᴜᴇꜱᴛɪᴏɴꜱ

A. Allegheny, Nordlinger, *and the Equal Protection Clause.* The Court's decisions in *Allegheny* and *Nordlinger* raise a series of questions bearing on the relationship between a taxpayer's federal right to equal protection and the underlying state classification scheme. If a state can classify property for ad valorem tax purposes on the basis of sales price, then, as the Court has stated in an analogous context, "the only question relevant for us is whether the state has done so." Nashville, C. & St. L. Ry. v. Browning, 310 U.S. 362, 369, 60 S.Ct. 968 (1940). The Court's conclusion in *Allegheny*, of course, was based on its determination that the state had not done so. Does this mean, however, that if West Virginia tomorrow were formally to adopt an ad valorem tax system based on recent sales prices that the preexisting practice of the Webster County assessor would satisfy equal protection strictures? Apparently so, in light of *Nordlinger.*

But why should the result be any different merely because the classification in West Virginia was de facto rather than de jure? As the Court declared in *Nashville, C. & St. L. Ry.*, in dismissing an equal protection challenge by railroads to the valuation of its property which was overvalued by comparison to the valuation of other property in Tennessee:

> If the discrimination of which the Railway complains had been formally written into the statutes of Tennessee, a challenge to its constitutionality would be frivolous. If the state supreme court had construed the requirement of uniformity in the Tennessee Constitution so as to permit recognition of these diversities, no appeal could successfully be made to the Fourteenth Amendment. Here * * * all the organs of the state are conforming to a practice, systematic, unbroken for more than forty years, and now questioned for the first time. It would be a narrow conception of jurisprudence to confine the notion of "laws" to what is found written on the statute books, and to disregard the gloss which life has written upon it. Settled state practice cannot supplant constitutional guarantees, but it can establish what is state law. * * * And if the state supreme court chooses to cover up under a formal veneer of uniformity the established system of differentiation between two classes of property, an exposure of that fiction is not enough to establish its unconstitutionality. * * * The Equal Protection Clause is not a command of candor.

Id., 310 U.S. at 369.

The Court's answer to the question raised in the preceding paragraph would presumably be the one it gave in *Allegheny*: "There is no suggestion in the opinion of the Supreme Court of West Virginia, or from any other authoritative source, that the State may have adopted a different system in practice from that specified by statute." Allegheny, 488 U.S. at 345. But it is difficult to reconcile this view with the West Virginia Supreme Court's declaration that "[t]he uniform use of recent deed values as the basis for appraising property subject to ad valorem taxation does not violate W. Va. Const., art I, § 1 ['taxation shall be equal and uniform throughout the

State']." In re 1975 Tax Assessments Against Oneida Coal Co., 178 W.Va. 485, 360 S.E.2d 560, 564 (1987). If the Tennessee Supreme Court may "cover up under a formal veneer of uniformity the established system of differentiation between two classes of property," Nashville, C. & St. L. Ry., 310 U.S. at 369, why may not the West Virginia Supreme Court do so? Perhaps the evidence of the adoption of an implicit policy applied evenhandedly to all similarly situated property in the state was not as strong in West Virginia as it was in Tennessee. In any event, the Court's opinion in *Allegheny* leaves us with this perplexing question: When does "intentional systematic undervaluation by state officials of property in the same class," Sunday Lake Iron, 247 U.S. at 352–53, which is nevertheless sanctioned by the highest court of the state as satisfying that state's uniformity and equality requirement, amount merely to a covering up "under a formal veneer of uniformity the established system of differentiation between two classes of property"? Nashville, C. & St. L. Ry., 310 U.S. at 369.

B. *State Court Equal Protection Decisions.* State courts are, of course, bound by the Supreme Court's precedents when they construe the *federal* Equal Protection Clause. When construing equal protection clauses of state constitutions, however, the state courts are free to depart from the Supreme Court's views of equal protection. Indeed, the Iowa Supreme Court in 2004 struck down as offensive to the state's equality provision the very same tax classification that the U.S. Supreme Court had sustained over federal equal protection objections in 2003 in *Fitzgerald*. Notwithstanding the U.S. Supreme Court's determination that the Iowa legislature's higher tax on race-track gambling than on riverboat gambling had a rational basis and therefore passed muster under the federal Equal Protection Clause, the Iowa Supreme Court concluded on remand that the tax was invalid under Iowa's equality clause because "the classifications * * * lack a rational basis in the constitutional sense." Racing Ass'n of Cent. Iowa v. Fitzgerald, 675 N.W.2d 1, 16 (Iowa 2004).

State courts have also departed from the Supreme Court's equal protection doctrine in the school financing cases, in which some courts have struck down, under their states' equal protection clauses, property taxes that would have been sustained by the Supreme Court. Relying on the Equal Protection Clause of the state constitution, the Texas Supreme Court struck down a provision of the state's property tax law that denied preferential "open-space land" designation to property owned by nonresident aliens. HL Farm Corp. v. Self, 877 S.W.2d 288 (Tex. 1994). The court concluded that the distinction drawn between foreign and domestic owners was not rationally related to the purpose of the statute, which was to promote and preserve open-space land. Yet a Texas court had previously sustained the very same statute over federal equal protection objections. Alexander Ranch, Inc. v. Central Appraisal Dist., 733 S.W.2d 303, 307 (Tex. App. 1987), cert. denied, 486 U.S. 1026, 108 S.Ct. 2005 (1988).

Most state courts do not carefully distinguish between federal and state constitutional provisions or criteria when adjudicating equal protection issues. Although it is possible that the U.S. Supreme Court would have reached the same result the state courts have reached in these equal protection cases, some state courts appear to be more sympathetic than the U.S. Supreme

Court to equal protection challenges to state tax classifications. Consider the following cases: In Northern Natural Gas Co. v. State Bd. of Equalization & Assessment, 232 Neb. 806, 443 N.W.2d 249 (1989), cert. denied, 493 U.S. 1078, 110 S.Ct. 1130 (1990), the Nebraska Supreme Court held that a pipeline had a right under the Equal Protection Clause to ad valorem tax treatment identical to that accorded to railroads. The railroads' tax assessments had been reduced pursuant to a federal statute protecting railroads (but not pipelines) from property taxes that exceeded those generally applicable to most other commercial and industrial property in the state. In MCI Telecommunications Corp. v. Limbach, 68 Ohio St.3d 195, 625 N.E.2d 597, cert. denied, 513 U.S. 818, 115 S.Ct. 77 (1994), the Ohio Supreme Court held that a long-distance "interexchange" carrier, which owned the same type of equipment as a reseller of telecommunications services, was entitled under the Equal Protection Clause to be treated in the same manner as the reseller for ad valorem tax purposes. The long-distance carrier was considered to be a utility under state law but the reseller was not. And the Vermont Supreme Court held in Oxx v. Vermont Dep't of Taxes, 159 Vt. 371, 618 A.2d 1321 (1992), that the state violated the Equal Protection Clause when it compelled a taxpayer to follow federal income tax reporting requirements thereby forcing him to "recapture" a federal investment tax credit for state income tax purposes for which he received no state tax benefit. In the court's view, there was no rational basis for requiring the taxpayer to pay the same amount of tax as a comparably situated taxpayer, also subject to recapture, who had derived a state income tax benefit in a prior year. Wholly apart from the wisdom of the legislative lines drawn in these cases, can you think of a "rational basis" related to a "legitimate state purpose" that the state might have had in these cases for drawing the tax classification in question? For a comment on the *Northern Natural Gas* case, see Walter Hellerstein, "Equal Protection Run Amok: An Analysis of the Nebraska Supreme Court's Decision in the *Northern Natural Gas* Case," Tax Notes, Nov. 20, 1989, p. 995.

C. *School Finance Litigation and the Equal Protection Clause.* When states rely on local property taxes to fund public schools, interdistrict disparities in property tax wealth can give rise to both unequal levels of school spending and differences in property tax burdens. For example, imagine a state with two school districts—Rich District and Poor District. Assume that the per pupil assessed valuation of property in Rich District is $100,000, while the same figure in Poor District is $20,000. Applying the same tax rate of, say, 10 percent, will generate $10,000 per pupil in Rich District, but only $2,000 in Poor District. Alternatively, generating comparable revenues of $5,000 would require a tax rate of 25 percent in Poor District but only 5 percent in Rich District. These disparities have spawned litigation under both federal and state equal protection clauses. As you may have learned in earlier courses in constitutional law, the U.S. Supreme Court put an end to federal challenges in San Antonio Independent School Dist. v. Rodriguez, 411 U.S. 1, 93 S.Ct. 1278 (1973); however, school financing systems that rely on local property taxation have been and continue to be assailed on state grounds.[s]

---

s. For a summary of developments in this area, see Table 3.3, School finance litigation, by year, case, and status, by state: 1970–99, p. 41, in David Hurst, et al., National Center for

The New Jersey experience with the legality of school financing is a fascinating illustration of the interaction between the legal and political processes. In Robinson v. Cahill, 62 N.J. 473, 303 A.2d 273, cert. denied, 414 U.S. 976, 94 S.Ct. 292 (1973) (*Robinson I*), the New Jersey Supreme Court ruled that New Jersey's system of financing public education by local property taxation violated the state's obligation to furnish a thorough and efficient system of free public schools. However, in Robinson v. Cahill, 63 N.J. 196, 306 A.2d 65, cert. denied, 414 U.S. 976, 94 S.Ct. 292 (1973) (*Robinson II*), the court decided to take no action if the state legislature acted by December 31, 1974 to enact a comprehensive constitutional plan for state public education. When the legislature refused to change the system of school financing from one based on local property taxation to one funded by some other means, the court first delayed action and then ordered the disbursement of funds to finance the schools in accordance with specific criteria approved by the court. Robinson v. Cahill, 67 N.J. 35, 335 A.2d 6 (1975) (*Robinson III*); Robinson v. Cahill, 67 N.J. 333, 339 A.2d 193 (1975), republished at 69 N.J. 133, 351 A.2d 713 (1975) (*Robinson IV*). In response to this judicial action, the state legislature passed the Public School Education Act of 1975, which was designed to equalize payments among schools; the legislature, however, did not specifically provide for funding of the Act. The Act was held to be constitutional on its face, on the assumption that it would be fully funded. Robinson v. Cahill, 69 N.J. 449, 355 A.2d 129 (1976) (*Robinson V*). When the state legislature refused to enact an income tax to fund the Act, the court enjoined state public officials from operating the schools under existing financing schemes. Robinson v. Cahill, 70 N.J. 155, 358 A.2d 457 (1976) (*Robinson VI*). Resistance to a state income tax was very strong in New Jersey, but when the state's public schools closed and a federal court refused to lift the state court's injunction, the legislature adopted a modified type of income tax to fund the Public School Education Act. The New Jersey Supreme Court then lifted its own injunction. Robinson v. Cahill, 70 N.J. 464, 360 A.2d 400 (1976) (*Robinson VII*). In Abbott v. Burke, 119 N.J. 287, 575 A.2d 359 (1990) (*Abbott I*), the court invalidated the system approved in *Robinson V* on the ground that stark failures of poor urban school districts prevented students from competing with those from wealthier suburban school districts, and it ordered funding of poor urban districts at levels commensurate with wealthy districts. In Abbott v. Burke, 136 N.J. 444, 643 A.2d 575 (1994) (*Abbott II*), the court invalidated the system adopted by the New Jersey legislature in response to *Abbott I* on the grounds that it failed to achieve "parity" or "substantial equivalence" of funding between rich and poor districts and therefore failed to meet the mandate of *Abbott I*.

3. SEPARATE CLASSIFICATION OF FOREIGN AND DOMESTIC CORPORATIONS: THE INSURANCE COMPANY CASES

Taxes levied on foreign insurance companies for the privilege of doing business in the state have played a large role in the development of equal

---

Education Statistics, U.S. Dept. of Education, Overview and Inventory of State Education Reforms: 1990–2000, July 2003, available at http://nces.ed.gov/pubs2003/2003020.pdf.

protection principles under the Fourteenth Amendment. While the Commerce Clause has generally prevented the states from imposing burdensome or discriminatory taxes upon foreign corporations that seek to engage in interstate commerce within the state, the insurance industry falls within an exception to this rule. In Paul v. Virginia, 75 U.S. (8 Wall.) 168 (1869), the U.S. Supreme Court held that the insurance business did not constitute "commerce" within the meaning of the Commerce Clause, because "[i]ssuing a policy of insurance is not a transaction of commerce" and insurance "contracts are not articles of commerce within any proper meaning of the word." Id. at 183. Consequently, for much of our constitutional history, the insurance industry has been deprived of the protection of the Commerce Clause. Instead, it has been compelled to rely principally on the Equal Protection Clause as a defense against discriminatory state tax laws. Indeed, even though the Court ultimately overturned *Paul v. Virginia* and held that insurance was "commerce" within the meaning of the Commerce Clause, United States v. South–Eastern Underwriters Ass'n, 322 U.S. 533, 64 S.Ct. 1162 (1944), Congress quickly restored the status quo ante by enacting the McCarran–Ferguson Act, 15 U.S.C. §§ 1011–1015, which once again left the states free of Commerce Clause restraints in taxing the insurance industry.

The protection that the insurance industry has actually enjoyed from discriminatory state taxes under the Equal Protection Clause has been uneven at best because of the narrow reading that the Court gave to the Equal Protection Clause. The Court held that the Equal Protection Clause afforded no protection to a foreign corporation that had not yet entered the state to do business on the ground that, until the corporation had entered the state, it was not "a person within [the state's] jurisdiction" and was not, therefore, entitled to the equal protection of the state's laws. Philadelphia Fire Ass'n v. New York, 119 U.S. 110, 7 S.Ct. 108 (1886). As a consequence, the Court upheld fees imposed on foreign insurers as a condition to obtaining licenses to operate in the state, even though the state levied no comparable fees on domestic insurers. Id.; Lincoln Nat. Life Ins. Co. v. Read, 325 U.S. 673, 65 S.Ct. 1220 (1945). Once the foreign corporation had been licensed and had entered the state, however, it became entitled to equal protection of the laws as a person within the state's jurisdiction. Southern Ry. v. Greene, 216 U.S. 400, 30 S.Ct. 287 (1910). On this theory, the Court relied on the Equal Protection Clause in striking down a number of levies that favored domestic over foreign insurers. See Concordia Fire Ins. Co. v. Illinois, 292 U.S. 535, 54 S.Ct. 830 (1934); Hanover Fire Ins. Co. v. Carr, 272 U.S. 494, 47 S.Ct. 179 (1926).

METROPOLITAN LIFE INSURANCE COMPANY v. WARD

Supreme Court of the United States, 1985.
470 U.S. 869, 105 S.Ct. 1676.

JUSTICE POWELL delivered the opinion of the Court.

This case presents the question whether Alabama's domestic preference tax statute, Ala.Code §§ 27–4–4 and 27–4–5 (1975), that taxes out-of-state insurance companies at a higher rate than domestic insurance companies, violates the Equal Protection Clause.

I

Since 1955, the State of Alabama has granted a preference to its domestic insurance companies by imposing a substantially lower gross premiums tax rate on them than on out-of-state (foreign) companies.[2] Under the current statutory provisions, foreign life insurance companies pay a tax on their gross premiums received from business conducted in Alabama at a rate of 3 percent, and foreign companies selling other types of insurance pay at a rate of 4 percent. Ala.Code § 27–4–4(a) (1975). All domestic insurance companies, in contrast, pay at a rate of only 1 percent on all types of insurance premiums. § 27–4–5(a). As a result, a foreign insurance company doing the same type and volume of business in Alabama as a domestic company generally will pay three to four times as much in gross premiums taxes as its domestic competitor.

Alabama's domestic preference tax statute does provide that foreign companies may reduce the differential in gross premiums taxes by investing prescribed percentages of their worldwide assets in specified Alabama assets and securities. § 27–4–4(b). By investing 10 percent or more of its total assets in Alabama investments, for example, a foreign life insurer may reduce its gross premiums tax rate from 3 to 2 percent. Similarly, a foreign property and casualty insurer may reduce its tax rate from 4 to 3 percent. Smaller tax reductions are available based on investment of smaller percentages of a company's assets. Regardless of how much of its total assets a foreign company places in Alabama investments, it can never reduce its gross premiums tax rate to the same level paid by comparable domestic companies. These are entitled to the 1 percent tax rate even if they have no investments in the State. Thus, the investment provision permits foreign insurance companies to reduce, but never to eliminate, the discrimination inherent in the domestic preference tax statute.

II

Appellants, a group of insurance companies incorporated outside of the State of Alabama, filed claims with the Alabama Department of Insurance in 1981, contending that the domestic preference tax statute, as applied to them, violated the Equal Protection Clause. They sought refunds of taxes paid for the tax years 1977 through 1980. The Commissioner of Insurance denied all of their claims on July 8, 1981.

Appellants appealed to the Circuit Court for Montgomery County, seeking a judgment declaring the statute to be unconstitutional and requiring the Commissioner to make the appropriate refunds. Several domestic companies intervened, and the court consolidated all of the

---

2. For domestic preference tax purposes, Alabama defines a domestic insurer as a company that both is incorporated in Alabama and has its principal office and chief place of business within the State. Ala.Code § 27–4–1(3) (1975). A corporation that does not meet both of these criteria is characterized as a foreign insurer. § 27–4–1(2).

appeals, selecting two claims as lead cases to be tried and binding on all claimants. On cross-motions for summary judgment, the court ruled on May 17, 1982, that the statute was constitutional. Relying on this Court's opinion in Western & Southern Life Ins. Co. v. State Board of Equalization of California, 451 U.S. 648, 101 S.Ct. 2070 (1981), the court ruled that the Alabama statute did not violate the Equal Protection Clause because it served "at least two purposes, in addition to raising revenue: (1) encouraging the formation of new insurance companies in Alabama, and (2) encouraging capital investment by foreign insurance companies in the Alabama assets and governmental securities set forth in the statute." The court also found that the distinction the statute created between foreign and domestic companies was rationally related to those two purposes and that the Alabama Legislature reasonably could have believed that the classification would have promoted those purposes.

After their motion for a new trial was denied, appellants appealed to the Court of Civil Appeals. It affirmed the Circuit Court's rulings as to the existence of the two legitimate state purposes, but remanded for an evidentiary hearing on the issue of rational relationship, concluding that summary judgment was inappropriate on that question because the evidence was in conflict. Appellants petitioned the Supreme Court of Alabama for certiorari on the affirmance of the legitimate state purpose issue, and the State and the intervenors petitioned for review of the remand order. Appellants then waived their right to an evidentiary hearing on the issue whether the statute's classification bore a rational relationship to the two purposes found by the Circuit Court to be legitimate, and they requested a final determination of the legal issues with respect to their equal protection challenge to the statute. The Supreme Court denied certiorari on all claims. Appellants again waived their rights to an evidentiary hearing on the rational relationship issue and filed a joint motion with the other parties seeking rehearing and entry of a final judgment. The motion was granted, and judgment was entered for the State and the intervenors. This appeal followed, and we noted probable jurisdiction. We now reverse.

III

Prior to our decision in Western & Southern Life Ins. Co. v. State Board of Equalization of California, supra, the jurisprudence of the applicability of the Equal Protection Clause to discriminatory tax statutes had a somewhat checkered history. Lincoln National Life Ins. Co. v. Read, 325 U.S. 673, 65 S.Ct. 1220 (1945), held that so-called "privilege" taxes, required to be paid by a foreign corporation before it would be permitted to do business within a State, were immune from equal protection challenge. That case stood in stark contrast, however, to the Court's prior decisions in Southern R. Co. v. Greene, 216 U.S. 400, 30 S.Ct. 287 (1910), and Hanover Fire Ins. Co. v. Harding, 272 U.S. 494, 47 S.Ct. 179 (1926), as well as to later decisions, in which the Court had recognized that the Equal Protection Clause placed limits on other forms of discriminatory taxation imposed on out-of-state corporations solely because of their residence. See, e.g., WHYY, Inc. v. Glassboro, 393 U.S. 117, 89 S.Ct. 286 (1968); Allied Stores of Ohio, Inc. v. Bowers, 358 U.S. 522, 79 S.Ct. 437 (1959); Wheeling Steel Corp. v. Glander, 337 U.S. 562, 69 S.Ct. 1291 (1949).

In Western & Southern, supra, we reviewed all of these cases for the purpose of deciding whether to permit an equal protection challenge to a California statute imposing a retaliatory tax on foreign insurance companies doing business within the State, when the home States of those companies imposed a similar tax on California insurers entering their borders. We concluded that *Lincoln* was no more than "a surprising throwback" to the days before enactment of the Fourteenth Amendment and in which incorporation of a domestic corporation or entry of a foreign one had been granted only as a matter of privilege by the State in its unfettered discretion. 451 U.S., at 665, 101 S.Ct., at 2081. We therefore rejected the longstanding but "anachronis[tic]" rule of *Lincoln* and explicitly held that the Equal Protection Clause imposes limits upon a State's power to condition the right of a foreign corporation to do business within its borders. Id., at 667, 101 S.Ct., at 2082. We held that "[w]e consider it now established that, whatever the extent of a State's authority to exclude foreign corporations from doing business within its boundaries, that authority does not justify imposition of more onerous taxes or other burdens on foreign corporations than those imposed on domestic corporations, unless the discrimination between foreign and domestic corporations bears a rational relation to a legitimate state purpose." Id., at 667–668, 101 S.Ct., at 2082–2083.

Because appellants waived their right to an evidentiary hearing on the issue whether the classification in the Alabama domestic preference tax statute bears a rational relation to the two purposes upheld by the Circuit Court, the only question before us is whether those purposes are legitimate.[5]

A

(1)

The first of the purposes found by the trial court to be a legitimate reason for the statute's classification between foreign and domestic corporations is that it encourages the formation of new domestic insurance companies in Alabama. The State, agreeing with the Court of Civil Appeals, contends that this Court has long held that the promotion of domestic industry, in and of itself, is a legitimate state purpose that will survive equal protection scrutiny. In so contending, it relies on a series of cases, including *Western & Southern*, that are said to have upheld discrim-

---

5. The State and the intervenors advanced some 15 additional purposes in support of the Alabama statute. As neither the Circuit Court nor the Court of Civil Appeals ruled on the legitimacy of those purposes, that question is not before us, and we express no view as to it. On remand, the State will be free to advance again its arguments relating to the legitimacy of those purposes.

inatory taxes. See Bacchus Imports, Ltd. v. Dias, 104 S.Ct. 3049 (1984); Pike v. Bruce Church, Inc., 397 U.S. 137, 90 S.Ct. 844 (1970); Allied Stores of Ohio, Inc. v. Bowers, supra; Parker v. Brown, 317 U.S. 341, 63 S.Ct. 307 (1943); Carmichael v. Southern Coal & Coke Co., 301 U.S. 495, 57 S.Ct. 868 (1937); Board of Education v. Illinois, 203 U.S. 553, 27 S.Ct. 171 (1906).

The cases cited lend little or no support to the State's contention. In *Western & Southern,* the case principally relied upon, we did not hold as a general rule that promotion of domestic industry is a legitimate state purpose under equal protection analysis. Rather, we held that California's purpose in enacting the retaliatory tax—to promote the *interstate* business of domestic insurers by deterring *other States* from enacting discriminatory or excessive taxes—was a legitimate one. 451 U.S., at 668, 101 S.Ct., at 2083. In contrast, Alabama asks us to approve its purpose of promoting the business of its domestic insurers *in Alabama* by penalizing foreign insurers who also want to do business in the State. Alabama has made no attempt, as California did, to influence the policies of other States in order to enhance its domestic companies' ability to operate interstate; rather, it has erected barriers to foreign companies who wish to do interstate business in order to improve its domestic insurers' ability to compete at home.

The crucial distinction between the two cases lies in the fact that Alabama's aim to promote domestic industry is purely and completely discriminatory, designed only to favor domestic industry within the State, no matter what the cost to foreign corporations also seeking to do business there. Alabama's purpose, contrary to California's, constitutes the very sort of parochial discrimination that the Equal Protection Clause was intended to prevent. As Justice Brennan, joined by Justice Harlan, observed in his concurrence in Allied Stores of Ohio, Inc. v. Bowers, 358 U.S. 522, 79 S.Ct. 437 (1959), this Court always has held that the Equal Protection Clause forbids a State to discriminate in favor of its own residents solely by burdening "the residents of other state members of our federation." Id., at 533, 79 S.Ct., at 444. Unlike the retaliatory tax involved in *Western & Southern,* which only burdens residents of a State that imposes its own discriminatory tax on outsiders, the domestic preference tax gives the "home team" an advantage by burdening *all* foreign corporations seeking to do business within the State, no matter what they or their States do.

The validity of the view that a State may not constitutionally favor its own residents by taxing foreign corporations at a higher rate solely because of their residence is confirmed by a long line of this Court's cases so holding. WHYY, Inc. v. Glassboro, 393 U.S., at 119–120, 89 S.Ct., at 287; Wheeling Steel Corp. v. Glander, 337 U.S., at 571, 69 S.Ct., at 1296; Hanover Fire Ins. Co. v. Harding, 272 U.S., at 511, 47 S.Ct., at 183; Southern R. Co. v. Greene, 216 U.S., at 417, 30 S.Ct., at 291. See Reserve Life Ins. Co. v. Bowers, 380 U.S. 258, 85 S.Ct. 951 (1965) (per curiam). As the Court stated in *Hanover Fire Ins. Co.,* with respect to general tax burdens on business, "the foreign corporation stands equal, and is to be classified with domestic corporations of the same kind." 272 U.S., at 511, 47 S.Ct., at 183. In all of these cases, the discriminatory tax was imposed by the State on foreign corporations doing business within the State solely because of their residence, presumably to promote domestic industry within the State.[7] In relying on these cases and rejecting *Lincoln* in *Western & Southern,* we reaffirmed the continuing viability of the Equal Protection Clause as a means of challenging a statute that seeks to benefit domestic industry within the State only by grossly discriminating against foreign competitors.

The State contends that Allied Stores of Ohio, Inc. v. Bowers, supra, shows that this principle has not always held true. In that case, a domestic merchandiser challenged on equal protection grounds an Ohio statute that exempted foreign corporations from a tax on the value of merchandise held for storage within the State. The Court upheld the tax, finding that the purpose of encouraging foreign companies to build warehouses within Ohio was a legitimate state purpose. The State contends that this case shows that promotion of domestic business *is* a legitimate state purpose under equal protection analysis.

We disagree with the State's interpretation of *Allied Stores* and find that the case is not inconsistent with the other cases on which we rely. We agree with the holding of *Allied Stores* that a State's goal of bringing in new business is legitimate and often admirable. *Allied Stores* does not, however, hold that promotion of domestic business by *discriminating* against foreign corporations is legitimate. The case involves instead a statute that *encourages non-residents*—who are not competitors of residents—to build warehouses within the State. The discriminatory tax involved did not favor residents by burdening outsiders; rather, it granted the non-resident business an exemption that residents did not share. Since the foreign and domestic companies involved were not competing to provide warehousing services, granting the former an exemption did not even directly affect adversely the domestic companies subject to the tax. On its facts, then, *Allied Stores* is not inconsistent with our holding here that promotion of domestic business within a State, by discriminating against foreign corporations that wish to compete by doing business there, is not a legitimate state purpose. See 358 U.S., at 532–533, 79 S.Ct., at 443–444 (Brennan, J., concurring).

(2)

The State argues nonetheless that it is impermissible to view a discriminatory tax such as the one at issue here as violative of the Equal Protection Clause. This approach, it contends, amounts to no more than "Commerce Clause rhetoric in equal protection clothing." Brief for Appellee Ward 22. The State maintains that because Congress, in enacting the

---

7. Although the promotion of domestic business was not a purpose advanced by the States in support of their taxes in these cases, such promotion is logically the primary reason for enacting discriminatory taxes such as those at issue here.

McCarran–Ferguson Act, 15 U.S.C. §§ 1011–1015, intended to authorize States to impose taxes that burden interstate commerce in the insurance field, the tax at issue here must stand. Our concerns are much more fundamental than as characterized by the State. Although the McCarran–Ferguson Act exempts the insurance industry from Commerce Clause restrictions, it does not purport to limit in any way the applicability of the Equal Protection Clause. As noted above, our opinion in Western & Southern expressly reaffirmed the viability of equal protection restraints on discriminatory taxes in the insurance context.[8]

* * *

In whatever light the State's position is cast, acceptance of its contention that promotion of domestic industry is always a legitimate state purpose under equal protection analysis would eviscerate the Equal Protection Clause in this context. A State's natural inclination frequently would be to prefer domestic business over foreign. If we accept the State's view here, then any discriminatory tax would be valid if the State could show it reasonably was intended to benefit domestic business.[10] A discriminatory tax would stand or fall depending primarily on how a State framed its purpose—as benefiting one group or as harming another. This is a distinction without a difference, and one that we rejected last term in an analogous context arising under the Commerce Clause. Bacchus Imports, Ltd. v. Dias, 468 U.S., at 273, 104 S.Ct., at 3056. We hold that under the circumstances of this case, promotion of domestic business by discriminating against non-resident competitors is not a legitimate state purpose.

B

The second purpose found by the courts below to be legitimate was the encouragement of capital investment in the Alabama assets and governmental securities specified in the statute. We do not agree that this is a legitimate state purpose when furthered by discrimination. Domestic insurers remain entitled to the more favorable rate of tax regardless of whether they invest in Alabama assets. Moreover, the investment incentive provision of the Alabama statute does not enable foreign insurance companies to eliminate the discriminatory effect of the statute. No matter how much of their assets they invest in Alabama, foreign insurance companies are still required to pay a higher gross premiums tax than

---

8. In fact, as we noted in *Western & Southern,* the legislative history of the McCarran–Ferguson Act reveals that the Act was Congress's response only to United States v. South-Eastern Underwriters Assn., 322 U.S. 533, 64 S.Ct. 1162 (1944), and that Congress did not intend thereby to give the States any power to tax or regulate the insurance industry other than what they had previously possessed. Thus Congress expressly left undisturbed this Court's decisions holding that the Equal Protection Clause places limits on a State's ability to tax out-of-state corporations. See 451 U.S., at 655, n. 6, 101 S.Ct., at 2076, n. 6.

10. Indeed, under the State's analysis, *any* discrimination subject to the rational relation level of scrutiny could be justified simply on the ground that it favored one group at the expense of another. This case does not involve or question, as the dissent suggests, the broad authority of a State to promote and regulate its own economy. We hold only that such regulation may not be accomplished by imposing discriminatorily higher taxes on non-resident corporations solely because they are non-residents.

ty in which such classifications had been invalidated on equal protection grounds were inapposite because in none of those cases had the "tax statutes at issue rested on relevant differences between domestic and foreign corporations or had purposes other than raising of revenue at the out-of-state corporation's expense." By contrast, in her view, "Alabama does *not* tax at a higher rate solely on the basis of residence; it taxes insurers, domestic as well as foreign, who do not maintain a principal place of business or substantial assets in Alabama, based on conceded distinctions in the contributions of these insurers *as a class* to the State's insurance objectives." (Emphasis in original.)]

IV

* * *

Western & Southern established that a State may validly tax out-of-state corporations at a higher rate if its goal is to promote the ability of its domestic businesses to compete in *interstate* markets. Nevertheless, the Court today concludes that the converse policy is forbidden, striking down legislation whose purpose is to encourage the *intrastate* activities of local business concerns by permitting them to compete effectively on their home turf. In essence, the Court declares: "We will excuse an unequal burden on foreign insurers if the State's purpose is to foster its domestic insurers activities in *other* States, but the same unequal burden will be unconstitutional when employed to further a policy that places a higher social value on the domestic insurer's *home State* than interstate activities." This conclusion is not drawn from the Commerce Clause, the textual source of constitutional restrictions on state interference with interstate competition. Reliance on the Commerce Clause would, of course, be unavailing here in view of the McCarran–Ferguson Act. Instead the Court engrafts its own economic values on the Equal Protection Clause. Beyond guarding against arbitrary or irrational discrimination, as interpreted by the Court today this Clause now prohibits the effectuation of economic policies, even where sanctioned by Congress, that elevate local concerns over interstate competition. "But a constitution is not intended to embody a particular economic theory. * * * It is made for people of fundamentally differing views." Lochner v. New York, 198 U.S. 45, 75–76, 25 S.Ct. 539, 546–547 (1905) (Holmes, J., dissenting). In the heyday of economic due process, Justice Holmes warned:

"Courts should be careful not to extend [the express] prohibitions [of the Constitution] beyond their obvious meaning by reading into them conceptions of public policy that the particular Court may happen to entertain." Tyson & Brother v. Banton, 273 U.S. 418, 445–446, 47 S.Ct. 426, 433 (1927) (Holmes, J., dissenting, joined by Brandeis, J.) (emphasis added).

Ignoring the wisdom of this observation, the Court fashions its own brand of economic equal protection. In so doing, it supplants a legislative policy endorsed by both Congress and the individual States that explicitly sanctioned the very parochialism in regulation and taxation of insurance that the Court's decision holds illegitimate. This newly unveiled power of the Equal Protection Clause would come as a surprise to the Congress that passed the McCarran–Ferguson Act and the Court that sustained the Act against constitutional attack. In the McCarran–Ferguson Act, Congress expressly sanctioned such economic parochialism in the context of state regulation and taxation of insurance.

The doctrine adopted by the majority threatens the freedom not only of the States but also of the Federal Government to formulate economic policy. The dangers in discerning in the Equal Protection Clause a prohibition against barriers to interstate business irrespective of the Commerce Clause should be self-evident. The Commerce Clause is a flexible tool of economic policy that Congress may use as it sees fit, letting it lie dormant or invoking it to limit as well as promote the free flow of commerce. Doctrines of equal protection are constitutional limits that constrain the acts of federal and state legislatures alike. See, e.g., Califano v. Webster, 430 U.S. 313, 97 S.Ct. 1192 (1977); Cohen, Congressional Power to Validate Unconstitutional State Laws: A Forgotten Solution to an Old Enigma, 35 Stan.L.Rev. 387, 400–413 (1983). The Court's analysis casts a shadow over numerous congressional enactments that adopted as federal policy "the type of parochial favoritism" the Court today finds unconstitutional. White v. Massachusetts Council of Construction Employers, 460 U.S., at 213, 103 S.Ct., at 1047. Contrary to the reasoning in *Benjamin,* the Court today indicates the Equal Protection Clause stands as an independent barrier if courts should determine that either Congress or a State has ventured the "wrong" direction down what has become, by judicial fiat, the one-way street of the Commerce Clause. Nothing in the Constitution or our past decisions supports forcing such an economic straightjacket on the federal system.

V

Today's opinion charts an ominous course. I can only hope this unfortunate adventure away from the safety of our precedents will be an isolated episode. I had thought the Court had finally accepted that

> "the judiciary may not sit as a superlegislature to judge the wisdom or desirability of legislative policy determinations made in areas that neither affect fundamental rights nor proceed along suspect lines; in the local economic sphere, it is only the invidious discrimination, the wholly arbitrary act, which cannot stand consistently with the Fourteenth Amendment." New Orleans v. Dukes, 427 U.S., at 303–304, 96 S.Ct., at 2516–2517 (citations omitted).

Because I believe that the Alabama law at issue here serves legitimate state purposes through concededly rational means, and thus is neither invidious nor arbitrary, I would affirm the court below. I respectfully dissent.

NOTES AND QUESTIONS

A. In Western & Southern Life Ins. Co. v. State Board of Equalization, 451 U.S. 648, 101 S.Ct. 2070 (1981), which the Court discusses in *Metropolitan Life*, the Court sustained a retaliatory insurance tax that discriminated against out-of-state insurers. Applying its "rational basis" equal protection standard—that a tax must be "rationally related to a legitimate state purpose"—the Court held that the California Legislature rationally could have believed that a discriminatory tax could promote the legitimate state purpose of promoting domestic insurers in interstate commerce by deterring other states from enacting discriminatory or excessive taxes.

The Court's decision in *Western & Southern* was significant for two reasons. First, it discarded the Court's earlier doctrine approving discriminatory taxes predicated upon the states' power to condition an insurance company's entry into the state to do business. Second, it sanctioned discriminatory taxation of foreign corporations under the Equal Protection Clause if that discrimination was rationally related to a legitimate state purpose. The Court's earlier decisions had established a much broader requirement of equality in taxation than that enunciated in *Western & Southern*. In *Metropolitan Life,* the Court appears to have returned to the sound principle of constitutional adjudication supported by its pre-*Western & Southern* precedents that the Equal Protection Clause forbids the states from "imposing discriminatorily higher taxes on non-residents solely because they are non-residents."

Was the Court's distinction of *Western & Southern* in *Metropolitan Life* persuasive? Could not Alabama's purpose in *Metropolitan Life* have been characterized as promoting the domestic insurance industry by inducing insurers to incorporate and maintain their principal place of business in Alabama in order to serve the needs of local residents that were inadequately served by out-of-state insurers? If thus characterized, would such a purpose be any less legitimate than the purpose of California's retaliatory tax?

B. *The Permissible Scope of Retaliation Under* Western & Southern. The operation of retaliatory insurance taxes can best be explained by illustration. Suppose that State A imposes a general insurance premiums tax at the rate of two percent (as most states do), but that State B imposes a general insurance premiums tax at the rate of three percent. If an insurer from State B collects premiums from insureds in State A, State A will subject the State B insurer to (1) its general premiums tax of two percent and (2) an additional retaliatory tax of one percent. The net result of the retaliatory tax scheme is to impose on the State B insurer in State A an aggregate tax burden of three percent—the same premiums tax burden that the State A insurer will bear in State B. As noted above, see Note A supra, the U.S. Supreme Court sustained a retaliatory tax regime in *Western & Southern* on the ground that it promoted the retaliating state's legitimate interest in attempting to persuade other states to reduce their insurance premiums rates.

But consider the following variation on retaliatory taxation. Suppose that State A decides that it wants to raise its general premiums tax to three percent. If it does so, it will receive no additional revenues from State B insurers. They will pay State A's revised general premiums tax of three percent, but will no longer be subject to the one percent retaliatory tax, because there will no longer be any basis for retaliation against the State B tax. Suppose further, however, that a clever state fiscal advisor, desiring to avoid the loss in retaliatory tax revenues while enjoying the increase in revenues attributable to the increase in the general premiums tax rate, proposes the following: We will designate the additional one percent levy a "fee" to be used for insurance-related regulation (including promotion of good health and avoidance of accidents to keep insurance rates down); since "fees" are not "taxes," we will continue to be able to collect the retaliatory tax from insurers from State B, since the State B three percent tax rate will continue to exceed our two percent tax rate. Will such a scheme pass muster under the Equal Protection Clause as construed by the U.S. Supreme Court in *Western & Southern* and *Metropolitan Life*? See State Farm Mut. Auto. Ins. Co. v. Long, 129 N.C.App. 164, 497 S.E.2d 451 (1998), aff'd per curiam, 350 N.C. 84, 511 S.E.2d 303 (1999) (state need not consider "regulatory charge" measured by insurance premiums in determining relative tax burdens for retaliatory tax purposes). Cf. Prudential Ins. Co. v. Commissioner of Revenue, 429 Mass. 560, 709 N.E.2d 1096 (1999) (state need not aggregate all the premiums taxes imposed on out-of-state insurers, rather than considering insurance taxes on an insurance-line by insurance-line basis, in determining relative tax burdens for retaliatory tax purposes).

The Michigan Supreme Court sustained, over equal protection objections, a retaliatory tax that excluded payments that insurers made to various private insurance associations and facilities from the determination of the tax burden that Michigan imposed on insurance companies. TIG Ins. Co. v. Department of Treasury, 464 Mich. 548, 629 N.W.2d 402, cert. denied, 534 U.S. 1056, 122 S.Ct. 647 (2001). The Michigan Court of Appeals had found that the tax violated the Equal Protection Clause, because the exclusion of the payments in question was designed to raise funds in response to a projected shortfall in insurance tax revenues and this was "not a valid reason for discriminating against foreign insurers." TIG Ins. Co. v. Department of Treasury, 237 Mich.App. 219, 602 N.W.2d 839, 845 (1999) The Michigan Supreme Court, however, found that the exclusion satisfied the "rational basis" standard for adjudicating equal protection challenges: The legislature could have believed that excluding payments to private insurance associations and facilities from the retaliatory tax calculation would encourage other states to establish similar associations and facilities, because the payments to such organizations would not affect retaliatory taxes that their domestic insurers paid to other states.

C. *References.* The *Metropolitan Life* and *Western & Southern* cases are critically analyzed in William Cohen, "Federalism in Equality Clothing: A Comment on Metropolitan Life Insurance Company v. Ward," 38 Stan. L. Rev. 1 (1985); David W. Haller, "Within the States' Jurisdiction: *Metropolitan, Northeast Bancorp,* and the Equal Protection Clause," 96 Yale L.J. 2110 (1987); Walter Hellerstein & Ruurd Leegstra, "Supreme Court in *Metropolitan Life* Strikes Down Discriminatory State Insurance Tax," 63 J. Tax'n 108 (1985); Walter Hellerstein, "Supreme Court Bars Louisiana's First Use Tax,

Upholds California's Retaliatory Insurance Tax," 55 J. Tax'n 106 (1981); and Note, "Taxing Out-of-State Corporations After *Western & Southern:* An Equal Protection Analysis," 34 Stan. L. Rev. 877 (1982).

4. SEPARATE CLASSIFICATION OF FOREIGN AND DOMESTIC CORPORATIONS: THE NON–INSURANCE CASES

Notes and Questions

A. *Discriminatory Taxation of Domestic Corporations as Compared to Foreign Corporations.* In Allied Stores of Ohio, Inc. v. Bowers, 358 U.S. 522, 79 S.Ct. 437 (1959), which is discussed in *Metropolitan Life*, the Court sustained over equal protection objections an ad valorem property tax exemption for property stored in warehouses by foreign—but not by domestic— corporations. The Court found that the discrimination was not arbitrary because it was based on factors other than the residence of the corporation— namely encouraging the location of industry within the state. The Court distinguished an earlier case, Wheeling Steel Corp. v. Glander, 337 U.S. 562, 69 S.Ct. 1291 (1949), which had struck down a tax exemption for accounts receivable owned by residents on the grounds that it arbitrarily discriminated against nonresidents, even though the state argued that the exemption was designed to create a scheme of reciprocal exemptions with other states. Justice Brennan, joined by Justice Harlan, wrote the following concurring opinion:

> We hold today that Ohio's ad valorem tax law does not violate the Equal Protection Clause in subjecting the property of Ohio corporations to a tax not applied to identical property of non-Ohio corporations. Yet in Wheeling Steel Corp. v. Glander, 337 U.S. 562, 69 S.Ct. 1291, the Court struck down, as violating the Equal Protection Clause, another provision of Ohio's ad valorem tax law which subjected the property of non-Ohio corporations to a tax not applied to identical property of Ohio corporations.

> The question presented in the two cases, if stated generally, and as I shall show, somewhat superficially, is: Measured by the demands of the Equal Protection Clause, is a State constitutionally permitted separately to classify domestic and foreign corporations for the purposes of payment of or exemption from an ad valorem tax? In both cases the distinction complained of as denying equal protection of the laws is that the incidence of the tax in fact turns on "the different residence of the owner." With due respect to my Brethren's view, I think that if this were all that the matter was, *Wheeling* and this case would be indistinguishable.[3] Therefore, while I agree with my Brethren that the classification is valid

---

3. The statute in *Wheeling* "discriminated" against non-residents in the same way that the present statute "discriminates" against residents. What my Brethren describe as the forbidden purpose of the distinction in *Wheeling* seems to me clearly to be only a rejected argument made by the State to show that there was no discrimination in fact. 337 U.S. at pages 572–574, 69 S.Ct. at pages 1296–1297. I see no indication in *Wheeling* that the Court's condemnation of the tax was based solely on its rejection of the "reciprocity" argument.

in this case, I cannot reach that conclusion without developing the ground on which *Wheeling* is distinguishable.

Why is the "different residence of the owner" a constitutionally valid basis for Ohio's freeing the property of the foreign corporation from the tax in this case and an invalid basis for its freeing the property of the domestic corporation from the tax involved in the *Wheeling* case?

I think that the answer lies in remembering that our Constitution is an instrument of federalism. The Constitution furnishes the structure for the operation of the States with respect to the National Government and with respect to each other. The maintenance of the principles of federalism is a foremost consideration in interpreting any of the pertinent constitutional provisions under which this Court examines state action. Because there are 49 States and much of the Nation's commercial activity is carried on by enterprises having contacts with more States than one, a common and continuing problem of constitutional interpretation has been that of adjusting the demands of individual States to regulate and tax these enterprises in light of the multistate nature of our federation. While the most ready examples of the Court's function in this field are furnished by the innumerable cases in which the Court has examined state taxation and regulation under the Commerce and Due Process Clauses, still the Equal Protection Clause, among its other roles, operates to maintain this principle of federalism.

Viewing the Equal Protection Clause as an instrument of federalism, the distinction between *Wheeling* and this case seems to me to be apparent. My Brethren's opinion today demonstrates that in dealing with as practical and complex a matter as taxation, the utmost latitude, under the Equal Protection Clause, must be afforded a State in defining categories of classification. But in the case of an ad valorem property tax, *Wheeling* teaches that a distinction which burdens the property of nonresidents but not like property of residents is outside the constitutional pale. But this is not because no rational ground can be conceived for a classification which discriminates against non-residents solely because they are non-residents: could not such a ground be found in the State's benign and beneficent desire to favor its own residents, to increase their prosperity at the expense of outlanders, to protect them from, and give them an advantage over, "foreign" competition? These bases of legislative distinction are adopted in the national policies of too many countries, including from time to time our own, to say that, absolutely considered, they are arbitrary or irrational. The proper analysis, it seems to me, is that *Wheeling* applied the Equal Protection Clause to give effect to its role to protect our federalism by denying Ohio the power constitutionally to discriminate in favor of its own residents against the residents of other state members of our federation. On the other hand, in the present case, Ohio's classification based on residence operates *against* Ohio residents and clearly presents no state action disruptive of the federal pattern. There is, therefore, no reason to judge the State action mechanically by the same principles as state efforts to favor residents. As my Brethren's opinion makes clear, a rational basis can be found for this exercise by Ohio of the latitude permitted it to define classifications under the Equal

Protection Clause. One could, in fact, be found in the concept that it is proper that those who are bound to a State by the tie of residence and accordingly the more permanently receive its benefits are proper persons to bear the primary share of its costs. Accordingly, in this context, it is proper to say that any relief forthcoming must be obtained from the State Legislature.

Allied Stores, 358 U.S. at 530–33.

Does Justice Brennan's concurrence provide a plausible explanation for the Court's decision in *Metropolitan Life*, as well as in Williams v. Vermont, 472 U.S. 14, 105 S.Ct. 2465 (1985), discussed in Section B(5), Note A, p. 279 infra, and in Hooper v. Bernalillo County Assessor, 472 U.S. 612, 105 S.Ct. 2862 (1985), discussed in Section B(5), Note B, pp. 279–80 infra, in which the Court struck down residence-based tax classifications on the ostensible ground that they could not survive "rational basis" scrutiny? In other words, is the real engine driving the Court's decisions in these cases its concern with discrimination against out-of-state corporations and individuals rather than the Court's belief that the state legislature was really acting irrationally? If so, the Court is doing so sub silentio because Justice Brennan himself, writing for the Court in *Western & Southern Life* (discussed in Section B(3), Note A, p. 273 supra), explicitly noted that the Court "has required no more than a rational basis for discrimination against out-of-state interests in the context of equal protection litigation." Western & Southern Life, 451 U.S. at 667. In that case, of course, the Court sustained a retaliatory insurance tax that discriminated against out-of-state insurance companies. Moreover, Justice Brennan joined Justice O'Connor's dissent in *Metropolitan Life*, which suggests that Justice Brennan abandoned the approach he articulated in *Allied Stores*, even if the Court has not.

B. *Discriminatory Taxation of Foreign Corporations as Compared to Domestic Corporations.* States sometimes grant exemptions to domestic corporations that they do not extend to foreign corporations. For example, New Jersey denied a property tax exemption to a foreign corporation, which was engaged in non-commercial educational television and which owned and maintained a station and transmission tower in the state. Thirty percent of the television station's audience was in that state. Admittedly, a New Jersey corporation would have been exempt from all state real and personal property taxes, if it had conducted the same activities in the state. The state court upheld the denial of exemption on the ground that it was permissible for the legislature to "decide that the State should not be burdened with the administrative problem of checking the status of foreign corporations under foreign laws and evaluating them with our requirements." WHYY, Inc. v. Borough of Glassboro, 50 N.J. 6, 231 A.2d 608, 612 (1967). The U.S. Supreme Court reversed on the ground that once foreign corporations are admitted to the state, "the adopted corporations are entitled to equal protection with the state's own corporate progeny, at least to the extent that their property is entitled to an equally favorable *ad valorem* tax basis." WHYY, Inc. v. Borough of Glassboro, 393 U.S. 117, 119, 89 S.Ct. 286 (1968) (quoting Wheeling Steel Corp. v. Glander, 337 U.S. 562, 571–72, 69 S.Ct. 1291 (1949)).

There are decisions indicating that a state may deny tax exemptions to out-of-state charitable, educational, and other organizations that do not conduct their operations within the state, without running afoul of the Equal Protection Clause. See Board of Educ. v. Illinois, 203 U.S. 553, 27 S.Ct. 171 (1906). The opinion in that case, which sustained a denial of an inheritance tax exemption for a gift to an educational organization that was organized and operated outside the state, was largely based on "the greater control and direction the State had over domestic than over foreign corporations." Id., 203 U.S. at 562. The *WHYY* case put the Illinois holding on a different footing, one that was mentioned briefly at the end of the Illinois case, by characterizing it as

> [a] case in which the exemption was withheld by reason of the foreign corporation's failure or inability to benefit the State in the same measure as do domestic nonprofit corporations. Compare Board of Educ. v. Illinois
> * * *

WHYY, 393 U.S. at 120.

The rationale behind such decisions is that the out-of-state organizations do not meet the condition underlying the grant of tax exemptions to charities, namely, that they relieve the state of the costs and burdens of public functions it would otherwise have to perform and that they perform other services benefiting the people of the state. That policy ought to suffice as a justification under the Equal Protection Clause for the denial to out-of-state charities of the benefits of exemptions or deductions for property, death, or income taxes. Query, however, whether such discrimination can pass muster under the Commerce Clause? State taxes discriminating against foreign corporations ordinarily constitute a quintessential violation of the Commerce Clause. See South Central Bell Telephone Co. v. Alabama, 526 U.S. 160, 119 S.Ct. 1180 (1999). The critical question, then, is whether the discrimination implicates the Commerce Clause at all, on the theory that the denial of the deduction does not substantially affect interstate commerce. But see Camps Newfound/Owatonna, Inc. v. Town of Harrison, Maine, 520 U.S. 564, 117 S.Ct. 1590 (1997), set out at pp. 131–43 supra (invalidating under Commerce Clause exemption for charitable institution limited to organizations operating principally for benefits of residents).

State courts have invalidated a number of provisions that discriminated against foreign corporations when the states were unable to advance any persuasive justifications for the unequal treatment of the foreign corporation. The Florida Supreme Court struck down a provision of the state's intangibles tax that limited the privilege of filing consolidated returns to affiliated groups of corporations whose parent company was either incorporated or maintained its commercial domicile in the state. Department of Revenue v. Amrep Corp., 358 So.2d 1343 (Fla. 1978). The Florida Court of Appeals invalidated a tax exemption for homes for the aged limited to such homes owned by Florida nonprofit corporations. Miller v. Board of Pensions, 431 So.2d 350 (Fla. App. 1983). The Missouri Supreme Court struck down an organization tax that would have been $50 if imposed on a domestic corporation but came to $96,600 as applied to a foreign corporation. Missouri Pacific R.R. v. Kirkpatrick, 652 S.W.2d 128 (Mo. 1983). The New York courts have likewise invalidated a license tax on foreign corporations imposed at higher rates than the organization tax on domestic corporations, even though the disparity had existed for more than half a century. In re Aurora Corp. v. Tully, 60 N.Y.2d 338, 457 N.E.2d 735, 469 N.Y.S.2d 630 (1983). And the Pennsylvania Supreme Court struck down a provision of the state's capital stock tax that granted an election to domestic corporations to apportion their income by either of two alternative methods but limited foreign corporations to a single method of apportionment. Gilbert Associates, Inc. v. Commonwealth, 498 Pa. 514, 447 A.2d 944 (1982). As suggested in the preceding paragraph, provisions discriminating against foreign corporations will often raise Commerce Clause issues as well.

5. DISCRIMINATION AGAINST NONRESIDENT INDIVIDUALS

NOTES AND QUESTIONS

A. *Denial of Use Tax Credit for Sales Taxes Paid by Nonresidents.* Vermont imposes a use tax on cars purchased elsewhere and subsequently registered in Vermont. Although Vermont, like most states, generally grants a credit against the use tax for sales taxes paid to other states, Vermont did not grant a credit for sales taxes paid on cars purchased in other states if the taxpayer was not a resident of Vermont when she purchased the car. In Williams v. Vermont, 472 U.S. 14, 105 S.Ct. 2465 (1985), the Supreme Court held that the discrimination against nonresidents in Vermont's taxing scheme violated the Equal Protection Clause. The Court found that the discrimination was not justified by the only plausible legitimate state purpose advanced in its defense—that those using the roads should pay for them. Residents purchasing cars elsewhere likewise used Vermont roads yet they were permitted a credit against their out-of-state sales tax. The Court dismissed the other allegedly legitimate state purposes, such as encouraging out-of-staters to purchase in Vermont and enabling Vermont residents to shop without penalty, as fanciful. The Court concluded that:

> [W]e can see no relevant difference between motor vehicle registrants who purchased their cars out-of-state while they were Vermont residents and those who only came to Vermont after buying a car elsewhere. To free one group and not the other from the otherwise applicable tax burden violates the Equal Protection Clause.

Id., 472 U.S. at 27.

B. *Limiting Tax Exemption to Long-term State Residents.* Closely allied to the question of discrimination against nonresidents is the question of discrimination against short-term in favor of long-term residents. In Zobel v. Williams, 457 U.S. 55, 102 S.Ct. 2309 (1982), the Court held that the Equal Protection Clause forbids a state from making cash distributions to its residents, when such distributions are graduated according to the number of years that the individual has been a resident of the state. In Hooper v. Bernalillo County Assessor, 472 U.S. 612, 105 S.Ct. 2862 (1985), the Court considered the constitutionality of a New Mexico property tax exemption for Vietnam War veterans who were residents of the state before May 8, 1976.

Vietnam veterans who became residents of the state after that date were ineligible for the exemption. The Court held that the distinction between the two classes of resident veterans was not rationally related to the purposes New Mexico offered to support the classification, and it struck the classification down under the Equal Protection Clause. New Mexico sought to justify the classification as an incentive to encourage Vietnam veterans to move to New Mexico. But the Court observed that the legislature established the eligibility date long after the triggering date occurred and that "[t]he legislature cannot plausibly encourage veterans to move to the State by passing such retroactive legislation." Id., 472 U.S. at 619. The state also sought to defend the statute on the ground that it was designed to reward veterans who resided in the state before May 8, 1976. But the Court again found that the distinction drawn was not rationally related to the asserted purpose:

> Even assuming that the State may legitimately grant benefits on the basis of a coincidence between military service and past residence, the New Mexico statute's distinction between resident veterans is not rationally related to the State's asserted legislative goal. The statute is not written to require any connection between the veteran's prior residence and military service. Indeed, the veteran who resided in New Mexico as an infant long ago would immediately qualify for the exemption upon settling in the State at any time in the future regardless of where he resided before, during, or after military service.

Id. at 621–22.

C. PRIVILEGES AND IMMUNITIES

1. INTRODUCTION

As you may recall from earlier courses in constitutional law, there are two clauses in the Federal Constitution dealing with privileges and immunities. Article IV, Section 2 is the "interstate" Privileges and Immunities Clause, which provides that the "Citizens of each State shall be entitled to all Privileges and Immunities of Citizens in the several States." We will examine this provision in further detail below.

The second Privileges and Immunities Clause, which is in the Fourteenth Amendment, provides that "No State shall make or enforce any law which shall abridge the privileges or immunities of citizens of the United States." The Slaughter–House Cases, 83 U.S. (16 Wall.) 36 (1873), established the principle that the Privileges and Immunities Clause of the Fourteenth Amendment created no new rights of national citizenship, but merely furnished an additional guaranty of rights which citizens of the United States already possessed. Although the U.S. Supreme Court had considered some 50 cases involving constitutional challenges to state statutes under the Privileges and Immunities Clause of the Fourteenth Amendment, the Court had never found that a state statute violated that clause until the 1935 decision in Colgate v. Harvey, 296 U.S. 404, 56 S.Ct. 252 (1935). In that case a Vermont statute imposed an income tax on interest from notes and mortgages but allowed a deduction for such interest paid on in-state loans. Colgate, a Vermont resident, successfully attacked this discrimination against interest on out-of-state loans under the Privileges and Immunities Clause of the Fourteenth Amendment. The Court rested its decision on the theory that "the right of a citizen of the United States to engage in business, to transact any lawful business, or to make a lawful loan of money in any state other than that in which he resides" (id., 296 U.S. at 430) is a privilege of a citizen of the United States protected by the Fourteenth Amendment. Justices Stone, Brandeis, and Cardozo dissented.

Five years later in Madden v. Kentucky, 309 U.S. 83, 60 S.Ct. 406 (1940), the Court considered a Kentucky statute that imposed an ad valorem tax on bank deposits of its citizens at the rate of 10 cents per $100 for deposits within the state and 50 cents per $100 on deposits outside the state. Madden, a resident of Kentucky, had substantial deposits in New York banks. In a suit involving the validity of the higher tax on such deposits during Madden's lifetime, his executors challenged the levy. The Supreme Court, after sustaining the classification as reasonable under the Equal Protection Clause on the ground that collection of tax on out-of-state deposits is more difficult and more expensive than on local deposits, went on to hold that the tax did not violate the Privileges and Immunities Clause of the Fourteenth Amendment. In so holding, the Court explicitly overruled *Colgate v. Harvey*, and it repudiated the view that "the right to carry out an incident to a trade, business or calling such as a deposit of money" is a privilege of national citizenship. Id., 309 U.S. at 91. As a consequence, for most of the twentieth century, courts and commentators viewed the Fourteenth Amendment as creating no new privileges or immunities for citizens of the United States, but rather as protecting only those rights otherwise granted by the Constitution.

But the final chapter of Fourteenth Amendment Privileges and Immunities Clause jurisprudence has not yet been written. In 1999, the U.S. Supreme Court relied on the Privileges and Immunities Clause of the Fourteenth Amendment as a source of the "right to travel" in striking down limitations on welfare benefits for newly arrived residents. Saenz v. Roe, 526 U.S. 489, 119 S.Ct. 1518 (1999). The case arguably "breathes new life into the previously dormant Privileges and Immunities Clause of the Fourteenth Amendment." Id., 526 U.S. at 511 (Rehnquist, C.J., dissenting). It remains to be seen, however, whether this rediscovered source of individual rights will have a significant impact on the states' power to legislate. See generally Laurence H. Tribe, 1 American Constitutional Law §§ 6–37, 7–5 (3d ed. 2000).

2. LIMITATIONS ON STATE TAXATION UNDER ARTICLE IV, SECTION 2

In the field of state taxation, it is Article IV, Section 2, of the Constitution, the so-called "interstate" Privileges and Immunities Clause, that has been the principal basis for a claim of denial of privileges and immunities since 1940. As noted above, the clause provides that the "Citizens of each State shall be entitled to all Privileges and Immunities of Citizens in the several States." In the early case of Ward v. Maryland, 79 U.S. (12 Wall.) 418, 430 (1870), the Supreme Court indicated that the clause "plainly and unmistakably secures and protects the right of a citizen of one State to pass into any other State of the Union for the purpose of engaging in lawful commerce, trade, or business without molestation." Among other things, the Court indicated that the clause entitles nonresidents "to be exempt from any higher taxes or excises than are imposed by the State upon its own citizens." Id. Consider the application of this principle in the two cases below.

AUSTIN v. NEW HAMPSHIRE

Supreme Court of the United States, 1975.
420 U.S. 656, 95 S.Ct. 1191.

JUSTICE MARSHALL delivered the opinion of the Court.

Appellants are residents of Maine who were employed in New Hampshire during the 1970 tax year and as such were subject to the New Hampshire Commuters Income Tax. On behalf of themselves and others similarly situated, they petitioned the New Hampshire Superior Court for a declaration that the tax violates the Privileges and Immunities and Equal Protection Clauses of the Constitutions of New Hampshire and of the United States. The cause was transferred directly to the New Hampshire Supreme Court, which upheld the tax. We noted probable jurisdiction of the federal constitutional claims, and on the basis of the Privileges and Immunities Clause of Art. IV, we now reverse.

I

The New Hampshire Commuters Income Tax imposes a tax on nonresidents' New Hampshire-derived income in excess of $2,000.[1] The tax rate is 4% except that if the nonresident taxpayer's State of residence would impose a lesser tax had the income been earned in that State, the New Hampshire tax is reduced to the amount of the tax that the State of residence would impose. Employers are required to withhold 4% of the nonresident's income, however, even if his home State would tax him at less than the full 4%. Any excess tax withheld is refunded to the nonresident upon his filing a New Hampshire tax return after the close of the tax year showing that he is entitled to be taxed at a rate less than 4%.

The Commuters Income Tax initially imposes a tax of 4% as well on the income earned by New Hampshire residents outside the State. It then exempts such income from the tax, however: (1) if it is taxed by the State

---

1. N.H. Rev. Stat. Ann. § 77–B:2 II (1971) provides: "A tax is hereby imposed upon every taxable nonresident, which shall be levied, collected and paid annually at the rate of four percent of their New Hampshire derived income ... less an exemption of two thousand dollars; provided, however, that if the tax hereby imposed exceeds the tax which would be imposed upon such income by the state of residence of the taxpayer, if such income were earned in such state, the tax hereby imposed shall be reduced to equal the tax which would be imposed by such other state."

from which it is derived; (2) if it is exempted from taxation by the State from which it is derived; or (3) if the State from which it is derived does not tax such income.[2] The effect of these imposition and exemption features is that no resident of New Hampshire is taxed on his out-of-state income. Nor is the domestic earned income of New Hampshire residents taxed. In effect, then, the State taxes only the incomes of nonresidents working in New Hampshire;[3] it is on the basis of this disparate treatment of residents and nonresidents that appellants challenge New Hampshire's right to tax their income from employment in that State.[4]

II

The Privileges and Immunities Clause of Art. IV, § 2, cl. 1, provides: "The Citizens of each State shall be entitled to all Privileges and Immunities of Citizens in the several States." The Clause thus establishes a norm of comity without specifying the particular subjects as to which citizens of one State coming within the jurisdiction of another are guaranteed equality of treatment. The origins of the Clause do reveal, however, the concerns of central import to the Framers. During the preconstitutional period, the practice of some States denying to outlanders the treatment that its citizens demanded for themselves was widespread. The fourth of the Articles of Confederation was intended to arrest this centrifugal tendency with some particularity. It provided:

---

2. N.H. Rev. Stat. Ann. § 77–B:2 I (1971) provides: "A tax is hereby imposed upon every resident of the state, which shall be levied, collected and paid annually at the rate of four percent of their income which is derived outside the state of New Hampshire . . . ; provided, however, that if such income shall be subject to a tax in the state in which it is derived, such tax shall constitute full satisfaction of the tax hereby imposed; and provided further, that if such income is exempt from taxation because of statutory or constitutional provisions in the state in which it is derived, or because the state in which it is derived does not impose an income tax on such income, it shall be exempt from taxation under this paragraph."

3. New Hampshire residents pay a 4.5% tax on interest (other than interest on notes and bonds of the State and on bank deposits) and dividends (other than cash dividends on stock in national banks and New Hampshire banks and thrift institutions) in excess of $600. N.H. Rev. Stat. Ann. §§ 77:1–5 (1971). Residents also pay a $10 annual "resident tax" for the use of their town or city of residence. N.H. Rev. Stat. Ann. §§ 72:1, 5–a (1973). Other state taxes, such as those on business profits, real estate transfers, and property, are paid by residents and nonresidents alike. State income tax revenues from the tax on residents' unearned income in fiscal year 1970 were $3,462,000. In fiscal year 1971, the first in which the State taxed the earned income of nonresidents, total income tax revenues rose to $5,238,000. U.S. Dept. of Commerce, Bureau of the Census, State Tax Collections in 1970 (Series GF70 No. 1) and in 1971 (Series GF71 No. 1), p. 26.

4. Appellees challenge appellants' standing to maintain this action on the theory that their economic position was unchanged despite the imposition of the Commuters Income Tax because they received an offsetting credit under the tax laws of Maine, Me. Rev. Stat. Ann., Tit. 36, § 5127 (Supp. 1973), against income taxes owing to that State; the appellants' total tax liability, that is, was unaffected. We think the question is covered, however, by the holding of Allied Stores of Ohio, Inc. v. Bowers, 358 U.S. 522, 79 S.Ct 437 (1959). In addition, appellants are affected by the requirements that they file a New Hampshire tax return and that their employers withhold 4% of their earnings; since the appellees do not suggest that appellants are subject to the tax at the 4% rate, at the very least the withholding requirement deprives them of the use value of the excess withheld over their ultimate tax liability, if any. These effects may not be substantial, but they establish appellants' status as parties "adversely affected" by the State's tax laws, giving them "a direct stake in the outcome" of this litigation. Sierra Club v. Morton, 405 U.S. 727, 740, 92 S.Ct. 1361, 1368 (1972).

"The better to secure and perpetuate mutual friendship and intercourse among the people of the different States in this Union, the free inhabitants of each of these States, paupers, vagabonds and fugitives from justice excepted, shall be entitled to all privileges and immunities of free citizens in the several States; and the people of each State shall have free ingress and regress to and from any other State, and shall enjoy therein all the privileges of trade and commerce, subject to the same duties, impositions and restrictions as the inhabitants thereof respectively."

The discriminations at which this Clause was aimed by no means eradicated during the short life of the Confederation, and the provision was carried over into the comity article of the Constitution in briefer form but with no change of substance or intent, unless it was to strengthen the force of the Clause in fashioning a single nation. Thus, in the first, and long the leading, explication of the Clause, Mr. Justice Washington, sitting as Circuit Justice, deemed the fundamental privileges and immunities protected by the Clause to be essentially coextensive with those calculated to achieve the purpose of forming a more perfect Union, including "an exemption from higher taxes or impositions than are paid by the other citizens of the state." Corfield v. Coryell, 6 F.Cas pp. 546, 552 (No. 3,230) (CCED Pa. 1825).

In resolving constitutional challenges to state tax measures this Court has made it clear that "in taxation, even more than in other fields, legislatures possess the greatest freedom in classification." Madden v. Kentucky, 309 U.S. 83, 88, 60 S.Ct 406, 408 (1940). See Lehnhausen v. Lake Shore Auto Parts Co. 410 U.S. 356, 93 S.Ct. 1001 (1973). Our review of tax classifications has generally been concomitantly narrow, therefore, to fit the broad discretion vested in the state legislatures. When a tax measure is challenged as an undue burden on an activity granted special constitutional recognition, however, the appropriate degree of inquiry is that necessary to protect the competing constitutional value from erosion.

This consideration applies equally to the protection of individual liberties, see Grosjean v. American Press Co., 297 U.S. 233, 56 S.Ct. 444 (1936), and to the maintenance of our constitutional federalism. See Michigan–Wisconsin Pipe Line Co. v. Calvert, 347 U.S. 157, 164, 74 S.Ct. 396, 399 (1954). The Privileges and Immunities Clause, by making noncitizenship or nonresidence an improper basis for locating a special burden, implicates not only the individual's right to nondiscriminatory treatment but also, perhaps more so, the structural balance essential to the concept of federalism. Since nonresidents are not represented in the taxing State's legislative halls, cf. Allied Stores of Ohio, Inc. v. Bowers, 358 U.S. 522, 532–533, 79 S.Ct. 437, 443–444 (1959) (Brennan, J., concurring), judicial acquiescence in taxation schemes that burden them particularly would remit them to such redress as they could secure through their own State; but "to prevent (retaliation) was one of the chief ends sought to be accomplished by the adoption of the Constitution." Travis v. Yale & Towne Mfg. Co., 252 U.S. 60, 82, 40 S.Ct. 228, 233 (1920). Our prior cases, therefore, reflect an appropriately heightened concern for the integrity of the Privileges and Immunities Clause by erecting a standard of review substantially more rigorous than that applied to state tax distinctions among, say forms of business organizations or different trades and professions.

The first such case was Ward v. Maryland, 12 Wall. 418 (1871), challenging a statute under which nonresidents were required to pay $300 per year for a license to trade in goods not manufactured in Maryland, while resident traders paid a fee varying from $12 to $150, depending upon the value of their inventory. The State attempted to justify this disparity as a response to the practice of "runners" from industrial States selling by sample in Maryland, free from local taxation and other overhead expenses incurred by resident merchants. It portrayed the fee as a "tax upon a particular business or trade, carried on in a particular mode," rather than a discrimination against traders from other States. Although the tax may not have been "palpably arbitrary," see Allied Stores of Ohio, Inc. v. Bowers, supra, 358 U.S. at 530, 79 S.Ct. at 442, the discrimination could not be denied and the Court held that it violated the guarantee of the Privileges and Immunities Clause against "being subjected to any higher tax or excise than that exacted by law of ... permanent residents."

In Travellers' Insurance Co. v. Connecticut, 185 U.S. 364, 22 S.Ct. 673 (1902), the Court considered a tax laid on the value of stock in local insurance corporations. The shares of nonresident stockholders were assessed at their market value, while those owned by residents were assessed at market value less the proportionate value of all real estate held by the corporation and on which it had already paid a local property tax. In analyzing the apparent discrimination thus worked against nonresidents, the Court took account of the overall distribution of the tax burden between resident and nonresident stockholders. Finding that nonresidents paid no local property taxes, while residents paid those taxes at an average rate approximating or exceeding the rate imposed by the State on nonresidents' stock, the Court upheld the scheme. While more precise equality between the two classes could have been obtained, it was "enough that the state has secured a reasonably fair distribution of burdens, and that no intentional discrimination has been made against nonresidents." Their contribution to state and local property tax revenues, that is, was no more than the ratable share of their property within the State.

The principles of *Ward* and *Travellers'* were applied to taxes on nonresidents' local incomes in Shaffer v. Carter, 252 U.S. 37, 40 S.Ct. 221 (1920), and Travis v. Yale & Towne Mfg. Co., supra. *Shaffer* upheld the Oklahoma tax on income derived from local property and business by a nonresident where the State also taxed the income-from wherever derived-of its own citizens. Putting aside "theoretical distinctions" and looking to "the practical effect and operation" of the scheme, the nonresident was not treated more onerously than the resident in any particular, and in fact was called upon to make no more than his ratable contribution to the support of the state government. The New York tax on residents' and nonresidents' income at issue in Travis, by contrast, could not be sustained when its actual effect was considered. The tax there granted personal exemptions to each resident taxpayer for himself and each dependent, but it made no similar provision for nonresidents. The disparity could not be "deemed to be counterbalanced" by an exemption for nonresidents' interest and dividend income because it was not likely "to benefit nonresidents to a degree corresponding to the discrimination against them." Looking to "the concrete, the particular incidence" of the tax, therefore, the Court said of the many New Jersey and Connecticut residents who worked in New York:

> "They pursue their several occupations side by side with residents of the state of New York-in effect competing with them as to wages, salaries, and other terms of employment. Whether they must pay a tax upon the first $1,000 or $2,000 of income, while their associates and competitors who reside in New York do not, makes a substantial difference.... This is not a case of occasional or accidental inequality due to circumstances personal to the taxpayer ... but a general rule, operating to the disadvantage of all nonresidents ... and favoring all residents ..." 252 U.S., at 80–81, 40 S.Ct., at 232 (citations omitted).

III

Against this background establishing a rule of substantial equality of treatment for the citizens of the taxing State and nonresident taxpayers, the New Hampshire Commuters Income Tax cannot be sustained. The overwhelming fact, as the State concedes, is that the tax falls exclusively on the income of nonresidents; and it is not offset even approximately by other taxes imposed upon residents alone.[10] Rather, the argument advanced in favor of the tax is that the ultimate burden it imposes is "not more onerous in effect," Shaffer v. Carter, supra, on nonresidents because their total state tax liability is unchanged once the tax credit they receive from their State of residence is taken into account. While this argument has an initial appeal, it cannot be squared with the underlying policy of comity to which the Privileges and Immunities Clause commits us.

According to the State's theory of the case, the only practical effect of the tax is to divert to New Hampshire tax revenues that would otherwise be paid to Maine, an effect entirely within Maine's power to terminate by repeal of its credit provision for income taxes paid to another State. The

---

10. The $10 annual resident tax and the tax on certain unearned income in excess of $600 would rarely equal, much less exceed, the 4% tax on nonresidents' incomes over $2,000. Appellant Logan, for example, with $33,000 of New Hampshire-derived income, paid $252 in taxes to that State; a resident with the same earned income would have paid only the $10 resident tax. Against this disparity and the disparities among nonresidents' tax rates depending on their State of residence, we find no support in the record for the assertion of the court below that the Commuters Income Tax creates no more than a "practical equality" between residents and nonresidents when the taxes paid only by residents are taken into account. "[S]omething more is required than bald assertion"—by the state court or by counsel here—to establish the validity of a taxing statute that on its face discriminates against nonresidents. Mullaney v. Anderson, 342 U.S. 415, 418, 72 S.Ct 428, 430 (1952).

Maine Legislature could do this, presumably, by amending the provision so as to deny a credit for taxes paid to New Hampshire while retaining it for the other 48 States. Putting aside the acceptability of such a scheme, and the relevance of any increase in appellants' home state taxes that the diversionary effect is said to have,[11] we do not think the possibility that Maine could shield its residents from New Hampshire's tax cures the constitutional defect of the discrimination in that tax. In fact, it compounds it. For New Hampshire in effect invites appellants to induce their representatives, if they can, to retaliate against it.

A similar, though much less disruptive, invitation was extended by New York in support of the discriminatory personal exemption at issue in *Travis*. The statute granted the nonresident a credit for taxes paid to his State of residence on New York-derived income only if that State granted a substantially similar credit to New York residents subject to its income tax. New York contended that it thus "looked forward to the speedy adoption of an income tax by the adjoining States," which would eliminate the discrimination "by providing similar exemptions similarly conditioned." To this the Court responded in terms fully applicable to the present case. Referring to the anticipated legislative response of the neighboring States, it stated:

> "This, however, is wholly speculative; New York has no authority to legislate for the adjoining States; and we must pass upon its statute with respect to its effect and operation in the existing situation. ... A State may not barter away the right, conferred upon its citizens by the Constitution of the United States, to enjoy the privileges and immunities of citizens when they go into other States. Nor can discrimination be corrected by retaliation; to prevent this was one of the chief ends sought to be accomplished by the adoption of the Constitution." 252 U.S., at 82, 40 S.Ct., at 233.

Nor, we may add, can the constitutionality of one State's statutes affecting nonresidents depend upon the present configuration of the statutes of another State.

Since we dispose of this case under Art. IV, § 2, of the Constitution, we have no occasion to address the equal protection arguments directed at the disparate treatment of residents and nonresidents and at that feature of the statute that causes the rate of taxation imposed upon nonresidents to vary among them depending upon the rate established by their State of residence.

Reversed.

MR. JUSTICE DOUGLAS took no part in the consideration or decision of this case.

---

11. The States of Maine and Vermont, amici curiae, point out that at least $400,000 was diverted from Maine to New Hampshire by reason of the challenged tax and Maine's tax credit in 1971, and that the average Maine taxpayer, appellants included, thereby bore an additional burden of 40 cents in Maine taxes. While the inference is strong, we deem the present record insufficient to demonstrate that Maine taxes were actually higher than they otherwise would have been but for this revenue loss.

MR. JUSTICE BLACKMUN, dissenting.

For me, this is a noncase. I would dismiss the appeal for want of a substantial federal question. We have far more urgent demands upon our limited time than this kind of litigation.

Because the New Hampshire income tax statutes operate in such a way that no New Hampshire resident is ultimately subjected to the State's income tax, the case at first glance appears to have some attraction. That attraction, however, is superficial and, upon careful analysis, promptly fades and disappears entirely. The reason these appellants, who are residents of Maine, not of New Hampshire, pay a New Hampshire tax is because the Maine Legislature—the appellants' own duly elected representatives—has given New Hampshire the option to divert this increment of tax (on a Maine resident's income earned in New Hampshire) from Maine to New Hampshire, and New Hampshire willingly has picked up that option. All that New Hampshire has done is what Maine specifically permits and, indeed, invites it to do. If Maine should become disenchanted with its bestowed bounty, its legislature may change the Maine statute. The crux is the statute of Maine, not the statute of New Hampshire. The appellants, therefore, are really complaining about their own statute. It is ironic that the State of Maine, which allows the credit, has made an appearance in this case as an amicus urging, in effect, the denial of the credit by an adjudication of unconstitutionality of New Hampshire's statute. It seems to me that Maine should be here seeking to uphold its own legislatively devised plan or turn its attention to its own legislature.

* * *

One wonders whether this is just a lawyers' lawsuit. Certainly, the appellants, upon prevailing today, have no direct or apparent financial gain. Relief for them from the New Hampshire income tax results only in a corresponding, pro tanto, increase in their Maine income tax. Dollarwise, they emerge at exactly the same point. The single difference is that their State, Maine, enjoys the tax on the New Hampshire-earned income, rather than New Hampshire. Where, then, is the injury? If there is an element of injury, it is Maine-imposed.

We waste our time, therefore, by theorizing and agonizing about the Privileges and Immunities Clause and equal protection in this case. But if that exercise in futility is nevertheless indicated, I see little merit in the appellants' quest for relief. It is settled that absolute equality is not a requisite under the Privileges and Immunities Clause. And I fail to perceive unconstitutional unequal protection on New Hampshire's part. If inequality exists, it is due to differences in the respective income tax rates of the States that border upon New Hampshire.

I say again that this is a noncase, made seemingly attractive by high-sounding suggestions of inequality and unfairness. The State of Maine has the cure within its grasp, and if the cure is of importance to it and to its citizens, such as appellants, it and they should be about adjusting Maine's house rather than coming here complaining of a collateral effect of its own statute.

NOTES AND QUESTIONS

A. *The Scope of the Protection.* Note that corporations are not "citizens," and the Privileges and Immunities Clause therefore provides no protection for corporations. See Western Turf Ass'n v. Greenberg, 204 U.S. 359, 27 S.Ct. 384 (1907). In this respect, the Privileges and Immunities Clause should be contrasted with the Due Process and Equal Protection Clauses, which protect all "person[s]" including corporate persons. The Privileges and Immunities Clause is also limited by the fact that it embraces only "fundamental" rights. "Only with respect to those 'privileges and immunities' bearing upon the vitality of the Nation as a single entity must the State treat all citizens, resident and nonresident, equally." Baldwin v. Montana Fish and Game Commission, 436 U.S. 371, 383, 98 S.Ct. 1852 (1978). The Court therefore upheld an elk-hunting license scheme that imposed substantially higher fees on nonresidents than on residents because access by nonresidents to recreational big game hunting in Montana did not fall within the category of fundamental rights protected by the Privileges and Immunities Clause. On other occasions, however, the Court has struck down differential license fees for nonresidents. In Toomer v. Witsell, 334 U.S. 385, 68 S.Ct. 1156 (1948), South Carolina imposed a license fee on shrimp fishing boats in its coastal waters at the rate of $25 for each resident-owned boat and $2,500 for each boat owned by a nonresident. The Court invalidated the levy under the Privileges and Immunities Clause of Article IV, concluding that the purpose and effect of the fee were not to conserve shrimp but to exclude nonresidents and thereby create a commercial shrimp monopoly for South Carolina residents.

B. *Personal Income Taxation of Nonresidents.* The New York Court of Appeals followed *Austin* in striking down legislation that exempted New York State resident commuters, but not out-of-state commuters, from the application of New York City's income tax. City of New York v. State, 94 N.Y.2d 577, 730 N.E.2d 920, 709 N.Y.S.2d 122 (2000). By contrast, the Maryland Court of Special Appeals upheld Maryland's "special nonresident tax" (SNRT). Enacted by the Maryland General Assembly in 2004, the SNRT applies only to individuals subject to the state income tax but not subject to county or local income taxes in the state, which generally apply only to state residents. Timothy Frey, a Pennsylvania resident with Maryland income arising from the operation of his law practice, challenged the tax, arguing that it violated the Privileges and Immunities Clause since it applied only to nonresidents. The Court of Special Appeals rejected that challenge, reasoning that the SNRT was designed to approximate the local income tax burden on Maryland residents. The court concluded that "the SNRT places nonresidents and residents on an equal footing because nonresidents pay no more Maryland income tax than residents. Although the SNRT is imposed only on nonresidents, residents also pay the county income tax. There is no violation of the Privileges and Immunities Clause." Frey v. Comptroller of the Treasury, 184 Md.App. 315, 965 A.2d 923 (2009).

LUNDING v. NEW YORK TAX APPEALS TRIBUNAL

Supreme Court of the United States, 1998.
522 U.S. 287, 118 S.Ct. 766.

JUSTICE O'CONNOR delivered the opinion of the Court.

The Privileges and Immunities Clause, U.S. Const., Art. IV, § 2, provides that "[t]he Citizens of each State shall be entitled to all Privileges and Immunities of Citizens in the several States." In this case, we consider whether a provision of New York law that effectively denies only nonresident taxpayers an income tax deduction for alimony paid is consistent with that constitutional command. We conclude that because New York has not adequately justified the discriminatory treatment of nonresidents effected by N.Y. Tax Law § 631(b)(6), the challenged provision violates the Privileges and Immunities Clause.

I

A

New York law requires nonresident individuals to pay tax on net income from New York real property or tangible personalty and net income from employment or business, trade, or professional operations in New York. See N.Y. Tax Law § 631(a), (b) (McKinney 1987). Under provisions enacted by the New York Legislature in 1987, the tax on such income is determined according to a method that takes into consideration the relationship between a nonresident taxpayer's New York source income and the taxpayer's total income, as reported to the Federal Government. § 601(e)(1).

Computation of the income tax nonresidents owe New York involves several steps. First, nonresidents must compute their tax liability "as if" they resided in New York. The starting point for this computation is federal adjusted gross income, which, in accordance with the Internal Revenue Code, 26 U.S.C. § 215, includes a deduction for alimony payments. After various adjustments to federal adjusted gross income, nonresidents derive their "as if" resident taxable income from which "as if" resident tax is computed, using the same tax rates applicable to residents. Once the "as if" resident tax has been computed, nonresidents derive an "apportionment percentage" to be applied to that amount, based on the ratio of New York source income to federal adjusted gross income. N.Y. Tax Law § 601(e)(1). The denominator of the ratio, federal adjusted gross income, includes a deduction for alimony paid, by virtue of 26 U.S.C. § 215, as incorporated into New York law by N.Y. Tax Law § 612(a). The numerator, New York source income, includes the net income from property, employment, or business operations in New York, but, by operation of § 631(b)(6), specifically disallows any deduction for alimony paid. In the last step of the computation, nonresidents multiply the "as if" resident tax by the apportionment percentage, thereby computing their actual New York income tax liability. There is no upper limit on the apportionment percentage. Thus, in circumstances where a nonresident's New York income, which does not include a deduction for alimony paid, exceeds federal adjusted gross income, which does, the nonresident will be liable for more than 100% of the "as if" resident tax.

* * *

B

In 1990, petitioners Christopher Lunding and his wife, Barbara, were residents of Connecticut. During that year, Christopher Lunding earned substantial income from the practice of law in New York. That year, he also incurred alimony expenses relating to the dissolution of a previous marriage. In accordance with New York law, petitioners filed a New York Nonresident Income Tax Return to report the New York earnings. Petitioners did not comply with the limitation in § 631(b)(6), however, instead deducting a pro rata portion of alimony paid in computing their New York income based on their determination that approximately 48% of Christopher's business income was attributable to New York.

The Audit Division of the New York Department of Taxation and Finance denied that deduction and recomputed petitioners' tax liability. After recalculation without the pro rata alimony deduction, petitioners owed an additional $3,724 in New York income taxes, plus interest. Petitioners appealed the additional assessment to the New York Division of Tax Appeals, asserting that § 631(b)(6) discriminates against New York nonresidents in violation of the Privileges and Immunities, Equal Protection, and Commerce Clauses of the Federal Constitution.* * *

* * *

* * *[T]he New York Court of Appeals * * * upheld the constitutionality of § 631(b)(6). In its decision, the New York Court of Appeals found that Shaffer v. Carter, 252 U.S. 37, 40 S.Ct. 221 (1920), and Travis v. Yale & Towne Mfg. Co., 252 U.S. 60, 40 S.Ct. 228 (1920), "established that limiting taxation of nonresidents to their in-State income [is] a sufficient justification for similarly limiting their deductions to expenses derived from sources producing that in-State income," and that the constitutionality of a tax law should be determined based on its " 'practical effect.' " 89 N.Y.2d, at 288, 653 N.Y.S.2d, at 65, 675 N.E.2d, at 819. The court noted that "the Privileges and Immunities Clause does not mandate absolute equality in tax treatment," and quoted from Supreme Court of N.H. v. Piper, 470 U.S. 274, 284, 105 S.Ct. 1272, 1278 (1985), in explaining that the Clause is not violated where " '(i) there is a substantial reason for the difference in treatment; and (ii) the discrimination practiced against nonresidents bears a substantial relationship to the State's objective.' " 89 N.Y.2d, at 289, 653 N.Y.S.2d, at 66, 675 N.E.2d, at 820.

Applying those principles to § 631(b)(6), the court determined that the constitutionality of not allowing nonresidents to deduct personal expenses had been settled by Goodwin v. State Tax Comm'n, 286 App.Div.

694, 146 N.Y.S.2d 172 (1955), aff'd, 1 N.Y.2d 680, 150 N.Y.S.2d 203, 133 N.E.2d 711, appeal dism'd, 352 U.S. 805, 77 S.Ct. 47 (1956), in which a New Jersey resident unsuccessfully challenged New York's denial of tax deductions respecting New Jersey real estate taxes, interest payments, medical expenses, and life insurance premiums. The *Lunding* court adopted two rationales from *Goodwin* in concluding that § 631(b)(6) was adequately justified. First, the court reasoned that because New York residents are subject to the burden of taxation on all of their income regardless of source, they should be entitled to the benefit of full deduction of expenses. Second, the court concluded that where deductions represent personal expenses of a nonresident taxpayer, they are more appropriately allocated to the State of residence. 89 N.Y.2d, at 289–290, 653 N.Y.S.2d, at 66, 675 N.E.2d, at 820.

* * *

Recognizing that the ruling of the New York Court of Appeals in this case creates a clear conflict with the Oregon Supreme Court's decision in Wood v. Department of Revenue, 305 Or. 23, 749 P.2d 1169 (1988), and is in tension with the South Carolina Supreme Court's ruling in Spencer v. South Carolina Tax Comm'n, 281 S.C. 492, 316 S.E.2d 386 (1984), aff'd by an equally divided Court, 471 U.S. 82, 105 S.Ct. 1859 (1985), we granted certiorari. We conclude that, in the absence of a substantial reason for the difference in treatment of nonresidents, § 631(b)(6) violates the Privileges and Immunities Clause by denying only nonresidents an income tax deduction for alimony payments.

II

A

* * *

* * * [W]hen confronted with a challenge under the Privileges and Immunities Clause to a law distinguishing between residents and nonresidents, a State may defend its position by demonstrating that "(i) there is a substantial reason for the difference in treatment; and (ii) the discrimination practiced against nonresidents bears a substantial relationship to the State's objective." Piper, 470 U.S., at 284, 105 S.Ct., at 1278.

* * *

B

Our review of the State's justification for § 631(b)(6) is informed by this Court's precedent respecting Privileges and Immunities Clause challenges to nonresident income tax provisions. In Shaffer v. Carter, the Court upheld Oklahoma's denial of deductions for out-of-state losses to nonresidents who were subject to Oklahoma's tax on in-state income. The Court explained:

"The difference ... is only such as arises naturally from the extent of the jurisdiction of the State in the two classes of cases, and cannot be regarded as an unfriendly or unreasonable discrimination. As to residents, it may, and does, exert its taxing power over their income from all sources, whether within or without the State, and it accords to them a corresponding privilege of deducting their losses, wherever these accrue. As to nonresidents, the jurisdiction extends only to their property owned within the State and their business, trade, or profession carried on therein, and the tax is only on such income as is derived from those sources. Hence there is no obligation to accord to them a deduction by reason of losses elsewhere incurred." 252 U.S., at 57, 40 S.Ct., at 227.

In so holding, the Court emphasized the practical effect of the provision, concluding that "the nonresident was not treated more onerously than the resident in any particular, and in fact was called upon to make no more than his ratable contribution to the support of the state government." Austin [v. New Hampshire], supra, [420 U.S.] at 664, 95 S.Ct., at 1196 [(1975)].

Shaffer involved a challenge to the State's denial of business-related deductions. The record in *Shaffer* discloses that, while Oklahoma law specified that nonresidents were liable for Oklahoma income tax on "the entire net income from all property owned, and of every business, trade or profession carried on in [Oklahoma]," there was no express statutory bar preventing nonresidents from claiming the same nonbusiness exemptions and deductions as were available to resident taxpayers. * * *

In *Travis v. Yale & Towne Mfg. Co.*, a Connecticut corporation doing business in New York sought to enjoin enforcement of New York's nonresident income tax laws on behalf of its employees, who were residents of Connecticut and New Jersey. In an opinion issued on the same day as *Shaffer*, the Court affirmed *Shaffer*'s holding that a State may limit the deductions of nonresidents to those related to the production of in-state income. See Travis, 252 U.S., at 75–76, 40 S.Ct., at 230 (describing *Shaffer* as settling that "there is no unconstitutional discrimination against citizens of other States in confining the deduction of expenses, losses, etc., in the case of non-resident taxpayers, to such as are connected with income arising from sources within the taxing State"). * * * [T]he statutory provisions disallowing nonresidents' tax deductions at issue in *Travis* essentially mirrored those at issue in *Shaffer* because they tied nonresidents' deductions to their in-state activities.

Another provision of New York's nonresident tax law challenged in *Travis* did not survive scrutiny under the Privileges and Immunities Clause, however. Evincing the same concern with practical effect that animated the *Shaffer* decision, the *Travis* Court struck down a provision that denied only nonresidents an exemption from tax on a certain threshold of income, even though New York law allowed nonresidents a corresponding credit against New York taxes in the event that they paid resident income taxes in some other State providing a similar credit to New York residents. * * *

In *Austin*, a more recent decision reviewing a State's taxation of nonresidents, we considered a commuter tax imposed by New Hampshire, the effect of which was to tax only nonresidents working in that State. The Court described its previous decisions, including *Shaffer* and *Travis*, as "establishing a rule of substantial equality of treatment for the citizens of the taxing State and nonresident taxpayers," under which New Hampshire's one-sided tax failed. 420 U.S., at 665, 95 S.Ct., at 1197.

Travis and *Austin* make clear that the Privileges and Immunities Clause prohibits a State from denying nonresidents a general tax exemption provided to residents, while *Shaffer* and *Travis* establish that States may limit nonresidents' deductions of business expenses and nonbusiness deductions based on the relationship between those expenses and in-state property or income. While the latter decisions provide States a considerable amount of leeway in aligning the tax burden of nonresidents to in-state activities, neither they nor *Austin* can be fairly read as holding that the Privileges and Immunities Clause permits States to categorically deny personal deductions to a nonresident taxpayer, without a substantial justification for the difference in treatment.

III

In this case, New York acknowledges the right of nonresidents to pursue their livelihood on terms of substantial equality with residents. * * * In attempting to justify the discrimination against nonresidents effected by § 631(b)(6), respondents assert that because the State only has jurisdiction over nonresidents' in-state activities, its limitation on nonresidents' deduction of alimony payments is valid. Invoking *Shaffer* and *Travis*, the State maintains that it should not be required to consider expenses "wholly linked to personal activities outside New York." Brief for Respondent Commissioner of Taxation and Finance 24. We must consider whether that assertion suffices to substantially justify the challenged statute.

A

Looking first at the rationale the New York Court of Appeals adopted in upholding § 631(b)(6), we do not find in the court's decision any reasonable explanation or substantial justification for the discriminatory provision. Although the court purported to apply the two-part inquiry derived from *Toomer* [v. Witsell, 334 U.S. 385, 68 S.Ct. 1156 (1948)] and *Piper*, in the end, the justification for § 631(b)(6) was based on rationales borrowed from another case, Goodwin v. State Tax Comm'n, 286 App.Div. 694, 146 N.Y.S.2d 172, aff'd, 1 N.Y.2d 680, 150 N.Y.S.2d 203, 133 N.E.2d 711 (1956), appeal dism'd, 352 U.S. 805, 77 S.Ct. 47 (1956). There, a New Jersey resident challenged New York's denial of deductions for real estate taxes and mortgage interest on his New Jersey home, and his medical expenses and life insurance premiums. The challenge in that case, however, was to a provision of New York tax law substantially similar to that considered in *Travis*, under which nonresident taxpayers were allowed deductions " 'only if and to the extent that, they are connected with [taxable] income arising from sources within the state.' " 286 App.Div., at 695, 146 N.Y.S.2d, at 175 (quoting then N.Y. Tax Law § 360(11)).

There is no analogous provision in § 631(b)(6), which plainly limits nonresidents' deduction of alimony payments, irrespective of whether those payments might somehow relate to New York-source income. * * *

In summarizing its holding, the New York Court of Appeals explained that, because "there can be no serious argument that petitioners' alimony deductions are legitimate business expenses[,] . . . the approximate equality of tax treatment required by the Constitution is satisfied, and greater fine-tuning in this tax scheme is not constitutionally mandated." 89 N.Y.2d, at 291, 653 N.Y.S.2d, at 67, 675 N.E.2d, at 821. This Court's precedent, however, should not be read to suggest that tax schemes allowing nonresidents to deduct only their business expenses are per se constitutional, and we must accordingly inquire further into the State's justification for § 631(b)(6) in light of its practical effect.

B

* * *

As a practical matter, the Court's interpretation of the Privileges and Immunities Clause in *Travis* and *Shaffer* implies that States may effectively limit nonresidents' deduction of certain personal expenses based on a reason as simple as the fact that those expenses are clearly related to residence in another State. But here, § 631(b)(6) does not incorporate such analysis on its face or, according to the New York Court of Appeals, through legislative history, see 89 N.Y.2d, at 290–291, 653 N.Y.S.2d at 67, 675 N.E.2d, at 821. Moreover, there are situations in which § 631(b)(6) could operate to require nonresidents to pay significantly more tax than identically situated residents. For example, if a nonresident's earnings were derived primarily from New York sources, the effect of § 631(b)(6) could be to raise the tax apportionment percentage above 100%, thereby requiring that individual to pay more tax than an identically situated resident, solely because of the disallowed alimony deduction. Under certain circumstances, the taxpayer could even be liable for New York taxes approaching or even exceeding net income.

There is no doubt that similar circumstances could arise respecting the apportionment for tax purposes of income or expenses based on in-state activities without a violation of the Privileges and Immunities Clause. Such was the case in *Shaffer*, despite the petitioner's attempt to argue that he should be allowed to offset net business income taxed by Oklahoma with business losses incurred in other States. See 252 U.S., at 57, 40 S.Ct., at 227. It is one thing, however, for an anomalous situation to arise because an individual has greater profits from business activities or property owned in one particular State than in another. An entirely different situation is presented by a facially inequitable and essentially unsubstantiated taxing scheme that denies only nonresidents a tax deduction for alimony payments, which while surely a personal matter, see United States v. Gilmore, 372 U.S. 39, 44, 83 S.Ct. 623, 626–627 (1963), arguably bear some relationship to a taxpayer's overall earnings. Alimony payments also differ from other types of personal deductions, such as mortgage interest and property tax payments, whose situs can be determined based on the location of the underlying property. Thus, unlike the expenses discussed in *Shaffer*, alimony payments cannot be so easily characterized as "losses elsewhere incurred." 252 U.S., at 57, 40 S.Ct., at 227. Rather, alimony payments reflect an obligation of some duration that is determined in large measure by an individual's income generally, wherever it is earned. The alimony obligation may be of a "personal" nature, but it cannot be viewed as geographically fixed in the manner that other expenses, such as business losses, mortgage interest payments, or real estate taxes, might be.

Accordingly, contrary to the dissent's suggestion, post, at 785, 788, we do not propose that States are required to allow nonresidents a deduction for all manner of personal expenses, such as taxes paid to other States or mortgage interest relating to an out-of-state residence. Nor do we imply that States invariably must provide to nonresidents the same manner of tax credits available to residents. Our precedent allows States to adopt justified and reasonable distinctions between residents and nonresidents in the provision of tax benefits, whether in the form of tax deductions or tax credits. In this case, however, we are not satisfied by the State's argument that it need not consider the impact of disallowing nonresidents a deduction for alimony paid merely because alimony expenses are personal in nature, particularly in light of the inequities that could result when a nonresident with alimony obligations derives nearly all of her income from New York, a scenario that may be "typical," see Travis, supra, at 80, 40 S.Ct., at 232. By requiring nonresidents to pay more tax than similarly situated residents solely on the basis of whether or not the nonresidents are liable for alimony payments, § 631(b)(6) violates the "rule of substantial equality of treatment" this Court described in Austin, 420 U.S., at 665, 95 S.Ct., at 1197. * * *

IV

In sum, we find that the State's inability to tax a nonresident's entire income is not sufficient, in and of itself, to justify the discrimination imposed by § 631(b)(6). While States have considerable discretion in formulating their income tax laws, that power must be exercised within the limits of the Federal Constitution. Tax provisions imposing discriminatory treatment on nonresident individuals must be reasonable in effect and based on a substantial justification other than the fact of nonresidence.

Although the Privileges and Immunities Clause does not prevent States from requiring nonresidents to allocate income and deductions based on their in-state activities in the manner described in *Shaffer* and *Travis*, those opinions do not automatically guarantee that a State may disallow nonresident taxpayers every manner of nonbusiness deduction on the assumption that such amounts are inevitably allocable to the State in which the taxpayer resides. Alimony obligations are unlike other expenses that can be related to activities conducted in a particular State or property held there. And as a personal obligation that generally correlates with a taxpayer's total income or wealth, alimony bears some relationship to earnings regardless of their source. Further, the manner in which New York taxes nonresidents, based on an allocation of an "as if" resident tax liability, not only imposes upon nonresidents' income the effect of New York's graduated tax rates but also imports a corresponding element of fairness in allowing nonresidents a pro rata deduction of other types of personal expenses. It would seem more consistent with that taxing scheme and with notions of fairness for the State to allow nonresidents a pro rata deduction for alimony paid, as well.

Under the circumstances, we find that respondents have not presented a substantial justification for the categorical denial of alimony deductions to nonresidents. The State's failure to provide more than a cursory justification for § 631(b)(6) smacks of an effort to "penaliz[e] the citizens of other States by subjecting them to heavier taxation merely because they are such citizens," Toomer, 334 U.S., at 408, 68 S.Ct., at 1168 (Frankfurter, J., concurring). We thus hold that § 631(b)(6) is an unwarranted denial to the citizens of other States of the privileges and immunities enjoyed by the citizens of New York.

Accordingly, the decision of the New York Court of Appeals is reversed, and the case is remanded for proceedings not inconsistent with this opinion.

It is so ordered.

JUSTICE GINSBURG, with whom THE CHIEF JUSTICE and JUSTICE KENNEDY join, dissenting.

* * *

I

To put this case in proper perspective, it is helpful to recognize not only that alimony payments are "surely a personal matter," ante, at 780; in addition, alimony payments are "unlike other.... personal obligation[s]," ante, at 782. Under federal tax law, mirrored in state tax regimes, alimony is included in the recipient's gross income, 26 U.S.C. § 71(a), and the payer is allowed a corresponding deduction, §§ 215(a), 62(a)(10), for payments taxable to the recipient. This scheme "can best be seen as a determination with respect to choice of taxable person rather than as rules relating to the definition of income or expense. In effect, the [alimony payer] is treated as a conduit for gross income that legally belongs to the [alimony recipient] under the divorce decree." M. Chirelstein, Federal Income Taxation ¶ 9.05, p. 230 (8th ed.1997) (hereinafter

Chirelstein); see also B. Bittker & M. McMahon, Federal Income Taxation of Individuals ¶ 36.7, p. 36–18 (2d ed. 1995) ("Unlike most other personal deductions, [the deduction for alimony payments] is best viewed as a method of designating the proper taxpayer for a given amount of income, rather than a tax allowance for particular expenditures. In combination, § 71 [allowing a deduction to the alimony payer] and § 215 [requiring the alimony recipient to include the payment in gross income] treat part of the [payer]'s income as though it were received subject to an offsetting duty to pay it to the payee."). New York applies this scheme to resident alimony payers. But N.Y. Tax Law § 631(b)(6) (McKinney 1987) declares that, in the case of a nonresident with New York source income, the alimony deduction for which federal law provides "shall not constitute a deduction derived from New York sources."

Thus, if petitioner Christopher Lunding and his former spouse were New York residents, his alimony payments would be included in his former spouse's gross income for state as well as federal income tax purposes, and he would receive a deduction for the payments. In other words, New York would tax the income once, but not twice. In fact, however, though Lunding derives a substantial part of his gross income from New York sources, he and his former spouse reside in Connecticut. That means, he urges, that New York may not tax the alimony payments at all. Compared to New York divorced spouses, in short, Lunding seeks a windfall, not an escape from double taxation, but a total exemption from New York's tax for the income in question. This beneficence to nonresidents earning income in New York, he insists, is what the Privileges and Immunities Clause of Article IV, § 2, of the United States Constitution demands.

Explaining why New York must so favor Connecticut residents over New York residents, Lunding invites comparisons with other broken marriages—cases in which one of the former spouses resides in New York and the other resides elsewhere. First, had Lunding's former spouse moved from Connecticut to New York, New York would count the alimony payments as income to her, but would nonetheless deny him, because of his out-of-state residence, any deduction. In such a case, New York would effectively tax the same income twice, first to the payer by giving him no deduction, then to the recipient, by taxing the payments as gross income to her. Of course, that is not Lunding's situation, and one may question his standing to demand that New York take nothing from him in order to offset the State's arguably excessive taxation of others.

More engagingly, Lunding compares his situation to that of a New York resident who pays alimony to a former spouse living in another State. In such a case, New York would permit the New Yorker to deduct the alimony payments, even though the recipient pays no tax to New York on the income transferred to her. New York's choice, according to Lunding, is to deny the alimony deduction to the New Yorker whose former spouse resides out of state, or else extend the deduction to him. The Court apparently agrees. At least, the Court holds, New York "has not adequately justified" the line it has drawn. Ante, at 771.

The Court's condemnation of New York's law seems to me unwarranted. As applied to a universe of former marital partners who, like Lunding and his former spouse, reside in the same State, New York's attribution of income to someone (either payer or recipient) is hardly unfair. True, an occasional New York resident will be afforded a deduction though his former spouse, because she resides elsewhere, will not be chased by New York's tax collector. And an occasional New York alimony recipient will be taxed despite the nonresidence of her former spouse. But New York could legitimately assume that in most cases, as in the Lundings' case, payer and recipient will reside in the same State. Moreover, in cases in which the State's system is overly generous (New York payer, nonresident recipient) or insufficiently generous (nonresident payer, New York recipient), there is no systematic discrimination discretely against nonresidents, for the pairs of former spouses in both cases include a resident and a nonresident.

In reviewing state tax classifications, we have previously held it sufficient under the Privileges and Immunities Clause that "the State has secured a reasonably fair distribution of burdens, and that no intentional discrimination has been made against non-residents." Travellers' Ins. Co. v. Connecticut, 185 U.S. 364, 371, 22 S.Ct. 673, 676 (1902).* * *

* * *

I would affirm the judgment of the New York Court of Appeals as consistent with the Court's precedent, and would not cast doubt, as today's decision does, on state tax provisions long considered secure.

* * *

NOTES AND QUESTIONS

A. *The Constitutionality of Denying Personal Income Tax Deductions and Exemptions to Nonresidents After* Lunding. *Lunding* makes it clear that a state may not "categorically deny" a nonresident a deduction for alimony. *Lunding* makes it equally clear that states are on solid constitutional ground in limiting nonresidents' deductions or exemptions to those that are proportional to, or connected with, their income taxable by the state, as most states do. What remains unclear after *Lunding* is the extent to which a state may wholly deny deductions other than alimony to nonresidents. For example, in Goodwin v. State Tax Comm'n, 286 App.Div. 694, 146 N.Y.S.2d 172 (3d Dep't 1955), aff'd mem., 1 N.Y.2d 680, 133 N.E.2d 711, 150 N.Y.S.2d 203, appeal dismissed, 352 U.S. 805, 77 S.Ct. 47 (1956), discussed in *Lunding,* the New York courts sustained the complete denial to a New Jersey resident of deductions for real estate taxes on his New Jersey residence, interest on his home mortgage, medical expenses, and life insurance premiums. Is *Goodwin* still good law after *Lunding* in categorically denying a nonresident a deduction for such expenses? What about Anderson v. Tiemann, 182 Neb. 393, 155

N.W.2d 322 (1967), appeal dismissed, 390 U.S. 714, 88 S.Ct. 1418 (1968) (sustaining food sales tax credit against residents'—but not nonresidents'—personal income tax liability over Privileges and Immunities Clause objections)? What about Harris v. Commissioner, 257 N.W.2d 568 (Minn. 1977) and Taylor v. Conta, 106 Wis.2d 321, 316 N.W.2d 814 (1982) (both denying nonresidents, who were former residents, the right to deduct moving expenses incurred in their moves to other states)?

B. *Limiting Nonrecognition Treatment on Exchanges of Like–Kind Property to Residents.* The Oregon Tax Court held that Oregon's limitation to residents of nonrecognition treatment in connection with like-kind exchanges (see I.R.C. § 1031) when the newly acquired property is located outside of Oregon discriminated against nonresidents in violation of the Privileges and Immunities Clause. Fisher v. Department of Revenue, 16 Or. Tax 323 (2001). Oregon sought to defend the discriminatory treatment on the ground that it was necessary to deal with the difficulties associated with collecting tax on the deferred gain from the nonresidents when the gain would be triggered only upon a nonqualifying disposition of the out-of-state property. The court dismissed this claim as speculative, because there was no evidence supporting the assertion of collection difficulties. The court also noted that an Oregon resident (who qualified for nonrecognition treatment) presented the same collection difficulties if he or she later moved outside the state. Finally, the court pointed out that the state had reasonable nondiscriminatory alternatives for attaining its objectives (e.g., conditioning nonrecognition treatment for residents and nonresidents alike on the filing of information returns). For a general consideration of the problems raised by the Oregon case, see James C. Smith & Walter Hellerstein, "State Taxation of Federally Deferred Income: The Interstate Dimension," 44 Tax L. Rev. 349 (1989).

C. *Limiting Homestead Exemption to Owner's Principal or Permanent Residence.* States with homestead exemptions typically limit them to the homeowner's "principal" or "permanent" residence. This limitation has a particular bite in Florida, where many nonresidents own vacation homes. Two out-of-state residents, who owned second homes in Florida, challenged the limitation of Florida's homestead exemption to the owner's "permanent residence" on the ground, among others, that it violated the Privileges and Immunities Clause because it effectively discriminated against nonresidents. In rejecting this contention, the court observed that

> [t]he difference in taxation treatment between the real property of nonresidents and the property of *some* Florida residents (those who meet the "permanent residence" requirement) is only incidentally related to state residency, and it is explained by the practical effect of a provision that that was intended to provide financial assistance to owners who make the Florida property their permanent residence.

Reinish v. Clark, 765 So.2d 197, 210 (Fla. Dist. Ct. App. 2000) (emphasis in original), review denied, 790 So.2d 1107 (Fla.), cert. denied, 534 U.S. 993, 122 S.Ct. 458 (2001).

In so concluding, the court echoed the sentiments of an earlier New Jersey decision that had rejected a similar claim. Rubin v. Glaser, 83 N.J. 299, 416 A.2d 382 (1980). In *Rubin*, the court extracted the following principle from its review of the Privileges and Immunities Clause decisions of the Supreme Court and other state tribunals: "state taxing statutes, conferring a benefit or advantage only on residents, do not run afoul of the Privileges and Immunities Clause, provided they bear a 'close' or 'substantial relationship' to a legitimate purpose independent of discrimination against nonresidents." Id., 416 A.2d at 386. Applying this principle, the court found that the act's application solely to principal places of residence was closely related to the beneficent purpose of alleviating the heavy realty tax burden. It also observed that the statutory purpose was not directed against nonresidents.

> New Jersey residents who do not own a principal residence in the State are on the same footing as nonresidents. For example, a New Jersey resident whose principal place of residence is a rented apartment would not receive a rebate on a home he owned at the New Jersey shore. Moreover no one is entitled to a rebate of taxes paid on a second home. Thus, plaintiffs are treated the same as New Jersey residents who own a second home for summer vacations in New Jersey with respect to rebates on that second home.

Id. Accord Markham v. Comstock, 272 A.D.2d 971, 708 N.Y.S.2d 674 (4th Dep't), appeal denied, 95 N.Y.2d 886, 738 N.E.2d 781, 715 N.Y.S.2d 377 (2000), cert. denied, 531 U.S. 1079, 121 S.Ct. 778 (2001).

D. *Permitting Homeowners to Retain Assessment Benefits on Intrastate Moves.* Recall that in *Nordlinger* (pp. 243–57 supra), the petitioner alleged that exemptions from reassessment under California's Proposition 13 for transfers by owners over 55 and for transfers between parents and children were unconstitutional because they classified on the basis of California residency and impeded the right to travel across state lines. Nordlinger v. Hahn, 505 U.S. 1, 10–11, 112 S.Ct. 2326 (1992). The Court refused to consider the contention because the petitioner herself had made an intrastate move and therefore lacked standing to raise the claim under the Court's prudential standing principles. In 2008, however, the Florida voters approved an even broader exemption applicable to the state's "Save Our Homes" provision—a constitutionally based assessment limitation analogous to Proposition 13, but limited to homesteads. Under the constitutional amendment, Florida homeowners who move from one homestead to another in Florida generally may retain an assessment benefit equal to the difference between the assessed value and market value of their previous homestead. Homeowners moving to Florida from outside the state, however, enjoy no such benefit. Is the Florida regime vulnerable to attack under the Privileges and Immunities Clause or other constitutional provisions? For an extended answer to that question based on a study prepared for the Florida Legislature, see Walter Hellerstein, "Federal Constitutional Restraints on Property Tax Assessment Limitations: An Analysis of Florida's Portability Proposals," State Tax Notes, June 11, 2007, p. 789.

CHAPTER 5

IMMUNITY OF FEDERAL INSTRUMENTALITIES FROM STATE TAXATION

■ ■ ■

A. SALES, USE, GROSS RECEIPTS, AND OTHER EXCISE TAXES

UNITED STATES v. NEW MEXICO

Supreme Court of the United States, 1982.
455 U.S. 720, 102 S.Ct. 1373.

JUSTICE BLACKMUN delivered the opinion of the Court.

We are presented here with a recurring problem: to what extent may a State impose taxes on contractors that conduct business with the Federal Government?

I

A

This case concerns the contractual relationships between three private entities and the United States. The three agreements involved are typical in most respects of management contracts devised by the Atomic Energy Commission (AEC), now the Department of Energy (DOE).* * *

The first of the contractors, Sandia Corporation, was organized in 1949 as a subsidiary of Western Electric Company, Inc. Sandia manages the Government-owned Sandia Laboratories in Albuquerque, N. M., and engages exclusively in federally sponsored research. It receives no fee under its contract, and owns no property except for $1,000 in United States bonds that constitute its paid-in capital. But Sandia and Western Electric are guaranteed royalty-free, irrevocable licenses for any communications-related discoveries or inventions developed by most Sandia employees during the course of the contract, and the company receives complete reimbursements for salary outlays and other expenditures.

The Zia Company, another of the contractors, is a subsidiary of Santa Fe Industries, Inc. Since 1946, Zia has performed a variety of management, maintenance, and related functions at the Government's Los Alamos Scientific Laboratory, for which it receives its costs as well as a fixed annual fee. While Zia owns property and performs private work, virtually none of its property is used in the performance of its contract with the Government, and all of its private activities are conducted away from Los Alamos by a separate work force.

The third contractor is Los Alamos Constructors, Inc. (LACI), since 1953 a subsidiary of Zia. LACI's operations are limited to construction and repair work at the Los Alamos facility. The company owns no tangible personal property and makes no purchases; it procures needed property and equipment through its parent, Zia. And like Zia, LACI receives its costs plus a fixed annual fee from the Government. The management contracts between the Government and the three contractors have a number of significant features in common. As in most DOE atomic facility management agreements, the contracts provide that title to all tangible personal property purchased by the contractors passes directly from the vendor to the Government.[1] Similarly, the Government bears the risk of loss for property procured by the contractors. Zia and LACI must submit an annual voucher of expenditures for Government approval. And the agreements give the Government control over the disposition of all property purchased under the contracts, as well as over each contractor's property management procedures. Disputes under the contracts are to be resolved by a DOE contracting official.

On the other hand, the contractors place orders with third-party suppliers in their own names, and identify themselves as the buyers. Indeed, the Government acknowledged during discovery that Sandia, Zia, and LACI "may be ... 'independent contractor[s],' rather than ... 'servant[s]' for ... given 'function[s] under' the contract[s] (e.g., directing the details of day-to-day ... operations and the hiring and direct supervision of employees)," and the Government does not claim that the contractors are federal instrumentalities. Similarly, the United States disclaims responsibility for torts committed by the contractors' employees, and maintains that such employees have no claim against the United States for labor-related grievances.

Finally, and most importantly, the contracts use a so-called "advanced funding" procedure to meet contractor costs. Advanced funding, an accounting device developed shortly after the conclusion of the Manhattan Project, is designed to provide "up-to-date meaningful records of costs and controls of property," as well as to "speed up reimbursement of contractors." The procedure allows contractors to pay creditors and employees with drafts drawn on a special bank account in which United States Treasury funds are deposited.

To put the advanced funding mechanism in place, the United States, the contractor, and a bank establish a designated bank account, pursuant to a three-party contract. The Government dispatches a letter of credit to a Federal Reserve Bank in favor of the contractor, making Treasury funds

---

1. LACI does not purchase goods, and the Government retains title to property it furnishes to the company.

available in the designated account. The contractor pays its expenses by drawing on the account, at which time the bank or the contractor executes a payment voucher in an amount sufficient to cover the draft. The voucher is forwarded to the Federal Reserve Bank. The United States owns the account balance. As a result of all this, only federal funds are expended when the contractor makes purchases. If the Government fails to provide funding, the contractor is excused from performance of the contract, and the Government is liable for all properly incurred claims.

Prior to July 1, 1977, the Government's contracts with Sandia, Zia, and LACI did not refer to the contractors as federal "agents." On that date—some two years after the commencement of this litigation—the agreements were modified to state that each contractor "acts as an agent [of the Government] ... for certain purposes," including the disbursement of Government funds and the "purchase, lease, or other acquisition" of property. This was designed to recognize what was described as the "long-standing agency status and authority" of the contractors. Thus it was made clear that Sandia and Zia were authorized to "pledge the credit of the United States," and the Government declared that it "considers all obligations properly incurred" in accordance with the contractual provisions to be Government obligations "from their inception." At the same time, however, the United States denied any intent "formally and directly [to] designat[e] the contractors as agents," and each modification stated that it did not "create rights or obligations not otherwise provided for in the contract."

<h1 style="text-align:center">B</h1>

New Mexico imposes a gross receipts tax and a compensating use tax on those doing business within the State. With limited exceptions, "[f]or the privilege of engaging in business, an excise tax equal to four per cent [4%] of gross receipts is imposed on any person engaging in business in New Mexico." N.M.Stat.Ann. § 72–16A–4 (Supp.1975). In effect, the gross receipts tax operates as a tax on the sale of goods and services. The State also levies a compensating use tax, equivalent in amount to the gross receipts tax, "[f]or the privilege of using property in New Mexico." § 72–16A–7. This is imposed on property acquired out-of-state in a "transaction that would have been subject to the gross receipts tax had it occurred within [New Mexico]." § 72–16A–7(A)(2). Thus the compensating use tax functions as an enforcement mechanism for the gross receipts tax by imposing a levy on the use of all property that has not already been taxed; the State collects the same percentage regardless of where the property is purchased. Neither tax, however, is imposed on the "receipts of the United States or any agency or instrumentality thereof," or on the "use of property by the United States or any agency or instrumentality thereof." §§ 72–16A–12.1, 72–16A–12.2.

Without objection, Zia and LACI each year paid the New Mexico gross receipts tax on the fixed fees they received from the Federal Government. But the Government argued that the contractors' other expenditures and operations are constitutionally immune from state taxation. In July 1975 the United States therefore initiated this suit in the United States District Court for the District of New Mexico, seeking a declaratory judgment that advanced funds are not taxable gross receipts to the contractors; that the receipts of vendors selling tangible property to the United States through the contractors cannot be taxed by the State; and that the use of Government-owned property by the contractors is not subject to the State's compensating use tax.

The District Court granted the United States summary judgment. * * *

The United States Court of Appeals for the Tenth Circuit reversed. 624 F.2d 111 (1980). * * *

The United States sought certiorari, and we granted the writ to consider the seemingly intractable problems posed by state taxation of federal contractors.

II

A

With the famous declaration that "the power to tax involves the power to destroy," McCulloch v. Maryland, 4 Wheat. 316, 431 (1819), Chief Justice Marshall announced for the Court the doctrine of federal immunity from state taxation. In so doing he introduced the Court to what has become a "much litigated and often confused field," United States v. City of Detroit, 355 U.S. 466, 473, 78 S.Ct. 474, 478 (1958), one that has been marked from the beginning by inconsistent decisions and excessively delicate distinctions.

McCulloch itself relied on generalized notions of federal supremacy to invalidate a state tax on the Second Bank of the United States. The Court gave broad scope to state power: the opinion declined to "deprive the States of any resources which they originally possessed. It does not extend to . . . a tax imposed on the interest which the citizens of Maryland may hold in [the Bank], in common with other property of the same description throughout the State." 4 Wheat., at 436. Not long afterwards, however, Chief Justice Marshall, speaking for the Court, seemingly disregarded the *McCulloch* dictum in striking down a state tax on interest income from federal bonds, explaining that such levies cannot constitutionally fall on an "operation essential to the important objects for which the government was created." Weston v. City Council of Charleston, 2 Pet. 449, 467 (1829). During the following century the Court took to heart *Weston*'s expansive analysis of federal tax immunity, invalidating, among many others, state taxes on the income of federal employees, Dobbins v. Commissioners of Erie County, 16 Pet. 435 (1842); on income derived from property leased from the Federal Government, Gillespie v. Oklahoma, 257 U.S. 501, 42 S.Ct. 171 (1922); and on sales to the United States, Panhandle Oil Co. v. Mississippi ex rel. Knox, 277 U.S. 218, 48 S.Ct. 451 (1928).

These decisions, it has been said, were increasingly divorced both from the constitutional foundations of the immunity doctrine and from "the actual workings of our federalism," Graves v. New York ex rel. O'Keefe, 306 U.S. 466, 490, 59 S.Ct. 595, 603 (1939) (Frankfurter, J., concurring), and in James v. Dravo Contracting Co., 302 U.S. 134, 58 S.Ct. 208 (1937), by a 5–4 vote, the Court marked a major change in course. Over the dissent's justifiable objections that it was "overrul[ing], sub silentio, a century of precedents," id., at 161, 58 S.Ct., at 221, the Court upheld a state tax on the gross receipts of a contractor providing services to the Federal Government:

> " '[I]t is not necessary to cripple [the State's power to tax] by extending the constitutional exemption from taxation to those subjects which fall within the general application of non-discriminatory laws, and where no direct burden is laid upon the governmental instrumentality, and there is only a remote, if any, influence upon the exercise of the functions of government.' " Id., at 150, 58 S.Ct., at 216, quoting Willcuts v. Bunn, 282 U.S. 216, 225, 51 S.Ct. 125, 126 (1931).

The Court's more recent cases involving federal contractors generally have hewed to the *James* analysis. Alabama v. King & Boozer, 314 U.S. 1, 62 S.Ct. 43 (1941), upheld a state tax on sales to a federal contractor, overruling Panhandle Oil Co. v. Mississippi ex rel. Knox, supra. Decisions such as United States v. City of Detroit, supra, have validated state use taxes on private entities holding federal property.

Even the Court's post-*James* decisions, however, cannot be set in an entirely unwavering line. United States v. Allegheny County, 322 U.S. 174, 64 S.Ct. 908 (1944), invalidated a state property tax that included in the assessment the value of federal machinery held by a private party; 14 years later that decision in large part was overruled by United States v. City of Detroit, supra. In Livingston v. United States, 364 U.S. 281, 80 S.Ct. 1611 (1960), summarily aff'g 179 F.Supp. 9 (E.D.S.C.1959), the Court, without opinion or citation, approved the invalidation of a state use tax as applied to a federal contractor. Yet United States v. Boyd, supra, upheld a virtually identical state tax, seemingly confining *Livingston* to its "extraordinary" facts. 378 U.S., at 45, n. 6, 84 S.Ct., at 1522.

Similarly, the decisions fail to speak with one voice on the relevance of traditional agency rules in determining the tax-immunity status of federal contractors. Thus, Alabama v. King & Boozer, supra, declined to find immunity in part because the contractors involved lacked the "status of agents," 314 U.S., at 13, 62 S.Ct., at 47, and United States v. Township of Muskegon, 355 U.S. 484, 486, 78 S.Ct. 483, 485 (1958), upheld a use tax on a federal contractor with the caveat that the "case might well be different if [the contractor] ... could properly be called a 'servant' of the United States in agency terms." See Kern–Limerick, Inc. v. Scurlock, 347 U.S. 110, 74 S.Ct. 403 (1954). Yet James v. Dravo Contracting Co., supra, stated flatly that tax immunity is not dependent " 'upon the nature of the agents, or upon the mode of their constitution, or upon the fact that they are agents.' " 302 U.S., at 154, 58 S.Ct., at 218, quoting Railroad Co. v. Peniston, 18 Wall. 5, 36 (1873) (plurality opinion). And United States v. Boyd, supra, rejected the Government's argument that its contractors were federal agents and therefore tax immune, stating simply that the private entities were not "instrumentalities of the United States." 378 U.S., at 48, 84 S.Ct., at 1524.

B

We have concluded that the confusing nature of our precedents counsels a return to the underlying constitutional principle. The one constant here, of course, is simple enough to express: a State may not, consistent with the Supremacy Clause, U.S.Const., Art. VI, cl. 2, lay a tax "directly upon the United States." Mayo v. United States, 319 U.S. 441, 447, 63 S.Ct. 1137, 1140 (1943). While "[o]ne could, and perhaps should, read *M'Culloch* ... simply for the principle that the Constitution prohibits a State from taxing discriminatorily a federally established instrumentality," First Agricultural Bank v. State Tax Comm'n, 392 U.S. 339, 350, 88 S.Ct. 2173, 2179 (1968) (dissenting opinion), the Court has never questioned the propriety of absolute federal immunity from state taxation. And after 160 years, the doctrine has gathered "a momentum of authority that reflects, if not a detailed exposition of considerations of policy demanded by our federal system, certainly a deep instinct that there are such considerations...." City of Detroit v. Murray Corp., 355 U.S. 489, 503–504, 78 S.Ct. 458, 491 (1958) (opinion of Frankfurter, J.).

But the limits on the immunity doctrine are, for present purposes, as significant as the rule itself. Thus, immunity may not be conferred simply because the tax has an effect on the United States, or even because the Federal Government shoulders the entire economic burden of the levy. That is the import of Alabama v. King & Boozer, where a sales tax was imposed on the gross receipts of a vendor selling to a cost-plus Government contractor. The Court found it constitutionally irrelevant that the United States reimbursed all the contractor's expenditures, including those going to meet the tax: the Government's right to be free from state taxation "does not spell immunity from paying the added costs, attributable to the taxation of those who furnish supplies to the Government and who have been granted no tax immunity." 314 U.S., at 9, 62 S.Ct., at 45. That the contractor is purchasing property for the Government is similarly irrelevant; in *King & Boozer*, title to goods purchased by the contractor vested in the United States immediately upon shipment by the seller. Id., at 13, 62 S.Ct., at 47.

Similarly, immunity cannot be conferred simply because the state tax falls on the earnings of a contractor providing services to the Government. James v. Dravo Contracting Co., supra. And where a use tax is involved, immunity cannot be conferred simply because the State is levying the tax on the use of federal property in private hands, United States v. City of Detroit, supra, even if the private entity is using the Government property to provide the United States with goods, United States v. Township of

Muskegon, supra; City of Detroit v. Murray Corp., supra, or services, Curry v. United States, 314 U.S. 14, 62 S.Ct. 48 (1941). In such a situation the contractor's use of the property "in connection with commercial activities carried on for profit," is "a separate and distinct taxable activity." United States v. Boyd, 378 U.S., at 44, 84 S.Ct., at 1521–22. Indeed, immunity cannot be conferred simply because the tax is paid with Government funds; that was apparently the case in *Boyd*, where the contractor made expenditures under an advanced funding arrangement similar to the one involved here. Id., at 41, 84 S.Ct., at 1520.

What the Court's cases leave room for, then, is the conclusion that tax immunity is appropriate in only one circumstance: when the levy falls on the United States itself, or on an agency or instrumentality so closely connected to the Government that the two cannot realistically be viewed as separate entities, at least insofar as the activity being taxed is concerned. This view, we believe, comports with the principal purpose of the immunity doctrine, that of forestalling "clashing sovereignty," McCulloch v. Maryland, 4 Wheat., at 430, by preventing the States from laying demands directly on the Federal Government. See City of Detroit v. Murray Corp., 355 U.S., at 504–505, 78 S.Ct., at 491–492 (opinion of Frankfurter, J.). As the federal structure—along with the workings of the tax immunity doctrine[11]—has evolved, this command has taken on essentially symbolic importance, as the visible "consequence of that [federal] supremacy which the constitution has declared." McCulloch v. Maryland, 4 Wheat. At the same time, a narrow approach to governmental tax immunity accords with competing constitutional imperatives, by giving full range to each sovereign's taxing authority.

Thus, a finding of constitutional tax immunity requires something more than the invocation of traditional agency notions: to resist the State's taxing power, a private taxpayer must actually "stand in the Government's shoes." City of Detroit v. Murray Corp., 355 U.S., at 503, 78 S.Ct., at 491 (opinion of Frankfurter, J.). That conclusion is compelled by the Court's principal decisions exploring the nature of the Constitution's immunity guarantee. Chief Justice Hughes' opinion for the Court in *James*, which set the doctrine on its modern course, suggested that a state tax is impermissible when the taxed entity is "so intimately connected with the exercise of a power or the performance of a duty" by the Government that taxation of it would be " 'a direct interference with the functions of government itself.' " 302 U.S., at 157, 58 S.Ct., at 219, quoting Metcalf & Eddy v. Mitchell, 269 U.S. 514, 524, 46 S.Ct. 172, 174–75 (1926). And the point is settled by *Boyd*, the Court's most recent decision in the field. There, the Government argued that its contractors were tax-exempt because they were federal agents. Without any discussion

---

11. With the abandonment of the notion that the economic—as opposed to the legal—incidence of the tax is relevant, it becomes difficult to maintain that federal tax immunity is designed to insulate federal operations from the effects of state taxation. It remains true, of course, that state taxes on contractors are constitutionally invalid if they discriminate against the Federal Government, or substantially interfere with its activities. New Mexico, however, is not discriminating here.

of traditional agency rules the Court rejected that suggestion out-of-hand, declaring that "we cannot believe that [the contractors are] 'so assimilated by the Government as to become one of its constituent parts.' " 378 U.S., at 47, 84 S.Ct., at 1523, quoting United States v. Township of Muskegon, 355 U.S., at 486, 78 S.Ct., at 485. And the Court continued:

> "Should the [Atomic Energy] Commission intend to build or operate the plant with its own servants and employees, it is well aware that it may do so and familiar with the ways of doing it. It chose not to do so here. We cannot conclude that [the contractors], both cost-plus contractors for profit, have been so incorporated into the government structure as to become instrumentalities of the United States and thus enjoy governmental immunity." 378 U.S., at 48, 84 S.Ct., at 1524.

The Court's other cases describing the nature of a federal instrumentality have used similar language: "virtually . . . an arm of the Government," Department of Employment v. United States, 385 U.S., at 359–360, 87 S.Ct., at 467–468; "integral parts of [a governmental department]," and "arms of the Government deemed by it essential for the performance of governmental functions," Standard Oil Co. v. Johnson, 316 U.S. 481, 485, 62 S.Ct. 1168, 1170 (1942).

Granting tax immunity only to entities that have been "incorporated into the government structure" can forestall, at least to a degree, some of the manipulation and wooden formalism that occasionally have marked tax litigation—and that have no proper place in determining the allocation of power between coexisting sovereignties. In this case, for example, the Government and its contractors modified their agreements two years into the litigation in an obvious attempt to strengthen the case for nonliability. Yet the Government resists using its own employees for the tasks at hand—or, indeed, even formally designating Sandia, Zia, and LACI as agents—because it seeks to tap the expertise of industry, without subjecting its contractors to burdensome federal procurement regulations. Instead, the Government earnestly argues that its contractors are entitled to tax immunity because, among other things, they draw checks directly on federal funds, instead of waiting a time for reimbursement. We cannot believe that an immunity of constitutional stature rests on such technical considerations, for that approach allows "any government functionary to draw the constitutional line by changing a few words in a contract." Kern–Limerick, Inc. v. Scurlock, 347 U.S., at 126, 74 S.Ct., at 412–413 (dissenting opinion).

If the immunity of federal contractors is to be expanded beyond its narrow constitutional limits, it is Congress that must take responsibility for the decision, by so expressly providing as respects contracts in a particular form, or contracts under particular programs. And this allocation of responsibility is wholly appropriate, for the political process is "uniquely adapted to accommodating the competing demands" in this area. Massachusetts v. United States, 435 U.S. 444, 456, 98 S.Ct. 1153,

1161 (1978) (plurality opinion). But absent congressional action, we have emphasized that the States' power to tax can be denied only under "the clearest constitutional mandate." Michelin Tire Corp. v. Wages, 423 U.S. 276, 293, 96 S.Ct. 535, 544 (1976).

III

It remains to apply these principles to the Sandia, Zia, and LACI contracts. The Government concedes that the legal incidence of the gross receipts and use taxes falls on the contractors, and we do not disagree. The issue, then, is whether the contractors can realistically be considered entities independent of the United States. If so, a tax on them cannot be viewed as a tax on the United States itself.

So far as the use tax is concerned, United States v. Boyd, supra, controls this case. The contracts at issue in *Boyd* were standard AEC management contracts, in all relevant respects identical to the ones here. The contractors performed maintenance and construction work at Government facilities, under the general direction of the Government. They procured materials, and paid for the goods with Government funds under an advanced funding arrangement; title passed directly from the vendor to the United States. The contractors owned none of the property involved, and received a fixed annual fee. Indeed, one of the contractor's purchase orders stated that it made purchases "for and on behalf of the Government." 378 U.S., at 42, n. 4, 84 S.Ct., at 1520, n. 4. And the Tennessee use tax did not differ in any significant way from the use tax now before us.

As noted above, the Government argued that this close contractual relationship made the contractors federal agents, and therefore tax immune. Yet the Court had no difficulty upholding the application of the Tennessee tax, concluding that " '[t]he vital thing' is that [the contractors are] 'using the property in connection with [their] own commercial activities.' " Id., at 45, 84 S.Ct., at 1522, quoting United States v. Township of Muskegon, 355 U.S., at 486, 78 S.Ct., at 485. That the federal property involved was being used for the Government's benefit—something that by definition will be true in virtually every management contract—was irrelevant, for the contractors remained distinct entities pursuing "private ends," and their actions remained "commercial activities carried on for profit." 378 U.S., at 44, 84 S.Ct., at 1521–1522. For that reason, the contractors had not become "instrumentalities" of the United States. Id., at 48, 84 S.Ct., at 1524.

The same factors are at work here. The tax, the taxed activity, and the contractual relationships do not differ from those involved in *Boyd*. The contractors here are privately owned corporations; "Government officials do not run [their] day-to-day operations nor does the Government have any ownership interest." First Agricultural Bank v. State Tax Comm'n, 392 U.S., at 354, 88 S.Ct., at 2181 (dissenting opinion). In contrast to federal employees, then, Sandia and its fellow contractors cannot be termed "constituent parts" of the Federal Government. It is true, of course, that employees are a special type of agent, and like the contractors here employees are paid for their services. But the differences between an employee and one of these contractors are crucial. The congruence of professional interests between the contractors and the Federal Government is not complete; their relationships with the Government have been created for limited and carefully defined purposes. Allowing the States to apply use taxes to such entities does not offend the notion of federal supremacy.

For similar reasons, the New Mexico gross receipts tax must be upheld as applied to funds received by the contractors to meet salaries and internal costs. Once it is conceded that the contractors are independent taxable entities, it cannot be disputed that their gross income is taxable. This conclusion follows directly from James v. Dravo Contracting Co., supra, where the Court upheld a state tax reaching "gross amounts received from the United States." 302 U.S., at 137, 58 S.Ct., at 211. In any event, incurring obligations to achieve contractual ends is not significantly different from using property for the same purposes. And despite the Government's arguments, the use of advanced funding does not change the analysis. That device is, at heart, an efficient method of reimbursing contractors—something the Government has apparently recognized in contexts other than tax litigation. If receipt of advanced funding is coextensive with status as a federal instrumentality, virtually every federal contractor is, or could easily become, immune from state taxation.

New Mexico's tax on sales to the contractors presents a more complex problem. So far as the use tax discussed above is concerned, the subject of the levy is the taxed entity's beneficial use of the property involved. Unless the entity as a whole is one of the Government's "constituent parts," then, a tax on its use of property should not be seen as falling on the United States; in that situation the property is being used in furtherance of the contractor's essentially independent commercial enterprise. In the case of a sales tax, however, it is arguable that an entity serving as a federal procurement agent can be so closely associated with the Government, and so lack an independent role in the purchase, as to make the sale—in both a real and a symbolic sense—a sale to the United States, even though the purchasing agent has not otherwise been incorporated into the Government structure.

Such was the Court's conclusion in Kern–Limerick, Inc. v. Scurlock, supra, a decision on which the Government heavily relies. The contractor in that case identified itself as a federal procurement agent, and when it made purchases title passed directly to the Government; the purchase orders themselves declared that the purchase was made by the Government and that the United States was liable on the sale. Equally as important, the contractor itself was not liable for the purchase price, and it required specific Government approval for each transaction. And, as the Court emphasized, the statutory procurement scheme envisioned the use of federal purchasing agents. The Court concluded that a sale to the contractor was in effect a sale to the United States, and therefore not a proper subject for the Arkansas sales tax. As we have noted elsewhere,

Kern–Limerick "stands only for the proposition that the State may not impose a tax the legal incidence of which falls on the Federal Government." United States v. County of Fresno, 429 U.S., at 459–460, n. 7, 97 S.Ct., at 703.

We think it evident that the *Kern–Limerick* principle does not invalidate New Mexico's sales tax as applied to purchases made by the contractors here. Even accepting the Government's representation that it is directly liable to vendors for the purchase price, Sandia and Zia nevertheless make purchases in their own names—Sandia, in fact, is contractually obligated to do so,—and presumably they are themselves liable to the vendors. Vendors are not informed that the Government is the only party with an independent interest in the purchase, as was true in *Kern–Limerick*, and the Government disclaims any formal intention to denominate the contractors as purchasing agents. Similarly, Sandia and Zia need not obtain advance Government approval for each purchase. These factors demonstrate that the contractors have a substantial independent role in making purchases, and that the identity of interests between the Government and the contractors is far from complete. As a result, sales to Zia and Sandia are in neither a real nor a symbolic sense sales to the "United States itself." It is true that title passes directly from the vendor to the Federal Government, but that factor alone cannot make the transaction a purchase by the United States, so long as the purchasing entity, in its role as a purchaser, is sufficiently distinct from the Government.

* * *

* * * For the reasons set out above, we conclude that the contractors here are not protected by the Constitution's guarantee of federal supremacy. If political or economic considerations suggest that a broader immunity rule is appropriate, "[s]uch complex problems are ones which Congress is best qualified to resolve." United States v. City of Detroit, 355 U.S., at 474, 78 S.Ct., at 478.

Accordingly, the judgment of the Court of Appeals is

Affirmed.

NOTES AND QUESTIONS

A. *Historical Overview.* The Court's opinion in *United States v. New Mexico* lucidly traces the evolution of the doctrine that the Federal Government and its instrumentalities are immune from state taxation. As the Court observes, the origins of the doctrine lie in the seminal case of McCulloch v. Maryland, 17 U.S. (4 Wheat.) 316 (1819). In *McCulloch,* the Court confronted a Maryland tax levied on notes issued by any bank not chartered by the state. No equivalent levy was imposed on Maryland banks. The only bank in Maryland actually fitting the statutory description was the Bank of the United States, created and incorporated by an act of Congress. In Chief Justice Marshall's landmark opinion, the Court held that Congress had constitutional authority to create the Bank and that Maryland's levy upon it was invalid under the Supremacy Clause:

The question is, in truth, a question of supremacy; and if the right of the States to tax the means employed by the general government be conceded, the declaration that the constitution, and the laws made in pursuance thereof, shall be the supreme law of the land, is empty and unmeaning declamation.

Id. at 320–21.

McCulloch involved a tax that discriminated against the operations of the Federal Government, and Chief Justice Marshall was careful to point out that the implied prohibition against state taxation of the Federal Government would

not extend to a tax paid by the real property of the bank, in common with other real property within the state, nor to a tax imposed on the interest which citizens of Maryland may hold in this institution in common with other property of the same description throughout the state.

Id. at 436.

Nevertheless, as the Court observed in *United States v. New Mexico*, decisions following *McCulloch* broadened the scope of the immunity into a prohibition against state taxes upon the Federal Government and its instrumentalities, and, for a period, even to the invalidation of taxes on the receipts or income of persons who contracted with or worked for the Federal Government. The pressure on the Court to narrow Chief Justice Marshall's "rhetorical absolute" (New York v. United States, 326 U.S. 572, 576, 66 S.Ct. 310 (1946) (Frankfurter, J., concurring))—namely, that "the power to tax involves the power to destroy," id. at 431—intensified as the Federal Government's commercial role increased and with it the volume of activity exempt from state taxation. The Court's opinion in *United States v. New Mexico* explains how the Court gradually reformulated the doctrine of federal immunity from state taxation and dramatically cut back on its scope, especially with regard to the derivative immunity that the Court had accorded to the private sector in its dealing with the Federal Government and its agencies.

The process of delineating the precise bounds of the Federal Government's immunity from state taxation continues with every term of the Court. Broadly speaking, however, modern case law has narrowed the immunity to a proscription against taxes whose legal incidence falls on the United States and its instrumentalities and to levies that discriminate against the Federal Government. See generally Walter Hellerstein, "State Taxation and the Supreme Court: Toward a More Unified Approach to Constitutional Adjudication," 75 Mich. L. Rev. 1426, 1434–41, 1446–54 (1977).

B. *The Scope of the Immunity of Federal Contractors From State Sales, Use, and Gross Receipts Taxes.* Could the Federal Government have structured its contracts with the three federal contractors in *United States v. New Mexico* to avoid the use, gross receipts, or sales taxes imposed by New Mexico in the case? In other words, what, if anything, could the Federal Government and the federal contractors have done to bring the transactions at issue within the principle of *Kern–Limerick* rather than *James* or *King & Boozer*?

C. *Substance Versus Form in Federal Immunity Cases.* Doesn't the Federal Government bear the economic impact of the taxes sustained in cases like *James, Boyd, King & Boozer*, and *United States v. New Mexico*, and is not the practical effect of those cases to let the states tax the Federal Government? How, then, can you reconcile the Court's analysis in *United States v. New Mexico* with its analysis in other areas of its state tax jurisprudence where the Court emphasizes "economic realities" (Complete Auto Transit, Inc. v. Brady, 430 U.S. 274, 279, 97 S.Ct. 1076 (1977)), and considers the "practical or economic effect of the tax." Goldberg v. Sweet, 488 U.S. 252, 262, 109 S.Ct. 582 (1989)? Does not the Court's analysis in *United States v. New Mexico* allow form to triumph over substance?

D. *"Legal Incidence" Test as Criterion for Determining Federal Immunity From State Taxation.* In light of the Court's explicit rejection of the "economic burden" test as a criterion for determining the constitutional immunity of the Federal Government from state taxation in cases like *King & Boozer* and *United States v. New Mexico*, the critical constitutional issue—apart from any question of discrimination—becomes whether the "legal incidence" of the tax falls on the Federal Government or its instrumentalities. In Kern–Limerick, Inc. v. Scurlock, 347 U.S. 110, 74 S.Ct. 403 (1954), discussed in *United States v. New Mexico*, the Court struck down the application of a sales tax to a Federal Government contractor. Even though the substance of the underlying transaction in *Kern–Limerick* was in all essential respects identical to the transaction in *King & Boozer*, the Court struck down the tax because the contractor was deemed, under the applicable contract, to be a "purchasing agent" for the Federal Government. Hence the "legal incidence" of the tax fell on the Federal Government as purchaser rather than on the contractor. The Court acknowledged that the contract in *Kern–Limerick* "differs in form but not in economic substance" from the contract in *King & Boozer* and that "the form of contracts, when governmental immunity is not waived by Congress, may determine the effect of state taxation on federal agencies, for decisions consistently prohibit taxes levied on the property or purchases of the Government itself." Id., 347 U.S. at 122–23. See also United States v. Boyd, 378 U.S. 39, 44, 84 S.Ct. 1518 (1964), discussed in *United States v. New Mexico* (sustaining tax on use of tangible personal property by contractor, even though property was owned by the Federal Government, because "legal incidence is upon a contractor doing business with the United States, even though the economic burden of the tax * * * is ultimately borne by the United States").

In United States v. State Tax Comm'n, 421 U.S. 599, 95 S.Ct. 1872 (1975), the Court found that a Mississippi regulation requiring out-of-state liquor distillers and suppliers to collect a wholesale markup on liquor sold to military installations amounted to an unconstitutional state tax on federal instrumentalities. The Court perceived no difference between the markup and a sales tax, and it found that the legal incidence of the tax was intended to rest and did rest upon the federal purchasers. In response to the state's contention that the wholesalers and not the federal installations were liable for the tax, the Court noted that it had "squarely rejected the proposition that the legal incidence of a tax falls always upon the person legally liable for its payment." Id., 421 U.S. at 607. Where, as in the case before it, "a state requires that its sales tax be passed on to the purchaser and be collected by the vendor from him, this establishes as a matter of law that the legal incidence of the tax falls upon the purchaser." Id. at 608.

E. *Scope of a Tax–Immune "Federal Instrumentality" Under the Constitutional Immunity Doctrine.* The identification of what constitutes a tax-immune "federal instrumentality" has been a source of controversy in some cases. The Supreme Court has declared that "there is no simple test for determining whether an institution is so closely related to governmental activity as to become a tax-immune instrumentality." Department of Employment v. United States, 385 U.S. 355, 358–59, 87 S.Ct. 464 (1966). Thus, in determining that the Red Cross constituted a federal instrumentality and hence was immune from any state taxes imposed "directly" upon it, the Court relied on the federal charter of the Red Cross, its obligation to perform a wide variety of functions indispensable to the workings of the armed forces, its receipt of substantial material assistance from the Federal Government, and its recognized "status virtually as an arm of the Government." Id., 385 U.S. at 359–60.

As *United States v. New Mexico* reveals, the problem of determining what constitutes a tax-immune federal instrumentality also arises in cases in which the legal incidence falls on a private contractor working for the Federal Government. If the contractors in United States v. New Mexico had been tax-immune federal instrumentalities, the taxes would have been invalid, since their legal incidence fell on the contractors. The contractors, however, failed to meet the Court's stringent test for determining whether private parties constitute tax-immune federal instrumentalities: They must be "an agency or instrumentality so closely connected to the Government that the two cannot realistically be viewed as separate entities, at least insofar as the activity being taxed is concerned." In other words, as the Court elaborated in *United States v. New Mexico*, "a finding of constitutional tax immunity requires something more than the invocation of traditional agency notions: to resist the State's taxing power, a private taxpayer must actually 'stand in the Government's shoes.'"

It is important to keep in mind two limitations on the constitutional tax immunity of federal instrumentalities. First, the United States may waive the immunity of its instrumentalities, as it often has, in delineating through legislation the precise scope of state tax immunity that it wishes to accord to its instrumentalities. See Section D infra (addressing federal statutory rules governing federal immunity from state taxation). Second, there may be some question whether mere designation of an entity as a "federal instrumentality" carries with it the implication that the entity is, in the absence of any further congressional direction, immune from all state taxes. As noted in the preceding paragraph, the Court has been careful to describe a *tax-immune* federal instrumentality as "an agency or instrumentality *so closely connected to the Government that the two cannot realistically be viewed as separate entities*, at least insofar as the activity being taxed is concerned" (emphasis supplied). Moreover, in a related context, the Court has held that although Production Credit Associations are "federal instrumentalities," they do not fall within the exception to the Tax Injunction Act for suits brought by the United States or federal agencies, because their "business is making commercial loans," "all their stock is owned by private entities," and "[t]heir interests are not coterminous with those of the Government any more than most commercial interests." Arkansas v. Farm Credit Services of Central Arkansas, 520 U.S. 821, 831, 117 S.Ct. 1776 (1997).[a] Cf. Shawnee Bank, Inc. v. Paige, 200 W.Va. 20, 488 S.E.2d 20 (1997) (state may tax income from securities issued by Federal National Mortgage Association without violating intergovernmental tax immunity doctrine or West Virginia statutory exemption for income from obligations of "federal instrumentalities").

F. *Federal Employees' Purchases.* When federal employees pay for car rentals, hotel rooms, and other purchases in the course of their official business, are they subject to state sales and use tax in light of the immunity of federal instrumentalities from state taxation? Some courts have held that when federal employees pay for automobile and hotel rentals with cash or personal credit cards, the legal incidence of the tax falls on the employee and the purchases are therefore taxable. Comptroller of the Treasury v. World Inns, Inc., 310 Md. 154, 528 A.2d 477 (1987); Keystone Auto Leasing, Inc. v. Norberg, 486 A.2d 613 (R.I. 1985). Others have held that such purchase are immune from taxation because the employees are federal instrumentalities. Chestnut Fleet Rentals, Inc. v. Department of Revenue, 559 So.2d 264 (Fla. App. 1990); Egner v. Commonwealth, 125 Pa.Cmwlth. 434, 557 A.2d 1157 (1989). Which courts have the better of the argument? Can federal contractors be distinguished from federal employees under United States v. New Mexico? If you were in charge of employee travel for a federal agency, what steps might you take to minimize payments of state taxes?

B. PROPERTY TAXES

1. PROPERTY OWNED BY THE FEDERAL GOVERNMENT

It is settled that the Constitution forbids the states from imposing property taxes on property owned by the Federal Government or its instrumentalities since the legal incidence of such a levy falls on "directly on the United States," Mayo v. United States, 319 U.S. 441, 447, 63 S.Ct. 1137 (1943), or "on an instrumentality so closely connected with the United States that the two cannot realistically be viewed as separate entities." United States v. New Mexico, supra, 455 U.S. at 720. To limit the erosion of the ad valorem property tax base resulting from the ownership of property by the Federal Government and other exempt entities, as well as to equalize the tax burden of competing commercial enterprises, whether they use tax-exempt or taxable property in the operation of their businesses, many states have enacted statutes imposing taxes on leasehold or other interests possessed by private profit-seeking entities in tax-exempt property.

---

a. The *Farm Credit Services* case is considered further in Chapter 11 infra, p. 968, in connection with the discussion of the Tax Injunction Act.

NOTES AND QUESTIONS

A. *The Michigan Cases.* In three companion cases, the U.S. Supreme Court considered claims by federal contractors that the imposition of property taxes on their interests in property owned by the Federal Government conflicted with the Federal Government's immunity from state taxation. United States v. City of Detroit, 355 U.S. 466, 78 S.Ct. 474 (1958) (*Detroit*); United States v. Township of Muskegon, 355 U.S. 484, 78 S.Ct. 483 (1958) (*Muskegon*); City of Detroit v. Murray Corp., 355 U.S. 489, 78 S.Ct. 458 (1958) (*Murray*). *Detroit* and *Muskegon* presented essentially the same question under a Michigan statute providing that tax-exempt property used by a private party in a business conducted for profit shall be subject to taxation in the same amount and to the same extent as though the lessee or user were the owner of such property. The contractor in *Detroit* leased property from the Federal Government for use in its private business. The contractor in *Muskegon* used the Federal Government's property under a permit in the performance of its contracts with the Federal Government. In both cases, the tax was imposed on the contractor and measured by the value of the tax-exempt property.

The Court sustained both taxes. In *Detroit*, the Court rejected the Federal Government's argument "that since the tax is measured by the value of the property used it should be treated as nothing but a contrivance to lay a tax on the property." Detroit, supra, 355 U.S. at 470. The Court observed that "it may be permissible for a State to measure a tax imposed on a valid subject of state taxation by taking into account Government property which is itself tax exempt." Id. at 471. On this ground, the Court distinguished its earlier decision in United States v. Allegheny County, 322 U.S. 174, 64 S.Ct. 908 (1944), in which it had invalidated an ad valorem property tax on Federal Government property used by federal contractors. A dissenting opinion, relying on *Allegheny,* accused the Court of elevating form over substance, declaring that it was "crystal clear" that the tax is a "direct imposition upon the Government's property interests." Detroit, supra, 355 U.S. at 478.

In upholding the levy in *Muskegon,* the Court held that it was controlled by the principles articulated in *Detroit*. There were only two factual differences between *Detroit* and *Muskegon:* the taxpayer in *Muskegon* was not using the federal property under a formal lease, as was the case in *Detroit,* but under a "permit"; and the taxpayer, unlike the taxpayer in *Detroit,* was using the property in performance of its contracts with the Federal Government. With regard to the lease versus permit issue, the Court declared that "[c]onstitutional immunity from state taxation does not rest on such insubstantial formalities as whether the party using government property is formally designated a 'lessee,' " Muskegon, supra, 355 U.S. at 486, because immunity could then be conferred "by a simple stroke of a draftsman's pen." Id. What was critical was that the taxpayer was using the property in connection with its own commercial activities. With regard to the fact that the taxpayer was using the property in the performance of Federal Government contracts, the Court also found the distinction immaterial. The taxpayer "was not so assimilated by the Government to become one of its constituent parts," id., and although "[i]n a certain loose way it might be called an 'instrumentality' of the United States," it would be "no more so than any other private party supplying goods for his own gain to the Government." Id. at 486–87.

Murray presented a slightly different issue. The case again involved a federal contractor that used federally owned property in performing its contracts, but the statute provided that "[t]he owners or persons in possession of any personal property shall pay all taxes assessed thereon." Murray, supra, 355 U.S. at 489. The Court again rejected the argument that this amounted to a direct tax on the Federal Government's property, finding the case indistinguishable in substance from *Detroit* and *Muskegon:* "We see no essential difference so far as constitutional tax immunity is concerned between taxing a person for using property he possesses and taxing him for possessing property he uses when in both instances he uses the property for his own private ends." Id. at 493.

Many states have exercised their constitutional power, as delineated in the *Detroit–Muskegon–Murray* trilogy, to tax private contractors' beneficial interest in property owned by the federal government. For example, after the U.S. Court of Appeals for the Ninth Circuit held that Nevada's tax on federal property used by federal contractors violated the intergovernmental immunity doctrine because the tax was imposed on the property as such, United States v. Nye County, Nevada, 938 F.2d 1040 (9th Cir. 1991) (*Nye I*), the state revised its statutes to authorize a tax on the "leasehold interest, possessory interest, beneficial interest or beneficial use" of such property. United States v. Nye County, Nevada, 178 F.3d 1080, 1084 (9th Cir. 1999) (*Nye II*) (quoting the statute). In *Nye I*, the court had said: "[T]he wording of a tax measure is significant * * * [W]hen a statute says it taxes property it probably does. And when it says it doesn't, it probably doesn't." *Nye I,* supra, 938 F.2d at 1043. In *Nye II*, the court found the change in the statutory language dispositive, and it sustained the tax. Could a state avoid the restraints of the Commerce Clause by declaring in a statute that it is not taxing "interstate commerce," but rather some "local" event? If not, why should it be able to avoid the restraints of the Supremacy Clause (and the intergovernmental immunity doctrine) by declaring in a statute that it is not taxing "federal property" but merely the "beneficial use" of federal property?

B. *State Tax on Federal Employees' Possessory Interests in Federal Housing Rented From Federal Government.* In United States v. County of Fresno, 429 U.S. 452, 97 S.Ct. 699 (1977), the Court invoked the principles of the *Detroit–Muskegon–Murray* trilogy in sustaining the constitutionality of a local tax on possessory interests in houses owned by the U.S. Government that were rented to federal employees. The taxpayers, who were employees of the U.S. Forest Service, and worked in national forests, were required to live in Government houses in the forests. The Forest Service deducted from salaries of the employees the fair rental value of the housing. The Court found that the legal incidence of the tax fell on the employees, not on the Federal Government, and that the *Detroit–Muskegon–Murray* cases are equally applicable to federal property used for personal purposes, as to property used in a business.

C. *Vendee in Possession Under Contract of Purchase From Federal Agency.* When the Federal Government has entered into a contract for the sale of realty and the purchaser has taken possession but has not yet completed the payment of the purchase price, a condition which must be met before it receives the deed to the property, is the property subject to local ad valorem taxation? See S.R.A., Inc. v. State of Minnesota, 327 U.S. 558, 66 S.Ct. 749 (1946).

2. THE MAGNITUDE OF TAX–IMMUNE FEDERAL PROPERTY

PAYMENTS IN LIEU OF TAXES ON FEDERAL REAL PROPERTY

United States Advisory Commission on Intergovernmental Relations.
Report A–90, 1981, pp. 1–18.

The federal government is the single largest owner of real property in the United States. It currently owns 775.3 million acres, more than one-third of the country's entire land area. In addition, it owns 23,988 installations, 2,598 million square feet of floor area, and various other buildings and structures and facilities. In 1978, the total value of U.S. real property was valued at approximately $279 billion, 23% in land, 53% in buildings, and 24% in structures and facilities.

These holdings include forest reserves, office buildings, harbors, housing projects, grazing lands, waterways, airports, cemeteries, hospitals, defense bases, parks, power lines, utility systems, museums, industrial facilities, communications systems, railroads, navigation and traffic aids, monuments and memorials, and even islands used for military target practice. Moreover, the magnitude of these holdings can be expected to grow. * * *

The incidence of federally owned properties varies widely across the 50 states. They are located in both rural and urban areas, and are industrial and nonindustrial, residential and commercial, permanent and semipermanent. Some of them provide largely local services, while others are regionally or nationally oriented. Some profoundly affect the fiscal and economic base of their communities, while others have only the most minor of impacts.

The one generalization that can best be made regarding the array of federally owned property is that there is no guiding principle regarding the extent to which the federal government as a property owner should contribute to the financial support of state and local governments. Some local governments share in the revenues generated by federal establishments operating within their borders, primarily from mineral leasing or from the sale of grazing, farming, and forestry rights to private interests. On other properties, Congress has recognized a responsibility for a partial or full payment in lieu of taxes (PILOT) to state and local governments as compensation for property taxes foregone. For some of its instrumentalities, such as its various banking and credit institutions, the federal government has authorized the full range of direct state/local taxation.

Most commonly, however, the Congress has declared the U.S. government exempt from both direct state/local taxation as well as from any in lieu of tax responsibility. This is true despite the fact that, over the years, its own committees and study groups have recommended enactment of some form of uniform payment system to compensate all states and localities for the effect of the federal presence on property tax revenues. Indeed, in 1969, the Joint Economic Committee of the U.S. Congress, arguing "only basic equity," urged that Congress make payments in lieu of real property taxes on property owned by both the U.S. government and foreign governments (embassies, consulates, missions) in the U.S.

* * *

Major Conclusions

A number of major conclusions have been drawn by the Commission staff based on the research findings associated with the broad scope of this study. These conclusions are:

A.   The federal government lacks any procedure that permits it to know the current value of its real property holdings in the U.S. Except for the estimates for 1978 made in this report, there is no inventory of the total value of tax immune federal property. In order to receive useful information for policy regarding the federal government's property wealth, Congress must require that the General Services Administration make major adjustments in its methods of collecting information.

* * *

B.   The Nature of the Legal Framework for Property Tax Immunity Has Changed Over Time.

* * *

C.   Federal tax exemptions erode a large part of state and local tax bases.

Several arguments can be marshaled both for and against any type of institutional exemption from a comprehensive tax base. The justification given for exemptions range from the "need" to provide locational incentives to some private firms, to the simple fact that the exemption is mandated by a higher level of government and therefore is beyond local control. The arguments against exemptions usually center on the concerns for taxpayer equity and economic efficiency, and the erosion of the local tax base. Each of these topics has been examined in this report as it relates specifically to the immunity of the federal government from state and local taxation.

From an overall local policy perspective, perhaps the most important of these issues centers on the local government revenue loss from real property tax exemption. In the context of the federal immunity issue, this loss is, indeed, quite large. In 1978, the current dollar value of all federally owned property in the U.S. that was exempt from real property taxation amounted to $279 billion. If one excludes "open space" lands (as is proposed in Chapter 3 of this study), the total erosion amounts to $210 billion. To put this in perspective, if this $210 billion were fully taxable, and no other adjustments were made in current property tax rates or federal payment programs, $3.65 billion would have been added to state and, primarily, local treasuries (96%). This is equivalent to an increase in total local property collections of almost 6%.

If local governments could make up for this revenue loss by simply using nonproperty tax sources more extensively, the policy concern regarding this erosion of the revenue base might not be so important. However, the "open economy"* characteristic of subnational government virtually dictates that local governments must employ taxes on immovable property as the mainstay of their own-source revenues. Moreover, in the present fiscal environment, which provides for a growing local dependency upon outside—state and federal—aid to local governments, the maintenance of own-source revenues to meet both traditional and recently mandated costs at the local level has become more important.

Stated otherwise, if an accepted goal of U.S. federalism is to have a financially strong and independent local government sector that is able to carry out peculiarly local functions—such as the provisions of police, fire, and judicial protection, public education, and low to moderate income housing services—then a closer look at the policy of federal real property tax immunity is clearly warranted.

   D.   The federal immunity from state and local taxes violates major equity principles of public finance.

Because the federal government is exempt from paying state and local taxes on most of its activities and properties, a basic equity principle of public finance is violated: that "taxpayers" (herein, institutions) in similar circumstances should be treated similarly. This equity violation arises both when the direct property taxpaying status of private institutions is juxtaposed with that of federal government agencies and instrumentalities and when the indirect taxable status of federal leasehold activity is contrasted with the exempt nature of federal property ownership.

* * *

   E.   Although Congress has recognized a responsibility to some local governments for making some form of in lieu tax payment to "compensate" for the federal presence, the result has been a patchwork of uncoordinated and ad hoc federal payment programs that has developed over the years.

* * *

---

* An open economy is characterized by a high degree of mobility of goods and factor movements across jurisdictional borders—activities which a local government cannot constrain.

F. In general, existing federal grant programs are not designed to compensate subnational governments for revenue losses which result from the federal government tax immunity.

* * *

G. Authorization for either full real property taxation of the federal government or a full tax equivalency system of payments in lieu of real property taxes is an appropriate policy response to the status quo.

* * *

H. Real property taxation of the federal government or a full tax equivalency system of payments in lieu of real property taxes is a workable policy response to the status quo.

Notes and Questions

A. *Payments in Lieu of Taxes: 2008 Data.* For fiscal 2008, the Federal Government made payments of in lieu of taxes (PILOTs) of $228.5 million to approximately 1,850 local government jurisdictions across the United States. U.S. Dep't of the Interior, FY 2008 Payment Bulletin, available at www.doi. gov/pilt/index.html. Eligibility for PILOTs is reserved for local governments (usually counties) that contain nontaxable federal lands and provide government services related to public safety, housing, social services, transportation, and the environment. Id. There is a wide variation among the states in the amount of PILOTs received by their respective localities. The western states' localities receive the lion's share of the PILOTs. The top five recipients for 2008 were New Mexico ($22.5 million); Utah ($20.0 million); Arizona ($19.1 million); Colorado ($17.6 million); and Idaho ($16.1 million). U.S. Dep't of the Interior, "228 Million Paid to County Governments as Compensation for Lost Taxes on Federal Lands," June 12, 2008, available at /www.doi.gov/news/08_News_Releases/080612d.html. Localities in Rhode Island did not receive a single penny of PILOTs in 2008, and localities in Connecticut and Delaware received less than $20,000 per state. Id.

B. *Relief From Immunity of Federal Property by Congressional Action.* Congress employs three principal methods to provide relief to state and local jurisdictions from the tax immunity enjoyed by federal property:

(1) Federal payments to states and localities of a specified percentage of revenues from federal operations. This method is used with respect to national forests, grazing and mineral lands, and other large tracts from which the Federal Government derives revenues from its own operations or from leasing, etc. The Tennessee Valley Authority pays to the local taxing authorities a percentage of its gross revenues from power sales, with a guaranteed minimum equal to the former property taxes paid on the acquired property.

(2) Federal payment of a tax equivalent out of revenue receipts or appropriations. Federal housing projects are the outstanding example for the use of this method.

(3) Waiver of federal tax immunity by act of Congress. Real property acquired by the Reconstruction Finance Corporation on foreclosure are subject to local property tax as a result of congressional action. Generally speaking, however, Congress has made no provision for payments to or taxation by the states or localities for office buildings, court houses, post offices, hospitals, prisons, military and naval installations, and other property used for general governmental administration. Federal payments are often made, however, to local school districts containing military bases.

It is not surprising to find that many state and local taxing officials, particularly in the western states where federal land holdings are most extensive, do not believe that the Federal Government has gone far enough in relieving its property from tax immunity.

C. STATE TAXES DISCRIMINATING AGAINST THE FEDERAL GOVERNMENT

DAVIS v. MICHIGAN DEPARTMENT OF TREASURY

Supreme Court of the United States, 1989.
489 U.S. 803, 109 S.Ct. 1500.

JUSTICE KENNEDY delivered the opinion of the Court.

The State of Michigan exempts from taxation all retirement benefits paid by the State or its political subdivisions, but levies an income tax on retirement benefits paid by all other employers, including the Federal Government. The question presented by this case is whether Michigan's tax scheme violates federal law.

I

Appellant Paul S. Davis, a Michigan resident, is a former employee of the United States Government. He receives retirement benefits pursuant to the Civil Service Retirement Act, 5 U.S.C. § 8331 et seq. In each of the years 1979 through 1984, appellant paid Michigan state income tax on his federal retirement benefits in accordance with Mich.Comp.Laws Ann. § 206.30(1)(f) (Supp.1988). That statute defines taxable income in a manner that excludes all retirement benefits received from the State or its political subdivisions, but includes most other forms of retirement benefits. The effect of this definition is that the retirement benefits of retired state employees are exempt from state taxation while the benefits received by retired federal employees are not.

In 1984, appellant petitioned for refunds of state taxes paid on his federal retirement benefits between 1979 and 1983. After his request was denied, appellant filed suit in the Michigan Court of Claims. Appellant's complaint * * * averred that his federal retirement benefits were "not legally taxable under the Michigan Income Tax Law" and that the State's inconsistent treatment of state and federal retirement benefits discriminated against federal retirees in violation of 4 U.S.C. § 111, which preserves federal employees' immunity from discriminatory state taxation. The Court of Claims, however, denied relief.

The Michigan Court of Appeals affirmed. * * *

The Supreme Court of Michigan denied appellant's application for leave to appeal. We noted probable jurisdiction.

II

Appellant places principal reliance on 4 U.S.C. § 111. In relevant part, that section provides:

> "The United States consents to the taxation of pay or compensation for personal service as an officer or employee of the United States ... by a duly constituted taxing authority having jurisdiction, if the taxation does not discriminate against the officer or employee because of the source of the pay or compensation."

* * *

III

Section 111 was enacted as part of the Public Salary Tax Act of 1939, the primary purpose of which was to impose federal income tax on the salaries of all state and local government employees. Prior to adoption of the Act, salaries of most government employees, both state and federal, generally were thought to be exempt from taxation by another sovereign under the doctrine of intergovernmental tax immunity. * * *

For a time, *McCulloch* was read broadly to bar most taxation by one sovereign of the employees of another. See Collector v. Day, 11 Wall. 113, 124–128 (1871) (invalidating federal income tax on salary of state judge); Dobbins v. Commissioners of Erie County, 16 Pet. 435 (1842) (invalidating state tax on federal officer). This rule "was based on the rationale that any tax on income a party received under a contract with the government was a tax on the contract and thus a tax 'on' the government because it burdened the government's power to enter into the contract." South Carolina v. Baker, 485 U.S. 505, 518, 108 S.Ct. 1355, 1364 (1988).

In subsequent cases, however, the Court began to turn away from its more expansive applications of the immunity doctrine. Thus, in Helvering v. Gerhardt, 304 U.S. 405, 58 S.Ct. 969 (1938), the Court held that the Federal Government could levy nondiscriminatory taxes on the incomes of most state employees. The following year, Graves v. New York ex rel. O'Keefe, 306 U.S. 466, 486–487, 59 S.Ct. 595, 601–602 (1939), overruled the *Day–Dobbins* line of cases that had exempted government employees from nondiscriminatory taxation. After *Graves*, therefore, intergovernmental tax immunity barred only those taxes that were imposed directly on one sovereign by the other or that discriminated against a sovereign or those with whom it dealt.

It was in the midst of this judicial revision of the immunity doctrine that Congress decided to extend the federal income tax to state and local government employees. The Public Salary Tax Act was enacted after Helvering v. Gerhardt, supra, had upheld the imposition of federal income taxes on state civil servants, and Congress relied on that decision as support for its broad assertion of federal taxing authority. However, the Act was drafted, considered in Committee, and passed by the House of Representatives before the announcement of the decision in Graves v. New York ex rel. O'Keefe, supra, which for the first time permitted state taxation of federal employees. * * *

By the time the statute was enacted * * * the decision in *Graves* had been announced, so the constitutional immunity doctrine no longer proscribed nondiscriminatory state taxation of federal employees. In effect, § 111 simply codified the result in *Graves* and foreclosed the possibility that subsequent judicial reconsideration of that case might reestablish the broader interpretation of the immunity doctrine.

* * *

* * * Regardless of whether § 111 provides an independent basis for finding immunity or merely preserves the traditional constitutional prohibition against discriminatory taxes * * * the inquiry is the same. In either case, the scope of the immunity granted or retained by the nondiscrimination clause is to be determined by reference to the constitutional doctrine. Thus, the dispositive question in this case is whether the tax imposed on appellant is barred by the doctrine of intergovernmental tax immunity.

IV

It is undisputed that Michigan's tax system discriminates in favor of retired state employees and against retired federal employees. The State argues, however, that appellant is not entitled to claim the protection of the immunity doctrine, and that in any event the State's inconsistent treatment of Federal and State Government retirees is justified by meaningful differences between the two classes.

A

In support of its first contention, the State points out that the purpose of the immunity doctrine is to protect governments and not private entities or individuals. As a result, so long as the challenged tax does not interfere with the Federal Government's ability to perform its governmental functions, the constitutional doctrine has not been violated.

It is true that intergovernmental tax immunity is based on the need to protect each sovereign's governmental operations from undue interference by the other. But it does not follow that private entities or individuals who are subjected to discriminatory taxation on account of their dealings with a sovereign cannot themselves receive the protection of the constitutional doctrine. Indeed, all precedent is to the contrary. In Phillips Chemical Co. [v. Dumas Independent School District, 361 U.S. 376 (1960)], supra, for example, we considered a private corporation's claim that a state tax discriminated against private lessees of federal land. We concluded that the tax "discriminate[d] unconstitutionally against the United States *and its lessee,*" and accordingly held that the tax could not be exacted. Id., 361 U.S., at 387, 80 S.Ct., at 481 (emphasis added). The State offers no reasons for departing from this settled rule, and we decline to do so.[4]

We also take issue with the dissent's assertion that "it is peculiarly inappropriate to focus solely on the treatment of state governmental employees" because "[t]he State may always compensate in pay or salary for what it assesses in taxes." Post, at 1512. In order to provide the same after-tax benefits to all retired state employees by means of increased salaries or benefit payments instead of a tax exemption, the State would have to increase its outlays by more than the cost of the current tax exemption, since the increased payments to retirees would result in higher federal income tax payments in some circumstances. This fact serves to illustrate the impact on the Federal Government of the State's discriminatory tax exemption for state retirees. Taxes enacted to reduce the State's employment costs at the expense of the federal treasury are the type of discriminatory legislation that the doctrine of intergovernmental tax immunity is intended to bar.

B

Under our precedents, "[t]he imposition of a heavier tax burden on [those who deal with one sovereign] than is imposed on [those who deal with the other] must be justified by significant differences between the two classes." Phillips Chemical Co. v. Dumas Independent School Dist., 361 U.S., at 383, 80 S.Ct., at 479. In determining whether this standard of justification has been met, it is inappropriate to rely solely on the mode of analysis developed in our equal protection cases. We have previously observed that "our decisions in [the equal protection] field are not necessarily controlling where problems of intergovernmental tax immunity are involved," because "the Government's interests must be weighed in the balance." Id., at 385, 80 S.Ct., at 480. Instead, the relevant inquiry is whether the inconsistent tax treatment is directly related to, and justified by, "significant differences between the two classes." Id., at 383–385, 80 S.Ct., at 479–480.

The State points to two allegedly significant differences between federal and state retirees. First, the State suggests that its interest in

---

4. The dissent argues that this tax is nondiscriminatory, and thus constitutional, because it "draws no distinction between the federal employees or retirees and the vast majority of voters in the State." Post, at 1512. In Phillips Chemical Co., however, we faced that precise situation: an equal tax burden was imposed on lessees of private, tax-exempt property and lessees of federal property, while lessees of state property paid a lesser tax, or in some circumstances none at all. Although we concluded that "[u]nder these circumstances, there appears to be no discrimination between the Government's lessees and lessees of private property," 361 U.S., at 381, 80 S.Ct., at 478, we nonetheless invalidated the State's tax. This result is consistent with the underlying rationale for the doctrine of intergovernmental tax immunity. The danger that a State is engaging in impermissible discrimination against the Federal Government is greatest when the State acts to benefit itself and those in privity with it. As we observed in Phillips Chemical Co., "it does not seem too much to require that the State treat those who deal with the Government as well as it treats those with whom it deals itself." Id., at 385, 80 S.Ct., at 480.

hiring and retaining qualified civil servants through the inducement of a tax exemption for retirement benefits is sufficient to justify the preferential treatment of its retired employees. This argument is wholly beside the point, however, for it does nothing to demonstrate that there are "significant differences between the two classes" themselves; rather, it merely demonstrates that the State has a rational reason for discriminating between two similar groups of retirees. The State's interest in adopting the discriminatory tax, no matter how substantial, is simply irrelevant to an inquiry into the nature of the two classes receiving inconsistent treatment.

Second, the State argues that its retirement benefits are significantly less munificent than those offered by the Federal Government, in terms of vesting requirements, rate of accrual, and computation of benefit amounts. The substantial differences in the value of the retirement benefits paid the two classes should, in the State's view, justify the inconsistent tax treatment.

Even assuming the State's estimate of the relative value of state and federal retirement benefits is generally correct, we do not believe this difference suffices to justify the type of blanket exemption at issue in this case. While the average retired federal civil servant receives a larger pension than his state counterpart, there are undoubtedly many individual instances in which the opposite holds true. A tax exemption truly intended to account for differences in retirement benefits would not discriminate on the basis of the source of those benefits, as Michigan's statute does; rather, it would discriminate on the basis of the amount of benefits received by individual retirees. Cf. Phillips Chemical Co., supra, at 384–385, 80 S.Ct., at 479–480 (rejecting proffered rationale for State's unfavorable tax treatment of lessees of federal property, because an evenhanded application of the rationale would have resulted in inclusion of some lessees of State property in the disfavored class as well).

V

For these reasons, we conclude that the Michigan Income Tax Act violates principles of intergovernmental tax immunity by favoring retired state and local government employees over retired federal employees. * * *

It is so ordered.

JUSTICE STEVENS, dissenting.

The States can tax federal employees or private parties who do business with the United States so long as the tax does not discriminate against the United States. The Court today strikes down a state tax that applies equally to the vast majority of Michigan residents, including federal employees, because it treats retired state employees differently from retired federal employees. The Court's holding is not supported by the rationale for the intergovernmental immunity doctrine and is not compelled by our previous decisions. I cannot join the unjustified, court-imposed restriction on a State's power to administer its own affairs.

* * *

The nondiscrimination rule recognizes the fact that the Federal Government has no voice in the policy decisions made by the several States. The Federal Government's protection against state taxation that singles out federal agencies for special burdens is therefore provided by the Supremacy Clause of the Federal Constitution, the doctrine of intergovernmental tax immunity, and statutes such as 4 U.S.C. § 111. When the tax burden is shared equally by federal agents and the vast majority of a State's citizens, however, the nondiscrimination principle is not applicable and constitutional protection is not necessary. As the Court explained in United States v. County of Fresno:

> "The rule to be derived from the Court's more recent decisions, then, is that the economic burden on a federal function of a state tax imposed on those who deal with the Federal Government does not render the tax unconstitutional so long as the tax is imposed equally on the other similarly situated constituents of the State. This rule returns to the original intent of M'Culloch v. Maryland. The political check against abuse of the taxing power found lacking in *M'Culloch*, where the tax was imposed solely on the Bank of the United States, is present where the State imposes a nondiscriminatory tax only on its constituents or their artificially owned entities; and *M'Culloch* foresaw the unfairness in forcing a State to exempt private individuals with beneficial interests in federal property from taxes imposed on similar interests held by others in private property. Accordingly, *M'Culloch* expressly excluded from its rule a tax on 'the interest which the citizens of Maryland may hold [in a federal instrumentality] in common with other property of the same description throughout the State.' 4 Wheat., at 436." 429 U.S., at 462–464, 97 S.Ct., at 704–706.[2]

The Court has repeatedly emphasized that the rationale of the nondiscrimination rule is met when there is a political check against excessive taxation. See South Carolina v. Baker, 485 U.S. 505, 526, n. 15, 108 S.Ct. 1355, 1368, n. 15 (1988) ("[T]he best safeguard against excessive taxation (and the most judicially manageable) is the requirement that the government tax in a nondiscriminatory fashion. For where a government imposes a nondiscriminatory tax, judges can term the tax 'excessive' only by second-guessing the extent to which the taxing government and its people have taxed themselves, and the threat of destroying another government

---

2. The quotation in the text omits one footnote, but this footnote is relevant:

"A tax on the income of federal employees, or a tax on the possessory interest of federal employees in Government houses, if imposed only on them, could be escalated by a State so as to destroy the federal function performed by them either by making the Federal Government unable to hire anyone or by causing the Federal Government to pay prohibitively high salaries. This danger would never arise, however, if the tax is also imposed on the income and property interests of all other residents and voters of the State." 429 U.S., at 463, 97 S.Ct., at 705.

can be realized only if the taxing government is willing to impose taxes that will also destroy itself or its constituents"); Washington v. United States, 460 U.S. 536, 545, 103 S.Ct. 1344, 1350 (1983) ("A 'political check' is provided when a state tax falls on a significant group of state citizens who can be counted upon to use their votes to keep the State from raising the tax excessively, and thus placing an unfair burden on the Federal Government. It has been thought necessary because the United States does not have a direct voice in the state legislatures").

If Michigan were to tax the income of federal employees without imposing a like tax on others, the tax would be plainly unconstitutional. On the other hand, if the State taxes the income of all its residents equally, federal employees must pay the tax. Graves v. New York ex rel. O'Keefe, 306 U.S. 466, 59 S.Ct. 595 (1939). The Michigan tax here applies to approximately 4½ million individual taxpayers in the State, including the 24,000 retired federal employees. It exempts only the 130,000 retired state employees. Once one understands the underlying reason for the *McCulloch* holding, it is plain that this tax does not unconstitutionally discriminate against federal employees.

The Court reaches the opposite result only by examining whether the tax treatment of federal employees is equal to that of one discrete group of Michigan residents—retired state employees. It states: "It is undisputed that Michigan's tax system discriminates in favor of retired state employees and against retired federal employees." * * *

To be sure, there is discrimination against federal employees—and all other Michigan taxpayers—if a small group of residents is granted an exemption. If the size of the exempt group remains the same—say, no more than 10% of the populace—the burden on federal interests also remains the same, regardless of how the exempt class is defined. Whether it includes school teachers, church employees, state judges, or perhaps handicapped persons, is a matter of indifference to the Federal Government as long as it can fairly be said that federal employees are treated like other ordinary residents of the State.

* * *

When the Court rejected the claim that a federal employee's income is immune from state taxation in Graves v. New York ex rel. O'Keefe, 306 U.S. 466, 59 S.Ct. 595 (1939), Justice Frankfurter wrote separately to explain how a "seductive cliche" had infected the doctrine of intergovernmental immunity, which had been "moving in the realm of what Lincoln called 'pernicious abstractions.' " He correctly noted that only a "web of unreality" could explain how the "[f]ailure to exempt public functionaries from the universal duties of citizenship to pay for the costs of government was hypothetically transmuted into hostile action of one government against the other." Id., at 489–490, 59 S.Ct. at 603.

Today, it is not the great Chief Justice's dictum about how the power to tax includes the power to destroy that obscures the issue in a web of unreality; it is the virtually automatic rejection of anything that can be labeled "discriminatory." The question in this case deserves more careful consideration than is provided by the mere use of that label. It should be answered by considering whether the ratio decidendi of our holding in McCulloch v. Maryland is applicable to this quite different case. It is not. I, therefore, respectfully dissent.

NOTES AND QUESTIONS

A. *The Rule Forbidding Taxes That Discriminate Against the Federal Government.* From the very beginning of our constitutional history, it has been clear that the states may not impose taxes discriminating against the Federal Government. The narrowing of the Federal Government's immunity in cases involving nondiscriminatory taxes has not undermined this fundamental principle. For example, in Phillips Chemical Co. v. Dumas Independent School District, 361 U.S. 376, 80 S.Ct. 474 (1960), discussed in the *Davis* case, the Court held that a tax assessed against a private lessee of federally owned property was unconstitutional because no tax was assessed against private lessees of property owned by Texas or its political subdivisions. The Court reached a similar conclusion in striking down a Tennessee tax on the net earnings of banks that included interest received on federal but not on Tennessee obligations. Memphis Bank & Trust Co. v. Garner, 459 U.S. 392, 103 S.Ct. 692 (1983).[b] Could an exemption for gain resulting from the sale of state—but not federal—obligations pass constitutional muster under these rulings? See NACCO Industries, Inc. v. Tracy, 79 Ohio St.3d 314, 681 N.E.2d 900 (1997), cert. denied, 522 U.S. 1091, 118 S.Ct. 882 (1998).

What are the limits to the principle articulated in *Phillips Chemical* and reiterated in *Davis* (see footnote 4 to the Court's opinion) that "it does not seem too much to require that the State treat those who deal with the Government as well as it treats those with whom it deals itself"? Does it require that any exemption for those who deal with the state be extended to all those who deal with the Federal Government? In United States v. Nye County, Nevada, 178 F.3d 1080 (9th Cir. 1999), discussed at p. 318 supra, for example, Nevada imposed a tax on the beneficial use of exempt property. In addition to the contention that the levy amounted to an unconstitutional state tax on the Federal Government's property—a contention the court rejected under the *Detroit–Muskegon–Murray* trilogy (see pp. 317–18 supra)—the United States argued that the statute discriminated against the Federal Government because it exempted those who use the property of any state-supported educational institution. In response, the court declared:

> Does this provision, standing alone, in fact discriminate against the federal government? While it appears to do so by its terms, in fact, it does not because Nevada has no federally-supported educational institutions, while Nevada has a very fine state university system. Therefore there are

---

b. Although the issue technically involved the question whether the tax violated the statutory prohibition against state taxation of federal obligations, 31 U.S.C. § 742 (now 31 U.S.C. § 3124), see Section D infra, the Court noted that "[o]ur decisions have treated 742 as principally a restatement of the constitutional rule." Id., 459 U.S. at 397.

no federal contractors analogous to the state contractors who benefit from [the exemption].

Id. at 1088. Would the result be different in New York, Maryland, or Colorado, the respective homes of the Army, Navy, and Air Force Academies?

In United States v. County of Fresno, 429 U.S. 452, 97 S.Ct. 699 (1977), discussed in Section B(1), Note B, p. 318 supra, the Court also addressed the claim that the possessory interest tax on the interests of the U.S. Forest Service employees in their federally owned residences violated the Supremacy Clause, because it discriminated against federal employees. The Court found the levy nondiscriminatory, because it did not tax federal employees living in federally owned houses differently from state employees living in state-owned houses.

B. *Constitutionality of Increase in State Retirees' Pension Benefits Equal to Reduction in State Retirees' Tax Benefits Required to Create Nondiscrimination Under* Davis. In the aftermath of the Supreme Court's decision in *Davis* striking down Michigan's exemption of retirement income for state, but not federal, employees, several states responded by reducing or eliminating the exemption for state retirees to match the treatment of federal retirees, but at the same time increasing the amount of the state retirees' pension benefits to approximate their loss of tax benefits. Does this coordinated tax and benefit increase, which leaves state retirees in essentially the same position that they were in under the preexisting discriminatory tax regime, survive constitutional scrutiny under *Davis*? The cases are split on this issue, although arguably one may distinguish them on the basis of how closely the benefit increase tracks the tax increase. Compare Sheehy v. Public Employees Retirement Division, 262 Mont. 129, 864 P.2d 762 (1993) and Vogl v. Department of Revenue, 327 Or. 193, 960 P.2d 373 (1998) (invalidating coordinated action as in substance a tax rebate that left preexisting tax discrimination in place) with Ragsdale v. Department of Revenue, 321 Or. 216, 895 P.2d 1348 (1995), cert. denied, 516 U.S. 1011, 116 S.Ct. 569 (1995), Ward v. State, 356 S.C. 449, 590 S.E.2d 30 (2003), cert. denied, 543 U.S. 808, 125 S.Ct. 31 (2004), and Thompson v. Utah State Tax Comm'n, 2004 UT 107, 112 P.3d 1205 (2004) (sustaining coordinated taxing and spending provisions because they were not precisely correlated). For a detailed analysis of these issues, see Dan T. Coenen & Walter Hellerstein, "Suspect Linkage: The Interplay of State Taxing and Spending Measures in the Application of Constitutional Antidiscrimination Rules," 95 Mich. L. Rev. 2167 (1997).

C. *The Federal Immunity Principle and the Complementary Tax Doctrine.* In Washington v. United States, 460 U.S. 536, 103 S.Ct. 1344 (1983), the Court considered a claim of discrimination against the Federal Government in the context of the State of Washington's sales and use tax as applied to federal contractors. Washington generally places the legal incidence of its sales and use tax on the landowner who purchases construction work from the contractor. The tax is measured by the full cost of the construction contract, including markups. When construction work is performed for the United States on its property, however, the Supremacy Clause precludes the state from applying the tax to the United States as landowner. To prevent federal contractors from escaping the state's sales tax, Washington provided that federal contractors should pay a sales tax on their purchases of materials.

The United States attacked this levy claiming that it discriminated against the Federal Government and those who deal with it by imposing a sales tax on purchases made by federal contractors but not on purchases made by other contractors. The Court, while acknowledging the surface plausibility of the argument, responded:

> Washington does, however, impose a sales tax on all purchases from contractors who do not deal with the Federal Government. The tax is imposed on every construction transaction, and the tax rate is the same for everyone. The only deviation from equality between the Federal Government and federal contractors on the one hand, and every other taxpayer on the other, is that the former are taxed on a smaller percentage of the value of the project than the latter. * * * This hardly seems * * * to be the mistreatment of the Federal Government against which the Supremacy Clause protects.

Id., 460 U.S. at 541–42.

In upholding the levy, the Court refused to focus solely on the tax that the contractor is required to pay, as the United States had urged, because it viewed the critical question to be "whether a contractor who is considering working for the Federal Government is faced with a cost he would not have to bear if he were to do the same thing for a private party." Id. at 541 n.4. This required the Court to consider the economic burden on the contractor and the owner together. Citing the *Detroit–Muskegon–Murray* trilogy (see pp. 317–18 supra) and *County of Fresno,* the Court declared that the "important consideration * * * is not whether the State differentiates in determining what entity shall bear the legal incidence of the tax, but whether the tax is discriminatory with regard to the economic burdens that result." Id. at 544. The Court further observed that Washington, rather than discriminating against the Federal Government, was "merely accommodat[ing] for the fact that it may not impose a tax directly on the United States as project owner." Id. at 546. Can *Washington v. United States* be squared with the Court's more recent "complementary tax doctrine" cases decided under the Commerce Clause? See pp. 148–49 supra. Does it need to be? See generally Walter Hellerstein, "Complementary Taxes as a Defense to Unconstitutional State Tax Discrimination," 39 Tax Law. 405 (1986).

D. FEDERAL STATUTORY RULES GOVERNING FEDERAL IMMUNITY FROM STATE TAXATION

The preceding discussion has dealt primarily with the implied *constitutional* immunity that the Federal Government and its instrumentalities enjoy from state taxation without regard to congressional legislation. Congress has the power to expand, modify, or waive that immunity by specific legislation. Indeed, it is settled law that Congress has full power to define the scope of immunity from state taxation for its agencies and instrumentalities employed in carrying out its powers under the Constitution. See Federal Land Bank of St. Paul v. Bismarck Lumber Co., 314 U.S.

95, 62 S.Ct. 1 (1941) (Congress has the power under the Necessary and Proper Clause in furtherance of its lending functions to immunize federal land banks from state sales taxes).

The most important congressional legislation providing immunity for the Federal Government and its instrumentalities from state taxation is directed at state taxation of federal obligations and state taxation of national banks.

1. STATE TAXATION OF FEDERAL OBLIGATIONS

NOTES AND QUESTIONS

A. *Historical Overview of the Statutory Immunity of Federal Obligations and Their Income From State Taxation.* The statutory immunity of federal obligations from state taxation is rooted in the constitutional doctrine that the obligations of the United States are immune from state taxation. See Weston v. City Council of Charleston, 27 U.S. (2 Pet.) 449 (1829) (invalidating on constitutional grounds local property tax on federal securities in the hands of the owner). In 1862, in order to assure the immunity of the increasing amount of federal obligations that were issued in connection with the Civil War, Congress enacted a statute embodying the rule of *Weston.* The statute, as amended in 1864, appeared for many years as Revised Statutes § 3701, 31 U.S.C. § 742, and provided:

> All stocks, bonds, Treasury notes, and other obligations of the United States, shall be exempt from taxation by or under State or municipal or local authority.

In construing this statute, the Supreme Court consistently held that the language prohibited state taxes imposed on federal obligations as part of a tax on the taxpayer's property or assets. See, e.g., Society for Savings v. Bowers, 349 U.S. 143, 75 S.Ct. 607 (1955) (tax on total assets of a corporation is a tax on federal obligations it owns).

At the same time, however, the Court held that Revised Statutes § 3701 did not prevent the states from imposing nondiscriminatory taxes on discrete property interests, such as corporate shares or corporate franchises, even though the value of the interest was measured in part by U.S. obligations. As a consequence, corporate franchise taxes have long been measured by net income that includes income from U.S. Government obligations that may not be taxed directly. See, e.g., Reuben L. Anderson–Cherne, Inc. v. Commissioner, 303 Minn. 124, 226 N.W.2d 611, appeal dismissed, 423 U.S. 886, 96 S.Ct. 181 (1975). The same is true of corporate franchise taxes measured by capital stock, which may include the value of U.S. Government obligations without violating the bar on state taxation of federal obligations. See, e.g., Home Ins. Co. v. New York, 134 U.S. 594, 10 S.Ct. 593 (1890). Similarly, the Court interpreted the statute as permitting taxes imposed on the right to take property by inheritance, even though the value of the inheritance was measured by the value of the federal obligation transferred. Plummer v. Coler, 178 U.S. 115, 20 S.Ct. 829 (1900) (inheritance tax measured by value of the property passing).

The foregoing cases turned on the formal distinction between the subject and the measure of the taxes involved. The federal obligations, and the income therefrom, could not be the subject of a state tax, but they could be included in its measure. In 1956, the Court declared that this formal but economically meaningless distinction between taxes on federal obligations and taxes on separate interests was "firmly embedded in the law." Society for Savings v. Bowers, supra, 349 U.S. at 148.

Despite the Supreme Court's recognition that Revised Statutes § 3701 precluded direct taxation of the interest on federal obligations as well as taxation of the underlying obligations themselves, see New Jersey Realty Title Ins. Co. v. Division of Tax Appeals, 338 U.S. 665, 675–76, 70 S.Ct. 413 (1950), the State of Idaho had taken the position that it could avoid the import of this holding by imposing a tax on individuals measured by such interest rather than imposing a tax on the interest itself. See American Bank and Trust Co. v. Dallas County, 463 U.S. 855, 866, 103 S.Ct. 3369 (1983) (discussing legislative history of Revised Statutes § 3701). In response to this potential frustration of the purposes of Revised Statutes § 3701, Congress added the following language to the statute in 1959:

> This exemption extends to every form of taxation that would require that either the obligations or the interest thereon or both, be considered, directly or indirectly, in the computation of the tax, except nondiscriminatory franchise or other nonproperty taxes in lieu thereof imposed on corporations and except estate or inheritance taxes.[c]

In American Bank & Trust Co. v. Dallas County, supra, the Court considered the impact of the 1959 amendment on a state property tax on bank shares computed on the basis of the bank's net assets without any deduction for tax-exempt U.S. obligations held by the bank. The Court observed that the exemption for federal obligations under the amended statute is "sweeping," extending to " '*every form*' of taxation that would require that either the obligations or the interest thereon, or both, *be considered, directly or indirectly, in the computation* of the tax." Id., 463 U.S. at 862 (emphasis in original). Under this reading of the statute, the bank shares statute could not stand because federal obligations were considered in computing the bank shares tax at issue. The tax was computed by the use of an "equity capital formula," which involved determining the amount of the bank's capital assets (including federal obligations), subtracting from that figure the bank's liabilities and the assessed value of the bank's real estate, and then dividing the result by the number of shares.

---

c. In 1982, Revised Statutes § 3701, 31 U.S.C. § 742, was "reformulated without substantive change," see American Bank & Trust Co. v. Dallas County, supra, 463 U.S. at 859 n. 1, as 31 U.S.C. § 3124. The statute now reads:

Stocks and obligations of the United States Government are exempt from taxation by a state or political subdivision of a state. The exemption applies to each form of taxation that would require the obligation, the interest on the obligation, or both, to be considered in computing a tax except—

(1) a nondiscriminatory franchise tax or another nonproperty tax instead of a franchise tax, imposed on a corporation; and

(2) an estate or inheritance tax.

In holding that Revised Statutes § 3701, as amended, barred a bank shares tax measured by federal obligations, the Court left open the question whether a state must permit a bank to deduct from its net worth the full value of federal obligations it holds or whether the state may limit the deduction to the portion of federal obligations attributable to assets rather than liabilities. In Missouri ex rel. Missouri Insurance Co. v. Gehner, 281 U.S. 313, 50 S.Ct. 326 (1930), the Court had held that Revised Statutes § 3701 prohibited a state from increasing an insurance company's personal property tax base by the liabilities proportionate to the amount of its tax-exempt federal obligations, which had been subtracted from its taxable assets. The Court reasoned that the pro rata deduction violated Revised Statutes § 3701 because it made ownership of federal bonds the basis for denying a full deduction of liabilities, and thereby increased the tax burden of the taxpayer.

In First National Bank of Atlanta v. Bartow County Board of Tax Assessors, 470 U.S. 583, 105 S.Ct. 1516 (1985), the Court revisited this question in connection with a Georgia bank shares tax. As construed prior to the *American Bank* case, Georgia's bank shares tax, which was measured by the fair market value of a bank's shares, included the value of U.S. obligations held by the bank. The Georgia Supreme Court sought to save the statute by construing it to allow a bank to deduct from its net worth the percentage of assets attributable to federal obligations. The court rejected the bank's argument that the total value of the federal obligations had to be subtracted from net worth under Revised Statutes § 3701, observing that such a deduction would not merely insulate federal obligations from the tax but would go beyond the requirements of Revised Statutes § 3701 by sheltering the bank's taxable assets from tax.

The Supreme Court agreed with the Georgia court and sustained the proportionate deduction. The Court recognized that if *Gehner* were controlling, the bank's argument would prevail because *Gehner* held that anything less than a full deduction for federal obligations failed to satisfy the requirements of Revised Statutes § 3701. Id., 470 U.S. at 590–91. After reexamining *Gehner*, however, the Court concluded that its reasoning had been undermined by cases raising analogous issues. See United States v. Atlas Life Ins. Co., 381 U.S. 233, 85 S.Ct. 1379 (1965) (insurance company required to apportion tax-exempt interest between its gross income and policy holders' income). The Court therefore upheld the proportionate deduction of federal obligations from the bank shares tax base declaring that Revised Statutes § 3701, as amended, requires only that " 'a State may not subject one to a greater tax burden upon his property because he owns tax-exempt government securities,' " Id. at 590 (quoting National Life Ins. Co. v. United States, 277 U.S. 508, 48 S.Ct. 591 (1928)). Cf. Hunt–Wesson, Inc. v. Franchise Tax Bd., 528 U.S. 458, 120 S.Ct. 1022 (2000) (invalidating, under Commerce and Due Process Clauses, California's denial of interest expense deduction equal to taxpayer's nontaxable income, but suggesting that pro-rata denial would pass constitutional muster) (citing *First National Bank*). The *Hunt–Wesson* case is set out at pp. 436–41 infra.

B. *Delineation of "Federal Obligation": Open Accounts, Ginnie Maes, and Repos.* The question sometimes arises whether a debt or a payment constitutes a federal obligation or interest from such an obligation. In Smith

v. Davis, 323 U.S. 111, 65 S.Ct. 157 (1944), the taxpayers, who had engaged in construction work for the United States, had a claim against the Government in the amount of approximately $30,000. The balance owing "was in the nature of an open account and represented an account receivable." Id., 323 U.S. at 112. The taxpayers assailed a Georgia personal property tax assessed on this open account on the ground that it was a levy on a federal obligation. The Court rejected the contention, holding that an open account claim against the United States "does not represent a credit instrumentality of the federal government within the meaning of this constitutional immunity." Id. at 113. It held that the obligations of the United States which are subject to the rule had been limited to interest bearing indebtedness issued to public creditors pursuant to act of Congress. The Court also pointed out that the taxation of the open account claim can in no sense embarrass the credit of the United States or its ability to secure aid from independent contractors for military and civilian construction projects.

"Ginnie Maes" are financial instruments issued by private financial institutions and guaranteed by the Government National Mortgage Association (otherwise known as GNMA or Ginnie Mae). In Rockford Life Insurance Co. v. Illinois, 482 U.S. 182, 107 S.Ct. 2312 (1987), the Court considered the question whether these standard securities were exempt from Illinois personal property taxes applied to an insurance company's capital stock, whose value reflected its holding of Ginnie Maes. The Court held that Ginnie Maes are not "obligations of the United States" because the primary obligation to make payment falls on the private issuer of the certificate. Unless the issuer defaults in its payments to the holder, no federal funds are used in connection with the payments of principal and interest set forth in the certificate.

A "repo" is a repurchase agreement whereby a seller of a security agrees to repurchase the security at an agreed price at a later date. The repurchase price is higher than the original sale price, and the difference reflects interest. Taxpayers who have engaged in these repurchase agreements involving Treasury notes have argued that they are owners of "federal obligations" and that they earn exempt federal interest from these obligations during the time that they hold them. In Nebraska Department of Revenue v. Loewenstein, 513 U.S. 123, 115 S.Ct. 557 (1994), the U.S. Supreme Court held that interest from repos involving federal securities was not exempt federal obligation interest. Rather, the interest was earned on a loan from the "purchaser" of the federal obligation to the "seller," not on the underlying federal security, which merely served as collateral for the loan.

2. STATE TAXATION OF NATIONAL BANKS

NOTES AND QUESTIONS

A. *Historical Overview of the Immunity of National Banks From State Taxation.* The immunity of national banks from state taxation, like the immunity of federal obligations, has constitutional roots that go back to McCulloch v. Maryland, 17 U.S. (4 Wheat.) 316 (1819). Shortly after enacting the National Banking Act in 1863, Congress provided that the states could tax national banks only on their real estate and shares. 13 Stat. 111 (1864). This statute, which became known as Revised Statutes § 5219 (codified at 12 U.S.C. § 548), was amended in 1926 to provide that the states could tax national banks in four ways: (1) by taxing bank shares, (2) by including bank share dividends in the taxable income of a shareholder, (3) by taxing national banks on their net income, and (4) by levying a franchise tax on national banks measured by their net income. 44 Stat. 223 (1926).

In 1968, the Supreme Court held that 12 U.S.C. § 548 forbade the states from imposing sales and use taxes on a national bank's purchase of waste paper baskets, office supplies, and similar items. First Agricultural National Bank of Berkshire County v. State Tax Commission, 392 U.S. 339, 88 S.Ct. 2173 (1968). The Supreme Court recognized the force of the contention that national banks, under present day conditions, were essentially indistinguishable from state banks and should not enjoy immunity from taxation as federal instrumentalities. It nevertheless felt that the legislative history of 12 U.S.C. § 548 was clear in prescribing the only way in which the states may tax national banks and that "if a change is to be made in state taxation of national banks it must come from the Congress." Id., 392 U.S. at 346. Justice Marshall vigorously dissented from the Court's opinion on the ground that national banks should no longer be considered as tax-immune federal instrumentalities and that 12 U.S.C. § 548 should be construed as limiting only the types of taxes specifically mentioned in the statute. See also Dickinson v. First National Bank of Homestead, 393 U.S. 409, 89 S.Ct. 685 (1969) (invalidating Florida's mortgage recording and documentary stamp taxes on a national bank).

These cases induced Congress to reexamine the existing immunities of national banks from state taxation. In 1969, Congress enacted legislation directing the Federal Reserve Board to study state and local taxation of banks and to report to Congress its recommendations as to what, if any, further legislation "may be needed to reconcile the promotion of the economic efficiency of the banking systems of the nation with the achievement of effectiveness and local autonomy in meeting the fiscal needs of the States and their political subdivisions." P.L. 91–156, 83 Stat. 434 (1969). For the interim period, Congress enacted a temporary amendment to 12 U.S.C. § 548, which authorized state and local governments to subject national banks to nondiscriminatory sales and use taxes, real and tangible personal property taxes, documentary stamp taxes, and levies on the ownership or use of tangible personal property located within the jurisdiction. Id. § 1. The temporary amendment also empowered the states to apply to national banks having their principal offices in the state whatever taxes (other than taxes on intangible personal property) they levied generally on their own domestic state banks. Id.

At the same time, Congress adopted a permanent amendment to the statute, which terminated, as of January 1, 1972, all congressionally granted immunity of national banks from state taxation. Id. § 2. (For purposes of the permanent amendment, 12 U.S.C. § 548 was also amended to provide that a national bank is to be treated as a bank organized under the laws of the state or other jurisdiction in which its principal office is located.) The effectiveness of the permanent amendment was postponed until September 12, 1976, because of the sharp conflicts between and among the commercial banks, savings banks, savings and loan associations, and the states as to how far the states should be permitted by Congress to tax nondomiciliary depository institutions. See P.L. 92–213, 85 Stat. 775 (1971); P.L. 93–100, 87 Stat. 342 (1973); P.L. 94–222, 90 Stat. 197 (1976). Legislation further restricting the states' power to tax national banks was never enacted. Accordingly, since 1976 states have been free to tax national banks just as they tax state banks. See generally Sandra B. McCray, "State Taxation of Interstate Banking," 21 Ga. L. Rev. 283 (1986); Jerome R. Hellerstein, "Current Issues in Multistate Taxation of Banks," 30 Tax L. Rev. 155, 156–58 (1975).

3. OTHER CONGRESSIONAL LEGISLATION CREATING FEDERAL IMMUNITY FROM STATE TAXATION

NOTES AND QUESTIONS

A. *The Buck Act.* The Buck Act of 1940, 4 U.S.C. § 105 et seq., provides for a waiver of the federal immunity that might otherwise be asserted with respect to state sales, use, and income taxes imposed on activities occurring within federal areas. The most significant impact of the Buck Act occurs with respect to federal enclaves, where the states lack any power to tax in the absence of a congressional waiver of immunity.[d]

The Buck Act provides in part that

[n]o person shall be relieved from liability for any income tax levied by any State, or by any duly constituted taxing authority therein, having jurisdiction to levy such a tax, by reason of his residing within a Federal area or receiving income from transactions occurring or services performed in such area.

4 U.S.C. § 106(a). The Buck Act defines "income tax" as "any tax levied on, with respect to, or measured by, net income, gross income, or gross receipts." Id. § 110(c).

In Howard v. Commissioners of Sinking Fund of Louisville, 344 U.S. 624, 73 S.Ct. 465 (1953), employees at a federal ordnance plant located on federal land within the City of Louisville challenged the validity of a Louisville tax imposed on persons engaged in any trade, occupation or profession within the city. The tax was an annual "license fee for the privilege of engaging in said activities" (id., 344 U.S. at 625) measured by one percent of salaries, wages, and the net profits of trades, businesses or professions. The taxpayers argued that the state and localities were not authorized to tax the privilege of working on federal land although located within a state. The Court held that the tax was an "income tax" within the meaning of the Buck Act since it was

---

d. As the term is generally employed in constitutional parlance, a "federal enclave" is a territory that the United States has acquired pursuant to the Jurisdiction Clause. U.S. Const. art. I, § 8, cl. 17. That clause provides in pertinent part that "Congress shall have the power to exercise exclusive Legislation in all cases whatsoever * * * over all places purchased by the Consent of the Legislature of the State in which the Same shall be, for the Erection of Forts, Magazines, Arsenals, Dock–Yards and other needful buildings." Most federally owned lands fall outside this provision because they have been reserved from the original public domain, purchased without the consent of a state, or acquired by eminent domain.

measured by gross receipts, despite the holding of the Kentucky court that the levy was not an income tax within the meaning of the Kentucky Constitution.

Many controversies have arisen as to how far Congress has waived immunity under the Buck Act. In Alaska v. Baker, 64 Wash.2d 207, 390 P.2d 1009 (1964), appeal dismissed, 380 U.S. 260, 85 S.Ct. 952 (1965), the court held that Alaska's business license tax, measured by gross receipts, was an "income tax" within the meaning of Buck Act and hence was properly applied to a federal contractor that performed work exclusively on a U.S. military reservation. Similarly, in Burns v. State, Bureau of Revenue, 79 N.M. 53, 439 P.2d 702, cert. denied, 393 U.S. 841, 89 S.Ct. 119 (1968), the court applied the Buck Act to deny immunity from New Mexico's income tax to Texas residents who worked as civilian employees of the Federal Government at the White Sands Missile Range in New Mexico.

The Supreme Court of Texas reached a dubious conclusion in construing the Texas franchise tax, which was measured essentially by capital stock, as an "income tax" within the meaning of the Buck Act. The court reasoned that "the granting of the privilege to transact business in Texas represents the realization of gross income" and that the franchise tax was "measured by * * * gross receipts," since the apportionment formula included a receipts factor. General Dynamics Corp. v. Bullock, 547 S.W.2d 255, 259 (Tex. 1976), cert. denied, 434 U.S. 1009, 98 S.Ct. 717 (1978). See also Humble Oil & Refining Co. v. Calvert, 478 S.W.2d 926 (Tex. 1972) (occupation taxes measured by the value of oil and gas produced constitute "income taxes" for purposes of the Buck Act).

From time to time, Congress acts to provide protection to employees working at specific federal sites. In 1998, for example, Congress preempted Kentucky, Nebraska, and Oregon from taxing the income of nonresident employees who worked in federal enclaves that lay in part in those states. Pub. L. No. 105–261, 112 Stat. 1920 (1998). Congressional delegations from the non-income tax states of Tennessee, South Dakota, and Washington sought the legislation. In all three instances, they represented regions where the federal enclave straddled two states: the Fort Campbell military base in Kentucky and Tennessee; a dam on the Missouri River in Nebraska and South Dakota; and a dam on the Columbia river in Oregon and Washington. In all three cases, the workers would cross state lines many times during the day. Congress evidently believed that the nonresident workers did not receive services or benefits from the states sufficient to subject them to income taxation and that the administrative burden in filing returns in those states would be excessive. During the debate over the legislation, lawmakers drew a clear distinction between the cross-border situations under consideration and other federal enclaves located entirely within a single state.

B. *Soldiers and Sailors Relief Act.* The Soldiers and Sailors Relief Act of 1940, 50 U.S.C. App. § 574, prohibits, among other things, state taxation of personal property, owned by military personnel who are in the state (other than the state of domicile) by reason of military orders, if the property is not used in a trade or business. See Dameron v. Brodhead, 345 U.S. 322, 73 S.Ct. 721 (1953) (invalidating Denver personal property tax on household furnishings of officer located in rented apartment near airfield where he was stationed). In Sullivan v. United States, 395 U.S. 169, 89 S.Ct. 1648 (1969), the Supreme Court held that the Soldiers and Sailors Relief Act did not bar a state from imposing sales and use taxes on tangible personal property purchased by nonresident servicemen present in a state under military orders. The Court found that the statutory language limiting "taxation in respect of the personal property" (50 U.S.C. App. § 574) of nonresident servicemen did not include or exclude sales taxes. The Court relied instead on the statute's legislative history, which reflected a congressional purpose to relieve nonresident servicemen of the risk of double taxation from annually recurring property taxes but not to shield them from sales or use taxes of the host state.

C. *The Public Salary Tax Act.* The Public Salary Tax Act, 4 U.S.C. § 111, considered in Davis v. Michigan Dep't of Treasury, 489 U.S. 803, 109 S.Ct. 1500 (1989), set out at pp. 323–30 supra, allows a state and its political subdivisions to tax the pay or compensation of federal employees "if the taxation does not discriminate against the [federal] employee because of the source of the pay or compensation." In Jefferson County, Alabama v. Acker, 527 U.S. 423, 119 S.Ct. 2069 (1999), two federal district court judges from Alabama challenged the application of a county occupational license tax to their judicial salaries. The levy was measured by one-half percent of the "gross receipts" of the person subject to tax. The judges acknowledged that the Public Salary Tax Act would defeat their claim if the county tax were a nondiscriminatory income tax. They argued, however, that the levy was in fact an unconstitutional licensing scheme and, even if a tax, one that discriminated against federal judges. The Court rejected both contentions. It found that "[i]n practice, Jefferson County's license tax serves a revenue-raising, not a regulatory purpose," id., 527 U.S. at 440, and that "Jefferson County neither issues licenses to taxpayers, nor in any way regulates them in the performance of their duties based on their status as license taxpayers." Id. In rejecting the claim that the occupational tax discriminated against federal judges because of the availability of exemptions for those who held licenses under other state or county laws, the Court observed:

> In *Davis*, the Court held that a state tax exempting retirement benefits paid by the State but not those paid by the Federal Government violated the Public Salary Tax Act's nondiscrimination requirement. Jefferson County's tax, by contrast, does not discriminate against federal judges in particular, or federal officeholders in general, based on the federal source of their pay or compensation. The tax is paid by all State District and Circuit Court judges in Jefferson County and the three State Supreme Court justices who have satellite offices in the county.

Id. at 442–43.

E. STATE TAXATION OF INDIAN TRIBES

"State laws generally are not applicable to tribal Indians on an Indian reservation except where Congress has expressly provided that State laws shall apply. It follows that Indians and Indian property on an Indian reservation are not subject to state taxation except by virtue of express authority conferred upon the State by act of Congress." U.S. Dep't of the

Interior, Federal Indian Law 845 (1958), quoted with approval in McClanahan v. State Tax Comm'n, 411 U.S. 164, 171, 93 S.Ct. 1257 (1973). In *McClanahan,* the Court, after examining the relevant treaties and statutes, held that Arizona had no power to impose a tax on the income of Navajo Indians on the Navajo Reservation when the income was wholly derived from reservation sources. In another case decided on the same day, the Court, construing the applicable provision of the Indian Reorganization Act, 25 U.S.C. § 465, held that New Mexico could impose a nondiscriminatory gross receipts tax on a ski resort operated by an Indian Tribe on non-reservation land leased from the Federal Government; but it denied the state power to impose a use tax on personalty installed in the construction of ski lifts. Mescalero Apache Tribe v. Jones, 411 U.S. 145, 93 S.Ct. 1267 (1973). In *Mescalero,* the Court articulated the operating legal principle governing state taxation of Indians as follows:

> [I]n the special area of state taxation, absent cession of jurisdiction or other federal statutes permitting it, there has been no satisfactory authority for taxing Indian reservation lands or Indian income from activities carried on within the boundaries of the reservation, and *McClanahan* * * * lays to rest any doubt in this respect by holding that such taxation is not permissible absent congressional consent.

Id., 411 U.S. at 148.

Beginning in the 1980s and continuing over the past few decades, the Court handed down a number of cases concerning the states' power to tax Indians and Indian-related activity. The resolution of these cases turned largely on the Court's reading of the complex web of specific treaties, laws, and administrative rulings governing the relationship between the states and the Indian Tribes. Montana v. Blackfeet Tribe of Indians, 471 U.S. 759, 105 S.Ct. 2399 (1985), is illustrative. In that case, the Court held that a state could not levy taxes on a tribe's royalty interests in oil and gas produced under leases issued by the tribe. The critical question was whether the provision of a 1924 federal statute, which authorized state taxation of such royalty payments, was implicitly repealed by the Indian Mineral Leasing Act of 1938, 25 U.S.C. § 396a et seq., which was silent on the question. In rejecting the state's argument that repeal by implication is not favored, the Court noted that ordinary principles of statutory construction did not have their usual force in Indian cases, and that "[t]he canons of construction applicable * * * are rooted in the unique trust relationship between the United States and the Indians." Id., 471 U.S. at 766. Because the states may tax Indians only when explicit congressional authorization exists, and such authorization was not granted by the 1938 Act, the Court denied Montana the power to tax the royalty payments.

Other cases construing Indian immunity from state taxation include Wagnon v. Prairie Band Potawatomi Nation, 546 U.S. 95, 126 S.Ct. 676 (2005) (off-reservation sale of motor fuel between non-Indians did not enjoy Indian immunity even though economic burden of tax fell on Indian retailer who sold fuel on reservation); City of Sherrill, N.Y. v. Oneida

Indian Nation of New York, 544 U.S. 197, 125 S.Ct. 1478 (2005) (tribal land sold to non-Indian purchasers in 1807 and repurchased by tribe in 1997 and 1998 did not enjoy tribal property immunity); Arizona Dep't of Revenue v. Blaze Construction Co., 526 U.S. 32, 119 S.Ct. 957 (1999) (state may impose a nondiscriminatory tax upon a private company's proceeds from contracts with the Federal Government, regardless of whether the federal contractor renders its services on an Indian reservation); Oklahoma Tax Commission v. Chickasaw Nation, 515 U.S. 450, 115 S.Ct. 2214 (1995) (states may not, absent congressional authorization, impose excise tax on motor fuel sold by Indian retailers on tribal lands when legal incidence of tax falls on the Indian tribe); Department of Taxation & Finance v. Milhelm Attea Bros., Inc., 512 U.S. 61, 114 S.Ct. 2028 (1994) (state may impose record-keeping requirements and quantity limitations on cigarette wholesalers who sell untaxed cigarettes to reservation Indians); Oklahoma Tax Commission v. Sac & Fox Nation, 508 U.S. 114, 113 S.Ct. 1985 (1993) (extending rule of *McClanahan* to Native Americans living in "Indian country," whether or not they reside within the boundaries of a formal reservation); County of Yakima v. Confederated Tribes & Bands of Yakima Indian Nation, 502 U.S. 251, 112 S.Ct. 683 (1992) (county may impose ad valorem taxes on patented lands owned by tribe and its members, but not excise taxes on sale of such lands, because the former, but not the latter, were authorized by federal legislation); Oklahoma Tax Commission v. Citizen Band Potawatomi Indian Tribe of Oklahoma, 498 U.S. 505, 111 S.Ct. 905 (1991) (state may not impose sales tax on sales of cigarettes by Indian tribe to tribal members on land held in trust for Indians by Federal Government but may impose taxes on sales to nontribal members); Ramah Navajo School Board, Inc. v. Bureau of Revenue, 458 U.S. 832, 102 S.Ct. 3394 (1982) (Federal statutes encouraging the development of Indian-controlled institutions, and detailed federal regulations governing school construction on reservation, preempt state tax on gross receipts received by non-Indian construction company from tribal school board for constructing school on Indian reservation); White Mountain Apache Tribe v. Bracker, 448 U.S. 136, 100 S.Ct. 2578 (1980) (pervasive federal regulation of commercial timber activity on tribal lands preempts state tax on non-Indian enterprise harvesting timber on Indian reservation); Washington v. Confederated Tribes of the Colville Indian Reservation, 447 U.S. 134, 100 S.Ct. 2069 (1980) (Washington may impose sales tax on purchases of cigarettes made on Indian reservations by nonmembers of the tribe).

F. REFERENCES

For general analyses of federal immunity from state and local taxation, see 2 Jerome R. Hellerstein & Walter Hellerstein, State Taxation ch. 22 (3d ed. 2001 & Cum. Supp. 2009) and Paul J. Hartman, Federal Limitations on State and Local Taxation ch. 6 (1981). The classic treatments of the doctrine remain Thomas R. Powell, "The Waning of Intergovernmental Tax Immunities," 58 Harv. L. Rev. 633 (1945) and Thomas R. Powell, "The Remnant of Intergovernmental Immunities," 58 Harv. L. Rev. 757 (1945). For more recent discussions of federal immunity, see 1 Laurence H. Tribe, American Constitutional Law §§ 6–33, 6–34 (3d ed. 2000); Sealy H. Cavin, Jr., "Federal Immunity of Government Contractors from State and Local Taxation," 61 Denver L. Rev. 797 (1984); Note, "Federal Immunity from State Taxation: A Reassessment," 45 U. Chi. L. Rev. 695 (1978).

For references dealing with state taxation of Indians, see generally Rennard Strickland, ed., Felix S. Cohen's Handbook of Federal Indian Law 405–31 (1982); see also Milner S. Ball, "Constitution, Court, Indian Tribes," 1987 Am. Bar Found. Res. J. 1, 100–110; William S. Dockins, "Limitations on State Power to Tax Natural Resource Development on Indian Reservations," 43 Mont. L. Rev. 217 (1982); Robert Laurence, "The Indian Commerce Clause," 23 Ariz. L. Rev. 203 (1981).

PART 2

MAJOR STATE AND LOCAL TAXES

■ ■ ■

CHAPTER 6

PERSONAL INCOME TAXES

■ ■ ■

The personal income tax has roots deep in colonial America. The colonial "faculty taxes" combined property and income as the tax base, and the income element of the faculty tax persisted after 1776 in several states. The panic of 1837 resulted in the adoption of income taxes in a number of states. In 1840, for example, Pennsylvania levied a tax of one percent on salaries and a tax of one-tenth of one percent on other incomes. During the Civil War, all the Confederate states and several Union states enacted income taxes. Without exception, however, the nineteenth century income taxes were administrative failures, and their revenue yields were trifling.

In 1911, Wisconsin opened a new chapter in American fiscal history with an income tax administered by a state tax commission.[a] The new tax featured progressive marginal rates, beginning at one percent over a moderate exemption and rising to six percent on the excess over $12,000. The success of the Wisconsin income tax was immediately apparent, and several other states enacted income tax laws shortly thereafter. The Wisconsin experience, along with the adoption of the federal income tax in 1913, demonstrated that a centrally administered income tax could be a practicable source of revenue. Scholars had long pointed to the income tax as a highly desirable form of taxation because of its close conformity to the principle of taxation according to ability to pay.

In the early 1920s, many observers believed that personal income taxes would soon become a universal form of state taxation, but the movement that began with New York's and North Dakota's income taxes in 1919 soon waned. Beginning in 1929, however, there was another wave of state income tax enactments. During the next decade, 13 more states instituted personal income taxes. By the middle of the twentieth century, the overwhelming majority of states had personal income taxes. Today, 41 states and the District of Columbia levy broad-based personal income taxes.[b]

---

a. See W. Eliot Brownlee, Progressivism and Economic Growth: The Wisconsin Income Tax 1911–1929 (1974).

b. Alaska, Florida, Nevada, South Dakota, Texas, Washington, and Wyoming impose no personal income taxes; New Hampshire and Tennessee impose taxes on only limited types of personal income.

During the last decade of the twentieth century and the first decade of the twenty-first, personal income taxes emerged as the single most important source of state tax revenues, rising from roughly 30 percent of state tax revenues in 1988 to more than 36 percent of state tax revenues in 2008. The total yield of state personal income taxes for 2008 was $280 billion. Local governments collected over $21 billion in personal income tax revenue during 2008, although property taxes remain the most important source of revenues for local governments.[c] Total personal income tax revenues collected by state and local governments for 2008 thus amounted to roughly $301 billion.

A. CONFORMITY OF STATE INCOME TAXES TO THE FEDERAL INCOME TAX

Most state personal income taxes conform closely to the federal personal income tax. At one time, some states adopted the most extreme form of federal conformity, under which the state tax was simply a percentage of the federal tax. Although no state embraces that method today, the overwhelming majority of states with broad-based income taxes employ federal adjusted gross income or federal taxable income as the computational starting point for determining state taxable income. The states then provide for various adjustments (additions and subtractions) to the federal figure in determining state taxable income. Some of these adjustments, such as provisions permitting a deduction for interest from federal obligations, are compelled by federal law.[d] Others reflect local concerns of—or political pressures on—state legislatures. For example, all but a handful of states require that federally exempt interest from state or municipal bonds issued by other states or their political subdivisions be added back to the state personal income tax base. Other common adjustments to federal adjusted gross or taxable income in determining the state personal income tax base include (1) additions for lump-sum distributions from pension plans and percentage depletion allowances and (2) subtractions for certain forms of retirement income and the taxable portion of Social Security and Railroad Retirement Fund benefits. In addition, many states provide variations from the standard and itemized deductions permitted under federal law. For example, some states provide no deduction for charitable contributions, most deny a deduction for state income taxes, and others provide a deduction for federal income taxes.[e]

---

c. Data cited in the text can be found on the Census Bureau's website. See U.S. Census Bureau, National Totals of State Tax Revenues by Type of Tax (Table 2) and U.S. Census Bureau, National Totals of State and Local Tax Revenues by Type of Tax (Table 1), available at http://ftp 2.census.gov/govs/qtax/.

d. 31 U.S.C. § 3124.

e. Provisions referenced in this paragraph are discussed in the All States Tax Guide (RIA) ¶¶ 221, 228–A.5, 228–C, 228–C—228–F, 230, 237 (2009) (chart), available at www.checkpoint.riag. com.

NOTES AND QUESTIONS

A. *Challenges to Conformity Provisions.* In Alaska Steamship Company v. Mullaney, 180 F.2d 805 (9th Cir. 1950), taxpayers challenged the Alaska territorial legislature's effort to base Alaska's personal income tax on " 'the Internal Revenue Code of the United States ... as now in effect *or hereafter amended.*' " Id. at 814 (quoting the statute, emphasis in original). While observing that no taxpayers were currently affected by any such changes since no changes had yet been made, the court proceeded to address the question whether incorporation by reference of future changes constituted an unconstitutional delegation of legislative power:

> We do not overlook the fact that if the words "or hereafter amended" were dropped from the Act, what remains would, in the long run, be unworkable under the legislative scheme here devised, for if the federal income tax requirements were changed substantially by future amendments, it would be impossible, administratively, to calculate the Alaska income tax merely by dividing the tax shown on the federal return by 10.
> * * *

> We think it is far from clear that any invalid delegation is attempted. There are of course many cases which have held attempts by a legislative body to incorporate provisions into its enactments, by reference to future acts or amendments by other legislatures, to be invalid. But where it can be said that the attempt to make the local law conform to future changes elsewhere is not a mere labor-saving device for the legislators, but is undertaken in order to attain a uniformity which is in itself an important object of the proposed legislative scheme, there are a number of precedents for an approval of this sort of thing. Reciprocal and retaliatory legislation falls in this category.

> Similarly the efforts of the states to take advantage, in their inheritance tax laws, of the 80 percent credit provision in the federal laws relating to Estate Tax, 44 Stat. 70, now 26 U.S.C. 813(b), have been carried out by simple reference to the federal estate tax law. Brown v. State, 323 Mo. 138, 19 S.W.2d 12. Perhaps the best-known instance of action by Congress encompassing within its regulation the laws of states, then or thereafter enacted, was the Conformity Act, 17 Stat. 196, 197. There, also, making the procedure in common law actions conform to that prevailing in the states was a prime object of the legislation.

> The effort of the Alaska legislature to make its territorial income tax machinery conform to the federal act, and to preserve and continue such conformity, makes sense. It makes for convenience to the taxpayer and for simplicity of administration. A similar coordination has been recommended by students of income tax problems for adoption by the states generally. Since the attainment of this uniformity was in itself a major objective of the Alaska legislature, in enacting that the local law must conform, the Alaska legislature, which alone could make this decision, was itself acting, and was not abdicating its functions, nor, in our opinion, making an invalid delegation to Congress.

> There are two other ways in which, it is asserted, an invalid delegation is made. One is the provision that "rules and regulations promulgat-

ed by the United States Commissioner of Internal Revenue . . . shall be regarded as regulations promulgated by the Tax Commissioner under . . . this Act." We think what we have said concerning incorporation of the Internal Revenue Code sufficiently disposes of this question. If the one is valid, the other is also.

Id. at 816–17.

The statute involved in the *Alaska Steamship* case reflects the most complete type of federalization of the state personal income tax, which no state currently employs. The constitutional objections raised in the case, however, namely the alleged impropriety of incorporation of another statute by reference, and the claimed illegality of the delegation by a state legislature of its powers to Congress, apply as well to less comprehensive conformity statutes, and these objections have impeded the growth of conformity. To be sure, in many states incorporation of other statutes by reference (even including future changes) has had a long history of statutory or judicial acceptance. In other states, however, serious doubts as to the propriety of such legislative delegation persists. As a result, some states, in order to maintain their conformity to the Internal Revenue Code, are required to enact provisions incorporating any changes that Congress may have made during the preceding year. State legislatures that are required to take such action typically do so on an annual basis with little controversy. Other states have adopted constitutional amendments permitting full conformity to the federal income tax base. See, e.g., Haw. Const. art. VII, § 2 ("In enacting any law imposing a tax on or measured by income, the legislature may define income by reference to provisions of the laws of the United States as they may be or become effective at any time or from time to time * * * ").

B. *Policy Questions Raised by Conformity to the Federal Income Tax Base.* Conformity to the federal income tax base—whether defined as federal adjusted gross income or federal taxable income—raises fundamental policy questions. Why should a state accept a federal determination as to the delineation of taxable income, the availability of particular deductions, or the treatment of capital gains? Even if a state generally accepts the federal approach to these questions, why should a state automatically allow nonresidents a pro rata deduction for personal expenses unconnected to their income-producing activity in the state, which it effectively will do by adopting the federal tax base? However, if a state insists on making these determinations on an independent basis, will it not frustrate the basic goal of conformity—namely, allowing state taxpayers to report their state income tax simply and efficiently? What aspects of the state tax structure can most easily be adapted to state-specific goals without creating time-consuming and complex compliance issues for state taxpayers?

There are also significant revenue issues raised by conformity. Base-broadening or base-narrowing at the federal level tends to generate a response at the state level, because failure to respond ordinarily increases or decreases state revenues in the absence of a state rate adjustment. The Federal Tax Reform Act of 1986, for example, broadened the federal personal income tax while lowering its rates. In response, twenty-seven of the then forty states[f]

---

f. Connecticut did not enact its income tax until 1991, becoming the forty-first state to adopt a broad-based income tax. See text accompanying note a supra.

with broad-based personal income taxes enacted changes to their own tax regimes, with most returning at least a portion of the so-called revenue windfall to state taxpayers. National Governors Ass'n, The Impact of Federal Tax Reform on the States (1987). More recently, with the enactment of the base-narrowing provisions of the American Recovery and Reinvestment Act of 2009, P.L. 111–5, 115 Stat. 123 (Feb. 17, 2009), many states have moved to "decouple" their tax regimes from the federal tax model to avoid revenue losses. See, e.g., Steven Roll, "Georgia Law Updates Federal Conformity, but Decouples from Latest Stimulus Bill," BNA Daily Tax Report (May 7, 2009).

C. *Controversies Arising Under State Conformity Provisions.* Controversies sometimes arise over the relationship between the state personal income tax laws and the federal personal income tax provisions upon which they rely. The Minnesota Supreme Court held that the disallowance of a deduction on the taxpayer's federal personal income tax return by the U.S. Tax Court estops the taxpayer from relitigating the state's disallowance of the same deduction on the state tax return. Tarutis v. Commissioner of Revenue, 393 N.W.2d 667 (Minn. 1986). A California court likewise held that taxpayers were estopped from relitigating in state court the amount of their gross income for state income tax purposes when gross income had already been determined in a prior federal tax case. Calhoun v. Franchise Tax Bd., 20 Cal.3d 881, 574 P.2d 763, 143 Cal.Rptr. 692 (1978).

The Missouri Supreme Court, on the other hand, held that the compromise and settlement of a taxpayer's federal tax liability did not have a conclusive effect on his state tax liability. Buder v. Director of Revenue, 869 S.W.2d 752 (Mo. 1994). The Internal Revenue Service (IRS) had sought to disallow certain of the taxpayer's claimed deductions for farming operations and for charitable contributions. The taxpayer and the IRS ultimately settled the dispute, with the taxpayer paying approximately 50 percent of the tax that would have been due had the IRS prevailed. Based on this settlement, the Missouri Director of Revenue took the position that the taxpayer owed additional Missouri taxes and interest. The taxpayer contended that he was not bound by the settlement because it compromised only the federal tax liability and did not constitute an adjustment to his federal adjusted gross income on which Missouri tax liability is based. The court rejected the Director's claim that failing to give the federal settlement preclusive effect "will undo the 'coupling'" between Missouri income tax law and its federal counterpart. Id. at 753. The court concluded that the taxpayer's compromise and settlement did not constitute a conclusive admission of Missouri tax liability and that "the unilateral IRS adjustment to the [taxpayer's] taxable income may be challenged in the determination of Missouri tax liability." Id. at 754. Suppose the taxpayer and the IRS had settled by reducing the taxpayer's adjusted gross income by 50 percent. Would the result have been the same as in the *Buder* case?

In contrast to cases holding that issues litigated at the federal level are binding for state tax purposes, a number of state courts have held that state tax administrators have the authority to make adjustments to amounts *reported* for federal income tax purposes. For example, in holding that the state taxing authority properly disallowed, for state tax purposes, a deduction for contingent liabilities that the taxpayer had taken on his federal tax return in determining his federal adjusted gross income, on which the Maine tax is based, the Maine Supreme Judicial Court said:

> The Assessor's audit power includes the authority to interpret the applicable federal tax provisions and ensure that the taxpayer reports a federal adjusted gross income figure that comports with federal law. Section 5121 [of the Maine statutes] expressly requires a taxpayer to report a legally accurate federal adjusted gross income. Interpreting section 5121 to require the Assessor to accept the federal adjusted income figure *as reported* on the taxpayer's state tax return would contradict section 5121's express language in cases when that figure is contrary to federal law. Moreover, such an interpretation would unduly restrict the Assessor's audit powers and render him powerless to correct a fraudulent or erroneously reported federal adjusted gross income figure.

Williams v. State Tax Assessor, 812 A.2d 245, 248–249 (Me. 2002) (emphasis in original); see also Maxitrol Co. v. Department of Treasury, 217 Mich.App. 366, 551 N.W.2d 471 (1996) (state tax administrator has authority to assess validity of taxpayer's claimed federal deductions).

B. DETERMINATION OF RESIDENCE FOR STATE TAX PURPOSES

The states possess (and generally exercise) the power to tax the personal income of their residents regardless of its source. They are constitutionally restrained, however, from taxing the income of nonresidents except insofar as it is derived from sources within the state. The determination of a taxpayer's residence is therefore a crucial factor in delimiting the extent of a taxpayer's personal income tax liability.

NOTES AND QUESTIONS

A. *The Definition of Resident Under State Income Tax Laws.* Altman and Keesling classify the definitions of "residence" used by the states as including one or more of five concepts:

(1) Domicile;

(2) Presence in the state for other than a temporary or transitory purpose;

(3) Presence in the state for a specified period of time—either six, seven or nine months;

(4) Maintenance of a permanent place of abode or a place of abode for a specified period of time; and

(5) A combination of (3) and (4), i.e., presence in the state for a specified period of time accompanied by the maintenance of a permanent place of abode.

George T. Altman & Frank M. Keesling, Allocation of Income in State Taxation 43 (2d ed. 1950).

The definition of resident includes "domicile" in most states. Some states, however, exclude from the definition of "resident" persons domiciled in the state provided they meet other qualifications.[g] The Restatement of Conflicts defines domicile as "a place, usually person's home, to which the rules of Conflict of Laws sometimes accord significance because of the person's identification with that place." The Restatement goes on to note that "[e]very person has a domicil at all times and, at least for the same purpose, no person has more than one domicil at a time."[h]

Where a person is domiciled is principally a question of fact, although the elements to be considered in locating a domicile present a question of law. The cases addressing the question whether a taxpayer is domiciled in a state are legion, and they generally focus on the objective indicia of the taxpayer's subjective intention to make a particular state her home. These include such factors as the extent to which the taxpayer is physically present in the state; the nature and locations of the taxpayer's abodes, especially the one in which her family resides; whether the taxpayer owns property in the state; the state in which the taxpayer votes, registers her car, maintains her bank accounts; and the state in which the taxpayer maintains club memberships, seeks professional services (medical, legal, accounting), and establishes professional and social relationships.

The factors that generally determine residence apart from domicile—presence in the state for more than a temporary purpose or for a specific length of time and maintenance of a permanent abode in the state—overlap with some of the factors that determine whether a taxpayer is domiciled in the state, but they can provide an independent basis for finding that a taxpayer is a state resident. For example, under the New York statute, cited above, a taxpayer may be a statutory resident, whose income is subject to tax regardless of source, if the taxpayer either is domiciled in the state or spends more than 183 days in the state and maintains a permanent abode in the state.

Suppose a New York investment banker, who is domiciled in New Jersey, is a New York resident by virtue of the fact that she spends more than 183 days in New York and maintains a permanent abode there. If every state (including New Jersey) adopted such a statute, the taxpayer would plainly be subject to multiple taxation that an investment banker confining all of her activity to a single state would avoid, at least in the absence of a credit for taxes paid to other states. Does this violate the Due Process Clause? See Sections C and D infra. Does it violate the Commerce Clause and its "internal consistency" test? See Chapter 3, pp. 145–48 supra. In answering the latter question, you must first resolve the question whether the taxpayer's complaint implicates the Commerce Clause at all. See Luther v. Commissioner of Revenue, 588 N.W.2d 502 (Minn.), cert. denied, 528 U.S. 821, 120 S.Ct. 66 (1999) (Commerce Clause, not implicated by allegedly internally inconsistent definition of resident); Tamagni v. New York State Tax Tribunal, 91 N.Y.2d

---

g. See, e.g., N.Y. Tax Law § 605(b) (Westlaw 2009) (excluding from definition of resident a person domiciled in the state except those who (1) retain no permanent abode in the state (2) retain a permanent abode elsewhere, and (3) spend 30 days or less in the state); Pa. Stat. Ann. tit. 72, § 7301(p) (Westlaw 2009) (same).

h. Restatement (Second) of Conflicts § 11(1) (1969).

530, 695 N.E.2d 1125, 673 N.Y.S.2d 44, cert. denied, 525 U.S. 931, 119 S.Ct. 340 (1998) (same); p. 144 supra (discussing this aspect of *Luther* and *Tamagni*). Does the applicability of the Commerce Clause depend on whether the taxpayer's difficulty is traceable, on the one hand, to the demands of her business that she be in New York or, on the other hand, to her personal choice to live in New Jersey? How would you resolve that question? Does the provision of a credit for taxes paid to other states (see Section H infra) remove the "internal consistency" problem in any event? See generally Note, "Resident Taxpayers: Internal Consistency, Due Process, and State Income Taxation," 91 Colum. L. Rev. 119 (1991).

B. *The Constitutionality of Double Taxation Based on Inconsistent Determinations of Domicile.* In Texas v. Florida, 306 U.S. 398, 59 S.Ct. 563 (1938), the Court noted: "That two or more States may each constitutionally assess death taxes on a decedent's intangibles upon a judicial determination that the decedent was domiciled within it in proceedings binding upon the representatives of the estate * * * is an established principle of our federal jurisprudence." Id., 306 U.S. at 410. Moreover, the Court has observed that "[n]either the Fourteenth Amendment nor the full faith and credit clause requires uniformity of different states as to the place of domicile, where the exertion of state power is dependent upon domicile within its boundaries." Worcester County Trust Co. v. Riley, 302 U.S. 292, 299, 58 S.Ct. 185 (1937). The same doctrine presumably applies to double taxation of personal income based on inconsistent determinations of domicile.

The result of such a doctrine as applied to personal income and death taxes can be harsh and oppressive. The situation is further exacerbated by the fact that residence in addition to domicile may provide a basis for taxing all of a taxpayer's income (see Note A supra; Section C infra), and the definition of residence may vary from state to state. The Court could resolve this issue more equitably by holding that, under the Due Process Clause, only one state possesses the extraordinary power of taxing all of a taxpayer's income or intangibles. See Section C infra. The issue of "domicile" or "residence," whichever test were used, would then become a constitutional question, and only one state would be able to tax all a taxpayer's income wherever earned or his intangibles wherever located. Justice Powell espoused this position in his dissenting opinion in Cory v. White, 457 U.S. 85, 97–102, 102 S.Ct. 2325 (1982).

C. *Residence of Military Personnel.* Section 514 of the Soldiers and Sailors Relief Act of 1940, 50 U.S.C. App. § 574, provides:

For the purposes of taxation in respect of any person, or of his personal property, income or gross income, by any State, * * * such person shall not be deemed to have lost a residence or domicile in any State * * * solely by reason of being absent therefrom in compliance with military or naval orders, or to have become resident in, or resident of, any other State * * * while, and solely, by reason of being so absent. For purposes of taxation in respect of the * * * income or gross income of any such person by any State * * * of which a person is not a resident or in which he is not domiciled, compensation for military or naval service shall not be deemed income for services performed within, or from sources, within, such State * * *.

The normal rules that apply to determining the residence of most taxpayers therefore do not apply to service personnel when they are stationed in particular states pursuant to military orders. Taxpayers who would normally be deemed residents under typical provisions defining a resident as one who maintains a physical presence in the state for an extended period may not, under the federal statute, be treated as residents simply because of their presence in the state.[i] The effect is to prohibit the state in which the serviceman is stationed from taxing him on income earned from sources outside the state, including income from intangibles. Moreover, the normal rules that apply to taxing the income of nonresidents do not apply to the compensation of military personnel. While nonresidents are normally taxable on their compensation earned within the state, nonresident service personnel may not be taxed on such income. Consequently, states in which nonresident service personnel are stationed are confined to taxing them on non-compensation income derived from sources within the state.

As a result of the Soldiers and Sailors Relief Act, a disproportionate number of the nation's military personnel claim legal residence in states that do not tax personal income. Once stationed in a state like Texas or Florida, which do not tax such income, military personnel tend to claim the state as their permanent residence thus shielding some, if not all, of their personal income from taxation even upon future changes in duty stations. According to a report of the General Accounting Office, 52 percent of generals and admirals, 58 percent of colonels, lieutenant colonels, and majors, and 43 percent of senior sergeants claimed their legal residence in states that did not tax income, even though only 13, 21, and 25 percent of the respective categories of personnel were actually stationed in those states.[j] While the federal statute provides that military personnel will not be deemed to have abandoned their former domicile and acquired a new domicile *solely* by reason of their presence in a state pursuant to military orders, if a servicewoman in fact intends to make her present duty station her permanent home, she may be found to be a domiciliary in the state in which she is currently stationed.

Do you regard the claim by military personnel that they are domiciliaries of states like Texas and Florida an abuse of the statutory protection that Congress provided them in the Soldiers and Sailors Relief Act? If so, how would you amend the statute to curb that abuse while still serving the purpose for which it was designed? Do you think such an amendment would command widespread support in Congress?

---

i. The states do not appear to have adopted the converse of this proposition, namely, treating as residents taxpayers who are absent from the state solely by reason of military orders. In many states, such taxpayers would normally be deemed *not* to be residents under provisions that exclude from the definition of residents taxpayers maintaining no permanent physical presence in the state. Cf. Ryan v. Chapman, 273 App.Div. 99, 76 N.Y.S.2d 341 (3d Dep't 1948) (commissioned army officer who was domiciled in New York but was stationed in California was not a resident for state tax purposes).

j. The New York Times, Nov. 3, 1987, p. A9, col. 1.

C. THE TAXATION OF INCOME OF RESIDENTS

1. STATE POWER TO TAX RESIDENTS' INCOME REGARDLESS OF ITS SOURCE

The states' constitutional power to tax residents on all their personal income regardless of its source is well established. In Oklahoma Tax Comm'n v. Chickasaw Nation, 515 U.S. 450, 115 S.Ct. 2214 (1995), the Court referred to the "well established principle of interstate and international taxation—namely, that a jurisdiction, such as Oklahoma, may tax *all* the income of its residents, even income earned outside the taxing jurisdiction." Id., 515 U.S. at 463 (emphasis in original). The Court had earlier made it clear that residence in a state provides a sufficient basis under the Due Process Clause to permit a state to tax all of the resident's income without regard to source:

> That the receipt of income by a resident of the territory of a taxing sovereignty is a taxable event is universally recognized. Domicil itself affords a basis for such taxation. Enjoyment of the privileges of residence in the state and the attendant right to invoke the protection of its laws are inseparable from responsibility for sharing the costs of government. "Taxes are what we pay for civilized society ...," see Compania Gen. de Tabacos v. Collector, 275 U.S. 87, 100, 48 S.Ct. 100. A tax measured by the net income of residents is an equitable method of distributing the burdens of government among those who are privileged to enjoy its benefits. The tax, which is apportioned to the ability of the taxpayer to pay it, is founded upon the protection afforded by the state to the recipient of the income in his person, in his right to receive the income and in his enjoyment of it when received. These are rights and privileges which attach to domicil within the state. To them and to the equitable distribution of the tax burden, the economic advantage realized by the receipt of income and represented by the power to control it, bears a direct relationship.
>
> Neither the privilege nor the burden is affected by the character of the source from which the income is derived. For that reason income is not necessarily clothed with the tax immunity enjoyed by its source. A state may tax its residents upon net income from a business whose physical assets, located wholly without the state, are beyond its taxing power. It may tax net income from bonds held in trust and administered in another state, although the taxpayer's equitable interest may not be subjected to the tax. It may tax net income from operations in interstate commerce, although a tax on the commerce is forbidden. Congress may lay a tax on net income derived from the business of exporting merchandise in foreign commerce, although a tax upon articles exported is prohibited by constitutional provision (Art. I, § 9, Cl. 5).

New York ex rel. Cohn v. Graves, 300 U.S. 308, 312–13, 57 S.Ct. 466 (1937).

Notes and Questions

A. *Rentals from Out-of-State Realty.* In New York ex rel. Cohn v. Graves, supra, the Court upheld an income tax on a resident, which included rentals from out-of-state real estate. In so holding, the Court rejected "the contention that a tax on income is a tax on the land which produces it," id., 300 U.S. at 313, and continued:

> The incidence of a tax on income differs from that of a tax on property. Neither tax is dependent upon the possession by the taxpayer of the subject of the other. His income may be taxed, although he owns no property, and his property may be taxed, although it produces no income. The two taxes are measured by different standards, the one by the amount of income received over a period of time, the other by the value of the property at a particular date. Income is taxed but once; the same property may be taxed recurrently. The tax on each is predicated upon different governmental benefits; the protection offered to the property in one state does not extend to the receipt and enjoyment of income from it in another.
>
> It would be pressing the protection which the due process clause throws around the taxpayer too far to say that because a state is prohibited from taxing land which it neither protects nor controls, it is likewise prohibited from taxing the receipt and command of income from the land by its resident, who is subject to its control and enjoys the benefits of its laws. The imposition of these different taxes, by the same or different states, upon these distinct and separable taxable interests, is not subject to the objection of double taxation, which has been successfully urged in those cases where two or more states have laid the same tax upon the same property interest in intangibles or upon its transfer at death. * * * These considerations lead to the conclusion that income derived from real estate may be taxed to the recipient at the place of his domicil, irrespective of the location of the land, and that the state court rightly upheld the tax.
>
> Nothing which was said or decided in Pollock v. Farmers' Loan & Trust Co., 157 U.S. 429, 15 S.Ct. 673, calls for a different conclusion. There the question for decision was whether a federal tax on income derived from rents of land is a direct tax requiring apportionment under Art. I, § 2, Cl. 3, of the Constitution. In holding that the tax was "direct," the Court did not rest its decision upon the ground that the tax was a tax on the land, or that it was subject to every limitation which the Constitution imposes on property taxes. It determined only that for purposes of apportionment there were similarities in the operation of the two kinds of tax which made it appropriate to classify both as direct, and within the constitutional command.

Id. at 313–15.

B. *Income From Services Rendered Outside the State*. In Lawrence v. State Tax Commission, 286 U.S. 276, 52 S.Ct. 556 (1932), a Mississippi resident who earned income from building highways in Tennessee contended that Mississippi's taxation of such income violated the Due Process Clause, because the tax was imposed on income from activities carried on wholly outside the state. The Court responded:

> The obligation of one domiciled within a state to pay taxes there, arises from unilateral action of the state government in the exercise of the most plenary of sovereign powers, that to raise revenue to defray the expenses of government and to distribute its burdens equally among those who enjoy its benefits. Hence, domicile in itself establishes a basis for taxation.* * *

> * * *

> It is enough, so far as the constitutional power of the state to levy it is concerned, that the tax is imposed by Mississippi on its own citizens with reference to the receipt and enjoyment of income derived from the conduct of business, regardless of the place where it is carried on.

Id., 286 U.S. at 279–80.

2. STATE STATUTORY TREATMENT OF RESIDENTS' PERSONAL INCOME

Most states with broad-based personal income taxes impose their levies on all of a resident's income wherever earned. To avoid double taxation of their residents' income that is attributable to and taxed in other states, all states with broad-based personal income taxes provide a credit for taxes paid by their residents to other states.[k] In some instances, states have not exerted their full constitutional power over residents' personal income and have excluded from the resident personal income tax base specific items of income attributable to out-of-state property or activities. Oklahoma, for example, does not tax residents on income from real or tangible personal property or from business carried on in other states.[l]

D. THE TAXATION OF INCOME OF NONRESIDENTS

1. STATE POWER TO TAX NONRESIDENTS' INCOME FROM SOURCES WITHIN THE STATE

The seminal cases sustaining the states' power to tax nonresidents on income derived from sources within the state were decided on the same

---

k.   See All States Tax Guide (RIA) ¶ 236–A (2009) (chart), available at www.checkpoint.riag.com.

l.   Okla. Stat. Ann. tit. 68, § 2358(A)(4) (Westlaw 2009).

day in 1920. In Shaffer v. Carter, 252 U.S. 37, 40 S.Ct. 221 (1920), the Court sustained an Oklahoma income tax on income derived by a nonresident individual from the ownership and operation of oil- and gas-producing properties and oil and gas leases located in the state. Emphasizing the nature of the tax as a levy on income and not property, the taxpayer had contended that because he conducted the business at his office in Illinois, Oklahoma could not tax him on his income. The Court responded:

> [W]e deem it clear, upon principle as well as authority, that just as a State may impose general income taxes upon its own citizens and residents whose persons are subject to its control, it may, as a necessary consequence, levy a duty of like character, and not more onerous in its effect, upon incomes accruing to nonresidents from their property or business within the State, or their occupations carried on therein.

Id., 252 U.S. at 52. As the Court's statement implies, however, a state's power to tax nonresidents is more limited than its power to tax residents:

> As to residents it may, and does, exert its taxing power over their income from all sources, whether within or without the State. * * * As to nonresidents, the jurisdiction extends only to their property owned within the State and their business, trade, or profession carried on therein, and the tax is only on such income as is derived from those sources.

Id. at 57.

In the companion case of Travis v. Yale & Towne Manufacturing Co., 252 U.S. 60, 40 S.Ct. 228 (1920), the issue was New York's power to tax the wages and salaries of nonresident employees working in New York. The taxpayer had argued that a state lacks jurisdiction to tax the income of nonresidents from business or occupations conducted within its borders, as distinguished from income derived from property located in the state, whose taxability it conceded. In Shaffer v. Carter, the Court put the contentions made in *Yale & Towne* as follows:

> [I]t was contended, in substance, that while a State may tax the property of a nonresident situate within its borders, or may tax the incomes of its own citizens and residents because of the privileges they enjoy under its constitution and laws and the protection they receive from the State, yet a nonresident, although conducting a business or carrying on an occupation there, cannot be required through income taxation to contribute to the governmental expenses of the State whence his income is derived; that an income tax, as against nonresidents, is not only not a property tax but is not an excise or privilege tax, since no privilege is granted; the right of the noncitizen to carry on his business or occupation in the taxing State being derived, it is said, from the provisions of the federal Constitution.

Shaffer v. Carter, supra, 252 U.S. at 49–50.

The Court summarily rejected this view of state taxing power, declaring:

> This radical contention is easily answered by reference to fundamental principles. In our system of government the States have general dominion, and, saving as restricted by particular provisions of the Federal Constitution, complete dominion over all persons, property, and business transactions within their borders; they assume and perform the duty of preserving and protecting all such persons, property, and business, and, in consequence, have the power normally pertaining to governments to resort to all reasonable forms of taxation in order to defray the governmental expenses. Certainly they are not restricted to property taxation, nor to any particular form of excises. In well-ordered society, property has value chiefly for what it is capable of producing, and the activities of mankind are devoted largely to making recurrent gains from the use and development of property, from tillage, mining, manufacture, from the employment of human skill and labor, or from a combination of some of these; gains capable of being devoted to their own support, and the surplus accumulated as an increase of capital. That the State, from whose laws property and business and industry derive the protection and security without which production and gainful occupation would be impossible, is debarred from exacting a share of those gains in the form of income taxes for the support of the government, is a proposition so wholly inconsistent with fundamental principles as to be refuted by its mere statement.

Id. at 50.

NOTES AND QUESTIONS

A. *Due Process Clause Limitations on Double Taxation of Personal Income on the Basis of Residence and Source.* As we observed in Chapter 2 dealing with the general principles underlying jurisdiction to tax income, the existence of the power to tax on the basis of residence (see Section C supra) coupled with the power to tax on the basis of source can lead to double taxation. See pp. 65–67 supra. It is well established, however, that the Due Process Clause imposes no restraints on such double taxation. See Curry v. McCanless, 307 U.S. 357, 368, 59 S.Ct. 900 (1939) ("income may be taxed both by the state where it is earned and by the state of the recipient's domicile. Protection, benefit, and power over the subject matter are not confined to either state."); Guaranty Trust Co. v. Virginia, 305 U.S. 19, 22–23, 59 S.Ct. 1 (1938) (Due Process Clause does not bar multiple taxation of income from trust). To deal with the problem of double taxation resulting from the overlapping claims of power to tax on the basis of residence and source, all states with broad-based personal income taxes provide a credit for taxes paid by their residents to other states. See Section H infra.

B. *Commerce Clause Limitations on Double Taxation of Personal Income on the Basis of Residence and Source.* Despite the absence of any due process objection to double taxation of personal income resulting from the overlapping claims of states that seek to tax on the basis of both residence and source, can one successfully argue that the Commerce Clause nevertheless bars such taxation? See Chapter 3 supra. Does the answer to this question depend on the precise cause of the double taxation, cf. Section B, Note A, pp. 351–53 supra, or on the nature of the income that is exposed to double taxation? If the Commerce Clause bars a state from taxing a domiciliary corporation on all of its income on a residence basis when another state possesses the power to tax the same corporation on an apportioned share of its income on a source basis, see pp. 65–67 supra and pp. 73–89 infra, why would it not likewise prevent a state from taxing an individual resident on all of her income on a residence basis when another state possesses the power to tax the resident on a portion of her income on a source basis? The practical significance of this question may be limited by the fact that resident states provide credits for taxes paid to other states (see Note A supra), but is the question completely academic? See Sections G and H infra (discussing credits for income taxes paid to other states and the limitations on the availability of such credits).

In thinking about the response to the last question, consider the following: A taxpayer, T, residing in State A makes a loan secured by property located in State B. The mortgagor pays interest on the loan to T in State A. Is the interest on the mortgage taxable by State A or State B or both? Suppose that T conducts an active mortgage loan business in State C, negotiating the loans there and receiving interest there. May State C tax the mortgage interest?

C. *Profit Derived by Nonresident From Sale of a "Right" to Seat on Stock Exchange Located in the State.* T, a broker residing in Massachusetts, owned a seat on the New York Stock Exchange. His firm used the seat to enable it to effect sales on the Exchange at reduced commission rates for members. Neither T nor his firm had a New York office, and they carried on no business in New York, except for the operations through the Stock Exchange. When the number of Exchange seats was increased in 1929, each member obtained a "right" to one fourth of a new seat. T sold his "right." New York imposed an income tax on the sale, which the Court sustained over due process objections. The Court held that the "dominant feature" of the seat was the "privilege of conducting the business of buying and selling securities on the floor of the Exchange," which "localizes it at the Exchange." New York ex rel. Whitney v. Graves, 299 U.S. 366, 373, 57 S.Ct. 237 (1937). The *Whitney* case reflects the general rule that states may tax the income from intangibles owned by a nonresident if the intangibles are used in connection with a business in the state or have acquired a business situs there.

D. *Dividends Received by Nonresident Shareholder from Corporation Doing Business in the State.* In International Harvester Co. v. Wisconsin Department of Taxation, 322 U.S. 435, 64 S.Ct. 1060 (1944), Wisconsin imposed a tax "[f]or the privilege of declaring and receiving dividends, out of income derived from property located and business transacted in this state * * *" Wis. Stat. § 71.60 (1941), quoted in id., 322 U.S. at 446. The tax was measured by the proportion of the corporation's dividends attributable to Wisconsin, determined by applying its corporate income tax apportionment percentage to the dividends. The dividend payors were required to deduct the tax from the dividends payable to both resident and nonresident shareholders. Because of this withholding provision, the Court had previously sustained the levy on the ground that "the practical operation of the tax is to impose an additional tax on corporate earnings within Wisconsin, but to postpone the liability for payment of the tax until such earnings are paid out in dividends." Wisconsin v. J.C. Penney Co., 311 U.S. 435, 442, 61 S.Ct. 246 (1940). The Wisconsin courts, however, subsequently construed the state taxing statute as imposing the levy upon the shareholders. In *International Harvester*, the Court revisited the constitutional questions raised by the tax on the assumption

> that the statute, by directing deduction of the tax from declared dividends, distributes the tax burden among the stockholders differently than if the corporation had merely paid the tax from its treasury *and that the tax is thus in point of substance, laid upon and paid by the stockholders* * * *.

Id. at 440 (emphasis supplied).

International Harvester challenged the statute on the ground that it violated the Due Process Clause by taxing (1) the act of declaring dividends and (2) the act of receiving dividends, both of which occurred outside Wisconsin, since Harvester declared its dividends in Chicago and 98 percent of its shareholders were nonresidents of Wisconsin. Id. at 446 (Jackson, J., dissenting). The Court rejected this claim and sustained the tax in liberal terms:

> The power to impose a tax on the corporation's earnings includes the power to postpone the tax until the distribution of those earnings, and to measure it by the amounts distributed. In taxing such distributions, Wisconsin may impose the burden of the tax either upon the corporation or upon the stockholders who derive the ultimate benefit from the corporation's Wisconsin activities. Personal residence within the state of the stockholders-taxpayers is not essential to the constitutional levy of a tax out of so much of the corporation's Wisconsin earnings as is distributed to them. A state may tax such part of the income of a non-resident as is fairly attributable either to property located in the state or to events or transactions which, occurring there, are subject to state regulation and which are within the protection of the state and entitled to the numerous other benefits which it confers. And the privilege of receiving dividends derived from corporate activities within the state can have no greater immunity than the privilege of receiving any other income from sources there.

Id. at 441–42.

Wisconsin had plainly afforded "protection and benefits to appellants' corporate activities and transactions within the state." Id. at 442. Accordingly, Wisconsin was entitled to tax the dividends because "[t]hese activities have given rise to the dividend income of appellants' stockholders and this income fairly measures the benefits they have derived from these Wisconsin activities." Id. Finally, so long as the earnings actually arose in the state, the fact that "some practically effective device [may] be necessary in order to enable the state to collect the tax—here by imposing on the corporation the duty to withhold" (id. at 444)**ᵐ**—did not deprive the state of power to impose the levy on the nonresident shareholder.

Suppose Wisconsin had not provided for withholding of the dividend tax by the corporate payor. Could it have enforced its right to tax the income that an out-of-state investor derives from her investment in a corporation doing business in the state? In the absence of voluntary compliance, how would the state collect the tax? By a default judgment, based on the out-of-state investor's failure to pay the tax due? But would Wisconsin have jurisdiction over the out-of-state investor? Cf. Quill Corp. v. North Dakota, 504 U.S. 298, 112 S.Ct. 1904 (1992), pp. 24–38 supra; Geoffrey, Inc. v. State Tax Commission, 313 S.C. 15, 437 S.E.2d 13, cert. denied, 510 U.S. 992, 114 S.Ct. 550 (1993), pp. 68–76 supra. If not, is it proper for Wisconsin to collect a tax due from a nonresident investor over whom it has no personal jurisdiction? It may be worth observing that the taxpayer in *International Harvester* rested entirely on the Due Process Clause, without invoking the Commerce Clause. For a detailed consideration of the questions raised by *International Harvester*, see Walter Hellerstein, "State Taxation of Corporate Income From Intangibles: *Allied–Signal* and Beyond," 48 Tax L. Rev. 739, 824–26 n.446 (1993).

2. APPLICATION OF THE SOURCE PRINCIPLE: STATUTORY AND CONSTITUTIONAL ISSUES

Most state personal income tax statutes reflect the constitutional restraints on the states' power to tax nonresidents' income and are therefore limited to income derived from sources within the state. The California personal income tax, for example, is imposed on nonresidents' income "derived from sources within this state." Cal. Rev. & Tax. Code § 17041(i) (Westlaw 2009). The New York statute applies to nonresidents' income "derived from or connected with New York sources." N.Y. Tax Law § 631 (Westlaw 2009). In elaborating on the concept of income derived from sources within the state, the state statutes typically point to income derived from compensation earned in the state, services performed in the state, trade or business carried on in the state, or property located in the state. See, e.g., Ga. Code Ann. § 48–7–20 (Westlaw 2009); N.J. Stat. Ann. § 54A:5–8(a) (Westlaw 2009); N.C. Gen. Stat. § 105–134.5(b) (Westlaw 2009). As the following cases and materials reveal, the issues arising in connection with the application of the state statutory rules to nonresidents' personal income are often intertwined with the constitutional restraints on the states' power to tax such income.

---

m. Wisconsin's taxing scheme was thus analogous to the federal scheme for taxing U.S. source interest, dividends, rents, annuities and "other fixed or determinable annual or periodical gains, profits, and income" earned by nonresident alien individuals or by foreign corporations. I.R.C. §§ 871, 881. The Internal Revenue Code imposes a 30 percent tax on such income, which is withheld by the U.S. payor. I.R.C. §§ 1441, 1442.

ZELINSKY v. TAX APPEALS TRIBUNAL OF THE STATE OF NEW YORK

Court of Appeals of New York, 2003.
1 N.Y.3d 85, 801 N.E.2d 840, 769 N.Y.S.2d 464, cert.
denied, 541 U.S. 1009, 124 S.Ct. 2068 (2004).

KAYE, CHIEF JUDGE.

The taxpayer, a professor at Cardozo School of Law in New York City, contends that New York State may not constitutionally tax the entirety of his income because he performed some of his work at his home in Connecticut. We disagree and uphold the challenged tax.

I.

During the academic semesters in 1994 and 1995, petitioner-taxpayer commuted to New York three days each work week to teach his classes and meet with students. On the other two days, he stayed at home, where he prepared examinations, wrote student recommendations, and conducted scholarly research and writing. When school was not in session, and during his sabbatical leave in the fall semester of 1995, he worked exclusively at home.

On the 1994 and 1995 New York State nonresident income tax returns filed jointly by the taxpayer and his wife, he apportioned to New York the percentage of his total salary that reflected the number of days he commuted to the law school, allocating the remainder to Connecticut. The New York State Department of Taxation and Finance issued notices of deficiency for both years, maintaining that the entire law school salary was subject to taxation by New York. Applying the "convenience of the employer" test, the Department determined that the days that the taxpayer worked at his Connecticut residence should be counted as New York work days because he stayed at home for his own convenience and was not obligated by his employer to work outside New York. The portion of his salary that he allocated to the days he worked at home was also taxed by Connecticut, which did not provide a credit for the taxes assessed by New York.

Petitioner contested the deficiencies and also sought a refund for taxes paid on salary earned during his sabbatical leave, which he had forgotten to allocate to Connecticut. He claimed, as he does now, that application of the convenience of the employer test to him, resulting in New York's taxation of salary earned on the days he worked at home, violates the Commerce and Due Process Clauses of the Federal Constitution. An Administrative Law Judge rejected those constitutional challenges, as did the Tax Appeals Tribunal. The taxpayer then commenced an article 78 proceeding in the Appellate Division, pursuant to Tax Law § 2016. The Appellate Division confirmed the administrative determination and dismissed the petition. We now affirm.

II.

Although a state may tax all the income of its residents, even income earned outside the taxing jurisdiction, it may constitutionally tax nonresidents only on their income derived from sources within the state (see Shaffer v. Carter, 252 U.S. 37, 57, 40 S.Ct. 221 [1920]). In New York, the income of nonresidents is thus taxed by the State if it is "derived from or connected with New York sources" (see Tax Law § 601[e][1]; § 631[a][1]).[2] New York source income includes income attributable to a business, trade, profession or occupation carried on in this state (see Tax Law § 631[b][1][B]). When a nonresident works partly in New York and partly in another state, the New York source income must be determined by apportionment and allocation according to regulations of the Commissioner of Taxation and Finance (see Tax Law § 631[c]).

The Commissioner's regulations generally provide that if a nonresident employee performs services for an employer both within and without New York State, the portion of his or her income derived from New York sources, and thus apportioned and allocated to New York, consists of the ratio of total days worked in New York to total days worked both in and out of the state (see 20 NYCRR 132.18[a]). Such apportionment and allocation, however, are limited by the convenience of the employer test, which states that "any allowance claimed for days worked outside New York State must be based upon the performance of services which of necessity, as distinguished from convenience, obligate the employee to out-of-state duties in the service of his employer" (20 NYCRR 132.18[a]).[3] Accordingly, nonresidents employed in New York who work at home when not required to do so by their employers must treat those days as if they had been present at their workstation in New York, resulting in New York source income. That is the proposition being tested by the present appeal.

III.

Although the dormant Commerce Clause limits the power of states to erect barriers against interstate trade, a challenged tax will generally satisfy constitutional requirements if it "is applied to an activity with a substantial nexus with the taxing State, is fairly apportioned, does not discriminate against interstate commerce, and is fairly related to the services provided by the State" (Complete Auto Tr., Inc. v. Brady, 430 U.S. 274, 279, 97 S.Ct. 1076 [1977]).

Here, the taxpayer challenges only the second prong of this four-part test—that the tax be fairly apportioned—conceding that the remaining three criteria are met. The central purposes of the fair apportionment requirement are "to ensure that each State taxes only its fair share of an interstate transaction" (Goldberg v. Sweet, 488 U.S. 252, 260–261, 109 S.Ct. 582 [1989]) and to "minimize the likelihood that an interstate transaction will be improperly burdened by multiple taxation" (Tennessee Gas Pipeline Co. v. Urbach, 96 N.Y.2d 124, 133, 726 N.Y.S.2d 350, 750 N.E.2d 52 [2001]).

---

2. New York residents, by contrast, are taxed on their worldwide income (see Tax Law § 611[a]; § 612[a]; Internal Revenue Code [26 USC] § 61[a]; § 62[a]).

3. The "convenience of the employer" would therefore more aptly be called the "necessity of the employer" test.

A tax is fairly apportioned if it is both internally and externally consistent. To be internally consistent, the tax must be structured so that if every state were to impose an identical tax, no multiple taxation would result. Here, the taxpayer concedes that if Connecticut were to adopt the convenience of the employer test, he would not be subject to double taxation, because in that case Connecticut, after initially taxing the worldwide income of its resident, would provide a credit for the taxes paid to New York for the days he worked at home for his own convenience. His sole claim, therefore, is that the challenged tax is not externally consistent.

External consistency looks "to the economic justification for the State's claim upon the value taxed, to discover whether a State's tax reaches beyond that portion of value that is fairly attributable to economic activity within the taxing State.... [T]he threat of real multiple taxation ... may indicate a State's impermissible overreaching" (Oklahoma Tax Commn. v. Jefferson Lines, Inc., 514 U.S. 175, 185, 115 S.Ct. 1331 [1995] [internal citations omitted]). External consistency is "essentially a practical inquiry" (Goldberg, 488 U.S. at 264, 109 S.Ct. 582) for determining "whether the State has taxed only that portion of the revenues from the interstate activity which reasonably reflects the in-state component of the activity being taxed" (id. at 262, 109 S.Ct. 582). No particular apportionment formula or method need be used to satisfy constitutional requirements, "and when a State has chosen one, an objecting taxpayer has the burden to demonstrate 'by clear and cogent evidence' that 'the income attributed to the State is in fact out of all appropriate proportions to the business transacted ... in that State, or has led to a grossly distorted result'" (Jefferson Lines, 514 U.S. at 195, 115 S.Ct. 1331, quoting Moorman Mfg. Co. v. Bair, 437 U.S. 267, 274, 98 S.Ct. 2340 [1978] [other internal quotation marks omitted]).

IV.

In applying these principles, we need decide only whether the convenience of the employer test is constitutional as applied to the facts of this case. The convenience test was originally adopted to prevent abuses arising from commuters who spent an hour working at home every Saturday and Sunday and then claimed that two sevenths of their work days were non-New York days and that two sevenths of their income was thus non-New York income, and either free of tax (if the state of their residence had no income tax) or subject to a lower rate than New York's.[4] In the present case, the taxpayer's efforts to reduce the amount of tax owed to New York on his New York source income earned during the work week raise similar concerns.[5]

---

4. Of course, in the absence of the convenience test, opportunities for fraud are great and administrative difficulties in verifying whether an employee has actually performed a full day's work while at home are readily apparent.

5. We reject his claim that the convenience test no longer has any justifiable basis because Connecticut has since 1991 imposed an income tax. Insofar as the test "serves to protect the integrity of the apportionment scheme by including income as taxable" when the income results

We note at the outset that many busy professionals, at the conclusion of a full day, routinely bring work home for the evenings or weekends. Even when undertaken by an out-of-state commuter such as petitioner, this work cannot transform employment that takes place wholly within New York into an interstate business activity subject to the Commerce Clause. Cardozo Law School provides educational services to its students in New York City, which is where the taxpayer performs the primary duties of his occupation—teaching classes and meeting with students. The work he chooses to do at home is thus inextricably intertwined with the business of his New York law school, and cannot convert his employer's New York business into an interstate one when Cardozo did not employ him to carry out any of the school's business activities in Connecticut.

The taxpayer's reliance on City of New York v. State of New York, 94 N.Y.2d 577, 709 N.Y.S.2d 122, 730 N.E.2d 920 [2000] is therefore misplaced. In that case, we rejected the claim that a tax on out-of-state commuters did not implicate the Commerce Clause, explaining that the commute of tens of thousands of out-of-state residents "into New York City on a daily basis, earning and spending part of their income in New York City, while paying the commuter tax" clearly impacted interstate commerce (94 N.Y.2d at 597, 709 N.Y.S.2d 122, 730 N.E.2d 920). The critical distinction between *City of New York* and the instant case, however, is that in *City of New York*, the tax at issue was imposed on the activity of commuting, not on the individual as a commuter. Here, the tax is imposed on income derived from the activity of teaching, not on the individual who is reading in his study in Connecticut.

Nor can petitioner's circumstances be likened to the bus in Central Greyhound Lines of N.Y. v. Mealey, 334 U.S. 653, 68 S.Ct. 1260 [1948], where the Supreme Court struck down an unapportioned gross receipts tax imposed on the sale of transportation services between points within New York because the bus traveled in large part over routes using out-of-state highways. In *Central Greyhound*, the risk of multiple taxation imposed by each of the various states through which the bus of necessity passed unfairly burdened interstate commerce, which was clearly impacted by the interstate travel of the bus. Here, by contrast, all of petitioner's teaching is accomplished in New York and his voluntary choice to bring auxiliary work home to Connecticut cannot transform him into an interstate actor.

"The dormant Commerce Clause protects markets and participants in markets, not taxpayers as such" (General Motors Corp. v. Tracy, 519 U.S. 278, 300, 117 S.Ct. 811 [1997]). The taxpayer's crossing of state lines to do his work at home simply does not impact upon any interstate market in which residents and nonresidents compete so as to implicate the Commerce Clause. On these facts, the convenience of the employer test neither

from services derived from New York sources but performed out-of-state "to effect a subterfuge" (Matter of Colleary v. Tully, 69 A.D.2d 922, 923, 415 N.Y.S.2d 266 [3d Dept.1979]), the same incentive for tax avoidance exists when, as here, a neighboring state imposes tax at a lower rate than New York as when the state imposes no income tax at all.

unfairly burdens interstate commerce nor discriminates against the free flow of goods in the marketplace. Nor does it result in differential treatment benefitting in-state interests at the expense of out-of-state interests. Rather, the convenience test serves merely to equalize tax obligations among residents and nonresidents, preventing nonresidents from manipulating their New York tax liability by choice of auxiliary work location in a manner unavailable to similarly situated New York resident employees. Since a New York resident would not be entitled to any special tax benefits for similar work performed at home, neither should a nonresident.

Allowing this taxpayer to allocate his income to Connecticut when he stays home to do his work in connection with his teaching activity would enable him to avoid paying taxes that his colleagues who do that work at home in New York—or at the law school—pay. The Constitution does not require that a nonresident who does not opt for the personal convenience of taking work home rather than traveling into work every day be taxed at a higher effective tax rate than one who does. The State need not subsidize such personal convenience, while at the same time discouraging commuting into New York City and facilitating erosion of the tax base.

Even presuming that petitioner's work at home sufficiently impacts upon interstate business activity as to implicate the Commerce Clause, because the entirety of the taxpayer's salary is derived from New York sources, New York's tax on his non-resident income is fairly apportioned. As a law professor, the taxpayer is primarily engaged in the business of teaching. It is for this that Cardozo hired him and for this that he is paid. It is thus readily apparent that he is not paid his salary in exchange for working five days per week, or three, or seven. Nor is he paid an hourly or daily wage. As long as his work is completed, he receives his full salary, whether he completes his work during the three days he comes to the office, or at home, or on the weekend. If he finishes all his work during the three days he commutes to the law school, and stays home without working on the other two days, he is paid no less. And if he ends up working five days a week in addition to every weekend, he is paid no more. From the perspective of his employer, as long as he performs his teaching responsibilities as scheduled, it matters not when or where he performs his ancillary functions.

The taxpayer is able to earn his salary—all of it—because of the benefits he receives every day from New York. He benefits directly from an employment opportunity and an office here. He benefits from a salary on every day that he works, which he is able to earn entirely within this state if he so chooses. As the Appellate Division noted, even his scholarly writings, drafted at home, attach prominence to his position as a professor at Cardozo Law School. New York thus provides a host of tangible and intangible protections, benefits and values to the taxpayer and his employer, including police, fire and emergency health services, and public utilities. Petitioner's election to absent himself from the locus of his New York employment does not diminish what New York provides in order to enable him to earn that income. New York may require contributions from him because he thus "realiz[ed] current pecuniary benefits under the protection of the government" (Shaffer v. Carter, 252 U.S. 37, 51, 40 S.Ct. 221 [1920]), and the tax imposed need not "bear an exact relation to the services actually provided to the individual taxpayer" (Matter of Tamagni v. Tax Appeals Trib., 91 N.Y.2d 530, 544, 673 N.Y.S.2d 44, 695 N.E.2d 1125 [1998]).

Nevertheless, petitioner maintains that a constitutional violation is evident because his income has been taxed by two jurisdictions. But the mere potential for or actual existence of double taxation does not automatically transgress the Commerce Clause if, as here, the challenged tax is in fact fairly apportioned. For as the Tax Appeals Tribunal recognized, it was his own choice to allocate his income that created the threat of double taxation, not the convenience rule.

In *Tamagni*, we upheld the application of New York's resident income tax to statutory residents of this state who, as domiciliaries of New Jersey, were subject to resident income tax in New Jersey on certain income also taxed by New York. Since each tax was permissibly imposed under a different theory—New York validly taxed its statutory residents and New Jersey validly taxed its domiciliaries—the New York tax did not violate the Commerce Clause, even though its effect was double taxation. Similarly, in the instant case, New York has validly taxed the income of a nonresident derived from New York sources, while Connecticut has, as it may, taxed the income of its resident.[7] "The multiple taxation placed upon interstate commerce by such a confluence of taxes is not a structural evil that flows from either tax individually, but it is rather the accidental incident of interstate commerce being subject to two different taxing jurisdictions" (Jefferson Lines, 514 U.S. at 192, 115 S.Ct. 1331 [citations and internal quotation marks omitted]).

Since the New York tax is fairly apportioned, the resultant double taxation does not serve to invalidate the tax. For while a state may indeed constitutionally tax the worldwide income of its residents, it will typically provide a credit for income tax paid to another state—as New York does. Here, it is Connecticut's refusal to provide a credit to its resident for all of the nonresident income tax that the taxpayer paid to New York that has created the threat of double taxation. It is not, however, the "purpose of the Commerce Clause to protect state residents from their own state taxes" (Goldberg, 488 U.S. at 266, 109 S.Ct. 582).

Since the New York tax imposed did not "reach[ ] beyond that portion of value ... fairly attributable to economic activity within the taxing State" (Jefferson Lines, 514 U.S. at 185, 115 S.Ct. 1331), the taxpayer has failed to demonstrate by clear and cogent evidence that the income attributed to New York was in fact out of all appropriate proportion to the business transacted here or has led to a grossly distorted result.

---

7. Connecticut may and does tax petitioner's income because he is its resident, not because two out of five of his work days were allegedly sourced in Connecticut.

V.

The Due Process Clause places two restrictions on a state's power to tax income generated by interstate activities. First, it "requires some definite link, some minimum connection, between a state and the person, property or transaction it seeks to tax" (Quill Corp. v. North Dakota, 504 U.S. 298, 306, 112 S.Ct. 1904 [1992] [citation omitted]). Second, the "income attributed to the State for tax purposes must be rationally related to values connected with the taxing State" (Moorman, 437 U.S. at 273, 98 S.Ct. 2340 [citation and internal quotation marks omitted]). A state, therefore, may not tax value earned outside its borders. Rather, the tax imposed must "bear[ ] fiscal relation" to "opportunities which [the state] has given, to protection which it has afforded, to benefits which it has conferred by the fact of being an orderly, civilized society.... The simple but controlling question is whether the state has given anything for which it can ask return" (Wisconsin v. J.C. Penney Co., 311 U.S. 435, 444, 61 S.Ct. 246 [1940]).

Here, petitioner—both because of his physical presence in New York and because he has "purposefully avail[ed][him]self of the benefits of an economic market in the forum State" (Quill, 504 U.S. at 307, 112 S.Ct. 1904)—clearly has a "minimum connection" to New York by virtue of his employment at Cardozo School of Law. Moreover, based on the same protections, opportunities and benefits conferred on him by New York as to satisfy the Commerce Clause, the convenience of the employer test as applied here does not tax "extraterritorial values" (Container Corp. of Am. v. Franchise Tax Bd., 463 U.S. 159, 164, 103 S.Ct. 2933 [1983] [internal quotation marks omitted]). Rather, as the Appellate Division recognized, an ample foundation to justify the tax is provided by the host of tangible and intangible benefits flowing directly and indirectly to petitioner from New York, the location of the law school that supplies his total relevant income.

Accordingly, the judgment of the Appellate Division should be affirmed, with costs.

JUDGES SMITH, CIPARICK, ROSENBLATT, GRAFFEO, and READ concur.

NOTES AND QUESTIONS

A. *The Statutory Basis for the "Convenience of the Employer" Test.* Under the statutory test of taxing a nonresident only on income "derived from or connected with New York sources" what bearing do the taxpayer's reasons for working at home instead of at his office have on the "source" of the income? Would the New York income tax of two nonresident employees vary because Employee A, who happens to live in the same community in New Jersey as his employer, confers (at the employer's request) with the employer about business in the employer's home, while Employee B works evenings at his own home in New Jersey on his employer's business? In short, wholly apart from the constitutional questions addressed in *Zelinsky*, was the "convenience of the employer" regulation a reasonable interpretation of the statute? Nebraska and Pennsylvania have administrative rules adopting a "convenience of the employer" test similar to New York's. See 316 Neb. Admin. Code § 22–003.01C(1) (Westlaw 2009); 61 Pa. Code § 109.8. (Westlaw 2009).

B. *The* Zelinsky *Court's Constitutional Analysis.* Was the *Zelinsky* court's constitutional analysis persuasive? The court distinguished *Central Greyhound*, where the Supreme Court struck down an unapportioned gross receipts tax on an interstate bus line under the Commerce Clause, on the ground that the risk of multiple taxation in *Central Greyhound* "was clearly impacted by the interstate travel of the bus." The court found Zelinsky's case distinguishable by the fact that "all of petitioner's teaching is accomplished in New York and his voluntary choice to bring auxiliary work home to Connecticut cannot transform him into an interstate actor." But did teaching constitute all of the duties for which Zelinsky was compensated? Was the court correct in characterizing Zelinsky's scholarly and other non-teaching responsibilities as "auxiliary" and "ancillary"? Do you think such activities had any bearing on his tenure or salary? If Zelinsky was in fact compensated in part for activities performed in Connecticut, why is multiple taxation any less of a burden on interstate commerce when one crosses state lines to conduct economic activity out of choice rather than out of necessity?

In dismissing Zelinsky's claim that New York's tax was not fairly apportioned, the court was on solid ground in observing (based on the doctrine of which you should be aware after having read *Norfolk & Western* in Chapter 3 (pp. 124–30 supra) and that you will study in detail in Chapter 7) that:

> No particular apportionment formula or method need be used to satisfy constitutional requirements, "and when a State has chosen one, an objecting taxpayer has the burden to demonstrate 'by clear and cogent evidence' that 'the income attributed to the State is in fact out of all appropriate proportions to the business transacted . . . in that State, or has led to a grossly distorted result.' "

But is that observation relevant to the "convenience of the employer" test? Does that test recognize *any* fiscal claim of the state in which a nonresident performs his or her services to the income from such services when they are performed there out of choice rather than necessity? If not, what are the implications for the analysis of the "fair apportionment" question?

What due process "protections, opportunities and benefits" did the court believe New York was providing to Zelinsky while he was working in Connecticut that justified the state's taxation of all of Zelinsky's Cardozo income? What is the relevance of the court's statement that "[f]rom the perspective of his employer, as long as [Zelinsky] performs his teaching responsibilities as scheduled, it matters not when or where he performs his ancillary functions"? Is it the benefits provided to Zelinsky or to Cardozo that should be the touchstone of the constitutional analysis?

C. *The* Zelinsky *Court's Policy Analysis.* Does the *Zelinsky* court's policy analysis withstand critical scrutiny? The court declared that "[s]ince a New York resident would not be entitled to any special tax benefits for similar work at home, neither should a nonresident." But does the court's view that "the convenience test serves merely to equalize tax obligations among residents and nonresidents" reflect the respective limitations on a state's power to tax the personal income of residents and nonresidents? The court also suggested that the "convenience of the employer" test was justified as an antidote to "fraud" and the "administrative difficulties in verifying whether an employee has actually performed a full day's work while at home." (See footnote 4 of the court's opinion.) Is this a legitimate concern? If so, is the appropriate response to deny altogether the possibility that the nonresident is in fact working outside New York? Can you think of any alternatives to such an approach that would satisfy the state's concern while also recognizing the possibility that the nonresident was performing services outside New York?

D. *The "Convenience of the Employer" Test and Telecommuting.* Perhaps the most controversial aspect of the "convenience of the employer" rule, particularly as implemented by the New York taxing authorities, is its extension to telecommuters. Not only is telecommuting an increasingly common phenomenon, especially in the New York area where physical commutes to work can be costly and time consuming, but the defensibility of the "convenience of the employer" doctrine in this context is at its weakest. In Phillips v. State Department of Taxation & Finance, 267 A.D.2d 927, 700 N.Y.S.2d 566 (3d Dep't 1999), appeal denied, 94 N.Y.2d 763, 729 N.E.2d 709, 708 N.Y.S.2d 52 (2000), for example, Phillips, a Lehman Brothers employee and a Pennsylvania resident, was a bond salesman in Lehman's municipal bond department in New York. Because his "unique services *required* that he be able to analyze and monitor markets and execute trades at any time of the day or night," id., 700 N.Y.S.2d at 567 (emphasis supplied), Lehman provided Phillips with a home office equipped with computers, fax machines, information systems, and 25 telephone lines. Moreover, Phillips submitted a letter from Lehman Brothers attesting to the fact that " '[b]ecause of the unusual hours [petitioner] maintains and the services he provides, his presence [in Lehman's New York office] is not feasible or practical on a daily basis." Id. at 568.

Despite this evidence, the court found that the New York State Tax Tribunal's "conclusion that the evidence submitted by petitioner failed to meet the strict standard required for establishing employer necessity [was] by no means irrational." Id. The court was "not persuaded that Lehman's offices could not be reasonably adapted to serve petitioner's needs." Id. at 569. Based on the 342 days that Phillips had worked in Lehman's New York City office during the years at issue, the court found that the Tax Appeals Tribunal could reasonably conclude that he was able to function from that office. Consequently, the court sustained the determination that the days Phillips spent working in Pennsylvania should be treated as days worked in New York. See also Huckaby v. State Tax Appeals Tribunal, 4 N.Y.3d 427, 829 N.E.2d 276, 796 N.Y.S.2d 312 (2005) (sustaining tax on all of the employment income of a Tennessee-based computer programmer, who spent approximately 25 percent of his time working in New York at his employer's location), cert. denied, 546 U.S. 976, 126 S.Ct. 546 (2005).

Does the *Phillips* case represent an appropriate application of the "convenience of the employer" doctrine? What standard did the employee need to satisfy to demonstrate that the work was performed at home out of "necessity" rather than "convenience"? Was that standard consistent with the constitutional restraints limiting states' power to tax nonresidents' income?

E. *The Outer Limits of the "Convenience of the Employer" Doctrine.* What are the limits to the reasoning of cases like *Zelinsky* and *Phillips* that a nonresident's income derived from personal services performed outside the state can be taxed at the employee's principal business location? Could the states provide, for example, that a nonresident employee's income will be taxed entirely by the state in which the employee's office is located regardless of where she performs her personal services? Thus, a nonresident traveling salesman attached to a New York office, but who spends virtually all of her time in other states, would be taxed by New York on her entire salary.

In the end, the question is whether, as a constitutional matter, the states have the power under the Due Process Clause and the Commerce Clause to tax personal income from services performed outside the state by a nonresident whose base of business operations lies within the state. Under the Due Process Clause, the question is whether there is a sufficient connection between the nonresident's services performed outside the taxing state and her base of operations within the taxing state to warrant taxation of her entire income from her business or employment. Does an affirmative answer this question reflect a confusion of residence-based taxing principles with source-based taxing principles?

Under the Commerce Clause, the principal question is whether such taxation will create a burden on commerce by exposing the taxpayer to the risk of multiple taxation. Plainly the state in which the nonresident performs her services will have the power to tax them. Consequently, in the absence of a credit provided either by the state in which taxpayer performs her services or by the state in which the taxpayer's operations are based, the risk would appear to be substantial. While most states do provide credits to residents for taxes paid to other states, see Section H infra, those credits generally are provided only by the state of *residence* against taxes imposed by the state of *source*. Id.; see also Section G infra. Accordingly, there could be a serious Commerce Clause claim under each of the following two circumstances: (1) if the taxpayer was not a resident either of the state in which she performed her services or of the state in which her operations were based, i.e., if both states were seeking to tax her income on the basis of source without credit for other states' source-based taxes; (2) if the taxpayer's state of residence refused to grant a credit for taxes paid to the state of her base of operations on the ground that the base of operations was not the state of source since the taxpayer did not perform her services in that state.

Would it be an answer to such a claim, however, that the origin of the problem lies in different sourcing rules adopted by the various states (e.g., a sourcing rule based on physical presence in the state vis-à-vis a sourcing rule based on the "convenience of the employer" test)? Could one argue that, as long as the state's own sourcing rules are "internally consistent" (e.g., as long as New York would source income from activity physically performed in New York to other states if such activity was not performed within New York for the convenience of the employer), the state is on constitutionally defensible ground in sourcing income from activity physically performed in other states to itself when such activity is not performed outside the state for the convenience of the employer? This was essentially the answer offered by the *Zelinsky* court. Do you agree with it?

For a consideration of these and other questions raised by the *Zelinsky* case, see Walter Hellerstein, "Reconsidering the Constitutionality of the 'Convenience of the Employer' Doctrine," State Tax Notes, May 12, 2003, p. 535; 2 Jerome R. Hellerstein & Walter Hellerstein, State Taxation ¶ 20.05[4][e] (3rd ed. 2003 & Cum. Supp. 2009); Robert Plattner, "New York's 'Convenience of the Employer' Doctrine–A Role for *Complete Auto Transit's* Fourth Prong," State Tax Notes, July 7, 2003, p. 55 (arguing that the "convenience of employer doctrine" is unconstitutional on the grounds that it violates the Commerce Clause requirement that taxes be "fairly related to services provided by the state" because it ignores the taxpayer's physical presence in the state); Edward Zelinsky, "New York's 'Convenience of the Employer' Rule is Unconstitutional," State Tax Notes, May 19, 2008, p. 553 (Zelinksy on *Zelinsky*).

F. *Apportionment of Nonresidents' Personal Income.* Personal income tax laws, or implementing regulations, commonly provide for apportioning a portion of the nonresident's income to the taxing state, where the income is derived from services rendered, or business done, both within and without the state. Thus, if an employee works within and without the state, an apportionment is typically made by reference to the number of days' work performed in the state, as compared to the total number of days worked during the year. For example, the Pennsylvania regulations provide:

> If a nonresident employee * * * performs services for an employer * * * both within and without this Commonwealth, his income derived from Commonwealth sources includes that proportion of his total compensation for services rendered as an employee * * * which the total number of working days employed within this Commonwealth bears to the total number of working days employed both within and without this Commonwealth.

61 Pa. Code § 109.8 (Westlaw 2009). As noted above, Pennsylvania, utilizes a "convenience of the employer" test for determining working days performed outside the state. Id. ("[A]ny allowance claimed for days worked outside of this Commonwealth shall be based upon the performance of services which, of necessity, obligate the employee * * * to perform out-of-State duties in the service of his employer.").

G. *Taxation of Nonresident Athletes.* Many states have adopted specific regulations for allocating and apportioning the compensation of nonresident athletes. Of the states adopting such regulations, most have followed the rules suggested by the Federation of Tax Administrators in 1994 for apportioning the income of nonresident professional team members. Federation of Tax Administrators, "State Income Taxation of Nonresident Team Athletes: A Uniform Approach" (1994), reprinted in State Tax Notes, May 9, 1994, p. 1215. Under these rules, the nonresident professional athlete must apportion his compensation to the state based on the ratio of the "duty days" spent within the state rendering services for the team over the total number of duty days during the year. The term duty days includes both official pre-season training and post-season play, as well as other days on which the team member renders services to the team. In the past, a few states employed a "games played" formula, but no state appears to do so today. For non-team athletes (such as golfers, tennis players, boxers, and jockeys), states often attribute income to the state on the basis of compensation received for the specific performance or by reference to the ratio of in-state performances to total performances. Should a nonresident's signing bonuses be treated in the same manner as his regular compensation? What about the income that an athlete receives from endorsing products?

H. *Employees Working in Interstate Transportation.* May a state tax the income earned by nonresident railroad workers working on nonstop transcontinental freight trains traveling across the state? In Blangers v. State, Department of Revenue & Taxation, 114 Idaho 944, 763 P.2d 1052 (1988), cert. denied, 489 U.S. 1090, 109 S.Ct. 1557 (1989), the question was whether Idaho's income tax could constitutionally be applied to such workers, when between 25 and 40 percent of their wages (on a time or mileage basis) was attributable to Idaho. One opinion from the Idaho Supreme Court declared:

> [T]here is no showing that the presence of the train crews in Idaho cause the state, in the words of the Court in *J.C. Penney Co.*, to give "anything for which it can ask return." * * *
>
> If the due process clause allows Idaho to tax income earned by train crews while in Idaho, then we must be prepared to sustain the taxes on the income earned by any person who crosses Idaho by any means without stopping or transacting business here. We are not prepared to say that the Constitution permits taxation by the state in this fashion.

Id., 763 P.2d at 1059–60.

A second opinion in the same case observed that not a single case from other jurisdictions "holds this tax on the railroaders improper or unconstitutional," id. at 1063; that the U.S. Supreme Court had made it clear that "[a] state is free to pursue its own fiscal policies, unembarrassed by the Constitution, if by the practical operation of a tax the state has exerted its power in relation to opportunities which it has give, to protection which it has afforded, to benefits it which it has conferred by the fact of being an orderly, civilized society," id. (quoting Wisconsin v. J.C. Penney Co., 311 U.S. 435, 444, 61 S.Ct. 246 (1940)); and it inquired:

> [A]s our train traverses Idaho, are those benefits, protections, and opportunities provided by Washington, Idaho, or Montana; or are the employees in *no state at all* for income tax purposes because wheels and tracks magically separate them from *terra firma* and the Idaho income tax?

Id. at 1062 (emphasis in original).

Which opinion was the majority and which was the dissent? Which opinion should have been the majority? Federal statutory law now substantially limits states' power to tax the compensation of nonresident employees engaged in interstate transportation within the state. Federal statutes prohibit a state, other than the state of the employee's residence, from taxing the employee's compensation from an interstate rail carrier, motor carrier, or merchant mariner. See 49 U.S.C. § 11502 (railroad employees); 49 U.S.C.

§ 14503 (motor carrier employees); 46 U.S.C. § 11108(b) (merchant mariner employees). Federal law limits the states' power to tax the compensation of employees who perform regularly assigned duties on interstate air carriers in more than one state to the state of the employee's residence and to the state in which the employee earns more than 50 percent of the compensation paid by the carrier to such employee. 49 U.S.C. § 40116(f)(2). Federal law also imposes limits on the states' authority to require withholding of income taxes from certain employees of water carriers. 46 U.S.C. § 11108(a).

I. *Income from Intangible Property.* The states do not—and constitutionally could not—tax the personal income that a nonresident derives from intangible property, unless the intangible property is used in a business in the state or has acquired a business situs there. See New York ex rel. Whitney v. Graves, 299 U.S. 366, 373, 57 S.Ct. 237 (1937) (sustaining tax on income derived by nonresident from sale of right to stock exchange seat located in state), discussed at p. 360 supra. Controversies arise, however, as to the proper characterization, and, consequently, the proper rule for attribution of income from intangible property, on the one hand, and income from tangible property or from services, on the other.

Because states generally tax nonresidents on their income from the sale of tangible property located in the state, but not on their income from intangible property without a business situs in the state, the question has arisen whether the interest received by nonresidents on the deferred payments from a sale of real or tangible personal property located in the state is taxable by such state. New York, for example, taxes nonresidents' income from "the ownership of any interest in real or tangible personal property in this state," N.Y. Tax Law § 631(b) (Westlaw 2009), but it excludes nonresidents' income from intangible property unless "such income is from property employed in a business, trade, profession, or occupation carried on in this state," id. § 631(b)(2), or from New York lottery winnings in excess of $5,000. Id. Two nonresidents of New York sold an apartment building in New York and took back a purchase-money mortgage for the unpaid balance of the purchase price. The mortgage note provided for quarterly payments to amortize the loan, with interest. To the extent the quarterly payments represented the taxpayers' gain from the sale of the property, the taxpayers reported the amount as New York income. They did not, however, include the portion of the payments reflecting interest in their New York nonresident returns. The court held that the taxpayers properly excluded the interest income from their New York return because the income-producing property was the intangible mortgage note, not the real estate apartment building secured by the mortgage. Epstein v. State Tax Comm'n, 89 A.D.2d 256, 456 N.Y.S.2d 454 (3d Dep't 1982). The court applied the same principle to sustain the exclusion from taxable income of interest payable on an installment note arising out of the sale of a seat on the New York Stock Exchange. Delmhorst v. State Tax Comm'n, 92 A.D.2d 981, 461 N.Y.S.2d 499 (3d Dep't), aff'd, 60 N.Y.2d 628, 454 N.E.2d 935, 467 N.Y.S.2d 352 (1983).

A Massachusetts court reached a contrary conclusion in a case involving interest on a deferred payment note received by a nonresident on a sale of Massachusetts realty. Horst v. Commissioner of Revenue, 389 Mass. 177, 449 N.E.2d 667 (Mass. App. 1983). The court rejected the taxpayer's contention that the interest was not "income derived from * * * the ownership of any interest in real or tangible personal property located in the commonwealth," Mass. Gen. Laws ch. 62, § 5A(a)(3) (Westlaw 2009), but rather was income from an intangible asset. The court stated that "the time of the taxpayer's transfer of his interest in the property does not alter the derivative nature of that income or transform the transaction into one involving an intangible asset unrelated in origin to an interest in property located within the Commonwealth." Id., 449 N.E.2d at 670–71. In Commissioner of Revenue v. Chinchillo, 417 Mass. 219, 629 N.E.2d 974 (1994), the court approved the reasoning in *Horst* and extended it to a case in which the taxpayer had reported all of the income from the disposition in the year of sale:

> In this case, the taxpayers, unlike *Horst*, have a mortgage on Massachusetts real estate to secure the debt. The benefit and protection that the law of the Commonwealth extends to taxpayers is sufficient to justify the tax on the taxpayers' interest income. The fact that the taxpayers chose to pay the Massachusetts tax on the entire gain in the year of sale rather than to effect installment treatment of the gain makes no difference in the constitutional sense.

Id., 629 N.E.2d at 977.

Just as the determination of whether income is derived from tangible property, on the one hand, or from intangible property, on the other, can substantially affect its taxability to a nonresident, so the determination of whether income is derived from services, on the one hand, or from intangible property, on the other, has analogous ramifications for nonresident taxpayers. The issue arises in connection with income that may plausibly be characterized as either payments for personal services, normally taxable where the services are performed, or as payments for an intangible right, normally taxable only by the taxpayer's state of residence. In Michaelsen v. New York State Tax Comm'n, 67 N.Y.2d 579, 496 N.E.2d 674, 505 N.Y.S.2d 585 (1986), for example, the question was whether a nonresident was taxable on income from the sale of stock acquired pursuant to stock options granted in the course of the taxpayer's employment in the state. The taxpayer, who lived in Connecticut, worked in New York City as a senior executive for Avon Products. He was granted options to purchase Avon stock, which he later exercised, and he sold the stock at a profit. He reported no income for New York state tax purposes on the ground that the income derived from intangible property that was not employed in a business in the state. The New York State Tax Commission took the position that the stock was connected with the taxpayer's employment, and it taxed the gain. The New York Court of Appeals held that a portion of the gain realized was taxable by the state, namely, the difference between the option price and the fair market value of the stock on the date the option was exercised. The court held that this portion of the gain constituted compensation taxable as personal service income earned in New York. Id., 505 N.Y.S.2d at 587 ("The employee's compensation comes from the employer's willingness to let the employee benefit from market appreciation in the stock without risk to his own capital."). The remainder of the gain, however, which was due to an increase in the market value of the stock between the time the option was exercised and the time it was sold, "is clearly investment income rather than compensation and, as a nonresident, petitioner cannot be taxed on this amount." Id. at 588. See also McBroom v. Department of Revenue, 14 Or. Tax 239 (1997) (sustaining tax on gain realized by nonresident from exercise of stock options granted while a resident).

For a detailed discussion of the issues raised in connection with state taxation of nonresidents' personal income from intangibles, including employee stock options, covenants not to compete, employment termination agreements, and other deferred compensation arrangements, see 2 Jerome R. Hellerstein & Walter Hellerstein, State Taxation ¶ 20.05[7][b] (3rd ed. 2003 & Cum. Supp. 2009); see also Michael J. Nathanson, et al., "Multistate Taxation of Stock Options: An Undiscovered Territory," State Tax Notes, Jan. 19, 2004, p. 179; Timothy Noonan & Paul Comeau, "Multistate Taxation of Stock Option Income—Time for a National Solution?," State Tax Notes, June 30, 2008, p. 1063; Richard Reichler, State Taxation of Compensation Benefits, Tax Mgmt. (BNA) Multistate Tax Portfolio, 1750 T.M.

3. APPLICATION OF PROGRESSIVE MARGINAL TAX RATES TO NONRESIDENT INCOME

WHEELER v. STATE OF VERMONT

Supreme Court of Vermont, 1969.
127 Vt. 361, 249 A.2d 887, appeal dismissed 396 U.S. 4, 90 S.Ct. 24 (1969).

BARNEY, JUSTICE.

The plaintiff is a Vermont taxpayer and a New Hampshire resident. He is seeking reduction of tax levies against his Vermont-earned income on the grounds that they are so formulated as to be unconstitutionally discriminatory. The tax commissioner and then the lower court denied relief and he has appealed.

The facts are not in dispute. The plaintiff lives in Enfield, New Hampshire, and is employed as a salesman by Ward Foods, Inc., of White River Junction, Vermont. He solicits orders from retail food outlets in both Vermont and New Hampshire, and receives commissions based on his sales. These commissions were his only income during 1966, the year involved in this litigation, and totaled $7,714.47. This income was the "adjusted gross income" for the plaintiff for 1966, under the definition in 32 V.S.A. sec. 5811(1) * * *. Of this total income, $1,928.62 represented compensation earned in Vermont, and is his "Vermont derived income" under 32 V.S.A. sec. 5811(17). It amounts to 25% of his total compensation of $7,714.47.

Under Vermont taxing procedure for the year 1966, all individual taxpayers commenced the computation of their income taxes in the same way. Starting with "adjusted gross income," which is defined in 32 V.S.A. sec. 5811(1) as the adjusted gross income determined under the laws of the United States, except for capital gains and losses and certain exempt income not applicable here, the "Vermont taxable income" is arrived at. This is the taxable income of the taxpayer under the laws of the United

States, but again excluding any consideration of capital gains or losses or exempt income. In other words, it is the adjusted gross income less all deductions available to the taxpayer on his federal return, without distinguishing their Vermont, New Hampshire or other derivation. From this is also deducted the appropriate personal exemptions allowed by Vermont law. With Vermont taxable income arrived at, every individual taxpayer, resident or non-resident, * * * [computed his 1966 tax at graduated rates beginning at 2% of the first $1,000 of Vermont taxable income and reaching 7.5% on such income in excess of $5,000.]

For the Vermont resident, this final figure is the tax he pays. For the non-resident, this tax figure is further reduced by the application of 32 V.S.A. sec. 5823, which provides:

> The tax imposed upon the income of a non-resident under section 5822 of this title is reduced by a percentage equal to the percentage of his adjusted gross income for the taxable year which is not Vermont derived income.

For the further protection of the non-resident taxpayer, 32 V.S.A. sec. 5827 allows a credit to avoid double taxation of income by the income tax law of another state, provided that state accords a reciprocal credit. Since New Hampshire assesses no general income tax based on ordinary earned income, this credit is not involved in this case. This leaves as the plaintiff's tax, the amount arrived at by applying the percentage relationship between his Vermont income and his total income to the tax figure based on his full income.

* * *

The plaintiff * * * argues that a New Hampshire taxpayer with some New Hampshire income pays a higher tax on his Vermont-earned portion than a Vermont taxpayer whose total income is the same as the Vermont income of the New Hampshire taxpayer. Reference to two of his examples may make his argument clearer:

	Vt. Taxpayer	N.H. Taxpayer	
Adjusted gross income	$4,000.	$6,000.	($4000. Vt. earned)
Two exemptions	1000.	1000.	
10% standard deduction	400.		600.
Vermont taxable income	$2,600.		$4,400.
Vermont tax	$ 84.		$ 184.
⅔ ratio Vt./N.H. earnings			67%
Adjusted Vermont tax			$ 122.28

It is his contention that the true comparison lies, not between taxpayers with the same adjusted gross income, but between taxpayers having identical Vermont income. He further complains that an increase in the New Hampshire taxpayer's income from New Hampshire sources will increase the amount of tax he pays on his Vermont earnings, if it moves him up another tax bracket.

This last is, of course, true. In fact an increase in adjusted gross income from any taxable source might do the same thing. It is conceivable that this New Hampshire resident with Vermont earnings could be in the same predicament if he had no New Hampshire income at all, but did have income from someplace outside of Vermont that put his adjusted gross income at the level in question, and was not of a sort to be eligible for any reciprocal income tax credit.

It is the argument of the plaintiff that, since the addition of New Hampshire income increases the tax, it must be New Hampshire income that is being taxed. However, in reality what is happening is that Vermont income is being taxed at an increased rate, and nothing more.

If the contention of the plaintiff is sound, at some point as progressive tax rates advanced, the measure of the tax payable would begin to go beyond the total Vermont income earned and require resort to money earned in New Hampshire. This certainly would be true if progressive rates in Vermont began to reach the highest levels applicable in federal income taxation.

This is made abundantly clear if, in any of these situations, we assume a totally confiscatory tax rate on Vermont income of 100%. As, we have said, if New Hampshire income were in fact being taxed, the application of such a rate would necessarily, at some point, create a tax liability larger than the total Vermont income. But this cannot occur, because even with no deductions and that confiscatory rate, the provisions of 32 V.S.A. sec. 5823 will impose a limit measured by the Vermont derived income. This illustrates that the contention that the Vermont procedure taxes property beyond its jurisdiction cannot be supported. With it falls the argument that the Due Process Clause has been violated. McCutchan v. Oklahoma Tax Commission, 191 Okl. 578, 579, 132 P.2d 337.

It is also arithmetically obvious that the plaintiff would have no cause to complain if the Vermont income tax was a flat rate rather than progressive, since the variations in the size of his adjusted gross income would not affect the tax on his Vermont earnings. An evaluation of all of his contentions makes it clear that it is the progressive nature of the tax rate which is truly under attack.

Progressive tax rates on income, widespread among the United States and firmly imbedded in the federal tax structure, are intended to make more equitable the tax burden as it falls upon citizens of various states of affluence. It is their purpose to take into account variations in ability to pay. As such they found early and complete constitutional acceptance in Brushaber v. Union Pacific, 240 U.S. 1, 25, 36 S.Ct. 236, dealing with the 1913 federal income tax, and the question has remained at rest in that area. Shaffer v. Carter, 252 U.S. 37, 51, 40 S.Ct. 221, in 1920 indicated that it is within the taxing power of state governments to levy income taxes with progressive rates. We view this aspect of the matter as constitutionally settled.

We must then determine whether the application of these tax rates, applied to the plaintiff as a non-resident, is a transgression of constitutional bounds. His arguments are framed in terms of discriminatory treatment which he claims violates his privileges and immunities under Article 4, Section 2 of the United States Constitution, and also his right to equal protection of the laws under the Fourteenth Amendment. He contends that since he, as a non-resident, is taxed at a higher rate on his Vermont derived income than a Vermont resident whose total income is of Vermont derivation, he has been treated with such unfair diversity as to violate these constitutional prohibitions. To show such a violation, it is his burden to demonstrate discrimination to the extent that it is arbitrary and unreasonable. Underwood Typewriter Co. v. Chamberlain, 254 U.S. 113, 121, 41 S.Ct. 45, 47.

If the principle of ability to pay is accepted, his contention is misleading, for he limits his comparison to a taxpayer of lower income than his. Going back to the examples already set out, if, in any of them relating to a combination of Vermont and New Hampshire income, the taxpayer were a Vermont resident, he would pay the full assessed tax on his combined Vermont and New Hampshire incomes, with no percentage reduction. To show discrimination, the plaintiff must first demonstrate that he is disadvantaged compared to another in an equivalent position. He has made no such showing. There is no place where his burden is increased over that of a resident in an equivalent income position. Even if it were, the taxpayer would still be confronted with the burden of showing such discrimination, nonexistent here, to be such an invidious inequality as to be arbitrary, for it to be condemned as unconstitutional. Maxwell v. Bugbee, 250 U.S. 525, 543, 40 S.Ct. 2.

But, again, his real objection is the operation of the taxing progression. He objects to the importation of his total income for rate determination purposes. Yet this principle, too, has already been approved as constitutional. Maxwell v. Bugbee, supra, 250 U.S. 525, 539, 40 S.Ct. 2; Great Atlantic & Pacific Tea Co. v. Grosjean, 301 U.S. 412, 425, 57 S.Ct. 772. A similar principle was recognized and accepted in our own case of Gulf Oil Corp. v. Morrison, 120 Vt. 324, 330, 141 A.2d 671, which states the necessity of establishing by appropriate evidence any claim that extraterritorial values are being taxed.

It was for the plaintiff to show that the Vermont taxing system was arbitrary and unreasonable in its classification to sustain a violation of the Equal Protection Clause. Maxwell v. Bugbee, supra, 250 U.S. 525, 543, 40 S.Ct. 2. It was for the plaintiff to demonstrate diversity of treatment without reasonable basis to sustain an abridgment of his constitutional privileges and immunities. Travis v. Yale and Towne Mfg. Co., 252 U.S. 60, 79, 40 S.Ct. 228. He has not done so.

Judgment affirmed.

NOTES AND QUESTIONS

A. Was *Wheeler* correctly decided? Consider a rich Texas oilman who summers in Vermont, where he owns a small antique store from which he derives a modest income. Is there not something troubling (if not unconstitutional) about the thought that for every barrel of oil that the taxpayer extracts in Texas his Vermont tax increases? Is this not "in substance" taxing out-of-state activities in violation of basic due process restraints? On the other hand, consider a wandering minstrel, residing in some state other than Vermont, who wanders through 50 states earning $2,000 in each state. Must every state (except her state of residence) consider her as a $2,000–per-year minstrel rather than a $100,000–per-year minstrel and tax her at the lowest marginal rates (if at all) based on the fiction that she earns only $2,000? In other words, does the Due Process Clause require that the states blind themselves to ability to pay when that ability derives from out-of-state activities? Is ability to pay a jurisdictionally limited concept? For an examination of this and other questions raised by *Wheeler*, see Walter Hellerstein, "Some Reflections on the State Taxation of a Nonresident's Personal Income," 74 Mich. L. Rev. 1309 (1974).

Whatever doubts you may harbor about the correctness of *Wheeler*, the courts have not shared them. The basic holding of *Wheeler* has been reaffirmed in Stevens v. Tax Assessor, 571 A.2d 1195 (Me.), cert. denied, 498 U.S. 819, 111 S.Ct. 65 (1990); Matteson v. Director of Revenue, 909 S.W.2d 356 (Mo. 1995); and in Brady v. State, 80 N.Y.2d 596, 607 N.E.2d 1060, 592 N.Y.S.2d 955 (1992), cert. denied, 509 U.S. 905, 113 S.Ct. 2998 (1993). Cf. United States v. Kansas, 810 F.2d 935 (10th Cir. 1987) (sustaining the consideration of income exempt from taxation under the Soldiers and Sailors Relief Act, pp. 339–40 supra, in determining the rate at which nonresident military personnel pay tax on their income taxable by Kansas). Moreover, many states, including California and New York, calculate a nonresident's income tax in a manner that takes account of a nonresident's entire income in determining the effective marginal rate at which the nonresident's income is taxed.

B. In Landgraf v. Vermont Commissioner, 130 Vt. 589, 298 A.2d 551 (1972), the court considered the provision of the statute that a taxpayer's net "Vermont income tax" should not under any circumstances exceed "4½ percent of the total income of the taxpayer for that taxable year." In calculating the 4.5 percent ceiling, a nonresident was required to look to his "total income" *wherever earned;* but in determining whether the ceiling limited his Vermont tax bill, the nonresident was required to look to his actual "net" Vermont tax liability, which had been reduced to reflect only income *earned in Vermont.* As a result, the nonresident would in some circumstances be deprived of the benefit of the 4.5 percent limitation even though a resident with the same "total income" who paid Vermont tax on all such income would benefit by it. The provision, which has since been repealed, was sustained on the ground that the nonresident "taxpayer would never pay any greater tax than his Vermont counterpart." Id., 298 A.2d at 556. Did the ceiling destroy the premise on which the approval of the Vermont method of taxation was predicated, namely, that the resident and nonresident taxpayer with the same ability to pay ought to pay to Vermont the same percentage of their income taxable by Vermont? See Walter Hellerstein, "Some Reflections on the State Taxation of a Nonresident's Personal Income," 74 Mich. L. Rev. 1309 (1974).

4. DISCRIMINATION AGAINST NONRESIDENTS

State and local tax provisions that discriminate against nonresidents are often subject to challenge under the Privileges and Immunities Clause of Article IV, Section 2 of the U.S. Constitution. For a discussion, see Chapter 4, Section C (pp. 280–301 supra).

E. CHANGE OF RESIDENCE

When a taxpayer changes residence during the taxable year, most states tax her as a resident for the period of residence and as a nonresident for the period of nonresidence. In some states a taxpayer is required to file two returns, one as a resident reporting all income, from whatever source, during the period of residence, and the other as a nonresident, reporting income only from sources within the state during the period of nonresidence. Exemptions during the period of residence typically are prorated on the basis of months of residence; exemptions during the period of nonresidence are prorated on the basis of in-state income over total income for the period of nonresidence as well as the months of residence. In other states, it is not necessary for part-year residents to file two returns, but they must nevertheless determine their income as residents for the period of residence and as nonresidents for the period of nonresidence. In many states, the personal deductions and exemptions for part-year residents are determined on the basis of the ratio of income taxable by the state to the taxpayer's total income without distinguishing between exemptions attributable to the period of residence and those attributable to the period of nonresidence.

NOTES AND QUESTIONS

A. *Taxation of New Residents on Income Earned in State of Former Residence.* Cash-basis taxpayers who receive compensation in their new state of residence for work performed in the former state of residence usually are taxed on this income in the new state. The courts uniformly have sustained the states' power to tax such income over taxpayers' constitutional objections. See, e.g., Rogers v. Chilivis, 141 Ga.App. 407, 233 S.E.2d 451, cert. denied, 434 U.S. 891, 98 S.Ct. 266 (1977); Evans v. Comptroller, 273 Md. 172, 328 A.2d 272 (1974); Hardy v. State Tax Comm'r, 258 N.W.2d 249 (N.D. 1977). These holdings combine two well-established principles, one of constitutional law and the other of tax accounting. First, a resident is taxable on all of his income from whatever source derived (see pp. 355–57 supra); second, a cash-basis taxpayer recognizes as income all items of income actually or constructively received during the taxable year. Treas. Reg. § 1.466–1(c)(1)(i).

Controversies involving arriving residents have arisen over the proper treatment of pensions, annuities, and other deferred compensation. The Oregon Supreme Court held that a taxpayer who contributed amounts to a tax-deferred annuity through a salary reduction agreement while working in

California was taxable by Oregon when he withdrew his contributions after retirement when he was a resident of Oregon. Petersen v. Department of Revenue, 301 Or. 144, 719 P.2d 869 (1986). The California Court of Appeal sustained the inclusion of a resident taxpayer's pension income from a deferred compensation plan based on employment in other states at a time when the taxpayer was a resident of other states. Daks v. Franchise Tax Bd., 73 Cal.App.4th 31, 85 Cal.Rptr.2d 927 (2d Dist. 1999). The Idaho and Maine Supreme Courts likewise held that former residents of other states who made individual retirement account (IRA) contributions while residents of those states were taxable on the income they recognized for federal income tax purposes when they received an IRA distribution after becoming Idaho and Maine residents. Idaho State Tax Comm'n v. Stang, 135 Idaho 800, 25 P.3d 113 (2001); Smith v. State Tax Assessor, 860 A.2d 387 (Me. 2004).

The holdings of these cases are not inconsistent with the holdings of a number of other cases that the states may not tax the income of new residents received from sources outside the state during the taxable year but *prior* to the time they became residents. Courts have rejected states' assertion that their right to tax residents on their income from all sources extends to income earned and received before they were residents, and they have observed that so to hold would create constitutional concerns. In District of Columbia v. Davis, 371 F.2d 964 (D.C. Cir.), cert. denied, 386 U.S. 1034, 87 S.Ct. 1487 (1967), for example, the lower court had held that the statute's effort to reach the full year's income, where the taxpayer resided in the District for nine months of the year, violated the Due Process Clause. The U.S. Court of Appeals avoided the constitutional point by holding that the taxing statute did not, by its terms, subject the income to taxation. See also Forrester v. Culpepper, 194 Ga. 744, 22 S.E.2d 595 (1942); Martin v. Gage, 281 Ky. 95, 134 S.W.2d 966 (1939).

B. *Taxation of Former Residents on Income Earned in the State but Received or Recognized After Establishing Residence Elsewhere.* States plainly possess the constitutional power to tax income that a taxpayer earns in or derives from the state but does not receive or recognize until after she establishes residence in another state. For example, if a resident of State A realizes, but does not recognize, gain under I.R.C. § 1031 in Year 1 from a like kind exchange of real property located in State A and, in Year 2, after she has established her residence in State B, recognizes the gain from the disposition of the State A property, it is clear that State A has the power to tax such gain. See generally James C. Smith & Walter Hellerstein, "State Taxation of Federally Deferred Income: The Interstate Dimension," 44 Tax L. Rev. 349 (1989). Moreover, the state statutes in principle extend to such income because they generally apply to all income that a nonresident derives from sources within the state, when first recognized for federal tax purposes, without regard to whether the income is reported in the same tax year as it is earned. As a practical matter, however, such income may escape taxation because taxpayers will fail, perhaps through ignorance, to file a tax return reporting such income to their state of former residence. If they did file such a return, they would not be subject to double taxation, because their state of current residence would grant a credit against the tax imposed by the state in which the income was earned. See Section H infra.

The efforts of some states to exercise their right to tax nonresidents on pension income derived from their prior employment within the state created a political controversy in the 1990s. Marching under the banner of "taxation without representation," organizations such as RESIST (Retirees to Eliminate State Income Source Tax) railed against states whose "Gestapo tactics" allegedly were forcing retired workers into "financial slavery" by taxing the pensions of former residents. "The Thin Blue Line" 21 (reprinted from Retirement Life (May 1989)). Responding to these pleas, Congress in 1995 limited the power of states to tax former residents on their pension income attributable to services performed in the state by prohibiting a state from imposing "an income tax on any retirement income of an individual who is not a resident or domiciliary of such State * * *" 4 U.S.C. § 114. Although there is no sound constitutional basis for depriving states in which deferred income is earned of the right to tax such income, are there nevertheless sound policy reasons for the congressional legislation?[n]

F. TAXATION OF INCOME FROM PARTNERSHIPS

Most states follow the basic federal rules governing personal income taxation of partners and partnerships. I.R.C. §§ 701 et seq. Under the federal rules, partnerships are treated as conduits and are not themselves subject to tax, but partners are directly taxable with respect to their distributive shares of partnership items of income, gains, loss, deductions, and credits. As under federal law, partnership items normally retain their character when passed through to the partners as though realized directly by the partners from their source.

Most states tax resident individual partners on their entire distributive shares of partnership income regardless of the source of such income or the state to which it is attributed. This is an application to partnership income of the general principle that residents are taxable on their income from whatever source derived. Nonresident individual partners, like nonresident individuals generally, are taxable on their share of partnership income derived from property, business operations, or other activities of the partnership in the state.

State taxation of the income that nonresident partners earn from their partnership interests raises two basic questions. First, does the state have jurisdiction to tax the nonresident partner on the basis of the partnership's activities in the state? Second, if the answer to the first question is yes, what portion of the nonresident's partner's income is subject to tax by the state? With respect to the first question, if a partnership has nexus with the state, the general rule is that state has jurisdiction over the nonresident partner. See, e.g, Borden Chems. & Plastics, L.P. v. Zehnder, 312 Ill.App.3d 35, 244 Ill.Dec. 477, 726 N.E.2d

n. See Walter Hellerstein & James C. Smith, "State Taxation of Nonresidents' Pension Income," Tax Notes, July 13, 1992, p. 221; Note, "Take the Money and Run: State Source Taxation of Pension Plan Distributions to Nonresidents," 14 Va. Tax Rev. 645 (1995).

73, 81 (1st Dist. 2000); People ex rel. Badische Anilin & Soda Fabrik v. Roberts, 11 A.D. 310, 42 N.Y.S. 502 (1896), aff'd, 152 N.Y. 59, 46 N.E. 161 (1897). The same rule typically applies to limited partners, id., but some states have carved out statutory exceptions for certain limited partners. With respect to the second question, the nonresident is generally taxable on the portion of his distributive share that has its source within the taxing state, based on the partnership's activities in the state. The following case is addressed to both of these questions.

WEIL v. CHU

Supreme Court, Appellate Division, Third Department, 1986.
120 A.D.2d 781, 501 N.Y.S.2d 515 aff'd, 70 N.Y.2d 783, 521 N.Y.S.2d 223, 515
N.E.2d 908, appeal dismissed, 485 U.S. 901, 108 S.Ct. 1069 (1988).

MIKOLL, JUSTICE.

* * *

Petitioners Russell T. Weil, Stuart S. Dye, Robert J. Hickey and Ronald A. Capone are attorneys in the Washington, D.C., office of the law firm of Kirlin, Campbell & Keating (hereinafter the law firm), which also has an office in New York City. * * * [D]eficiencies were issued on the basis that a portion of petitioners' distributive shares of partnership income from the law firm were derived from or connected with New York State and were therefore taxable.

* * *

Petitioners' contention that none of their income was derived from or connected with New York and that, therefore, they are not liable for New York State income tax pursuant to Tax Law § 601(b), § 632(a)(1) and § 637[o] is not persuasive. Petitioners assert that they have never practiced

---

o. [The relevant provisions of the New York Tax Law as they read today are as follows:

(a) General. The New York source income of a nonresident individual shall be the sum of the following:

　(1) The net amount of items of income, gain, loss and deduction entering into his federal adjusted gross income, as defined in the laws of the United States for the taxable year, derived from or connected with New York sources, including: (A) his distributive share of partnership income, gain, loss and deduction * * *.

* * *

(c) Income and deductions partly from New York sources. If a business, trade, profession or occupation is carried on partly within and partly without this state, as determined under regulations of the tax commission, the items of income, gain, loss and deduction derived from or connected with New York sources shall be determined by apportionment and allocation under such regulations.

N.Y. Tax Law § 631 (Westlaw 2009).

(a) Portion derived from New York sources.

　(1) In determining New York source income of a nonresident partner of any partnership, there shall be included only the portion derived from or connected with New York sources of such partner's distributive share of items of partnership income, gain, loss and deduction entering into his federal adjusted gross income, as such portion shall be determined under regulations of the tax commission * * *.

N.Y. Tax Law § 632 (Westlaw 2009).]

law or been authorized to practice law in New York, that they have practiced law exclusively in Washington and that almost all of their clients and fees were generated in Washington. They also claim that the "source" of a taxpayer's income is the place where the services were actually performed.

Although the Tax Commission adopted most of petitioners' allegations as to the nature of the law firm's Washington law practice in its findings of fact, it nevertheless rejected petitioners' conclusion that none of their income was derived or connected with New York. * * * The Tax Commission * * * allocated petitioners' income according to the proportion that partnership net income from sources outside New York bore to partnership net income from all sources. The record demonstrates that petitioners are members of a partnership which derives most of its income from New York.

* * *

Petitioners' contention that application of the tax violates the due process clauses of both the State and Federal Constitutions (U.S. Const., 14th amend; N.Y. Const., art. I, § 6), on the basis that there is no appreciable connection between petitioners and New York, is without merit. The connection is significant. Petitioners are partners in a law firm that maintains a considerable permanent practice in New York. Thus, there is a sufficient nexus between their income and New York to validate the tax in question (see, Matter of Knapp v. State Tax Comm., 67 A.D.2d 1024, 413 N.Y.S.2d 237).

Petitioners' claim that the imposition of the tax violates the commerce clause of the Federal Constitution (U.S. Const., art. I, § 8) also lacks merit. Their entire argument is based on the assertion that they worked only in the firm's Washington office, ignoring the fact that the partnership also practiced in New York. The requirements necessary to pass constitutional muster are set out in the decision in Complete Auto Transit v. Brady, 430 U.S. 274, 97 S.Ct. 1076, and they are met in this case. There is a sufficient nexus to New York. The tax does not discriminate against interstate commerce since only that portion of petitioners' income which represents partnership earnings in New York is taxed. The tax is fairly apportioned since it is only levied on the percentage of the law firm's income that was earned in New York. And, lastly, the tax is fairly related to services provided by New York.

We reject petitioners' argument that the imposition of the tax in this case would violate the privileges and immunities clause (U.S. Const., art. IV, § 2; 14th amend.), in that New York residents are granted a credit against their New York taxes for any income tax paid to other jurisdictions but nonresidents subject to New York income taxes are denied a comparable credit (see, Tax Law §§ 620, 635). Tax Law § 620(a) applies only to non-New York income. Petitioners' income which is taxed is New York income. They are not being denied any benefit which inures to New York residents. New York residents are taxable on New York income by virtue of their residency in New York. Non–New Yorkers, however, are not taxed on non-New York income.

Petitioners' assertion that the taxing of their income violates their right to equal protection, since they as a group are being treated less favorably than others under similar circumstances (U.S. Const., 14th amend.; N.Y. Const., art. I, § 11), is not persuasive. Petitioners, as partners in a law firm with its main office in New York, are carrying on a profession in this State (see, Tax Law § 632[b][1][B]). This is not true of employees of the Washington office or of out-of-state attorneys who are not members of a New York law firm. Thus, petitioners are not treated less favorably than others in similar circumstances.

Finally, the argument that, in any event, petitioners Hickey and Dye are exempt from the tax in question since they were employees of the law firm rather than partners, also lacks merit. It is argued that they were "junior partners" and that junior partners were not true partners, but employees. However, the Tax Commission found that Hickey and Dye were partners for tax purposes. This finding is supported by substantial evidence. A partnership is defined as "an association of two or more persons to carry on as co-owners a business for profit" (Partnership Law § 10[1]). In determining the existence of a partnership, "[t]he receipt by a person of a share of the profits of a business is prima facie evidence that he is a partner in the business" (Partnership Law § 11[4]).

In the instant case, it is clear that junior partners received a share of the profits, albeit a small share, in addition to their salary. Junior partners were also subject to liability for law firm losses, a significant element of a partnership. Hickey and Dye also chose to hold themselves out as partners and, having done so in circumstances such as these, can be required to accept the tax consequences of their decision. Thus, Hickey and Dye were properly held subject to the tax as nonresident partners of the firm (see, Tax Law § 637[a][1]).

Determination confirmed, and petition dismissed, without costs.

NOTES AND QUESTIONS

A. *Receipt by Nonresident Partners of Nonpartnership Income from Partnership.* If a nonresident partner receives a payment from the partnership for services she renders to the partnership in her individual capacity (rather than in her capacity as a partner), such income is taxed under the rules governing nonresidents' earning of personal service income rather than partnership income. Taxpayers generally have been unsuccessful in arguing that they fall within this rule, however. Thus a nonresident partner of a New York law firm sought to exclude from his distributive share of partnership income amounts received for nonlegal services performed outside of New York for foreign corporations that neither maintained offices nor did any business in New York. These services could not have been performed satisfactorily in New York, but the fees they generated were paid directly to the New York law firm. The court held that the taxpayer was not entitled to reduce his New York taxable income by the amounts in question, because the New York law firm was retained to serve the foreign clients and, in rendering the services at issue, the taxpayer acted as an agent of the firm and not in his individual capacity. Knapp v. State Tax Comm'n, 67 A.D.2d 1024, 413 N.Y.S.2d 237 (3d Dep't 1979). See also Jablin v. State Tax Comm'n, 65 A.D.2d 891, 410 N.Y.S.2d 414 (3d Dep't 1978) (rejecting a nonresident partner's contention that amounts he received from the partnership were commission income not derived from or connected with New York sources rather than a share of partnership profits).

B. *S Corporations.* Under I.R.C. §§ 1361–1378, a corporation meeting specified conditions (e.g., shareholders limited to U.S. resident individuals, estates, and certain trusts; one class of stock; no more than 100 shareholders) may elect to be treated as an S corporation. In general, an S corporation is treated like a partnership for federal income tax purposes: it pays no income tax and its income and deductions are allocated and passed through to its shareholders. In Dupee v. Tracy, 85 Ohio St.3d 350, 708 N.E.2d 698 (1999), the Ohio Supreme Court rejected the contention of nonresident shareholders of an S corporation conducting business in Ohio that they should not be subject to Ohio personal income tax on their distributive shares of S corporation income on the theory that the S corporation rather than the shareholder earned the income. The court concluded that the taxpayers' position ignored the flow-through nature of an S corporation. See also Kulick v. Department of Revenue, 290 Or. 507, 624 P.2d 93 (1981), appeal dismissed, 454 U.S. 803, 102 S.Ct. 76 (1981) (sustaining tax on nonresidents' share of the distributed and undistributed taxable income of the S corporation derived from sources within the state).

C. *Composite Returns.* The obligation of nonresident partners (and owners of interests in similar flow-through entities such as S corporations and limited liability companies (LLCs)) to file returns and pay taxes in every state in which the flow-through entity does business creates potentially burdensome administrative problems, both for states attempting to enforce that obligation and for flow-through entities and flow-through entity owners attempting to comply. Indeed, in the case of large multistate partnerships, including limited partnerships, partners may well be obligated to file returns and pay taxes in virtually every state, even if their individual shares of the partnership's income are small. Most states have responded to this problem by allowing flow-through entities, under specified conditions, to file "composite" returns on behalf of nonresident flow-through entity owners. Among the conditions often imposed by states for accepting the filing of composite returns are that each nonresident joining in the composite return provide written consent to inclusion in the return; that taxes be paid at the highest marginal rate applicable in the state; and that no deductions, exemptions, or credits unrelated to the flow-through entity be claimed by the nonresident; and that the nonresident have no other in-state income (or have only specified categories of other in-state income).

The Ohio provision governing composite returns is typical:

> Except as otherwise provided * * *, any pass-through entity may file a single return on behalf of one or more of the entity's investors other than an investor that is a person subject to the [corporate income tax]. The single return shall set forth the name, address, and social security number * * * of each of those pass-through entity investors and shall indicate the distributive share of each of those pass-through entity investor's income taxable in this state. * * * Such pass-through entity investors for whom the pass-through entity elects to file a single return are not entitled to the exemption or credit provided for by [the personal income tax]; shall calculate the tax before business credits at the highest rate of tax set forth in [the personal income tax]; and are entitled to only their distributive share of the business credits. * * * A single check drawn by the pass-through entity shall accompany the return in full payment of the tax due for such investors other than investors who are persons subject to the tax imposed under [the corporate income tax].

Ohio Rev. Code Ann. § 5747.08(D)(1)(a) (Westlaw 2009).

D. *Sale of Partnership Interest.* Because resident partners are normally taxable on all of their income whatever its source, they are subject to tax on the gain on disposition of their partnership interests regardless of the source of the gain. When a nonresident realizes gain from the sale of a partnership interest, the states usually treat the transaction under the general rules governing taxation of income from intangibles, that is, the income is taxable by the state of the partner's domicile under the principle of *mobilia sequuntur personam* ("movables follow the person") unless the intangible has acquired a business situs in another state. See Section D(2), Note I, p. 375 supra; Appeals of Amyas & Ames, 1987 WL 50165 (Cal. St. Bd. Eq. June 17, 1987) (nonresident not taxable on gain realized from the sale of interests in partnership owning and renting real estate in the state because transaction was sales by nonresident of intangible interests that had not acquired a business situs in the state); Cohen v. Commissioner of Revenue, 1995 WL 575131 (Mass. App. Tax Bd. Aug. 30, 1995) (same).

The rule that a nonresident partner is selling an intangible when he disposes of his partnership interest, rather than a portion of the underlying business itself, is based on an entity theory of partnership. In substance, the partnership is viewed as an entity separate from the partner, and the partner is viewed as selling his intangible interest in that entity just as if he were selling his intangible interest in a corporation by selling his shares in the corporation. This is the theory employed for federal income tax purposes in the sale of an interest in a partnership, even though the Code, like state statutes, generally taxes partnership income under the aggregate approach. See I.R.C. § 741; William McKee, et al., Federal Taxation of Partnerships and Partners ¶ 16.01 (4th ed. 2007). These principles are equally applicable to the disposition by an S corporation shareholder of his interest in an S corporation or an LLC member's disposition of her interest in an LLC. Commissioner of Revenue v. Dupee, 423 Mass. 617, 670 N.E.2d 173 (1996) (nonresident not taxable on sale of S corporation shares in Boston Celtics, because pass-through nature of S corporation, like pass-through nature of partnership, applies only to distributive share income, not to income from the sale of an interest in the S corporation or partnership).

E. *References.* 2 Jerome R. Hellerstein & Walter Hellerstein, State Taxation ¶ 20.08 (3rd ed. 2003 & Cum. Supp. 2009); Michael McLoughlin & Walter Hellerstein, "State Tax Treatment of Foreign Corporate Partners and LLC Members After Check-the-Box," 8 St. & Loc. Tax Law 1 (2003); Scott Salmon, et at., State Taxation of Pass-Through Entities and Their Owners (2006).

G. TAXATION OF INCOME OF TRUSTS AND ESTATES

Most states follow the basic federal rules for taxing the income of trusts, estates, and their beneficiaries. I.R.C. §§ 641–78. Under these rules, the trust or estate is considered a conduit for income tax purposes, with the result that the trust or estate is not taxable with respect to income required to be distributed currently, but such income is taxable to the beneficiary. With respect to income accumulated by the trustee under discretionary provisions, the trust ordinarily pays the tax, and when the distribution of the accumulated income is made, the beneficiary effectively receives a credit for the tax previously paid on such income by the trust.

The income tax laws of many states distinguish between resident and nonresident trusts and estates. As in the case of resident and nonresident individuals, resident trusts and estates are taxable on all their income from whatever source derived, whereas nonresident trusts and estates are taxed only on income derived from sources within the state. Trust and estate beneficiaries are taxable on the income they earn from the trust or estate under the general rules governing the taxation of resident and nonresident individuals. Although the taxation of resident and nonresident trusts, estates, and beneficiaries would otherwise create the risk of multiple taxation of the same income, the credits that the states provide for personal income taxes paid to other states reduce this risk. See Section H infra.

NOTES AND QUESTIONS

A. *The* Chase Manhattan *case.* In Chase Manhattan Bank v. Gavin, 249 Conn. 172, 733 A.2d 782, cert. denied, 528 U.S. 965, 120 S.Ct. 401 (1999), Chase was the trustee of four testamentary trusts and an inter vivos trust. The trusts were all "resident" Connecticut trusts. The testamentary trusts were "resident" trusts because the decedent was a Connecticut resident at the time of his death. The inter vivos trust was a "resident" trust because the settlor was a Connecticut resident when he irrevocably transferred property to the trust. During the tax year at issue, Chase had no presence in Connecticut; no asset of any trust was located in Connecticut; no aspect of trust administration was conducted in Connecticut; and, except for periodic accountings with respect to some of the trusts, Chase was not involved in any judicial or administrative proceedings in Connecticut. The assets of all of the trusts consisted solely of cash and securities held in Chase's trustee accounts in New York. With respect to two of the testamentary trusts, none of the beneficiaries was a resident or a domiciliary of Connecticut. The other two testamentary trusts and the inter vivos trust had Connecticut domiciliaries as beneficiaries. Connecticut taxed "resident" trusts on their undistributed income, regardless of its source. The question was whether Connecticut could tax this income under the Due Process and Commerce Clauses.

With respect to Connecticut's power to tax the undistributed income of the testamentary trusts under the Due Process Clause, Chase argued that Connecticut did not provide the trusts with contemporaneous benefits, protections, and opportunities sufficient to characterize the trusts as residents because for each trust, the trustees, the trust assets, and the trust administration were located outside of Connecticut. The court rejected this argument. The court reasoned that the state could constitutionally take the practical position of treating the seats of the trusts—where they were established, and where their principal legal protections and benefits were provided—as residents of the state. For due process purposes, the court saw nothing less compelling about the benefits and opportunities provided by Connecticut to these trusts by its legal and judicial systems than those benefits provided by states in which either the trustee or the administration of a trust might be located.

The court reached a similar conclusion with respect to the inter vivos trust, although in so doing it effectively held that the U.S. Supreme Court's decision in Safe Deposit & Trust Co. v. Virginia, 280 U.S. 83, 50 S.Ct. 59 (1929) was no longer good law. In *Safe Deposit & Trust*, a Virginia domiciliary had created an inter vivos trust of intangible personalty—stocks and bonds— of which a Maryland bank was trustee, and the stock and bond certificates were located in Maryland. The beneficiaries, however, were Virginia domiciliaries. The Court held that the Due Process Clause prohibited Virginia from imposing an ad valorem tax on the value of the intangibles the evidence of which was located in Maryland. Central to the Court's reasoning was that the adoption of a contrary rule would lead to double taxation of intangibles. The Court, of course, has since abandoned the notion that the Due Process Clause precludes double taxation of intangibles. The state court concluded that "[i]t is unlikely that the Supreme Court would now hold, on the weakened authority of the *Safe Deposit & Trust* case and under the later Due Process Clause cases, that the Due Process Clause bars the State of a resident trust or estate from taxing a nonresident trustee on income accumulated by the trust from intangibles held by the trustee who resides outside the State and administers the trust there." Chase Manhattan, 733 A.2d at 803 (quoting 2 Jerome R. Hellerstein & Walter Hellerstein, State Taxation ¶ 20.09[2], p. 20–68 (1992)).

Finally, Chase claimed that Connecticut's taxation scheme as applied to all the trusts violated the Commerce Clause because (1) there was an undue risk of multiple taxation on the income of the trusts; and (2) Connecticut did not provide a tax credit for any taxes paid to any other state by the trusts. As a consequence, Chase argued, testators and settlers will have an incentive to appoint only Connecticut trustees because appointing a trustee in another state would subject the trust to the risk of multiple taxation. Such an incentive, the argument concluded, violated the Commerce Clause by favoring in-state over out-of-state trustees. While acknowledging that there were some risks of multiple taxation as a result of Connecticut's taxing scheme, the court concluded they were too remote and speculative to constitute a dormant Commerce Clause violation.

    B. *Due Process Limitations on State Taxation of Income from Trusts and Estates.* The *Chase Manhattan* case raises two due process issues. The first is whether the Due Process Clause forbids a state from taxing undistributed income earned by a trust created by a resident decedent or settlor when the trust assets, trustee, and trust beneficiaries are located outside the state and all the income subject to taxation is derived from sources outside the state.[p] There is currently a sharp division of authority in state courts over this issue. Compare District of Columbia v. Chase Manhattan Bank, 689 A.2d 539 (D.C. App. 1997) and First National Bank of Boston v. Harvey, 111 Vt. 281, 16 A.2d 184 (1940) (in accord with position of *Chase Manhattan*) with Swift v. Director of Revenue, 727 S.W.2d 880 (Mo. 1987); Pennoyer v. Director of Revenue, 5 N.J. Tax 386 (1983); and Taylor v. State Tax Commission, 85 App.Div. 2d 821, 445 N.Y.S.2d 648 (3d Dep't 1981) (contra to position of *Chase Manhattan*). The second due process issue raised by *Chase Manhattan* is the continuing vitality of the U.S. Supreme Court's decision in *Safe Deposit & Trust*.

    Consider the dilemma facing trust administrators given the uncertainty in the current case law. Their fiduciary obligations require them to pay only those taxes that are *lawfully* imposed on the trusts that they administer. Consequently, if they follow the teachings of *Chase Manhattan* (and the supporting precedent it cited from the District of Columbia and Vermont), they will be paying a tax that courts in Missouri, New Jersey, and New York have said may not constitutionally be imposed. They therefore could be subjected to personal liability for such payment if the tax is later struck down. If, however, they rely on the Missouri, New Jersey, and New York precedents in refusing to pay the tax (or even file the return), they expose themselves to the risk of personal liability for interest and penalties if the tax is ultimately sustained on the strength of *Chase Manhattan* and kindred cases. In light of the split of authority among the state courts on the due process issue, the conflict between the Connecticut Supreme Court's decision and the Court's own decision in *Safe Deposit & Trust*, the Hobson's choice that this uncertainty creates for trust administrators, and the Commerce Clause issues described in Note C infra, why did the Court deny certiorari in the *Chase Manhattan* case?

    C. *Commerce Clause Limitations on State Taxation of Income from Trusts and Estates.* In evaluating the Court's resolution of the Commerce Clause issue raised by *Chase Manhattan*, consider the following excerpt from the amicus curiae brief filed by the American Bankers Association and a number of state bankers' associations urging the Court to grant certiorari in the case:[q]

---

p. Only two of the five trusts in *Chase Manhattan* raised the precise issue described in the text, since three of them had Connecticut beneficiaries.

q. In the interest of full disclosure, it should be noted that Walter Hellerstein was the principal author of the brief. Most of the citations from the brief have been omitted.

Whether or not Connecticut may tax the undistributed trust income at issue in this case, no one would doubt that New York (where the trustees resided, where the trust property was located, and where the trusts were administered) may do so. Accordingly, if this Court leaves undisturbed the Connecticut Supreme Court's determination that the Due Process Clause is no obstacle to Connecticut's taxing the undistributed income of one or more of the trusts at issue here, a second question of abiding concern to amici is presented. The concern stems from Connecticut's failure to make any accommodation for the fact that other States have an equal or greater entitlement to tax the trusts' intangible investment income. As a consequence, Connecticut's taxing scheme creates a substantial risk of multiple taxation of trusts that have contacts with more than one State. It thereby undermines our national common market, in direct contradiction of fundamental Commerce Clause principles.

To appreciate the nature and magnitude of the problem created by Connecticut's regime for taxing income of trusts, one may usefully compare it with state income taxation of individuals. States have traditionally used two alternative predicates to tax income (whether of individuals or trusts): residence and source. Neither predicate offends due process. * * * Accordingly, States generally tax residents (whether individuals or trusts) on all income wherever earned, while taxing nonresidents on income from sources within the State.

In the case of income earned outside a taxpayer's State of residence, the confluence of the two alternative predicates for taxation may lead to *multiple* taxation—i.e., the same income may be subjected to source-based taxation by one State and residence-based taxation by another State. Without more, multiple taxation would plainly inhibit interstate commerce, thereby raising grave Commerce Clause problems. But States have generally recognized and addressed this problem. When both the State of residence and the State of source have a legitimate claim to tax income, the State of residence (implicitly acknowledging its inferior entitlement to tax) ordinarily yields to the State of source to avoid double taxation. It does so by providing credits against income taxes for taxes paid to the State of source. Indeed, every State with a broad-based personal income tax provides a credit for taxes that their resident individuals and trusts pay to other States.

But the credit statutes of many of these States (including Connecticut) limit the credit to taxes paid on "income derived from sources" in other States. [Citing statutes.] And, for purposes of these statutes, investment income from intangibles is usually deemed not to have a "source" in other States; thus, States with credit statutes like Connecticut's will deny a resident a credit for taxes paid to other States on investment income derived from intangibles.

In the context of income taxation of individuals, this refusal to grant a credit may be tolerable. States tax nonresidents only on income from sources within the State, and States generally do not consider intangible investment income earned by a nonresident as being derived from sources within the State. Consequently, a State's failure to grant its individual residents a credit for taxes paid on intangible investment income to other States usually imposes no hardship on such taxpayers, because other States have not taxed such income. It is only in those rare instances in which an individual is deemed to be a resident of more than one State simultaneously—*e.g.*, because she has a domicile in one State while maintaining a substantial presence in another—that the individual would face even the possibility of double taxation of her intangible investment income. And, at any rate, intangible investment income comprises a relatively modest portion of the earnings of most individuals.

Where income taxation of *trusts* is concerned, however, more serious problems arise. Whereas individual taxpayers almost invariably are considered to be resident in only one State at any given time, trusts frequently are considered to be resident in several States simultaneously: they may be considered to be resident where the trustee resides, where the beneficiaries reside, where the trust's assets are located, or where a combination of these factors applies. These States' claim to the residence of the trust may be equal or greater than Connecticut's claim based on the domicile of the settlor or the testator. Moreover, because each of these States, like Connecticut, will be taxing the trust's income on a "residence" basis, they will subject the trust's undistributed investment income to tax regardless of its source. And they will provide no credit for other States' taxes on such income: the income (being investment income from intangibles) was not "derived from sources" within those States.

The resulting problem is obvious. For example, Connecticut's claim of an entitlement to tax 100 percent of a resident taxpayer's undistributed investment income gives rise to double or triple or even quadruple taxation if other States likewise assert an entitlement to tax such income without providing a credit for taxes paid to other States or some form of apportionment. If a Connecticut resident decedent established a testamentary trust with an Arizona resident trustee, who arranged for the trust to be administered in Virginia for the benefit of the trust's California resident beneficiaries, Connecticut, Arizona, Virginia, and California each would tax the trust on its undistributed investment income. Yet none of these States would provide a credit for the taxes paid on the same investment income to the other States.

These conflicting claims have a direct and pernicious impact on interstate commerce. Testators, settlors, and their advisers are induced to confine trust-related activities to a single jurisdiction in order to avoid the untoward tax consequences of crossing state lines. This balkanizing effect is illustrated by the advice offered by sophisticated trust-and-estate counsel, who urge that "the settlor must be advised of the tax consequences of selecting a person or trust company residing or situated out of state to serve as trustee of the proposed trust." Max Gutierrez, "Oops! The State Income Taxation of Multi–Jurisdictional Trusts," 25th Annual Philip E. Heckerling Institute on Estate Planning ¶ 1204.1, at 12–19 (1991). Indeed, the court below agreed with petitioners' contention that, under the Connecticut statute, "testators will have an incentive to appoint only Connecticut trustees because appointing a trustee in another state 'necessarily subjects the testamentary trust to the risk of a second income tax in that State.' "

Despite this risk of multiple taxation and its balkanizing effect, the Connecticut decision denies the existence of a Commerce Clause problem. It thereby flies in the face of settled Commerce Clause doctrine: this Court has repeatedly and abundantly made clear that no State may tax 100 percent of a tax base to which other States may lay some legitimate claim. The logical underpinning for this rule is irrefutable: if a taxpayer is subject to tax in more than one State, permitting either State to tax the entire base without apportionment or a credit for taxes imposed by other States would expose the taxpayer to multiple taxation, which the Court has long condemned under the Commerce Clause. * * *

Thus, in Standard Oil Co. v. Peck, 342 U.S. 382 (1952), the Court rejected Ohio's contention—analogous to Connecticut's here—that, as Standard Oil's domicile, it was entitled to tax 100 percent of Standard Oil's personal property, even though other States had authority to tax at least a portion of such property:

> The rule which permits taxation by two or more states on an apportionment basis precludes taxation of all the property by the state of the domicile. Otherwise there would be multiple taxation of interstate operations and the tax would have no relation to the opportunities, benefits, or protection which the taxing state gives those operations.

Id. at 384–85 (internal citation omitted). The Court has reiterated this principle, rejecting claims that domiciliary States may tax 100 percent of a taxpayer's income or property when other States have a right to tax such property. See Mobil Oil Corp. v. Commissioner of Taxes, 445 U.S. 425, 444 (1980) ("[t]axation by apportionment and taxation by allocation to a single situs are theoretically incommensurate"); Japan Line, Ltd. v. County of Los Angeles, 441 U.S. 434, 447 (1979) ("The corollary of the apportionment principle, of course, is that no jurisdiction may tax the instrumentality in full.").

In short, the multiple tax burdens to which Connecticut's taxing scheme exposes multistate trusts plainly offends the teachings of this Court's Commerce Clause cases: it "forecloses tax-neutral decisions," Boston Stock Exchange v. State Tax Comm'n, 429 U.S. 318, 331 (1977), and creates a competitive advantage for local over out-of-state trustees, cf. South Central Bell Tel. Co. v. Alabama, 526 U.S. 160 (1999) (invalidating state tax favoring local over out-of-state corporations). This Court's review of the Connecticut decision is essential to reaffirm the fundamental Commerce Clause principle that, "if a taxpayer located in State A can demonstrate that it is taxable in State B, the taxpayer has a constitutional right to insist that State A attribute at least a portion of the taxpayer's overall tax base—whether it be property, income, or receipts—to State B." 1 Hellerstein & Hellerstein, State Taxation ¶ 8.02[1] at 8–10 (3d ed. 1998).

Does the amicus curiae brief overstate the Commerce Clause issue? To what extent do you believe trusts are actually subject to multiple taxation?

Was there any multiple taxation in fact in the *Chase Manhattan* case? Why not? In Zunamon v. Zehnder, 308 Ill.App.3d 69, 241 Ill.Dec. 269, 719 N.E.2d 130 (1999), appeal denied, 187 Ill.2d 593, 244 Ill.Dec. 191, 724 N.E.2d 1275, cert. denied, 530 U.S. 1244, 120 S.Ct. 2692 (2000), there was actual multiple taxation of trust income, resulting from the fact that Illinois, the state of the trust's domicile, did not provide a full credit for other states' taxes levied on income earned by the trust from real property located in those states.[r] The Illinois Court of Appeals perfunctorily dismissed the Commerce Clause claims with the observation that "[t]he trusts fail to cite any case in which the *Complete Auto* test has been applied to bar a state from taxing all of the income of its own residents," id., 719 N.E.2d at 137, and that "[t]he trusts have also failed to identify the interstate market or transaction purportedly implicated here." Id. at 138. How would you respond to these observations if you were representing the taxpayer?

D. *The Taxation of Revocable Trusts.* Section 676(a) of the Internal Revenue Code provides that "[t]he grantor shall be treated as the owner of any portion of a trust * * * where at any time the power to revest in the grantor title to such portion is exercisable by the grantor or a nonadverse party, or both." Insofar as the states follow the federal rules, grantor trusts raise no significant state tax issues, because the trust is essentially ignored, and the grantor is taxable directly on the income that is earned by the trust. If the states fail to follow the federal grantor trust rules, however, questions may arise as to whether the grantor or the trust is taxable on the income, which plainly may have state tax consequences. In Bruner v. Wisconsin Dept. of Revenue, 57 Wis.2d 70, 203 N.W.2d 663 (1973), the court held that a resident grantor of a revocable trust administered outside the state was not taxable on capital gains that were accumulated by the trustee. The Wisconsin court refused to follow the federal rule and held that the trustee was the legal recipient of the income, despite the fact that under the laws of many states the result would be to allow the income to go untaxed. It was not clear whether Illinois, the state where the trust was administered, would tax the trustee under these circumstances.

E. *Income Taxation of Beneficiaries of a Trust.* A resident beneficiary of a trust is taxable by the state of his residence on income distributed to him by the trustee, although the trust was created by a nonresident and its assets are held by a nonresident trustee, who administers the trust outside the state. Guaranty Trust Co. of New York v. Commonwealth of Virginia, 305 U.S. 19, 59 S.Ct. 1 (1938). This holding is an application of the familiar principle, established by Lawrence v. State Tax Comm'n, 286 U.S. 276, 52 S.Ct. 556 (1932), that the state of domicile may tax an individual on all income from whatever source derived. In State Tax Comm'n v. Fine, 356 Mass. 51, 247 N.E.2d 701 (1969), however, the court held that a resident holder of shares in an out-of-state real estate trust was exempt from Massachusetts income tax. Because the Massachusetts income tax had been construed as a tax on the

---

r. Although Illinois, like all other states, generally grants a credit against its personal income tax for taxes that its residents pay to other states on income derived from sources in those states, it did not permit such a credit against its Personal Property Tax Replacement Income Tax, levied on corporations, partnerships, and trusts to replace revenues lost from the repeal of Illinois' personal property tax.

underlying property, see p. 231 supra, the application of the tax on income from out-of-state realty was deemed to violate principles of extraterritorial taxation.

Since nonresidents are taxed only on income from sources within the state, nonresident trust beneficiaries generally are not taxed by the state in which a securities portfolio is managed on distributions made by a resident trustee. They are, however, typically taxed by the state in which the trust holds real and tangible personal property on income from those assets. In short, the usual underlying source rules normally govern taxability to the nonresident beneficiary of income from a resident trust. In Matter of McCormac, 64 Hawaii 258, 640 P.2d 282 (1982), however, the court held that nonresident beneficiaries of a trust consisting entirely of intangible property were nevertheless taxable on the income from the trust, because the property generating the income had acquired a "business situs" in Hawaii.

H. CREDIT OR ALLOWANCE FOR TAXES PAID TO OTHER STATES

Because the states generally tax residents on their income from all sources while taxing nonresidents on income from sources within the state, and because the Due Process Clause and, in some cases, even the Commerce Clause, do not forbid multiple taxation of personal income, taxpayers deriving income from states other than their own are exposed to the risk that their income will be subjected to duplicative taxation. To deal with this problem, the states provide credits against their personal income taxes for personal income taxes paid to other states. Indeed, every state with a broad-based personal income tax provides a credit for taxes that their residents pay to other states, All States Tax Guide (RIA) ¶ 236–A (2009), available at www.checkpoint.riag.com. The result is to revert the final tax to the state that is the source of the taxed income. Some states also provide credits for nonresidents for taxes paid to their home states on income derived from sources within the state of nonresidence, id., thereby reverting the final tax to the taxpayer's state of residence. Credits may be taken only with respect to the income that is subject to tax by both states, and the credit for the tax paid on the out-of-state income may not exceed the tax imposed on such income by the state granting the credit. In addition, states generally limit the credit to taxes paid to other states during the taxable year for which the credit is claimed.

NOTES AND QUESTIONS

A. *Limitation of Credit Granted by Resident State to Income Derived From Sources Within the Taxing the State.* States generally limit their credit to taxes imposed by other states on income from "sources within" such state. For example, New York provides a resident tax credit for "any income tax imposed * * * by another state * * * upon income both *derived therefrom* and subject to tax under this article." N.Y. Tax Law § 620 (Westlaw 2009) (emphasis supplied). The rationale for this limitation—like the rationale for limitation of the U.S. foreign tax credit to taxes paid on "foreign source" income (see I.R.C. § 904)—arises out of the underlying rationale for credit. As the American Law Institute explains:

> When one country taxes on the basis of domiciliary jurisdiction and another country taxes on the basis of source, the same income will be taxed twice. Under internationally accepted practice, it is incumbent on the domiciliary jurisdiction to alleviate this double taxation by some reasonable means. The foreign tax credit, under which the U.S. allows a credit against U.S. tax for foreign income taxes imposed on the income of U.S. domiciliary taxpayers, satisfies this requirement; *and it is appropriate to fashion the credit so that it does not offset that portion of the U.S. tax which is attributable to U.S.-source income.*

American Law Institute, Federal Income Tax Project: International Aspects of United States Income Taxation 6 (1987) (emphasis supplied).

In general, it is the credit-granting state that determines the sourcing rules that are employed to determine whether the state that is purporting to tax on a source basis is taxing income that has its source in that country for tax credit purposes. As the cases below reveal, this can result in double taxation, and it may appear unfair to the individual taxpayer who is compelled to pay tax on the same income to two states. Nevertheless, as a leading text observes, this approach, which is the approach embraced by the United States in determining the source of income for foreign tax credit purposes under the Internal Revenue Code) "is not necessarily wrong":

> When a country undertakes to mitigate double taxation for its residents, it gives up primary jurisdiction over income its residents earn in other countries. This undertaking need not extend to whatever income other countries choose to tax. A country's source rules are a means of classifying income between income the country claims primary jurisdiction to tax and income as to which it yields primary jurisdiction to other countries. When countries disagree on source characterizations, the country of the taxpayer's residence, even though generally committed to a policy of eliminating double taxation of its residents, is not necessarily the country that should concede the disputed point.

Boris I. Bittker & Lawrence Lokken, Federal Taxation of Income, Estates & Gifts ¶ 72.6.1 (2009) (Westlaw version).

As noted above, New York provides a resident tax credit for "any income tax imposed * * * by another state * * * upon income both derived therefrom and subject to tax under this article." N.Y. Tax Law § 620 (Westlaw 2009). A New York resident sought a credit for taxes paid to Missouri from income earned from a Missouri resident trust of which she was a beneficiary. The New York Tax Appeals Tribunal denied the credit, despite the resulting double taxation, because the trust income, though constitutionally taxable by Missouri, was not "derived" from Missouri within the meaning of the New York statute. In re Mallinckrodt, 1992 WL 346998 (N.Y. Tax App. Tribunal Nov. 12, 1992). The tribunal relied on the New York regulation that denied a credit for taxes imposed by other jurisdictions upon income from intangibles except where such income is from property employed in a business, trade, or profession carried on in such jurisdiction. N.Y. Comp. Codes R. & Regs. tit. 20,

§ 120.4(d) (Westlaw 2009). Relying on this same regulation, an administrative law judge observed that a New York resident would not be entitled to a credit for any taxes paid to New Jersey for gambling winnings in New Jersey, unless, of course, he was a professional gambler. In re Katz, 1994 WL 109447 (N.Y. Div. of Tax Appeals, Admin. Law Judge Div. Mar. 24, 1994).

In Boulet v. State Tax Assessor, 626 A.2d 33 (Me. 1993), the Maine Supreme Court permitted a resident a credit against the tax imposed by Massachusetts on an annuity payment received as a result of winning the Massachusetts lottery. The court rejected the Tax Assessor's view that the source of the income was in Maine under the principle that intangibles have their situs at the owner's domicile. Although Maine would not have taxed the lottery winnings of a nonresident derived from Maine lottery winnings under similar circumstances because Maine taxes nonresidents on income from intangibles only to the extent derived from intangible property employed in a business, trade, or occupation carried on in Maine, the court observed that there were constitutional limitations on Maine's power to tax income of nonresidents and concluded that "it is * * * not unreasonable to assume that the legislature intended a tighter definition of those sources of Maine income taxable to nonresidents than those sources of foreign income for which Maine residents receive a credit for taxes paid to that foreign jurisdiction." Id. at 35.

While the Maine court's approach to the definition of "source" for foreign tax credit purposes has the salutary effect of relieving residents of double taxation, it is not consistent with the prevailing approaches to this issue, namely, defining "source" in terms of the rules that the state would apply in determining the taxability of nonresidents' income. Indeed, in 2003, the Maine Legislature amended its credit legislation to make it clear that, in determining whether income is derived from sources within another state, the State Tax Assessor must look to Maine sourcing rules, rather than the rules of the state to which the tax was paid, thereby effectively reversing the result in the lottery case described above. Me. Rev. Stat. Ann. tit. 36, § 5217–A (Westlaw 2009) ("[i]n determining whether income is derived from sources in another jurisdiction, the assessor may not employ the law of the other jurisdiction but shall instead assume that a statute equivalent to [Maine's income tax statute] applies in that jurisdiction").

B. *Credits for Taxes Paid by Trusts and Trust Beneficiaries on the Same Income.* A trust administered in Massachusetts paid income taxes on amounts earned by the trust and subsequently distributed to a New York beneficiary. The beneficiary paid New York income tax on the amounts distributed by the trust and sought to take a credit against her New York tax liability for the taxes paid by the trust. The State Tax Commission took the position that she was not entitled to the credit on the ground that, since Massachusetts had imposed the tax upon the trust, the taxpayer had not paid any income tax to Massachusetts. The court reversed:

> [R]espondent required Mrs. Smith to include the taxes which were paid by the trust in her New York adjusted gross income. The resultant effect of this is that Mrs. Smith has borne the burden of paying the Massachusetts taxes. Having so borne the burden of the income taxes paid to Massachusetts, petitioners have constructively paid "income tax imposed

for the taxable year by another state" and are thus entitled to a credit under Tax Law § 620(a).

Smith v. New York State Tax Comm'n, 120 A.D.2d 907, 503 N.Y.S.2d 169, 170–71 (3d Dep't 1986).

In an earlier case, however, the Massachusetts Supreme Court refused to treat a trust and its beneficiary as essentially a single taxpayer when the question arose whether the trust was entitled to a credit against Massachusetts income taxes paid on income distributed to a Massachusetts beneficiary who had paid personal income tax to California on amounts distributed to him. Whiteside v. Commissioner of Revenue, 394 Mass. 206, 474 N.E.2d 1128 (1985). For tax credit purposes, the trust and the beneficiary were treated as separate taxable entities under the statute.

C. *Nature of the Tax to Which the Credit Applies.* Most of the crediting provisions permit a credit only for "income" taxes paid to other jurisdictions. Under such a provision, the Maryland Supreme Court denied a taxpayer a credit for the District of Columbia tax on unincorporated businesses, levied at the rate of five percent of taxable income, on the privilege of carrying on trade or business in the District. The court held that the levy was a privilege or franchise tax and not an income tax and hence not subject to the crediting provision. The Virginia Supreme Court, on the other hand, concluded that the District of Columbia levy was an income tax and allowed a Virginia resident a credit for the District tax. King v. Forst, 239 Va. 557, 391 S.E.2d 60 (1990). Thereafter, the Maryland Supreme Court reached the same result as the Virginia Supreme Court had reached, distinguishing its earlier decision on the basis of a change in the District statute, which a District court had construed as being an income tax rather than a franchise tax. Roach v. Comptroller, 327 Md. 438, 610 A.2d 754 (1992). Subsequently, the Virginia legislature amended the Virginia credit provision to eliminate the credit for the District's unincorporated business tax. Va. Code Ann. § 58.1–332(A) (Westlaw 2009).

D. *Credit for Tax Paid to Foreign Countries and Municipalities.* Under state statutory provisions providing a credit for taxes paid to other "states," the courts have held that the term does not embrace taxes paid to other countries. See Ludka v. Department of Treasury, 155 Mich.App. 250, 399 N.W.2d 490 (1986); cf. Shulevitz v. Michigan Department of Treasury, 78 Mich.App. 655, 261 N.W.2d 31 (1977) (denying credit for tax paid to Puerto Rico). The Virginia Supreme Court has likewise held that the credit for an "income tax [paid] to the state where [the nonresident] resides" does not include local Maryland income taxes. Department of Taxation v. Smith, 232 Va. 407, 350 S.E.2d 645 (1986). Does denying a credit for income taxes paid to foreign countries, while permitting such a credit for income taxes paid to other states, discriminate against foreign commerce in violation of the Commerce Clause? See In re Barton–Dobenin, 269 Kan. 851, 9 P.3d 9 (2000), cert. denied, 531 U.S. 1073, 121 S.Ct. 765 (2001) (recognizing that a state income tax can have substantial effect on foreign commerce, but dismissing claim of discrimination against foreign commerce because "taxpayers in this case have not met their burden to prove that the tax involved in this case is subject to the Foreign Commerce Clause").

CHAPTER 7

CORPORATE INCOME TAXES

■ ■ ■

The Development of State Corporate Taxes. Most states impose annual franchise or privilege taxes on corporations. The states impose these taxes on the right to exist as a domestic corporation, on the privilege of doing business in the state as a foreign corporation, or on the actual conduct or carrying on of business in the state by a corporation. These taxes may be measured by the corporation's net income or by its capital stock. Corporate franchise taxes are frequently described by their measure rather than their subject. Accordingly, a franchise tax measured by net income is frequently referred to as a "net income" tax, and a franchise tax measured by capital stock is frequently referred to as a "capital stock" tax. In addition (or as an alternative) to franchise taxes measured by net income or capital stock, many states have adopted "direct" corporate net income taxes. These taxes are imposed directly on a corporation's net income attributable to the state rather than on the privilege of exercising a corporate franchise in the state, measured by net income.[a]

The development of the existing structure of state corporate franchise taxation has its roots in the property tax. The earliest form of general corporation tax in this country, the corporate excess tax, was not a special tax but a modification of the general property tax. It was a levy on the value of a corporate business in excess of the appraised value of its assets including good will, going-concern value, and other factors that are reflected in the market value of the corporation's stock. At first states assessed and taxed this intangible "corporate excess" value to the shareholders. Subsequently, they levied the tax on the corporations themselves. This form of corporate taxation largely gave way to the capital stock tax.[b]

The capital stock tax is typically an annual franchise tax, imposed on domestic corporations for the privilege of existing as a corporation and on

---

a. The distinction between privilege taxes measured by net income and direct net income taxes—now largely of historical significance for Commerce Clause purposes—was considered in Chapter 3. See pp. 104–20 supra. The distinction retains its significance for purposes of federal immunity from state taxation, however. Income from federal obligations may be included in the measure of a nondiscriminatory franchise tax (because the state is not imposing a "direct" tax on the Federal Government) but not in the measure of direct net income taxes (because the state is imposing a "direct" tax on the Federal Government). See Chapter 5.

b. For a historical account of the development of state corporate taxation in this country, see Edwin R.A. Seligman, Essays in Taxation 137 et seq. (1st ed. 1895).

foreign corporations for the privilege of doing business (or on the actual conduct of business) within the taxing state. The measures employed fall into two general classifications. In one category are "capital-account" levies that have narrow bases taken from the corporation's statement of capital, either authorized shares or outstanding (or issued) shares. In the other category are broader, "capital-value" based levies, that reflect in a variety of ways historical earning capacity or value as a continuing business enterprise. The capital stock tax has a long history in state taxation; its development paralleled the growth of the American corporation. Such levies developed in the early nineteenth century, when incorporation was a special privilege or franchise for which a separate tax was regarded as appropriate. Around the turn of the century, capital stock taxes grew rapidly. In 1902, 13 states imposed capital stock taxes; by 1912, the number had reached 25; and by 1929, 33 states imposed such levies. Today roughly half the states impose franchise taxes measured by capital stock. States generally impose franchise taxes measured by capital stock in addition to their general corporate income tax, except for those states that impose no corporate income taxes. All States Tax Guide (RIA) ¶ 210 (2009) (chart).

The most widely used measure of state corporation taxes is net income—the latest arrival in the family of corporate tax measures. During the nineteenth century, the states occasionally taxed corporate income. Virginia imposed an income tax on corporations in 1844, and Georgia did so in 1863. Most of the states, however, did not enter this area of taxation until the twentieth century. In 1911, Wisconsin inaugurated the modern era of income taxation by enacting a corporate (and personal) income tax, and thereafter other states followed suit. Today, almost all states and the District of Columbia impose broad-based taxes measured by corporate net income. A few states impose both a direct net income tax and a franchise tax measured by net income, although taxpayers subject to one tax are exempt from the other.[c] Only Michigan, Nevada, Ohio, South Dakota, Texas, Washington, and Wyoming have no broad-based corporate income tax, although Michigan, Ohio, Texas and Washington impose broad-based taxes on corporate gross receipts. All States Tax Guide (RIA) ¶ 210 (2009) (chart). The features of these corporate gross receipts taxes vary greatly from state to state.

Special Taxes on Selected Businesses. States have traditionally singled out public utilities for special levies. States and localities experienced difficulties in applying simple property tax assessment techniques to a railroad or a power company, whose special franchises and properties are spread over the state or country. This, coupled with political considerations and other factors, led to the widespread imposition on public utilities of gross income taxes apportioned to the state, often in lieu of property, franchise, and income taxes. Similarly, states rich in natural

---

c. The reason for the existence of these "double-barreled" net income measures stems from the different constitutional restraints imposed on "direct" and "indirect" income taxes. See footnote **a** supra.

resources frequently impose severance taxes, which are levies on the extraction of natural resources. Severance taxes are typically measured by the gross receipts from, or gross value of, the product, although some severance taxes are imposed on a per unit basis (e.g., so many dollars per barrel of oil or ton of coal). Almost all states subject insurance companies to special taxes on their gross premiums apportioned to the state. The states impose these levies as a substitute for the more general corporate net income tax imposed on most other businesses. Some states also impose special levies on banks and other financial institutions.

Organization and Entrance Taxes. During the nineteenth century, states customarily collected flat fees to cover the costs of incorporation. After the Civil War, these fees gradually increased and evolved into taxes. These levies are based on the par value of authorized stock and a flat rate on each share of authorized no-par value stock. The states collect these levies at the time the incorporation papers are filed. Upon the subsequent filing of a certificate increasing the corporation's authorized capital, the state collects an additional fee.

In 1894, Ohio extended this principle to foreign corporations by imposing a tax on the grant of a license to do business in the state, measured by the amount of capital stock to be employed in the state. This type of entrance tax spread throughout the country. Some states impose the tax at a flat rate, which may more nearly resemble a fee than a tax. Many states, however, measure the tax by the amount of authorized or issued capital stock apportioned to the state. Unlike the corporate franchise tax, these entrance taxes are not annually recurring levies. They come into play after the initial entrance only if the amount of authorized or issued capital is increased, or if the amount of property or volume of business in the state, or other apportionment factor, increases.

The problems addressed in this chapter concern principally the measures of corporate income, franchise, and capital stock taxes, and, particularly, apportionment and allocation issues. With the inevitable overlapping of legal materials, we have already adverted to apportionment issues in Chapter 3 (dealing with the Commerce Clause) and in Chapter 2 (dealing with jurisdiction to tax). In this chapter, however, we will undertake a more detailed and systematic exploration of apportionment and allocation problems arising in the application of state levies.

A. THE STATE CORPORATE INCOME TAX BASE

As you might expect from your study of state personal income taxes (Chapter 6, Section A supra), the outstanding characteristic of state corporate income taxes (whether denominated "franchise taxes" or "direct net income taxes") is their broad conformity to the federal corporate income tax. The prime force responsible for this conformity has been pressure from taxpayers for easing compliance and auditing burdens. The simplest method of achieving federal conformity short of complete piggy-backing (i.e., calculating the state tax as a percentage of the federal tax) is to incorporate into the state statute the key operative terms from the federal statute, such as "gross income" and "taxable income," and then to make such specific adjustments as state policy and federal law may dictate. Today every state with a corporate income tax except Arkansas and Mississippi uses federal taxable income as the starting point for the determination of state corporate income tax liability. Federal Income Tax Rules Used in the States, All States Tax Guide (RIA) ¶ 221 (2009) (chart). Even these states' corporate tax bases conform substantially to the federal corporate income tax base through the adoption of detailed definitions of "gross income," "net income," and other terms that largely track the federal provisions. Id.

Some state legislatures have been unwilling to incorporate the provisions of the Internal Revenue Code by reference. There are several reasons for this reluctance. First, there is the concern that such legislation might constitute an unconstitutional delegation to Congress of state legislative powers. Second, incorporation by reference may run afoul of state constitutional provisions requiring clear identification of the precise law being enacted. Third, as a matter of policy, legislators may be unwilling to empower Congress to change the state's tax laws without having had an opportunity to review the changes. To be sure, the state legislature can always reject any amendment to the Internal Revenue Code, but that is a cumbersome procedure requiring affirmative action by the legislature, and there may be a time lag between the enactment of the federal change and the state's decision whether to incorporate the change.

In the early 1980s, the states were jolted into a realization of the risks to state revenues attendant upon adoption of the federal tax base (along with any changes that may be effectuated from year to year) by the Reagan Administration's dramatic federal income tax cutting program. The sharp increases in depreciation under the Accelerated Cost Recovery System (ACRS), for example, had a significant impact on state revenues for states that conformed to the federal tax base. As a consequence, a number of states "decoupled" their corporate tax bases from the federal model, at least with respect to specific provisions such as ACRS and safe harbor leases. The Federal Tax Reform Act of 1986 likewise had substantial repercussions on state corporate income taxes, but this time the result was to increase revenues. As a result of the 1986 Act, a number of states that had "decoupled" their tax bases from the federal model reconformed their taxes to the federal scheme, thereby simplifying taxpayers' compliance burdens.

More recently, Congress's post–9/11 economic stimulus package gave rise to conformity issues for the states. In the Job Creation and Worker Assistance Act of 2002, Congress provided for an additional first-year depreciation allowance equal to 30 percent of the adjusted basis of qualified property placed in service between September 10, 2001 and September 10, 2004. See I.R.C. § 168(k). The impact of this so-called "bonus depreciation" on state revenues—assuming they took no action to decouple their tax regimes from the federal model—was substantial. Facing severe budget shortfalls even without the revenue impact of bonus depreciation, many states reacted by decoupling their tax regimes from the federal tax regime insofar as bonus depreciation was concerned. Some states enacted legislation completely decoupling from the bonus depreciation provisions, other states partially decoupled, and yet other states conformed to the federal rules. To get a sense of the complexity confronting taxpayers doing business in many states, consider the legislative landscape shortly after the enactment (and the state response) to bonus depreciation: sixteen states permitted bonus depreciation; twenty-five states did not; one state (Oklahoma) spread bonus depreciation over five years and another (Ohio) spread it over six years; Nebraska taxpayers had to add back 85 percent of the bonus depreciation claimed on their federal return, claiming 20 percent of the addback beginning in 2005 and for the next four taxable years; North Carolina taxpayers had to add back all bonus depreciation claimed on the federal return in 2001 and 2002, 70 percent in 2003, and thereafter could deduct the amount of the previously disallowed deduction over a five year period. John M. Majowka, "The New Federal Bonus Depreciation Rules: A BNA Survey Shows Most States Do Not Conform," Tax Mgmt. (BNA), Multistate Tax Report, Vol 9, No. 10, Oct. 25, 2002, p. 875. See generally LeAnn Luna and Ann Boyd Watts, "Federal Tax Legislative Changes and State Conformity," State Tax Notes, Feb. 25, 2008, p. 619.

From a policy perspective, how would you reconcile the competing concerns reflected in the preceding discussion? Doesn't the states' failure to conform to the federal rules create a compliance nightmare for multistate businesses and, to a lesser extent, for taxpayers in individual states that must separately determine depreciation for federal and state tax purposes? At the same time, what recourse is open for states that, unlike the Federal Government, are almost universally under a state constitutional obligation to balance their budgets and cannot simply ignore the revenue consequences of major changes at the federal level?

B. DIVISION OF THE TAX BASE

The Problem. Dividing the tax base of the multistate enterprise is among the most troublesome and complex problems in the field of state taxation. The problem relates to taxpayers who own property, earn income, or derive receipts in more than one state and who, ordinarily, are subject to the jurisdiction of the various states in which the property is owned, the income is earned, or the receipts are derived. How do we determine the portion of the total value of the taxpayer's property, income, or receipts that each state is entitled to tax?

It would be nice, of course, if we could resolve this question simply by attributing the amount of property, income, or receipts to each state based on their location or source. Real property, for example, would be taxable where it was physically situated; income from services would presumably be taxable where the services were performed; and gross receipts from sales of tangible personal property would be taxable where the property was delivered.

There are two basic problems with this solution to dividing the tax base of the multistate enterprise. First, it may not always be possible to determine a precise location for the property, income, or receipts that are potentially subject to tax in several states. While it is easy enough to determine the situs of real property, where should railroad rolling stock, which may pass through dozens of states during the tax year, be taxable? While some services may be performed in a single state, many services— including those in the burgeoning fields of telecommunications, data processing, and information retrieval—involve activities performed (often simultaneously) in several states. Where are such services "located"? And even receipts from sales of tangible personal property, while easily attributable to the state of destination, may also be attributed to the state where the seller accepted the sales order, or the state from which the property was shipped, or the state where the contract for the sale was negotiated. Which state ought to tax the receipts?

Second, wholly apart from the difficulty of determining—at least in many cases—a single appropriate physical situs for property, income, or receipts of a multistate business, there is a more fundamental problem in assigning the tax base to a particular situs. Even if one can determine a single tax situs for property, income, or receipts, it may be inappropriate to assign all of the value attributable to the property, income, or receipts to that single location. For example, if a railroad owns terminals in New York and California, but the terminals would have little value without the track connecting the two terminals, it may well be more appropriate for tax purposes to spread the value of the terminals (along with the railroad's other operating property) among all the states in which the railroad operates rather than attempting to determine and assign the value to a single situs based on physical location.

As we shall see, there is no single "solution" to the problem of dividing the tax base of the multistate enterprise. Rather there are a number of approaches the states have adopted over the years to assigning for tax purposes the property, income, and receipts of businesses that cross state lines. Many of those approaches continue to exist in one form or another under current law and practice, although particular approaches may be applicable only in narrowly defined circumstances.

The states have broad leeway in adopting particular division-of-tax-base methodologies. In so doing, however, they are ultimately subject to the constraints of the Due Process and Commerce Clauses in taxing no more than their fair share of the property, income, or receipts of a multistate enterprise. The materials that you will study in this chapter therefore involve not only the state statutes and regulations designed to divide the tax base but also the constitutional limitations on the states' efforts to do so, and, perhaps most importantly, the interplay between the two.

Allocation, Apportionment, and Separate Accounting. There are essentially three different methods that the states have adopted to divide the tax base of a multistate enterprise: allocation, apportionment, and separate accounting.[d]

Allocation. "Allocation" (or "specific allocation") attempts to trace the property, income, or receipt to the state of its source and to include the item in full in the measure of that state's tax. For example, in a corporate capital stock tax, which ordinarily employs as its measure the value of the corporation's assets in the state (as reflected in the value of its capital stock attributable to the state), the real and tangible personal property located in the state would be treated as a part of the corporation's property used in and allocated to the state. Where, however, the property is intangible, the problem is more difficult. Suppose the intangible is an account receivable owed to the taxpayer, which maintains its plant and executive offices in State A, by a customer in State B, and arising out of a sale of goods manufactured in and shipped from State A. If both states tax the account receivable in full, the corporation dividing its operations between two states would be subject to a more onerous tax burden than the local manufacturer selling its goods in one state. If only one state should include the intangible in the measure of its tax, which state should that be? State A affords the taxpayer the benefits and protection of conducting its manufacturing operations and of maintaining its executive offices in that state, and, therefore, it has a strong basis for regarding the proceeds of the manufacturer as part of the assets attributable to its state. Likewise, the state of the market, State B, can make a persuasive case for levying the tax. It furnishes the market for the sale. The customer-debtor is located in State B, whose courts may be used to enable the taxpayer to collect the amount owing. Moreover, unless State B imposes the tax on out-of-state vendors who do business in State B, they may have a competitive advantage over local manufacturer-vendors, since State A may not in fact impose a similar tax.

Similar and indeed more complex problems are presented by income and gross receipts taxes. T manufactures goods in State A, where it maintains its executive offices. It warehouses the goods in State B and

---

d. The terms "allocation" and "apportionment" are often used interchangeably in state statutes and decisions in referring to the formulary method of dividing income or other tax measures. The term "allocation" (or "specific allocation") is also used to refer to non-formulary attribution of income to a state or states, such as the assignment of rents from property to the state in which the property is located or the assignment of a corporation's interest and dividend income to the state of its commercial domicile. Increasingly, however, the term "allocation" is being used to refer exclusively to the attribution of a particular type of property, income, or receipt to a particular state, whereas "apportionment" refers to the division of the tax base by formula. That is the terminology that we employ in the editorial materials in this book. It is also the terminology employed by the Uniform Division of Income for Tax Purposes Act ("UDITPA"), and by most of the state income tax statutes, many of which have adopted UDITPA. See pp. 527–35 infra.

sells them in States A, B, C, and D. Where should the income or receipts from the sale be allocated? To State A, where the order is accepted, or to State B, where the stock of goods is located from which the order is filled, or to State C or D where the goods are delivered to the customers? Whatever the law of contracts as to where the contract is made, or the law of sales as to where title passes—considerations which may have some bearing on the constitutional power of the states to impose certain laws— these considerations would appear to have little importance in determining state fiscal policy as to where the income or receipts should be taxed. Each state, A, B, C, and D, would appear to have a legitimate claim to a portion of the income or receipts.

It is because of such competing claims of the states—the difficulty of fixing a single situs of intangible assets and of attaching the entire income or receipts from sales to a single state—that the states have largely rejected allocation of intangible assets under capital stock taxes and allocation of sales income under net income taxes. A number of states, however, apply allocation to rents and royalties from real estate and tangible personal property, including oil and mineral royalties; to patent and copyright royalties; to dividends and interest; to capital gains and losses; and, in some states, to compensation for services. Under the Uniform Division of Income for Tax Purposes Act ("UDITPA") and similar statutes, which have been adopted by most states with corporate income taxes, income of the above description is allocated, but only if such income does not arise out of transactions in the ordinary course of the taxpayer's trade or business. See pp. 544–57 infra.

Apportionment. For the reasons suggested above, it is apparent that the operating property or income of a multistate business often cannot be allocated satisfactorily by source. To deal with this problem, the states developed the method of apportioning the tax base by formula. The theory of apportionment by formula is that certain factors or elements of a business will fairly reflect the measure of the tax attributable to a state. Thus, in capital stock taxes, which employ essentially a property measure, an apportionment method used in some states is a single-factor formula of the ratio of the corporation's real and tangible personal property within the state to the corporation's entire real and tangible personal property wherever located. For example, suppose the value of T's entire real and personal property is $1,000,000 and its factory and inventory and other tangibles within the State A are valued at $750,000. Seventy-five percent of its capital stock will be apportioned to State A, where it will be taxed. If all the other states in which T does business utilize a similar method of apportionment and find the same values for T's property and capital stock, T's entire capital stock will be taxed, in full, but only once, by all the states in which it does business.

While states still occasionally utilize the single-factor property formula in apportioning capital stock taxes, they have generally discarded it in apportioning net income and, in many cases, in apportioning capital stock. The most widely used formula the states employ, the so-called Massachusetts formula, utilizes three factors: real and tangible personal property, payroll, and sales. Historically, the three factors were averaged, so that if a corporation had 40 percent of its property, 35 percent of its payroll and 15 percent of its sales in the state, its apportionment percentage would be 30 ([40 + 35 + 15] ÷ 3); and it would apportion 30 percent of its income or capital stock or other measure of the tax to the state. Today roughly half the states put additional weight (usually double) on the sales factor, so that the corporation described in the preceding sentence would have an apportionment factor of approximately 26 percent ([40 + 35 + 15 + 15] ÷ 4). The three factors of property, payroll, and sales can be justified as a rough indicator of either the source of a corporation's income or capital stock value or of the social costs that the corporation generates.

Separate Accounting. The separate accounting method is generally limited to the division of *income* as distinguished from other tax bases of the multistate business. Separate accounting seeks to treat the taxpayer's business activities conducted within the state separately from its out-of-state business activities and to compute its income as if the income-producing activities were confined to the taxing state. When income taxation of corporations began in this country, separate accounting for multistate operations was regarded as the most precise method of determining the income derived from various states. Early state income tax laws permitted corporations to treat separately the income earned in each state as long as they maintained separate geographic accounting records that enabled them to ascertain that income with reasonable accuracy. The essential problem with separate accounting, as the U.S. Supreme Court has observed, is that "separate accounting, while it purports to isolate portions of income received in various States, may fail to account for contributions to income resulting from functional integration, centralization of management, and economies of scale." Mobil Oil Corp. v. Commissioner of Taxes, 445 U.S. 425, 438, 100 S.Ct. 1223 (1980).

1. APPORTIONMENT BY FORMULA IN GENERAL: FEDERAL CONSTITUTIONAL LIMITATIONS

Most of the ensuing materials involve questions relating to formulary apportionment, particularly of corporate net income taxes. In this connection, it is critically important for you to understand at the outset that there are two fundamental inquiries that underlie these questions. The first is the determination of the *apportionable tax base*, i.e., what property, income, or receipts are properly includable in the "pie" of which the state is attempting to take its fair "slice" by means of an apportionment formula? Since much of the taxpayer's property, income, or receipts may be "located" outside the state in a territorial sense, the question becomes whether the state is justified in looking to such out-of-state property, income, or receipts for purposes of determining the property, income, or receipts that are taxable by the state. As we shall see, the answer to this question depends largely on whether the property, income, or receipts derive from the "unitary business" that the taxpayer carries on within the taxing state.

Once one has delineated the apportionable tax base, the second problem is to determine the actual percentage of the tax base that should be apportioned to the state. This is no mere mechanical inquiry. It involves not only the application of detailed and sometimes complex statutory and regulatory rules that the states have developed to apportion income and other tax bases to the state, it also, in many cases, raises the fundamental constitutional question whether the tax base has been *fairly apportioned* to the taxing state. This inquiry depends on whether the "slice" of the taxpayer's apportionable "pie" that the state has attributed to itself by formula in fact reasonably reflects the activities that the taxpayer is carrying on within the state with respect to that tax base. If the taxpayer can demonstrate that the property, or income, or receipts assigned to the state by formula bear no reasonable relationship to the taxpayer's local presence or activities, the Due Process and Commerce Clauses will bar the state from taxing the tax base assigned to the state by formula. As we shall see, however, the taxpayer has an extremely heavy burden of proof on this issue.

Finally, you should be aware that these two questions—(1) what is the apportionable tax base?, and (2) is the apportionment fair?—are not always clearly articulated or differentiated in the judicial opinions, even though they are analytically distinct.

a. The Apportionable Tax Base

Although this chapter is entitled "Corporate Income Taxes," the first apportionment case set out below is an ad valorem property tax case as are a number of the other cases considered in the ensuing materials. There is a reason for this. The U.S. Supreme Court first articulated the constitutional principles governing apportionability and fair apportionment in the context of ad valorem property taxes on interstate railroads, express companies, and other instrumentalities of interstate commerce. Thus while the Court has declared that "the linchpin of apportionability in the field of state *income* taxation is the unitary business principle," Mobil Oil Corp. v. Commissioner of Taxes, 445 U.S. 425, 439, 100 S.Ct. 1223 (1980) (emphasis supplied), the unitary business principle derives from the "unit rule" developed in the late nineteenth century for apportioning property values of railroad, telegraph, and express companies to state and local taxing jurisdictions.

To ascertain the value of a company's property that was properly attributable to the taxing jurisdiction, states and localities would determine the value of the entire operating system and then assign to the state or locality a proportion of the system value based on the ratio of the amount of some identifiable factor within the state to the amount of such factor in the entire system. See, e.g., Western Union Tel. Co. v. Taggart, 163 U.S. 1, 18, 16 S.Ct. 1054 (1896) (telegraph line mileage); Pullmans

Palace Car Co. v. Pennsylvania, 141 U.S. 18, 26, 11 S.Ct. 876 (1891) (track mileage). When taxpayers complained that taxing jurisdictions were exceeding their power by taking account of extraterritorial values for purposes of determining the proper value of the taxpayer's property attributable to the taxing state or locality, the Court responded:

> But * * * a railroad must be regarded for many, indeed for most purposes, as a unit. The track of the road is but one track from one end of it to the other, and, except in its use as one track, is of little value. In this track as a whole each county through which it passes has an interest much more important than it has in the limited part of it lying within its boundary. * * * It may well be doubted whether any better mode of determining the value of that portion of the track within any one county has been devised than to ascertain the value of the whole road, and apportion the value within the county by its relative length to the whole.

State Railroad Tax Cases, 92 U.S. (2 Otto) 575, 608 (1875). While the Court's articulation of the unit rule quoted above was addressed to the apportionment of the railroad's property among counties rather than among states, the Court subsequently applied the same principles to disputes involving interstate values.

FARGO v. HART

Supreme Court of the United States, 1904.
193 U.S. 490, 24 S.Ct. 498.

MR. JUSTICE HOLMES delivered the opinion of the Court:

This is an appeal from a decree of the United States circuit court dismissing the plaintiff's bill and supplemental bills. The bill was brought by the president of the American Express Company, a joint stock company of New York, on behalf of himself and the other members of the company, to enjoin the auditor of the state of Indiana from certifying an assessment for 1898 to the auditor of the several counties of the state. Supplemental bills sought the like remedy in respect of the assessments for the following years through 1901. The ground of relief is that the assessments will result in unconstitutional interferences with commerce among the states and also are contrary to the 14th Amendment. The plaintiff's case may be stated in a few words. The American Express Company is engaged in commerce among the states, including Indiana. It has real estate of a market value of nearly two million dollars, which is outside of Indiana, and which it says is not used in its business, and fifteen million and a half dollars' worth of personal property in New York, as to which it says the same; over three million dollars' worth of real estate used in connection with the business, and about a million and a half dollars' worth of personal property used in the business, of which there was less than eight thousand dollars' worth in Indiana. It has paid the local taxes on this last. The total value of the property for 1898 was $22,059,055.35. The market value of what, for brevity, we may call its stock, was $21,600,000. The state board of tax commissioners has undertaken to tax the property of the company under the law which was upheld in American Exp. Co. v. Indiana, 165 U. S. 255, 17 Sup. Ct. Rep. 991, by treating the whole business as a unit and assessing the company on a proportion of the total value of its property, determined by the ratio of the mileage in Indiana to the total mileage of the company, excluding its ocean mileage for foreign express business, which the company says should have been included. The company relies on the fact that it made a return to the board, setting forth in detail what its property was, where it was situated, and how used, and that the value and nature of the property was not disputed; and it contends that when these facts appeared the board was not at liberty to spread the whole value over the whole line equally, and tax by mileage. The auditor in his answer sets up that the said sum of fifteen and a half million dollars in securities is used by the company as a part of the necessary capital of its business, and denies that the board assesses personal property not used in connection with its business. Thus, he admits, by implication, that the above sum did enter into the assessment made, and this would be obvious unless we should assume the intended tax to be wholly arbitrary, as the assessment was at the rate of $450 a mile for 1,798 and a fraction miles, amounting to $809,253, as against less than eight thousand dollars' worth of tangible property in the state. * * *

We come, then, to the real question of the case: whether, the tax provided for by the statute being a tax on property, it sufficiently appears that the board took into account property which it had no right to take into account in fixing the assessment at the large sum which we have mentioned. We already have stated reasons for assuming that the personal property in New York did enter into the valuation. * * * The ground taken before the board, and insisted on in argument before us, was that the property ought to enter into the valuation, because, wherever situated, it was used in the business; if not otherwise, at least as giving the credit necessary for carrying the business on. We shall assume that the question before us is narrowed to whether that ground can be maintained. * * *

The general principles to be applied are settled. A state cannot tax the privilege of carrying on commerce among the states. Neither can it tax property outside of its jurisdiction belonging to persons domiciled elsewhere. On the other hand, it can tax property permanently within its jurisdiction although belonging to persons domiciled elsewhere and used in commerce among the states. And when that property is part of a system and has its actual uses only in connection with other parts of the system, that fact may be considered by the state in taxing, even though the other parts of the system are outside of the state. The sleepers and rails of a railroad, or the posts and wires of a telegraph company, are worth more than the prepared wood and the bars of steel or coils of wire, from their organic connection with other rails or wires and the rest of the apparatus of a working whole. This being clear, it is held reasonable and constitutional to get at the worth of such a line, in the absence of anything more special, by a mileage proportion. The tax is a tax on property, not on the privilege of doing the business, but it is intended to reach the intangible value due to what we have called the organic relation of the property in the state to the whole system. Western U. Teleg. Co. v. Taggart, 163 U. S. 1, 21, 22, 16 Sup. Ct. Rep. 1054. And this principle, established by many cases, has been extended by the cases first cited above to the lines of express companies, although those lines are not material lines upon the face of the earth. There is the same organic connection as in the other cases.

It is obvious, however, that this notion of organic unity may be made a means of unlawfully taxing the privilege, or property outside the state, under the name of enhanced value or good will, if it is not closely confined to its true meaning. So long as it fairly may be assumed that the different parts of a line are about equal in value, a division by mileage is justifiable. But it is recognized in the cases that if, for instance, a railroad company had terminals in one state equal in value to all the rest of the line through another, the latter state could not make use of the unity of the road to equalize the value of every mile. That would be taxing property outside of the state under a pretense. The same principle applies to personal property which the state would not have the right to tax directly. * * *

We come back to the question whether the taking of personal property outside the state into the assessment can be justified on the ground that it gives credit necessary for the business in the state. The testimony was that the property was not necessary for that purpose, and, in fact, was not used. We may assume that the board was of a different opinion, so far as that was concerned, and still we may hold its action unjustified. It will be seen that we are dealing with much more attenuated relations than when there is a physical line of rails or wires to be valued, every mile of which is a necessary condition of the use of the rest of the lines beyond, and therefore a reflex condition of the value of the line behind it. The case is stronger even than one of terminals having a large value as real estate independent of their use to the road. The express business added nothing to the value of the bonds in New York. Conversely, the utmost extent to which those bonds entered into the value of property in Indiana was in so far as they helped to make the public believe that the express company could be trusted, and therefore increased its good will. That they made a part of the public more willing to buy interests in the company because they were an assurance against personal liability was no concern of Indiana. * * *

But again, suppose that the state of the assets of the company had been published in every newspaper in Indiana, can it be imagined that it would have had an appreciable effect upon the company's business? Certainly it is absurd to say that the business of such companies will bear an exact or any proportion to the stocks and bonds which they may own. Unless we are much mistaken, most people who want to send things by express employ a company simply because it is there, and they see its sign is out. The only effect that knowledge of the capital of the company could have would be to produce the conviction that the company was safe to employ. Assume that something is to be added to the good will of a company because it is safe, and that the good will, or a part of it, of the express business in Indiana may be considered in assessing its property there, this is very different from measuring the good will by the capital, when the facts appear as they do in this case. The difference is not a mere difference in valuation, it is a difference in principle, and in our opinion the principle adopted by the board was wrong. It involved an attempt to tax property beyond the jurisdiction of the state, and to throw an unconstitutional burden on commerce among the states. * * *

Decree reversed.

The CHIEF JUSTICE, MR. JUSTICE BREWER, and MR. JUSTICE DAY dissented.

NOTES AND QUESTIONS

A. Why were the $15.5 million in bonds that American Express owned deemed to be personal property "in New York"? Was it the fact that the bonds were deemed to be "in New York" that precluded them from being included in American Express's "unitary" tax base for Indiana ad valorem property tax purposes? If not, what was it that prevented them from being included in the apportionable "pie" of which Indiana was seeking to tax its fair "slice"? If American Express had owned $15.5 million of horses, wagons, and furniture that were located in New York but were used in its express business, could Indiana have included the value of such property in American Express's apportionable tax base? See American Express Co. v. Indiana, 165 U.S. 255, 17 S.Ct. 991 (1897), which the Court cites in *Fargo v. Hart*. If so, is it the fact that the bonds were intangible rather than tangible that led to their exclusion? Suppose the bonds had been part of American Express's working capital, which was used to purchase operating equipment and to meet short-term obligations. Would the result in the case have been the same? Why were the bonds not characterized as working capital?

EXXON CORPORATION v. WISCONSIN DEPARTMENT OF REVENUE

Supreme Court of the United States, 1980.
447 U.S. 207, 100 S.Ct. 2109.

MR. JUSTICE MARSHALL delivered the opinion of the Court.

This case raises three important questions regarding state taxation of the income of a vertically integrated corporation doing business in several States. The first issue is whether the Due Process Clause of the Fourteenth Amendment prevents a State from applying its statutory apportionment formula to the total corporate income of the taxpayer when the taxpayer's functional accounting separates its income into the three distinct categories of marketing, exploration and production, and refining, and when the taxpayer performs only marketing operations within the State. * * *

I

A

Appellant, Exxon Corp., a vertically integrated petroleum company, is organized under the laws of Delaware, with its general offices located in Houston, Tex. During the years in question here, 1965 through 1968, appellant's corporate organization structure consisted of three parts: Corporate Management, Coordination and Services Management, and Operations Management.

Corporate Management, which was the highest order of management for the entire corporation, consisted of the board of directors, the executive committee, the chairman of the board (who was also the chief executive officer), the president, and various directors-in-charge who were members of the board of directors. Coordination and Services Management was composed of corporate staff departments which provided specialized corporate services. These services included long-range planning for the company, maximization of overall company operations, development of financial policy and procedures, financing of corporate activities, maintenance of the accounting system, legal advice, public relations, labor relations, purchase and sale of raw crude oil and raw materials, and coordination between the refining and other operating functions "so as to obtain an optimum short range operating program." App. 189; id., at 187–192.

The third level of management within the corporation was Operations Management, which was responsible for directing the operating activities of the functional departments of the company. These functional departments were Exploration and Production, Refining, Marketing, Marine, Coal and Shale Oil, Minerals, and Land Management. Each functional department was organized as a separate unit operating independently of the other operating segments, and each department had its own separate management responsible for the proper conduct of the operation. These departments were treated as separate investment centers by the company, and a profit was determined for each functional department.

At all relevant times each operating department was independently responsible for its performance. This arrangement permitted centralized management to evaluate each operation separately. Each department was therefore required to compete with the other departments for available investment funds, and with other members of the industry performing the same function for the company's raw materials and refined products. There was no requirement that appellant's crude oil go to its own refineries or that the refined products sold through marketing be produced from appellant's crude oil.

Transfers of products and raw materials among the three major functional departments—Exploration and Production, Refining, and Marketing—were theoretically based on competitive wholesale market prices. For purposes of separate functional accounting, transfers of crude oil from Exploration and Production to Refining were treated as sales at posted industry prices; transfers of products from Refining to Marketing were also based on wholesale market prices. If no readily available wholesale market value existed for a product, then representatives of the two departments involved would negotiate as to the appropriate internal transfer value.

Appellant had no exploration and production operations or refining operations in Wisconsin; the only activity carried out in that State was marketing. The Wisconsin marketing district reported administratively to the central region office in Chicago, which in turn was responsible to the Marketing Department headquarters in Houston. The motor oils, greases, and other packaged materials sold by appellant in Wisconsin during this period were manufactured outside the State and then shipped into that State from central warehouse facilities in Chicago. Tires, batteries, and accessories were centrally purchased through the Houston office and then shipped into Wisconsin for resale. The gasoline sold in Wisconsin was not produced by Exxon but rather was obtained from Pure Oil Co. in Illinois under an exchange agreement, permitting Exxon to reduce the cost of transporting the gasoline from its source to the retail outlets. This exchange agreement was negotiated by the Supply and Refining Departments. Additives were put into the Pure Oil gasoline in order to make the final product conform to uniform Exxon standards.

Exxon used a nationwide uniform credit card system, which was administered out of the national headquarters in Houston. Uniform packaging and brand names were used, and the overall plan for distribution of products was developed in Houston. Promotional display equipment was designed by the engineering staff at the marketing headquarters.

B

Because appellant marketed its products in Wisconsin during the calendar years 1965 through 1968, it was required to file corporate income and franchise tax returns in that State for those years. Exxon prepared the returns based on separate state accounting methods, reflecting only the Wisconsin marketing operation. The returns showed losses in the amounts of $821,320 for 1965, $1,159,830 for 1966, $1,026,224 for 1967, and $919,575 for 1968. Accordingly, no tax was shown as being due for any of those years.

Appellee Wisconsin Department of Revenue audited Exxon for the years in question, and on June 25, 1971, the Department sent the taxpayer a notice of assessment of additional income and franchise tax. The Department concluded that pursuant to Wis.Stat. § 71.07(2) (1967) the Wisconsin marketing operation was "an integral part of a unitary business," and therefore Exxon's taxable income in Wisconsin must be determined by application of the State's apportionment formula to the taxpayer's total income. The Department's calculation revealed an additional taxable income of $4,532,155 for the period 1965 through 1968.

Additional taxes in the amount of $316,470.85 were assessed against appellant.

* * *

The Wisconsin Supreme Court * * * concluded that the test for what constituted a unitary business was " 'whether or not the operation of the portion of the business within the state is dependent upon or contributory to the operation of the business outside the state. If there is such a relationship the business is unitary.' " Id., at 711, 281 N.W.2d, at 100, quoting G. Altman & F. Keesling, Allocation of Income in State Taxation 101 (2d ed. 1950). Reviewing the organizational structure and business operations of Exxon, the court reasoned that Exxon's production and refining functions were dependent on its marketing operation to provide an outlet for its products, and Wisconsin was a part of that marketing system. In a high capital investment industry such as the petroleum industry, the court found, the existence of a stable marketing system was important for the full utilization of refining capacity. Accordingly, the court concluded that Exxon's Wisconsin marketing operations were an integral part of one unitary business and therefore its total corporate income was subject to the statutory apportionment formula.

* * *

II

We recently set forth at some length the basic principles for state taxation of the income of a business operating in interstate commerce, see Mobil Oil Corp. v. Commissioner of Taxes, 445 U.S. 425, 436–442, 100 S.Ct. 1223, 1231–1234 (1980), and need not repeat them here in great detail. It has long been settled that "the entire net income of a corporation, generated by interstate as well as intrastate activities, may be fairly apportioned among the States for tax purposes by formulas utilizing in-state aspects of interstate affairs." Northwestern States Portland Cement Co. v. Minnesota, 358 U.S. 450, 460, 79 S.Ct. 357, 363 (1959); Mobil Oil Corp. v. Commissioner of Taxes, supra, at 436, 100 S.Ct., at 1231. The Due Process Clause of the Fourteenth Amendment imposes two requirements for such state taxation: a "minimal connection" or "nexus" between the interstate activities and the taxing State, and "a rational relationship between the income attributed to the State and the intrastate values of the enterprise." Mobil Oil Corp. v. Commissioner of Taxes, supra, at 436, 437, 100 S.Ct., at 1231. The tax cannot be "out of all appropriate proportion to the business transacted by the appellant in that State." Hans Rees' Sons v. North Carolina ex rel. Maxwell, supra, 283 U.S., at 135, 51 S.Ct., at 389.

The nexus is established if the corporation "avails itself of the 'substantial privilege of carrying on business' within the State." Mobil Oil Corp. v. Commissioner of Taxes, supra, at 437, 100 S.Ct., at 1231, quoting Wisconsin v. J. C. Penney Co., 311 U.S. 435, 444–445, 61 S.Ct. 246, 249–50 (1940). In the present case, Exxon does not dispute that it avails itself of that privilege through its marketing operations within Wisconsin. Appellant contends, however, that this nexus is insufficient to permit inclusion of all of Exxon's corporate income within the apportionment formula. While appellant appears to concede that Wisconsin may properly apply its apportionment statute to Exxon's Marketing Department income as established by its separate functional accounting, see Brief for Appellant 18, 29, 33; Reply Brief for Appellant 2–3, it argues that it has demonstrated through its accounting method what portion of its income is derived from exploration and production and from refining—functions which do not occur in Wisconsin and of which the marketing operation in that State is not an integral part.

* * *

The "linchpin of apportionability" for state income taxation of an interstate enterprise is the "unitary-business principle." Mobil Oil Corp. v. Commissioner of Taxes, supra, at 439, 100 S.Ct., at 1232. If a company is a unitary business, then a State may apply an apportionment formula to the taxpayer's total income in order to obtain a "rough approximation" of the corporate income that is "reasonably related to the activities conducted within the taxing State." Moorman Mfg. Co. v. Bair, 437 U.S., at 273, 98 S.Ct., at 2341. In order to exclude certain income from the apportionment formula, the company must prove that "the income was earned in the course of activities unrelated to the sale of petroleum products in that State." Mobil Oil Corp. v. Commissioner of Taxes, supra, at 439, 100 S.Ct., at 1232. The court looks to the "underlying economic realities of a unitary business," and the income must derive from "unrelated business activity" which constitutes a "discrete business enterprise," 445 U.S., at 441, 442, 439, 100 S.Ct., at 1233, 1234, 1232.

We agree with the Wisconsin Supreme Court that Exxon is such a unitary business and that Exxon has not carried its burden of showing that its functional departments are "discrete business enterprises" whose income is beyond the apportionment statute of the State. While Exxon may treat its operational departments as independent profit centers, it is nonetheless true that this case involves a highly integrated business which benefits from an umbrella of centralized management and controlled interaction.

As has already been noted, Exxon's Coordination and Services Management provided many essential corporate services for the entire company, including the coordination of the refining and other operational functions "to obtain an optimum short range operating program." App. 189. Many of the items sold by appellant in Wisconsin were obtained through a centralized purchasing office in Houston whose obvious purpose was to increase overall corporate profits through bulk purchases and efficient allocation of supplies among retailers. Cf. Butler Bros. v. McColgan, 315 U.S., at 508, 62 S.Ct. at 705 ("the operation of the central buying division alone demonstrates that functionally the various branches are closely integrated"). Even the gasoline sold in Wisconsin was available only because of an exchange agreement with another company arranged by the Supply Department, part of Coordination and Services Management, and the Refining Department. Similarly, sales were facilitated through the use of a uniform credit card system, uniform packaging, brand names, and promotional displays, all run from the national headquarters.

The important link among the three main operating departments of appellant was stated most clearly in the testimony of an Exxon senior vice president. This official testified that:

"[I]n any industry which is highly capital intensive, such as the petroleum industry, the fixed operating costs are highly relative to total operating costs, and for this reason the profitability of such an industry is very sensitive and directly related to the full utilization of the capacity of the facilities.

"So, in the case of the petroleum industry it is—where you have high capital investments in refineries, the existence of an assured supply of raw materials and crude is important and the assured and stable outlet for products is important, and therefore when there are—when these segments are under a single corporate entity, it provides for some assurance that the risk of disruptions in refining operations are minimized due to supply and demand imbalances that may occur from time to time.

* * *

"[T]he placing individual segments under one corporate entity does provide greater profits stability for the reason that ... nonparallel and nonmutual economic factors which may affect one department may be offset by the factors existing in another department." App. 224–225.

The evidence fully supports the conclusion of the court below that appellant's marketing operation in Wisconsin is an integral part of a unitary business. Exxon's use of separate functional accounting, and its decision for purposes of corporate accountability to assign wholesale market values to interdepartmental transfers of products and supplies, does not defeat the clear and sufficient nexus between appellant's interstate activities and the taxing State.

* * *

The judgment of the Supreme Court of Wisconsin is

Affirmed.

MR. JUSTICE STEWART took no part in the consideration or decision of this case.

NOTES AND QUESTIONS

A. Why did the Court frame the question presented as arising under the Due Process Clause rather than (or in addition to) the Commerce Clause? Did Exxon's separate accounting evidence go to the question of apportionability or fair apportionment? The U.S. Supreme Court observed in *Exxon* that "[t]he Wisconsin Supreme Court * * * concluded that the test for what constituted a unitary business was ' "whether or not the operation of the portion of the business within the state is dependent upon or contributory to the operation of the business outside the state." ' " Is this definition of a unitary business different from the definition the Court articulated in Mobil Oil Corp. v. Commissioner of Taxes, 445 U.S. 425, 100 S.Ct. 1223 (1980), discussed in *Exxon*, namely, a business characterized by "functional integration, centralization of management, and economies of scale"? Id., 445 U.S. at 438. May a state adopt a definition of a unitary business that is different from the definition adopted by the U.S. Supreme Court? See Section B(3) infra (dealing with the delineation of the unitary business concept under state law).

ALLIED–SIGNAL, INC. v. DIRECTOR, DIVISION OF TAXATION

Supreme Court of the United States, 1992.
504 U.S. 768, 112 S.Ct. 2251.

JUSTICE KENNEDY delivered the opinion of the Court.

Among the limitations the Constitution sets on the power of a single State to tax the multi-state income of a nondomiciliary corporation are these: there must be "a 'minimal connection' between the interstate activities and the taxing State," Mobil Oil Corp. v. Commissioner of Taxes of Vt., 445 U.S. 425, 436–437, 100 S.Ct. 1223, 1231–1232 (1980) (quoting Moorman Mfg. Co. v. Bair, 437 U.S. 267, 273, 98 S.Ct. 2340, 2344 (1978)), and there must be a rational relation between the income attributed to the taxing State and the intrastate value of the corporate business. Under our precedents, a State need not attempt to isolate the intrastate income-producing activities from the rest of the business; it may tax an apportioned sum of the corporation's multistate business if the business is unitary. E.g. ASARCO Inc. v. Idaho State Tax Comm'n, 458 U.S. 307, 317, 102 S.Ct. 3103, 3109 (1982). A State may not tax a nondomiciliary corporation's income, however, if it is "derive[d] from 'unrelated business activity' which constitutes a 'discrete business enterprise.' " Exxon Corp. v. Wisconsin Dept. of Revenue, 447 U.S. 207, 224, 100 S.Ct. 2109, 2120 (1980) (quoting Mobil Oil, supra, 445 U.S., at 442, 439, 100 S.Ct., at 1234, 1232). This case presents the questions: (1) whether the unitary business principle remains an appropriate device for ascertaining whether a State has transgressed its constitutional limitations; and if so, (2) whether, under the unitary business principle, the State of New Jersey has the constitutional power to include in petitioner's apportionable tax base certain income which, petitioner maintains, was not generated in the course of its unitary business.

I

Petitioner Allied–Signal, Inc., is the successor-in-interest to the Bendix Corporation (Bendix). The present dispute concerns Bendix's corporate business tax liability to the State of New Jersey for the fiscal year ending September 30, 1981. Although three items of income were contested earlier, the controversy in this Court involves only one item: the gain of $211.5 million realized by Bendix on the sale of its 20.6% stock interest in ASARCO Inc. (ASARCO). The case was submitted below on stipulated facts, and we begin with a summary.

During the times in question, Bendix was a Delaware corporation with its commercial domicile and corporate headquarters in Michigan. Bendix conducted business in all 50 States and 22 foreign countries. Having started business in 1929 as a manufacturer of aviation and automotive parts, from 1970 through 1981, Bendix was organized in four major operating groups: automotive; aerospace/electronics; industrial/energy; and forest products. Each operating group was under separate management, but the chief executive of each group reported to the chairman and chief executive officer of Bendix. In this period Bendix's primary operations in New Jersey were the development and manufacture of aerospace products.

ASARCO is a New Jersey corporation with its principal offices in New York. It is one of the world's leading producers of nonferrous metals, treating ore taken from its own mines and ore it obtains from others. From December 1977 through November 1978, Bendix acquired 20.6% of ASARCO's stock by purchases on the open market. In the first half of 1981, Bendix sold its stock back to ASARCO, generating a gain of $211.5 million. The issue before us is whether New Jersey can tax an apportionable part of this income.

Our determination of the question whether the business can be called "unitary" is all but controlled by the terms of a stipulation between the taxpayer and the State. They stipulated: "During the period that Bendix held its investment in ASARCO, Bendix and ASARCO were unrelated business enterprises each of whose activities had nothing to do with the other." Furthermore,

> "[p]rior to and after its investment in ASARCO, no business or activity of Bendix (in New Jersey or otherwise), either directly or indirectly (other than the investment itself), was involved in the nonferrous metal production business or any other business or activity (in New Jersey or otherwise) in which ASARCO was involved. On its part, ASARCO had no business or activity (in New Jersey or otherwise) which, directly or indirectly, was involved in any of the businesses or activities (in New Jersey or otherwise) in which Bendix was involved. None of ASARCO's activities, businesses or income (in New Jersey or otherwise) were related to or connected with Bendix's activities, business or income (in New Jersey or otherwise)."

The stipulation gives the following examples of the independence of the businesses:

"There were no common management, officers, or employees of Bendix and Asarco. There was no use by Bendix of Asarco's corporate plant, offices or facilities and no use by Asarco of Bendix's corporate plant, offices or facilities. There was no rent or lease of any property by Bendix from Asarco and no rent or lease of any property by Asarco from Bendix. Bendix and Asarco were each responsible for providing their own legal services, contracting services, tax services, finance services and insurance. Bendix and Asarco had separate personnel and hiring policies ... and separate pension and employee benefit plans. Bendix did not lend monies to Asarco and Asarco did not lend monies to Bendix. There were no joint borrowings by Bendix and Asarco. Bendix did not guaranty any of Asarco's debt and Asarco did not guaranty any of Bendix's debt. Asarco had no representative on Bendix's Board of Directors. Bendix did not pledge its Asarco stock. As far as can be determined there were no sales of product by Asarco itself to Bendix or by Bendix to Asarco. There were certain sales of product in the ordinary course of business by Asarco subsidiaries to Bendix but these sales were minute compared to Asarco's total sales.... These open market sales were at arms length prices and did not come about due to the Bendix investment in ASARCO. There were no transfers of employees between Bendix and Asarco."

While Bendix held its ASARCO stock, ASARCO agreed to recommend that two seats on the 14–member ASARCO Board of Directors be filled by Bendix representatives. The seats were filled by Bendix chief executive officer W.M. Agee and a Bendix outside director. Nonetheless, "Bendix did not exert any control over ASARCO."

After respondent assessed Bendix for taxes on an apportioned amount which included in the base the gain realized upon Bendix's disposition of its ASARCO stock, Bendix sued for a refund in New Jersey Tax Court. The case was decided based upon the stipulated record we have described, and the Tax Court held that the assessment was proper. The Appellate Division affirmed, and so, in turn, did the New Jersey Supreme Court. Bendix Corp. v. Director, Div. of Taxation, 125 N.J. 20, 592 A.2d 536 (1991).

The New Jersey Supreme Court held it was constitutional to consider the gain realized from the sale of the ASARCO stock as earned in Bendix's unitary business, drawing from our decision in Container Corp. of America v. Franchise Tax Bd., 463 U.S. 159, 166, 103 S.Ct. 2933, 2940 (1983), the principle that "the context for determining whether a unitary business exists has, as an overriding consideration, the exchange or transfer of value, which may be evidenced by functional integration, centralization of management, and economies of scale." 125 N.J., at 34, 592 A.2d, at 543–544. The New Jersey Supreme Court went on to state: "The tests for determining a unitary business are not controlled, however, by the relationship between the taxpayer recipient and the affiliate generator of the income that becomes the subject of State tax." Id., at 35, 592 A.2d, at 544. Based upon Bendix documents setting out corporate strategy, the court found that the acquisition and sale of ASARCO "went well beyond . . . passive investments in business enterprises," id., at 36, 592 A.2d, at 544, and Bendix "essentially had a business function of corporate acquisitions and divestitures that was an integral operational activity." Ibid. As support for its conclusion that the proceeds from the sale of the ASARCO stock were attributable to a unitary business, the New Jersey Supreme Court relied in part on the fact that Bendix intended to use those proceeds in what later proved to be an unsuccessful bid to acquire Martin Marietta, a company whose aerospace business, it was hoped, would complement Bendix's aerospace/electronics business.

We granted certiorari. At the initial oral argument in this case New Jersey advanced the proposition that all income earned by a nondomiciliary corporation could be apportioned by any State in which the corporation does business. To understand better the consequences of this theory we requested rebriefing and reargument. Our order asked the parties to address three questions:

"1. Should the Court overrule ASARCO Inc. v. Idaho State Tax Comm'n, 458 U.S. 307 [102 S.Ct. 3103] (1982), and F.W. Woolworth Co. v. Taxation and Revenue Dept. of New Mexico, 458 U.S. 354 [102 S.Ct. 3128] (1982)?

"2. If *ASARCO* and *Woolworth* were overruled, should the decision apply retroactively?

"3. If *ASARCO* and *Woolworth* were overruled, what constitutional principles should govern state taxation of corporations doing business in several states?" 112 S.Ct. 1461 (1992).

Because we give a negative answer to the first question, see infra, at 783–786, we need not address the second and third.

II

The principle that a State may not tax value earned outside its borders rests on the fundamental requirement of both the Due Process and Commerce Clauses that there be "some definite link, some minimum connection, between a state and the person, property or transaction it seeks to tax." Miller Bros. Co. v. Maryland, 347 U.S. 340, 344–345, 74 S.Ct. 535, 539 (1954). The reason the Commerce Clause includes this limit is self-evident: in a Union of 50 States, to permit each State to tax activities outside its borders would have drastic consequences for the national economy, as businesses could be subjected to severe multiple taxation. But the Due Process Clause also underlies our decisions in this area. Although our modern due process jurisprudence rejects a rigid, formalistic definition of minimum connection, we have not abandoned the requirement that, in the case of a tax on an activity, there must be a connection to the activity itself, rather than a connection only to the actor the State seeks to tax. See Quill Corp. v. North Dakota, 504 U.S. 298, 306–308, 112 S.Ct. 1904, 1909–1910 (1992). The constitutional question in a case such as *Quill Corp.* is whether the State has the authority to tax the corporation at all. The present inquiry, by contrast, focuses on the guidelines necessary to circumscribe the reach of the State's legitimate power to tax. We are guided by the basic principle that the State's power to tax an individual's or corporation's activities is justified by the "protection, opportunities and benefits" the State confers on those activities. Wisconsin v. J.C. Penney Co., 311 U.S. 435, 444, 61 S.Ct. 246, 250 (1940).

Because of the complications and uncertainties in allocating the income of multistate businesses to the several States, we permit States to tax a corporation on an apportionable share of the multistate business carried on in part in the taxing State. That is the unitary business principle. It is not a novel construct, but one which we approved within a short time after the passage of the Fourteenth Amendment's Due Process Clause. We now give a brief summary of its development.

When States attempted to value railroad or telegraph companies for property tax purposes, they encountered the difficulty that what makes such a business valuable is the enterprise as a whole, rather than the track or wires which happen to be located within a State's borders. The Court held that, consistent with the Due Process Clause, a State could base its tax assessments upon "the proportionate part of the value resulting from the combination of the means by which the business was carried on, a value existing to an appreciable extent throughout the entire domain of operation." Adams Express Co. v. Ohio State Auditor, 165 U.S. 194, 220–221, 17 S.Ct. 305, 309 (1897) * * * Pullmans Palace Car Co. v. Pennsylvania, 141 U.S. 18, 11 S.Ct. 876 (1891).

Adams Express recognized that the principles which permit a State to levy a tax on the capital stock of a railroad, telegraph, or sleeping car company by reference to its unitary business also allow proportional valuation of a unitary business in enterprises of other sorts. As the Court explained: "The physical unity existing in the former is lacking in the latter; but there is the same unity in the use of the entire property for the specific purpose, and there are the same elements of value arising from such use." 165 U.S., at 221, 17 S.Ct., at 309.

The unitary business principle was later permitted for state taxation of corporate income as well as property and capital. * * * Underwood Typewriter Co. v. Chamberlain, 254 U.S. 113, 120–121, 41 S.Ct. 45, 47 (1920).

* * *

As these cases make clear, the unitary business rule is a recognition of two imperatives: the States' wide authority to devise formulae for an accurate assessment of a corporation's intrastate value or income; and the necessary limit on the States' authority to tax value or income which cannot in fairness be attributed to the taxpayer's activities within the

State. It is this second component, the necessity for a limiting principle, that underlies this case.

As we indicated in Mobil Oil Corp. v. Commissioner of Taxes, 445 U.S., at 442, 100 S.Ct., at 1234: "Where the business activities of the dividend payor have nothing to do with the activities of the recipient in the taxing State, due process considerations might well preclude apportionability, because there would be no underlying unitary business." The constitutional question becomes whether the income "derive[s] from 'unrelated business activity' which constitutes a 'discrete business enterprise.'" Exxon Corp. v. Wisconsin Dept. of Revenue, 447 U.S. 207, 224, 100 S.Ct. 2109, 2120 (1980) (quoting Mobil Oil, supra, 445 U.S., at 442, 439, 100 S.Ct., at 1234, 1232).

Although *Mobil Oil* and *Exxon* made clear that the unitary business principle limits the States' taxing power, it was not until our decisions in ASARCO Inc. v. Idaho State Tax Comm'n, 458 U.S. 307, 102 S.Ct. 3103 (1982), and F.W. Woolworth Co. v. Taxation and Revenue Dept. of N.M., 458 U.S. 354, 102 S.Ct. 3128 (1982), that we struck down a state attempt to include in the apportionable tax base income not derived from the unitary business. In those cases the States sought to tax unrelated business activity.

The principal question in *ASARCO* concerned Idaho's attempt to include in the apportionable tax base of ASARCO certain dividends received from, among other companies, the Southern Peru Copper Corp. The analysis is of direct relevance for us because we have held that for constitutional purposes capital gains should be treated as no different from dividends. The ASARCO in the 1982 case was the same company as the ASARCO here. It was one of four of Southern Peru's shareholders, owning 51.5% of its stock. Under an agreement with the other shareholders, ASARCO was prevented from dominating Southern Peru's board of directors. ASARCO had the right to appoint 6 of Southern Peru's 13 directors, while 8 votes were required for the passage of any resolution. Southern Peru was in the business of producing unrefined copper (a nonferrous ore), some of which it sold to its shareholders. ASARCO purchased approximately 35% of Southern Peru's output, at average representative trade prices quoted in a trade publication and over which neither Southern Peru nor ASARCO had any control. We concluded that "ASARCO's Idaho silver mining and Southern Peru's autonomous business [were] insufficiently connected to permit the two companies to be classified as a unitary business." Id., at 322, 102 S.Ct., at 3112.

On the same day we decided *ASARCO*, we decided *Woolworth*. In that case, the taxpayer company was domiciled in New York and operated a chain of retail variety stores in the United States. In the company's apportionable state tax base, New Mexico sought to include earnings from four subsidiaries operating in foreign countries. The subsidiaries also engaged in chainstore retailing. We observed that although the parent company had the potential to operate the subsidiaries as integrated divisions of a single unitary business, that potential was not significant if the subsidiaries in fact comprise discrete business operations. Following the indicia of a unitary business defined in *Mobil Oil,* we inquired whether any of the three objective factors were present. The factors were: (1) functional integration; (2) centralization of management; and (3) economies of scale. Woolworth, supra, at 364, 102 S.Ct., at 3135. We found that "[e]xcept for the type of occasional oversight—with respect to capital structure, major debt, and dividends—that any parent gives to an investment in a subsidiary," id., at 369, 102 S.Ct., at 3138, none of these factors was present. The subsidiaries were found not to be part of a unitary business. Ibid.

Our most recent case applying the unitary business principle was Container Corp. of America v. Franchise Tax Bd., 463 U.S. 159, 103 S.Ct. 2933 (1983). The taxpayer there was a vertically integrated corporation which manufactured custom-ordered paperboard packaging. California sought to tax income it received from its wholly owned and mostly owned foreign subsidiaries, each of which was in the same business as the parent. The foreign subsidiaries were given a fair degree of autonomy: they purchased only 1% of their materials from the parent and personnel transfers from the parent to the subsidiaries were rare. We recognized, however:

> "[I]n certain respects, the relationship between appellant and its subsidiaries was decidedly close. For example, approximately half of the subsidiaries' long-term debt was either held directly, or guaranteed, by appellant. Appellant also provided advice and consultation regarding manufacturing techniques, engineering, design, architecture, insurance, and cost accounting to a number of its subsidiaries, either by entering into technical service agreements with them or by informal arrangement. Finally, appellant occasionally assisted its subsidiaries in their procurement of equipment, either by selling them used equipment of its own or by employing its own purchasing department to act as an agent for the subsidiaries." Id., at 173, 103 S.Ct., at 2944.

Based on these facts, we found that the taxpayer had not met its burden of showing by " ' "clear and cogent evidence" ' " that the State sought to tax extraterritorial values. Id., at 175, 164, 103 S.Ct., at 2945, 2939 (quoting Exxon Corp., supra, 447 U.S., at 221, 100 S.Ct., at 2119, in turn quoting Butler Bros. v. McColgan, 315 U.S. 501, 507, 62 S.Ct. 701, 704 (1942), in turn quoting Norfolk Western R. Co. v. North Carolina ex rel. Maxwell, 297 U.S. 682, 688, 56 S.Ct. 625, 628 (1936)).

In the course of our decision in *Container Corp.,* we reaffirmed that the constitutional test focuses on functional integration, centralization of management, and economies of scale. 463 U.S., at 179, 103 S.Ct., at 2947 (citing Woolworth, supra, 458 U.S., at 364, 102 S.Ct., at 3135; Mobil Oil, supra, 445 U.S., at 438, 100 S.Ct., at 1232). We also reiterated that a unitary business may exist without a flow of goods between the parent and subsidiary, if instead there is a flow of value between the entities. Id., at 178, 103 S.Ct., at 2947. The principal virtue of the unitary business principle of taxation is that it does a better job of accounting for "the many subtle and largely unquantifiable transfers of value that take place among the components of a single enterprise" than, for example, geographical or transactional accounting. Id., at 164–165, 103 S.Ct., at 2940 (citing Mobil Oil Corp., 445 U.S., at 438–439, 100 S.Ct., at 1232–1233).

Notwithstanding the Court's long experience in applying the unitary business principle, New Jersey and several amici curiae argue that it is not an appropriate means for distinguishing between income generated within a State and income generated without. New Jersey has not persuaded us to depart from the doctrine of *stare decisis* by overruling our cases which announce and follow the unitary business standard. In deciding whether to depart from a prior decision, one relevant consideration is whether the decision is "unsound in principle." Garcia v. San Antonio Metropolitan Transit Authority, 469 U.S. 528, 546, 105 S.Ct. 1005, 1015 (1985). Another is whether it is "unworkable in practice." Ibid. And, of course, reliance interests are of particular relevance because "[a]dherence to precedent promotes stability, predictability, and respect for judicial authority." Hilton v. South Carolina Public Railways Comm'n, 112 S.Ct. 560, 564 (1991) * * *. See also Quill Corp. v. North Dakota, 504 U.S., at 316, 112 S.Ct., at 1915 (industry's reliance justifies adherence to precedent); id., at 320, 112 S.Ct., at 1923 (SCALIA, J., concurring in part and concurring in judgment) (same). Against this background we address the arguments of New Jersey and its amici.

New Jersey contends that the unitary business principle must be abandoned in its entirety, arguing that a nondomiciliary State should be permitted "to apportion all the income of a separate multistate corporate taxpayer." Brief for Respondent on Reargument 27. According to New Jersey, the unitary business principle does not reflect economic reality, while its proposed theory does. We are not convinced.

New Jersey does not appear to dispute the basic proposition that a State may not tax value earned outside its borders. It contends instead that all income of a corporation doing any business in a State is, by virtue of common ownership, part of the corporation's unitary business and apportionable. See Tr. of Oral Arg. 25–26 (Apr. 22, 1992). New Jersey's sweeping theory cannot be reconciled with the concept that the Constitution places limits on a State's power to tax value earned outside of its borders. To be sure, our cases give States wide latitude to fashion formulae designed to approximate the instate portion of value produced by a corporation's truly multi-state activity. But that is far removed from New Jersey's theory that any business in the State, no matter how small or unprofitable, subjects all of a corporation's out-of-state income, no matter how discrete, to apportionment.

According to New Jersey, Brief for Respondent on Reargument 11, there is no logical distinction between short term investment of working capital, which all concede is apportionable, see Reply Brief for Petitioner on Reargument 4–5 and n. 3; Tr. of Oral Arg. 7–8 (Apr. 22, 1992); Container Corp., 463 U.S., at 180, n. 19, 103 S.Ct., at 2948, n. 19, and all other investments. The same point was advanced by the dissent in ASARCO, 458 U.S., at 337, 102 S.Ct., at 3119 (opinion of O'CONNOR, J.). New Jersey's basic theory is that multi-state corporations like Bendix regard all of their holdings as pools of assets, used for maximum long-term profitability, and that any distinction between operational and investment assets is artificial. We may assume, arguendo, that the managers of Bendix cared most about the profits entry on a financial statement, but that state of mind sheds little light on the question whether in pursuing maximum profits they treated particular intangible assets as serving, on the one hand, an investment function, or, on the other, an operational function. See Container Corp., supra, 463 U.S., at 180, n. 19, 103 S.Ct. at 2948, n. 19. That is the relevant unitary business inquiry, one which focuses on the objective characteristics of the asset's use and its relation to the taxpayer and its activities within the taxing State. It is an inquiry to which our cases give content, and which is necessary if the limits of the Due Process and Commerce Clauses are to have substance in a modern economy. In short, New Jersey's suggestion is not in accord with the well-established and substantial case law interpreting the Due Process and Commerce Clauses.

Our precedents are workable in practice; indeed, New Jersey conceded as much. See Tr. of Oral Arg. 37–38 (Apr. 22, 1992). If lower courts have reached divergent results in applying the unitary business principle to different factual circumstances, that is because, as we have said, any number of variations on the unitary business theme "are logically consistent with the underlying principles motivating the approach," Container Corp., supra, at 167, 103 S.Ct., at 2941, and also because the constitutional test is quite fact-sensitive.

Indeed, if anything would be unworkable in practice, it would be for us now to abandon our settled jurisprudence defining the limits of state power to tax under the unitary business principle. State legislatures have relied upon our precedents by enacting tax codes which allocate intangible non-business income to the domiciliary State, see App. to Brief for Petitioner on Reargument 1a–7a (collecting statutes). Were we to adopt New Jersey's theory, we would be required either to invalidate those statutes or authorize what would be certain double taxation. And, of course, we would defeat the reliance interest of those corporations which have structured their activities and paid their taxes based upon the well-established rules we here confirm. Difficult questions respecting the retroactive effect of our decision would also be presented. See James B. Beam Distilling Co. v. Georgia, 111 S.Ct. 2439 (1991). New Jersey's proposal would disrupt settled expectations in an area of the law in which the demands of the national economy require stability.

Not willing to go quite so far as New Jersey, some amici curiae urge us to modify, rather than abandon, the unitary business principle. See, e.g., Brief for Multistate Tax Commission as Amicus Curiae; Brief for Multistate Tax Commission as Amicus Curiae on Reargument; Brief for Chevron Corporation as Amicus Curiae. They urge us to hold that the Constitution does not require a unitary business relation between the payor and the payee in order for a State to apportion the income the payee corporation receives from an investment in the payor. Rather, they urge us to adopt as the constitutional test the standard set forth in the business income definition in section 1(a) of the Uniform Division of Income for Tax Purposes Act (UDITPA), 7A U.L.A. 331, 336 (1985). Under UDITPA, "business income," which is apportioned, is defined as: "income arising from transactions and activity in the regular course of the taxpayer's trade or business and includes income from tangible and intangible property if the acquisition, management and disposition of the property constitute integral parts of the taxpayer's regular trade or business operations." UDITPA § 1(a). "Non-business income," which is allocated, is defined as "all income other than business income." UDITPA § 1(e).

In the abstract, these definitions may be quite compatible with the unitary business principle. See Container Corp., supra, 463 U.S., at 167, 103 S.Ct., at 2941 (noting that most of the relevant provisions of the California statute under which we sustained the challenged tax there were derived from UDITPA). Furthermore, the unitary business principle is not so inflexible that as new methods of finance and new forms of business evolve it cannot be modified or supplemented where appropriate. It does not follow, though, that apportionment of all income is permitted by the mere fact of corporate presence within the State; and New Jersey offers little more in support of the decision of the State Supreme Court.

We agree that the payee and the payor need not be engaged in the same unitary business as a prerequisite to apportionment in all cases. *Container Corp.* says as much. What is required instead is that the capital transaction serve an operational rather than an investment function. 463 U.S., at 180, n. 19, 103 S.Ct., at 2948, n. 19. Hence, in *ASARCO,* although we rejected the dissent's factual contention that the stock investments there constituted "interim uses of idle funds 'accumulated for the future operation of [the taxpayer's] ... business [operation],'" we did not dispute the suggestion that had that been so the income would have been apportionable. 458 U.S., at 325, n. 21, 102 S.Ct., at 3113, n. 21.

To be sure, the existence of a unitary relation between the payor and the payee is one means of meeting the constitutional requirement. Thus, in *ASARCO* and *Woolworth* we focused on the question whether there was such a relation. We did not purport, however, to establish a general requirement that there be a unitary relation between the payor and the payee to justify apportionment, nor do we do so today.

It remains the case that "[i]n order to exclude certain income from the apportionment formula, the company must prove that 'the income was earned in the course of activities unrelated to [those carried out in the taxing] State.'" Exxon Corp. v. Wisconsin Dept. of Revenue, 447 U.S. 207,

223, 100 S.Ct. 2109, 2120 (1980) (quoting Mobil Oil Corp. v. Commissioner of Taxes, 445 U.S. 425, 439, 100 S.Ct. 1223, 1232 (1980)). The existence of a unitary relation between payee and payor is one justification for apportionment, but not the only one. Hence, for example, a State may include within the apportionable income of a nondomiciliary corporation the interest earned on short-term deposits in a bank located in another state if that income forms part of the working capital of the corporation's unitary business, notwithstanding the absence of a unitary relationship between the corporation and the bank. That circumstance, of course, is not at all presented here. See infra, at 789.

III

Application of the foregoing principles to the present case yields a clear result: the stipulated factual record now before us presents an even weaker basis for inferring a unitary business than existed in either *ASARCO* or *Woolworth,* making this an *a fortiori* case. There is no serious contention that any of the three factors upon which we focused in *Woolworth* were present. Functional integration and economies of scale could not exist because, as the parties have stipulated, "Bendix and ASARCO were unrelated business enterprises each of whose activities had nothing to do with the other." App. 169. Moreover, because Bendix owned only 20.6% of ASARCO's stock, it did not have the potential to operate ASARCO as an integrated division of a single unitary business, and of course, even potential control is not sufficient. Woolworth, 458 U.S., at 362, 102 S.Ct., at 3134. There was no centralization of management.

Furthermore, contrary to the view expressed below by the New Jersey Supreme Court, see 125 N.J., at 36–37, 592 A.2d, at 544–545, the mere fact that an intangible asset was acquired pursuant to a long-term corporate strategy of acquisitions and dispositions does not convert an otherwise passive investment into an integral operational one. Indeed, in *Container Corp.* we noted the important distinction between a capital transaction which serves an investment function and one which serves an operational function. 463 U.S., at 180, n. 19, 103 S.Ct., at 2948, n. 19 (citing Corn Products Refining Co. v. Commissioner, 350 U.S. 46, 50–53, 76 S.Ct. 20, 23–25 (1955)). If that distinction is to retain its vitality, then, as we held in *ASARCO,* the fact that a transaction was undertaken for a business purpose does not change its character. 458 U.S., at 326, 102 S.Ct., at 3114. Idaho had argued that intangible income could be treated as earned in the course of a unitary business if the intangible property which produced that income is " 'acquired, managed or disposed of for purposes relating or contributing to the taxpayer's business.' " Ibid. (quoting Brief for Appellee 4). In rejecting the argument we observed:

> "This definition of unitary business would destroy the concept. The business of a corporation requires that it earn money to continue operations and to provide a return on its invested capital. Consequently *all* of its operations, including any investment made, in some sense can be said to be 'for purposes related to or contributing to the

[corporation's] business.' When pressed to its logical limit, this conception of the 'unitary business' limitation becomes no limitation at all." 458 U.S., at 326, 102 S.Ct., at 3114.

Apart from semantics, we see no distinction between the "purpose" test we rejected in *ASARCO* and the "ingrained acquisition-divestiture policy" approach adopted by the New Jersey Supreme Court. 125 N.J., at 36, 592 A.2d, at 544. The hallmarks of an acquisition which is part of the taxpayer's unitary business continue to be functional integration, centralization of management, and economies of scale. *Container Corp.* clarified that these essentials could respectively be shown by: transactions not undertaken at arm's length, 463 U.S., at 180, n. 19, 103 S.Ct., at 2948, n. 19; a management role by the parent which is grounded in its own operational expertise and operational strategy, ibid.; and the fact that the corporations are engaged in the same line of business. Id., at 178, 103 S.Ct., at 2947. It is undisputed that none of these circumstances existed here.

The New Jersey Supreme Court also erred in relying on the fact that Bendix intended to use the proceeds of its gain from the sale of ASARCO to acquire Martin Marietta. Even if we were to assume that Martin Marietta, once acquired, would have been operated as part of Bendix's unitary business, that reveals little about whether ASARCO was run as part of Bendix's unitary business. Nor can it be maintained that Bendix's shares of ASARCO stock, which it held for over two years, amounted to a short-term investment of working capital analogous to a bank account or certificate of deposit. See Container Corp., supra, at 180, n. 19, 103 S.Ct., at 2948, n. 19; ASARCO, supra, 458 U.S., at 325, n. 21, 102 S.Ct., at 3113, n. 21.

In sum, the agreed-upon facts make clear that under our precedents New Jersey was not permitted to include the gain realized on the sale of Bendix's ASARCO stock in the former's apportionable tax base.

The judgment of the New Jersey Supreme Court is reversed, and the case is remanded for further proceedings not inconsistent with this opinion.

It is so ordered.

Jᴜsᴛɪᴄᴇ O'Cᴏɴɴᴏʀ, with whom the Cʜɪᴇғ Jᴜsᴛɪᴄᴇ, Jᴜsᴛɪᴄᴇ Bʟᴀᴄᴋᴍᴜɴ, and Jᴜsᴛɪᴄᴇ Tʜᴏᴍᴀs join, dissenting.

In my view, petitioner has not shown by "clear and cogent evidence" that its investment in ASARCO was not operationally related to the aerospace business petitioner conducted in New Jersey. Exxon Corp. v. Wisconsin Dept. of Revenue, 447 U.S. 207, 221, 100 S.Ct. 2109, 2119 (1980) (internal quotation marks omitted). Though I am largely in agreement with the Court's analysis, I part company on the application of it here.

I agree with the Court that we cannot adopt New Jersey's suggestion that the unitary business principle be replaced by a rule allowing a State to tax a proportionate share of all the income generated by any corporation doing business there.

* * *

I also agree with the Court that there need not be a unitary relationship between the underlying business of a taxpayer and the companies in which it invests in order for a State to tax investment income.

* * *

In this connection, I agree with the Court that out-of-state investments serving an operational function in the nondomiciliary taxpayer's in-state business are sufficiently related to that business to be taxed. In particular, I agree that " 'interim uses of idle funds "accumulated for the future operation of [the taxpayer's] business [operation]," ' may be taxed. Ante, at 2263 (quoting ASARCO, supra, 458 U.S., at 325, n. 21, 102 S.Ct., at 3113, n. 21). The Court, however, leaves "operational function" largely undefined. I presume that the Court's test allows taxation in at least those circumstances in which it is allowed by the Uniform Division of Income for Tax Purposes Act (UDITPA). UDITPA counts as apportionable business income from "tangible and intangible property if the acquisition, management, and disposition of the property constitute *integral parts* of the taxpayer's regular trade or business operations." UDITPA § 1(a), 7A U.L.A. 336 (1985) (emphasis added). Presumably, investment income serves an operational function if it is, to give only some examples, intended to be used by the time it is realized for making the business' anticipated payments; for expanding or replacing plants and equipment; or for acquiring other unitary businesses that will serve the in-state business as stable sources of supply or demand, or that will generate economies of scale or savings in administration.

In its application of these principles to this case, however, I diverge from the Court's analysis. The Court explains that while "interest earned on short-term deposits in a bank located in another State" may be taxed "if that income forms part of the working capital of the corporation's unitary business," petitioner's longer-term investment in ASARCO may not be taxed. Ante, at 2263. The Court finds the investment here not to be operational because it was not analogous to a "short-term investment of working capital analogous to a bank account or certificate of deposit." Ante, at 2264.

Any distinction between short-term and long-term investments cannot be of constitutional dimension. Whether an investment is short-term or long-term, what matters for due process purposes is whether the investment is operationally related to the in-state business. "The interim investment of retained earnings prior to their commitment to a major corporate project ... merely recapitulates on a grander scale the short-term investment of working capital prior to its commitment to the daily financial needs of the company." ASARCO, supra, at 338, 102 S.Ct., at 3120 (dissenting opinion). I see no distinction relevant to due process between investing in a company in order to build capital to acquire a second company related to the in-state business and, for example, "leas[ing] for a term of years the areas of [the taxpayer's] office buildings into which it intends ultimately to expand," which could hardly be claimed to set up a "separate and unrelated leasing business." Id., at 338, n. 6, 102 S.Ct. at 3120, n. 6.

The link between the ASARCO investment here and the in-state business is closer than the Court suggests. It is not just that the ASARCO investment was made to benefit Bendix as a corporate entity. As the Court points out, any investment a corporation makes is intended to benefit the corporation in general. Ante, at 2264. The proper question is rather: Was the income New Jersey seeks to tax intended to be used to benefit a unitary business of which Bendix's New Jersey operations were a part?

Petitioner has not carried the heavy burden of showing by clear and cogent evidence that the capital gains from ASARCO were not operationally related to its in-state business. See Container Corp., supra, 463 U.S., at 175, 103 S.Ct., at 2945. Though this case comes to us on a stipulated record, there is no stipulation that the ASARCO capital gains were not intended to be used to benefit a unitary business, part of which operated in New Jersey. Instead, the record suggests that, by the time the capital gains were realized, at least some of the income was intended to be used in the attempt to acquire a corporation also engaged in the aerospace industry. App. 70–71, 81, 193. The acquisition of Martin Marietta, had it succeeded, would have been part of petitioner's unitary aerospace business, part of which operated in New Jersey. Id., at 194. As the New Jersey Supreme Court found: "[T]he purpose of acquiring Martin Marietta was to complement the aerospace-electronics facets of Bendix business, some of which are located in New Jersey.... Even though the Martin Marietta takeover never came to fruition, the fact that it served as a goal for part of the capital generated by the sales of ASARCO ... stock nurtures the premise that Bendix's ingrained policy of acquisitions and divestitures projected the existence of a unitary business." Bendix Corp. v. Director, Division of Taxation, 125 N.J. 20, 38, 592 A.2d 536, 545 (1991). We will, "if reasonably possible, defer to the judgment of state courts in deciding whether a particular set of activities constitutes a 'unitary business.'" Container Corp., supra, 463 U.S., at 175, 103 S.Ct., at 2945. Because petitioner has failed to show by clear and cogent evidence that the income derived from the ASARCO investment was not related to the operations of its unitary aerospace business, part of which was in New Jersey, New Jersey should be able to apportion and tax that income. As the Court holds that it may not, I must respectfully dissent.

NOTES AND QUESTIONS

A. *The Scope of the Unitary Business in Light of* Allied–Signal. Did the Court's opinion in *Allied–Signal* broaden the unitary business principle as articulated in prior cases? If so, how? Does the unitary business principle differ depending on which of the following two questions is being asked: (1) Is income from one portion of the taxpayer's business includable in the taxpayer's apportionable tax base (the question in *Exxon*); (2) Is income from a particular transaction includable in the taxpayer's apportionable tax base (the question in *Allied–Signal*)? Suppose the question is whether income from two separate corporate entities is includable in a single apportionable tax base. Does this affect the unitary business analysis? Reserve your answer to the last question until you have considered the cases in the next section dealing with apportionment of income from multicorporate enterprises. For a detailed analysis of the *Allied–Signal* case, see Walter Hellerstein, "State Taxation of Corporate Income From Intangibles: *Allied–Signal* and Beyond," 48 Tax L. Rev. 739 (1993).

B. *The Definition of an "Operational" Function.* In adopting an apportionability standard based on whether the asset serves an "operational" rather than an "investment" function in the taxpayer's business, the Court in *Allied–Signal* declared that the operational-function criterion is "one which focuses on the objective characteristics of the asset's use and its relation to the taxpayer's activities within the taxing State." Yet the Court also declared that "in *ASARCO,* although we rejected the dissent's factual contention that the stock investments there constituted 'interim uses of idle funds "accumulated for the future operation of [the taxpayer's] ... business [operation]," ' we did not dispute the suggestion that had that been so the income would have been apportionable." Is this comment consistent with the Court's own definition of an "operational" asset in *Allied–Signal?* Should the critical question be whether the asset is used in the taxpayer's current operations or its future operations? If income from interim uses of idle funds accumulated for future operation of the taxpayer's business is apportionable, why wasn't the income from Bendix's sale of its ASARCO stock apportionable since the proceeds of the sale were used to acquire stock in Martin Marietta, a company that clearly would have been part of Bendix's unitary business once it was acquired?

C. *Short-term Versus Long-term Investments.* In *Allied–Signal*, the Court appears to emphasize the short-term character of an investment as affecting whether it serves an "operational" or an "investment" function. Is there any justification for equating the distinction between short-term and long-term investments with the distinction between investments serving an "operational" rather than an "investment" function? Does it make any difference from a constitutional standpoint whether a corporation's working capital takes the form of 30–year Treasury bills or 30–day commercial paper? If not, why did the Court refer to a "*short-term* investment of working capital" (emphasis supplied) as being a paradigmatic example of an "operational" investment? Would income from a portfolio of overnight loans (so-called "repos") held exclusively to finance future business expansion be apportionable?

D. *Relationship Between the Unitary Business Principle and the Operational Function Test of Apportionability.* In MeadWestvaco Corp. v. Illinois Department of Revenue, ___ U.S. ___, 128 S.Ct. 1498 (2008), the Mead Corporation, whose successor in interest was MeadWestvaco, was in the business of producing and selling paper, packaging, and school and office supplies. Mead had its commercial domicile in Ohio and was engaged in business in Illinois. In 1968, Mead acquired Data Corporation, which later evolved into Lexis/Nexis (Lexis). Lexis was subject to Mead's oversight, but Mead did not manage Lexis's day-to-day affairs. The two businesses maintained separate manufacturing, sales, and distribution facilities, as well as separate accounting, legal, human resources, credit and collections, purchasing, and marketing departments. Mead's involvement was generally limited to approving Lexis's annual business plan and significant corporate transactions. In 1994, Mead sold Lexis, which was then a division, for $1.5 billion, realizing a gain of about $1 billion. Mead used the proceeds to repurchase stock, retire debt, and pay taxes. Mead took the position that the gain from its disposition of Lexis was not includible in its Illinois apportionable tax base. The Illinois taxing authority disagreed. The trial court found that Mead and Lexis were not engaged in a unitary business in an "enterprise" sense, because there was no functional integration, centralized management, or economies of scale between the two businesses. Id., 128 S.Ct. at 1504. Nevertheless, the trial court found that Lexis served an "operational purpose" in Mead's business, and it therefore held the gain to be apportionable on that ground. The Illinois Appellate Court affirmed on the same ground.

The Supreme Court never reached the merits of the question of whether Lexis served an operational function in Mead's business. According to the Court, "the state courts erred in considering whether Lexis served an 'operational purpose' in Mead's business after determining that Lexis and Mead were not unitary." Id. at 1505. The Court observed:

> [O]ur references to "operational function" in *Container Corp.* and *Allied–Signal* were not intended to modify the unitary business principle by adding a new ground for apportionment. The concept of operational function simply recognizes that an asset can be part of a taxpayer's unitary business even if what we may term a unitary relationship does not exist between the "payor and payee."

Id. at 1507–08.

The Court elaborated on this fundamental point by adverting to examples of assets that were operationally related to the taxpayer's unitary business, and thus properly viewed as giving rise to apportionable income, even though there was no "enterprise" unity between the parties involved. Id. at 1508. Thus, in the example set forth in *Allied–Signal* (see p. 430 supra), the taxpayer was not unitary, in an enterprise sense, with its banker, "but the taxpayer's deposits, which represented working capital and thus operational assets, were clearly unitary with the taxpayer's business." Id. The Illinois courts' error in applying the operational-function test, then, was not that the operational-function test has no role to play once it is determined that two businesses are not unitary in the enterprise sense. The fatal flaw in the Illinois courts' analysis was that they applied the operational-function test to another business on an enterprise basis rather than to a discrete asset of the business or to the business as a discrete asset. As the court declared: "Where, as here *the asset in question is another business*, we have described the 'hallmarks' of a unitary relationship as functional integration, centralized management, and economies of scale." Id. (emphasis supplied).

In sum, the holding of *MeadWestvaco* is that one does not inquire into enterprise unity under both the traditional unitary factors (first articulated in *Mobil*) and again under the operational-function test. Because the only question before the state courts was enterprise unity—there was no claim to apportionability of income from a discrete asset of Lexis or as Lexis being employed as discrete asset—there simply was no place for application of the operational-function criterion. Id. at 1508. For further discussion of *MeadWestvaco*, see Walter Hellerstein, "*MeadWestvaco* and the Scope of the Unitary Business Principle," 108 J. Tax'n 261 (2008).

E. *Allocation of Expenses to Unitary and Nonunitary Income.* If a nondomiciliary taxpayer earns income that is not derived from a unitary business conducted in the taxing state and therefore is constitutionally exempt from tax under the principles articulated in *Allied–Signal*, it is clear as a matter of sound income tax policy, and, indeed, as a matter of constitutional law, that the state may deny the taxpayer a deduction for expenses incurred in earning that income. Thus, if Bendix had incurred expenses in selling its investment in ASARCO, which generated income that New Jersey could not constitutionally tax, New Jersey could have required Bendix to reduce its otherwise allowable expense deductions by the expenses attributable to the sale of its ASARCO stock. The Internal Revenue Code adopts the same principle in providing that "[n]o deduction shall be allowed for * * * [a]ny amount otherwise allowable as a deduction which is allocable to * * * income * * * wholly exempt from the taxes imposed by this subtitle * * *" I.R.C. § 265. But suppose a state takes the position that *all* expenses should be attributed to the generation of nontaxable, nonunitary income before they are permitted as a deduction from taxable, unitary income? This, in simplified terms, is the question raised by the *Hunt–Wesson* case.

HUNT–WESSON, INC. v. FRANCHISE TAX BOARD OF CALIFORNIA

Supreme Court of the United States, 2000.
528 U.S. 458, 120 S.Ct. 1022.

JUSTICE BREYER delivered the opinion of the Court.

A State may tax a proportionate share of the income of a nondomiciliary corporation that carries out a particular business both inside and outside that State. Allied–Signal, Inc. v. Director, Div. of Taxation, 504 U.S. 768, 772, 112 S.Ct. 2251 (1992). The State, however, may not tax income received by a corporation from an " ' "unrelated business activity' " which constitutes a " 'discrete business enterprise." ' " Id., at 773, 112 S.Ct. 2251 (quoting Exxon Corp. v. Department of Revenue of Wis., 447 U.S. 207, 224, 100 S.Ct. 2109 (1980), in turn quoting Mobil Oil Corp. v. Commissioner of Taxes of Vt., 445 U.S. 425, 442, 439, 100 S.Ct. 1223 (1980)). California's rules for taxing its share of a multistate corporation's income authorize a deduction for interest expense. But they permit (with one adjustment) use of that deduction only to the extent that the amount exceeds certain out-of-state income arising from the unrelated business activity of a discrete business enterprise, i.e., income that the State could not otherwise tax. We must decide whether those rules violate the Constitution's Due Process and Commerce Clauses. We conclude that they do.

I

The legal issue is less complicated than may first appear, as examples will help to show. California, like many other States, uses what is called a "unitary business" income-calculation system for determining its taxable share of a multistate corporation's business income. In effect, that system first determines the corporation's total income from its nationwide business. During the years at issue, it then averaged three ratios—those of the firm's California property, payroll, and sales to total property, payroll, and sales—to make a combined ratio. Finally, it multiplies total income by the combined ratio. The result is "California's share," to which California then applies its corporate income tax. If, for example, an Illinois tin can manufacturer, doing business in California and elsewhere, earns $10 million from its total nationwide tin can sales, and if California's formula determines that the manufacturer does 10% of its business in California, then California will impose its income tax upon 10% of the corporation's tin can income, $1 million.

The income of which California taxes a percentage is constitutionally limited to a corporation's "unitary" income. Unitary income normally includes all income from a corporation's business activities, but excludes income that "derive[s] from unrelated business activity which constitutes a discrete business enterprise," Allied–Signal, 504 U.S., at 773, 112 S.Ct. 2251 (internal quotation marks omitted). As we have said, this latter "nonunitary" income normally is not taxable by any State except the corporation's State of domicile (and the states in which the "discrete enterprise" carries out its business).

Any income tax system must have rules for determining the amount of net income to be taxed. California's system, like others, basically does so by asking the corporation to add up its gross income and then deduct costs. One of the costs that California permits the corporation to deduct is interest expense. The statutory language that authorizes that deduction—the language here at issue—contains an important limitation. It says that the amount of "interest deductible" shall be the amount by which "interest expense *exceeds* interest and dividend income . . . not subject to allocation by formula," i.e., the amount by which the interest expense exceeds the interest and dividends that the nondomiciliary corporation has received from nonunitary business or investment. Cal. Rev. & Tax. Code Ann. § 24344 (West 1979) (emphasis added). Suppose the Illinois tin can manufacturer has interest expense of $150,000; and suppose it receives $100,000 in dividend income from a nonunitary New Zealand sheep-farming subsidiary. California's rule authorizes an interest deduction, not of $150,000, but of $50,000, for the deduction is allowed only insofar as the interest expense "exceeds" this other unrelated income.

* * *

The question before us then is reasonably straightforward: Does the Constitution permit California to carve out an exception to its interest expense deduction, which it measures by the amount of nonunitary dividend and interest income that the nondomiciliary corporation has received? Petitioner, Hunt–Wesson, is successor in interest to a nondomiciliary corporation. That corporation incurred interest expense during the years at issue. California disallowed the deduction for that expense insofar as the corporation had received relevant nonunitary dividend and interest income. Hunt–Wesson challenged the constitutional validity of the disallowance. The California Court of Appeal found it constitutional, and the California Supreme Court denied review. We granted certiorari to consider the question.

II

Relevant precedent makes clear that California's rule violates the Due Process and Commerce Clauses of the Federal Constitution. In Container Corp. of America v. Franchise Tax Bd., 463 U.S. 159, 103 S.Ct. 2933 (1983), this Court wrote that the "Due Process and Commerce Clauses . . . do not allow a State to tax income arising out of interstate activities—even on a proportional basis—unless there is a ' "minimal connection" or "nexus" between the interstate activities and the taxing State, and "a rational relationship between the income attributed to the State and the intrastate values of the enterprise." ' " Id., at 165–166, 103 S.Ct. 2933 (quoting Exxon Corp., 447 U.S., at 219–220, 100 S.Ct. 2109, in turn quoting Mobil Oil Corp., 445 U.S., at 436, 437, 100 S.Ct. 1223). The parties concede that the relevant income here—that which falls within the scope of the statutory phrase "not allocable by formula"—is income that, like the New Zealand sheep farm in our example, by itself bears no "rational relationship" or "nexus" to California. Under our precedent, this "nonunitary" income may not constitutionally be taxed by a State other than the corporation's domicile, unless there is some other connection between the taxing state and the income.

California's statute does not directly impose a tax on nonunitary income. Rather, it simply denies the taxpayer use of a portion of a deduction from unitary income (income like that from tin can manufacture in our example), income which does bear a "rational relationship" or "nexus" to California. But, as this Court once put the matter, a " 'tax on sleeping measured by the number of pairs of shoes you have in your closet is a tax on shoes.' " Trinova Corp. v. Michigan Dept. of Treasury, 498 U.S. 358, 374, 111 S.Ct. 818 (1991) (quoting Jenkins, State Taxation of Interstate Commerce, 27 Tenn. L. Rev. 239, 242 (1960)). California's rule measures the amount of additional unitary income that becomes subject to its taxation (through reducing the deduction) by precisely the amount of nonunitary income that the taxpayer has received. And for that reason, that which California calls a deduction limitation would seem, in fact, to amount to an impermissible tax. National Life Ins. Co. v. United States, 277 U.S. 508, 48 S.Ct. 591 (1928) (finding that a federal statute that reduced an insurance company's tax deduction for reserves by the amount of tax-exempt interest the company received from a holding of "tax-free" municipal bonds constituted unlawful taxation of tax-exempt income).

However, this principle does not end the matter. California offers a justification for its rule that seeks to relate the deduction limit to collection of California's tax on unitary income. If California could show that its deduction limit actually reflected the portion of the expense properly related to nonunitary income, the limit would not, in fact, be a tax on nonunitary income. Rather, it would merely be a proper allocation of the deduction. See Denman v. Slayton, 282 U.S. 514, 51 S.Ct. 269 (1931) (upholding federal tax code's denial of interest expense deduction where borrowing is incurred to "purchase or carry" tax-exempt obligations).

California points out that money is fungible, and that consequently it is often difficult to say whether a particular borrowing is "really" for the purpose of generating unitary income or for the purpose of generating nonunitary income. California's rule prevents a firm from claiming that it paid interest on borrowing for the first purpose (say, to build a tin can plant) when the borrowing is "really" for the second (say, to buy shares in the New Zealand sheep farm). Without some such rule, firms might borrow up to the hilt to support their (more highly taxed) unitary business needs, and use the freed unitary business resources to purchase (less highly taxed) nonunitary business assets. This "tax arbitrage" problem, California argues, is why this Court upheld the precursor of 26 U.S.C. § 265(a)(2), which denies the taxpayer an interest deduction insofar as the interest expense was "incurred or continued to purchase or carry" tax-exempt obligations or securities. Denman v. Slayton, supra, at 519, 51 S.Ct. 269. This Court has consistently upheld deduction denials that represent reasonable efforts properly to allocate a deduction between taxable and tax-exempt income, even though such denials mean that the taxpayer owes more than he would without the denial. E.g., First Nat. Bank of Atlanta v. Bartow County Bd. of Tax Assessors, 470 U.S. 583, 105 S.Ct. 1516 (1985).

The California statute, however, pushes this concept past reasonable bounds. In effect, it assumes that a corporation that borrows any money at all has really borrowed that money to "purchase or carry," cf. 26 U.S.C. § 265(a)(2), its nonunitary investments (as long as the corporation has such investments), even if the corporation has put no money at all into nonunitary business that year. Presumably California believes that, in such a case, the unitary borrowing supports the nonunitary business to the extent that the corporation has any nonunitary investment because the corporation might have, for example, sold the sheep farm and used the proceeds to help its tin can operation instead of borrowing.

At the very least, this last assumption is unrealistic. And that lack of practical realism helps explain why California's rule goes too far. A state tax code that unrealistically assumes that *every* tin can borrowing first helps the sheep farm (or the contrary view that *every* sheep farm borrowing first helps the tin can business) simply because of the theoretical possibility of a hypothetical sale of either business is a code that fails to "actually reflect a reasonable sense of how income is generated," Container Corp., 463 U.S., at 169, 103 S.Ct. 2933, and in doing so assesses a tax upon constitutionally protected nonunitary income.* * *

No other taxing jurisdiction, whether federal or state, has taken so absolute an approach to the tax arbitrage problem that California presents. Federal law in comparable circumstances (allocating interest expense between domestic and foreign source income) uses a ratio of assets and gross income to allocate a corporation's total interest expense. See 26 CFR §§ 1.861–9T(f), (g) (1999). In a similar, but much more limited, set of circumstances, the federal rules use a kind of modified tracing approach—requiring that a certain amount of interest expense be allocated to foreign income in situations where a United States business group's loans to foreign subsidiaries and the group's total borrowing have increased relative to recent years (subject to a number of adjustments), and both loans and borrowing exceed certain amounts relative to total assets. See § 1.861–10. Some States other than California follow a tracing approach. See, e.g., D.C. Mun. Regs., tit. 9, § 123.4 (1998); Ga. Rules and Regs. § 560–7–7.03(3) (1999). Some use a set of ratio-based formulas to allocate borrowing between the generation of unitary and nonunitary income. See, e.g., Ala.Code § 40–18–35(a)(2) (1998); La. Reg. § 1130(B)(1) (1988). And some use a combination of the two approaches. See, e.g., N.M. Admin. Code, Tit. 3, § 5.5.8 (1999); Utah Code Ann. § 59–7–101(19) (1999). No other jurisdiction uses a rule like California's.

Ratio-based rules like the one used by the Federal Government and those used by many States recognize that borrowing, even if supposedly undertaken for the unitary business, may also (as California argues) support the generation of nonunitary income. However, unlike the California rule, ratio-based rules do not assume that all borrowing first supports nonunitary investment. Rather, they allocate each borrowing between the two types of income. Although they may not reflect every firm's specific actions in any given year, it is reasonable to expect that, over some period of time, the ratios used will reflect approximately the amount of borrowing that firms have actually devoted to generating each type of income. Conversely, it is simply not reasonable to expect that a rule that attributes all borrowing first to nonunitary investment will accurately reflect the amount of borrowing that has actually been devoted to generating each type of income.

Because California's offset provision is not a reasonable allocation of expense deductions to the income that the expense generates, it constitutes impermissible taxation of income outside its jurisdictional reach. The provision therefore violates the Due Process and Commerce Clauses of the Constitution.

The determination of the California Court of Appeals is reversed, and the case remanded for proceedings not inconsistent with this opinion.

It is so ordered.

NOTES AND QUESTIONS

A. *The States' Approaches to Expense Allocation.* As the Court observed in *Hunt–Wesson,* the states employ a variety of methods for assigning expenses to taxable and nontaxable income. Some states employ direct tracing rules under which expenses are denied when they can be traced directly to the generation of exempt income. Other states employ pro rata rules (based, for example, on the ratio of nontaxable income to total income or to assets generating nontaxable income to total income-producing assets). And still other states employ somewhat arbitrary percentage allocations or some combination of direct tracing and pro rata allocation. See Marilyn W. Wethekam & Craig B. Fields, *"Hunt–Wesson* and Excessive Disallowance Issues," State Tax Notes, July 24, 2000, p. 245.

B. *References.* Walter Hellerstein, "Constitutional Restraints on State Interest Expense Allocation After *Hunt–Wesson,*" 92 J. Tax'n 241 (2000); Michael J. McIntyre, "Constitutional Limitations on State Power to Combat Tax Arbitrage: An Evaluation of the *Hunt–Wesson* Case," State Tax Notes, Jan. 3, 2000, p. 51; Michael J. McIntyre, "What May States Do to Combat Tax Arbitrage After *Hunt–Wesson?,*" 6 State and Loc. Tax Law. 57; (2001); Kathleen Wright, "California's *Hunt–Wesson*—The Aftermath," State Tax Notes, July 24, 2000, p. 231.

b. *Fair Apportionment*

The materials in the preceding subsection focused on the question of apportionability, i.e., how we define the "pie" of which the states may tax an appropriate "slice" determined according to an apportionment formula. The materials in this subsection address the question whether the "slice" that the state seeks to tax is fair. Needless to say, cases do not all come neatly prepackaged in "apportionability" and "fair apportionment" categories. Indeed, many cases involve both issues, with courts considering the fair apportionment issue only after they have considered, and resolved in the state's favor, the apportionability issue. The *Exxon* case set forth in the preceding section was just such a case, but we omitted the fair apportionment discussion because we felt that it was preferable, at least in introducing the subject, to separate the apportionability questions from the fair apportionment questions.

The cases in this subsection are addressed largely to the fair apportionment requirement. They are confined in this manner, however, not because we have omitted the discussion of apportionability,[e] but rather

---

e. To the contrary, we have retained the Court's discussion of apportionability insofar as the opinions addressed the issue.

because apportionability was never in controversy in many of these cases. In reading these cases, you should nevertheless ask yourselves whether there was any argument that could have been made that the tax base was not apportionable because the income did not arise from (or the property was not part of) the taxpayer's unitary business.

UNDERWOOD TYPEWRITER CO. v. CHAMBERLAIN

Supreme Court of the United States, 1920.
254 U.S. 113, 41 S.Ct. 45.

MR. JUSTICE BRANDEIS delivered the opinion of the Court.

This action was brought by the Underwood Typewriter Company, a Delaware corporation, in the superior court for the county of Hartford, Conn., to recover the amount of a tax assessed upon it by the latter state and paid under protest. * * *

Connecticut established in 1915 a comprehensive system of taxation, applicable alike to all foreign and domestic corporations carrying on business within the state. This system prescribes practically the only method by which such corporations are taxed, other than the general property tax to which all property located within the state, whether the owner be a resident or a nonresident, an individual or a corporation, is subject. The act divides business corporations into four classes, and the several classes are taxed by somewhat different methods. The fourth class, "Miscellaneous Corporations," includes, among others, manufacturing and trading companies, and with these alone are we concerned here. Upon their net income earned during the preceding year from business carried on within the state a tax of 2 per cent. is imposed annually. The amount of the net income is ascertained by reference to the income come upon which the corporation is required to pay a tax to the United States. If the company carries on business also outside the state of Connecticut, the proportion of its net income earned from business carried on within the state is ascertained by apportionment in the following manner: The corporation is required to state in its annual return to the tax commissioner from what general source its profits are principally derived. If the company's net profits are derived principally from ownership, sale, or rental of real property, or from the sale or use of tangible personal property, the tax is imposed on such proportion of the whole net income as the fair cash value of the real and the tangible personal property within the state bears to the fair cash value of all the real and tangible personal property of the company. If the net profits of the company are derived principally from intangible property, the tax is imposed upon such proportion of the whole net income as the gross receipts within the state bear to the total gross receipts of the company. * * *

The Underwood Typewriter Company is engaged in the business of manufacturing typewriters and kindred articles; in selling its product, and also certain accessories and supplies, which it purchases; and in repairing and renting such machines. Its main office is in New York City. All its manufacturing is done in Connecticut. It has branch offices in other states for the sale, lease, and repair of machines and the sale of supplies, and it has one such branch office in Connecticut. All articles made by it—and some which it purchases—are stored in Connecticut until shipped direct to the branch offices, purchasers, or lessees. In its return to the tax commissioner of Connecticut, made in 1916 under the above law, the company declared that its net profits during the preceding year had been derived principally from tangible personal property; that these profits amounted to $1,336,586.13; that the fair cash value of the real estate and tangible personal property in Connecticut was $2,977,827.67, and the fair cash value of the real estate and tangible personal property outside that state was $3,343,155.11. The proportion of the real estate and tangible personal property within the state was thus 47 per cent. The tax commissioner apportioned that percentage of the net profits, namely $629,668.50, as having been earned from the business done within the state, and assessed thereon a tax of $12,593.37, being at the rate of 2 per cent. The company, having paid the tax under protest, brought this action in the superior court for the county of Hartford to recover the whole amount.

* * *

It is contended that the tax violates the Fourteenth Amendment because, directly or indirectly, it is imposed on income arising from business conducted beyond the boundaries of the state. * * * In support of its objection that business outside the state is taxed, plaintiff rests solely upon the showing that of its net profits $1,293,643.95 was received in other states and $42,942.18 in Connecticut, while under the method of apportionment of net income required by the statute 47 per cent. of its net income is attributable to operations in Connecticut. But this showing wholly fails to sustain the objection. The profits of the corporation were largely earned by a series of transactions beginning with manufacture in Connecticut and ending with sale in other states. In this it was typical of a large part of the manufacturing business conducted in the state. The legislature, in attempting to put upon this business its fair share of the burden of taxation, was faced with the impossibility of allocating specifically the profits earned by the processes conducted within its borders. It, therefore, adopted a method of apportionment which, for all that appears in this record, reached, and was meant to reach, only the profits earned within the state. "The plaintiff's argument on this branch of the case," as stated by the Supreme Court of Errors, "carries the burden of showing that 47 per cent. of its net income is not reasonably attributable, for purposes of taxation, to the manufacture of products from the sale of which 80 per cent. of its gross earnings was derived after paying manufacturing costs." The corporation has not even attempted to show this; and for aught that appears the percentage of net profits earned in Connecticut may have been much larger than 47 per cent. There is, consequently, nothing in this record to show that the method of apportionment adopted by the state was inherently arbitrary, or that its application to this corporation produced an unreasonable result.

* * *

Affirmed.

NOTES AND QUESTIONS

A. Could the taxpayer in *Underwood* have made a persuasive argument that the income at issue was not apportionable? How did the taxpayer attempt to establish that the apportionment of income to Connecticut was not fair? Was the formula that the state employed for apportioning the income a fair one? How do you determine whether a formula is fair? Can you think of a fairer formula for apportioning income than the one employed by Connecticut? If you can, does that mean that Connecticut's formula is unconstitutional? Is the question "Is the formula fair?" the same question as "Is the apportionment fair?" What are the standards for determining the answer to each of these questions?

B. *Apportionment of Net Income to Loss State.* In Bass, Ratcliff & Gretton v. State Tax Commission, 266 U.S. 271, 45 S.Ct. 82 (1924), an English company engaged in brewing ale in England sold its product both in England and in the United States. The company maintained sales offices in Chicago and New York. Its federal income tax return showed a loss from United States operations, although the business as a whole operated at a profit. The New York State Tax Commission, in accordance with the state's franchise tax formula, assigned to the state the portion of the total net income of the business which the value of certain assets within New York bore to the total value of all such assets wherever located. The company contended that the state tax commission was attempting to assign income derived from its operations outside the United States to New York, when it actually operated at a loss in that state. In upholding the state tax commission, the Court took the position that since the business profits were derived from the operations of the company as a whole, a portion could be attributed to New York through the state's apportionment formula. Whatever one may say about the fairness of an apportionment formula that attributes more income to a state than that determined by the taxpayer's separate accounting methods (as in *Underwood*), how does one square with the concept of fairness the result in *Bass, Ratcliff*, which turns a loss into a gain? Or is that an inaccurate characterization of what happened in the case?

BUTLER BROS. v. McCOLGAN

Supreme Court of the United States, 1942.
315 U.S. 501, 62 S.Ct. 701.

MR. JUSTICE DOUGLAS delivered the opinion of the Court.

This is an appeal (Judicial Code § 237(a) 28 U.S.C. § 344(a)) from a final judgment of the Supreme Court of California sustaining the validity of a statute of California against the claim that as construed and applied to appellant it violated the Fourteenth Amendment. 17 Cal.2d 664, 111 P.2d 334. The statute in question is the Bank and Corporation Franchise Tax Act * * * [that] provides for an annual corporate franchise tax payable by a corporation doing business within the State. The tax is measured by the corporation's net income and is at the rate of four per cent "upon the basis of its net income" for the preceding year. The minimum annual tax is $25. Sec. 10 prescribes the method for computing the net income on which the tax is laid. It provides in part:

> "If the entire business of the bank or corporation is done within this State, the tax shall be according to or measured by its entire net income; and if the entire business of such bank or corporation is not done within this State, the tax shall be according to or measured by that portion thereof which is derived from business done within this State. The portion of net income derived from business done within this State, shall be determined by an allocation upon the basis of sales, purchases, expenses of manufacture, pay roll, value and situs of tangible property, or by reference to these or other factors, or by such other method of allocation as is fairly calculated to assign to the State the portion of net income reasonably attributable to the business done within this State and to avoid subjecting the taxpayer to double taxation."

The tax in dispute is for the calendar year 1936. Appellant paid the minimum tax of $25, asserting that it operated in California during 1935 at a loss of $82,851. The tax commissioner made an additional assessment of $3,798.43 which appellant paid, together with interest, under protest. This suit was brought to recover back the amount so paid on the theory that the method of allocation employed by the tax commissioner attributed to California income derived wholly from business done without that State.

The facts are stipulated and show the following. Appellant is an Illinois corporation qualified to do business in California. Its home office is in Chicago, Ill. It is engaged in the wholesale dry goods and general merchandise business, purchasing from manufacturers and others and selling to retailers only. It has wholesale distributing houses in seven states, including one at San Francisco, California. Each of its houses in the seven states maintains stocks of goods, serves a separate territory, has its own sales force, handles its own sales and all solicitation, credit and collection arrangements in connection therewith, and keeps its own books of account. For the period in question, all receipts from sales in California were credited to the San Francisco house. Appellant maintains a central buying division through which goods for resale are ordered, the goods being shipped by manufacturers to the houses for which they are ordered. All purchases made by appellant for sale at its various houses are made through that central buying division. The cost of the goods and the transportation charges are entered on the books of the house which receives the goods. No charges are made against any house for the benefit of appellant or any of its other houses by reason of the centralized purchasing. But the actual cost of operating the centralized buying division is allocated among the houses. The greater part of appellant's other operating expenses is incurred directly and exclusively at the respective houses. Certain items of expense are incurred and paid by appellant for the benefit of all the houses and allocated to them. No question exists as to the accuracy of the amounts of such expense or the method of allocation. The latter admittedly followed recognized accounting principles. For the year 1935 the amount of such allocated expense charged to the San Francisco house was $100,091. For purposes of this suit it was agreed that approximately 75% of that amount would have been incurred even though the San Francisco house was not operated. The accuracy and propriety of the basis of allocation of those common expenses for 1935 were admitted. Included in such expenses were executive salaries, certain accounting expenses, the cost of operating a central buying division, and a central advertising division. Except for such common expenses, each house is operated independently of each other house. Appellant computed its income from the San Francisco house for the period in question by deducting from the gross receipts from sales in California the cost of such merchandise, the direct expense of the San Francisco house, and the indirect expense allocated to it. By that computation a loss of $82,851 was determined. In the year 1935 the operations of all houses of appellant produced a profit of $1,149,677. The tax commissioner allocated to California 8.1372 per cent of that amount. That percentage was determined by averaging the percentages which (a) value of real and tangible personal property (b) wages, salaries, commissions and other compensation of employees, and (c) gross sales, less returns and allowances, attributable to the San Francisco house bore to the corresponding items of all houses of appellant. No other factor or method of allocation was considered. The propriety of the use of that formula is not questioned if by reason of the stipulated facts a formula for allocation to California of a portion of appellant's income from all sources is proper.

The stipulation also states that in the year 1935 the total sales made by appellant at all its houses amounted to $66,326,000, of which $5,206,000 were made by the San Francisco house. The purchases made for the account of that house were substantially in the same proportion to total purchases. By reason of the volume of purchases made by appellant "more favorable prices are obtained than would be obtainable in respect of purchases for the account of any individual house." The addition of purchases "in an amount equal to the purchases made for the account of the San Francisco house results in no more favorable prices than could be obtainable in respect of purchases in an amount equal to the purchases which would be made" by appellant for its other houses if the San Francisco house was not in existence; and "a reduction in the volume of purchases in an amount equal to the purchases made for the San Francisco house would result in no less favorable prices being obtainable in respect of the purchases which would be made for the remaining houses" of appellant.

Hans Rees' Sons v. North Carolina, 283 U.S. 123, 51 S.Ct. 385, constitutes appellant's chief support in its attack on the formula employed and the tax imposed by California. Appellant maintains that the use of the formula in question, resulted in converting a loss of $82,851 into a profit of over $93,500 and that the difference of some $175,000 has either been created out of nothing or has been appropriated by California from other states.

We take a different view. We read the statute as calling for a method of allocation which is "fairly calculated" to assign to California that portion of the net income "reasonably attributable" to the business done there. The test, not here challenged, which has been reflected in prior decisions of this Court, is certainly not more exacting. Bass, Ratcliff & Gretton v. Tax Commission, 266 U.S. 271, 45 S.Ct. 82; Ford Motor Co. v. Beauchamp, 308 U.S. 331, 60 S.Ct. 273. Hence if the formula which was employed meets those standards, any constitutional question arising under the Fourteenth Amendment is at an end.

One who attacks a formula of apportionment carries a distinct burden of showing by "clear and cogent evidence" that it results in extraterritorial values being taxed. See Norfolk & Western Ry. Co. v. North Carolina, 297 U.S. 682, 688, 56 S.Ct. 625. This Court held in Hans Rees' Sons v. North Carolina, supra, p. 135, that that burden had been maintained on a showing by the taxpayer that "in any aspect of the evidence" its income attributable to North Carolina was "out of all appropriate proportion to the business" transacted by the taxpayer in that State. No such showing has been made here.

It is true that appellant's separate accounting system for its San Francisco branch attributed no net income to California. But we need not impeach the integrity of that accounting system to say that it does not prove appellant's assertion that extraterritorial values are being taxed. Accounting practices for income statements may vary considerably according to the problem at hand. Sanders, Hatfield & Moore, A Statement of Accounting Principles (1938), p. 26. A particular accounting system, though useful or necessary as a business aid, may not fit the different requirements when a State seeks to tax values created by business within its borders. Cf. Hamilton, Cost as a Standard for Price, 4 Law & Contemporary Problems 321. That may be due to the fact, as stated by Mr. Justice Brandeis in Underwood Typewriter Co. v. Chamberlain, 254 U.S. 113, 121, 41 S.Ct. 45, that a State in attempting to place upon a business extending into several States "its fair share of the burden of taxation" is "faced with the impossibility of allocating specifically the profits earned by the processes conducted within its borders." Furthermore, the particular system used may not reveal the facts basic to the State's determination. Bass, Ratcliff & Gretton v. Tax Commission, supra, p. 283. In either aspect of the matter the results of the accounting system employed by appellant do not impeach the validity or propriety of the formula which California has applied here.

At least since Adams Express Co. v. Ohio, 165 U.S. 194, 17 S.Ct. 305, this Court has recognized that unity of use and management of a business which is scattered through several States may be considered when a State attempts to impose a tax on an apportionment basis. As stated in Hans Rees' Sons v. North Carolina, supra, p. 133, "... the enterprise of a corporation which manufactures and sells its manufactured product is ordinarily a unitary business, and all the factors in that enterprise are essential to the realization of profits." And see Bass, Ratcliff & Gretton v. Tax Commission, supra, p. 282. By the same token, California may properly treat appellant's business as a unitary one. There is unity of ownership and management. And the operation of the central buying division alone demonstrates that functionally the various branches are closely integrated. Admittedly, centralized purchasing results in more favorable prices being obtained than if the purchases were separately made for the account of any one branch. What the savings were and what portion is fairly attributable to the volume contributed by the San Francisco branch do not appear. But the concession that a reduction or addition of purchases "in an amount equal to the purchases made for the San Francisco house" would not result in higher or lower purchase prices respectively does not aid appellant's case. There is no justification on this record for singling out the San Francisco branch rather than another and concluding that it made no contribution to those savings. As aptly stated by the Supreme Court of California, "If the omission of the California sales would have no effect on the purchasing power, the omission of sales in an equal amount wherever made would likewise have no effect on the company's ability to purchase at a saving. Thus, by proceeding in turn from state to state, it could be shown that none of the sales in any of the states should be credited with the income resulting from the purchasing of goods in large quantities." Nor are there any facts shown which permit the conclusion that the other advantages of centralized management are attributable to other branches but not to the one in California. The fact of the matter is that appellant has not shown the precise sources of its net income of $1,149,677. If factors which are responsible for that net income are present in other States but not present in California, they have not been revealed. At least in absence of that proof, California was justified in assuming that the San Francisco branch contributed its aliquot share to the advantages of centralized management of this unitary enterprise and to the net income earned.

We cannot say that property, pay roll, and sales are inappropriate ingredients of an apportionment formula. We agree with the Supreme Court of California that these factors may properly be deemed to reflect "the relative contribution of the activities in the various states to the production of the total unitary income," so as to allocate to California its just proportion of the profits earned by appellant from this unitary business. And no showing has been made that income unconnected with the unitary business has been used in the formula.

Affirmed.

* * *

Notes and Questions

A. In Hans Rees' Sons, Inc. v. North Carolina, 283 U.S. 123, 51 S.Ct. 385 (1931), on which the taxpayer relied in *Butler Brothers* to support its position, the taxpayer was engaged in tanning and manufacturing leather. Its tannery and manufacturing plant were located in North Carolina, and it engaged in some leather finishing in New York, where the company's sales office and warehouse were located. The state used a single-factor property formula to apportion the measure of the net income tax assessed, with the result that the North Carolina apportionment fraction ranged from 83 to 85 percent for three of the years at issue and was 66 percent for the fourth year. The taxpayer contended, however, that only about 17 percent of its income, which was derived from the manufacturing and tanning operations in North Carolina, was properly attributable to the state for the years at issue. To support this contention, the company offered evidence designed to show that it derived its income from three sources: buying profit, manufacturing profit, and selling profit. It computed its asserted 17 percent apportionment by attributing only the manufacturing profit and the profit from wholesale sales to North Carolina. Hans Rees, 283 U.S. at 127–28. The trial court, however, struck this evidence from the record on the ground that the apportionment formula was "valid upon its face," and that since the taxpayer was "conducting a unitary business, * * * it was not permissible to lop off certain elements of the business constituting a single unit, in order to place the income beyond the taxing jurisdiction of the State." Id. at 131–32 (quoting the trial court). The Supreme Court of North Carolina sustained the trial court's decision.

The U.S. Supreme Court reversed, declaring:

> We are unable to agree with this view. Evidence which was found to be lacking in the *Underwood* and *Bass* cases is present here. These decisions are not authority for the conclusion that, where a corporation manufactures in one state and sells in another, the net profits of the entire transaction, as a unitary enterprise, may be attributed, regardless of evidence, to either state. * * * In both instances, a method of apportionment was involved which, as was said in the *Underwood* case, "for all that appears in this record, reached, and was meant to reach, only the profits earned within the state." The difficulty with the evidence offered in the *Underwood* case was that it failed to establish that the amount of net income with which the corporation was charged in Connecticut under the method adopted was not reasonably attributable to the processes conducted within the borders of that State; and in the *Bass* case, the court found a similar defect in proof with respect to the transactions in New York.

> Undoubtedly the enterprise of a corporation which manufactures and sells its manufactured product is ordinarily a unitary business, and all the factors in that enterprise are essential to the realization of profits. The difficulty of making an exact apportionment is apparent, and hence, when the state has adopted a method not intrinsically arbitrary, it will be sustained until proof is offered of an unreasonable and arbitrary applica-

tion in particular cases. But the fact that the corporate enterprise is a unitary one, in the sense that the ultimate gain is derived from the entire business, does not mean that for the purpose of taxation the activities which are conducted in different jurisdictions are to be regarded as "component parts of a single unit" so that the entire net income may be taxed in one state regardless of the extent to which it may be derived from the conduct of the enterprise in another state. * * * When, as in this case, there are different taxing jurisdictions, each competent to lay a tax with respect to what lies within, and is done within, its own borders, and the question is necessarily one of apportionment, evidence may always be received which tends to show that a state has applied a method, which, albeit fair on its face, operates so as to reach profits which are in no just sense attributable to transactions within its jurisdiction.

* * *

For the present purpose, in determining the validity of the statutory method as applied to the appellant, it is not necessary to review the evidence in detail, or to determine as a matter of fact the precise part of the income which should be regarded as attributable to the business conducted in North Carolina. It is sufficient to say that, in any aspect of the evidence, and upon the assumption made by the state court with respect to the facts shown, the statutory method, as applied to the appellant's business for the years in question operated unreasonably and arbitrarily, in attributing to North Carolina a percentage of income out of all appropriate proportion to the business transacted by the appellant in that state. In this view, the taxes as laid were beyond the state's authority.

Id. at 132–36.

Can *Butler Brothers* be reconciled with *Hans Rees*? More fundamentally, under the rationale of *Butler Brothers*, when would separate accounting *ever* be a basis for undermining the fairness of the apportionment of the income of a unitary enterprise? Was there anything technically deficient with the taxpayer's separate accounting evidence in *Butler Brothers*? If not, how could it fail to demonstrate the arbitrariness and unreasonableness of the result, which transmuted a loss into a gain? In percentage terms, is not the amount of distortion infinite?

B. *The History of the Use of Separate Accounting.* When corporation income taxation first developed in this country, separate accounting for multistate operations was regarded as the most precise and accurate method of determining the income derived from various states. Consequently the usual practice under the early state income taxes permitted corporations to use separate accounting, if they maintained accounting records enabling them to ascertain with reasonable accuracy the net income in each of the states in which they operated. "Report of Committee on the Apportionment between States of Taxes on Mercantile and Manufacturing Business," 1922 Procs. of the Nat'l Tax Ass'n 198, 214–15. Indeed, for several decades, the Committees of the National Tax Association ("NTA") preferred separate accounting for corporate income taxes, if the taxpayer's records were maintained in a manner adequate to permit a state-by-state breakdown of data. "Report of the

Committee of the NTA on Allocation of Income," 1939 Procs. of the Nat'l Tax Ass'n 190, 204. This was not, however, the only view. See Frank M. Keesling, id. at 220. A survey by the NTA Committee in 1939 disclosed that a majority of the corporate respondents preferred apportionment by formula to separate accounting. See id. at 220–30. Today most state statutes require apportionment of income from operations carried on within and without the state and authorize separate accounting or "any other method to effectuate an equitable allocation and apportionment" of income *only* if the prescribed methods do not "fairly represent the extent of the taxpayer's business activity in this state." Uniform Division of Income for Tax Purposes Act § 18 (emphasis supplied). (The state statutes and the uniform act are considered in detail in Sections B(4)–B(10) infra.) The courts have interpreted such provisions as preferring formulary apportionment to separate accounting.

From the outset, many observers recognized that the disproportionate expense of separate accounting was a serious deterrent to its use. As one NTA Committee put it, "[s]eparate accounting * * * is very expensive and in most cases would probably be so costly that the tax found to be due" by formulary apportionment "would be less than the cost of arriving at the tax if this method were used." Charles W. Gerstenberg, "Allocation of Business Income," 1931 Procs. of the Nat'l Tax Ass'n 301, 306. He further observed that "a system of separate accounts for branches or subsidiaries is, in the majority of cases, impracticable." Id.

Over the years, separate accounting has also come in for increased criticism on the merits. As one study concluded:

> The concepts of separate accounting and unitary business, i.e., a business wherein different components of the activity are interrelated and benefitted by each by the other, are incompatible by their very natures. Except in the simplest of cases, * * * determination by the separate accounting method of the economic effect within prescribed geographical limits of any particular phase of a unitary business is artificial and extremely awkward.

Controllership Foundation, "Apportionment and Allocation Formulae and Factors Used by States in Levying Taxes Based on or Measured by Net Income of Manufacturing, Distributive and Extractive Corporations" 8 (1954). As multistate businesses have come to dominate the economies of all 50 states in which they manufacture, produce, process, warehouse, and market a large number and variety of products and services, separate accounting for unitary businesses has become even less viable, less warranted in principle, and, as a consequence, it is now seldom used in state corporate income taxation. 1 Willis Comm. Rep. 160–67.

C. *Distributing Profits Under Separate Accounting.* The taxpayer in the *Hans Rees* case offered to establish the portion of the profit allocable to buying, to manufacturing, and to selling. What methods are available for apportioning the profit of a unitary business which buys, manufactures, and sells? Two methods often used to separate the manufacturing profit from selling profit are these:

(1) Ascertain the actual cost of manufacturing and add a "reasonable" profit determined by reference to profit made by other corporations,

by the opinions of businessmen, and so forth. The goods are then deemed to have been sold by the manufacturing department to the selling department at the price indicated. Specific costs of each department are determined and overhead, administrative, and other general expenses are charged to the various departments. Thereupon, the allocable profit is determined.

(2) Ascertain the price at which the articles manufactured may be purchased from other manufacturers in the quantities desired. Utilize this figure as the cost of goods and otherwise proceed as indicated in (1) above.

Do such methods produce a satisfactory norm for drawing the line between manufacturing costs at which the goods can be bought elsewhere, manufacturing profit, selling costs, and selling profits? Is it possible with any degree of accuracy to obtain truly comparable prices at which the goods can be bought elsewhere—considering quantities, delivery dates, terms of payment, and devotion of the entire output to a single customer? Is it possible, without speculation and arbitrary assumptions, to establish a reasonable markup over manufacturing costs as the manufacturer's share of an integrated sales operation? What source data could be used that would not suffer from the same defects as the taxpayer's own records? Even if a satisfactory constructive profit can be allocated to each branch of the business, i.e., manufacturing, selling, and so on, does not the entire method proceed on a false assumption that the business should be treated as if it sells not to the trade but to an intermediary (i.e., the taxpayer), which in turn resells?

D. *Attributing Income from Sales Under the Separate Accounting Method.* Under the separate accounting method, a taxpayer which buys and sells goods normally charges each branch of the business with the actual cost of the merchandise sold. The following illustration (taken from George T. Altman & Frank M. Keesling, Allocation of Income in State Taxation 96 (2d ed. 1950)) raises an important question as to the soundness of this method of cost allocation. X, a dealer in mules, has a customer in New Jersey, A, who wants to buy a mule, for which he will pay $100. X can purchase a mule in Missouri, but it will cost him $100 delivered to A. He scouts around and finds B, in New York, who also wants to buy a mule, but B will pay only $75. X then finds that he can buy two mules in Missouri for a total price of $150, including delivery to A and B. X makes the deals and realizes a total profit of $25. X, a resident of Connecticut, does business in both New York and New Jersey and is subject to income tax in both states. To which state or states should the $25 profit be allocated?

E. *Invocation of Separate Accounting by Tax Administrators.* In Texas Co. v. Cooper, 236 La. 380, 107 So.2d 676 (1958), an oil company sought to use the three-factor apportionment formula under the Louisiana income tax. Under the statute, the state tax administrator may resort to separate accounting if this method will more equitably determine net income from sources within the state, but he or she must bear the burden of showing that the formula would produce a "manifestly unfair result." La. Rev. Stat. Ann. § 47:287.94(C) (Westlaw 2009). The taxpayer's principal business in the state was the production of crude oil from its wells and leases; it used most of the oil in its refineries outside the state, but it sold some crude in the market in Louisiana. The taxpayer argued that the tax administrator had erred in utilizing separate accounting in making the assessment, since it was a unitary business whose Louisiana net income could not properly be determined except by formula. Declaring that there was no authority requiring it to treat the oil business as unitary, the court sustained the tax administrator. It looked to sales of crude oil on the local market as the means of establishing the profit attributable to every barrel of oil produced by the taxpayer in Louisiana as it left the state for refining elsewhere.

Does such a method—measuring the profit on sales of crude oil on the local market of a comparatively small portion of a producer's output—fairly determine the profit allocable to the Louisiana oil production in the operation of an integrated producer-refiner-distributor, which sells the final products— gasoline, fuel oil, lubricating oil, and other products—throughout the country and abroad under the Texaco trade-name? There is little doubt that if the taxpayer sought to compel separate accounting under the Louisiana statutory standards, it would fail.

F. *The Weaknesses of Separate Accounting as a Basis for Challenging Unitary Apportionment.* As we have noted above, separate accounting was historically the method that both tax administrators and taxpayers preferred for dividing the income of corporations doing business within and without the state. The method was largely abandoned, however, because it proved to be unworkable in practice. The Achilles heel of separate accounting is the inability to establish fair arm's-length prices for goods transferred, or basic operational services rendered, between controlled branches or subsidiaries of an enterprise. Taxpayers have long contended that the transfer price problem of multinational enterprises is effectively handled by the IRS in auditing federal income tax returns that require a separation of foreign from U.S. source income, and that under section 482 of the Internal Revenue Code, fair arm's-length prices are regularly established. The General Accounting Office (GAO) dealt that argument a body blow in a report it published based on its study of the determination of transfer prices by the IRS under section 482. Comptroller General of the United States, General Accounting Office, Report to the House Ways and Means Committee on the Internal Revenue Service's Administration of Section 482 of the Internal Revenue Code (1981). The GAO concluded that the current system is not working satisfactorily, and it recommended that the Treasury study the possible substitution of unitary apportionment for the current separate accounting method under section 482.

Separate accounting is also vulnerable on its merits when applied to a unitary business because it operates in a universe of unreality. For the essence of the separate accounting technique of dividing the income of a unitary business is to ignore the interdependence and integration of the business operations conducted in the various taxing jurisdictions and treat them, instead, as if they were separate, independent, and nonintegrated. Thus, a business that owns and operates its own rubber plantations, produces rubber and related raw materials, manufactures a variety of products, ranging from automobile tires and airplane parts to raincoats and galoshes, and sells them to manufacturers, wholesalers, and retailers, is a very different enterprise from the sum total of a rubber plantation owner, a rubber products manufacturer, and a wholesaler, each separate, unaffiliated, and independent, and each owning and operating one piece of the business. The differences between such separate businesses and the national and multinational unitary businesses that dominate our economy are crucial and, to a considerable extent, the wealth, power, and profits of the latter group are attributable to the very fact that they are integrated, unitary businesses. That is why separate accounting, which ignores the unitary character of businesses, is not in general a satisfactory method of division of taxable income among the states.

G. *Disparities in Wage and Property Costs in Various Jurisdictions as Distorting Apportionment.* Taxpayers have also contended that the substantial disparities in wage rates and property costs in the various jurisdictions in which a multistate or multinational unitary business operates require a modification or rejection of the standard formula. This type of challenge to formulary apportionment does not depend on the use of a technique, such as separate accounting, which departs from the formulary approach adopted by the state legislature, or promulgated by the tax administrator. Instead, the taxpayer's contention is that with respect to two of the factors, property and payroll, the formula itself is based on the premise that every dollar of payroll spent and every dollar of property cost incurred in one state will produce roughly the same amount of income as a dollar of property or payroll expended in the other jurisdictions in which the corporation may be taxed. A substantial overage of State A's wage and property costs, as compared to those prevailing in other states, perverts this premise, with the consequence, as taxpayers contend, that State A thereby taxes income that is attributable to other taxing jurisdictions under the rationale of the formula itself.

The major problem with this type of demonstration is one of proof. A showing, for example, that wage rates are higher in the taxpayer's manufacturing plants in the Northeast than in the South does not establish distortion of income. Labor productivity, which may depend not only on the comparative skill and efficiency of workers in the various plants, but also on the character and efficiency of the machinery being used and on energy, environmental protection costs, and the like must be taken into account. Consequently, unit labor costs and unit property costs, i.e., the labor and property costs of producing a single unit of the same article in the plants located in varying taxing jurisdictions, must be established. Moreover, if one plant produces, for example, one model or type of automobile and other plants produce different models or types of automobiles, if one produces subcompacts in large volume and another large luxury cars in smaller volume, the unit wage and property costs may not be comparable. And the comparability problem would be greatly magnified if the taxpayer produces a variety of products, such as TV sets in one state, DVD players in another, and cell phones in a third.

NORFOLK AND WESTERN RAILWAY COMPANY
v. MISSOURI STATE TAX COMMISSION

Supreme Court of the United States, 1968.
390 U.S. 317, 88 S.Ct. 995.

[Reread *Norfolk & Western*, Chapter 3, pp. 124–30 supra, before considering the following Notes and Questions.]

NOTES AND QUESTIONS

A. *Norfolk & Western* is a property tax case, not an income tax case. As the Court's discussion reveals, however, the constitutional principles underlying the fair apportionment requirement are essentially the same in the context of property taxation as they are in the context of income taxation. The Court struck down the apportionment in *Norfolk & Western* on the ground that the tax was unfairly apportioned, i.e., that the apportionment formula yielded a "grossly distorted result." But should the Court even have reached the fair apportionment issue? What was the basis for including the Norfolk & Western rolling stock in the apportionable tax base? Although the Court frequently cites *Fargo v. Hart* (pp. 411–14 supra), did the Court correctly apply the principle of that case to the facts in *Norfolk & Western*? In short, why did the Court not address the question of apportionability and, if it had addressed that question, how should the Court have resolved it?

B. *Facial Attacks on Apportionment Formulas: The Single–Factor Gross Receipts Formula for Apportioning Income.* Up to this juncture, we have been considering "as applied" rather than "facial" attacks on the fairness of state tax apportionments. In other words, the issue in cases like *Underwood, Hans Rees, Butler Brothers*, and *Norfolk & Western* was whether the particular apportionment formula in question produced a "grossly distorted result" or an apportionment "out of all appropriate proportion" to the taxpayer's activities in the taxing state. The answer to that question depended in part on a fact-sensitive inquiry into a comparison of the taxpayer's income actually earned (or its property actually located) in the state to the taxpayer's income (or its property) attributed to the state by formula. When the disparity was demonstrated with sufficient specificity and was too great, as in *Hans Rees* and *Norfolk & Western*, the Court invalidated the apportionment as to the particular taxpayer on the facts of the case. Yet there was no suggestion in those cases that the formulas at issue were intrinsically unconstitutional. To the contrary, the Court in *Hans Rees* invalidated the application of a single-factor property formula substantially the same as the single-factor property formula whose application it sustained in *Underwood*. And in *Norfolk & Western*, the Court explicitly acknowledged that "[t]his Court has, in various contexts, permitted mileage formulas as a basis for taxation," even while striking down the application of the mileage formula in the case at hand.

As a matter of logic, however, a question that should be resolved before a court addresses the fairness of the application of an apportionment formula is whether the formula is fair on its face. Indeed, as a theoretical matter, the Court has insisted that an apportionment formula not be "inherently" (Underwood, 254 U.S. at 121) or "intrinsically" (Hans Rees, 283 U.S. at 133) arbitrary. But the Court has never held an apportionment formula unconstitutional on its face. The closest it came to doing so was in General Motors Corp. v. District of Columbia, 380 U.S. 553, 85 S.Ct. 1156 (1965). In *General Motors*, the Court considered an attack upon the single-factor sales formula promulgated by the District's tax commissioners. The formula was adopted by the commissioners pursuant to a statute authorizing them to prescribe apportionment and allocation regulations determining "the portion of the net income of the corporation * * * as is fairly attributable to any trade or business carried on or engaged in within the District." Id., 380 U.S. at 554. The formula provided that if income is derived from the manufacture and sale, or purchase and sale, of tangible personal property, the income was to be apportioned to the District in the percentage of District sales to sales everywhere.

General Motors, which manufactured motor vehicles, parts, and accessories outside the District and sold them within the District, challenged its tax based on the formula as unauthorized by the statute and as violative of the Due Process and Commerce Clauses. The Court agreed with the taxpayer's statutory argument, i.e., that in a case in which "the company carries on business both inside and outside the District," the statute requires that some portion of the income derived from the sales made in the District "be deemed to arise from sources outside the District," and must accordingly be apportioned outside the District. Id. at 559.

Although the Court explicitly disavowed deciding the case on constitutional grounds, it stated:

> The conclusion which we reach by analysis of the plain language of the statute also finds support in the consequences which a contrary view would have for the overall pattern of taxation of income derived from interstate commerce. The great majority of States imposing corporate income taxes apportion the total income of a corporation by application of a three-factor formula which gives equal weight to the geographical distribution of plant, payroll, and sales. The use of an apportionment formula based wholly on the sales factor, in the context of general use of the three-factor formula, will ordinarily result in multiple taxation of corporate income.

Id. at 559. Furthermore, the Court went on to observe that "[t]he standard three-factor formula can be justified as a rough, practical approximation of the distribution of either a corporation's sources of income or the social costs which it generates" whereas "the geographical distribution of a corporation's sales is, by itself, of dubious significance in indicating the locus of either factor." Id. at 561. Although some observers understandably read these remarks as casting doubt on the facial constitutionality of a single-factor sales formula for apportioning net income, see Jerome R. Hellerstein, "State Tax Discrimination Against Out-of-Staters," 30 Nat'l Tax J. 113, 122 (1977), the Court repudiated the constitutional overtones of *General Motors* in Moorman Manufacturing Co. v. Bair, which follows.

MOORMAN MANUFACTURING CO. v. BAIR

Supreme Court of the United States, 1978.
437 U.S. 267, 98 S.Ct. 2340.

MR. JUSTICE STEVENS delivered the opinion of the Court.

The question in this case is whether the single-factor sales formula employed by Iowa to apportion the income of an interstate business for income tax purposes is prohibited by the Federal Constitution.

I

Appellant, Moorman Manufacturing Company, is an Illinois corporation engaged in the manufacture and sale of animal feeds. Although the products it sells to Iowa customers are manufactured in Illinois, appellant has over 500 salesmen in Iowa and it owns six warehouses in the State from which deliveries are made to Iowa customers. Iowa sales account for about 20% of appellant's total sales.

Corporations, both foreign and domestic, doing business in Iowa are subject to the State's income tax. The taxable income for federal income tax purposes, with certain adjustments, is treated as the corporation's "net income" under the Iowa statute. If a corporation's business is not conducted entirely within Iowa, the statute imposes a tax only on the portion of its income "reasonably attributable" to the business within the State.

There are essentially two steps in computing the share of a corporation's income "reasonably attributable" to Iowa. First, certain income, "the geographical source of which is easily identifiable," is attributed entirely to a particular State.[1] Second, if the remaining income is derived from the manufacture or sale of tangible personal property, "the part thereof attributable to business within the state shall be in that proportion which the gross sales made within the state bear to the total gross sales."[2] This is the single-factor formula that appellant challenges in this case.

* * *

During the fiscal years 1949 through 1960, the State Tax Commission allowed appellant to compute its Iowa income on the basis of a formula consisting of three, equally weighted factors—property, payroll and sales—

---

1. The statute provides:

"Interest, dividends, rents and royalties (less related expenses) received in connection with business in the state, shall be allocated to the state, and where received in connection with business outside the state, shall be allocated outside of the state." Iowa Code § 422.33(1)(a).

In describing this section, the Iowa Supreme Court stated that "certain income, the geographical source of which is easily identifiable, is allocated to the appropriate state." 254 N.W.2d 737, 739. Thus, for example, rental income would be attributed to the State where the property was located. And in appellant's case, this section operated to exclude its investment income from the tax base.

2. Iowa Code § 422.33(1)(b).

rather than the formula prescribed by statute.[3] For the fiscal years 1961 through 1964, appellant complied with a directive of the State Tax Commission to compute its income in accordance with the statutory formula. Since 1965, however, appellant has resorted to the three-factor formula without the consent of the Commission.

In 1974, the Iowa Director of Revenue revised appellant's tax assessment for the fiscal years 1968 through 1972. This assessment was based on the statutory formula, which produced a higher percentage of taxable income than appellant, using the three-factor formula, had reported on its return in each of the disputed years.[4] The higher percentages, of course produced a correspondingly greater tax obligation for those years.[5]

After the Tax Commission had rejected Moorman's appeal from the revised assessment, appellant challenged the constitutionality of the single-factor formula in the Iowa District Court for Polk County. That court held the formula invalid under the Due Process Clause and the Commerce Clause. The Supreme Court of Iowa reversed, holding that an apportionment formula that is necessarily only a rough approximation of the income properly attributable to the taxing State is not subject to constitutional attack unless the taxpayer proves that the formula has produced an income attribution "out of all proportion to the business transacted" within the State. The court concluded that appellant had not made such a showing.

We noted probable jurisdiction of Moorman's appeal and now affirm.

II

Appellant contends that Iowa's single-factor formula results in extraterritorial taxation in violation of the Due Process Clause. This argument rests on two premises: first, that appellant's Illinois operations were responsible for some of the profits generated by sales in Iowa; and, second, that a formula that reaches any income not in fact earned within the borders of the taxing State violates due process. The first premise is speculative and the second is foreclosed by prior decisions of this Court.

---

3. The operation of the two formulas may be briefly described. The single-factor sales formula yields a percentage representing a ratio of gross sales in Iowa to total gross sales. The three-factor formula yields a percentage representing an average of three ratios: property within the State to total property, payroll within the State to total payroll, and sales within the State to total sales.

These percentages are multiplied by the adjusted total net income to arrive at Iowa taxable net income. This net income figure is then multiplied by the tax rate to compute the actual tax obligation of the taxpayer.

4. For those years the two formulas resulted in the following percentages:

Fiscal Year Ended	Sales Factor Percentage	Three–Factor Percentage
3/31/68	21.8792%	14.1088%
3/31/69	21.2134%	14.3856%
3/31/70	19.9492%	14.0200%
3/31/71	18.9544%	13.2186%
3/31/72	18.6713%	12.2343%

For a description of how these percentages are computed, see n. 3, supra.

5. Thus, in 1968, for example, Moorman's three-factor computation resulted in a tax of $81,466, whereas the Director's single-factor computation resulted in a tax of $121,363.

Appellant does not suggest that it has shown that a significant portion of the income attributed to Iowa in fact was generated by its Illinois operations; the record does not contain any separate accounting analysis showing what portion of appellant's profits was attributable to sales, to manufacturing, or to any other phase of the company's operations. But appellant contends that we should proceed on the assumption that at least some portion of the income from Iowa sales was generated by Illinois activities.

Whatever merit such an assumption might have from the standpoint of economic theory or legislative policy, it cannot support a claim in this litigation that Iowa in fact taxed profits not attributable to activities within the State during the years 1968 through 1972. For all this record reveals, appellant's manufacturing operations in Illinois were only marginally profitable during those years and the high volume sales to Iowa customers from Iowa warehouses were responsible for the lion's share of the income generated by those sales. Indeed, a separate accounting analysis might have revealed that losses in Illinois operations prevented appellant from earning more income from exploitation of a highly favorable Iowa market. Yet even were we to assume that the Illinois activities made some contribution to the profitability of the Iowa sales, appellant's claim that the Constitution invalidates an apportionment formula whenever it may result in taxation of some income that did not have its source in the taxing State is incorrect.

The Due Process Clause places two restrictions on a State's power to tax income generated by the activities of an interstate business. First, no tax may be imposed, unless there is some minimal connection between those activities and the taxing State. National Bellas Hess, Inc. v. Department of Revenue, 386 U.S. 753, 756, 87 S.Ct. 1389, 1390. This requirement was plainly satisfied here. Second, the income attributed to the State for tax purposes must be rationally related to "values connected with the taxing state." Norfolk & Western R. Co. v. Missouri, 390 U.S. 317, 325, 88 S.Ct. 995, 1001.

Since 1934 Iowa has used the formula method of computing taxable income. This method, unlike separate accounting, does not purport to identify the precise geographical source of a corporation's profits; rather, it is employed as a rough approximation of a corporation's income that is reasonably related to the activities conducted within the taxing State. The single-factor formula used by Iowa, therefore, generally will not produce a figure that represents the actual profits earned within the State. But the same is true of the Illinois three-factor formula. Both will occasionally over-reflect or under-reflect income attributable to the taxing State. Yet despite this imprecision, the Court has refused to impose strict constitutional restraints on a State's selection of a particular formula.[6]

---

6. See, e.g., Underwood Typewriter Co. v. Chamberlain, 254 U.S. 113, 41 S.Ct. 45; Bass, Ratcliff & Gretton v. State Tax Comm'n, 266 U.S. 271, 45 S.Ct. 82; Ford Motor Co. v. Beauchamp, 308 U.S. 331, 60 S.Ct. 273.

Thus, we have repeatedly held that a single-factor formula is presumptively valid. * * * [discussing *Underwood Typewriter*, pp. 442–44 supra].

In individual cases, it is true, the Court has found that the *application* of a single-factor formula to a particular taxpayer violated due process. See Hans Rees' Sons v. North Carolina, 283 U.S. 123, 51 S.Ct. 385; Norfolk & Western R. Co. v. State Tax Commission, 390 U.S. 317, 88 S.Ct. 995. In *Hans Rees'*, for example, the Court concluded that proof that the formula produced a tax on 83% of the taxpayer's income when only 17% of that income actually had its source in the State would suffice to invalidate the assessment under the Due Process Clause. But in neither *Hans Rees'* nor *Norfolk & Western* did the Court depart from the basic principles that the States have wide latitude in the selection of apportionment formulas and that a formula-produced assessment will only be disturbed when the taxpayer has proved by "clear and cogent evidence" that the income attributed to the State is in fact "out of all appropriate proportion to the business transacted ... in that State," 283 U.S., at 135, 51 S.Ct., at 389, or has "led to a grossly distorted result." 390 U.S., at 326, 88 S.Ct., at 1002.

* * *

[The Court also discussed *General Motors Corp. v. District of Columbia*, see p. 456 supra, and concluded that] the Court in *General Motors* made clear that it did "not mean to take any position on the constitutionality of a state income tax based on the sales factor alone." 380 U.S., at 561, 85 S.Ct., at 1161.

The Iowa statute afforded appellant an opportunity to demonstrate that the single-factor formula produced an arbitrary result in its case. But this record contains no such showing and therefore the Director's assessment is not subject to challenge under the Due Process Clause.[9]

III

Appellant also contends that during the relevant years Iowa and Illinois imposed a tax on a portion of the income derived from the Iowa sales that was also taxed by the other State in violation of the Commerce Clause. Since most States use the three-factor formula that Illinois adopted in 1970, appellant argues that Iowa's longstanding single-factor

---

9. In his concurring opinion, Justice McCormick of the Iowa Supreme Court made this point:

"In the present case, Moorman did not attempt to prove the amount of its actual net income from Iowa activities in the years involved. Therefore no basis was presented for comparison of the corporation's Iowa income and the income apportioned to Iowa under the formula. In this era of sophisticated accounting techniques, it should not be impossible for a unitary corporation to prove its actual income from activities in a particular state. However, Moorman showed only that its tax liability would be substantially less if Iowa employed a three-factor apportionment formula. We have no basis to assume that the three-factor formula produced a result equivalent to the corporation's actual income from Iowa activities. Having failed to establish a basis for comparison of its actual income in Iowa with the income apportioned to Iowa under the single-factor formula, Moorman did not demonstrate that the single-factor formula produced a grossly unfair result. Thus it did not prove unconstitutionality of the formula as applied." 254 N.W.2d, at 757.

formula must be held responsible for the alleged duplication and declared unconstitutional. We cannot agree.

In the first place, this record does not establish the essential factual predicate for a claim of duplicative taxation. Appellant's net income during the years in question was approximately $9 million. Since appellant did not prove the portion derived from sales to Iowa customers, rather than sales to customers in other States, we do not know whether Illinois and Iowa together imposed a tax on more than 100% of the relevant net income. The income figure that appellant contends was subject to duplicative taxation was computed by comparing gross sales in Iowa to total gross sales. As already noted, however, this figure does not represent *actual* profits earned from Iowa sales. Obviously, all sales are not equally profitable. Sales in Iowa, although only 20% of gross sales, may have yielded a much higher percentage of appellant's profits. Thus, profits from Iowa sales may well have exceeded the $2.5 million figure that appellant contends was taxed by the two States. If so, there was no duplicative taxation of the net income generated by Iowa sales. In any event, on this record its existence is speculative.[11]

Even assuming some overlap, we could not accept appellant's argument that Iowa, rather Illinois, was necessarily at fault in a constitutional sense. It is of course true that if Iowa had used Illinois' three-factor formula, a risk of duplication in the figures computed by the two States might have been avoided. But the same would be true had Illinois used the Iowa formula. Since the record does not reveal the sources of appellant's profits, its Commerce Clause claim cannot rest on the premise that profits earned in Illinois were included in its Iowa taxable income and therefore the Iowa formula was at fault for whatever overlap may have existed. Rather, the claim must be that even if the presumptively valid Iowa formula yielded no profits other than those properly attributable to appellant's activities within Iowa, the importance of avoiding any risk of duplication in the taxable income of an interstate concern justifies invalidation of the Iowa statute.

Appellant contends that to the extent this overlap is permitted the corporation that does business in more than one State shoulders a tax burden not shared by those operating entirely within a State.[12] To alleviate the burden, appellant invites us to hold that the Commerce Clause itself, without implementing legislation by Congress, requires Iowa to compute corporate net income under the Illinois equally weighted,

---

11. Since there is no evidence in the record regarding the percentages of its total net income taxed in the other States in which it did business during those years, any claim that appellant was taxed on more than 100% of its total net income would also be speculative.

12. Appellant also contends that the Iowa formula discriminates against interstate commerce in violation of the Commerce Clause and the Equal Protection Clause, because an Illinois corporation doing business in Iowa must pay tax on a greater portion of its income than a local Iowa company, and an Iowa company doing business in Illinois will pay tax on less of its income than an Illinois corporation doing business in Iowa. The simple answer, however, is that whatever disparity may have existed is not attributable to the Iowa statute. It treats both local and foreign concerns with an even hand; the alleged disparity can only be the consequence of the combined effect of the Iowa *and* Illinois statutes, and Iowa is not responsible for the latter.

three-factor formula. For the reasons that follow, we hold that the Constitution does not require such a result.

The only conceivable constitutional basis for invalidating the Iowa statute would be that the Commerce Clause prohibits any overlap in the computation of taxable income by the States. If the Constitution were read to mandate such precision in interstate taxation, the consequences would extend far beyond this particular case. For some risk of duplicative taxation exists whenever the States in which a corporation does business do not follow identical rules for the division of income. Accepting appellant's view of the Constitution, therefore, would require extensive judicial law-making. Its logic is not limited to a prohibition on use of a single-factor apportionment formula. The asserted constitutional flaw in that formula is that it is different from that presently employed by a majority of States and that difference creates a risk of duplicative taxation. But a host of other division of income problems create precisely the same risk and would similarly rise to constitutional proportions.

Thus, it would be necessary for this Court to prescribe a uniform definition of each category in the three-factor formula. For if the States in which a corporation does business have different rules regarding where a "sale" takes place, and each includes the same sale in its three-factor computation of the corporation's income, there will be duplicative taxation despite the apparent identity of the formulas employed.[13] A similar risk of multiple taxation is created by the diversity among the States in the attribution of "non-business" income, generally defined as that portion of a taxpayer's income that does not arise from activities in the regular course of its business.[14] Some States do not distinguish between business and nonbusiness income for apportionment purposes. Other States, however, have adopted special rules that attribute nonbusiness income to specific locations. Moreover, even among the latter, there is diversity in the definition of nonbusiness income and in the designation of the locations to which it is deemed attributable. The potential for attribution of the same income to more than one State is plain.[15]

The prevention of duplicative taxation, therefore, would require national uniform rules for the division of income. Although the adoption of a uniform code would undeniably advance the policies that underlie the Commerce Clause, it would require a policy decision based on political and economic considerations that vary from State to State. The Constitution,

---

13. Thus, while some States such as Iowa assign sales by destination, "sales can be assigned to the state ... of origin, the state in which the sales office is located, the state where an employee of the business making the sale carries on his activities or where the order is first accepted, or the state in which an interstate shipment is made." Note, State Taxation of Interstate Businesses and the Multistate Tax Compact: The Search for a Delicate Uniformity, 11 Colum.J.Law & Soc.Prob. 231, 237 n. 20 (1975) (citation omitted).

14. See, e.g., Uniform Division of Income for Tax Purposes Act § 1(a).

15. Thus, one State in which a corporation does business may consider a particular type of income business income and simply include it in its apportionment formula; a second State may deem that same income nonbusiness income and attribute it to itself as the "commercial domicile" of the company; and a third State, though also considering it nonbusiness income, may attribute it to itself as the "legal domicile" of the company. See Note, supra n. 13, at 239.

however, is neutral with respect to the content of any uniform rule. If division of income problems were to be constitutionalized, therefore, they would have to be resolved in the manner suggested by appellant for resolution of formula diversity—the prevalent practice would be endorsed as the constitutional rule. This rule would at best be an amalgam of independent State decisions, based on considerations unique to each State. Of most importance, it could not reflect the national interest, because the interests of those States whose policies are subordinated in the quest for uniformity would be excluded from the calculation.

While the freedom of the States to formulate independent policy in this area may have to yield to an overriding national interest in uniformity, the content of any uniform rules to which they must subscribe should be determined only after due consideration is given to the interests of all affected States. It is clear that the legislative power granted to Congress by the Commerce Clause of the Constitution would amply justify the enactment of legislation requiring all States to adhere to uniform rules for the division of income. It is to that body, and not this Court, that the Constitution has committed such policy decisions.

Finally, it would be an exercise in formalism to declare appellant's income tax assessment unconstitutional based on speculative concerns with multiple taxation. For it is evident that appellant would have had no basis for complaint if, instead of an income tax, Iowa had imposed a more burdensome gross receipts tax on the gross receipts from sales to Iowa customers. In Standard Pressed Steel Co. v. Department of Revenue, 419 U.S. 560, 95 S.Ct. 706, the Court sustained a tax on the entire gross receipts from sales made by the taxpayer into Washington State. Because receipts from sales made to States other than Washington were not included in Standard Steel's taxable gross receipts, the Court concluded that the tax was " 'apportioned exactly to the activities taxed.' " Id., at 564, 95 S.Ct. at 709.

In this case appellant's actual income tax obligation was the rough equivalent of a 1% tax on the entire gross receipts from its Iowa sales. Thus, the actual burden on interstate commerce would have been the same had Iowa imposed a plainly valid gross receipts tax instead of the challenged income tax. Of more significance, the gross receipts tax sustained in *Standard Pressed Steel* and General Motors Corp. v. Washington, 377 U.S. 436, 84 S.Ct. 1564, is inherently more burdensome than the Iowa income tax. It applies whether or not the interstate concern is profitable and its imposition may make the difference between profit and loss. In contrast, the income tax is only imposed on enterprises showing a profit and the tax obligation is not heavy unless the profits are high.

Accordingly, until Congress prescribes a different rule, Iowa is not constitutionally prohibited from requiring taxpayers to prove that application of the single-factor formula has produced arbitrary results in a particular case.

The judgment of the Iowa Supreme Court is affirmed.

[The dissenting opinion of JUSTICE BRENNAN has been omitted.]

MR. JUSTICE BLACKMUN, dissenting.

The unspoken, but obvious, premise of the majority opinion is the fear that a Commerce Clause invalidation of Iowa's single-factor sales formula will lead the Court into problems and difficulties in other cases yet to come. I reject that premise.

I agree generally with the content of Mr. Justice Powell's opinion in dissent. I join that opinion because I, too, feel that the Court has a duty to resolve, not to avoid, these problems of "delicate adjustment," Boston Stock Exchange v. State Tax Comm'n, 429 U.S. 318, 329, 97 S.Ct. 599, 606 (1977), and because the opinion well demonstrates that Iowa's now anachronistic single-factor sales formula runs headlong into overriding Commerce Clause considerations and demands.

Today's decision is bound to be regressive. Single-factor formulas are relics of the early days of state income taxation. The three-factor formulas were inevitable improvements and, while not perfect, reflect more accurately the realities of the business and tax world. With their almost universal adoption by the States, the Iowa system's adverse and parochial impact on commerce comes vividly into focus. But with its single-factor formula now upheld by the Court, there is little reason why other States, perceiving or imagining a similar advantage to local interests, may not go back to the old ways. The end result, in any event, is to exacerbate what the Commerce Clause, absent governing congressional action, was devised to avoid.

MR. JUSTICE POWELL, with whom MR. JUSTICE BLACKMUN joins, dissenting.

It is the duty of this Court "to make the delicate adjustment between the national interest in free and open trade and the legitimate interest of the individual States in exercising their taxing powers." Boston Stock Exchange v. State Tax Commission, 429 U.S. 318, 329, 97 S.Ct. 599, 606 (1977). This duty must be performed with careful attention to the settings of particular cases and consideration of their special facts. See Raymond Motor Transp., Inc. v. Rice, 434 U.S. 429, 447–448 n. 25, 98 S.Ct. 787, 797 (1978). Consideration of all the circumstances of this case leads me to conclude that Iowa's use of a single-factor sales formula to apportion the net income of multistate corporations results in the imposition of "a tax which discriminates against interstate commerce ... by providing a direct commercial advantage to local business." Northwestern States Portland Cement Co. v. Minnesota, 358 U.S. 450, 458, 79 S.Ct. 357, 362 (1959). I therefore dissent.

I

Iowa's use of a single-factor sales apportionment formula—though facially neutral—operates as a tariff on goods manufactured in other States and as a subsidy to Iowa manufacturers selling their goods outside of Iowa. Because 44 of the 45 other States which impose corporate income taxes use a three-factor formula involving property, payroll, and sales, Iowa's practice insures that out-of-state businesses selling in Iowa will have higher total tax payments than local businesses. This result follows from the fact that Iowa attributes to itself all of the income derived from sales in Iowa, while other taxing States—using the three-factor formula—are also taxing some portion of the same income through attribution to property or payroll in those States.

This surcharge on Iowa sales increases to the extent that a business' plant and labor force are located outside Iowa. It can be avoided altogether only by locating all property and payroll in Iowa; an Iowa manufacturer selling only in Iowa will never have any portion of its income attributed to any other State. And to the extent that an Iowa manufacturer makes its sales in States other than Iowa, its overall state tax liability will be reduced. Assuming comparable tax rates, its liability to other States, in which sales constitute only one-third of the apportionment formula, will be far less than the amount it would have owed with a comparable volume of sales in Iowa, where sales are the exclusive mode of apportioning income. The effect of Iowa's formula, then, is to penalize out-of-state manufacturers for selling in Iowa and to subsidize Iowa manufacturers for selling in other States.

This appeal requires us to determine whether these economic effects of the Iowa apportionment formula violate either the Due Process Clause or the Commerce Clause. I now turn to those questions.

II

For the reasons given by the Court, * * * I agree that application of Iowa's formula does not violate the Due Process Clause. * * *

This conclusion does not *ipso facto* mean that Commerce Clause strictures are satisfied as well. This Court's decisions dealing with state levies that discriminate against out-of-state business, as Iowa's formula does, compel a more detailed inquiry.

III

A

It is a basic principle of Commerce Clause jurisprudence that "[n]either the power to tax nor the police power may be used by the state of destination with the aim and effect of establishing an economic barrier against competition with the products of another state or the labor of the residents."

* * *

One form of such unreasonable restrictions is "discriminating State legislation." Welton v. Missouri, 91 U.S. 275, 280 (1876). This Court consistently has struck down state and local taxes which unjustifiably benefit local businesses at the expense of out-of-state businesses.

* * *

This ban applies not only to state levies that by their terms are limited to products of out-of-state business, or which explicitly tax out-of-state sellers at higher rates than local sellers. It also reaches those taxes that "in their practical operation [work] discriminatorily against interstate commerce to impose upon it a burden, either in fact or by the very threat of its incidence." Nippert v. Richmond, supra, 327 U.S., at 425, 66 S.Ct., at 590. For example, this Court has invalidated a facially neutral fixed-fee license tax collected from all local and out-of-state "drummers," where it appeared the tax fell far more heavily upon out-of-state businesses, since local businesses had little or no occasion to solicit sales in that manner. * * * Thus, the constitutional inquiry relates not simply to the form of the particular tax, but to its effect on competition in the several States.

As indicated in Part I above, application of Iowa's single-factor-sales apportionment formula, in the context of general use of three-factor formulae, inevitably handicaps out-of-state businesses competing for sales in Iowa. The handicap will diminish to the extent that the corporation locates its plant and labor force in Iowa, but some competitive disadvantage will remain unless all of the corporate property and payroll are relocated in Iowa. In the absence of congressional action, the Commerce Clause constrains us to view the State's interest in retaining this particular levy as against the constitutional preference for an open economy. * * *

B

Iowa's interest in any particular level of tax revenues is not affected by the use of the single-factor sales formula. It cannot be predicted with certainty that its application will result in higher revenues than any other formula. If Iowa needs more revenue, it can adjust its tax rates. That adjustment would not have the discriminatory impact necessarily flowing from the choice of the single-factor sales formula. Hence, if Iowa's choice is to be sustained, it cannot be by virtue of the State's interest in protecting its fisc or its power to tax. No other justification is offered. If we are to uphold Iowa's apportionment formula, it must be because no consistent principle can be developed that could account for the invalidation of the Iowa formula, yet support application of other States' imprecise formulae.

C

It is argued that since this Court on several occasions has upheld the use of single-factor formulae, Iowa's scheme cannot be regarded as suspect simply because it does not embody the prevalent three-factor theory. Consideration of the decisions dealing with single-factor formulae, however, reveals that each is distinguishable.

* * *

[After discussing the *Underwood Typewriter* and *Bass, Ratcliff* cases, pp. 442–44 supra, Justice Powell turned to other single-factor apportionment formula cases].

Somewhat more troublesome is Ford Motor Co. v. Beauchamp, 308 U.S. 331, 60 S.Ct. 273 (1939). In that case, the Court sustained Texas' use of a single-factor sales formula to apportion the outstanding capital stock, surplus, undivided profits, and long-term obligations of corporations subject to the state franchise tax. While this case may be seen as standing for the proposition that single-factor sales formulae are not *per se* illegal, it is not controlling in the present case. In *Ford Motor Co.*, as in *Underwood Typewriter* and *Bass,* there was no showing of virtually universal use of a conflicting type of formula for determining the same tax. Thus it could not be said that the Texas formula inevitably imposed a competitive disadvantage on out-of-state corporations. Discrimination not being shown, there was no basis for invalidating the Texas scheme under the Commerce Clause.

The opposite is true here. In the context of virtually universal use of the basic three-factor formula, Iowa's use of the single-factor sales formula necessarily discriminates against out-of-state manufacturers. The only remaining question, then, is whether Iowa's scheme may be saved by the fact that its discriminatory nature depends on context: If other States were not virtually unanimous in their use of an opposing formula, past decisions would make it difficult to single out Iowa's scheme as more offensive than any other.

D

On several occasions, this Court has compared a state statutory requirement against the practice in other States in determining the statute's validity under the Commerce Clause. In Southern Pacific Co. v. Arizona ex rel. Sullivan, 325 U.S. 761, 65 S.Ct. 1515 (1945), the Court struck down a state statute limiting passenger trains to 14 cars and freight trains to 70 cars. Noting that only one State other than Arizona enforced a restriction on train lengths, the *Southern Pacific* Court specifically considered the Arizona law against the background of the activities in other States.

* * *

The Court also looked to the practices of other States in holding unconstitutional Illinois' mudguard requirement in Bibb v. Navajo Freight Lines, Inc., 359 U.S. 520, 79 S.Ct. 962 (1959). * * *

[Justice Powell referred to General Motors Corp. v. District of Columbia, discussed at p. 456 supra, and emphasized the Court's reference to the widespread use of the three-factor formula, quoting the Court's statement that the]

"use of an apportionment formula based wholly on the sales factor, in the context of general use of the three-factor approach, will ordinarily result in multiple taxation of corporate net income.... In any case, the sheer inconsistency of the District formula with that generally prevailing may tend to result in the unhealthy fragmentation of enterprise and an uneconomic pattern of plant location, and so presents an added reason why this Court must give proper meaning to the relevant provisions of the District Code." Id., at 559–560, 85 S.Ct. at 1160.

The *General Motors* Court, then, expressly evaluated the single-factor sales formula in the context of general use of the three-factor method and concluded that the former created dangers for interstate commerce.

These cases lead me to believe that it is not only proper but essential to determine the validity of the Iowa formula against the background of practices in the other States. If one State's regulatory or taxing statute is significantly "out of line" with other States' rules, Bibb, 359 U.S., at 530, 79 S.Ct. at 968, and if by virtue of that departure from the general practice it burdens or discriminates against interstate commerce, Commerce Clause scrutiny is triggered, and this Court must invalidate it unless it is justified by a legitimate local purpose outweighing the harm to interstate commerce, Pike v. Bruce Church, Inc., supra, 397 U.S. at 142, 90 S.Ct. at 847; accord, Hughes v. Alexandria Scrap Corp., 426 U.S. 794, 804, 96 S.Ct. 2488, 2495 (1976). There probably can be no fixed rule as to how nearly uniform the countervailing state policies must be; that is, there can be no rule of 26 States, of 35, or of 45. Commerce Clause inquiries generally do not run in such precise channels. The degree of conflict and its resulting impact on commerce must be weighed in the circumstances of each case. But the difficulty of engaging in that weighing process does not permit this Court to avoid its constitutional duty and allow an individual State to erect "an unreasonable clog upon the mobility of commerce," Baldwin v. G.A.F. Seelig Inc., 294 U.S., at 527, 55 S.Ct. at 502, by taking advantage of the other States' commendable trend toward uniformity.

Such is the case before us. Forty-four of the 45 States, other than Iowa, that impose a corporate income tax utilize a similar three-factor apportionment formula. The 45th State, West Virginia, uses a two-factor formula based on property and payroll. Those formulae individually may be no more rational as means of apportioning the income of a multistate business than Iowa's single-factor sales formula. But see General Motors Corp. v. District of Columbia, 380 U.S., at 561, 85 S.Ct. at 1161. Past decisions upheld differing formulae because of this inability to determine that any of the various methods of apportionment in use was the best; so long as a State's choice was not shown to be grossly unfair, it would be upheld. Compare *Underwood Typewriter,* supra, with *Hans Rees' Sons,* supra. The more recent trend toward uniformity, however, permits identification of Iowa's formula, like the mudguard requirement in *Bibb,* as "out of line," if not *per se* irrational. Since Iowa's formula inevitably discriminates against out-of-state sellers, and since it has not been justified on any fiscal or administrative basis, I would hold it invalid under the Commerce Clause.

NOTES AND QUESTIONS

A. During the more than three decades following *Moorman,* the states have moved decidedly away from the uniformity that characterized their income tax apportionment formulas as of 1978. Approximately 10 other states have joined Iowa in adopting single-factor sales formulas, and many other states given added (often double) weight to the sales factor when computed the state's apportionment ratio. Factors of Apportionment Fractions, All States Tax Guide (RIA) ¶ 223 (2009) (chart). Do these changes strengthen or undercut the force of Justice Powell's dissent?

B. *The Significance of Separate Accounting Evidence to Attack Formulary Apportionment after* Moorman. In *Moorman,* the Court faulted the taxpayer for failing to show that "a significant portion of the income attributed to Iowa in fact was generated by its Illinois operations" and for failing to provide "any separate accounting analysis showing what portion of appellant's profits was attributable to sales, to manufacturing, or to any other phase of the company's operations." In Exxon Corp. v. Wisconsin Dept. of Revenue, 447 U.S. 207, 100 S.Ct. 2109 (1980), set out in part at pp. 414–19 supra, the taxpayer attacked the application of Wisconsin's three-factor formula to its income on the basis of detailed separate accounting evidence that purportedly demonstrated that significantly less income was earned in the state than was apportioned to the state by the formula. In the course of rejecting the taxpayer's claim, which relied on the above quoted language from *Moorman,* the Court denigrated its remarks in *Moorman* as "dicta" and declared:

> In *Moorman* we simply noted that the taxpayer had made no showing that its Illinois operations were responsible for profits from sales in Iowa. This hardly leads to the conclusion, urged by Exxon here, that a taxpayer's separate functional accounting, if it purports to separate out income from various aspects of the business, must be accepted as a matter of constitutional law for state tax purposes. Such evidence may be helpful, but *Moorman* in no sense renders such accounting conclusive.

Id., 447 U.S. at 223.

C. *Apportionment of Value Added Tax: The* Trinova *Case.* Until the recent repeal of the Michigan Single Business Tax (SBT), Michigan was unique among American states in having as its principal form of business tax an exaction on "value added." In contrast to the typical corporate net income tax, which is measured by a corporation's profits during the taxable year, the SBT was roughly measured by the increase in the value of goods and services attributable to the taxpayer's business activity during the taxable year. The essential components of the SBT were the value added by the contributions of labor, capital, and entrepreneurial skill that the taxpayer makes in producing its goods or services. The value added by the taxpayer's labor, which made up more than 75 percent of the SBT base, was measured by compensation paid by the taxpayer. The value added by the taxpayer's capital was measured by the depreciation, interest, dividends, and royalties paid by the taxpayer. The value added by the taxpayer's entrepreneurial skill was measured by the taxpayer's federal taxable income as adjusted for SBT purposes. The profit component made up less than six percent of the SBT base.

In Trinova Corp. v. Michigan Department of Treasury, 498 U.S. 358, 111 S.Ct. 818 (1991), the taxpayer challenged the application of Michigan's three-factor formula to its value-added tax base. The gravamen of Trinova's constitutional argument was that Michigan's application of the three-factor apportionment formula to Trinova's SBT base apportioned to Michigan value added outside the state in violation of the Commerce and Due Process Clauses. Trinova's case rested on the premise that its SBT base—unlike an income tax base—was comprised largely of components that could be readily identified on a geographic basis. Thus Trinova could specifically identify the locus of its value-adding activities that constituted the compensation element of the SBT tax base, namely, the state in which the labor was performed. Trinova could likewise identify the locus of its value-adding activities that constituted the depreciation element of the SBT base, namely, the state in which the property was located.

The Supreme Court rejected Trinova's claim. The fact that Trinova could identify the location of its plant and equipment and much of its compensation did not, in the Court's eyes, establish the geographic location of its SBT base. "The Michigan SBT * * * is not three separate and independent taxes [on compensation, depreciation, and profit]." Trinova, 498 U.S. at 375. Rather, it was a single tax imposed on the result of integrated activities—including the demand provided by the Michigan market—that the state was constitutionally entitled to view as a whole rather than the sum of its constituent parts.

Once the Court made the essential determination that identifying the precise source of value added, like identifying the precise source of income, was not "feasible," its conclusion that Michigan could properly apportion Trinova's SBT base followed inexorably from the Court's income tax precedents.

> The same factors that prevent determination of the geographic location where income is generated, factors such as functional integration, centralization of management, and economies of scale, make it impossible to determine the location of value added with exact precision. In concluding that Michigan can apportion the SBT, we merely reaffirm what we have written before: "in the case of a more-or-less integrated business enterprise operating in more than one State, ... arriving at precise territorial allocations of 'value' is often an elusive goal, both in theory and in practice."

Id. at 379.

D. *The "Big" Question.* In light of all the decisions you have now considered in this chapter involving taxpayers' efforts to challenge the apportionment of the income (or property) by a separate accounting demonstration, under what circumstances will a taxpayer's separate accounting evidence be sufficient to invalidate the application of the state's formula as a matter of constitutional law? Does the answer to this question depend on the detail with which the separate accounting evidence is presented? On the disparity the separate accounting evidence demonstrates between the result under separate accounting and the result under formulary apportionment? On whether the apportionment being challenged is a single-factor formula or a three-factor formula? On whether the apportionment being challenged involves income, or property, or some other base? On whether the base being apportioned should have been held apportionable in the first place? Would it be overstating the case to say that a taxpayer will *never* be able to challenge a three-factor apportionment of the income of a unitary business on the ground that its separate accounting evidence shows a "grossly distorted result"? If so, can you describe the circumstances (considering in particular the Court's opinions in *Butler Brothers, Exxon,* and *Trinova*) under which this statement would be false?

    E. *Establishing That Formulary Apportionment Results in Extraterritorial Taxation: Beyond Separate Accounting.* Whatever may be the difficulty of establishing by separate accounting evidence that formulary apportionment of a unitary business results in unconstitutional distortion, there may well be other evidence which, along with separate accounting, can make such a showing. In British Land (Md.), Inc. v. Tax Appeals Tribunal, 85 N.Y.2d 139, 647 N.E.2d 1280, 623 N.Y.S.2d 772 (1995), a taxpayer, who owned office buildings in Baltimore and New York, received a gain from the sale of the Baltimore building that was includable in its New York apportionable tax base because it arose from a unitary business conducted in part in New York. The taxpayer was nevertheless able to prove that allowing New York to tax the gain would create unconstitutional distortion. The New York Court of Appeals observed that New York's three-factor formula was "fair on its face" (id., 647 N.E.2d at 1284) and that a tax on extraterritorial values cannot "be established simply by showing that the taxpayer's formula-based intrastate income is many times greater than the income reflected in separate geographical accounting." Id. at 1285. (The taxpayer had demonstrated that application of the formula resulted in increasing its New York tax bill by 2,200 percent by comparison with the result reached under separate accounting.)

    The Court of Appeals declared, however, that

    [i]n addition to the marked discrepancy revealed by separate accounting, the evidence showed * * * four factors principally responsible for the appreciation in the value of petitioner's Baltimore property giving rise to the gain from its sale: (1) an improved economic climate in downtown Baltimore * * *; (2) sound management * * *, resulting in high occupancy rates; (3) renovations to the building; and (4) acquisition of the fee interest in the property. The record clearly points to the conclusion that these factors, and any corporate decision-making involving them, occurred and had their economic impact on the Baltimore office building prior to the commencement of the petitioner's activities in New York * * * In this respect, therefore, and particularly because the single gain from the sale of the Baltimore property so dwarfed petitioner's other net income, clear and cogent evidence supports the conclusion that two-thirds of petitioner's $13 million gain on the sale of the Baltimore property "cannot in fairness be attributed to [petitioner's] activities within [New York] State." Allied–Signal, Inc. v. Director, Div. of Taxation, 504 U.S. at 780, 112 S. Ct. at 2259.

Id.

The court also identified one further area of proof demonstrating that the application of the formula taxed extraterritorial values. It observed that the taxpayer's unitary real estate business consisted of only two properties, one in New York and one in Baltimore, and that the New York property was a relatively recent acquisition, but with a significantly greater cost than the Maryland property. "Under these circumstances, the extremely marked differences in value inevitably had a distorting effect on the application of the statutory apportionment formula." Id. at 1286.

Should *British Land* provide comfort to taxpayers who are seeking to attack the result of a formulary apportionment of a unitary business on the ground that it results in unconstitutional distortion? What are the lessons you can draw from *British Land* in mounting such an attack? If the taxpayers in *Underwood, Bass, Butler Brothers, Moorman, Exxon,* and *Trinova* had had the benefit of the *British Land* opinion, would they have been able to fashion an argument that would have established unconstitutional distortion? Would you take an unconstitutional distortion case on a contingency?

2. APPORTIONMENT BY FORMULA AS APPLIED TO MULTICORPORATE ENTERPRISES: CONSTITUTIONAL LIMITATIONS

The materials in the preceding section focused on the development of the constitutional restraints on apportionability and fair apportionment in the context of a single corporate entity. In *Exxon* (pp. 414–19 and 469 supra), for example, the apportionability and fair apportionment issues arose in connection with a vertically integrated oil company that conducted its operations through different functional departments. Although some of those departments (exploration and production, and refining) did no business in the state, all of the income at issue was the operating income of a single entity (Exxon). Moreover, all of the apportionment factors of that entity (property, payroll, and sales) were included in the apportionment formula employed to apportion Exxon's income to Wisconsin.

Suppose, however, that Exxon had separately incorporated each of its departments, and that each of the departments (now a separate Exxon subsidiary) reported its own operating income, which it paid out in dividends to its corporate parent. Although in substance Exxon may still have been operating as the same integrated oil company that it was prior to the incorporation of its departments, much of Exxon's income will now take the form of dividends earned by separate corporations (e.g., Exxon Exploration & Production Corporation and Exxon Refining Corporation) conducting no business within the state. Moreover, Exxon's apportionment factors will reflect only its own property, payroll, and sales, not the property, payroll, and sales of the subsidiaries that are producing its dividend income. What happens, then, if a state like Wisconsin in which Exxon does business (but is not headquartered) seeks to tax an apportioned share of Exxon's income (including its dividend income)? May the state require Exxon to include the dividend income in Exxon's apportionable tax base, even though the subsidiaries do no business in the state and Exxon manages its subsidiaries at its out-of-state corporate headquarters where it receives the dividends? And if it may, must the state permit Exxon to include the factors of Exxon's subsidiaries in its apportionment formula to reflect the contributions that the subsidiaries make to its apportionable income in order to assure that the apportionment formula, and the resulting apportionment, is fair? Furthermore, what if the subsidiaries are foreign? Does *Japan Line* preclude taxation of those dividends under the Foreign Commerce Clause?

The *Mobil* case, set out immediately below, addresses some of these issues, and they are further explored in the cases and materials that follow. Keep in mind that the focus in this section is on the broad, federal constitutional constraints on apportionability and fair apportionment of the multicorporate enterprise. We will consider state law issues arising in connection with apportionment of the income of multicorporate enterprises in Section 3 infra.

MOBIL OIL CORPORATION v. COMMISSIONER OF TAXES OF VERMONT

Supreme Court of the United States, 1980.
445 U.S. 425, 100 S.Ct. 1223.

MR. JUSTICE BLACKMUN delivered the opinion of the Court.

In this case we are called upon to consider constitutional limits on a nondomiciliary State's taxation of income received by a domestic corporation in the form of dividends from subsidiaries and affiliates doing business abroad. The State of Vermont imposed a tax, calculated by means of an apportionment formula, upon appellant's so-called "foreign source" dividend income for the taxable years 1970, 1971, and 1972. The Supreme Court of Vermont sustained that tax.

I

A

Appellant Mobil Oil Corporation is a corporation organized under the laws of the State of New York. It has its principal place of business and its "commercial domicile" in New York City. It is authorized to do business in Vermont.

Mobil engages in an integrated petroleum business, ranging from exploration for petroleum reserves to production, refining, transportation, and distribution and sale of petroleum and petroleum products. It also engages in related chemical and mining enterprises. It does business in over 40 of our States and in the District of Columbia as well as in a number of foreign countries.

Much of appellant's business abroad is conducted through wholly and partly owned subsidiaries and affiliates. Many of these are corporations organized under the laws of foreign nations; a number, however, are domestically incorporated in States other than Vermont. None of appellant's subsidiaries or affiliates conducts business in Vermont, and appellant's shareholdings in those corporations are controlled and managed elsewhere, presumably from the headquarters in New York City.

In Vermont, appellant's business activities are confined to wholesale and retail marketing of petroleum and related products. Mobil has no oil or gas production or refineries within the State. Although appellant's business activity in Vermont is by no means insignificant, it forms but a small part of the corporation's worldwide enterprise. According to the Vermont corporate income tax returns Mobil filed for the three taxable years in issue appellant's Vermont sales were $8,554,200, $9,175,931, and $9,589,447 respectively; its payroll in the State was $236,553, $244,577, and $254,938, respectively; and the value of its property in Vermont was $3,930,100, $6,707,534, and $8,236,792 respectively. App. 35–36, 49–50, 63–64. Substantial as these figures are, they too, represent only tiny portions of the corporation's total sales, payroll, and property.

Vermont imposes an annual net income tax on every corporation doing business within the State. Under its scheme, net income is defined as the taxable income of the taxpayer "under the laws of the United States." Vt.Stat.Ann., Tit. 32, § 5811(18) (1970 and Supp.1978). If a taxpayer corporation does business both within and without Vermont, the State taxes only that portion of the net income attributable to it under a three-factor apportionment formula. In order to determine that portion, net income is multiplied by a fraction representing the arithmetic average of the ratios of sales, payroll, and property values within Vermont to those of the corporation as a whole. § 5833(a).

Appellant's net income for 1970, 1971, and 1972, as defined by the Federal Internal Revenue Code, included substantial amounts received as dividends from its subsidiaries and affiliates operating abroad. Mobil's federal income tax returns for the three years showed taxable income of approximately $220 million, $308 million, and $233 million, respectively, of which approximately $174 million, $283 million, and $280 million was net dividend income. On its Vermont returns for these years, however, appellant subtracted from federal taxable income items it regarded as "nonapportionable," including the net dividends. As a result of these subtractions, Mobil's Vermont returns showed a net income of approximately $23 million for 1970 and losses for the two succeeding years. After application of Vermont's apportionment formula, an aggregate tax liability of $1,871.90 to Vermont remained for the three-year period; except for a minimum tax of $25 for each of 1971 and 1972, all of this was attributable to 1970.

The Vermont Department of Taxes recalculated appellant's income by restoring the asserted nonapportionable items to the preapportionment tax base. It determined that Mobil's aggregate tax liability for the three years was $76,418.77, and deficiencies plus interest were assessed accordingly. Appellant challenged the deficiency assessments before the Commissioner of Taxes. It argued, among other things, that taxation of the dividend receipts under Vermont's corporate income tax violated the Due Process Clause of the Fourteenth Amendment, as well as the Interstate and Foreign Commerce Clause, U.S. Const., Art. 1, § 8, cl. 3. Appellant also argued that inclusion of the dividend income in its tax base was inconsistent with the terms of the Vermont tax statute, because it would not result in a "fair" and "equitable" apportionment, and it petitioned for modification of the apportionment. See Vt.Stat.Ann., Tit. 32, § 5833(b). It is evident from the transcript of the hearing before the Commissioner that appellant's principal object was to achieve the subtraction of the asserted nonapportionable income from the preapportionment tax base; the alternative request for modification of the apportionment formula went largely undeveloped.

The Commissioner held that inclusion of dividend income in the tax base was required by the Vermont statute, and he rejected appellant's Due Process Clause and Commerce Clause arguments.

Mobil sought review by the Superior Court of Washington County. That court reversed the Commissioner's ruling. It held that inclusion of dividend income in the tax base unconstitutionally subjected appellant to prohibitive multiple taxation because New York, the State of appellant's commercial domicile, had the authority to tax the dividends in their entirety. Since New York could tax without apportionment, the court concluded, Vermont's use of an apportionment formula would not be an adequate safeguard against multiple taxation. It agreed with appellant that subtraction of dividend income from the Vermont tax base was the only acceptable approach.

The Commissioner, in his turn, appealed to the Supreme Court of Vermont. That court reversed the judgment of the Superior Court. 136 Vt. 545, 394 A.2d 1147 (1978). The court noted that appellant's quarrel was with the calculation of the tax base and not with the method or accuracy of the statutory apportionment formula. Id., at 547, 394 A.2d, at 1148. It found a sufficient "nexus" between the corporation and the State to justify an apportioned tax on both appellant's investment income and its operating income. The court rejected the "multiple taxation" theory that had prevailed in the Superior Court. In its view, appellant had failed to prove that multiple taxation would actually ensue. New York did not tax the dividend income during the taxable years in question, and "[i]n a conflict between Vermont's apportioned tax on Mobil's investment income and an attempt on New York's part to tax that same income without apportionment, New York might very well have to yield." Id., at 552, 394 A.2d, at 1151. Accordingly, the court held that no constitutional defect had been established. It remanded the case for reinstatement of the deficiency assessments.

The substantial federal question involved prompted us to note probable jurisdiction.

B

In keeping with its litigation strategy, appellant has disclaimed any dispute with the accuracy or fairness of Vermont's apportionment formula. See Juris. Statement 10; Brief for Appellant 11. Instead, it claims that dividends from a "foreign source" by their very nature are not apportionable income. This election to attack the tax base rather than the formula substantially narrows the issues before us. In deciding this appeal, we do not consider whether application of Vermont's formula produced a fair attribution of appellant's dividend income to that State. Our inquiry is confined to the question whether there is something about the character of income earned from investments in affiliates and subsidiaries operating abroad that precludes, as a constitutional matter, state taxation of that income by the apportionment method.

In addressing this question, moreover, it is necessary to bear in mind that Mobil's "foreign source" dividend income is of two distinct types. The first consists of dividends from domestic corporations, organized under the laws of States other than Vermont, that conduct all their operations, and hence earn their income, outside the United States.[12] The second type consists of dividends from corporations both organized and operating abroad. The record in this case fails to supply much detail concerning the activities of the corporations whose dividends allegedly fall into these two categories, but it is apparent, from perusal of such documents in the record as appellant's corporate reports for the years in question, that many of these subsidiaries and affiliates, including the principal contributors to appellant's dividend income, engage in business activities that form part of Mobil's integrated petroleum enterprise. Indeed, although appellant is unwilling to concede the legal conclusion that these activities form part of a "unitary business," see Reply Brief for Appellant 2, n. 1, it has offered no evidence that would determine the conclusion that most, if not all, of its subsidiaries and affiliates contribute to appellant's worldwide petroleum enterprise.

To justify exclusion of the dividends from income subject to apportionment in Vermont, Mobil offers three principal arguments. First, it argues that the dividends may not be taxed in Vermont because there is no "nexus" between that State and either appellant's management of its investments or the business activities of the payor corporations. Second, it argues that taxation of the dividends in Vermont would create an unconstitutional burden of multiple taxation because the dividends would be taxable in full in New York, the State of commercial domicile. In this context, appellant relies on the traditional rule that dividends are taxable at their "business situs," a rule which it suggests is of constitutional

---

12. Under the Vermont tax scheme, income falling into this category is subject to apportionment only in part. Because Vermont's statute is geared to the definition of taxable income under federal law, it excludes from the preapportionment tax base 85% of all dividends earned from domestic corporations in which the taxpayer owns less than 80% of the capital stock, and 100% of all dividends earned from domestic corporations in which the taxpayer owns 80% or more of the capital stock. See § 243 of the Internal Revenue Code of 1954, as amended, 26 U.S.C. § 243; Vt.Stat.Ann., Tit. 32, § 5811(18) (1970 and Supp.1978).

dimension. Third, Mobil argues that the "foreign source" of the dividends precludes state income taxation in this country, at least in States other than the commercial domicile, because of the risk of multiple taxation at the international level. In a related argument, appellant contends that local taxation of the sort undertaken in Vermont prevents the Nation from speaking with a single voice in foreign commercial affairs. We consider each of these arguments in turn.

II

It long has been established that the income of a business operating in interstate commerce is not immune from fairly apportioned state taxation. Northwestern States Portland Cement Co. v. Minnesota, 358 U.S. 450, 458–462, 79 S.Ct. 357, 362–364 (1959) * * *. "[T]he entire net income of a corporation, generated by interstate as well as intrastate activities, may be fairly apportioned among the States for tax purposes by formulas utilizing instate aspects of interstate affairs." Northwestern States Portland Cement Co. v. Minnesota, 358 U.S., at 460, 79 S.Ct., at 363. For a State to tax income generated in interstate commerce, the Due Process Clause of the Fourteenth Amendment imposes two requirements: a "minimal connection" between the interstate activities and the taxing State, and a rational relationship between the income attributed to the State and the intrastate values of the enterprise. * * * The requisite "nexus" is supplied if the corporation avails itself of the "substantial privilege of carrying on business" within the State; and "[t]he fact that a tax is contingent upon events brought to pass without a state does not destroy the nexus between such a tax and transactions within a state for which the tax is an exaction." Wisconsin v. J.C. Penney Co., 311 U.S. 435, 444–445, 61 S.Ct. 246, 250 (1940).

We do not understand appellant to contest these general principles. Indeed, in its Vermont tax returns for the years in question, Mobil included all its operating income in apportionable net income, without regard to the locality in which it was earned. Nor has appellant undertaken to prove that the amount of its tax liability as determined by Vermont is "out of all appropriate proportion to the business transacted by the appellant in that State." Hans Rees' Sons v. North Carolina ex rel. Maxwell, 283 U.S. 123, 135, 51 S.Ct. 385, 389 (1931).[13] What appellant does seek to establish, in the due process phase of its argument, is that its *dividend* income must be excepted from the general principle of apportionability because it lacks a satisfactory nexus with appellant's business activities in Vermont. To carve that out as an exception, appellant must demonstrate something about the nature of this income that distinguishes it from operating income, a proper portion of which the State concededly

---

13. Application of the Vermont three-factor formula for the three years resulted in attributing to the State the following percentages of the corporation's net income:

1970	0.146032%
1971	0.173647%
1972	0.182151%

App. 36, 50, 64.

may tax. From appellant's argument we discern two potential differentiating factors: the "foreign source" of the income, and the fact that it is received in the form of dividends from subsidiaries and affiliates.

The argument that the source of the income precludes its taxability runs contrary to precedent. In the past, apportionability often has been challenged by the contention that income earned in one State may not be taxed in another if the source of the income may be ascertained by separate geographical accounting. The Court has rejected that contention so long as the intra-state and extra-state activities formed part of a single unitary business. See Butler Bros. v. McColgan, 315 U.S. 501, 506–508, 62 S.Ct. 701, 703–704 (1942); Ford Motor Co. v. Beauchamp, 308 U.S. 331, 336, 60 S.Ct. 273, 276 (1939); cf. Moorman Mfg. Co. v. Bair, 437 U.S., at 272, 98 S.Ct., at 2344. In these circumstances, the Court has noted that separate accounting, while it purports to isolate portions of income received in various States, may fail to account for contributions to income resulting from functional integration, centralization of management, and economies of scale. Butler Bros. v. McColgan, 315 U.S., at 508–509, 62 S.Ct., at 704–705. Because these factors of profitability arise from the operation of the business as a whole, it becomes misleading to characterize the income of the business as having a single identifiable "source." Although separate geographical accounting may be useful for internal auditing, for purposes of state taxation it is not constitutionally required.

The Court has applied the same rationale to businesses operating both here and abroad. Bass, Ratcliff & Gretton, Ltd. v. State Tax Comm'n, 266 U.S. 271, 45 S.Ct. 82 (1924), is the leading example. A British corporation manufactured ale in Great Britain and sold some of it in New York. The corporation objected on due process grounds to New York's imposition of an apportioned franchise tax on the corporation's net income. The Court sustained the tax on the strength of its earlier decision in Underwood Typewriter Co. v. Chamberlain, supra, where it had upheld a similar tax as applied to a business operating in several of our States. It ruled that the brewer carried on a unitary business, involving "a series of transactions beginning with the manufacture in England and ending in sales in New York and other places," and that "the State was justified in attributing to New York a just proportion of the profits earned by the Company from such unitary business." 266 U.S., at 282, 45 S.Ct., at 84.

As these cases indicate, the linchpin of apportionability in the field of state income taxation is the unitary business principle. In accord with this principle, what appellant must show, in order to establish that its dividend income is not subject to an apportioned tax in Vermont, is that the income was earned in the course of activities unrelated to the sale of petroleum products in that State. *Bass, Ratcliff & Gretton* forecloses the contention that the foreign source of the dividend income alone suffices for this purpose. Moreover, appellant has made no effort to demonstrate that the foreign operations of its subsidiaries and affiliates are distinct in any business or economic sense from its petroleum sales activities in Vermont. Indeed all indications in the record are to the contrary, since it appears that these foreign activities are part of appellant's integrated petroleum enterprise. In the absence of any proof of discrete business enterprise, Vermont was entitled to conclude that the dividend income's foreign source did not destroy the requisite nexus with in-state activities.

It remains to be considered whether the form in which the income was received serves to drive a wedge between Mobil's foreign enterprise and its activities in Vermont. In support of the contention that dividend income ought to be excluded from apportionment, Mobil has attempted to characterize its ownership and management of subsidiaries and affiliates as a business distinct from its sale of petroleum products in this country. Various *amici* also have suggested that the division between parent and subsidiary should be treated as a break in the scope of unitary business, and that the receipt of dividends is a discrete "taxable event" bearing no relation to Vermont.

At the outset, we reject the suggestion that anything is to be gained by characterizing receipt of the dividends as a separate "taxable event." In Wisconsin v. J.C. Penney Co., supra, the Court observed that "tags" of this kind "are not instruments of adjudication but statements of result," and that they add little to analysis. 311 U.S., at 444, 61 S.Ct., at 250. Mobil's business entails numerous "taxable events" that occur outside Vermont. That fact alone does not prevent the State from including income earned from those events in the preapportionment tax base.

Nor do we find particularly persuasive Mobil's attempt to identify a separate business in its holding company function. So long as dividends from subsidiaries and affiliates reflect profits derived from a functionally integrated enterprise, those dividends are income to the parent earned in a unitary business. One must look principally at the underlying activity, not at the form of investment, to determine the propriety of apportionability.

Superficially, intercorporate division might appear to be a more attractive basis for limiting apportionability. But the form of business organization may have nothing to do with the underlying unity or diversity of business enterprise. Had appellant chosen to operate its foreign subsidiaries as separate divisions of a legally as well as a functionally integrated enterprise, there is little doubt that the income derived from those divisions would meet due process requirements for apportionability. Cf. General Motors Corp. v. Washington, 377 U.S. 436, 441, 84 S.Ct. 1564, 1568 (1964). Transforming the same income into dividends from legally separate entities works no change in the underlying economic realities of a unitary business, and accordingly it ought not to affect the apportionability of income the parent receives.[15]

---

15. In its reply brief, Mobil submits a new due process argument based on Vermont's failure to require "combined apportionment" which, while including the income of subsidiaries and affiliates as part of appellant's net income, would eliminate intercorporate transfers, such as appellant's dividend income, from that calculation. A necessary concomitant of this would be inclusion of the subsidiaries' and affiliates' sales, payroll, and property in the calculation of the apportionment formula. Reply Brief for Appellant 1–6. The result, presumably, would be advanta-

We do not mean to suggest that all dividend income received by corporations operating in interstate commerce is necessarily taxable in each State where that corporation does business. Where the business activities of the dividend payor have nothing to do with the activities of the recipient in the taxing State, due process considerations might well preclude apportionability, because there would be no underlying unitary business. We need not decide, however, whether Vermont's tax statute would reach extraterritorial values in an instance of that kind. Cf. Underwood Typewriter Co. v. Chamberlain, 254 U.S., at 121, 41 S.Ct., at 47. Mobil has failed to sustain its burden of proving any unrelated business activity on the part of its subsidiaries and affiliates that would raise the question of nonapportionability. See Norton Co. v. Department of Revenue, 340 U.S. 534, 537, 71 S.Ct. 377, 380 (1951); Butler Bros. v. McColgan, 315 U.S., at 507, 62 S.Ct., at 704. We therefore hold that its foreign source dividends have not been shown to be exempt, as a matter of due process, from apportionment for state income taxation by the State of Vermont.

III

In addition to its due process challenge, appellant contends that Vermont's tax imposes a burden on interstate and foreign commerce by subjecting appellant's dividend income to a substantial risk of multiple taxation. We approach this argument in two steps. First, we consider whether there was a burden on interstate commerce by virtue of the effect of the Vermont tax relative to appellant's income tax liability in other States. Next, we determine whether constitutional protections for foreign commerce pose additional considerations that alter the result.

A

The effect of the Commerce Clause on state taxation of interstate commerce is a frequently litigated subject that appears to be undergoing a revival of sorts. In several recent cases, this Court has addressed the issue and has attempted to clarify the apparently conflicting precedents it has spawned. See, e.g., Moorman Mfg. Co. v. Bair, 437 U.S., at 276–281, 98 S.Ct., at 2346–2348 (1978); Washington Revenue Dept. v. Association of Wash. Stevedoring Cos., 435 U.S. 734, 743–751, 98 S.Ct. 1388, 1395–1400 (1978); Complete Auto Transit, Inc. v. Brady, 430 U.S. 274, 97 S.Ct. 1076 (1977). In an endeavor to establish a consistent and rational method of inquiry, we have examined the practical effect of a challenged tax to determine whether it "is applied to an activity with a substantial nexus with the taxing State, is fairly apportioned, does not discriminate against interstate commerce, and is fairly related to the services provided by the State." Id., at 279, 97 S.Ct., at 1079.

Appellant asserts that Vermont's tax is discriminatory because it subjects interstate business to a burden of duplicative taxation that an

---

geous to appellant, since virtually nothing would be added to the "Vermont" numerators of the apportionment factors, while there would be substantial increases in the "everywhere" denominators, resulting in a diminution of the apportionment fraction.

intrastate taxpayer would not bear. Mobil does not base this claim on a comparison of Vermont's apportionment formula with those used in other States where appellant pays income taxes. Rather, it contends that *any* apportioned tax on its dividends will place an undue burden on that specific source of income, because New York, the State of commercial domicile, has the power to tax dividend income without apportionment. For the latter proposition, appellant cites property tax cases that hold that intangible property is to be taxed either by the State of commercial domicile or by the State where the property has a "business situs." See, e.g., First Bank Stock Corp. v. Minnesota, 301 U.S. 234, 237, 57 S.Ct. 677, 678 (1937).

Inasmuch as New York does not presently tax the dividends in question, actual multiple taxation is not demonstrated on this record. The Vermont courts placed some reliance on this fact, and much of the debate in this Court has aired the question whether an actual burden need be shown. We agree with Mobil that the constitutionality of a Vermont tax should not depend on the vagaries of New York tax policy. But the absence of any existing duplicative tax does alter the nature of appellant's claim. Instead of seeking relief from a present tax burden, appellant seeks to establish a theoretical constitutional preference for one method of taxation over another. In appellant's view, the Commerce Clause requires allocation of dividend income to a single situs rather than apportionment among the States.

Taxation by apportionment and taxation by allocation to a single situs are theoretically incommensurate, and if the latter method is constitutionally preferred, a tax based on the former cannot be sustained. See Standard Oil Co. v. Peck, 342 U.S. 382, 384, 72 S.Ct. 309, 310 (1952). We find no adequate justification, however, for such a preference. Although a fictionalized situs for intangible property sometimes has been invoked to avoid multiple taxation of ownership, there is nothing talismanic about the concepts of "business situs" or "commercial domicile" that automatically renders those concepts applicable when taxation of income from intangibles is at issue. The Court has observed that the maxim *mobilia sequuntur personam,* upon which these fictions of situs are based, "states a rule without disclosing the reasons for it." First Bank Stock Corp. v. Minnesota, 301 U.S., at 241, 57 S.Ct., at 680 (1937). The Court also has recognized that "the reason for a single place of taxation no longer obtains" when the taxpayer's activities with respect to the intangible property involve relations with more than one jurisdiction. Curry v. McCanless, 307 U.S. 357, 367, 59 S.Ct. 900, 906 (1939). Even for property or franchise taxes, apportionment of intangible values is not unknown. See Adams Express Co. v. Ohio, 166 U.S. 185, 222, 17 S.Ct. 604, 606 (1897). Moreover, cases upholding allocation to a single situs for property tax purposes have distinguished income tax situations where the apportionment principle prevails. See Wheeling Steel Corp. v. Fox, 298 U.S., at 212, 56 S.Ct., at 778.

The reasons for allocation to a single situs that often apply in the case of property taxation carry little force in the present context. Mobil no doubt enjoys privileges and protections conferred by New York law with respect to ownership of its stock holdings, and its activities in that State no doubt supply some nexus for jurisdiction to tax. Cf. First Bank Stock Corp. v. Minnesota, 301 U.S., at 240–241, 57 S.Ct., at 679–680. Although we do not now presume to pass on the constitutionality of a hypothetical New York tax, we may assume, for present purposes, that the State of commercial domicile has the authority to lay some tax on appellant's dividend income as well as on the value of its stock. But there is no reason in theory why that power should be exclusive when the dividends reflect income from a unitary business, part of which is conducted in other States. In that situation, the income bears relation to benefits and privileges conferred by several States. These are the circumstances in which apportionment is ordinarily the accepted method. Since Vermont seeks to tax income, not ownership, we hold that its interest in taxing a proportionate share of appellant's dividend income is not overridden by any interest of the State of commercial domicile.

B

What has been said thus far does not fully dispose of appellant's additional contention that the Vermont tax imposes a burden on foreign commerce. Relying upon the Court's decision last Term in Japan Line, Ltd. v. County of Los Angeles, 441 U.S. 434, 99 S.Ct. 1813 (1979), Mobil suggests that dividends from foreign sources must be allocated to the State of commercial domicile, even if dividends from subsidiaries and affiliates operating domestically are not. By accepting the power of the State of commercial domicile to tax foreign source dividend income, appellant eschews the broad proposition that foreign source dividends are immune from state taxation. It presses the narrower contention that, because of the risk of multiple taxation abroad, allocation of foreign source income to a single situs is required at home. Appellant's reasoning tracks the rationale of *Japan Line,* that is, that allocation is required because apportionment necessarily entails some inaccuracy and duplication. This inaccuracy may be tolerable for businesses operating solely within the United States, it is said, because this Court has power to correct any gross overreaching. The same inaccuracy, however, becomes intolerable when it is added to the risk of duplicative taxation abroad, which this Court is powerless to control. Accordingly, the only means of alleviating the burden of overlapping taxes is to adopt an allocation rule.

This argument is unpersuasive in the present context for several reasons. First, it attempts to focus attention on the effect of foreign taxation when the effect of domestic taxation is the only real issue. By admitting the power of the State of commercial domicile to tax foreign source dividends *in full,* Mobil necessarily forgoes any contention that local duplication of foreign taxes is proscribed. Thus, the only inquiry of constitutional dimension is the familiar question whether taxation by apportionment at home produces significantly greater tax burdens than taxation by allocation. Once appellant's argument is placed in this perspective, the presence or absence of taxation abroad diminishes in importance.

Second, nothing about the logic of Mobil's position is limited to dividend income. The same contention could be advanced about any income arguably earned from foreign commerce. If appellant's argument were accepted, state taxing commissions would face substantial difficulties in attempting to determine what income does or does not have a foreign source.

Third, appellant's argument underestimates the power of this Court to correct excessive taxation on the field where appellant has chosen to pitch its battle. A discriminatory effect on foreign commerce as a result of multiple state taxation is just as detectable and corrigible as a similar effect on commerce among the States. Accordingly, we see no reason why the standard for identifying impermissible discrimination should differ in the two instances.

Finally, acceptance of appellant's argument would provide no guarantee that allocation will result in a lesser domestic tax burden on dividend income from foreign sources. By appellant's own admission, allocation would give the State of commercial domicile the power to tax that income in full, without regard to the extent of taxation abroad. Unless we indulge in the speculation that a State will volunteer to become a tax haven for multinational enterprises, there is no reason to suspect that a State of commercial domicile will be any less vigorous in taxing the whole of the dividend income than a State like Vermont will be in taxing a proportionate share.

Appellant's attempted analogy between this case and *Japan Line* strikes us as forced. That case involved ad valorem property taxes assessed directly upon instrumentalities of foreign commerce. As has been noted, the factors favoring use of the allocation method in property taxation have no immediate applicability to an income tax. *Japan Line* moreover, focused on problems of duplicative taxation at the international level, while appellant here has confined its argument to the wholly different sphere of multiple taxation among our States. Finally, in *Japan Line* the Court was confronted with actual multiple taxation that could be remedied only by adoption of an allocation approach. As has already been explained, in the present case we are not similarly impelled.

Nor does federal tax policy lend additional weight to appellant's arguments. The federal statutes and treaties that Mobil cites, Brief for Appellant 38–43, concern problems of multiple taxation at the international level and simply are not germane to the issue of multiple state taxation that appellant has framed. Concurrent federal and state taxation of income, of course, is a well-established norm. Absent some explicit directive from Congress, we cannot infer that treatment of foreign income at the federal level mandates identical treatment by the States. The absence of any explicit directive to that effect is attested by the fact that Congress has long debated, but has not enacted, legislation designed to regulate state taxation of income. See H.R.Rep. No. 1480, 88th Cong., 2d Sess. (1964); H.R.Rep. No. 565, 89th Cong., 1st Sess. (1965); H.R.Rep. No. 952, 89th Cong., 1st Sess. (1965). Legislative proposals have provoked debate over issues closely related to the present controversy. Congress in the future may see fit to enact legislation requiring a uniform method for state taxation of foreign dividends. To date, however, it has not done so.

IV

In sum, appellant has failed to demonstrate any sound basis, under either the Due Process Clause or the Commerce Clause, for establishing a constitutional preference for allocation of its foreign source dividend income to the State of commercial domicile. Because the issue has not been presented, we need not, and do not, decide what the constituent elements of a fair apportionment formula applicable to such income would be. We do hold, however, that Vermont is not precluded from taxing its proportionate share.

The judgment of the Supreme Court of Vermont is affirmed.

It is so ordered.

MR. JUSTICE STEWART and MR. JUSTICE MARSHALL took no part in the consideration or decision of this case.

MR. JUSTICE STEVENS, dissenting.

The Court today decides one substantive question and two procedural questions. Because of the way in which it resolves the procedural issues, the Court's substantive holding is extremely narrow. It is carefully "confined to the question whether there is something about the character of income earned from investments in affiliates and subsidiaries operating abroad that precludes, as a constitutional matter, state taxation of that income by the apportionment method." * * * Since that question has long since been answered in the negative, see, e.g., Bass, Ratcliff & Gretton, Ltd. v. State Tax Commission, 266 U.S. 271, 45 S.Ct. 82, the Court's principal holding is unexceptional.

The Court's substantive holding rests on the assumed premises (1) that Mobil's investment income and its income from operations in Vermont are inseparable parts of one unitary business and (2) that the entire income of that unitary business has been accurately and fairly apportioned between Vermont and the rest of the world—assuming the constitutional validity of including any foreign income in the allocation formula. The Court holds—as I understand its opinion—that Mobil "offered no evidence" challenging the first premise, and that it expressly disclaimed any attack on the second.

I disagree with both of these procedural holdings. I am persuaded that the record before us demonstrates either (1) that Mobil's income from its investments and its income from the sale of petroleum products in

Vermont are not parts of the same "unitary business," as that concept has developed in this Court's cases; or (2) if the unitary business is defined to include both kinds of income, that Vermont's apportionment formula has been applied in an arbitrary and unconstitutional way. To explain my position, it is necessary first to recall the limited purpose that the unitary business concept serves in this kind of case, then to identify the two quite different formulations of Mobil's "unitary business" that could arguably support Vermont's application of its apportionment formula to Mobil's investment income, and finally to show why on this record Mobil is entitled to relief using either formulation. Because I also believe that Mobil has done nothing to waive its entitlement, I conclude that the Court's substantive holding is inadequate to dispose of Mobil's contentions.

I

It is fundamental that a State has no power to impose a tax on income earned outside of the State. The out-of-state income of a business that operates in more than one State is subject to examination by the taxing State only because of "the impossibility of allocating specifically the profits earned by the processes conducted within its borders." Underwood Typewriter Co. v. Chamberlain, 254 U.S. 113, 121, 41 S.Ct. 45, 47. An apportionment formula is an imperfect, but nevertheless acceptable, method of measuring the in-state earnings of an integrated business. "It owes its existence to the fact that with respect to a business earning income through a series of transactions beginning with manufacturing in one State and ending with a sale in another, a precise—or even wholly logical—determination of the State in which any specific portion of the income was earned is impossible." Moorman Mfg. Co. v. Bair, supra, 437 U.S., at 286, 98 S.Ct., at 2351 (Powell, J., dissenting).

In the absence of any decision by Congress to prescribe uniform rules for allocating the income of interstate businesses to the appropriate geographical source, the Court has construed the Constitution as allowing the States wide latitude in the selection and application of apportionment formulas. See, e.g., Moorman Mfg. Co., supra, at 278–280, 98 S.Ct., at 2347–2348. Thus an acceptable formula may allocate income on the basis of the location of tangible assets, Underwood Typewriter, supra, on the basis of gross sales. Moorman, supra, or—as is more typical today—by an averaging of three factors: payroll, sales and tangible properties. * * *

The justification for using an apportionment formula to measure the in-state earnings of a unitary business is inapplicable to out-of-state earnings from a source that is unconnected to the business conducted within the State. This rather obvious proposition is recognized by the commentators[5] and is noted in our opinions. If a taxpayer proves by clear

---

5. See, e.g., Keesling and Warren, The Unitary Concept in the Allocation of Income, 12 Hastings L.J. 42, 48 (1960):

"In applying the foregoing definitions, it must be kept clearly in mind that although in particular instances all the activities of a given taxpayer may constitute a single business, in

and cogent evidence that the income attributed to the State by an apportionment formula is " 'out of all appropriate proportion to the business transacted . . . in that State,' " see Moorman, supra, 437 U.S., at 274, 98 S.Ct., at 2345, the assessment cannot stand.

As Mr. Justice Holmes wrote, with respect to an Indiana property tax on the unitary business conducted by an express company:

> "It is obvious, however, that this notion of organic unity may be made a means of unlawfully taxing the privilege [of carrying on commerce among the States], or property outside the State, under the name of enhanced value or good will, if it is not closely confined to its true meaning. So long as it fairly may be assumed that the different parts of a line are about equal in value a division by mileage is justifiable. But it is recognized in the cases that if, for instance, a railroad company had terminals in one State equal in value to all the rest of the line through another, the latter State could not make use of the unity of the road to equalize the value of every mile. That would be taxing property outside of the State under a pretense." Fargo v. Hart, 193 U.S. 490, 499–500, 24 S.Ct. 498, 500.

In this case the "notion of organic unity" of Mobil's far flung operations is applied solely for the purpose of making a fair determination of its Vermont earnings. Mobil does not dispute Vermont's right to treat its operations in Vermont as part of a unitary business and to measure the income attributable to Vermont on the basis of the three-factor formula that compares payroll, sales and tangible properties in that State with the values of those factors in the whole of the unitary business. Mobil's position, simply stated, is that it is grossly unfair to assign any part of its investment income to Vermont on the basis of those factors. To evaluate that position, it is necessary to identify the unitary business that produces the income subject to taxation by Vermont.

II

Mobil's operations in Vermont consist solely of wholesale and retail marketing of petroleum products. Those operations are a tiny part of a huge unitary business that might be defined in at least three different ways.

First, as Mobil contends, the business might be defined to include all of its operations, but to exclude the income derived from dividends paid by legally separate entities.

Second, as the Supreme Court of Vermont seems to have done, the unitary business might be defined to include not only all of Mobil's operations, but also the income received from all of its investments in other corporations, regardless of whether those other corporations are

---

other instances the activities may be segregated or divided into a number of separate businesses. It is only where the activities within and without the state constitute inseparable parts of a single business that the classification of unitary should be used."

engaged in the same kind of business as Mobil, and regardless of whether Mobil has a controlling interest in those corporations.

Third, Mobil's unitary business might be defined as encompassing not only the operations of the taxpayer itself but also the operations of all affiliates that are directly or indirectly engaged in the petroleum business. The Court seems to assume that this definition justifies Vermont's assessment in this case.

Mobil does not contend that it would be unfair for Vermont to apply its three-factor formula to the first definition of its unitary business. It has no quarrel with apportionment formulas generally, not even Vermont's. But by consistently arguing that its income from dividends should be entirely excluded from the apportionment calculation, Mobil has directly challenged any *application* of Vermont's formula based on either the second or the third definition of its unitary business. I shall briefly explain why the record is sufficient to support that challenge.

III

Under the Supreme Court of Vermont's conception of the relevant unitary business—the second of the three alternative definitions just posited—there is no need to consider the character of the operations of the corporations that have paid dividends to Mobil. For Vermont automatically included all of the taxpaying entity's investment income in the tax base. Such an approach simply ignores the *raison d'etre* for apportionment formulas.

We may assume that there are cases in which it would be appropriate to regard modest amounts of investment income as an incidental part of a company's overall operations and to allocate it between the taxing State and other jurisdictions on the basis of the same factors as are used to allocate operating income.[11] But this is not such a case. Mobil's investment income is far greater than its operating income. Clearly, it is improper simply to lump huge quantities of investment income that have no special connection with the taxpayer's operations in the taxing State into the tax base and to apportion it on the basis of factors that are used to allocate operating income. The Court does not reject this reasoning; rather, its opinion at least partly disclaims reliance on any such theory.

The Court appears to rely squarely on the third alternative approach to defining a unitary business. It assumes that Vermont's inclusion of the dividends in Mobil's apportionable tax base is predicated on the notion that the dividends represent the income of what would be the operating divisions of the Mobil Oil Corporation if Mobil and its affiliates were a single, legally integrated enterprise, rather than a corporation with numerous interests in other, separate corporations that pay it dividends.

---

11. Because there is no necessary correlation between the levels of profitability of investment income and marketing income, if more than incidental amounts of investment income are used in an averaging formula intended to measure marketing income, inaccuracy is sure to result.

* * * Theoretically, that sort of definition is unquestionably acceptable.[16] But there are at least three objections to its use in this case.

First, notwithstanding the Court's characterization of the record, it is readily apparent that a large number of the corporations in which Mobil has small minority interests and from which it derived significant dividend income would seem neither to be engaged in the petroleum business nor to have any connection whatsoever with Mobil's marketing business in Vermont. Second the record does not disclose whether the earnings of the companies that pay dividends to Mobil are even approximately equal to the amount of the dividends.

But of greatest importance, the record contains no information about the payrolls, sales or property values of any of those corporations, and Vermont has made no attempt to incorporate them into the apportionment formula computations. Unless the sales, payroll and property values connected with the production of income by the payor corporations are added to the denominator of the apportionment formula, the inclusion of earnings attributable to those corporations in the apportionable tax base will inevitably cause Mobil's Vermont income to be overstated.

Either Mobil's "world-wide petroleum enterprise" is all part of one unitary business, or it is not; if it is, Vermont must evaluate the entire enterprise in a consistent manner. As it is, it has indefensibly used its apportionment methodology artificially to multiply its share of Mobil's 1970 taxable income perhaps as much as ten-fold. In my judgment, the record is clearly sufficient to establish the validity of Mobil's objections to what Vermont has done here.

IV

The Court does not confront these problems because it concludes that Mobil has in effect waived any objections with respect to them. Although the Court's effort to avoid constitutional issues by narrowly constricting its holding is commendable, I believe it has seriously erred in its assessment of the procedural posture of this case.

It is true that appellant has disclaimed any dispute with "Vermont's method of apportionment." Brief for Appellant, at 11. And, admittedly, appellant has confused its cause by variously characterizing its attack in its main brief and reply brief. But contrary to the Court's assertions, see nn. 1, 3, supra, appellant did not disclaim any dispute with the accuracy or

---

16. "It seems clear, strictly as a logical proposition, that foreign source income is no different from any other income when it comes to determining, by formulary apportionment, the appropriate share of the income of a unitary business taxable by a particular state. This does not involve state taxation of foreign source income any more than does apportionment—in the case of a multistate business—involve the taxation of income arising in other states. In both situations the total income of the unitary business simply provides the starting point for computing the in-state income taxable by the particular state. . . .

"Obviously, if the foreign source income is included in the base for apportionment, foreign property, payrolls and sales must be included in the apportionment fractions. This was recognized in Bass [Ratcliff & Gretton, Ltd. v. State Tax Commission, supra]. . . ." State Taxation, supra, at 205. [State Taxation refers to E. George Rudolph, "State Taxation of Interstate Business: The Unitary Business Concept and Affiliated Corporate Groups," 25 Tax L. Rev. 171 (1980). Eds.]

fairness of the application of the formula in this case. Mobil merely disclaimed any attack on Vermont's *method* of apportionment generally to contrast its claims in this case with the sort of challenge to Iowa's single-factor formula that was rejected in *Moorman.*

The question whether Vermont may include investment income in the apportionable tax base should not be answered in the abstract without consideration of the other factors in the allocation formula. The apportionable tax base is but one multiplicand in the formula. Appellant's challenge to the inclusion of investment income in that component necessarily carries with it a challenge to the product.

Because of the inherent interdependence of the issues in a case of this kind, it seems clear to me that Mobil has not waived its Due Process objections to Vermont's assessment. Appellant's disclaimer of a *Moorman* style attack cannot fairly be interpreted as a concession that makes its entire appeal a project without a purpose. On the contrary, its argument convincingly demonstrates that the inclusion of its dividend income in the apportionable tax base has produced a palpably arbitrary measure of its Vermont income.

In sum, if Vermont is to reject Mobil's calculation of its tax liability, two courses are open to it: (1) it may exclude Mobil's investment income from the apportionable tax base and also exclude the payroll and property used in managing the investments from the denominator of the apportionment factor; or (2) it may undertake the more difficult and risky task of trying to create a consolidated income statement of Mobil's entire unitary business, properly defined. The latter alternative is permissible only if the statement fairly summarizes consolidated earnings, and takes the payroll, sales and property of the payor corporations into account. Because Vermont has employed neither of these alternatives, but has used a method that inevitably overstates Mobil's earnings in the State, I would reverse the judgment of the Supreme Court of Vermont.

NOTES AND QUESTIONS

A. Why did the taxpayer in *Mobil* focus on the apportionability rather than the fair apportionment question? If Mobil had established a separate subsidiary in Delaware to receive and manage its dividends from its foreign subsidiaries (cf. Geoffrey, Inc. v. South Carolina Tax Commission, 313 S.C. 15, 437 S.E.2d 13, cert. denied, 510 U.S. 992, 114 S.Ct. 550 (1993), set out in Chapter 2, pp. 68–73 supra), would Vermont have had the constitutional power to include those dividends in Mobil's apportionable tax base under the Court's rationale in *Mobil*? If so, would Vermont have been in a position under its own statutes to tax an apportioned share of those dividends? Why did New York, Mobil's commercial domicile, not seek to tax its dividends? If it had done so, would the result in *Mobil* have been different? Does *Mobil* hold that a domiciliary state's power to tax dividends on a residence basis must yield to a nondomiciliary state's power to tax dividends on a source basis? The *Mobil* case is analyzed in Walter Hellerstein, "State Income Taxation of

Multijurisdictional Corporations: Reflections on *Mobil, Exxon,* and H.R. 5076," 79 Mich. L. Rev. 113 (1980); see also Jerome R. Hellerstein, "Allocation and Apportionment of Dividends and the Delineation of the Unitary Business," Tax Notes, Jan. 25, 1982, p. 155; Note, "State Taxation of Foreign–Source Income: *Mobil Corp. v. Commissioner of Taxes,*" 66 Cornell L. Rev. 805 (1981).

B. *Factor Representation.* Suppose the Court had found that Mobil had indeed challenged the fairness of the apportionment rather than just the apportionability of its dividends. Would the Court have then agreed with Justice Stevens that Vermont would have been required to "undertake the * * * risky task of trying to create a consolidated income statement of Mobil's entire unitary business," which "is permissible only if the statement fairly summarizes consolidated earnings, and takes the payroll, sales and property of the payor corporations into account"? Invoking Justice Stevens's opinion, corporate taxpayers have vigorously contended that if dividend income from their subsidiaries is included in the apportionable tax base on the theory that such income derives from a unitary business carried on in part in the taxing state, then they are entitled to "factor representation," i.e., inclusion of some or all of the subsidiaries' factors in the parent's apportionment formula. Most courts have rejected this argument, usually on the ground that the taxpayer failed to show unconstitutional distortion from the state's failure to provide for factor representation. See, e.g., NCR Corp. v. Taxation and Revenue Dep't, 115 N.M. 612, 856 P.2d 982, cert. denied, 115 N.M. 612, 856 P.2d 982 (Ct. App. 1993), cert. denied, 512 U.S. 1245, 114 S.Ct. 2763 (1994); NCR Corp. v. South Carolina Tax Comm'n, 312 S.C. 52, 439 S.E.2d 254 (1993), cert. denied, 512 U.S. 1245, 114 S.Ct. 2763 (1994). Other courts have recognized the right of a parent to factor representation in this context, but have failed to indicate precisely how that right should be implemented. See, e.g., Tambrands, Inc. v. State Tax Assessor, 595 A.2d 1039, 1044 (Me. 1991); American Tel. & Tel. Co. v. Wisconsin Dep't of Revenue, 143 Wis.2d 533, 422 N.W.2d 629, 634–37 (1988). In the most comprehensive state court analysis to date of the issues raised by factor representation, a sharply divided Pennsylvania Supreme Court rejected the taxpayer's claim of a right to factor representation under Pennsylvania's capital stock tax. Unisys Corp. v. Commonwealth, Board of Finance and Revenue, 571 Pa. 139, 812 A.2d 448 (2002), cert. denied, 540 U.S. 812, 124 S.Ct. 54 (2003).

Is there any basis, as a matter of principle, for rejecting the right of a taxpayer to include the subsidiary's factors in the parent's apportionment formula when the income from the subsidiary is included in the parent's apportionable tax base on the theory that the corporations are engaged in a unitary business? Put another way, would such a formulary apportionment be "inherently" or "intrinsically" arbitrary as the Court employed those terms in Underwood, 254 U.S. at 113 (pp. 442–44 supra) and in Hans Rees, 283 U.S. at 133 (pp. 449–50 supra)? Does the defense that the result is not "grossly distorted" under Norfolk & Western, 390 U.S. at 326 (pp. 124–30 supra), respond to the theoretical objection to the failure to provide for factor representation? Can it be maintained that this defense is designed to provide the states with a reasonable amount of leeway in implementing apportionment formulas that are fair on their face but allegedly unfair in application, and that it cannot properly be invoked as a safe harbor for analytically indefensible apportionment regimes that happen to produce results that are not "grossly distorted" in a constitutional sense?

Does the argument for factor representation extend to dividend income that is apportionable not because the subsidiaries are engaged in a unitary business with their parent (as in *Mobil*) but because the corporate stock serves an operational function (under *Allied–Signal*, pp. 420–33 supra) in the parent's business (e.g., small holdings of utility stocks employed as working capital)? How about to other forms of apportionable income derived from unitary subsidiaries or from investments that serve an operational function in the taxpayer's business, such as interest, royalties, and capital gains? These questions are addressed in detail in Walter Hellerstein, "State Taxation of Corporate Income From Intangibles: *Allied–Signal* and Beyond," 48 Tax L. Rev. 739, 829–57 (1993).

C. *Foreign Commerce Clause Restraints on Apportionability of Foreign Source Income.* What distinguished *Mobil* from *Japan Line* (pp. 187–95 supra)? Was it that *Mobil* involved a tax on income rather than property? Why should that make a difference? Is multiple international taxation of income any more acceptable than multiple international taxation of property? Or was it that no foreign jurisdiction was actually seeking to tax the dividend income in full so that there was no actual multiple taxation? But did not the Court say that the *risk* rather than the *actuality* of multiple taxation is the standard for determining the constitutionality of the tax under the Commerce Clause? Or was it simply that the Court felt uncomfortable with a broad reading of *Japan Line* and was using *Mobil* as a vehicle for limiting its scope? Keep these questions in mind when considering Container Corp. of America v. Franchise Tax Board, 463 U.S. 159, 103 S.Ct. 2933 (1983), pp. 496–517 infra, and Barclays Bank PLC v. Franchise Tax Board, 512 U.S. 298, 114 S.Ct. 2268 (1994), pp. 518–20 infra.

D. ASARCO. ASARCO, Inc. v. Idaho State Tax Commission, 458 U.S. 307, 102 S.Ct. 3103 (1982), which the Court discussed in *Allied–Signal* (pp. 420–33 supra), raised essentially the same question as *Mobil*—whether a state (Idaho) could include within the apportionable tax base of a nondomiciliary corporation (ASARCO) the intangible income (dividends, interests, and capital gains) that the corporation derived from its investments in subsidiaries. The Court accordingly approached *ASARCO* within the analytical framework it had constructed in *Mobil*. The Court described its task as determining whether, on the record before it, "ASARCO * * * has succeeded where the taxpayer[] in *Mobil* * * * failed, in proving that the dividend payors at issue are not part of its unitary business, but rather are 'discrete business enterprises.' " Id., 458 U.S. at 320.

Despite the similarity of the broad questions presented by *Mobil* and *ASARCO*, the latter was a much more difficult case because ASARCO's relationship to its subsidiaries was considerably more attenuated than Mobil's vertically integrated relationship to its subsidiaries. ASARCO was in the business of mining, smelting, refining, and selling nonferrous metals. ASARCO's principal activity in Idaho was the mining of silver. The intangible income at issue arose out of ASARCO's investments in five subsidiaries, all of which were engaged in various aspects of the nonferrous metals industry but none of which conducted any business in Idaho: M.I.M. Holdings, Ltd. (production and processing of nonferrous metals in Australia and England); General Cable Corporation (manufacture of cable); Revere Copper and Brass, Inc. (manufacture of copper products); ASARCO Mexicana (production, smelting, refining and sale of nonferrous metals in Mexico); and Southern Peru Copper Company (production and smelting of copper in Peru). ASARCO received dividends from all five corporations; it received interest on Revere's convertible debentures, on a note acquired in connection with an earlier sale of Mexicana stock, and on a note acquired in connection with an earlier sale of General Cable stock; and it received capital gains from the sale of General Cable and M.I.M. stock.

Reviewing the relationship between ASARCO and its subsidiaries in light of the unitary-business factors the Court had identified in *Mobil*—"functional integration, centralization of management, and economies of scale" (Mobil, 445 U.S. at 438)—the Court found that ASARCO was not unitary with any of its subsidiaries. Southern Peru, which was 51.5 percent owned by ASARCO, presented the "closest question." ASARCO, 458 U.S. at 320. Although Southern Peru sold ASARCO 35 percent of its output and was potentially subject to its control, the Court, after examining the details of management contracts, cited trial court findings and evidence to the effect that ASARCO did not "control Southern Peru in any sense of that term." Id. at 322. The Court therefore concluded that "ASARCO's Idaho silver mining and Southern Peru's autonomous business are insufficiently connected to permit the two companies to be classified as a unitary business." Id.

The Court likewise found that the "relationship of each of the other four subsidiaries to ASARCO falls far short of bringing any of them within its unitary business." Id. M.I.M., which was 52.7 percent owned by ASARCO, failed the test because it was never actually controlled by ASARCO, operated "entirely independently of and ha[d] minimal contact with" ASARCO (id. at 323), and sold ASARCO only one percent of its output. General Cable and Revere Copper, which were 34 percent owned by ASARCO, were not unitary with ASARCO because the intercompany purchases and sales never exceeded six percent of the totals involved, and "[n]either Revere's nor General Cable's management seeks direction or approval from ASARCO on operational or other management decisions." Id. at 324. ASARCO Mexicana, which was 49 percent owned by ASARCO, was not engaged in a unitary business with ASARCO because there were only "insignificant" intercompany sales during the years in question and Mexicana "operate[d] independently of [ASARCO]." Id.

In sustaining the taxpayer's claim in *ASARCO*, the Court focused on two features of the unitary business principle that precluded apportionability of the income at issue. The Court declared no less than six times in the course of its opinion that proof of a "discrete business enterprise" conducted by the out-of-state payor prevents the apportionability of dividends, interest, and capital gains by the state in which the nondomiciliary taxpayer-payee conducts its business (id. at 317, 319, 320, 328, and 329 n.4.). And the Court four times repeated the admonition that the Constitution bars the apportionment of income from intangibles when the business activities of the payor "have nothing to do with the activities of the recipient in the taxing State." Id. at 317–18, 327, 328, and 329 n.4.

In addition, the Court rejected Idaho's contention that "intangible income should be considered part of a unitary business if the intangible property (the shares of stock) is 'acquired, managed, or disposed of for purposes relating or contributing to the taxpayer's business.'" Id. at 326 (quoting Brief for Appellee at 4). Characterizing Idaho's position as having "corporate *purpose* * * * define unitary business," id. at 326 (emphasis in original), the Court invoked the internal logic of the unitary business principle itself in refuting it:

> This definition of unitary business would destroy the concept. The business of a corporation requires that it earn money to continue operations and to provide a return on its invested capital. Consequently *all* of its operations, including any investment made, in some sense can be said to be "for purposes related to or contributing to the [corporation's] business." When pressed to its logical limit, this conception of the "unitary business" limitation becomes no limitation at all. When less ambitious interpretations are employed, the result is simply arbitrary.

Id. (emphasis in original).

The Court thus viewed ASARCO's dividend-paying subsidiaries as an intangible investment that merely "'adds to the riches of the corporation but does not affect the [taxing State's] part of the [business].'" Id. at 328 (quoting Wallace v. Hines, 253 U.S. 66, 69–70, 40 S.Ct. 435 (1920)). Idaho therefore lacked the minimum connection with ASARCO's dividend-producing activities to justify the state's inclusion of the dividend income in the taxpayer's apportionable tax base. Without inquiring into the possible differences between income from dividends, interest, and capital gains—no doubt because the parties agreed "that interest and capital gains income derived from these companies should be treated in the same manner as the dividend income," id. at 330, the Court concluded that all three forms of intangible income should be handled similarly. Consequently, because ASARCO was not engaged in a unitary business with the corporations that were the source of its interest and capital gain income, such income, like the dividend income, was not apportionable. The *ASARCO* case is analyzed in detail in Walter Hellerstein, "State Income Taxation of Multijurisdictional Corporations, Part II: Reflections on *ASARCO* and *Woolworth*," 81 Mich. L. Rev. 157 (1982).

E. Woolworth. F.W. Woolworth Co. v. Taxation and Revenue Department, 458 U.S. 354, 102 S.Ct. 3128 (1982) was a companion case to *ASARCO*, and it raised essentially the same question: whether a state (New Mexico) could include within the apportionable tax base of a nondomiciliary corporation (Woolworth) the intangible income (dividends) that the corporation derived from its investments in subsidiaries.

F.W. Woolworth Company was engaged in the general retail merchandise business. It was domiciled in New York and made substantial retail sales throughout the United States, including New Mexico. The dispute centered on the dividends that Woolworth received from four foreign subsidiaries, which operated in Canada, Germany, Mexico, and England. Woolworth owned 100 percent of the stock of the Canadian, German, and Mexican subsidiaries and a majority of the stock of the English subsidiary. The subsidiaries conducted the same general type of business in their respective countries as Woolworth conducted in the United States. Woolworth sought to exclude the dividends from its apportionable tax base in New Mexico on the grounds that the income did not derive from the unitary retail business it conducted there. New Mexico contended that the dividends were apportionable both because the investments were "motivated by business considerations" (Brief for Appellee at 16, id., 458 U.S. 354) and were therefore an "integral part" (id.) of Woolworth's unitary business in New Mexico, and because the dividends arose from an underlying unitary business conducted by Woolworth and its subsidiaries.

In rejecting New Mexico's arguments and holding that the state lacked the constitutional power to include Woolworth's dividends in its apportionable tax base, the Court reinforced the fundamental lessons of *ASARCO*. It chided New Mexico, as it had chided Idaho, for advancing a definition of a unitary business that would, in the Court's view, emasculate the concept. New Mexico had contended that its investments in its subsidiaries could be considered part of its unitary business because, as the state court had reasoned:

> "The possession of large assets by subsidiaries, is a business advantage of great value to the parent; it may give credit which will result in more economical business methods; it may give a standing which shall facilitate purchases; it may enable the corporation to enlarge the field of its activities and in many ways give it business standing and prestige."

Id. at 363 (quoting Taxation and Revenue Dep't v. F.W. Woolworth Co., 95 N.M. 519, 624 P.2d 28, 38 (1981)).

As it had done in *ASARCO*, the Court in *Woolworth* squarely rejected the notion that the income from a nondomiciliary taxpayer's investments arose out of its unitary business merely because the investment advanced the taxpayer's business purposes:

> The state court's reasoning would trivialize this due process limitation by holding it satisfied if the income in question "adds to the riches of the corporation...." Income from whatever source, always is a "business advantage" to a corporation. Our cases demand more.

Id.

The Court also rejected the contention that income from intangibles may be regarded as unitary when it is commingled with the corporation's general funds and used for general corporate operating purposes:

> This analysis likewise subverts the unitary-business limitation. *All* dividend income—irrespective of whether it is generated by a "discrete business enterprise"—would become part of a unitary business if the test were whether the corporation commingled dividends from other corporations, whether unitary or not.

Id. at 364 n.11 (emphasis in original).

With regard to the question whether Woolworth's underlying relationship to its dividend-paying subsidiaries warranted the conclusion that they were engaged in unitary business, the Court, as in *ASARCO*, found little evidence of the key unitary factors—"functional integration, centralization of management, and economies of scale." Id. at 364 (quoting Mobil, 445 U.S. at 438 (1980)). The Court found that "the record is persuasive that Woolworth's operations were not functionally integrated with its subsidiaries" (id. at 366) in light of the absence of "centralized purchasing, manufacturing, or warehousing of merchandise," id. at 365; autonomous decisionmaking by subsidiaries with respect to such matters as site selection, advertising, and accounting control, id; and independent responsibility by each subsidiary for obtaining financing. Id. at 366.

The Court similarly found little evidence of centralized management or economies of scale. Each subsidiary operated as a distinct business enterprise at the management level; there was little interchange of personnel; each subsidiary enjoyed autonomy in retailing policy; and Woolworth had no formal organization for overseeing the operations of its foreign subsidiaries. Id. at 366–70. While there were some managerial links, the Court discounted them as insignificant when compared to the type of business integration that typified enterprises it had characterized as unitary in other cases. The Court therefore concluded that "[e]xcept for the type of occasional oversight—with respect to capital structure, major debt, and dividends—that any parent gives to an investment in a subsidiary, there is little or no integration of the business activities or centralization of management of these five corporations." Id. at 369. The *Woolworth* case is analyzed in detail in Walter Hellerstein, "State Income Taxation of Multijurisdictional Corporations, Part II: Reflections on *ASARCO* and *Woolworth*," 81 Mich. L. Rev. 157 (1982).

F. *Combined Reporting.* In *Mobil*, *ASARCO*, and *Woolworth*, the questions of apportionability and fair apportionment arose in the context of taxing regimes that taxed corporate income on a separate company basis. In *Mobil*, for example, Vermont never sought to characterize the income that Mobil received from its subsidiaries as anything other than dividends paid to it by other—albeit affiliated—corporations. It was for that reason that Vermont did not permit Mobil to include the subsidiaries' factors in the parent's apportionment formula. By its lights, Vermont was taxing only Mobil's income—operating income as well as dividend income—on a separate company basis, and therefore only Mobil's factors ought to be taken into account. Even though the ground for including the dividends in Mobil's apportionable tax base may have been the underlying unitary enterprise Mobil was conducting with its subsidiaries, Vermont's approach did not seek to apportion the income as if Mobil were conducting its unitary business as a single entity.

In many states, however, when a group of affiliated corporations is conducting a unitary business, it is required to report its income on a "combined" basis, by combining the operating income of all of the unitary affiliates and apportioning this income on the basis of the combined property, payroll, and sales factors of the unitary corporate group. Under combined reporting, the apportionable income of a group of corporations conducting a unitary business is the income derived by members of the multicorporate unitary enterprise from dealings with nonmembers of the group. Dividends paid by one member of the group to other members of the group, insofar as they reflect income from the unitary business, are eliminated altogether from the tax base. See generally 1 Jerome R. Hellerstein & Walter Hellerstein,

State Taxation ¶ 8.11 (3d ed. 1998); E. George Rudolph, "State Taxation of Interstate Business: The Unitary Business Concept and Affiliated Corporate Groups," 25 Tax L. Rev. 171, 194–200 (1970).

The landmark case of *Container Corp. of America v. Franchise Tax Board*, which is set out immediately below, considers the federal constitutional limitations on apportionability and fair apportionment in the context of a multicorporate enterprise that is required to file on a combined basis, under both the constitutional principles generally governing apportionability and fair apportionment and under the constitutional principles specifically directed to state taxation of foreign commerce.

CONTAINER CORPORATION OF AMERICA v. FRANCHISE TAX BOARD

Supreme Court of the United States, 1983.
463 U.S. 159, 103 S.Ct. 2933.

JUSTICE BRENNAN delivered the opinion of the Court.

This is another appeal claiming that the application of a state taxing scheme violates the Due Process and Commerce Clauses of the Federal Constitution. California imposes a corporate franchise tax geared to income. In common with a large number of other States, it employs the "unitary business" principle and formula apportionment in applying that tax to corporations doing business both inside and outside the State. Appellant is a Delaware corporation headquartered in Illinois and doing business in California and elsewhere. It also has a number of overseas subsidiaries incorporated in the countries in which they operate. Appellee is the California authority charged with administering the State's franchise tax. This appeal presents three questions for review: (1) Was it improper for appellee and the state courts to find that appellant and its overseas subsidiaries constituted a "unitary business" for purposes of the state tax? (2) Even if the unitary business finding was proper, do certain salient differences among national economies render the standard three-factor apportionment formula used by California so inaccurate as applied to the multinational enterprise consisting of appellant and its subsidiaries as to violate the constitutional requirement of "fair apportionment"? (3) In any event, did California have an obligation under the Foreign Commerce Clause, U.S. Const., Art. I, § 8, cl. 3, to employ the "arm's-length" analysis used by the Federal Government and most foreign nations in evaluating the tax consequences of intercorporate relationships?

I

A

Various aspects of state tax systems based on the "unitary business" principle and formula apportionment have provoked repeated constitutional litigation in this Court. See, e.g., ASARCO Inc. v. Idaho State Tax Comm'n, 458 U.S. 307, 102 S.Ct. 3103 (1982); F.W. Woolworth Co. v. Taxation & Revenue Dept., 458 U.S. 354, 102 S.Ct. 3128 (1982); Exxon

Corp. v. Wisconsin Dept. of Revenue, 447 U.S. 207, 100 S.Ct. 2109 (1980); Mobil Oil Corp. v. Commissioner of Taxes, 445 U.S. 425, 100 S.Ct. 1223 (1980); Moorman Mfg. Co. v. Bair, 437 U.S. 267, 98 S.Ct. 2340 (1978); Butler Bros. v. McColgan, 315 U.S. 501, 62 S.Ct. 701 (1942); Bass, Ratcliff & Gretton, Ltd. v. State Tax Comm'n, 266 U.S. 271, 45 S.Ct. 82 (1924); Underwood Typewriter Co. v. Chamberlain, 254 U.S. 113, 41 S.Ct. 45 (1920).

Under both the Due Process and the Commerce Clauses of the Constitution, a State may not, when imposing an income-based tax, "tax value earned outside its borders." ASARCO, supra, 458 U.S., at 315, 102 S.Ct., at 3108. In the case of a more-or-less integrated business enterprise operating in more than one State, however, arriving at precise territorial allocations of "value" is often an elusive goal, both in theory and in practice. See Mobil Oil Corp. v. Commissioner of Taxes, supra, 445 U.S., at 438, 100 S.Ct., at 1232; Butler Bros. v. McColgan, supra, 315 U.S., at 507–509, 62 S.Ct., at 704–705; Underwood Typewriter Co. v. Chamberlain, supra, 254 U.S., at 121, 41 S.Ct., at 47. For this reason and others, we have long held that the Constitution imposes no single formula on the States and that the taxpayer has the " 'distinct burden of showing by 'clear and cogent evidence' that [the state tax] results in extraterritorial values being taxed. ...' " Exxon Corp., supra, 447 U.S., at 221, 100 S.Ct., at 2119, quoting Butler Bros. v. McColgan, supra, 315 U.S., at 507, 62 S.Ct., at 704, in turn quoting Norfolk & Western R. Co. v. North Carolina ex rel. Maxwell, 297 U.S. 682, 688, 56 S.Ct. 625, 628 (1936).

One way of deriving locally taxable income is on the basis of formal geographical or transactional accounting. The problem with this method is that formal accounting is subject to manipulation and imprecision, and often ignores or captures inadequately the many subtle and largely unquantifiable transfers of value that take place among the components of a single enterprise. See generally Mobil Oil Corp., supra, 445 U.S., at 438–439, 100 S.Ct., at 1232, and sources cited. The unitary business/formula apportionment method is a very different approach to the problem of taxing businesses operating in more than one jurisdiction. It rejects geographical or transactional accounting, and instead calculates the local tax base by first defining the scope of the "unitary business" of which the taxed enterprise's activities in the taxing jurisdiction form one part, and then apportioning the total income of that "unitary business" between the taxing jurisdiction and the rest of the world on the basis of a formula taking into account objective measures of the corporation's activities within and without the jurisdiction. This Court long ago upheld the constitutionality of the unitary business/formula apportionment method, although subject to certain constraints. See, e.g., Hans Rees' Sons, Inc. v. North Carolina ex rel. Maxwell, 283 U.S. 123, 51 S.Ct. 385 (1931); Bass, Ratcliff & Gretton, Ltd. v. State Tax Comm'n, supra; Underwood Typewriter Co. v. Chamberlain, supra. The method has now gained wide acceptance, and is in one of its forms the basis for the Uniform Division of

Income for Tax Purposes Act (Uniform Act), which has at last count been substantially adopted by 23 States, including California.

B

Two aspects of the unitary business/formula apportionment method have traditionally attracted judicial attention. These are, as one might easily guess, the notions of "unitary business" and "formula apportionment," respectively.

(1)

The Due Process and Commerce Clauses of the Constitution do not allow a State to tax income arising out of interstate activities—even on a proportional basis—unless there is a " 'minimal connection' or 'nexus' between the interstate activities and the taxing State, and 'a rational relationship between the income attributed to the State and the intrastate values of the enterprise.' " Exxon Corp. v. Wisconsin Dept. of Revenue, supra, 447 U.S., at 219–220, 100 S.Ct., at 2118, quoting Mobil Oil Corp. v. Commissioner of Taxes, supra, 445 U.S., at 436, 437, 100 S.Ct., at 1231. At the very least, this set of principles imposes the obvious and largely self-executing limitation that a State not tax a purported "unitary business" unless at least some part of it is conducted in the State. See Exxon Corp., supra, 447 U.S., at 220, 100 S.Ct., at 2118; Wisconsin v. J.C. Penney Co., supra, 311 U.S., at 444, 61 S.Ct., at 249. It also requires that there be some bond of ownership or control uniting the purported "unitary business." See ASARCO, supra, 458 U.S., at 316–317, 102 S.Ct., at 3109.

In addition, the principles we have quoted require that the out-of-state activities of the purported "unitary business" be related in some concrete way to the in-state activities. The functional meaning of this requirement is that there be some sharing or exchange of value not capable of precise identification or measurement—beyond the mere flow of funds arising out of a passive investment or a distinct business operation—which renders formula apportionment a reasonable method of taxation. See generally ASARCO, supra, at 317, 102 S.Ct., at 3115; Mobil Oil Corp., supra, 445 U.S., at 438–442, 100 S.Ct., at 1232–1234. In Underwood Typewriter Co. v. Chamberlain, supra, we held that a State could tax on an apportioned basis the combined income of a vertically integrated business whose various components (manufacturing, sales, etc.) operated in different States. In Bass, Ratcliff & Gretton, supra, we applied the same principle to a vertically integrated business operating across national boundaries. In Butler Bros. v. McColgan, supra, we recognized that the unitary business principle could apply, not only to vertically integrated enterprises, but also to a series of similar enterprises operating separately in various jurisdictions but linked by common managerial or operational resources that produced economies of scale and transfers of value. More recently, we have further refined the "unitary business" concept in Exxon Corp. v. Wisconsin Dept. of Revenue, 447 U.S. 207, 100 S.Ct. 2109 (1980), and Mobil Oil Corp. v. Commissioner of Taxes, 445 U.S. 425, 100 S.Ct.

1223 (1980), where we upheld the States' unitary business findings, and in ASARCO Inc. v. Idaho State Tax Comm'n, 458 U.S. 307, 102 S.Ct. 3103 (1982), and F.W. Woolworth Co. v. Taxation & Revenue Dept., 458 U.S. 354, 102 S.Ct. 3128 (1982), in which we found such findings to have been improper.

The California statute at issue in this case, and the Uniform Act from which most of its relevant provisions are derived, track in large part the principles we have just discussed. In particular, the statute distinguishes between the "business income" of a multijurisdictional enterprise, which is apportioned by formula, Cal.Rev. & Tax.Code Ann. §§ 25128–25136 (West 1979), and its "nonbusiness" income, which is not.[1] Although the statute does not explicitly require that income from distinct business enterprises be apportioned separately, this requirement antedated adoption of the Uniform Act, and has not been abandoned.

A final point that needs to be made about the unitary business concept is that it is not, so to speak, unitary: there are variations on the theme, and any number of them are logically consistent with the underlying principles motivating the approach. For example, a State might decide to respect formal corporate lines and treat the ownership of a corporate subsidiary as *per se* a passive investment.[4] In Mobil Oil Corp., 445 U.S., at 440–441, 100 S.Ct., at 1233, however, we made clear that, as a general matter, such a *per se* rule is not constitutionally required:

> "Superficially, intercorporate division might appear to be a[n] ... attractive basis for limiting apportionability. But the form of business organization may have nothing to do with the underlying unity or diversity of business enterprise." Id., at 440, 100 S.Ct., at 1233.

Thus, for example, California law provides:

> "In the case of a corporation ... owning or controlling, either directly or indirectly, another corporation, or other corporations, and in the case of a corporation ... owned or controlled, either directly or indirectly, by another corporation, the Franchise Tax Board may require a consolidated report showing the combined net income or such other facts as it deems necessary." Cal.Rev. & Tax.Code Ann. § 25104 (West 1979).[5]

---

1. Certain forms of nonbusiness income, such as dividends, are allocated on the basis of the taxpayer's commercial domicile. Other forms of nonbusiness income, such as capital gains on sales of real property, are allocated on the basis of situs. See Cal.Rev. & Tax.Code Ann. §§ 25123–25127 (West 1979).

4. We note that the Uniform Act does not speak to this question one way or the other.

5. See also Cal.Rev. & Tax.Code Ann. § 25105 (West 1979) (defining "ownership or control"). A necessary corollary of the California approach, of course, is that intercorporate dividends in a unitary business *not* be included in gross income, since such inclusion would result in double-counting of a portion of the subsidiary's income (first as income attributed to the unitary business, and second as dividend income to the parent). See § 25106.

Some States, it should be noted, have adopted a hybrid approach. In *Mobil* itself, for example, a nondomiciliary State invoked a unitary business justification to include an apportioned share of certain corporate dividends in the gross income of the taxpayer, but did not require a combined return and combined apportionment. The Court in *Mobil* held that the taxpayer's objection to

Even among States that take this approach, however, only some apply it in taxing American corporations with subsidiaries located in foreign countries. The difficult question we address in Part v. of this opinion is whether, for reasons not implicated in *Mobil*,[7] that particular variation on the theme is constitutionally barred.

(2)

Having determined that a certain set of activities constitute a "unitary business," a State must then apply a formula apportioning the income of that business within and without the State. Such an apportionment formula must, under both the Due Process and Commerce Clauses, be fair. See Exxon Corp., supra, 447 U.S., at 219, 227–228, 100 S.Ct., at 2118, 2122–2123; Moorman Mfg. Co., 437 U.S., at 272–273, 98 S.Ct., at 2343–2344; Hans Rees' Sons, Inc., 283 U.S., at 134, 51 S.Ct., at 389. The first, and again obvious, component of fairness in an apportionment formula is what might be called internal consistency—that is, the formula must be such that, if applied by every jurisdiction, it would result in no more than all of the unitary business income being taxed. The second and more difficult requirement is what might be called external consistency— the factor or factors used in the apportionment formula must actually reflect a reasonable sense of how income is generated. The Constitution does not "invalidat[e] an apportionment formula whenever it *may* result in taxation of some income that did not have its source in the taxing State...." Moorman Mfg. Co., supra, 437 U.S., at 272, 98 S.Ct., at 2344 (emphasis added). See Underwood Typewriter Co., 254 U.S., at 120–121, 41 S.Ct., at 46–47. Nevertheless, we will strike down the application of an apportionment formula if the taxpayer can prove "by 'clear and cogent evidence' that the income attributed to the State is in fact 'out of all appropriate proportions to the business transacted ... in that State,' [Hans Rees' Sons, Inc.,] 283 U.S., at 135, 51 S.Ct., at 389, or has 'led to a grossly distorted result,' [Norfolk & Western R. Co. v. Missouri State Tax Comm'n, 390 U.S. 317, 326, 88 S.Ct. 995, 1001 (1968)]." Moorman Mfg. Co., supra, 437 U.S., at 274, 98 S.Ct., at 2345.

California and the other States that have adopted the Uniform Act use a formula—commonly called the "three-factor" formula—which is based, in equal parts, on the proportion of a unitary business' total

---

this approach had not been properly raised in the state proceedings. 445 U.S., at 441, n. 15, 100 S.Ct., at 1233, n. 15. Justice Stevens, however, reached the merits, stating in part: "Either Mobil's worldwide 'petroleum enterprise' is all part of one unitary business, or it is not; if it is, Vermont must evaluate the entire enterprise in a consistent manner." Id., at 461, 100 S.Ct., at 1243 (citation omitted). See id., at 462, 100 S.Ct., at 1244 (Stevens, J., dissenting) (outlining alternative approaches available to State); cf. The Supreme Court, 1981 Term, 96 Harv.L.Rev. 62, 93–96 (1982).

7. *Mobil* did, in fact, involve income from foreign subsidiaries, but that fact was of little importance to the case for two reasons. First, as discussed in n. 5, supra, the State in that case included *dividends* from the subsidiaries to the parent in its calculation of the parent's apportionable taxable income, but did not include the underlying income of the subsidiaries themselves. Second, the taxpayer in that case conceded that the dividends could be taxed *somewhere* in the United States, so the actual issue before the Court was merely whether a particular State could be barred from imposing some portion of that tax. See 445 U.S., at 447, 100 S.Ct., at 1236.

payroll, property, and sales which are located in the taxing State. See Cal.Rev. & Tax.Code Ann. §§ 25128–25136 (West 1979). We approved the three-factor formula in Butler Bros. v. McColgan, 315 U.S. 501, 62 S.Ct. 701 (1942). Indeed, not only has the three-factor formula met our approval, but it has become, for reasons we discuss in more detail infra, at 2949, something of a benchmark against which other apportionment formulas are judged. See Moorman Mfg. Co., supra, at 282, 98 S.Ct., at 2349 (Blackmun, J., dissenting); cf. General Motors Corp. v. District of Columbia, 380 U.S. 553, 561, 85 S.Ct. 1156, 1161 (1965).

Besides being fair, an apportionment formula must, under the Commerce Clause, also not result in discrimination against interstate or foreign commerce. See Mobil Oil Corp., supra, 445 U.S., at 444, 100 S.Ct., at 1235; cf. Japan Line, Ltd. v. County of Los Angeles, 441 U.S. 434, 444–448, 99 S.Ct. 1813, 1819–1821 (1979) (property tax). Aside from forbidding the obvious types of discrimination against interstate or foreign commerce, this principle might have been construed to require that a state apportionment formula not differ so substantially from methods of allocation used by other jurisdictions in which the taxpayer is subject to taxation so as to produce double taxation of the same income, and a resultant tax burden higher than the taxpayer would incur if its business were limited to any one jurisdiction. At least in the interstate commerce context, however, the anti-discrimination principle has not in practice required much in addition to the requirement of fair apportionment. In Moorman Mfg. Co. v. Bair, supra, in particular, we explained that eliminating all overlapping taxation would require this Court to establish not only a single constitutionally mandated method of taxation, but also rules regarding the application of that method in particular cases. Because that task was thought to be essentially legislative, we declined to undertake it, and held that a fairly apportioned tax would not be found invalid simply because it differed from the prevailing approach adopted by the States. As we discuss infra, however, a more searching inquiry is necessary when we are confronted with the possibility of international double taxation.

II

A

Appellant is in the business of manufacturing custom-ordered paperboard packaging. Its operation is vertically integrated, and includes the production of paperboard from raw timber and wastepaper as well as its composition into the finished products ordered by customers. The operation is also largely domestic. During the years at issue in this case—1963, 1964, and 1965—appellant controlled 20 foreign subsidiaries located in four Latin American and four European countries. Its percentage ownership of the subsidiaries (either directly or through other subsidiaries) ranged between 66.7% and 100%. In those instances (about half) in which appellant did not own a 100% interest in the subsidiary, the remainder was owned by local nationals. One of the subsidiaries was a holding company that had no payroll, sales, or property, but did have book income.

Another was inactive. The rest were all engaged—in their respective local markets—in essentially the same business as appellant.

Most of appellant's subsidiaries were, like appellant itself, fully integrated, although a few bought paperboard and other intermediate products elsewhere. Sales of materials from appellant to its subsidiaries accounted for only about 1% of the subsidiaries' total purchases. The subsidiaries were also relatively autonomous with respect to matters of personnel and day-to-day management. For example, transfers of personnel from appellant to its subsidiaries were rare, and occurred only when a subsidiary could not fill a position locally. There was no formal United States training program for the subsidiaries' employees, although groups of foreign employees occasionally visited the United States for 2–6 week periods to familiarize themselves with appellant's methods of operation. Appellant charged one senior vice president and four other officers with the task of overseeing the operations of the subsidiaries. These officers established general standards of professionalism, profitability, and ethical practices and dealt with major problems and long-term decisions; day-to-day management of the subsidiaries, however, was left in the hands of local executives who were always citizens of the host country. Although local decisions regarding capital expenditures were subject to review by appellant, problems were generally worked out by consensus rather than outright domination. Appellant also had a number of its directors and officers on the boards of directors of the subsidiaries, but they did not generally play an active role in management decisions.

Nevertheless, in certain respects, the relationship between appellant and its subsidiaries was decidedly close. For example, approximately half of the subsidiaries' long-term debt was either held directly, or guaranteed, by appellant. Appellant also provided advice and consultation regarding manufacturing techniques, engineering, design, architecture, insurance, and cost accounting to a number of its subsidiaries, either by entering into technical service agreements with them or by informal arrangement. Finally, appellant occasionally assisted its subsidiaries in their procurement of equipment, either by selling them used equipment of its own or by employing its own purchasing department to act as an agent for the subsidiaries.

B

During the tax years at issue in this case, appellant filed California franchise tax returns. In 1969, after conducting an audit of appellant's returns for the years in question, appellee issued notices of additional assessments for each of those years. The respective approaches and results reflected in appellant's initial returns and in appellee's notices of additional assessments capture the legal differences at issue in this case.

In calculating the total unapportioned taxable income of its unitary business, appellant included its own corporate net earnings as derived from its federal tax form (subject to certain adjustments not relevant here), but did not include any income of its subsidiaries. It also deducted—

as it was authorized to do under state law—all dividend income, non-business interest income, and gains on sales of assets not related to the unitary business. In calculating the share of its net income which was apportionable to California under the three-factor formula, appellant omitted all of its subsidiaries' payroll, property, and sales. The results of these calculations are summarized in the margin.[11]

The gravamen of the notices issued by appellee in 1969 was that appellant should have treated its overseas subsidiaries as part of its unitary business rather than as passive investments. Including the overseas subsidiaries in appellant's unitary business had two primary effects: it increased the income subject to apportionment by an amount equal to the total income of those subsidiaries (less intersubsidiary dividends, see n. 5, supra), and it decreased the percentage of that income which was apportionable to California. The net effect, however, was to increase appellant's tax liability in each of the three years.[12]

Appellant paid the additional amounts under protest, and then sued in California Superior Court for a refund, raising the issues now before this Court. The case was tried on stipulated facts, and the Superior Court upheld appellee's assessments. On appeal, the California Court of Appeal affirmed, and the California Supreme Court refused to exercise discretionary review. We noted probable jurisdiction.

III

A

We address the unitary business issue first. As previously noted, the taxpayer always has the "distinct burden of showing by 'clear and cogent evidence' that [the state tax] results in extraterritorial values being taxed." One necessary corollary of that principle is that this Court will, if

---

11.

	Total income of unitary business	Percentage attributed to California	Amount attributed to California	Tax (5.5%)
1963.....	$26,870,427.00	11.041	$2,966,763.85	$163,172.01
1964.....	28,774,320.48	10.6422	3,062,220.73	168,422.14
1965.....	32,280,842.90	9.8336	3,174,368.97	174,590.29

See Exhibit A–7 to Stipulation; Record 36, 76, 77, 79, 104, 126.

12. According to the notices, appellant's actual tax obligations were as follows:

	Total income of unitary business	Percentage attributed to California	Amount attributed to California	Tax (5.5%)
1963.....	$37,348,183.00	8.6886	$3,245,034.23	$178,476.88
1964.....	44,245,879.00	8.3135	3,673,381.15	202,310.95
1965.....	46,884,966.00	7.6528	3,588,012.68	197,340.70

See Exhibit A–7 to Stipulation; Record 76, 77, 79.

reasonably possible, defer to the judgment of state courts in deciding whether a particular set of activities constitutes a "unitary business." As we said in a closely related context in Norton Co. v. Department of Revenue, 340 U.S. 534, 71 S.Ct. 377 (1951):

> "The general rule, applicable here, is that a taxpayer claiming immunity from a tax has the burden of establishing his exemption.
>
> *"This burden is never met merely by showing a fair difference of opinion which as an original matter might be decided differently. ...* Of course, in constitutional cases, we have power to examine the whole record to arrive at an independent judgment as to whether constitutional rights have been invaded, but that does not mean that we will re-examine, as a court of first instance, findings of fact supported by substantial evidence." Id., at 537–538, 71 S.Ct., at 380 (footnotes omitted; emphasis added).

See id., at 538, 71 S.Ct., at 380 (concluding that, "in light of all the evidence, the [state] judgment [on a question of whether income should be attributed to the State] was within the realm of permissible judgment"). The legal principles defining the constitutional limits on the unitary business principle are now well established. The factual records in such cases, even when the parties enter into a stipulation, tend to be long and complex, and the line between "historical fact" and "constitutional fact" is often fuzzy at best. Cf. ASARCO, 458 U.S., at 326–328, nn. 22, 23, 102 S.Ct., at 3114–3115, nn. 22, 23. It will do the cause of legal certainty little good if this Court turns every colorable claim that a state court erred in a particular application of those principles into a *de novo* adjudication, whose unintended nuances would then spawn further litigation and an avalanche of critical comment. Rather, our task must be to determine whether the state court applied the correct standards to the case; and if it did, whether its judgment "was within the realm of permissible judgment."[15]

B

In this case, we are singularly unconvinced by appellant's argument that the State Court of Appeal "in important part analyzed this case under a different legal standard," F.W. Woolworth, 458 U.S., at 363, 102

---

15. *ASARCO* and *F.W. Woolworth* are consistent with this standard of review. *ASARCO* involved a claim that a parent and certain of its partial subsidiaries, in which it held either minority interests or bare majority interests, were part of the same unitary business. The State Supreme Court upheld the claim. We concluded, *relying on factual findings made by the state courts,* that a unitary business finding was impermissible because the partial subsidiaries were not realistically subject to even minimal control by ASARCO, and were therefore passive investments in the most basic sense of the term. We held specifically that to accept the State's theory of the case would not only constitute a misapplication of the unitary business concept, but would "destroy" the concept entirely.

F.W. Woolworth was a much closer case, involving one partially owned subsidiary and three wholly owned subsidiaries. We examined the evidence in some detail, and reversed the state court's unitary business finding, but only after concluding that the state court had made specific and crucial legal errors, not merely in the conclusions it drew, but in the legal standard it applied in analyzing the case.

S.Ct., at 3134, from the one articulated by this Court. Appellant argues that the state court here, like the state court in *F.W. Woolworth,* improperly relied on appellant's mere *potential* to control the operations of its subsidiaries as a dispositive factor in reaching its unitary business finding. In fact, although the state court mentioned that "major policy decisions of the subsidiaries were subject to review by appellant," 117 Cal.App.3d, at 998, 173 Cal.Rptr., at 127, it relied principally, in discussing the management relationship between appellant and its subsidiaries, on the more concrete observation that "[h]igh officials of appellant gave directions to subsidiaries for compliance with the parent's standard of professionalism, profitability, and ethical practices." Id., at 998, 173 Cal.Rptr., at 127–128.[16]

Appellant also argues that the state court erred in endorsing an administrative presumption that corporations engaged in the same line of business are unitary. This presumption affected the state court's reasoning, but only as one element among many. Moreover, considering the limited use to which it was put, we find the "presumption" criticized by appellant to be reasonable. Investment in a business enterprise truly "distinct" from a corporation's main line of business often serves the primary function of diversifying the corporate portfolio and reducing the risks inherent in being tied to one industry's business cycle. When a corporation invests in a subsidiary that engages in the same line of work as itself, it becomes much more likely that one function of the investment is to make better use—either through economies of scale or through operational integration or sharing of expertise—of the parent's existing business-related resources.

Finally, appellant urges us to adopt a bright-line rule requiring as a prerequisite to a finding that a mercantile or manufacturing enterprise is unitary that it be characterized by "a substantial flow of goods." Brief for Appellant 47. We decline this invitation. The prerequisite to a constitutionally acceptable finding of unitary business is a flow of *value,* not a flow of goods. As we reiterated in *F.W. Woolworth,* a relevant question in the unitary business inquiry is whether " 'contributions to income [of the subsidiaries] result[ed] from functional integration, centralization of management, and economies of scale.' " 458 U.S., at 364, 102 S.Ct., at 3135, quoting Mobil, 445 U.S., at 438, 100 S.Ct., at 1232. "[S]ubstantial mutual interdependence," F.W. Woolworth, supra, 458 U.S., at 371, 102 S.Ct., at 3139, can arise in any number of ways; a substantial flow of goods is clearly one but just as clearly not the only one.[17]

---

16. In any event, although potential control is, as we said in *F.W. Woolworth,* not *"dispositive"* of the unitary business issue, id., at 362, 102 S.Ct., at 3134 (emphasis added), it is *relevant,* both to whether or not the components of the purported unitary business share that degree of common ownership which is a prerequisite to a finding of unitariness, and also to whether there might exist a degree of implicit control sufficient to render the parent and the subsidiary an integrated enterprise.

17. As we state supra, there is a wide range of constitutionally acceptable variations on the unitary business theme. Thus, a leading scholar has suggested that a "flow of goods" requirement would provide a reasonable and workable bright-line test for unitary business, see Hellerstein, Recent Developments in State Tax Apportionment and the Circumscription of Unitary Business,

C

The State Court of Appeal relied on a large number of factors in reaching its judgment that appellant and its foreign subsidiaries constituted a unitary business. These included appellant's assistance to its subsidiaries in obtaining used and new equipment and in filling personnel needs that could not be met locally, the substantial role played by appellant in loaning funds to the subsidiaries and guaranteeing loans provided by others, the "considerable interplay between appellant and its foreign subsidiaries in the area of corporate expansion," 117 Cal.App.3d, at 997, 173 Cal.Rptr., at 128, the "substantial" technical assistance provided by appellant to the subsidiaries, id., at 998–999, 173 Cal.Rptr., at 127–128, and the supervisory role played by appellant's officers in providing general guidance to the subsidiaries. In each of these respects, this case differs from *ASARCO* and *F.W. Woolworth,*[18] and clearly comes closer than those cases did to presenting a "functionally integrated enterprise," Mobil, supra, 445 U.S., at 440, 100 S.Ct., at 1233, which the State is entitled to tax as a single entity. We need not decide whether any one of these factors would be sufficient as a constitutional matter to prove the existence of a unitary business. Taken in combination, at least, they clearly demonstrate that the state court reached a conclusion "within the realm of permissible judgment."[19]

---

21 Nat.Tax J. 487, 501–502 (1968); Hellerstein, Allocation and Apportionment of Dividends and the Delineation of the Unitary Business, 14 Tax Notes 155 (Jan. 25, 1982), and some state courts have adopted such a test, see, e.g., Commonwealth v. ACF Industries, Inc., 441 Pa. 129, 271 A.2d 273 (1970). But see, e.g., McLure, Operational Interdependence Is Not the Appropriate "Bright Line Test" of a Unitary Business—At Least Not Now, 18 Tax Notes 107 (Jan. 10, 1983). However sensible such a test may be as a policy matter, however, we see no reason to impose it on all the States as a requirement of constitutional law. Cf. Wisconsin v. J.C. Penney Co., 311 U.S. 435, 445, 61 S.Ct. 246, 250 (1940).

18. See n. 15, supra. See also, e.g., F.W. Woolworth, 458 U.S., at 365, 102 S.Ct., at 3135–3136 ("*no* phase of any subsidiary's business was integrated with the parent's"), ibid. (undisputed testimony stated that each subsidiary made business decisions independently of parent); id., at 366, 102 S.Ct., at 3135 ("each subsidiary was responsible for obtaining its own financing from sources other than the parent"); ibid. ("With one possible exception, none of the subsidiaries' officers during the year in question was a current or former employee of the parent.") (footnote omitted).

19. Two of the factors relied on by the state court deserve particular mention. The first of these is the flow of capital resources from appellant to its subsidiaries through loans and loan guarantees. There is no indication that any of these capital transactions were conducted at arm's length, and the resulting flow of value is obvious. As we made clear in another context in Corn Products Refining Co. v. Commissioner, 350 U.S. 46, 50–53, 76 S.Ct. 20, 23–24 (1955), capital transactions can serve either an investment function or an operational function. In this case, appellant's loans and loan guarantees were clearly part of an effort to ensure that "[t]he overseas operations of [appellant] continue to grow and to become a more substantial part of the company's strength and profitability." Container Corporation of America, 1964 Annual Report 6, reproduced in Exhibit I to Stipulation of Facts.

The second noteworthy factor is the managerial role played by appellant in its subsidiaries' affairs. We made clear in *F.W. Woolworth Co.* that a unitary business finding could not be based merely on "the type of occasional oversight—with respect to capital structure, major debt, and dividends—that any parent gives to an investment in a subsidiary...." 458 U.S., at 369, 102 S.Ct., at 3138. As *Exxon* illustrates, however, mere decentralization of day-to-day management responsibility and accountability cannot defeat a unitary business finding. 447 U.S., at 224, 100 S.Ct., at 2120. The difference lies in whether the management role that the parent does play is grounded in its own operational expertise and its overall operational strategy. In this case, the business "guidelines" established by appellant for its subsidiaries, the "consensus" process by

IV

We turn now to the question of fair apportionment. Once again, appellant has the burden of proof; it must demonstrate that there is " 'no rational relationship between the income attributed to the State and the intrastate values of the enterprise,' " Exxon Corp., 447 U.S., at 220, 100 S.Ct., at 2118, quoting Mobil, supra, 445 U.S., at 437, 100 S.Ct., at 1231, by proving that the income apportioned to California under the statute is "out of all appropriate proportion to the business transacted by the appellant in that State," Hans Rees' Sons, Inc., 283 U.S., at 135, 51 S.Ct., at 389.

Appellant challenges the application of California's three-factor formula to its business on two related grounds, both arising as a practical (although not a theoretical) matter out of the international character of the enterprise. First, appellant argues that its foreign subsidiaries are significantly more profitable than it is, and that the three-factor formula, by ignoring that fact and relying instead on indirect measures of income such as payroll, property, and sales, systematically distorts the true allocation of income between appellant and the subsidiaries. The problem with this argument is obvious: the profit figures relied on by appellant are based on precisely the sort of formal geographical accounting whose basic theoretical weaknesses justify resort to formula apportionment in the first place. Indeed, we considered and rejected a very similar argument in *Mobil,* pointing out that whenever a unitary business exists,

> "separate [geographical] accounting, while it purports to isolate portions of income received in various States, may fail to account for contributions to income resulting from functional integration, centralization of management, and economies of scale. Because these factors of profitability arise from the operation of the business as a whole, it becomes misleading to characterize the income of the business as having a single identifiable 'source.' Although separate geographical accounting may be useful for internal auditing, for purposes of state taxation it is not constitutionally required." 445 U.S., at 438, 100 S.Ct., at 1232 (citation omitted).

Appellant's second argument is related, and can be answered in the same way. Appellant contends:

> "The costs of production in foreign countries are generally significantly lower than in the United States, primarily as a result of the lower wage rates of workers in countries other than the United States. Because wages are one of the three factors used in formulary apportionment, the use of the formula unfairly inflates the amount of income apportioned to United States operations, where wages are higher." Brief for Appellant 12.

which appellant's management was involved in the subsidiaries' business decisions, and the sometimes uncompensated technical assistance provided by appellant, all point to precisely the sort of operational role we found lacking in *F.W. Woolworth.*

Appellant supports this argument with various statistics that appear to demonstrate, not only that wage rates are generally lower in the foreign countries in which its subsidiaries operate, but also that those lower wages are not offset by lower levels of productivity. Indeed, it is able to show that at least one foreign plant had labor costs per thousand square feet of corrugated container that were approximately 40% of the same costs in appellant's California plants.

The problem with all this evidence, however, is that it does not by itself come close to impeaching the basic rationale behind the three-factor formula. Appellant and its foreign subsidiaries have been determined to be a unitary business. It therefore may well be that in addition to the foreign payroll going into the production of any given corrugated container by a foreign subsidiary, there is also California payroll, as well as other California factors, contributing—albeit more indirectly—to the same production. The mere fact that this possibility is not reflected in appellant's accounting does not disturb the underlying premises of the formula apportionment method.

Both geographical accounting and formula apportionment are imperfect proxies for an ideal which is not only difficult to achieve in practice, but also difficult to describe in theory. Some methods of formula apportionment are particularly problematic because they focus on only a small part of the spectrum of activities by which value is generated. Although we have generally upheld the use of such formulas, see, e.g., Moorman Mfg. Co. v. Bair, 437 U.S. 267, 98 S.Ct. 2340 (1978); Underwood Typewriter Co. v. Chamberlain, 254 U.S. 113, 41 S.Ct. 45 (1920), we have on occasion found the distortive effect of focusing on only one factor so outrageous in a particular case as to require reversal. In Hans Rees' Sons, Inc. v. North Carolina ex rel. Maxwell, supra, for example, an apportionment method based entirely on ownership of tangible property resulted in an attribution to North Carolina of between 66% and 85% of the taxpayer's income over the course of a number of years, while a separate accounting analysis purposely skewed to resolve all doubts in favor of the State resulted in an attribution of no more than 21.7%. We struck down the application of the one-factor formula to that particular business, holding that the method, "albeit fair on its face, operates so as to reach profits which are in no just sense attributable to transactions within its jurisdiction." Id., at 134, 51 S.Ct., at 389.

The three-factor formula used by California has gained wide approval precisely because payroll, property, and sales appear in combination to reflect a very large share of the activities by which value is generated. It is therefore able to avoid the sorts of distortions that were present in *Hans Rees' Sons, Inc.*

Of course, even the three-factor formula is necessarily imperfect.[20] But we have seen no evidence demonstrating that the margin of error

---

20. First, the one-third-each weight given to the three factors is essentially arbitrary. Second, payroll, property, and sales still do not exhaust the entire set of factors arguably relevant to the (systematic or not) inherent in the three-factor formula is greater than the margin of error (systematic or not) inherent in the sort of separate accounting urged upon us by appellant. Indeed, it would be difficult to come to such a conclusion on the basis of the figures in this case: for all of appellant's statistics showing allegedly enormous distortions caused by the three-factor formula, the tables we set out at nn. 11, 12, supra, reveal that the percentage increase in taxable income attributable to California between the methodology employed by appellant and the methodology employed by appellee comes to approximately 14%, a far cry from the more than 250% difference which led us to strike down the state tax in *Hans Rees' Sons, Inc.,* and a figure certainly within the substantial margin of error inherent in any method of attributing income among the components of a unitary business.

V

For the reasons we have just outlined, we conclude that California's application of the unitary business principle to appellant and its foreign subsidiaries was proper, and that its use of the standard three-factor formula to apportion the income of that unitary business was fair. This proper and fair method of taxation happens, however, to be quite different from the method employed both by the Federal Government in taxing appellant's business, and by each of the relevant foreign jurisdictions in taxing the business of appellant's subsidiaries. Each of these other taxing jurisdictions has adopted a qualified separate accounting approach—often referred to as the "arm's-length" approach—to the taxation of related corporations.[21] Under the "arms-length" approach every corporation even if closely tied to other corporations, is treated for most—but decidedly not all—purposes as if it were an independent entity dealing at arm's length with its affiliated corporations, and subject to taxation only by the jurisdictions in which it operates and only for the income it realizes on its own books.

If the unitary business consisting of appellant and its subsidiaries were entirely domestic, the fact that different jurisdictions applied different methods of taxation to it would probably make little constitutional difference, for the reasons we discuss supra. Given that it is international, however, we must subject this case to the additional scrutiny required by the Foreign Commerce Clause. See Mobil Oil Corp., 445 U.S., at 446, 100

---

production of income. Finally, the relationship between each of the factors and income is by no means exact. The three-factor formula, as applied to horizontally linked enterprises, is based in part on the very rough economic assumption that rates of return on property and payroll—as such rates of return would be measured by an ideal accounting method that took all transfers of value into account—are roughly the same in different taxing jurisdictions. This assumption has a powerful basis in economic theory: if true rates of return were radically different in different jurisdictions, one might expect a significant shift in investment resources to take advantage of that difference. On the other hand, the assumption has admitted weaknesses: an enterprise's willingness to invest simultaneously in two jurisdictions with very different true rates of return might be adequately explained by, for example, the difficulty of shifting resources, the decreasing marginal value of additional investment, and portfolio-balancing considerations.

21. The "arm's-length" approach is also often applied to geographically distinct divisions of a single corporation.

S.Ct., at 1236; Japan Line, Ltd., 441 U.S., at 446, 99 S.Ct., at 1820; Bowman v. Chicago & N.W.R. Co., 125 U.S. 465, 482, 8 S.Ct. 689, 696 (1888). The case most relevant to our inquiry is *Japan Line*.

A

Japan Line involved an attempt by California to impose an apparently fairly apportioned, nondiscriminatory, ad valorem property tax on cargo containers which were instrumentalities of foreign commerce and which were temporarily located in various California ports. The same cargo containers, however, were subject to an unapportioned property tax in their home port of Japan. Moreover, a convention signed by the United States and Japan made clear, at least, that neither National Government could impose a tax on temporarily imported cargo containers whose home port was in the other nation. We held that "[w]hen a State seeks to tax the instrumentalities of foreign commerce, two additional considerations, beyond those articulated in [the doctrine governing the Interstate Commerce Clause], come into play." 441 U.S., at 446, 99 S.Ct., at 1820. The first is the enhanced risk of multiple taxation. Although consistent application of the fair apportionment standard can generally mitigate, if not eliminate, double taxation in the domestic context,

> "neither this Court nor this Nation can ensure full apportionment when one of the taxing entities is a foreign sovereign. If an instrumentality of commerce is domiciled abroad, the country of domicile may have the right, consistently with the custom of nations, to impose a tax on its full value. If a State should seek to tax the same instrumentality on an apportioned basis, multiple taxation inevitably results. ... Due to the absence of an authoritative tribunal capable of ensuring that the aggregation of taxes is computed on no more than one full value, a state tax, even though 'fairly apportioned' to reflect an instrumentality's presence within the State, may subject foreign commerce ' "to the risk of a double tax burden to which [domestic] commerce is not exposed, and which the commerce clause forbids." ' " Id., at 447–448, 99 S.Ct., at 1821.

The second additional consideration that arises in the foreign commerce context is the possibility that a state tax will "impair federal uniformity in an area where federal uniformity is essential." 441 U.S., at 448, 99 S.Ct., at 1821.* * * On the basis of the facts in *Japan Line*, we concluded that the California tax at issue was constitutionally improper because it failed to meet either of the additional tests mandated by the Foreign Commerce Clause.

This case is similar to *Japan Line* in a number of important respects. First, the tax imposed here, like the tax imposed in *Japan Line,* has resulted in actual double taxation, in the sense that some of the income taxed without apportionment by foreign nations as attributable to appellant's foreign subsidiaries was also taxed by California as attributable to the State's share of the total income of the unitary business of which those subsidiaries are a part.[22] Second, that double taxation stems from a serious divergence in the taxing schemes adopted by California and the foreign taxing authorities. Third, the taxing method adopted by those foreign taxing authorities is consistent with accepted international practice. Finally, our own Federal Government, to the degree it has spoken, seems to prefer the taxing method adopted by the international community to the taxing method adopted by California.

Nevertheless, there are also a number of ways in which this case is clearly distinguishable from *Japan Line*.[24] First, it involves a tax on income rather than a tax on property. We distinguished property from income taxation in Mobil Oil Corp., 445 U.S., at 444–446, 100 S.Ct., at 1235–1236, and Exxon Corp., 447 U.S., at 228–229, 100 S.Ct., at 2122–2123, suggesting that "[t]he reasons for allocation to a single situs that often apply in the case of property taxation carry little force" in the case of income taxation. 445 U.S., at 445, 100 S.Ct., at 1235. Second, the double taxation in this case, although real, is not the "inevitabl[e]" result of the California taxing scheme. Cf. Japan Line, 441 U.S., at 447, 99 S.Ct., at 1820. In *Japan Line,* we relied strongly on the fact that one taxing jurisdiction claimed the right to tax a given value in full, and another taxing jurisdiction claimed the right to tax the same entity in part—a combination resulting necessarily in double taxation. Here, by contrast, we are faced with two distinct methods of allocating the income of a multinational enterprise. The "arm's-length" approach divides the pie on the basis of formal accounting principles. The formula apportionment method divides the same pie on the basis of a mathematical generalization. Whether the combination of the two methods results in the same income being taxed twice or in some portion of income not being taxed at all is dependent solely on the facts of the individual case. The third difference between this case and *Japan Line* is that the tax here falls, not on the foreign owners of an instrumentality of foreign commerce, but on a corporation domiciled and headquartered in the United States. We specifically left open in *Japan Line* the application of that case to "domestically owned instrumentalities engaged in foreign commerce," id., at 444, n. 7, 99 S.Ct., at 1819, n. 7, and—to the extent that corporations can be

---

22. The stipulation of facts indicates that the tax returns filed by appellant's subsidiaries in their foreign domiciles took into account "only the applicable income and deductions incurred by the subsidiary or subsidiaries in that country and not . . . the income and deductions of [appellant] or the subsidiaries operating in other countries." App. 72. This does not conclusively demonstrate the existence of double taxation because appellant has not produced its foreign tax returns, and it is entirely possible that deductions, exemptions, or adjustments in those returns eliminated whatever overlap in taxable income resulted from the application of the California apportionment method. Nevertheless, appellee does not seriously dispute the existence of actual double taxation as we have defined it, Brief for Appellee 114–121, but cf. Tr. of Oral Arg. 28–29, and we assume its existence for the purposes of our analysis. Cf. Japan Line, 441 U.S., at 452, n. 17, 99 S.Ct., at 1823, n. 17.

24. Note that we deliberately emphasized in *Japan Line* the narrowness of the question presented: "whether instrumentalities of commerce that are owned, based, and registered abroad and that are used exclusively in international commerce, may be subjected to apportioned ad valorem property taxation by a State." 441 U.S., at 444, 99 S.Ct., at 1819.

analogized to cargo containers in the first place—this case falls clearly within that reservation.[26]

In light of these considerations, our task in this case must be to determine whether the distinctions between the present tax and the tax at issue in *Japan Line* add up to a constitutionally significant difference. For the reasons we are about to explain, we conclude that they do.

B

In *Japan Line,* we said that "[e]ven a slight overlapping of tax—a problem that might be deemed *de minimis* in a domestic context— assumes importance when sensitive matters of foreign relations and national sovereignty are concerned." Id., at 456, 99 S.Ct., at 1825 (foot- note omitted). If we were to take that statement as an absolute prohibi- tion on state-induced double taxation in the international context, then our analysis here would be at an end. But, in fact, such an absolute rule is no more appropriate here than it was in *Japan Line* itself, where we relied on much more than the mere fact of double taxation to strike down the state tax at issue. Although double taxation in the foreign commerce context deserves to receive close scrutiny, that scrutiny must take into account the context in which the double taxation takes place and the alternatives reasonably available to the taxing State.

In *Japan Line,* the taxing State could entirely eliminate one impor- tant source of double taxation simply by adhering to one bright-line rule: do not tax, to any extent whatsoever, cargo containers "that are owned, based, and registered abroad and that are used exclusively in international commerce...." Id., at 444, 99 S.Ct., at 1819. To require that the State adhere to this rule was by no means unfair, because the rule did no more than reflect consistent international practice and express federal policy. In this case, California could try to avoid double taxation simply by not taxing appellant's income at all, even though a good deal of it is plainly domestic. But no party has suggested such a rule, and its obvious unfair- ness requires no elaboration. Or California could try to avoid double taxation by adopting some version of the "arm's-length" approach. That course, however, would not by any means guarantee an end to double taxation.

As we have already noted, the "arm's-length" approach is generally based, in the first instance, on a multicorporate enterprise's own formal accounting. But, despite that initial reliance, the "arm's-length" approach recognizes, as much as the formula apportionment approach, that closely related corporations can engage in a transfer of values that is not fully reflected in their formal ledgers. Thus, for example, 26 U.S.C. § 482 provides:

---

26. We have no need to address in this opinion the constitutionality of combined apportion- ment with respect to state taxation of domestic corporations with foreign parents or foreign corporations with either foreign parents or foreign subsidiaries.

"In any case of two or more ... businesses (whether or not incorporated, whether or not organized in the United States, and whether or not affiliated) owned or controlled directly or indirectly by the same interests, the Secretary [of the Treasury] may distribute, apportion, or allocate gross income, deductions, credits, or allowances between or among such ... businesses, if he determines that such distribution, apportionment, or allocation is necessary in order to prevent evasion of taxes or clearly to reflect the income of any of such ... businesses."

And, as one might expect, the United States Internal Revenue Service has developed elaborate regulations in order to give content to this general provision. Many other countries have similar provisions. A serious problem, however, is that even though most nations have adopted the "arm's-length" approach in its general outlines, the precise rules under which they reallocate income among affiliated corporations often differ substantially, and whenever that difference exists, the possibility of double taxation also exists. Thus, even if California were to adopt some version of the "arm's-length" approach, it could not eliminate the risk of double taxation of corporations subject to its franchise tax, and might in some cases end up subjecting those corporations to more serious double taxation than would occur under formula apportionment.

That California would have trouble avoiding double taxation even if it adopted the "arm's-length" approach is, we think, a product of the difference between a tax on income and a tax on tangible property. Allocating income among various taxing jurisdictions bears some resemblance, as we have emphasized throughout this opinion, to slicing a shadow. In the absence of a central coordinating authority, absolute consistency, even among taxing authorities whose basic approach to the task is quite similar, may just be too much to ask. If California's method of formula apportionment "inevitably" led to double taxation that might be reason enough to render it suspect. But since it does not, it would be perverse, simply for the sake of avoiding double taxation, to require California to give up one allocation method that sometimes results in double taxation in favor of another allocation method that also sometimes results in double taxation. Cf. Moorman Mfg. Co., 437 U.S., at 278–280, 98 S.Ct., at 2347–2348.

It could be argued that even if the Foreign Commerce Clause does not require California to adopt the "arm's-length" approach to foreign subsidiaries of domestic corporations, it does require that whatever system of taxation California adopts must not result in double taxation in any particular case. The implication of such a rule, however, would be that even if California adopted the "arm's-length" method, it would be required to defer, not merely to a single internationally accepted bright-line standard, as was the case in *Japan Line,* but to a variety of § 482–type reallocation decisions made by individual foreign countries in individual cases. Although double taxation is a constitutionally disfavored state of affairs, particularly in the international context, *Japan Line* does not require forbearance so extreme or so one-sided.

C

We come finally to the second inquiry suggested by *Japan Line*— whether California's decision to adopt formula apportionment in the international context was impermissible because it "may impair federal uniformity in an area where federal uniformity is essential," 441 U.S., at 448, 99 S.Ct., at 1821, and "prevents the Federal Government from 'speaking with one voice' in international trade," id., at 453, 99 S.Ct., at 1824, quoting Michelin Tire Corp. v. Wages, 423 U.S. 276, 285, 96 S.Ct. 535, 540 (1976). In conducting this inquiry, however, we must keep in mind that if a state tax merely has foreign resonances, but does not implicate foreign affairs, we cannot infer, "[a]bsent some explicit directive from Congress, . . . that treatment of foreign income at the federal level mandates identical treatment by the States." Mobil, 445 U.S., at 448, 100 S.Ct., at 1237. Thus, a state tax at variance with federal policy will violate the "one voice" standard if it *either* implicates foreign policy issues which must be left to the Federal Government *or* violates a clear federal directive. The second of these considerations is, of course, essentially a species of pre-emption analysis.

(1)

The most obvious foreign policy implication of a state tax is the threat it might pose of offending our foreign trading partners and leading them to retaliate against the Nation as a whole. 441 U.S., at 450, 99 S.Ct., at 1822. In considering this issue, however, we are faced with a distinct problem. This Court has little competence in determining precisely when foreign nations will be offended by particular acts, and even less competence in deciding how to balance a particular risk of retaliation against the sovereign right of the United States as a whole to let the States tax as they please. The best that we can do, in the absence of explicit action by Congress, is to attempt to develop objective standards that reflect very general observations about the imperatives of international trade and international relations.

This case is not like *Mobil,* in which the real issue came down to a question of interstate rather than foreign commerce. 445 U.S., at 446–449, 100 S.Ct., at 1236–1237. Nevertheless, three distinct factors, which we have already discussed in one way or another, seem to us to weigh strongly against the conclusion that the tax imposed by California might justifiably lead to significant foreign retaliation. First, the tax here does not create an *automatic* "asymmetry," Japan Line, supra, 441 U.S., at 453, 99 S.Ct., at 1824, in international taxation. See supra, at 2952, 2954– 2955. Second, the tax here was imposed, not on a foreign entity as was the case in *Japan Line,* but on a domestic corporation. Although, California "counts" income arguably attributable to foreign corporations in calculating the taxable income of that domestic corporation, the legal incidence of the tax falls on the domestic corporation. Third, even if foreign nations have a legitimate interest in reducing the tax burden of domestic corporations, the fact remains that appellant is without a doubt amenable to be taxed in California in one way or another, and that the amount of tax it pays is much more the function of California's tax rate than of its allocation method. Although a foreign nation might be more offended by what it considers unorthodox treatment of appellant than it would be if California simply raised its general tax rate to achieve the same economic result, we can only assume that the offense involved in either event would be attenuated at best.

A state tax may, of course, have foreign policy implications other than the threat of retaliation. We note, however, that in this case, unlike *Japan Line,* the Executive Branch has decided not to file an *amicus curiae* brief in opposition to the state tax.[33] The lack of such a submission is by no means dispositive. Nevertheless, when combined with all the other considerations we have discussed, it does suggest that the foreign policy of the United States—whose nuances, we must emphasize again, are much more the province of the Executive Branch and Congress than of this Court—is not seriously threatened by California's decision to apply the unitary business concept and formula apportionment in calculating appellant's taxable income.

(2)

When we turn to specific indications of congressional intent, appellant's position fares no better. First, there is no claim here that the federal tax statutes themselves provide the necessary pre-emptive force. Second, although the United States is a party to a great number of tax treaties that require the Federal Government to adopt some form of "arm's-length" analysis in taxing the domestic income of multi-national enterprises, that requirement is generally waived with respect to the taxes imposed by each of the contracting nations on its own domestic corporations. This fact, if nothing else, confirms our view that such taxation is in reality of local rather than international concern. Third, the tax treaties into which the United States has entered do not generally cover the taxing activities of subnational governmental units such as States, and in none of the treaties does the restriction on "non-arm's length" methods of taxation apply to the States. Moreover, the Senate has on at least one occasion, in considering a proposed treaty, attached a reservation declining to give its consent to a provision in the treaty that would have extended that restriction to the States. Finally, it remains true, as we said in *Mobil,* that "Congress has long debated, but has not enacted, legislation designed to

---

33. The Solicitor General did submit a memorandum opposing worldwide formula apportionment by a State in Chicago Bridge & Iron Co. v. Caterpillar Tractor Co., No. 81–349, a case that was argued last Term, and carried over to this Term. Although there is no need for us to speculate as to the reasons for the Solicitor General's decision not to submit a similar memorandum or brief in this case, cf. Brief for National Governors' Association et al. as Amici Curiae 6–7, there has been no indication that the position taken by the Government in *Chicago Bridge & Iron Co.* still represents its views, or that we should regard the brief in that case as applying to this case.

regulate state taxation of income." 445 U.S., at 448, 100 S.Ct., at 1237. Thus, whether we apply the "explicit directive" standard articulated in *Mobil,* or some more relaxed standard which takes into account our residual concern about the foreign policy implications of California's tax, we cannot conclude that the California tax at issue here is pre-empted by federal law or fatally inconsistent with federal policy.

VI

The judgment of the California Court of Appeal is

Affirmed.

JUSTICE STEVENS took no part in the consideration or decision of this case.

JUSTICE POWELL, with whom THE CHIEF JUSTICE and JUSTICE O'CONNOR join, dissenting.

The Court's opinion addresses the several questions presented in this case with commendable thoroughness. In my view, however, the California tax clearly violates the Foreign Commerce Clause—just as did the tax in Japan Line, Ltd. v. County of Los Angeles, 441 U.S. 434, 99 S.Ct. 1813 (1979). I therefore do not consider whether appellant and its foreign subsidiaries constitute a "unitary business" or whether the State's apportionment formula is fair.

With respect to the Foreign Commerce Clause issue, the Court candidly concedes: (i) "double taxation is a constitutionally disfavored state of affairs, particularly in the international context," ante, at 193; (ii) "like the tax imposed in *Japan Line,* [California's tax] has resulted in actual double taxation," ante, at 187; and therefore (iii) this tax "deserves to receive close scrutiny," ante, at 189. The Court also concedes that "[t]his case is similar to *Japan Line* in a number of important respects," ante, at 187, and that the Federal Government "seems to prefer the ['arm's-length'] taxing method adopted by the international community," ante, at 189. The Court identifies several distinctions between this case and *Japan Line,* however, and sustains the validity of the California tax despite the inevitable double taxation and the incompatibility with the method of taxation accepted by the international community.

In reaching its result, the Court fails to apply "close scrutiny" in a manner that meets the requirements of that exacting standard of review. Although the facts of *Japan Line* differ in some respects, they are identical on the critical questions of double taxation and federal uniformity. The principles enunciated in that case should be controlling here: a state tax is unconstitutional if it either "creates a substantial risk of international multiple taxation" or "prevents the Federal Government from 'speaking with one voice when regulating commercial relations with foreign governments.'" 441 U.S., at 451, 99 S.Ct., at 1823.

* * *

In *Japan Line* we identified two constraints that a state tax on an international business must satisfy to comply with the Foreign Commerce Clause. We explicitly declared that "[i]f a state tax contravenes either of these precepts, it is unconstitutional." 441 U.S., at 451, 99 S.Ct., at 1823. In my view, the California tax before us today violates *both* requirements. I would declare it unconstitutional.

NOTES AND QUESTIONS

A. In *Container*, the Court declared that "[t]he prerequisite to a constitutionally acceptable finding of unitary business is a flow of *value*." Under this standard, why were not the affiliated corporations under consideration in *ASARCO* and *Woolworth* unitary? Was there not a flow of value between those corporate affiliates indistinguishable from the flow of value the Court found dispositive in *Container*? Moreover, if the standard for review of state court determinations regarding the existence of a unitary business is the relaxed "within-the-realm-of permissible-judgment" criterion the Court endorsed in *Container*, why was that standard not met in *ASARCO* and *Woolworth*? Indeed, in terms of the interdependence of the corporate affiliates, was *Container* a stronger or weaker case than *ASARCO*?

Did *Container* implicitly overrule *ASARCO* and *Woolworth,* or at least limit them so narrowly to their facts as to deprive them of precedential significance? Although this was a hotly debated issue during the decade that elapsed between the Court's decision in *Container* and its decision in *Allied–Signal* (pp. 420–33 supra), you should have no difficulty answering this question, if you read *Allied–Signal*. Are *Allied–Signal* and *Container* reconcilable? Why was there no "flow of value" between Bendix's operations in New Jersey and the income it derived from its investment in ASARCO to justify the inclusion of the gain from the sale of the stock in Bendix's New Jersey apportionable tax base? Now that you have considered all of the Court's significant modern cases on apportionability of income—namely, *Mobil, Exxon, ASARCO, Woolworth, Container,* and *Allied–Signal*—can you state in a succinct paragraph the essential constitutional limits on apportionability established by these cases?

B. *Worldwide Combined Reporting and Sound Tax Policy.* Whatever may be said about the *Container* Court's resolution of the Foreign Commerce Clause issue as a matter of constitutional law—and, in this regard, you should keep in mind that the Constitution is not concerned with the wisdom of (or economic justification for) state legislation—unitary apportionment may become a questionable yardstick as a fair measure of a state's share of the earnings of an enterprise when it is extended worldwide, at least from the standpoint of sound tax policy. Some companies may earn considerably higher rates of profit abroad than in the United States, and relative ratios of property, payroll, and receipts may be an extremely crude method of ascribing profits actually earned in the various countries. The large differences in wage rates paid in the United States and many foreign countries, particularly in Latin America, Africa, and Asia, where wage scales for the same type of work may amount to as little as one-fifth or one-tenth of those in the United States, tend to produce serious distortions in the apportionment. Of course, the monetary wage rates need to be adjusted for differences in productivity, but it is likely that in some industries unit wage costs vary so markedly as to result in such distortion.

The underlying premise of formulary apportionment under the standard three-factor formula is that, by and large, every dollar of wages or property spent in one taxing jurisdiction, along with receipts from sales in the area, will produce the same amount of profit in all taxing jurisdictions. Wide disparities in unit labor or unit property costs between taxing jurisdictions tend to attribute to the high wage-property cost jurisdictions, such as the United States, income which is attributable to other jurisdictions. To be sure, the Court in *Container* was reciting familiar law when it adverted to the "substantial margin of error inherent in any method of attributing income among the components of a unitary business" as a basis for sustaining California's apportionment. And this "substantial margin of error" may preclude taxpayers from mounting successful challenges to most state tax apportionments in the domestic (United States) context. In the international context, however, that "substantial margin of error" may well be exceeded when large disparities in unit costs between U.S. and foreign jurisdictions tend to attribute to the United States income that is almost certainly earned elsewhere. These problems are compounded by the difficulties of obtaining accurate and verifiable data from foreign countries as to assets, payroll, and sales and by the fact that accounting techniques and methods in foreign jurisdictions frequently vary sharply from those prevailing in the United States, especially in the case of subsidiaries or branches of U.S. corporations operating in the developing countries.

C. *State "Water's Edge" Legislation Limiting Combined Reporting.* The initial reaction of some state legislatures to *Container*'s approval of worldwide combined reporting was to adopt expanded definitions, both conceptually and geographically, of the scope of a unitary business. By the mid–1980s, however, a clear countertrend had emerged. The change in legislative direction was attributable in large part to the successful lobbying campaign of the business community which predicted dire economic consequences for states that jumped on (or failed to jump off) the worldwide unitary combination band-wagon. Thus, while Florida and Maine broadened their definitions of a unitary business in 1983 after *Container* was handed down, by 1987 Florida had reversed course, repealing its previous adoption of worldwide unitary combination; Arizona, Colorado, Idaho, Indiana, Oregon, and Utah had endorsed a water's edge approach to the unitary business principle; and, most significantly, California—the principal source of the controversy over worldwide unitary combination—had adopted water's edge legislation effective January 1, 1988. By 1992, every state had adopted a limitation on world-wide combination, although in a number of states the limitation was elective.

D. *Foreign Commerce Clause Restraints on Worldwide Combined Reporting of a Foreign–Based Multinational Corporate Group: The* Barclays Bank *Case.* In *Container*, the Court declared that "[w]e have no need to address in this opinion the constitutionality of combined apportionment with respect to state taxation of domestic corporations with foreign parents or foreign corporations with either foreign parents or foreign subsidiaries." See footnote 26 of the Court's opinion. In Barclays Bank PLC v. Franchise Tax

Bd., 512 U.S. 298, 114 S.Ct. 2268 (1994), the Court did address that issue. The Barclays Group was a multinational banking enterprise including more than 220 corporations in some 60 nations. Two corporate members of the Barclays Group did business in California, and California sought to determine their California tax liability on the basis of worldwide combined reporting. Barclays conceded that it was engaged in a worldwide unitary business. Accordingly, apart from the foreign nature of its operations, there was no question that California could require Barclays to report on a combined basis. The principal question before the Court, then, was whether worldwide combined reporting as applied to a *foreign*-based multinational was consonant with the Court's *Foreign* Commerce Clause jurisprudence.

With respect to the first of the two additional factors that must be addressed when a state tax implicates Foreign Commerce Clause concerns— the enhanced risk of multiple taxation—the Court considered Barclays's contention that there was a more aggravated risk of international multiple taxation with a foreign-based than with a U.S.-based multinational (as in *Container*) because foreign-based multinationals typically have more of their operations outside the United States. Consequently, a higher proportion of their income is subject to tax abroad with a concomitantly enhanced risk of international multiple taxation when such income is included in California's apportionable tax base.

Without questioning Barclays's premises, the Court found that *Container* had nevertheless answered Barclays's multiple taxation argument. The Court observed that *Container*'s holding rejecting the taxpayer's multiple taxation argument rested on two considerations. First, the multiple taxation in *Container* though "real" (id., 512 U.S. at 318 n.17 (quoting *Container*)) was not "inevitabl[e]" (id.) because it resulted from the overlap of two different methods of dividing a tax base and could as easily result in undertaxation as overtaxation. Second, the alternative method available to the taxing state (arm's-length, separate accounting) would not eliminate the risk of multiple taxation because different jurisdictions apply the arm's-length separate accounting method differently. The Court stated:

> And if, as we have held, adoption of a separate accounting system does not dispositively lessen the risk of multiple taxation of the income earned by foreign affiliates of *domestic*-owned corporations, we see no reason why it would do so in respect of the income earned by foreign affiliates of *foreign*-owned corporations. We refused in *Container Corp.* "to require California to give up one allocation method that sometimes results in double taxation in favor of another allocation method that also sometimes results in double taxation." The foreign domicile of the taxpayer (or the taxpayer's parent) is a factor inadequate to warrant retraction of that position.

Id. at 319 (emphasis in original).

Turning to the question whether worldwide combined reporting " 'impair[ed] uniformity in an area where federal uniformity is essential,' " (id. at 320, quoting Japan Line, 441 U.S. at 448) and, in particular, whether the state's taxing regime prevented the Federal Government "from 'speaking with one voice' in international trade," (id., quoting Japan Line, 441 U.S. at

453) the Court relied largely on *Container* and on Wardair Canada, Inc. v. Florida Department of Revenue, 477 U.S. 1, 106 S.Ct. 2369 (1986), in answering the question in the negative. The Court found that the considerations which had led to its conclusion in *Container* likewise applied in the context of a foreign-based multinational. These considerations were that (1) California's method did not create an automatic asymmetry in international taxation; (2) the taxpayers were plainly subject to tax in California in one way or another, and the amount of tax they pay is therefore much more the function of California's tax rate than of its allocation method; and, most significantly, (3) there were no specific indications of congressional intent to preempt California's tax.

Similarly, in *Wardair*, where the Court rejected a challenge to Florida's tax on the sale of fuel to foreign airlines on the ground that it "threaten[ed] the ability of the Federal Government to speak with one voice," Barclays, 512 U.S. at 322 (quoting Wardair, 477 U.S. at 9), the Court found its analysis relevant to the controversy now before it. Specifically, the Court in *Wardair* had examined international agreements which barred taxation of aviation fuel at the national level, but not at the subnational level. The *Wardair* Court concluded that "[b]y negative implication arising out of [these international accords,] the United States has at least acquiesced in state taxation of fuel used by foreign carriers in international travel." Wardair, 477 U.S. at 9.

A critical lesson that the Court in *Barclays* drew from *Container* and *Wardair* was that "Congress may more passively indicate that certain state practices do *not* 'impair federal uniformity in an area where federal uniformity is essential'; it need not convey its intent with the unmistakable clarity required to permit state regulation that discriminates against interstate commerce or otherwise falls short under *Complete Auto* inspection." Barclays, 512 U.S. at 323 (quoting Japan Line, 441 U.S. at 448 (emphasis in original)). Under this relaxed standard, the Court had little difficulty concluding that the "one voice" criterion was satisfied in *Barclays*. As in *Container* and *Wardair*, there were no specific indications of congressional intent to the bar the state tax in question. Moreover, the Court felt that its decision in *Container* had

> left the ball in Congress's court: had Congress * * * considered nationally uniform use of separate accounting 'essential,' it could have enacted legislation prohibiting the States from taxing corporate income based on the worldwide combined reporting method. In the 11 years that have elapsed since our decision in *Container Corp.*, Congress has failed to enact such legislation.

Id. at 324. In light of these "indicia of Congress's willingness to tolerate States' worldwide combined reporting mandates, even when those mandates are applied to foreign corporations and domestic corporations with foreign parents," id. at 327, and given the Court's firm conviction that these questions are "much more the province of the Executive Branch and Congress than of this Court," id., the Court concluded that there was no basis for its intervention.

E. *References.* There is an extensive literature on the legal, economic, and policy issues associated with worldwide combined reporting in general and with the *Container* and *Barclays* cases in particular. See, e.g., Christina

M. Lyons, "The Constitutionality of the Worldwide Combined Reporting Method of Taxation of Multinational Corporations," 37 B.C.L. Rev. 183 (1995); Charles E. McLure, Jr., Economic Perspectives on State Taxation of Multijurisdictional Corporations (1986); Charles E. McLure, Jr., ed., The State Corporation Income Tax: Issues in Worldwide Unitary Combination (1984); U.S. General Accounting Office, California Taxes on Multinational Corporations and Related Federal Issues, GAO/GCD–95–171 (1995).

3. STATE COURT APPROACHES TO THE UNITARY BUSINESS PRINCIPLE AND COMBINED REPORTING: LAW AND POLICY

NOTES AND QUESTIONS

A. *State Law Variations on the Definition of a Unitary Business.* As the Supreme Court recognized in *Container*, "the unitary business concept is not * * * so to speak, unitary: there are variations on the theme, and any number of them are logically consistent with the underlying principles motivating the approach." This observation has particularly important implications for the delineation of the unitary business principle under state law. While the Supreme Court's decisions establish the outer limits of apportionability as a matter of federal constitutional law, they plainly do not require state courts (or legislatures) to embrace approaches to the unitary business concept that extend to these limits. Indeed, as the ensuing discussion reveals, there are compelling arguments from the standpoint of tax policy for confining the unitary business principle within bounds that are narrower than those approved by the Supreme Court.

The most obvious circumstance in which states stop short of constitutionally allowable limits is when they choose to allow (or require) separate company reporting rather than combined reporting. Indeed, close to half of the states either allow or require separate reporting rather than combined reporting. All States Tax Guide (RIA) ¶ 222–A (2009) (chart). Additionally, states have varying views on the proper scope of a unitary business, ranging from restrictive, to intermediate, to expansive. See 1 Jerome R. Hellerstein & Walter Hellerstein, State Taxation ¶ 8.09 (3d ed. 1998–2009).

In State ex rel. Arizona Department of Revenue v. Talley Industries, Inc., 182 Ariz. 17, 893 P.2d 17 (Ct. App. 1994), the Arizona Court of Appeals adopted the intermediate "operational interdependence" test:

> According to a respected authority on state taxation:
>
> > The cases are replete with varying attempts by the courts to define "unitary business" for formulary apportionment purposes. Perhaps the most frequently repeated definition is that of the California Supreme Court:
> >
> > > If the operation of the portion of the business done within the state is dependent upon or contributes to the operation of the business without the state, the operations are unitary.

A more particular statement of the test is that a business is unitary if these circumstances are present: "(1) Unity of ownership; (2) Unity of operation as evidenced by central purchasing, advertising, accounting and management divisions; and (3) Unity of use of its centralized executive force and general system of operation."

I Hellerstein, supra, ¶ 8.11[1] [2d ed. 1993] (footnotes omitted).

The California three-unities test for "unitary business" is at one end of a continuum of alternative formulae, see id. ¶ 8.11[3], the narrowest of which is exemplified by Louisiana and Mississippi. See id. ¶ 8.11[2]. In an example of a narrow test for unitary business, the Louisiana Supreme Court, in Texas Co. v. Cooper, 236 La. 380, 107 So.2d 676 (1958), held that an oil company that produced, refined, and sold oil products across a number of states was not unitary, and, accordingly, was required to report its instate production income to Louisiana on a separate accounting basis. Hellerstein criticizes the *Texas Co.* approach as overly "restrictive." We agree.

We similarly agree with a number of Hellerstein's criticisms of the prevailing California "three-unities" approach. Hellerstein states that "[s]uch generalizations ... offer little practical guidance in deciding unitary business controversies." I Hellerstein, supra, ¶ 8.11[1]. According to the treatise, the "three-unities" approach has been used both by courts who have applied the test in a highly restrictive manner and by others who have applied it very broadly. Id. In those states that apply the "unitary business" test broadly, there is "an extensive, time consuming, and burdensome (to the taxpayer at least) detailed examination of virtually every aspect of the interrelations of the various constituents of the enterprise." Id. ¶ 8.11[5] (footnote omitted). This has been compared to a " 'psychoanalysis of the business.' " Id. The tax administrator then makes a subjective judgment about "whether the requisite centralized control, management, and unity of operation exists (centralized ownership is usually a simple matter to establish or disprove)." Id. Hellerstein asserts that because of the magnitude and complexity of the record produced by this extensive inquiry, on review judges are reluctant to set aside the assessment. Id.

As a rational compromise between the broad California three-unities test and the unduly restrictive approach at the other end of the spectrum, Hellerstein advocates * * * [an] "intermediate approach" * * *

* * *

Hellerstein persuasively characterizes the features and advantages of this intermediate approach. The treatise states: "The recognition that an enterprise is not unitary unless, inter alia, there is a substantial interdependence of basic operations among the various affiliates or branches of the business provides a quantifiable, objective test of the unitary business." I Hellerstein, supra, ¶ 8.11[5], at 8–92. The writers further state:

> Minor or insubstantial transactions or interrelations between segments of a business ought not suffice for treatment as a unitary business. *Inherent in the concept that a business is sufficiently integrated and interdependent to warrant apportionment by a formula that is applied to the entire tax base of the multi-state or multi-national enterprise is the assumption that the interrelations and interdependence are substantial....* Substantiality is subsumed in many cases by the court's detailing the extent of interdependent operations taking place in the various states. In point of fact, in most of the cases in which the businesses have been found unitary, interdependence of the basic operations has been substantial, by any reasonable measure of substantiality.

Id. ¶ 8.11[4][c], at 8–90 to 8–91 (emphasis added) (footnote omitted).

In drawing the line between basic operations that make a business unitary and those that do not, we take note of the considerations that gave rise to the unitary business doctrine in the first place. The doctrine was originally derived from the unit rule as it developed in the nineteenth century with respect to enterprises such as railroads and telegraph companies. Id. ¶ 8.11[4][b]. These organizations were horizontally integrated; typically, a segment of the railroad was operated in each of several states. Id. The unitary business doctrine was also applied to manufacturing, producing, and mercantile companies doing business across state lines. The latter organizations normally involve vertically integrated businesses. Both vertically and horizontally integrated organizations are generally held to be unitary, "because of the inability to determine, under any practicable separate accounting method, the amount of income properly attributable to the various stages of the enterprise conducted in particular states." Id.

Thus, under the formulary method of apportionment applicable to unitary businesses, no need exists "to determine a fair arm's-length price for goods transferred to a branch or affiliate, as must be done in a separate accounting." Id. The problem with separate accounting in a unitary business is the "inability to establish fair arms'-length prices for goods transferred, or basic operational services rendered, between controlled branches or subsidiaries of an enterprise." Id. ¶ 8.10[1][a].

The unitary business rule, then, essentially rests on the difficulty of determining the amount of income attributable to various stages of producing, refining, manufacturing, transporting, buying, selling, and the like, conducted in different states. This consideration does not exist, at least to the same extent, to centralized management or control, financing, research, legal, accounting, or other internal services rendered by one branch or affiliate to another. Id. ¶ 8.11[4][b]. Such services are not contained in the product or its delivery to the customer and may be considered as an accessory to the operations of the business. Id. Furthermore, "unlike the elusive efforts to determine the proper cost to be attributed to articles produced or manufactured by one branch or affiliate and sold to another," management costs and other services can be charged to the various operations by using generally accepted accounting methods. Id. The result is that the same state tax avoidance opportunities afforded by intercompany transfer pricing, which are inherent in transfers of materials, products, or goods between branches or affiliates, are not present in attributing to various states management costs and the costs of other types of internal services and facilities. Id.

B. The Proper Definition of a Unitary Business. The Arizona Court of Appeals' opinion in *Talley Industries* sets forth the position taken by the senior author of this casebook, and vigorously advanced by his late father, regarding the proper definition of a unitary business. But is this position warranted? The U.S. Supreme Court implicitly rejected the "operational interdependence" test in *Container*, observing that for constitutional purposes a "flow of value" not a "flow of goods" should be the touchstone of unitariness. And many state courts, including those in California, have done the same. In evaluating the merits of the various approaches to the unitary business definition, consider the following case for a broader definition than that proposed by your casebook authors and adopted by the Arizona Court of Appeals.

The unitary business principle serves to define a set of interrelated activities the income from which may properly be assigned to a state by apportionment rather than by separate accounting. The rationale for apportioning income by formula—rather than separately accounting for it on a state-by-state basis—is that the income cannot be satisfactorily identified on a geographic basis. The same rationale extends across corporate lines. If a group of commonly owned corporations is engaged in a set of interrelated activities giving rise to income that cannot satisfactorily be identified on an entity-by-entity basis, the income of the group is properly determined by apportioning the group's income as a single enterprise rather than determining it on the basis of formal corporate lines that have no economic meaning. Consequently, the critical consideration in determining whether a business is unitary is whether the income from the purported unitary business can meaningfully be determined by separating out various components of the business—on a state-by-state or an entity-by-entity basis—or whether it is intrinsically inseparable and must therefore be viewed as a whole.

It is in this respect that the operational-interdependence test fails to perform the function that the unitary business principle was designed to serve. By narrowly confining its focus to 'substantial interdependence of basic operations' " (Talley Industries, supra, (quoting 1 J. Hellerstein & W. Hellerstein, ¶ 8.11[5] at 8–92 (2d ed. 1993)), the test ignores other significant economic relationships among commonly controlled business activities that contribute to the production of income, which is no more easily identifiable on a geographic or separate company basis than is income derived from interdependent basic operations.

Charles E. McLure, Jr. demonstrated the inadequacies of the operational interdependence test as the defining feature of a unitary business in his critique of the test in "Operational Interdependence Is Not the Appropriate 'Bright Line Test' of a Unitary Business—at Least, Not Now," Tax Notes, Jan. 10, 1983, p. 107. McLure pointed out that the essential feature of a unitary business is not whether there is operational interdependence but rather whether there is *economic interdependence* among members of a commonly controlled group of corporations. If any of the common forms of economic interdependence (e.g., shared expenses, other economies of scale or scope, and intra-group transactions) exist, then the question is whether they are substantial enough so that "separate accounting would fail to produce a satisfactory division of profits between members of the group." Id. This, after all, is why one resorts to combined reporting in the first place, and a unitary business definition should reflect that fundamental point.

The operational-interdependence test, by contrast, simply ignores those economic interdependencies which do not manifest themselves in the group's basic operations. Thus, McLure observes that

> Hellerstein argues that centralized management, in and of itself, should never justify a finding of unitariness, since its costs are small and they can be allocated arbitrarily among the firms in the group without materially affecting the division of income between them. But this fails to address the potential role of management in maximizing group profits when demand is interdependent and in determining the division of profits between parts of a unitary business under those circumstances.

Id. at 108.

McLure provides further examples of why "operational interdependence * * * is not essential to the existence of a unitary business" (id.) in both the transfer of information among commonly controlled affiliates and in their horizontal diversification. Thus, the transfer of "technological knowhow, [and] * * * managerial and organizational skills and goodwill (including brand loyalty) have been identified as areas where it is sufficiently difficult to quantify the advantages of intra-group transfer of information that separate accounting is likely to fail and a finding of unitariness is appropriate." Id. at 110. Yet, as McLure observes, "in none of these cases is there necessarily any flow of transactions between affiliates." Id. Similarly, horizontal diversification itself provides a vehicle for the transfer of proprietary information that may not, as a practical matter, ever be transferred among unrelated parties. Under these circumstances, "it would be impossible to attribute the profits accurately to the several activities drawing on the common pool of technology," (id.) and separate entity accounting would therefore be inappropriate despite the lack of operational interdependence. Id. Indeed, in other writings

McLure has gone so far to suggest that "centralization of important decisions * * * should * * * be considered prima facie evidence that a unitary business exists." Charles E. McLure, Jr., "Defining a Unitary Business: An Economist's View," in Charles E. McLure, Jr., ed., The State Corporation Income Tax: Issues in Worldwide Unitary Combination 105 (1984).

Who, in your judgment, has the better of argument? Jerome R. Hellerstein responded to McLure's critique in "The Basic Operations Interdependence Requirement of a Unitary Business: A Reply to Charles E. McLure, Jr.," Tax Notes, Feb. 28, 1983, p. 723. McLure responded in turn in "The Basic Operational Interdependence Test of a Unitary Business: A Rejoinder," Tax Notes, October 10, 1983, p. 91. For a provocative series of articles contending that "classical" unitary business doctrine fails to reflect the economic characteristics of the contemporary firm, and that, as a consequence, "classical unitary law is peppered with inconsistencies and contradictions that separate its practice from theory, and as a result, makes it no less arbitrary than separate accounting," William H. Weissman, "Does Classical Unitary Law Really Provide a Cure for Separate Accounting's Ills," State Tax Notes, August 30, 2004, pp. 641, 647, see id; William H. Weissman, "A Review of the Unitary Business Theory in Light of the Firm Today," State Tax Notes, July 26, 2004, p. 267; William H. Weissman, "Defining the Contours of the Trades or Businesses in a Unitary Enterprise," State Tax Notes, August 2, 2004, p. 373; William H. Weissman, "Is Equity Ownership Really Necessary for Control?," State Tax Notes, August 9, 2004, p. 473; William H. Weissman, "Does Centralized Management Really Create Unquantifiable Flows of Value in a Unitary Enterprise?," State Tax Notes, August 16, 2004, p. 519; and William H. Weissman, "How Do You Measure Substantiality in a Unitary Determination?," State Tax Notes, August 23, 2004, p. 589.

4. THE STATE STATUTORY FRAMEWORK GOVERNING DIVISION OF CORPORATE INCOME

The federal constitutional restraints bearing on state division-of-income issues have largely shaped the state statutory framework governing division of corporate income. The two principal constitutional restraints with special relevance to division of the corporate income tax base—the unitary business principle and the fair apportionment requirement (see Sections B(1) and B(2) supra)—are reflected in most states' corporate income tax regimes. The unitary business principle finds expression in the line the states have drawn between allocable and apportionable income; the fair apportionment requirement is embodied in the formulas the states have adopted to divide apportionable income among the states with power to tax it.

The overwhelming majority of states have sought to discharge their constitutional obligation to confine their corporate income taxes to income derived from the corporation's activities in the taxing state by adopting the Uniform Division of Income for Tax Purposes Act (UDITPA) or a substantially similar statute. See Table 1, pp. 537–39 infra, These taxing regimes provide rules that attribute the income of a taxpayer whose income is taxable both within and without the state to the various states in which the taxpayer is taxable. In a few of the states adopting UDITPA, taxpayers have an option to apply the state's alternative apportionment or allocation methods. Moreover, many states have enacted modifications to UDITPA, particularly with regard to the weight to be given to the three factors of UDITPA's equally-weighted three-factor formula of property, payroll, and sales, see Tables 1 and 2, pp. 539–41 infra, and, to a lesser extent, with regard to the definition of those factors. Some state statutes provide that all income is apportionable (e.g., Connecticut, Maine, Maryland, Massachusetts, Rhode Island, and Vermont). In these states the limits on apportionability are provided entirely by federal constitutional restraints and by administrative pronouncements reflecting those restraints.

UDITPA was developed by the National Conference of Commissioners on Uniform State Laws, and it was approved by the 66th Annual Conference in July 1957 and by the House of Delegates of the American Bar Association during the same year. For a brief analysis of the provisions of UDITPA by one of its drafters, see William J. Pierce, "The Uniform Division of Income for State Tax Purposes," 35 Taxes 747 (1957); see also Fred L. Cox, "The NCCUSL Uniform Apportionment Formula," 42 Taxes 530 (1964); Walter Hellerstein, "Construing the Uniform Division of Income for Tax Purposes Act: Reflections on the Illinois Supreme Court's Reading of the Throwback Rule," 45 U. Chi. L. Rev. 768 (1978); Frank M. Keesling & John S. Warren, "California's Uniform Division of Income for Tax Purposes Act," 15 U.C.L.A. L. Rev. (1968); Arthur D. Lynn, "The Uniform Division of Income for Tax Purposes Act Re–Examined," 46 Va. L. Rev. 1257 (1960); Arthur D. Lynn, "The Uniform Division of Income for Tax Purposes Act," 19 Ohio St. L.J. 41 (1958); John A. Wilkie, "Uniform Division of Income for Tax Purposes," 37 Taxes 65 (1959). The following text of UDITPA includes the comments of the Commissioners who drafted it.

UNIFORM DIVISION OF INCOME FOR TAX PURPOSES ACT

Sec. 1. As used in this Act, unless the context otherwise requires:

(a) "Business income" means income arising from transactions and activity in the regular course of the taxpayer's trade or business and includes income from tangible and intangible property if the acquisition, management, and disposition of the property constitute integral parts of the taxpayer's regular trade or business operations.

COMMENT

This definition refers to "the" taxpayer's trade or business as if he had one business. It is not intended by this language to require a taxpayer having several "businesses" to use the same allocation and apportionment methods for the businesses. The language permits separate treatment of different businesses of a single taxpayer. Section 18 clearly permits separate treatment.

Income from the disposition of property used in a trade or business of the taxpayer is includible within the meaning of business income.

(b) "Commercial domicile" means the principal place from which the trade or business of the taxpayer is directed or managed.

COMMENT

The phrase "directed or managed" is not intended to permit both the state where the board of directors meets and the state where the company is managed to claim the commercial domicile. The phrase "directed or managed" is intended as two words serving the same end; not as two separate comments.

(c) "Compensation" means wages, salaries, commissions and any other form of remuneration paid to employees for personal services.

COMMENT

This definition is derived from the Model Unemployment Compensation Act which has been adopted in all states.

Compensation paid to "employees" becomes important in the payroll fraction in section 13. If a corporation is employed to provide personal services, section 18 may be used to include compensation paid to corporations in the fraction if exclusion of compensation paid to corporate agents failed to reflect adequately the business activity in the state.

(d) "Financial organization" means any bank, trust company, savings bank, [industrial bank, land bank, safe deposit company], private banker, savings and loan association, credit union, [cooperative bank], investment company, or any type of insurance company.

COMMENT

This definition and the definition of "public utility" in subsection (f) is necessary because section 2 excludes from allocation and apportionment under this Act, income from these two types of business activity. The exclusion is proposed because some states have separate legislation for apportionment and allocation of income of such taxpayers. If not, and the state proposes to change subsection (2) so as to apply the Act to such taxpayers, this would not necessarily detract from the uniformity objective of the Act.

(e) "Non-business income" means all income other than business income.

(f) "Public utility" means [any business entity which owns or operates for public use any plant, equipment, property, franchise, or license for the transmission of communications, transportation of goods or persons, or the production, storage, transmission, sale, delivery, or furnishing of electricity, water, steam, oil, oil products or gas.]

COMMENT

It is expected that "public utility" will be defined to include all taxpayers subject to the control of the state's regulatory bodies on the theory that separate legislation will provide for the apportionment and allocation of the income of such taxpayers.

See Comment to the definition of "financial organization" for purpose of this definition. "Oil, oil products, or gas" is not intended to be so restrictive as to treat differently a public utility, if any, which transmits or produces "gas products." The essential point of the definition is the requirement that the business excluded by this definition and subsection 2 be a "public utility." Private transmission lines and private production or storage companies are thus not excluded.

(g) "Sales" means all gross receipts of the taxpayer not allocated under sections 4 through 8 of this Act.

COMMENT

This all inclusive definition of sales is intended to make apportionable all income not allocated under sections 4 through 8. As indicated in the Comment to subsection 1(a), income from sales or property used in trade or business is included in apportionable income.

(h) "State" means any state of the United States, the District of Columbia, the Commonwealth of Puerto Rico, any territory or possession of the United States, and any foreign country or political subdivision thereof.

Sec. 2. Any taxpayer having income from business activity which is taxable both within and without this state, other than activity as a financial organization or public utility or the rendering of purely personal services by an individual, shall allocate and apportion his net income as provided in this Act.

Sec. 3. For purposes of allocation and apportionment of income under this Act, a taxpayer is taxable in another state if (1) in that state he is subject to a net income tax, a franchise tax measured by net income, a franchise tax for the privilege of doing business, or a corporate stock tax, or (2) that state has jurisdiction to subject the taxpayer to a net income tax regardless of whether, in fact, the state does or does not.

COMMENT

This section defines, for purposes of section 2, where a taxpayer is "taxable both within and without this state." To bring this Act into operation a taxpayer must have income from business activity, and he must be taxable in this state, and also in some other state.

Two tests are used by this section to determine when a taxpayer is "taxable in another state." The first test is a fairly obvious one, the taxpayer is taxable in another state if he is actually subjected to the type of taxes listed in subparagraph (1).

The second test, in subparagraph (2), uses a "notional" or "hypothetical" standard rather than the actual one. Thus, if a corporation has its commercial domicile in state X, which has only a sales tax and no tax measured by net income, but that corporation has business activity in state A, which has this apportionment Act, state A must apportion the business income as provided in this Act so that some of it is allocated to state X, even though as a result of the tax system of state X a portion of the business income escapes income taxation. This is desirable in order to treat the businesses of all states equally, and in order to avoid having this Act as a factor in inducing a state to have an income tax. If it does not wish to tax income, that is no reason for a state which does wish to tax income to attempt to obtain more than its share of taxable income.

It should be noted that in subsection 1(h) the word "state" is defined broadly enough to include a foreign country. This means that "taxable in another state" within section 3 may mean a foreign country. The apportioning state, however, need consider only whether the foreign country "could have" taxed the income under the constitution of the United States if it had been a state.

While subparagraph (1) lists several types of taxes which might be actually in effect in another state, the reference in subparagraph (2) only to a "net income" tax is not intended to be more restricted than the hypothetical tax than the section is with respect to the actual tax.

Sec. 4. Rents and royalties from real or tangible personal property, capital gains, interest, dividends, or patent or copyright royalties, to the extent that they constitute non-business income, shall be allocated as provided in sections 5 through 8 of this Act.

COMMENT

This section is the general section on "allocating" nonbusiness income to a state just as section 9 is the general section on apportionment of business income. Section 2 refers to an allocation and an apportionment of "net income." In "allocating" nonbusiness income to a state, the states concerned with this allocation may desire to allocate the expenses properly attributable to nonbusiness but allocable income in the same way that income is allocated so that these expenses will not be involved in determining net income from business activity where apportionment is used. Section 18 of this Code empowers the state to make this adjustment if it wishes.

Sec. 5. (a) Net rents and royalties from real property located in this state are allocable to this state.

(b) Net rents and royalties from tangible personal property are allocable to this state:

(1) if and to the extent that the property is utilized in this state, or

(2) in their entirety if the taxpayer's commercial domicile is in this state and the taxpayer is not organized under the laws of or taxable in the state in which the property is utilized.

(c) The extent of utilization of tangible personal property in a state is determined by multiplying the rents and royalties by a fraction, the numerator of which is the number of days of physical location of the property in the state during the rental or royalty period in the taxable year and the denominator of which is the number of days of physical location of the property everywhere during all rental or royalty periods in the taxable year. If the physical location of the property during the rental or royalty period is unknown or unascertainable by the taxpayer tangible personal property is utilized in the state in which the property was located at the time the rental or royalty payer obtained possession.

COMMENT

Rents from mobile tangible property are to be allocated in accordance with section 5(c). This subsection apportions rents by a fraction based on the number of days in the state on the assumption that the rents are generally based on time of use. If the rent itself is calculated on the basis of some factor other than time, section 18 would permit a state to substitute a fraction based on this substitute factor. Thus, if the rent for a drilling rig is calculated on the basis of the number of feet drilled, the "extent of utilization" in the state might also be determined on the basis of a fraction which uses "feet drilled" rather than days in the state.

Sec. 6. (a) Capital gains and losses from sales of real property located in this state are allocable to this state.

(b) Capital gains and losses from sales of tangible personal property are allocable to this state if

(1) the property had a situs in this state at the time of the sale, or

(2) the taxpayer's commercial domicile is in this state and the taxpayer is not taxable in the state in which the property had a situs.

(c) Capital gains and losses from sales of intangible personal property are allocable to this state if the taxpayer's commercial domicile is in this state.

Sec. 7. Interest and dividends are allocable to this state if the taxpayer's commercial domicile is in this state.

Sec. 8. (a) Patent and copyright royalties are allocable to this state:

(1) if and to the extent that the patent or copyright is utilized by the payer in this state, or

(2) if and to the extent that the patent or copyright is utilized by the payer in a state in which the taxpayer is not taxable and the taxpayer's commercial domicile is in this state.

(b) A patent is utilized in a state to the extent that it is employed in production, fabrication, manufacturing, or other processing in the state or to the extent that a patented product is produced in the state. If the basis of receipts from patent royalties does not permit allocation to states or if the accounting procedures do not reflect states of utilization, the patent is utilized in the state in which the taxpayer's commercial domicile is located.

(c) A copyright is utilized in a state to the extent that printing or other publication originates in the state. If the basis of receipts from copyright royalties does not permit allocation to states or if the accounting procedures do not reflect states of utilization, the copyright is utilized in the state in which the taxpayer's commercial domicile is located.

Sec. 9. All business income shall be apportioned to this state by multiplying the income by a fraction, the numerator of which is the property factor plus the payroll factor plus the sales factor, and the denominator of which is three.

Sec. 10. The property factor is a fraction, the numerator of which is the average value of the taxpayer's real and tangible personal property owned or rented and used in this state during the tax period and the denominator of which is the average value of all the taxpayer's real and tangible personal property owned or rented and used during the tax period.

COMMENT

The property to be included in the numerator and denominator is property producing the net income to be apportioned. If net income from property is allocated property under sections 5 through 8 such property should be excluded in constructing the fraction.

Sec. 11. Property owned by the taxpayer is valued at its original cost. Property rented by the taxpayer is valued at eight times the net annual rental rate. Net annual rental rate is the annual rental rate paid by the taxpayer less any annual rental rate received by the taxpayer from sub-rentals.

COMMENT

This section is admittedly arbitrary in using original cost rather than depreciated cost, and in valuing rented property as eight times the annual rental. This approach is justified because the act does not impose a tax, nor prescribe the depreciation allowable in computing the tax, but merely provides a basis for division of the taxable income among the several states. The use of original cost obviates any differences due to varying methods of depreciation, and has the advantage that the basic figure is readily ascertainable from the taxpayer's books. No method of valuing the property would probably be universally acceptable.

In any situation where it is impossible to ascertain original cost, section 18 may be used to determine a fair market value of such property. Section 18 may also be necessary to aid in determining "net annual rental value" of tangible personal property where the actual rent is so related to services that the part attributable to the object is difficult to determine.

Section 18 may also be used to determine a reasonable rental rate for this fraction where the actual rent is zero or nominal as may be the case where a local government in attempting to induce an industry to come to a community supplies the property at a nominal rent.

Sec. 12. The average value of property shall be determined by averaging the values at the beginning and ending of the tax period but the [tax administrator] may require the averaging of monthly values during the tax period if reasonably required to reflect properly the average value of the taxpayer's property.

Sec. 13. The payroll factor is a fraction, the numerator of which is the total amount paid in this state during the tax period by the taxpayer for compensation, and the denominator of which is the total compensation paid everywhere during the tax period.

COMMENT

Payroll attributable to management or maintenance or otherwise allocable to nonbusiness property should be excluded from the fraction.

Payroll "paid" should be determined by the normal accounting methods of the business so that if the taxpayer "accrues" such matters the payroll should be treated as "paid" for purpose of this section.

Sec. 14. Compensation is paid in this state if:

(a) the individual's service is performed entirely within the state; or

(b) the individual's service is performed both within and without the state, but the service performed without the state is incidental to the individual's service within the state; or

(c) some of the service is performed in the state and (1) the base of operations or, if there is no base of operations, the place from which the service is directed or controlled is in the state, or (2) the base of operations or the place from which the service is directed or controlled is not in any state in which some part of the service is performed, but the individual's residence is in this state.

COMMENT

This section is derived from the Model Unemployment Compensation Act. This is the same figure which will be used by taxpayers for unemployment compensation purposes.

Sec. 15. The sales factor is a fraction, the numerator of which is the total sales of the taxpayer in this state during the tax period, and the denominator of which is the total sales of the taxpayer everywhere during the tax period.

COMMENT

The sales to be included in the fraction are only the sales which produce business income. Sales which produce "capital gains" are under section 6 and are to be allocated rather than apportioned.

"Total sales" means "total net sales" after discounts and returns.

Sec. 16. Sales of tangible personal property are in this state if:

(a) the property is delivered or shipped to a purchaser, other than the United States government, within this state regardless of the f.o.b. point or other conditions of the sale; or

(b) the property is shipped from an office, store, warehouse, factory, or other place of storage in this state and (1) the purchaser is the United States government or (2) the taxpayer is not taxable in the state of the purchaser.

COMMENT

The phrase "delivered or shipped to a purchaser" in this state includes shipments, at the designation of the purchaser, to a person in this state such as designating, while a shipment is enroute, the ultimate recipient.

Sales to the United States are treated separately. It is thought that this is justified because sales to the United States are not necessarily attributable to a market existing in the state to which the goods are originally shipped. This different treatment may also be justified because, if the goods are defense or war materials, it may be impossible to determine whether the goods ever come to rest in the state due to use of coded delivery instructions.

This section does not specify how sales from a subsidiary in the state to an out-of-state parent, such as a marketing corporation who thereupon redirects the goods back into the state, should be treated. If returns are not consolidated under existing state tax law, it may be necessary to use section 18 to make a fair representation of the business income in this situation.

Sec. 17. Sales, other than sales of tangible personal property, are in this state if:

(a) the income-producing activity is performed in this state; or

(b) the income-producing activity is performed both in and outside this state and a greater proportion of the income-producing activity is performed in this state than in any other state, based on costs of performance.

Sec. 18. If the allocation and apportionment provisions of this Act do not fairly represent the extent of the taxpayer's business activity in this state, the taxpayer may petition for or the [tax administrator] may require, in respect to all or any part of the taxpayer's business activity, if reasonable:

(a) separate accounting;

(b) the exclusion of any one or more of the factors;

(c) the inclusion of one or more additional factors which will fairly represent the taxpayer's business activity in this state; or

(d) the employment of any other method to effectuate an equitable allocation and apportionment of the taxpayer's income.

COMMENT

It is anticipated that this act will be made a part of the income tax acts of the several states. For that reason, this section does not spell out the procedure to be followed in the event of a disagreement

Section 18 is intended as a broad authority, within the principle of apportioning business income fairly among the states which have contact with the income, to the tax administrator to vary the apportionment formula and to vary the system of allocation where the provisions of the Act do not fairly represent the extent of the taxpayer's business activity in the state. The phrases in section 18(d) do not foreclose the use of one method for some business activity and a different method for a different business activity. Neither does the phrase "method" limit the administrator to substituting factors in the formula. The phrase means any other method of fairly representing the extent of the taxpayer's business activity in the state.

Sec. 19. This Act shall be so construed as to effectuate its general purpose to make uniform the law of those states which enact it.

Sec. 20. This Act may be cited as the Uniform Division of Income for Tax Purposes Act.

5. THE MULTISTATE TAX COMPACT

The Multistate Tax Compact was developed in 1967 under the aegis of the Council of State Governments in part at least to offset the severe criticism the Willis Committee Report (see Chapter 2, note h, p. 82 supra) leveled against the widespread diversity in state apportionment and allocation methods. The Compact became effective in 1967 on adoption by seven between the taxpayer and the tax administrator. The income tax acts of each state presumably outline the procedure to be followed.states. As of late 2009, there were 20 member states (and the District of Columbia); seven sovereignty member states; and 21 associate and project member states. See www.mtc.gov. The 20 member states have adopted the Compact to which they are bound; they have voting rights; and they have dues obligations. The five sovereignty member states have not adopted the Compact but pay dues as if they had adopted the Compact and fully participate in Compact activities. The associate member states are not bound by the terms of the Compact, have no voting powers, and are under no obligation to contribute to the financial support of the work of the Multistate Tax Commission. Associate members have, however, participated in the activities carried out under the Compact. Project member states participate in particular projects carried on under the auspices of the Compact. See 2000 Multistate Tax Comm'n Rev. 33.

In furtherance of the Compact's stated purpose to "promote uniformity or compatibility in significant components of tax systems," the Compact incorporates UDITPA. The Multistate Tax Commission (MTC), composed of one member from each member state, is the governing and administering agency of the Compact. It is empowered to adopt uniform regulations relating to income, capital stock, gross receipts and sales or use taxes, if two or more member states have uniform or similar provisions. These regulations are merely advisory and not binding on any state, unless it adopts them itself. See www.mtc.gov (complete text of MTC regulations). The MTC is also authorized to conduct joint audits on behalf of member states requesting them and to issue subpoenas and seek their judicial enforcement, in order to enable the Commission to examine taxpayers' books, records, and other documents.

The U.S. Supreme Court sustained the constitutionality of the Multistate Tax Compact in United States Steel Corp. v. Multistate Tax Comm'n, 434 U.S. 452, 98 S.Ct. 799 (1978). The plaintiffs contended, among other things, that the Compact violated the Compact Clause of the Federal Constitution (U.S. Const. art. I, § 10), which provides that "[n]o State shall, without the Consent of Congress * * * enter into any Agreement or Compact with another State, or with a foreign power * * *." The Supreme Court rejected this contention. It construed the Compact Clause, in accordance with the principle established by the Supreme Court in a dictum in 1893, that congressional consent is required for the validity of a compact or agreement between states only if it "is directed to the formation of any combination tending to the increase of political power in the States, which may encroach upon or interfere with the just supremacy of the United States." Virginia v. Tennessee, 148 U.S. 503, 519, 13 S.Ct. 728 (1893). The Court found no such encroachment, and it likewise dismissed the taxpayers' Commerce, Due Process, and Equal Protection Clause arguments.

TABLE 1

States Adopting UDITPA, the Multistate Tax Commission Regulations, and the Multistate Tax Compact[f]

In the table below, those states listed as having adopted UDITPA and the MTC regulations include not only those that have formally adopted them, but also those that have enacted statutory or regulatory provisions that substantially duplicate them.

State	Adoption of UDITPA	Adoption of MTC Regs	Membership in Multistate Tax Compact
Alabama	Yes	Substantially all	Yes (full member)
Alaska	Yes	Substantially all	Yes (full member)
Arizona	Yes	Substantially all	No (assoc./project member)
Arkansas	Yes, with modifications	Adopted the business/non-business income regs.	Yes (full member)
California	Yes, with modifications	Substantially all	Yes (full member)
Colorado	Yes, for corporations electing to apportion income under UDITPA rather than under Colo. income tax act	Yes, for corporations electing to apportion income using the MTC apportionment schedule, as opposed to the method prescribed by the CO income tax act. Legislation enacted in 2008 repealed provisions that permitted taxpayers to apportion income using the three-factor formula available under the MTC	Yes (full member)
Connecticut	No	None	No (assoc./project member)
Delaware	No, but similar statute	None	No
District of Columbia	No, but some substantially similar provisions	Yes	Yes (full member)

f. See Multistate Corporate Income Tax Guide (CCH) ¶ 600–830 (2009) (chart, and the Multistate Tax Commission's web site, www.mtc.gov, on which Table 1 is based. (©2009 CCH. All Rights Reserved. Reprinted with permission from MULTISTATE CORPORATE INCOME TAX GUIDE).

State	Adoption of UDITPA	Adoption of MTC Regs	Membership in Multistate Tax Compact
Florida	No, but many similar provisions	None	No (assoc./project member)
Georgia	No, but many similar provisions	None, but some similar provisions	No (sovereignty member)
Hawaii	Yes, with some modifications	Substantially all	Yes (full member)
Idaho	Yes	All except airline reg.	Yes (full member)
Illinois	No	None	No (assoc./project member)
Indiana	No, but many similar provisions	Only business rents/royalty income reg.	No (assoc./project member)
Iowa	No, but statute contains some similar provisions	Only business rents/royalty income reg.	No (assoc./project member)
Kansas	Yes, with some modifications	Most	Yes (full member)
Kentucky	Yes, with many variations	None, but many similar provisions	No (sovereignty member)
Louisiana	No, but similar statutory provisions	None	No (sovereignty member)
Maine	Yes, with modifications (allocation provisions deleted; use of double-weighted sales factor)	Abbreviated version	No (assoc./project member)
Maryland	No, but similar apportionment factor rules	None	No (sovereignty member)
Massachusetts	No	None	No (assoc./project member)
Michigan	No, but similar apportionment provisions	None	Yes (full member)
Minnesota	No	None, but generally consistent provisions	Yes (full member)
Mississippi	No, but many similar provisions	None	No (assoc./project member)
Missouri	Yes, but option to apply state's one-factor formula or separate accounting	Substantially all	Yes (full member)
Montana	Yes, except provisions dealing with exemptions for financial organizations and public utilities	Substantially all	Yes (full member)
Nebraska	No, but several similar provisions	None, but some similar provisions	No (assoc./project member)
New Hampshire	No, but several similar provisions	None, but similar factor provisions	No (assoc./project member)

State	Adoption of UDITPA	Adoption of MTC Regs	Membership in Multistate Tax Compact
New Jersey	No	None	No (sovereignty member)
New Mexico	Yes	None, but generally consistent provisions	Yes (full member)
New York	No	None, but several comparable NY regs.	No (assoc./project member)
North Carolina	No, but substantially similar provisions	None	No (assoc./project member)
North Dakota	Yes, except provisions dealing with financial institutions, public utilities, broadcasting, and some transportation	Substantially all	Yes (full member)
Ohio	No, but similar provisions	None	No (assoc./project member)
Oklahoma	No, but many similar provisions	None	No (assoc./project member)
Oregon	Yes, with modified sales factor	Substantially all	Yes (full member)
Pennsylvania	Yes, with some exceptions	None, but generally consistent allocation and apportionment provisions	No (assoc./project member)
Rhode Island	No, but some similar provisions	None	No (assoc./project member)
South Carolina	No Generally consistent provisions; no UDITPA option		No (assoc./project member)
Tennessee	Yes	Yes, substantially similar version	No (assoc./project member)
Texas	No	None	Yes (full member)
Utah	Yes, with some modifications	Most	Yes (full member)
Vermont	No, but some similar provisions	None	No (assoc./project member)
Virginia	No	None	No
West Virginia	No	None	No (sovereignty. member)
Wisconsin	No, but many similar provisions	Some, including business/nonbusiness income regs.	No (assoc./project member)

TABLE 2

State Income Tax Apportionment Formulas[g]

State	Formula
Alabama	Evenly weighted three-factor formula
Alaska	Evenly weighted three-factor formula
Arizona	Enhanced receipts factor formula 80–10–10 (receipts, property, payroll)
Arkansas	Three-factor formula with double-weighted receipts factor
California	Three-factor formula with double-weighted receipts factor
Colorado	One factor receipts formula
Connecticut	One-factor gross receipts formula for income other than that derived from the sale or use of tangible personal or real property, and three-factor formula with double-weighted sales factor for income derived from the sale or use of tangible personal or real property
Delaware	Evenly weighted three-factor formula
Dist. of Col.	Evenly weighted three-factor formula
Florida	Three-factor formula with double-weighted receipts factor
Georgia	Three-factor formula 90–5–5 (receipts, property, payroll)
Hawaii	Evenly weighted three-factor formula
Idaho	Three-factor formula with double-weighted receipts factor
Illinois	Single-factor receipts formula
Indiana	Three-factor formula with double-weighted receipts factor. Property and payroll factors phased out by 10% each year from 2008 through 2011. Single receipts factor apportionment formula effective in tax year 2011
Iowa	Single-factor receipts formula
Kansas	Evenly weighted three-factor formula
Kentucky	Three-factor formula with double-weighted receipts factor
Louisiana	Evenly weighted three-factor formula for corporations without a specific formula (i.e., businesses other than manufacturing, merchandising, transportation, or services, etc.)
Maine	One-factor receipts formula
Maryland	Three-factor formula with double-weighted receipts factor; single-factor receipts formula for manufacturers
Massachusetts	Three-factor formula with double-weighted receipts factor
Michigan	Three-factor formula 92–3.75–3.75 (receipts-payroll-property) for purposes of computing Single Business Tax (SBT). One-factor receipts formula for purposes of computing Michigan Business Tax (MBT), effective for tax years after 2007
Minnesota	Three-factor formula 84–8–8 (receipts-payroll-property) in 2009; 87–6.5–6.5 in 2010; 90–5–5 in 2011; 93–3.5–3.5 in 2012; 96–2–2 in 2013; one-factor receipts factor after 2013

---

g. Table 2 is based on Multistate Corporate Income Tax Guide (CCH) ¶ 600–200 (2009) (chart), available in CCH Internet Tax Research Network (©2009 CCH. All Rights Reserved. Reprinted with permission from MULTISTATE CORPORATE INCOME TAX GUIDE).

State	Formula
Mississippi	No general formula. One-factor receipts formula for taxpayers that are not required to use a designated apportionment formula based on specific type or line of in-state business activity
Missouri	Evenly-weighted three-factor formula or optional one-factor formula for coporations other than public utilities and transportation companies
Montana	Evenly weighted three-factor formula
Nebraska	Single-factor receipts formula
New Hampshire	Three-factor formula with double weighted receipts factor
New Jersey	Three-factor formula with double-weighted receipts factor
New Mexico	Evenly weighted three-factor formula
New York	One-factor receipts formula
North Carolina	Three-factor formula with double-weighted receipts factor
North Dakota	Evenly weighted three-factor formula
Ohio	Three-factor formula with triple-weighted receipts factor
Oklahoma	Evenly weighted three-factor formula; corporations meeting investment criteria allowed to double-weight the receipts factor
Oregon	One-factor receipts formula
Pennsylvania	Three-factor formula 70–15–15 (receipts, property, payroll)
Rhode Island	Evenly weighted three-factor formula
South Carolina	Single-factor receipts formula, subject, through 2011, to certain adjustments if less income is apportioned to state than would be apportioned under the traditional three-factor formula
Tennessee	Three-factor formula with double-weighted receipts factor
Texas	Single-factor receipts formula
Utah	Evenly weighted three-factor formula, unless election is made to use double-weighted receipts factor
Vermont	Three-factor formula, with double-weighted receipts factor
Virginia	Three-factor formula with double-weighted receipts factor
West Virginia	Three-factor formula with double-weighted receipts factor
Wisconsin	One-factor receipts formula

6. THE RIGHT TO APPORTION OR ALLOCATE THE TAX BASE

Under UDITPA and most other states' corporate income and franchise taxes, the right to apportion or allocate the tax base is granted only when the taxpayer is taxable or doing business in other states. The requirement is based on the sensible premise that a taxpayer has no legitimate claim to apportionment or allocation if it is not taxable or doing business in other states, since, under those circumstances, its tax base is not likely to be exposed to taxation by other states. What may be logical in principle, however, is not always so simple in practice.

NOTES AND QUESTIONS

A. *The Right to Apportion and Allocate the Tax Base Under UDITPA.* Under UDITPA, a taxpayer is entitled to allocate and apportion its net income only when it has "income from business activity which is taxable both within and without this state." UDITPA § 2. UDITPA goes on to provide that:

> For purposes of allocation and apportionment of income under this Act, a taxpayer is taxable in another state if (1) in that state he is subject to a net income tax, a franchise tax measured by net income, a franchise tax for the privilege of doing business, or a corporate stock tax, or (2) that state has jurisdiction to subject the taxpayer to a net income tax regardless of whether, in fact, the state does or does not.

UDITPA § 3.

Why did the UDITPA draftsmen include clause (1) in § 2 of UDITPA? Could there ever be a case in which a taxpayer is "subject to" the taxes listed in clause (1) in a state that nevertheless lacks jurisdiction to subject the taxpayer to a net income tax under clause (2)? If not, isn't clause (1) superfluous? If so, can you describe the conditions under which such a case would arise? Might the answer to these questions change over time? In particular, consider that (a) UDITPA was drafted in the 1950s and adopted in 1957; (b) *Northwestern* (p. 109 supra) was decided in 1959; (c) Public Law 86–272 was enacted in 1959; (d) *Complete Auto* (pp. 110–19 supra) was decided in 1977; and (e) the Court's constitutional standards governing jurisdiction to tax have evolved considerably since 1957 (see Chapter 2).

What is the policy justification for clause (2) of § 2 of UDITPA? Why shouldn't the right to apportion depend on whether a taxpayer has in fact been subjected to an income tax by another state rather than merely whether that state has the power to impose an income tax on the taxpayer, even if the state has failed to exercise that power? Is UDITPA's approach consistent with the constitutional restraints on multiple taxation? In other words, is a tax unconstitutional merely because it exposes the taxpayer to a risk of multiple taxation or must the taxpayer demonstrate actual multiple taxation to make out a case of constitutional proportions? See *Mobil* (pp. 473–89 supra). Put slightly differently, is the failure of one state to exercise its constitutional power to tax relevant to the constitutional power of another state to tax?

Can a taxpayer obtain the right to apportion under clause (1) of § 2 of UDITPA by the simple expedient of voluntarily paying a "franchise tax for the privilege of doing business, or a corporate stock tax" in a state which imposes only a nominal tax of that kind? In Richardson Investment Management, Inc. v. New Hampshire Board of Taxation, 119 N.H. 159, 399 A.2d 968 (1979), the taxpayer contended it was entitled to apportionment of New Hampshire's business profits tax because Delaware had subjected it to a capital stock tax. The Delaware tax, imposed on authorized capital stock, amounted to $20. In rejecting the taxpayer's claim that it was entitled to apportion the New Hampshire tax, the court declared:

> [T]he New Hampshire business profits tax * * * is similar to a corporate income tax. The reason for the apportionment provisions * * * is to avoid

taxing in this State corporate *income* or *property* which is subject to taxation in another state. The possibility of double taxation is thereby eliminated. * * * The Delaware franchise tax is neither based on the value of the corporate stock of plaintiff's corporation nor on any of the corporate property. Therefore, taxing the gross income of the corporation at its commercial domicile, New Hampshire, does not constitute double taxation, and the plaintiff cannot apportion its income. * * * The plaintiff has not claimed that it is subject to income tax in Delaware or any other State that would subject it to double taxation.

Id., 399 A.2d at 969 (emphasis in original).

7. DISTINGUISHING APPORTIONABLE FROM ALLOCABLE INCOME UNDER STATE STATUTES

The states generally provide two mechanisms for attributing a taxpayer's income to the various states in which it is taxable: allocation and apportionment.[h] When income is allocated, it is attributed to the particular state or states that are considered to be the source of the income, often on the basis of the location of the property that gave rise to the income or on the basis of the taxpayer's commercial domicile. For example, when rents, royalties, and capital gains from real property are allocated, they are typically allocated in their entirety to the state in which the property is located. UDITPA §§ 5, 6. When interest and dividends are allocable, they are allocated in their entirety to the taxpayer's commercial domicile. UDITPA § 7.

When income is apportioned, on the other hand, it is divided among the various states in which the taxpayer derives such apportionable income. The mechanism for apportioning income among the states under UDITPA is the familiar three-factor apportionment formula of property, payroll, and sales. UDITPA § 9. Under this formula, a taxpayer's income is attributed to the state on the basis of a percentage determined by averaging the ratios of the taxpayer's property, payroll, and sales within the state to its property, payroll, and sales everywhere. UDITPA §§ 10–17.

The division of income process usually begins with the taxpayer's federal income tax base (federal taxable income). The statutes typically require that specific categories of income be allocated to a single state or, occasionally, to several states.[i] The balance of the taxpayer's income, i.e.,

---

h. At the outset of this chapter, we identified *three* different methods that the states have adopted to divide the tax base of a multistate enterprise—allocation, apportionment, and separate accounting. Under the state statutes, however, separate accounting is generally permissible only when the allocation and apportionment provisions do not fairly represent the extent of the taxpayer's business activity in the state. See UDITPA § 18 (the "equitable apportionment" or "relief" provision). As a practical matter, then, taxpayers must either allocate or apportion their income, unless they are able to persuade the taxing authority or the courts that the standard allocation and apportionment provisions produce unfair results and that separate accounting is an appropriate alternative. See Section B(9) infra.

i. In some instances, income may be allocated to more than one state, as in the case of income from tangible personal property that may be allocated to a state based on the relative number of days it is physically located in such state. UDITPA §§ 5(b), 5(c).

the federal taxable income less allocable income, is apportioned among the states by formula. The determination whether a taxpayer's income is allocated under rules that generally attribute the income to a single state or is apportioned under rules that attribute the income to all of the states in which the taxpayer has property, payroll, or sales depends on the question whether the income is determined to be "business income" or "nonbusiness income." Under UDITPA and similar taxing regimes, all "business income" is apportioned; all "nonbusiness income" is allocated. UDITPA §§ 4, 9.

As noted above, the statutes of some states provide that all income is apportionable. Needless to say, these statutes are limited by federal constitutional restraints on apportionability. Tax administrators from many of these states have issued statements acknowledging that their statutes do not extend to income that cannot constitutionally be apportioned.

a. The Business–Nonbusiness Income Distinction Under UDITPA

UDITPA defines "business income" as

income arising from transactions and activity in the regular course of the taxpayer's trade or business and includes income from tangible and intangible property if the acquisition, management, and disposition of the property constitute integral parts of the taxpayer's regular trade or business operations.

UDITPA § 1(a). UDITPA defines "nonbusiness income" as "all income other than business income." UDITPA § 1(e).

The regulations issued by the Multistate Tax Commission (MTC), the administrative agency of the Multistate Tax Compact (see Section B(5), pp. 535–36 supra), which embodies UDITPA, state that "[i]ncome of any type or class and from any source is business income if it arises from transactions and activity occurring in the regular course of a trade or business." MTC Reg. IV.1.(a), available at www.mtc.gov. In general the regulations consider "all transactions and activities of the taxpayer which are dependent upon or contribute to the operations of the taxpayer's economic enterprise as a whole" as "arising in the regular course of, and * * * constitut[ing] integral parts of, a trade or business." Id. The MTC regulations also construe UDITPA as establishing a presumption in favor of apportionment, stating that "the income of the taxpayer is business income unless clearly classifiable as nonbusiness income." Id.

The MTC regulations are extremely influential in the construction of UDITPA, even though they have no legal force in any state unless that state adopts the regulations in accordance with its own rulemaking procedures. Multistate Tax Compact art. VII(3). In fact, however, many UDITPA states have adopted the MTC regulations in whole or in part. See Table 1, pp. 537–39 supra. Because of the wide variation among the states in the extent to which they have adopted (or, in some instances, modified) the MTC regulations, one must carefully examine each state's regulations in order to ascertain the extent to which the MTC regulations are applicable in a particular state.

How does UDITPA's definition of business income differ from the constitutional definition of apportionable income? In answering this question, consider the U.S. Supreme Court's observations about the relationship between the UDITPA definition and the constitutional standard in *Allied–Signal* (pp. 420–33 supra). Can the state law definition of business income ever be more expansive than the constitutional definition of apportionable income? Do the MTC's regulations, which take an expansive view of the business income definition, fairly interpret the language of UDITPA? In particular, what basis is there for presuming that income is business income, unless clearly classifiable as nonbusiness income? Even assuming that the MTC regulations reflect a correct reading of UDITPA, can their emphasis on corporate "purpose" be squared with *Allied–Signal* as well as the Court's decisions in *ASARCO* (pp. 491–93 supra) and *Woolworth* (pp. 493–95 supra) limiting the scope of apportionable income? As the ensuing materials make clear, courts have not always accepted the MTC's broad definition of the business income concept.

In determining whether income is apportionable or allocable, courts have divided sharply over the proper construction of UDITPA's business income definition. The following case explores that controversy.

EX PARTE UNIROYAL TIRE COMPANY

Supreme Court of Alabama, 2000.
779 So.2d 227.

COOK, JUSTICE.

We granted the petition of Uniroyal Tire Company ("Uniroyal") for certiorari review of a judgment of the Court of Civil Appeals. That court affirmed a judgment in favor of the State Department of Revenue (the "Department"), holding that Uniroyal was liable for $2,148,178 in corporate income taxes and interest, on a capital gain of $99.7 million it realized from the liquidation in 1990 of all its business assets.

The essentially undisputed facts are set forth in the opinion of the Court of Civil Appeals as follows:

"In 1986, Uniroyal entered into a partnership with the B.F. Goodrich Company, wherein both corporations transferred their assets to the partnership and each received a 50% partnership interest. *Thereafter, Uniroyal's only asset was its partnership interest, and between 1986 and 1989 Uniroyal treated income received from the partnership as business income.* Then, in 1988, the partnership was recapitalized, resulting in Uniroyal's percentage of ownership in the partnership being reduced and in Uniroyal's receiving $80 million in cash.

"Later, in 1990, Uniroyal sold its entire partnership interest for approximately $260,600,000 and realized a capital gain of approximately $99.7 million. On its 1990 Alabama tax return, Uniroyal treated the $99.7 million as nonbusiness income. The Department contested the return, maintaining that the $99.7 million was business income, and assessed corporate income tax accordingly. Uniroyal appealed to the Department's Administrative Law Division...."

Uniroyal Tire Co. v. State Dep't of Revenue, 779 So.2d 221, 222 (Ala.Civ. App. 1999).

The Department assessed the tax on the basis of the term "business income," as it is defined in Ala.Code 1975, § 40–27–1, Art. IV, 1.(a), and in the Revenue Department Regulations then in effect, specifically, Ala.Admin.Code r. 810–3–31–.02(1)(a)4.(ii):

"[§ 40–27–1, Art. IV, 1.(a)] 'Business income' means income arising from transactions and activity in the regular course of the taxpayer's trade or business and includes income from tangible and intangible property if the acquisition, management, and disposition of the property constitute integral parts of the taxpayer's regular trade or business operations."

"[Reg. 810–3–31–.02(1)(a)4.(ii)] As a general rule, gain ... from the sale, exchange or other disposition of real or tangible or intangible personal property constitutes business income if the property while owned by the taxpayer was used to produce business income."

Uniroyal appealed the assessment to the Department's Administrative Law Division. The administrative law judge ("the ALJ") defined the issue as follows:

"The primary issue is whether [Uniroyal's] gain from the sale of a partnership interest in 1990 was business income, as defined by the above statute, and thus *apportionable to Alabama*, or 'nonbusiness income,' and thus allocable entirely to [Uniroyal's] state of commercial domicile, Connecticut."....

"Generally speaking, [the statute] requires a corporation to apportion its business income among the various states in which the corporation does business using a standard three-factor formula of property, payroll, and sales. All other nonbusiness income is allocated directly to the corporation's state of commercial domicile...."

(Emphasis added.) The ALJ ruled in favor of Uniroyal, holding that the capital gain from the liquidation of partnership assets was "nonbusiness" income.

The Department appealed to the Montgomery Circuit Court, which entered a summary judgment in favor of the Department. Relying on Reg. § 810–3–31–.02(1)(a)4.(ii), the trial court explained:

" 'Here, Uniroyal admitted that its partnership interest produced 'business' income while it was owned by Uniroyal. Contrary to the implication of the [ALJ], this regulation does not conflict with the statutory definition of 'business' income and is not inconsistent with that definition. Instead, the regulation is reasonable.' "

Uniroyal appealed to the Court of Civil Appeals, which, over the strenuous dissent of two judges, affirmed the summary judgment. The majority stated: "We agree with the analysis of the North Carolina Supreme Court in Polaroid Corp. v. Offerman, 349 N.C. 290, 507 S.E.2d 284 (1998), and we find no conflict between the regulation and the statute." 779 So.2d at 223. Uniroyal then sought certiorari review in this Court. We reverse and remand.

The construction of § 40–27–1, Art. IV, 1.(a), and its relationship with the Department regulations are questions of first impression in this Court. Section 40–27–1, Art. IV, 1.(a), is a provision of the Multistate Tax Compact (the "MTC"), as enacted by the Alabama Legislature in Act No. 395, 1967 Ala.Acts 982 (Reg.Session). The MTC "was created in 1966 to establish a uniform system for taxing multistate taxpayers and became effective in 1967 after various states had adopted it." State Dep't of Revenue v. MGH Management, Inc., 627 So.2d 408, 409 (Ala.Civ.App. 1993). To date, there are 21 "compact member states"—including Alabama—that is, states that have adopted the MTC. 1 All States Tax Guide (RIA) ¶ 564 (June 6, 2000). Article IV of the MTC incorporated the Uniform Division of Income for Tax Purposes Act (the "UDITPA").

The UDITPA was "approved" in 1957 by the National Conference of Commissioners on Uniform State Laws and the American Bar Association and "recommended . . . for adoption by the states." Comment, A Matter of (Statutory) Interpretation: North Carolina Recognizes the Functional Test of Corporate Taxation in Polaroid Corp. v. Offerman, 77 N.C.L.Rev. 2326, 2327 (1999). Its purpose was similar to that of the MTC, namely, "to address the problem of multiple taxation and to create a uniform method for allocating corporate income among the states entitled to tax a portion thereof." Id. The Alabama Legislature took *verbatim* from the UDITPA, § 1(a), the definition of "business income" in § 40–27–1, Art. IV, 1.(a), which is at issue in this case.

But the uniformity sought by the proponents of the UDITPA/MTC has been compromised by judicial disagreement over the definition of the term "business income." This disagreement has evolved into what is essentially a dichotomy in judicial construction of the definition. Indeed, two separate "tests" have developed as a result of the judiciary's attempts to determine when a gain is "business income."

A number of courts construing language functionally identical to that of § 40–27–1, Art. IV, 1.(a), have concluded that their statute contained only what is popularly described as the "transactional" test. See, e.g., Phillips Petroleum Co. v. Iowa Dep't of Revenue & Fin., 511 N.W.2d 608 (Iowa 1993); Western Natural Gas Co. v. McDonald, 202 Kan. 98, 446 P.2d 781, 783 (1968); McVean & Barlow, Inc. v. New Mexico Bureau of Revenue, 88 N.M. 521, 543 P.2d 489 (Ct.App.), cert. denied, 89 N.M. 6,

546 P.2d 71 (N.M.1975); General Care Corp. v. Olsen, 705 S.W.2d 642 (Tenn. 1986). Proponents of the transactional test find it "rooted in the statutory phrase, 'earnings arising from transactions and activity in the *regular course* of the taxpayer's trade or business.'" General Care, 705 S.W.2d at 644 (emphasis added in *General Care*). "Thus, under the transactional test, the 'controlling factor by which business income [is defined] is the nature of the particular transaction giving rise to the income.' ... The frequency and regularity of similar transactions and the former practices of the business are pertinent considerations." Id. (quoting McDonald, supra).

Other courts construing the same language have concluded that their statute *also* contains an *alternative* test, which is popularly known as the "functional" test. See, e.g., Pledger v. Getty Oil Exploration Co., 309 Ark. 257, 831 S.W.2d 121 (1992); Texaco–Cities Serv. Pipeline Co. v. McGaw, 182 Ill.2d 262, 230 Ill.Dec. 991, 695 N.E.2d 481 (1998); and Laurel Pipe Line Co. v. Commonwealth, 537 Pa. 205, 642 A.2d 472 (1994); cf. Simpson Timber Co. v. Department of Revenue, 326 Ore. 370, 953 P.2d 366 (1998) (Durham, J., concurring). Proponents of the functional test find it rooted in that second clause of the statute, which reads: "and includes income from tangible and intangible property if the acquisition, management, and disposition of the property constitute integral parts of the taxpayer's regular trade or business operations." "*More broadly* [than under the transactional test], under the functional test, all gain from the disposition of a capital asset is considered business income if the asset disposed of was '*used by the taxpayer* in its regular trade or business operations.'" Texaco–Cities Serv., 182 Ill.2d at 269, 230 Ill.Dec. 991, 695 N.E.2d at 484 (emphasis added). "Under the functional test ..., the extraordinary nature or infrequency of the sale is irrelevant." Id., 182 Ill.2d at 269, 230 Ill.Dec. 991, 695 N.E.2d at 484. Proponents of this view hold that "income constitutes business income if *either one* of the above tests is met." Id. (emphasis added).

The "functional test" is embodied in revenue department *regulations* adopted by various states. See Appeal of Chief Indus., Inc., 255 Kan. 640, 646–47, 875 P.2d 278, 283 (1994). Specifically, 15 states have adopted regulations promulgated by the Multistate Tax Commission "on allocation and apportionment of income generally and for specialized businesses" (the "Model Regulations"). 1 All States Tax Guide (RIA) ¶ 226–B (October 19, 1999). Alabama is among these 15 states. Id.; see also Bradley J. Sklar & W. Todd Carlisle, The Alabama Limited Liability Company Act, 45 Ala.L.Rev. 145, 175 n. 202 (1993) ("[t]he provisions of income tax regulation 810–3–31–.02 are virtually identical to the model regulations promulgated by the Multistate Tax Commission under the [MTC]"). The Model Regulations were "intended to set forth rules concerning the application of the apportionment and allocation provisions of Article IV of the Multistate Tax Compact." 1 All States Tax Guide, at ¶ 630 (June 6, 2000). Under the Model Regulations and their state-revenue-department counterparts, "[g]ain or loss from the sale, exchange or other disposition of real property or of tangible or intangible personal property constitutes business income if the property while owned by the taxpayer was used in the taxpayer's trade or business." Id. at ¶ 633 (Mod.Reg.IV.1.(c)(2)); see Ala.Admin.Code r. 810–3–31–.02(1)(a)4.(ii). "In essence," under these regulations, "all income which arises from the conduct of trade or business operations of a taxpayer is business income." 1 All States Tax Guide, at ¶ 631 (Mod.Reg.IV.1(a)).

The Department urges us to adopt the view that § 40–27–1, Art. IV, 1.(a), contains *both* tests, and argues that gain from the sale of Uniroyal's partnership interest constitutes "business income" under either test. Uniroyal, on the other hand, contends that the statute contains only the transactional test and that gain from the sale of its partnership interest was not "business income" under that test. We agree with Uniroyal.

We consider this case within the context of two well-settled rules. First, "[t]axing statutes must be construed most strictly against the taxing authority and most favorably for the taxpayer." City of Arab v. Cherokee Elec. Co-op., 673 So.2d 751, 761 (Ala. 1995). The second rule was succinctly stated by the ALJ: "[W]hile a Department regulation interpreting a statute should be given weight, it must be rejected if it conflicts with the language of the statute." Uniroyal Tire Co. v. State Dep't of Revenue, 779 So.2d at 232.

" 'The starting point in every case involving construction of a statute is the language itself.' " * * * To facilitate discussion, we shall parse § 40–27–1, Art. IV, 1.(a), into its two disputed clauses, referring to the first clause—"income arising from transactions and activity in the regular course of the taxpayer's trade or business"—as ¶ 1, and the remainder of the section as ¶ 2. It is undisputed that ¶ 1 contains the transactional test. The only question is whether ¶ 2 contains the alternative test.

Grammatically speaking, construction of the UDITPA definition of "business income" is a field that has been thoroughly plowed. Those courts that have construed their statute as containing *both* the transactional test and the functional test have done so on the rationale that ¶ 2 may operate independently of ¶ 1, and they have concluded that the grammatical structure of the statute supports that construction. As the North Carolina Supreme Court has explained it:

> "First, grammatically speaking, business income constitutes the *subject of the sentence*, which is thereafter defined by two independent clauses, each with its own verb and subsequent definitional language. In fact, the statute could grammatically be read as stating: 'Business income means income arising from transactions and activity in the regular course of the corporation's trade or business, and [business income] includes income from tangible and intangible property....' That is, N.C.G.S. § 105–130.4(a)(1) does not contain a misplaced modifier, but rather utilizes a compound predicate to illustrate that 'business income' includes the definitions set forth in both the first and second clauses."

Polaroid Corp. v. Offerman, 349 N.C. 290, 297–98, 507 S.E.2d 284, 290–91 (1998) (adopting the functional-test alternative) (emphasis added).

Those courts that have construed their statute as containing only the transactional test, however, have "read [¶ 2] as simply *modifying* [¶ 1]," Polaroid Corp. v. Offerman, 349 N.C. at 295, 507 S.E.2d at 289 (emphasis added). See also Phillips Petroleum Co. v. Iowa Dep't of Revenue & Fin., 511 N.W.2d 608 (Iowa 1993). Under this approach, ¶ 2 is a "subset" of ¶ 1, in accord with the rule of construction known as the doctrine of the "last antecedent." See Kroger Co. v. Department of Revenue, 284 Ill.App.3d 473, 478, 220 Ill.Dec. 566, 673 N.E.2d 710, 713 (1996) (rejecting this construction and applying the functional test). In other words, ¶ 2 serves to exemplify "what fits within the definition." Polaroid, 349 N.C. at 297, 507 S.E.2d at 290.

These courts conclude that construing ¶ 2 to operate independently of ¶ 1 does *not* comport with the grammatical structure of the statute. For example, in General Care, supra, the court stated:

> "We likewise reject the Commissioner's argument that income from the sale of property is to be considered business earnings if the property sold constituted an integral part of the taxpayer's business [regardless of whether it was a transaction or an activity 'in the regular course of the taxpayer's trade or business]'. . . . In our opinion the Commissioner disregards the statute's clear grammatical structure by attempting to make the word 'property' the *subject of the clause* upon which she bases her argument. The literal terms of the statute cannot be read to make the integral role of an asset in the taxpayer's business the controlling factor by which business earnings are identified without doing violence to the elementary rules of grammar. The language the Commissioner relies upon cannot be lifted out of its context and construed without reference to the balance of the statute."

705 S.W.2d at 648 (emphasis added).

We agree with these observations of the Tennessee Supreme Court. But that court identified another, more troubling, weakness in the functional-test rationale—the fact that ¶ 2 is written in the *con*junctive, not the *dis*junctive. Specifically, "income from . . . property" is business income only if the "acquisition, management, *and* disposition . . . constitute integral parts of the taxpayer's . . . business." (Emphasis added.) The court explained:

> "We find the Commissioner's position that the 'disposition' of property need not be within the scope of the taxpayer's regular business operations in order to give rise to business income contrary to the plain language of the statute. The drafters' use of the conjunction 'and' clearly indicates that the disposition, *as well as* the acquisition and management of property must be an integral part of the taxpayer's regular trade or business operations in order to produce business earnings. This Court will presume that every word used in a

statute was intended by the General Assembly to convey meaning and purpose. . . . 'Where, as here, in a legislative act, words are used in a series, effect must be given to every word, and it must be presumed that the Legislature did not use three words where one would do. . . .' R.J. Reynolds Tobacco Co. v. Carson, 187 Tenn. 157, 213 S.W.2d 45, 48 (1948). It is the duty of the Court 'to construe a statute so that no part will be inoperative, superfluous, void, or insignificant . . . and further to give effect to every word, phrase, clause and sentence of the act in order to carry out the legislative intent.' Tidwell v. Collins, 522 S.W.2d 674, 676–77 (Tenn. 1975)."

General Care, 705 S.W.2d at 646 (emphasis added).

This construction of the statute is shared by tax commentators * * *:

* * *

" '[W]e believe that, as a matter of statutory construction, courts adopting the transactional test have the better of the argument. The language of UDITPA, after all, says that business income "includes income from tangible and intangible property if the acquisition, management, *and* disposition of the property constitute integral parts of the taxpayer's regular trade or business." The plain language of the statute thus requires that the "disposition" (as well as the acquisition and management) of the property constitute an integral part of the taxpayer's trade or business. If the transaction is an extraordinary one, it is hard to see how the disposition can constitute an integral part of the taxpayer's regular trade or business.' "

Brief of Amicus Curiae Committee on State Taxation (see note 2) at 10 (quoting J. Hellerstein & W. Hellerstein, State Taxation ¶ 9.05[2][c] (3d ed. 1998) (emphasis in State Taxation). * * * We agree with these comments, and we add the following observations in regard to the use of the conjunction in ¶ 2.

We recognize the fact that "the legislature's use of the disjunctive conjunction 'or,' as opposed to the conjunctive conjunction 'and,' is not *conclusive* with respect to the legislature's intent," and that "this Court is at liberty in ascertaining the intent of the legislature to construe the disjunctive conjunction 'or' and the conjunctive conjunction 'and' interchangeably." Ex parte Jordan, 592 So.2d 579, 581 (Ala. 1992) (emphasis added). However, "[w]hile there may be circumstances which call for an interpretation of the words 'and' and 'or,' ordinarily these words are *not* interchangeable." 1A Norman J. Singer, Sutherland Statutory Construction § 21.14 (5th ed. 1993) (emphasis added). "The *literal meaning of these terms should be followed* unless it renders the statute inoperable or the meaning becomes questionable." Id. at 26 (Supp.2000) (emphasis added). To substitute by judicial construction the word "or" for the word "and" would significantly impact the scope of this statute.

Indeed, this distinction in statutory language formed one of the bases of the court's decision in Polaroid Corp. v. Offerman, 349 N.C. 290, 507

S.E.2d 284—the case on which the Court of Civil Appeals primarily relied. *Polaroid* adopted and applied the functional-test analysis and concluded that proceeds the Polaroid Corporation derived from a judgment in its favor in a patent-infringement action against Eastman Kodak Company were taxable as business income. However, unlike the Alabama statute, § 40–27–1, Art. IV, 1.(a), the North Carolina statute, N.C.Gen.Stat. § 105–130.4(a)(1)—North Carolina's version of the UDITPA—contains the words "and/or" in place of "and" in ¶ 2 of § 40–27–1, Art. IV, 1.(a).

In adopting the functional test, the court noted that "North Carolina's definition of business income is . . . *broader* than the definition found under the Uniform Act." 349 N.C. at 294 n. 3, 507 S.E.2d at 288 n. 3. "Specifically," it explained, "North Carolina's definition reads 'acquisition, management, and/or disposition of the property,' as opposed to the definition in UDITPA [and the definition in § 40–27–1, Art. IV, 1.(a)], which uses the conjunction '*and*' rather than '*and/or.*'" Id. (emphasis added). Thus, under *Polaroid*'s functional-test analysis, the income was taxable if it was either (1) acquired as a part of the taxpayer's "regular trade or business operations"; (2) managed as a part of the taxpayer's "regular trade or business operations"; or (3) disposed of as a part of the taxpayer's "regular trade or business operations."

We also deem it significant that, after their state courts failed to find the functional test in their statutes, two state legislatures amended their definition of "business income" by striking out the word "and" in ¶ 2, and substituting the word "or." N.M.Stat.Ann.1978, § 7–4–2 (responding to McVean & Barlow, Inc. v. New Mexico Bureau of Revenue, 88 N.M. 521, 543 P.2d 489, supra; Tenn.Code Ann., § 67–4–2004(1) (responding to General Care Corp. v. Olsen, 705 S.W.2d 642 (Tenn. 1986), and its progeny). Similarly, in response to Phillips Petroleum Co. v. Iowa Dep't of Revenue & Fin., 511 N.W.2d 608 (Iowa 1993), the Iowa legislature amended its statute to read as follows:

> " 'Business income' means income arising from transactions and activity in the regular course of the taxpayer's trade or business; or income from tangible and intangible property if the acquisition, management, and disposition of the property constitute integral parts of the taxpayer's regular trade or business operations; *or* gain or loss resulting from the sale, exchange, or other disposition of real property or of tangible or intangible personal property, if the property while owned by the taxpayer was operationally related to the taxpayer's trade or business carried on in Iowa or operationally related to sources within Iowa, or the property was operationally related to sources outside this state and to the taxpayer's trade or business carried on in Iowa; or gain or loss resulting from the sale, exchange, or other disposition of stock in another corporation if the activities of the other corporation were operationally related to the taxpayer's trade or business carried on in Iowa while the stock was owned by the taxpayer."

Iowa Code § 422.32.2 (emphasis added).

We agree with *Polaroid* that the use of the word "or" in place of "and" in ¶ 2 broadens the scope of the statute. Considering all the circumstances, we decline the invitation to ignore the ordinary distinction between the words "and" and "or." With the substitution of the word "or" for "and" in ¶ 2, the statute could be construed—if not as broadly as the proponents of the functional test construe it—at least so broadly as to *eclipse entirely the transactional test in* ¶ 1. Therein lies our greatest reservation about the Department's argument, which is that § 40–27–1, Art. IV, 1.(a), contains two *alternative* tests. The functional test, as embodied in Reg. 810–3–31–.02(1)(a)4.(ii), is so broad that it essentially renders nugatory the transactional test. Under the functional test as represented by Reg. 810–3–31–.02(1)(a)4.(ii), "all gain from the disposition of a capital asset is considered business income if the asset disposed of was *'used by the taxpayer* in its regular trade or business operations.'" Texaco–Cities Serv., 182 Ill.2d at 268, 230 Ill.Dec. 991, 695 N.E.2d at 484 (emphasis added). Indeed, we know of no case in which it was held that gain *was* business income under the *transactional test*, but was not business income under the functional test, nor can we conceive of such a case. If income is business income under the transactional test, then, a fortiori, it is business income under the functional test. In other words, the functional test would include everything that the transactional test includes—and much more. Thus, under the alternative-test approach, ¶ 1 is a mere appendage without any real purpose.

"It must be presumed," however, that statutes are enacted with a "meaningful purpose." Adams v. Mathis, 350 So.2d 381, 385–86 (Ala. 1977). "The Legislature will not be presumed to have done a futile thing in enacting a statute." Ex parte Watley, 708 So.2d 890, 892 (Ala. 1997). "There is a presumption that every word, sentence, or provision was intended for some useful purpose, has some force and effect, and that some effect is to be given to each, and also that no superfluous words or provisions were used." Sheffield v. State, 708 So.2d 899, 909 (Ala.Crim. App.), cert. denied, 708 So.2d 911 (Ala. 1997). For the reasons discussed above, we decline to hold that § 40–27–1, Art. IV, 1.(a), also contains a functional test.

From this conclusion, it follows that Reg. 81 0–3–31–.02(1)(a) 4.(ii), cannot constitute authority for the collection of the tax in this case. This is so, because, as the embodiment of the broader functional test, it would authorize tax that § 40–27–1, Art. IV, 1.(a), does not. To the extent that it would do so, it directly conflicts with the statute. This, it may not do.

A complete liquidation and cessation of business do not generate business income under the transaction test. Associated Partnership I, Inc. v. Huddleston, 889 S.W.2d 190 (Tenn. 1994). This is so, because, by definition, such events are most extraordinary; they do not occur in the "regular course of the taxpayer's trade or business."

* * *

Moreover, even courts applying the functional test have excepted true liquidations from its application. For example, *Polaroid*, on which the Court of Civil Appeals relied, stated: "We do note, however, that cases involving liquidation are in a category by themselves. Indeed, true liquidation cases are inapplicable to these situations because the asset and transaction at issue are not in furtherance of the unitary business, but rather a means of cessation." 349 N.C. at 306 n. 6, 507 S.E.2d at 296 n. 6.

Other courts agree with this distinction. In Laurel Pipe Line Co. v. Commonwealth, 537 Pa. at 205, 642 A.2d 472, supra, for example, the Pennsylvania Supreme Court held that gain from the sale by a "[m]ulti-state corporate taxpayer engaged in pipeline transportation of petroleum products," 642 A.2d at 472 (West synopsis of case), of an "idle pipeline and related assets," id., 537 Pa. at 207, 642 A.2d at 473, amounted to a liquidation of "a portion of its assets," and, consequently, was not business income. Id., 537 Pa. at 211, 642 A.2d at 475.

The Pennsylvania court first concluded that the sale did not satisfy the "transactional" test. In discussing the "functional" test, the court noted: "Income meets the functional test if the gain arises from the sale of an asset which produced business income while it was owned by the taxpayer." Id. The court then explained:

> "The Aliquippa–Cleveland pipeline had been idle for over three years prior to the time that it was sold. In our view, *the pipeline was not disposed of as an integral part of Laurel's regular trade or business*. Rather, the effect of the sale was that the company liquidated a portion of its assets. This is evidenced by the fact that the proceeds of the sale were not reinvested back into the operations of the business, but were distributed entirely to the stockholders of the corporation. Although Laurel continued to operate a second, independent pipeline, the sale of the . . . pipeline constituted a liquidation of a separate and distinct aspect of its business."

Id. (emphasis added). Thus, the court concluded that the gain from the sale of the pipeline was business income under *neither* test. See also McVean & Barlow, Inc. v. New Mexico Bureau of Revenue, 88 N.M. 521, 543 P.2d 489 (Ct.App.) (holding that gain from the sale of pipeline equipment in *partial* liquidation of taxpayer's business did not constitute business income; the dissent of Lopez, J., conceding that a true liquidation and cessation of business does not yield business income), cert. denied, 89 N.M. 6, 546 P.2d 71 (N.M.1975); cf. Texaco–Cities Serv. Pipeline Co. v. McGaw, 182 Ill.2d 262, 273, 695 N.E.2d 481, 486 (1998) (distinguishing *Laurel* on the ground that *Laurel* represented a true liquidation of a "separate and distinct aspect" of the taxpayer's business). But see Huddleston, 889 S.W.2d at 196 (holding that liquidation of a partnership did not produce business income, but stating in dicta that "no significance is attached to the fact that a transaction involves a liquidation" under the functional test). Indeed, the Department has not directed us to *any* case holding that gains realized from a complete liquidation and cessation of business operations produced business income.

We express no opinion as to how an amendment of the statute to substitute the disjunctive "or" for the conjunctive "and" might affect cases involving true liquidations. However, we are clear to the conclusion that under our statute as it is currently constituted, *true liquidations* do not generate "business income" within the meaning of § 40–27–1, Art. IV, 1.(a).

In summary, we hold (1) that § 40–27–1, Art. IV, 1.(a), contains the transactional test for determining when gain from multistate business operations may be taxed as "business income"; (2) that the 1990 disposition of the Uniroyal partnership interest was not "business income" as determined by that test; (3) that § 40–27–1, Art. IV, 1.(a), does not contain the "functional test"; and (4) that Reg. 810–3–31–.02(1)(a)4.(ii), to the extent it does embody the functional test, conflicts with § 40–27–1, Art. IV, 1.(a), and is, therefore, inapplicable. For these reasons, the judgment of the Court of Civil Appeals is reversed and the cause is remanded for an order or proceedings consistent with this opinion.

REVERSED AND REMANDED.

HOOPER, C.J., and MADDOX, SEE, LYONS, JOHNSTONE, and ENGLAND, JJ., concur.

HOUSTON, J., dissents.

HOUSTON, JUSTICE (dissenting).

I agree with the State Department of Revenue, the Alabama Court of Civil Appeals, and Polaroid Corp. v. Offerman, 349 N.C. 290, 507 S.E.2d 284 (1998). * * *

NOTES AND QUESTIONS

A. *The "Transactional" and "Functional" Tests of Business Income Under UDITPA.* As the *Uniroyal* opinion recognized, there is a sharp division among the state courts as to whether UDITPA's business income definition embraces a "functional" as well as a "transactional test." As the opinion also recognized, the widespread use of the functional test of business income is due in large part to the fact that the MTC regulations embrace it. The MTC regulations, which Alabama had adopted, provide:

> Gain or loss from the sale, exchange or other disposition of real property or of tangible or intangible personal property constitutes business income if the property while owned by the taxpayer was used in the taxpayer's trade or business. However, if the property was utilized for the production of nonbusiness income or otherwise was removed from the property factor before its sale, exchange or other disposition, the gain or loss will constitute nonbusiness income.

MTC Reg. IV.1.(c)(2).

Do the MTC regulations go beyond a fair reading of UDITPA's language as the *Uniroyal* court held? Or should the court have deferred to the construction of a technical statute by the expert agency charged with its administration?

B. *Policy Justification for the Functional Test of Business Income.* Wholly apart from the question of statutory interpretation, does the functional test make sense as a matter of tax policy? What are the policies underlying the business/nonbusiness income distinction? Does the functional test create constitutional difficulties? What authority would you cite for your answer to that question? What is the relevance to the business income determination of the MTC regulations' focus on whether the property produced nonbusiness income or was included in the property factor? Is it relevant whether the taxpayer deducted expenses associated with the property (e.g., depreciation) from apportionable business income during the time the taxpayer owned the property? Why?

C. *Statutory Modifications of UDITPA's Business Income Definition.* As the *Uniroyal* court observed, several states (including Iowa, New Mexico, and Tennessee) have modified their definitions of business income to overturn judicial rulings that UDITPA's business income definition embodies only a transactional test. Thus the Tennessee legislature amended its statute in 1993 to provide that "business earnings" means:

> earnings arising from transactions and activity in the regular course of the taxpayer's trade or business or earnings from tangible and intangible property if the acquisition, use, management, *or* disposition of the property constitutes an integral part of the taxpayer's regular trade or business operations.

1993 Tenn. Laws, Ch. 282, p. 442, codified at Tenn. Code Ann. § 67–4–2004(3) (Westlaw 2009) (emphasis supplied). Indeed, following the decision in *Uniroyal*, the Alabama legislature effectively overruled it by providing that that business income includes income from the disposition of property that was operationally related to the taxpayer's business. 2002 Ala. Acts (H.B. 7), codified at Ala. Code 40–27–1, Art. IV, 1(a) (Westlaw 2009). Furthermore, both the North Carolina and Pennsylvania legislatures have provided simply that business income means all income that is constitutionally apportionable. N.C. Gen. Stat. § 105–130.4(a)(1) (Westlaw 2009) (defining "apportionable income" as "all income that is apportionable under the United States Constitution"); Pa. Stat. Ann. tit. 72, § 7401(3)(2)(a)(1)(A) (Westlaw 2009). See also Iowa Code Ann. § 422.32.2 (Westlaw 2009) ("It is the intent of the General Assembly to treat as apportionable income all income that may be treated as apportionable business income under the Constitution of the United States").

D. *Should the Business–Nonbusiness Income Distinction Be Abolished Altogether?* Is there any justification for an "independent" state statutory definition of apportionable income that differs from the constitutional definition of apportionability? In other words, is there any justification for a business-nonbusiness income distinction that is discrete from the constitutional line between apportionable and nonapportionable income? For one answer to that question, see Walter Hellerstein, "The Business–Nonbusiness Income Distinction and the Case for Its Abolition," State Tax Notes, Sept. 3, 2001, p. 725. The article contends that there is no policy-based justification for an independent statutory inquiry into apportionability. It further maintains that the existence of such an independent standard has created uncertainty, unfairness, and inconsistency in the law. It concludes that states should adopt of a definition of business income based solely on the constitutional standard of apportionability, as several states have already done. See Note C supra.

b. Apportionment and Allocation of Income From Real and Tangible Personal Property

Apportionment and Allocation of Income from Real and Tangible Personal Property Under UDITPA. Under UDITPA and similar division-of-income statutes, allocable income from real and tangible personal property is attributed to the state in which the property is located. UDITPA §§ 5, 6. Apportionable income from real and tangible personal property is combined with the taxpayer's other apportionable income and apportioned among the states in which the taxpayer carries on the business in which the real or tangible personal property is employed. UDITPA § 9.

Apportionment and Allocation of Income from Real and Tangible Personal Property in Non–UDITPA States. Most—but not all—states have statutes that draw the line between apportionable and allocable income on the basis of UDITPA's business income definition or on a definition of apportionable income that is substantially equivalent to UDITPA's business income definition. Some states, however, allocate income from real and tangible personal property to the state in which it is located regardless of whether the income from the property arises in transactions in the regular course of the taxpayer's trade or business. In Oklahoma, for example, income from mineral leases, royalty interests, oil payments, or other mineral interests is attributed to the state where the mineral property is located. Okla. Stat. Ann. tit. 68, § 2358(A)(4) (Westlaw 2009). In Louisiana, rents and royalties from real and tangible personal property are allocated directly to the state or states where the property is located. La. Rev. Stat. Ann. § 47:287.93(A)(1) (Westlaw 2009).

c. Apportionment and Allocation of Income From Intangible Property in General

Historical Background. Historically, the states treated corporate income from intangibles in one of three ways: (1) they allocated intangible income to a single situs, often to the corporation's legal or commercial domicile,[j] but also to other states where the intangible was deemed to have its "tax situs"; (2) they allocated the intangible income that was not connected with the corporation's business to a single situs and apportioned the intangible income that was connected with the business among all the states in which the corporation carried on its business; or (3) they

---

j. A corporation's legal domicile is the state of its incorporation. A corporation's commercial domicile is "the actual seat of its corporate government." Wheeling Steel Corp. v. Fox, 298 U.S. 193, 56 S.Ct. 773 (1936). UDITPA defines commercial domicile as "the principal place from which the trade or business of the taxpayer is directed or managed." UDITPA § 1(b).

apportioned all intangible income (along with all of the corporation's other income) regardless of its connection to the corporation's business.[k]

There were several established rules for allocating income from intangibles to a single situs. The rule assigning income from intangibles to the owner's domicile had the widest application. It was based on the premise that intangibles were located at their owner's domicile, a notion that grew out of the medieval maxim *mobilia sequuntur personam* (movables follow the person). During the maxim's heyday, the Court could declare that the "maxim * * * is so fixed in the common law of this country * * *, in so far as it relates to intangible property, * * * that it must be treated as settled * * * whether it approve itself to legal philosophic test or not." Blodgett v. Silberman, 277 U.S. 1, 9–10, 48 S.Ct. 410 (1928). Courts routinely invoked the principle as a basis for allocating income from stocks, bonds, patents, copyrights, partnerships, and other intangibles to the owner's domicile. Although the rule came under increasing criticism, see, e.g., First Bank Stock Corp. v. Minnesota, 301 U.S. 234, 237, 57 S.Ct. 677 (1937); Curry v. McCanless, 307 U.S. 357, 367, 59 S.Ct. 900 (1939), and was rejected as an *exclusive* basis for determining states' constitutional power to tax intangibles, Curry, 307 U.S. at 367–74, it nevertheless provided the theoretical underpinning—or, at least the historical explanation—for the state corporate income statutes that assigned intangible income to the taxpayer's domicile. In the context of state corporate income taxation, the corporation's "commercial domicile"—"the actual seat of its corporate government" where "the management functioned" (Wheeling Steel Corp. v. Fox, 298 U.S. 193, 211–12, 56 S.Ct. 773 (1936))—gradually replaced the corporation's "legal domicile"—the state of its incorporation—as the situs to which intangible income was assigned under the *mobilia* principle.

States also allocated income from intangibles to the "business situs" of the intangible on the theory that intangibles "may acquire a situs for taxation other than that of the domicile of their owner if they have become integral parts of some local business." Farmers' Loan & Trust Co. v. Minnesota, 280 U.S. 204, 213, 50 S.Ct. 98 (1930). For example, the Supreme Court held that New York could tax the gain from the sale of a seat on the New York Stock Exchange, even though its owner was domiciled outside the state, because the seat had acquired a business situs in New York apart from its owner. New York ex rel. Whitney v. Graves, 299 U.S. 366, 57 S.Ct. 237 (1937). Trade receivables and other credits arising from the course of business in a state, Liverpool & London & Globe Ins. Co. v. Board of Assessors, 221 U.S. 346, 31 S.Ct. 550 (1911), stock investments actively managed in a state, First Bank Stock Corp. v. Minnesota, 301 U.S. 234, 237–38, 57 S.Ct. 677 (1937), and loans secured by property in a state were likewise found to have a business situs apart from their owner's domicile. In addition to the commercial domicile and business situs principles, the states sometimes relied on other rules for

---

k. Needless to say, the apportionment of nondomiciliary corporations' intangible income was subject to federal constitutional constraints.

allocating corporate income from intangibles such as the location of the payor of interest or dividends or the state in which the transaction creating the obligation occurred.

The Current Framework. The line that most states currently draw between allocable and apportionable income in their corporate income tax regimes in principle makes no distinction between income from intangibles and income from other sources. Under UDITPA and similar statutes that are in force in the majority of states, income is apportionable if it is "business income," i.e., "income arising from transactions and activity in the regular course of the taxpayer's trade or business." UDITPA § 1(a). "Business income" is specifically defined to include "income from * * * *intangible property* if the acquisition, management, and disposition of the property constitute integral parts of the taxpayer's regular trade or business operations." Id. (emphasis supplied).

Under UDITPA and kindred taxing schemes, then, the apportionability of income from intangibles turns entirely on the question whether the income is "business income." When income from intangibles does not constitute "business income," UDITPA and similar statutes usually allocate the income to the taxpayer's commercial domicile. Thus "nonbusiness" interest, dividends, and capital gains from the sale of intangible property are allocated to the taxpayer's commercial domicile. UDITPA §§ 6(a), 7. "Nonbusiness" patent and copyright royalties, on the other hand, are allocable to the state in which the patent or copyright is utilized by the royalty payor, unless the taxpayer is not taxable in such state, in which case the royalties are allocated to the taxpayer's commercial domicile. UDITPA § 8.

Some states do not conform to the UDITPA model. For example, several states continue to allocate all income from intangibles (or from selected intangibles) to a specific state, usually the taxpayer's commercial domicile, Va. Code Ann. §§ 58.1–407,–408 (Westlaw 2009) (dividends), or the business situs of the intangible. Okla. Stat. Ann. tit. 68, § 2358(A)(4)(b) (Westlaw 2005). Other states continue to treat all income (including income from intangibles) as apportionable, see, e.g., Conn. Gen. Stat. Ann. § 12–218 (Westlaw 2009) although their power to do so is subject to constitutional restraints on apportionability.

d. *Apportionment and Allocation of Interest Income*

Traditionally, interest, like most other intangible income, was allocated to the state of the taxpayer's commercial domicile under the *mobilia* principle. Today, while a few states still follow that rule, most states, under UDITPA and similar statutes, allocate only interest earned on assets that are not part of the taxpayer's regular trade or business, and they apportion other interest income.

The Multistate Tax Commission regulations provide:

Interest. Interest income is business income where the intangible with respect to which the interest was received arises out of or was created in the regular course of the taxpayer's trade or business operations or where the purpose for acquiring and holding the intangible is related to or incidental to such trade or business operations.

Example (i): The taxpayer operates a multistate chain of department stores, selling for cash and on credit. Service charges, interest, or time-price differentials and the like are received with respect to installment sales and revolving charge accounts. These amounts are business income.

* * *

Example (v): The taxpayer is engaged in a multistate manufacturing and selling business. The taxpayer usually has working capital and extra cash totaling $200,000 which it regularly invests in short-term interest-bearing securities. The interest income is business income.

Example (vi): In January the taxpayer sold all the stock of a subsidiary for $20,000,000. The funds are placed in an interest-bearing account pending a decision by management as to how the funds are to be utilized. The interest income is nonbusiness income.

MTC Reg. IV.1(c)(3). Can the MTC regulation's position that interest income is business income if the purpose for acquiring or holding the intangible is "incidental" to the taxpayer's trade or business be squared with the language of UDITPA defining business income? Cf. Willamette Industries, Inc. v. Department of Revenue, 331 Or. 311, 15 P.3d 18, 20 (2000) ("We cannot reconcile the statutory standard 'integral' with the disparate standard in the rule 'incidental.'").

SPERRY AND HUTCHINSON CO. v. DEPARTMENT OF REVENUE

Supreme Court of Oregon, 1974.
270 Or. 329, 527 P.2d 729.

O'CONNELL, CHIEF JUSTICE.

This is an appeal under ORS 305.425 from a decree of the Oregon Tax Court. Sperry & Hutchinson Co. v. Dept. of Rev., 5 OTR Adv.Sh. 301 (1973). The question presented is whether income received by plaintiff in the tax years 1961, 1963, 1964 and 1965 as interest on investment securities is apportionable in part to Oregon.

The Sperry & Hutchinson Company (S & H) is incorporated in New Jersey, domiciled in New York, and does business in 48 states including Oregon. S & H's primary business and the only business conducted in Oregon is the sale of a trading stamp promotional service to retailers. During the years in question this enterprise produced substantial revenues, a large part of which S & H invested in fixed income securities. Plaintiff's investment portfolio is divided into three categories: short-term[1] securities held pending use of the funds in the green stamp business; short-term securities held pending acquisition of other companies or favorable developments in the long-term money market, and long-term securities held as an investment. Plaintiff reported the interest received on all three categories as allocable to its domicile rather than apportionable to all states in which it does business. The Department of Revenue held all of the interest to be apportionable, and imposed an additional corporate excise tax for the years in question.

Plaintiff appealed to the Tax Court which held that the interest on the long-term and short-term securities held for investment was not apportionable, but that the interest on short-term securities used in the stamp business was apportionable. The Department of Revenue appeals from the first holding and S & H cross-appeals from the second. We affirm the Tax Court on both the appeal and cross-appeal.

The income from S & H's long-term investments are not apportionable to Oregon because neither the capital invested nor the income derived therefrom is a part of the trading stamp business conducted in this state. This is equally true both under the current Uniform Division of Income for Tax Purposes Act (ORS 314.605 to 314.670) which became effective beginning 1965 and under the pre-existing statute (ORS 314.280). Both statutes impose a tax on an interstate corporation only as to income attributable to Oregon and do so through minor variations on the concept of "unitary business." We hold that because S & H's long-term investment income was neither "closely connected or necessary" under the old statute, nor "income arising from transactions . . . in the regular course of the taxpayer's" trading stamp business under the new statute, the interest is not apportionable. The Department of Revenue seeks to avoid this conclusion by emphasizing that liquidation of the trading stamp enterprise would require S & H to use its long-term investment to redeem all outstanding stamps. Although this may be true, as a factual matter S & H did not draw on this portion of its investment to satisfy its stamp obligations and there is nothing in the record to indicate it shall ever be required to do so.

The short-term securities held pending favorable developments in the long-term money market or acquisition of other businesses are in precisely the same position as the long-term investments. They are not a part of the stamp business and, therefore, not apportionable to Oregon.

The short-term securities held to satisfy the needs for liquid capital in the stamp business are apportionable. These securities are purchased during periods of cash flow surplus and are liquidated when the proceeds, both interest and capital, are needed to meet business obligations during periods of cash flow deficit. Thus, this is business income "arising from transactions and activity in the regular course of the taxpayer's trade or business" and is part of S & H's unitary business.

---

1.   Securities bearing a maturity of less than 12 months.

S & H argues that because this income is the return on an intangible it must be allocated to the legal situs. Nothing in our former law requires such an arbitrary result and our current law expressly prohibits it.[9]

As decreed by the Tax Court, the case must be remanded to the defendant to redetermine the amount of corporate excise tax and interest due the state of Oregon by excluding from plaintiff's apportionable income the interest received on long-term investments and such of plaintiff's short-term holdings as it can show were not used in or held for use in its trading stamp business.

Affirmed.

NOTES AND QUESTIONS

A. *Apportionment and Allocation of Interest in UDITPA States.* Other courts construing UDITPA have followed *Sperry and Hutchinson* when confronted with the question whether interest income is apportionable or allocable. For example, the Colorado Supreme Court relied on *Sperry and Hutchinson* in holding that interest income on short-term loans made to the taxpayer's parent company, out of surplus funds not immediately needed for current operations, was apportionable. Lone Star Steel Co. v. Dolan, 668 P.2d 916 (Colo. 1983). Similarly, the Kentucky Court of Appeals held that the income that railroad companies received from short-term securities purchased with revenue from their railroad business constituted business income. Cincinnati, N.O. & T.P. Ry. v. Kentucky Department of Revenue, 684 S.W.2d 303 (Ky. App. 1984). To the railroads' argument that they were "in the railroad business, not in the securities business," the court responded that "the statute does not limit business income to income from the taxpayers' trade" and that the railroads' "investments are an integral part of their regular business operations." Id. at 305.

In *Sperry and Hutchinson* and in the other cases described in the preceding paragraph, it was the state that sought to characterize the interest income as apportionable business income and the taxpayer that sought to characterize the interest income as allocable. Why was that so? The positions of the taxpayer and the state on this issue, however, are sometimes reversed. In Holiday Inns, Inc. v. Olsen, 692 S.W.2d 850 (Tenn. 1985), for example, it

9. ORS 314.610 provides:

"(1) 'Business income' means income arising from transactions and activity in the regular course of the taxpayer's trade or business and includes income from tangible and intangible property if the acquisition, the management, use or rental, and the disposition of the property constitute integral parts of the taxpayer's regular trade or business operations.

" . . .

"(5) 'Nonbusiness income' means all income other than business income."

ORS 314.625 is fully consistent with this result.

"314.625. Rents and royalties from real or tangible personal property, capital gains, interest, dividends, or patent or copyright royalties, *to the extent that they constitute nonbusiness income,* shall be allocated as provided in ORS 314.630 to 314.645." (Emphasis added.)

S & H also contends that California has reached the opposite conclusion in interpreting its similar law. This is incorrect. The California decisions holding interest income must be allocated are expressly based on a statute unique to that jurisdiction. Fibreboard Paper Products Corp. v. Franchise Tax Bd., 268 Cal.App.2d 363, 370, 74 Cal.Rptr. 46 (1968).

was the taxpayer that sought to have its interest from short-term investments treated as apportionable business income. What does that tell you about Holiday Inns? The court, relying on *Sperry and Hutchinson* and *Cincinnati, N.O. & T.P. Ry.* agreed with Holiday Inns that its interest income was apportionable.

Are these decisions consistent with *Allied–Signal*'s delineation of the constitutional limits on the apportionability of income from intangibles? Is the critical distinction in these cases whether the interest derives from short-term or long-term obligations? Suppose all the securities in *Sperry and Hutchinson* had been 30–year Treasury notes. Any difference in result?

B. *Apportionment and Allocation of Interest Income in Non–UDITPA States.* Although the Minnesota Legislature has amended the state's division-of-income statutes on numerous occasions over the years, the current statute (Minn. Stat. Ann. § 290.17(Subd. 4) (Westlaw 2009)), reflects the long-standing rule in that state that all income that is part of a unitary business is apportionable. In Montgomery Ward & Co. v. Commissioner of Taxation, 276 Minn. 479, 151 N.W.2d 294 (1967), the taxpayer, whose commercial domicile was located outside Minnesota, had accumulated some $300 million in cash out of the earnings of its nationwide general retailing business "in anticipation of a change in the economic climate which would make expansion of the business operation profitable." Id., 151 N.W.2d at 295. Pending this development, the taxpayer invested the funds outside Minnesota in liquid securities, and it did not segregate the funds from its current operating income. The statute provided that income derived from a trade or business carried on within and without the state "including income from intangible property employed in such business" was apportionable. Id. In sustaining the tax commissioner's inclusion of the income from the securities in the apportionable base, the court employed the unitary business principle in determining whether the securities constituted "intangible property employed in" the interstate business.

Montgomery Ward's major contention was that the income, gain, and principal of the securities at issue were not used to pay the expenses and obligations of the business activities, but instead "the primary purpose for which it acquired the intangibles was the *expansion* of its business." Id. at 296 (emphasis in original). The court referred to the facts that the taxpayer carried the intangibles on the corporate balance sheet as current assets and that it commingled the income from the investments with other corporate business income in accounts used to pay ordinary business obligations. The court concluded that the taxpayer had "failed to sustain its burden of proving that the intangibles were not employed in its principal business." Id. The court evidently regarded the income in controversy as on the borderline between apportionable and non-apportionable income, because it remanded the case to give the taxpayer an opportunity to show that "for all practical purposes some part of the amounts up to $300,000,000 held during the period in question and invested in liquid securities was not actually used or usable in its merchandising operation in any significant sense." Id. Accord, Qualls v. Montgomery Ward & Co., Inc., 266 Ark. 207, 585 S.W.2d 18 (1979), in which the court reached the same result under UDITPA.

Is the Minnesota court's reliance on the taxpayer's failure to segregate the investment accounts from its operating accounts a sensible test of whether income from intangibles constitutes apportionable income? If a taxpayer commingles its investment income with its operating income, does this make the income apportionable as a matter of federal constitutional law? See *Woolworth* (discussed pp. 493–95 supra). If a taxpayer separately classifies funds as "long-term investments" on its balance sheet, does this prevent a nondomiciliary state from including the income from such investments in a taxpayer's apportionable tax base as a matter of federal constitutional law? If balance sheet classification should not be the decisive test of apportionability of interest as a matter of federal constitutional or state statutory law, how can taxpayers and taxing authorities deal with the uncertainties created by borderline situations like *Montgomery Ward*? Can you articulate a bright-line test that would avoid these uncertainties but be more responsive to the justification for apportionment?

e. Apportionment and Allocation of Dividend Income

Most of the states exclude some or all dividends from the net income measure of their corporate taxes. The state laws usually adopt, as the starting point for the determination of the corporate income measure, taxable income as defined for federal income tax purposes. In defining taxable income, the Internal Revenue Code allows a deduction from gross income of 100 percent of the dividends received from U.S. domestic corporations with which it could have elected to file a consolidated return. This generally includes corporations 80 percent or more of whose voting stock is owned by the group. I.R.C. §§ 243(a)(3), 1501 et seq. Seventy percent of the dividends received from other domestic corporations are deductible from gross income. I.R.C. § 243(a)(1). Dividends received from foreign corporations are taxable in full, with exceptions in the case of dividends paid by foreign corporations taxable in the United States, foreign personal holding companies, and the like.

In adjusting federal taxable income to state taxable income (before apportionment or allocation), a number of states depart in one way or another from the federal rules. For example, some states exempt all intercorporate dividends (thus providing a more generous rule than that provided by the Internal Revenue Code) and other states provide a dividend deduction more limited than that provided at the federal level. Some states, including California, granted a deduction for intercorporate dividends only if (or to the extent that) the paying corporation was taxable in the state. But such limitations have been struck down as unconstitutionally discriminatory. See, e.g., Farmer Bros. Co. v. Franchise Tax Bd., 108 Cal.App.4th 976, 134 Cal.Rptr.2d 390 (2003), cert. denied, 540 U.S. 1178, 124 S.Ct. 1411 (2004); D.D.I., Inc. v. State, 657 N.W.2d 228 (N.D. 2003).

Under UDITPA and similar statutes, dividends (like interest) are apportioned if they constitute business income and allocated to the taxpayer's commercial domicile if they constitute nonbusiness income. UDITPA

§§ 7, 9. Although some states allocate all dividends (see, e.g., Va. Code Ann. §§ 58.1–407, 58.1–408 (Westlaw 2009)), the overwhelming majority of states provide for both apportionment and allocation of dividends. When dividends are allocated, they are almost always allocated to the taxpayer's commercial domicile.

NOTES AND QUESTIONS

A. *Apportionment and Allocation of Dividends Under UDITPA.* As noted above, dividends are apportionable or allocable under UDITPA depending on whether they constitute business or nonbusiness income. The Multistate Tax Commission's apportionment regulations contain the following provisions interpreting business and nonbusiness dividend income:

> **Dividends.** Dividends are business income where the stock with respect to which the dividends are received arises out of or was acquired in the regular course of the taxpayer's trade or business operations or where the purpose for acquiring and holding the stock is related to or incidental to such trade or business operations.
>
> * * *
>
> Example (ii): The taxpayer is engaged in a multistate manufacturing and wholesaling business. In connection with that business the taxpayer maintains special accounts to cover such items as workmen's compensation claims, etc. A portion of the moneys in those accounts is invested in interest-bearing bonds. The remainder is invested in various common stocks listed on national stock exchanges. Both the interest income and any dividends are business income.
>
> * * *
>
> Example (v): The taxpayer receives dividends from the stock of its subsidiary or affiliate which acts as the marketing agency for products manufactured by the taxpayer. The dividends are business income.
>
> Example (vi): The taxpayer is engaged in a multistate glass manufacturing business. It also holds a portfolio of stock and interest-bearing securities, the acquisition and holding of which are unrelated to the manufacturing business. The dividends and interest income received are nonbusiness income.

MTC Reg. IV.1.(c).(4).

Do these regulations fairly reflect the language of UDITPA's business income definition? Do they accurately reflect constitutional limitations on the apportionment of dividends under *Mobil, ASARCO, Woolworth,* and *Allied–Signal*? In this regard, consider, in particular, the position of the regulations that dividends constitute business income "where the purpose for acquiring and holding the stock is related to or incidental to such trade or business operations."

B. *Allocation of Dividends to the Commercial Domicile.* The rationale behind the allocation of dividends (as well as other income from intangibles) to the state of the recipient's commercial domicile rests squarely on the residence principle of taxation. In substance, it substitutes the commercial domicile—"the actual seat of its corporate government" where "the management function[s]" (Wheeling Steel Corp. v. Fox, 298 U.S. 193, 211–12, 56 S.Ct. 773 (1936))—for the corporation's legal domicile—the state of its incorporation—as the corporation's residence for tax purposes. The justification for allocating a corporation's intangible income to its commercial domicile is simply the application of the established doctrine that a state may tax its residents on their income without regard to its source.

This is not to suggest, however, that the allocation of intangibles to the taxpayer's commercial domicile may not in some cases be reinforced by, if not independently justified by, source-based considerations. Thus if a corporation's investment portfolio, unrelated to its operations, is actively managed at its commercial domicile, as it typically would be, one could justify assigning the income from such portfolio to the commercial domicile under a source-based rationale, namely, that the income-producing activity—the portfolio management—occurred in the state of commercial domicile. It is important to recognize, however, that this is *not* the theoretical basis for the commercial domicile rule. For if the corporation managed its investment portfolio in some state other than its commercial domicile, the commercial domicile would retain its power to tax such income regardless of source, except insofar as the other state's power to tax the portfolio income under source-based principles confines the domiciliary state's power. See Walter Hellerstein, "State Taxation of Corporate Income from Intangibles: *Allied–Signal* and Beyond," 48 Tax L. Rev. 739, 811 (1993).

C. *Separate Investment Business.* When a taxpayer carries on an investment business separate from its operating business, how should dividends, as well as other investment income, be treated? Should the income be apportioned along with the taxpayer's other operating income? Allocated to the taxpayer's commercial domicile? Apportioned separately from the taxpayer's other income? In Louis Dreyfus Corp. v. Huddleston, 933 S.W.2d 460 (Tenn. App. 1996), the court held that a taxpayer could not be required to include income from its out-of-state securities trading business in its apportionable tax base when the only activity conducted in the state was a commodities trading operation.

D. *Apportionment of Dividends by Reference to the State in Which the Dividend Paying Corporation Conducts Its Business.* The theory on which virtually all states rest their power to tax intangible income earned by nondomiciliary corporations is that the income is connected in one way or another with the corporations' activities in the taxing state. There is, however, a theoretical basis for taxing some forms of intangible income that has nothing to do with the corporate taxpayer's activities in the taxing state. A few jurisdictions, most significantly New York State and New York City, focus on the "investee's" rather than the investor's activities as the basis for taxing intangible investment income such as dividends, interest, and capital gains. N.Y. Tax Law § 210(3)(b) (Westlaw 2009); N.Y. City Admin. Code § 11–604(3)(b) (Westlaw 2009). The New York franchise tax law is based on the concept that stock and the income it produces should be attributed to the state in which the corporation whose stock is held conducts its business. Dividends from stocks of nonsubsidiary corporations (New York does not tax dividends paid by subsidiaries), as well as other "investment income," are attributed to New York by reference to the payor corporation's apportionment percentage. N.Y. Tax Law § 210(3)(b) (Westlaw 2009).

E. *A Critique of Allocation Allocating and Apportioning Dividends.* Consider the following testimony before a congressional committee considering federal legislation concerning state tax apportionment:

> The controversy concerning the taxation of intercorporate dividends and the definition of business and nonbusiness income, as those terms are used in UDITPA, needs to be approached by recognizing that there are dividends and dividends. Thus, if a manufacturing company receives dividends from its wholly-owned subsidiary which is engaged principally in selling the product of the parent company, the dividends constitute a part of the profits derived from the parent-subsidiary unitary business. Such profits constitute operating income, income of the business, just as they would if the enterprise were conducted through sales branches, instead of a subsidiary. Such dividends ought to be apportioned as part of the basic operating income of the enterprise and, therefore, should fall within the UDITPA classification as business income.
>
> As I have already indicated [in the earlier part of the testimony], the realistic and fiscally sound tax treatment of such an enterprise is to combine or consolidate the income of the parent and selling subsidiary for purposes of unitary apportionment. The dividend issue would then disappear, since the dividends would be eliminated as an intercompany item. If, however, neither the State nor the taxpayer exercises the option granted by the type of statute which it is assumed would be in force to utilize the combined or consolidated approach, or, if for one reason or another, the taxpayer does not qualify under the statutory provision for combination, the character of the dividend income on a separate parent company basis, nevertheless, does not, in my thinking, change; it is still operating income which ought to be apportioned in taxing the recipient.
>
> When we turn, however, to dividends paid by nonaffiliates, or by corporations which are not integral parts of the unitary enterprise, the situation will ordinarily be different. Apart from a corporation engaged in the securities business, dividends received from investments in nonaffiliated corporations, or from affiliates in a conglomerate, which are not a part of the unitary enterprise, constitute investment income. Such income does not flow from the unitary basic operating activities, of which the taxpayer is a part. To apportion that type of dividend income by reference to factors such as the location of the taxpayer's plant and inventory of goods, the States in which its manufacturing employees and its salesmen operate, the location of its customers, would appear to me to be distorting, and simply would not reflect the activities of the taxpayer which produced the non-unitary dividends, or other factors relevant to the attribution of the dividends to particular States.
>
> If this conclusion is accepted, the commercial domicile rule which has been traditionally applied to income from intangibles, reflects a good deal of wisdom. For that State has the dominant claim to tax such non-operating dividend income, since the activities relating to the investment,

the control and management of the stocks which produced the dividend income typically take place at the executive offices, where the financial work is carried on. Consequently, in the language of UDITPA, such investment or non-operating dividend income ought to be treated as nonbusiness income and be allocated to the commercial domicile.

Hearings Before the Subcomm. on State Taxation of Interstate Commerce of the Senate Finance Committee, 93rd Cong., 1st Sess. 154, 163 (1973) (testimony of Jerome R. Hellerstein).

In *Mobil Oil* (pp. 473–89 supra), the Supreme Court approved the principle that dividends are not apportionable to a nondomiciliary state unless the dividend payors are engaged in a unitary business with the dividend recipients. In *ASARCO* (discussed pp. 491–93 supra) and *Woolworth* (discussed pp. 493–95 supra), the Court applied this principle and invalidated taxes imposed by a nondomiciliary state on dividends received by foreign corporations, on the ground that the payors were not part of the unitary business of the dividend recipients. In *Allied–Signal* (pp. 420–33 supra), however, the Court made it clear that the apportionability of intangible income (including dividends) was not limited to the case in which there was "payor-payee" unity. Other types of dividends—namely, those arising from investments that serve an "operational function" in the payee's business—are apportionable even if the payor is not engaged in a unitary business with the payee. Accordingly, dividends from temporary investments of working capital or other current funds held for normal operating uses and dividends received from stocks falling within the *Corn Products* doctrine are plainly apportionable, even if the payor of the dividends is not unitary with the payee.[1]

f. Apportionment and Allocation of Capital Gains and Losses

The rules for apportioning and allocating capital gains and losses from sales of intangible personal property are essentially the same as the rules applicable to interest and dividends. In states adopting UDITPA and similar statutes, such gains are apportioned if they constitute business income and allocated to the taxpayer's commercial domicile if they constitute nonbusiness income. UDITPA §§ 6(c), 9. A few states treat all capital gains from intangibles as allocable. See, e.g., Okla. Stat. Ann. tit. 68, § 2358(A)(4)(b) (Westlaw 2009). In those states whose statutes provide for apportionment of all income, the apportionability of intangible capital gains income is determined by constitutional restraints. Indeed, *Allied–*

---

1. In Corn Products Refining Co. v. Commissioner, 350 U.S. 46, 76 S.Ct. 20 (1955), the Court held that "profits and losses arising from the everyday operation of a business" should be treated as ordinary income rather than capital gain for federal income tax purposes, even if those profits arose from the sale of property that constituted a capital asset under a literal reading of the Internal Revenue Code. Id., 350 U.S. at 52. In Container Corp. of America v. Franchise Tax Bd., 463 U.S. 159, 103 S.Ct. 2933 (1983), the Court cited *Corn Products* in adverting to the fact that "capital transactions can serve either an investment function or an operational function." Id., 463 U.S. at 180 n.19. Hence income from intangible assets used in the present conduct of the business—for example, stock in a corporation acquired to secure a source of supply—is apportionable *Corn Products* income. Although the Court subsequently limited the scope of the *Corn Products* doctrine for federal income tax purposes in Arkansas Best Corp. v. Commissioner, 485 U.S. 212, 108 S.Ct. 971 (1988), this limitation has no effect on its application to apportionability of income for state tax purposes.

Signal (pp. 420–33 supra), the leading case on this question, involved the New Jersey statute, which then provided that all income of a multistate business is apportionable. The New Jersey statute has since been amended to recognize the constitutional limitations on the state's power to treat all income as apportionable and to provide, in addition, that "100% of the nonoperational income of a taxpayer that has its principal place from which the trade or business of the taxpayer is directed or managed in this State shall be specifically assigned to this State to the extent permitted under the Constitution and statutes of the United States." N.J. Rev. Stat. Ann. § 54:10A–6.1 (Westlaw 2009).

One of the most hotly contested issues in recent years involving capital gains from intangibles is whether the extraordinary or unusual disposition of stock in a subsidiary or affiliate constitutes business or nonbusiness income under the "transactional" or "functional" test of business income under UDITPA. See Section B(7)(a) supra. If the affiliate whose stock the taxpayer sold was part of the taxpayer's business, then the gain will ordinarily constitute business income under the "functional" test. But suppose the state has adopted the transactional test. Under what circumstances, if any, would the capital gains be apportionable? See Atlantic Richfield Co. v. State, 198 Colo. 413, 601 P.2d 628 (1979).

g. *Apportionment and Allocation of Income From Patents, Copyrights, and Similar Intangibles*

Under UDITPA and similar statutes, the business/nonbusiness income distinction determines whether patent and copyright royalties are apportionable or allocable. When patent and copyright royalties are allocable, they are not automatically assigned to the taxpayer's commercial domicile, as in the case of interest, dividends, and capital gains from intangibles. Rather they are allocated to a state "if and to the extent that the patent or copyright is utilized by the payer in the state" (UDITPA § 8(a)), unless the taxpayer is not taxable in that state, in which case they are allocated to the taxpayer's commercial domicile. Id. Why are patent and copyright royalties treated differently from other intangible income (interest, dividends, and capital gains) for allocation purposes?

The Multistate Tax Commission regulations concerning patent and copyright royalties provide as follows:

> **Patent and copyright royalties**. Patent and copyright royalties are business income where the patent or copyright with respect to which the royalties were received arises out of or was created in the regular course of the taxpayer's trade or business operations or where the purpose for acquiring and holding the patent or copyright is related to or incidental to such trade or business operations.
>
> Example (i): The taxpayer is engaged in the multistate business of manufacturing and selling industrial chemicals. In connection with that business the taxpayer obtained patents on certain of its products. The taxpayer licensed the production of the chemicals in foreign

countries, in return for which the taxpayer receives royalties. The royalties received by the taxpayer are business income.

Example (ii): The taxpayer is engaged in the music publishing business and holds copyrights on numerous songs. The taxpayer acquires the assets of a smaller publishing company, including music copyrights. These acquired copyrights are thereafter used by the taxpayer in its business. Any royalties received on these copyrights are business income.

Example (iii): Same as example (ii), except that the acquired company also held the patent on a type of phonograph needle. The taxpayer does not manufacture or sell phonographs or phonograph equipment. Any royalties received on the patent would be nonbusiness income.

MTC Reg. IV.1(c)(5). Do these regulations fairly implement the language of UDITPA? Do they fall within federal constitutional limitations on apportionability?

The Montana Supreme Court followed the MTC regulations in holding that royalties derived from patents and copyrights developed by a mining company's research department constituted apportionable business income. The court concluded that "[t]his income is derived from sources that are integral portions of * * * [the taxpayer's] business." Montana Dept. of Revenue v. American Smelting & Refining Co. (ASARCO), 173 Mont. 316, 567 P.2d 901, 907 (1977), appeal dismissed, 434 U.S. 1042, 98 S.Ct. 884 (1978). Similarly, the Maryland Court of Appeals, construing a non-UDITPA statute, sustained the apportionability of royalties that Xerox received from out-of-state licensees for the use of its patents, trademarks, and copyrights, because of the close relationship of these royalties to Xerox's in-state copier-related operations. Xerox Corp. v. Comptroller, 290 Md. 126, 428 A.2d 1208 (1981).

8. THE APPORTIONMENT FORMULA: DELINEATION OF THE FACTORS

Once a taxpayer has determined its apportionable income under the state division-of-income rules described above, the taxpayer must then apportion this tax base among the states in which it carries on its activities. We have already considered the federal constitutional "fair apportionment" limitations on the states' application of formulas to a unitary tax base—limitations that are loose at best. See pp. 441–521 supra. In this section, we examine the individual factors of the apportionment formulas and the issues that they raise.

Although a the growing number of states have adopted single-factor sales formulas (see *Moorman*, pp. 457–69 supra), most states continue to employ the familiar three-factor formula of property, payroll, and receipts for apportioning net income. See Table 2 supra. As noted above, however, the weight that the states accord to these factors, as well as their precise

CK

ЛО

definition, can vary from state to state. Id. Moreover, even when states have adopted identical apportionment factors, state courts and tax administrators sometimes construe them in different ways.

a. Property Factor

STATE OF ALASKA, DEPARTMENT OF REVENUE v. AMOCO PRODUCTION COMPANY

Supreme Court of Alaska, 1984.
676 P.2d 595.

BURKE, CHIEF JUSTICE.

Amoco Production Company [Amoco], a wholly owned subsidiary of Standard Oil Company of Indiana, is incorporated in Delaware and licensed to do business in Alaska. Amoco's principal activities in Alaska are the exploration for and the production of oil and gas. * * *

* * *

II. Inclusion of Non–Producing Leaseholds in the Apportionment Formula.

Amoco contends that the value of its leaseholds in Alaska that are not producing oil or gas should not have been included in the apportionment formula's property factor. It argues first that such leaseholds are not included within the statutory definition of the property factor, which requires property to be "used." Alternatively, even if within the statute, Amoco argues that inclusion of their value in the apportionment formula violates Amoco's due process rights.

The Department of Revenue rejected both these arguments. The superior court, however, reversed the Department of Revenue. It found that non-producing leaseholds were not "used" as required by the statute. It therefore remanded the case to the Department to recompute income tax liability with these leases excluded from the property factor. For the reasons discussed below, we reverse on this issue. We hold the non-producing leases were properly included in the property factor under the statute, and that such inclusion is constitutional.

A. Statutory Analysis

In 1959, Alaska substantially adopted the Uniform Division of Income for Tax Purposes Act [UDITPA] which was contained in AS 43.20.051–.150 (repealed 1975). AS 43.20.130 provided for the allocation of business income through use of a three factor apportionment formula. AS 43.20.130 provided in part:

(a) All business income which cannot be directly apportioned and allocated to this state shall be apportioned to this state by multiplying the income by a fraction, the numerator of which is the property factor plus the payroll factor plus the sales factor, and the denominator which is three.

(b) *The property factor is a fraction, the numerator of which is the average value of the taxpayer's real and tangible personal property owned or rented and used* in this state during the tax period and the denominator of which is the average value of all the taxpayer's real and tangible personal property *owned or rented and used* during the tax period....

(Emphasis added).

The relevant regulations in effect during most of the tax years in question were 15 AAC 10.100 and .120 (effective 5/25/72, repealed 1978). 15 AAC 10.100 provided in part:

(b) The term "real and tangible personal property" includes lands, buildings, machinery, stocks of goods, equipment, and other real and tangible personal property *used in connection with the production of business income....*

(Emphasis added). 15 AAC 10.120 provided in part:

(a) The numerator of the property factor shall include the average value of the taxpayer's real and tangible personal property in this state during the tax period *used, is available for use, or is capable of being used for the production of business income.* (Emphasis added).[4]

The issue, therefore, is whether oil and gas leaseholds on which no recoverable quantities of oil and gas have yet been discovered are "used" for purposes of AS 43.20.130(b). We conclude that when the objective of the apportionment formula is considered, such leaseholds are properly included.

The economic theory underlying the formula is that the dollar value of the unitary business' capital investments, labor costs, and sales within the state, when compared to the business' total capital investments, labor costs and sales everywhere will roughly reflect the fraction of total income that is attributable to the business' in-state activities. These property, payroll and sales factors are merely indicative of the business' income producing capabilities. They are not intended to reflect the business' precise sources of income for any particular year. "The factors in an apportionment formula represent an attempt to relate the taxpayer's presence within the state to his presence everywhere." Peckron, Apportionment Factors Employed by States in the Computation of Corporate Income Tax, 3 J. Corp. Tax'n 388, 392 (1977); See State Taxation of Interstate Businesses and the Multistate Tax Compact: The Search for a Delicate Uniformity, 11 Colum.J.L. & Soc.Probs. 231, 236 (1975). "[E]con-

---

4. These regulations were repealed and replaced in 1978 with 15 AAC 19.141, .151 and .171. Amoco relied heavily upon the 1978 regulation, which states that property under construction during the tax period must be excluded from the property factor until the property is actually used in the regular course of the taxpayer's business. 15 AAC 19.151(b). This regulation, however, is of little relevance to the issue before the court since it was not effective during the tax years in question.

omists agree that property, representing the cost of capital, is one element in the production of income." Note, State Taxation of Interstate Commerce and Apportionment of Income: The Iowa Formula Under Attack, 4 J.Corp.L. 125, 134 (1978). "Furthermore, the value of property used by a taxpayer in a particular state, whether owned or leased, is some measure of the relative importance of the taxpayer's activities in that state." Keesling and Warren, California's Uniform Division of Income for Tax Purposes Act, 15 UCLA L.Rev. 655, 657 (1967).

* * *

The non-producing oil and gas leases are an example of nonobvious contributions to Amoco's production of income. The exploration and development of what later turn out to be unproductive oil or gas wells is a necessary and integral part of Amoco's eventual discovery and exploration of productive oil and gas wells. To say that only property values associated with oil and gas leases which are known to contain recoverable quantities of oil and gas should be included within the property factor is to ignore the actual business activities that lead up to Amoco's ability to derive oil and gas income.[7] As was stated in Superior Oil Co. v. Franchise Tax Board, 60 Cal.2d 406, 34 Cal.Rptr. 545, 551, 386 P.2d 33, 39 (1963), "[i]t must also be considered that each producing well in a particular state is the end product of interstate activities which may involve many other unproductive wells in many other states."[8]

The value of non-producing leaseholds is includable in the property factor of the apportionment formula. To interpret the word "used" contained in AS 43.20.130(b) to exclude such leaseholds is overly restrictive and not consonant with the realities of oil and gas production. We therefore reverse the superior court's holding on this issue and instead affirm the agency's decision that non-producing oil and gas leases are "used" by Amoco within the meaning of AS 43.20.130(b).

---

7. Of some relevance is the fact that the value included in the apportionment formula reflects the fact that the leases are not producing. AS 43.20.130(b) provided that rented property includable within the property factor is valued at "eight times the net annual rental rate." In the years in which the lessee has not drilled and obtained production, a flat rate delay rental is assessed. Only after a well is successfully drilled will the lessee pay additional rental in the form of a royalty. In addition to these two separate rents, the lessee pays a lease bonus at the outset which is added to the property factor but not multiplied by eight.

8. The California State Board of Equalization found non-producing leaseholds to be "used" within the meaning of the formulary apportionment statute in that state. Appeal of Richfield Oil Corporation, (California State Board of Equalization, November 17, 1964); Appeal of Union Oil Company of California, (California State Board of Equalization, November 17, 1964). In the *Richfield Oil* decision, the California Board noted the value of non-producing leases:

Aside from the fact that the acquisition of new lands, much of which will prove to be unproductive, is an essential element in the process of discovering new oil sources, appellant has vividly demonstrated the many other contributions that such acreage makes to the ultimate realization of income. Appellant is not simply acquiring land and blindly drilling holes. Every investment that it makes is a reasoned decision, a decision made on the best available information. Without the information derived from unproductive as well as productive areas, it is reasonable to believe that the effectiveness and efficiency of appellant's exploration program would be diminished with a resulting increase in the cost of producing crude oil.

B. Constitutionality

* * *

When the non-producing leaseholds are included in the property factor, the result is the apportionment of approximately .3% more world-wide income to Alaska. Such increase does not result in income attribution to Alaska out of all appropriate proportions to the business transacted in the state. * * *

AFFIRMED in part; REVERSED in part.

NOTES AND QUESTIONS

A. *Inclusion in Property Factor of Property "Available for Use" or "Capable of Being Used" to Produce Apportionable Income.* Insofar as the Alaska regulations required the inclusion in the property factor of property that "is available for use, or is capable of being used for the production of business income," do they go beyond the plain language of UDITPA? Is the inclusion of such property in the property factor consistent with the underlying theory of the property factor? What is that theory? If property is not actually being used to produce business income, why should it be used to apportion such income?

The Multistate Tax Commission's regulations are consistent with the Alaska regulation quoted in the *Amoco* case. They provide that "[p]roperty shall be included in the property factor if it is actually used or is available for or capable of being used during the tax period in the regular course of the trade or business of the taxpayer." MTC Reg. IV.10.(b). At the same time, however, these regulations provide that "[p]roperty or equipment under construction * * * shall be excluded from the factor until such property is actually used in the regular course of the trade or business of the taxpayer." Id. Are these two positions taken by the MTC regulations logically consistent? Why should "actual use" be the standard for inclusion in the latter case but not in the former? Wholly apart from the merits of the MTC and Alaska regulations, did the court in *Amoco* rely on those regulations in reaching its conclusion?

In Commissioner of Revenue v. Exxon Corp., 407 Mass. 17, 551 N.E.2d 36 (1990), the Massachusetts Supreme Court did rely on regulations substantially identical to the MTC regulations in reaching a conclusion similar to that reached by the *Amoco* court. In *Exxon*, it was the *taxpayer*—not the state (as in *Amoco*)—that invoked the regulations? Why? Does it surprise you that Massachusetts subsequently eliminated the regulation in question? What does that tell you about the relationship of state fiscal policy to sound apportionment theory?

B. *The Limitation of the Property Factor to Real and Tangible Personal Property.* The property factor normally includes only real and tangible personal property. See UDITPA § 10. Indeed, except in the case of special industries (e.g., banking), see Section B(10) infra, no state takes account of intangible property in the property factor of the standard three-factor formula. The historical explanation for the exclusion of intangible property from the property factor lies in the fact that states adopted apportionment formulas to divide the operating income of mercantile and manufacturing businesses. States typically regarded the intangible income of such businesses as discrete from their "trading income," and they generally assigned it to a single situs under the doctrine of *mobilia sequuntur personam* or the "business situs" doctrine. See pp. 558–59 supra. In short, since states generally excluded income from intangibles from the apportionable tax base, there was no necessity of taking account of intangible property in the apportionment factor. Moreover, the selection of the state to which intangibles are to be attributed, if they are included in the property factor, is fraught with exceptional complications. Nevertheless, with the growing importance of income from intangibles, the exclusion of intangible property from the property factor has come under increasing challenge, particularly in cases in which intangible income is a significant component of a taxpayer's tax base. See, e.g., Crocker Equipment Leasing, Inc. v. Department of Revenue, 314 Or. 122, 838 P.2d 552 (1992) (taxpayer deriving most of its income from intangible property was entitled under "equitable apportionment" provision (UDITPA § 18) to adjust property factor by including value of intangible property); see generally Walter Hellerstein, "State Taxation of Corporate Income From Intangibles: *Allied–Signal* and Beyond," 48 Tax L. Rev. 739, 841–48 (1993).

C. *Rented Property in the Property Factor.* Traditionally, the property factor did not take account of rented property; it included only property owned by the taxpayer. This tended to create unwarranted discrepancies between taxpayers that owned the plants, stores, or office buildings they used in their operations, and those that leased the property. With the extensive employment of sale-leasebacks and the widespread use of leasing, in form if not in substance, of trucks, airplanes, duplicating equipment, computers, and other personalty, many states changed their laws to include in the property factor rented property used in the business. See, e.g., UDITPA § 10. The value of rented property is usually determined by a multiple of net rents (gross rents paid less rents received on subrentals of the property), almost always at eight times rentals. All States Tax Guide (RIA) ¶ 226–A (2009) (chart).

If L rents property to T, UDITPA makes it clear that T must include the property in its property factor at eight times rentals. But what about L? The Ohio Supreme Court held that a taxpayer, which rented property to lessees in the state, was not required to include the property in its property factor because the property, although "owned or rented" by the taxpayer, was not "used in the trade or business in this state" by the taxpayer under Ohio's UDITPA-type property factor. Illinois Tool Works v. Lindley, 70 Ohio St.2d 175, 436 N.E.2d 220 (1982). The court agreed with the taxpayer that since it did not physically use the property in the state and the lessee was required to include the leased property in the property numerator, the value of the property was not includable in the taxpayer's Ohio property numerator. The court was impressed by the argument that "two people cannot own the same property," id., 436 N.E.2d at 222, and concerned by the fact that to require the lessor to include the property in its numerator would be a form of double counting.

But was the court right? Does the fact that T uses leased property in its business to generate apportionable income carry with it the implication that L *cannot* use the same property in its business to generate its own apportionable income? If L is in the business of purchasing and renting fleets of automobiles to others, and L leases a fleet of cars to T for T to use in its rent-a-car business, is L using the property any less than T is? From a theoretical standpoint, insofar as L has apportionable rental income from the lease of its automobiles, should not the location of the property that produces such income be used to apportion L's income among the states?[m]

D. *Property in Transit and Mobile Property.* The MTC regulations provide that

> [p]roperty in transit between locations of the taxpayer to which it belongs shall be considered to be at the destination for purposes of the property factor. Property in transit between a buyer and seller which is included by a taxpayer in the denominator of its property factor in accordance with its regular accounting practices shall be included in the numerator according to the state of destination.

MTC Reg. IV.10.(d). The laws and regulations of many states, however, are silent on the question of how to treat inventory in transit between the states. In some states, inventory in transit between the taxing state and any other state is excluded from both the numerator and the denominator of the factor.

A related question arises in the case of mobile property, such as trucks, automobiles, construction equipment, and airplanes used in the conduct of the taxpayer's business. Some states apportion the value of the equipment to the numerator to the extent the equipment is used in the states, by methods such as percentage, mileage, or time factors, and include the full value of the property in the denominator. The language of most state statutes, including UDITPA, which defines the property factor as the ratio of "the taxpayer's real and tangible personal property owned or rented and used in this state during the tax period" to the total everywhere (UDITPA § 10), appears to lend itself to such apportionment. Indeed, the MTC regulations provide that "[t]he value of mobile or movable property * * * located within and without this state during the tax period shall be determined for purposes of the numerator of the factor on the basis of total time within the state during the tax period." MTC Reg. IV.10.(d).

E. *Valuation of Property.* Most states determine the value of the property in the property factor at original cost. Multistate Corporate Income Tax Guide (CCH) ¶ 600–710 (2009) (chart), available in CCH Internet Tax Research Network; UDITPA § 11. A few states use depreciated book value or fair market value as the valuation standard. The National Conference of Commissioners on Uniform State Laws, which drafted UDITPA, justified its use of original cost, although "admittedly arbitrary," on the ground of ease of compliance. UDITPA § 11 (comment). This figure is usually readily ascertain-

---

m. In 2003, Ohio modified its property factor specifically to include in the lessor's property factor property that the lessor rents to others when the property generates business income, thereby effectively reversing the *Illinois Tool Works* decision. See Ohio Rev. Code Ann. 5733.05(B)(2)(a) (Westlaw 2009).

able, and its use eliminates "any differences due to varying methods of depreciation." Id. Moreover, since the same standard applies to both in-state and out-of-state property, any distortion resulting from the use of undepreciated cost would not ordinarily be significant. Most statutes provide that property values are to be determined by averaging values at the beginning and end of the taxable year, but the tax administrator is usually authorized, in appropriate cases, to permit or require monthly or other averaging of values over the year. UDITPA § 12.

b. *Payroll Factor*

Except for those states using single-factor sales formulas, all the states that impose corporate taxes measured by net income use a payroll factor, either in the regular state formula, or in the optional formula that is occasionally authorized. Table 2, pp. 540–41 supra. The payroll factor, which is somewhat more varied over the country than the property factor, raises fewer controversial questions. "Compensation," the usual statutory term used, is defined by UDITPA as "wages, salaries, commissions and any other form of remuneration paid to employees for personal services," UDITPA § 1(c), and most other state laws adopt essentially the same language. These provisions track the definition of wages in the Federal Unemployment Tax Act and are generally construed in accordance with the interpretation of that Act by the Internal Revenue Service, as embracing all compensation for services as an employee, whether paid in cash or in kind, which is treated as gross income for federal income tax purposes.

UDITPA and most other state statutes attribute payroll to the taxing state if (1) the services are performed entirely within the state; or (2) the services are performed both within and without the state and (a) the service performed without the state is incidental to the service performed within the state, (b) the base of operations, or, if there is no base of operations, the place from which the service is directed or controlled, is in the state, or (c) the base of operations, or the place from which the service is directed or controlled, is not in any state in which the employee performs services, but his residence is in the state. UDITPA § 14. This test does not fractionate the compensation of any individual employee who renders services in more than one state, as is done, for example, in some states with respect to the property factor in dealing with construction equipment and other movable property.

In a few states compensation paid to executive officers is not taken into account in the payroll factor, All States Tax Guide (RIA) ¶ 226 (2009) (chart), presumably on the theory that high executive salaries tend to distort the payroll factor. The states are divided on the question whether deferred compensation (e.g., income from I.R.C. § 401(k) plans) is reflected in the payroll factor.

CINCINNATI, NEW ORLEANS AND TEXAS PACIFIC RAILWAY COMPANY v. KENTUCKY DEPARTMENT OF REVENUE

Court of Appeals of Kentucky, 1984.
684 S.W.2d 303, discretionary review denied Feb. 21, 1985.

COMBS, JUDGE.

The appellants, Southern Railway Company, and its wholly-owned subsidiary, Cincinnati, New Orleans and Texas Pacific Railway Company, operated railroads in Kentucky and other states.

* * *

Because the appellants do business in Kentucky and other states, their income must be apportioned for income tax purposes. KRS 141.120 is the Kentucky version of the Uniform Division of Income for Tax Purposes Act. Generally, the statute provides that income taxable by Kentucky is a proportion of business income that is attributable to the taxpayer's business activities in Kentucky. The proportion is determined by a formula in which property, payroll and sales in Kentucky are compared with the total property, payroll and sales of the multi-state business. Non-business income is taxable by Kentucky to the extent that the income-producing property is located or used in this state.

The appellants along with other subsidiaries of Southern operate their railroads by "pooling." The corporations have common management and the employees of one company may do work for another. When an employee of one company does work for another, the company compensating the employee is reimbursed by the company for whom the labor is performed.

The trial court held that compensation of Southern's employees for services performed for the benefit of the subsidiary is to be included in the apportionment of Southern's income, and not in the apportionment of the subsidiary's income. Appellants argue that the compensation should be included in the formula of the company for which the service was performed.

Although we have found no case law on point, the Department has interpreted in prior audits the statute in the manner urged by appellants. An administrative agency's interpretation of the law is of great weight, and in this case the General Assembly has not by amendment or adoption of superseding statutes mandated a different interpretation.

The purpose of KRS 141.120 is to adopt a formula to determine the business income attributable to activity in Kentucky. To include the compensation of the employees in the formula of the company for whom service was performed would promote this purpose.

The payroll factor is determined by comparing the "compensation" paid in Kentucky and the total "compensation" paid. KRS 141.120(1)(c) defines compensation as follows:

... wages, salaries, commissions, and any other form of remuneration paid or payable to employees for personal service.

Because the subsidiary indirectly compensated the employees whose activities they controlled when the employees performed services for them and because Southern did not profit from loaning their employees to the subsidiary, we find that the subsidiary was the employer of Southern's employees when they performed services for the subsidiary. On this issue we agree with the board and reverse the trial court.

* * *

NOTES AND QUESTIONS

A. Is *Cincinnati, New Orleans* faithful to the language of UDITPA? To the policy underlying the payroll factor? What is that policy? How far does the principle of the *Cincinnati, New Orleans* case extend? If payroll should be attributed to the taxpayer for which services are actually performed rather than to the taxpayer that pays the employees, should not the services of independent contractors be included in the taxpayer's payroll factor? For example, if a company outsources its word processing operations to Kelly Services, Inc., should not the amounts paid to Kelly Services be included in the taxpayer's payroll factor? How is the Kelly Services hypothetical different from *Cincinnati, New Orleans*? What are the limits of a payroll attribution test based on an inquiry into the question whether a taxpayer "indirectly compensated the employees whose activities they controlled when the employees performed services for them"?

Does the *Cincinnati, New Orleans* opinion pay sufficient attention to the administrative benefits of a payroll factor based largely on a "paper" inquiry? Does not the abandonment of the simple inquiry into which entity issues an employee its checks, withholds taxes, issues W–2 forms, and makes contributions to state unemployment compensation funds lead to serious administrative problems under the payroll factor? Can you articulate a narrower view of *Cincinnati, New Orleans* that would avoid the administrative difficulties suggested by the foregoing questions?

In contrast to *Cincinnati, New Orleans*, the Missouri Supreme Court took a more formalistic approach to the payroll attribution issue in Philip Morris, Inc. v. Director of Revenue, 760 S.W.2d 888 (Mo. 1988). Phillip Morris Company had elected to pay the salaries of the top officials of its subsidiary, the Seven–Up Company. It nevertheless argued that their compensation should be attributed to Seven–Up for payroll purposes because "the evidence shows that the employees are Seven–Up's employees, and not its employees, because they perform all of their duties for the benefit of Seven–Up, and that that corporation has the sole right of control over them." Id. at 890. The court rejected this claim on the ground that the objective indicia of employment—including the fact that the compensation was reported by Phillip Morris for unemployment compensation purposes—justified the tax administrator's position that the compensation should be attributed to Phillip Morris for payroll purposes. Are *Cincinnati, New Orleans* and *Philip Morris* reconcilable? If not, which court got it right?

B. *Taxpayers Using Independent Contractors in Lieu of Employees.* Most states exclude payments to independent contractors from the payroll factor. All States Tax Guide (RIA) ¶ 226 (2009) (chart). In UPS Worldwide Forwarding, Inc. v. Commonwealth, 843 A.2d 438 (Pa. Commw. 2004), UPS had no employees. All of its services were performed by affiliated companies and independent contractors. UPS argued that it should be permitted to use a payroll factor (along with the sales and property factor) to apportion its income on the theory that the amounts it transferred to its affiliate, whose employees performed services for the taxpayer, in substance amounted to payroll expenses. The court rejected the argument and agreed with the state that the payroll factor should be eliminated. The court observed: "Because Taxpayer did not have any employees, we agree with the Commonwealth that, although Taxpayer had an expense charged to it, it could not have paid compensation as that term is defined in the [statute] and had no *payroll* expenses." Id. at 442 (emphasis in original). As a matter of good tax policy, should payments to independent contractors be given weight in computing a taxpayer's apportionment ratio? If your answer is yes, should the taxpayer's other expenses (not already included in the property or payroll factors) also be given weight in some manner, for example, in a separate "expense factor"?

c. *Receipts or Sales Factor*

The receipts or sales factor has been at the center of the major controversies that have arisen in the implementation of the apportionment factors. All of the states with corporate taxes measured by net income use a receipts or sales factor. The terminology varies. UDITPA and some non-UDITPA state statutes use the narrow term "sales factor"; others use the broader term "receipts factor." Whatever the terminology, the factor has a much broader scope than receipts from sales of property. It covers income from services, rentals, royalties, and business operations generally. See UDITPA § 1(g) ("'sales' means all gross receipts of the taxpayer not allocated * * * "). The drafters of UDITPA and similar statutes may have adopted the narrow term "sales factor" because the three-factor formula was originally designed to apportion the "trading income" of mercantile and manufacturing companies.

Historically, the states used four different methods for attributing receipts to the numerator of a state's sales factor: (1) *the destination test,* attribution to the state in which the goods are shipped to the customer, or in which they are delivered to the customer; (2) *the origin test,* attribution to the state of the factory, warehouse, or office from which the goods are shipped; (3) *the sales office negotiation test,* attribution to the state of the sales office from or through which the sale was principally negotiated; (4) *the sales activity test,* attribution to the state in which the sales employees principally conducted selling activities. See 1 Willis Comm. Rep., supra Chapter 2, note h, at 182–83 (Table 7–2).

The destination test for attributing receipts from sales of tangible personal property has spread so rapidly that it is now in use in every state with a broad-based corporate income tax. See All States Tax Guide (RIA) ¶ 224 (2009) (chart). Attribution of receipts from sales to the state of origin has its major current importance under the so-called throwback rule, where sales are assigned to the state of origin when the taxpayer is not taxable in the state of destination or the sale is to the U.S. Government. UDITPA § 16(b). Receipts from sales other than sales of tangible personal property (e.g., services) are typically assigned to the state in which most of the income-producing activity is performed. UDITPA § 17; All States Tax Guide (RIA) ¶ 224 (2009) (chart).

COMMONWEALTH OF PENNSYLVANIA v. GILMOUR MANUFACTURING COMPANY

Supreme Court of Pennsylvania, 2003.
573 Pa. 143, 822 A.2d 676.

JUSTICE CASTILLE.

This appeal presents a tax issue of first impression for this Court: whether a Pennsylvania corporation's sales of goods to out-of-state purchasers, who retrieve the goods at the seller's place of business in Pennsylvania and then transport the goods outside of Pennsylvania, should be included in the Pennsylvania corporation's calculation of corporate net income ("CNI") tax under the Tax Reform Code of 1971. For the reasons that follow, we agree with the Commonwealth Court that the Pennsylvania Department of Revenue's regulation, which treats such sales as in-state sales, is contrary to the Code and, accordingly, we affirm.

This matter proceeded in Commonwealth Court based upon a stipulation of facts * * * Gilmour Manufacturing Company, a Pennsylvania corporation, manufactures lawn and garden products at a facility in Somerset County, Pennsylvania. * * * Gilmour sells its goods throughout the United States, most often shipping them to out-of-state purchasers through common carriers and paying the freight charges for the shipping. Some of Gilmour's out-of-state customers, however, prefer to retrieve the products themselves at Gilmour's Pennsylvania loading dock. Gilmour refers to these customer pick-up transactions as "dock sales," for which Gilmour provides a freight allowance to its customers. Gilmour generally knows the destination to which its out-of-state "dock sale" customers transport the products. The proper tax treatment of Gilmour's "dock sales" income is the issue before this Court.

By way of background, Section 401 of the Tax Reform Code permits a company that does not transact all of its business within the Commonwealth, such as Gilmour, to apportion its tax liability based upon the ratio of the company's business transacted in the Commonwealth to its total business. The apportionment formula is an arithmetic average of three factors, i.e., property, payroll and sales factors. * * * [I]t is the sales factor, and more particularly the numerator of that factor (i.e., sales conducted in Pennsylvania), which is at issue.

In 1991, the year pertinent to this appeal, Gilmour * * * excluded its "dock sales" to out-of-state purchasers from its calculation of the numerator of its sales factor, considering those sales to be out-of-state. The

Department of Revenue, however, disagreed with Gilmour's calculations. Consistently with its interpretation of the relevant existing regulation, the Department recalculated Gilmour's taxes to include as sales in Pennsylvania dock sales where out-of-state purchasers retrieved the goods themselves.[1] Gilmour's out-of-state dock sales for 1991 totaled $2,385,362. Inclusion of the sales as Pennsylvania sales resulted in a $17,912 increase in the tax due.

* * * The issue in the Commonwealth Court was the proper construction of Section 401(3)2(a)(16) of the Code, which provides as follows:

> Sales of tangible personal property are in this State if the property is delivered or shipped to a purchaser, within this State regardless of the f.o.b. point or other conditions of the sale.[2]

The dispute centered on the meaning of the phrase "within this State." Gilmour essentially argued that the statute set forth a "destination" rule, while the Commonwealth maintained that the statute set forth a "delivery" rule. A divided three-judge panel of the Commonwealth Court found in favor of the Commonwealth (*Gilmour I*). * * * Judge Doyle dissented without opinion. Gilmour filed exceptions which the Commonwealth Court, sitting en banc, granted. The en banc majority, in an opinion by Judge Doyle, * * * entered judgment in favor of Gilmour (*Gilmour II*).* * * Judge Smith, joined by Judge Flaherty, dissented, reiterating the position taken in her earlier panel majority opinion in *Gilmour I*.

* * *

The Commonwealth correctly argues that administrative interpretations of a statute, such as the Department's regulation interpreting the Tax Reform Code at issue here, are entitled to some deference, particularly where a statute is technical or complex. But, as the Commonwealth also concedes, and the Commonwealth Court properly recognized, such deference will exist only where the reviewing court is satisfied that the regulation tracks the meaning of the statute, as narrowly construed, and does not violate the intent of the legislation. * * *.

The Commonwealth argues that the Department's regulation is a reasonable interpretation of the Tax Reform Code; the regulation has been in existence since 1976 without the General Assembly modifying the statute; and the regulation is a valid exercise of the Department's rule-making authority. Since the regulation is neither clearly inconsistent with the Tax Code nor unreasonable, the Commonwealth argues, the Commonwealth Court erred in failing to defer to the Department and by substituting its own judgment. In addition, the Commonwealth argues that its "delivery rule" interpretation is sensible because the focus should be on

---

1. The Department's regulation states, as the "general rule," that: "Sales of tangible personal property are in the state in which delivery to a purchaser occurs." 61 Pa.Code § 153.26(b)(2). Since the out-of-state purchaser takes delivery in Pennsylvania when a "dock sale" is consummated, the Department treats those sales as Pennsylvania sales.

2. F.O.B. is an abbreviation for "free on board." The significance of the designation is that it sets the point at which title for goods passes to the purchaser. * * *

the Pennsylvania taxpayer (here Gilmour), not on the buyer and, therefore, "completed sales" in Pennsylvania should be deemed sales within the state. The Commonwealth also notes that the delivery rule it advocates offers the added benefit of ease of administration, since it is "far simpler" to determine where physical delivery occurs than to ascertain the ultimate destination of goods once the goods leave the seller's dock. Finally, the Commonwealth argues that the Commonwealth Court's reliance upon decisions from other jurisdictions was misplaced.

Gilmour responds that the Commonwealth Court correctly interpreted the statute and, since the Department's regulation is inconsistent with the statute, the court was not required to defer to it. Citing to cases from California, Connecticut, Florida, Kentucky, Minnesota, and Wisconsin,[3] Gilmour notes that the reported cases reveal that every other state court which has interpreted language identical or substantially identical to the Pennsylvania statute in question here has construed the provision as the Commonwealth Court did—i.e., as excluding dock sales to out-of-state purchasers from the sales factor numerator—while no state court has deemed such sales to be sales within the state where the dock was located. Gilmour further notes that the statute here, like the statutes at issue in the other jurisdictions which considered the question, derives from the Uniform Division of Income for Tax Purposes Act (UDITPA). The courts in those jurisdictions have all interpreted the phrase "within this state" as modifying the word "purchaser" and not the word "delivered." Even though Pennsylvania has not specifically adopted UDITPA in this instance, Gilmour argues that since the General Assembly enacted language substantially identical to the language contained in the Uniform Act, that fact weighs in favor of following the courts of other jurisdictions and hewing to the prevailing judicial interpretation. See 1 Pa.C.S. § 1927 ("statutes uniform with those of other states shall be interpreted and construed to effect their general purpose to make uniform the laws of those states which enact them").

Gilmour further argues that the Department's regulation, and the Commonwealth's corresponding construction of the statute, ignores that the statute speaks not only to property "delivered" to purchasers but also to property "shipped." The Commonwealth's "delivery rule," Gilmour maintains, would allow the Commonwealth "to have its cake and eat it too" since the construction applies only to goods "delivered" in Pennsylvania and not to goods "shipped." Gilmour also argues that the Commonwealth's focus on the fact that the dock is located in Pennsylvania ignores the statutory mandate to ignore delivery or f.o.b. terms. Finally, Gilmour argues that the statute should properly be understood as establishing a

---

3. See McDonnell Douglas Corp. v. Franchise Tax Bd., 26 Cal.App.4th 1789, 33 Cal.Rptr.2d 129 (1994); Texaco, Inc. v. Groppo, 215 Conn. 134, 574 A.2d 1293 (1990); Florida Dept. of Revenue v. Parker Banana Co., 391 So.2d 762 (Fla.Ct.App.2d Dist.1980); Revenue Cabinet v. Rohm & Haas, 929 S.W.2d 741 (Ky.Ct.App.1996); Olympia Brewing Co. v. Commissioner of Revenue, 326 N.W.2d 642 (Minn.1982); Pabst Brewing Co. v. Wisconsin Dept. of Revenue, 130 Wis.2d 291, 387 N.W.2d 121 (Wis.App.1986), review denied, 130 Wis.2d 544, 391 N.W.2d 209 (1986).

"destination test" because weighting the sales factor in favor of the out-of-state contribution to gross income acts as a counterbalance to the fact that the other two factors involved in computing the CNI tax, i.e., property and payroll, are "biased" the other way, in favor of in-state activity.

* * *

Notwithstanding the age of the Department's regulation, which was apparently promulgated in 1976, this case has presented the first opportunity for the Commonwealth Court, and this Court, to determine whether the regulation is consonant with the statutory command. After careful consideration, we agree with the *Gilmour II* court's holding and reasoning. The *Gilmour II* court found that the phrase "within this State" modifies the immediately preceding word "purchaser," and thus only sales to Pennsylvania purchasers are includable in the numerator of the sales factor for CNI tax purposes. Viewing the plain language of the statutory provision in a common sense fashion, we agree that, as a matter of basic sentence construction, the phrase "within this State" was intended to modify the immediately preceding word "purchaser." This logical construction of the statute also gives effect to all of its terms, including the term "shipped" and the concluding remonstration that the "f.o.b. point or other conditions of the sale," which obviously could encompass delivery terms, are not to be deemed controlling. Moreover, if the General Assembly had intended "within this state" to modify "delivered," as urged by the Commonwealth, the statute could have been drafted to accomplish that purpose simply by omitting the misplaced comma and inserting the phrase immediately after the word "delivered."

Notably, however, that would have required the General Assembly to deviate significantly from the language it obviously adopted from the UDITPA. The statute would then read as follows given the above:

> Sales of tangible personal property are in this State if the property is delivered within this State or shipped to a purchaser within this State, regardless of the f.o.b. point or other conditions of the sale.

As so constructed, the statute would be congruent with the Department's interpretation and inconsistent with Gilmour's interpretation. The problem with the statute as written is that, using the rules of grammar, as we must, one cannot easily ascertain what actions (the verbs) or what parties (the nouns) the phrase "within this State" modifies or references. Since we must apply the rules of grammar and since we must construe the taxing statute in favor of the taxpayer, then Gilmour must, perforce, prevail.

We also agree with the *Gilmour II* court that the fact that other jurisdictions have uniformly interpreted corresponding statutes as employing a destination test, while not controlling, weighs heavily in favor of Gilmour's construction. This is so not only because a uniform interpretation of legislation affecting multistate matters is preferable, but also because those courts have persuasively explained why their construction is commanded by the language and intent of the legislation. For example, in the *Olympia Brewing* case, the Minnesota Supreme Court noted that "practical considerations" weighed in favor of a destination rule. Those practical considerations included the Minnesota taxing authority's "inability to justify treating differently" sales where the out-of-state purchaser picked up the goods at the seller's dock and sales where the same purchasers have the goods picked up by common or contract carriers at the same dock:

> This result makes the selection of mode of transportation dispositive, which, as even the commissioner concedes, would be contrary to the statutory language.... We think that to distinguish between a sale within or without a state on the basis of the mode of transportation— whose truck does the transporting—is an untenable distinction.

326 N.W.2d at 647. Similar practical considerations were cited in the *Parker Banana* case as warranting a destination rule. See 391 So.2d at 763 (Florida Revenue Department's interpretation would have words "within this state" apply to word "delivered" but not to word "shipped" since it would not treat sales to out-of-state purchasers as in-state sales if shipment was made by common carrier; in rejecting that "tortured construction," court notes that "we see no way in the world that the statute can logically or grammatically be construed so that the words 'within this state' apply only to the word 'delivered' "). The Department's regulation here erects no less valid a distinction which cannot be supported by the plain language of the statute.

We are also persuaded that the purpose of the CNI tax is furthered by this construction. As the *Gilmour II* court reasoned:

> [T]he tax is designed to measure the amount of commercial activity that an entity engages in during a given year and tax it accordingly.... [S]tatutes permitting a corporation to apportion its sales for purposes of the CNI are designed to represent the contribution of various consumers and purchasers to the entity's overall sales. Specifically, in Pennsylvania, the numerator of the sales factor represents the contribution of Pennsylvania consumers and purchasers to the entity's sales, while the denominator represents the contribution of all consumers and purchasers. Accordingly, including in a corporation's Pennsylvania sales transactions out-of-state purchasers who come into the Commonwealth, pick-up a product and leave the Commonwealth, as the Commonwealth argues, artificially inflates the contribution of Pennsylvania consumers and purchasers to the entity's sales.

750 A.2d at 953 (citation omitted).

With respect to the Commonwealth's argument that the administrative ease in enforcing a delivery rule supports its construction, we note that mere administrative ease cannot justify a regulation which is inconsistent with the language and purpose of the statute. Moreover, since, as the *Gilmour II* court properly noted, the burden falls on the taxpayer to prove an error in the Commonwealth's settlement of the CNI tax, there is no undue administrative burden arising from a proper, plain language interpretation of the statute.

* * *

For the foregoing reasons, we agree with the *Gilmour II* court that the Department of Revenue's regulation is contrary to the clear wording of Section 401(3)2(a)(16) of the Tax Reform Code. Accordingly, we affirm the order below entering judgment in favor of Gilmour.

NOTES AND QUESTIONS

A. *Dock Sales and the Sales Destination Test.* As the *Gilmour* case indicates, most courts construing UDITPA and similar statutes have likewise concluded that dock sales to out-of-state purchasers are not in-state sales under UDITPA's sales destination provision. In these cases, the courts took the position that attributing the sale to the final destination of the goods more faithfully served the purpose of the sales destination provision and that the terms of delivery should not control the sales attribution rule.

Despite the *Gilmour* case and similar decisions, however, UDITPA can fairly be construed as attributing dock sales to the state where the purchaser picks up the goods. Indeed, this is apparently the position taken in the Multistate Tax Commission regulations, which provide that "[p]roperty is delivered or shipped to a purchaser within this state if the shipment terminates in this state, even though the property is subsequently transferred by the purchaser to another state." MTC Reg. IV.16.(a).(3).

The statutory question as to whether the ultimate-destination rule or the place-of-delivery rule represents a proper construction of UDITPA § 16(a) is a close one that

> one can reasonably answer * * * either way. Consequently, in determining what is the destination of the goods, the decisive consideration should be the facilitation of simple and inexpensive taxpayer compliance and administration by the taxing authorities. For we are here dealing with a vast number of transactions that occur annually over the country, and it is unlikely that any significant shift of revenues among the states will be produced by whatever rule is adopted as to the destination of the goods in the types of transactions under discussion.

> The MTC construction of UDITPA enables the vendor to classify the destination of sales by the buyer's invoice address, without making it necessary for it to examine the facts as to the purchaser's reshipment or transshipment of the goods, except for reshipments by common carrier, which should not be difficult to identify. The * * * *ultimately received* rule * * * introduce[s] time-consuming and burdensome complexities that require vendors to inquire into the course of a product's journey after it is turned over to the customer, the local trucker, or the like. These practical considerations should outweigh the * * * court's desire—

albeit a legitimate one—to attribute sales to the market for the goods, which will typically be the state of ultimate destination.

1 Jerome R. Hellerstein & Walter Hellerstein, State Taxation ¶ 9.18[1][a] (3d ed. 1998–2009) (emphasis in original).

Is this criticism of the ultimate destination rule well taken? Courts following the ultimate destination rule have responded to this argument by observing that "administrative ease, while a legitimate concern, does not justify an interpretation of a statute which is inconsistent with its purpose (here to recognize the contribution of the consumer's or purchaser's state)." McDonnell Douglas Corp. v. Franchise Tax Bd., 26 Cal.App.4th 1789, 33 Cal.Rptr.2d 129, 133 (2d Dist. 1994) (quoting Olympia Brewing Co. v. Commissioner of Revenue, 326 N.W.2d 642, 648 (Minn. 1982)). Moreover, as the *Gilmour* court observed, the taxpayer bears the burden of proof in establishing the proper sales factor, so a state may continue to assert that products received within the state are in-state sales and leave it to the taxpayer to demonstrate through shipping records or other evidence that the tangible personal property was taken outside of the state for resale in another jurisdiction.

Some states' sales destination provisions specifically provide for an ultimately-received rather than a place-of-delivery rule for attribution purposes. For, example, the Louisiana statute provides that "[i]n the case of delivery of goods by common carrier or by other means of transportation, including transportation by the purchaser, the place at which the goods are *ultimately received* after all transportation has been completed shall be considered as the place at which the goods are received by the purchaser." La. Rev. Stat. Ann. § 47:245.F(3) (Westlaw 2009) (emphasis supplied).

B. *"Throwback" and "Throwout" Rules.* In order to prevent any part of the tax base from being assigned to states in which the taxpayer is not taxable, and thus from escaping taxation by any state, UDITPA contains a so-called "throwback" rule. Under the "throwback" rule, sales into states in which the taxpayer is not taxable (e.g., because of Public Law 86–272) are reassigned—or "thrown back"—from the state of destination to the state of origin. UDITPA § 16(a) (attributing sales of tangible personal property to the state of origin when "the taxpayer is not taxable in the state of the purchaser"). Consistently with the language of UDITPA § 2(a) (defining when a taxpayer is "taxable in another state"), courts have construed the term "taxable in the state of the purchaser" as referring to the power of the purchaser's state to tax the vendor, whether or not the power has been exercised. Miles Laboratories, Inc. v. Department of Revenue, 274 Or. 395, 546 P.2d 1081 (1976). In Covington Fabrics Corp. v. South Carolina Tax Commission, 264 S.C. 59, 212 S.E.2d 574, appeal dismissed, 423 U.S. 805, 96 S.Ct. 14 (1975), the court sustained the constitutionality of the "throwback" rule.

Wholly apart from its constitutionality, which seems to be firmly established, is the "throwback" rule justifiable as a matter of policy? Is it logical to posit a method for apportioning income based on the assumption that the market state contributes to its production and then to abandon that assumption as a result of some extraneous factor such as the taxpayer's invulnerability to taxation in the market state? The "throwback" rule assumes a correlation between the factors that render a taxpayer taxable in a state and the factors that contribute to its production of income there. But whether a taxpayer has the requisite contacts with a state to render it taxable there would in fact seem to have no necessary relation to whether the existence of a market in that state contributed to the production of the taxpayer's income.

In terms of the underlying basis for apportioning income, isn't it a non sequitur to suggest, as UDITPA implicitly does, that "if" the taxpayer has no taxable nexus with the market state, "then" it is "proper" to attribute income from sales into that state to states with the requisite nexus? It is only "proper" to do so because of the consideration, which is logically distinct from the question of where income is earned, that multistate businesses should be taxable on 100 percent of their income. Apportionment principles designed to achieve that objective—generally known as "full accountability" or "full apportionment"—may be inconsistent with a theoretically sound approach to the question of where income is earned. To tamper with basic apportionment doctrine in this manner, it may be contended, is unsound policy. See Walter Hellerstein, "Construing the Uniform Division of Income for Tax Purposes Act: Reflections on the Illinois Supreme Court's Reading of the 'Throwback' Rule," 45 U. Chi. L. Rev. 768, 779 (1978).

In the end one's views as to the propriety of the "throwback" rule will depend on whether one believes that the "full accountability" principle ought to override a theoretically consistent approach to apportioning income. Although there is something a little unseemly about a state's changing apportionment theories "in the middle of the stream," the alternative may be equally unpalatable—assigning income to a jurisdiction where it cannot be taxed. It is worth noting that some of the states, in enacting or amending UDITPA, have eliminated the "throwback" rule. See All States Tax Guide (RIA) ¶ 224 (2009) (chart).

A "throwout" rule provides an alternative to the "throwback" rule. Under the "throwout" rule, receipts otherwise assigned to a state in which the taxpayer is not taxable are eliminated from—or "thrown out" of—both the numerator and denominator of the sales factor. Such a rule results in "full accountability" for all the taxpayer's income to the states in which the corporation is taxable. The Pennsylvania Supreme Court initially sustained the Department of Revenue's use of the "throwout" rule as a proper exercise of the power to vary the statutory formula under the state's relief provision. Hellertown Manufacturing Co. v. Commonwealth, 480 Pa. 358, 390 A.2d 732 (1978). Six years later, however, the court overruled its earlier decision and held that the tax administrator lacked authority under Pennsylvania's version of UDITPA to modify the state's apportionment provisions in this fashion. Paris Manufacturing Co., Inc. v. Commonwealth, 505 Pa. 15, 476 A.2d 890 (1984). For a consideration of the apportionment relief or variation provisions, see Section B(9) infra. As a matter of policy, does the "throwback" rule or the "throwout" rule represent a sounder means of achieving "full accountability"?

Does UDITPA's "throwback" rule apply to sales destined to customers located in foreign countries? See UDITPA § 1(h). If it does, are U.S. standards, based on our jurisdictional traditions and concepts and in part on the Constitution of the United States, to be employed in determining taxability in foreign countries? Should Public Law 86–272 be taken into account? See Appeal of Dresser Industries, 1982 WL 11983 (Cal. St. Bd. Eq. June 29, 1982) (U.S. jurisdictional standards, but not Public Law 86–272, should be taken into account in determining whether a foreign country has jurisdiction to tax for purposes of the "throwback" rule); contra Scott & Williams, Inc. v. Board of Taxation, 117 N.H. 189, 372 A.2d 1305 (1977) (jurisdiction of foreign country to tax, for purposes of "throwback" rule, must be determined by laws of the country in question). See generally 1 Jerome R. Hellerstein & Walter Hellerstein, State Taxation ¶ 9.18[1][b] (3d. ed. 1998–2009).

UDITPA's "throwback" rule also applies to sales to the Federal Government on the theory that "they are not necessarily attributable to a market existing in the state to which the goods are originally shipped." UDITPA § 16 (comment). Does "throwback" to the state of origin produce a disproportionate attribution of income from defense and other governmental contracts to the manufacturing states? Would a "throwout" rule produce more satisfactory attribution of the income among the states involved? See John A. Wilkie, "Uniform Division of Income for Tax Purposes," 37 Taxes 65 (1959).

C. *Drop Shipments.* T, a corporation engaged in business in Illinois, makes sales of goods to customers in State X, in which T is not taxable. T orders the goods in question from a supplier, S, located in State Y, in which T likewise is not taxable, and, at T's request, S delivers the goods directly to T's customer in State X. Are T's receipts from such so-called "drop shipment" sales includable in the numerator of its Illinois sales factor under Illinois's UDITPA-based apportionment formula? Recall that the language of UDITPA provides for a "throwback" to the state of origin only when "the property is *shipped from * * * this state*." UDITPA § 16(b) (emphasis supplied). Although the Illinois court answered the question in the affirmative in reliance on UDITPA's relief provision (see Section 9 infra), GTE Automatic Electric, Inc. v. Allphin, 68 Ill.2d 326, 12 Ill.Dec. 134, 369 N.E.2d 841 (1977), the court's opinion is open to criticism. See Walter Hellerstein, "Construing the Uniform Division of Income for Tax Purposes Act: Reflections on the Illinois Supreme Court's Reading of the 'Throwback' Rule," 45 U. Chi. L. Rev. 768 (1978). In a similar case, the Colorado Supreme Court refused to countenance the Department of Revenue's resort to the state's equitable apportionment provision to read a "throwback" rule into the apportionment formula. Miller International, Inc. v. State, Dep't of Revenue, 646 P.2d 341 (Colo. 1982).

From the standpoint of the manufacturer or wholesaler, a drop shipment sale raises the question whether the taxpayer should assign the receipts from the sale to the state to which the goods are physically shipped (i.e., the state of the retailer's customer) or to the state in which the manufacturer's or wholesaler's customer, the retailer, is located. In terms of the broad policy underlying the sales factor—to attribute a portion of a taxpayer's income to the market state—one should assign the sale to the state in which the retailer is located, since the retailer constitutes the manufacturer's or wholesaler's "market." Nevertheless, the language of UDITPA and most other state statutes does not lend itself to that result because it requires that the property be "delivered or shipped to a purchaser * * * within this state."

UDITPA § 16(a). Unless one reads "delivered" or "shipped" as *constructively* delivered" or *"constructively* shipped" to a purchaser within this state, it is hard to see how a drop shipment transaction can be assigned to the state of the retailer, to whom property is never actually "delivered" or "shipped."

In fact, most states that have considered this issue have taken the position that a manufacturer or wholesaler should assign receipts from a drop shipment to the state to which the goods are physically shipped. For example, California, a UDITPA state, provides by regulation that, in the context of a drop shipment, "a purchaser within this state" includes the purchaser's customer. Cal. Code Regs. tit. 18, § 25135(a)(4) (Westlaw 2009). Similarly, Pennsylvania, whose sales factor is identical to UDITPA's, provides by regulation that receipts are assigned to the ultimate recipient of the property "if the taxpayer, at the designation of the purchaser, delivers property in this Commonwealth to the ultimate recipient." 61 Pa. Code § 153.26(b)(3)(ii)(A) (Westlaw 2009). The New Jersey Tax Court likewise found that a manufacturer's drop shipment sales to the non-New Jersey designees of the manufacturer's New Jersey customer did not generate New Jersey receipts under a statute assigning receipts to New Jersey "where shipments are made to points within this State." Stryker Corp. v. Director, Div. of Taxation, 18 N.J.Tax 270 (1999), aff'd on other grounds, 333 N.J.Super. 413, 755 A.2d 1200 (App. Div. 2000), aff'd, 168 N.J. 138, 773 A.2d 674 (2001); N.J. Stat. Ann. § 54:10A–6(B)(1), (2) (Westlaw 2009). The court observed that there was never any physical transfer of the products in question to the manufacturer's customer in New Jersey; that "[t]he concepts of constructive delivery and constructive shipment * * * are inconsistent with the actual physical transfer which the word 'shipment,' as used in the statute implies" (Stryker, 18 N.J.Tax at 283–84); and that similar statutes "have been interpreted consistently to refer to the shipment to the ultimate customer." Id. at 284.

D. *Rents and Royalties From Real and Tangible Personal Property.* Prior to the emergence of UDITPA, the states generally allocated rents and royalties from real and tangible personal property to the state in which the property was located. The Willis Committee reported (as of 1963) that 29 states allocated rents and royalties from real estate and that 27 of the 29 states allocated such rent and royalties to the state in which the property was located. 1 Willis Comm. Rep., supra Chapter 2, note h, at 206–07. A few states apportioned rents and royalties, and those states usually included the receipts in the numerator of their receipts factors if the property was located in the state. In allocating or apportioning rents and royalties from mobile tangible personal property, or other tangibles which are situated in more than one state during the taxable year, states usually attributed the income or receipts to the state to the extent of its use within the state. These allocation and apportionment principles are still in effect in some of the states that have not adopted UDITPA.

UDITPA follows the traditional rule of allocating rents and royalties to the state where the real property is located if the rents and royalties constitute nonbusiness income. UDITPA § 5. But if they constitute business income, rentals and royalties from real property are apportioned. UDITPA § 9. The attribution of apportionable rents and royalties for sales factor purposes is governed by the catch-all provision of the UDITPA sales factor.

UDITPA § 17. Hence, such rents and royalties come into the numerator of a state's sales factor only if the greater proportion of the "income-producing activity is performed in this state." Id.

Suppose that T, a real estate company whose commercial domicile is in Denver, owns an office building in Omaha. The operations of the building, including leasing, maintenance, collection of the rents and the like, are handled by an Omaha independent managing agent, under contract with T. T carries on all of its own activities relating to the building at its Denver office. UDITPA would classify the rents T receives as business income. Should T's rental receipts be assigned to Colorado or Nebraska, both of which have adopted UDITPA?

The Multistate Tax Commission's regulations interpreting UDITPA take the position that "income producing activity" does not include "activities performed on behalf of a taxpayer, such as those conducted on its behalf by an independent contractor" for purposes of determining where "income producing activity" occurs under Section 17 of UDITPA. MTC Reg. IV.17(2). If this is a proper construction of the statute, the rentals derived from the Nebraska building would be attributed to Colorado. Is this an acceptable result? Is it a sufficient answer to Nebraska's claim to inclusion of the rentals in its receipts factor that the value of the property is included in that state's property factor? Should the UDITPA rule of allocating nonbusiness rentals to the state in which real property is located also be made applicable to business rentals?

E. *Receipts From Services: The Basic Rules.* The receipts factors of the state apportionment provisions typically include receipts from the rendition of services. Prior to the adoption of UDITPA, many states included receipts from services in the numerator of the receipts factors to the extent that the services were performed in the state. See 1 Willis Comm. Rep., supra Chapter 2, note h, at 180, 188–89; "Final Report of the Committee on Tax Situs and Allocation," 1951 Nat'l Tax Ass'n Procs. 456, 463. That rule still applies in some states. Accordingly, if a taxpayer receives a lump sum for services rendered both within and without the state, the receipts are assigned on a comparative time base, the relative values of the services in the various states, and similar factors. See, e.g., N.J. Admin. Code tit. 18, § 18:7–8.10 (Westlaw 2009); N.Y. Comp. Codes R. & Regs. tit. 20, § 4–4.1 (Westlaw 2009).

UDITPA contains no separate provision dealing explicitly with either the allocation or apportionment of income from services, or with the assignment of receipts from services for sales factor purposes. Sections 4–8 of UDITPA, which provide for allocation of specific types of income (including rents and royalties, interest, dividends, and the like, to the extent that they constitute non-business income), do not refer to service income. As a consequence, receipts from the rendition of services are dealt with by UDITPA only through the general definition of "business income" and the catch-all attribution to the taxing state of "sales other than sales of tangible personal property." UDITPA § 17. (Verify this conclusion for yourself by tracing through UDITPA §§ 1(a) and 1(c), 4–8, 15, and 17.) Hence, receipts from services fall within the numerator of the state's sales factor if "the income-producing activity is performed in this state," or if performed in more than one state and "a greater proportion of the income-producing activity is performed in this state than in any other state." The test of the proportion of income-producing activity within a state is its cost of performance. UDITPA § 17.

The UDITPA rule can give rise to questions in determining the state in which the "greater proportion of the income-producing activity is performed." Does UDITPA provide an acceptable basis for attributing receipts from services? Would a more equitable result be obtained by fractionating the receipts from services on a time or cost basis, so that where substantial work is done in more than one state, each state would benefit? See John A. Wilkie, "Uniform Division of Income for Tax Purposes," 37 Taxes 65, 73 (1959). The experience of the states over the years with apportionment and allocation of service income indicates the virtue of a statutory standard that employs a variety of factors, which can be adapted to the broad diversity of business operations. The drafters of UDITPA were aware of this problem and expressed the view that the adjustment or relief provision of UDITPA could be employed in order to deal with what it regarded as exceptional situations. See Section 9 infra; William J. Pierce, "The Uniform Division of Income for State Tax Purposes," 35 Taxes 747 (1957).

F. *A Possible Gap in UDITPA.* Suppose one determines that income from a particular type of services does not constitute "business income" under UDITPA. Is such income subtracted from the apportionable tax base and allocated? If so, to which state? Examine UDITPA § 4. If such service income is not allocable, is it apportioned? Examine UDITPA § 9. Is service income which is nonbusiness income excluded from tax by UDITPA? See Wilkie, supra Note E.

G. *Receipts From Intangibles.* When intangible income is included in a corporation's apportionable tax base, under UDITPA and similar statutory schemes the attribution of receipts from intangibles for sales factor purposes falls under the general provision for the attribution of "[s]ales, other than sales of tangible personal property." UDITPA § 17. As noted above, this provision attributes sales to a state if "the income-producing activity is performed in th[e] state," id., or, if the income-producing activity is performed both within and without the state, then to the state in which the greatest proportion of the income-producing activity is performed, based on costs of performance.

If the income-producing activity with respect to income from an intangible is deemed to be the activity associated with acquiring, managing, and disposing of the intangible, receipts from intangible property will ordinarily be assigned to the state of the taxpayer's commercial domicile. In fact, based on this reading of the UDITPA and similar statutes, taxpayers routinely assign receipts from intangibles to the numerator of their commercial domicile's sales factor, especially where the commercial domicile taxes little or none of such income.

Despite the general statutory rule under UDITPA for assigning receipts from sales other than sales of tangible personal property, however, the Multistate Tax Commission has adopted a special sales factor regulation for intangibles, which is followed by a large number of states:

Where the income producing activity in respect to business income from intangible personal property can be readily identified, such income is included in the denominator of the sales factor and, if the income producing activity occurs in this state, in the numerator of the sales factor as well.* * *

Where business income from intangible property cannot readily be attributed to any particular income producing activity of the taxpayer, such income cannot be assigned to the numerator of the sales factor for any state and shall be excluded from the denominator of the sales factor. For example, where business income in the form of dividends received on stock, royalties received on patents or copyrights, or interest received on bonds, debentures or government securities results from the mere holding of the intangible personal property by the taxpayer, such dividends and interest shall be excluded from the denominator of the sales factor.

MTC Reg. IV.18.(c)(3). Under this regulation, when the intangible income cannot be attributed to any particular income-producing activity of the taxpayer, the receipts from the intangibles are "thrown out" of the sales factor, with the result that the intangible income is effectively assigned according to a formula that takes no account of the intangible property or the receipts that it generates.

Aside from states that have adopted UDITPA and similar statutes, states that include income from intangibles in the apportionable tax base generally assign the associated receipts to the state of the commercial domicile. For example, Connecticut, which apportions all income that is constitutionally apportionable, assigns gains from the sale or other disposition of intangible assets managed or controlled within the state to that state's sales factor numerator. Conn. Gen. Stat. § 12–218(c) (Westlaw 2009). New Jersey, which likewise apportions all constitutionally apportionable income, generally assigns receipts from intangibles to the sales factor numerator of the owner's domicile, unless the intangible has acquired a business situs in the state, in which case they are assigned to the business situs. N.J. Stat. Ann. § 54:10A–6(B) (Westlaw 2009); N.J. Admin. Code tit. 18, § 18:7–8.12(e) (Westlaw 2009).

There are also variations in the quantum of receipts from intangibles that are reflected in the sales factor. While the sales factors of most states' apportionment formulas require that the "gross receipts" from the transaction be included in the factor, see, e.g., UDITPA §§ 1(g), 17, a number of states include only the *net* income from intangibles in the sales factor. In some instances states have so provided by statute or regulation, see, e.g., R.I. Gen. Laws § 44–11–14(a)(2)(iv), (v) (Westlaw 2009); Ill. Admin. Code § 100.3380(c)(5) (Westlaw 2009); in some instances they have done so through the "equitable apportionment" or relief provision, see, e.g., American Tel. & Tel. Co. v. State Tax Appeal Bd., 241 Mont. 440, 787 P.2d 754 (1990), and Section B(9) infra; and in some instances they have done so simply as a matter of practice.

H. *Receipts from Services and Intangibles and the Destination Principle.* Suppose that a seller located in state A sells or licenses electronically delivered music files to customers in State B. Or suppose that this seller makes information available on-line to customers in State B for a fee. To which state will the seller's receipts be attributed for receipts factor purposes if they are characterized as receipts from the sale of tangible personal property? To which state will the sales be attributed if they are characterized as receipts from sale of an intangible (or a service)? From a tax policy perspective, should the answers be the same or different? If the answers should be the same, which answer should it be? See John A. Swain, "Reforming the State Corporate Income Tax: A Market State Approach to the Sourcing of Service Receipts," 83 Tul. L. Rev. 285 (2008). A growing number of states have begun to attribute receipts from services and intangibles on a destination basis. See, e.g., 35 Ill. Comp. Stat. § 5/304(a)(3)(C5)(iv) (Westlaw 2009); 36 Me. Rev. Stat. Ann. tit. 36, § 5221(16–A) (Westlaw 2009).

I. *Receipts From Extraordinary Transactions.* The Multistate Tax Commission's regulations provide:

> Where substantial amounts of gross receipts arise from an incidental or occasional sale of a fixed asset used in the regular course of the taxpayer's trade or business, those gross receipts shall be excluded from the sales factor. For example, gross receipts from the sale of a factory or plant will be excluded.

MTC Reg. IV.18.(c)(1). Is this regulation consistent with the language of UDITPA? Compare the MTC's position on attributing receipts from occasional sales with its position on classifying the income from such sales as business income. See pp. 544–45 supra. If the income in question would be classified as business income under the "functional" test and MTC Reg. IV.1.(c)(2) (p. 555 supra), why shouldn't receipts be included in the sales factor? Isn't inclusion of income in the apportionable tax base without inclusion of the factors that produced such income inherently distorting? Cf. Justice Stevens's dissent in *Mobil* (pp. 484–89 supra). If not, why not?

9. RELIEF PROVISIONS FOR VARYING STATUTORY FORMULAS

TWENTIETH CENTURY–FOX FILM CORPORATION v. DEPARTMENT OF REVENUE

Supreme Court of Oregon, 1985.
299 Or. 220, 700 P.2d 1035.

ROBERTS, JUSTICE.

The Department of Revenue (department) appeals the decision of the Tax Court in favor of Twentieth Century Fox (taxpayer). There is one dispositive issue: whether the department proved that the statutory three-factor apportionment formula used to apportion income to Oregon for purposes of corporate excise taxation did not fairly represent the extent of taxpayer's business activity in this state thus permitting the department to employ a different method.

Taxpayer produces and distributes motion pictures. Its only business activity in Oregon during the years in question was the licensing of motion pictures for exhibition by independent theaters. Taxpayer filed

Oregon corporate excise tax returns for 1975, 1976 and 1977, using the statutory three-factor formula for apportionment of income to Oregon. ORS 314.650 to 314.665. ORS 314.650 through 314.665 are taken from the Uniform Division of Income for Tax Purposes Act (UDITPA), ORS 314.605 et seq. * * *

The three-factor formula * * * typically produces fair taxation in that it fairly approximates the portion of taxpayer's business activity that was conducted in Oregon. The three-factor apportionment formula is the standard for covered industries in all the states that have adopted UDIT-PA. A variation of it is used in some non-UDITPA jurisdictions. There is no claim that it is 100 percent accurate for each taxpayer or taxing jurisdiction. However, if every taxing jurisdiction used this formula, the slight inequities would be balanced to a great extent and no more and no less than 100 percent of taxpayer's income would be taxed. Even though the UDITPA formula is not used universally, the inequities inherent in any apportionment formula are balanced to a certain extent, by the widespread usage of these three factors to apportion income.

In this case, taxpayer included in the numerator of the property factor the cost of positive prints[1] of its films, which are the only tangible property of taxpayer that enters Oregon. Department's auditor modified the property factor numerator to include a portion of the value of taxpayer's film negatives, which are stored in California. Film negatives are valued at the cost of producing the film. Their value varies greatly, but is generally between $5 million and $20 million.

Taxpayer challenged the proposed modification, but department upheld its auditor's assessment. Thus, taxpayer owed approximately $22,000 more for the three tax years than was indicated by the original returns. Taxpayer appealed to the Tax Court, which held that department had not met its burden of proof to establish that the statutory apportionment formula did not fairly represent the extent of taxpayer's business activity in Oregon. Department acknowledges that it must meet this burden in order to apply a different formula from the three-factor apportionment formula. Donald M. Drake Co. v. Dept. of Rev., 263 Or. 26, 32, 500 P.2d 1041 (1972), established that "the use of any method other than apportionment should be exceptional and the party—the taxpayer or the Department of Revenue—who seeks to invoke the applicability of ORS 314.670 has the burden of proof." Although this language leaves room for argument, it mandates that the burden of proof be placed on department in the instant case.

* * *

---

1. Taxpayer and department entered into a stipulation which included the following definitions:

"1. A film 'negative' is the original exposed film that is created by photographing a movie production. A film negative cannot be displayed for public viewing.

"2. A film 'print' is a positive print made from a film negative. Film prints are distributed to theaters for exhibition for public viewing."

Department appealed. We review under ORS 305.445, which provides that appeals from the Tax Court to this court "shall be in accordance with the procedure in equity cases on appeal from a circuit court." We thus review under ORS 19.125(3), which provides that "the cause shall be tried anew upon the record." See Oregon Broadcasting Co. v. Dept. of Revenue, 287 Or. 267, 270–71, 598 P.2d 689 (1979).

I

This review will focus on ORS 314.670 (Section 18 of UDITPA), which provides:

> "If the allocation and apportionment provisions of ORS 314.610 to 314.665 do not fairly represent the extent of the taxpayer's business activity in this state, the taxpayer may petition for and the department may permit, or the department may require, in respect to all or any part of the taxpayer's activity, if reasonable:

> "(1) Separate accounting;

> "(2) The exclusion of any one or more of the factors;

> "(3) The inclusion of one or more additional factors which will fairly represent the taxpayer's business activity in this state; or

> "(4) The employment of any other method to effectuate an equitable allocation and apportionment of the taxpayer's income."

We examine this section of the uniform act in connection with the act as a whole.

Professor William J. Pierce, the drafter of UDITPA, offered explanations of the purpose and nature of the act. He wrote: "The uniform act, if adopted in every state having a net income tax or a tax measured by net income, would assure that 100 per cent of income, and no more or no less, would be taxed." Pierce, The Uniform Division of Income for State Tax Purposes, 35 Taxes 747, 748 (1957). He refers to the allocation and apportionment sections of the uniform act as "a formula designed for manufacturing and merchandising businesses." Pierce, supra, at 749. He states that section 18 of the uniform act

> "necessarily must be used where the statute reaches arbitrary or unreasonable results so that its application could be attacked successfully on constitutional grounds. Furthermore, it gives both the tax collection agency and the taxpayer some latitude for showing that for the particular business activity, some more equitable method of allocation and apportionment could be achieved. Of course, departures from the basic formula should be avoided except where reasonableness requires. Nonetheless, some alternative method must be available to handle the constitutional problem as well as the unusual cases, because no statutory pattern could ever resolve satisfactorily the problems for the multitude of taxpayers with individual business characteristics." Pierce, supra, at 781.

Other commentators have discussed the purpose and interpretation of section 18 of UDITPA:

"It must be recognized, of course, that the Uniform Act does contain an express grant of discretion to the administrator to select allocation [and apportionment] methods other than those prescribed. In the allocation [and apportionment] of income, unusual situations, which should be excepted from the application of general rules, frequently arise. Such situations may be impossible to anticipate or difficult to describe with sufficient precision to permit drafting of a provision in the statute setting forth precisely the rules to be applied. Accordingly, it is common in allocation statutes to include a general relief provision authorizing the administrator to depart from the general rule if necessary to obtain fair or equitable results. ...."
Keesling & Warren, California's Uniform Division of Income for Tax Purposes Act (Part I), 15 UCLA L Rev 156, 170 (1967).

Two basic goals of UDITPA, and thus of ORS 314.605 et seq, emerge: (1) fair apportionment of income among the taxing jurisdictions; and (2) uniformity of application of the statutes.[5] In this case, these two purposes are seemingly in conflict. Taxpayer argues for uniformity in adhering to the statutory apportionment formula. Department argues for fair apportionment by recognizing the economic reality of the film industry and taxpayer's business activity in Oregon.

* * *

III

Although the specific facts of this case present an issue of first impression, prior caselaw has discussed apportionment and section 18 of UDITPA (ORS 314.670), Donald M. Drake Co. v. Dept. of Rev., supra. Statutory three-factor apportionment is the favored method of attributing income for purposes of Oregon corporate excise taxation. The party who desires a different method has the burden of proof. Drake, supra, 263 Or. at 32, 500 P.2d 1041. Two things must be proved.

First, department must demonstrate that the statutory formula as a whole does not "fairly represent the extent of the taxpayer's business activity in this state." It is necessary to establish that the application of the three factors does not fairly represent business activity, not merely that one factor fails to meet this standard. This is so because in certain cases one factor may be unreasonably high and another unreasonably low but the application of the three factors together fairly represents business activity. See Donovan Construction Co. v. Treasury Dep't., 126 Mich.App. 11, 337 N.W.2d 297, 301 (1983). It is also important to note that it must be established that statutory apportionment does not adequately reflect business activity, not merely that it does not adequately reflect income

---

5. ORS 314.605(2) (Section 19 of UDITPA) provides:

"ORS 314.610 to 314.670 shall be so construed as to effectuate its general purpose to make uniform the law of those states which enact it."

earned in the state. See Amoco Production Co. v. Armold, Director of Taxation, 213 Kan. 636, 518 P.2d 453 (1974).

Second, the party with the burden of proof must establish that its alternative method of allocating income is "reasonable." We believe that in the context of UDITPA, reasonableness has at least three components: (1) the division of income fairly represents business activity and if applied uniformly would result in taxation of no more or no less than 100 percent of taxpayer's income; (2) the division of income does not create or foster lack of uniformity among UDITPA jurisdictions; and (3) the division of income reflects the economic reality of the business activity engaged in by the taxpayer in Oregon.

With regard to the first requirement, we initially examine the extent of taxpayer's business activity in the state. This is the factual predicate for application of the three-factor formula.

Taxpayer is in the business of producing and distributing films. The tangible properties of taxpayer which enter Oregon are prints made from the negatives of taxpayer's motion pictures. The prints, as reels of exposed film, have a value ranging from $800 to $1000, depending on footage. The negatives from which the prints derive are valued at production cost and could vary in value from under $5 million to over $20 million. It would be inaccurate to describe taxpayer's business activity as distributing reels of prints without reference to the negatives from which they are made. Without the negative, the distribution prints could not be made. The business activity of taxpayer in Oregon is the distribution for display of the embodiment of a story or theme, photographed, edited, acted and captured on film.

The question posed by the first requirement is whether the statutory apportionment formula fairly represents the extent of the taxpayer's business activity in this state. We have already stated that department must show not just that one factor fails to meet this standard, but that the entire formula taken together does not fairly reflect taxpayer's business activity.

The evidence establishes the following: The payroll factors for these three years are zero. This factor cannot be a minus or negative number. Thus, the taxpayer enjoys the lowest possible payroll factor. It is also established that the sales factors for each year accurately reflects taxpayer's receipts in Oregon. Because both the payroll factor and the sales factor are either accurate or not capable of being inaccurately high, these factors will not offset any under-evaluation in the property factor. Whatever inaccuracy and unfairness exist in the property factor may establish that the three-factor statutory apportionment formula does not fairly represent business activity.

The statutory property numerator is calculated solely with reference to the prints (as opposed to prints and negatives) because the prints, the reels of films, are the only tangible property to enter the state. Their value reflects only the cost by foot of film on a reel without regard to the contents of the film. This figure substantially underrepresents the business activity of taxpayer in this state. The statutory apportionment formula's use of the value of prints to the exclusion of the value of negatives in the Oregon property factor numerator is woefully inadequate to "fairly represent" the extent of that business activity. Thus, department has proved that "the apportionment provisions of ORS 314.610 to 314.665 do not fairly represent the extent of the taxpayer's business activity in this state . . . ." ORS 314.670.

The second requirement of proof involves the reasonableness of department's substituted apportionment formula. Department's auditor originally calculated a percentage of all films in inventory but the department's hearing officer expressly determined that this was not proper. Opinion and Order No. I 83–48, Twentieth Century–Fox Film Corporation, p. 10, dated April 12, 1983. Pursuant to this order, department was to follow the California guidelines in their entirety to calculate the property factor. These guidelines provide:

> "The numerator of the property factor includes the following to the extent the property is in California.
>
> " . . .
>
> "(c) The total value of films in release . . . are attributed to this state in the same ratio in which the total California receipts from such films . . . bears to the total of such receipts everywhere."

Substituting "Oregon" for "California," the effect of the hearing officer's ruling is to limit the Oregon property factor numerator to a percentage (Oregon receipts over receipts everywhere) of the value of those films distributed in Oregon during each tax year in question.

We find department's modified apportionment formula, as defined in the preceding paragraph, to be reasonable under ORS 314.670. The apportionment was proposed by department and does not result in more than 100 percent of taxpayer's income being taxed. The apportionment fairly represents taxpayer's business activity in Oregon in that it accurately reflects the cost or value of films owned by taxpayer and distributed for display in Oregon. The apportionment fosters uniformity among UDITPA jurisdictions in that it conforms to the California guidelines, which could serve as a model for other states with less experience with the motion picture industry. The apportionment reflects the economic reality of the distribution of motion pictures by taxpayer by discarding an artificial distinction between prints and negatives and attributing to a film the costs of production, which more accurately reflects the business activity of taxpayer.

Department has met its burden of proof by a preponderance of the evidence, ORS 305.427. It may properly utilize ORS 314.670(4) in avoidance of the statutory apportionment formula in this case. Department has also proved that its modification of the property factor numerator is reasonable.

* * *

The decision of the Tax Court is reversed and remanded with instructions to remand to the Department of Revenue.

NOTES AND QUESTIONS

A. Most statutes prescribing the use of apportionment formulas provide for variations if the "provisions * * * do not fairly represent the extent of the taxpayer's business activity in this state." UDITPA § 18. In such cases, the statutes usually authorize the tax administrator, on his own initiative or on petition by the taxpayer, to apply separate accounting, to exclude or add one or more factors, or to use "any other method to effectuate an equitable allocation and apportionment of the taxpayer's income." Id. As the *Twentieth Century–Fox* case indicates, the burden of proof rests on the party seeking to invoke the relief provision. See also Union Pacific Corp. v. Idaho State Tax Comm'n, 139 Idaho 572, 83 P.3d 116 (2004); Montana Department of Revenue v. United Parcel Service, Inc., 252 Mont. 476, 830 P.2d 1259 (1992).

B. *Standards for Relief Under the Equitable Apportionment Provisions.* In most states, the taxpayer cannot establish a right under the equitable apportionment provision to substitute separate accounting for formulary apportionment merely by showing that separate accounting produces a lower tax. See, e.g., Commonwealth v. Lucky Stores, Inc., 217 Va. 121, 225 S.E.2d 870 (1976) (to succeed in obtaining relief under the equitable apportionment provision, taxpayer must establish, by evidence other than separate accounting, that distortion results from the statutory method). On the other hand, the taxpayer need not show that the distortion created by the formula exceeds constitutional bounds. The *Twentieth Century–Fox* case so held in a portion of the opinion not reproduced. The court's conclusion on this issue is unassailable, since the statute would otherwise be superfluous. One does not need a statute to have a right of protection from unconstitutional state taxing measures.

The Michigan Court of Appeals has taken the position that use of an alternative to the formulary apportionment cannot be justified even on the basis of a "gross disparity" in the results between the different methods because this does not necessarily show that the method proposed under the relief provision "more accurately reflects the corporate taxpayer's unitary business in the state." Donovan Construction Co. v. Michigan, Dept. of Treasury, 126 Mich.App. 11, 337 N.W.2d 297, 300 n. 2 (1983). The critical question in Michigan is qualitative rather than quantitative: "Only if formulary apportionment does not fairly represent *the extent of business activity in the state* may a different method, such as separate accounting, be employed." Id. (emphasis supplied).

By way of contrast, the Supreme Court of Kansas upheld the tax director's reliance on that state's UDITPA relief provisions, in applying separate accounting to the income of a wholly owned subsidiary of Standard

Oil Company of Indiana in lieu of the combined apportionment method sought by the taxpayer. Amoco Production Co. v. Armold, 213 Kan. 636, 518 P.2d 453 (1974). The taxpayer, Amoco, was engaged in the exploration and production of crude oil and natural gas in 21 states, including Kansas. As the principal source of crude oil for Standard and its subsidiaries, Amoco was clearly part of an integrated unitary oil enterprise. Nevertheless, the court sustained the tax director's use of the separate accounting method applied to Amoco on the basis of the relief provision, stating that "the majority of this court is unable to say an apportionment of 2.78 or 2.71 percent of Amoco's business income fairly represents the extent of its business activities in Kansas, when those activities actually generated a grossly disproportionate 23 or 24 percent of its total net income." Id., 518 P.2d at 464.

The Kansas court evidently relied for its conclusion regarding the percentage of income "actually generated" within the state on the tax director's separate accounting figures, a reliance that the *Lucky Stores* case rejected. Three Justices dissented in the Kansas case on the ground that "the use of any method other than apportionment should be exceptional," and that by the use of separate accounting figures, the director had not borne his burden of providing "a factual basis" for his contention that the preferred apportionment method "does not clearly reflect the extent of the taxpayer's Kansas business activity." Id. at 468. Skeptical tax counsel for multistate enterprises may be inclined to regard the crucial difference between the two decisions to be that in the Virginia case the taxpayer sought a variation from the statutory formula, whereas in the Kansas case, the tax director sought the variation.

C. *Disparity Between Factors as a Basis for Relief.* Taxpayers have sought relief under the equitable apportionment provisions based on disparities between the different factors of the three-factor apportionment formula. In GATX Corp. v. Limbach, 21 Ohio App.3d 59, 486 N.E.2d 840 (1984), the taxpayer, which was engaged primarily in the business of leasing railroad rolling stock, also manufactured railroad cars for use in its leasing business. Its single manufacturing facility was located in Ohio. GATX sought relief from the application of the three-factor formula to its Ohio income tax base on the ground that inclusion of the wage factor resulted in distortion of its income "since the sales factor * * * was 1.10 percent, the property factor was 3.01 percent, and the wage factor was 27.84 percent." Id., 486 N.E.2d at 842. The court granted the taxpayer's request under the relief provision to eliminate the payroll factor because of its view that "the payroll factor which is thirteen times the property factor and twenty-seven times the sales factor puts the entire apportionment formula out of focus." Id. at 843. Is the Ohio court's view that a disparity between different factors provides a basis for relief under the equitable apportionment provisions warranted? Compare Paris Manufacturing Co., Inc. v. Commonwealth and Doe Spun, Inc. v. Commonwealth, 505 Pa. 15, 476 A.2d 890, 893 (1984), where the Pennsylvania Supreme Court rejected "the assertion that mere disparity between the magnitudes of the property, payroll, and sales fractions is, in itself, indicative of a failure of the apportionment fairly to reflect the loci of business activities."

D. *Requirement of "Unusual Case" as Prerequisite to Equitable Relief.* Invoking the remarks of Professor William Pierce, UDITPA's principal draftsman, that the equitable apportionment provision should be limited to the "unusual case" (quoted in *Twentieth Century–Fox*), courts and administrative tribunals sometimes have insisted that the central question under UDITPA's relief provision "is not whether some quantitative comparison has produced a large-enough 'distortive' figure," but rather "whether there is an unusual fact situation that leads to an unfair reflection of business activity under the standard apportionment formula." Appeal of Crisa Corporation, 2002 WL 1400003 at *10 (Cal. St. Bd. Eq. June 20, 2002). See also MTC Reg. IV.18(b). As the California State Board of Equalization (SBE) elaborated in *Crisa* after making the foregoing observation:

> The answer to this question lies in an analysis of the relationship between the structure and function of the standard apportionment formula and the circumstances of a particular taxpayer. If the analysis reveals some manner in which the standard formula does not adequately deal with the taxpayer's circumstances, then [UDITPA § 18] may apply.

Crisa, 2002 WL 1400003 at *10. The SBE further observed that "there is no bright line rule that determines when the standard formula does not adequately deal with a particular situation," id., and that these cases must be analyzed on a case-by-case basis. However, it did offer five examples, based on its prior opinions, of unusual factual situations that may trigger relief under the equitable apportionment provision.

1. A corporation does substantial business in California, but the standard formula does not apportion any income to California. For example, the employees of a professional sports franchise render services in California while playing "away" games, but the standard formula apportions all income to the team's home state (citing Appeal of New York Football Giants, 1977 WL 3825 (Cal. St. Bd. Eq. Feb. 3, 1977), and Appeal of Milwaukee Professional Sports and Services, Inc., 1979 WL 4134 (Cal. St. Bd. Eq. June 28, 1979)).

2. The factors in the standard formula are mismatched to the time during which the income is generated. For example, a construction contractor reports income when long-term contracts are completed, but the standard formula requires income to be reported currently (citing Appeal of Donald M. Drake Co., 1977 WL 3823 (Cal. St. Bd. Eq. Feb. 3, 1977)).

3. The standard formula creates "nowhere income" that does not fall under the taxing authority of any jurisdiction. For example, a company owns equipment the value of which is attributed to the high seas or outer space, where it cannot be taxed by any jurisdiction (citing Appeal of American Telephone and Telegraph Co., 1982 WL 11771 (Cal. St. Bd. Eq. June 29, 1982)).

4. One or more of the standard factors is biased by a substantial activity that is not related to the taxpayer's main line of business. For example, the taxpayer continuously reinvests a large pool of "working capital," generating large receipts that are allocated to the site of the investment activity. However, the investments are unrelated to the services provided by the taxpayer as its primary activity (citing. Appeal of Pacific Telephone and Telegraph Co., 1978 WL 3941 (Cal. St. Bd. Eq. May 4, 1978)).

5. A particular factor does not have material representation in either the numerator or the denominator, rendering that factor useless as a means of reflecting business activity. For example, because a company does not own or rent any tangible or real personal property, the numerator and the denominator of the property factor are zero (citing Appeal of Oscar Enterprises, LTD, 1987 WL 50197 (Cal. St. Bd. Eq. Oct. 6, 1987)).

In none of these cases, the SBE stressed, did numerical comparisons play a significant role in the Board's determination. Rather, the cases analyzed the relationship between the structure and function of the standard apportionment formula and the circumstances of the particular taxpayer at issue.

10. METHODS OF APPORTIONMENT FOR SPECIAL INDUSTRIES

The three-factor apportionment formula of property, payroll, and receipts was developed for mercantile and manufacturing businesses. See "Model Business Income Tax," 6 Nat'l Tax Ass'n Bull. 113 (Nov. 1920). In a 1939 survey of the operation of the formula, the National Tax Association Committee on Allocation of Income pointed out: "It is obvious, however, from the studies conducted by the present Committee * * * that such a formula would not be suited to taxpayers other than those engaged in manufacturing or conducting mercantile businesses." 1939 Nat'l Tax Ass'n Procs. 190, 205. Legislatures usually exclude public utilities (e.g., transportation, communication, gas, and electric utilities) from the scope of the general statutory formula. See UDITPA § 2. The same is true in many states of other specialized industries, e.g., insurance companies, which are typically taxed on their gross premiums attributable to the state, and financial businesses, which are often subject to bank-specific taxing regimes. Nevertheless, the failure of some statutes to restrict the formula to such businesses, or to enact (or to authorize tax administrators to promulgate) methods especially adapted to the characteristics of non-manufacturing and non-mercantile businesses, has sometimes resulted in awkward and inappropriate apportionment under the general formula.

The states have developed special formulas adapted to the characteristics of particular industries. For example, many states have special apportionment rules for the transportation industry, including railroads, motor carriers, airlines, and pipelines. They include such factors as track mileage, revenue miles, flight time, and barrel miles to reflect the economic activities of the particular industry in question. Similarly, the states have developed special formulas for banking, broadcasting, publishing, and construction with factors reflecting the special characteristics of those industries, such as intangible property, audience, and circulation. The Multistate Tax Commission, usually working with industry groups, has been instrumental in developing these specialized apportionment formulas that it has promulgated as special regulations under UDITPA § 18. See MTC Reg. IV.18.(d) (construction contractors); MTC Reg. IV.18.(e) (airlines); MTC Reg. IV.18.(f) (railroads); MTC Reg. IV.18.(g) (trucking companies); MTC Reg. IV.1.(h) (television and radio broadcasting); MTC Reg. IV.18.(i) (financial institutions); MTC Reg. IV.18.(j) (publishing). These can be found at www.mtc.gov. There is an excellent study of the apportionment of public utility income in John A. Wilkie, "Income Apportionment of Unitary Public Utility Corporations," 15 Tax L. Rev. 467 (1960).

Detailed consideration of the division of income of special industries is beyond the scope of this book. Such consideration is provided in 1 Jerome R. Hellerstein & Walter Hellerstein, State Taxation ch. 10 (3d ed. 1998–2009).

CHAPTER 8

SALES TAXATION

■ ■ ■

A. INTRODUCTION

1. THE CLASSIFICATION AND NATURE OF SALES TAXES

The term "sales tax" embraces a large variety of levies in force in the United States. Haig and Shoup[a] have defined a sales tax as "any tax which includes within its scope all business sales of tangible personal property at either the retailing, wholesaling, or manufacturing stage, with the exceptions noted in the taxing law." Robert M. Haig & Carl S. Shoup, The Sales Tax in the American States 3 (1934). They classify sales taxes as:

(a) *Retail Sales Tax,* which is imposed only on sales of tangible personal property at retail or for use or consumption. This tax also includes sales of utility services and levies on admissions.

(b) *General Sales Tax,* which reaches sales of tangible personal property both at retail and for resale, and also the acts of extracting natural resources and of manufacturing.

(c) *Gross Receipts Tax,* which has the essential elements of the general sales tax and in addition is levied upon sales of personal and professional services, and in some cases sales of intangibles.

(d) *Gross Income Taxes,* which include (a), (b), and (c), above, and in addition receipts from non-business activities such as rents, interest, salaries.

Haig & Shoup, supra, at 3–4.

The most significant form of sales taxation in this country—and the form to which most of the materials in this chapter are devoted—is the retail sales tax. In principle, a retail sales tax is a single-stage levy on consumer expenditures, i.e., it applies only to final sales for personal use and consumption. John F. Due & John L. Mikesell, Sales Taxation: State and Local Structure and Administration 16 (2d ed. 1994). Accordingly, a

---

a. The excerpts from Haig and Shoup's work are reprinted with the permission of Columbia University Press.

theoretically ideal retail sales tax would exclude business inputs from the tax base. In fact, however, the American retail sales tax deviates substantially from this norm: roughly 40 percent of state sales tax revenues are attributable to business purchases. Robert Cline, et al., "Sales Taxation of Business Inputs: Existing Tax Distortions and the Consequences of Extending the Sales Tax to Business Services," State Tax Notes, Feb. 14, 2005, p. 457; Raymond J. Ring, Jr., "Consumers' Share and Producers' Share of the General Sales Tax," 52 Nat'l Tax J. 79 (1999); Raymond J. Ring, Jr., "The Proportion of Consumers' and Producers' Goods in the General Sales Tax," 42 Nat'l Tax J. 167, 175 (1989).

While no state has adopted a theoretically pure retail sales tax, all states have provisions that are designed to achieve its underlying theoretical purposes. Every state excludes sales for resale from the retail sales tax base. Similarly, states commonly exclude sales of ingredients or components of property produced for sale from the retail sales tax. These types of exclusions typically require that the business input retain its physical form as it moves through the production process. Other provisions reflect the broader view that all business inputs should be excluded from the retail sales tax base, even though such costs cannot be tied directly to the item ultimately sold or some component part of that item. Exclusions or exemptions for purchases of machinery and equipment used to produce tangible personal property for sale illustrate these sorts of provisions.

State retail sales taxes (hereafter simply "state sales taxes") share a number of administrative features that reflect, and in some cases are intended to further, the underlying philosophy of the tax as a levy imposed on the purchaser's use or consumption of the item sold, with the tax burden resting on the consumer. To make it more likely that the economic incidence of the tax is borne by the consumer,[b] state sales taxes usually are separately stated, and most states prohibit vendors from advertising that they will absorb the tax. Due & Mikesell, supra, at 30. Further, the tax itself is excluded from the base of the tax. In addition, sales taxes are collected from the purchaser by the seller and are imposed on a transaction-by-transaction basis. These features effectuate the understanding that the sales tax is a discrete charge, apart from the price of an item, that is paid by the consumer and collected by the vendor.

Although state sales taxes display significant common features and generally operate in a uniform manner, they nevertheless may be subdivided into three categories—vendor taxes, consumer taxes, and hybrid taxes. Id. at 28–29. Vendor taxes are sales taxes whose legal incidence rests on the vendor (e.g., for the privilege of making retail sales), and the vendor therefore has primary legal responsibility for paying the tax. Illinois, for example, imposes a "Retailers' Occupation Tax" on "persons engaged in the business of selling at retail tangible personal property" measured by the "gross receipts from [such] sales * * * made in the

---

b. See Section A(3) infra regarding the economic incidence and the distribution of the burden of the state sales tax.

course of business." 35 Ill. Comp. Stat. Ann. §§ 120/2, 120/2–10 (Westlaw 2009). Consumer taxes are sales taxes imposed upon the retail "sale" of property or services, and they are measured by the sales price of the goods or services. The measure of consumer taxes (sales price to the buyer) may therefore be contrasted—at least in a formal sense—with the measure of vendor taxes (gross receipts of the seller). Hybrid taxes contain features of both vendor and consumer levies. Notwithstanding these variations among state sales taxes, they all operate in essentially the same manner as levies intended and designed to fall on consumers (even when denominated as "vendor taxes").

Some states have significant nonretail elements in their sales tax structures. See Due & Mikesell, supra, at 54–56 (listing Arizona, Hawaii, Louisiana, and Mississippi). In addition, all states impose selective sales taxes on specific commodities, such as gasoline, alcohol, and tobacco. Finally, several states use a gross receipts taxes as their general business levy. Most other states have adopted a corporate income tax for this purpose. See Chapter 7.

2. THE GROWING FISCAL IMPORTANCE OF STATE AND LOCAL SALES TAXES

States' increasing reliance on sales taxes is one of the most significant developments in state finances during the twentieth century. The sales tax was a child of the Depression. With traditional sources of revenue, such as income and property taxes, providing lower and lower yields, the states turned to a new form of financing basic functions—the sales tax—as "a desperation measure." Due & Mikesell, supra, at 1. Mississippi enacted the first state sales tax in 1932, although levies in a few states had some features of sales taxes prior to that date. Many other states quickly followed Mississippi's lead so that by 1935 more than half the states had adopted sales taxes. Special Subcomm. on State Taxation of the House Comm. on the Judiciary, State Taxation of Interstate Commerce, H.R. Rep. No. 565, 89th Cong., 1st Sess. 610 (1965) ("Willis Comm. Rep."). Today, the general sales tax is in force in 45 states and the District of Columbia. Only Alaska, Delaware, Montana, New Hampshire, and Oregon have no general retail sales tax, although Alaska makes extensive use of the sales tax at the local level. For 2008, such general sales and use taxes produced $237 billion, or 31 percent of total state tax collections. See U.S. Census Bureau, National Totals of State Tax Revenue, By Type of Tax, available at www.census.gov/govs/www/qtax.html.

Municipalities and other local subdivisions of state governments have increasingly relied on sales taxes to supplement the revenues from the property tax, their traditional principal source of revenue. See U.S. Census Bureau, United States State & Local Government Finances by Level of Government, available at www.census.gov/govs/www/html. Today local governments in roughly two-thirds of the states levy sales taxes. Due & Mikesell, supra, at 277. Most local sales taxes are integrated with the state sales tax and are administered by the state. The state then distributes the local portion of the sales tax, sometimes after deducting a fee for administration, to the locality whose tax it has collected. Id. at 311–14.

References. John F. Due & John L. Mikesell, Sales Taxation: State and Local Structure and Administration (2d ed. 1994); John F. Due, Sales Taxation (1959); William F. Fox, ed., Sales Taxation: Critical Issues in Policy and Administration (1992); 2 Jerome R. Hellerstein & Walter Hellerstein, State Taxation ch. 12 (3d ed. 1999 & Cum. Supp. 2009); Daniel C. Morgan, Jr., Retail Sales Tax (1964); Jerome R. Hellerstein, "Significant Sales and Use Tax Developments During the Past Half Century," 39 Vand. L. Rev. 961 (1986); Herman C. McCloud, "Sales Tax and Use Tax: Historical Developments and Differing Features," 22 Duquesne L. Rev. 823 (1984). Volume 3 of the Willis Committee Report, Special Subcomm. on State Taxation of the House Comm. on the Judiciary, State Taxation of Interstate Commerce, H.R. Rep. No. 565, 89th Cong., 1st Sess. 610 (1965), contains an exhaustive, if somewhat dated, study of sales and use taxes.

3. DISTRIBUTION OF THE BURDEN OF RETAIL SALES AND USE TAX

It is generally assumed that sales taxes on consumer purchases are shifted forward to consumers. Due & Mikesell, supra, at 7. This is not always the case, however. See Timothy J. Besley & Harvey S. Rosen, "Sales Taxes and Prices: An Empirical Analysis," 52 Nat'l Tax J. 157 (1999) (empirical data show a variety of shifting patterns depending on the particular commodity involved). For example, if the demand for a product is relatively elastic, i.e., if an increase in the price of the product induces a relatively larger decrease in the demand for it, a tax on the product is likely to be borne by the seller of the product rather than by the consumer of it—regardless of whether the sales tax is separately stated and nominally passed on to the consumer. Assuming that consumers are unwilling to pay more than $5 for a pound of filet mignon, a five percent tax on the sale of filet mignon will not affect the after-tax price of the filet mignon, which will remain at $5. Instead the butcher will have to reduce its price to a little over $4.75, and it will absorb the economic burden of the tax (or pass it back to its suppliers). On the other hand, if the demand is relatively inelastic, i.e. if an increase in the price of the product induces a comparatively smaller decrease in the demand for it, a tax on the product is likely to be borne by its consumers rather than by sellers of the product. Assuming that consumers will not alter their pattern of purchasing salt even in the face of a price increase, a five percent tax on a box of salt selling for $1 will increase the price of the salt to $1.05, thereby requiring the purchaser to absorb the tax.

The usual assumption that retail sales taxes are generally passed on to consumers becomes more complicated when the tax is applied to business purchases. Despite the theoretical premise that the retail sales tax is a single-stage levy on consumer expenditures, and despite the existence of statutory provisions that exclude intermediate purchases in the economic process from the retail sales tax, business inputs in fact make up a healthy portion of most states' sales tax bases, as we observed above. See Section (A)(1) supra. Specifically, a nationwide study concluded that business inputs as a share of the sales tax base averaged 40 percent for 45 states and the District of Columbia. Raymond J. Ring, Jr., "Consumers' Share and Producers' Share of the General Sales Tax," 52 Nat'l Tax J. 79 (1999); Raymond J. Ring, Jr., "The Proportion of Consumers' and Producers' Goods in the General Sales Tax," 42 Nat'l Tax J. 167, 175 (1989). Typical taxable business inputs are those in which the business is deemed to be the ultimate consumer of the particular item purchased, even though the cost of the item will likely constitute part of the price of the product that the producer sells. For example, transportation equipment, office furniture, advertising catalogs, and supplies purchased by manufacturers and other businesses are usually taxable under state sales taxes. The ultimate distribution of the burden of sales taxes on business purchases of this nature is much less certain. Nevertheless, "one could reasonably assume that a large portion of the tax is ultimately reflected in higher prices for the consumption goods produced, directly or indirectly, but in a very uneven pattern relative to consumer spending." Due & Mikesell, supra, at 7–8.

On the assumption that sales taxes are generally shifted forward to consumers, many observers have long criticized sales taxes on the ground that they are "regressive," i.e., that sales taxes constitute a larger proportion of the income of low-income groups than of high-income groups. A Minnesota study, for example, found that for the portion of the retail sales tax borne by households, the tax constitutes 5.2 percent of the incomes of persons in the lowest ten percent of income earners while constituting just 1.3 percent of income persons in the top ten percent of income earners. Minnesota Department of Revenue, Tax Research Division, Minnesota Tax Incidence Study (1993), cited in Due & Mikesell, supra, at 9. Similarly, a Connecticut study revealed that the sales and use tax as a percentage of income falls from 8.15 percent at the under $5,000 income level to 5.03 percent at the $10,000 to $15,000 level, to 2.18 percent at the $100,000 to $200,000 level. KPMG Peat Marwick, The Connecticut Sales and Use Tax: Analysis of Tax Revision Alternatives, report prepared for State of Connecticut Task Force on State Tax Revenue (1990) (Table 11–4), cited in Due & Mikesell, supra, at 9. A 1988 study concluded that "[s]ales and excise taxes everywhere are regressive, often shockingly so: they can create unconscionable hardships for people living in poverty, they represent real financial burdens for middle-class families, and they let the rich, particularly the super rich, off the hook almost entirely." Citizens for Tax Justice, Nickels and Dimes: How Sales and Excise Taxes Add Up in the 50 States 3 (1988).

An earlier Connecticut survey, however, came to a different conclusion:

The consumer sales tax * * * can be shown to have a substantial element of progressivity in view of the greater benefit of exemptions to taxpayers of lesser consumption as compared with those of greater consumption. * * * For example * * * 78 per cent of the expenditures of a family in the lowest disposable income group is excluded from taxation by the exemption of food, housing and medical care. The same exemptions exclude only 53 per cent of the taxable expenditures of a family in the $5,000 and up disposable income group. In other words, major sales tax exemptions reduce the potential tax liability between 61 per cent and 78 per cent for those families having annual incomes (after Federal income tax) of less than $3,000, while the reduction in tax liability for families with $3,000 and more disposable income would run downward from 60 per cent.

Report of the Connecticut Tax Survey Committee 85 (1949).

Later studies reinforce the doubts expressed in the above quoted Connecticut report questioning the accepted wisdom that sales taxes are regressive. Some scholars have argued that one should judge the regressivity of the sales tax over the lifetime of the consumer and that, from this perspective, the sales tax is less regressive than indicated by annual income studies, Don Fullerton & Diane Lim Rogers, Who Bears the Lifetime Tax Burden? (1993), and might even be progressive. Gilbert E. Metcalf, "The Lifetime Incidence of State and Local Sales Taxes," National Bureau of Economic Research, Working Paper 4252 (1993). Another scholar maintains that since Social Security and welfare payments to lower income groups are indexed for price-level changes, the relative burden on the poor is much less than appears in many studies and, consequently, the regressivity is less. Edgar K. Browning, "Tax Incidence, Indirect Taxes, and Transfers," 38 Nat'l Tax J. 525 (1985). Yet another scholar concludes that the extent of regressivity of a sales tax depends significantly on the manner in which one measures savings by income level. John Sabelhaus, "What Is the Distributional Burden in Taxing Consumption?," 46 Nat'l Tax J. 46 (1993).

In the end, the consensus remains that sales taxes are regressive. See, e.g., Donald Phares, Who Pays State and Local Taxes 96 (1980) ("there is little question about its regressive incidence"). Nevertheless, while "[t]he absolute sales tax burden on the poor remains a significant consideration," this conclusion is "mitigated" by the fact that "many families are in low-income brackets only temporarily, or are in the high spending phases of the life cycle, and many welfare measures are primarily aimed at the benefiting the lowest income groups." Due & Mikesell, supra, at 12. Furthermore, the criticisms of the sales tax on the basis of regressivity are weakened both by the exemptions in many states for basic expenditures (e.g., food, clothing, gas, electricity, and prescription drugs) and by the substantial degree of progressivity in other portions of most states' taxing regimes. Id.

References. In addition to the secondary sources cited in the preceding discussion, see John F. Due, "Tax Incidence, Indirect Taxes, and Transfers—A Comment," 39 Nat'l Tax J. 539 (1986); John F. Due, "Sales Taxation and Consumer," 53 Am. Econ. Rev. 1078 (1963); William F. Fox & Charles Campbell, "Stability of the State Sales Tax Income Elasticity," 37 Nat'l Tax J. 201 (1984); William Hamovitch, "Sales Taxation: An Analysis of the Effects of Rate Increases in Two Contrasting Cases," 19 Nat'l Tax J. 411 (1966); James W. McGrew, "Food Exemption and Incidence of Sales Tax," 2 Nat'l Tax J. 362 (1949) (concluding that "a retail sales tax with food exempt is substantially proportional in burden"); Daniel C. Morgan, "Reappraisal of Sales Taxation: Some Recent Arguments," 16 Nat'l Tax J. 89 (1963); Gerhard Rostvold, "Distribution of Property, Retail Sales, and Personal Income Tax Burdens in California," 19 Nat'l Tax J. 38 (1966).

4. STRUCTURAL FLAWS IN THE RETAIL SALES TAX: IMPLICATIONS FOR LEGAL ANALYSIS

Many of the most troublesome legal questions that arise again and again in the course of sales tax adjudication can be traced directly to two fundamental structural flaws in the sales tax as it is currently in force in most states. The first flaw, to which we have alluded above (see p. 606 supra), is that the retail sales tax does not live up to the normative ideal of a tax on household consumption, but in fact includes substantial business purchases within the tax base. The second flaw, which is considered in more detail below (see pp. 612–13 infra), is that the sales tax base is confined largely to sales of tangible personal property and does not generally extend to sales of services or intangible property.

A. *The Taxation of Business Purchases.* If states limited the retail sales tax to final purchases for personal consumption, they would not tax business inputs, and the whole range of problems raised by business purchases now constituting close to half of the tax base[c] would simply disappear. Thus we would not have to struggle with such questions as whether an enterprise's purchase of a particular item was for its own use or for resale. See pp. 646–54 infra. We would not need to consider whether manufacturers' purchases of materials used in the manufacturing process were taxable, on the theory that they were "consumed" in the manufacturing process, or were exempt, on the theory that they became an ingredient or component part of an article produced for sale. See pp. 654–65 infra. Nor would we have to wrestle with the question whether machinery or equipment was used "directly" in manufacturing, in which

---

c. As we have already observed, business purchases are estimated to constitute 40 percent of the retail sales tax base. Robert Cline, et al., "Sales Taxation of Business Inputs: Existing Tax Distortions and the Consequences of Extending the Sales Tax to Business Services," State Tax Notes, Feb. 14, 2005, p. 457; Raymond J. Ring, Jr., "Consumers' Share and Producers' Share of the General Sales Tax," 52 Nat'l Tax J. 79 (1999); Raymond J. Ring, Jr., "The Proportion of Consumers' and Producers' Goods in the General Sales Tax," 42 Nat'l Tax J. 167, 175 (1989).

case it would be exempt from tax, or used only indirectly in manufacturing, in which case it would be taxable. See pp. 665–77 infra.

Indeed, from a normative standpoint, the very notion of "business consumption" is an oxymoron. Since the sales tax base is designed to be a tax on personal consumption, "business consumption" by definition lies outside its scope. Hence there is simply no need to inquire into the question whether any business purchases are taxable, since, on the basis of first principles, they are exempt. Accordingly, the difficulty that courts have in finding sensible answers to the questions raised in the preceding paragraph is due in part to the fact that, from the standpoint of sales tax theory, we should not be asking those questions in the first place. Moreover, when we do ask those questions, we have no intellectually satisfactory guiding principle by which to resolve them, since the concept of "business consumption" is based on statutory language that is not rooted in any sound principle of tax policy.

For example, how can one sensibly go about determining whether the purchase of particular materials—say, coke purchased by a steel manufacturer—should be taxed on the ground that it is "consumed" by the steel manufacturer in producing heat to fire its furnaces or, alternatively, should be exempt because a portion of the coke is infused into the iron and becomes an "ingredient or component part" of a product produced for sale? As an economic matter, of course, the price of all the materials that the steel manufacturer purchases will be reflected in the charge paid by the ultimate purchaser of the product, and it is that transaction—not the intermediate transaction in the economic process—that should be taxed, assuming that the product is purchased for personal consumption.[d] The notion of "business consumption" thus becomes an inquiry into physical rather than economic consumption, an inquiry that has little to do with the underlying purposes of a retail sales tax and one that predictably leads to confusing and inconsistent results in the cases. See pp. 654–65 infra.

B. *The Limitation of the Sales Tax Base to Sales of Tangible Personal Property.* If states included the retail sale of services and of intangible property—along with the retail sale of tangible personal property—in the sales tax base, they would eliminate many of the most difficult legal controversies spawned by the retail sales tax. It would no longer be necessary to determine whether the "true object" or "dominant purpose" of a transaction was the purchase of tangible personal property, on the

---

d. All goods and services are ultimately designed for personal consumption, although some goods and services (namely, so-called "public goods" such as national defense, public education, and fire and police protection) are not "sold" to consumers on a transaction-by-transaction basis, but rather are purchased indirectly by consumers through the tax system. Wholly apart from federal and state constitutional immunities from sales taxation, one may contend that it makes little sense to impose sales taxes upon expenditures for public goods—e.g., the purchase of arms by the Defense Department, or automobiles by a police department, or personal services by a board of education—since the tax revenues simply have to be increased to pay the taxes in question. Of course, there may still be an incentive to impose such taxes when the governmental body making the expenditure is not the same governmental body imposing the sales tax. Moreover, failure to impose sales taxes on public goods creates a tax advantage for such goods that might lead to overconsumption of such goods by comparison to the amount of public goods that would be purchased in a tax-neutral environment.

one hand, or the purchase of services or intangible content, on the other, when both the tangible property and services or intangibles are inseparable elements of a single transaction. See pp.618–29 infra. The only question would be whether the goods or services/intangibles were purchased for household consumption. If they were, the entire transaction would be taxable; if they were not, the entire transaction would be exempt.

Under these circumstances, the extensive body of case law distinguishing taxable sales or rentals of tangible personal property from nontaxable sales of services or intangibles would be rendered irrelevant. Taxpayers and state taxing authorities would no longer have to contend with such questions as whether the "true object" of the subscriber to a diaper service is getting the diaper (rental of tangible personal property) or getting the diaper cleaned (purchase of a service). See Saverio v. Carson, 186 Tenn. 166, 208 S.W.2d 1018 (1948). The difficulty of answering such questions is that there is no sound principle of tax policy on which the distinction rests and, consequently, no sound analytical basis for drawing a line that should not, as a normative matter, be drawn in the first place. The subscriber to a diaper service obviously wants both the diaper *and* the diaper cleaned, and it simply makes no sense from the standpoint of retail sales tax policy to try to separate two inextricably intertwined aspects of a transaction each of which provides personal consumption. The confusion and inconsistency in the cases arising under the retail sales tax is in large part attributable to the fact that tribunals are compelled to draw a line between taxable sales of tangible personal property and nontaxable sales of services or intangible property that is unrelated to any intellectually defensible principle of tax or economic policy.

C. *Legal Analysis in the Context of a Normatively Flawed Sales Tax.* Needless to say, the failure of state legislatures to conform the sales tax to the theoretical ideal of a single-stage levy on the final sale of goods and services to the consumer does not permit lawyers to ignore the law as written and to engage in legal advocacy based on the sales tax as it should have been designed. Taxpayers, taxing authorities, and adjudicative bodies must deal with the sales tax as it written. Accordingly, they must address issues raised by taxation of "business consumption" and by the distinction between taxable sales of personal property and nontaxable sales of services or intangibles, even if such concepts or distinctions are theoretically or analytically unsatisfactory.

It is nevertheless useful to keep the basic structural defects of the sales tax in mind when one approaches the legal questions that the retail sales tax raises. Although the resolution of legal controversies does not generally turn on normative principles that legislatures have not adopted, these broader normative considerations may have a role to play in the proper resolution of a controversy when the laws that the legislatures have adopted do not provide clear answers to whether a particular transaction is taxable. Moreover, if one recognizes that there is no sound policy basis for taxing business inputs or for distinguishing between sales of tangible personal property and sales of services or intangibles, it may inform the search for workable legal rules in this domain. If courts and tax administrators understand that they are drawing lines that are not tied to any guiding theoretical principle, they may concentrate their efforts on devising rules that are clear and workable rather than engaging in a futile effort to prescribe rules that are theoretically sound.

Once you have studied the existing sales and use tax framework, you will have an opportunity to reconsider the tax policy questions raised above in the final section of this chapter devoted to fundamental sales tax reform. See Section L infra.

B.   DELINEATION OF TAXABLE SALE

States have generally confined their retail sales taxes to sales of tangible personal property. Although most states tax some services, and some states tax many services, the inclusion of services in the sales tax base remains the exception rather than the rule. As a consequence, courts frequently confront the question whether a particular transaction constitutes a taxable sale of tangible personal property, on the one hand, or a nontaxable sale of services, intangibles, or real property, on the other. The cases and materials in this section consider these definitional issues.

1.   DISTINGUISHING TANGIBLE PERSONAL PROPERTY FROM SERVICES OR INTANGIBLES

If a sale involves a transfer that is limited to tangible personal property (e.g., the typical purchase of goods at a retail store) or a transfer that is limited to services or intangibles (e.g., a haircut or a right to display an image), its taxability under a traditional retail sales tax is not in doubt. The former transaction will be taxable as a sale of tangible personal property; the latter transactions will be exempt as a sale of services or intangibles. But many transactions do not fall squarely into one category or another. For example, the hairdresser may transfer tangible personal property to his or her customer in the form of shampoo or coloring agents in the course of providing hairdressing services. Similarly, a vendor of the right to reproduce photographic images may transfer a hard copy of the image to its customer along with the right to reproduce it. While one might regard the transfers of tangible personal property described above as insignificant to the overall transaction, in many circumstances the resolution of the question whether the transfer involves essentially tangible personal property, on the one hand, or essentially services or intangible property, on the other, is far from self-evident (e.g., the transfer of commercial artwork or a disk containing computer software).

To deal with this problem, many states have adopted a specific statutory exemption from the sales tax base for "personal service transactions which involve sales as inconsequential elements for which no separate charges are made." As the following case reveals, however, such exemptions do not resolve the difficulties of drawing the line between taxable and nontaxable transactions involving both taxable and nontaxable elements. Moreover, although the statutory exemptions in question are directed to the distinction between sales of tangible personal property and sales of services, the cases lend themselves to an alternative (but parallel) analysis based on the distinction between the sale of tangible personal property and the sale of (or license to use) an intangible.

WASHINGTON TIMES–HERALD v.
DISTRICT OF COLUMBIA

United States Court of Appeals, District of Columbia Circuit, 1954.
94 U.S.App.D.C. 154, 213 F.2d 23.

WILBUR K. MILLER, CIRCUIT JUDGE.

We are asked to review a decision of the District of Columbia Tax Court under the District of Columbia Use Tax Act.[1] Petitioner, a newspaper publishing company, contracted with several syndicates for its supply of comic strips. The syndicates carry out these contracts by sending the petitioner, at intervals, fiber matrices (mats) bearing impressions of the current sequence of strips. These mats are manufactured by the syndicates, from the original drawings, by a photo-engraving process. Petitioner uses the mats in the first of a series of operations culminating in the production of a metal plate from which the comic page is printed.[2] The petitioner pays the syndicates for the comic strip mats sums which are greatly in excess of the price of blank mats. For example, the Times–Herald purchased blank mats the size of newspaper page for twenty-two cents each, but for a mat containing six daily strips of the "Gump Family," with the right to use each strip one time, it paid the sum of $30.00.

The Tax Court held the transactions with the syndicates were sales at retail within the meaning of § 201 of the Act,[3] and upheld taxation thereof on the basis of the substantial prices paid the syndicates for mats which, had they been blank, could have been bought at a small fraction of those prices.

Section 47–2701, subd. 1(b)(3) of the Code exempts from sales and use taxes "Professional, insurance, or personal service transactions which involve sales as inconsequential elements for which no separate charges

---

1. 63 Stat. 124 et seq., § 47–2701 et seq., D.C.Code 1951.

2. Metal casts are made from the mats; these casts are combined in the sequence desired for the newspaper page; a mat is made of the whole page; an impression from this mat is transferred to a metal plate; this plate is put on the printing press, and the comic page is then printed.

3. Section 47–2701, subd. 1, D.C.Code 1951.

are made." An implementing Regulation[4] provides that a sale is an "inconsequential element" where the price of the tangible personal property is less than ten per cent of the amount charged for the services rendered. The Tax Court found as a fact that

> "The value and sales price of the matrices (also known as 'mats') ... were less than ten per cent of the amount charged for the services rendered the petitioner under the contracts [with the syndicates]...."

This finding, which was disregarded by the Tax Court in its decision holding the transactions taxable, was a sufficient basis for reaching the opposite conclusion. The syndicates sold to the Times–Herald the right to reproduce one time the work of artists who make the drawings. They simply sold the professional and personal services of the artists whom they had under contract and in so doing transferred title to the mats, of inconsequential value, from which the drawings could be reproduced. The price was paid for the artists' work, i.e., for the right to reproduce the impressions on the mats—not for the mats themselves. The newspaper bought the creation of the artist—not the material on which it was impressed—and the right to reproduce it. Without that right, the comic strip mats would be entirely worthless.

The transactions in question are clearly exempt under § 47–2701, subd. 1(b)(3).

Reversed.

S<small>TEPHENS</small>, C<small>HIEF</small> J<small>UDGE</small>. I concur in the result for the following reason: I think that, in essence, what the Times–Herald contracted with the Syndicates for was a right to reproduce, once, the artist-created comic strip ideas expressed, for the purpose of reproduction, in "mat" form. That, in my view, is not a "use ... or consumption of any tangible personal property" and is not the purchase or sale of "services" and is therefore not taxable under Section 47–2702 of the D.C.Code.

I am authorized to state that C<small>IRCUIT</small> J<small>UDGES</small> F<small>AHY</small> and W<small>ASHINGTON</small> concur in the foregoing.

N<small>OTES AND</small> Q<small>UESTIONS</small>

A. Does the majority face the question in the case when it declares that the "sale" of the mats was an inconsequential element in the case? Under the court's test—the value of the materials as compared with the value of the services going into the final product—would the sale of a Rembrandt painting be free of sales tax, since the canvas and the paint are inconsequential elements in the cost of the article? In fact, courts and tax administrators have typically construed sales tax laws to cover transactions involving works of art, originally designed dresses, and other items in which the cost of the materials used is inconsequential. Does the court ever address the question whether the

---

4. Section 202(b) of the Regulations Pertaining to Sales and Use Taxes, promulgated July 12, 1949, by the Commissioners of the District of Columbia.

transaction in question is a "personal service" transaction? Or does it simply assume that, if the cost of materials is inconsequential, the transaction is in essence one of personal service? Can this assumption be squared with the statutory exemption for "[p]rofessional, insurance, or personal service transactions which involve sales as inconsequential elements for which no separate charges are made"?

B. *Relative Cost of Tangible Personal Property as the Determining Factor Whether a Transaction Involves a Taxable Sale.* As suggested above, many courts disagree with the position taken in the *Washington Times–Herald* opinion that there is a sale of a service rather than a sale of tangible personal property if the value or price of the materials that go into the product furnished to the consumer is inconsequential as compared to the charge for the services involved. As the North Dakota Supreme Court pointed out long ago, in a statement that many courts have quoted:

> There is no article, fabricated by a machine or fashioned by the human hand, that is not the fruit of the exercise and application of individual ability and skill. And few, indeed, are the instances where the greater part of the cost thereof is not chargeable to personal service directly or remotely applied.

Voss v. Gray, 70 N.D. 727, 298 N.W. 1, 4 (1941).

The court expressed similar sentiments in Craig–Tourial Leather Co. v. Reynolds, 87 Ga.App. 360, 73 S.E.2d 749 (1952), in construing a "sales as inconsequential elements" provision in a shoe repairer's case:

> We do not think that the actual cost or monetary value of the materials used is determinative. * * * However, we think that the main consideration should be the purpose of the customer, who primarily wishes to buy the skilled services of the shoe repairman * * * Under such circumstances, the sale of various grades or qualities of materials by the shoe repairman is really incidental to and but a means of rendering the services which his customers want.

Id., 73 S.E.2d at 752.

C. *Sale of Tangible Personal Property as Distinguished From the Sale or License to Use Intangibles.* As suggested by the concurring opinion in *Washington Times–Herald*, a transaction involving the distinction between the taxable sale of tangible personal property (associated with the transfer of an "inconsequential" service) and the nontaxable sale of a service (associated with the transfer of "inconsequential" tangible personal property) may also, or alternatively, be viewed as involving the distinction between the taxable sale of tangible personal property and the nontaxable sale or license to use an intangible. Indeed, courts frequently use the term "service" and "intangible" interchangeably (and indiscriminately) in this context. Although these two categories are not airtight, and the conclusion that a transaction involves the sale of a service or the sale or license to use an intangible leads to the same result (as in *Washington Times–Herald*), you should keep in mind the distinction between services and intangibles, because it can be significant in some circumstances (e.g., if a state taxes the sale of services but not of intangible rights). Moreover, some courts use different criteria for drawing the distinction between sales of tangible personal property and sales of services, on the one hand, and sales of tangible personal property and sales of intangibles, on the other. See, e.g., Navistar International Transportation Corp. v. State Board of Equalization, 8 Cal.4th 868, 35 Cal.Rptr.2d 651, 884 P.2d 108 (1994) ("true object" test applied only to the distinction between the sale of tangible personal property "incidental to the performance of a service," not to the sale of tangible personal property incidental to the sale of an intangible).

2. THE "TRUE OBJECT" AND SIMILAR TESTS

If the *Washington Times–Herald* case demonstrates nothing else, it shows that the legislative effort to distinguish between taxable and nontaxable sales involving transfers of tangible personal property in conjunction with the transfer of services or intangibles has not put an end to controversies over this question. Indeed, such exemptions often do little more than provide the framework within which courts and administrative tribunals undertake the analysis of these issues. Regardless of the statutory or regulatory guidance that state legislatures and state tax administrators may provide to help draw the line between taxable sales of tangible personal property and nontaxable sales of services and intangibles, courts often fashion their own criteria for resolving the question of whether a transaction is taxable or not. The ensuing case and materials focus on the judicially developed rules in this area, although these rules often reflect legislative or administrative guidance.

CITY OF BOULDER v. LEANIN' TREE, INC.

Supreme Court of Colorado, 2003. En Banc.
72 P.3d 361.

JUSTICE COATS delivered the Opinion of the Court.

* * *

I.

In April 1997, Boulder conducted a tax audit of Leanin' Tree, a Boulder business manufacturing and selling greeting cards and other gift products, for the period of February 1, 1994 through January 31, 1997. As a result of the audit, the city issued a notice of assessment for various items. * * * [T]he parties filed cross-motions for summary judgment. For purposes of summary judgment, the parties entered a joint statement of undisputed facts.

The greeting cards and other gift products manufactured and sold by Leanin' Tree contain images of original artwork created by independent artists. Leanin' Tree entered into license agreements with these artists whereby it borrowed their artwork and received the exclusive right to reproduce and publish the images. To obtain the artwork, Leanin' Tree borrowed the original piece, a photographic negative of the original artwork, or a digital image on a computer disk of the original piece.

Because the original image, in most cases, was much larger than the five to seven square-inch size available on greeting cards or other products, Leanin' Tree created a color separation of the artwork, negative, or digital image, transforming the image from its original size to a product-usable size. In addition, Leanin' Tree routinely added borders or verse or both, almost always changed the contrast of the image, often changed the composition of the image by adding or deleting elements in the image, and frequently cropped the image to best fit the product. The derivative image on the color separation was then burned onto metal plates that were used along with colored inks to print the image of the artwork onto greeting cards. In every case, Leanin' Tree returned the original artwork to the artist after it created the color separation.

If Leanin' Tree manufactured and sold merchandise containing an artist's ideas, it paid the artist royalties as a percentage of the revenues received for the product. In cases where Leanin' Tree borrowed a piece of artwork and made a color separation, and then decided not to manufacture any products with the image or sell any products with the image, Leanin' Tree owed nothing to the artist under the license agreement.

The district court entered summary judgment in favor of Leanin' Tree, holding that the right it acquired through these license agreements was an intangible right that was not subject to the use tax. In an unpublished opinion, the court of appeals affirmed on other grounds, holding that the transactions were not taxable under the manufacturer's processing exemption, which exempts from taxation tangible personal property sold at wholesale that enters into the processing and becomes an ingredient or component part of the product or service being manufactured or furnished. Boulder petitioned this court for a writ of certiorari.

II.

Boulder's tax code requires the payment of a sales or use tax on the purchase price paid or charged for tangible personal property or taxable services sold or used in the city. It defines "tangible personal property," in pertinent part, as "corporeal personal property that may be seen, weighed, measured, felt, or touched or is in any manner perceptible to the senses." B.R.C. § 3–1–1(ss). The code makes no attempt to define services[2] or personal property that is other-than-tangible.

The price of a purchase often includes a combination of tangible personal property and services or rights that are other-than-tangible. See, e.g., Babcock v. Nudelman, 367 Ill. 626, 12 N.E.2d 635, 637 (1937) (practice of optometry involves both providing a service and furnishing tangible property). If the price of the tangible property involved in a transaction can be meaningfully separated from the price commanded by the intangible portion of the transaction, the sales or use tax must be calculated on the purchase price of only the tangible property. Cf. A.D.

---

2. It does of course enumerate the services that are taxable, none of which have the parties claimed to be applicable here.

Store Company, Inc. v. Exec. Dir. of the Dept. of Rev., 19 P.3d 680, 684 (Colo.2001) (construing state sales tax statute with regard to the sale and alteration of clothing: "If they are separable, then the service is not taxable."). If, however, the various portions of the transaction are not meaningfully separable, the ordinance, like the corresponding state statute, provides no more express guidance for taxing the transaction.

Rather than imposing a sales or use tax on the full purchase price of every inseparably mixed transaction, the City Manager of Boulder has, by implementing regulation,[3] construed the ordinance to require characterization of each transaction according to its "true" or "real object."

> The test for determining whether a particular transaction involves a sale of tangible personal property or the transfer of tangible personal property incidental to the performance of a service is one of the true objects of the contract. If the true object sought by the buyer is the service per se, the transaction is not subject to tax even though some tangible personal property is transferred.... [A]n idea may be expressed in the form of tangible personal property and that property may be transferred for a consideration from one person to another; however, the person transferring the property may still be regarded as the consumer of the property. *Thus, the transfer to a publisher of an original manuscript by the author thereof for the purpose of publication is not subject to taxation.* The author is the consumer of the paper on which is recorded the text of the creation. However, the tax would apply to the sale of mere copies of an author's works or the sale of manuscripts written by other authors where the manuscript itself is of particular value as an item of tangible personal property and the purchaser's primary interest is in the physical property. Tax would also apply to the sale of artistic expressions in the form of paintings and sculptures even though the work of art may express an original idea since the purchaser desires the tangible object itself; that is, since the true object of the contract is the work of art in its physical form.

Special Industry Regulation, SR–31(2) (emphasis added).

Although not binding on courts, such interpretative regulations are entitled to deference with regard to implementation, as long as they do not misapply or misconstrue the statute or ordinance. The regulation's mandate to tax inseparably mixed transactions only when the object of the transaction is fairly characterized as the sale or use of tangible personal property is clearly consistent with the mandate of the ordinance itself to tax only tangible personal property. It is less clear that the regulation prescribes any practical method, much less one that reflects the legislative intent embodied in the ordinance, for making that determination in individual cases.

A number of jurisdictions have similar provisions in either their statutes or regulations for determining the true character, object, or

---

3. The city manager has the authority to adopt legislative and interpretive rules to implement the tax provisions in the code.

purpose of inseparably mixed transactions for purposes of their taxability. Attempts to apply these provisions in a consistent and meaningful way have led to a variety of approaches, with emphasis on a variety of different factors. See, e.g., Emery Indust., Inc. v. Limbach, 43 Ohio St.3d 134, 539 N.E.2d 608, 613 (1989) ("overriding purpose" test); Hasbro Indus., Inc. v. Norberg, 487 A.2d 124, 126 (R.I.1985) ("real object" of the transaction); Quotron Systems, Inc. v. Comptroller of Treasury, 287 Md. 178, 411 A.2d 439, 443 (1980) ("predominant purpose" test); Bullock v. Statistical Tabulating Corp., 549 S.W.2d 166, 167 (Tex.1977) ("essence-of-the-transaction" test); WTAR Radio–TV Corp. v. Commonwealth, 217 Va. 877, 883, 234 S.E.2d 245, 249 (1977) ("true object" test). This court has not before expressly considered the taxability of inseparably mixed transactions.

III.

The transactions for which Boulder assessed a use tax against Leanin' Tree clearly involved purchases of other-than-tangible personal property, even if they included the transfer of tangible personal property as well; and the tangible and other-than-tangible portions of the transaction were not meaningfully separable. Although Leanin' Tree used in its manufacturing process the tangible medium upon which the artists' representations appeared, the transactions never permitted Leanin' Tree to keep, sell, display, or otherwise benefit from the artwork as a finished product. Furthermore, the arrangements for compensating the artists clearly reflected a transaction other than a traditional sale of goods. The transactions normally did not involve direct payment to the artists for the use of their artwork but involved compensation in the nature of royalties for cards or products sold by Leanin' Tree. Short of simply separating the cost of raw materials, which is more appropriately taxed to the artists in the absence of contrary directions in the tax law, there is no meaningful way to separate the value of the tangible medium from the value of the right to reproduce the image appearing on it. The taxability of these transactions therefore must depend upon the intent of the Boulder ordinance to treat transactions of this kind as the sale or use of tangible personal property or as something else.

Faced with a virtually identical interpretative regulation (although substantially different tax provisions), California has resolved the matter by reference to the single consideration of physical usefulness. See Preston v. State Bd. of Equalization, 25 Cal.4th 197, 105 Cal.Rptr.2d 407, 19 P.3d 1148, 1158 (2001) ("Together, these decisions establish that any transfer of tangible property *physically useful* in the manufacturing process is subject to sales tax even though the true object of the transfer is an intangible property right like a copyright.") (emphasis in original); see also Simplicity v. State Bd. of Equalization, 27 Cal.3d 900, 167 Cal.Rptr. 366, 615 P.2d 555, 562 (1980) (holding that film negatives and master recordings were tangible personal property, even though they were valued in part for their intellectual content, because they were also physically useful in the manufacturing process). Boulder urges that its tax provisions be implemented similarly.

While such a standard has the clear advantages of simplicity and relative consistency of application, it does little to further an expressed legislative intent to tax only the purchase or use of tangible personal property. Rather, by postulating, in effect, that the tangible aspect of the transaction is necessarily an object of the transaction and cannot be incidental, as long as the intangible right can be acquired and used only in conjunction with or through the use of tangible property, it reduces virtually all inseparable transactions to transactions for the purchase of tangible personal property, to be taxed in their entirety.

Furthermore, to the extent that reliance upon "physical usefulness" as the determining factor does not render a tax exemption for intangible rights (like copyrights) completely illusory, its desirability as tax policy, and the corresponding intent of the ordinance, is far from clear. Distinguishing a manuscript that merely provides "verbal guidance"—in the sense that it can be read and retyped—from one that is filmed or photocopied, on the grounds that in the latter cases the tangible manuscript is physically useful in the manufacturing process, is both conceptually tenuous and discriminatory for reasons that have little, if any, justification in tax policy. Accepted normative principles requiring functionally equivalent transactions to be taxed similarly, see generally 2 Jerome R. Hellerstein & Walter Hellerstein, State Taxation, ¶ 12.08[3] (3d ed.2002), would be thwarted by the disparate treatment of technologies, like photocopying and scanning, that serve similar purposes. And to the extent that scanning a manuscript could be treated as rendering it physically useful, too, it is not readily apparent why the manuscript would not similarly be physically useful as a medium for communicating the author's words to a typist for retyping. Seductive as the single-factor, physical usefulness test may be, it is an extremely blunt tool for implementing a legislative intent to tax only tangible personal property, given the variety of situations to which it must be applied.

Whether couched in terms of the true object, dominant purpose, or essence of the transaction, or of the consequential or incidental nature of the transfer of tangible property, the rationales of most courts attempting to characterize inseparably mixed transactions acknowledge, either explicitly or implicitly, that they are not reducible to a single, dispositive factor. See, e.g., New England Telephone & Telegraph Co. v. Clark, 624 A.2d 298, 302 (R.I.1993) ("The real-object test must be applied to the totality of the transaction."); Mr. B's, Inc. v. City of Chicago, 302 Ill.App.3d 930, 236 Ill.Dec. 127, 706 N.E.2d 1001, 1005 (1998) ("When tangible goods or items are provided in conjunction with services, courts examine the totality of the transaction to determine its taxability.") (internal quotation omitted); Bullock, 549 S.W.2d at 169 (because resolution of consequential or inconsequential inquiry can turn on many factors, issue must be decided on case by case basis). While there has been no clear emergence of a comprehensive and consistent theory that more expressly articulates the goals of the analysis, a veritable plethora of factors have been relied on under the circumstances of individual cases.

Some courts have compared the value of the tangible property with that of the intangible property or service. See, e.g., Washington Times–Herald v. District of Columbia, 213 F.2d 23, 24 (D.C.Cir.1954) (sale of one-time-use cartoon mats was sale of professional and personal services rather than of mats because their value when blank was inconsequential compared with their value after the artwork was complete); Fingerhut Prods. Co. v. Comm'r of Revenue, 258 N.W.2d 606, 609 (Minn.1977) (value of mailing lists in tangible format was slight compared to price paid for names themselves). Other decisions have considered whether there was an alternative method of transfer. See, e.g., Commerce Union Bank v. Tidwell, 538 S.W.2d 405, 408 (Tenn.1976) (no taxable transfer where computer programming information conveyed by magnetic tape could have been transmitted by telephone lines or fed directly into the computer). The length of time the information provided retains its value has also been considered significant. See, e.g., Fingerhut, 258 N.W.2d at 609 (mailing lists containing names of potential buyers had limited useful life expectancy); Williams & Lee Scouting Service, Inc. v. Calvert, 452 S.W.2d 789, 792 (Tex.App.1970) (statistical data provided to oil companies had very short useful life unless reported at least weekly). Some decisions have looked for constraints on the buyer's ability to use the tangible property. See, e.g., Dun & Bradstreet v. City of New York, 276 N.Y. 198, 204–05, 11 N.E.2d 728, 731 (1937) (significant that subscriber of confidential information was not allowed to share it with public); Fingerhut, 258 N.W.2d at 609 (significant that provider of mailing lists allowed them to be used only once, between set dates). Yet others have examined what is actually done with the tangible property after it has yielded the intangible component. See, e.g., Commerce Union Bank, 538 S.W.2d at 408 (sale of computer software not tangible personal property where once information was transferred into computer, tangible property was returned or destroyed); Sneary v. Director of Revenue, 865 S.W.2d 342, 346 (Mo.1993) (architectural illustrations were consequential because buyer did not dispose of illustrations after using them). Finally, several jurisdictions have considered whether the tangible property represents the finished product sought by the buyer. See, e.g., Columbus Coated Fabrics Div. v. Porterfield, 30 Ohio St.2d 307, 285 N.E.2d 50, 53 (1972) (finding that end product of the service, rather than service itself, that taxpayer was after); Hasbro Indus., Inc., 487 A.2d at 126–27 (taxpayer's real object was mechanical artwork as an end product from which its product packaging could be fabricated in finished form for ultimate sale).

In circumstances not unlike those at issue here, the Missouri Supreme Court emphasized that the skill and expertise used to create a color separated film and color keys were the true objects of a sale and that a color separation served only as a medium to convey the transparency colors and had no value after having done so. K & A Litho Process, Inc. v. Director of Revenue, 653 S.W.2d 195 (Mo.1983) (where taxpayer received film transparencies and by highly technical and scientific process created color separation and key for making printing plates). It also distinguished the taxpayer's separated film from motion pictures, the latter being finished products which a buyer could use in the form sold. In a later case, the same court distinguished transactions involving architectural illustrations, finding them not merely disposable conduits, where the architectural information was not transferred from them and they were not disposed of, and where the architect's clients desired, used, and valued the illustrations in the same form as sold, making them more like finished motion pictures. Sneary v. Director of Revenue, 865 S.W.2d 342 (Mo.1993).

Varied as these analyses may be, they largely share in common some attempt to identify characteristics of the transaction at issue that make it either more analogous to what is reasonably and commonly understood to be a sale of goods, or more analogous to what is generally understood to be the purchase of a service or intangible right. Perhaps the quintessential transaction for the purchase of an intangible right is the marketing of literary works, in which the clear object, around which the entire transaction is structured, is the right to publish the author's work. Although the transactions by Leanin' Tree may superficially appear to be akin to the purchase of artwork, which is normally considered to be the sale of a tangible object, upon closer examination the transactions between Leanin' Tree and its artists have much more in common with a transaction for the right to publish.

Unlike the typical purchase of a work of art, the transactions structured by Leanin' Tree do not include the transfer of title and possession with a right to resell or exhibit the artwork. In fact, they do not entitle Leanin' Tree to the enjoyment or profit from the finished product of the artist at all. Instead they grant it a right to use the image created by the artist in creating a new tangible object, which may be subject to sales and use tax. Consistent with this objective, the artist is not paid a lump-sum for his artwork or even for the use of his artwork as a lease agreement. Rather, he is compensated for his contribution to the production of the finished product, in the form of royalties or entitlement to a percentage of the ultimate sales. Despite having provided his artwork to Leanin' Tree for its use, the artist receives no compensation unless his image is ultimately incorporated into and sold as a new product. In all essential respects, the transactions structured by Leanin' Tree resemble the purchase of a right to edit and publish rather than the sale of artwork.

Unless the attempt to distinguish tangible from other-than-tangible property is abandoned altogether, some multi-factor or totality of circumstances test, permitting characterization of the transaction according to a reasonable and common understanding of those concepts, is virtually unavoidable. See generally 2 Hellerstein, supra at ¶ 12.08[2]. The necessary flexibility of such an analysis will inevitably leave the characterization of some transactions in doubt. It is a longstanding rule of construction in this jurisdiction that tax statutes "will not be extended beyond the clear import of the language used, nor will their operation be extended by analogy. . . . All doubts will be construed against the government and in favor of the taxpayer." Transponder Corp. v. Property Tax Admin., 681 P.2d 499, 504 (Colo.1984). To the extent that any doubt remains that the transactions by Leanin' Tree should be characterized as other than the purchase of tangible personal property, that doubt is therefore resolved in favor of Leanin' Tree.

IV.

Considered in their totality, the challenged transactions, for which Leanin' Tree was assessed use tax, do not constitute transactions for the sale or use of tangible personal property within the contemplation of Boulder's tax code. Without considering the merits of the court of appeals' rationale, we therefore affirm its judgment affirming the district court.

CHIEF JUSTICE MULLARKEY, concurring in part and dissenting in part:

I agree with the majority that we should apply a multi-factor or totality-of-the-circumstances test to determine whether the transaction involved here is the sale or use of tangible personal property under the Boulder ordinance. I also agree that in applying the test, we should apply a practical, common sense understanding to determine the nature of the transaction. This is the approach advocated by 2 Jerome R. Hellerstein & Walter Hellerstein, State Taxation, ¶ 12.08[2] (3d ed.2002). As the authors point out, courts will have to untangle transactions that have both tangible and intangible qualities as long as legislative bodies continue to make artificial distinctions between tangible property that is taxed and services that are not taxed.

However, I disagree with the majority's application of the test. Leanin' Tree purchases finished paintings from freelance artists. These are tangible, touchable objects that Boulder can tax under its ordinance. I respectfully concur in part and dissent in part from the majority opinion.

The *State Taxation* treatise cited above makes it clear that most states distinguish between written works which are not taxed, and photographs and artwork which are taxed. The reason for the distinction is simple enough. Unless the writing involves a rare manuscript or something similar, the form of the writing has no significance. A publisher is purchasing the contents of the writing, that is, the purchaser buys the abstract ideas expressed in the writing.

A piece of visual art is treated quite differently. The purchaser buys a photograph or an artwork as a physical object that embodies the artist's ideas. The form is the substance of the work.

Although we have no relevant cases in Colorado, the regulations construing the state sales and use tax are helpful by analogy. Under these regulations, the services of photographers and photofinishers are taxable where the primary purpose of the transaction is the resulting physical photograph. The regulation concerning photofinishers specifically states that "[p]hotofinishers are engaged in the business of selling tangible personal property to their customers and such sales are taxable." 1 C.C.R.

201–5, Special Regulations, SR–34 "Photofinishers". Under the regulation governing photographers, their services are likewise taxable unless the services are specifically bargained for and the tangible personal property is irrelevant in the transaction.

With respect to transactions for the use of photography and art in a commercial setting, many states treat the transaction as a sale of taxable tangible personal property rather than a sale of nontaxable services. Preston v. State Bd. Of Equalization, 25 Cal.4th 197, 105 Cal.Rptr.2d 407, 19 P.3d 1148 (2001); State Taxation, at ¶ 13.05[2] (citing Federated Dep't Stores v. Kosydar, 45 Ohio St.2d 1, 340 N.E.2d 840 (1976)); Southern Bell Tel. & Tel. Co. v. Dep't of Revenue, 366 So.2d 30 (Fla.Dist.Ct.App.1978); Hillman Periodicals, Inc. v. Gerosa, 285 A.D. 441, 137 N.Y.S.2d 863 (1955); Voss v. Gray, 70 N.D. 727, 298 N.W. 1 (1941)).

Helpful in understanding the taxation distinction between written works and visual arts is the California Supreme Court's decision in *Preston* which found the taxation of an artist's work permissible in circumstances very similar to the case at hand. In *Preston,* an artist appealed taxes assessed against her, arguing that her agreements with publishers and a manufacturer for the right to reproduce her artwork were not taxable under a state regulation that exempted taxation on intangible personal property. This regulation gave the publishing of a manuscript as an example for when the exemption would apply. The artist specifically argued that an exemption would be proper in her case because, although the right to reproduce the artwork had been transferred, the artwork remained with her and thus no sale of artwork had occurred. Pursuant to these agreements, the artist would transfer her finished pieces to the respective clients who would copy and reproduce the pieces and use the images in their finished products as illustrations in books or on rubber stamps. The artwork would then be returned to the artist, who would receive royalties on sales of the products.

In rejecting the artist's contentions, the California court distinguished artwork from a manuscript, explaining that tangible artwork was physically useful and necessary to the production process while a manuscript simply provided verbal guidance and was not essential to the manufacturing process. Although focusing on physical usefulness, essentially, the court found artwork distinguishable from written work because of the greater physical value of artwork to a purchaser that is not present in a manuscript.

Keeping in mind this distinction between a writing and an artwork, I now turn to the circumstances of this case. As stipulated by both parties, Leanin' Tree manufactures and sells greeting cards and other gift products that contain images of original artwork produced independently by artists. Pursuant to license agreements, Leanin' Tree is given the exclusive right to reproduce that artwork and "may incorporate such reductions, enlargements or modifications to individual original Artworks as Leanin' Tree, in its business judgment, may determine." In compensation, the artists are paid a royalty dependent on the volume of sales of the products displaying their artwork. In order to incorporate the artwork into its products, Leanin' Tree must physically obtain the artwork in order to create a color separation necessary to reproduce the artwork on the greeting cards and other products.

Under the facts presented in this case, it is clear that the purpose of the transactions in question was the use of the artists' actual tangible personal property. Similar to the case in *Preston*, Leanin' Tree's possession and use of the physical artwork in the manufacturing of its products was a key element in its transactions and necessary for the creation of its products. Although the transactions engaged in by Leanin' Tree are not typical transactions for the purchase of artwork, the fact that Leanin' Tree returns the artwork to the artists and pays them royalties contingent on the sales of items bearing their artwork has no significance. The transaction that Boulder seeks to tax is the same regardless of the purpose or nature of the transfer of the artwork and regardless of the form of payment agreed upon.

In my view, the Colorado regulations and the *Preston* decision provide a practical, common sense result that is consistent with the test adopted by the majority. Therefore, I would hold that payments made by Leanin' Tree, Inc. to artists for the right to reproduce their finished, original works of art on greeting cards and related products are subject to the City of Boulder's sales and use tax on tangible, personal property.

I am authorized to say that JUSTICE MARTINEZ and JUSTICE BENDER join in this concurrence and dissent.

NOTES AND QUESTIONS

A. *The "True Object" and Similar Tests for Distinguishing Sales of Tangible Personal Property from Sales of Services.* As noted in *Leanin' Tree*, many state courts have articulated a "true object" or similar test for distinguishing taxable sales of tangible personal property from exempt sales of services even in the absence of statutory or regulatory adoption of such a test. For example, the Virginia Supreme Court has declared:

> The test applied by a preponderance of the authorities from other jurisdictions with sales tax statutes similar to our statute is: If the "true object" sought by the taxpayer is the services per se, the exemption is available, but if the true object of the buyer is to obtain the property produced by the service, the exemption is not available.

WTAR Radio–TV Corp. v. Commonwealth, 217 Va. 877, 234 S.E.2d 245, 249 (1977). Two semantic variations on the "true object" test are the "dominant purpose" test and the "essence of the transaction" test. If the "dominant purpose" of the transaction is the transfer of tangible personal property, the transaction will constitute a taxable sale of tangible personal property; if the "dominant purpose" of the transaction is the transfer of services, the transaction will constitute a nontaxable sale of services. Similarly, if the "essence of the transaction" is a sale of property, it will be taxable; if the "essence of the transaction" is the sale of service, it will be exempt. These formulations are in substance the same as the "true object" test.

There are literally hundreds of cases applying these tests to various transactions. See, e.g., Sneary v. Director of Revenue, 865 S.W.2d 342 (Mo. 1993) ("true object" of transaction is the receipt of architectural illustrations, not the architect's services); State ex rel. Clayburgh v. American West Community Promotions, Inc. 645 N.W.2d 196 (N.D. 2002) ("true object" of transaction was the intangible right to discounts and free products and services, not coupon books that served merely as tangible means for the transmission of intangible right); Mark O. Haroldsen, Inc. v. State Tax Comm'n, 805 P.2d 176 (Utah 1990) (taxpayer's "real object" is the receipt of mailing lists, not the personal service of creating the list); Wisconsin Department of Revenue v. Dow Jones & Co., 148 Wis.2d 872, 436 N.W.2d 921 (App. 1989) ("real objective" of transaction is receipt of news services, not possession of teleprinter).

B. *Application of the "True Object" and Similar Tests to Distinguishing Sales of Tangible Personal Property from Sales of Intangibles.* The "true object" and similar tests typically have been articulated in the context of distinguishing between sales of tangible personal property and sales of services, perhaps because the tangible personal property/service issue arises more frequently than does the tangible personal property/intangible issue. Many courts, however, including the court in *Leanin' Tree*, would apply the "true object" and similar tests to any transaction involving a "mixed" transaction of both taxable and nontaxable elements, whether the latter were services or intangibles. Indeed, as we have already observed throughout the preceding materials, courts frequently do not clearly differentiate between services and intangibles when dealing with "mixed" transactions, and they therefore effectively apply the "true object" or similar test to services and intangibles.

C. *Evaluation of the "True Object" Test.* Is the "true object" test a useful mechanism for distinguishing sales of tangible personal property from sales of services or intangibles? Does it have a high predictive value, i.e., would you feel confident (in the absence of a precedent on point) in providing advice to a client as to whether a court is likely to find the "true object" of a transaction to be the sale of tangible personal property or the sale of services or intangibles? If not, why not? When dealing with such items as art work, records, tapes, disks, and architectural drawings, can the customer's needs be satisfied without having the benefit of both the services or intangible content and the tangible personal property in which they are embodied? If not, does it make any sense even to attempt to identify the services/intangibles or tangible personal property as the "true object" of the transaction since the truth of the matter is that *both* the services or intangibles *and* the tangible personal property are the "true object" of the transaction? In the end, what objective or other basis is there for determining the purchaser's "true object"? Does it depend on the court's "gut reaction"?

D. *The "common understanding" test.* Both the majority and the dissent in *Leanin' Tree* purport to apply the test advanced in 2 Jerome R. Hellerstein & Walter Hellerstein, State Taxation ¶ 12.08[2] (3d ed. 1999 & Cum. Supp. 2009)), based on a "common understanding" of whether the transaction involves the sale of tangible personal property or the sale of services or intangibles. Yet the two opinions disagree over the proper application of the test. What does that tell you about the usefulness of the test?

3.　COMPUTER SOFTWARE

A. *Historical Overview*. The characterization of computer software for sales tax purposes as tangible (and thus taxable) or intangible (and thus nontaxable) has given rise to an enormous amount of controversy. Commerce Union Bank v. Tidwell, 538 S.W.2d 405 (Tenn. 1976), was the first state supreme court decision to consider the taxability of computer software for sales tax purposes. In that case, a bank purchased computer programs relating to its payroll and loan amortization payments. Some of the programs were of standard design and required only minor modifications to fit the bank's needs, while others were specialized and unique. Although the software vendors could have transmitted the programs electronically from their own computers to the bank's computers using telecommunications facilities, the vendors in fact transmitted the programs by means of punch cards, magnetic tapes, or disks. The vendors frequently provided manuals, services, and consultation in order to instruct the bank's employees in handling the programs.

The bank contended that "while the intellectual processes may be embodied" in the punch cards and magnetic tapes, "the logic or intelligence of the program is an intangible property right," id. at 407, and that is what it purchased. The court agreed, saying:

> In the case at bar * * * no product is created. What is created and sold here is information, and the magnetic tapes which contain this information are only a method of transmitting these intellectual creations from the original to the user. It is merely incidental that these intangibles are transmitted by way of a tangible reel of tape that is not even retained by the user.

Id. Although tax administrators contended that computer software is no different from phonograph records, music tapes, and rentals of motion picture films, whose sale is normally taxable, a number of state court opinions, especially those handed down shortly after *Commerce Union Bank* in the late 1970s and early 1980s, adopted the view of software expressed in the *Commerce Union Bank* case.

In 1983, however, the highest courts of Maryland and Vermont rejected the view of the earlier cases and held that canned, standardized computer software programs are subject to sales tax. Comptroller of the Treasury v. Equitable Trust Co., 296 Md. 459, 464 A.2d 248 (1983); Chittenden Trust Co. v. King, 143 Vt. 271, 465 A.2d 1100 (1983). In South Central Bell Telephone Co. v. Barthelemy, 643 So.2d 1240 (La. 1994), the Louisiana Supreme Court, in a wide-ranging opinion that canvassed much of the case law and commentary dealing with the taxation of computer software, concluded that any software, whether canned or custom made, is tangible property "once the 'information' or 'knowledge' is transformed into physical existence and recorded in physical form." Id. at 1250. Accordingly, it held that the sale of switching system software and data processing software was subject to sales tax. Alabama, the last state to exempt canned software (based on an earlier decision of the Alabama Supreme Court), fell into line with the other states in 1996 when the Alabama Supreme Court overruled the earlier decision, relying heavily on the reasoning of the *South Central Bell* case. Wal–Mart Stores, Inc. v. City of Mobile, 696 So.2d 290 (Ala. 1996).

In recent years, many states have dealt specifically with the taxability of computer software, through legislation or administrative regulations, in an effort to resolve the questions raised by the computer software cases. The trend has been to tax canned but not custom-made software. As of 2009, every sales tax state taxed canned software, roughly half those states taxed modified canned software, and about one-third of those states taxed custom software. All States Tax Guide (RIA) ¶ 259–A (2009) (chart), available at www.checkpoint.riag.com. The Streamlined Sales and Use Tax Agreement, see pp. 784–99 infra, simply includes "pre-written software" within the definition of "tangible personal property." Streamlined Sales and Use Tax Agreement, App. C, pt. 1. For a more detailed discussion of the computer software cases, and the issues they raise, see 2 Jerome R. Hellerstein & Walter Hellerstein, State Taxation ¶ 13.06 (3d ed. 1999 & Cum. Supp. 2009); Robert L. Cowdrey, "Software and Sales Tax: The Illusory Intangible," 63 B.U.L. Rev. 181 (1983); Robert D. Crockett, "Software Taxation: A Critical Reevaluation of the Notion of Intangibility," 1980 B.Y.U.L. Rev. 859; John M. Shontz, "Computer Software: Time to Pay a Fair Share," 68 Taxes 162 (1990).

B. *Canned as Compared to Custom–Made Software.* The practice of taxing canned but not custom-made software collides with the widely applied principle under the sales tax that there is no justification for exempting custom-made articles from tax, as long as the same article, when bought off the rack, is taxable. If states did not tax custom-made articles, they would tax a dress bought in a department store but not a specially designed gown made by a fashionable couturier. Moreover, exempting custom-made computer software programs, while taxing canned programs, tends to favor larger businesses at the expense of smaller ones. Larger businesses are generally better able to afford sophisticated software programs, designed to meet the special needs of the business, whereas smaller businesses are more likely to be able to afford only canned programs, bought off the shelf, which require only minor, if any, modifications. Finally, the line between custom and canned software is often so thin that reliance on it a basis for taxability creates uncertainty, controversy, and difficulties in administration. The explanation for the treatment of custom-made software as nontaxable may lie in the fact that custom-made software, whose design and installation can involve considerable interaction between the vendor and purchaser, is more plausibly characterized as a nontaxable service than is canned software. See Note D infra.

C. *Electronically Delivered Software and other Digital Products.* It is now commonplace for sellers to transfer software, music, videos, books, magazines, and similar products electronically without using tangible delivery media, such as CDs, DVDs, videotapes, or paper. The question naturally arises as to whether these transactions are taxable under traditional sales tax definitions of retail sales, which usually require the transfer of title or possession of tangible personal property. Regarding software in particular, some states distinguish between software delivered via tangible storage media and software delivered electronically, taxing the former but not the latter. Compare 86 Ill. Admin. Code 130.1935(a) (Westlaw 2009) (canned software taxable "regardless of the form in which it is delivered") with Va. Code Ann. § 58.1–609.5 (Westlaw 2009) (excluding software "not involving an exchange of tangible personal property").

The states are also split in their treatment of other digital products. A Texas letter ruling advises that digitally delivered music, video games, and ringtones are taxable tangible personal property. Policy Ltr. Rul. No. 200605591 (Tex. Comptroller of Public Accounts May 17, 2006). In contrast, the New York taxing authority has advised that electronically delivered videos are not subject to sales tax, observing that while electronically delivered software is taxable under an express statutory provision, "sales of music and photographs delivered electronically are not considered to be sales of software." TSB–A–07(11)S, 2007 WL 1610057, at *3 (N.Y. State Dep't of Tax'n and Finance April 12, 2007). Following a similar line of reasoning, the Missouri Department of Revenue issued a letter ruling advising that "online" newspaper subscription charges are not subject to sales or use tax, because they are neither for the sale of tangible personal property nor for a statutorily enumerated taxable service. Ltr. Rul. No. LR4060 (Mo. Dep't Rev. Sept. 26, 2007). A New Jersey statute expressly taxes the retail sale of "digital property," which is defined to mean "electronically delivered music, ringtones, movies, books, audio and video works and similar products, where the customer is granted a right or license to use, retain or make a copy of such item." NJ Rev. Stat. §§ 54:32B–2(vv), 54:32B–3 (Westlaw 2009).

How can it be argued, as a matter of statutory interpretation, that the electronic transfer of a digital product is the sale of "tangible personal property"? What policy arguments support this characterization?

D. *Computer Software and Digital Products as Tangible Personal Property, Intangible Personal Property, or Services.* Depending on the particular type of software or digital product under consideration, one may plausibly characterize the software or digital product in one of three different ways. For example, one may reasonably characterize a word processing program purchased off the shelf as tangible personal property indistinguishable for practical purposes from a book, record, or compact disk. On the other hand, one may reasonably characterize the purchase of a series of complex computer commands, transferred electronically to the purchaser's computer or digital playback device, as a transaction involving intangible property. Finally, if a business contracts with a software company for the company to develop and install a software program that will handle the business's accounts receivable, one may reasonably characterize the transaction as involving the purchase of services.

Although the distinction between canned and customized software is sometimes evanescent, at least when the "customization" amounts to little more than routine configuration of a program for a customer's preexisting software platform, there is clearly a real distinction between the three transactions described above. But, as a matter of sound tax policy, is there any justification for treating these transactions differently? Why should the first be taxable, when the second and third are tax free? Is there some economic policy reason why transactions involving intangibles or services should be favored over transactions involving tangibles? Whatever the answer to these questions, the fact remains that in most jurisdictions—at least for the moment—transactions involving intangibles and transactions involving services are not subject to sales and use taxation whereas transactions involving tangible personal property are. In light of this fact, can you devise guidelines that will provide taxpayers and taxing authorities with a clear line between taxable and tax-free computer software and digital products?

ASSIGNMENT

Analyze the sales and use tax statutes of your state and the rules and regulations bearing on the distinction between sales of tangible personal property and sales of services. Classify the treatment of transactions involving (a) professionals, (b) the graphic arts, (c) computer software, (d) digital products, and (e) others. What tests are used for distinguishing tangible personal property from services for purposes of your state's sales or use tax?

4. SALES OF A "BUNDLE" OF DISTINCT PROPERTY AND SERVICES IN A SINGLE CONTRACT

The "true object" and similar tests typically result in the characterization of a transaction as either a taxable sale of tangible personal property or as a nontaxable sale of a service or intangible property. Indeed, both of the cases you have read (*Washington Times–Herald* and *Leanin' Tree*) resulted in an all-or-nothing determination of the transaction as taxable or nontaxable. But not every transaction involving the sale of both tangible personal property and services or intangibles requires an all-or-nothing analysis. In some circumstances, it may be possible to "unbundle" the sale of what appears to be a "mixed" transaction into two separate transactions, which are treatable as taxable or nontaxable in their own right. The following case illustrates the application of this principle.

DELL, INC. v. SUPERIOR COURT

California Court of Appeal, First District, 2008.
159 Cal.App.4th 911, 71 Cal.Rptr.3d 905.

SEPULVEDA, J.

Several consumers brought actions contesting imposition of sales and use taxes on optional service contracts sold with computers. In this action, plaintiffs sued Dell for unfair and deceptive business practices for collecting tax on the service contracts, and Dell cross-complained against the California State Board of Equalization (SBE) for a refund of the disputed taxes Dell remitted to the tax agency. The parties agreed to a bench trial on the discrete issue of whether the sales of service contracts to plaintiffs were subject to California sales or use tax. The trial court concluded that the sales were not subject to tax. Dell and the other defendants petitioned this court for a writ of mandate. Defendants asked us to review and to reverse the trial court's decision.

We have reviewed the decision and, following briefing and oral argument, conclude that the trial court correctly found that the sales were not taxable. California taxes the retail sale and use of tangible personal property but not the sale or use of intangible personal property or the performance of services. Dell and SBE concede that optional service contracts are not tangible personal property and are generally exempt from taxation. Dell and SBE claim that taxation of Dell service contracts is nevertheless proper because Dell sells its computers and service contracts for a single lump-sum price, without a separate statement on the invoice of the charge for the service contract. We reject the claim.

While Dell computers and service contracts are sold concurrently for an aggregate price, they are distinct consumer items and each is a significant object of the transaction. Dell service contracts have readily ascertainable values, even without itemized invoices. Accordingly, SBE cannot decree that the exclusive means to establish a tax exemption for an optional service contract sold together with a taxable product is that its value be separately stated on the retailer's invoice, absent a statute, regulation, or consistent administrative interpretation of the laws mandating a separate statement of value.

I. FACTS

Dell sells computer systems and services to individuals, businesses, and governmental agencies. Dell operates on a direct-sales business model, rather than through traditional retail outlets. Customers primarily order products directly from Dell by telephone, over an Internet website, or by other direct means. Dell products are marketed in various packages, which consist of hardware, software, a warranty, and a service contract. Each configuration bears a single, lump-sum price: the components are itemized but not separately priced. The customer has the option of changing the configuration of a package by switching hardware, software, or service contract components in exchange for an increase or decrease in the lump-sum price. * * *

The statement of the purchase price to the customer is either an acknowledgement of the purchase if the customer pays in full at the time of the order, or an invoice if money is due. An invoice or acknowledgement identifies the computer's components and states the total sales price for the aggregate of the components selected by the customer. The invoices and acknowledgements generally do not list separate unit prices for the computer's various components (e.g., memory, hard drive, monitor, service contract). Internally, Dell does assign unit prices to many of the computer systems' components. Those unit prices appear, among other places, in price lists and Dell's computerized record database.

Computer systems sold by Dell are warranted at no additional cost to the customer. The warranties cover defects in materials and workmanship in Dell-branded products. The warranties are "return to facility" warranties requiring the consumer to return the defective product or part to Dell for repair or replacement. Computer systems sold by Dell also typically include computer service contracts. Many such service contracts provide for the dispatch of an on-site repair technician, while others provide for repair or replacement within certain time frames.

A standard service contract is included in every initial package (the package before the customer customizes its configuration). A customer can eliminate this standard service contract from the package and receive a reduction of the lump-sum purchase price. Extended service contracts are available that vary in duration, coverage and benefits. The selection of an extended service contract will have a varying effect on the lump-sum price based upon the contract's duration and other terms. It is not necessary that any of these extended service contracts be included in order for a customer to purchase a package of hardware, software, and basic warranty. Dell's internal price list specifies a particular dollar figure for each type of standard and extended service contract. On every invoiced sale, Dell keeps records showing a separate and exact amount for the service contract.

* * *

III. DISCUSSION

California applies sales and use tax to tangible personal property but not to intangible property and services. Dell computers are taxable tangible personal property. Service contracts are nontaxable intangible property or services. The question presented here is whether a mixed sale in which a Dell computer and service contract sold at the same time, for a single undifferentiated price on the invoice, is wholly taxable (as Dell and SBE claim) or only partially taxable (as plaintiffs claim). We conclude that the transaction is only partially taxable—the computer is taxed and the service contract is not taxed. A service contract for a Dell computer is a distinct and separately identifiable component of the transaction entitled to individual tax treatment. Guiding principles of tax law lay the path to that conclusion.

* * *

The taxation of bundled and mixed transactions

Drawing the line between taxable sales of tangible property and nontaxable sales of services or intangibles is sometimes difficult, especially where property that was largely created by personal services is transferred. (Hellerstein, State Taxation (3d ed. 2007) ¶ 12.08[1], p. 1.) Where services and tangible property are inseparably bundled together, determination of the taxability of the transaction turns upon whether the purchaser's "true object" was to obtain the finished product or the service.

As an example, the true object in purchasing a sculpture is acquisition of the finished product, and thus the transaction is taxable without reduction for the service embodied in the product. (Cal.Code Regs., tit. 18, § 1501.) In contrast, the true object in purchasing tax advice is the performance of a service, so the entire transaction is not taxable despite the incidental furnishing of forms, binders or other tangible property. (Ibid.) In Culligan Water Conditioning. v. State Bd. of Equalization (1976) 17 Cal.3d 86, 96, 130 Cal.Rptr. 321, 550 P.2d 593, the court held that the true object of a water conditioning contract—in which water softening equipment is attached to a customer's home plumbing and periodically serviced—is the furnishing of the tangible equipment "which, by itself and without requiring any performance of human labor, softens the water."

The above examples involve so-called bundled transactions in which goods and services are inextricably intertwined in a single sale. (Hellerstein, State Taxation, supra, ¶ 12.08[1][c], pp. 6–8.) For bundled transactions of goods and services, the true object test applies and the entire transaction is generally taxed or not taxed as a whole. * * *

Tax rules sometimes allow allocation between taxable and nontaxable items bundled together if the value of the nontaxable item is separately stated. (Hellerstein, State Taxation, supra, ¶ 17.03[4] pp. 1–2 & ¶ 19A.04[2][a] [iv], pp. 1–2, 5.) In California, for example, separately stated charges for specified transportation costs of goods are statutorily exempted from sales and use tax. (§§ 6011, subd. (c)(7), 6012, subd. (c)(7).) Transportation charges are regarded as separately stated "only if they are separately set forth in the contract for sale or in a document reflecting that contract, issued contemporaneously with the sale, such as the retailer's invoice." (Cal.Code Regs., tit. 18, § 1628, subd. (a).)

* * *

Bundled transactions are distinguishable from transactions in which goods and services are sold together yet are readily separable-so-called mixed transactions. One respected commentator has stated that "a 'mixed transaction' involving separately identifiable transfers of goods and services can and should be distinguished from a 'bundled transaction' involving goods and services that are inextricably intertwined in a single sale." (Hellerstein, State Taxation, *supra,* ¶ 12.08[1], p. 7[c] & ¶ 19A.04 [2][a][iv], pp. 1–3.)

Unlike bundled transactions, the goods and services in a mixed transaction are distinct (not intertwined) and each is a significant object of the transaction (not one incidental to the other). (Rylander, [v. San Antonio SMSA Limited Partnership] supra, 11 S.W.3d [484] at pp. 487–488 [Tex. App.–Austin 2000].) In mixed transactions, the separate elements of the transaction are analyzed as separate transactions for tax purposes. The tangible property aspect of the transaction is taxed and the service aspect of the transaction is not taxed.

Several examples of mixed transactions are illustrative. In Overly Mfg. Co. v. State Bd. of Equalization (1961) 191 Cal.App.2d 20, 21–28, 12 Cal.Rptr. 391, the court found that a lump-sum contract for steel door frames and doors was divisible into taxable tangible property (the manufactured frames) and nontaxable services (installation of the doors). The court noted the "dual nature" of the contract, which supplied products and provided separate services, and contrasted the transaction from those where an entire bundled transaction is taxable because service is incidental to the sale of goods.

In *Advance Schools,* an out-of-state correspondence school provided California students with both educational services and lesson materials in the form of books, printed lessons, training kits, and tools. (Advance Schools, [Inc. v. California State Bd. of Equalization,] supra, 2 B.R. [231] at pp. 232, 237 [N.D. Ill. 1980].) The school charged a single tuition fee, with no separate charge for the lesson materials. The court held the school liable for use taxes on that portion of the tuition attributable to the sale of the lesson materials. The court rejected the school's argument that the entire transaction was not taxable because a student's true object in paying tuition was to obtain educational services.

The federal bankruptcy court in *Advance Schools* noted that California recognizes "three possible situations with regard to mixed sales of services and property." (Advance Schools, supra, 2 B.R. at p. 235; see In re Los Angeles Internat. Airport Hotel Associates (9th Cir.BAP 1996) 196 B.R. 134, 138 [approving *Advance Schools* analysis].) First, tangible property is the primary item or true object of the transaction, in which case tax applies to the entire sales price. Second, service is the primary item or true object of the transaction, in which case no tax applies to the transaction. Third is "the truly mixed transaction," where property and services are distinct and consequential elements of the transaction, in which case the transaction is severable into its taxable and nontaxable components. The school's reliance on the true object test was misplaced because that test applies only to the first two described situations where services rendered are inseparable from the property transferred. The court found the lesson materials provided by the school to be separate from the educational services, and both the materials and services significant aspects of the transaction. The court severed the transaction for tax purposes, and allocated tax upon the market price of the materials.

* * *

The taxation of Dell service contracts

* * *

SBE concedes that service contracts generally are not taxable and justifies its taxation of Dell service contracts on the fact that the service contracts are sold without a separate statement of the value of the contracts on the sales invoice. It is the so-called ''bundled sale'' of computers (tangible personal property) with service contracts (intangibles or services) that render the latter taxable, according to SBE. Dell and plaintiffs likewise construe the subject transactions as bundled sales of taxable and nontaxable items. In this respect, all parties err, and that error has misdirected the analysis of the taxation issue.

The subject transactions are not bundled sales, but rather mixed transactions. As noted above, ''a 'mixed transaction' involving separately identifiable transfers of goods and services can and should be distinguished from a 'bundled transaction' involving goods and services that are inextricably intertwined in a single sale.'' (Hellerstein, State Taxation, supra, ¶ 12.08[1], p. 7[c] & ¶ 19A.04[2][a][iv], pp. 1–3.). So, too, is a mixed transaction involving separately identifiable transfers of tangible and intangible property distinguishable from a bundled sale of intertwined property. Dell's sale of computers with service contracts is not, properly speaking, a bundled sale.

The service contracts are readily separable from the computers Dell sells. Dell, for marketing purposes, presents particular product configurations to its customers but these configurations are not fixed. Dell proudly advertises: ''At Dell, you can custom-build your dream system from the ground up.'' As a Dell tax manager explained in her declaration submitted at trial: Dell ''typically offer[s] to their customers various models of Dell-branded computer systems. Each different model is often available in a basic configuration of computer components (which may include, for example, a microprocessor, memory, hard drive, monitor, warranty, service contract, etc.) sold for a single, total price for the basic configuration. Dell customers typically have the option to customize a computer model by upgrading or downgrading various computer components in exchange for an increase or decrease in the single, total price for the customer's order.''

It is also clear that the computer and service contract are each significant aspects of the transaction, and not one incidental to the other. Dell touts its ''award-winning service,'' as well as its computer equipment, and the cost of service contracts is far from de minimis. In plaintiff Mohan's purchase of a computer and service contract, for example, the service contract was valued at over 20 percent of the total price of the transaction. In Advance Schools, Inc., supra, 2 B.R. at 237, where the court severed tuition paid for nontaxable education services from taxable lesson materials, the court found that materials valued at close to 20 percent of the total tuition charged could not "be deemed an insignificant aspect of the transaction."

We conclude that the proper approach under California law is to tax the computer (tangible personal property) and not the service contract (service or intangible property). As other courts have recognized, "when there is a fixed and an ascertainable relationship between the value of the article and the value of the services rendered, and each is a consequential element capable of a separate and distinct transaction, then the elements must be analyzed as separate transactions for tax purposes." ([New England Tel. & Tel. Co. v.] Clark, supra, 624 A.2d [298] at p. 301 [(R.I. 1993)].)

* * *

Dell service contracts are not taxable even without separate invoicing

SBE and Dell maintain that it is proper to treat Dell service contracts as taxable because the value of the contracts is not separately stated on an invoice. SBE contends that, in a concurrent sale of tangible personal property and services, the generally nontaxable service element is taxable unless its purchase is optional *and* its value is separately stated on an invoice. SBE and Dell present the so-called separate statement rule as a "general principle" or "general rule" in sales and use tax administration, and argue that it should be upheld because it promotes the efficient administration of the tax code.

While tax administrators may properly apply the separate statement rule in a number of contexts, this is not one of them. The primary sources of the separate statement rule are tax statutes that expressly require separately stated charges. In California, the sales price of tangible personal property, upon which tax is imposed, is defined to exclude "[s]eparately stated charges for transportation." (§ 6011, subd. (c)(7).) Other states statutorily exclude various charges from taxation if separately stated or identified. (E.g. Tex. Tax Code Ann. § 151.007; see generally Hellerstein, State Taxation, supra, ¶ 17.01[1], quoting the Streamlined Sales and Use Tax Agreement definition of "sales price.") As SBE conceded at trial, there is no California statute or regulation that requires service contract charges to be separately stated to avoid taxation.

Another alleged source of the separate statement rule is the administrative enforcement of statutes carrying a presumption of taxability. "[T]he burden of proof concerning the right to a tax exemption is on the taxpayer" because "the taxpayer is in the best position to create and maintain records of his transactions and to destroy or conceal such records." When property and services are purchased together, separate invoices or separate itemization on the same invoice are useful in meeting the taxpayer's evidentiary burden of proving tax exemption for the service item in the transaction. In many transactions, separate itemization may be the only practical means of proof. But no [California] statute or regulation demands a separate statement of a service contract's value on an invoice as the exclusive means of meeting the taxpayer's evidentiary burden. In the unusual situation presented here, the value of Dell service contracts is readily ascertainable without an itemized invoice, as discussed above.

* * *

* * * The petition for a peremptory writ of mandate is denied.

NOTES AND QUESTIONS

A. *Distinguishing Between "Bundled" and "Mixed" Transactions.* The *Dell* court, relying on the analysis in Rylander v. San Antonio SMSA Limited Partnership, 11 S.W.3d 484 (Tex. App.—Austin 2000), distinguished mixed transactions from bundled transactions:

> Unlike bundled transactions, the goods and services in a mixed transaction are distinct (not intertwined) and each is a significant object of the transaction (not one incidental to the other). In mixed transactions, the separate elements of the transaction are analyzed as separate transactions for tax purposes. The tangible property aspect of the transaction is taxed and the service aspect of the transaction is not taxed.

But how does one draw the line between these two classes of transactions? Does it depend on the relative values of the property element and the service element? On whether the property element serves any function if it is made available without the service element or vice versa? On whether there is a separate statement on the invoice of the charge for the property element and the charge for the service element?

B. *The Separate Statement Rule.* As the *Dell* court conceded, its decision was unusual in that it allowed the "unbundling" of a transaction even though the taxable and nontaxable charges had not been separately stated on the customers' invoices. The general rule, however, is that the vendor must separately state the charges for the respective sales in order for the sales to receive separate treatment. For example, the Kentucky regulations provide:

> If the labor and other services are not separately stated from the selling price of the property furnished * * *, it shall be presumed that the entire charge represents the sale price of the property and the tax shall apply to the entire charge.

103 Ky. Admin. Regs. 27:150(4) (Westlaw 2009). Why did the *Dell* the court deviate from the general rule?

C. *Consumer class actions refund claims. Dell* involved a class action lawsuit brought by consumers who claimed they had been overcharged sales tax on their purchases of computers that were bundled with service contracts. Thus, Dell was in the unusual position of aligning with the taxing authority in arguing that no tax refund was due. In the alternative, it argued that if it had overcharged sales tax, then it was entitled to a refund from the state. Why hadn't Dell simply separately stated a charge for service contracts and not collected tax on those charges, thereby reducing the total price it charged consumers without reducing its net receipts from these sales? If Dell had been your client, what would you have advised? More generally, what would you advise a seller if the sales and use tax consequences of a transaction are uncertain?

5. LEASES OF TANGIBLE PERSONAL PROPERTY AS A SALE

If sales taxes were confined to actual sales of tangible personal property, i.e., transactions in which title to the property passes from the seller to the purchaser, they would not capture many transfers of tangible personal property for a consideration in which title does not pass to the buyer. In particular, rental payments for leases of tangible personal property would escape sales taxation. As a consequence, almost all state sales taxes apply to receipts from leases and other transfers of tangible personal property for a consideration. All States Tax Guide (RIA) ¶ 253 (2009) (chart), available at www.checkpoint.riag.com. The Florida statute contains a typical broadened definition of a sale: " 'Sale' means and includes: (a) any transfer of title or possession or both, exchange, barter, license, lease, or rental, conditional or otherwise, in any manner or by any means whatsoever, of tangible personal property for a consideration." Fla. Stat. Ann. § 212.02(15) (Westlaw 2009). Just as courts have struggled with the distinction between traditional sales of tangible personal property and sales of services or intangible property, so they have struggled with the distinction between taxable leases of tangible personal property and nontaxable payments for services or for the license to use intangibles.

NOTES AND QUESTIONS

A. *Holdings Under Provisions Extending the Sales Tax to Leases of Tangible Personal Property.* Under broad definitions of "sale" covering leases, rentals, or licenses to use tangible personal property, courts have found the following payments taxable: payments for mops and mats supplied to building owners, which the supplier regularly picked up, laundered, treated chemically, and returned to the building owners, Servi–Clean Indus., Inc. v. Collins, 50 Ohio St.2d 80, 362 N.E.2d 648 (1977); payments to a diaper service, Saverio v. Carson, 186 Tenn. 166, 208 S.W.2d 1018 (1948); payments to an ice skating rink for rentals of skates, Pla Mor, Inc. v. Glander, 149 Ohio St. 295, 78 N.E.2d 725 (1948); and payments to a supplier of office coats and towels, Philadelphia Ass'n of Linen Suppliers v. Philadelphia, 139 Pa.Super. 560, 12 A.2d 789 (1940). Why were the payments in *Servi–Clean* and *Saverio* not properly characterizable, respectively, as payments for a cleaning service and a diaper service? What was the "true object" of those transactions? Does the subscriber to a diaper service care more about getting the diaper or getting the diaper cleaned? Does the answer to this question depend on whether you have ever washed a dirty diaper? Would the subscriber to the diaper service pay for the service without the assurance that he or she would receive not only a diaper, but also a *clean* diaper? Are these questions that people who have spent four years in college and three years in law school should be arguing about at rates well exceeding $100 per hour? If not, how would you structure the sales tax to avoid this issue?

Would payments for the use of the ice skating rink—as distinguished from the rental of the skates (as in *Pla Mor*)—be taxable under a broad sale definition such as that contained in the Florida statute (quoted at the beginning of this subsection)? Suppose the skater paid a single charge that included both the skates and the right to use the rink? If the diaper service had charged separately in *Saverio* for the rental of the diapers and for the service of cleaning them, would the result have been different? If so, doesn't this mean that form (the way the charges are stated) would govern over substance (the "true object" or "essence" of the transaction)?

B. *Rental of Coin–Operated Facilities.* Is the rental of lockers in railroad stations and other public places a "sale" within the meaning of a license to use provision of a sales tax? In American Locker Co. v. City of New York, 308 N.Y. 264, 125 N.E.2d 421 (1955), the plaintiff owned coin-operated lockers in which baggage and other personal belongings could be checked for a dime or a quarter for no more than 24 hours. The court held that the charge for locker use did not constitute a payment for a "license to use" tangible personal property because the New York City statute covered only transactions in which there is a transfer of title or possession of the article. The court concluded that the company's patrons do not obtain "possession" of the locker. In State Tax Comm'n v. Peck, 106 Ariz. 394, 476 P.2d 849 (1970), however, the court held that proceeds from coin-operated laundromats and car-washing machines were taxable under a definition of taxable sales that included "[l]easing or renting tangible personal property for a consideration." The Arizona legislature subsequently amended the statute to exclude "[o]perating coin operated washing, drying and dry cleaning machines or coin operated car washing machines" from the tax on "leasing or renting tangible personal property." Ariz. Rev. Stat. Ann. § 42–5071(A)(4) (Westlaw 2009).

Consider along with the locker rental cases the taxability of outdoor billboard advertising. Must the owner of the billboard collect sales tax on the payments it receives for exhibiting its customers' advertisements on its billboards or other signs? Courts have reached opposite answers to that question depending on their view as to whether "possession" or "control" of the signs is transferred to the customer. Compare Federal Sign & Signal Corp. v. Bowers, 172 Ohio St. 161, 174 N.E.2d 91 (1961) (receipts from leasing advertising signs not taxable) with Register Mobile Advertising, Inc. v. Strickland, 242 Ga. 604, 250 S.E.2d 468 (1978) (receipts from leasing advertising signs taxable).

Should the issue as to whether there is a taxable lease or license to use tangible personal property in these cases depend on whether there is a transfer of "possession" of the article? The possession concept has its usefulness for various purposes of property law, but should it be the key issue in determining sales tax liability? The purpose of the license to use provisions is to sweep into the sales tax base rental or leasing substitutes for sales, such as the now widespread leasing of vehicles and office machinery in industrial and commercial businesses. In addition, it encompasses the short-term use of the article by various users, such as rentals of automobiles, tuxedos, and other articles. The economic consumption of the articles is made by the renter. Should that rather than "possession" be the test of taxability? To be sure, the transfer of possession will in many cases provide a good proxy for determining whether the transferee is consuming the thing transferred. But, as the locker and billboard cases reveal, this may not always be the case. Is the sounder test for determining whether payment for the use of a locker or a billboard is nontaxable whether the locker or billboard owner is providing a storage or advertising service rather than transferring possession of tangible property? Indeed, in *American Locker*, the court analogized the case to the "service" rendered in a railroad station when luggage is hand-checked in the baggage room in holding the receipts for locker rentals nontaxable. The cases you have already read, however, suggest that the sales/service distinction may be no more effective than the transfer-of-possession test for resolving these issues. Does the statute itself justify a focus on the transfer of possession as being a key to sales tax liability?

C. *Sale–Leaseback Transactions.* In order to finance the purchase of equipment, a purchaser may enter into an arrangement whereby it sells the equipment it has purchased to a third party which immediately leases back the equipment to the original purchaser. In substance, these arrangements amount to little more than a loan transaction, whereby the "lessee" (borrower) amortizes the loan by paying "rent" to the "lessor" over the term of the loan. The "lessee" retains all of the substantial indicia of ownership, including risk of loss, liability for taxes, and obligation to maintain and insure the property. The question arises whether the rental payments made pursuant to such a sale-leaseback arrangement are nevertheless taxable under a sales and use tax scheme that generally taxes rentals of tangible personal property. Some courts have held that, despite the formal transfer of title to property, these are merely financing transactions that fall outside the intent of the sales tax. As the California Supreme Court declared in Cedars–Sinai Medical Center v. State Board of Equalization, 162 Cal.App.3d 1182, 208 Cal.Rptr. 837 (2d Dist. 1984), in holding that rental payments pursuant to a sale-leaseback were not taxable:

> As a practical matter plaintiff had no reason to "sell" the equipment to the companies and "rent" it back from them at a total cost to plaintiff of approximately $1,426,400 more than the original cost of the equipment. Viewed in their entirety plaintiff's transactions with the leasing companies were devices by which plaintiff in effect borrowed from them the money necessary to pay the full purchase price of the equipment to the vendors; the leasing companies reimbursed plaintiff for that portion of the purchase price it had paid to the vendors and then paid the balance of the price to the vendors on plaintiff's behalf; plaintiff, in the form of rent, repaid the companies the total amount of the purchase price plus interest.

Id., 208 Cal.Rptr. at 841. On similar facts, other courts have reached similar conclusions. See Rockwell Int'l Corp. v. Commonwealth, 99 Pa. Cmwlth. 130, 512 A.2d 1332 (1986); Bullock v. Citizens National Bank of Waco, 663 S.W.2d 923 (Tex. App. 1984).

Some courts, however, have held that sale-leasebacks are taxable. For example, in Apex Custom Lease Corp. v. State Tax Assessor, 677 A.2d 530 (Me. 1996), the court held that a sales tax was due on a sale-leaseback transaction that an automobile dealership entered into with an affiliated leasing company. The court observed that the taxpayer derived a benefit from the transaction, namely, freeing the dealership of debt burdens that allowed its line of credit to be used for other purposes. See also Midwest Federal Savings & Loan Ass'n v. Commissioner of Revenue, 259 N.W.2d 596 (Minn. 1977).

D. *License to Use Intangible Property as Distinguished From a Sale or License to Use Tangible Property: Exhibition of Motion Pictures, Television Films, and Video Tapes.* When a movie theater or television station receives a film or video tape with the right to exhibit or broadcast it, the question arises whether the payments made by the theater or the station to the producer or distributor of the film or tape are taxable sales under statutes taxing the "rental, lease, or license to use" tangible personal property. In answering this question in the affirmative, the Vermont Supreme Court declared:

> We are persuaded by the reasoning of the more recent decisions in this area which have embraced the theory now advanced by the Department of Taxes. We find particularly germane the point made by the Supreme Court of Arkansas that "the right to use property cannot be separated from the property itself." American Television Co. v. Hervey, 253 Ark. 1010, 1014, 490 S.W.2d 796, 799 (1973). The right of which taxpayer speaks is simply of no value to it without the use of the video tape or film itself.

Mount Mansfield Television, Inc. v. Vermont Commissioner of Taxes, 133 Vt. 284, 336 A.2d 193, 194–95 (1975). Most of the cases have adopted the view reflected in the *Mount Mansfield* case that licenses to exhibit motion pictures or television films are taxable sales. But is the majority rule right?

In WDKY–TV, Inc. v. Revenue Cabinet, Commonwealth of Kentucky, 838 S.W.2d 431 (Ky. App. 1992), the court declared:

> The [Revenue] Cabinet and the cases on which it relies have simply failed to perceive the distinction between the right to own an object and the right to make use of an object that one owns. For example, a bookstore buys individual copies of a book for resale, while a publishing house buys the right to make copies of a book; and an appliance store sells certain brand name appliances, while a manufacturer buys the right to make a brand of appliances. In each example, one party buys things and one party buys the intangible * * * right to make reproductions of a thing.

> Contrary to the Cabinet's arguments, we believe it to be obvious that one who purchases a Bart Simpson t-shirt, or a Pepsi, or a Cadillac does not thereby accede to any intangible rights. By purchasing a t-shirt, for example, one acquires the right to use that individual t-shirt; one does not acquire the right to make 10,000 copies and sell them to the public. The fact that the thing produced is the result of some intangible flash of inspiration by the inventor is simply irrelevant. In the case of a video-tape, the right to put the taxed images upon the TV screens of the

populace is distinct from the right, inherent in ownership of the thing, to put the tape into a VCR for one's own enjoyment.

Id. at 434–35.

In the *Crescent Amusement* case, which the Vermont Supreme Court cites in *Mount Mansfield*, the Tennessee Supreme Court held that operators of motion picture theaters were liable for sales tax on film rented from producers, and it declared:

> There is scarcely to be found any article susceptible to sale or rent that is not the result of an idea, genius, skill and labor applied to a physical substance. * * * If these elements should be separated from the finished product and the sales tax applied only to the cost of the raw material, the sales tax would, for all practical purposes, be entirely destroyed.

Crescent Amusement Co. v. Carson, 187 Tenn. 112, 213 S.W.2d 27, 29 (1948).

Does this policy-based argument truly respond to the narrower point reflected in *WDKY–TV* that there is a specific, separately identifiable intangible property right associated with a movie or TV film that can be—and traditionally has been—segregated from the tangible property through which that right is typically exploited? Moreover, if the key to taxing the payments made by the television station to the film producer or distributor is that the television station receives something tangible (the film or tape) that is inseparable from the intangible, does it make sense that there is no tax when the television station receives what is functionally the same thing but with no transfer of tangible personal property, namely, a satellite transmission of the film which the station records on its own blank tape?

Does the underlying philosophy of a *retail* sales tax—a tax on the ultimate consumer—assist in determining the right answer to these questions? Doesn't the *Crescent Amusement* court's legitimate concern with the destruction of the sales tax base bear principally on the specter of consumers of automobiles, appliances, and other quintessentially taxable items successfully contending that the "true object" of their purchases is the nontaxable labor and patented technology embodied in the tangible personal property they are acquiring? We would clearly have an equal concern if consumers could avoid paying tax on their video rentals at Blockbuster by arguing that they are acquiring a license to view a film and that the hard copy is merely an inconsequential incident to the payment for that intangible right. But is a movie theater or television station the ultimate consumer of the film it receives? And, whether it is or is not, perhaps we cannot arrive at a sensible answer to any of these questions without knowing whether the proceeds that the movie theater or television studio receives from its exhibition or broadcast of the film will themselves be subject to a sales or use tax.

E. *Receipts from Rental of Rooms or Lodgings.* Because the sales tax does not apply to transfers of realty, the rental of realty does not ordinarily fall within the scope of a sales tax. The vast majority of states, however, subject receipts from the rental of rooms and lodging by hotels and motels to sales taxation. Those states that fail to reach such receipts through their sales tax often have a special excise tax on hotel or motel occupancy. Why do you think states have treated this particular form of real estate rental—rental of transient lodging—differently from other forms of real estate rental under the sales tax?

There is considerable controversy over whether online travel companies such as Hotels.com are taxable as hotel or motel operators. It is not uncommon for these companies to contract for the right to acquire rooms at a reduced rate and then offer those rooms at a higher rate to their online customers. Taxing authorities argue that occupancy tax is due on the total amount charged by the online travel companies to their customers, while the online travel companies argue that tax is due only on the amount they pay to the actual operator of the lodging facility. See generally 2 Jerome R. Hellerstein & Walter Hellerstein, State Taxation ¶ 19.03[6] (3d ed. 2008 & Cum. Supp. 2009). As with the above discussion in note D supra regarding the exhibition of motion pictures and the like, does the underlying philosophy of the retail sales tax as tax on the ultimate consumer assist in determining correct resolution of this controversy? We turn to this and similar questions in the next section of this chapter.

C. RETAIL SALE

A retail sales tax in principle reaches only sales to the ultimate consumer. In accord with this principle, state sales taxes exclude or exempt many intermediate transactions in the economic process from sales taxation. Every state retail sales tax statute, for example, contains a sale for resale exclusion or exemption. Most sales taxes also exclude sales of components or ingredients of property produced for sale. Similarly, many states exempt the purchase of machinery and equipment used in manufacturing property for sale as well as property consumed in the manufacture of articles for sale. The purpose of all these provisions is to ensure that only the final sale to the consumer gets taxed and that there is no pyramiding of the tax by imposing it on intermediate purchases as well.

Despite the theoretical premise that the retail sales tax is a single-stage levy on consumer expenditures, and the existence of provisions (like those described in the preceding paragraph) designed to implement that premise, it is important to recognize from the outset that the sales tax in practice falls far short of that goal. It does so because the anti-pyramiding provisions of the typical retail sales tax focus more on physical than on economic concepts. In other words, the retail sales tax often treats a business purchaser as the ultimate consumer of property or services it purchases, even though the price of that property or those services will be reflected in property or services that are subsequently sold and taxed. As a consequence, business purchases comprise a substantial portion of the "retail" sales tax base (see p. 609 supra), and many of these business purchases are subjected—in an economic sense at least—to a second sales tax.

It is also important to keep in mind that the provisions designed to eliminate intermediate transactions from the sales tax base may sometimes be overinclusive. If a purchaser of property engaged in a service occupation persuades a tax administrator or court that it is reselling the property purchased to its customers, while at the same time taking the position that its resale of the property is merely "incidental" to a transaction whose "real object" is the purchase of nontaxable services (see Section B supra), the sale of the property may escape taxation altogether.

In studying the ensuing materials delineating the scope of a retail sale under state sales tax statutes, you should try to identify those instances in which the tax fails to conform to the an economically sound approach to retail sales taxation and to articulate the reasons why the tax fails to live up to its theoretical promise. Of course, even if you systematically subject each case to a rigorous analysis based on the underlying policy of a retail sales tax, you should be prepared to find that many of the cases can be explained only by the particular language that the legislature, wittingly or unwittingly, has chosen to implement the retail sales tax.

1. SALE FOR RESALE EXEMPTION

McDONALD'S RESTAURANTS OF MASSACHUSETTS, INC. v. COMMISSIONER OF REVENUE

Appellate Tax Board, Commonwealth of Massachusetts, 2005.
Docket No. C262528, 2005 WL 941510.

* * *

FINDINGS OF FACT AND REPORT

* * *

During the periods at issue, McDonald's Restaurants of Massachusetts, Inc. ("MRM") was a wholly-owned subsidiary of McDonald's Corporation ("McDonald's") engaged in the business of operating a McDonald's franchise in Massachusetts. The items at issue in this appeal were toys ("Happy Meal Toys") that MRM included as part of a Happy Meal, a branded bundle of products that was designed for children under the age of ten. Happy Meals consisted of a McDonald's hamburger, cheeseburger, or chicken nuggets entrée, a small order of McDonald's French fries, a twelve-ounce beverage, and a Happy Meal Toy. Happy Meals were contained in a box or a bag designed to fit the theme of the particular Happy Meal promotion and the Happy Meal Toy placed inside. Every Happy Meal included exactly one Happy Meal Toy.

MRM purchased the Happy Meal Toys, as well as other supplies, from Martin–Brower, an unrelated vendor. MRM gave Martin–Brower a blanket Form ST–4 Sales Tax Resale Certificate for its purchases of "Food & Merchandise/Toys" believed to be exempt from sales and use taxes as items resold to its customers in the regular course of MRM's business. The issue in the instant appeal was whether MRM owed a use tax on its purchases of Happy Meal Toys which it included in the Happy Meals sold during the periods at issue. Stated another way, MRM maintained that it sold the Happy Meal Toys in the regular course of its business while the Commissioner argued that MRM used the Happy Meal Toys to promote the conduct of its restaurant business.

Karlin Linhardt, head of the National Marketing Group for McDonald's, testified to the extensive process involved in developing and producing the Happy Meal Toys. He explained that McDonald's selected the Happy Meal Toys which would be available at all participating franchises as part of a uniform Happy Meal promotion throughout the country. Each Happy Meal promotion generally lasted for approximately three to four weeks. Mr. Linhardt explained how his group researched trends in children's entertainment and developed Happy Meal promotions to coincide with these trends. Virtually all of the Happy Meal Toys involved pre-existing characters, for example, action figures based on the "Inspector Gadget" motion picture showing in movie theaters contemporaneously with that Happy Meal promotion. Some of the Happy Meal Toys promoted during the periods at issue were especially popular with customers, particularly the Teenie Beanie Babies and the Furbies, which Mr. Linhardt claimed were viewed as highly collectable.

McDonald's advertised each Happy Meal program principally on national television. McDonald's also promoted the sale of Happy Meals through the use of advertising posters and in-store display cases located within the restaurants. Transcripts and a video cassette of the television commercials, a picture of an advertising poster, and two display cases containing Happy Meal Toys were introduced as evidence. The Board found that the commercials, poster, and display cases, which advertised the Happy Meals, devoted primary attention to the Happy Meal Toy.

Mr. Linhardt testified that on average McDonald's sold about eight hundred thousand toys annually as part of the various Happy Meal promotions. During the periods at issue, McDonald's franchisees, including MRM, also made separate sales of Happy Meal Toys. While a Happy Meal Toy was not an item listed separately on its in-store menus, McDonald's cash registers included a separate key for Happy Meal Toys sold separately. Mr. Linhardt testified that about three to five percent of the total eight hundred thousand Happy Meal Toy sales he cited were separate sales outside of the Happy Meals. MRM collected and remitted a sales tax on these separate sales of Happy Meal Toys, and the Commissioner did not contend that MRM owed additional sales or use tax on these separate sales. MRM also collected and remitted sales tax to the Commissioner based on the full sale price of the Happy Meal, which included the Happy Meal Toys.

* * *

The Commissioner based its audit on the contention that MRM did not sell the Happy Meal Toys but instead used the toys to promote its business of selling food at its restaurants. During the course of the hearing, the Commissioner argued, *inter alia*, that MRM's business contracts and practice failed to support its claim that the Happy Meal Toys were sold.

* * *

OPINION

The principal issue before the Board was whether the Happy Meal Toys contained in Happy Meals were sold by MRM in the regular course of its business, or whether MRM consumed those toys in operating its business and thus owed a use tax on its purchase of the toys from its distributor. The governing statute, G.L. c. 64I, § 2, imposes "an excise . . . upon the storage, use or other consumption of tangible personal property . . . purchased from any vendor for storage, use or other consumption within the commonwealth at the rate of five percent of the sales price of the property . . . ." "Use" is defined as "the exercise of any right or power over tangible personal property incident to the ownership of that property, *except that it does not include the sale of that property in the regular course of business* . . . ." G.L. c. 64I, § 1 (emphasis added). Therefore, if MRM met its burden of proving that it sold the Happy Meal Toys in the regular course of its business, and that it collected and remitted a tax on the sale price of its toys, then the Commissioner's assessment of use taxes on the Happy Meal Toys was invalid.

Key facts distinguished the instant appeal from cases where the Supreme Judicial Court has found that the taxpayer consumed the item in question in the conduct of its business. In each of these cases, namely Clark Franklin Press Corp. v. State Tax Commission, 364 Mass. 598 (1974), Prince v. State Tax Commission, 366 Mass. 470 (1974), and Jan Co. Central, Inc. v. Commissioner of Revenue, 405 Mass. 686 (1989), the Supreme Judicial Court noted that the transferred item was merely a promotional item that served to induce the customer to engage in a particular transaction or an incidental item that facilitated a purchase of the predominant item or items. In none of these cases was the item in question an integral component of the sale, as the Happy Meal Toy was to the sale of the Happy Meal.

Clark Franklin Press addressed the taxability of travel brochures sold by the taxpayer to its parent, a travel company, AITS, which distributed the brochures to its customers. The Supreme Judicial Court found that "AITS [was] in the business of selling travel services, not brochures." Id. at 602. Brochures were transferred to customers to advertise and promote the travel services that AITS sold and "in and of themselves had no consumer value." Id. Instead, their transfer "constituted only an insignificant part of AITS's transactions with its customers, and it is obvious that the services provided by AITS were the predominant factor in the charges made to its customers." Id. Accordingly, the Supreme Judicial Court ruled that AITS did not resell the brochures in the regular course of its travel business, and therefore, Clark Franklin Press should have collected and remitted a sales tax on the value of the brochures sold to AITS.

Prince addressed the taxability of items distributed by an amusement park operator to customers as prizes for "games of skill." 366 Mass. at 470. Customers purchased tickets entitling them to play the various games, and "[o]nly those contestants who [were] successful in the games [were] entitled to prizes." Id. The taxpayer remitted sales tax based only on the transactions in which a customer won a prize. The Commissioner, however, contended that the taxpayer owed a use tax on its purchases of all of the prizes. Id. at 471. The Supreme Judicial Court agreed with the Commissioner that the fees paid by customers "are like greens fees at golf courses and fees at bowling alleys and pool tables" and that "such fees or charges are not taxable under the sales tax law." Id. at 473. Therefore, "[t]he prize awarded is an inducement to play the game and is not a sale at retail." Id. Accordingly, the Court ruled that the taxpayer owed a use tax on its cost to purchase those prizes.

Jan Co. addressed the taxability of certain paper and plastic products, including napkins, utensils, sandwich cartons and wrappers, and French fry sleeves, which the taxpayer, the owner and operator of a Burger King restaurant franchise, purchased from its suppliers. 405 Mass. at 686–87. The taxpayer contended that these items were resold to its customers in the regular course of its restaurant business. It was uncontested that "Jan Co. charge[d] a single price for each of the food products and drinks" and that "[t]his price [did] not differ depending on whether the customer consume[d] the products on or off the premises, nor [did] it differ depending on whether the customer use[d] the various paper and plastic products (knives, forks, spoons, straws, napkins, stirrers) available on the premises." Id. at 687. The Supreme Judicial Court reviewed its earlier findings, including *Clark Franklin Press* and *Prince*, and concluded that "certain transfers of tangible personal property (brochures and prizes) are not resales in the regular course of the transferor's business but are incidental to the transferor's business, serving to facilitate the consummation of the principal transactions." Id. at 689. Based on its earlier cases, the Supreme Judicial Court ruled that "[t]he providing of paper and plastic products and accessories may be an inducement to the customer who wants a quick, convenient meal and may facilitate the customer's consumption of the meal, but it is, nevertheless, incidental to the basic purpose of the transaction, the sale of food and drink." Id. at 689–90. Accordingly, the Supreme Judicial Court ruled that Jan Co. did not sell the items in the regular course of its business, but instead consumed the items in the operation of its restaurant business and, accordingly, owed a use tax on its purchases of those items.

In the instant appeal, the Commissioner focused on language from these cases concerning the inherent nature of a taxpayer's business and argued that, as in *Clark Franklin Press*, MRM's distribution of the items in question "constituted only an insignificant part of [its] transactions with its customers," because MRM "[was] in the business of selling [food], not [toys]." 364 Mass. at 602. Thus, the items at issue served merely as an "inducement" to MRM's customers to purchase food. See Prince, 366 Mass. at 473; Jan Co., 405 Mass. at 689–90.

The Board, however, found that the sale of eight hundred thousand Happy Meals, which included eight hundred thousand Happy Meal Toys, was not an "insignificant" part of McDonald's business. Moreover, the Board has previously found that a narrow interpretation of "regular course of business," which requires the taxpayer to be "primarily engaged" or "principally engaged" in the sale of specific merchandise, "improperly narrows" that term. International Business Machines Corp. v. Commissioner of Revenue, 1997 Mass. A.T.B. Adv. Sh. 1028, 1045 (Docket Nos. 170420–26). The determination of whether an item is purchased for resale does not simply "end[] with a determination of the seller's primary line of business," but instead must focus on the "dominant purpose" of the particular transaction involved. Id. at 1051 (citing Coca Cola Bottling Company of Northampton v. Commissioner of Revenue, 393 Mass. 726, 729 (1985)).

Based on its view of the dominant purpose of the particular transaction, namely the sale of Happy Meals, the Board ruled that MRM's distribution of Happy Meal Toys amounted to a sale of those toys in the regular course of its business. The Board found that the evidence concerning the planning and marketing of the Happy Meal Toys, including the commercials which showcased those toys, established that the Happy Meal Toys were intended to be, and were, a popular commodity with intrinsic value to the customers of McDonald's and its franchisees. Thus, unlike the napkins and wrappers transferred to customers in *Jan Co.* or the travel brochures in *Clark Franklin*, the Happy Meal Toys were a significant part of the Happy Meals which MRM sold in the regular course of its business. Moreover, unlike *Prince*, MRM established that the transactions at issue involved the transfer of tangible personal property, namely the Happy Meal, to its customers, and that every Happy Meal included exactly one Happy Meal Toy. MRM collected and remitted a sales tax on the sale price of the entire Happy Meal package. Therefore, the Happy Meal Toy was not merely used as an inducement to engage the customer in a nontaxable transaction, but was instead an integral part of the tangible personal property that was transferred to the customer and for which the customer was charged a sales tax on the total cost. Accordingly, the Board ruled that the transfer to its customers of Happy Meal Toys constituted a sale of those toys in MRM's regular course of business.

* * *

CONCLUSION

* * * [T]he Happy Meal Toys were not "give away" items. The Board thus ruled that MRM met its burden of proving that it sold Happy Meal Toys in the course of its business of operating a McDonald's franchise and, therefore, the Commissioner's assessment of use taxes on MRM's purchases of Happy Meal Toys from its distributor was invalid. Accordingly, the Board issued a decision for MRM in this appeal.

By: Frank J. Scharaffa, Commissioner

Notes and Questions

A. Do the results in *McDonalds* and the cases cited in *McDonalds* (*Clark Franklin Press*, *Prince*, and *Jan Co.*) reflect sound retail sales tax policy? To answer that question, it may be helpful to answer several other questions. First, what is the ultimate sale in the economic process to which the transaction at issue relates? Second, will the retail sales tax reach the receipts from that transaction? If not, are the receipts at issue within the scope of the retail sales tax (i.e., are they receipts from a transaction the legislature intended to tax)?

B. *Other Promotional Items Distributed "Free."* The Milwaukee Brewers baseball club purchased bats and jackets outside the state that it distributed to fans at its home games in connection with their purchase of tickets. The state asserted that the club owed a use tax on the articles. The club contended that the promotional items were free of the tax, contending that it purchased them for resale. The court sustained the assessment on the ground that the baseball club did not resell the bats and jackets because they were given away to the fans. Wisconsin Dep't of Revenue v. Milwaukee Brewers Baseball Club, 111 Wis.2d 571, 331 N.W.2d 383 (1983). The court relied in part on a provision of the Wisconsin statute specifying that "no part of the charge for a service may be deemed a sale * * * of tangible personal property," id., 331 N.W.2d at 386 (quoting the statute), and in part on the fact that Wisconsin taxed admissions to baseball games as services. Accord, Minnesota Twins Partnership v. Commissioner of Revenue, 587 N.W.2d 287 (Minn. 1998). As in *McDonalds*, however, the Missouri Supreme Court held that "[a]lthough the promotional items are ostensibly given away, the cost of purchasing these items is factored into the price charged for each ticket of admission to a Royals game." Kansas City Royals v. Director of Revenue, 32 S.W.3d 560, 563 (Mo. banc. 2000).

C. *Sales for Resale and the Rendition of Services.* As the *Milwaukee Brewers* case suggests, the question whether a transaction is a nontaxable sale for resale or a taxable sale for use or consumption is often intimately connected to the question whether the purchaser is engaged in rendering services or in selling tangible personal property. For example, courts have held that sales of linens, soap, paper towels, napkins, cups, and stationery to hotels for use by their guests are retail sales for consumption by the purchaser in rendering services to their customers. Hotels, these courts conclude, do not resell these articles to their guests. See, e.g., Adamar of New Jersey v. Director, Division of Taxation, 17 N.J.Tax 80, 89 (1997), aff'd, 18 N.J.Tax 70 (Super. Ct., App. Div. 1999), aff'd per curiam, 167 N.J. 67, 768 A.2d 1054 (2001) (observing that "[t]his conclusion is consistent * * * with the weight of authority throughout the United States") (citing cases); Helmsley Enterprises, Inc. v. Tax Appeals Tribunal, 187 A.D.2d 64, 592 N.Y.S.2d 851 (3d Dep't), appeal denied, 81 N.Y.2d 710, 616 N.E.2d 854, 600 N.Y.S.2d 197

(1993). But see Kansas City Power and Light Co. v. Director of Revenue, 83 S.W.3d 548 (Mo. banc. 2002) (hotel's purchases of electricity for customer space constitute exempt sale for resale). See also Nashville Clubhouse Inn v. Johnson, 27 S.W.3d 542 (Tenn. App. 2000) (upscale hotel's purchases of beverages and food that it provided to registered guests on a "complimentary" basis constitute nontaxable purchases for resale).

Professionals are generally treated as rendering services. Accordingly, lawyers are taxable on the paper they purchase for preparing contracts, wills, and other documents, although they turn these legal documents over to their clients. Likewise, dentists generally must pay tax on the crowns, bridges, dentures, cements, and other materials they purchase because they use these materials in the course of rendering services and do not resell them to their patients. See, e.g., Kilbane v. Director, Department of Revenue, 544 S.W.2d 9 (Mo. 1976); Hardy v. State Tax Comm'n, 561 P.2d 1064 (Utah 1977); but see Wisconsin Department of Revenue v. Milwaukee Refining Corp., 80 Wis.2d 44, 257 N.W.2d 855 (1977) (sales of gold to dentists are not retail sales).

D. *Restaurant Purchases of Disposable Cups, Napkins, and Similar Items.* There is a split of authority on the question whether fast-food restaurants, cafeterias, and other vendors of meals are taxable on their purchases of disposable wrappers, cups, napkins, and plastic eating utensils they transfer to their customers with the meals. The Illinois Supreme Court held a Dairy Queen franchisee (Sta–Ru Corp.) taxable on its purchases of disposable plastic containers, declaring:

> Obviously, Sta–Ru is in the business of selling food and beverages, not disposable containers, and it is the food or beverage which its customers come to purchase. * * * Sta–Ru provides the plastic and paper containers as part of its standard method of doing business. There is no resale of the containers to the customers within the meaning of the [sales tax statute]. Rather, the cost of the containers used to serve food on its premises is a cost of doing business as would be the cost of permanent dinnerware.

Sta–Ru Corp. v. Mahin, 64 Ill.2d 330, 1 Ill.Dec. 67, 356 N.E.2d 67, 70 (1976). Accord, e.g., Jan Co. Cent., Inc. v. Commissioner of Revenue, 405 Mass. 686, 544 N.E.2d 586 (1989) (discussed in *McDonald*'s); Covenco, Inc. v. Commonwealth, 134 Pa.Cmwlth. 314, 579 A.2d 434 (1990), aff'd, 530 Pa. 206, 607 A.2d 1077 (1992).

The New York Court of Appeals, on the other hand, held that Burger King purchased its disposable hamburger wrappers, beverage cups, and french fry "sleeves" for resale. Burger King v. State Tax Commission, 51 N.Y.2d 614, 416 N.E.2d 1024, 435 N.Y.S.2d 689 (1980). Because the packaging "is such a critical element of the final product sold to the customers," the court concluded that

> the packaging material is as much a part of the final price as is the food or drink item itself. It would be exalting form over substance, therefore, to hold that resale of these paper products does not take place merely because Burger King does not list a separate price.

Id., 435 N.Y.S.2d at 693. See also Shamrock Foods Co. v. City of Phoenix, 157 Ariz. 286, 757 P.2d 90 (1988); Macke Co. v. Comptroller of the Treasury, 302 Md. 18, 485 A.2d 254 (1984).

Is *Sta–Ru* or *Burger King* more consistent with the underlying policy of the retail sales tax? As we have suggested above, the answer to that question arguably depends on whether the subsequent sale of the meal (along with the disposable packaging and utensils) will be subject to sales tax.

E. *Intention to Resell After Use of Article.* Does the purchase of an article qualify under a resale provision if it is purchased with the intention to use it and then to resell it? In Baltimore Foundry and Machine Corp. v. Comptroller, 211 Md. 316, 127 A.2d 368 (1956), a foundry purchased patterns or molds that it used to make steel castings, which it sold to its customers. After it made the castings, the foundry sold the patterns to its customers. The foundry agreed to sell the patterns to its customers at the time the customers ordered the castings. The state argued that the resale provision is inapplicable unless the *only* purpose of the use is resale. The court disagreed, holding that the resale provision applied in view of the contemporaneous resale intention.

The California Court of Appeal, on the other hand, held a computer manufacturer liable for use tax on computer components used for testing purposes and then refurbished and sold to its customers. Burroughs Corp. v. State Board of Equalization, 153 Cal.App.3d 1152, 200 Cal.Rptr. 816 (3d Dist. 1984). The Georgia Supreme Court likewise held that cars used as "demonstrators" by auto dealerships are subject to sales tax when purchased by the dealer, even though they are ultimately resold to customers. Law Lincoln Mercury, Inc. v. Strickland, 246 Ga. 237, 271 S.E.2d 152 (1980).

As a matter of retail sales tax policy, should the use of property by the purchaser deprive the purchaser of the sale-for-resale exemption? If the retail sales tax is designed to be a tax on consumption, what does this suggest about the appropriate treatment of property that is purchased for both use and resale? Assume, for example, that a car dealer purchases a new vehicle from the manufacturer for $15,000 and, after using the car as a demonstrator for six months, sells the vehicle to the customer for $10,000. What is the proper measure of the sales tax on the sale to the dealer and the dealer's customer respectively? Would a tax imposed in a theoretically sound manner be difficult to administer? See generally Richard D. Pomp & Oliver Oldman, "A Normative Inquiry into the Base of a Retail Sales Tax: Casual Sales, Used Goods, and Trade–Ins," 43 Nat'l Tax J. 427 (1990).

F. *Purchase of Property for Rental as a Sale for Resale.* Because almost all states include the rental of tangible personal property within the definition of a taxable sale (see pp. 640–45 supra), they should treat the purchase of property for rental as an exempt sale for resale to avoid pyramiding of the tax. In fact, many states treat a purchase of property for rental or leasing as a sale for resale in order to avoid double taxation. In other states, one who purchases property for the purpose of renting or leasing it may either pay sales tax on the purchase or collect tax on the rental receipts. See, e.g., Cal. Rev. & Tax. Code §§ 6006(g)(5), 6010(e)(5) (Westlaw 2009). In some states, however, there is no explicit provision in the statute eliminating double taxation, with the result that states sometimes impose tax on both the purchase and lease of the property by the lessor.

In Ryder Truck Rental, Inc. v. Bryant, 170 So.2d 822 (Fla. 1964), the court sustained a two percent sales tax on a car rental agency's purchase of motor vehicles, despite the imposition of a three percent tax on the vehicle rental fees that the agency received from its customers. The court determined that the legislature had levied the sales tax on the vendor for the privilege of selling while levying the rental tax on the taxpayer for the privilege of renting the cars. Since both taxes are levied under Florida's sales and use tax and collected from the customer, is not the court's argument that "there is no 'pyramiding' or duplication of the tax since each is a separate and distinct taxable privilege" (id. at 825) true only in the most formalistic sense? Nevertheless, both the legislative history and the language of the statute suggest that the court's decision was sound, not for the reason given by the court, but on the ground that the Florida Legislature did in fact intend to impose the challenged double taxation.

As a matter of sound retail sales tax policy, what is the appropriate sales tax treatment of a rent-a-car company that purchases, leases, and ultimately sells a fleet of cars? Compare your answer with your answer to the problem posed in the last paragraph of Note E supra. Are your answers consistent?

G. *Limitation of Resale Exemption to Resales Taxable by the State.* May a state limit its exclusion from tax for sales for resale to cases in which the resale transaction will take place within its boundaries? Can the state reasonably defend such a rule on the theory that the resale exclusion is granted only to avoid pyramiding of tax on the subsequent resale and, in cases in which the resale occurs outside the state, there will be no taxable resale insofar as the taxing state is concerned? See Don McCullagh, Inc. v. State, 354 Mich. 413, 93 N.W.2d 252 (1958), appeal dismissed, 359 U.S. 343, 79 S.Ct. 897 (1959) (denying resale exemption to purchaser of cars for out-of-state rental under statute limiting resale exemption to leases "when rental receipts are taxable" by state); Mayo Collaborative Servs., Inc. v. Commissioner of Revenue, 698 N.W.2d 408 (Minn. 2005), cert. denied, 546 U.S. 1171, 126 S.Ct. 1334 (2006) (denying sale for resale exemption under health care provider tax for items sold to providers who are not subject to the tax for items sold to out-of-state providers). What arguments would you make against the validity of these statutes? Would you prevail?

2. MANUFACTURING, PROCESSING, AND FABRICATION EXEMPTIONS

The sales tax provisions of every state exclude or exempt purchases of materials for use in the manufacturing, processing, or fabricating of tangible personal property for sale. All States Tax Guide (RIA) ¶ 254 (2009) (chart), available at www.checkpoint.riag.com. The theory underlying these exclusions or exemptions is the same theory that underlies the sale-for-resale provisions considered above: the materials in question are not purchased for final consumption but rather for resale in the form of the final manufactured product. For this reason, these provisions often require that the materials purchased become an integral or component part of the product that is ultimately to be sold at retail. For example, the Arkansas statute provides that

> [g]oods, wares, merchandise, and property sold for use in manufacturing, compounding, processing, assembling or preparing for sale can be classified as having been sold for the purposes of resale * * * only in the event the goods, wares, merchandise, or property becomes a recognizable integral part of the manufactured, compounded, processed, assembled, or prepared products.

Ark. Code Ann. § 26–52–401(12)(B)(i) (Westlaw 2009). In some states, the manufacturing and processing provisions are written more broadly to include materials used or consumed in manufacturing or processing tangible personal property for resale, even if not physically incorporated in the final product sold at retail.

In the ensuing materials (as in the materials you have already studied in this chapter), there is a often a palpable tension in the cases between the theoretically sound result (assuming that the retail sales tax is viewed as a tax on final consumption) and the result dictated by the precise language of the statute or by administrative and revenue concerns. Indeed, from a theoretical standpoint, one may ask why it *ever* should make any difference whether the property purchased by a business is physically incorporated in the property that the business resells, or is used in "manufacturing" or "processing," as long as the price of the purchased property will be reflected in the price of the property that is resold (and taxed) at retail. The challenge for you is to wend your way through the frequently conflicting cases with a sensitivity both to the statutory provisions and legal doctrine that inform the decisions in particular cases as well as to the broader tax policy concerns to which the decisions may or may not be faithful.

KAISER STEEL CORPORATION v. STATE BOARD OF EQUALIZATION

Supreme Court of California, 1979.
24 Cal.3d 188, 593 P.2d 864, 154 Cal.Rptr. 919.

Manuel, Justice.

Plaintiff Kaiser Steel Corporation (Kaiser) appeals from a judgment denying recovery of certain sales and use taxes paid to defendant State Board of Equalization (Board) in the period October 31, 1967, through December 31, 1973. We conclude that Kaiser purchased the materials which are the subject of the disputed taxes for a "purpose other than resale" and that the transactions were "retail sales" within the provisions of Revenue and Taxation Code, section 6007. We therefore affirm the judgment.

The case was tried by the court upon stipulated facts as follows: At its plant in Fontana, Kaiser is engaged in the manufacture and production for sale of steel, pig iron, and other products. Kaiser purchased certain materials to charge its furnaces and to remove impurities from the molten metal, namely, limestone, burnt lime, fluorspar, raw dolomite, burnt dolomite, bentonite, aluminum bar and shot, gravel, and aluminum magnesium alloy (materials). The removal of impurities is accomplished by combining them with the materials to form slag.

Portions of the materials were incorporated in the steel to achieve a specific quality; portions simply remained in the finished steel; portions were dissipated or lost in the manufacturing process; and portions, ranging from 52 percent to 97 percent of various materials, became components of the slag. None of the aluminum magnesium alloy became part of the slag; 80 percent remained in the steel product and 20 percent was dissipated. Forty percent of the aluminum bar and shot was incorporated into the steel, giving it a fine grained quality; the remaining 60 percent ended up in the slag. Only those portions of those materials which became components of the slag are at issue in this litigation.

An independent company removed the slag from Kaiser's premises, paid Kaiser 1 cent for each ton removed, reprocessed the slag, and remitted to Kaiser a 10 percent royalty on the net sales price of the reprocessed slag, which is used in a wide variety of businesses and for a number of differing purposes. Through this arrangement Kaiser recovered 8.7 percent of the cost of the raw materials (including the value of removing the slag).[2]

When it purchased the materials Kaiser either paid the sales tax (§ 6052) or gave the vendors a resale certificate (§ 6091) and later paid a use tax (§ 6094, subd. (a)). Kaiser filed claims for refund with the Board for sales and use taxes paid with respect to the materials that combined to form slag, alleging that the materials had been purchased for the purpose of resale. The company brought the instant action pursuant to section 6934 when the Board failed to take action on the claims.

The Board took the position that Kaiser purchased the materials for a purpose other than resale, namely to aid in the manufacture of steel, and that therefore the purchases were not tax exempt. Kaiser contended that it purchased the materials for the purpose of resale in the form of slag, a by-product in the manufacture of steel. Kaiser asked the court to order an apportionment of the cost of the materials between the exempt and nonexempt uses of the materials.

The trial court construed the pertinent authorities and concluded that Kaiser's "primary purpose" for purchasing the raw materials determines their taxability. It found the Board's conclusion that Kaiser purchased the materials primarily to aid in manufacturing steel was reasonable. The

---

2. In a typical year, 1971, Kaiser paid approximately $3.8 million for the materials and produced almost 2,500,000 tons of steel which it sold for approximately $255 million; in the same year Kaiser produced almost 1,250,000 tons of slag for which it received approximately $99,000 in royalties. (Kaiser credited the 1 cent per ton purchase price against the royalty). The value to Kaiser in having the slag removed from its premises was $233,000.

court therefore held that the purchases of raw materials were subject to sales and use tax. We agree.

Section 6051 provides for a tax on all retail sales. Section 6007 defines a retail sale as "a sale for any purpose other than resale in the regular course of business in the form of tangible personal property." Normally, the tax is collected by the retailer from the purchaser. (§ 6052.) If the purchaser pays the tax, then resells the property "prior to making any use of the property other than retention, demonstration, or display while holding it for sale in the regular course of business," a deduction is allowed. (§ 6012, subd. (a)(1).) On the other hand, if the purchaser gives a resale certificate to the seller (§ 6091) and thereafter makes use of the property before reselling it, a "use" tax is imposed on the original purchase price. (§ 6094, subd. (a).)

A Board regulation generally applicable to manufacturers, producers, and processors provides:

> "(a) Tax applies to the sale of tangible personal property to persons who purchase it for the purpose of use in manufacturing, producing or processing tangible personal property and not for the purpose of physically incorporating it into the manufactured article to be sold. Examples of such property are machinery, * * * and chemicals used as catalysts or otherwise to produce a chemical or physical reaction such as the production of heat or the removal of impurities.

> "(b) Tax does not apply to sales of tangible personal property to persons who purchase it for the purpose of incorporating it into the manufactured article to be sold, as, for example, any raw material becoming an ingredient or component part of the manufactured article." (Reg. 1525.)

In determining whether a sale is taxable as a retail sale or exempt as a sale for resale, the California courts have consistently looked to the primary intent of the purchaser or primary purpose of the purchase. (People v. Puritan Ice Co. (1944) 24 Cal.2d 645, 151 P.2d 1; * * *). In *Puritan,* ice was sold to vegetable packers and shippers for use in preserving perishable products. This court held that the sales to packers and shippers were retail sales and taxable despite the fact that the packers and shippers separately charged their customers for the ice. "The essence of the matter is that the purchasers of the ice are acquiring it for purpose other than resale. They are not engaged in the ice selling business. They are selling vegetables and the use of the ice or purported sale thereof to the purchasers of the vegetables is merely an incident of that activity. It is common knowledge that the dominant purpose for the use of ice in shipping perishable produce is to preserve the produce by means of refrigeration ..." (24 Cal.2d at pp. 651–652, 151 P.2d at p. 4; accord Good Humor Co., supra, 152 Cal.App.2d at p. 877, 313 P.2d 640 [dry ice merely passed on "as an incident" of ice cream product sales activity]; Monterey Ice & Dev. Co., supra, 29 Cal.App.2d at p. 424, 84 P.2d 1069 ["real purpose" of ice purchase was to furnish refrigeration as a "necessary incident" of business of selling lettuce].)

In Kirk v. Johnson, supra, 37 Cal.App.2d 224, 99 P.2d 279, the "primary purpose" test was applied where cows, purchased for milk production, were eventually sold for beef. The original purchase was taxable in full because the primary purpose was dairy use, not resale for beef. In Safeway Stores, supra, 148 Cal.App.2d 299, 306 P.2d 597, the company purchased cartons which were used to ship products from the warehouse to retail stores; 80 percent remained in good condition and were eventually used for crating retail customers' grocery purchases, an exempt use. The court held that the total carton purchase was subject to sales tax because Safeway first used all of them for a nonexempt purpose.

We recognize that none of the cases discussed thus far involve the purchase of materials for manufacturing. We cannot agree with Kaiser, however, that the primary purpose test has no application in the manufacturing industries. In our view, regulation 1525, quoted earlier, *is* a statement of the primary-purpose test. Thus, if property is purchased as an aid in the manufacturing process, it is taxable despite the fact that some portion remains in the finished product or that an incidental waste or by-product results. Conversely, if the property is purchased for incorporation as a component of the finished product, it is not taxable despite the fact that some portion may be lost or otherwise dissipated in the manufacturing process.

Our interpretation of the regulation accords with the interpretation of the Board in its tax counsel rulings. * * *

Significantly, burnt lime, limestone, and aluminum (in several forms) were among the products purchased by Kaiser and either used as an aid to manufacture the steel (all of the lime, limestone and aluminum in alloy form and 60 percent of the aluminum bar and shot) or incorporated into the steel (40 percent of the aluminum bar and shot). As in the prior rulings, the Board here considered the purpose for which the materials were purchased; its conclusion that Kaiser purchased all the materials which eventually ended up in the slag primarily for aid in the manufacture of the steel is eminently reasonable.

Given the economics of steel versus slag production, the resale of the slag is as collateral to the production of steel as the resale of cows in *Kirk* was collateral to dairy farming. It is as incidental to Kaiser's business as the resale of ice in *Puritan* * * *. The primary-purpose test of *Puritan* and *Kirk* is applicable to the manufacturing industries.

Kaiser attempts to distinguish *Kirk* and *Puritan* on grounds that the uses there were successive rather than simultaneous. The argument is not persuasive. The Board has made no distinction in its rulings based upon simultaneous as contrasted to successive use. Where there are simultaneous uses but only one or primary purpose for the purchase, the entire unit of material is taxed or not taxed, depending on that purpose: "If the primary purpose of purchasing chromic acid is to supply the chrome which is applied through a plating process to articles to be sold, the chromic acid is purchased for resale, even though the acid contains ingredients which aid in the application of the chrome to the articles." (C.C.H. 60–118.31; Tax Counsel Ruling 6/29/51.) Conversely, use of forged steel balls to grind silica sand to a desired fineness determines the taxability of the purchase of the balls as a retail sale, even though in the course of the grinding the balls wear out and all of the steel from the balls eventually becomes a part of the product. (C.C.H. 60–118.41; Tax Counsel Ruling 5/16/52.)

Similarly, when the entire unit is first utilized as an aid in processing or manufacturing and subsequently incorporated into a manufactured product to be sold, the entire unit is taxable. For example, paper pulp and wood fiber, first used in a filtration process, is later incorporated into cattle feed and sold. The purchases of pulp and fiber are taxable. (C.C.H. 60–118.693; Tax Counsel Ruling 3/25/65.) Also, the sale of sulfuric acid, first used as a dehydrating agent, is a retail sale and subject to tax even though it is subsequently incorporated into other tangible personal property which is sold. (C.C.H. 60–118.121; Tax Counsel Ruling 5/26/55.)

It is evident from the record that Kaiser's dominant motive or purpose in purchasing the materials in question was to use them in removing the impurities from its molten steel, a "purpose other than resale." (§ 6007.) Although Kaiser intended to eventually resell the materials in the form of slag, Kaiser first *used* all of the materials in question in a nonexempt manner, thereby determining their taxability. (§ 6012, subd. (a)(1) and § 6094, subd. (a).)

Kaiser suggests that in the manufacturing field, the courts should, as the Board has done, apportion the tax according to uses made of the materials purchased. Indeed, the Board has apportioned the tax in some circumstances, not here applicable. When the purchaser buys a quantity of materials and has two purposes in mind (within the meaning of § 6007), the Board permits apportionment of the tax if the purchaser can establish what portion he is using for the exempt purpose and what portion for the nonexempt purpose. This is so even though the portions will be utilized at the same time. Thus, in the instant case Kaiser had purchased a quantity of aluminum bar and shot and was able to establish that 60 percent was used as an aid in manufacturing and 40 percent was incorporated into the steel.[5] Tax counsel rulings are in accord: "Where scrap carbon or graphite is added to the charge in addition to the normal coke charge, and is used solely to add carbon to the iron and is not used as a fuel, the sale of the scrap carbon or graphite would be exempt from tax as a sale for resale. If, however, any portion of such scrap carbon or graphite does in fact oxidize or burn and, therefore, provide heat which aids the manufacturing process, that proportion would be considered as sold for consumption as is the

---

5. The parties stipulated and the court found that upon auditing Kaiser's tax returns, the Board accepted Kaiser's claim that "a portion of the aluminum bar and shot is purchased to incorporate it into steel according to customer specifications." The customer wanted a special fine grained quality. We are not here concerned with the 40 percent incorporated into the steel. As noted earlier our issue relates only to the taxation of the materials which became slag.

case of the 55% of the coke considered used by Ruling 17." (C.C.H. 60–118.481; Tax Counsel Ruling 7/19/55.) Tax Ruling 17, referred to in the above quoted ruling, has been adopted as regulation 1530. It applies to foundries in general and determines the taxability of coke in terms of proportions utilized for the dual purposes of aid in manufacture and for resale. The industry has apparently been able to establish to the satisfaction of the Board that any purchase of a quantity of coke in that industry is for dual purposes and utilized thus in the proportions provided by the section. Likewise, the fur dressers and dyers have been able to establish that certain dyestuffs and chemicals used by them are for incorporation into skins and furs which they process. The Board has noted, however, that two of the materials (sodium chloride and hydrogen peroxide) are also commonly used for "fleshing" and "bleaching" respectively, and insofar as the furriers give the vendor resale certificates and then "consume" any portion of the materials for fleshing or bleaching, the entire purchase of the material is taxable unless the furrier keeps accurate records showing the respective amounts used for each purpose. (Reg.1531.)

Apportionment has no place in the instant case because Kaiser did not have dual purposes for the quantities purchased. *All* quantities of the materials which ended up in the slag and are the subject of the instant dispute were purchased for use as an aid in the manufacturing process. It is settled law that the eventual resale of personal property by a person who purchases such property for use will not prevent the original sale of such property from being a retail sale subject to tax. (§§ 6009, 6094, subd. (a).)

Kaiser cites out-of-state cases which support its position. Since the sales tax schemes in states where those cases arise differ from California's, no purpose is served in reviewing them here.

The primary-purpose test, which we reaffirm in this decision, finds support in tax policy. The test assures that the entire amount of materials will be taxed at its highest value. Permitting an exemption when materials are incorporated into the finished product is rational, since the materials enhance the value of the product which will eventually be sold and taxed at its highest value. Kaiser's position would permit use of materials costing millions of dollars in aid of manufacturing a profitable article, while avoiding taxation in the reselling of a relatively worthless waste by-product. In other words, instead of materials being taxed at their highest value, they will be taxed at a tiny fraction of that value. Such a result does not comport with the legislative scheme as indicated by the court decisions and administrative interpretations.

The judgment is affirmed.

BIRD, C.J., and TOBRINER, MOSK, CLARK, RICHARDSON and NEWMAN, JJ., concur.

NOTES AND QUESTIONS

A. Was not the price of all the materials that Kaiser purchased reflected in the price that Kaiser (or some subsequent seller) charged to the ultimate consumer of the steel product in a taxable transaction? If so, why should Kaiser have paid tax on any of the materials? Why did Kaiser seek to avoid taxation on only an apportioned share of the costs of its raw materials? The court in *Kaiser Steel* declares that "[t]he primary purpose test, which we reaffirm in this decision, finds support in tax policy," namely, to tax materials "at their highest value" rather than "at a tiny fraction of that value." How does this policy, at least as applied to business purchases whose price will be reflected in the subsequent taxable sale of other goods, square with the underlying policy of a retail sales tax? If we must tax a substantial portion of business purchases in order to generate the revenues that we anticipate from the retail sales tax without raising the rates to politically unpalatable levels, and we know that the legislature has made a conscious decision to do so, does it make any sense even to ask the question whether the outcome of a particular case comports with the theory of a simon-pure consumption tax?

B. *Ingredient or Component Part of Manufactured Product: Other Steel Production Cases.* Other courts have confronted essentially the same question raised by *Kaiser Steel*, with diverse results. In Granite City Steel Co. v. Department of Revenue, 30 Ill.2d 552, 198 N.E.2d 507 (1964), the court approved the revenue department's construction of an ingredient-component part exemption that divided the purchased property between the exempt and taxable portion. A producer of pig iron and steel used coke for two distinct purposes: it burned the coke (1) to generate heat which was necessary to melt the iron and induce the desired chemical reaction, and (2) to infuse the iron with an essential ingredient—carbon. The taxpayer argued that the entire cost of property is exempt as an ingredient if "any portion * * * however small that portion may be, is intended to and does become a necessary ingredient in a furnished product." Id., 198 N.E.2d at 511. The court disagreed and sustained the Department's exemption of roughly one-third of the coke that was infused as carbon into the iron.

The Nebraska Supreme Court adopted a different rule in Nucor Steel v. Herrington, 212 Neb. 310, 322 N.W.2d 647 (1982). The court held that if a substantial part of the material becomes an ingredient of the finished product—even though there are other primary uses for the material—and the rest is consumed in the manufacturing process, all of the material constitutes an exempt ingredient. The court reasoned:

> On the facts in the present record the trial court correctly determined that the graphite electrodes were used in this case for two primary purposes and functions and that a substantial amount of the graphite electrodes entered into and remained an ingredient and component part of the finished steel product. The electrodes involved here were within the specific terms of the statute and we see no reason to read into the statute a requirement that a majority of the substance used must remain in the finished product in order to make the purpose of its use primary. There is no justification for holding that the purpose of using a substance

which is an essential and critical ingredient of the finished product is not a primary and important purpose simply because there is also another reason for using the substance which is also important. It is tacitly conceded that if the graphite involved here was used in a form other than an electrode, it would not be subject to tax. The fact that the same substance can serve an additional purpose in the manufacturing process if it is in the form of an electrode does not change the factual reality or the terms of the tax statute.

Where graphite electrodes are used in the manufacture of steel for the dual purpose of providing essential carbon for the steel manufacturing process and for the conduction of electricity which provides heat for the process, and where a substantial part of the graphite electrodes enters into and becomes an essential ingredient or component part of the finished steel and the remainder is consumed in the manufacturing and refining process, the use of such graphite electrodes in the manufacturing and processing of steel for ultimate sale at retail is not subject to taxation under the provisions of §§ 77–2702 and 77–2703.

Id., 322 N.W.2d at 651.

The Washington Court of Appeals adopted an even more generous view of the exemption when it ruled that the purchase of coke used in manufacturing iron was exempt from tax on the ground that "[t]he important fact for application of the ingredient exemption is that a necessary ingredient is supplied, not that the quantity is small." Van Dyk v. Department of Revenue, 41 Wash.App. 71, 702 P.2d 472 (1985); see also State v. Alabama Metallurgical Corp., 446 So.2d 41 (Ala. Civ. App. 1984). On the other hand, the Louisiana Supreme Court held that coke purchased by a manufacturer of manhole covers was taxable under a statute exempting "sale of materials for further processing into articles of tangible personal property for sale at retail" (La. Rev. Stat. Ann. § 47:301(10)(c)(i)(aa) (Westlaw 2009)) because the coke was used primarily as a fuel, and the small amount of coke absorbed by the iron was incidental. Vulcan Foundry, Inc. v. McNamara, 414 So.2d 1193 (La. 1981).

On the reasonable assumption that the state legislatures in these cases have adopted the view that the exemption issue is to be decided by reference to physical rather than economic concepts, which of the tests articulated by the cases described above best serves the legislature's purpose? The "primary purpose" test of *Kaiser Steel*? The "substantiality" test of *Nucor Steel*? The "necessary ingredient" test of *Van Dyk*? The split-the-baby approach of *Granite City Steel*? Why?

C. *Ingredient or Component Part of Manufactured Product: Other Cases.* Nebraska excludes from the definition of a retail sale the sale of "[p]roperty which will enter into and become an ingredient or component part of property manufactured, processed, or fabricated for ultimate sale at retail." Neb. Rev. Stat. § 77–2704.45 (Westlaw 2009). In American Stores Packing Co. v. Peters, 203 Neb. 76, 277 N.W.2d 544 (1979), a meat packer bought cellulose casing for use in making skinless frankfurters and luncheon meats. The meat packer stuffed the prepared meat mechanically into the casings and then cooked and treated the meat along with the casings. During the cooking and treatment process, "an undetermined amount of the glycerine with which the casing is impregnated, moves by osmosis from the casing into the meat." Id., 277 N.W.2d at 546. The casing was then split, blown off, and discarded. The taxpayer argued that " 'enough [of the glycerine] goes in [to the product] to make a difference' and this should be the test of whether the casing enters into or becomes an ingredient or component part of the product." Id. at 546. The court reviewed the cases from other jurisdictions and sustained the tax on the casings, saying:

> The determination of whether or not tangible property enters into or becomes an ingredient or component part of other property does not ordinarily offer any difficulty. The lumber which goes into the manufacture of a piece of furniture obviously becomes a component part of that furniture, i.e., the function of the lumber is that of being a component and it serves no other purpose. In the case before us, the casing served the apparently indispensable function of a mold. In the end, the casing is discarded. It does not become an ingredient or component in any real sense, as it does not reach the ultimate consumer of the meat product. If one judges solely by the physical evidence, i.e., a sample of unused casing and a sample of used casing, the answer seems almost obvious. The casing remains after the manufacture. The principal function of the glycerine and moisture is to enable the casing to serve its function. The transfer of some part of the glycerine into meat which already contains glycerine appears incidental.

Id. at 548.

In American Distilling Co. v. Department of Revenue, 53 Ill.App.3d 42, 10 Ill.Dec. 946, 368 N.E.2d 541 (1977), a distiller purchased oak barrels for use in aging bourbon whiskey. The distillers reuse the barrels and sell them after the aging process is completed. In ruling that the barrels were a nontaxable ingredient in the manufacture of whiskey, the court declared:

> The function of the barrels is to impart the tannins and other wood extractives to the raw alcohol which cause the bourbon to take on its distinctive color, bouquet, and taste. Without the use of these barrels, there could be no bourbon whiskey, for it was the uncontroverted evidence below there is no known scientific means for man to artificially create bourbon whiskey. It is clear the barrels' function is vital to the production of bourbon whiskey.

Id., 368 N.E.2d at 543.

Can you reconcile the *American Stores* and the *American Distilling* cases? Should there be a de minimis rule that excludes from the ingredient exemption purchases of materials when only small amounts of those products appear in the final product? Or should the test be a qualitative one—whether the material—regardless of its amount—is essential to the final product? But are the casings any less essential to the production of frankfurters than the tannin is to the production of bourbon? In Container Corp. of America v. Wagner, 293 Ill.App.3d 1089, 228 Ill.Dec. 387, 689 N.E.2d 259 (1997), the court distinguished *American Distilling* in holding that a manufacturer's purchase of solvents for use in diluting inks and lacquers utilized in the manufacturing process did not fall within an exclusion for property "resold as an ingredient of" a manufactured product. The court declared:

> In *American Distilling*, the barrels and tannins were not consumed in the manufacturing process as the solvents are here; rather, the tannins and barrels were passed onto subsequent users albeit in altered form. In this case, in contrast, the solvent used to dilute the base inks and lacquers are not passed in tangible form to the ultimate consumer because * * * the solvents evaporate during the drying process.

Id., 689 N.E.2d at 263.

D. *Coal Purchased to Generate Electricity*. A California case illustrates the courts' typical focus on physical flows and the precise language of the statute rather than on theoretical or policy considerations in resolving sales tax controversies. The taxpayer was in the business of selling electricity to California consumers, and it purchased coal from out-of-state suppliers for this purpose. The coal was burned to heat boilers that generated steam; the steam, in turn, caused turbines to rotate a magnet inside a generator that produced electricity. The statute exempted sales of tangible personal property for resale, which California by regulation had interpreted to include ingredients and component parts. Although the court agreed with the taxpayer's contentions that electricity is tangible personal property and that the primary purpose of the coal was to provide fuel to be used to generate electricity, the court held that the taxpayer failed to show that the coal was "physically incorporated" into the electricity. Accordingly the court disallowed the taxpayer's claim for exemption. Searles Valley Minerals Operations, Inc. v. State Bd. of Equalization, 160 Cal.App.4th 514, 72 Cal.Rptr.3d 857 (2008).

E. *Property Used or Consumed in Manufacturing Products for Sale*. As noted at the outset of this subsection, some manufacturing and processing exemptions are not limited to property that becomes an ingredient or component part of the property sold. They embrace, in addition, property that is used or consumed in the manufacturing process. The Minnesota exemption, for example, excludes from sales tax "[m]aterials stored, used, or consumed in industrial production of personal property intended to be sold ultimately at retail * * * whether or not the item so used becomes an ingredient or constituent part of the property produced." Minn. Stat. § 297A.68(Subd. 2(a)) (Westlaw 2009). In Midwestern Press, Inc. v. Commissioner, 295 Minn. 59, 203 N.W.2d 344 (1972), the court held that a publisher's purchases of lithographic plates were exempt from tax, even though the plates were not physically destroyed during the printing process, because

> the term "consumed" as used in our statute does not necessarily mean physical consumption but is broad enough to include economic consumption of the subject property. It is the opinion of this Court that the lithographic plates are "economically consumed" in the printing process, having only junk value at the end of their run.

Id., 203 N.W.2d at 347.

In Bonnar–Vawter, Inc. v. Johnson, 157 Me. 380, 173 A.2d 141 (1961), on the other hand, the Maine Supreme Court held that a printer's purchases of metal plates used in the printing process did not qualify for the exemption for sales of "[t]angible personal property * * * that is consumed or destroyed or loses its identity directly and primarily in * * * the production of tangible personal property for later sale or lease." Me. Rev. Stat. Ann. tit. 36, § 1760(74) (Westlaw 2009). Because the printer stored the plates and reused them in making subsequent reprints of the same copy, the court held that the plates were not consumed in the process and, hence, were not covered by the exemption.

In Standard Packaging Corp. v. Commissioner of Revenue, 288 N.W.2d 234, 237 (Minn. 1979), the taxpayer, which manufactured playing cards, calendars, and other advertising specialties, purchased paintings and other art work from artists for reproduction in its products. The taxpayer photographed the art work and used the resulting color transparencies in the printing of the products. The court (construing the Minnesota statute quoted above) held that the purchases of the paintings and other art work were not taxable. It stated:

> We do not * * * agree that the right of reproduction is not "used or consumed in industrial production" within the meaning of the statute. The statutory scheme is to devise a unitary tax which exempts intermediate transactions and imposes it only on sales when the finished product is purchased by the ultimate user. The items here for consideration, in our opinion, fall into that category.

Id. at 239. Could a similar contention be made that the purchase by a printer or publisher of art work and the right of reproduction are exempt under a state's ingredient and component provision, on the ground that the art work becomes a physical ingredient in a component part of the printed article by reproduction?

3. MACHINERY AND EQUIPMENT EXEMPTIONS

Although the early sales taxes generally applied to purchases of industrial machinery and equipment, the modern trend is to exempt such purchases when made for use in manufacturing tangible personal property that is to be sold. Today, over half the states with sales taxes exempt purchases of industrial machinery and equipment. Some states also exempt tools and parts used in the manufacture of tangible personal property for sale. A number of states apply a lower tax rate to such purchases; still others limit the exemption to purchases of new and expanded machinery and equipment; and a few provide partial exemptions. A handful of states provide no exemptions specifically aimed at the purchase of machinery and equipment used to produce tangible personal property. See generally John Due & John Mikesell, Sales Taxation: State and Local Structure and Administration 63–64 (2d ed. 1994); All States Tax Guide (RIA) ¶ 254 (2009) (chart), available at www.checkpoint.riag. com.

The theoretical justification for exempting machinery, equipment, and other property purchased for use in production is the same as the sale-for-resale exemption generally, and the analogous exemptions and exclusions we have considered above, namely, to avoid pyramiding of the tax. As Due and Mikesell observe:

> [E]xemption of machinery is warranted because the category constitutes a major element in the cost of manufacturing, with no logic for taxing it. * * * Directly and immediately this taxation constitutes an addition to the cost of real investment, and presumably has some influence in lessening total real investment. This is completely contrary to the philosophy of a sales tax of taxing consumer spending.

Due & Mikesell, supra, at 65. Perhaps a more practical justification for these exemptions—and one that may explain their existence—is that machinery and equipment exemptions encourage economic activity—and, specifically, the location of industrial plants—in the state.

The critical legal problems raised by the machinery and equipment exemptions lie in the limitations that the states impose upon such exemptions. There is a good deal of diversity among the states in the scope and requirements for exclusion or exemption from sales tax of machinery and equipment. Many of the statutes exclude or exempt from sales tax only "machinery or equipment," or "machinery, equipment or tools," purchased for use "directly," or in some states, for use "directly and predominantly," in "manufacturing" or "producing" personal property. In other states, the statutory exclusion is not limited to machinery, equipment, and tools, but applies either to property generally or to "industrial materials" purchased for use in the fabrication of tangible personal property for sale. The exemption or exclusion in some states applies only to machinery and equipment used to create new plants or facilities within the state.

The designation of the types of operations to which the machinery and equipment provisions extend likewise varies among the states. In lieu of the exemption or exclusion from tax that some statutes provide for purchases of machinery or equipment for use in "manufacturing or production," some statutes explicitly cover not only "manufacturing" or "production," but also "processing" or "fabrication, assembly, extraction, mining, processing, refining, or finishing of * * * tangible personal property." Ind. Code Ann. § 6-2.5-5-3 (Westlaw 2009). A good many states have exempted purchases of agricultural machinery, equipment, or tools purchased for use in farming or in processing agricultural commodities. See generally Due & Mikesell, supra, at 65–66; Jordan Goodman, et al., Sales and Use Taxes: The Machinery and Equipment Exemption, Tax Mgmt. (BNA) Multistate Tax Portfolio Series, 1330 T.M; All States Tax Guide (RIA) ¶ 254 (2009) (chart), available at www.checkpoint.riag.com.

CONCORD PUBLISHING HOUSE, INC.
v. DIRECTOR OF REVENUE
Supreme Court of Missouri, 1996. En Banc.
916 S.W.2d 186.

PRICE, JUDGE.

The Director of Revenue appeals the Administrative Hearing Commission ("AHC") decision exempting Concord Publishing Company ("Concord") and Cape Mississippi Development, Inc. ("Cape") from sales and use tax on computers and computer equipment the companies purchased and used to implement changes in the production process and format of the newspaper and to increase the number of newspapers sold. We affirm * * *.

I.

Cape and Concord have been under common ownership since 1986. Before 1992, Concord's primary business was commercial printing. One division of Concord operated a printing press which was used to print a number of newspapers, including the Southeast Missourian ("SEMO"). Cape owned and published SEMO. Cape became the owner of the press division sometime in 1990. On July 31, 1992, Cape formally merged into Concord.

Before and during the audit periods Cape used a "tiling," or overlaying process to prepare SEMO for print. Text was entered into computers and printed off on laser printers. It was then manually arranged on a sample page, and a photograph was taken to create a negative. Color photographs were processed manually by aligning separate negatives of the photo for each of the four basic colors. The negatives were sent to Concord's press which used them to print the newspapers Cape sold to the public. Cape entered the cost of the printing as an expense on its books and Concord entered the cost as revenue.

SEMO is now published using the "pagination" process which eliminates much of the manual work involved in creating a layout. Newspaper pages are assembled on a computer network and the negative is electronically produced. Photographs are aligned by computer as well, resulting in sharper images at a lower cost. More color pictures are now used by SEMO and there is a new masthead. Because of pagination, SEMO is assembled more quickly, extending the deadlines for reporters and including more current news. SEMO is now published seven days a week instead of six.

In 1993 the Director audited Concord for the period September 1, 1989 through August 31, 1992, and Cape for the period September 16, 1989 through April 28, 1992. During the audit periods both companies purchased computer equipment that is now used in pagination. The equipment was not purchased to replace old, worn out, or obsolete equipment but to upgrade the publication system in order to implement pagination and expand production.

Because of the significant capital expense involved, the necessary equipment for pagination was purchased over time as finances would allow. A requirement for each item purchased was the capability of working with all other present and future components in the pagination system. Pagination was not implemented until October, 1993. Until then, some of the equipment was used on an interim basis in the tiling process.

The Director assessed sales and use tax on the equipment, which Cape and Concord paid under protest.[1]

This Court has jurisdiction pursuant to Mo. Const. art. V, § 3 and reviews the AHC's interpretation of revenue law de novo. L & R Egg Co. v. Director of Revenue, 796 S.W.2d 624, 625 (Mo.banc 1990). Factual determinations are upheld if supported by "substantial evidence upon the whole record." Id.; § 621.193, RSMo 1994.[2] In accordance with this standard we essentially adopt the factual findings of the AHC.[3]

II.

This case involves the assessment of sales and use taxes for items purchased or used in Missouri. § 144.020; § 144.610. Apparently Concord and Cape issued exemption certificates to the sellers of the equipment and are therefore the proper parties to this action. Conagra Poultry Co. v. Director of Revenue, 862 S.W.2d 915, 918 (Mo.banc 1993); § 144.210.1.

Cape and Concord, now merged as Concord, argue that the computer equipment should be exempt from sales tax under § 144.030.2(4) and (5). These exemptions also apply to use taxes. § 144.615(3). We find the purchases are governed by § 144.030.2(4) and (5) which exempt the following:

> (4) Machinery and equipment, and the materials and supplies solely required for the installation or construction of such machinery and equipment, replacing and used for the same purposes as the machinery and equipment replaced by reason of design or product changes,

---

1. Cape paid $9,417.67 and Concord paid $12,389.60.

2. All statutory references are to the 1994 Missouri Revised Statutes unless otherwise indicated.

3. The AHC exempted the following items from sales and use taxes:

Concord purchased for the publication of SEMO:

1. Powerbook, laptop computer (12/91)
2. Daisy CD Rom (6/92)
3. Syncmaster, monitor (6/92)

Cape purchased for the publication of SEMO:

1. Equity, VGA Bund, ARC crd, computer (4/90)
2. Macintosh II FX, SCSI, and keyboard, computer (5/90)
3. Macintosh SE computer, keyboard, and PAR, computer (5/90)
4. Memory Simm, memory expansion (12/90)
5. Logic Board and Macintosh II FX, computer (3/91)
6. Travelmate, laptop computer (3/91)
7. Maxtor, disk drive (3/91)
8. Power Flex notebook, Multisync, laptop computer and color monitor (3/91)
9. Notebook, laptop computer (3/91)
10. Power Flex, Multisync, PM9, M26, computers (3/91)
11. Computer (4/91)
12. Power Flex notebook, laptop computer (6/91)
13. Five Arcnet memory boards (6/91)
14. Phonet Connectors, connects computers (5/90)

which is purchased for and used directly for manufacturing or fabricating a product which is intended to be sold ultimately for final use or consumption;

(5) Machinery and equipment, and the materials and supplies solely required for the installation or construction of such machinery and equipment, purchased and used to establish new or to expand existing manufacturing, mining or fabricating plants in the state if such machinery and equipment is used directly in manufacturing, mining or fabricating a product which is intended to be sold ultimately for final use or consumption.

Neither sales nor use tax is due on machinery and equipment (1) used directly (2) in manufacturing (3) a product which is intended to be sold ultimately for final use or consumption (4) if the machinery or equipment was purchased (a) to replace existing equipment by reason of design or product changes or (b) to expand existing manufacturing. These statutes were enacted by the legislature to encourage the production of items ultimately subject to sales tax and to encourage the location and expansion of industry in Missouri. Bridge Data Co. v. Director of Revenue, 794 S.W.2d 204, 206 (Mo.banc 1990); *State ex rel.* Ozark Lead Co. v. Goldberg, 610 S.W.2d 954, 957 (Mo.1981); Floyd Charcoal Co. v. Director of Revenue, 599 S.W.2d 173, 177 (Mo.1980); Heidelberg Central, Inc. v. Director of Dept. of Revenue, 476 S.W.2d 502, 506 (Mo.1972); West Lake Quarry & Material Co. v. Schaffner, 451 S.W.2d 140, 142 (Mo.1970).

The Director does not contest that the listed items are machinery and equipment. Nor does she dispute that the newspaper is a product intended to be sold for final use or consumption and on which sales tax is properly collected. The Director, however, claims that the computers purchased and used in the publication of SEMO (1) were not used in manufacturing the newspaper, (2) the computers were not used in "directly" manufacturing the newspaper, (3) the changes in the post-pagination SEMO were not a "product change," (4) even if there was a "product change," the change did not occur until after the audit period, [and] (5) increased production volume is not expanded manufacturing * * *.

III.   Used Directly in Manufacturing

(A) Manufacturing

The Director claims that the computer equipment was not used directly in manufacturing SEMO. Although she concedes that printing presses, or presumably other equipment that involve the printing of words and pictures on the actual paper sold, are used in manufacturing a newspaper, she claims that gathering, storing, and arranging the information printed is not manufacturing. We disagree.

Newspaper publication involves the mechanical processing of words and pictures. It begins when words are put into the network. Manufacturing occurs as those words are manipulated and finally affixed onto a printed page, creating a new edition "through the use of machinery, labor and skill." Heidelberg Central, 476 S.W.2d at 506.[5]

We have already established that organizing information through computer technology is "manufacturing." Bridge Data Co., 794 S.W.2d at 206. In *Bridge Data*, we held that the hardware in the taxpayer's computer system, used to collect raw financial data and transmit the data to customers, qualified for an exemption even though the final product was intangible. We concluded that "what comes out of the system is clearly different from what went into it"; therefore, the computers were involved in "manufacturing." Id.

We find the present case indistinguishable from *Bridge Data*. The computer layout system here is also used to process data and convey information to customers. The final product is clearly different from what is put into the system. The present case is even stronger because the computer network produces a tangible, taxable product, a newspaper.

The Director's argument that the only manufacturing that occurs in the publishing of a newspaper is the process of putting ink on paper is artificially limited. It ignores the labor, skill, and complex machinery required to generate daily newspapers and the transformation that took place when the taxpayers adopted the pagination system. We hold that the computers in the present case were used in "manufacturing" a newspaper.

(B) Directly Used

The Director claims that even if the pagination system is considered manufacturing, it does not directly manufacture the newspaper, which is the item intended to be "sold ultimately for final use or consumption." The Director makes four arguments. First, she claims the computer equipment is used merely to produce a negative which is not sold and has no retail value. Second, she claims that the "integrated plant doctrine" does not apply between separate corporate entities. Third, the Director argues that because the newspaper is produced in two different locations it cannot be considered a single integrated process. Finally, she claims that laptop computers used by reporters are not integrally used in the pagination process. Consistent with our holding above, we disagree with the Director on all four points.

(i)

The Director claims that the computers directly produce a negative, not a newspaper, and because the negative is not the final product Cape and Concord do not qualify for either exemption. Although some courts strictly interpret the phrase "directly used" to exempt only those ma-

---

5. In *Heidelberg* it was noted that cases from other jurisdictions have held that the publication and circulation of a newspaper is not "manufacturing." Heidelberg, 476 S.W.2d at 505. However, this Court has recently construed "manufacturing" more liberally. See Bridge Data, 794 S.W.2d 204; 2 Jerome R. Hellerstein & Walter Hellerstein, State Taxation § 14.05[2][d] (1992).

chines that physically alter raw materials to a finished product, Missouri has adopted the "integrated plant doctrine," viewing manufacturing operations as "continuous and indivisible." Floyd, 599 S.W.2d at 178 (citing Niagara Mohawk Power Corp. v. Wanamaker, 286 A.D. 446, 144 N.Y.S.2d 458, 462 (N.Y.Sup.Ct.1955)); Noranda Aluminum, Inc. v. Missouri Dept. of Revenue, 599 S.W.2d 1, 4 (Mo.1980). In Floyd we rejected a contention similar to that made by the Director in this case. "To limit the exemption to those items of machinery or equipment which produce a change in the composition of the raw materials involved in the manufacturing process would ignore the essential contribution of the devices required for such operation." Floyd, 599 S.W.2d at 178.

By holding the computers are used in manufacturing a newspaper, we also find they are directly used in manufacturing because they are an integral part of the publication process. The computers are as essential to the printing of the paper as the printing presses themselves. A more limited view of the process would arguably exclude the most important step in manufacturing a newspaper, the composition and editing of its contents.

(ii)

The Director also argues that the integrated plant doctrine connects machinery, not corporations. She maintains that for the period of time when Cape and the press division of Concord were separately operated, the computer equipment Cape used did not directly manufacture the newspaper because the final step, printing, was completed by Concord.

The Director cites Copperweld Steel Co. v. Lindley, 31 Ohio St.3d 207, 509 N.E.2d 1242 (Ohio 1987), claiming involvement by two corporations in "manufacturing" a product breaks the direct link. In *Copperweld* the Ohio Supreme Court essentially held that transporting waste to a separate corporation was not a part of the manufacturing process. Id. 509 N.E.2d at 1248. Likewise, this Court has also held that merely transporting a finished product is not manufacturing. See West Lake Quarry, 451 S.W.2d at 143. However, these holdings have nothing to do with the present case. Concord was not a mere recipient of waste or an end product, but was an essential participant in the effort to manufacture a newspaper. The exchange between Cape and Concord occurred as a coordinated and necessary step in the manufacturing process, not as mere by-product disposal.

The reasoning of Central Paving Co. v. Idaho Tax Commission, 126 Idaho 174, 879 P.2d 1107 (Idaho 1994), is more persuasive and more analogous to our own situation. In *Central Paving* the Idaho Supreme Court held a rock crushing machine owned by one company and used to crush another company's rock for the second company's use in manufacturing cement was tax exempt. "If the statute's purpose is to exempt materials and equipment used in the manufacture of items ultimately sold at retail then it makes no difference whether the manufacturing process is contracted out to various parties who never obtain title to or ownership of the product being manufactured and items ultimately sold." Id. at 177, 879 P.2d at 1110.

In the present case Cape merely contracted Concord's press division to print the newspaper from the negative. The negative was useless without the final step of printing, and the newspaper likewise could not have been printed without the negative. The operations, even by separate corporate entities, were "integrated and synchronized" to the single purpose of producing and selling SEMO. 12 CSR 10–3.326(3). The integrated plant doctrine can span two corporate entities as long as both businesses work together to manufacture a single product. Both Cape and Concord manufactured SEMO and both qualify for manufacturing exemptions.

(iii)

The Director also suggests that because the publishing operation is physically separated from the printing press the computer equipment is not an integral part of manufacturing the newspaper. The Department of Revenue's regulations instruct us to consider physical location when deciding whether machinery is "directly used" in manufacturing. 12 CSR 10–3.326(2). However, physical distance alone is not determinative. We have previously permitted the exemption for equipment used in a different location from a manufacturing plant. See Noranda, 599 S.W.2d at 4 (exemption allowed for laboratory equipment located in separate building). We have also recognized that portions of a newspaper may be produced in separate locations and by separate corporations, but still be considered part of one publication. Daily Record Co. v. James, 629 S.W.2d 348, 351 (Mo.banc 1982).

The composition and editing process is as essential to manufacturing a newspaper as the printing press, regardless of whether it is located in the same building or across town. We find the physical distance between the operations in this case does not break the direct tie between the composition and printing of SEMO.

(iv)

Finally, the Director argues that even if the pagination system directly manufactures the newspaper, the laptop or portable computers were only used to take notes at an event, not to process the information and were, therefore, not necessary or integral to the pagination process. She argues they merely deliver the information to the editing computers and are not themselves involved in the editing process. We believe equipment used to record information is part of the manufacturing process as well. Recording is the first step in processing words into a newspaper.

In the present case, the laptop computers not only record information but allow for its immediate editing, even in the field. In essence, the laptop computers extend SEMO's editing process to locations where news events occur, speeding up the editing process. As the AHC found, "The portable computers allow the reporter to convert his or her account of events immediately to electronic transmissions that the reporter can deliver to the office computer network via telephone modem or after he or she gets back to the office." AHC opinion at 16. Because of this capability, SEMO is able to carry more current news. Like the other equipment at issue, the laptop computers are an integral part of manufacturing the SEMO.

* * *

[The court also held that the changes in the post-pagination SEMO were "product changes" that occurred during the audit period and that served to "expand existing manufacturing," thereby satisfying the other requirements of the machinery and equipment exemption statute.]

* * *

We affirm the decision of the Administrative Hearing Commission * * *.

NOTES AND QUESTIONS

A. In *Concord Publishing*, the court construed the statute as exempting from sales and use tax "machinery and equipment (1) used directly (2) in manufacturing (3) a product which is intended to be sold ultimately for final use or consumption (4) if the machinery or equipment was purchased (a) to replace existing equipment by reason of design or product changes or (b) to expand existing manufacturing." What is the legislative purpose behind each of these conditions?

B. *Scope of Manufacturing.* As the *Concord Publishing* opinion observed, there is a split of authority among the states as to whether newspaper publishing constitutes "manufacturing" under machinery and equipment exemptions. See note 5 of the court's opinion. Some courts, like the court in *Concord Publishing*, have held that newspaper publishing constitutes "manufacturing" or "processing" and have therefore sustained exemptions for purchases of machinery and parts of a newspaper printing plant, State v. Advertiser Co., 257 Ala. 423, 59 So.2d 576 (1952); Hearst v. State Department of Assessments and Taxation, 269 Md. 625, 308 A.2d 679 (1973), and for purchases of flashbulbs, film, and tapes in connection with newsgathering activity. McClure Newspapers, Inc. v. Vermont Department of Taxes, 132 Vt. 169, 315 A.2d 452 (1974). Other courts, however, have agreed with the Arkansas Supreme Court that "[i]n the ordinary use of the term we do not think of printing, photography, and binding as manufacturing." Western Paper Co. v. Qualls, 272 Ark. 466, 615 S.W.2d 369, 370 (1981). These courts have sustained taxes on purchases of newspaper printing equipment, Chicago Tribune Co. v. Johnson, 106 Ill.2d 63, 87 Ill.Dec. 505, 477 N.E.2d 482 (1985), appeal dismissed, 474 U.S. 915, 106 S.Ct. 241 (1985), and on photofinishing equipment. Colorcraft Corp. v. Department of Revenue, 112 Ill.2d 473, 98 Ill.Dec. 45, 493 N.E.2d 1066 (1986). (The Illinois statute was subsequently amended to exempt graphic arts and photoprocessing equipment from sales and use taxation. 35 Ill. Comp. Stat. Ann. 120/2–5(4), 120/2–5(20) (Westlaw 2009)).

State courts, legislatures, and tax administrators have developed a variety of tests for determining what constitutes "manufacturing." The *physical change test* defines manufacturing as the process of changing the form or composition of materials. Under this test, which the Ohio courts adopted, National Tube Co. v. Glander, 157 Ohio St. 407, 105 N.E.2d 648 (1952), and the Ohio legislature subsequently codified, Ohio Rev. Code § 5739.01(S) (Westlaw 2009), "manufacturing" is "essentially the transformation or conversion of materials or things into a different state or form from that in which they originally existed." National Tube, 105 N.E.2d at 650. Under this test, the court held that unloading and blending of iron ore prior to its introduction in the taxpayer's blast furnace did not constitute manufacturing. In Comptroller of the Treasury v. Disclosure, Inc., 340 Md. 675, 667 A.2d 910 (1995), on the other hand, the court held that a company that compiles, collates, and organizes data, which it transfers onto CD–ROMs that it sells, is engaged in "manufacturing" under the physical change test. In the court's view, converting paper documents into electronic documents and then into a format for computer-readable compact disks constitutes a "substantial transformation" of the property.

Some courts have adopted the view that manufacturing constitutes the *adaptation of materials to commercial use*. Under this test, the Kentucky Supreme Court held that a recycler of used metal drums was engaged in manufacturing. Department of Revenue v. Allied Drum Service, Inc., 561 S.W.2d 323, 326 (Ky. 1978). "This is not a case of taking a used drum and ending up with a used drum but is one where the Appellee takes a virtually unusable and non-marketable damaged drum and converts it into a serviceable and marketable commodity." Id. at 326.

The New York courts originated the *integrated plant test* of manufacturing, which a number of other courts have followed (including the Missouri courts, as noted in *Concord Publishing*). In Niagara Mohawk Power Corp. v. Wanamaker, 286 App.Div. 446, 144 N.Y.S.2d 458 (4th Dep't 1955), aff'd, 2 N.Y.2d 764, 139 N.E.2d 150, 157 N.Y.S.2d 972 (1956), the power company contended that equipment used in handling the disposition of ash in its power plant was directly used in manufacturing. In holding that the equipment fell within the statutory exemption, the court articulated the view that manufacturing should encompass all equipment that is an integral part of the production process:

> After much study of the matter, we have concluded that the purchase or use of the coal and ash handling equipment is not taxable. The equipment is as essential to production as the generator itself. A serious breakdown in it would quickly stop or impair the output of electricity. We are further impressed with the synchronization and integration of the boiler and coal and ash equipment. The one could not operate without the other. Working together they make up a system which supplies the power from which electricity is produced. A taxing statute should receive a practical construction. * * * It is not practical to divide a generating plant into "distinct" states. It was not built that way, and it does not

operate that way. The words "directly and exclusively" should not be construed to require the division into theoretically distinct stages of what is in fact continuous and indivisible.

Id., 144 N.Y.S.2d at 461–62.

Which of these tests best serves the theoretical and fiscal policies underlying the retail sales tax? Can that question be answered intelligently since, as the *Niagara Mohawk* court recognized, *none* of a manufacturer's purchases of machinery or equipment would *ever* be taxable "[i]f the policy of avoidance of multiple taxation were pursued to its natural and logical limits," id. at 460, whereas *all* of a manufacturer's purchases of machinery and equipment would *always* be taxable if one's goal was to maximize revenue? If a court's role is to "strike a balance between the policy of avoiding multiple taxation and the need for raising revenue" (id.), how should that balance be struck?

C. *Animal Farming as "Manufacturing" or "Processing."* A commercial hatchery that purchased incubators for hatching eggs contended that it fell within Arkansas's exemption for equipment used in "manufacturing" and "processing." In Peterson Produce Co. v. Cheney, 237 Ark. 600, 374 S.W.2d 809 (1964), the court denied the exemption, declaring:

> We agree with the learned Chancellor, who delivered an excellent opinion at the conclusion of the case, to the effect that one does not "manufacture" a baby chick, and the use of incubators is not a "processing" step therein. As he stated,
>
> > "Thus, by plaintiff's [appellant's] view, if he chose to hatch his eggs in the old-fashioned way, by having brooder hens sit on them, his purchase of hens * * * would be exempt from use tax, because such hens were 'processing' the eggs into chicks. An incubator merely aids and abets the natural course of hatching, and is not a process in itself."

Id., 374 S.W.2d at 810. Accord State Tax Com'r v. Flow Research Animals, Inc., 221 Va. 817, 273 S.E.2d 811 (1981) (raising and breeding laboratory animals does not constitute "manufacturing" or "processing"). But see Wilson & Co. v. Department of Revenue, 531 S.W.2d 752 (Mo. 1976) (hog butchering constitutes "manufacturing"); Master Hatcheries, Inc. v. Coble, 286 N.C. 518, 212 S.E.2d 150 (1975) (chicken processing constitutes "manufacturing"); Hawthorn Mellody, Inc. v. Lindley, 65 Ohio St.2d 47, 417 N.E.2d 1257 (1981) (milk processing constitutes "manufacturing").

D. *Machinery and Equipment Purchased for Use "Directly" in Manufacturing, Producing, or Processing.* The requirement in many of the machinery and equipment exemption statutes that the machinery or equipment must be used "directly" in manufacturing, production, or processing has spawned an enormous amount of litigation. The problem is illustrated by cases like *Concord Publishing* involving the question whether computers purchased to assist in manufacturing are used "directly" in the manufacturing process. For example, the Kentucky Supreme Court held that a computer purchased by a manufacturer of transformers was not machinery used "directly" in manufacturing. Although the computer "expedited the means of production, it did not participate in the physical production of the transformers," and, accordingly, "was not machinery used directly in the manufacturing process." Commonwealth v. Kuhlman Corp., 564 S.W.2d 14, 16 (Ky. 1978). Similarly, the Arkansas Supreme Court held that an environmental control system installed to reduce breakdowns of computerized production equipment was not "directly" used in manufacturing, Pledger v. Baldor Int'l, Inc., 309 Ark. 30, 827 S.W.2d 646 (1992); the Georgia Supreme Court held that climate control equipment used by a textile manufacturer was not used "directly" in manufacturing, Blackmon v. Screven County Industrial Development Authority, 131 Ga.App. 265, 205 S.E.2d 497 (1974); the Pennsylvania Supreme Court held that equipment purchased by a manufacturer of electronic devices for use in its distribution facility was not "directly used" in manufacturing, AMP, Inc. v. Commonwealth, 578 Pa. 366, 852 A.2d 1161 (2004); and the Rhode Island Supreme Court held that a computer was not used "directly" in manufacturing when it produced photographs for customer approval prior to production, Rhode Island Lithograph Corporation v. Clark, 519 A.2d 589 (R.I.1987).

Despite its decision in the *Baldor* case, on the other hand, the Arkansas Supreme Court in an earlier case had held that a computer system employed by a hand tool manufacturer to produce dies the manufacturer used to create hand tools was used "directly" in manufacturing. Pledger v. EASCO Hand Tools, Inc., 304 Ark. 47, 800 S.W.2d 690 (1990). The Oklahoma Supreme Court likewise held that machinery and equipment used in an integrated manufacturing process is "directly used" in manufacturing. Dolese Bros. v. Oklahoma Tax Comm'n, 64 P.3d 1093 (Okla. 2003).

E. *Purchase for Use in "Actual" Manufacturing*. Texas exempts from sales tax purchases of equipment "used or consumed in the actual manufacturing, processing, fabrication, or repair of tangible personal property for ultimate sale * * * " Tex. Tax Code Ann. § 151.318(a)(5) (Westlaw 2009). A manufacturer of cast-iron pipe claimed an exemption for equipment used for making sand molds to be employed in the manufacture of the pipe. Noting the split among jurisdictions between those that have adopted the "integrated plant theory," which gives similar exemptions a broader construction, and those following the "Ohio rule" or "physical change rule," which gives such exemptions a narrower reading, the court adopted the broader view and permitted the exemption. Sharp v. Tyler Pipe Industries, Inc., 919 S.W.2d 157 (Tex. App.–Austin 1996). The court observed that the Texas statute contains no restriction that the equipment be used "directly" in manufacturing, and it did "not construe the term 'actual' to prohibit the existence of any intervening medium or agent in the manufacturing process." Id. at 162. Furthermore, it noted that the overwhelming majority of jurisdictions that have addressed similar tax exemption statutes, even those containing the term "directly," have rejected Ohio's physical-change theory in favor of the broader reading. The court also found its broader interpretation of the exemption was consistent with the legislature's general purposes in enacting it:

> (1) to encourage economic development in this state; (2) to avoid pyramiding the sales tax on successive buyers and sellers, which would result in the ultimate consumer paying sales tax on sales tax; and (3) to strike a balance between the policy of avoiding multiple taxation and the need to raise revenue for the state.

Id. at 161.

F. *Concluding Questions.* Are the results reached in the cases discussed in this section, with the inevitable refinements industry by industry, growing out of the choice of standards employed by courts, legislatures, and tax administrators in drawing the line between exempt and non-exempt purchases, adequately adapted to determining how the states' sales and use tax burden ought to be distributed? How would you draw an exemption provision better adapted (and if possible with fewer niceties and refinements) to accomplish what you regard as the fiscal and economic objectives of the provisions under consideration?

G. *References.* There is a state-by-state analysis of the machinery and equipment exemption in Jordan Goodman, et al., Sales and Use Taxes: The Machinery and Equipment Exemption, Tax Mgmt. (BNA) Multistate Tax Portfolio Series, 1330 T.M.

4. CONTAINERS AND PACKAGING

A. *Exemption of Containers and Packaging Under Resale Provisions.* In those states that have no explicit statutory provision dealing with the taxability of containers or packaging, their taxability is usually decided under the resale exemption. Compare, e.g., Burger King v. State Tax Commission, 51 N.Y.2d 614, 416 N.E.2d 1024, 435 N.Y.S.2d 689 (1980) (food wrappings not taxable under resale provisions) with Sta–Ru Corp. v. Mahin, 64 Ill.2d 330, 1 Ill.Dec. 67, 356 N.E.2d 67 (1976) (containers taxable under resale provisions), considered at pp. 652–53 supra. The issue in these cases usually turns on the court's view as to whether the taxpayer is using the container or packaging in the course of delivering its product or is separately selling the container or packaging. In District of Columbia v. Seven–Up Washington, 214 F.2d 197 (D.C. Cir. 1954), cert. denied, 347 U.S. 989, 74 S.Ct. 851 (1954), for example, the court held that cardboard cartons, wooden cases, and bottles purchased by soft drink bottlers for use in delivering their products were purchased for use, not for resale.

> [W]e think the Tax Court erred in holding that purchases of the bottles and cases by respondents were for the purpose of resale to their customers. The purpose was to use them, not to resell them. Respondents are not in the business of selling bottles or cases but of using them as a means of marketing their soft drinks.

Id. at 200.

B. *Reusable Bottles, Cases, and Other Containers.* When bottles, cases, and other containers are reusable, courts generally hold they are taxable. See, e.g., Arkansas Beverage Co. v. Heath, 257 Ark. 991, 521 S.W.2d 835 (1975) (reusable soft drink bottles); Albany Calcium Light Co. v. State Tax Comm'n, 44 N.Y.2d 986, 380 N.E.2d 165, 408 N.Y.S.2d 333 (1978) (reusable gas cylinders). Some courts, however, have held that reusable soft drink bottles are purchased for resale by the bottlers. See, e.g., Coca–Cola Bottling Works Co. v. Kentucky Department of Revenue,

517 S.W.2d 746 (Ky. 1974). These courts usually stress the fact that title to the bottle passes to the purchaser, who is free to do with the bottles whatever she pleases.

C. *Statutory Exemption of Containers and Packaging Materials.* Because of the difficult issues raised by containers and packaging under the resale provisions, most states have addressed the issue by statute. John F. Due & John L. Mikesell, Sales Taxation: State and Local Structure and Administration 62 (2d ed. 1994). The statutes typically provide that the sale of the container to the vendor is a nontaxable sale for resale. The term container generally embraces all forms of packaging, including wrapping paper, twine, etc. For example, Florida excludes from the definition of a retail sale

> materials, containers, labels, sacks, bags or similar items intended to accompany a product sold to a customer without which delivery of the product would be impracticable because of the character of the contents and be used one time only for packaging tangible personal property for sale.

Fla. Stat. § 212.02(14)(c) (Westlaw 2009). Some statutes, however, expressly exclude certain shipping materials and containers from the resale exemption. See e.g. Tex. Tax Code Ann. § 151,302(d) (Westlaw 2009) (excluding items such as bags, cartons, crates, tape, and twine, as well as "property used inside a package to shape, form, stabilize, preserve or protect the contents").

D. SERVICES

When state legislatures first enacted general sales taxes during the 1930s, they restricted the tax base largely to sales of tangible personal property. Although most states traditionally taxed some services (e.g., public utility services and hotel services), and a few states (e.g., Hawaii and New Mexico) always taxed a broad range of services, the states historically limited the sales tax base to tangible personal property and selected services. The original explanation for the limited scope of the sales tax base lies partly in the desire to create a simple and easily administrable tax and partly in the perception that a tax on services would have constituted a tax on labor. Once so limited, however, political resistance to additional taxes helped confine the sales tax principally to sales of tangible personal property, at least until relatively recently.

Whatever the historical explanation for the limitation of the sales tax base to sales of tangible personal property, it certainly does not lie in the dictates of sound fiscal or economic policy. Indeed, tax economists long have deplored the exclusion of consumer services other than health and, in some cases, utility services from sales taxation. As Professor John Due of the University of Illinois, a leading economic authority on sales taxation, observed many years ago:

Most of the American state sales taxes do not apply to any services or to only a few categories. * * * From an economic standpoint, the distinction between a service and a commodity is not a very significant one, since both satisfy personal wants. A haircut, an opera concert, or a plane ride satisfy persons' desires in the same manner as a loaf of bread, a piano, or an automobile. Obviously services rendered to business firms, whether by employees or commercial service establishments, are not suitable bases for a sales tax, since they are essentially producers' goods, and do not in themselves satisfy personal wants. But the failure to include services rendered to consumers gives rise to the same objectionable results as the exemption of specific commodities. Persons making relatively high expenditures for services are favored compared to those concentrating their purchases on tangible goods, resource allocation may be distorted, and in some cases administrative complications are created. This is particularly true when services are rendered by establishments also selling commodities; the line of distinction between service and commodity is by no means a sharp one, and the two may be provided jointly, particularly in the case of repair and fabrication service. Any sale, of course, involves the rendering of some services (that of the merchant, for example, with a retail tax); when services, as such, are not taxed, the line of demarkation is not actually made between commodity sale and the rendering of service, but between the type of service regarded as typical merchandising activity and another type, which is not so regarded. The drawing of this line of distinction is highly arbitrary, and gives rise to a number of administrative problems.

John F. Due, Sales Taxation 374–75 (1957).[e] See also John F. Due, "Proposed Application of the Illinois Sales Tax to Services," 44 Ill. Bus. Rev. 3 (June 1987).

Despite the states' historical reluctance to extend the sales tax to services, economic and fiscal pressures are pushing them strongly in that direction. The significant shift in economic activity toward the service sector has had the effect of eroding the sales tax base relative to total consumption expenditures. Thus from 1960 to 1991, the share of personal consumption expenditures for services (excluding housing) increased from 26 percent to 42 percent. National Council of State Legislatures & National Governors' Association, Financing State Government in the 1990s 34 (1993). During the same period, the share of personal consumption expenditures for tangible goods fell from 60 percent to 44 percent. Id. By 2002, expenditures for services had reached 59.1 percent of total consumer expenditures. William F. Fox, "The Ongoing Evolution of State Revenue Systems," 88 Marq. L. Rev. 19, 41 (2004). As a leading state tax administrator observed, "[t]he inexorable shift in consumer expenditures from the purchase of goods to the purchase of services continues to raise concerns about the long-term vitality of state retail sales taxes which

---

e. This material is used with the consent of the copyright owner, Routledge and Kegan Paul, Ltd.

traditionally are applied primarily to the sale of tangible personal property." Federation of Tax Administrators, Sales Taxation of Services: An Update i (1994).

In response to these developments in the American economy, there has been a gradual but piecemeal expansion of the sales tax base to selected services. These include (in addition to utility, admissions, and hotel and motel services that most states tax), services such as repair of tangible personal property; repair of real property; data processing services; information services; and cleaning services. See John Due & J. Mikesell, Sales Taxation: State and Local Structure and Administration 92–97 (2d ed. 1994); All States Tax Guide (RIA) ¶ 259–A (2009) (chart), available at www.checkpoint.riag.com. In general, however, the states have not extended the sales tax base to the services that would generate the greatest revenues—such as construction, professional services, and health care. William F. Fox, "Importance of the Sales Tax in the 21st Century" in Matthew N. Murray & William F. Fox, eds., The Sales Tax in the 21st Century 1, 3 (1997). Moreover, the attempts of two states (Florida and Massachusetts) to expand the sales tax base broadly to include most services were repealed shortly after they were enacted. Samuel B. Bruskin & Kathleen K. Parker, "State Sales Taxes on Services: Massachusetts as a Case Study," 45 Tax Law. 49 (1991); Walter Hellerstein, "Florida's Sales Tax on Services," 41 Nat'l Tax J. 1 (1988).

1. REPAIR, ALTERATION, AND SERVICING OF TANGIBLE PERSONAL PROPERTY

COVINGTON PIKE TOYOTA, INC. v. CARDWELL

Supreme Court of Tennessee, 1992.
829 S.W.2d 132.

ANDERSON, JUSTICE.

The issue presented in this sales tax appeal is whether sale of extended warranty contracts on automobiles constitutes "the performing for a consideration of any repair services" within the meaning of Tenn. Code Ann. § 67–6–102(22)(F)(iv), thus making it subject to sales tax. The Commissioner of Revenue assessed sales taxes upon sales of extended warranty contracts to purchasers of new and used automobiles. The assessment was challenged in this action; the Chancellor granted the taxpayer's motion for summary judgment, reduced the tax assessment by the amount imposed upon the extended warranty sales, and found that the Commissioner exceeded his statutory rule-making authority by including such contracts as a repair service. The Commissioner has appealed, contending that the legislature's statutory scheme was to tax warranty contracts, and that the rule was within the Commissioner's rule-making authority.

We disagree and affirm.

Factual History

Covington Pike Toyota, Inc. is a Tennessee corporation with its principal place of business in Memphis, Tennessee. In addition to engaging in the business of selling new and used automobiles, Covington sells extended warranty service contracts to cover the cars purchased from them. These contracts, sold by Covington for Toyota Motor Insurance Services pursuant to a written Administrative Services Agreement, entitle the purchasers to certain repair services free of charge at participating Toyota dealerships all over the United States after expiration of the original manufacturer's warranty.

After being audited by the Tennessee Department of Revenue for the period of March 31, 1986, through December 31, 1988, the taxpayer was assessed a deficiency in sales and use taxes, penalty, and interest in the amount of $107,555.00. Most of the deficiency, $106,458.00, was for taxes on sales of extended warranty service contracts * * * [T]he Commissioner taxed Covington's sales of extended warranty service contracts to cover those cars on the basis of Tenn.Code Ann. § 67–6–102(22)(F)(iv) and (vi) (1983 & Supp. 1987).[2] That section provides that taxable retail sales shall include:

> (iv) The *performing* for a consideration of any *repair services* with respect to any kind of tangible personal property; [and]
>
> . . .
>
> (vi) The installation of tangible personal property . . . where a charge is made for such installation whether or not such installation is made as an incident to the sale. . . .

The Commissioner interpreted the statute by promulgating Sales and Use Tax Rule 1320–5–1–.54(2) ("Rule 54"), which provides that:

> (2) For the purposes of this rule, *"repair services"* and "repairs" of tangible personal property shall mean and include any one or all of the following for a user and consumer: work done to preserve or restore to or near the original condition made necessary by wear, normal use, wastage, injury, decay, partial destruction, or dilapidation; the mending, correction, or adjustment made for any defect or defective portion; alterations; refinishing; maintenance, preventive maintenance, or *warranty contracts*; any cleaning that is a necessary part of any repair work; "service calls" where any repair work is done or contemplated; and changes in the size, shape, or content.

The taxpayer brought this action to challenge the assessment in the Shelby County Chancery Court. Following a hearing on July 20, 1990, the Chancellor granted the taxpayer's motion for summary judgment, finding that the Commissioner exceeded his statutory rule-making authority by including warranty contracts in Rule 54 as a taxable repair service under

---

2. The Retailer's Sales Tax Act was amended, effective March 26, 1991, to expressly make "[c]harges for warranty or service contracts" taxable. See Tenn.Code Ann. § 67–6–102(22)(F)(ix) (Supp. 1991).

Tenn.Code Ann. § 67–6–102(22)(F)(iv) and (vi). The Chancellor ordered the Commissioner to reduce the total assessment by $106,458.00, and awarded the taxpayer attorneys' fees and expenses pursuant to Tenn.Code Ann. § 67–1–1803 (1983 & Supp. 1987).

Analysis

Under Tenn.Code Ann. § 67–1–102 (1983 & Supp. 1987) and § 67–6–402 (1983), the Commissioner of Revenue is authorized to prescribe reasonable rules and regulations not inconsistent with the taxing statutes. In the absence of a clear showing that a rule is arbitrary or contrary to statute, a court should not substitute its judgment for the Commissioner's. However, it is fundamental that the Commissioner cannot enlarge the scope of a taxing statute by regulation, and rules contrary to the express directives of a taxing statute are void.

The Commissioner contends that the inclusion of automobile warranty contracts in Rule 54 is entirely consistent with the taxing statutes. The Commissioner argues that the legislature's enactment of Tenn.Code Ann. § 67–6–102(13)(F) and § 67–6–324 in 1963 evidences a clear legislative intent to tax warranty contracts. The Commissioner also argues that this Court should defer to Department of Revenue's interpretation of the statutes in Rule 54 because the rule was promulgated in 1964 and has never been challenged or changed.

* * *

Tennessee Code Annotated § 67–6–102(13)(F) (1983 & Supp. 1987) lists a number of taxable services and includes in the list "[t]he performing for a consideration of any repair services" and "[t]he installing of tangible personal property." On the other hand, Tenn.Code Ann. § 67–6–324 (1983) exempts from taxation replacement parts or goods provided under warranty:

> There shall be exempt from sales tax any replacement parts or goods transferred without cost to a purchaser for the replacement of faulty parts or equipment which prior thereto had been sold under a warranty or guarantee or condition and upon which original purchase or importation a sales or use tax was paid.

The Commissioner contends it is clear from reading these two statutes together that the legislature intended to tax warranty contracts like the ones at issue in this case. We disagree.

Without the exemption for replacement parts or goods provided in § 67–6–324, the providing of such goods would be subject to sales taxes even though they are transferred without cost pursuant to a warranty. This is because the sales tax imposed on selling tangible personal property is imposed, pursuant to Tenn.Code Ann. § 67–6–202, on "the sales price of each item or article of tangible personal property." "Sales price" is defined, in § 67–6–102(24), as "the total amount for which ... tangible personal property is sold ... valued in money, whether paid in money or otherwise." In the absence of § 67–6–324, the satisfaction of a contractual commitment to provide replacement parts would constitute "the total amount for which [such] tangible property is sold."

Although both of these statutes were first passed in 1963, they were enacted by separate Public Acts at separate times with separate legislative sponsors. Moreover, one is a taxing statute and the other is an exemption statute. Taxation and exemption statutes are construed differently. Taxation statutes must be liberally construed in favor of the taxpayer and strictly construed against the taxing authority. Sky Transpo, Inc. v. City of Knoxville, 703 S.W.2d 126, 129 (Tenn. 1985). Conversely, exemptions are construed against the taxpayer, who bears the burden of proving entitlement to the exemption. Hyatt v. Taylor, 788 S.W.2d 554, 556 (Tenn. 1990).

Words employed by the legislature in the enactment of tax statutes are to be taken in their natural and ordinary sense. Western Pipe Line Constr., Inc. v. Dickinson, 203 Tenn. (7 McCanless) 248, 254, 310 S.W.2d 455, 458 (1958). The words "performing" and "installing," taken in their natural and ordinary sense, mean the carrying out of physical acts. Performing repair services does not include the act of entering into a contractual commitment to provide in the future and on a contingent basis repair services. Under the statute, "[t]he taxable event is the rendering of repair services in Tennessee," LeTourneau Sales & Serv., Inc. v. Olsen, 691 S.W.2d 531, 536 (Tenn. 1985), not the future and uncertain prospect of having repair services performed in Tennessee. The taxable activity described in § 67–6–102(22)(F)(iv) is a physical activity performed with respect to tangible personal property, and does not include the undertaking of a contractual commitment whereby such services may, or may not, be provided in the future.

Statutes levying taxes will not be extended by implication beyond the clear import of the language used, nor will their operation be enlarged so as to embrace matters not specifically pointed out, although standing on a close analogy. Union Carbide Corp. v. Alexander, 679 S.W.2d 938, 942 (Tenn. 1984). We conclude that the undertaking of contractual commitments by entering into an extended warranty contract does not constitute "the performing for a consideration of any repair services" within the meaning of Tenn.Code Ann. § 67–6–102(22)(F)(iv); that the inclusion of "warranty contracts" in a list of "repair services" or "repairs" in Department of Revenue Rule 1320–5–1–.54(2) is beyond the Commissioner of Revenue's rule-making authority; and that the foregoing rule is, to the extent of such inclusion, invalid.

Accordingly, we affirm the Chancellor's judgment. The costs of this appeal are taxed to the defendant, Commissioner of Revenue, and this case is remanded to the Chancery Court for a determination of the attorneys' fees and litigation expenses to which the taxpayer is entitled under Tenn.Code Ann. § 67–1–1803.

REID, C.J., and DROWOTA, O'BRIEN and DAUGHTREY, JJ.

A. *Taxable Repair Services and the Sale of Extended Warranties.* Whatever one may say about the Tennessee court's analysis as a matter of statutory construction, does it make sense as a matter of policy? In substance, the taxpayer who buys an extended warranty is paying in advance for future repair services, even though the receipt of such services is contingent upon future events. From an administrative standpoint, it makes sense to impose the tax at the time that the warranty is sold, just as it is imposed on the value of the warranty that comes with the original purchase of the warranted items. By holding that the purchase of an extended warranty falls outside the statute imposing a tax on repair services, the court forces the tax administrator to seek to impose the tax at the time the services are rendered. But at that time, will any consideration change hands? How will the tax on the repair services be valued? How will most customers react when they are presented with a tax bill for the "free" services covered by the warranty? Is the alternative, imposing no tax on the extended warranty service, consistent with the legislative intention to tax repair services? Or can one argue that the purchase of an extended warranty should be viewed as the purchase of insurance, which no state subjects to sales taxation? See Department of Finance & Administration v. Staton, 325 Ark. 341, 942 S.W.2d 804, 805 (1996) (rejecting claim that the sale of an extended warranty was taxable as a repair service in part because there is "a considerable difference between a prepayment for services to be rendered and a payment for something like insurance against the need for services which may or may not arise"). But see South Central Utah Telephone Ass'n, Inc. v. Auditing Division, 951 P.2d 218 (Utah 1997) (holding sale of extended warranties taxable as "repairs or renovations of tangible personal property"). As noted in the *Covington* case (see note 2 of the court's opinion), the Tennessee legislature amended its sales tax statute to include warranty and maintenance contracts within the definition of taxable services. Tenn. Code Ann. § 67–6–102(45)(F)(ix) (Westlaw 2009). See generally Walter Hellerstein, "The Treatment of Warranties and Associated Repair Work Under State Sales and Use Taxes," State Tax Notes, June 19, 2000, p. 2095 (observing, among other things, that roughly half the states with sales taxes apply them to optional or extended warranties).

B. *Alteration Services.* The Kansas sales tax applies to the "service of repairing, servicing, altering, or maintaining tangible personal property" not held for resale. Kan. Stat. Ann. § 79–3603(q) (Westlaw 2009). A welder who produced drilling rigs also constructed a pipeline. In so doing he welded sections of pipe together to create a "continuous conduit." He attacked the sales tax on his services on the ground that he created a new product—a pipeline—but the court disagreed, holding that he merely altered the pipes. The court defined "altering" as meaning:

> To make a change in; to modify; to vary in some degree; to change some of the elements or ingredients or details without substituting an entirely new thing or destroying the identity of the thing affected. To change partially. To change on one or more respects, but without destruction of existence or identity of the thing changed; to increase or diminish.

Appeal of Black, 9 Kan.App.2d 666, 684 P.2d 1036, 1039 (1984) (quoting Black's Law Dictionary). In sustaining the tax, the court said:

> In constructing drilling rigs from angle iron, appellant has made no qualitative change in the angle iron itself; all he has done is take a quantity of angle iron and rearrange its spatial arrangement. Despite being put to use as a component part of a completed product, each piece of angle iron retains its identity as angle iron. Thus, appellant has merely altered the angle iron.
>
> The same reasoning holds true for the welding of individual sections of pipe into a continuous and unbroken pipeline. The inherent nature of each segment of pipe is not changed by the simple act of connecting the segments into a continuous conduit; both before and after interconnection, the pipe remains pipe.

Id. Does the court's holding fairly reflect the common understanding of the service of "altering * * * tangible personal property"? Does it reflect sound retail sales tax policy?

2. COMPUTER, DATA PROCESSING, AND INFORMATION SERVICES

NOTES AND QUESTIONS

A. *The Delineation of Taxable Computer, Data Processing, and Information Services.* While the tangible results of computer, data processing, and information services are often taxable under familiar sales tax principles applicable to sales of tangible personal property, a number of states have explicitly extended their traditional sales tax base to include the taxation of computer, data processing, and information services. See generally J. Elaine Bialczak, Sales and Use Taxes: Information Services, Tax Mgmt. (BNA) Multistate Tax Portfolio Series, 1320 T.M.; All States Tax Guide (RIA) ¶ 259–A (2009) (chart), available at www.checkpoint.riag.com. For example, Texas imposes a tax on specified taxable services, including "information services," Tex. Tax Code Ann. § 151.0101(a)(10) (Westlaw 2009), and "data processing services." Tex. Tax Code Ann. § 151.0101(a)(12) (Westlaw 2009). New York's sales tax applies to the "furnishing * * * of an * * * information service * * * delivered by means of telephony or telegraphy or telephone or telegraph service" and which would "otherwise be subject to taxation" as the sale of tangible personal property "if it were furnished by printed, mimeographed, or multigraphed matter." N.Y. Tax Law § 1105(c)(9) (Westlaw 2009). And Ohio defines a taxable sale to include all transactions by which

> [a]utomatic data processing, computer services, or electronic information services are or are to be provided for use in business when the true object of the transaction is the receipt by the consumer of automatic data processing, computer services, or electronic information services rather than the receipt of personal or professional services to which automatic data processing, computer services, or electronic information services are incidental or supplemental.

Ohio Rev. Code § 5739.01(B)(3)(e) (Westlaw 2009).

These provisions have given rise to numerous controversies, most of which revolve around the question whether the service at issue falls within the definition of a taxable computer, data processing, or information service. For example, the Ohio statute defines taxable "automatic data processing" as "processing of others' data, including keypunching or similar data entry services together with verification thereof, or providing access to computer equipment for the purpose of processing data." Ohio Rev. Code § 5739.01(Y)(1)(a) (Westlaw 2009). In Quotron Systems, Inc. v. Limbach, 62 Ohio St.3d 447, 584 N.E.2d 658 (1992), the Ohio Supreme Court held that the taxpayer, which provided price information on stocks and commodities to its subscribers by means of computer terminals in its subscribers' offices, was rendering a taxable automatic data processing service because the subscriber had access to the computers for purposes of acquiring information.

The court rejected Quotron's argument that the statute imposes the tax on the services only when the vendor rendering the service processes another's data or permits the customer to use the vendor's equipment to process the customer's data. The court declared:

> The statute's language does not support this reading. The statute includes as an adp [automatic data processing] or computer service the service that Quotron provides—access to Quotron's computer equipment to examine or acquire stock price data stored in or accessible to that computer equipment.

Id., 584 N.E.2d at 659.

The Ohio Board of Tax Appeals, on the other hand, found *Quotron* distinguishable in concluding that payments made by a bank to a provider of credit card authorization services did not constitute the purchase of taxable automatic data processing and computer services. PNC Bank, Ohio v. Tracy, 1995 WL 412414 (Ohio Bd. Tax App. July 7, 1995). The bank, rather than the credit card authorization company, performed the actual data processing because the bank processed the information received from the credit card authorization company. Moreover, in contrast to the facts in *Quotron*, no access was provided to the credit card authorization company's computer equipment.

The Ohio Supreme Court likewise found that litigation support services are distinct from taxable data processing and computer services. Community Mutual Ins. Co. v. Tracy, 73 Ohio St.3d 371, 653 N.E.2d 220 (1995). The litigation support activities included receiving, reviewing, analyzing, coding, categorizing, interpreting, and summarizing documents. The litigation support provider employed data processing and computer equipment in performing its services. Although the litigation support company's name—Document Automation Services—might have suggested that its services fell squarely within the definition of "automatic data processing services" that Ohio subjects to tax, the court found that the activities performed were professional legal services to which data processing and computer services were only incidental. As to the argument that only lawyers can render legal services, the court responded that "laypersons can perform legal services if accomplished under an attorney's supervision." Id., 653 N.E.2d at 223.

In a Texas administrative decision, an Internet employment service that created a "web brochure" for employers was subject to the Texas sales tax on data processing services. The decision likewise held that the employment service's receipts from allowing prospective employers to search a prospective employee data base and from providing market information designed to assist employers in technology workforce decisions were taxable. The administrative law judge noted that although the applicable Texas regulation provides that the sales of information compiled for a particular client are not subject to information services tax, it also provides that the compilation of information for the use of the general public or a specific industry is subject to the tax. 34 Tax. Admin Code §§ 3.342(5), 3.342(6) (Westlaw 2009). Here, the employment service "gathers, maintains, and compiles information that is made available to the public, specifically technology workers, for which it charges its customers." Hearing No. 45,694, 2006 WL 3532395 (Tex. Comptroller of Public Accounts Aug. 30, 2006).

3. TELECOMMUNICATIONS SERVICES

All but a handful of the states with broad-based sales taxes impose sales taxes on telecommunications services. While the imposition of a sales tax on telecommunications services is an exception to the general rule that state sales taxes are limited to sales of tangible personal property, it is consistent with the widespread exception to that rule for utility services. See J. Due & J. Mikesell, Sales Taxation: State and Local Structure and Administration 93 (2d ed. 1994). The telecommunications sales tax base invariably includes charges for intrastate services; in some instances it also includes the intrastate portion of interstate services; and, in recent years, many states have extended the sales tax base to the full charges for interstate telecommunications services if the telecommunication originates or terminates in the state and is charged to a local service address. Furthermore, many states have broadened the definition of taxable telecommunications well beyond traditional telephone communications to include virtually any interactive two-way electromagnetic communications, including beeper services, custom calling services, answering services, and 900 number services.

In Chapter 3, you were exposed to the Commerce Clause issues raised by state taxation of interstate telecommunications services in *Goldberg v. Sweet* (pp. 176–85 supra). Here we consider the statutory issues raised by sales taxation of telecommunications services. In particular, we focus on these issues in the context of three rulings, each addressing the same question—the taxability of the purchase of prepaid calling cards—but each taking a strikingly different approach to the question.

RULING NO. 95–10

Connecticut Department of Revenue.
August 10, 1995.

Facts

A company that owns and operates a chain of convenience stores (the "Company") plans to sell units of long distance service provided by a telecommunications service provider (the "Telecommunications Provider"). Each unit, which costs the Company twenty cents, will equal one minute of domestic long distance telephone service, and will be represented by a card with a value of 15, 30 or 60 units (a "phone card"). As orders are placed through the Company's phone card distributor, the Company will pay the Telecommunications Provider for the prepaid long distance telecommunications services associated with each order. Customers (the "Users") purchase the phone cards at one of the Company's convenience stores, at a charge of twenty-five or thirty cents per unit. No personal information from a User is required when purchasing a phone card. Users will redeem the phone cards through use of an "800" number and a validation code to access the Telecommunications Provider's telecommunications equipment through which the call is routed and rated and the call details are recorded. The Telecommunications Provider monitors the length of each call and, upon completion of the call, informs the User about the number of units used and remaining on the card. The Telecommunications Provider generates a call detail record of each call (consisting of the call's origin, destination and time), in the same manner as if the call had been made on a pay telephone using a standard "calling card." The Telecommunications Provider sends the call detail records to another company to be processed as if the calls were being billed instead of debited, calculating and remitting state taxes as required.

Issue

Whether the sale of prepaid long distance telephone cards is taxable under either Conn. Gen. Stat. § 12–407(2)(a) as the sale of tangible personal property or Conn. Gen. Stat. § 12–407(2)(k) as the sale of telecommunications services?

Discussion

Following Dine Out Tonight Club, Inc. v. Dept. of Revenue Services, 210 Conn. 567 (1989), Bulletin 24 (rev. 1/90) was issued by the Department, indicating that the sale of a "cash equivalent" (such as a voucher, gift certificate or trading stamp) is not taxable because its true object is the sale of the intangible right to purchase tangible personal property or a service in the future. However, purchases made by redeeming such a cash equivalent are taxable if the property or service being purchased is taxable, based on the sales price of such property or service "valued in money, whether received in money or otherwise" (Conn. Gen. Stat. § 12–

407(8)). A prepaid phone card operates in a manner similar to the cash equivalents discussed in Bulletin 24, in that all or a portion of the purchase price of an item or service to be purchased in the future is prepaid. Therefore, a phone card is also a cash equivalent subject to the rules set forth in the Bulletin.

The general rule for imposing tax on telecommunications services is described in Conn. Gen. Stat. § 12–407a. Such services are taxable when a call (1) both originates and terminates in Connecticut; (2) originates in Connecticut and terminates outside Connecticut and is charged to a telephone number, customer or account located in Connecticut or to the account of any transmission instrument in Connecticut; or (3) originates outside Connecticut and terminates within Connecticut and is charged to a telephone number, customer or account located in Connecticut or to the account of any transmission instrument in Connecticut.

The rules for taxing the sale of cash equivalents and telecommunications services combine to require that, while no tax is due on the sale of the prepaid phone cards, tax is due on the telecommunications services when a phone card is used to make a call both originating and terminating in Connecticut or originating in Connecticut and terminating outside Connecticut. In the latter case, the call is "charged" to the User (the customer) at the location from which the User makes the call. (It follows that calls originating outside Connecticut and terminating in Connecticut made with a prepaid phone card are not subject to tax, since they are not charged to a customer located in Connecticut.) The tax, based on the *full* sales price of the telecommunications service that would have been paid without the use of a prepaid phone card, must be remitted by the Telecommunications Provider at the time the call is made, and should be "charged" to the User by debiting the amount of tax from the prepaid units remaining on the User's card. Tax is not due on prepaid telecommunications services where a call originates outside Connecticut and terminates in Connecticut, because the requirement that the call is charged to a telephone number, customer or account located in Connecticut or to the account of any transmission instrument in Connecticut is not met when a call is made by a User on a telephone outside Connecticut using a prepaid phone card.

Ruling

Although the sale of the prepaid phone cards at the Company's stores is not taxable under Conn. Gen. Stat. § 12–407(2)(a) as the sale of tangible personal property, the telecommunications services rendered when such cards are used to make calls either originating and terminating within Connecticut or originating within Connecticut and terminating outside Connecticut are subject to tax under Conn. Gen. Stat. § 12–407(2)(k). Tax must be included in the Telecommunications Provider's calculation of the amount to be debited from the phone card, and must be remitted to the Department by the Telecommunications Provider.

PRIVATE LETTER RULING NO. 95–0431

Illinois Department of Revenue.
October 30, 1995.

* * *

* * * [M]y client is investigating the sale of telephone credit cards. A customer would prepay a certain amount and then be able to use the credit card in place of cash when making a telephone call. Prepaid Debit Card is the more common name of the service. There are many of them on the market under a variety of names.

The question—is there any Illinois Sales Tax on the card (i.e., the amount that the customer prepays and is credited with in [his or her] name on the card or on the adding of dollars of credit to the card when the original amount is used up)? Also, is anything associated with the card subject to any other tax, understanding that the income would be subject to Illinois income tax.

The Telecommunications Excise Tax Act, 35 ILCS 630/1 et seq. (1994 State Bar Edition), imposes a tax upon the act or privilege of originating or receiving intrastate or interstate telecommunications by a person in this state for those telecommunications purchased at retail from a retailer. The tax applies to the gross charges for intrastate or interstate telecommunications that originate or are received in Illinois. Gross charges means the amount paid for the act or privilege of originating or receiving telecommunications in this State. This amount includes all payments whether made in cash, credits, or services.

Assuming that your client may be purchasing telecommunications units from the telephone service provider and selling them at retail, such situation is similar to hotels that sell telecommunications service. See 86 Ill. Adm. Code 495.110. If this is the case, your client would be required to register as a telecommunications retailer and collect and remit Illinois Telecommunications Excise Tax to the Department. The tax base would be the amount charged to the card purchaser for the taxable service subsequently provided, i.e., calls that originate or terminate in Illinois.

When the cards are sold in Illinois, the Department presumes that the calls will originate or terminate in this State. Your client would have the burden of establishing that the charges are exempt from the Telecommunications Excise Tax. The only way to properly document such an exemption would be through telephone service provider records. Practically speaking, since your client will not know at the time of sale what taxable service the cardholder will actually consume after purchase of the card, your client will need to charge tax on the full amount of the card.

SALES TAX NEWSLETTER

Office of North Dakota State Tax Commissioner.
Volume 23, No. 1, March 1996.

* * *

Taxability of Prepaid Telephone Calling Cards

We continue to receive questions concerning the taxability of sales by retailers and telephone companies of prepaid telephone calling cards. The calling cards generally provide access numbers that allow the holders of the cards to use a predetermined number of minutes, or a set dollar amount of long distance service.

Sales of prepaid telephone calling cards are sales of tangible personal property. Prepaid telephone cards sold within the State of North Dakota are subject to sales tax, regardless of where the long distance calls purchased with the cards original or terminate.

* * *

NOTES AND QUESTIONS

A. The foregoing rulings raise three sets of questions: whether the sale of the telephone card is the sale of tangible personal property, services, or intangible property; whether the sale of the telephone card is taxable at the point of sale or at the time the prepaid telephone service is used; and whether the tax base constitutes the amount charged to the retailer of the card by the registered long distance providers or the amount charged to the customer or ultimate user of the card. How does each one of the rulings resolve each one of those questions?

Which of the foregoing rulings most accurately reflects the substance of the underlying transaction? Which is most sensitive to administrative concerns? To constitutional concerns? Suppose an Illinois resident purchases a prepaid telephone card in Illinois and uses it while on a business trip in Connecticut to call home. What will be the tax consequences of those transactions? Suppose a Connecticut resident purchases a prepaid telephone card in Connecticut and uses it while on a business trip in Illinois to call home. What will be the tax consequences of those transactions? Can the North Dakota approach to the sale of prepaid telephone calling cards be squared with economic reality? With the constitutional restraints articulated in *Goldberg v. Sweet* (pp. 176–85 supra)?

B. *Prepaid Telephone Calling Cards.* Whatever the theoretical merits of Connecticut's approach to taxing prepaid calling cards, it is administratively awkward at best. As a consequence, the telephone industry has made a concerted effort to persuade states to tax such cards at the point of sale. Today the overwhelming majority of states tax prepaid cards at the point of sale with only a handful imposing a tax where the card is used. Indeed, Connecticut amended its statute statute in 2000 to provide for taxation of telephone cards at the point of sale, see Conn. Gen. Stat. § 12–407(a)(2)(O) (Westlaw 2009), and Illinois amended its statute to provide that "prepaid telephone calling arrangements shall be considered tangible personal property subject to the tax imposed under this Act regardless of the form in which those arrangements may be embodied, transmitted, or fixed by any method now known or hereafter developed." 35 Ill. Comp. Stat. Ann. §§ 105/3, 115/3, 120/2 (Westlaw 2009). What impact does this amendment have on the analysis in *Private Letter Ruling No. 95–0431?*

C. *Gift Cards.* The purchase of a prepaid calling card is very similar in principle to the purchase of a gift card or certificate. In each case, the purchaser acquires the right to make future purchases of a certain kind in a certain amount. In contrast to their treatment of prepaid calling cards, however, states generally treat the purchase of a gift card or gift certificate as the nontaxable purchase of an intangible (a "cash equivalent"). Tax is not due until the card is later used to make a taxable purchase, at which time sales tax is due on the dollar amount of the transaction. See, e.g., Fla. Admin. Code Ann. § 12A–1.089 (Westlaw 2009). What explains the difference in the tax treatment of these essentially identical types of purchases?

D. *Sale for Resale of Telecommunications Services Used in Conjunction with the Provision of Other Services.* When telecommunications services are purchased by a company engaged in the business of providing other services, the question sometimes arises whether the company is "consuming" the telecommunications service in its business or is "reselling" the telecommunications service to its customers. For example, the Connecticut Department of Revenue considered the question whether a company that provided data processing and computer services to banks was "consuming" or "reselling" the telecommunications services it purchased for transmitting data to and from the banks. The banks would enter the data at their computer terminals, which were linked to the taxpayer's computers through the telecommunications network. The taxpayer, which separately stated its charge for the telecommunications services on the invoices it sent to the banks, contended that it should pay no tax on its purchases of the telecommunications services because it was purchasing them for resale. The Department of Revenue disagreed and found that the telecommunications services were "merely incidental" to the company's business of providing data processing services. Hence it concluded:

> Where telecommunications service is needed by a company engaged in the business of providing computer and data processing services in order to provide such services to its customers, the company is using the telecommunications service, and it is not purchasing such service for resale to its customers.

Ruling 91–16, 1991 WL 157533, at *2 (Conn. Dep't of Rev. June 5, 1991). Massachusetts's position on sales for resale of telecommunications services is similar to Connecticut's. Technical Information Release 1991–1 (Mass. Dep't of Rev. March 29, 1991).

Does the Connecticut ruling make sense? While the position of Connecticut and Massachusetts is consistent with cases holding that business purchases are taxable when they can be characterized as being "consumed" rather than "resold" by the business, how does that position square with the theory of the retail sales tax? Will the telecommunications services that the taxpayer purchases from the telecommunications provider be taxed again, directly or indirectly, when the taxpayer bills its clients for data processing or telecommunications services? If so, won't taxing the services when purchased by the data processing company result in a pyramiding of the tax? Should these questions be resolved by asking whether the resale in fact will be subject to tax? Compare City of Tucson v. Tucson Hotel Equity Limited Partnership, 196 Ariz. 551, 2 P.3d 110 (App. 2000) (hotel may claim resale exemption for purchase of telecommunications services it marks up and includes in its guests' taxable hotel bills) with Sales and Use Tax Ruling No. SUT–98–084 (Pa. Dep't of Rev. Aug. 27, 1999) (Internet access provider "cannot claim resale of its purchase of * * * telecommunication service * * * because it uses the service in order to provide its nontaxable Internet access service").

In any event, is it not also true that the taxpayer in the Connecticut ruling was engaged not in the business of selling telecommunications, but rather in the business of selling data processing services that it transmitted by telecommunications? The fact that the cost to the taxpayer of the telecommunications services it used was charged to its customers does not necessarily mean that the taxpayer "resold" the telecommunications services any more than a lawyer who gives her client legal advice over the telephone is reselling telephone services, even though she charges the client the telephone expense. The situation arguably is no different from that of a retailer that has paid a sales tax on a truck it purchased for use in delivering merchandise to its customers. The retailer ordinarily includes a portion of the cost of the delivery truck in the price of the goods it sells. While the result is to tax the cost of the truck twice under the retail sales tax, such "double taxation" is a well ingrained feature of the existing sales tax base.

4. TAXABLE SERVICES AND THE SALE-FOR-RESALE EXCLUSION

As the immediately preceding Note reveals, the sale-for-resale issue that we explored in conjunction with sales of tangible personal property arises as well in the context of sales of services. However, it is often more difficult to trace services than tangible personal property in time and space. For this reason, the resale issue can be more complex in the services context—at least when state legislatures insist on tying the resale exclusion to physical rather than economic concepts of taxing the same thing twice.

NOTES AND QUESTIONS

A. *The Sale of Tangible Personal Property to a Taxpayer Engaged in Providing Taxable Services.* The sale-for-resale exclusion is designed to avoid pyramiding of the sales tax by ensuring that no tax applies to intermediate transactions in the economic process when the tax will apply to the final transaction involving the item in question. In the context of a sales tax base that reaches most sales of tangible personal property while exempting most sales of services, the sale-for-resale exclusion generally excludes the sale of tangible personal property when the property itself will ultimately be subject to a further tax. The exclusion generally does not apply, on the other hand, when tangible personal property is transferred to a service provider who consumes the property in rendering *nontaxable* services. See Section C supra. When the services provided by the purchaser of tangible personal property are themselves *taxable*, however, the logic of the sale-for-resale exclusion would suggest that such purchases should fall within the resale exclusion because their cost will be reflected in the measure of the service provider's taxable services. A number of states, especially those that tax substantial number of services, specifically broaden the resale provision to deal with this issue. Thus, Iowa exempts from sales tax sales "for resale of tangible personal property or taxable services, *or for resale of tangible personal property in connection with taxable services.*" Iowa Code Ann. § 423.3(2) (Westlaw 2009) (emphasis supplied). Similarly, New Jersey's definition of a "retail sale" excludes sales of tangible personal property

> for use * * * in performing * * * services subject to tax * * * where the property so sold becomes a physical component part of the property upon which the services are performed or where the property so sold is later actually transferred to the purchaser of the service in conjunction with the performance of the service subject to tax.

N.J. Stat. Ann. § 54:32B–2(e)(1) (Westlaw 2009). Nevertheless, in the absence of a statutory provision granting an exclusion or exemption for sales of tangible personal property to providers of taxable services, such transactions may be deemed taxable on the ground that the service provider is consuming rather than reselling the property.

B.   *The Sale of Taxable Services to a Taxpayer Engaged in Providing Taxable Services.* States that tax services usually recognize that the sale-for-resale exemption should apply to the resale of services just as it applies to the resale of tangible personal property. Thus the New York statute taxing specified services applies to the "receipts from every sale, *except for resale*, of the following services * * * " N.Y. Tax Law § 1105(c) (Westlaw 2009) (emphasis supplied). However, whether services are resold, rather than consumed by the purchaser, can be a much more troublesome inquiry than whether tangible personal property is consumed, because services, by their very nature, are often more difficult to trace in a physical sense than are items of tangible personal property.

Recognizing this problem, some states have modified the resale exemption in its application to services. The Ohio definition of a retail sale, for example, provides that it does not include a sale "in which the purpose of the consumer is to resell the thing transferred *or the benefit of the service provided * * * in the form in which the same is, or is to be, received by him.*" Ohio Rev. Code § 5739.01(E) (Westlaw 2009) (emphasis supplied). Construing this provision, the Ohio Supreme Court held that a hotel's purchase of cleaning services for room and restaurant linens fell within the resale exemption because the hotel "purchased this service, normally a taxable transaction, and its guests received the benefit of this service in being able to use clean linen." Hyatt Corp.

v. Limbach, 69 Ohio St.3d 537, 634 N.E.2d 995, 996 (1994). Similarly, the court held that a company that prepared computer-generated tax returns and was engaged in the sale of automatic data processing services could sell those services for resale because the benefit of the service (the tax returns) would be resold by the taxpayer's customers in the same form in which the customer received them. CCH Computax v. Tracy, 68 Ohio St.3d 86, 623 N.E.2d 1178 (1993). But a company's purchase of temporary employment services for assistance in manufacturing automobile wheel assemblies did not fall within the resale exemption because the company did not transfer the benefit of the work force in the same form to its customers. Bellemar Parts Industries, Inc. v. Tracy, 88 Ohio St.3d 351, 725 N.E.2d 1132 (2000).

Can these decisions be reconciled? The court thought so, declaring:

> In *Hyatt*, the taxpayer purchased laundry services, received laundered linens as the benefit of those services, and resold them in that form to the customers. Likewise, in *CCH*, the taxpayer purchased tax return preparation, received completed tax returns as the benefit, and resold the returns unchanged to its customers.

Id., 725 N.E.2d at 1135. But could not one just as easily say that in *Bellemar* the taxpayer purchased employment services, received the benefit of those services in the form of completed wheel assemblies, and resold the "benefit of the service provided * * * in the form * * * received"? See also Corporate Staffing Resources, Inc. v. Zaino, 95 Ohio St.3d 1, 764 N.E.2d 1006 (2002) (relying on *Bellemar* in rejecting claim that purchase of temporary employment services for repairing customers' computers was a sale for resale over a dissent that contended the taxpayer resold the labor to its customers).

The New Jersey Tax Court considered the question whether the purchase by a cable television company of installation services from a subcontractor was exempt from tax under a sale-for-resale provision. Futurevision Cable Enter., Inc. v. Division of Taxation, 9 N.J.Tax 165 (1987). The cable company contended that the installation services were resold to its customers in the form of a hook-up fee. The court held that the taxpayer's purchases of installation services were exempt under the resale exemption only if the cable company could specifically identify particular installation services that were resold, through the hook-up fee, to particular subscribers. The court observed that "if a subcontractor has separately billed [the cable company] for installation of a drop line for a particular subscriber and this subcontractor drop line charge has been passed on to the subscriber in whole or in part as a hook-up fee, the service * * * has been resold." Id. at 176–77. In the absence of such proof, however, the cable company's purchase of installation services would be taxable.

Is the New Jersey Tax Court justified in insisting that, in order for a sale of services to qualify for the sale-for-resale exclusion, there must be an exact matching of the individual acquisition of services to a sale of that acquired service? Is such a matching of purchases and sales on a transaction-by-transaction basis necessary to qualify for the resale exclusion when sales of tangible personal property are involved? For example, can one successfully maintain that a printer who purchases large quantities of paper must identify the purchaser of a particular quantity of paper with the sale of a particular printed product in order to qualify for the resale exclusion? If not, is there any reason why there should be a different rule in the context of the resale of services?

ASSIGNMENT

Analyze the sales and use tax laws and regulations of your state and prepare a report as to how the following transactions would be treated:

(1) A has new rubber heels and soles put on his shoes. He receives a bill of $10 for heels and the leather used in his soles and $10 for labor and miscellaneous materials, such as glue and thread. What is the base, if any, of the tax?

(2) B has her fur coat relined and is billed $400 for the lining and $600 for labor, thread, and miscellaneous materials. What is the base, if any, of the tax?

(3) C's car is damaged in an accident; he receives a bill as follows:

(a) new front fender—materials $500, labor $400;

(b) new radiator—materials $300, labor $200;

(c) straightening back fender and doors—labor $150, bolts, hinges, etc. $90;

(d) repainting—paint $100, labor $500.

What is the base, if any, of the tax?

E.   REAL ESTATE CONSTRUCTION AND REPAIR

NOTES AND QUESTIONS

A. *Construction Contracting.* The basic structure of the retail sales tax creates a number of problems with respect to the taxation of sales to and by construction contractors. First, because the retail sales tax does not apply to the sale of real estate, any sale by a construction contractor that is characterized as a sale of real estate will escape sales taxation. Second, because in many states the retail sales tax does not apply to the services sold by construction contractors, sales of construction services generally will escape taxation along with any "incidental" transfers of tangible personal property that construction contractors make along with their services. Consequently, even though construction contractors plainly "resell" the tangible personal property that they purchase in the sense that they dispose of it in transactions for which they receive consideration, such property could escape sales taxation altogether if the contractors' purchases are exempt under the resale exemption. This is because the resale may escape tax, either as the nontaxable sale of real estate or as the nontaxable sale of services with an "incidental" transfer of tangible personal property.

The solution to this problem, which the overwhelming majority of states have adopted, is to treat the construction contractor as the consumer of the building materials it purchases and uses in constructing or adding improvements to real estate. All States Tax Guide (RIA) ¶ 254 (2009) (chart), available at www.checkpoint.riag.com; John F. Due & John L. Mikesell, Sales Taxation: State and Local Structure and Administration 97 (2d ed. 1994). The construction contractor accordingly must pay tax on its purchases of building materials. This comports with the underlying policy of the retail sales tax to tax the final consumption of tangible personal property.[f] This treatment becomes problematic, however, when construction contractors are treated as reselling tangible personal property in a taxable transaction or when the construction contractor's own services (along with the property it transfers) are taxable. In fact, insofar as contractors are deemed to be selling at retail (e.g., when they separately state the price for the materials they transfer to the purchaser), they may purchase those materials tax free under a resale certificate but then must collect tax on their resale of those materials.

The large amount of construction that is done for tax-immune federal, state, and local governments, as well as tax-exempt universities, hospitals, and churches, has also influenced the sales tax treatment of the real estate construction industry. Many states treat the construction contractor as the taxable consumer of its purchases because the subsequent sale to the purchaser would not be taxable in any event. The U.S. Supreme Court has sustained this practice with regard to Federal Government contractors, see Washington v. United States, 460 U.S. 536, 103 S.Ct. 1344 (1983), over the objection that it discriminates against the Federal Government by imposing a tax on purchases made by federal contractors but not by other contractors. See Chapter 5.

B. *Traditional Property Law Distinctions As Applied to Sales Taxation of Real Estate Contractors.* In State ex rel. Otis Elevator Co. v. Smith, 357 Mo. 1055, 212 S.W.2d 580 (1948), the court held that a corporation constructing and installing elevators was engaged in selling tangible personal property at retail and, therefore, was required to collect sales tax. The decision turned largely on provisions in the contracts retaining in the taxpayer title to the elevators and other apparatus until final payment was made. To buttress this security, the contracts provided that the apparatus "can be removed without material damage to the freehold." Id., 212 S.W.2d at 581. In light of these clauses of the contracts, the court concluded that there is not an "inseparable commingling of labor and material that produced the finished product," but instead a taxable sale of tangible personal property. Id. In a later case, the court held that charges made for the construction and installation of wooden cabinets in homes did not constitute receipts from sales of tangible personal property; the installation, said the court, was an integral part of the contract, and the transfer was consummated when the cabinets were affixed to the real

---

f. On a more fundamental level, of course, the taxation of construction contractors' purchases of building materials cannot be justified, even if their resales are nontaxable sales of real estate or services, when those sales are to business purchasers, whose own sales will be subject to retail sales tax. Under these circumstances, the value of the building materials will be taxed twice, once to the construction contractors and again to the ultimate consumers of the products sold by the construction contractors' customers. As we have already pointed out on a number of occasions in this chapter, however, the retail sales tax in force in this country is a far cry from the theoretical norm of a uniform levy on consumer expenditures. While it is important to be sensitive to the levy's deviation from that norm, those deviations, as often as not, reflect conscious legislative policy.

estate; there was therefore no transfer of tangible personalty. Marsh v. Spradling, 537 S.W.2d 402 (Mo. 1976). The court distinguished *Otis Elevator* on the ground that the general principle—"that upon the installation of personal property into real estate as a part of a general construction contract the article becomes a part of the real estate," id. at 406—was inapplicable due to the agreement in the *Otis Elevator* case by which title was retained in the property even after installation.

Should real property concepts (e.g., the question whether property constitutes a "fixture" and therefore is real property at the time of sale) determine the outcome of sales tax cases? In U.S. Lines, Inc. v. State Board of Equalization, 182 Cal.App.3d 529, 227 Cal.Rptr. 347 (1st Dist. 1986), a shipping company contested the application of California's sales tax to the transfer of massive cranes installed at the Port of Oakland on the ground that at the time it transferred title to the cranes they had become affixed to real property and therefore had become nontaxable fixtures. The court rejected the taxpayer's "myopic focus on the stipulated real property character of the cranes for purposes of local tax assessment and property tax payment" which "overlooks the fact that classification of affixed equipment as real property 'fixtures' for property taxation does not preclude classification of the same equipment as tangible personal property for sales tax purposes." Id., 227 Cal.Rptr. at 350. In holding the transfer of the cranes subject to sales tax, the court declared:

> In the context of sales tax, two discrete situations are presented in which sale of personal property is cloaked with the indicia of real property. First, when the object is installed by the seller on the buyer's land and becomes affixed thereto, the courts generally have held the object is personal property in the hands of the seller even thought it is real property to the owner of the land. Second, when the object is transferred by the seller together with the real property, the test is whether removal of the object is contemplated; if so it is personalty; if not, the object remains part of the realty. * * * [T]he court below correctly determined that the sale of the cranes was a sale of personal property. U.S. Lines did *not* transfer the cranes along with the land; rather it installed the cranes on land already owned by the Port. Although the cranes became an integral part of the Port's real property, the cranes were personal property in the hands of U.S. Lines at the time of sale. Ordinarily, when personal property is affixed to the land of another, it belongs to the owner of the land (Civ. Code, § 1013) and cannot be removed. For purposes of *sales* tax, the sale and installation of personal objects are nonetheless subject to sales tax even though affixed to the buyer's land.

Id. at 536 (emphasis in original). See also Indiana Department of State Revenue v. Trump Indiana, Inc., 814 N.E.2d 1017 (Ind. 2004) (boat assembled in Florida and transferred to Indiana for use as a casino riverboat is tangible personal property for purposes of Indiana sales and use tax even though it is also subject to property tax as real property once it is in place as a riverboat).

C. *Sales of Prefabricated Homes.* Are sales of prefabricated homes sales of tangible personal property under a retail sales tax? In Idaho State Tax Comm'n v. Boise Cascade Corp., 97 Idaho 312, 543 P.2d 865 (1975), landowners entered into contracts with the Boise Cascade Corporation for the construction of prefabricated buildings. Boise Cascade proceeded to construct the building in its factories. When it completed its work, Boise Cascade transported the building to the owner's site, where it placed the building on the foundation and performed various related tasks. Title to the building did not pass to the landowner until Boise Cascade placed the building on his site and attached the building to its foundation. After a detailed consideration of the legislative history of the Idaho Sales Tax Act, the court concluded that Boise Cascade was engaged in improving real property and not in making retail sales of personalty. The court said:

> The only distinction between Boise Cascade's method of construction and that of the traditional on-site contractor is that Boise Cascade does a majority of its construction at their plant while a majority of the traditional contractor's work is done at the homeowner's lot. The legislature considered the process of construction to be a service and enacted I.C. § 63–3609(a) to tax the contractor for the materials consumed in the building process. The fact that Boise Cascade's method of construction involves hauling the nearly completed home to the buyer's lot does not change the end result, that is, the landowner having a home on his previously unimproved lot.

Id., 543 P.2d at 868. As a consequence, Boise Cascade was liable for tax on its purchases of materials used in its operations, but it did not have to collect tax on its sale to the owner of the site.

In Sterling Custom Homes Corp. v. Commissioner of Revenue, 391 N.W.2d 523 (Minn. 1986), on the other hand, the court held that a company that prepares plans for custom-designed homes, then constructs components of those homes and delivers them to the construction site of the home, unloads the components and oversees the erection of the component, but that does not assume responsibility for construction, is a supplier of building materials. It is not a construction contractor; consequently, it is taxable on the sale of its homes and not on the purchase of the materials. See also Adrian Housing Corp. v. Collins, 253 Ga. 263, 319 S.E.2d 852 (1984) (sales of modular homes taxable). But in Wisconsin Dep't of Revenue v. Sterling Custom Homes Corp., 91 Wis.2d 675, 283 N.W.2d 573 (1979), the court held that the same company involved in the Minnesota case was a construction contractor, taxable on its purchases of building materials but not on its sales of the prefabricated homes.

Sales of prefabricated and mobile raise not only the technical question of whether the transfer constitutes a taxable sale of tangible personal property or a nontaxable transfer of realty, they also raise fundamental questions of tax equity. If prefabricated and mobile homes are subject to sales tax whereas the construction of more traditional (and more expensive) housing is not, the sales tax will clearly discriminate against low-end purchases of prefabricated housing as compared with more upscale on-site construction. Even though the on-site construction contractor may have paid taxes on its purchases of supplies and passed the economic burden of those taxes on to its purchasers, the labor component of the on-site construction will nevertheless escape sales taxation in most instances. By contrast, the labor component of the prefabricated housing will be fully taxed if the transaction is characterized as a retail sale. To deal with this problem, many states tax only a portion of the sales price of prefabricated housing or tax it at a lower rate. See, e.g., Cal. Rev. & Tax. Code § 6012.7(a) (Westlaw 2009) (receipts from sales of "factory-built housing" taxed at 40 percent of sales price); Cal. Rev. & Tax. Code § 6012.8(a) (Westlaw 2009) (receipts from sales of mobile homes taxed at 75 percent of sales price). John F. Due & John L. Mikesell, Sales Taxation: State and Local Structure and Administration 99 (2d ed. 1994).

D. *References.* John F. Due & John L. Mikesell, Sales Taxation: State and Local Structure and Administration 97–100 (2d ed. 1994); 2 Jerome R. Hellerstein & Walter Hellerstein, State Taxation ¶ 15.08 (3d ed. 2000 & Cum. Supp. 2009).

ASSIGNMENT

Analyze the provisions of your state's sales and use tax laws and regulations, and consider the taxability of the building supplier and contractor under: (a) a lump sum contract, and (b) a contract requiring the contractor to sell the materials and supplies at the usual retail price and to render services for an additional consideration. In this connection, consider the function and purpose of the exemption of sales for resale, or the limitation of the tax to retail sales, sales at retail, and the like.

Assuming that you represent the following persons in the negotiation of the building contracts enumerated below, what provisions would you recommend as to price, billings, and so forth, of materials and services?

Client	**Type of Contract**
(a) Supplier of contractor	Contract to build a church for
(b) Contractor	religious organization.
(c) Church	
(a) Supplier of contractor	Contract to build apartment house
(b) Contractor	for private realty corporation.
(c) Realty corporation	

F. USE TAXES

When states first adopted sales taxes during the 1930s, they encountered a troublesome gap in the sales tax structure attributable to the constitutional strictures prohibiting them from taxing sales consummated outside their borders or in interstate commerce. The gap created two concerns. First, states feared the loss of business that local merchants would suffer when prospective customers made out-of-state or interstate purchases to avoid local sales tax liability. Second, states feared the loss of revenue they would incur as a result of the diversion of sales tax to nontax states. To deal with this potential loss of business and revenue, states enacted "complementary" or "compensating" use taxes.

Compensating use taxes are functionally equivalent to sales taxes. They are typically levied upon the use, storage, or other consumption in the state of tangible personal property that has not been subjected to a sales tax. The use tax imposes an exaction equal in amount to the sales tax that would have been imposed on the sale of the property in question if the sale had occurred within the state's taxing jurisdiction. The state overcomes the constitutional hurdle of taxing an out-of-state or interstate sale by imposing the tax on a subject within its taxing power—the use, storage, or consumption of property within the state. In principle, then, the in-state consumer stands to gain nothing by making an out-of-state or interstate purchase free of sales tax because she will ultimately be saddled with an identical use tax when the property is brought into the taxing state.[g]

The Supreme Court of Tennessee has described the use tax as follows:

> The use tax is a compensating tax, designed to prevent the avoidance of sales taxes and ensure that Tennessee manufacturers and merchants remain on equal competitive footing with nonresidents who enter this state to do business. Taken together, the sales and use taxes provide a uniform scheme of taxation on goods (tangible personal property) purchased within the state and goods purchased outside the state for "storage, use, or consumption" within the state.

> Broadly speaking, the use tax is a tax "on the enjoyment of that which was purchased, after a sale has spent its interstate character." McLeod v. Dilworth, 322 U.S. 327, 64 S.Ct. 1023 (1944). More specifically, the use tax is a tax on the "privilege of using, consuming, distributing or storing tangible personal property after it is brought into this State from without this State." Broadacre Dairies, Inc. v. Evans, 193 Tenn. 441, 444–45, 246 S.W.2d 78, 79 (1952). This definition is fairly uniform throughout the states. See 68 Am.Jur. Sales and Use Taxes § 171 (1953). Thus, it was the legislative intent, as manifested in Section 67–3005, T.C.A., to impose a use tax on all tangible personal property imported from other states and used and consumed in this state, provided a similar tax, equal to or greater, has not been paid in the exporting state.

Woods v. M.J. Kelley Co., 592 S.W.2d 567, 570 (Tenn. 1980).

Much of the material considered above with regard to retail sales taxes (pp. 605–700 supra) is equally applicable to use taxes, for example, determining what constitutes a taxable purchase of tangible personal property. The materials in this part deal with the special problems arising under use tax acts.

---

g. In practice, the critical question facing the taxing state is often whether it can require the out-of-state vendor to collect the use tax concededly due from the local consumer. See Quill Corp. v. North Dakota, 504 U.S. 298, 112 S.Ct. 1904 (1992), pp. 24–38 supra. The consumer is not likely to remit the tax voluntarily, and it is not administratively feasible for the state to collect small amounts of a tax from individual purchasers. We considered the constitutional restraints on the states' power to impose use tax obligations on out-of-state vendors in Chapter 2 and we consider them further in Section I infra.

COMMISSIONER OF REVENUE v.
J.C. Penney Company, Inc.
Supreme Judicial Court of Massachusetts, 2000.
431 Mass. 684, 730 N.E.2d 266.

LYNCH, J.

The Commissioner of Revenue (commissioner) appeals, pursuant to G.L. c. 58A, § 13, from a decision of the Appellate Tax Board (board) ordering an abatement of a use tax assessed on catalogs that J.C. Penney Company (taxpayer) mailed from out-of-State locations to Massachusetts residents between the years 1991 and 1993. The commissioner argues that the board erred in concluding that the taxpayer's distribution of these catalogs did not constitute a taxable "use" of property, as that term is statutorily defined. We transferred the case here on our own motion and now reverse the board's decision.

1. *Facts.* The taxpayer, a Delaware corporation with its principal place of business in Plano, Texas, is engaged in the business of retail merchandising. During the relevant tax periods, it operated retail stores in all fifty States, including ten stores in Massachusetts, and a direct mail catalog business, which it administered separately from the retail store division.

In connection with its catalog business, each year the taxpayer issued three major seasonal catalogs, as well as various small sale or specialty catalogs, that described and illustrated merchandise available for purchase by mail order. The planning, artwork, design, and layout for these catalogs were completed and paid for outside of Massachusetts, primarily in Texas, and the taxpayer contracted with independent printing companies located outside the Commonwealth to produce the catalogs. During the relevant time period, the three major catalogs were printed in Indiana, while the specialty catalogs were printed in South Carolina and Wisconsin. The taxpayer supplied the printers with paper, shipping wrappers, and address labels for the catalogs; the printers supplied the ink, binding materials, and labor. None of these materials was purchased in Massachusetts.

Printed catalogs, with address labels and postage affixed, were transported by a common carrier from the printer to a United States Postal Service office located outside Massachusetts, where they were sent to Massachusetts addressees via third or fourth class mail. Title to the catalogs passed from the printer to the taxpayer when the common carrier assumed possession. Although the taxpayer made no effort to recall or to change the time or method of delivery of the catalogs after they left the printers' facilities, it instructed the postal service, from its offices outside Massachusetts, to return any undeliverable catalogs to its catalog distribution center in Connecticut.

The catalogs advertised a broader range of merchandise than was available for purchase in the taxpayer's retail stores. The taxpayer's express purpose for mailing these catalogs, free of charge, to residents of, among other places, Massachusetts, was to solicit mail order purchases from current and potential customers. Catalog recipients were selected by the taxpayer at its offices outside Massachusetts. Purchases of catalog merchandise were made by telephoning or returning an order form to the taxpayer at a location outside Massachusetts, and the merchandise was shipped to customers from the taxpayer's Connecticut distribution center.

For each sales and use tax period in the years 1991–1993, the taxpayer filed Massachusetts sales and use tax returns and paid the taxes reflected thereon as due. On August 3, 1993, the commissioner notified the taxpayer that these tax returns had been selected for audit, and on April 26, 1995, assessed the taxpayer for unpaid use taxes, of which $314,674.42, plus interest and penalties, represented a tax on the value of the catalogs the taxpayer mailed to Massachusetts residents during the relevant tax periods. The taxpayer paid the assessment and applied for an abatement. Following the commissioner's denial of this application, the taxpayer appealed to the board. In ordering an abatement of the use tax assessed on the mailed catalogs, the board held that the taxpayer, in causing the catalogs to be mailed from out-of-State locations to Massachusetts residents, had not made a taxable "use" of these items of tangible personal property in Massachusetts, as required by the use tax statute, G.L. c. 64I, § 2.

2. *Discussion.* * * * The sole question presented by this appeal is whether the term "use" in G.L. c. 64I, § 2, as defined in G.L. c. 64I, § 1, encompasses a taxpayer's distribution of merchandise catalogs to Massachusetts addressees by means of interstate mail for the purpose of soliciting retail business. We answer this question in the affirmative and, therefore, reverse the board's decision.

General Laws c. 64I, § 2, imposes an excise tax, at the rate of five per cent, on "the storage, use or other consumption in the [C]ommonwealth of tangible personal property or services purchased from any vendor for storage, use, or other consumption within the [C]ommonwealth." "Use" is defined, in relevant part, to "mean and include ... the exercise of any right or power over tangible personal property incident to the ownership of that property, except that it does not include the sale of that property in the regular course of business." G.L. c. 64I, § 1. Significantly, tangible personal property shipped or brought into Massachusetts by the purchaser within six months after its out-of-State purchase is presumed to have been purchased for storage, use, or other consumption in the Commonwealth. G.L. c. 64I, § 8 (f). The use tax established by G.L. c. 64I, together with the sales tax in G.L. c. 64H, are complementary elements of a unitary taxing program intended to "reach all transactions, except those expressly exempted, 'in which tangible personal property is sold inside or outside the Commonwealth for storage, use, or other consumption within the Commonwealth.' " M & T Charters, Inc. v. Commissioner of Revenue, 404 Mass. 137, 140, 533 N.E.2d 1359 (1989). The use tax was thus designed "to prevent the loss of sales tax revenue from out-of-State purchases," M & T Charters, Inc. v. Commissioner of Revenue, supra, and to protect local merchants from loss of business to merchants in other States with lower or nonexistent sales taxes. See 2 J. & W. Hellerstein, State Taxation § 16.03[3] (3d ed.1998).

In concluding that the taxpayer had not made a taxable "use" of the catalogs mailed to Massachusetts residents, the board reasoned that the taxpayer's activities with respect to the catalogs did not constitute an exercise *in* the Commonwealth of a right or power incident to the ownership of tangible personal property situated in Massachusetts. In the board's view, the "exercise" of a right or power over property, such as control, equates with "some degree or form of activity," yet "none of the [taxpayer's] activities undertaken to arrange the in-State distribution of the catalogs occurred in Massachusetts [n]or did [the taxpayer's] relevant activities occur while the catalogs were in the Commonwealth." The board further reasoned that, had the Legislature intended a taxpayer's mailing of catalogs to Massachusetts residents to be subject to the use tax, it would have expressly designated the "distribution" of property as a taxable use in G.L. c. 64I, § 1, as other States have done. Finally, the board * * * rejected as unpersuasive numerous decisions from other jurisdictions that have held to the contrary.

In urging us to affirm the board's decision, the taxpayer argues that assessment of a use tax is improper where, as here, the taxpayer "did not do anything with the catalogs in Massachusetts."[2] While this proposition is not objectionable in principle, we reject its application to the undisputed facts of this case. For, contrary to the board's conclusion and the taxpayer's contention, the taxpayer here did, in a very real sense, "do something" with its catalogs in the Commonwealth by distributing them, via the United States Postal Service, to Massachusetts residents, thereby deploying them in the service of its Massachusetts direct mail retail business.

It is a settled principle of our taxation jurisprudence that tax statutes are "to be construed as imposing taxes with respect to matters of substance and not with respect to mere matters of form." Green v. Commissioner of Corps. & Taxation, 364 Mass. 389, 394, 305 N.E.2d 92 (1973). It is apparent from the board's findings that the taxpayer, even though it did not itself physically possess the catalogs in Massachusetts, nevertheless exercised substantive rights and powers over the catalogs in the Commonwealth by effectuating their delivery to Massachusetts addressees. As the board observed, citing its own precedent, although the acts constituting an

---

2. The taxpayer asserts, additionally, that it did not have any right or power over the catalogs while they were in the Commonwealth, which assertion is practically indistinguishable from a denial of ownership of the catalogs. This claim, however, is not supported by the board's findings that the taxpayer acquired title to the catalogs before they were mailed into Massachusetts and instructed the postal service to return any undelivered catalogs to its Connecticut distribution center, facts that indicate that the taxpayer never relinquished its title to, and right to possess, the catalogs in Massachusetts until such time as they were delivered to their intended recipients. Moreover, United States Postal Service regulations give the sender or its representative the exclusive right to recall mail prior to its delivery. See 39 C.F.R. § 111.5 (1999); United States Postal Service Domestic Mail Manual, D030, § 1.1 * * * Thus, we have no doubt that the taxpayer owned the catalogs within the Commonwealth and had rights and powers incident to that ownership. The sole issue, therefore, is whether the taxpayer *exercised in Massachusetts* any such right or power.

exercise of a right or power over property must occur in Massachusetts in order for a taxable "use" to occur, it is not necessary that the taxpayer itself directly perform these acts, but rather this requirement may be satisfied where another possesses and acts on property in the Commonwealth at the taxpayer's direction. See, e.g, Federal Express Corp. v. Commissioner of Revenue, 23 Mass.App. Tax Bd. 1, 3–4 (1997), aff'd, 427 Mass. 399, 693 N.E.2d 682 (1998) (taxpayer's directing, through in-State operator, travel of aircraft located in Massachusetts constituted taxable use). This principle is applicable here, as the United States Postal Service, which carried the catalogs into the Commonwealth and delivered them to Massachusetts residents, possessed and acted on the taxpayer's property in the Commonwealth at all times in accordance with the taxpayer's express instructions and on the taxpayer's behalf. The taxpayer, who acquired title to the catalogs prior to their entry into Massachusetts, directed the postal service, and paid it a fee, to deliver the catalogs to specified Massachusetts residents; absent these directions, the catalogs would never have made their way into the Commonwealth or, once here, into the hands of their addressees. Moreover, the taxpayer instructed the postal service regarding the disposition of undelivered catalogs, directing that they be carried out of Massachusetts and returned to its Connecticut distribution center. * * * [T]his indirect taxpayer control of the catalogs is indistinguishable, for purposes of determining the applicability of the use tax, from the control the taxpayer would have exercised had it chosen to ship the catalogs into the Commonwealth and to effectuate their delivery by means of a common carrier or its own employees.[4] Such taxpayer control by proxy over items of tangible personal property sent into Massachusetts via interstate mail thus constitutes an exercise within the Commonwealth of a right or power incident to ownership of that property and, therefore, a "use" of that property within the meaning of G.L. c. 64I, § 2.[5]

---

4. The taxpayer asserts that this conclusion "ignores the tradition in case law that honors for tax purposes the very real distinction between doing something oneself and having the Postal Service or common carrier do it for you." As support for this purported tradition, the taxpayer cites the decisions of the United States Supreme Court in Quill Corp. v. North Dakota, 504 U.S. 298, 311, 112 S.Ct. 1904 (1992), and National Bellas Hess, Inc. v. Department of Revenue of Ill., 386 U.S. 753, 759, 87 S.Ct. 1389 (1967). However, neither of these decisions stands for the rule asserted. Each case involved a constitutional challenge to a State's assessment of a use tax on goods purchased for use in the taxing State by an out-of-State mail order merchant that had no in-State retail outlets or sales representatives. The Supreme Court concluded that a State's assessment of a use tax in such circumstances violates the commerce clause of the Federal Constitution, art. 1, § 8, because "a vendor whose only contacts with the taxing State are by mail or common carrier lacks the 'substantial nexus' required by the Commerce Clause." Quill Corp. v. North Dakota, supra, citing National Bellas Hess, Inc. v. Department of Revenue of Ill., supra. This is a far cry from invoking a rule that the acts of a delivery agent cannot, for taxation purposes, be attributed to the sender of mailed items of tangible property. Indeed, in D.H. Holmes Co. v. McNamara, 486 U.S. 24, 32, 108 S.Ct. 1619 (1988), which was cited approvingly in Quill Corp. v. North Dakota, supra, the Supreme Court concluded, in circumstances similar to those present here, that it "verge[d] on the nonsensical" to claim that the taxpayer did not have control over catalogs that it directed the United States Postal Service to deliver to residents of the taxing State.

5. Of course, it remains the case that for an assessment of a use tax on mailed promotional material to be consistent with the commerce clause of the United States Constitution, art. 1, § 8, it must be shown, among other things, that the sender has a "substantial nexus" with the

Moreover, the economic and commercial reality of the taxpayer's distribution of the catalogs clearly warrants the conclusion that the taxpayer made a taxable "use" of the catalogs in Massachusetts. As the board found, the taxpayer's avowed purpose in mailing the catalogs to Massachusetts addressees was the solicitation of purchase orders from current and prospective customers. By means of the catalogs, then, the taxpayer advertised its merchandise and offered goods for sale in the Commonwealth, and provided Massachusetts residents the means for making purchases (i.e., toll-free telephone number and mail order forms). The catalogs were thus intended to, and did, serve as an instrument in the taxpayer's conduct of a commercial enterprise within the Commonwealth. We conclude that the term "use" in G.L. c. 64I, § 2, encompasses such a commercial utilization of direct mail catalogs and like promotional materials to conduct business in Massachusetts markets * * *.[6]

The absence of the term "distribution" from G.L. c. 64I, §§ 1, 2, does not preclude our construing the term "use" in these statutes to encompass an interstate mailing of promotional materials such as catalogs. Any significance which might be attributed to this absence is outweighed by the Legislature's having defined "use" broadly to "mean[ ] and include[ ] ... the exercise of any right or power over tangible personal property incident to the ownership of that property," G.L. c. 64I, § 1, a definition that plainly encompasses a taxpayer's directing another to deliver to intended recipients property to which the taxpayer holds legal title.[7]

* * *

The conclusion we reach today accords with the modern trend among jurisdictions that have addressed this issue. In D.H. Holmes Co. v. McNamara, 486 U.S. 24, 32, 108 S.Ct. 1619 (1988), the United States Supreme Court upheld Louisiana's assessment of a use tax on the taxpayer's in-State distribution of catalogs via interstate mail. While we recognize, as did the board below, that the *D.H. Holmes Co.* case involved a

---

Commonwealth, including a physical presence in Massachusetts. The taxpayer here, who operated retail stores in Massachusetts throughout the relevant tax periods, has not challenged the Commonwealth's constitutional authority to assess a use tax on its interstate mailings.

6. This conclusion is further supported by a leading authority on State taxation:

"In our view, physical control or possession of the catalogs or preprints ... are inappropriate measuring rods for determining whether a taxable use of the promotional materials in the state by the vendors took place. Use ought to be judged by economic standards.... '[A]dvertising is used by advertisers ... for the purpose of making sales.' The economic utilization of the promotional materials lies in getting them to the prospective customers in the state. The advertiser, which had the articles produced, delivered them to the prospects through its agents—the printer, the Post Office, the common carrier, or the private trucker. Such delivery in the state and such exploitation of the state's market by the taxpayer or its agents on its behalf ought to be treated as a taxable use of the catalogs or advertising supplements in the market state." 2 J. & W. Hellerstein, State Taxation, § 16.03[3][a], at 16–19 (3d ed.1998).

7. We note, additionally, that during the relevant tax period, the taxpayer self-assessed and paid the use tax on catalogs shipped to its Massachusetts retail stores and distributed to customers there. The taxpayer thus appears to concede that the distribution of catalogs, as such, falls within the statutory definition of a taxable "use." Its argument, therefore, reduces to its claim that the postal service, not the taxpayer, distributed the direct mail catalogs in Massachusetts, a claim which we have adequately addressed above.

Federal constitutional challenge to a State's authority to tax interstate commerce, we nevertheless consider the Supreme Court's reasoning instructive with respect to the issue of a taxpayer's control of property sent into a taxing State by means of the United States Postal Service. For in concluding that the taxpayer had a substantial nexus with Louisiana that would justify the State's assessment of a use tax on the taxpayer's interstate mailings, the Supreme Court reasoned, in part, that the taxpayer's claim that it lacked control over the catalogs' in-State distribution "verge[d] on the nonsensical," as the taxpayer "ordered and paid for the catalogs and supplied the list of customers to whom the catalogs were sent; any catalogs that could not be delivered were returned to it ... [and the taxpayer] admit[ted] that it initiated the distribution to improve its sales and name recognition among Louisiana residents.... The [taxpayer's] distribution of catalogs to ... Louisiana customers was directly aimed at expanding and enhancing its Louisiana business." Id. In the wake of the Supreme Court's decision, the overwhelming majority of State appellate courts that have considered the issue have concluded that a taxpayer's distribution of merchandise catalogs and other promotional materials via interstate mail constitutes a taxable "use" of those materials in the destination State. See, e.g., Service Merchandise Co. v. Arizona Dep't of Revenue, 188 Ariz. 414, 417, 937 P.2d 336 (1996); Talbots, Inc. v. Schwartzberg, 928 P.2d 822, 823–824 (Colo.App.1996); Sharper Image Corp. v. Miller, 240 Conn. 531, 540, 692 A.2d 774 (1997); Sharper Image Corp. v. Department of Revenue, 704 So.2d 657, 659–660 (Fla. 1st DCA 1997), cert. denied, 526 U.S. 1016, 119 S.Ct. 1249 (1999); Collins v. J.C. Penney Co., 218 Ga.App. 405, 407–410, 461 S.E.2d 582 (1995); American Express Travel Related Servs. Co. v. Tax Comm'n, 128 Idaho 902, 903–905, 920 P.2d 921 (1996); J.C. Penney Co. v. Balka, 254 Neb. 521, 527, 577 N.W.2d 283 (1998); J.C. Penney Co. v. Olsen, 796 S.W.2d 943, 945 (Tenn.1990). See also Sharper Image Corp. v. Comptroller of the Treasury, Md. Tax Ct. No. 582, 1993 WL 226248 (Feb. 18, 1993); Comfortably Yours, Inc. v. Director, Div. of Taxation, 12 N.J.Tax 570, 574–578 (1992).[9],[10]

---

9. Both the board and the taxpayer note that, in some instances where State appellate courts have held the use tax applicable to the interstate distribution by mail of catalogs and promotional materials, the use tax statute in question expressly denoted "distribution" either as a taxable activity or as an element of the definition of "use." However, our review of these cases reveals that, although the statutes at issue expressly mentioned "distribution," these courts nevertheless concluded that the taxpayer's distribution of merchandising and promotional materials was encompassed by the more general term "use."

10. The taxpayer cites numerous State appellate court decisions that have held the use tax inapplicable in circumstances comparable to those presented here. However, of these cases, only one postdates D.H. Holmes Co. v. McNamara, 486 U.S. 24, 108 S.Ct. 1619 (1988). In Sharper Image Corp. v. Department of Treasury, 216 Mich.App. 698, 702–703, 550 N.W.2d 596 (1996), on which the board relied in its decision, the Michigan Court of Appeals reasoned that, for that State's use tax to apply, "a taxpayer must perform in Michigan one of the activities listed in the definition of 'use,'" and because "distribution" was not included in that list, the tax could not be applied to the taxpayer's mailing of merchandise catalogs. As we have noted above, however, G.L. c. 64I, § 1, does not list specific examples of activities constituting a taxable "use" of property, but instead defines "use" broadly as "the exercise of any right or power" incident to the ownership of tangible personal property. Finally, after reviewing the cited appellate decisions that predate D.H. Holmes Co. v. McNamara, supra, we conclude that their reasoning is unpersuasive, as many rely on the untenable view that a taxpayer who utilizes the interstate mails to deliver

Finally, as we have already observed, the underlying policy of G.L. c. 64I, § 2, supports the assessment of a use tax on property purchased outside Massachusetts for, inter alia, "use" within the Commonwealth in order both to prevent the loss of sales tax revenue to neighboring States and to ensure that Massachusetts businesses may compete on an even footing with their counterparts in other States with lower or nonexistent sales taxes. To hold the use tax inapplicable to the circumstances of this case would frustrate each of these policy goals by allowing a merchant operating in Massachusetts to avoid taxes altogether on promotional materials it uses to generate retail business in the Commonwealth merely by arranging to have these materials produced in, and mailed to prospective Massachusetts customers from, other States that impose no sales tax on the purchase of these materials. Such an outcome, by encouraging Massachusetts merchants to have their promotional mailings produced out-of-State, would clearly result in a loss of sales tax revenue for the Commonwealth, and would put Massachusetts companies that produce such promotional materials under a competitive disadvantage relative to producers in those other States. Moreover, there is no danger that merchants subject to a Massachusetts use tax on their interstate promotional mailings will suffer from an excessive, cumulative tax burden, as the Legislature has provided a credit against assessed use taxes for any sales taxes paid to other jurisdictions that offer a similar credit for sales taxes paid to the Commonwealth. See G.L. c. 64I, § 7(c).

In sum, the assessment of a use tax on catalogs and other promotional materials that a Massachusetts merchant sends to residents of the Commonwealth by interstate mail is consistent both with the plain language of G.L. c. 64I, § 2, and its underlying policy. * * *

Decision of the Appellate Tax Board reversed.

NOTES AND QUESTIONS

A. As the *J.C. Penney* opinion indicates, there has been a considerable amount of controversy in the state courts over the question whether a vendor whose catalogs are distributed in the state has "used" such catalogs within the meaning of the state use tax provisions. The trend of the decisions, as the court observed, is to find a taxable use. Any constitutional objection to the imposition of a use tax under these circumstances—i.e., circumstances in which the taxpayer itself has nexus with the state—was removed by the *D.H. Holmes* decision, discussed in *J.C. Penney.*

B. *Delineation of Taxable Use, Storage, and Consumption: Overview.* The state statutes defining the words "use," "storage," and "consumption"

---

promotional materials to residents of the taxing State, because it does not itself have physical possession of the property in the State, lacks real or substantial control over the mailed materials. See, e.g., Modern Merchandising, Inc. v. Department of Revenue, 397 N.W.2d 470, 472 (S.D.1986); District of Columbia v. W. Bell & Co., 420 A.2d 1208, 1209 (D.C.Ct.App.1980); Bennett Bros. v. State Tax Comm'n, 62 A.D.2d 614, 615, 405 N.Y.S.2d 803 (N.Y.App.Div.1978); Mart Realty, Inc. v. Norberg, 111 R.I. 402, 410–411, 303 A.2d 361 (1973); Hoffmann–LaRoche, Inc. v. Porterfield, 16 Ohio St.2d 158, 162, 45 O.O.2d 486, 243 N.E.2d 72 (1968).

to which the use tax applies generally do so in sweeping terms. For example, Florida's statute defines "use" as "the exercise of any right or power over tangible personal property incident to the ownership thereof, or interest therein, * * *." Fla. Stat. Ann. § 212.02(20) (Westlaw 2009). It defines "storage" as "any keeping or retention in this state of tangible personal property for use or consumption in this state or for any purpose other than sale at retail in the regular course of business." Id. § 212.02(18). Most other state statutes contain similar definitions.

Despite the broad definitions of "use," "storage," and "consumption" in the state statutes, the scope of the use tax is not all-encompassing. First, because the use tax is complementary to the sales tax, it cannot, as a constitutional matter, apply to a broader set of transactions than those to which the sales tax applies. See, e.g., Associated Industries of Missouri v. Lohman, 511 U.S. 641, 114 S.Ct. 1815 (1994) (invalidating Missouri's state-wide use tax, which was designed to equalize local option sales taxes, insofar as it applied to Missouri localities without local option sales taxes or with local option sales taxes imposed at rates lower than state-wide use tax); Halliburton Oil Well Cementing Co. v. Reily, 373 U.S. 64, 83 S.Ct. 1201 (1963). As a consequence, any exemptions or exclusions applicable to the sales tax are likewise applicable to the use tax. For example, if a taxpayer purchases an item outside the state for resale, the use tax will not be applicable when the taxpayer brings the property into the state. Since the in-state purchase for resale is exempt from the state's sales tax, see pp. 646–54 supra, the out-of-state purchase for resale must likewise be exempt from the state's use tax. To do otherwise would unconstitutionally discriminate in favor of in-state purchases for resale over out-of-state purchases for resale. Most of the state statutes reflect this constitutional imperative by explicitly extending to the use tax whatever exemptions or exclusions apply to the sales tax.

Second, notwithstanding the complementary nature of sales and use taxes, there is no *constitutional* imperative that use taxes be as extensive as sales taxes. For example, states are free (subject to state uniformity and federal equal protection provisions) to exclude from use tax property purchased outside the state that it would tax if purchased within the state. Indeed, many states do not extend their use tax to services that are taxable if sold within the state.

C. *Construction of "Purchased for Use" Provisions.* Roughly half of the states confine their use tax to tangible personal property purchased for use within the state. John F. Due & John L. Mikesell, Sales Taxation: State and Local Structure and Administration 247–248 (2d ed. 1994). As a consequence, such states usually do not apply their use tax to goods purchased for use in other states but subsequently brought into the state for storage, use, or consumption there. The other half of the states, however, apply their use tax to tangible personal property brought into the state regardless of whether the property was originally purchased for use in the state or were used elsewhere before being brought into the state. To accommodate for the fact that the property may have been used elsewhere, some of these states reduce the use tax base from the original purchase price of the property to the value of the property when first brought into the state.

Iowa's statute contains the typical restriction on use taxes to property "purchased for use in this state." Iowa Code § 423.5 (Westlaw 2009). The statute was at issue in a case involving an Idaho-based company engaged in large construction jobs. The company brought heavy construction equipment into Iowa in 1945 to work on the Rock Island Railroad. It had purchased much of the equipment during a period of eight years prior to the commencement of the Iowa job in other states where it had used the equipment. The taxpayer conceded Iowa use tax liability for the equipment it had purchased immediately prior to commencing the Iowa job, but contested liability for the other equipment as not having been "purchased for use" in Iowa. The Iowa taxing authorities assessed the tax on the original purchase price of all the equipment. The court held that the statute does not "impose a tax upon personal property first used in this State for a limited period long after its purchase and use in other States, without prior intent to use it here." Morrison–Knudsen Co. v. State Tax Commission, 242 Iowa 33, 44 N.W.2d 449, 451 (1950).

D. *Use Tax Imposed Long After Initial Purchase in States Without "Purchased for Use" Provisions.* In Matter of Atlantic Gulf & Pacific Co. v. Gerosa, 16 N.Y.2d 1, 209 N.E.2d 86, 261 N.Y.S.2d 32 (1965), appeal dismissed, 382 U.S. 368, 86 S.Ct. 553 (1966), the court upheld the application of New York City's use tax to dredging equipment that the taxpayer (1) purchased outside the state and used in states other than New York for eight years, (2) subsequently brought into the city for dredging contracts in the city's harbor waters for about six weeks, and (3) thereafter again moved outside the state. The court noted the broad language of the use tax statute, which embraced within its scope the "exercise of any right or power over tangible personal property by the purchaser thereof and includes but is not limited to the receipt, storage or any keeping or retention *for any length of time.*" Id., 209 N.E.2d at 87 (emphasis in original). The court rejected the taxpayer's argument that the sole purpose of the statute was to eliminate sales tax avoidance by imposing a use tax identical with the sales tax only on property purchased outside the city and brought into the city within a reasonable period after the purchase. The court also observed that "[i]t appears that no sales or use tax (on these items) was paid to any other jurisdiction." Id. at 87 n.1. On facts similar to those at issue in the *Atlantic Gulf* case, the Rhode Island Supreme Court reached a similar conclusion. Great Lakes Dredge & Dock Co. v. Norberg, 117 R.I. 600, 369 A.2d 1101 (1977).

One can easily distinguish *Morrison–Knudsen* discussed in Note C supra from *Atlantic Gulf* on the basis of the statutory language. But which decision most fully comports with the purpose of the use tax? If a use tax is a tax on consumption within the state, should not the state apportion the use tax according to the consumption that actually takes place within the state? Would such an apportionment be administratively practicable? Is it constitutionally required? We will consider the latter question in detail in connection with Oklahoma Tax Commission v. Jefferson Lines, Inc., 514 U.S. 175, 115 S.Ct. 1331 (1995), pp. 743–58 infra. Apart from apportionment, is there any other way in which the state could impose a use tax on property used elsewhere that would more accurately reflect the in-state use?

E. *Temporary Use Within the State.* When a taxpayer purchases property outside the state and brings it into the state for a brief period before removing it from the state, or when the taxpayer uses the property in interstate commerce in the state, the applicability of the use tax to the taxpayer's use of the property in the state can raise both constitutional and statutory questions. From a federal constitutional perspective, the Court's repudiation of its earlier doctrine that immunized interstate commerce from state taxation, and its explicit holding that "for Commerce Clause analysis it is largely irrelevant" whether goods are "in the stream of interstate commerce," D.H. Holmes Co. v. McNamara, 486 U.S. 24, 31, 108 S.Ct. 1619 (1988) (discussed in the *J.C. Penney* case) have to a considerable extent removed the constitutional cloud over state taxes imposed on goods that are only temporarily in the state. Nevertheless, significant issues of state statutory construction remain. These issues generally take one of two forms: (1) whether the temporary presence of the property in the state rises to the level of a taxable use and (2) whether the transient use of the property in the state falls within an explicit statutory exemption for property that is used in the state only for a temporary purpose or in interstate commerce.

In Skelton v. Federal Express Corp., 259 Ark. 127, 531 S.W.2d 941 (1976), the taxpayer transported 18 of its jet aircraft into Arkansas, where they remained for approximately 50 days for modifications, prior to being used in the taxpayer's air carrier operations. They had not been placed in service in the state. Over the objection that the use tax statute was inapplicable since it did not apply to "any article of tangible personal property purchased, produced or manufactured outside this State until the transportation of such article has finally come to rest within this State," id., 531 S.W.2d at 944, the court declared:

> The extensive modification of the jets in Arkansas was "incidental" to the transportation of the aircraft * * * but it was for the purposes of the owner. So here the aircraft left the stream of commerce and "finally came to rest" in Arkansas and consequently were subject to taxation at this point.

Id.

There are literally scores of other cases involving the application of use tax statutes to planes, boats, and motor vehicles used briefly in the state, and the decisions are sharply divided. See 2 Jerome R. Hellerstein & Walter Hellerstein ¶ 18.03 (3d ed. 2002 & Cum. Supp. 2009) (collecting the cases). Following the Arkansas Supreme Court's decision in *Federal Express*, the Arkansas legislature amended the statute to exempt from use tax aircraft brought into the state for repairs for less than 60 days. Ark. Code Ann. § 26–53–115 (Westlaw 2009). If such an exemption is no longer required by constitutional restraints, why would a state enact such an exemption?

F. *Application of Use Tax to Property Distributed Without Charge.* When a taxpayer purchases property outside the state and distributes it without charge within the state, the issue arises in a variety of contexts whether the taxpayer's in-state distribution of the property constitutes a taxable use. Sometimes this issue is resolved by reference to the question whether the taxpayer is reselling the property distributed without charge—either on the theory that the "free" item is inextricably linked to an item for which the distributee has paid, and thus should be considered sold to the distributee along with the paid-for item, or on the theory that some third-party (e.g., an advertiser) is furnishing the consideration for the item. In such cases, the essential inquiry is whether the sale for resale exemption applies. See, e.g., Mercury Cellular Tel. Co. v. Calcasieu Parish, 773 So.2d 914, 918 (La. App. 2000), cert. denied, 787 So.2d 314 (La. 2001) (cellular phone service provider liable for use tax on cell phones distributed "free" to subscribers) (prior law). We have considered those issues above (see pp. 646–54 supra) and need not revisit them here.

A taxpayer's out-of-state purchase of tangible personal property for in-state distribution without charge may raise a second set of issues, however, that are peculiar to the use tax. Even if the distributed items are not exempt from tax under the resale exemption, the question remains whether the taxpayer's distribution of the items—or the distribution of the items on behalf of the taxpayer—constitutes a taxable "use," "storage," or "consumption" within the meaning of the statutes. State courts have generally held that taxpayers use free samples that they purchase outside the state and distribute to potential customers within the state. See, e.g., Ciba Vision Corp. v. Jackson, 248 Ga.App. 688, 548 S.E.2d 431 (2001) (contact drug and ophthalmic drug manufacturer liable for use tax on free samples distributed to licensed dispensers); International Thomson Publishing, Inc. v. Tracy, 79 Ohio St.3d 415, 683 N.E.2d 1091 (1997) (textbook publisher subject to use tax on free "examination copies" it furnishes to teachers).

G. *Use of Property Produced by Taxpayer.* When a manufacturer uses property it produces in its own business, a number of states treat the use as taxable—as if the manufacturer had purchased the property for its own use. If such uses are not taxable, it provides an economic advantage to those who can produce their own property vis-à-vis those who must purchase such property from third parties. For example, Denver's use tax statute provides that "[a] manufacturer of tangible personal property is taxable under this article upon the use or consumption by the manufacturer of items of tangible personal property manufactured by it that it also sells or installs for a price in the ordinary course of its business at retail * * * " Denver Rev. Mun. Code § 53–106, quoted in Western Paving Constr. Co. v. Beer, 917 P.2d 344, 346–47 (Colo. App. 1996). Construing this provision, a Colorado appellate court held that a highway construction company was taxable on aggregates (a mixture of loose rocks and sand) that it combined with asphaltic cement to make asphalt for use in its construction activities. The court declared:

> In effect, [taxpayer's] use of the asphalt it has manufactured is treated as the equivalent of a sale at retail. The resulting basis for imposition of the resulting tax liability is the gross value of all the materials, labor, and services employed in the production of the manufactured property, including the value of the aggregate.

Id. at 348.

H. *Legislative Relief From Multiple Sales and Use Taxes: Credits for Sales or Use Taxes Paid to Other States.* From a policy standpoint, there is no warrant for a double sales or use tax, merely because articles are bought in one jurisdiction and used in another or are used in more than one state. In fact, every state that imposes a use tax provides a credit for sales or use taxes paid to other states. All States Tax Guide (RIA) ¶ 256 (2009) (chart), available at www.checkpoint.riag.com. Article V. of the Multistate Tax Compact, which 20 states have adopted (see Chapter 7, pp. 535–36 supra), provides:

> Each purchaser liable for a use tax on tangible personal property shall be entitled to full credit for the combined amount or amounts of legally imposed sales or use taxes paid by him with respect to the same property to another State and any subdivision thereof. The credit shall be applied first against the amount of any use tax due the State, and any unused portion of the credit shall then be applied against the amount of any use tax due a subdivision.

In State v. Sinclair Pipeline Co., 605 P.2d 377 (Wyo. 1980), the taxpayer purchased pipe for delivery in Canada that it stored temporarily in Colorado, where the pipe was covered with a protective coating. The pipe was then shipped to Wyoming for use in the pipeline. After the taxpayer had paid use tax to Wyoming, Colorado issued a notice of deficiency claiming use taxes were due based on the use of the pipe in Colorado. The taxpayer paid the Colorado tax and sought a refund of the Wyoming tax, apparently conceding that Colorado was correct in its assertion of use tax liability. The court, construing the Multistate Tax Compact's credit provision, nevertheless denied the refund. It declared:

> The statute says that a taxpayer who has *"paid"* his tax to one state will receive a credit upon any tax which may be due another state on that same property. In the instant matter, Sinclair had *paid* the Wyoming tax before Colorado ever assessed the taxpayer. * * *
>
> We need not look to any general rules of use taxation to read this statute. Paid means paid. Nothing could be more clear. It is the past tense of pay. It means that payment has occurred. Under Article *v.* [of the Multistate Tax Compact], when a proper use-tax payment has occurred in one state, another taxing entity seeking to impose a use tax on the same property must give credit to the taxpayer for the first-paid tax. That is what the statute says and we are not allowed to give it another meaning.

Id. at 379–80 (emphasis in original).

Utah, like Wyoming, has adopted the Multistate Tax Compact's provision for a credit against the state's use taxes for sales or use taxes paid to other states with respect to the sale or use of tangible personal property. The Utah Supreme Court, however, has adopted a different approach to the ordering issue than that adopted in Wyoming by holding that "precedence in liability shall prevail over precedence in payment." Chicago Bridge & Iron Co. v. State Tax Comm'n, 839 P.2d 303, 309 (Utah 1992) (quoting Resolution of Multistate Tax Commission). Accordingly it refused to permit a taxpayer a credit against Utah use taxes for use taxes paid to other states, when the equipment subject to the use tax was first used in Utah. Broadcast International, Inc. v. Utah State Tax Commission, 882 P.2d 691 (Utah App. 1994).

Is the Wyoming court's ruling or the Utah court's ruling the sounder approach to the ordering issue raised by the cases? Does the language of the

Multistate Tax Compact point to one approach rather than the other? Which ruling is more in keeping with the purposes of the crediting provisions? With considerations of administrative ease? For a useful survey of the practice with regard to credits for sales or use taxes paid to other states, see Sandra B. McCray, "Commerce Clause Sanctions Against Taxation on Mail Order Sales: A Reevaluation," 17 Urb. Law. 529, 529–36 (1985).

Wholly apart from the policy considerations underlying the grant of a credit against use tax liability for sales or use taxes paid to other states, such a credit clearly seems to be required as a matter of constitutional law, at least if a state provides a credit against (or exemption from) the state's use tax for goods or services purchased within the state and taxed under the state's sales tax (as all states do). Otherwise there would be discrimination against out-of-state purchases. See Oklahoma Tax Commission v. Jefferson Lines, Inc., 514 U.S. 175, 115 S.Ct. 1331 (1995), pp. 743–58 infra; General Motors Corp. v. City and County of Denver, 990 P.2d 59, 70 (Colo. 1999); Walter Hellerstein, et al., "Commerce Clause Restraints on State Taxation After *Jefferson Lines*," 51 Tax L. Rev. 47 (1995); Walter Hellerstein, "Is 'Internal Consistency' Foolish?: Reflections on an Emerging Commerce Clause Restraint on State Taxation," 87 Mich. L. Rev. 138, 160–61 (1988).

I. *Border State Problems.* Every state imposing sales and use taxes encounters difficulties with its communities that border on neighboring tax-free states or states with substantially lower rates. Local merchants in the former states complain that they lose trade as a result of the levies because their customers go across state lines to purchase goods. While the customers are typically subject to the state's use tax when they bring the goods back into their home state there is, as a practical matter, ordinarily no ready means of checking most sales, and people are not usually given to reporting such purchases voluntarily. Where a customer goes to a store in one state and there buys goods which are delivered to her in her state of residence, that state cannot ordinarily impose a duty on the out-of-state vendor to collect the use tax. See Quill Corp. v. North Dakota, 504 U.S. 298, 112 S.Ct. 1904 (1992), pp. 24–38 supra; Miller Bros. Co. v. Maryland, 347 U.S. 340, 74 S.Ct. 535 (1954). Town Fair Tire Centers, Inc. v. Commissioner of Revenue, 454 Mass. 601, 911 N.E.2d 757 (2009) (prohibiting state from requiring retailer with stores both within and without state from collecting use tax on out-of-state over-the-counter sales to in-state customers, in the absence of a statutory presumption regarding in-state use). Some articles, however, such as automobiles, must be registered in the buyer's state of residence, and the state can enforce the use tax in connection with the registration. We consider the problem of requiring the out-of-state vendor to collect the use tax in more detail in Section I infra.

G. MISCELLANEOUS EXEMPTIONS AND EXCLUSIONS FROM SALES AND USE TAXES

All states provide for exemptions and exclusions from the retail sales and use tax base. We have already considered exemptions and exclusions built into the structure of the retail sales tax, including provisions dealing with sale for resale; manufacturing, processing, and fabrication; machinery or equipment used in the manufacture, production, or processing of tangible personal property to be sold; and containers and packaging. In addition, the states provide exemptions for other tax policy reasons, such as tax equity or the encouragement of industrial location in the state. States generally exempt purchases by charitable, religious, and educational organizations. Many states also exempt purchases of food, medical devices, prescription drugs, and consumer purchases of gas and electricity. See generally All States Tax Guide (RIA) ¶¶ 253–55 (2009) (charts), available at www.checkpoint.riag.com; John F. Due & John L. Mikesell, Sales Taxation: State and Local Structure and Administration 75–88 (2d ed. 1994).

Notes and Questions

A. *Casual, Occasional, or Isolated Sales.* Virtually all of the states exempt "casual," "occasional," or "isolated" sales. All States Tax Guide (RIA) ¶ 253 (2009) (chart), available at www.checkpoint.riag.com. These exemptions typically apply to sales by those who are not regularly engaged in the business of selling, although some states' exemptions exclude occasional sales of motor vehicles, vessels, and aircraft from the casual sales provisions. Id. In Arizona Dep't of Revenue v. Mountain States Tel. & Tel. Co., 113 Ariz. 467, 556 P.2d 1129 (1976), for example, the court held that the casual sale provision exempted from tax the sale by a telephone company of a telephone communications system to the U.S. Department of the Army. "The facts submitted by the parties clearly support the conclusion that Mountain Bell made an unanticipated and isolated sale of its equipment to the United States Government. We cannot say that Mountain Bell is in the business of selling telephone communications equipment on the basis of one sale." Id., 556 P.2d at 1131.

Washington's sales tax does not apply to a "casual or isolated sale," which is defined as "a sale made by a person who is not engaged in the business of selling the type of property involved." Wash. Rev. Code Ann. § 82.04.040(2) (Westlaw 2009). A rent-a-car agency contended that its resale of rental vehicles to the original dealer after 10,000 to 20,000 miles of use constituted casual sales and were therefore not taxable. The court rejected this argument, noting that it was irrelevant for purposes of the statute whether the taxpayer realized a profit on the transactions and that the sale of late-model used cars was a regular part of the taxpayer's business. Budget Rent–A–Car of Washington–Oregon, Inc. v. Washington State Department of Revenue, 81 Wash.2d 171, 500 P.2d 764 (1972).

What is the underlying rationale for the casual sale exemption? Is it the administrative impracticality of asking persons not generally engaged in retailing—such as a family conducting a garage sale—to collect the tax, or it is something more? Does the fact that the seller at a garage sale generally already paid tax when the item was purchased new help you answer this question? Compare the tax treatment of a retailer, both at the time inventory is purchased and the time it is resold to the ultimate consumer, with the tax treatment of a casual seller. Can these differing treatments be reconciled?

The California statute exempts "occasional sales" from tax and defines an "occasional sale" as including:

> A sale of property not held or used by the seller in the course of activities for which he or she is required to hold a seller's permit * * * provided that the sale is not one of a series of sales sufficient in number, scope and character to constitute an activity for which he or she is required to hold a seller's permit * * *.

Cal. Rev. & Tax. Code § 6006.5(a) (Westlaw 2009).

The California Supreme Court held that, under this statute, the sale by a paper mill and wire mill of all of their assets failed to qualify for the exemption, because the capital assets in question were "held or used" in the course of business for which the mills were required to hold sellers' permits. Davis Wire Corp. v. State Bd. of Equalization, 17 Cal.3d 761, 553 P.2d 229, 132 Cal.Rptr. 133 (1976). Accord Ramrod, Inc. v. Wisconsin Department of Revenue, 64 Wis.2d 499, 219 N.W.2d 604 (1974). Is such a construction consistent with the underlying purpose of such provisions? See generally Richard D. Pomp & Oliver Oldman, "A Normative Inquiry Into the Base of a Retail Sales Tax: Casual Sales, Used Goods, and Trade–Ins," 43 Nat'l Tax J. 427 (1990).

B. *Exemptions for the Press.* Many sales and use tax statutes provide exemptions for the sale or use of newspapers or periodicals. Multistate Sales Tax Guide (CCH) ¶ 900–500 (2009), available in CCH Internet Tax Research Network. These exemptions raise both statutory and constitutional issues. The statutory issues generally relate to the question whether the publication under review has met the specified criteria for the exemption (e.g., whether it has sufficient editorial, as distinguished from advertising, content or whether it appears with sufficient frequency). The constitutional issues generally relate to First Amendment concerns (e.g., whether the exemption discriminates against some segment of the media or discriminates on the basis of content). See, e.g., Leathers v. Medlock, 499 U.S. 439, 111 S.Ct. 1438 (1991) (sustaining sales tax that applied to cable television but not to satellite broadcast or print media, because it did not single out the press, or a narrow group within the press, or discriminate on the basis of content); Arkansas Writers' Project, Inc. v. Ragland, 481 U.S. 221, 107 S.Ct. 1722 (1987) (invalidating sales tax imposed on general interest magazines, but not on newspapers and specialized magazines, because it singled out a small group of magazines and discriminated on the basis of content); Department of Revenue v. Magazine Publishers of Am., 604 So.2d 459, 462 (Fla. 1992) (invalidating newspaper tax exemption because it required a content-based determination whether a publication contained "reports of current events and matters of general interest which appeal to a wide spectrum of the general public"); Stahlbrodt v. Commissioner of Taxation and Finance, 92 N.Y.2d 646, 707 N.E.2d 421, 684 N.Y.S.2d 466 (1998) (sustaining denial of exemption for publication that did not qualify as exempt newspaper because more than 90 percent of the publication's printed area was devoted to advertising). See generally Note, "First Amendment Limits on the Use of Taxes to Subsidize Selectively the Media," 78 Cornell L. Rev. 106 (1992).

C. *Mergers, Reorganizations, Liquidations, and Transfers Between Affiliated Corporations.* Many states exempt transfers of tangible personal property to a corporation in connection with a merger, reorganization, or liquidation. For example, the New York statute excludes from the sales tax base transfers for stock pursuant to a "merger or consolidation," transfers of property to a corporation for its stock upon its organization, and distributions in liquidations to stockholders. N.Y. Tax Law § 1101(b)(4)(iv) (Westlaw 2009). Other states achieve the same result through their occasional sale exemption. Transfers between affiliated corporations are generally subject to sales taxation, unless explicitly exempted. See, e.g., Pemco, Inc. v. Kansas Department of Revenue, 258 Kan. 717, 907 P.2d 863 (1995). See generally Sho Sato, "The Sales Tax and Capital Transactions," 45 Calif. L. Rev. 450 (1957).

ASSIGNMENT

Consider a manufacturing business making a cash sale of it assets to another company that is in the same line of business. The acquiring company intends to use the assets for the same purposes as did the seller. The assets include:

- Manufacturing equipment
- Raw materials used to make the company's end product
- Chemicals and other items consumed in the manufacturing process
- Finished inventory
- Office supplies and equipment
- Vehicles used in the conduct of business
- Land and buildings

Assuming you represented one of the parties to the transaction, how might you argue that the sale of these assets are exempt? Consider not only the casual sale and merger and reorganization exemptions, but also any relevant sales tax exemptions or exclusions that you have already studied.

H. MEASURE OF THE SALES AND USE TAX

The measure of sales and use taxes—i.e., the base against which the rate is applied—is generally the consideration paid for goods or services sold. The Streamlined Sales and Use Tax Agreement (SSUTA), discussed at pp. 784–99 infra, defines "sales price" generally as the amount

> subject to sales tax and means the total amount of consideration, including cash, credit, property, and services, for which personal property or services are sold, leased, or rented, valued in money, whether received in money or otherwise, without any deduction for the following:

A. The seller's cost of the property sold;

B. The cost of materials used, labor or service cost, interest, losses, all costs of transportation to the seller, all taxes imposed on the seller, and any other expense of the seller;

C. Charges by the seller for any services necessary to complete the sale, other than delivery and installation charges;

D. Delivery charges;

E. Installation charges; and

F. Credit for any trade-in, as determined by state law.

States may exclude from "sales price" the amounts received for charges included in paragraphs (C) through (F) above, if they are separately stated on the invoice, billing, or similar document given to the purchaser. * * *

"Sales price" shall not include:

A. Discounts, including cash, term, or coupons that are not reimbursed by a third party that are allowed by a seller and taken by a purchaser on a sale;

B. Interest, financing, and carrying charges from credit extended on the sale of personal property or services, if the amount is separately stated on the invoice, bill of sale or similar document given to the purchaser; and

C. Any taxes legally imposed directly on the consumer that are separately stated on the invoice, bill of sale or similar document given to the purchaser.

SSUTA, App. C, pt. 1 (definitions).

NOTES AND QUESTIONS

A. *Discounts, Coupons, and Rebates.* A cash discount given by the seller at the time of the sale, and not dependent on time of payment, volume of purchases, or the like, is usually excluded from the sales tax base, on the ground that the discount is not part of the price. SSUTA, for example, provides that " '[s]ales price' shall not include: * * * Discounts, including cash, term, or coupons that are not reimbursed by a third party that are allowed by a seller and taken by a purchaser on a sale." SSUTA, App. C, pt. 1 (definitions). Because manufacturers' coupons are reimbursed by "a third party" (the manufacturer), they do not reduce the sales tax base under SSUTA. Many non-SSUTA states also include manufacturers' coupons and rebates within the measure of the tax. See 2 Jerome R. Hellerstein & Walter Hellerstein, State Taxation ¶ 17.06[2] (3d ed. 2001 & Cum. Supp. 2009). Similar rules apply with respect to cash rebates made by third parties. The rationale for including rebates within the measure of the sales tax, as one court articulated it, is that

> [w]e see nothing in the Act or the regulations * * * permitting a seller to deduct from his gross receipts an amount paid by a third party directly to

the purchaser even though the purpose of the payment is to reimburse the purchaser for a part of the purchase price. The gross receipts of the seller remain the same whether or not a rebate is paid by someone not directly involved in the sale.

Keystone Chevrolet Co. v. Kirk, 69 Ill.2d 483, 14 Ill.Dec. 455, 372 N.E.2d 651, 653 (1978). See also Ortbals v. Director of Revenue, 871 S.W.2d 435 (Mo. 1993).

Does the distinction between retailers' coupons and rebates and manufacturers' coupons and rebates make sense in terms of retail sales tax policy? The answer to that question would seem to turn on whether the measure of the sales tax should be determined by reference to the consideration that the retailer receives or the consideration that the consumer ultimately pays. Which perspective is the proper one from the standpoint of a retail sales tax? See generally John A. Swain, "Sausage–Making Streamlining–Style: Coupons, Rebates, and Third–Party Payments," State Tax Notes, Sept. 13, 2004, p. 794.

B. *Taxes.* Should amounts representing payment of a tax be included in the measure of taxable receipts under a retail sales tax? For example, when a consumer purchases gasoline, alcohol, or tobacco, the total cost of which includes a federal excise tax, should the measure of the state retail sales tax include the amounts reflecting payment of the federal tax? The determination whether the tax is imposed on the consumer is an important factor in resolving this question. Thus, if the levy is imposed on the consumer, as is the case in the federal tax on transportation of persons (I.R.C. § 4261), there is no warrant for including the amount of such a tax in the vendor's sales price, for it is merely a collector of the federal tax. On the other hand, where the tax is imposed on the vendor, e.g., the federal excise tax on certain tires (I.R.C. § 4071), a stronger case can be made for regarding the entire purchase price, including the tax, as within the measure of the sales tax.

In Gurley v. Rhoden, 421 U.S. 200, 95 S.Ct. 1605 (1975), the Supreme Court held that the federal excise tax on gasoline and lubricating oils (see I.R.C. §§ 4081 et seq.) legally fell on statutory producers (which included gasoline vendors who purchased gasoline from producers) and not on purchaser-consumers, even though the latter may have borne the economic burden of the tax. It thus upheld the application of Mississippi's retail sales tax, whose legal incidence is on the vendor, to a producer-vendor's receipts, which included an amount corresponding to the federal excise tax. In American Oil Co. v. Mahin, 49 Ill.2d 199, 273 N.E.2d 818 (1971), on the other hand, the Illinois Supreme Court found the legal incidence of the Illinois Motor Fuel Tax fell on the consumer and therefore was not includable in the measure of the state's sales whose legal incidence fell on retailers. Note, however, that the Illinois court also held that the legal incidence of the *federal* excise tax on gasoline fell on the producer-distributor and therefore *was* includable in the measure of the Illinois sales tax base. Martin Oil Service, Inc. v. Department of Revenue, 49 Ill.2d 260, 273 N.E.2d 823 (1971).

How are taxes treated under SSUTA?

C. *Trade–Ins.* Trade-ins present interesting questions under the sales tax statutes. Where A goes to a dealer and trades in her old car for a new one, receiving an allowance of $1,000 on a $10,000 new car, are there two taxable sales? Is the sales tax on the new car measured by $10,000 or $9,000? And is the dealer required to collect a tax when he resells the car received in the trade-in? Historically, these issues produced extensive litigation. See 2 Jerome R. Hellerstein & Walter Hellerstein, State Taxation ¶ 17.10 (3d ed. 2001 & Cum. Supp. 2009). Today, the overwhelming majority of states exclude the value of trade-ins, either by statute or case law. All States Tax Guide (RIA) ¶ 256 (2009) (chart), available at www.checkpoint.riag.com. Several states, including California, Maryland, Michigan, and North Carolina, however, allow no reduction in the sales tax measure for the value of the trade-in. Id.

What is the theoretically proper treatment of the value of the trade-in in connection with the purchase of a new item? In answering that question, it may be helpful to consider the following hypothetical: A buys a new car from dealer D for $10,000 and pays tax of $500. Three years later A buys another new car from D, again for $10,000, but receives a $5000 trade-in allowance for her old car. D subsequently sells the car it purchased from A to B for $6000. What is the proper sales tax treatment of D's second sale of a new car to A (along with A's trade-in) and D's sale of A's traded car to B? Does the current law in most states (exempting the value of the trade-in on the sale from D to A but taxing the full value of the sale from D to B) reflect a theoretically sound solution to the problem? See generally Richard D. Pomp & Oliver Oldman, "A Normative Inquiry Into the Base of a Retail Sales Tax: Casual Sales, Used Goods, and Trade–Ins," 43 Nat'l Tax J. 427 (1990).

D. *Customer Loyalty Programs.* Businesses often use "points," "frequent flyer miles," "trading stamps," and similar awards to encourage customer loyalty and repeat business. When a customer redeems these awards to acquire otherwise taxable goods, has a taxable sale taken place? A Virginia ruling addressed a customer loyalty program administered by a company that owned and franchised hotels worldwide including Virginia. During their stay, participating customers would earn "points" that they later could redeem for complimentary accommodations at any of the taxpayer's hotels. In order to fund the complimentary stays, each hotel would pay a monthly fee to a reserve fund based on the number of points earned by a hotel's customers that month, and when a customer redeemed points for use at a hotel, the hotel would receive a certain amount of money from the reserve fund. Relying on an earlier ruling that analogized hotel customer loyalty points to a retailer's discount coupon, the Virginia Tax Commissioner ruled that no tax was due on the exchange of points for a room. The taxing authority further ruled that no tax was due in connection with payments to or distributions from the reserve fund, reasoning that transfers in and out of the fund do not involve the exchange of taxable personal property or services. The Commissioner also observed that "the money contributed to the fund was taxed upon receipt from the hotel's customers. The hotel is merely receiving back the money contributed to the fund following a qualified sale." Ruling of the Tax Commissioner, P.D. 07–12, 2007 WL 1101290, at *1 (Va. Dep't Rev. March 23, 2007)

A New York administrative law judge (ALJ) rejected a taxpayer's claim that the credit she received against the purchase price of an automobile from points earned using her General Motors credit card should be excluded from the taxable sales price. As in the Virginia ruling, the ALJ reasoned by analogy from the rules governing coupons. In this case, however, because the dealer was not the issuer of the points but was instead being reimbursed by the manufacturer, General Motors, the apt analogy was with manufacturers' coupons, which are treated in New York (and in most other states) as includable in the taxable sales price. In re Nan S. Zavoski, No. 819119, 2003 WL 22162455 (NY Div. Tax App. September 11, 2003). See Note A supra for a discussion of the sales tax treatment of coupons.

Some states treat trading stamps as in substance a cash discount and accordingly reduce the measure of the tax by the value of the trading stamps. When the stamps are redeemed, a sales tax becomes payable on the value of the articles transferred. See Cal. Code Regs. tit. 18, § 1671 (Westlaw 2009) ("Trading stamps and related promotional plans").

E. *Transportation Charges.* The states generally do not tax transportation or delivery services as such. For example, if a business hires a common carrier to ship its products, or if an individual hires a moving company to transport his or her household goods, the states generally do not tax those transportation services. John F. Due & John L. Mikesell, Sales Taxation: State and Local Structure and Administration 95 (2d ed. 1994). The major sales tax controversies involving transportation and delivery services relate to the charges for the transportation or delivery of the goods by the retailer to its customer. Although some states tax the services of transporting and delivering tangible personal property, whether or not separately stated and charged to the consumer of the property, the general rule is that transportation and delivery charges, if quoted separately to the buyer, are not included in the taxable price. If they are not separately stated, however, they are included in the taxable figure. All States Tax Guide (RIA) ¶ 256 (2009) (chart), available at www.checkpoint.riag.com.

Some of the states that exempt separately stated transportation or delivery charges to the purchaser, however, also insist that the delivery be made f.o.b. store or other distribution point or that the customer actually make the payment for the transportation charge directly to the carrier. Due & Mikesell, supra, at 95; All States Tax Guide (RIA) ¶ 256 (2009) (chart), available at www.checkpoint.riag.com. Additionally, the states virtually always impose sales tax on transportation or delivery "charges in" (i.e., those made by a manufacturer or wholesaler to a retailer before the buyer takes title to the property) even if separately rebilled by the retailer to its customer. For example, the sticker on a new automobile will normally show a separately stated "destination charge," representing transportation costs to the dealer, but such destination charges are invariably included in the taxable retail sales price of the automobile. For a detailed consideration of transportation charges, see 2 Jerome R. Hellerstein & Walter Hellerstein, State Taxation ¶ 15.06 (3d ed. 2000 & Cum Supp. 2009).

F. *Installment Sales.* At what point is the tax to be collected in an installment or conditional sale—when the goods are delivered, or as the price is paid, or at the time the final payment is made? According to Due and Mikesell,

the actual practice of the states in this matter is not easy to ascertain. Frequently, the issue is not mentioned in the acts or even in the rulings and regulations. Even when it is mentioned, practice does not always agree with the wording of the published material. Twenty-five of the 45 sales tax states and the District of Columbia require the sales (accrual) basis as the standard procedure for determining tax liability. Arkansas, Maine, Mississippi, North Dakota, and Wyoming permit vendors to request a cash basis. Vermont offers vendors a choice * * * New Jersey, New York, and Washington laws provide that administrators may provide regulations for cash reporting on installment sales, but none have chosen to do so.

John F. Due & John L. Mikesell, Sales Taxation: State and Local Structure and Administration 38 (2d ed. 1994). Which approach is preferable from a theoretical standpoint? From an administrative standpoint? Are the considerations justifying installment sale reporting of income for federal income tax purposes equally applicable to installment sale reporting of "receipts" for sales tax purposes?

G. *Tips and Service Charges.* Are tips and service charges includable in the measure of a retail sales tax? Some cases turn on the question whether the employer derives any benefit from the tips or charges at issue. Thus, in Anders v. State Bd. of Equalization, 82 Cal.App.2d 88, 185 P.2d 883 (1947), the court held that tips to waitresses were includable in the measure of the tax to the extent that they were credited against the minimum wages due and payable to the waitresses; but the excess was not taxable. In St. Paul Hilton Hotel v. Commissioner, 298 Minn. 202, 214 N.W.2d 351 (1974), the court held the sales tax inapplicable to service charges added to customers' bills and apportioned among hotel employees, no part of which went to the hotel as operating revenue. Other cases turn on the question whether the tips or service charges are mandatory or voluntary. In Cohen v. Playboy Clubs Int'l, Inc., 19 Ill.App.3d 215, 311 N.E.2d 336 (1974), the court held that a mandatory 15 percent service charge was includable within the measure of the tax. Where the only compulsion on the club members to observe the club's tipping schedule was social, the Tennessee Supreme Court held that the tips were voluntary and therefore not part of the "sale price" of the services. Memphis Country Club v. Tidwell, 503 S.W.2d 919 (Tenn. 1973).

I. COLLECTION OF THE TAX BY THE VENDOR

As anyone who has ever paid a sales tax knows, the sales tax is generally collected by the retail vendor from the purchaser. Retail vendors generally collect use taxes as well, at least when they are subject to the state's taxing jurisdiction. See Quill Corp. v. North Dakota, 504 U.S. 298, 112 S.Ct. 1904 (1992), pp. 24–38 supra. Although taxpayers sometimes make use tax payments directly to the state, e.g., in the case of large corporations that self-assess use taxes and in the case of items that must be registered with the state (e.g., motor vehicles), the overwhelming majority of sales and use tax collections are made by vendors, who must remit the taxes to the state. States therefore must establish administrative machinery for assuring proper collection and payment of the sales and use tax if the levy is to operate successfully.

All sales tax states have some system for registering vendors. John F. Due & John L. Mikesell, Sales Taxation: State and Local Structure and Administration 131 (2d ed. 1994). Once a vendor registers with the state, it is authorized to make sales at retail, and it is required to collect and remit taxes on taxable sales. Id. Most states require monthly returns, although some states require only quarterly filing. Id. at 159. A vendor generally must collect a sales or use tax on any taxable item, unless the purchaser provides the vendor with a certificate establishing that the sale is exempt (e.g., a resale certificate). A vendor is ordinarily liable (either primarily or secondarily) for tax on any taxable transaction, whether or not it collects the tax from the purchaser.

NOTES AND QUESTIONS

A. *Vendor's Duty to Verify Customer's Purchase as Being for Resale.* How far must a vendor go in verifying its customer's assertion that it is purchasing goods for resale? Traditionally, state statutes, regulations, or court decisions have held vendors to a "good faith" standard for accepting a purchaser's exemption certificate. See, e.g., Long Manufacturing Co. v. Johnson, 264 N.C. 12, 140 S.E.2d 744 (1965) (vendor has only the duty of making a reasonable and prudent inquiry to determine whether a resale certificate received from the vendee applied to the latter's intended use of the articles purchased). In some circumstances, however, a vendor's assertion that it acted in good faith in accepting a resale certificate must be viewed with skepticism. See Department of Revenue v. Warren Chemical & Janitor Supply Co., 562 S.W.2d 644, 646 (Ky. App. 1977) ("It is ludicrous that the appellee could have received in good faith the resale certificates from a funeral home which purchased a weed killer, or from the Kentucky State Police in the purchase of toilet bowl cleaner"). Some states have enacted provisions that exonerate a vendor from any duty to collect tax from a purchaser, if the vendor has received from the purchaser a resale certificate in proper form, containing the purchaser's registration number with the state. See N.Y. Tax Law § 1132(c)(1) (Westlaw 2009). The Streamlined Sales and Use Tax Agreement also takes this approach. SSUTA § 317 (2009).

Is the good faith standard a fair compromise between subjecting the vendor to absolute liability and relieving it of all liability so long as the resale certificate is in proper form? Or does it impose an unrealistic standard on, for example, a busy employee at a building supply store who must deal with hundreds of transactions a day and would be hard pressed to go behind the resale certificate she is handed at the time of sale? Moreover, as a practical matter, some employees of busy organizations will be careless and not satisfy standards of "good faith." In such cases, does it make good tax policy to require the seller to pay the tax to the state? The seller, after all, is an involuntary collection agent for the state. Allowing the seller to rely entirely on the proper form of the resale certificate as a defense to tax liability, on the other hand, could lead to substantial evasion of the tax.

B. *Liability of Officers and Shareholders of Corporate Vendor for Sales Tax.* Most states impose personal liability on corporate officers or other corporate employees responsible for filing of tax returns for the corporation's failure to collect and pay sales and use taxes. The Illinois statute, for example, provides that

> [a]ny officer or employee of any taxpayer subject to the provisions of a tax Act * * * who has the control, supervision or responsibility of filing returns and making payment of the amount of any trust tax * * * and who wilfully fails to file the return or to make the payment to the Department * * * shall be personally liable for a penalty equal to the total amount of tax unpaid by the taxpayer including interest and penalties thereon.

35 Ill. Comp. Stat. Ann. 735/3–7(a) (Westlaw 2009). In defending against a suit to recover taxes under the predecessor of this provision, corporate officers argued that they had used the taxes in question to pay other creditors and that their actions were not "wilful." The court rejected the argument, declaring that "a voluntary, conscious and intentional failure [to file] satisfies the requirement of 'wilfully fails' under [the statute]." Department of Revenue v. Heartland Investments, Inc., 124 Ill.App.3d 28, 79 Ill.Dec. 525, 463 N.E.2d 1079, 1081 (1984). The court further observed that "in a civil action wilful conduct does not require bad purpose or intent to defraud the government." Id., 463 N.E.2d at 1081.

In one case the court pierced the corporate veil to hold the shareholders personally liable for a corporation's delinquent sales and use taxes. People v. Clauson, 231 Cal.App.2d 374, 41 Cal.Rptr. 691 (2d Dist. 1964). The shareholders, who owned substantially all of the stock of the corporation, exercised complete control over the business of the corporation; they were its "alter ego."

J. THE TAXATION OF INTERSTATE SALES

1. TERRITORIAL RESTRICTIONS ON SALES TAXES

State sales taxes (as distinguished from use taxes) are limited to retail sales occurring within the state. Some sales taxes are so limited by the explicit terms of the statute. See, e.g., Md. Code Ann., Tax–Gen. § 11–102(a)(1) (Westlaw 2009) ("a tax is imposed on (1) a retail sale in the State * * *"). Even if not so limited, the constraints of the Commerce and Due Process Clauses would limit the states to taxing sales that occurred within their borders. In some states, the sales and use tax statutes make it clear that the legislature intends to exercise its full power to tax except as prohibited by the U.S. Constitution. See, e.g., Ga. Code Ann. § 48–8–1 (Westlaw 2009). In other states, however, the statutory definition of a sale may not encompass all sales that are constitutionally taxable. Moreover, the power of local jurisdictions to impose taxes on transactions occurring within the state, but arguably outside the locality, is entirely a matter of state statutory (and, in some instances, state constitutional) law.

Notes and Questions

A. *Limitation of Sales Taxes to Transactions "Consummated" Within the Taxing Jurisdiction.* In Matter of C.G. Gunther's Sons v. McGoldrick, 255 App.Div. 139, 5 N.Y.S.2d 303 (1st Dep't), aff'd, 279 N.Y. 148, 18 N.E.2d 12 (1938), a New York fur merchant frequently deferred delivery of furs that it sold during the warmer months until the customer requested delivery during the colder months. The legislation authorizing New York City to impose a sales tax forbade "the imposition of a tax on any transaction * * * consummated outside of the territorial limits of [the] city." Id., 5 N.Y.S.2d at 305 (quoting the statute). The New York City tax law at issue imposed a two percent tax upon the receipts from every retail sale of tangible personal property in the city, and it defined a sale as the transfer of title or possession or both "or any agreement therefor." Id. Relying on state personal property law, which provided that "property does not pass until goods have been delivered to the buyer or reached the place agreed upon," the court concluded that

> the transactions in question involving future delivery outside the city of New York were not taxable as they were not consummated until the merchandise was delivered to the petitioner's customers outside the territorial limits of the city, including merchandise delivered in interstate commerce to points outside the State of New York.

Id.

New York City does not seek to tax sales of goods "consummated" by delivery of goods outside the city. It does, however, seek to tax sales negotiated outside the city involving goods delivered into the city. Would such a levy have violated the then-prevailing state enabling act provision noted in the *Gunther* case forbidding the city from imposing a tax on "any transaction originating" outside the territorial limits of the city?

B. *Out-of-State Purchases of Property Delivered to Third Parties Within the State.* In Bloomingdale Brothers v. Chu, 70 N.Y.2d 218, 513 N.E.2d 233, 519 N.Y.S.2d 347 (1987), the court held that the state sales tax does not apply to out-of-state purchases of merchandise by nonresidents delivered, at the request of the purchasers, to third persons in New York. The taxing statute, essentially the same provision that was at issue in the *Gunther* case, Note A supra, defines sale as "[a]ny transfer of title or possession or both * * * in any manner or by any means * * * for a consideration, or any agreement therefor." N.Y. Tax Law § 1101(b)(5) (Westlaw 2009). The court declared that "the transactions at issue are not taxable as the purchasers' only control over the property was exercised out of state when they directed petitioner to send the merchandise to New York donees *after the sale was completed.*" Bloomingdale Brothers, 519 N.Y.S.2d at 348–49 (emphasis in original).

A dissenting opinion in the court below had declared:

> To an ordinary person, sales effected by acceptance of orders and payments for the merchandise at a non-resident vendor's out-of-state office might well be considered to have been consummated outside the jurisdiction of New York taxing authorities. Nevertheless, for more than

40 years, it has been the settled law of this State that such transactions are subject to sales tax here if they encompass ultimate physical delivery of the goods in New York, even by common carrier, and even when delivery was F.O.B. the vendor's out-of-state factory. * * *

* * *

* * * [T]he Legislature has broadly defined "sale" for sales tax purposes with the clear intent (1) " 'to encompass most transactions involving the transfer or use of commodities in the business world' " and (2) to defeat tax avoidance devices and to cover transactions essentially the same as others taxed as sales and which, therefore, should be taxed as a matter of economic justice.

Viewed in the light of these undisputably expansive legislative purposes in defining "sale," I have no difficulty in concluding that the sales under review here are taxable. Tax Law § 1101(b)(5) expressly imposes the sales tax on a "transfer of title or *possession* ... for a consideration" (emphasis supplied). Certainly, the Tax Commission could reasonably infer on the basis of the stipulated facts of direct shipment from petitioner's out-of-state stores to its customers' designees in New York that those customers bought and paid for the delivery of the goods in New York as part of their transactions. Each such customer was a "purchaser" who furnished "consideration" for "transfer of ... possession" in New York (Tax Law § 1101[b][5]). Thus, these transactions fall literally within the definitions of Tax Law § 1101. Why, in view of the broadly encompassing statutory language, it should make a difference that the ultimate recipients of the transfer of physical possession in New York are donees/consignees of the purchasers, eludes me. Tax Law § 1101(b)(5) does not expressly require that the transfer of possession in New York be made to the purchaser, and petitioner has not cited us to any statutory language or legislative history excluding a transfer of possession to a donee/consignee of the purchaser as a taxable event. We have previously upheld imposition of the sales tax on the basis of delivery to the New York designee of the purchaser. * * * As a practical matter, the majority's decision will enable purchasers of merchandise at out-of-state stores for delivery in New York to avoid the sales tax by the simple expedient of directing delivery to a designee.

Bloomingdale Brothers v. Chu, 119 A.D.2d 41, 505 N.Y.S.2d 258, 260–61 (3d Dep't 1986) (Levine, J., dissenting) (emphasis in original).

2. TAXATION OF INTERSTATE SALES AND THE OUT–OF–STATE VENDOR'S DUTY TO COLLECT SALES AND USE TAXES

In Chapter 3 we explored Commerce Clause limitations on state taxation, including those bearing on interstate sales activity. See pp. 120–23 supra (dealing with gross receipts taxes on interstate selling activity). In Chapter 2, we considered the jurisdictional limitations on state taxation, including those bearing on nexus sufficient to require an out-of-state mail-order seller to collect a use tax on sales to in-state consumers. See pp. 24–51 supra. In this section, we focus more specifically and systematically on the Commerce and Due Process Clause limitations on state power to tax interstate retail sales and to require an out-of-state vendor to collect taxes on such sales.

McLEOD v. J.E. DILWORTH CO.

Supreme Court of the United States, 1944.
322 U.S. 327, 64 S.Ct. 1023.

GENERAL TRADING CO. v. STATE TAX COMMISSION

Supreme Court of the United States, 1944.
322 U.S. 335, 64 S.Ct. 1028.

INTERNATIONAL HARVESTER CO. v. DEPARTMENT OF TREASURY

Supreme Court of the United States, 1944.
322 U.S. 340, 64 S.Ct. 1019.

[Justice Rutledge wrote the following illuminating opinion concurring and dissenting in the *Dilworth, General Trading,* and *International Harvester* cases, which established the essential constitutional framework for adjudicating the validity of state sales and use taxes on interstate retail sales. The essential facts and the majority's disposition of each of the three cases are set out in Justice Rutledge's opinion.]

MR. JUSTICE RUTLEDGE, concurring in No. 355 (this case) and No. 441, ante, p. 335, and dissenting in No. 311, ante, p. 327:

These three cases present in various applications the question of the power of a state to tax transactions having a close connection with interstate commerce.

In No. 311, McLeod v. J.E. Dilworth Co., ante, p. 327, Arkansas has construed its tax to be a sales tax, but has held this cannot be applied where a Tennessee corporation, having its home office and place of business in Memphis, solicits orders in Arkansas, by mail, telephone or sending solicitors regularly from Tennessee, accepts the orders in Memphis, and delivers the goods there to the carrier for shipment to the purchaser in Arkansas. This Court holds the tax invalid, because "the sale—the transfer of ownership—was made in Tennessee. For Arkansas to impose a tax on such transaction would be to project its powers beyond its boundaries and to tax an interstate transaction." Though an Arkansas "use tax" might be sustained in the same situation, "we are not dealing with matters of nomenclature even though they be matters of nicety." And the case is thought to be different from the Berwind–White case, 309

U.S. 33, where New York City levied the tax, because, in the Arkansas court's language, "the corporation maintained its sales office in New York City, took its contracts in New York City and made actual delivery in New York City...."

On the other hand, in No. 441, General Trading Co. v. State Tax Commission, ante, p. 335, Iowa applies its "use tax" to a transaction in which a Minnesota corporation ships goods from Minnesota, its only place of business, to Iowa purchasers on orders solicited in Iowa by salesmen sent there regularly from Minnesota for that purpose, the orders being accepted in Minnesota. This tax the Court sustains. While "no State can tax the privilege of doing interstate business, ... the mere fact that property is used for interstate commerce or has come into an owner's possession as a result of interstate commerce does not diminish the protection which it may draw from a State to the upkeep of which it may be asked to bear its fair share. But a fair share precludes legislation obviously hostile or practically discriminatory toward interstate commerce.... None of these infirmities affects the tax in this case...." And the foreign or nonresident seller who does no more than solicit orders in Iowa, as the Tennessee seller does in Arkansas, may be made the state's tax collector.

In No. 355, International Harvester Co. v. Dept. of Treasury, ante, p. 340, the state applies its gross income tax, among other situations to one (Class D) where a foreign corporation authorized to do and doing business in Indiana sells and delivers its product in Indiana to out-of-state customers who come into the state for the transaction. The Court sustains the tax as applied.

I

For constitutional purposes, I see no difference but one of words and possibly one of the scope of coverage between the Arkansas tax in No. 311 and the Iowa tax in No. 441. This is true whether the issue is one of due process or one of undue burden on interstate commerce. Each tax is imposed by the consuming state. On the records here, each has a due process connection with the transaction in that fact and in the regular, continuous solicitation there. Neither lays a greater burden on the interstate business involved than it does on wholly intrastate business of the same sort. Neither segregates the interstate transaction for separate or special treatment. In each instance therefore interstate and intrastate business reach these markets on identical terms, so far as the effects of the state taxes are concerned.

And in my opinion they do so under identical material circumstances. In both cases the sellers are "nonresidents" of the taxing state, foreign corporations. Neither seller maintains an office or a place of business there. Each has these facilities solely in the state of origin. In both cases the orders are taken by solicitors sent regularly to the taxing state for that purpose. In both the orders are accepted at the home office in the state of origin. And in both the goods are shipped by delivery to the carrier or the post in the state of origin for carriage across the state line and delivery by it to the purchaser in his taxing state.

In the face of such identities in connections and effects, it is hard to see how one tax can be upheld and the other voided. Surely the state's power to tax is not to turn on the technical legal effect, relevant for other purposes but not for this, that "title passes" on delivery to the carrier in Memphis and may or may not so pass, so far as the record shows, when the Minnesota shipment is made to Iowa. In the absence of other and more substantial difference, that irrelevant technical consideration should not control. However it may be determined for locating the incidence of loss in transit or other questions arising among buyer, seller and carrier, for purposes of taxation that factor alone is a will-o'-the-wisp, insufficient to crux a due process connection from selling to consuming state and incapable of increasing or reducing any burden the tax may place upon the interstate transaction.

The only other difference is in the terms used by Iowa and Arkansas, respectively, to describe their taxes. For reasons of her own Arkansas describes her tax as a "sales tax." Iowa calls hers a "use tax." This court now is committed to the validity of "use" taxes. Similarly, "sales taxes" on "interstate sales" have been sustained. In McGoldrick v. Berwind–White Coal Mining Co., 309 U.S. 33, 60 S.Ct. 388, such a tax applied by the state of the market was upheld. Other things being the same, constitutionality should not turn on whether one name or the other is applied by the state. Wisconsin v. J.C. Penney Co., 311 U.S. 435, 61 S.Ct. 246. * * *

II

The Court's different treatment of the two taxes does not result from any substantial difference in the facts under which they are levied or the effects they may have on interstate trade. It arises rather from applying different constitutional provisions to the substantially identical taxes, in the one case to invalidate that of Arkansas, in the other to sustain that of Iowa. Due process destroys the former. Absence of undue burden upon interstate commerce sustains the latter.

It would seem obvious that neither tax of its own force can impose a greater burden upon the interstate transaction to which it applies than it places upon the wholly local trade of the same character with which that transaction competes. By paying the Arkansas tax the Tennessee seller will pay no more than an Arkansas seller of the same goods to the same Arkansas buyer; and the latter will pay no more to the Tennessee seller than to an Arkansas vendor, on account of the tax, in absorbing its burden. The same thing is true of the Iowa tax in its incidence upon the sale by the Minnesota vendor. The cases are not different in the burden the two taxes place upon the interstate transactions. Nor in my opinion are they different in the existence of due process to sustain the taxes.

"Due process" and "commerce clause" conceptions are not always sharply separable in dealing with these problems. To some extent they overlap. If there is a want of due process to sustain the tax, by that fact alone any burden the tax imposes on the commerce among the states becomes "undue." But, though overlapping, the two conceptions are not identical. There may be more than sufficient factual connections, with economic and legal effects, between the transaction and the taxing state to sustain the tax as against due process objections. Yet it may fall because of its burdening effect upon the commerce. And, although the two notions cannot always be separated, clarity of consideration and of decision would be promoted if the two issues are approached, where they are presented, at least tentatively as if they were separate and distinct, not intermingled ones.

Thus, in the case from Arkansas no more than in that from Iowa should there be difficulty in finding due process connections with the taxing state sufficient to sustain the tax. As in the Iowa case, the goods are sold and shipped to Arkansas buyers. Arkansas is the consuming state, the market these goods seek and find. They find it by virtue of a continuous course of solicitation there by the Tennessee seller. The old notion that "mere solicitation" is not "doing business" when it is regular, continuous and persistent is fast losing its force. In the *General Trading* case it loses force altogether, for the Iowa statute defines this process in terms as "a retailer maintaining a place of business in this State." The Iowa Supreme Court sustains the definition and this Court gives effect to its decision in upholding the tax. Fiction the definition may be; but it is fiction with substance because, for every relevant constitutional consideration affecting taxation of transactions, regular, continuous, persistent solicitation has the same economic, and should have the same legal, consequences as does maintaining an office for soliciting and even contracting purposes or maintaining a place of business, where the goods actually are shipped into the state from without for delivery to the particular buyer. There is no difference between the Iowa and the Arkansas situations in this respect. Both involve continuous, regular, and not intermittent or casual courses of solicitation. Both involve the shipment of goods from without to a buyer within the state. Both involve taxation by the state of the market. And if these substantial connections are sufficient to underpin the tax with due process in the one case, they are also in the other.

That is true, if labels are not to control, unless something which happens or may happen outside the taxing state operates in the one case to defeat the jurisdiction, but does not defeat it in the other.

As I read the Court's opinion, though it does not explicitly so state, the Arkansas tax falls because Tennessee could tax the transaction and, as between the two states, has exclusive power to do so. This is because "the sale—the transfer of ownership—was made in Tennessee." Arkansas' relation to the transaction is constitutionally different from that of New York in the *Berwind-White* case, though both are the state of the market, because the Berwind–White Company "maintained its sales office in New York City, took its contracts in New York City and made actual delivery in New York City." This "constituted a sale in New York and accordingly we sustained a retail sales tax by New York." So here the company's "offices are maintained in Tennessee, the sale is made in Tennessee, and the delivery is consummated either in Tennessee or in interstate commerce. * * * " The inevitable conclusion, it seems to me, is that the Court is deciding not only that Arkansas cannot tax the transaction but that Tennessee can tax it and is the only state which can do so. To put the matter shortly, Arkansas cannot levy the tax because Tennessee can levy it. Hence "for Arkansas to impose a tax on such transaction would be to project its powers beyond its boundaries and to tax an interstate transaction."

This statement of the matter appears to be a composite of due process and commerce clause ideas. If so, it is hard to see why the same considerations do not nullify Iowa's power to levy her tax in the identical circumstances and vest exclusive jurisdiction in Minnesota to tax these transactions. For in the Iowa case the selling corporation maintains its office and place of business in Minnesota, accepts the orders there, and the delivery, which is to carrier or post, is consummated, so far as the record shows, exactly in the manner it is made in the Tennessee–Arkansas transaction. If these facts nullify Arkansas' power to tax the transaction by vesting exclusive jurisdiction in Tennessee, it would seem *a fortiori* they would nullify Iowa's power and give Minnesota exclusive jurisdiction to tax the transactions there involved. Unless the sheer difference in the terms "sale" and "use," and whatever difference these might make as a matter of legislative selection of the transactions which are to bear the tax, are to control upon the existence of the power to tax, the result should be the same in both cases.

Merely as a matter of due process, it is hard to see why any of the four states cannot tax the transactions these cases involve. Each has substantial relations and connections with the transaction, the state of market not less in either case than the state of origin. It "sounds better" for the state of origin to call its tax a "sales tax" and the state of market to name its tax a "use tax." But in the *Berwind–White* case the latter's "sales tax" was sustained, where it is true more of the incidents of sale conjoined with the location of the place of market than do in either No. 311 or No. 441. If this is the distinguishing factor, as it might be for selecting one of the two connected jurisdictions for exclusive taxing power, it is not one which applies to either of these transactions. The identity is not between the *Dilworth* case and *Berwind–White*. It is rather between *Dilworth* and *General Trading*, with *Berwind–White* differing from both. And, so far as due process alone is concerned, it should make no difference whether the tax in the one case is laid by Arkansas or Tennessee and in the other by Iowa or Minnesota. Each state has a sufficiently substantial and close connection with the transaction, whether by virtue of tax benefits conferred in general police protection and otherwise or on account of ideas of territorial sovereignty concerning occurrence of "taxable incidents" within its borders, to furnish the due process foundation necessary to sustain the exercise of its taxing power. Whether it exerts this by selecting for "impingement" of the tax some feature or incident of the transaction which it denominates "sale" or "use" is both illusory and unimportant in any bearing upon its constitutional authority as a matter of due process. If this has any substantive effect, it is merely one of legislative intent in selecting the transactions to bear the tax and thus fixing the scope of its coverage, not one of constitutional power. "Use" may cover more transactions with which a state has due process connections than "sale." But whenever sale occurs and is taxed the tax bears equally, in final incidence of burden, upon the use which follows immediately upon it.

The great difficulty in allocating taxing power as a matter of due process between the state of origin and the state of market arises from the fact that each state, considered without reference to the other, always has a sufficiently substantial relation in fact and in tax benefit conferred to the interstate transaction to sustain an exertion of its taxing power, a fact not always recognized. And from this failure, as well as from the terms in which statutes not directed specifically to reaching these transactions are cast, comes the search for some "taxable incident taking place within the state's boundaries" as a hook for hanging constitutionality under due process ideas. "Taxable incident" there must be. But to take what is in essence and totality an interstate transaction between a state of origin and one of market and hang the taxing power of either state upon some segmented incident of the whole and declare that this does or does not "tax an interstate transaction" is to do two things. It is first to ignore that any tax hung on such an incident is levied on an interstate transaction. For the part cannot be separated from the whole. It is also to ignore the fact that each state, whether of origin or of market, has by that one fact alone a relation to the whole transaction so substantial as to nullify any due process prohibition. Whether the tax is levied on the "sale" or on the "use," by the one state or by the other, it is in fact and effect a tax levied on an interstate transaction. Nothing in due process requirements prohibits either state to levy either sort of tax on such transactions. That Tennessee therefore may tax this transaction by a sales tax does not, in any proper conception of due process, deprive Arkansas of the same power.

III

When, however, the issue is turned from due process to the prohibitive effect of the commerce clause, more substantial considerations arise from the fact that both the state of origin and that of market exert or may exert their taxing powers upon the interstate transaction. The long history of this problem boils down in general statement to the formula that the states, by virtue of the force of the commerce clause, may not unduly burden interstate commerce. This resolves itself into various corollary formulations. One is that a state may not single out interstate commerce for special tax burden. McGoldrick v. Berwind–White Coal Mining Co., 309 U.S. 33, 55–56, 60 S.Ct. 388, 397, 398. Nor may it discriminate against interstate commerce and in favor of its local trade. Welton v. Missouri, 91 U.S. at 275; Guy v. Baltimore, 100 U.S. 434; Voight v. Wright, 141 U.S. 62, 11 S.Ct. 855. Again, the state may not impose cumulative burdens upon interstate trade or commerce. Gwin, White & Prince v. Henneford, 305 U.S. 434, 59 S.Ct. 325; Adams Mfg. Co. v. Storen, 304 U.S. 307, 58 S.Ct. 913. Thus, the state may not impose certain taxes on interstate commerce, its incidents or instrumentalities, which are no more in amount or burden than it places on its local business, not because this of itself is discriminatory, cumulative or special or would violate due process, but because other states also may have the right constitutionally, apart from the commerce clause, to tax the same thing and either the actuality or the risk of their doing so makes the total burden cumulative, discriminatory or special.

In these interstate transactions cases involving taxation by the state of origin or that of market, the trouble arises, under the commerce clause, not from any danger that either tax taken alone, whether characterized as "sales" or "use" tax, will put interstate trade at a disadvantage which will burden unduly its competition with the local trade. So long as only one tax is applied and at the same rate as to wholly local transactions, no unduly discriminatory clog actually attaches to the interstate transaction of business.

The real danger arises most obviously when both states levy the tax. Thus, if in the instant cases it were shown that, on the one hand, Arkansas and Iowa actually were applying a "use" tax and Tennessee and Minnesota a "sales" tax, so that in each case the interstate transaction were taxed at both ends, the heavier cumulative burden thus borne by the interstate business in comparison with the local trade in either state would be obvious. If in each case the state of origin were shown to impose a sales tax of three per cent and the state of market a use tax of the same amount, interstate transactions between the two obviously would bear double the local tax burden borne by local trade in each state. This is a difference of substance, not merely one of names, relevant to the problem created by the commerce clause, though not to that of "jurisdiction" under due process conceptions. And the difference would be no less substantial if the taxes levied by both the state of origin and that of market were called "sales" taxes or if, indeed, both were called "use" taxes.

The Iowa tax in No. 441 avoids this problem by allowing credit for any sales tax shown to be levied upon the transaction whether in Iowa or elsewhere. Clearly therefore that tax cannot in fact put the interstate transaction at a tax disadvantage with local trade done in Iowa or elsewhere.

However, the Arkansas tax in No. 311 provides for no such credit. But in that case there is no showing that Tennessee actually imposes any tax upon the transaction. If there is a burden or clog on commerce, therefore, it arises from the fact that Tennessee has power constitutionally to impose a tax, may exercise it, and when this occurs the cumulative effect of both taxes will be discriminatorily burdensome, though neither tax singles out the transaction or bears upon it more heavily than upon the local trade to which it applies. In short, the risk of multiple taxation creates the unconstitutional burden which actual taxation by both states would impose in fact.

In my opinion this is the real question and the only one presented in No. 311. And in my judgment it is determined the wrong way, not on commerce clause grounds but upon an unsustainable application of the due process prohibition.

Where the cumulative effect of two taxes, by whatever name called, one imposed by the state of origin, the other by the state of market, actually bears in practical effect upon such an interstate transaction, there is no escape under the doctrine of undue burden from one of two possible alternatives. Either one tax must fall or, what is the same thing, be required to give way to the other by allowing credit as the Iowa tax does, or there must be apportionment. Either solution presents an awkward alternative. But one or the other must be accepted unless that doctrine is to be discarded and one of two extreme positions taken, namely, that neither state can tax the interstate transaction or that both may do so until Congress intervenes to give its solution for the problem. It is too late to accept the former extreme, too early even if it were clearly desirable or permissible to follow the latter.

As between apportionment and requiring one tax to fall or allow credit, the latter perhaps would be the preferable solution. And in my opinion it is the one which the Court in effect, though not in specific statement, adopts. That the decision is cast more largely in terms of due process than in those of the commerce clause does not nullify that effect.

If in this case it were necessary to choose between the state of origin and that of market for the exercise of exclusive power to tax, or for requiring allowance of credit in order to avoid the cumulative burden, in my opinion the choice should lie in favor of the state of market rather than the state of origin. The former is the state where the goods must come in competition with those sold locally. It is the one where the burden of the tax necessarily will fall equally on both classes of trade. To choose the tax of the state of origin presents at least some possibilities that the burden it imposes on its local trade, with which the interstate traffic does not compete, at any rate directly, will be heavier than that placed by the consuming state on its local business of the same character. If therefore choice has to be made, whether as a matter of exclusive power to tax or as one of allowing credit, it should be in favor of the state of market or consumption as the one most certain to place the same tax load on both the interstate and competing local business. Hence, if the risk of taxation by both states may be said to have the same constitutional consequences, under the commerce clause, as taxation in actuality by both, the Arkansas tax, rather than the power of Tennessee to tax, should stand.

It may be that the mere risk of double taxation would not have the same consequences, given always of course a sufficient due process connection with the taxing states, that actual double taxation has, or may have, for application of the commerce clause prohibition. Risk of course is not irrelevant to burden or to the clogging effect the rule against undue burden is intended to prevent. But in these situations it may be doubted, on entirely practical grounds, that the mere risk Tennessee may apply its taxing power to these transactions will have any substantial effect in restraining the commerce such as the actual application of that power would have. In any event, whether or not the choice must be made now or, as I think, has been made, it should go in favor of Arkansas, not Tennessee.

For all practical purposes Indiana's gross income tax in No. 355 may be regarded as either a sales tax or a use tax laid in the state of market, comparable in all respects (except in words) to the Arkansas tax laid in No. 311 and to the Iowa tax imposed in No. 441, except that here the seller as well as the buyer does business and concludes the transaction in Indiana, the state of the market. This is clearly true of Classes C and E. It is true also of Class D, in my opinion, although the buyer there resided in Illinois but went to Indiana to enter into the transaction and take delivery of the goods. That he at once removed them on completion of the transaction there, to Illinois, intended to do this from the beginning and this fact may have been known to the seller, does not take from the transaction its character as one entered into and completed in Indiana. Whether or not Illinois, in these circumstances, could impose a use tax or some other as a property tax is not presented and need not be determined. If the Arkansas and Iowa taxes stand, as either does, *a fortiori* the Indiana tax stands in these applications.

Accordingly, I concur in the decisions in Nos. 441 and 355, but dissent from the decision in No. 311.

NOTES AND QUESTIONS

A. The Court's decisions in *Dilworth, General Trading,* and *International Harvester*—and, particularly in *Dilworth* and *General Trading*—established the basic constitutional ground rules governing state sales and use taxation of interstate retail sales transactions. The Commerce Clause forbade the taxation of interstate sales because (under the Court's pre-*Complete Auto* understanding of the Commerce Clause) the states could not tax interstate commerce, and a tax on interstate sales was a tax on interstate commerce. Neither the Commerce Clause nor the Due Process Clause, on the other hand, forbade a use tax on property that was the subject of an interstate sale, because the taxable event was the local use of property that lay within the state's taxing power. The critical question regarding the taxation of interstate retail sales transactions therefore became whether the out-of-state vendor had sufficient connection with the state to enable the state to require the vendor to collect the use tax from the in-state customer. Over the next half-century, the Court struggled with that question in a series of cases culminating in Quill Corp. v. North Dakota, 504 U.S. 298, 112 S.Ct. 1904 (1992), pp. 24–38 supra.

Although you have already studied the latest episode in this story in Chapter 2 (which considers *Quill* and the post-*Quill* cases), the ensuing Notes briefly survey the pre-*Quill* case law, which is essential to a full understanding of the present state of the law regarding jurisdiction to require an out-of-state seller to collect a use tax.

B. Miller Brothers v. Maryland: *Use Tax on Out-of-State Over-the-Counter Goods Delivered to Customers in Retailer's Trucks.* A Wilmington, Delaware department store, with no offices or employees in Maryland, sold merchandise to Maryland customers, who came to the store to make their purchases. Some of the customers received delivery of the merchandise at the store. In other cases, the goods were delivered to them in Maryland by common carrier or by the store's trucks. The facts showed that the department store sold about $12,000 worth of merchandise over a 4½ year period to Maryland purchasers for use in Maryland. The department store delivered about two-thirds of this merchandise into Maryland in its own trucks. Maryland sought to require the department store to collect the state's use tax on all sales to its residents, no matter how delivery was made. Upon the department store's refusal to comply, Maryland seized one of the store's trucks while in the state to make deliveries. In a five-to-four decision, the Supreme Court held that the Maryland action violated the Due Process Clause and noted that it need not consider the Commerce Clause issue. Miller Bros. Co. v. Maryland, 347 U.S. 340, 74 S.Ct. 535 (1954).

Justice Jackson, writing for the majority, declared that

> little constructive discussion can be found in responsible commentary as to the grounds on which to rest a state's power to reach extraterritorial transactions on non-residents with tax liabilities. * * * But the course of decisions does reflect at least consistent adherence to one time-honored concept: that due process requires some definite link, some minimum connection between a state and the person, property or transaction it seeks to tax.

Id., 347 U.S. at 344–45.

After referring to the holding in McLeod v. J.E. Dilworth Co., supra, and concluding from that case that "Maryland could not have reached this Delaware vendor with a sales tax on these sales," the Court asked whether the same Delaware sale can be made

> a basis for imposing on the vendor liability for use taxes due from her own inhabitants? It would be strange law that would make appellant more vulnerable to liability for another's tax than to a tax on itself.

Id. at 346. Did not *General Trading* establish the precise result, which Justice Jackson refers to as "strange law," by imposing a tax-collection duty on a vendor in circumstances where the vendor could not have been made the taxpayer?

Justice Douglas dissented in an opinion joined by Chief Justice Warren and Justices Black and Clark. The dissent found

> no constitutional difficulty in making appellant a tax collector for Maryland under the general principles announced in General Trading Co. v. Tax Commission * * *.
>
> This is not a case of minimal contact between a vendor and the collecting State. Appellant did not sell cash-and-carry without knowledge of the destination of the goods; and its delivery truck was not in Maryland upon a casual, nonrecurring visit. Rather there has been a course of conduct in which the appellant has regularly injected advertising into media reaching Maryland consumers and regularly effected deliveries within Maryland by its own delivery trucks and by common carriers.

Id. at 357–58.

C. Scripto, Inc. v. Carson: *Presence of Independent Contractors in the State as the Basis for Imposition of Use Tax Collection Obligation on Out-of-State Vendor.* In Scripto, Inc. v. Carson, 362 U.S. 207, 80 S.Ct. 619 (1960), a Georgia corporation had no office or regular employees in Florida, but it employed wholesalers or jobbers to solicit sales of its products in Florida. The Court held that Florida could constitutionally impose upon the Georgia seller the duty of collecting a state use tax upon goods shipped to customers in Florida. Although the sales representatives in Florida were not Scripto's employees, the Court declared that whether Scripto's in-state representatives were characterized as "employees" or "independent contractors" was "a fine distinction without constitutional significance." Id., 362 U.S. at 207.

D. National Bellas Hess, Inc. v. Department of Revenue: *The Interstate Mail–Order Sale.* In National Bellas Hess, Inc. v. Department of Revenue, 386 U.S. 753, 87 S.Ct. 1389 (1967), the Court held that the Commerce and Due Process Clauses prohibited Illinois from imposing a use tax collection obligation on an out-of-state mail-order seller with no physical presence in state. In so holding, the Court declared:

> In order to uphold the power of Illinois to impose use tax burdens on National in this case, we would have to repudiate totally the sharp distinction which these and other decisions have drawn between mail order sellers with retail outlets, solicitors, or property within a State, and those who do no more than communicate with customers in the State by mail or common carrier as part of a general interstate business. But this basic distinction, which until now has been generally recognized by the state taxing authorities, is a valid one, and we decline to obliterate it.

Id., 386 U.S. at 758.

E. National Geographic Society v. State Board of Equalization: *In–State Presence Unrelated to Mail–Order Sales Activity as the Basis for Assertion of Use Tax Collection Obligation Over Out-of-State Seller.* In National Geographic Society v. State Bd. of Equalization, 430 U.S. 551, 97 S.Ct. 1386 (1977), the National Geographic Society, a District of Columbia corporation, made substantial mail-order sales of maps, atlases, globes, and books to California residents who responded to its magazine and direct mail solicitations. The Society also maintained two California offices, which solicited advertising for its magazine, but it conducted no activities relating to its mail-order business from those offices. California assessed a use tax against the Society on its mail-order sales to California customers. The California Supreme Court sustained the state's position, reasoning that the "slightest presence" of the seller within the state established a sufficient nexus to require the seller to collect use tax. Although the United States Supreme Court affirmed, it disavowed the state court's "slightest presence" test, stating:

> Our affirmance of the California Supreme Court is not to be understood as implying agreement with that court's "slightest presence" standard of constitutional nexus. Appellant's maintenance of two offices in the State, and solicitation by employees assigned to those offices of advertising copy in the range of one million dollars annually, establish a much more substantial presence than the expression "slightest presence" connotes. Our affirmance thus rests upon our conclusion that appellant's maintenance of the two offices in California and activities there adequately establish a relationship or "nexus" between the Society and the State that renders constitutional the obligations imposed upon appellant * * *

Id., 430 U.S. at 556.

In response to the Society's contention that the case was controlled by *Bellas Hess,* the Court said that its opinion in that case had

> carefully underscored * * * the "sharp distinction ... between mail order sellers with retail outlets, solicitors, or property within [the taxing] State, and those [like Bellas Hess] who do no more than communicate with customers in the State by mail or common carrier as part of a general interstate business." Appellant Society clearly falls into the former category.

Id. at 559.

The Court also rejected the Society's argument that the two California offices should be disregarded for purposes of determining whether the requisite nexus existed because such offices played no role with respect to the mail-order sales at issue:

> The Society argues in other words that there must exist a nexus or relationship not only between the seller and the taxing State, but also between the activity of the seller sought to be taxed and the seller's activity within the State. We disagree. However fatal to a direct tax a "showing that particular transactions are dissociated from the local business ...," Norton Co. v. Department of Revenue, supra, 340 U.S. 537, 71 S.Ct. 380, such dissociation does not bar the imposition of the use tax collection duty. * * * [T]he relevant constitutional test to establish the requisite nexus for requiring an out-of-state seller to collect and pay the use tax is not whether the duty to collect the use tax relates to the seller's activities carried on within the State, but simply whether the facts demonstrate "some definite link, some minimum connection, between [the State and] the *person* ... it seeks to tax." Miller Bros. v.

Maryland, supra, 347 U.S., at 344–345, 74 S.Ct., at 539. (Emphasis added.) Here the Society's two offices, without regard to the nature of their activities, had the advantage of the same municipal services—fire and police protection, and the like—as they would have had if their activities * * * included assistance to the mail order operations that generated the use taxes.

Id. at 560–61.

Would *National Geographic* have been decided the same way if National's advertising operations had been conducted by a separate corporate subsidiary in California?

F.   Quill Corp. v. North Dakota: *Reaffirmation of* National Bellas Hess *and the Bifurcation of Commerce and Due Process Nexus Analysis.* In Quill Corp. v. North Dakota, 504 U.S. 298, 112 S.Ct. 1904 (1992), set out at pp. 24–38 supra, the Court reaffirmed the holding of *Bellas Hess* that a state could not impose a use tax collection obligation on an out-of-state seller with no physical presence in the state. The Court rested its opinion entirely on the absence of "substantial nexus" under the Commerce Clause. The Court relied heavily on stare decisis considerations and was careful to limit its nexus holding to the mail-order sales context. Moreover, the Court found that the Due Process Clause did not bar the imposition of use tax collection responsibilities on physically absent vendors who purposefully availed themselves of the benefits of the state.

To complete your study of the constitutional limitations on the taxation of interstate sales and the out-of-state vendor's duty to collect sales and use taxes, you should reread *Quill* and the materials following the case (pp. 24–42 supra). Is *Miller Brothers v. Maryland* still good law after *Scripto, National Geographic,* and *Quill?*

G.   *Evasion of Use Taxes on Out-of-State Purchases.* With the exception of property that has to be registered, such as automobiles, boats, and airplanes, the practical problems of preventing use tax evasion in cases of goods bought in other states have proved extremely difficult. Congress took an important step in assisting states in enforcing use taxes in 1949 when it passed an act designed to eliminate avoidance of cigarette sales and use taxes through mail order purchases in non-sales tax states. 63 Stat. 884, Pub.L. No. 363, 1949, 81st Cong., 1st Sess. (1949), codified at 15 U.S.C. § 375. The act required persons selling cigarettes in interstate commerce shipped to persons other than licensed distributors to report all such sales to the taxing authority of the state into which the goods are shipped. The courts sustained the validity of this act in Consumer Mail Order Ass'n of America v. McGrath, 94 F.Supp. 705 (D.D.C. 1950), aff'd, 340 U.S. 925, 71 S.Ct. 500 (1951).

The most significant problem of evasion of use taxes is the states' inability to collect taxes on out-of-state mail order and Internet sales. Although there is considerable uncertainty about the precise revenue loss figures, because of the lack of reliable data and the ever changing Internet environment, there is no question that the losses are significant. One recent study, for example, conservatively estimates that annual revenue losses will reach $11.4 billion to $12.64 billion by 2012. Donald Bruce, William Fox & LeAnn Luna, "State and Local Government Sales Tax Revenue Losses from Electronic Commerce," State Tax Notes, May 18, 2009, p. 537.

The states' inability to force the out-of-state vendor to collect taxes on mail order sales, regardless of the volume of business conducted in the state by mail order seller, stems from the limits imposed on state tax power by *Bellas Hess* and *Quill*. Although legislation has been introduced in Congress from time to time that would authorize the states to require remote vendors to collect use taxes on mail-order sales, see, e.g., "The Sales Tax Fairness and Simplification Act," H.R.3396, 110th Cong., 1st Sess. (2007); "The Consumer and Main Street Protection Act of 1995," S. 545, 104th Cong., 1st Sess. (1995), and the U.S. Supreme Court virtually invited such legislation in *Quill*, a political stalemate between the states and the mail-order industry has thus far prevented the enactment of such legislation. The growth of electronic commerce has spurred renewed concern over these questions, and we consider them in more detail in Section K infra.

H. *Drop Shipments.* A drop shipment sale occurs when a retailer directs its supplier to ship goods directly to the retailer's customer. Drop shipment sales therefore involve two separate sales transactions: (1) the sale by Supplier to Retailer, and (2) the sale by Retailer to Customer. If all of the relevant events occur within a single state with which each of the parties has substantial nexus, the transaction raises no unusual sales and use tax issues. The sale by Supplier to Retailer is a sale for resale; the state recognizes the sale-for-resale certificate that Retailer provides to Supplier; and Supplier collects no tax from Retailer on the sale, because no tax is due. The sale by Retailer to Customer, however, is a retail sale, and Retailer collects a sales tax from Customer measured by the retail price of the product.

But now suppose that these events do not all occur in the same state and that Supplier, Retailer, and Customer do not each have nexus with the state in which the goods are delivered to Customer. Assume, for example, that Customer in State A orders goods from Retailer, which has no nexus in State A, and Retailer fulfills the order by directing Supplier, which has nexus in State A, to ship the goods directly to Customer in State A. While State A has no power to require Retailer to collect a use tax from Customer, because Retailer has no nexus with State A, can it require Supplier, which does have nexus with State A, to collect the tax? If it can, what will be the measure of the tax, the wholesale or the retail price? If it is the former, is not State A effectively imposing a tax on a wholesale transaction that is generally exempt from tax? If it is the latter, how will Supplier know the price at which Retailer has sold the goods to Customer, a transaction to which it is not a party?

In Steelcase, Inc. v. Crystal, 1994 WL 622100 (Conn. Super. Tax Oct. 26, 1994), aff'd on other grounds, 238 Conn. 571, 680 A.2d 289 (1996), Steelcase manufactured office furniture in Michigan. It sold its furniture to retailers located outside of Connecticut, and the retailers directed Steelcase to ship the furniture to their customers in Connecticut. Under the sales contract between Steelcase and the retailers, title to the furniture passed from Steelcase to the retailers upon delivery to a common carrier in Michigan. The Connecticut Department of Revenue Services (DRS) sought to impose a sales tax on Steelcase, although measured by the price that Steelcase charged to the retailer rather than on the price paid by the ultimate consumer. DRS's theory was that the delivery of furniture by Steelcase to the ultimate consumer in Connecticut was a retail sale under the Connecticut statute which provides:

The delivery in this state of tangible personal property by an owner or former owner thereof or by a factor, if the delivery is to a consumer pursuant to a retail sale made by a retailer not engaged in business in this state, is a retail sale in this state by the person making the delivery. Such person shall include the retail selling price of the property in such person's gross receipts.

Conn. Gen. Stat. Ann. § 12–407(a)(3)(A) (Westlaw 2009). The statute also provided, however, that sales for resale fell outside the scope of the tax, and Steelcase relied on this provision (along with its good faith receipt of a resale certificate from the retailer) in resisting application of the tax.

In a thoughtful opinion, the court held that "if the sales and use tax law is to be read as a coherent whole," the sales in question must be excluded as sales for resale. As the court observed:

[L]ooking at the overall transaction, it is clear that if Steelcase had shipped its furniture to the out-of-state retailers and those retailers had thereupon shipped the furniture to the ultimate Connecticut consumers, Connecticut could not tax Steelcase for its part in the transaction. Under these circumstances, the correct approach would plainly be to impose a use tax on the Connecticut consumer. Why should things be different if the furniture is shipped directly from Steelcase to the Connecticut consumer? This is an economically more efficient method of completing the transaction * * * But the actual flow of dollars remains the same. The most appropriate method to tax this transaction remains the imposition of a use tax on the consumer.

Steelcase, 1994 WL 622100, at *4.

The Connecticut Supreme Court affirmed the trial court's decision, although on a different ground. Steelcase, Inc. v. Crystal, 238 Conn. 571, 680 A.2d 289 (1996). While agreeing with the trial court that Steelcase was making exempt sales for resale, it observed that the statute nevertheless contemplates tax liability on a party other than the actual retailer (including a manufacturer who sells the property to a retailer for resale) when the "owner or former owner" of the property delivers it to a consumer pursuant to a retail sale and the retailer is not doing business in the state. Nevertheless, the court found that Connecticut could not assert tax liability over Steelcase on this basis because delivery occurred in Michigan, since the terms of the contract provided that delivery was "F.O.B. factory."

Construing a statute similar to Connecticut's, the California Court of Appeal held that an in-state wholesaler must charge and remit sales tax when it delivers goods sold by an out-of-state retailer to a local consumer. Lyon Metal Products, Inc. v. State Bd. of Equalization, 58 Cal.App.4th 906, 68 Cal.Rptr.2d 285 (1st Dist. 1997), review denied, (Cal.), cert. denied, 524 U.S. 916, 118 S.Ct. 2298 (1998). It thus reached a conclusion consistent with the views—but not the narrow holding of—the Connecticut Supreme Court in Steelcase.

The drop shipment issue raises troublesome problems from the standpoint of tax policy and tax administration. On the one hand, the state surely has a legitimate interest in using all appropriate means to assure that taxes are collected on sales to in-state consumers. On the other hand, there is something incongruous about imposing a tax on a retail sale but requiring a vendor one step removed from that transaction to undertake the collection responsibilities. What is the proper measure of the tax in a drop shipment transaction, the wholesale price or the retail price? If the former, what is the statutory authority for imposing a retail sales tax measured by the wholesale price? If the latter, how can the wholesaler determine the retail price if it has no knowledge of the price at which its customer (the retailer) billed the ultimate consumer to whom the wholesaler shipped the goods? In response to the latter objection raised by the drop-shipper in the *Lyon Metal* case discussed in the preceding paragraph, namely, that it "did not know how much the California consumer had agreed to pay the out-of-state [retailer] who bought the good from Lyon," the court responded that "[i]f that is true, * * * all Lyon had to do was to ask the [retailer] this question when the delivery in California was ordered." Lyon Metal, supra, 68 Cal.Rptr.2d at 288 n.3. Following the *Lyon* case, California amended its drop-shipment regulation to address this problem by providing:

> a drop shipper may calculate the retail selling price of its drop shipments of property based on its selling price of the property to the true retailer plus a mark-up of 10 percent (10%). A drop shipper may use a mark-up percentage lower than 10 percent if the drop shipper can document that the lower mark-up percentage accurately reflects the retail selling price charged by the true retailer to the California consumer.

Cal. Code Regs. tit. 18, § 1706(c)(2) (Westlaw 2009).

For a detailed treatment of drop shipment and related issues, see 2 Jerome R. Hellerstein & Walter Hellerstein, State Taxation ¶ 18.04[1][b] (3rd ed. 2002 & Cum. Supp. 2009); Walter Hellerstein, "Three–Party Multistate Sales Transactions: Drop Shipments and Similar Arrangements," State Tax Notes, May 13, 2002, p. 621; Marilyn Wethekam & Kendall Houghton, Sales and Use Taxes: Drop Shipments, Tax Mgmt. Multistate Tax Portfolio (BNA), 1340 T.M.

ASSIGNMENT

A foreign corporation not authorized to do business in your state sends a regional sales representative into your state to solicit orders for sales of college rings. The representative visits colleges in the state twice a year, spending about a week on each visit. The corporation maintains no office or place of business in the state. The sales representative receives a down payment on each order that he or she takes. The orders are forwarded to the main office of the corporation, located in State X, for acceptance. The rings are shipped from State X by Federal Express to the purchaser. The order slips recite that title to the goods will pass to the customer upon delivery by the taxpayer to the Federal Express office in in State X. The corporation advertises its product in college newspapers and on college billboards.

Analyze the statutes, regulations, and decisions under the sales and use tax laws of your state, and prepare a report setting forth your views as to whether the corporation is required to collect your state's sales or use tax on the sales of rings shipped to customers in your state.

3. APPORTIONMENT OF THE SALES TAX MEASURE

OKLAHOMA TAX COMMISSION v. JEFFERSON LINES, INC.

Supreme Court of the United States, 1995.
514 U.S. 175, 115 S.Ct. 1331.

JUSTICE SOUTER delivered the opinion of the Court.

This case raises the question whether Oklahoma's sales tax on the full price of a ticket for bus travel from Oklahoma to another State is consistent with the Commerce Clause, U.S. Const., Art. I, § 8, cl. 3. We hold that it is.

I

Oklahoma taxes sales in the State of certain goods and services, including transportation for hire. Okla.Stat., Tit. 68, § 1354(1)(C) (Supp. 1988).[1] The buyers of the taxable goods and services pay the taxes, which must be collected and remitted to the State by sellers. § 1361.

Respondent Jefferson Lines, Inc., is a Minnesota corporation that provided bus services as a common carrier in Oklahoma from 1988 to 1990. Jefferson did not collect or remit the sales taxes for tickets it had sold in Oklahoma for bus travel from Oklahoma to other States, although it did collect and remit the taxes for all tickets it had sold in Oklahoma for travel that originated and terminated within that State.

After Jefferson filed for bankruptcy protection on October 27, 1989, petitioner, Oklahoma Tax Commission, filed proof of claims in Bankruptcy Court for the uncollected taxes for tickets for interstate travel sold by Jefferson.[2] Jefferson cited the Commerce Clause in objecting to the claims, and argued that the tax imposes an undue burden on interstate commerce by permitting Oklahoma to collect a percentage of the full purchase price of all tickets for interstate bus travel, even though some of that value derives from bus travel through other States. The tax also presents the danger of multiple taxation, Jefferson claimed, because any other State through which a bus travels while providing the services sold in Oklahoma

---

1. At the time relevant to the taxes at issue here, section 1354 provided as follows: "There is hereby levied upon all sales ... an excise tax of four percent (4%) of the gross receipts or gross proceeds of each sale of the following ... (C) Transportation for hire to persons by common carriers, including railroads both steam and electric, motor transportation companies, taxicab companies, pullman car companies, airlines, and other means of transportation for hire." As a result of recent amendments, the statute presently provides for a 4½ percent tax rate.

2. The parties have stipulated that the dispute concerns only those taxes for Jefferson's in-state sales of tickets for travel starting in Oklahoma and ending in another State. The Commission does not seek to recover any taxes for tickets sold in Oklahoma for travel wholly outside of the State or for travel on routes originating in other States and terminating in Oklahoma. Accordingly, the validity of such taxes is not before us.

will be able to impose taxes of their own upon Jefferson or its passengers for use of the roads.

The Bankruptcy Court agreed with Jefferson, the District Court affirmed, and so did the United States Court of Appeals for the Eighth Circuit. In re Jefferson Lines, Inc., 15 F.3d 90 (1994). The Court of Appeals held that Oklahoma's tax was not fairly apportioned, as required under the established test for the constitutionality of a state tax on interstate commerce. See Complete Auto Transit, Inc. v. Brady, 430 U.S. 274, 279, 97 S.Ct. 1076, 1079 (1977). The Court of Appeals understood its holding to be compelled by our decision in Central Greyhound Lines, Inc. v. Mealey, 334 U.S. 653, 68 S.Ct. 1260 (1948), which held unconstitutional an unapportioned state tax on the gross receipts[3] of a company that sold tickets for interstate bus travel. The Court of Appeals rejected the Commission's position that the sale of a bus ticket is a wholly local transaction justifying a sales tax on the ticket's full value in the State where it is sold, reasoning that such a tax is indistinguishable from the unapportioned tax on gross receipts from interstate travel struck down in *Central Greyhound*. We granted certiorari and now reverse.

II

[The Court traced the development of its dormant Commerce Clause jurisprudence as applied to state taxes culminating in Complete Auto Transit, Inc. v. Brady, 430 U.S. 274, 97 S.Ct. 1076 (1977), where it embraced an approach that]

"considered not the formal language of the tax statute but rather its practical effect, and * * * sustained a tax against Commerce Clause challenge when the tax is applied to an activity with a substantial nexus with the taxing State, is fairly apportioned, does not discriminate against interstate commerce, and is fairly related to the services provided by the State." 430 U.S., at 279, 97 S.Ct., at 1079.

Since then, we have often applied, and somewhat refined, what has come to be known as *Complete Auto*'s four-part test. See, e.g., Goldberg v. Sweet, 488 U.S. 252, 109 S.Ct. 582 (1989) (tax on telephone calls); D.H. Holmes Co. v. McNamara, 486 U.S. 24, 108 S.Ct. 1619 (1988) (use tax); Container Corp. v. Franchise Tax Board, 463 U.S. 159, 103 S.Ct. 2933 (1983) (franchise tax); Commonwealth Edison Co. v. Montana, 453 U.S. 609, 101 S.Ct. 2946 (1981) (severance tax). We apply its criteria to the tax before us today.

III

A

It has long been settled that a sale of tangible goods has a sufficient nexus to the State in which the sale is consummated to be treated as a

---

3. We follow standard usage, under which gross receipts taxes are on the gross receipts from sales payable by the seller, in contrast to sales taxes, which are also levied on the gross receipts from sales but are payable by the buyer (although they are collected by the seller and remitted to the taxing entity). P. Hartman, Federal Limitations on State and Local Taxation §§ 8:1, 10:1 (1981).

local transaction taxable by that State. McGoldrick v. Berwind–White Coal Mining Co., 309 U.S. 33, 60 S.Ct. 388 (1940) (upholding tax on sale of coal shipped into taxing State by seller). So, too, in addressing the interstate provision of services, we recently held that a State in which an interstate telephone call originates or terminates has the requisite Commerce Clause nexus to tax a customer's purchase of that call as long as the call is billed or charged to a service address, or paid by an addressee, within the taxing State. Goldberg, supra, 488 U.S., at 263, 109 S.Ct., at 589–590. Oklahoma's tax falls comfortably within these rules. Oklahoma is where the ticket is purchased, and the service originates there. These facts are enough for concluding that "[t]here is 'nexus' aplenty here." See D.H. Holmes, supra, 486 U.S., at 33, 108 S.Ct., at 1624. Indeed, the taxpayer does not deny Oklahoma's substantial nexus to the in-state portion of the bus service, but rather argues that nexus to the State is insufficient as to the portion of travel outside its borders. This point, however, goes to the second prong of *Complete Auto*, to which we turn.

B

The difficult question in this case is whether the tax is properly apportioned within the meaning of the second prong of *Complete Auto*'s test, "the central purpose [of which] is to ensure that each State taxes only its fair share of an interstate transaction." Goldberg, supra, 488 U.S., at 260–261, 109 S.Ct., at 588. This principle of fair share is the lineal descendant of *Western Live Stock* [v. Bureau of Revenue, 303 U.S. 250, 58 S.Ct. 546 (1938)]'s prohibition of multiple taxation, which is threatened whenever one State's act of overreaching combines with the possibility that another State will claim its fair share of the value taxed: the portion of value by which one State exceeded its fair share would be taxed again by a State properly laying claim to it.

For over a decade now, we have assessed any threat of malapportionment by asking whether the tax is "internally consistent" and, if so, whether it is "externally consistent" as well. See id., at 261, 109 S.Ct., at 589; Container Corp., supra, 463 U.S., at 169, 103 S.Ct., at 2942. Internal consistency is preserved when the imposition of a tax identical to the one in question by every other State would add no burden to interstate commerce that intrastate commerce would not also bear. This test asks nothing about the degree of economic reality reflected by the tax, but simply looks to the structure of the tax at issue to see whether its identical application by every State in the Union would place interstate commerce at a disadvantage as compared with commerce intrastate. A failure of internal consistency shows as a matter of law that a State is attempting to take more than its fair share of taxes from the interstate transaction, since allowing such a tax in one State would place interstate commerce at the mercy of those remaining States that might impose an identical tax. There is no failure of it in this case, however. If every State were to impose a tax identical to Oklahoma's, that is, a tax on ticket sales within the State for travel originating there, no sale would be subject to more than one State's tax.

External consistency, on the other hand, looks not to the logical consequences of cloning, but to the economic justification for the State's claim upon the value taxed, to discover whether a State's tax reaches beyond that portion of value that is fairly attributable to economic activity within the taxing State. See Goldberg, supra, 488 U.S., at 262, 109 S.Ct., at 589; Container Corp., supra, 463 U.S., at 169–170, 103 S.Ct., at 2942–2943. Here, the threat of real multiple taxation (though not by literally identical statutes) may indicate a State's impermissible overreaching. It is to this less tidy world of real taxation that we turn now, and at length.

1

The very term "apportionment" tends to conjure up allocation by percentages, and where taxation of income from interstate business is in issue, apportionment disputes have often centered around specific formulas for slicing a taxable pie among several States in which the taxpayer's activities contributed to taxable value. In Moorman Mfg. Co. v. Bair, 437 U.S. 267, 98 S.Ct. 2340 (1978), for example, we considered whether Iowa could measure an interstate corporation's taxable income by attributing income to business within the State " 'in that proportion which the gross sales made within the state bear to the total gross sales.' " Id., at 270, 98 S.Ct., at 2342–2343. We held that it could. In *Container Corporation*, we decided whether California could constitutionally compute taxable income assignable to a multijurisdictional enterprise's instate activity by apportioning its combined business income according to a formula "based, in equal parts, on the proportion of [such] business' total payroll, property, and sales which are located in the taxing State." 463 U.S., at 170, 103 S.Ct., at 2943. Again, we held that it could. Finally, in *Central Greyhound*, we held that New York's taxation of an interstate busline's gross receipts was constitutionally limited to that portion reflecting miles traveled within the taxing jurisdiction. 334 U.S., at 663, 68 S.Ct., at 1266.

In reviewing sales taxes for fair share, however, we have had to set a different course. A sale of goods is most readily viewed as a discrete event facilitated by the laws and amenities of the place of sale, and the transaction itself does not readily reveal the extent to which completed or anticipated interstate activity affects the value on which a buyer is taxed. We have therefore consistently approved taxation of sales without any division of the tax base among different States, and have instead held such taxes properly measurable by the gross charge for the purchase, regardless of any activity outside the taxing jurisdiction that might have preceded the sale or might occur in the future. See, e.g., McGoldrick v. Berwind–White Coal Mining Co., 309 U.S. 33, 60 S.Ct. 388 (1940).

Such has been the rule even when the parties to a sales contract specifically contemplated interstate movement of the goods either immediately before, or after, the transfer of ownership. See, e.g., Wardair Canada Inc. v. Florida Dept. of Revenue, 477 U.S. 1, 106 S.Ct. 2369 (1986) (upholding sales tax on airplane fuel); State Tax Comm'n of Utah v. Pacific States Cast Iron Pipe Co., 372 U.S. 605, 83 S.Ct. 925 (1963) (per curiam) (upholding tax on sale that contemplated purchaser's interstate shipment of goods immediately after sale). The sale, we held, was "an activity which ... is subject to the state taxing power" so long as taxation did not "discriminat[e]" against or "obstruc[t]" interstate commerce, Berwind–White, 309 U.S., at 58, 60 S.Ct., at 398, and we found a sufficient safeguard against the risk of impermissible multiple taxation of a sale in the fact that it was consummated in only one State. As we put it in Berwind–White, a necessary condition for imposing the tax was the occurrence of "a local activity, delivery of goods within the State upon their purchase for consumption." Ibid. So conceived, a sales tax on coal, for example, could not be repeated by other States, for the same coal was not imagined ever to be delivered in two States at once. Conversely, we held that a sales tax could not validly be imposed if the purchaser already had obtained title to the goods as they were shipped from outside the taxing State into the taxing State by common carrier. McLeod v. J.E. Dilworth Co., 322 U.S. 327, 64 S.Ct. 1023 (1944). The out-of-state seller in that case "was through selling" outside the taxing State. Id., at 330, 64 S.Ct., at 1025. In other words, the very conception of the common sales tax on goods, operating on the transfer of ownership and possession at a particular time and place, insulated the buyer from any threat of further taxation of the transaction.

In deriving this rule covering taxation to a buyer on sales of goods we were not, of course, oblivious to the possibility of successive taxation of related events up and down the stream of commerce, and our cases are implicit with the understanding that the Commerce Clause does not forbid the actual assessment of a succession of taxes by different States on distinct events as the same tangible object flows along. Thus, it is a truism that a sales tax to the buyer does not preclude a tax to the seller upon the income earned from a sale, and there is no constitutional trouble inherent in the imposition of a sales tax in the State of delivery to the customer, even though the State of origin of the thing sold may have assessed a property or severance tax on it. See Berwind–White, supra, 309 U.S., at 53, 60 S.Ct., at 396; cf. Commonwealth Edison Co. v. Montana, 453 U.S. 609, 101 S.Ct. 2946 (1981) (upholding severance tax on coal mined within the taxing State). In light of this settled treatment of taxes on sales of goods and other successive taxes related through the stream of commerce, it is fair to say that because the taxable event of the consummated sale of goods has been found to be properly treated as unique, an internally consistent, conventional sales tax has long been held to be externally consistent as well.

2

A sale of services can ordinarily be treated as a local state event just as readily as a sale of tangible goods can be located solely within the State of delivery. Cf. Goldberg v. Sweet, 488 U.S. 252, 109 S.Ct. 582 (1989).

Although our decisional law on sales of services is less developed than on sales of goods, one category of cases dealing with taxation of gross sales receipts in the hands of a seller of services supports the view that the taxable event is wholly local. Thus we have held that the entire gross receipts derived from sales of services to be performed wholly in one State are taxable by that State, notwithstanding that the contract for performance of the services has been entered into across state lines with customers who reside outside the taxing State. Western Live Stock v. Bureau of Revenue, 303 U.S. 250, 58 S.Ct. 546 (1938). So, too, as we have already noted, even where interstate circulation contributes to the value of magazine advertising purchased by the customer, we have held that the Commerce Clause does not preclude a tax on its full value by the State of publication. Id., at 254, 258–259, 58 S.Ct., at 548, 549–550. And where the services are performed upon tangible items retrieved from and delivered to out-of-state customers, the business performing the services may be taxed on the full gross receipts from the services, because they were performed wholly within the taxing State. Department of Treasury of Ind. v. Ingram–Richardson Mfg. Co., 313 U.S. 252, 61 S.Ct. 866 (1941). Interstate activity may be essential to a substantial portion of the value of the services in the first case and essential to performance of the services in the second, but sales with at least partial performance in the taxing State justify that State's taxation of the transaction's entire gross receipts in the hands of the seller. On the analogy sometimes drawn between sales and gross receipts taxes, see International Harvester Co. v. Department of Treasury, 322 U.S. 340, 347–348, 64 S.Ct. 1019, 1022–1023 (1944), there would be no reason to suppose that a different apportionment would be feasible or required when the tax falls not on the seller but on the buyer.

Cases on gross receipts from sales of services include one falling into quite a different category, however, and it is on this decision that the taxpayer relies for an analogy said to control the resolution of the case before us. In 1948, the Court decided Central Greyhound Lines, Inc. v. Mealey, 334 U.S. 653, 68 S.Ct. 1260, striking down New York's gross receipts tax on transportation services imposed without further apportionment on the total receipts from New York sales of bus services, almost half of which were actually provided by carriage through neighboring New Jersey and Pennsylvania. The Court held the statute fatally flawed by the failure to apportion taxable receipts in the same proportions that miles traveled through the various States bore to the total. The similarity of *Central Greyhound* to this case is, of course, striking, and on the assumption that the economic significance of a gross receipts tax is indistinguishable from a tax on sales the Court of Appeals held that a similar mileage apportionment is required here, see 15 F.3d, at 92–93, as the taxpayer now argues.

We, however, think that *Central Greyhound* provides the wrong analogy for answering the sales tax apportionment question here. To be sure, the two cases involve the identical services, and apportionment by mileage per State is equally feasible in each. But the two diverge crucially in the identity of the taxpayers and the consequent opportunities that are understood to exist for multiple taxation of the same taxpayer. *Central Greyhound* did not rest simply on the mathematical and administrative feasibility of a mileage apportionment, but on the Court's express understanding that the seller-taxpayer was exposed to taxation by New Jersey and Pennsylvania on portions of the same receipts that New York was taxing in their entirety. The Court thus understood the gross receipts tax to be simply a variety of tax on income, which was required to be apportioned to reflect the location of the various interstate activities by which it was earned. This understanding is presumably the reason that the *Central Greyhound* Court said nothing about the arguably local character of the levy on the sales transaction.[5] Instead, the Court heeded *Berwind–White*'s warning about "[p]rivilege taxes requiring a percentage of the gross receipts from interstate transportation," which "if sustained, could be imposed wherever the interstate activity occurs...." 309 U.S., at 45–46, n. 2, 60 S.Ct., at 391, n. 2.

Here, in contrast, the tax falls on the buyer of the services, who is no more subject to double taxation on the sale of these services than the buyer of goods would be. The taxable event comprises agreement, payment, and delivery of some of the services in the taxing State; no other State can claim to be the site of the same combination. The economic activity represented by the receipt of the ticket for "consumption" in the form of commencement and partial provision of the transportation thus closely resembles *Berwind–White*'s "delivery of goods within the State upon their purchase for consumption," id., at 58, 60 S.Ct., at 398, especially given that full "consumption" or "use" of the purchased goods within the taxing State has never been a condition for taxing a sale of those goods. Although the taxpayer seeks to discount these resemblances by arguing that sale does not occur until delivery is made, nothing in our caselaw supports the view that when delivery is made by services provided over time and through space a separate sale occurs at each moment of delivery, or when each State's segment of transportation state-by-state is complete. The analysis should not lose touch with the common understanding of a sale, see Goldberg, 488 U.S., at 262, 109 S.Ct., at 589; the combined events of payment for a ticket and its delivery for present commencement of a trip are commonly understood to suffice for a sale.

In sum, the sales taxation here is not open to the double taxation analysis on which *Central Greyhound* turned, and that decision does not control. Before we classify the Oklahoma tax with standard taxes on sales of goods, and with the taxes on less complicated sales of services, however, two questions may helpfully be considered.

3

Although the sale with partial delivery cannot be duplicated as a taxable event in any other State, and multiple taxation under an identical

---

5. Although New York's tax reached the gross receipts only from ticket sales within New York State, 334 U.S., at 664, 666, 68 S.Ct., at 1266–1267, 1267–1268 (Murphy, J., dissenting), the majority makes no mention of this fact.

tax is thus precluded, is there a possibility of successive taxation so closely related to the transaction as to indicate potential unfairness of Oklahoma's tax on the full amount of sale? And if the answer to that question is no, is the very possibility of apportioning by mileage a sufficient reason to conclude that the tax exceeds the fair share of the State of sale?

a

The taxpayer argues that anything but a *Central Greyhound* mileage apportionment by State will expose it to the same threat of multiple taxation assumed to exist in that case: further taxation, that is, of some portion of the value already taxed, though not under a statute in every respect identical to Oklahoma's. But the claim does not hold up. The taxpayer has failed to raise any spectre of successive taxes that might require us to reconsider whether an internally consistent tax on sales of services could fail the external consistency test for lack of further apportionment (a result that no sales tax has ever suffered under our cases).

If, for example, in the face of Oklahoma's sales tax, Texas were to levy a sustainable, apportioned gross receipts tax on the Texas portion of travel from Oklahoma City to Dallas, interstate travel would not be exposed to multiple taxation in any sense different from coal for which the producer may be taxed first at point of severance by Montana and the customer may later be taxed upon its purchase in New York. The multiple taxation placed upon interstate commerce by such a confluence of taxes is not a structural evil that flows from either tax individually, but it is rather the "accidental incident of interstate commerce being subject to two different taxing jurisdictions." Lockhart [Gross Receipts Taxes on Interstate Transportation and Communication, 57 Harv. L. Rev. 40,] 75 ([1943)]; See Moorman Mfg. Co., 437 U.S., at 277, 98 S.Ct., at 2346–2347.[6]

---

6. Any additional gross receipts tax imposed upon the interstate bus line would, of course, itself have to respect well-understood constitutional strictures. Thus, for example, Texas could not tax the bus company on the full value of the bus service from Oklahoma City to Dallas when the ticket is sold in Oklahoma, because that tax would, among other things, be internally inconsistent. And if Texas were to impose a tax upon the bus company measured by the portion of gross receipts reflecting instate travel, it would have to impose taxes on in-state and interstate journeys alike. In the event Texas chose to limit the burden of successive taxes attributable to the same transaction by combining an apportioned gross receipts tax with a credit for sales taxes paid to Texas, for example, it would have to give equal treatment to service into Texas purchased subject to a sales tax in another State, which it could do by granting a credit for sales taxes paid to any State. See, e.g., Henneford v. Silas Mason Co., 300 U.S. 577, 583–584, 57 S.Ct. 524, 527–528 (1937) (upholding use tax which provided credit for sales taxes paid to any State); Halliburton Oil Well Cementing Co. v. Reily, 373 U.S. 64, 70, 83 S.Ct. 1201, 1204 (1963) ("[E]qual treatment for in-state and out-of-state taxpayers similarly situated is the condition precedent for a valid use tax on goods imported from out-of-state"); Maryland v. Louisiana, 451 U.S. 725, 759, 101 S.Ct. 2114, 2135 (1981) (striking down Louisiana's "first use" tax on imported gas because "the pattern of credits and exemptions allowed under the ... statute undeniably violates this principle of equality"); Tyler Pipe Industries, Inc. v. Washington State Dept. of Revenue, 483 U.S. 232, 240–248, 107 S.Ct. 2810, 2816–2820 (1987) (striking down Washington's gross receipts wholesaling tax exempting in-state, but not out-of-state, manufacturers); see also Boston Stock Exchange v. State Tax Comm'n, 429 U.S. 318, 331–332, 97 S.Ct. 599, 607–608 (1977).

Although we have not held that a State imposing an apportioned gross receipts tax that grants a credit for sales taxes paid in-state must also extend such a credit to sales taxes paid out-of-state, see, e.g., Associated Industries of Mo. v. Lohman, 511 U.S. 641, 643–644, and nn. 1 and 2, 114 S.Ct. 1815, 1819, and nn. 1 and 2 (1994); Halliburton, supra, 373 U.S., at 77, 83 S.Ct., at 1207–

Nor has the taxpayer made out a case that Oklahoma's sales tax exposes any buyer of a ticket in Oklahoma for travel into another State to multiple taxation from taxes imposed upon passengers by other States of passage. Since a use tax, or some equivalent on the consumption of services, is generally levied to compensate the taxing State for its incapacity to reach the corresponding sale, it is commonly paired with a sales tax, being applicable only when no sales tax has been paid or subject to a credit for any such tax paid. Since any use tax would have to comply with Commerce Clause requirements, the tax scheme could not apply differently to goods and services purchased out-of-state from those purchased domestically. Presumably, then, it would not apply when another State's sales tax had previously been paid, or would apply subject to credit for such payment. In either event, the Oklahoma ticket purchaser would be free from multiple taxation.

True, it is not Oklahoma that has offered to provide a credit for related taxes paid elsewhere, but in taxing sales Oklahoma may rely upon use-taxing States to do so. This is merely a practical consequence of the structure of use taxes as generally based upon the primacy of taxes on sales, in that use of goods is taxed only to the extent that their prior sale has escaped taxation. Indeed the District of Columbia and forty-four of the forty-five States that impose sales and use taxes permit such a credit or exemption for similar taxes paid to other States. See 2 Hellerstein & Hellerstein ¶ 18.08, p. 18–48; 1 All States Tax Guide ¶ 256 (1994). As one state court summarized the provisions in force:

> "These credit provisions create a national system under which the first state of purchase or use imposes the tax. Thereafter, no other state taxes the transaction unless there has been no prior tax imposed ... or if the tax rate of the prior taxing state is less, in which case the subsequent taxing state imposes a tax measured only by the differential rate." KSS Transportation Corp. v. Baldwin, 9 N.J.Tax 273, 285 (1987).

The case of threatened multiple taxation where a sales tax is followed by a use tax is thus distinguishable from the case of simultaneous sales taxes considered in *Goldberg*, where we were reassured to some degree by

1208 (Brennan, J., concurring), we have noted that equality of treatment of interstate and intrastate activity has been the common theme among the paired (or "compensating") tax schemes that have passed constitutional muster, see, e.g., Boston Stock Exchange, supra, 429 U.S., at 331–332, 97 S.Ct., at 607–608. We have indeed never upheld a tax in the face of a substantiated charge that it provided credits for the taxpayer's payment of in-state taxes but failed to extend such credit to payment of equivalent out-of-state taxes. To the contrary, in upholding tax schemes providing credits for taxes paid in-state and occasioned by the same transaction, we have often pointed to the concomitant credit provisions for taxes paid out-of-state as supporting our conclusion that a particular tax passed muster because it treated out-of-state and in-state taxpayers alike. See, e.g., Itel Containers Int'l Corp. v. Huddleston, 113 S.Ct. 1095, 1102–1103 (1993); D.H. Holmes Co. v. McNamara, 486 U.S. 24, 31, 108 S.Ct. 1619, 1623–1624 (1988) ("The ... taxing scheme is fairly apportioned, for it provides a credit against its use tax for sales taxes that have been paid in other States"); General Trading Co. v. State Tax Comm'n of Iowa, 322 U.S. 335, 64 S.Ct. 1028 (1944); Silas Mason, supra, 300 U.S., at 584, 57 S.Ct., at 527–528. A general requirement of equal treatment is thus amply clear from our precedent. We express no opinion on the need for equal treatment when a credit is allowed for payment of in-or out-of-state taxes by a third party. See Darnell v. Indiana, 226 U.S. 390, 33 S.Ct. 120 (1912).

the provision of a credit in the disputed tax itself for similar taxes placed upon the taxpayer by other States. See Goldberg, 488 U.S., at 264, 109 S.Ct., at 590–591 ("To the extent that other States' telecommunications taxes pose a risk of multiple taxation, the credit provision contained in the [t]ax [a]ct operates to avoid actual multiple taxation"). In that case, unlike the sales and use schemes posited for the sake of argument here, each of the competing sales taxes would presumably have laid an equal claim on the taxpayer's purse.

b

Finally, Jefferson points to the fact that in this case, unlike the telephone communication tax at issue in *Goldberg*, Oklahoma could feasibly apportion its sales tax on the basis of mileage as we required New York's gross receipts tax to do in *Central Greyhound*. Although *Goldberg* indeed noted that "[a]n apportionment formula based on mileage or some other geographic division of individual telephone calls would produce insurmountable administrative and technological barriers," 488 U.S., at 264–265, 109 S.Ct., at 590, and although we agree that no comparable barriers exist here, we nonetheless reject the idea that a particular apportionment formula must be used simply because it would be possible to use it. We have never required that any particular apportionment formula or method be used, and when a State has chosen one, an objecting taxpayer has the burden to demonstrate by " 'clear and cogent evidence,' " that " 'the income attributed to the State is in fact out of all appropriate proportions to the business transacted ... in that State, or has led to a grossly distorted result.' " Container Corp., 463 U.S., at 170, 103 S.Ct., at 2942, quoting Moorman Mfg. Co., 437 U.S., at 274, 98 S.Ct., at 2345 (internal quotation marks omitted; citations omitted). That is too much for Jefferson to bear in this case. It fails to show that Oklahoma's tax on the sale of transportation imputes economic activity to the State of sale in any way substantially different from that imputed by the garden-variety sales tax, which we have perennially sustained, even though levied on goods that have traveled in interstate commerce to the point of sale or that will move across state lines thereafter. See, e.g., Wardair Canada, Inc. v. Florida Dept. of Revenue, 477 U.S. 1, 106 S.Ct. 2369 (1986); see also Western Live Stock, 303 U.S., at 259, 58 S.Ct., at 550 (upholding tax where measure of the tax "include[s] the augmentation attributable to the [interstate] commerce in which [the object of the tax] is employed"); *Goldberg*, 488 U.S., at 262, 109 S.Ct., at 589 (upholding tax upon the purchase of an interstate telephone call which had "many of the characteristics of a sales tax ... [e]ven though such a retail purchase is not a purely local event since it triggers simultaneous activity in several States"). Nor does Oklahoma's tax raise any greater threat of multiple taxation than those sales taxes that have passed muster time and again. There is thus no reason to leave the line of longstanding precedent and lose the simplicity of our general rule sustaining sales taxes measured by full value, simply to carve out an exception for the subcategory of sales of interstate transportation services. We accordingly conclude that Oklahoma's tax on ticket sales for travel originating in Oklahoma is externally consistent, as reaching only the activity taking place within the taxing State, that is, the sale of the service. Cf. id., at 261–262, 109 S.Ct., at 588–589.[7]

C

We now turn to the remaining two portions of *Complete Auto*'s test, which require the tax must "not discriminate against interstate commerce," and must be "fairly related to the services provided by the State." 430 U.S., at 279, 97 S.Ct., at 1079. Oklahoma's tax meets these demands.

* * *

IV

Oklahoma's tax on the sale of transportation services does not contravene the Commerce Clause. The judgment of the Court of Appeals is reversed, accordingly, and the case is remanded for further proceedings consistent with this opinion.

It is so ordered.

JUSTICE SCALIA, with whom JUSTICE THOMAS joins, concurring in the judgment.

I agree with the Court's conclusion that Oklahoma's sales tax does not facially discriminate against interstate commerce. See ante, at 1345. That seems to me the most we can demand to certify compliance with the "negative Commerce Clause"—which is "negative" not only because it negates state regulation of commerce, but also because it does not appear in the Constitution. See Amerada Hess Corp. v. Director, Division of Taxation, New Jersey Department of the Treasury, 490 U.S. 66, 80, 109 S.Ct. 1617, 1625–1626 (1989) (SCALIA, J., concurring in judgment); Tyler Pipe Industries, Inc. v. Washington State Dept. of Revenue, 483 U.S. 232,

---

7. Justice BREYER would reject review of the tax under general sales tax principles in favor of an analogy between sales and gross receipts taxes which, in the dissent's view, are without "practical difference," post, at 1348. Although his dissenting opinion rightly counsels against the adoption of purely formal distinctions, economic equivalence alone has similarly not been (and should not be) the touchstone of commerce clause jurisprudence. Our decisions cannot be reconciled with the view that two taxes must inevitably be equated for purposes of constitutional analysis by virtue of the fact that both will ultimately be "pass[ed] ... along to the customer" or calculated in a similar fashion, ibid. Indeed, were that to be the case, we could not, for example, dismiss successive taxation of the extraction, sale, and income from the sale of coal as consistent with the Commerce Clause's prohibition against multiple taxation.

Justice BREYER's opinion illuminates the difference between his view and our own in its suggestion, post, at 1349, that our disagreement turns on differing assessments of the force of competing analogies. His analogy to *Central Greyhound* derives strength from characterizing the tax as falling on "interstate travel," post, at 1349, or "transportation," post, at 1347. Our analogy to prior cases on taxing sales of goods and services derives force from identifying the taxpayer in categorizing the tax and from the value of a uniform rule governing taxation on the occasion of what is generally understood as a sales transaction. The significance of the taxpayer's identity is, indeed, central to the Court's longstanding recognition of structural differences that permit successive taxation as an incident of multiple taxing jurisdictions. The decision today is only the latest example of such a recognition and brings us as close to simplicity as the conceptual distinction between sales and income taxation is likely to allow.

254, 259–265, 107 S.Ct. 2810, 2823–2824, 2826–2829 (1987) (SCALIA, J., concurring in part and dissenting in part).

I would not apply the remainder of the eminently unhelpful, so-called "four-part test" of Complete Auto Transit, Inc. v. Brady, 430 U.S. 274, 279, 97 S.Ct. 1076, 1079 (1977). Under the real Commerce Clause ("The Congress shall have Power ... To regulate Commerce ... among the several States," U.S. Const., Art. I, § 8), it is for Congress to make the judgment that interstate commerce must be immunized from certain sorts of nondiscriminatory state action—a judgment that may embrace (as ours ought not) such imponderables as how much "value [is] *fairly attributable* to economic activity within the taxing State," and what constitutes "*fair relation* between a tax and the benefits conferred upon the taxpayer by the State." Ante, at 1338, 1345 (emphases added). See Tyler Pipe, supra, 483 U.S., at 259, 107 S.Ct., at 2826. I look forward to the day when *Complete Auto* will take its rightful place in Part II of the Court's opinion, among the other useless and discarded tools of our negative-Commerce–Clause jurisprudence.

JUSTICE BREYER, with whom JUSTICE O'CONNOR joins, dissenting.

Despite the Court's lucid and thorough discussion of the relevant law, I am unable to join its conclusion for one simple reason. Like the judges of the Court of Appeals, I believe the tax at issue here and the tax that this Court held unconstitutional in Central Greyhound Lines, Inc. v. Mealey, 334 U.S. 653, 68 S.Ct. 1260 (1948), are, for all relevant purposes, identical. Both cases involve taxes imposed upon interstate bus transportation. In neither case did the State apportion the tax to avoid taxing that portion of the interstate activity performed in other States. And, I find no other distinguishing features. Hence, I would hold that the tax before us violates the Constitution for the reasons this Court set forth in Central Greyhound.

Central Greyhound considered a tax imposed by the State of New York on utilities doing business in New York—a tax called " '[e]mergency tax on the furnishing of utility services.' " Id., at 664, 68 S.Ct., at 1266 (Murphy, J., dissenting) (quoting New York Tax Law § 186–a). That tax was equal to "two per centum" of "gross income," defined to include "receipts received ... by reason of any sale ... made" in New York. 334 U.S., at 664, 68 S.Ct., at 1266–1267. The New York taxing authorities had applied the tax to gross receipts from sales (in New York) of bus transportation between New York City and cities in upstate New York over routes that cut across New Jersey and Pennsylvania. The out-of-state portion of the trips accounted for just over 40 percent of total mileage.

Justice Frankfurter wrote for the *Central Greyhound* Court that "it is interstate commerce which the State is seeking to reach," id., at 661, 68 S.Ct., at 1265; that the "real question [is] whether what the State is exacting is a constitutionally fair demand ... for that aspect of the interstate commerce to which the State bears a special relation," ibid.; and that by "its very nature an unapportioned gross receipts tax makes interstate transportation bear more than 'a fair share of the cost of the local government whose protection it enjoys,' " id., at 663, 68 S.Ct., at 1266 (quoting Freeman v. Hewit, 329 U.S. 249, 253, 67 S.Ct. 274, 277 (1946)). The Court noted that

> "[i]f New Jersey and Pennsylvania could claim their right to make appropriately apportioned claims against that substantial part of the business of appellant to which they afford protection, we do not see how on principle and in precedent such a claim could be denied. This being so, to allow New York to impose a tax on the gross receipts for the entire mileage—on the 57.47% within New York as well as the 42.53% without—would subject interstate commerce to the unfair burden of being taxed as to portions of its revenue by States which give protection to those portions, as well as to a State which does not." 334 U.S., at 662, 68 S.Ct., at 1265.

The Court essentially held that the tax lacked what it would later describe as "external consistency." Container Corp. of America v. Franchise Tax Bd., 463 U.S. 159, 169, 103 S.Ct. 2933, 2942 (1983). That is to say, the New York law violated the Commerce Clause because it tried to tax significantly more than "that portion of the revenues from the interstate activity which reasonably reflects the in-state component of the activity being taxed." Goldberg v. Sweet, 488 U.S. 252, 262, 109 S.Ct. 582, 589 (1989).

The tax before us bears an uncanny resemblance to the New York tax. The Oklahoma statute (as applied to "[t]ransportation ... by common carriers") imposes an "excise tax" of 4% on "the *gross receipts* or gross proceeds *of each sale*" made in Oklahoma. Okla.Stat., Tit. 68, § 1354(1)(C) (Supp. 1988) (emphasis added). The New York statute imposed a 2% tax on the "*receipts* received ... by reason of *any sale* ... made" in New York. See supra, at 1346 (emphasis added). Oklahoma imposes its tax on the total value of trips of which a large portion may take place in other States. New York imposed its tax on the total value of trips of which a large portion took place in other States. New York made no effort to apportion the tax to reflect the comparative cost or value of the in-state and out-of-state portions of the trips. Neither does Oklahoma. Where, then, can one find a critical difference?

Not in the language of the two statutes, which differs only slightly. Oklahoma calls its statute an "excise tax" and "levie[s]" the tax "upon all sales" of transportation. New York called its tax an "[e]mergency tax on ... services" and levied the tax on " 'gross income,' " defined to include " 'receipts ... of any sale.' " This linguistic difference, however, is not significant. As the majority properly recognizes, purely formal differences in terminology should not make a constitutional difference. Ante, at 1337–1338. In both instances, the State imposes the tax on gross receipts as measured by sales. Both taxes, then, would seem to have the same practical effect on the, inherently interstate, bus transportation activity. If the *Central Greyhound* Court was willing to look through New York's formal labels ("[e]mergency tax on ... services"; "gross income" tax) to the substance (a tax on gross receipts from sales), why should this Court not do the same?

The majority sees a number of reasons why the result here should be different from that in *Central Greyhound*, but I do not think any is persuasive. First, the majority points out that the New York law required a seller, the bus company, to pay the tax, whereas the Oklahoma law says that the "tax ... shall be paid by the consumer or user to the vendor." Okla.Stat., Tit. 68, § 1361(A) (Supp. 1988). This difference leads the majority to characterize the former as a "gross receipts" tax and the latter as a constitutionally distinguishable "sales tax." This difference, however, seems more a formal, than a practical difference. The Oklahoma law makes the bus company ("the vendor") and "each principal officer ... personally liable" for the tax, whether or not they collect it from the customer. Ibid. Oklahoma (as far as I can tell) has never tried to collect the tax directly from a customer. And, in any event, the statute tells the customer to pay the tax, not to the State, but "to the vendor." Ibid. The upshot is that, as a practical matter, in respect to both taxes, the State will calculate the tax bill by multiplying the rate times gross receipts from sales; the bus company will pay the tax bill; and, the company will pass the tax along to the customer.

Second, the majority believes that this case presents a significantly smaller likelihood than did *Central Greyhound* that the out-of-state portions of a bus trip will be taxed both "by States which give protection to those portions, as well as [by] ... a State which does not." Central Greyhound, 334 U.S., at 662, 68 S.Ct., at 1265–1266. There is at least a hint in the Court's opinion that this is so because the "taxable event" to which the Oklahoma tax attaches is not the interstate transportation of passengers but the sale of a bus ticket (combined, perhaps, with transportation to the state line). See ante, at 1341 ("The taxable event comprises agreement, payment, and delivery of some of the services in the taxing State...."). Thus, the majority suggests that a tax on transportation (as opposed to the sale of a bus ticket) by a different State might be "successive," ante, at 1341, but is not "double taxation" in a constitutionally relevant way, ibid.; see ante, at 1341 ("no other State can claim to be the site of the same combination"). I concede that Oklahoma could have a tax of the kind envisioned, namely one that would tax the bus company for the privilege of selling tickets. But, whether or not such a tax would pass constitutional muster should depend upon its practical effects. To suggest that the tax here is constitutional simply because it lends itself to recharacterizing the taxable event as a "sale" is to ignore economic reality. Because the sales tax is framed as a percentage of the ticket price, it seems clear that the activity Oklahoma intends to tax is the transportation of passengers—not some other kind of conduct (like selling tickets).

In any event, the majority itself does not seem to believe that Oklahoma is taxing something other than bus transportation; it seems to acknowledge the risk of multiple taxation. The Court creates an ingenious set of constitutionally-based taxing rules in footnote 6—designed to show that any other State that imposes, say, a gross receipts tax on its share of bus ticket sales would likely have to grant a credit for the Oklahoma sales tax (unless it forced its own citizens to pay both a sales tax and a gross receipts tax). But, one might have said the same in *Central Greyhound*. Instead of enforcing its apportionment requirement, the Court could have simply said that once one State, like New York, imposes a gross receipts tax on "receipts received ... by reason of any sale ... made" in that State, any other State, trying to tax the gross receipts of its share of bus ticket sales, might have to give some kind of credit. The difficulties with this approach lie in its complexity and our own inability to foresee all the ways in which other States might effectively tax their own portion of the journey now (also) taxed by Oklahoma. Under the Court's footnote rules, is not a traveler who buys a ticket in Oklahoma still threatened with a duplicative tax by a State that does *not* impose a sales tax on transportation (and thus, would not have to offer a credit for the sales tax paid in Oklahoma)? Even if that were not so, the constitutional problem would remain, namely that Oklahoma is imposing an unapportioned tax on the portion of travel outside the State, just as did New York.

Finally, the majority finds support in Goldberg v. Sweet, 488 U.S. 252, 109 S.Ct. 582 (1989), a case in which this Court permitted Illinois to tax interstate telephone calls that originated, or terminated, in that State. However, the *Goldberg* Court was careful to distinguish "cases [dealing] with the movement of large physical objects over identifiable routes, where it was practicable to keep track of the distance actually traveled within the taxing State," id., at 264, 109 S.Ct., at 590–591, and listed *Central Greyhound* as one of those cases, 488 U.S., at 264, 109 S.Ct., at 590–591. Telephone service, the *Goldberg* Court said, differed from movement of the kind at issue in *Central Greyhound*, in that, at least arguably, the service itself is consumed wholly within one State, or possibly two— those in which the call is charged to a service address or paid by an addressee. 488 U.S., at 263, 109 S.Ct., at 589–590. Regardless of whether telephones and buses are more alike than different, the *Goldberg* Court did not purport to modify *Central Greyhound*, nor does the majority. In any event, the *Goldberg* Court said, the tax at issue credited taxpayers for similar taxes assessed by other States. 488 U.S., at 264, 109 S.Ct., at 590– 591.

Ultimately, I may differ with the majority simply because I assess differently the comparative force of two competing analogies. The majority finds determinative this Court's case law concerning sales taxes applied to the sale of goods, which cases, for example, permit one State to impose a severance tax and another a sales tax on the same physical item (say, coal). In my view, however, the analogy to sales taxes is not as strong as the analogy to the tax at issue in *Central Greyhound*. After all, the tax before us is not a tax imposed upon a product that was made in a different State or was consumed in a different State or is made up of ingredients that come from a different State or has itself moved in interstate commerce. Rather, it is a tax imposed upon interstate travel itself—the very essence of interstate commerce. And, it is a fairly obvious effort to tax more than "that portion" of the "interstate activity['s]" revenue "which reasonably reflects the in-state component." Goldberg v. Sweet, supra, at 262, 109 S.Ct., at 589. I would reaffirm the *Central Greyhound* principle, even if doing so requires different treatment for the inherently interstate service of interstate transportation, and denies the possibility of having a single, formal constitutional rule for all self-described "sales taxes." The Court of Appeals wrote that this "is a classic instance of an unapportioned tax" upon interstate commerce. In re Jefferson Lines, Inc., 15 F.3d 90, 93 (C.A.8 1994). In my view, that is right. I respectfully dissent.

NOTES AND QUESTIONS

A. *Jefferson Lines* presented the Court with an uncomfortable dilemma. The signal characteristic of the Court's contemporary Commerce Clause opinions is their commitment to a jurisprudence based on pragmatism and economic reality. These two criteria typically reinforce one another, with the pragmatic outcome likewise being the outcome that makes economic sense. In *Jefferson Lines*, however, considerations of pragmatism and economic reality diverged. From a practical standpoint, Oklahoma's levy closely resembled the "garden-variety sales tax" on tangible personal property that the Court had "perennially sustained, even though levied on goods that have traveled in interstate commerce to the point of sale or that will move across state lines thereafter." Just as a state may impose a tax on the local sale of goods measured by their full sales price even though the price reflects value added outside the state, so it might seem that a state may impose a tax on the local sale of services measured by their full sales price even though the price reflects value added outside the state. From the standpoint of economic reality, however, there is no meaningful distinction between a tax imposed on the retail sale of interstate transportation services, measured by the unapportioned gross receipts from the sale of such services, and a tax imposed on the business of providing interstate transportation services, measured by the unapportioned gross receipts from the sale of such services. The Court had already condemned a levy of the latter description as incompatible with the Commerce Clause in *Central Greyhound*. If "economic realities" rather than "magic words and labels" were to govern the analysis, approval of the levy because it was denominated a retail sales tax rather than a business gross receipts tax would be difficult to justify. See generally Walter Hellerstein, et al., "Commerce Clause Restraints on State Taxation After *Jefferson Lines*," 51 Tax L. Rev. 47 (1995) on which the foregoing discussion is based.

B. Jefferson Lines *and "External Consistency."* Did the Court persuasively resolve the "external consistency" issue raised by *Jefferson Lines* (i.e., that the tax must be "fairly attributable to economic activity within the taxing state")? Consider an alternative, albeit unrealistic, method for Jefferson Lines to have charged for an interstate bus trip. Assume, for example, that Jefferson Lines dispensed with bus tickets and that passengers boarded busses on a first-come, first-serve basis for a trip from Oklahoma to Texas. Imagine that immediately after the bus crossed the Oklahoma/Texas border, it pulled over to the side of the road and the driver collected the fare for the Oklahoma leg of the trip, along with the appropriate Oklahoma sales tax. Then, after the bus reached its Texas destination, assume the driver collected the fare for the Texas leg of the trip as the passengers departed. Would the Court have upheld an Oklahoma sales tax on the fare collected in Texas for the Texas leg of the trip? How could an Oklahoma sales tax collected under these circumstances escape characterization as "reach[ing] beyond that portion of value that is fairly attributable to economic activity [within Oklahoma]"? How did the Oklahoma sales tax actually collected in *Jefferson Lines* differ in substance from the tax in hypothetical?

C. *The Fair Apportionment Criterion and the Structure of Retail Sales and Gross Receipts Taxes.* If *Jefferson Lines* can fairly be criticized as ignoring economic reality and allowing form to triumph over substance, it also can be defended, although not precisely for the reasons that the Court advanced in its opinion. Consider the following, which draws freely from Walter Hellerstein, et al., "Commerce Clause Restraints on State Taxation After *Jefferson Lines*," 51 Tax L. Rev. 47, 78–80 (1995):

The distinction between taxes that require apportionment and those that do not should *not* rest on whether the tax formally falls on the seller or the buyer, notwithstanding the Court's position to the contrary. Many retail sales taxes are formally imposed on the seller, but they should be viewed as "sales" taxes nonetheless rather than "gross receipts" taxes. This characterization reflects the way the legislature has framed them: they generally apply only to final sales and not to sales for resale; they are separately stated; they are imposed on a transaction-by-transaction basis; they are collected by the seller from the purchaser; and the seller may not claim that it is absorbing the tax. In other words, the legislature intended them to be consumption taxes, to be borne by the buyer, and not as measures of business activity, to be borne by the business.

In contrast to a retail sales tax, which is designed to tax the ultimate consumer, a gross receipts tax is intended to tax business activity, as measured by gross receipts, gross proceeds, or gross income. Because no reason exists to reach only the "final sale" of goods or services, gross receipts taxes typically incorporate none of the exclusions or exemptions found in a sales tax, such as the sale for resale exemption, the exemption for ingredient or component parts of products to be sold at retail, or the exemption for manufacturers' purchases. Unlike sales taxes, gross receipts tax statutes do not require that the tax be separately stated and the tax itself is not deductible from the tax base. Because there is no intent that the tax be borne by ultimate consumers, jurisdictions imposing gross receipts taxes do not require the seller to collect the tax from the purchaser, nor do they forbid the seller from advertising that it will absorb the tax. Moreover, gross receipts taxes are not collected on a transaction-by-transaction basis; instead, they are calculated and paid at regular intervals. In addition, gross receipts tax rates are generally much lower than the rates of retail sales taxes, and they frequently use multiple rates (e.g., for different business activities), which is a rare phenomenon in retail sales tax statutes.

Either a sales tax or a gross receipts tax is theoretically capable of being apportioned. Administrative considerations, however, make it much more likely that the latter rather than the former can be apportioned in practice. Because of these administrative differences, the dormant Commerce Clause rules for each type of tax have evolved quite differently, and properly so.

In the case of a sales tax, the practices of the states can be explained by the operating rule of thumb that consumption takes place in the state in which the goods are delivered. Because a sales tax is intended to tax consumption, the state of delivery rather than the state of origin is the state that levies a sales tax (or the functional equivalent—a use tax). For example, a person buying a product from a local store pays that state's sales tax, regardless of whether the goods were shipped in from outside the state. Similarly, goods purchased directly from an out-of-state vendor typically are not taxed by the state of origin but are subject to use tax in the state of delivery. In either case, the fact that the goods may subsequently be consumed in another state does not limit the right of the state of delivery to levy a consumption tax on the full amount of the sales price, without any type of apportionment. On the assumption that the goods will be consumed in the state in which they are delivered, a consumption tax levied on the transaction will be fairly apportioned because all of the consumption is deemed to occur in the taxing state.

Suppose, however, that consumption actually occurs in more than one state. For example, suppose that while T is a resident of State A, T purchases a car and uses it for half of its useful life in State A. Assume that T then moves to State B, where she consumes the remaining half of the car's useful life. Theoretically, T should receive a refund from State A for that part of the sales tax paid on the value of the car that will not be consumed in State A. Similarly, State B should be allowed to tax T only on the consumption of the car that will occur in State B. In this manner, the sales tax would effectively be apportioned to the amount of consumption occurring in each state.

Instead of this administratively cumbersome system, however, the rules that have evolved for sales taxation of tangible property implement a second-best approach in which State B levies a use tax, with a credit for the sales tax paid to State A. It is simply more convenient to allow State A to collect and keep the entire sales tax than it is to apportion it in a more precise way. Moreover, this second-best approach approximates the ideal pattern of apportionment that would exist if all states had nearly identical sales taxes and if, for every taxable product that leaves the state, an identical one enters.

This pattern of sales and use taxation arose in the context of sales of tangible personal property. The sale of tangible personal property can differ from the sale of services—or at least transportation services—in a fundamental respect. When tangible personal property is sold, it is difficult to determine where its consumption will occur. By contrast, when the transportation services in *Jefferson Lines* were sold, there was no comparable difficulty in determining where their consumption would occur because the ticket itself indicated the place of consumption.

Despite the possibility of apportioning Oklahoma's sales tax on transportation services without encountering the administrative difficulties that one would ordinarily face in seeking to apportion a sales tax on goods, the Court nevertheless adhered to the general rules it had developed for sales of goods. In effect, the Court decided to maintain and, arguably, to extend the second-best world of apportionment for sales taxes by treating the sale of transportation services as a subset of the more general rules governing sales of goods rather than using the case as a vehicle for creating a special tax regime involving true apportionment for certain types of services.

In short, the weakness in the Court's analysis in *Jefferson Lines* was not that it elevated legal form over economic substance. The Court candidly adopted this course for reasons that, in the sales tax context, outweigh the countervailing considerations that can be marshalled in favor of strict adherence to a Commerce Clause doctrine rooted in "economic reality." Rather, the weakness in the Court's analysis is that it adopted the wrong taxonomy for classifying levies that do (and do not) require true apportionment. While the suggested line between "sales" taxes and "gross receipts" taxes may not always be bright, it is nevertheless a more meaningful line than the one the Court drew in *Jefferson Lines*, and it is one that is implicit in the development of the applicable rules on apportionment.

D. *The Implications of* Jefferson Lines *for Sales Taxation of Interstate Services.* In *Jefferson Lines*, the Court conformed the treatment of sales taxation of transportation services to the treatment it had accorded sales taxation of tangible personal property. By characterizing the "taxable event" as "agreement, payment, and delivery of some of the services in the taxing State," the Court believed that it had eliminated the possibility of multiple sales taxation because "no other State can claim to be the site of the same combination."

Not all sales of interstate services can be so easily confined to a single state as those embodied in the sale of bus ticket, however. For example, a bank based in North Carolina may agree with a data processing firm in Texas to provide data processing services for the bank's branches all over the country. Assuming the "agreement" is reached in a law office in Atlanta, "payment" is made to the data processing firm's account in New York for services performed in Texas and "delivered" to the bank's branches across the country, where does the "sale" take place? And what is to prevent Georgia from taxing sales of data processing services based on where the agreement for the sale of such services is consummated, while Texas taxes the sale of services performed in the state, at the same time that New York taxes services where payment for the services is made, and the states where the services are delivered all tax the services based on delivery?

Does *Jefferson Lines* require that a state define a taxable sale of services so that it can only occur in one state, as did Oklahoma's sales tax at issue in that case? If not, would some or all of the states mentioned in the preceding paragraph have the power to tax the sale? If so, what would prevent a taxpayer purchasing the services described in the preceding paragraph from being subjected to multiple taxation? Does *Jefferson Lines* provide an answer to these questions? Reread Part III(B)(3)(a) of the Court's opinion. If that doesn't help, try Walter Hellerstein, et al., "Commerce Clause Restraints on State Taxation After *Jefferson Lines*," 51 Tax L. Rev. 47 (1995).

E. *The Congressional Overruling of* Jefferson Lines. Eight months after the Court's decision in *Jefferson Lines*, Congress passed legislation effectively overruling the decision by prohibiting the states from imposing sales or gross receipts taxes on interstate bus service. H.R. 2539, the Interstate Commerce Commission Termination Act, Pub. L. No. 104–88, 109 Stat. 803, Dec. 29, 1995, codified at 49 U.S.C. § 14505. While Congress thus overturned the particular result in *Jefferson Lines*, it did not thereby modify the broader implications of *Jefferson Lines* that we have explored above.

K.　TAXATION OF ELECTRONIC COMMERCE

The subject of taxation of electronic commerce could fill a separate volume, and the ensuing materials make no pretense of duplicating the more systematic, comprehensive, and detailed efforts that have been undertaken elsewhere to describe and address it.[h] Our purpose here is simply to introduce you to the problems raised by state taxation of electronic commerce. We have chosen to do so in the context of sales taxation, because that is the area of state taxation in which the problems raised by electronic commerce are most urgent and, consequently, have thus far received most attention.

WALTER HELLERSTEIN, ELECTRONIC COMMERCE AND THE CHALLENGE FOR TAX ADMINISTRATION

UN Document ST/SG/2000/L.7, Sept. 6, 2000.[i]

* * *

III.　ELECTRONIC COMMERCE AND CONSUMPTION TAXATION

In many respects, the most pressing problems of tax administration raised by taxation of electronic commerce are those raised by consumption

---

h. For the student who is interested in pursuing these matters in more depth, the following sources (as well as the sources cited in the ensuing discussion) should provide a useful starting point. Richard Doernberg Luc Hinnekens, Walter Hellerstein & Jinyan Li, Electronic Commerce and Multijurisdictional Taxation (2001); Karl Frieden, Cybertaxation: The Taxation of E–Commerce (2000); David E. Hardesty, Electronic Commerce: Taxation and Planning (1999). Moreover, legal and tax-related periodicals are filled with articles devoted to the particular problems raised by state taxation of electronic commerce. See, e.g., Walter Hellerstein, "Jurisdiction to Tax Income and Consumption in the New Economy: A Theoretical and Comparative Perspective," 38 Ga. L. Rev. 1 (2003); Walter Hellerstein, "Deconstructing the Debate Over State Taxation of Electronic Commerce," 13 Harv. J.L. & Tech. 549 (2000); Walter Hellerstein, "Federal Constitutional Limitations on Congressional Power to Legislate Regarding State Taxation of Electronic Commerce," 53 Nat'l Tax J. 1307 (2000); Walter Hellerstein, "Internet Tax Freedom Act Limits States' Power to Tax Internet Access and Electronic Commerce," 90 J. Tax'n 5 (1999); Walter Hellerstein, "State and Local Taxation of Electronic Commerce: Reflections on the Emerging Issues," 52 Miami L. Rev. 691 (1998); Walter Hellerstein, "State Taxation of Electronic Commerce," 52 Tax L. Rev. 425 (1997).

i. The ensuing discussion is is an updated adaptation of excerpts from the cited paper which was presented to the United Nations Ad Hoc Expert Group Meeting on Strategies for Improving Resource Mobilization in Developing Countries and Countries With Economies in Transition," Montreal, Canada, Oct. 4, 2000. Where the footnotes (as updated) are reproduced, the original footnote numbers have been retained.

taxes rather than income taxes. As the number of individual consumers with access to the Internet increases every day, and with more and more products—tangible and digital—being sold over the Internet, the challenges for tax administrations are immediate and real, because transactions involving individual consumers tend to be the weakest link in the chain of tax administration. Thus, during the course of its initial consideration of these issues, the OECD observed that "[t]he problems concerning the application of consumption taxes are generally recognised as having more immediacy than the issues concerning direct taxation."[53]

In examining the impact of electronic commerce on consumption taxes, one should distinguish between national and subnational consumption taxes and, more particularly, between value added taxes (VATs) like those adopted by members of the European Union (EU) and the retail sales tax (RST) in force in the American states. Although both levies in principle are consumption taxes, and both levies encounter certain common problems raised by electronic commerce, there are also dramatic differences between the VAT and the American RST that can lead to confusion and misconception when they are lumped together under the broad rubric of "consumption" taxes. I therefore propose first to discuss the electronic commerce issues raised by the VAT and then to turn to the special problems raised by the American RST.

A. VAT Issues

To put the implications of electronic commerce for consumption taxation in proper perspective, it is useful at the outset to identify four categories of transactions involving electronic commerce: first, transactions involving business-to-business (B2B) sales of tangible property consummated through electronic means (e.g., the purchase over the Internet of a computer by a business taxpayer from a remote computer vendor); second, transactions involving B2B sales of digital products (e.g., the purchase over the Internet of an electronic data base by a business taxpayer from a data base vendor); third, transactions involving business-to-consumer (B2C) sales of tangible property consummated through electronic means (e.g., the purchase over the Internet of clothing by an individual from a remote vendor); and fourth, transactions involving B2C sales of digital products (e.g., the purchase over the Internet of a downloadable video by an individual from a remote vendor). These four categories of transactions may be illustrated as follows:

B2B Tangible	B2B Digital
B2C Tangible	B2C Digital

53. OECD [Committee on Fiscal Affairs, Taxation of Electronic Commerce: A Discussion Paper on Taxation Issues (1998), hereinafter cited as] E–Commerce Discussion Paper, supra note 1, at 18.

There is really nothing new about the issues raised by transactions involving sales of tangible property effectuated through electronic means—whether B2B or B2C. Distance selling has existed for many years, and there is no difference in principle between a cross-border transaction in tangible goods effectuated by fax or a telephone call than one effectuated by the click of a mouse. Moreover, as the OECD has observed, "[m]ember countries ... have systems in place to ensure the taxation of imported tangible goods."[54] While electronic commerce plainly increases the opportunity for cross-border trade, and the increase in the volume of such transactions counsels that attention be paid to existing procedures to assure that they ensure the efficient collection of taxes as well as the speedy expedition of goods to their destination, electronic commerce does not raise any fundamental new challenges to operation of the VAT system insofar as tangible goods are concerned. As the EU concluded with respect to the likely increase in purchases of physical goods by private consumers over electronic networks:

> For VAT purposes, these are treated in the same way as any other form of distance sales (e.g., from catalogues, by phone, post, etc.). There are well established channels for taxing these transactions— goods purchased from third countries are taxed at import, exported goods are zero-rated and intra-Community sales of goods are taxed under a special regime for distance sales, either in the member State of the seller or the buyer (dependent largely on the volume of such trade carried out by the seller).[56]

Accordingly, it is not B2B or B2C sales of *tangible* products effectuated through electronic networks but rather B2B and B2C sales of *digital* products that raise novel and difficult questions for the VAT. These questions are in many respects analogous to those encountered in connection with direct taxation, namely questions of jurisdiction and questions of characterization, although they arise in a different context. In principle, of course, there is no question of jurisdiction over the ultimate VAT taxpayer—the consumer—because the taxing authority will always have jurisdiction over the consumer if the tax is imposed by the country of consumption. As a practical matter, however, unless the taxing authority has jurisdiction over the seller, it will not be able effectively to administer a consumption tax on B2C digital transactions.

Characterization is also important because liability for the VAT (at least in the EU, on which the following discussion is based) depends on the place where a supply is made, and the determination whether a supply is one of goods or services is critically important in determining if and when the VAT is due as well as establishing the party responsible for

---

54. OECD E–Commerce Discussion Paper, supra note 1, at 21.

56. Commission of the European Communities, Proposal for a Council Directive amending Directive 388/77/EEC as Regards the Value Added Tax Arrangements Applicable to Certain Services Supplied by Electronic Means, Explanatory Memorandum 4 (2000) [hereinafter cited as Explanatory Memorandum to EU E–Commerce Directive].

paying it to the taxing authorities. While the VAT rule for supply of goods is the destination principle, the rule for services is more complicated. Historically, the basic rule was that the place where a service is supplied is the place where the supplier has established its business or has a fixed establishment from which the service is supplied. However, there were a number of special rules for particular types of services, e.g., services relating to land, services relating to transport, services involving physical performance, and, most importantly for present purposes, services involving intangibles, consultancy services, and telecommunications.

[The ensuing portion of the article went on to explore the existing and proposed EU rules for the sourcing of service transactions. For an updated treatment of these issues, see Walter Hellerstein, "Consumption Taxation of Cross–Border Trade in Services in an Age of Globalization," in Arthur Cockfield, ed., Globalization and the Impact of Tax on International Investments (2010).]

* * *

B.   United States Subnational Retail Sales Tax (RST) Issues

There has been considerable national and international interest in the issues raised by the application of the American retail sales tax (RST) to electronic commerce. This interest, however, at least from an international perspective, is misplaced. As the ensuing discussion reveals, the Americans have very little to teach the world about consumption taxation, and the problems with which they are struggling vis-à-vis taxation of electronic commerce are largely problems of their own making, to wit, the unharmonized character of their state and local tax system and the consequent inability of the states to require distant sellers to collect taxes on sales to local consumers—upon tangible and digital products alike.

To appreciate the "American problem" of subnational (state and local) retail sales taxation of electronic commerce, one must first understand the nature of the American RST and the constitutional restraints that are imposed on its implementation. Forty-five states and the District of Columbia, as well as many of their political subdivisions, have adopted RSTs.[69] Probably the most significant feature of existing state RST laws insofar as they apply to electronic commerce is that state RSTs generally apply only to sales of tangible personal property and not to sales of services or of intangible property. While a few states tax a wide range of services (including information and data processing services), and most states tax some services (e.g., public utility services and hotel and motel services), most state sales taxes are limited to sales of tangible personal property. This makes the state RST a rather imperfect consumption tax— there is no sound reason for distinguishing between household consumption of goods and services for consumption tax purposes. More importantly

---

69.   2 Jerome R. Hellerstein & Walter Hellerstein ¶ 12.02 (3d ed. 1998). The local sales taxes are usually, but not always, identical to the state sales tax and in substance simply increase the rate of tax on the taxable sale.

for present purposes, it also makes the state RST an unlikely vehicle for concern about taxation of electronic commerce, since sales of digital products—the only novel issues raised by electronic commerce for a properly structured consumption tax—are largely excluded from the tax base.

Why, then, one might ask, are the Americans so concerned about the application of the RST to electronic commerce? To appreciate fully my somewhat extended answer to this question, we must start with an understanding of the constitutional structure governing the power of states to tax interstate sales. * * *

[The ensuing portion of the article describes the constitutional restraints on the ability of states to collect taxes on remote sales—restraints with which you should by now be familiar.]

* * *

In sum, the "American problem" with consumption taxation of electronic commerce has very little to do with electronic commerce everything to do with remote selling. And the problem is a self-inflicted wound. If the American states would harmonize their state and local tax systems, thereby removing the burden on the remote seller from complying with the inconsistent tax rules in 45 states and thousands of local taxing jurisdictions, there would no longer be any basis for prohibiting the states from requiring a remote vendor from collecting tax. And then the Americans could start to worry about the real problems raised by electronic commerce—taxation of digital products. But first they would have to include them in their tax base.[78]

NOTES AND QUESTIONS

A. *Consumption Tax Principles and Electronic Commerce.* Why should "[r]ules for the consumption taxation of cross-border trade * * * result in taxation in the jurisdiction where consumption takes place," as the Ottawa Framework Conditions promulgated by the OECD Finance Ministers declare? OECD, Committee on Fiscal Affairs, Electronic Commerce: Taxation Framework Conditions 5 (1998). Can't a consumption tax be administered *more* efficiently on an origin basis, especially in an e-commerce environment where destinations may be identifiable only by Internet Protocol (IP) addresses that often have no meaningful geographic significance? What would be the likely consequences of requiring vendors to collect taxes on Internet and other sales to the jurisdictions in which they were located?

B. *Further Exploration of Sourcing Issues.* The question of where a taxable sale of electronic products or services occurs is difficult because the transactions frequently have meaningful contacts with more than one jurisdiction. For example, an information provider in State A employing a server in State B can sell access to its data base through an Internet service provider in

---

78. As noted above, some states tax services and digital products, such as information services, computer services, and electronic data bases, but many states do not.

State C to a customer in State D who is billed by a financial intermediary in State E. Which state can, does, and should tax the sale?

To place this issue in proper perspective, it may be useful to begin with a general consideration of the principles underlying the situsing of sales for sales and use tax purposes, particularly as those principles relate to the sale of services. If goods are sold by a vendor in one state to a purchaser in another, it is apparent that both states have sufficient contact with the transaction to impose a tax on the transaction—although the tax imposed by the purchaser's state may be deemed a use tax rather than a sales tax to avoid constitutional problems. Generally speaking, however, perhaps because the states recognize that the sales tax is a consumption tax, perhaps because they do not wish to saddle local merchants with a tax on goods destined for other states, most states exempt from tax all sales for delivery outside the state.

Let us now shift the focus slightly to the sale of electronic services sold by a vendor in one state to a purchaser in another. Suppose, for example, that an oil company in Ohio uses the Internet to access the data base of an oil industry consulting firm in Texas. Assume further that both Ohio and Texas have decided, as a matter of principle, that information services are taxable. Will (or should) a Texas sales tax or, alternatively, an Ohio sales or use tax be added to the consulting firm's bill to the oil company?

Texas's claim to tax the services is based on the position that a sale of services should be deemed to occur where the services are performed rather than where they are consumed. The position is consistent with the rule applied to taxation of services by some states, namely, that the sale of services is taxed by the state in which the services are performed, even though the services are in effect "delivered" and consumed outside the state.[j] Moreover, this position may recommend itself from an administrative perspective because the taxing authorities of the state in which services are performed will always have jurisdiction over the service provider and will thus be in a position to enforce collection of the sales tax.

On the other hand, it must be recognized that a performance-based rule for taxing the sale of services is inconsistent with the general rule that the sale of tangible personal property is taxed by the state in which the goods are delivered to the purchaser. This rule reflects the view that goods are consumed in the state of the purchaser rather than in the state of the seller. A performance-based rule cannot be squared with the premise that a sales tax is a tax on consumption.

Consistently with this view, many states take the position that services should be taxed in the state in which they are delivered or enjoyed, and they exempt services if the use of the service occurs outside the state.[k] Moreover, a number of states by statute, regulation, or administrative pronouncement

---

j. See, e.g., Airwork Service Division v. Director, Division of Taxation, 2 N.J.Tax 329 (1981), aff'd, 4 N.J.Tax 532 (Super Ct., App. Div. 1982), aff'd, 97 N.J. 290, 478 A.2d 729 (1984), cert. denied, 471 U.S. 1127, 105 S.Ct. 2662 (1985) (sustaining tax on repair services performed in state on airplane engines delivered to customer outside the state); Matter of Airlift International, Inc. v. State Tax Commission, 52 A.D.2d 688, 382 N.Y.S.2d 572 (3d Dep't 1976) (sustaining use tax on repairs of airplanes used in interstate and international commerce).

k. In re State and Municipal Sales and Use Tax Liability of K.O. Lee Co., 489 N.W.2d 606 (S.D. 1992).

follow the rule—analogous to the rule prevailing with regard to sales of tangible personal property—that information, computer, and other electronically deliverable services are taxable where the purchaser is located with exemptions for services delivered to out-of-state purchasers.[1]

If, however, one adopts the view that a consumption-based rather than a performance-based approach to taxing services is appropriate, the question may be raised whether it is possible to implement such a rule since the "sale" of the service in the contractual sense will typically occur in the state in which it is performed, and the state in which the service is consumed will have no power to tax the "sale" of the service. The answer, of course, is the adoption of a "use" tax on services.

The theory underlying a use tax on services is identical to the theory underlying the use tax on the sale of tangible personal property. It is designed to counteract the potential loss of business and revenue the state might incur if in-state consumers of services sought to avoid the tax by purchasing services from out-of-state service providers. By imposing a use tax equal in amount to the sales tax that would have been imposed on the sale of the services if the sale had occurred within the state's taxing jurisdiction, the state removes the incentive for local consumers of services to purchase services outside the state.

There is yet a third possibility for "sourcing" sales in electronic commerce—apportionment of the sales tax base. During its brief lifetime, for example, Florida's broad-based sales tax on services (which taxed all services not explicitly exempted[m]) provided for the apportionment of certain services that were not situs-specific. Thus a corporation that purchased electronic data processing services for general use in its business would pay a sales tax to Florida on the percentage of the services that were presumed to be enjoyed in Florida, a percentage that would be determined by reference to the corporation's Florida income tax apportionment formula.[n] Under current law in Texas, if an information service is used to support a customer's business that is conducted at locations within and without the state, the service is taxable only to the extent that it is used within Texas, and the taxpayer "may use any reasonable method for allocation which is supported by business records."[o] The District of Columbia regulation provides that "[i]nformation services performed or delivered outside the District for use within other jurisdictions as well as for use within the District shall be subject to a prorated share of the

---

l. See, e.g., D.C. Mun. Regs. § 475.10 (Westlaw 2009) (exempting information services "sold and delivered by the vendor to locations outside of the District"); Pa. Rev. Pronouncement 60.13(b)(1) (1997) (sale of computer services subject to tax if predominant use of the service is in Pennsylvania; computer services delivered to a Pennsylvania location are presumed to be predominantly used in Pennsylvania); Tex. Tax Code Ann. §§ 151.010, 151.051, 151.101 (Westlaw 2009) (imposing tax on each "taxable item," defined to include taxable services, sold or used in this state); id. § 151.330(e) (exempting "[s]ervices performed for use outside this state").

m. See generally Walter Hellerstein, "Florida's Sales Tax on Services," 41 Nat'l Tax J. 1 (1988).

n. Id. at 5. Massachusetts adopted a similar apportionment regime during its similarly short-lived broad-based sales tax on services. See Samuel B. Bruskin & Kathleen K. Parker, "State Sales Taxes on Services: Massachusetts as a Case Study," 45 Tax Law. 49, 61–63 (1991).

o. 34 Tex. Admin. Code § 3.342(g)(2) (Westlaw 2009).

District use tax, provided that no sales tax was required to be paid on the prorated share to the other jurisdiction.''[p]

Needless to say, apportionment of a sales tax, often involving hundreds or thousands of individual transactions for a single taxpayer, is quite a different matter from apportionment of an income tax, which is filed on an annual basis. Indeed, it may not be feasible to administer an apportioned sales tax except for relatively large taxpayers, who are able to supply vendors with appropriate apportionment percentages or that "self-assess" sales and use taxes. It is clear, of course, after cases like *Goldberg v. Sweet*[q] and *Oklahoma Tax Commission v. Jefferson Lines, Inc.*[r] that states are not required to apportion sales taxes on services, any more than they are required to apportion sales taxes on sales of tangible personal property, at least in cases in which a sale can reasonably be deemed to occur in a particular jurisdiction.[s]

The question remains whether sourcing rules that look to the physical location of the seller or purchaser make good sense (and, therefore, good law) in the context of electronic commerce. For example, the physical location of the purchaser of access to a remote data base may be difficult, if not impossible, to identify, when the purchaser is accessing the data base from a laptop computer at various locations. Likewise with the increasing use of wireless phone systems as hand-held digital platforms for sending e-mail or faxes or connecting to the Internet, the location of the customer or of the "use" of the services will often be problematic.

Similar problems obtain when electronically delivered information is produced in one location, "delivered" or downloaded in another, and used in a third.

> The tendency to store both the data and application software at a remote location is likely to increase with the advent of network computers and Java "applets." The new technology allows consumers to access data and application software from a remote server on an "as needed" basis, reducing the need for large computer memory.[t]

Moreover, these "sourcing" problems are exacerbated when the information accessed is distributed by the purchaser to multiple locations throughout the country for use in the purchaser's own operations. In the following part of this chapter (pp. 781–801 infra), we explore the approach of the Streamlined Sales and Use Tax Agreement to resolving these sourcing issues and the problems that have been encountered in attempts to implement this approach.

---

p. D.C. Mun. Regs. § 475.9 (Westlaw 2009)

q. 488 U.S. 252, 109 S.Ct. 582 (1989), set out supra at pp. 176–85.

r. 514 U.S. 175, 115 S.Ct. 1331 (1995), set out supra at pp. 743–58.

s. This may not always be the case, however, in connection with transactions in electronic commerce. For example, software may be purchased by a nationwide enterprise and simultaneously delivered by the vendor to the purchaser's locations all across the country. Under those circumstances, it may not be appropriate to conclude that the sale occurs in a particular jurisdiction and apportionment of the base may be the only reasonable way to "source" the tax base.

t. Karl A. Frieden & Michael E. Porter, "The Taxation of Cyberspace: State Tax Issues Related to the Internet and Electronic Commerce," State Tax Notes, Nov. 11, 1996, pp. 1363, 1364.

C. *Comparing the E–Commerce Taxation Issues Raised by the American Retail Sales Tax and by the European Value Added Tax.* Why does the foregoing article claim that "the Americans have very little to teach the world about consumption taxation"? Why do the member countries of the EU not have the same problem of collecting value added taxes on remote sales of tangible personal property into member countries that the American states have with collecting use taxes on remote sales of tangible personal property into the states? Why should we be concerned about the sales tax issues raised by taxation of e-commerce, when most states do not even tax the paradigmatic e-commerce transaction—the sale of digital products? Why have your casebook authors burdened you with this esoterica regarding the EU VAT?

D. *The Internet Tax Freedom Act.* In 1998, Congress enacted the Internet Tax Freedom Act (ITFA). Pub. L. No. 105–277, tit. XI, 112 Stat. 2681 (1998). The Act imposes a three-year moratorium (subsequently extended through 2014) on three types of taxes: (1) taxes on Internet access; (2) discriminatory taxes on electronic commerce; and (3) multiple taxes on electronic commerce.

Taxes on Internet Access. The prohibition against taxes on Internet access forbids states from taxing charges for "a service that enables users to connect to the Internet to access content, information, or other services offered over the Internet." Pub. L. No. 105–277, § 1104(5) (1998), as amended by Internet Tax Freedom Act Amendments Act of 2007, Pub. L. No. 110–108, 121 Stat. 1024 (2007). The statute plainly forbids states from taxing the monthly fee that Internet access providers charge their customers for connecting to the Internet. The original prohibition contained a flat exclusion of telecommunications services from the definition of "Internet access." The 2004 extension of the moratorium added language making it clear that all forms of Internet access were covered by the moratorium, including high-speed wireline (DSL) and wireless service (i.e., telecommunications services "purchased, used, or sold by a provider of Internet access to provide Internet access"). Pub. L. No. 108–435, § 2(c), 118 Stat. 2615, 2616 (2004). The 2007 ITFA amendments expanded the definition of "Internet access" to include "a home page, electronic mail, and instant messaging (including voice-and video-capable electronic mail and instant messaging), video clips, and personal electronic storage capacity," whether packaged with Internet access or provided independently. The 2007 amendments further excluded from the definition of "tax on Internet access" taxes that Michigan, Ohio, and Texas impose on gross receipts or gross income from business activity (in lieu of the typical state-level corporate income tax). Pub. L. No. 110–108, § 4, 121 Stat. 1024 (2007).

The original act grandfathered preexisting state taxes on Internet access by excluding from ITFA's scope any tax that "was generally imposed and actually enforced prior to October 1, 1998." Pub. L. No. 105–277, § 1101(a)(1) (1998). Although that provision has been extended through 2014, a more limited grandfathering provision for states that were taxing the telecommunications services that were covered by the moratorium for the first time (i.e., telecommunications services purchased, used, or sold to provide Internet access) were grandfathered only through June 30, 2008. The 2004 extension of ITFA also made it clear that the prohibition does not apply to any tax on a voice or similar service using Internet Protocol (voice over Internet Protocol, or VOIP), except to the extent that the services are incidental to the Internet access (e.g., voice-capable email or instant messaging).

Discriminatory Taxes on Electronic Commerce. The Act's prohibition against discriminatory taxes on electronic commerce would have little impact if it were limited to that concept as it is generally understood, because there are no taxes that single out transactions in electronic commerce for invidious treatment. However, because Congress defined "discriminatory taxes" to include certain taxes in which a remote seller has only minimal nexus with a state, ITFA may have some impact with respect to use tax collection obligations. Specifically, the Act forbids states from relying on the existence of an in-state server as a basis for asserting use tax collection obligations.

Multiple Taxes on Electronic Commerce. The Internet Tax Freedom Act's prohibition of multiple taxation of electronic commerce is not a model of clarity. A "multiple tax" is defined as

> any tax that is imposed by one State * * *on the same or essentially the same electronic commerce that is also subject to another tax imposed by another State * * * (whether or not at the same rate or on the same basis), without a credit (for example, a resale exemption certificate) for taxes paid in other jurisdictions.

Pub. L. No. 105–277, § 1104(6)(A) (1998). Congress excluded from this definition sales or use taxes imposed concurrently by a state and its political subdivisions on the same electronic commerce and "a tax on persons engaged in electronic commerce which may also have been subject to a sales or use tax thereon." Id. § 1104(6)(B).

Although one can discern Congress's objective in enacting this provision (i.e., to prevent the same electronic commerce from being subject to tax by more than one state), the language that Congress chose to accomplish that goal is opaque at best. While preventing more than one state from taxing "the same electronic commerce" might leave some room for debate, the prevention of states from taxing "essentially the same electronic commerce" is almost an invitation for controversy. Indeed, it reads more like cocktail party conversation than a carefully thought out restraint on state taxing power.

Moreover, Congress apparently believes that two states can tax "the same" or "essentially the same" electronic commerce, even if the two levies are not imposed "on the same basis." Does this mean, for example, that Texas may not impose a sales or use tax on computer software transmitted via the Internet from a Washington State software producer, because "essentially the same electronic commerce" was subject to Washington's Business and Occupation Tax? See pp. 120–23 supra. Or is this the situation to which the "savings clause" was directed (i.e., "a tax on persons engaged in electronic commerce"), which is not regarded as a "multiple tax" even if the same electronic commerce is subject to sales or use tax? If it is, will the savings clause defeat Congress' objective? See p. 606 supra (describing the legal incidence of state sales taxes, which often fall on the vendor for the privilege of engaging in selling activities).

Bundled Services. The 2004 ITFA legislation addressed the thorny question of how one deals with sales of "bundled" services (i.e., a "bundle" of services that are both taxable and exempt under ITFA) in the following provision:

> If charges for Internet access are aggregated with and not separately stated from charges for telecommunications services or other charges that are subject to taxation, then the charges for Internet access may be subject to taxation unless the Internet access provider can reasonably identify the charges for Internet access from its books and records kept in the regular course of business.

Pub. L. No. 108–435, § 4, 118 Stat. 2615, 2617 (2004). This rule differs from the typical rule for "bundled sales" of taxable and nontaxable goods or services, which requires the vendor to state separately the charges for the respective components of the sale in order for them to receive separate treatment. The "books and records" approach embodied in ITFA represented a victory for vendors over state tax administrators, who much prefer the "separate statement rule" because of concerns about ease of tax administration and audit. Vendors, however, find the separate statement rule burdensome and, perhaps more importantly, inconsistent with their business model of selling a seamless bundle of goods and/or services. Reminding purchasers that they owe tax on a portion of the bundle through the separate statement rule undermines the vendors' marketing objective.

How does the "multiple tax" prohibition described above apply to "bundled" sales involving both "electronic commerce" and nonprotected commerce (e.g., telecommunications)? These services may be sold as a seamless package of services. Does the fact that the "electronic commerce" was previously subject to tax in one state mean that it may not be included in a "bundle" of services (including telecommunications) that is taxed in another state? Must the taxpayer "unbundle" the "electronic commerce" aspect of the service in order to take advantage of the prohibition or does the substantive rule of federal law preempt the rule of state tax administration? Does the "separate statement rule" or the "books and records" rule apply to such a bundle? For a general consideration of ITFA, see Walter Hellerstein, "Internet Tax Freedom Act Limits States' Power to Tax Internet Access and Electronic Commerce," 90 J. Tax'n 5 (1999).

L. FUNDAMENTAL SALES TAX REFORM AND THE STREAMLINED SALES AND USE TAX

1. FUNDAMENTAL SALES TAX REFORM

CHARLES E. McLURE, JR., THE NUTTINESS OF STATE AND LOCAL TAXES—AND THE NUTTINESS OF RESPONSES THERETO

State Tax Notes, Sept. 16, 2002, p. 841.u

I. Introduction

Many key elements of state and local taxes can only be described as nutty. Some nutty provisions may reflect the economic reality or the state of knowledge of economics that prevailed when the taxes were first enacted—or, of course, they may simply reflect the political realities of the time. Changes in economic reality and our understanding of the economic effects of unwise tax policy are sometimes reflected in improved tax policy. But policy response in the United States—when it has occurred—has often exhibited further nuttiness. Some of the nuttiness of the policy response to prior nuttiness can reasonably be interpreted as attempts to overcome the legacy of nutty policy, without eliminating the nuttiness directly, through fundamental reform.

The next section contains a short summary of key points in the theory of tax assignment, which will be useful as background for the ensuing discussion * * *.

* * *

II. Tax Assignment: A Short Course

The theory of tax assignment provides important lessons for the design of state and local taxes. Two aspects of that theory are worth emphasis here: the role of benefit-related taxes and the importance of compliance and administration in the rational design of a decentralized system of taxation.

A. The Role of Benefit–Related Taxes

The theory of tax assignment is rooted in the theory of fiscal federalism, in which subnational fiscal autonomy plays a crucial role. The theory of tax assignment suggests that, to the extent possible, subnational governments should rely on taxes that reflect the benefits of public services.[6] Benefit taxation has an advantage similar to that of using

---

u. Reprinted with the permission of the publisher and the author.

6. The use of benefit taxation should also be sought at the national level. But the national government may also be assigned a role in income redistribution—a role that is not ordinarily assigned to subnational governments—that requires the use of taxes not related to benefits.

market prices to determine what is produced and who pays for it: it promotes economic efficiency. (Many would argue that benefit taxation is also fair, but others might disagree; fairness is not essential to the case for benefit taxation.)

Aside from the use of taxes on motor fuels to pay for the construction and maintenance of roads and highways, it is difficult to design taxes that are closely related to benefits of public services. But the benefit principle does, none the less, yield some fairly straightforward lessons for the design of subnational taxes. The following are especially relevant for current purposes:

- Taxes on business that do not reflect benefits of public services provided to the taxpayer should be avoided. These include sales taxes on business purchases and corporate income taxes,[9] as well as taxes on business property that exceed benefits provided. Besides distorting production decisions, such taxes make a state an economically less attractive place to do business.

- Sales taxes should be levied primarily on a destination basis, not an origin basis—that is, by jurisdictions where consumption occurs, rather than where production occurs. The idea is that people consume public services predominantly where they consume private products, not where they produce them. Moreover, origin-based taxes that do not reflect benefits of public services distort the location of economic activity, making the taxing state less attractive to business. This principle means that products imported into the state should be taxed like those produced within the state and that exports from the state should not be taxed.

- Individual income taxes should be levied by the state where the taxpayer lives (that is, on the basis of residence), not where the taxpayer works (on the basis of source). The argument is similar to that for destination-based sales taxes; people consume public services primarily where they live, not where they work. * * *

- Tax competition among states can be beneficial, by protecting taxpayers from the tendency of politicians to levy taxes that exceed benefits provided to taxpayers.[12]

---

9. The basic point is that most public services are provided to households, not to businesses. * * * Beyond that, there is no reason to think that businesses require more public services because they purchase inputs, instead of producing the inputs themselves. Corporate income taxes are not likely to reflect benefits of public services because services are not provided only to businesses that are organized in corporate form, they are not likely to be provided only to corporations that are profitable, and they are not likely to increase in direct proportion to profits. * * *

12. Pogue writes, "Any single state will find it difficult to tax mobile businesses more heavily than other states, *unless it also provides services that are sufficiently valuable to offset its relatively high taxes.* Tax competition will thus tend to reduce interstate differences in taxes on mobile businesses *that are not matched by differences in government-provided services* (emphasis added)." He adds, however, "Tax competition will likely push business taxes below the levels required to offset external and public service costs." * * * [Thomas F. Pogue, "State and Local Business Taxation: Principles and Prospects," in David Brunori, The Future of State Taxation (Washington: Urban Institute Press, 1998), pp. 89–110.]

- Economic efficiency in government, as well as fairness, demands that subnational taxes not be exported to residents of other jurisdictions, unless they reflect benefits provided to nonresidents. (Residents of jurisdictions that are able to export taxes do not pay the full cost of the public services they receive and thus may demand an excessive amount of services.)

B. Compliance and Administration

Inconsistencies in the way different states impose a given tax can render tax administration and compliance needlessly complicated and costly, and it may create unacceptable inequities and economic distortions. The U.S. Supreme Court has implicitly recognized this important principle. In the *National Bellas Hess* decision (386 U.S. 753, 1967), the Court ruled that, due in large part to the complexity caused by the lack of uniformity of state sales taxes, a state can require a remote (out-of-of-state) vendor to collect its use tax (a substitute for the sales tax that is levied on the in-state "use" of a product bought outside the state) only if the vendor has a physical presence in the state.[13] This principle implies that certain aspects of subnational taxation should be coordinated, in order to facilitate administration and compliance and avoid inequities and distortions. Desirable aspects of uniformity include, *inter alia*, the definition of the tax base, means of dividing the tax base among states, the legal framework, and administrative procedures. *There is generally no persuasive case for requiring uniformity of tax rates*, which eliminates subnational fiscal autonomy, as well as any possibility of tax competition, without much affecting complexity. See, however, the discussion of local sales and use taxes below.

* * *

III. The Nuttiness of State Sales and Use Taxes

This section describes principles of sound sales tax policy, actual sales tax practices and the problems they create, and implications for policy.

A. Principles of Sound Sales Tax Policy

A fair and neutral system. A conceptually sound sales tax that is consistent with the principles of tax assignment outlined above would exhibit the following characteristics:

- All consumption would be taxed.
- No sales to business would be taxed.[20]

---

13. In affirming relevant aspects of this decision in *Quill*, the Court relied heavily on considerations of *stare decisis*, noting that a large and important industry had been built on the basis of the physical presence rule.

20. One might reasonably make an exception for products easily diverted to personal use, such as restaurant meals, entertainment, and automobiles. It would be possible to utilize a system in which all sales of many "dual use" products such as computers are initially subject to tax, requiring the buyer to submit a claim for a refund of tax on purchases made for business

- Exports would not be taxed.

- Sales by remote (out-of-state) vendors would be taxed like sales by local vendors (subject to *de minimis* rules to be considered below).

Such a system would be fair and economically neutral.[21] It would not discriminate between types of consumption, between ways of organizing production and distribution, or between local and remote vendors. It would not distort the location of economic activity. Nor would it discriminate between consumers who buy products that are subject to light and heavy taxation, as all products sold to consumers would be taxed the same.

Administrative features. There should be enough simplicity—which means interstate uniformity—that it is not unreasonable to require remote vendors to collect use tax if their sales in a state exceed a *de minimis* amount. Ideally there would be enough uniformity that a merchant in one state could easily comply with the sales and use tax of another state if it knew the laws of its own state, plus the destination of the sale and the tax rate of the other state. To achieve this objective, uniformity is required, *inter alia,* in:

- the tax base;

- definitions of products;

- rules for "sourcing" (determining the destination of) sales;

- exemption of purchases by business;

- statutes, regulations, and interpretations; and

- administrative procedures, including "one-stop" registration for all states.

Local jurisdictions within any state (and thus in all states) would follow the state definitions, legal frameworks, and procedures, and states would collect local taxes as surcharges on state taxes. Uniformity of state tax rates would not be required; indeed, as indicated above, state power to set tax rates is required for the exercise of fiscal autonomy. Diversity of local rates is considered below.

Nexus (duty to collect tax) should depend on having *either* a substantial physical presence or a non-*de minimis* amount of sales in a state, not merely on having a physical presence, as it does under *Quill*. This two-pronged test of nexus deserves comment. First, it would make no sense to force remote vendors that make only a small amount of sales in a state to collect tax. Thus the sales prong of the nexus test should depend on having non-*de minimis* sales in a state. Given the degree of uniformity inherent in the proposed system, the sales threshold could be set quite

---

purposes. This is, in essence the technique that underlies the credit-method VAT. Audits would be subject to the same uncertainty as federal income tax deductions for similar expenditures.

21. Some may wonder why I stress economic neutrality, rather than "optimal taxation." * * * Others may complain that such a tax would be regressive (that is, that it would take a smaller percentage of a household's income, the greater its income). This concern should be addressed by a progressive federal income tax and transfer payments, not by sales tax exemptions, which are a blunt instrument for achieving income distribution objectives.

low. Second, the physical presence test of *Quill* would be modified by the addition of the word "substantial." This would prevent remote vendors that have only an insubstantial physical presence and make only *de minimis* sales in a state from being forced to collect tax.[26] Finally, realistic vendor discounts would relieve the compliance burden of small firms, which is especially heavy.

Interaction between economic neutrality and simplicity. The economically neutral system described earlier would have the simplest possible tax base—or at least the simplest tax base that makes sense. It could be described in two sentences:

- If a household buys it, it is taxable;
- If a business buys it, it is exempt.

These rules allow focus to shift from the nature of the product to the nature of the purchaser. Whereas the former distinction is inevitably problematic, the latter is ordinarily straightforward. (There is, of course, some possibility of abuse by those who falsely characterize the purpose of purchases.)

Inevitable problems of local sales taxes. The imposition of sales and use taxes by local governments inevitably creates problems. (The same problems exist at the state level, but ordinarily in much attenuated form.)

First, remote vendors will experience compliance problems in:

- "sourcing" the sale to its destination;
- applying the proper tax rate(s); and
- channeling revenue to the right jurisdiction(s).

Note that solving the second problem, by requiring a single tax rate for remote sales made in a state, would not solve the other two problems, which are closely related.

Second, even if compliance problems can be overcome for remote commerce, the use of sales taxes by jurisdictions within a major metropolitan area can create other problems, because of cross-border shopping (making purchases in a jurisdiction other than that of residence):

- The exporting of taxes to nonresidents is unfair and distorts the price of local public services in the jurisdiction that exports taxes.

- Revenue does not go to jurisdictions of residence, which provide most public services provided by local governments.

- Local governments engage in unhealthy tax competition to attract stores and shopping malls that generate revenues from sales tax that is exported to households who live in other jurisdictions.[28]

---

26. It might be more sensible not to have a physical presence test. The word "substantial" invites uncertainty and litigation. If sales are not significant, not much revenue would be involved, whether or not the vendor has a physical presence in the state.

28. Unhealthy competition for cross-border shoppers can be distinguished from healthy competition for economic activity by the exporting of the tax to nonresidents of the taxing jurisdiction that occurs in the former case.

These inevitable problems lead some to conclude that local sales taxes should be avoided. This issue is considered further below.

B. The Nuttiness of Actual Sales Taxes

Extant sales taxes violate all the principles of sound tax policy stated above, with the adverse consequences indicated.

- Much consumption, especially of services, is not taxed.[31]
  - This distorts consumer choices and creates inequity among consumers.
  - The regressivity of the tax system is increased, because services are consumed disproportionately by the more affluent.
  - Tax rates must be higher than otherwise, to raise a given amount of revenue.
- Many sales to business are taxed.
  - This distorts business decisions on production and distribution.
  - Part of the cost of government is concealed.
- An origin-based element of taxation is interjected into the destination-based sales tax system.
  - Inputs employed in production for export are taxed.
  - There is a disincentive to produce in states that tax business purchases.
  - Producers in those states are disadvantaged, relative to foreign producers, in both foreign and domestic markets.
- There is substantial complexity because of the lack of uniformity in:
  - tax bases;
  - definitions of products;
  - exemptions of business purchases;
  - legal frameworks; and
  - administrative procedures.
  - Also, states do not exempt *de minimis* sales or provide realistic vendors' discounts.
- Local taxes are the source of much additional complexity.
  - It is necessary to "source" sales to local jurisdictions, apply the appropriate tax rate, and channel the revenue to the proper jurisdiction.
  - Local tax bases deviate from state bases in some states.
  - Local governments in some states administer their own taxes.

---

31. Many observe that taxation of purchases of business inputs by service providers partly offsets the failure to tax services. This is true, but, (a) business inputs are a relatively small cost of providing most consumer services and (b) to the extent business services (for example, legal and accounting expenses) are taxed in this indirect way, the tax constitutes an unjustified cost.

- Because of complexity, the U.S. Supreme Court has ruled that states can impose a duty to collect use tax only on vendors with a physical presence in the state (*National Bellas Hess* and *Quill* decisions).

    - This violates the destination principle.

    - This discriminates against "Main Street" merchants and their customers.

    - It leads to loss of revenue (or higher rates to raise a given amount of revenue).

C. Eliminating Nuttiness: Implications for Policy

The needed reforms. Some of the implications for policy are relatively straightforward. In order to eliminate nuttiness, it is necessary to:

- eliminate exemptions for consumer purchasers;

- exempt all business purchases;

- simplify the sales tax system by creating greater uniformity; and

- modify the physical presence test of nexus as suggested above.

The problem of local use taxes. As noted earlier, local sales taxes pose especially difficult problems. The proposal to eliminate local sales taxes and replace them with local income taxes seems hopelessly unrealistic. Not only are local sales taxes an important source of revenue for many local governments, revenues from them have been pledged to service bonds (e.g., for sports stadiums).

Local taxes could be simplified in various ways, particularly in the few states that deviate dramatically from the conceptual ideal. As a bare minimum, state and local taxes in a given state should be levied on the same tax base and states should collect local taxes. Beyond that, it should be possible to devise ways to reduce compliance costs for remote vendors, for example, by combining realistic *de minimis* rules and vendor discounts with a "technological fix" that would allow sales to be traced to the locality of buyers.

Requiring one use tax rate per state (combined with sales tax rates of local choosing and state allocation of use tax revenues among localities based on a formula, rather than attribution of individual sales by remote vendors to particular localities) would greatly simplify compliance for remote vendors, but would require congressional approval (because interstate sales would be taxed more heavily than sales by local merchants in jurisdictions with sales tax rates below the uniform use tax rate). One use tax rate per state would produce relatively little simplification if remote vendors were required to source sales and channel revenues to local jurisdictions.

D. Can a State 'Go It Alone' in Fixing Its Sales Tax?

The inability to require collection of use taxes on sales by remote vendors—and the complexity that underlies it—is currently the most vexing problem of sales taxation. If the states are to require vendors who lack an in-state physical presence to collect use tax, the Congress or the U.S. Supreme Court must override the *Quill* decision. This, in turn, is almost certain to require drastic simplification of the state sales tax "system." Because simplicity requires greater uniformity, no single state acting alone can achieve it. Rather, simplification requires the concerted effort of all the sales tax states—or at least enough of them to convince the Supreme Court or the Congress to reverse the *Quill* decision and allow those states to require remote vendors to collect use tax for them. This is a tall order because the complexity of the sales tax "system" is the evolutionary product of the independent actions of 45 states and the District of Columbia.

By comparison, any state could act unilaterally to rationalize its sales tax in the other ways mentioned. That is, a single state could extend the tax to services and other consumer products that are currently exempt and could exempt all sales to business. The second of these would have the salutary effect of removing a cost that impedes the ability of in-state firms to compete in both foreign and domestic markets, including the market of the taxing state, but it would have an enormous negative impact on revenues, unless rates were raised dramatically.

Some might decry the elimination of taxes on sales to business as a "race-to-the-bottom," using the pejorative term often employed to describe tax competition. But this form of tax competition is *good* tax competition, because the bottom—complete exemption of sales to business—is precisely what makes sense, both for the individual state and for the nation.[37] Moreover, if the legislatures and governors of all the states, acting independently, were to eliminate sales tax on all sales to business the result would be a substantial simplification of the entire system. State-by-state rules concerning what is exempt if bought by businesses (when engaged in particular activities) could be replaced by a single rule, and a single uniform tax exemption certificate could be used to implement the rule: "if a business buys it, it is exempt." One of the enduring mysteries is why business interests have not pressed for this reform, which has, in effect, been in place in Europe since the 1960s.

In theory the same type of state-specific action could also lead to a definition of the tax base that would be uniform across the nation, and therefore simple to implement: "If a consumer buys it, it is taxable." Realism suggests, however, that this reform is even less likely to result from the unilateral action of individual states. Whereas there should be powerful forces advocating elimination of tax on sales to business, there is no similar natural constituency for taxing all consumption—and plenty of constituencies that would oppose it.

* * *

---

37. To see this, consider the analogous situation under the income tax. Few would argue that not all reasonable costs of business should be deductible.

Notes and Questions

A. *Business Purchases.* What is McLure's argument for the exclusion of all business purchases from sales and use tax? Do you agree? McLure states that "[o]ne of the enduring mysteries is why business interests have not pressed for this reform, which has, in effect, been in place in Europe since the 1960s." Can this be explained?

B. *Taxation of Services and Sourcing.* McLure argues that services should be taxed in order to maintain neutrality. How do sourcing issues impede the expansion of the sales tax base to services? What might you do to overcome these obstacles?

C. *Local Taxes.* McLure recognizes the important role that local taxes have played in introducing complexity into the American retail sales tax, and their role in provoking the Court to limit the power of state and local governments to impose a use tax collection obligation on remote out-of-state sellers. If you were a city councilperson in a state which allowed the cities to establish their own tax base, set their own rates, and collect their own taxes (including the conduct of taxpayer audits), how would you feel about relinquishing these powers? Which powers would be most important to you? What arguments, if any, might persuade you to give them up voluntarily?

D. *Tax competition.* Try to understand and restate in your own words McLure arguments regarding beneficial tax competition among the states. Do you agree that tax competition is sometimes beneficial?

E. *Regressivity.* We noted earlier in this chapter that sales taxes are often criticized as being regressive (pp. 609–10), i.e., sales taxes constitute a larger proportion of the income of low-income persons than high-income persons. McLure argues that "[t]his concern should be addressed by a progressive federal income tax and transfer payments, not by sale tax exemptions, which are a blunt instrument for achieving distributional objectives." What makes a sales tax exemption a "blunt instrument" for this purpose? What makes a progressive income tax and transfer payments sharper instruments?

F. *Nuttiness.* What are the causes of the nuttiness of which McLure complains? Ignorance? Politics? Our federal governmental structure? Do you share McLure's pessimism about the prospects for the states to rationalize the sales tax through unilateral action?

2. THE STREAMLINED SALES AND USE TAX

If the preceding materials in this chapter reveal nothing else, they demonstrate that the retail sales tax in its current form is a complex, uncertain, and profoundly flawed mechanism that is peculiarly unsuited to an increasingly service oriented, digital, and borderless economy. We indicated at the outset of this chapter that a number of these difficulties are traceable to two structural defects in the retail sales tax: the levy's *overinclusiveness* in taxing many business purchases and the levy's *underinclusiveness* in excluding many services. See pp. 612–13 supra. But there are other difficulties as well. The existence of 46 independent state-level taxing regimes, along with more than 6,000 local taxing jurisdictions, has created a patchwork of rules of substantive tax liability and of tax administration that can make compliance a nightmare for the multistate vendor. The U.S. Supreme Court has reacted to this quagmire of different and often conflicting state and local tax rules by articulating, and then reaffirming, a nexus rule that relieves out-of-state vendors of use tax collection responsibilities in states in which they lack a physical presence. See pp. 24–38 supra. As a consequence, sales by remote vendors enjoy a de facto immunity from taxation, even though such purchases are frequently subject to use tax, and the failure to tax them provides a competitive advantage for out-of-state over local merchants.

How might we resolve these problems short of abandoning the sales tax or abolishing the federal system? The most fundamental solution would attack the problems at their root, namely, by eradicating the distinctions that tend to create the system's complexity. If the states were to transform their sales taxes into true consumption taxes in which all business purchases were exempt and all household purchases for personal consumption (whether of goods or services) were taxable, we would have gone a long way towards creating a simple and uniform sales tax that could be administered in a multistate environment with minimal burdens for interstate vendors. To determine whether a transaction was taxable, a vendor would need to know only whether the purchase was for personal consumption or for business purposes. To be sure, there could still be issues with respect to the identification of purchases for business as distinguished from personal use and of determining the proper "destination" state in connection with the sale of digital products for personal consumption. Nevertheless, these problems would pale by comparison to those that vendors confront under the existing sales and use tax system. Moreover, states could deal with these issues by adopting standard conventions for identifying business purchasers and for sourcing sales of digital products. Under such a simplified system, one could reasonably demand that mail-order and other remote vendors, at least those who exceeded a de minimis threshold of interstate sales, collect use taxes on such sales, thereby resolving one of the most contentious issues under the existing system. See generally Charles E. McLure, Jr., "Radical Reform of the State Sales and Use Tax: Achieving Simplicity, Economic Neutrality, and Fairness," 13 Harv. J.L. & Tech. 567 (2000).

As theoretically attractive as such a fundamental solution to the problems plaguing existing state and local tax regimes may be, they are— for the moment at least—politically unrealistic. The American public and, therefore, its representatives in state legislatures do not appear ready to endorse such a dramatic reconfiguration of the retail sales tax. Such a reform would lead not only to an expansion of the tax base to previously untaxed services, it would almost certainly lead to an increase in nominal tax rates to offset the decrease in revenues from business purchases that now constitute roughly 40 percent of the sales tax base.ᵛ See p. 609 supra. Recent experience with broad-based efforts to expand the sales tax to services provides little basis for thinking that the public is ready for radical reform of the sales tax base, as sensible as such reform may be. See p. 680 supra.

Although the states may be unready to embrace the radical reform of their retail sales taxes along the lines described above, they have nevertheless launched an unprecedented cooperative effort, under the auspices of the Streamlined Sales Tax Project (SSTP), to simplify and harmonize their sales and use tax regimes. The SSTP was organized in March 2000 to develop a simplified sales and use tax system to ease the burden of sales and use tax compliance for all types of retailers, particularly those operating on a multistate basis. There are a number of factors that are motivating the states to take such action. First, the states are acutely aware of the complexity of the present system and the burden that the system imposes on vendors and state tax administrators. Second, the states are no less aware of the threat that the growth of remote commerce poses to the future of the sales tax, particularly if steps are not taken to simplify the system to permit (or require) remote vendors to collect use taxes on interstate sales. Third, the states believe that the increased availability of modern technology will permit them to assist (or cooperate with) retail merchants in administering a simplified sales tax, leading to expanded voluntary compliance and, perhaps, to congressional or judicial relaxation of the constitutional rules that now prohibit them from forcing remote sellers to collect use taxes on interstate sales. For a comprehensive description and analysis of the SSTP, see Walter Hellerstein & John Swain, Streamlined Sales and Use Tax (2008–09), from which this discussion freely draws. See also 2 Jerome R. Hellerstein & Walter Hellerstein, State Taxation ch. 19A (3rd ed. 2008 & Cum. Supp. 2009).

The initial task of the SSTP was to draft a fundamental "constitutional" document—the Streamlined Sales and Use Tax Agreement (SSUTA or the Agreement)—containing the substantive, administrative, and governance rules to which states that are parties to SSUTA must adhere. The SSTP immediately undertook this task, which occupied the better part of two years. The working groups met formally and informally, often in consultation with business representatives, to address the principal issues at hand, and they produced valuable issue papers that analyzed the key concerns and made recommendations to the full SSTP.

In November 2002, the Streamlined Sales Tax Implementing States (SSTIS)—a deliberative body comprised of the states that had enacted legislation authorizing participation in the streamlining effort—adopted the Streamlined Sales and Use Tax Agreement that SSTP representatives had been drafting over the previous two years. Streamlined Sales and Use Tax Agreement, available at www.streamlinedsalestax.org. Despite the

---

v. We say "increase in nominal tax rates" because we are already paying sales taxes at a much higher level than the nominal rate insofar as we are bearing the effective tax burden imposed on business purchases in the price we pay for products purchased at retail.

significance of the Agreement, it is critical to keep in mind that SSUTA was in significant part no more than a blueprint whose basic requirements needed state by state implementation by adoption of more detailed legislation. As we go to press in late 2009, 20 states are Full Members of the Agreement, having brought themselves into full compliance with the Agreement.[w]

We have set out excerpts from the Agreement, as amended, below. As you consider the these excerpts, ask yourselves four basic questions: (1) What problem or problems is the particular provision attempting to address? (2) Does the provision address the problem effectively? (3) If not, how would you modify the provision to achieve the perceived objective more effectively? (4) Are there significant problems with the existing sales tax regime that the provisions do not address, and, if so, what are they and how would you address them?

STREAMLINED SALES AND USE TAX AGREEMENT

(As Adopted November 12, 2002 and amended through May 12, 2009).

ARTICLE I

PURPOSE AND PRINCIPLE

Section 101: TITLE

This multistate Agreement shall be referred to, cited, and known as the Streamlined Sales and Use Tax Agreement.

Section 102: FUNDAMENTAL PURPOSE

It is the purpose of this Agreement to simplify and modernize sales and use tax administration in the member states in order to substantially reduce the burden of tax compliance. The Agreement focuses on improving sales and use tax administration systems for all sellers and for all types of commerce through all of the following:

A. State level administration of sales and use tax collections.

B. Uniformity in the state and local tax bases.

C. Uniformity of major tax base definitions.

D. Central, electronic registration system for all member states.

E. Simplification of state and local tax rates.

F. Uniform sourcing rules for all taxable transactions.

G. Simplified administration of exemptions.

H. Simplified tax returns.

I. Simplification of tax remittances.

J. Protection of consumer privacy.

---

w. These states are Arkansas, Indiana, Iowa, Kansas, Kentucky, Michigan, Minnesota, Nebraska, Nevada, New Jersey, North Carolina, North Dakota, Oklahoma, Rhode Island, South Dakota, Vermont, Washington, West Virginia, Wisconsin, and Wyoming.

Section 103: TAXING AUTHORITY PRESERVED

This Agreement shall not be construed as intending to influence a member state to impose a tax on or provide an exemption from tax for any item or service. However, if a member state chooses to tax an item or exempt an item from tax, that state shall adhere to the provisions concerning definitions as set out in Article III of this Agreement.

* * *

ARTICLE II

DEFINITIONS

The following definitions apply in this Agreement:

* * *

Section 202: CERTIFIED AUTOMATED SYSTEM (CAS)

Software certified under the Agreement to calculate the tax imposed by each jurisdiction on a transaction, determine the amount of tax to remit to the appropriate state, and maintain a record of the transaction.

Section 203: CERTIFIED SERVICE PROVIDER (CSP)

An agent certified under the Agreement to perform all the seller's sales and use tax functions, other than the seller's obligation to remit tax on its own purchases.

Section 204: ENTITY–BASED EXEMPTION

An exemption based on who purchases the product or who sells the product. An exemption that is available to all individuals shall not be considered an entity-based exemption.

Section 205: MODEL 1 SELLER

A seller that has selected a CSP as its agent to perform all the seller's sales and use tax functions, other than the seller's obligation to remit tax on its own purchases.

Section 206: MODEL 2 SELLER

A seller that has selected a CAS to perform part of its sales and use tax functions, but retains responsibility for remitting the tax.

Section 207: MODEL 3 SELLER

A seller that has sales in at least five member states, has total annual sales revenue of at least five hundred million dollars, has a proprietary system that calculates the amount of tax due each jurisdiction, and has entered into a performance agreement with the member states that establishes a tax performance standard for the seller. As used in this definition, a seller includes an affiliated group of sellers using the same proprietary system.

* * *

Section 209: PRODUCT–BASED EXEMPTION

An exemption based on the description of the product and not based on who purchases the product or how the purchaser intends to use the product.

* * *

Section 214: USE–BASED EXEMPTION

An exemption based on a specified use of the product by the purchaser.

ARTICLE III

REQUIREMENTS EACH STATE MUST ACCEPT TO PARTICIPATE

Section 301: STATE LEVEL ADMINISTRATION

Each member state shall provide state level administration of sales and use taxes.

* * *

Section 302: STATE AND LOCAL TAX BASES

* * * [T]he tax base for local jurisdictions shall be identical to the state tax base unless otherwise prohibited by federal law. * * *

Section 303: SELLER REGISTRATION

Each member state shall participate in an online sales and use tax registration system in cooperation with the other member states. Under this system:

    A.   A seller registering under the Agreement is registered in each of the member states.

* * *

Section 308: STATE AND LOCAL TAX RATES

    A.   No member state shall have multiple state sales and use tax rates on items of personal property or services, except that a member state may impose a single additional rate, which may be zero, on food and food ingredients and drugs as defined by state law pursuant to the Agreement. * * *

    B.   A member state that has local jurisdictions that levy a sales or use tax shall not have more than one local sales tax rate or more than one local use tax rate per local jurisdiction. * * *

* * *

Section 310: GENERAL SOURCING RULES

A. Except as provided in Section 310.1, the retail sale, excluding lease or rental, of a product shall be sourced as follows:

1. When the product is received by the purchaser at a business location of the seller, the sale is sourced to that business location.

2. When the product is not received by the purchaser at a business location of the seller, the sale is sourced to the location where receipt by the purchaser (or the purchaser's donee, designated as such by the purchaser) occurs, including the location indicated by instructions for delivery to the purchaser (or donee), known to the seller.

3. When subsections (A)(1) and (A)(2) do not apply, the sale is sourced to the location indicated by an address for the purchaser that is available from the business records of the seller that are maintained in the ordinary course of the seller's business when use of this address does not constitute bad faith.

4.When subsections (A)(1), (A)(2), and (A)(3) do not apply, the sale is sourced to the location indicated by an address for the purchaser obtained during the consummation of the sale, including the address of a purchaser's payment instrument, if no other address is available, when use of this address does not constitute bad faith.

5. When none of the previous rules of subsections (A)(1), (A)(2), (A)(3), or (A)(4) apply, including the circumstance in which the seller is without sufficient information to apply the previous rules, then the location will be determined by the address from which tangible personal property was shipped, from which the digital good or the computer software delivered electronically was first available for transmission by the seller, or from which the service was provided (disregarding for these purposes any location that merely provided the digital transfer of the product sold).

* * *

Section 310.1: ELECTION FOR ORIGIN–BASED SOURCING (Effective January 1, 2010)

* * *

B. A member state may source retail sales, excluding lease or rental, of tangible personal property or digital goods to the location where the order is received by the seller if:

1. The order is received in the same state by the seller where receipt of the product by the purchaser (or the purchaser's donee, designated as such by the purchaser) occurs;

2. Location where receipt of the product by the purchaser occurs is determined pursuant to Section 310A (2), (3) and (4); and

3. At the time the order is received, the recordkeeping system of the seller used to calculate the proper amount of sales or use tax to be imposed captures the location where the order is received.

* * *

Section 312: MULTIPLE POINTS OF USE (Repealed on December 14, 2006)

* * *

Section 316: ENACTMENT OF EXEMPTIONS

A. A member state shall enact entity-based, use-based and product-based exemptions in accordance with the provisions of this section and shall utilize common definitions in accordance with the provisions of Section 327 and Library of Definitions in Appendix C of this Agreement.

B. (1) A member state may enact a product-based exemption without restriction if Part II of the Library of Definitions does not have a definition for such product.

* * *

C. (1) A member state may enact an entity-based or a use-based exemption for a product without restriction if Part II of the Library of Definitions does not have a definition for such product.

* * *

Section 317: ADMINISTRATION OF EXEMPTIONS

A. Each member state shall observe the following provisions when a purchaser claims an exemption:

1. The seller shall obtain identifying information of the purchaser and the reason for claiming a tax exemption at the time of the purchase as determined by the governing board.

* * *

B. Each member state shall relieve sellers that follow the requirements of this section from the tax otherwise applicable if it is determined that the purchaser improperly claimed an exemption and to hold the purchaser liable for the nonpayment of tax.

* * *

Section 318: UNIFORM TAX RETURNS

* * *

Section 326: DIRECT PAY PERMITS

Each member state shall provide for a direct pay authority that allows the holder of a direct pay permit to purchase otherwise taxable goods and services without payment of tax to the supplier at the time of purchase. * * *

Section 327: LIBRARY OF DEFINITIONS

Each member state shall utilize common definitions as provided in this section. The terms defined are set out in the Library of Definitions, in Appendix C of this Agreement. A member state shall adhere to the following principles:

A. If a term defined in the Library of Definitions appears in a member state's sales and use tax statutes or administrative rules or regulations, the member state shall enact or adopt the Library definition of the term in its statutes or administrative rules or regulations in substantially the same language as the Library definition.

B. A member state shall not use a Library definition in its sales or use tax statutes or administrative rules or regulations that is contrary to the meaning of the Library definition.

C. Except as specifically provided in Sections 316 and 332 and the Library of Definitions, a member state shall impose a sales or use tax on all products or services included within each Part II or Part III(B) definition or exempt from sales or use tax all products or services within each such definition. * * *

* * *

Section 330: BUNDLED TRANSACTIONS

A. A member state shall adopt and utilize to determine tax treatment, the core definition for a "bundled transaction" in Appendix C, Part I of the Library of Definitions in the Agreement.

* * *

Section 332: SPECIFIED DIGITAL PRODUCTS

A. A member state shall not include "specified digital products", "digital audio-visual works", "digital audio works" or "digital books" within its definition of "ancillary services", "computer software", "telecommunication services" or "tangible personal property." * * *

Section 333: USE OF SPECIFIED DIGITAL PRODUCTS (Effective January 1, 2010)

A member state shall not include any product transferred electronically in its definition of "tangible personal property." "Ancillary services", "computer software", and "telecommunication services" shall be excluded from the term "products transferred electronically." For purposes of this section, the term "transferred electronically" means obtained by the purchaser by means other than tangible storage media.

ARTICLE IV
SELLER REGISTRATION

Section 401: SELLER PARTICIPATION

A. The member states shall provide an online registration system that will allow sellers to register in all the member states.

B. By registering, the seller agrees to collect and remit sales and use taxes for all taxable sales into the member states, including member states joining after the seller's registration. Withdrawal or revocation of a member state shall not relieve a seller of its responsibility to remit taxes previously or subsequently collected on behalf of the state.

C. In member states where the seller has a requirement to register prior to registering under the Agreement, the seller may be required to provide additional information to complete the registration process or the seller may choose to register directly with those states.

* * *

Section 402: AMNESTY FOR REGISTRATION

A. Subject to the limitations in this section:

1. A member state shall provide amnesty for uncollected or unpaid sales or use tax to a seller who registers to pay or to collect and remit applicable sales or use tax on sales made to purchasers in the state in accordance with the terms of the Agreement, provided that the seller was not so registered in that state in the twelve-month period preceding the effective date of the state's participation in the Agreement.

* * *

Section 403: METHOD OF REMITTANCE

When registering, the seller may select one of the following methods of remittances or other method allowed by state law to remit the taxes collected:

A. MODEL 1, wherein a seller selects a CSP as an agent to perform all the seller's sales or use tax functions, other than the seller's obligation to remit tax on its own purchases.

B. MODEL 2, wherein a seller selects a CAS to use which calculates the amount of tax due on a transaction.

C. MODEL 3, wherein a seller utilizes its own proprietary automated sales tax system that has been certified as a CAS.

* * *

ARTICLE V

PROVIDER AND SYSTEM CERTIFICATION

Section 501: CERTIFICATION OF SERVICE PROVIDERS AND AUTOMATED SYSTEMS

A. The governing board shall certify automated systems and service providers to aid in the administration of sale and use tax collections.

* * *

ARTICLE VI

MONETARY ALLOWANCES FOR NEW TECHNOLOGICAL MODELS FOR SALES TAX COLLECTION

* * *

ARTICLE VII

AGREEMENT ORGANIZATION

* * *

Section 704: CONSIDERATION OF PETITIONS

A. A petitioning state that is found to be in compliance pursuant to Section 805 of the Agreement and the changes to their statutes, rules, regulations or other authorities necessary to bring them into compliance are in effect shall be designated a member state.

* * *

ARTICLE VIII

STATE ENTRY AND WITHDRAWAL

Section 801: ENTRY INTO AGREEMENT

A. After the effective date of the Agreement, a state may apply to become a party to the Agreement by submitting a petition for membership and certificate of compliance to the governing board. * * *

Section 804: REQUIREMENTS FOR MEMBERSHIP APPROVAL

The governing board shall determine if a petitioning state is in compliance with the Agreement. A three-fourths vote of the entire governing board is required to approve a state's petition for membership. * * *

Section 805: COMPLIANCE

A state is in compliance with the Agreement if the effect of the state's laws, rules, regulations, and policies is substantially compliant with each of the requirements set forth in the Agreement.

Section 806: AGREEMENT ADMINISTRATION

Authority to administer the Agreement shall rest with the governing board comprised of representatives of each member state. Each member state may appoint up to four representatives to the governing board. The representatives shall be members of the executive or legislative branches of the state. Each member state shall be entitled to one vote on the governing board. Except as otherwise provided in the Agreement, all actions taken by the governing board shall require an affirmative vote of a majority of the governing board present and voting. * * *

ARTICLE IX

AMENDMENTS AND INTERPRETATIONS

Section 901: AMENDMENTS TO AGREEMENT

Amendments to the Agreement may be brought before the governing board by any member state. The Agreement may be amended by a three-fourths vote of the entire governing board. * * *

Section 902: INTERPRETATIONS OF AGREEMENT

Matters involving interpretation of the Agreement, including all definitions in the Library of Definitions, may be brought before the governing board by any member state or by any other person. Interpretations * * * shall require a three-fourths vote of the entire governing board. * * *Interpretations shall be considered part of the Agreement and shall have the same effect as the Agreement. * * *

Section 903: DEFINITION REQUESTS

[A]ny member state or any other person may make requests for additional definitions or for interpretations on how an individual product or service fits within a * * * definition.

* * *

ARTICLE X

ISSUE RESOLUTION PROCESS

* * *

ARTICLE XI

RELATIONSHIP OF AGREEMENT TO MEMBER STATES AND PERSONS

Section 1101: COOPERATING SOVEREIGNS

This Agreement is among individual cooperating sovereigns in furtherance of their governmental functions. The Agreement provides a mechanism among the member states to establish and maintain a cooperative, simplified system for the application and administration of sales and use taxes under the duly adopted law of each member state.

Section 1102: RELATIONSHIP TO STATE LAW

No provision of the Agreement in whole or part invalidates or amends any provision of the law of a member state. Adoption of the Agreement by a member state does not amend or modify any law of the state. Implementation of any condition of the Agreement in a member state, whether adopted before, at, or after membership of a state, must be by the action of the member state. All member states remain subject to Article VIII.

Appendix C

LIBRARY OF DEFINITIONS

Part I. Administrative definitions including tangible personal property. Terms included in this Part are core terms that apply in imposing and administering sales and use taxes.

Part II. Product definitions. Terms included in this Part are used to impose sales and use taxes, exempt items from sales and use taxes or to impose tax on items by narrowing an exemption that otherwise includes these items.

Part III Sales tax holiday definitions. Terms included in this Part are core terms that apply in imposing and administering sales and use taxes during sales tax holidays.

PART I

Administrative Definitions

A **"bundled transaction"** is the retail sale of two or more products, except real property and services to real property, where (1) the products are otherwise distinct and identifiable, and (2) the products are sold for one non-itemized price. A "bundled transaction" does not include the sale of any products in which the "sales price" varies, or is negotiable, based on the selection by the purchaser of the products included in the transaction.

* * *

(C) A transaction that otherwise meets the definition of a "bundled transaction" as defined above, is not a "bundled transaction" if it is:

(1) The "retail sale" of tangible personal property and a service where the tangible personal property is essential to the use of the service, and is provided exclusively in connection with the service, and the true object of the transaction is the service; or

(2) The "retail sale" of services where one service is provided that is essential to the use or receipt of a second service and the first service is provided exclusively in connection with the second service and the true object of the transaction is the second service; or

(3) A transaction that includes taxable products and nontaxable products and the "purchase price" or "sales price" of the taxable products is de minimis. * * * or

(4) The "retail sale" of exempt tangible personal property and taxable tangible personal property where:

(a) the transaction includes "food and food ingredients", "drugs", "durable medical equipment", "mobility enhancing equipment", "over-the-counter drugs", "prosthetic devices" (all as defined in Appendix C) or medical supplies; and

(b) where the seller's "purchase price" or "sales price" of the taxable tangible personal property is fifty percent (50%) or less of the total "purchase price" or "sales price" of the bundled tangible personal property. * * *

"Delivery charges" * * *

"Direct mail" * * *

"Lease or rental" * * *

"Purchase price" applies to the measure subject to use tax and has the same meaning as sales price.

"Retail sale or Sale at retail" means any sale, lease, or rental for any purpose other than for resale, sublease, or subrent.

"Sales price" applies to the measure subject to sales tax and means the total amount of consideration, including cash, credit, property, and services, for which personal property or services are sold, leased, or rented, valued in money, whether received in money or otherwise, without any deduction for the following:

A. The seller's cost of the property sold;

B. The cost of materials used, labor or service cost, interest, losses, all costs of transportation to the seller, all taxes imposed on the seller, and any other expense of the seller;

C. Charges by the seller for any services necessary to complete the sale, other than delivery and installation charges;

D. Delivery charges;

E. Installation charges; and

F. Credit for any trade-in, as determined by state law.

States may exclude from "sales price" the amounts received for charges included in paragraphs (C) through (F) above, if they are separately stated on the invoice, billing, or similar document given to the purchaser. * * *

"Sales price" shall not include:

A. Discounts, including cash, term, or coupons that are not reimbursed by a third party that are allowed by a seller and taken by a purchaser on a sale;

B. Interest, financing, and carrying charges from credit extended on the sale of personal property or services, if the amount is separately stated on the invoice, bill of sale or similar document given to the purchaser; and

C. Any taxes legally imposed directly on the consumer that are separately stated on the invoice, bill of sale or similar document given to the purchaser.

"Sales price" shall include consideration received by the seller from third parties if:

A. The seller actually receives consideration from a party other than the purchaser and the consideration is directly related to a price reduction or discount on the sale;

B. The seller has an obligation to pass the price reduction or discount through to the purchaser;

C. The amount of the consideration attributable to the sale is fixed and determinable by the seller at the time of the sale of the item to the purchaser; and

D. One of the following criteria is met:

1. The purchaser presents a coupon, certificate or other documentation to the seller to claim a price reduction or discount where the coupon, certificate or documentation is authorized, distributed or granted by a third party with the understanding that the third party will reimburse any seller to whom the coupon, certificate or documentation is presented;

2. The purchaser identifies himself or herself to the seller as a member of a group or organization entitled to a price reduction or discount (a "preferred customer" card that is available to any patron does not constitute membership in such a group), or

3. The price reduction or discount is identified as a third party price reduction or discount on the invoice received by the purchaser or on a coupon, certificate or other documentation presented by the purchaser.

* * *

"Tangible personal property" means personal property that can be seen, weighed, measured, felt, or touched, or that is in any other manner perceptible to the senses. "Tangible personal property" includes electricity, water, gas, steam, and prewritten computer software.

PART II

Product Definitions

CLOTHING

"Clothing" means all human wearing apparel suitable for general use. The following list contains examples and is not intended to be an all-inclusive list.

A. "Clothing" shall include:

  1. Aprons, household and shop;

  2. Athletic supporters;

  3. Baby receiving blankets;

  * * *

  35. Wedding apparel.

B. "Clothing" shall not include:

  1. Belt buckles sold separately;

  2. Costume masks sold separately;

  3. Patches and emblems sold separately;

  4. Sewing equipment and supplies including, but not limited to, knitting needles, patterns, pins, scissors, sewing machines, sewing needles, tape measures, and thimbles; and

  5. Sewing materials that become part of "clothing" including, but not limited to, buttons, fabric, lace, thread, yarn, and zippers.

"Clothing accessories or equipment" means incidental items worn on the person or in conjunction with "clothing." "Clothing accessories or equipment" are mutually exclusive of and may be taxed differently than apparel within the definition of "clothing," "sport or recreational equipment," and "protective equipment." * * *

"Essential clothing" means any article of "clothing" with a sales price below a dollar threshold set by a member state if that state chooses to tax "essential clothing" differently from "clothing." * * *

"Fur clothing" * * *

"Protective equipment" * * *

"Sport or recreational equipment" * * *

COMPUTER RELATED

"Computer" means an electronic device that accepts information in digital or similar form and manipulates it for a result based on a sequence of instructions.

"Computer software" means a set of coded instructions designed to cause a "computer" or automatic data processing equipment to perform a task.

"Delivered electronically" means delivered to the purchaser by means other than tangible storage media.

"Electronic" means relating to technology having electrical, digital, magnetic, wireless, optical, electromagnetic, or similar capabilities.

"Load and leave" means delivery to the purchaser by use of a tangible storage media where the tangible storage media is not physically transferred to the purchaser.

"Prewritten computer software" means "computer software," including prewritten upgrades, which is not designed and developed by the author or other creator to the specifications of a specific purchaser. The combining of two or more "prewritten computer software" programs or prewritten portions thereof does not cause the combination to be other than "prewritten computer software." "Prewritten computer software" includes software designed and developed by the author or other creator to the specifications of a specific purchaser when it is sold to a person other than the specific purchaser. Where a person modifies or enhances "computer software" of which the person is not the author or creator, the person shall be deemed to be the author or creator only of such person's modifications or enhancements. "Prewritten computer software" or a prewritten portion thereof that is modified or enhanced to any degree, where such modification or enhancement is designed and developed to the specifications of a specific purchaser, remains "prewritten computer software;" provided, however, that where there is a reasonable, separately stated charge or an invoice or other statement of the price given to the purchaser for such modification or enhancement, such modification or enhancement shall not constitute "prewritten computer software." A member state may exempt "prewritten computer software" "delivered electronically" or by "load and leave."

Software Maintenance Contract Definitions:

A **"computer software maintenance contract"** is a contract that obligates a vendor of computer software to provide a customer with future updates or upgrades to computer software, support services with respect to computer software or both.

A **"mandatory computer software maintenance contract"** is a computer software maintenance contract that the customer is obligated by contract to purchase as a condition to the retail sale of computer software.

An **"optional computer maintenance contract"** is a computer software maintenance contract that a customer is not obligated to purchase as a condition to the retail sale of computer software.

* * *

DIGITAL PRODUCTS DEFINITIONS

"Specified digital products" means electronically transferred:

"Digital Audio–Visual Works" which means a series of related images which, when shown in succession, impart an impression of motion, together with accompanying sounds, if any,

"Digital Audio Works" which means works that result from the fixation of a series of musical, spoken, or other sounds, including ringtones, and

"Digital Books" which means works that are generally recognized in the ordinary and usual sense as "books".

For purposes of the definition of "digital audio works", "ringtones" means digitized sound files that are downloaded onto a device and that may be used to alert the customer with respect to a communication.

For purposes of the definitions of "specified digital products", "transferred electronically" means obtained by the purchaser by means other than tangible storage media.

FOOD AND FOOD PRODUCTS

"Alcoholic Beverages" * * *

"Candy" means a preparation of sugar, honey, or other natural or artificial sweeteners in combination with chocolate, fruits, nuts or other ingredients or flavorings in the form of bars, drops, or pieces. "Candy" shall not include any preparation containing flour and shall require no refrigeration.

"Dietary supplement" * * *

Food and food ingredients" means substances, whether in liquid, concentrated, solid, frozen, dried, or dehydrated form, that are sold for ingestion or chewing by humans and are consumed for their taste or nutritional value. "Food and food ingredients" does not include "alcoholic beverages" or "tobacco." A member state may exclude "candy," "dietary supplements" and "soft drinks" from this definition, which items are mutually exclusive of each other.

Notwithstanding the foregoing requirements of this definition or any other provision of the Agreement, a member state may maintain its tax treatment of food in a manner that differs from the definitions provided herein, provided its taxation or exemption of food is based on a prohibition or requirement of that state's Constitution that exists on the effective date of the Agreement.

"Food sold through vending machines" means food dispensed from a machine or other mechanical device that accepts payment.

"Prepared food" means:

A.   Food sold in a heated state or heated by the seller;

B.   Two or more food ingredients mixed or combined by the seller for sale as a single item; or

C.   Food sold with eating utensils provided by the seller, including plates, knives, forks, spoons, glasses, cups, napkins, or straws. A plate does not include a container or packaging used to transport the food.

* * *

"Soft drinks" means non-alcoholic beverages that contain natural or artificial sweeteners. "Soft drinks" do not include beverages that contain milk or milk products, soy, rice or similar milk substitutes, or greater than fifty percent of vegetable or fruit juice by volume.

"Tobacco" * * *

HEALTH–CARE

"Drug" * * *

"Durable medical equipment" * * *

"Grooming and hygiene products" * * *

"Mobility enhancing equipment" * * *

"Over-the-counter-drug" * * *

"Prescription" * * *

"Prosthetic device" * * *

TELECOMMUNICATIONS

* * *

PART III

Sales Tax Holiday Definitions

* * *

NOTES AND QUESTIONS

A. *The Role of Congress and the Achievement of the Goals of SSUTA.* One of the primary goals of SSUTA, if not the overriding goal, is to lay the groundwork for either the judicial or congressional repeal of the physical presence test as enunciated in the *Quill* decision, at least for states that have brought themselves into full compliance with the Agreement. Until that goal is reached, however, sellers are under no obligation to register under the Agreement to begin collecting tax on sales to customers in states with which the seller has no physical presence. Nevertheless, the Agreement does provide various enticements to *voluntary* registration, such as a limited amnesty period after a state becomes a full member, vendor compensation, and the availability of Certified Service Providers (CSPs) and certified software. SSU-TA §§ 402, 501, 601–03. Do you believe it is realistic to think that the states can effectively entice vendors to collect taxes on remote sales by means of the voluntary system reflected in SSUTA and without congressional (or judicial) intervention?

Assuming most vendors decline to join the system voluntarily, is the simplification and harmonization currently embodied in the Agreement sufficient to persuade Congress to reverse legislatively the rule of *Quill* and permit those states that have adopted the Agreement to require remote vendors to collect use taxes on sales into those states? What guarantees are there in the Agreement that such uniformity and harmonization will be maintained? Are those guarantees sufficient? If Congress determined that it wanted to legislate comprehensively in this area and in effect impose the essential provisions of SSUTA on willing and unwilling states and sellers alike, would it possess the constitutional authority to do so? See generally Walter Hellerstein, "Federal Constitutional Limitations on Congressional Power to Legislate Regarding State Taxation of Electronic Commerce," 53 Nat'l Tax J. 1307 (2000). See also

Charles E. McLure, Jr. & Walter Hellerstein, "Congressional Intervention in State Taxation: A Normative Analysis of Three Proposals," State Tax Notes, March 1, 2004, p. 721 (also in Tax Notes, March 15, 2004, p. 1375).

B. *General Sourcing Rules.* Do the uniform sourcing rules (set forth in Section 310(A)) change existing law in most states as you understand it? If so, how? How can Section 310(A)(5) be squared with the principle that the sales tax is a consumption tax to be imposed by the state of destination? Why did the Agreement adopt Section 310(A)(5)? Can you think of any analogy to Section 310(A)(5) in the income tax context? Can you think of any alternatives to Section 310(A)(5) that might be more consistent with the underlying purposes of the sales tax?

C. *Election for Origin–Based Sourcing on Intrastate Transactions.* As originally adopted, SSUTA did not include an origin-based sourcing option. Some states, however, have historically sourced intrastate transactions on an origin basis, while sourcing interstate transactions on a destination basis. For example, a sale originating from State A whose destination is City X in State B would be subject to tax at the rate applicable in City X. A sale originating from City Y in State B whose destination is City X in State B, however, would be taxed at the City Y rate—the origin rate—and not the rate applicable in City X, the destination rate. When there is only one rate applicable statewide, the amount of tax due would be the same. Sourcing rules still matter to the local taxing jurisdictions, however, because the sourcing rules determine which city receives the tax revenue. In addition, from the intrastate seller's perspective, the costs of collecting and remitting tax on an origin basis are generally lower, because the seller must report only to the jurisdiction in which it is located. Furthermore, if local tax rates differ, the sourcing rules can affect the amount of tax paid by the purchaser. For these reasons, states that historically have allowed origin-based sourcing of intrastate transactions met with stiff resistance from both local jurisdictions and local businesses when considering adopting SSUTA's destination-based sourcing rules. Although some states were able to overcome these political challenges and bring their tax codes into full compliance with SSUTA, other states could not, and either eventually fell out of compliance with SSUTA or were unable to bring themselves into full compliance in the first instance. As a result of these difficulties and the affect they had on attracting and retaining member states, the Governing Board amended SSUTA to allow members states to elect an origin-sourcing option for the purpose of sourcing *intrastate* transactions. SSUTA § 310.1. See John A. Swain & Walter Hellerstein, "The Streamlined Sales Tax Project and the Local Sourcing Conundrum," 104 J. Tax'n 230 (2006).

Consider the example given above involving Cities X and Y in State B. Assume that the tax rate in City Y is lower that the tax rate in City X, so that buyers in City X pay less tax when purchasing an item from an instate vendor located in City Y (for delivery to City X) than when purchasing from an out-of-state vendor. Is this constitutional? What might be the purchaser's use tax obligation to City X? Does the local origin-sourcing election option increase or lessen the compliance burdens of multistate retailers?

D. *Definitions.* One of the goals of SSUTA is to provide uniform definitions of terms that are central to delineating the tax base. Some of these definitions are administrative definitions, such as "delivery charge," "tangible personal property and "sales price," while others are product definitions, such as "clothing" and "prewritten computer software." With respect to product definitions, member states remain free to decide whether a defined product is taxable or not taxable. In doing so, however, they generally must employ the SSUTA definition. For example, if a member state wishes to exempt clothing, it must adopt the SSUTA definition of clothing and not its own idiosyncratic definition. Moreover, the state cannot exempt only a subset of clothing unless a definition of that subset (such as "protective equipment") is provided in the SSUTA library of definitions. Note that many of SSUTA's broad definitional categories include numerous "sub-definitions," which allow member states to do some fine tuning of their tax bases. For example, a broad definition of "food and food ingredients" includes candy, but a specific, separate definition of "candy" allows states both to exempt food generally and then to exclude candy from the general definition of exempt food. The Agreement does not purport to define every possible product that could be subject to taxation or exemption. How many other items must SSUTA define before it accomplishes its goal of "uniform definitions within tax bases"? Does every potentially taxable or nontaxable item have to be defined?

E. *Certification of Service Providers and Automated Systems.* Perhaps the most innovative aspect of SSUTA is the provision for a Certified Service Provider (CSP) and a Certified Automated System (CAS) as an integral part of the streamlined tax collection process. Review the definitions of a CSP and a CAS, as well as the definitions of Model 1, Model 2, and Model 3 Sellers in Article II of the Agreement, and identify the type of seller that is likely to use a CSP, a CAS, or a certified proprietary program. Why wouldn't every seller become a Model 1 Seller, since the state has assumed the full financial burden of paying for the CSP? The states responded to pressure from the business community in providing for some type of vendor compensation for all vendors who participate in the system. See Article VI. What other incentives are there in the Agreement for sellers to participate in the system? If your client were a seller with nexus in only one state, but selling into 49 others, would you advise it to register with states that had enacted the Agreement? Note that the Agreement provides that states may not "use registration with the central registration system and the collection of sales and use taxes in the member states as a factor in determining whether the seller has nexus with that state for any tax at any time." SSUTA § 401(D). It is also important to keep in mind that the Agreement is wholly voluntary. Any seller that does not wish to participate in the system need not do so. Needless to say, such a seller will not be entitled to the benefits of the system, such as reduced audit exposure and additional vendor compensation.

F. *Promise versus Performance.* Does SSUTA live up to its billing? Specifically, does it faithfully fulfill the "fundamental purposes" set out in Section 102? If not, which of the ten goals listed in Section 102 does the Agreement fail to accomplish? Of the ten goals listed, which do you believe are most critical to the proper functioning of the sales and use tax system? Which are the least critical?

CHAPTER 9

AD VALOREM PROPERTY TAXES

■ ■ ■

A. PROPERTY TAXATION AND PROPERTY RIGHTS

The property tax, one of the oldest taxes in the United States, is a mainstay of local government in this country. It provides about one-quarter of local revenue and more than one-third of revenue raised locally, as opposed to grants from the state and federal governments. It is also an endlessly controversial levy that serves as a frequent target for taxpayer discontent. In fact, the strengths of the property tax are related to its political liabilities. An independent source of revenue is essential if communities are to control some range of local activities, but state legislators often respond to pressure to reduce taxes by cutting county or municipal taxes rather than state-level taxes. The property tax is highly visible, clearly stated in bills delivered to taxpayers once or twice a year. It is therefore more unpopular than sales taxes that are collected in many transactions and never totaled for the taxpayer, or even income taxes that are withheld at the source. But a high profile also insures transparency and accountability. Voters can make informed decisions on local public spending only if they understand its costs and benefits.

The development of the contemporary property tax is closely inter-twined with changing concepts of property rights and the shifting relative importance of different types of property. In the United States, the property tax was often originally exactly that—a tax on all forms of property, real and personal, tangible and intangible, "upon every man according to his estate, and with consideration to all his other abilities whatsoever."[a] This was appropriate to an agrarian economy in which major elements of wealth, such as land, livestock, and farm equipment, were readily identifiable and could not easily be concealed or temporarily removed to another jurisdiction in order to evade tax. The nineteenth century saw enormous changes in the nation's economic structure, with a shift to new forms of capital, wealth, and property. Intangible property, including corporate stock and other securities, took on far greater impor-

---

a. Jens Jensen, Property Taxation in the United States 27 (1931) (quoting 1634 Massachusetts property tax statute).

tance, yet became ever more difficult for local officials to identify, locate, value, and assess. The evident injustice of farmers paying a tax that financiers could easily evade gave rise to an important reform movement that sought to restrict the property tax to tangible property and to reach intangible wealth through a tax on its income instead.

Today the property tax in the United States is limited largely to real estate, reaching only selected items of personal property. Most states tax automobiles, whose registration provides a basis for identification and assessment. Many states tax some business personal property, such as equipment and inventory, but allow broad exemptions. Exemption of personal property simplifies tax administration, for unlike land and buildings, it may have a tax situs in more than one jurisdiction over the course of a year.

Changing definitions of property also affect the tax base. Any calculation of fair market value relies, even if implicitly, on a prior decision as to which rights and interests constitute the property being valued. This inquiry can be confined to a single question, such as whether lease provisions affect valuation for tax purposes. It can also encompass a broad range of evolving issues concerning private rights and public restrictions, such as those concerning toxic contamination, responsibility for historic preservation or environmental protection. All of these issues influence the valuation and taxation of property.

KANKAKEE COUNTY BOARD OF REVIEW v. PROPERTY TAX APPEAL BOARD

Supreme Court of Illinois, 2007.
226 Ill.2d 36, 871 N.E.2d 38, 312 Ill.Dec. 638.

JUSTICE BURKE delivered the judgment of the court, with opinion.

Section 1–130 of the Property Tax Code (Code) defines taxable property as "[t]he land itself, with all things contained therein, and also all buildings, structures and improvements, and other permanent fixtures thereon, * * * and all rights and privileges belonging or pertaining thereto, except where otherwise specified by this Code." In the instant case, petitioner Kankakee County board of review assessed the property of respondent Natural Gas Pipeline Company of America for the tax years of 2000 and 2001. In its assessments, petitioner included the value of the rights and privileges taxpayer enjoys to two gas storage reservoirs that lie under the surface property of others. Taxpayer appealed these assessments before the Property Tax Appeal Board (PTAB) which found that the rights and privileges to the reservoirs should not have been assessed to taxpayer's property. The PTAB then reduced the property's assessed value for each year. The appellate court confirmed the decision of the PTAB. * * * For the reasons that follow, we find that the rights and privileges to the reservoirs should not be included in the assessment of taxpayer's property, and affirm the judgment of the appellate court.

BACKGROUND

Taxpayer, a subsidiary of Kinder Morgan, a Kansas corporation, owns a 75.976–acre parcel of land in Kankakee County (hereinafter, the subject property) on which it operates a multibuilding control center. The control center, known as Compressor Station 201, facilitates the piping of gas to a cross-country pipeline 16 miles away and the storage of natural gas in two underground storage facilities. The underground storage facilities, known as "reservoirs," are actually two separate layers of porous rock lying 1,700 and 2,400 feet below the surface, respectively. These reservoirs[2] lie below approximately 15,600 surface acres that surround and include the subject property. Taxpayer owns the portion of the reservoirs that lies directly below the subject property, but does not own any of the surrounding 15,600 acres or the reservoirs that lie below them.

For storage purposes, natural gas is injected into the reservoirs through a system of pipes that connect the pipeline to the compressor station, and connect the compressor station with 281 wells that reach down into the reservoirs at various surface points throughout the 15,600 acres. The injected gas displaces the water that naturally occurs within the porous rock. The displaced water then creates a natural "vessel" which keeps the gas from escaping laterally. The gas is prevented from exiting to the surface by a layer of nonporous rock that is likened to an upside-down soup bowl. The injection process is reversed when gas is removed from the reservoirs. Taxpayer charges its customers monthly reservation charges and tariffs based on gas volume transported.

In the early 1950s, before it acquired the subject property or began construction of the compressor station, taxpayer secured voluntary easements from the owners of the land that lay above and included the reservoirs so that it could install and operate the wells and pipes used in its storage system. The easements taxpayer acquired are similar for each granting owner. An easement identified as "the Dickman easement," which was found to be representative by the PTAB, reads in pertinent part: "This instrument made this [date] by record owner [name of the fee landowner], herein referred to as Grantors, is in favor of Natural Gas Storage Company of Illinois, a Delaware corporation, herein referred to as Grantee." The easements give taxpayer, as grantee, "the exclusive right, privilege and easement to introduce natural gas or other gases or vapors * * * into the [reservoirs] * * * to store gas in said storage reservoir and retain the possession of gas so stored as personal property, [and] to remove gas * * * from the storage reservoir."

The easements also give taxpayer the right to drill wells, construct and maintain those wells, lay pipes and electric lines on the grantees' properties, and to enter onto the grantees' properties to maintain the wells and pipes. In return, taxpayer pays each landowner an annual

---

2. The reservoirs are part of a much larger underground geological formation known as an aquifer. Any testimonial references to "the aquifer" can be inferred to be references to the reservoirs at issue.

monetary sum. Taxpayer also agrees to pay the landowners for any damage to crops, timber, or fences that its activities may cause, and to provide grantees with free city water.

In 1952, orders from the Illinois Commerce Commission (ICC) and Federal Power Commission (FPC) gave taxpayer the exclusive right to store gas in the reservoirs, to construct Compressor Station 201, to run approximately 16 miles of pipe from Compressor Station 201 to the cross-country pipeline, to dig the wells down to the reservoirs, and to lay the pipe that connects the wells with Compressor Station 201. Once the FPC and ICC orders were in place, taxpayer purchased the subject property from Otto Kruse and constructed Compressor Station 201. Operations began thereafter and continue to this day.

Petitioner assessed the subject property based on market values of $17,160,849 for the tax year of 2000, and $32,000,000 for the tax year of 2001. Market value is defined by the Uniform Standards of Professional Appraisal Practice as "the most probable price which a property should bring in a competitive and open market under all conditions requisite to a fair sale, the buyer and seller each acting prudently and knowledgeably, and assuming the price is not affected by undue stimulus." * * *

ANALYSIS

Before this court, petitioner characterizes the main issue of this case as the proper interpretation of section 1–130 of the Code, which holds that taxable real estate includes "all rights and privileges belonging or pertaining thereto." * * *

I. "Belonging or Pertaining"

Section 1–130 of the Code defines taxable property as "[t]he land itself, with all things contained therein, and also all buildings, structures and improvements, and other permanent fixtures thereon, * * * and all rights and privileges belonging or pertaining thereto, except where otherwise specified by this Code." Petitioner contends that, by choosing to include the words "belonging or pertaining" in the definition, the General Assembly intended another property right short of fee simple ownership. * * *

There is no dispute by either party that the reservoirs at issue belong, proportionately, to those who own the surface land directly above them. See Jilek v. Chicago, Wilmington & Franklin Coal Co., 382 Ill. 241, 248, 47 N.E.2d 96 (1943) ("The owner in fee owns to the center of the earth"). Petitioner argues, however, that the easements and governmental permits that allow taxpayer to utilize the portions of the reservoirs not under the subject property make up a "bundle of rights" that "pertains" to the subject property, thus enhancing its value beyond that of the neighboring industrial or farming property.

According to respondents, all of petitioners' arguments contain the same fundamental flaw: incorrectly assuming that the gas storage rights that taxpayer obtained and exercised benefitted the subject property, and not taxpayer's business. We agree with respondents and find that, while "pertain," for purposes of section 1–130 of the Code, might imply a less rigid connection than "belong," there still must be some direct relationship between the rights and the property at issue. For the following reasons, we find that petitioner has not established such a relationship.

A. Easements

The first components of the "bundle of rights" which petitioner contends pertain to the subject property are the easements that allow taxpayer to operate its pipes and wells on the 15,600 acres of property owned by others that surrounds Compressor Station 201. Petitioner concedes that these easements are easements in gross that name taxpayer, and not the subject property, as their beneficiary, but maintains that the classification of the easements is irrelevant because the easements "provide only part of the basis for Taxpayer's exclusive storage rights." Petitioner argues that, because the easements are only part of the "bundle of rights," their classification is not determinative. Further, according to petitioner, there is no legal authority to support the contention that easements in gross may not be considered as "rights and privileges" of a particular property.

An easement appurtenant is "created to benefit another tract of land, the use of easement being incident to the ownership of that other tract." Black's Law Dictionary 549 (8th ed. 2004). An easement appurtenant runs with the land and may be transferred. Traylor v. Parkinson, 355 Ill. 476, 479, 189 N.E. 307 (1934). An easement in gross is defined as "[a]n easement benefiting a particular person and not a particular piece of land." Black's Law Dictionary 549 (8th ed. 2004). See also Traylor, 355 Ill. at 479 (easement in gross is personal and nontransferable).

The Dickman easement, found to be representative, reads, "This instrument made this [date] by record owner [name of the fee landowner], herein referred to as Grantors, is in favor of Natural Gas Storage Company of Illinois, a Delaware corporation, herein referred to as Grantee." Such wording clearly indicates that these easements are in gross, and benefit taxpayer rather than the subject property, as petitioner concedes.

We find, contrary to petitioner's unsupported argument, that the classification of the easements in question is relevant here. Were the easements at issue here appurtenant, naming the subject property as the beneficiary of the right to place wells and pipes on the land of others, then such right would be attributed to the subject property and assessable by petitioner. The easements in question, however, are easements in gross, benefitting taxpayer, and not the subject property. Petitioner's contention that the legal effect of the easements is somehow negated by the fact that they are part of a "bundle of rights" has no support in logic or the law. Accordingly, we find that the easements in question do not pertain to the subject property.

B. ICC and FPC Permits

Petitioner next argues that certain passages in the orders of the ICC and FPC, as well as taxpayer's correspondence with those agencies, serve as evidence that the rights and privileges to the reservoirs that accrued to the taxpayer pertain to the subject property. Petitioner initially notes that the September 1952 order of the FPC, which granted taxpayer the right to construct Compressor Station 201 and utilize the reservoirs, includes the words "storage rights in approximately 15,000 acres * * * together with all necessary and appropriate consents, permits, contracts, easements, rights-of-way, and other interests in property pertaining to or used in connection with the storage project." Petitioner notes that the FPC used the term "pertaining," which is the statutory term at issue here. Petitioner argues that the PTAB incorrectly concluded that the method of assessing the subject property may not take account of these "pertaining" underground storage rights.

Petitioner also details the history of the creation of Compressor Station 201 and the use of the reservoirs, concluding that the history of regulatory approvals leading to the development of the gas storage project shows that the reservoirs were "intended to be operated as a single facility which would necessarily be managed and controlled" from one control center, wherever constructed. In support of its contention, petitioner cites two 1952 orders from the ICC and FPC, each granting taxpayer the right to "acquire ownership in fee simple or by other estate of parcels of real estate within or adjacent to the storage area necessary for the erection of compression plants, dehydration plants, and any structures appurtenant thereto, [and] lay gathering lines to connect them to the centrally located compressor station and dehydration plant." Petitioner also relies on a 1959 supplemental order from the ICC as well as a 1959 legal notice that ran in the Kankakee Daily Journal. These provide that taxpayer "owns and operates (under authority of certificates of public convenience and necessity issued to it by the FPC) an aquifer-type underground storage reservoir near Herscher."

Petitioner asserts that these passages from the recorded history of regulatory approval leading up to the development of the gas storage operation show plainly that the reservoirs were intended to be operated in union with a compressor station located in their vicinity. Petitioner contends that, since Compressor Station 201 is located on the subject property, the subject property cannot then be separated from the reservoirs for valuation purposes.

Illinois case law is consistent in holding that government permits, ordinances, licenses, orders, or regulatory approvals do not create assessable entities. See, e.g., Boland v. Walters, 346 Ill. 184, 188, 178 N.E. 359 (1931) (a license in respect to real property is merely a privilege to do certain things on land without being an estate itself); Dimucci Home Builders, Inc. v. Metropolitan Life Insurance Co., 312 Ill. App. 3d 779, 782, 728 N.E.2d 749, 245 Ill. Dec. 667 (2000) (permits are not conveyances of title); Pasquinelli v. Village of Mundelein, 257 Ill. App. 3d 1057, 1062–63, 1065, 630 N.E.2d 113, 196 Ill. Dec. 416 (1994) (permits and village board approvals to operate a sewer line are not indicia of ownership).

Central Illinois Public Service Co. v. Swartz, 284 Ill. 108, 119 N.E. 990 (1918), is instructive. In *Swartz*, the plaintiff was granted, by ordinance, the right to construct and maintain an electric plant as well as electric poles and wires in the town of Bushnell. Swartz, 284 Ill. at 110. When the property of the plaintiff was assessed for taxation, the assessor included the "franchise, got through an ordinance of the city of Bushnell, to operate a plant in the city." Swartz, 284 Ill. at 110. The *Swartz* court rejected the assessment of the franchise as tangible property. Swartz, 284 Ill. at 112. Specifically, it stated,

> "This permission or license exists independently of the poles, wire, apparatus, machinery or other means whereby it may be available. It attaches not to the tangible property of the corporation but to the franchise, and would remain and be available to the corporation if all its tangible property were destroyed." Swartz, 284 Ill. at 112.

In the instant case, all of the ICC and FPC orders attached to taxpayer, and not to the subject property. Just as in *Swartz*, should the taxpayer choose to leave the subject property, or suffer any destruction of its tangible property, the orders would remain in place, continuing to benefit taxpayer regardless of where its property was located. See also Quantum Pipeline Co. v. Illinois Commerce Comm'n, 304 Ill. App. 3d 310, 315–17, 709 N.E.2d 950, 237 Ill. Dec. 481 (1999) (permit issued by the ICC grants only a business right, not one of property). Accordingly, we find that the ICC and FPC orders did not, as petitioner alleges, create an indivisible union between the subject property and the reservoirs. Rather, the rights to the reservoirs accrue to taxpayer, and do not pertain to the subject property.

We note that petitioner attempts to draw an analogy between governmental orders such as those at issue in the instant case and property zoning. Petitioner argues that, just as zoning changes can affect the use of property and therefore its value, the rights to use the reservoir, which arise from easements and governmental rulings which have transpired over 50 years, enhance the value of the subject property. We find no merit in this argument.

Zoning regulations apply to particular properties and not their owners. See Lake Forest Chateau, Inc. v. City of Lake Forest, 133 Ill. 2d 129, 131, 549 N.E.2d 336, 139 Ill. Dec. 824 (1989) (zoning ordinances apply to property). As noted, the government orders at issue here accrue to taxpayer and not the subject property. Accordingly, petitioner's analogy to zoning is unpersuasive.

In light of our holdings above regarding easements and government permits, we find that the rights and privileges taxpayer enjoys to the reservoirs neither belong nor pertain to the subject property for purposes of section 1–130 of the Code.

II. Location

Petitioner next contends that regardless of whether the "rights and privileges" to the reservoirs are tied to it through any recorded basis or legal title, the subject parcel's proximity to the reservoirs enhances its value. Petitioner argues that Illinois courts routinely acknowledge that property value may increase or decrease due to elements that lay beyond the boundaries of the property. In support of its argument petitioner points to cases such as Lake County Board of Review v. Property Tax Appeal Board, 91 Ill. App. 3d 117, 122, 414 N.E.2d 173, 46 Ill. Dec. 451 (1980) ("property adjoining or in close proximity to a body of water, a park, golf course or other scenic view may well have an increased value because of its location"), O'Brien v. City of O'Fallon, 80 Ill. App. 3d 841, 400 N.E.2d 456, 36 Ill. Dec. 36 (1980) (value of house on lake impaired when sewage discharged into lake), and Illinois Light & Power Co. v. Bedard, 343 Ill. 618, 175 N.E. 851 (1931) (it is common knowledge that land located near a body of water is worth more than land located elsewhere).

Petitioner then cites Board of Education of Township High School District 205 v. Property Tax Appeal Board, 142 Ill. App. 3d 853, 491 N.E.2d 454, 96 Ill. Dec. 408 (1986), as an example of how location can enhance a property's value. In *Board of Education*, the property to be valued was a hydroelectric power plant. Board of Education, 142 Ill. App. 3d at 854–55. The *Board of Education* court held that the PTAB properly valued the plant by using the income approach applied to the power-generating capacity and potential income of the plant. Board of Education, 142 Ill. App. 3d at 857. Petitioner asserts that in both *Board of Education* and the instant case, the property at issue houses a "control center" type facility that utilizes a resource not found within the boundaries of that property. Petitioner maintains that the hydroelectric power plant in *Board of Education*, which takes its power from the river that begins and ends outside the boundaries of the property, is directly analogous to Compressor Station 201 here, which is used to access the natural gas stored in the reservoirs that lay mostly outside the subject property.

We do not dispute petitioner's argument that amenities or resources situated beyond a property's boundaries can increase its value. The difference between the properties in the cases petitioner relies on and the subject property, however, is one of market value. There is and will always be a market for properties with access to water, golf courses, and countless other features that hold value to prospective purchasers. There is no similar market for the subject property. Any purchaser who might acquire the subject property would not be able to utilize the reservoirs. This is because taxpayer, and not the subject property, holds exclusive rights, obtained through easements and government orders, to use the reservoirs. Thus, the right and privilege of being close to the reservoirs is not a marketable asset, and the market value of the subject property is not enhanced beyond that of other industrial or farming properties in the area.

Moreover, *Board of Education* does not support petitioner's contention. In *Board of Education*, the income approach to valuation was proper because the plant generated income due solely to its proximity to the river. The ability of a hydroelectric plant to generate income is directly tied to its location. A plant in a location away from the river would not be able to generate the same income. In the instant case, there is no similar need for the compressor station to be located on the subject property. Testimony has established that the compressor station could have been located anywhere in the area, even 16 miles away from the reservoirs along the main pipeline. In contrast to the hydroelectric plant, which derived its entire income value from its location on a river, the location of the compressor station, whether above the reservoirs or otherwise, has no real impact on the income it produces. Therefore, we find *Board of Education* to be inapplicable to the instant case.

Petitioner makes the argument that changes to the control center are forbidden without approval from FERC and the ICC, and that moving a gas storage control center with all its related equipment and connecting entities cannot be readily accomplished. This argument is misplaced. The issue is not whether Compressor Station 201 can be moved, but rather whether its income is derived from its location. Petitioner next contends that even if the compressor station were moved, the taxable character of the rights and privileges related to the reservoirs would not change, but would move with the compressor station. But this argument actually supports respondents' contention that the rights and privileges to the reservoirs do not pertain to the subject property. Accordingly, we find that the PTAB did not err when it relied on market value appraisals which did not attribute added value to the subject property due to its proximity to the reservoirs.

III. "A Broad Concept of Rights and Privileges"

Petitioner relies on People ex rel. City of Chicago v. Upham, 221 Ill. 555, 77 N.E. 931 (1906), as an example of this court interpreting the statutory definition of real property now found in section 1–130 of the Code and applying a "broad concept of rights and privileges." Petitioner contends that *Upham* provides sufficient authority to consider the rights and privileges of the reservoirs in the assessment of the subject property.

In *Upham*, the respondent telephone and telegraph companies, by virtue of city ordinances, constructed cement tunnels beneath Chicago city streets to facilitate their businesses. The ordinances authorized the corporations to maintain the tunnels for 30 years, at which time the tunnels could become the property of the city. The petitioner contended that the tunnels were taxable assets that it should assess. The respondent conceded that the tunnels were subject to assessment for taxation, but contended that since they were constructed below public streets, the taxable interest was one of intangible use, and not one of real property to be assessed by local assessors.

The *Upham* court found that "while it is true the title to the streets of Chicago is in the city, the [corporations], by virtue of said ordinances, clearly have 'rights and privileges' belonging and pertaining to the soil in which the tunnels are constructed, separate and apart from the fee of the streets, which rests in the city." The *Upham* court held that the tunnels had an existence separate from the city streets above and were real property in the same way that a bridge or a pier has a separate existence from the land upon which it is constructed. The fact that the tunnels were situated below city streets not subject to assessment for taxation had no bearing on this court's determination that the tunnels were real property. See also People ex rel. New York & Harlem R.R. Co. v. Commissioners of Taxes & Assessments, 101 N.Y. 322, 326, 4 N.E. 127, 128 (1886) (tunnels under city streets should be treated and assessed as real property).

We find *Upham* distinguishable and insufficient authority to support a finding that the rights and privileges taxpayer enjoys to the reservoirs are assessable to the subject property. The issue in *Upham* was whether the underground tunnels were real property or an intangible right. There is no disagreement in the instant case as to whether the reservoirs are real property or whether they have an existence separate from the land under which they lay. The issue here is whether respondents' rights to utilize the reservoirs pertain to and should be assessed to the subject property. *Upham* provides no guidance on this issue.

Further, there is a fundamental difference between the man-made tunnels in *Upham* and the naturally occurring reservoirs in the instant case. Piers, bridges, and underground tunnels "create" new property where none existed before, in spaces that were heretofore nonassessable. Piers extend into water, bridges soar into air, and tunnels create space below the surface of land. *Upham* holds that such man-made creations have a "separate existence from the land in which they are constructed," and are assessable real property belonging to their constructors. This differs greatly from the reservoirs at issue here, which are natural formations already owned by those who own the surface land above them. As such, we find that *Upham* has no bearing on the issues of the instant case and does not support petitioner's argument that taxpayer's right to utilize the reservoirs should be assessed to the subject property. * * *

CONCLUSION

In light of our holdings above, we find that the decision of the PTAB to disregard [the] appraisal, which attributed the rights and privileges of the reservoirs to the subject property, was correct. We need not address petitioner's contention that the PTAB erred in finding that petitioner failed to adequately describe the reservoirs it wished to be included in the valuation of the subject property. We find that, because neither the reservoirs, nor the rights to utilize them, can be attributed to the subject property, their description is irrelevant. For the foregoing reasons, the judgment of the appellate court is affirmed.

Appellate court judgment affirmed.

NOTES AND QUESTIONS

A. *Appurtenant Easements and Easements in Gross.* The court in the *Kankakee County* case placed great weight on the nature of the easements conveying rights to use the reservoirs for storage of natural gas. Because those rights were conveyed to the Natural Gas Storage Company of Illinois and thus constituted easements in gross rather than appurtenant easements benefiting specific real property, they were considered a business asset rather than a real property attribute enhancing the value of taxable property. This distinction has a long history in real property taxation. In an extremely influential case, People ex rel. Poor v. O'Donnel, 139 A.D. 83, 124 N.Y.S. 36 (1st Dep't 1910), aff'd mem., 200 N.Y. 518, 93 N.E. 1129 (1910), the New York Appellate Division found an appurtenant easement to reduce the value of the burdened or servient estate while raising the value of the benefited or dominant estate. That case dealt with Gramercy Park in Manhattan, a private park established by the real estate developer Samuel Ruggles in 1831. An easement preventing development of Gramercy Park ran in favor of the owners of neighboring lots. Ruggles was able to sell those lots at a premium because of their rights to the private park, a situation still in effect today. The New York court ruled that this arrangement deprived the park of taxable value. "[W]hen an easement is carved out of one property for the benefit of another, the market value of the servient estate is thereby lessened, and that of the dominant increased practically by just the value of the easement. The respective tenements should thereafter be assessed accordingly * * *." 124 N.Y.S. at 38. Needless to say, this approach has given rise to many complications and contradictions, but it has been restricted to appurtenant easements. Easements that favor an individual or entity rather than a parcel of property have not been considered to affect real property valuation. In that respect they resemble a lease, mortgage, or other division of interests not taken into account in assessing the underlying property for taxation.

B. *Property Rights and Property Values.* This emphasis on precise distinctions of property law should not obscure the market value basis for tax assessment. In the case of a private park, a nearby residence with no legal rights in the park might still rise in value because of its proximity to this amenity, while legal rights to a neglected park in an industrialized area might be of little value. In *Kankakee County*, the pipeline company owned 75 acres of land that lay above reservoirs of approximately 15,000 acres. Could this be a locational advantage for a natural gas company? What evidence would you require to establish an effect on market value?

C. *Valuation of the Servient Estate.* What implications does the court's approach have for the valuation of the "surface property" above the storage reservoirs? Note the court's statement that in exchange for the easements "taxpayer pays each landowner an annual monetary sum."

D. *Permits and Licenses.* Illinois does not assess permits or licenses as real property. Could these intangible rights still influence the value of the real property above the reservoirs, including the 75 acres held by the taxpayer here? In Susquehanna Power Co. v. State Tax Commission, 283 U.S. 291, 51 S.Ct. 434 (1931), the taxpayer argued that taxation of its lands at over $2 million constituted taxation of its Federal Power Commission license to produce electric power, since it was this that gave the dam and submerged lands their value. "The contention urged is that the lands are assessed at a higher value than they were before they were submerged, and higher than farm uplands in the neighborhood, and that, since their use as part of appellant's power project is rendered possible only by the federal license and by the water in the river, the assessment at higher value, in effect, involves a forbidden tax on the license, and taxation of appellant for the value of the waters of a navigable stream." Id., 283 U.S. at 295. The Court rejected that position: "An important element in the value of the land is the use to which it may be put. That may vary with its location and its relationship to the property * * *. A large part of the value of property in civilized communities has been built up by its inter-related uses; but it is a value ultimately reflected in earning capacity and the price at which the property may be sold, and hence is an element to which weight may appropriately be given in determining its taxable value. It has never been thought that the taxation of such property at its enhanced value is in effect taxation of its owner for the property of others." Id. at 296. Should the market value of such property be determined by reference to the price it would command from a purchaser with a license to use it for hydroelectric power generation, or to a purchaser without such a license? What about legal rights of use that do not require a special license? If the market value of a distillery rose upon the repeal of Prohibition, would an assessment at the higher value tax intangible rights? These are examples of the definitional issues underlying determinations of "fair market value," and of "taxable property."

E. *Special Franchises.* New York State sidestepped the distinction between tangible and intangible property that Illinois confronted in the 1906 *Upham* case discussed by the court. As subways, tunnels, and utilities put public ways to profitable commercial use, Governor Theodore Roosevelt made taxation of these rights a cornerstone of his legislative agenda. His efforts led to passage of legislation in 1899 that simply defined the privilege of such use as real property. In advising Governor Roosevelt on this matter, Professor E. R. A. Seligman of Columbia University wrote, "From an abstract point of view it is immaterial whether we class such a franchise as personalty or as real estate. It is both, and it is neither. The real estate of a corporation is made valuable by the existence of the franchise in the same way that the personalty of the same corporation is made valuable by the existence of the franchise. The franchise might therefore be classed as either real or as personal property* * *." He then suggested the term "Special Franchise" for this new type of taxable property. New York State Board of Equalization and Assessment, Report on Special Franchise Assessment Administration 8 (1983).

F. *"Property" as a Set of Intangible Interests.* Although it is a commonplace that "property" consists of a set of intangible rights in an object rather than the physical object itself, application of this reasoning to the taxation of less than fee interests can expand the range of the property tax in unexpected ways. At various times California courts have upheld property taxation of possessory interests, or rights to use otherwise untaxed government property, in the form of a defense contractor's right to use a government shipyard, Kaiser Co. v. Reid, 30 Cal.2d 610, 184 P.2d 879 (1947), a forest ranger's right to use government housing, United States v. County of Fresno, 50 Cal.App.3d 633, 123 Cal.Rptr. 548 (5th Dist. 1975), aff'd on other grounds, 429 U.S. 452, 97 S.Ct. 699 (1977), a refreshment company's right to operate concessions in a public stadium, Stadium Concessions, Inc. v. City of Los Angeles, 60 Cal. App.3d 215, 131 Cal.Rptr. 442 (2d Dist. 1976), and a company's right to rent television sets to patients in a county hospital, Wells Nat'l Services Corp. v. County of Santa Clara, 54 Cal.App.3d 579, 126 Cal.Rptr. 715 (1st Dist. 1976). The taxation of possessory interests has deep historic roots in California. An 1859 case, State v. Moore, 12 Cal. 56 (1859), held that a private mining claim on federal land could be taxed, even though federal immunity prevented taxation of the underlying title. Within a decade an even more contentious situation had arisen in People v. Shearer, 30 Cal. 645 (1866), where homesteaders refused to perfect title to their property because they wished to avoid taxation. The California Supreme Court found their right to possession sufficient to justify the tax even without complete legal title. "It is not the land itself, nor the title to the land, nor is it the identical estate held by the United States. It is not the pre-emption right, but it is the possession and valuable use of the land subsisting in the citizen. Why should it not contribute its proper share, according to the value of the interest, whatever it may be, of the taxes necessary to sustain the Government which recognizes and protects it?" Id. at 657. The homesteaders in question were refusing to take title to Marin County land at $1.25 an acre. Other early tax sales in Marin County included a 19,650 acre parcel "called Saucolito" sold for $745.27, thirty town lots in San Rafael sold for $141.39, and all of Angel Island sold for $160.50.

G. *The Property Tax as a Division of Property Rights.* A property tax may be viewed as a continuing public claim on a portion of the underlying property value. For example, if rental property yields a five percent annual return on investment, a tax of one percent of property value effectively constitutes a 20 percent public share of the property value. A public share of the property value is not the same as public ownership, since it does not carry rights to determine the use or disposition of the property. But it is akin to a limited partnership interest, with the titleholder maintaining control of the property but the public holding a right to a portion of its value. How would this perspective affect an analysis of the property tax? Consider, for example, the role a property tax might play when formerly public land is privatized, whether in post-Soviet Eastern Europe or in U.S. communities with decommissioned military bases offered for redevelopment.

1. ECONOMIC PERSPECTIVES: IS THE PROPERTY TAX REGRESSIVE?

The charge that the property tax is regressive is accepted without question in much public debate and yet is not accepted at all by many academic experts. Although it is common for non-economists to use the term "regressive" simply as a synonym for "unfair," regressive taxes are not always judged to be unfair. In fact, politically popular alternative revenue sources, from cigarette taxes to general sales taxes to lotteries, may be very regressive, while progressive taxes, such as the estate tax, are often unpopular and branded "unfair" by their opponents.

In economic terms, a regressive tax falls more heavily on low-income taxpayers, taking a larger percentage of their income than it takes from those with higher earnings. Thus, a tax of a specific dollar amount would be regressive, more burdensome for a low-income worker than for a highly compensated executive. Similarly, a flat-rate general sales tax will be regressive if low-income consumers spend a greater percentage of their incomes on taxable purchases than do wealthier households able to save and invest more. A progressive tax, by contrast, constitutes a higher percentage of income as income rises, and a proportional tax remains a constant percentage of income across different income levels.

It is important to note that a regressive tax or charge may be balanced by other methods of addressing income inequality, including subsidies and progressive taxes. Considering a single tax in isolation can be misleading if in fact it functions as one part of a complex fiscal system, with various roles for different taxes and different levels of government. A specific regressive tax would not necessarily be better replaced by a different method of raising revenue. However, even the charge of regressivity itself can be challenged in the case of the property tax. Whether the property tax takes a higher percentage of income from poorer households than from wealthier ones turns out to be a remarkably complex inquiry involving many component issues.

The legal incidence of a tax is determined by the person or entity officially designated as the taxpayer—the name on the tax bill. This may have very little to do with the economic incidence, the ultimate distribution of the actual tax burden. A tenant whose rent increases when property taxes rise bears an economic burden even if only the landlord receives a tax bill. Although legal incidence is critical to legal issues such as liability, enforcement, and exemption, it does not establish the progressivity or regressivity of a tax. That requires an investigation of economic incidence, which can rarely be observed directly. Usually some combination of data and theory provides a basis for estimating the final allocation of the economic burden.

Because regressivity measures the tax burden as a percentage of income, the definition of income is crucial, and controversial. Should tax-exempt income affect these calculations? Should unrealized gains? Should a graduate or professional student who anticipates greatly increased future earnings be considered as needy as a laborer with the same cash income who has already reached his peak wages? How should a wealthy retiree with substantial savings but modest current earnings be classified? Or a wealthy retiree with substantial income from tax-free municipal bonds? These questions are relevant to many non-tax issues as well. For example, a typical state formula for school aid to localities will consider, among other factors, the jurisdiction's property tax base, the average income of its residents, and its school enrollment. Should the low average earnings of university students increase the aid that college towns receive for their primary and secondary schools? The definition of income raises special questions in the case of the property tax because of the very long-term nature of home purchases and other housing decisions. If housing expenditures reflect income or prospects for income over many years, comparing the property tax burden to income in any single year may yield a distorted measure. This choice between annual income and long-term or "permanent" income is one specific issue that has divided professional opinion as to the regressivity of the property tax.

A property tax may also be analyzed according to its various components, each with a distinct economic impact. The tax on land can be distinguished from the tax on buildings, because for the most part the supply of land is fixed and cannot be altered. The economic burden of a tax shifts when producers and consumers respond to the tax by changing the amount of a taxed commodity that is produced and the price that is paid for it. In the long run, the supply of buildings can be increased through new construction or decreased through lack of maintenance and even eventual demolition. Because there is no similar opportunity to alter the supply of land (with very minor exceptions, as in the case of land reclamation), the burden of the tax on land, but not on buildings, is assumed to remain with the owner. Landowners are presumably already charging what the market will bear, and they have no option of raising the price by reducing the supply. The tax on buildings requires a further distinction between residences and business structures. Homeowners generally have no power to respond to a tax by changing either the prices they charge or the prices they pay, but businesses may be able to do either or both.

Because traditional analysis considered the burden of a tax on land to fall on landowners, this portion of the property tax was judged to be progressive, on the assumption that landholdings, like most capital, are concentrated among higher-income taxpayers. The residential portion of the tax on buildings was deemed regressive because housing expenditures were not thought to rise as rapidly as income—although substitution of long-term income data for annual income challenged this conclusion. The tax on business structures could be analyzed only in the context of specific taxpayers' opportunities for shifting the tax forward to purchasers (through higher prices) or backward to suppliers and employees (through lower payments and wages).

In the 1960s and 1970s a new view offered a different interpretation of the property tax, analyzing it as part of a nationwide tax on wealth and capital, with generally progressive effects. Professor Wallace Oates summarized the new view in this way: "The basic idea is that since nearly all communities are taxing local capital, the average rate of tax essentially becomes a national tax on capital. As such, it will likely be a progressive tax overall, since higher-income households own a disproportionately large share of the stock of capital."[b] Thus, just as a tax on land is assumed to be progressive because land ownership is concentrated among high-income

---

b. Wallace E. Oates, "An Overview and Some Reflections," in Wallace E. Oates, ed., Property Taxation and Local Government Finance 23 (2001) (footnote omitted).

households, a tax on capital is deemed progressive for the same reason. In recent decades this analysis has proved sufficiently convincing to form the new mainstream of economic opinion, "the predominant new conventional wisdom about the property tax among many economists and increasingly among policymakers as well."[c]

A third perspective offers yet another interpretation of the tax. It considers much residential property taxation to constitute a kind of consumer activity by which households purchase a specific mix of local services through their choices as to where to live. This benefit view accords with many policymakers' intuitive understanding of the property tax. For example, a Treasury Department study argued against the federal income tax deduction for state and local taxes on grounds that they constitute a type of personal consumption, "the cost paid by citizens for public services provided by State and local governments, such as public schools, roads, and police and fire protection. * * * To the extent that state and local taxes merely reflect the benefits of services provided to taxpayers, there is no more reason for a Federal subsidy for spending by state and local governments than for private spending."[d]

The benefit view alters the entire context for regressivity studies. If the property tax is the price for a bundle of local services, the net burden of the tax can be determined only by comparing what is paid with what is received. The concept of regressivity itself must be reexamined when the tax is analyzed as a payment for services. For example, it could readily be established that food, shelter, and other basic necessities require a diminishing proportion of income as household income rises. Increased discretionary income means that a lower proportion of income is devoted to non-discretionary necessities. But that does not imply that food or shelter prices are best analyzed as regressive taxes, or that society would be better served by substituting a different price system for these commodities. If the tax is viewed as part of consumer activity, the focus of the inquiry has shifted from a one-way payment—the government's collection of a specific amount from each taxpayer—to a market exchange of money for goods and services.

In this respect, both the new view and the benefit view suggest a complex interaction between considerations of regressivity and efficiency. The new view considers the property tax a levy on capital, and so generally progressive. This also means, however, that the tax distorts market signals and causes a corresponding loss of efficiency. The benefit view, which analyzes the tax as a payment for local services, accepts that this payment may constitute a diminishing percentage of income as income rises. However, the benefit view judges the property tax to be non-distortionary, and in fact extremely efficient. "If consumers treat the local property tax as a price for public services, then this price should not distort the housing market any more than the price of eggs should distort

---

c. Ronald C. Fisher, State and Local Public Finance 358 (3rd ed. 2007).

d. U.S. Dep't of Treasury, Report on Tax Simplification and Reform ch. 5, § IV(B)(1) (1984).

the housing market."[e] The fact that the proportion of income paid for an item decreases as income rises does not establish a failure in the price system. The best way of addressing income inequality may not be through price changes, but through transfer payments that permit low-income households to spend more on whatever goods or services are most useful to them.

Incidence, Exemptions, and Incentives. Consider the policy implications of the economic incidence of tax exemptions, whether offered to foster charitable activity, respect federal sovereignty, or to promote business growth. What would be the effect of a tax exemption for rental property owned by a charitable organization or by the federal government but leased to a private party for commercial purposes? If property taxes are capitalized into land prices, so that an increase in tax payments causes a drop in the purchase price, will this affect the impact of tax abatements intended to encourage business location in a particular jurisdiction? Tax-exempt institutions often contract to make payments in lieu of taxes to local governments in recognition of the services they receive. In Anderson Street Associates v. City of Boston, 442 Mass. 812, 817 N.E.2d 759 (2004), the Massachusetts Supreme Judicial Court held that developers who received a tax exemption in exchange for an agreement to pay an "urban redevelopment excise tax" could not renegotiate this obligation when later tax limitation measures reduced the property tax they avoided below the level of the excise tax.

References. A. For background on economic views of the property tax, see the first four chapters of Wallace E. Oates, ed., Property Taxation and Local Government Finance (2001), and Ronald Fisher, State and Local Public Finance (3rd ed. 2007). A clear and nontechnical explanation of the "old" and "new" views of the property tax is found in Henry Aaron, Who Pays the Property Tax? A New View (1975). On charitable property tax exemptions generally, see Evelyn Brody, ed., Property Tax Exemption for Charities (2002).

2. POLITICAL CHALLENGES TO MARKET–VALUE ASSESSMENT

The tax limitation measure known as "Proposition 13," approved by California voters in 1978, initiated a new era of restrictions on state and local taxes, with a particular focus on property taxes.[f] These limitations took a number of forms, including rate ceilings, restrictions on total collections, and changes in the calculation of assessed values. Proposition 13, for example, basically sets assessed value at the owner's purchase price

---

e. Bruce Hamilton, "Property Taxes and the Tiebout Hypothesis: Some Empirical Evidence," in Edwin S. Mills & Wallace E. Oates, eds., Fiscal Zoning and Land Use Controls: The Economic Issues 13 (1975) (quoted in Harvey S. Rosen, Public Finance 488 (1985)).

f. The U.S. Supreme Court's decision sustaining the constitutionality of Proposition 13 over the objection that it violated the Equal Protection Clause, Nordlinger v. Hahn, 505 U.S. 1, 112 S.Ct. 2326 (1992), is set out in Chapter 4, pp. 243–57 supra.

(or the 1975–76 tax value, if the property has not changed hands since then) with a maximum annual inflation adjustment of 2 percent. When property is sold, the sale price becomes the basis for the new owner's assessment. This system offers almost complete protection against unexpected assessment increases due to rising market values, which was a major concern in California in 1978. However, it imposes drastically different tax burdens on identical properties purchased at different times. It benefits long-term residents at the expense of homeowners who must move because of family or employment situations. The incentive for remaining in a residence, even if it is no longer suitable or efficient, was increased by a later provision allowing children to inherit their parents' tax assessments along with their houses. Proposition 13 might be viewed as not a property tax at all, but as a kind of sales tax payable in installments over the purchaser's term of ownership.

Variations on Proposition 13 have been enacted in a number of states, including Michigan, Oklahoma, and Florida. The 1992 Florida provision, called "Save Our Homes," is limited to homesteads, or principal residences, which means that owners of vacation property may pay many times the taxes due from neighboring year-round residents. Because those benefiting from Save Our Homes faced the possibility of sharp tax increases upon a change in residence, a 2008 referendum approved "portability" of the prior assessments to a new home. Again, this raises the question as to whether such a tax is best analyzed as a property tax or as a new excise on the ownership of real property.

A 1982 Colorado measure illustrates how complex assessment limitations can be. It restricts the residential portion of the total property tax base statewide to 45 percent. This means that after the value of all residential and non-residential property is computed, the state determines what percentage reduction in full-value assessment will achieve this balance. Immediately after this provision was approved, this assessment ratio for residential property was reduced from 30 percent to 21 percent, and the nonresidential assessment ratio was set at 29 percent. Every year a new ratio is computed for residential property, while the nonresidential ratio remains at 29 percent. The residential ratio fell to 15 percent in 1990, under 10 percent in 2000, and then below 8 percent when a 2003 ballot question to set the residential rate permanently at 8 percent failed by nearly a four-to-one margin. This statewide ratio is applied to taxable values in each county, so a county with a preponderance of residential property will have its tax base reduced with each drop in the residential ratio, while largely nonresidential areas will not experience the same reduction.

Property Tax Limitations by State			
State	Assessment Limits	Revenue Limits	Tax Rate Limits
Arizona	X	X	X
Arkansas	X	X	X
California	X		X

Property Tax Limitations by State			
State	Assessment Limits	Revenue Limits	Tax Rate Limits
Colorado	X	X	X
Connecticut	X		
District of Columbia	X		X
Florida	X		X
Georgia	X		X
Illinois	X	X	X
Iowa	X		X
Maryland	X		
Michigan	X	X	X
Minnesota	X	X	
Montana	X	X	X
New Mexico	X	X	X
New York	X		X
Oklahoma	X		X
Oregon	X		X
South Carolina	X		
Texas	X	X	X

Source: Nathan B. Anderson, "Property Tax Limitations: An Interpretative Review," 59 Nat'l Tax J. 685, 688 (2006).

Interestingly, restrictions on value increases can produce higher tax bills even for taxpayers within the classes favored by these limits. For example, the Minnesota Department of Revenue has studied the effect of that state's ceiling on assessment increases, which benefits four classes of property: residential, agricultural, seasonal recreational residential (e.g., cabins), and timberland. After computing the increase in tax rates necessary to maintain revenues when assessments were thus limited, the Department found that more than one-third of the properties in the favored categories and more than 84 percent of all residential homesteads in the state faced higher tax bills as a result:

> In 2007, the Limited Market Value law increased property taxes on 84% of the state's 1.4 million residential homesteads (1.2 million parcels), by $110 million (an average increase of $92 per parcel). For the other 16% of residential homesteads (227,000), the law decreased property taxes by $64 million (an average reduction of $282 per parcel). One-third of the parcels with limited value had an increase in tax. This seemingly counter-intuitive result occurs because the limitation on these residential homestead properties was overwhelmed by proportionately larger limitations on other properties. The net tax increase of $46 million on residential homesteads as a group results from shifts off of other limited classes of property.[g]

Limited values will not in and of themselves restrict the level of taxes if the tax rate is unconstrained. The example of "winners" and "losers"

---

g. Minnesota Department of Revenue, Limited Market Value Report: 2006 Assessment Year 15 (2007), available at www.taxes.state.mn.us/taxes/legal_policy/research_reports/content/2007_lmv_report.pdf.

demonstrates that assessment caps can have unintended consequences in their redistribution of the tax burden. The Florida experience shows that while an assessment freeze may be intended to allow seniors to stay in their homes, the "thaw" of revaluation upon sale can leave them feeling trapped and unable to move. Finally, all of these measures undermine transparency and accountability if they leave taxpayers unclear as to the basis for the tax or the computation of their bill.

There are methods to reduce burdens on individual taxpayers without undermining the market value basis for the tax. Some states limit tax rates or tax collections but assess property at full market value. "Circuit breakers" address tax burdens out of proportion to cash income by relieving some portion of the tax above a set percentage of income. Tax deferral programs permit a portion of senior citizens' property taxes to go unpaid, the debt accumulating with interest as a lien on the residence, to be paid when it is sold or the owner dies. This has traditionally has been considered unpalatable to senior citizens who would prefer to bequeath their property without encumbrances, but recent decades' experience with home equity loans and reverse mortgages may signal a change in that response.

Notes and Questions

A. *Alternate Tax Base Measures.* What would be the advantages and disadvantages of a property tax not based upon current sale value? Consider these alternatives: (a) a percentage of original acquisition cost; (b) a flat fee per household; (c) a tax on annual rental value rather than capital value, and (d) a tax measured by the physical characteristics of the property, such as length, front footage, land area, or building size. Physical characteristics of this type are frequently used to allocate special assessments for local improvements, such as sidewalks or street lights, not funded by general tax revenue. The British system of property taxes, or "rates," was long based on rental value rather than capital value, but taxes on residences there are now based on modified capital value.

3. ASSESSING AND COLLECTING THE TAX

An important advantage of a real property tax is the relative ease with which land and buildings can be located and identified. The immobility of real estate, as opposed to income or sales, prevents its simple migration in response to the tax, and avoids the problems of multijurisdictional tax-base allocation. An immovable asset also can serve as collateral for unpaid taxes, with potential foreclosure and sale to pay this debt. These features recommend the tax as a source of revenue for local governments, which often have neither the economic base nor the administrative capacity for efficient collection of more complex taxes. The distinctly local character of the property tax is due in part to constitutional limitations on federal taxation of property. Article I, § 9, cl. 4 of the

U.S. Constitution states: "No Capitation, or other direct, Tax shall be laid, unless in Proportion to the Census or Enumeration herein before directed to be taken." The Sixteenth Amendment exempted the federal income tax from this apportionment requirement. In New York Trust Co. v. Eisner, 256 U.S. 345, 349, 41 S.Ct. 506 (1921), Justice Holmes found that the federal estate tax was an excise on the transmission of property rather than a direct tax on the property itself, "not by an attempt to make some scientific distinction, which would be at least difficult, but on an interpretation of language by its traditional use. * * * Upon this point a page of history is worth a volume of logic." Note that customs receipts, which in some respects resemble non-recurrent ad valorem (i.e., value-based) tax revenue, were by far the most important source of federal funds until the Civil War.

The annual cycle of property taxation commonly begins with the assessor's computation of the total value of taxable property within the city, town, or other taxing entity. In many cases the tax rate for the year is then set at a level designed to raise the amount required by the jurisdiction, considering legislative and constitutional limitations as well as funds available through fees, charges, non-property taxes, and intergovernmental grants. The property tax is termed a "residual tax" if, as in this example, its rate is determined according to the revenue needed by the taxing jurisdiction after accounting for other sources of income. The property tax rate is frequently expressed in millage terms, a mill being one-tenth of a percent, or one one-thousandth. For example, a tax of twelve mills would be equivalent to a rate of 1.2 percent, or $12 for each $1,000 of assessed value.

The property tax rate, unlike income or sales tax rates, often rises or falls each year with changes in the tax base, the availability of other revenue, and local spending needs. This has important political and economic implications, for taxpayers perceive a direct connection between the total tax base, local government spending, and their annual property tax bills. The clarity of these relationships greatly enhances taxpayer awareness and public accountability, and also increases political controversy. For example, exemption of a major parcel of real estate can lead directly to a higher tax rate on the remaining taxpayers. By contrast, the theoretical relationship between the size of the charitable sector and the federal income tax rate schedule has a very attenuated political impact. Similarly, the local and visible property tax has often been the primary target for taxpayer revolts and tax-limitation measures.

The most challenging aspect of assessment, assigning a value to each taxable parcel, has been revolutionized in recent decades by the development of computerized methods for predicting market values. Computer-assisted mass appraisal (CAMA) compares the characteristics of properties that have been recently sold with those of other properties that have not changed hands in order to estimate the market value of properties in this second group. The availability of data on large numbers of comparable properties permits the correlation of characteristics such as location, size, design, and type of construction with selling price.

B. UNIFORMITY AND EQUALITY IN ASSESSMENT

In Chapter 4, we considered federal constitutional limitations on uniformity and equality in property tax assessments. See pp. 242–61 supra. In this Section, we consider state statutory and constitutional limitations on uniformity and equality in property tax assessments.

1. CLASSIFICATION AND FRACTIONAL ASSESSMENT

The amount of tax on any given property is the product of its assessed value and the tax rate. Several basic patterns link these two elements. The law may call for a single uniform rate of tax levied on the fair market value of the property, or for a uniform rate of tax on some specified fraction of fair market value. In the latter case the effective tax rate, or percentage of fair market value represented by the tax, would be a corresponding percentage of the stated or nominal rate. Finally, state law may call for a non-uniform system of taxation, with effective tax rates differing according to property type, such as residential, commercial, or industrial. Classification may be achieved through assessment at different fractions of fair market value, through non-uniform tax rates, through partial exemptions and abatements, or through a combination of these approaches.

In addition to statutory or constitutional classification systems, many instances of "extra-legal" classification, deliberate or not, vary the tax burden across property categories through inaccuracies in valuation. (Consider term "extra-legal" when reading the *Hellerstein* case, below at pp. 830–36.) A failure to revalue property periodically will produce assessment distortions as values rise in prosperous areas and fall in declining neighborhoods. If properties are revalued only when sales are recorded, parcels that once sold for similar amounts will continue to bear equivalent tax burdens even as their market values later diverge. Property owners who have suffered a loss in value will bear a heavier effective tax rate than owners of appreciating property because their tax bills will constitute a higher percentage of their property's market value, even though the nominal tax rate is the same in each case. *Relative* over-assessment is thus critical to the distribution of the tax burden. A taxpayer whose property is assessed at half its market value may be unlikely to protest this mistake. But if in fact most property in the jurisdiction is assessed at one-quarter of its full value, that taxpayer is bearing a disproportionate share of the total burden.

Such patterns are rarely the result of simple inadvertence. Owners of property in affluent neighborhoods may be more aware of property values and more likely to challenge an over-assessment than other taxpayers. The desire to benefit politically powerful groups has long motivated the relative over-and under-assessment of entire classes of property. This has resulted in over-assessment of property owned by nonresidents in vacation areas, under-assessment of farm property in the urban fringe, over-assessment of business property in mixed commercial and residential districts, and under-assessment of single-family homes nearly everywhere. Even uniform fractional assessment can produce distortions if the resulting values are used by another level of government, such as a school district, imposing a tax on multiple assessing jurisdictions. The assessing jurisdictions using a lower uniform fractional rate will appear to have less property wealth than equivalent jurisdictions assessing at a higher rate or at full market value. Because local property wealth is usually a factor in the distribution of state aid, state boards of equalization are often given the task of reviewing local assessments in order to correct such distortions.

When entire categories of property are subject to systematic under- and over-valuation the tax system has been classified even if no legal enactment prescribes different tax rates for different types of properties. However, an explicit, legal system of tax classification differs significantly from "extra-legal" practices reflecting assessor bias or inaccuracy in valuation. Consider, for example, a statute calling for one rate of tax for residential property and a second, higher rate for all other property, both imposed on a full market value base. If valuations are accurate, this system produces uniform tax burdens on all properties in a given class. By contrast, a system in which property values are updated only when a parcel is sold can produce an almost unlimited array of effective tax rates.

2. JUDICIAL AND LEGISLATIVE RESPONSES

Taxpayers seeking to challenge relative but not absolute over-assessment have long faced formidable obstacles. In the landmark case of Sioux City Bridge Co. v. Dakota County, 260 U.S. 441, 43 S.Ct. 190 (1923), the Supreme Court for the first time found a violation of federal equal protection guarantees in the case of a taxpayer whose property was assessed at a higher percentage of value than prevailed in the jurisdiction generally, even though the valuation was admittedly below full value. The Nebraska Supreme Court had held that the only remedy in such a situation was an action to require tax officials to raise the assessments of all undervalued parcels. The U.S. Supreme Court found this would

> deny the injured taxpayer any remedy at all because it is utterly impossible for him by any judicial proceeding to secure an increase in the assessment of the great mass of under-assessed property in the taxing district. * * * [W]here it is impossible to secure both the standard of the true value, and the uniformity and equality required by law, the latter requirement is to be preferred as the just and ultimate purpose of the law.

Id., 260 U.S. at 446.

The following case illustrates the obstacles taxpayers have sometimes encountered in challenging property tax systems on grounds of uniformity and equality.

PEOPLE EX REL. SCHLAEGER v. ALLYN

Supreme Court of Illinois, 1946.
393 Ill. 154, 65 N.E.2d 392.

FULTON, JUSTICE.

This matter comes to us on appeal from the judgment of the county court of Cook county overruling the objections of C.B. Allyn, hereafter referred to as the taxpayer, to the application of the ex officio county collector of Cook county, hereafter referred to as the collector, for judgment and order of sale on property belonging to the taxpayer for certain 1943 taxes paid under protest.

The taxpayer's property lies within the corporate limits of the village of Barrington, which municipality, while mainly located in Lake county, extends over into Cook county. Property in this village is subject to taxes for different counties, townships, and road and bridge districts, but the village of Barrington, Barrington park district and school district No. 4 are common taxing bodies. The objections herein are concerned only with the latter three tax levies. The levy is objected to as being discriminatory and constituting constructive fraud in violation of section 1 of article IX and section 2 of article II of the constitution of the State of Illinois, Smith–Hurd Stats., and of the due-process and equal-protection clauses of the fourteenth amendment to the constitution of the United States.

* * * By the stipulation it was agreed that for the year 1943 the tax rate for $100 of assessed valuation for the village of Barrington was $.65, for the Barrington park district, $.29 and for school district No. 4, $1.82; that the property of the taxpayer here was assessed by the Cook county assessor for the year 1943 at its fair cash value as of April 1, 1943, and the assessed value of the property was the amount determined by the assessor of Cook county as the fair cash value as of April 1, 1943; that the Department of Revenue determined the assessed value of all property throughout Cook county and throughout Lake county for the year 1943, and determined the ratio of assessed value to full cash valuation for each of said counties; that the ratio of assessed valuation to full valuation in Lake county as determined by the Department of Revenue was 21 per cent and that the ratio of assessed valuation to full valuation in Cook county for the year 1943 was 75 per cent; that the county clerk of Cook county and the county clerk of Lake county caused to be filed in the Department of Revenue an abstract of the assessed valuation of all the taxable property in their respective counties for the year 1943.

The only oral testimony produced at the hearing was by C. B. Allyn, the objecting taxpayer. It appears that Allyn, at the time of the hearing, was, and had been since 1943, head of the tax department of a large Chicago merchandising corporation. Prior to 1943, he had spent nineteen years with the Jewel Tea Company, the last nine years of which he was engaged as chief accountant and assistant comptroller in charge of accounting and taxes at the headquarters of the Jewel Tea Company in Barrington, Illinois; that, as a part of his duties in connection with the analysis of taxes for the Jewel Tea Company, he was familiar with the valuation methods used in Cuba township, Lake county, wherein the greater portion of the municipality of Barrington lies; that he was familiar with the report of the Department of Revenue disclosing the ratios of assessed valuation to full cash valuation for the year 1943, and that the figure of 21 per cent was a fair statement of the average as it existed in Cuba township in 1943; that he had made a study of assessment values from the records. He also testified that except for minor variations in the ratio of assessed value to full cash value, the ratio in Cuba township had been the same since 1930. Allyn further testified that the figure of 75 per cent of full value by the Department of Revenue as to Cook county was approximately correct as to the property in Barrington township, Cook county, and that this latter ratio has existed only starting in 1943. Prior thereto, an equalizing figure of 37 per cent had been applied to the previous 75 per cent of full value, which equalizing figure brought the assessed value down to 28 per cent.

Much of the testimony of Allyn was objected to by counsel for the collector on the ground of lack of qualification in Allyn to testify as to the assessment ratio used and that the testimony of Allyn was opinion evidence and conclusions. Over objection there was admitted in evidence taxpayer's exhibit 5, which was a computation of taxes as extended for the three taxing districts in question here on a sample piece of property worth $10,000 located in Cook county and in Lake county. For the three districts it appears that the $10,000 property in Cook county had been taxed at $207 and for Lake county, $57.96. The taxpayer also introduced as exhibit 6, over objection, his computation showing that the tax extended against his own property was $141.45 and that the tax extended against similar property in Lake county was $39.61.

Allyn further testified that in connection with exhibit 6, mentioned above, the property used as a comparison was a house built by a business associate of Allyn's the same year that Allyn built his house, that the same contractor and subcontractor were used and that the cost of the business associate's house exceeded Allyn's by 10 per cent. This same property, however, for the same municipal services paid a total tax of $39.61, whereas, Allyn's property was subject to a tax of $141.45. It further appears that a complaint was filed on the property here involved before the Board of Appeals based upon the grounds of lack of uniformity and the complainant asked for a hearing. No hearing was granted and on December 10, 1944, an order was entered by the Board of Appeals as follows: "No reduction."

* * *

While considerable emphasis is placed by counsel for the collector in his reply brief upon the fact that the proof and evidence in this case were not sufficient to overcome the stipulated prima facie case made by the collector, we are of the opinion from a reading of the whole record, including the stipulations entered into, that for the year 1943 the average assessed value of real property in the county of Cook was 75 per cent of the full, fair, cash, market value of said property, and that for the year 1943, the average assessed valuation of real property in Lake county was 21 per cent of the full, fair, cash, market value of said property. We are further of the opinion that on the average the above percentage figures applied to Barrington township in Cook county and to Cuba township in Lake county. We are called upon, therefore, to decide this question, Does a subsidiary corporate tax levy where the boundaries of the taxing unit extend into two or more counties violate the constitutional mandate of uniformity in taxation where the assessed valuation in one county is disproportionate to the assessed valuation in the other county?

The three common taxing bodies, Barrington village, Barrington park district, and school district No. 4, are each separate taxing bodies with statutory authority to levy taxes for their separate corporate purposes. These corporate purposes are separate and distinct from those for which counties are authorized to levy taxes and bear no relationship to corporate purposes of counties. The authorities of the three taxing bodies, however, have no power to assess and fix values of properties in their respective districts.

In support of his contention that a lack of uniformity exists in the above-mentioned taxing districts as required by section 1 of article IX of the constitution of 1870, the appellant has cited and quoted from a large number of Illinois cases where inequalities in taxation have been held improper and invalid. These cases have been so many times cited and analyzed that a detailed discussion of them is not necessary to this opinion. They all hold that courts will grant relief against inequality in taxation resulting from favoritism, fraud or intentional misconduct on the part of assessing bodies or officers. Most of them are cases where a given equalization factor has been applied to one class of property, or to property of one owner, and a different factor to another. * * *

They further hold that the great central and dominant idea of the constitution is uniformity of taxation. But it also can be said of those cases that the question arose over the misconduct of the assessor or the assessing bodies where the properties were State-wide or located in the same county and the factor adopted by the assessor was not applied equally to all property within the State or county. The rule of uniformity applies to property of like kind and character and similarly situated. * * * Section 1 of article IX of the constitution provides:

> The general assembly shall provide such revenue as may be needful by levying a tax, by valuation, so that every person and corporation shall pay a tax in proportion to the value of his, her or its property—

such value to be ascertained by some person or persons, to be elected or appointed in such manner as the general assembly shall direct, and not otherwise.

None of the cases relied upon by appellant presents a similar situation to that in the instant case. Here the values were fixed by the assessor or the assessing officers of the counties of Cook and Lake, respectively. The assessor is the officer who has been provided by the legislature for fixing the valuation of property for the purpose of taxation. In this record there is no suggestion of fraud made against the assessing bodies, nor any claim that the assessment was made on a wrong basis or an excessively high valuation placed thereon.

The appellant merely says he is paying a greater burden of the taxation for the three subsidiary corporations than like property similarly situated over in Lake county. In First National Bank v. Holmes, 246 Ill. 362, at page 367, 92 N.E. 893, at page 895, we said: "While the Constitution declares the rule of equality, it also provides that the value of property shall be ascertained by some person or persons to be elected or appointed in such manner as the General Assembly shall direct, and not otherwise. No system has ever been devised which has produced perfect equality and uniformity of taxation as between persons or corporations or different classes of property, and such a result cannot reasonably be expected. * * * Under the statute, the valuation is to be made by the assessor or board of review, and the judgments of such officers, when honestly exercised, will naturally differ. If their judgment is so exercised, the Constitution forbids a valuation by any other authority."

There is nothing in the briefs to indicate or suggest how uniformity might be maintained as between properties located in different counties but included within one park or school district. If he be correct in his position, it would necessitate all the property throughout the State being valued alike before absolute uniformity in overlapping districts, located partially in two or more counties, could be accomplished. In such situations, as long as the assessment and levy of taxes is based upon the judgment of the assessing officers in each separate county, absolute uniformity cannot be achieved. This matter is one exclusively for the legislature, and the relief, if any, in the several counties must come from the legislature and not from the courts. People ex rel. Hempen v. Baltimore & Ohio R. Co., 379 Ill. 543, at page 546, 42 N.E.2d 69.

In the case of People ex rel. Toman v. Olympia Fields Country Club, 374 Ill. 101, 28 N.E.2d 109, it was stated by this court that, concerning a taxpayer's claim of constructive fraud, the rule is that fraud in the valuation of property for purposes of taxation must be proved by clear and sufficient evidence. The presumption is that the tax is just and that the tax levying officers have performed their duties. The objector must establish by clear and convincing evidence that fraud has been committed.

In the present case there is nothing to show that the assessment was not made in the exercise of honest judgment, or that the assessor committed any act of discrimination against the appellant. There is no appearance of fraud or inequality between properties in either Lake or Cook counties.

"It is the law that the assessed value of property for taxation purposes cannot be impeached merely because of the difference of opinion as to values between the assessing bodies and the court," People ex rel. Wangelin v. Wiggins Ferry Co., 357 Ill. 173, 191 N.E. 296, 299. There is no claim, in the present case, that the valuation placed upon the property of the taxpayer was willful or arbitrary or at a valuation grossly in excess of its market value.

We do not feel that the taxpayer here has sustained the burden of proof imposed upon him by establishing by such clear and convincing evidence either actual or constructive fraud on the part of the taxing authorities such as would warrant a reversal of the judgment of the county court. The judgment of the county court of Cook county, is, therefore, affirmed.

Judgment affirmed.

NOTES AND QUESTIONS

A. *Nature of the Taxpayer's Complaint.* Was Allyn complaining that his property was overvalued? If not, what was his complaint? What is the difference between a property's fair market value and its assessed value? On which value does the taxing authority rely in determining the millage rate required to raise revenues sufficient to fund its budget? Would a taxpayer ever be concerned about fractional assessment if (contrary to the facts of *Allyn*) the assessment jurisdiction (e.g., the county) were coterminous with all taxing jurisdictions (e.g., the county, the school, district, and the park district)? Keep this question in mind when you read the *Hellerstein* case, below. To test your understanding of the mechanics of determining a property tax bill, explain precisely how the taxpayer arrived at his conclusion in Exhibit 5, i.e., that taxes for the three districts in question there would total $207 for a $10,000 property in Cook County and $57.96 for a $10,000 property in Lake County.

B. *Application of Uniformity and Equality Provisions to Different Assessment Methods.* In R. Cross, Inc. v. City of Newport News, 217 Va. 202, 228 S.E.2d 113 (1976), the court rejected the taxpayer's claim that the assessment of his tangible personal property by a method different from the assessment of other tangible personal property resulted in a higher effective rate of taxation on his property in violation of Article X, § 1 of the Virginia Constitution. That section provides: "All taxes * * * shall be uniform upon the same class of subjects within the territorial limits of the authority levying the tax." The court held that nothing in the relevant statute prescribes "the procedure to be followed by commissioners of the revenue in determining taxable values or prohibits the use of multiple methods" and that "there is no constitutional requirement that such methods be identical." Id., 228 S.E.2d at 116. Contra: State ex rel. Stephan v. Martin, 230 Kan. 759, 641 P.2d 1020 (1982) (assessing value of farm machinery by reference to "average loan value," while assessing other property by willing buyer/willing seller standard, violates uniformity and equality requirement); State Board of Equalization v. Barta, 124 Nev. 58, 188 P.3d 1092, 1095 (2008) (state constitutional requirement of uniformity in taxation not satisfied simply by showing property was not overvalued; "because the methods used to value a taxpayer's property are a material consideration in determining whether the property was justly and equitably valued, a taxpayer may challenge an assessment based on the use of unconstitutional methods even if the assessment does not exceed full cash value").

HELLERSTEIN v. ASSESSOR OF ISLIP

New York Court of Appeals, 1975.
37 N.Y.2d 1, 332 N.E.2d 279, 371 N.Y.S.2d 388.

WACHTLER, JUDGE.

Petitioner, an owner of real property located on Fire Island, claims that the entire assessment roll for the Town of Islip is void. The argument has been raised in a proceeding instituted pursuant to article 7 of the Real Property Tax Law, Consol. Laws, ch. 50a, which permits court review of an assessment upon a complaint of illegality, overvaluation or inequality (see Real Property Tax Law, sec. 706). There is no claim of overvaluation or unequal treatment in the assessment of petitioner's property. She argues only that the assessments are illegal because they were not made in accordance with section 306 of the Real Property Tax Law which states: "All real property in each assessing unit shall be assessed at the full value thereof." This, we have held, means market value, unless that cannot be established "and then other tests of full value must be used." (People ex rel. Parklin Operating Corp. v. Miller, 287 N.Y. 126, 129, 38 N.E.2d 465, 466.) Here it is conceded that all assessments throughout the township are based on a *percentage* of market value.

The Supreme Court, Suffolk County, in an opinion, dismissed the petition. The Appellate Division, Second Department, affirmed, without opinion. * * *

Section 306 of the Real Property Tax Law has an ancient lineage. In 1788 the New York Legislature directed "the assessors of each respective city, town and place in every county of this State (to) make out a true and exact list of the names of all the freeholders and inhabitants and opposite the name of every such person shall set down the real value of all his or her whole estate real and personal as near as they can discover the same." (See L.1788, ch. 65, March 7, 1788.) * * * Although the statute is one of the oldest in the State there does not appear to be any extant legislative history indicating what the full value requirement was intended to accomplish. And despite the fact that the custom of fractional assessments appears to be at least as old as the statute (see Kilmer, "Legal Requirements for Equality in Tax Assessments," 25 Albany L. Rev. 203, 210), it has prompted very little litigation. In several of the older cases the problem can be seen lurking in the background; but it is only during the last 10 years that we find the practice being directly challenged in the courts.

* * *

One of the most peculiar aspects of the township's case is the narrowness of their defense of the practice of fractional assessments. They are satisfied to rest on the theory "thus it has been, thus it always must be," without making any effort to explain how the custom began, whether it serves any useful purpose, and what would happen if the assessors complied, or were made to comply, with the strict letter of the law. Our own cases do not discuss these points; but they have been extensively reviewed and debated by scholarly commentators and by the courts in other jurisdictions.

The vast majority of States require assessors, either by statute or constitutional prescription, to assess at full value, true value, market value or some equivalent standard. * * *

Where full value is required, the standard has been almost universally disregarded. A 1957 study by the United States Census Bureau placed the average assessment ratio in the country at 30% of actual value (see Bird, The General Property Tax: Findings of the 1957 Census of Governments 40).

No one seems to know exactly how the practice of fractional assessment began. In an early case the Supreme Court suggested that: "If we look for the reason for this common consent to substitute a custom for the positive rule of the statute, it will probably be found in the difficulty of subjecting personal property, and especially invested capital, to the inspection of the assessor and the grasp of the collector. The effort of the landowner, whose property lies open to view, which can be subjected to the lien of a tax not to be escaped by removal, or hiding, to produce something like actual equality of burden by an underevaluation of his land, has led to this result" (Cummings v. Merchants' National Bank, 101 U.S. 153, 163).

This may well explain the origin of the rule, but it does not account for its remarkable powers of endurance, especially in a State like New York, which has removed personal property from the tax rolls (Real Property Tax Law, sec. 300). Its survival depends on other factors none of which are particularly commendable.

Bonbright, in his treatise, lists (p. 498):

"several reasons for the persistence of partial valuation. Gullible taxpayers associate a larger valuation with a larger tax, or at any rate are less contentious about a relatively excessive assessment if it does not exceed their estimate of true value. The ability to maintain a stable rate and to increase revenue by tampering with the tax base—a change which calls for less publicity and less opposition—is naturally desired by the party in power. Occasionally, partial valuation is intended as a substitute for a varied system of rates; i.e., different forms of property, while nominally taxed at the same rate, are in fact taxed at differing rates by being assessed at different proportions of full values. Undervaluation of realty is sometimes justified as compensating for the elusiveness of personalty; but even if the latter is assessed fully when caught, experience has shown that the net result is to furnish an additional incentive for evasion.

"Another inducement to undervaluation has been that, since the state relies on the property tax for part of its revenue, the county assessors seek to lighten their constituents' burden at the expense of the rest of the state by assessing the local property at a lower percentage than is applied elsewhere. This process has often resulted in a competition between counties as to which could most nearly approach the limit of nominal valuation. With the increasing trend in some states toward reserving the property tax for the support of the local communities, and in other states toward the creation of state boards of equalization, the enthusiasm for percentage valuation has been dampened."

Most of these considerations have probably served to perpetuate the custom in New York; but there may be other factors at work.

This State, of course, does not depend on real property taxes as a source of State revenue. However the State does supply financial aid to communities based primarily on assessed valuation (State Finance Law, sec. 54, subd. 1, par. c; sec. 54, subd. 2, pars. a, c, Consol.Laws, ch. 56) and this undoubtedly furnishes "another inducement to undervaluation." The activities of the State Equalization Board are meant to correct this problem but as one commentator observes "possibly local tax officials believe that there is no harm in trying" (Johnson, "Fractional Ratios and Their Effect on Achievement of Uniform Assessment," The Property Tax: Problems and Potentials, Tax Institute of America, p. 210).

Since the State Constitution provides that "[a]ssessments shall in no case exceed full value" (N.Y. State Const., art. XVI, sec. 2) assessing at a percentage of value discourages claims of unconstitutional overvaluation. Then the taxpayer is left with the far more difficult task of proving comparative inequality.

Obviously these reasons are all good reasons for abolishing the custom. As Bonbright observes (pp. 497–498): "Theoretically the taxpayer's pocket is not in the least affected by uniform undervaluation or overvaluation. Systematic undervaluation diminishes the tax base and the tax rate must therefore rise in order to supply the required government revenue. * * * The objections to the practice of undervaluation are patent. In the first place, except where sanctioned by statute, it involves a generally known and sanctioned disregard by officials of the law requiring them to assess property at its full and fair value. The other great vice is that the percentage of undervaluation is rarely a matter of common knowledge, so that it is extremely difficult to ascertain whether there is uniformity in the proportion or whether, through incompetence, favoritism, or corruption of the assessors, some portions of the taxpaying body are bearing the others' burdens, as between either individuals or local groups."

In recent years the high courts in several States, noting the mounting criticism, have held that full value means what it says and that the practice of fractional assessments is illegal (see, e.g., Switz v. Township of Middletown, 23 N.J. 580, 130 A.2d 15 [1957]; Ingraham v. Town & City of Bristol, 144 Conn. 374, 132 A.2d 563 [1957]; Russman v. Luckett, 391 S.W.2d 694 (Ky.) [1965]; Bettigole v. Assessors of Springfield, 343 Mass. 223, 178 N.E.2d 10 [1961]; Walter v. Schuler, 176 So.2d 81 (Fla.) [1965]; Southern Ry. Co. v. Clement, 57 Tenn. App. 54, 415 S.W.2d 146 [1966]).

In sum, for nearly 200 years our statutes have required assessments to be made at full value and for nearly 200 years assessments have been made on a percentage basis throughout the State. The practice has time on its side and nothing else. It has been tolerated by the Legislature, criticized by the commentators and found by our own court to involve a flagrant violation of the statute. Nevertheless the practice has become so widespread and been so consistently followed that it has acquired an aura of assumed legality. The assessors in Islip inherited the custom and it is conceded that they have continued it. Throughout the years taxes have been levied and paid, or upon default, tax liens have arisen, followed by foreclosure and ultimate transfer of title, all on reliance on the apparent legality of fractional assessments. Now we have before us a petition directly challenging the practice and seeking an order "declar[ing] the entire assessment roll of the Town of Islip for the year 1968–1969 as illegal, null and void." In the alternative the petitioner requests that we direct the township to "make future assessments of all property on the assessment rolls of said town at the full value."

The petitioner recognizes that if we invalidate the assessment roll this could bring "fiscal chaos to the Town of Islip." If the petitioner had sought mandamus this alone would be sufficient to deny relief, for we have long held that the courts should not act "so as to cause disorder and confusion in public affairs, even though there may be a strict legal right" (Andresen v. Rice, 277 N.Y. 271, 282, 14 N.E.2d 65, 70). We have not previously considered whether the same principle should apply to a claim of illegality brought pursuant to section 706 of the Real Property Tax Law. However since the nature of the relief and the public impact are identical, we believe it is incumbent on the courts, where their discretion is involved, to exercise the same degree of restraint whenever a settled assessment roll or property rights based thereon are challenged for illegality. And this should be true whether the proceeding be labeled mandamus or otherwise. It follows from this that we will not, in this action, on the equity side, disturb the settled assessment rolls. The taxes levied and paid, the tax liens, matured or pending, and completed transfers of foreclosed properties made in reliance on the assessment rolls are matters not now before the court and on which therefore it should not pass. We assume however that should these questions arise, the courts will exercise the sound discretion with which they are vested. To this extent we agree with the courts below that the petitioner was not entitled to have the past assessment rolls declared a nullity.

This does not mean however that we must indorse the practice or withhold relief insofar as future assessments are concerned. Future compliance with the full value requirement will undoubtedly cause some disruption of existing procedures, but time should cure the problem. The difficulty of transition is sufficient reason to defer relief, but not to deny it. The petitioner thus is entitled to an order directing the township to make future assessments at full value as required by section 306 of the Real Property Tax Law. The order however should not go into effect immediately. To make this transition, the township should be allowed a reasonable time, but not later than December 31, 1976. In the interim assessments may be made in accordance with the existing practice and any tax levies, liens, foreclosures or transfers based on such assessments shall not be subject to challenge for failing to comply with section 306 of the Real Property Tax Law.

Accordingly, the order of the Appellate Division should be modified to the extent of directing that, within a reasonable time, but in no event later than December 31, 1976, the respondent shall assess the real property within the township at full value.

JONES, JUDGE (dissenting).

I think the order of the Appellate Division should be affirmed.

While the long-standing practice of fractional assessments for real property taxation cannot be said to violate the constitutional mandate that "[a]ssessments shall in no case exceed full value" (N.Y. Const. art. XVI, sec. 2), there can be no blinking the fact that fractional assessment cannot be squared with the literal command of section 306 of the Real Property Tax Law—"All real property in each assessing unit shall be assessed at the full value thereof."

Were we now called on to interpret such a provision in a recently adopted statute or to pass on the propriety of an emerging practice of fractional valuation under an older enactment, we would be confronted with an entirely different question. Neither is the case now before us, however.

As is stated in the majority opinion, the literally explicit provision of section 306 which it is now sought for the first time in our court to enforce has an ancient lineage. As the majority also recognizes, however, paralleling the long history of statutory address to "full value" has been the equally venerable practice of fractional assessment. With but a few desultory exceptions, the custom of fractional assessment has been followed without challenge until recently. It appears that over the years a collector was held liable for taking property under a certificate based on a fractional assessment only in a single reported instance (Van Rensselaer v. Witbeck, 7 N.Y. 517). In People ex rel. Westchester County v. Fowler, 55

N.Y. 252, the supervisors of Westchester County sought unsuccessfully to compel full value assessment by requiring the assessors to file a proper certificate of assessment. The court, taking note of uncontroverted proof that it had been the custom at least for several years not to assess at full value but rather to assess at about one third or in some cases at one fourth of full value, refused to require the assessors precisely to track the statutory language. "Courts do not sit to compel man to take false oaths, and whatever duty the assessors may have omitted, they owe no duty to the public to commit crime, and no public exigency can require it of them." (55 N.Y. at p. 254.) While the *Fowler* court commented critically on the discrepancy between statutory language and practice, as did the Appellate Division, Third Department, in the later case of People ex rel. Congress Hall v. Ouderkirk, 120 App.Div. 650, 105 N.Y.S. 134. ("But it is a custom not only wholly repugnant to the plain mandates of the statute, but also radically at war with the official oaths of the assessors, and also with their oaths to the assessment rolls" (p. 655, 105 N.Y.S. p. 138)) no judicial mandate was sought or granted to enforce strict conformity with the statutory language. * * *

Although it may be accurate to say that our court has never squarely confronted the issue and held the practice of fractional assessment valid, more significant in my view, although obviously not conclusive, is the conspicuous fact that notwithstanding the ingenuity and dogged determination of taxpayers, sometimes on the flimsiest of arguments, to resist taxation thought to be illegal, the present is the first case in nearly 200 years in which our State's highest court has been invited to confront the issue head-on and to overturn fractional assessments.

* * *

In these circumstances and in the light of the history of both enactment and failure to enact on the part of our State Legislature, of the construction uniformly placed on the statutory assessment procedures by those charged with direct responsibility thereunder, and of what I can only characterize as the general acceptance by taxpayers and municipal authorities alike of fractional assessments, I conclude that it ill becomes the judiciary, in what I conceive to be an exaggerated emphasis on the literal but long-ignored terminology of the statute, to overturn a practice of such venerable and broadly accepted status. No one questions that the Legislature could explicitly authorize the present practice; there would be no constitutional impediment. I agree that it would be desirable from various points of view were the Legislature unmistakably to express its views with reference to fractional assessment. I see no sufficient reason, however, to invalidate present practice for the purpose of forcing the issue, opening as it inevitably will a veritable Pandora's box of both foreseeable and unforeseeable complications. Attractive and persuasive as are some of the arguments in support of the principle of full value assessment (more appropriately, however, to be addressed to the Legislature), it must be conceded as a practical matter that the implementation of such a system could be achieved only by the expenditure of very large sums of money to defray the expense of what would have to be nearly State-wide reassessment procedures. On the one hand I see no warrant for the judicial imposition of such costs in the historical circumstances of this case. On the other, I see no justification or useful purpose to be served in forcing the Legislature to go through the ceremony of formally expressing what I can only believe is at least its tacit approval of present fractional assessment procedures.

I would, therefore, affirm the order of the Appellate Division.

I am obliged additionally to observe that not only do I seriously question the wisdom of giving prospective-only effect to judicial determinations as does the majority in this case, more importantly I know of no sufficient legal authority for such a procedural disposition.

JASEN, FUCHSBERG and COOKE, JJ., concur with WACHTLER, J.

JONES, J., dissents and votes to affirm in a separate opinion in which BREITEL, C.J., and GABRIELLI, J., concur.

Order modified, without costs, in accordance with the opinion herein and, as so modified, affirmed.

NOTES AND QUESTIONS

A. Hellerstein, *Full–Value Assessments, and Limitations on Property Tax Assessments.* The *Hellerstein* decision was one of a series of cases in the 1960s and 1970s in which courts reversed their former tolerance of "extra-legal" fractional assessment practices. In some instances these decisions led to full-value assessment, in others they led to statutory or constitutional provisions for legal classification, and in California they helped set the stage for the Proposition 13 "tax revolt." In response to *Hellerstein*, New York State instituted a complex formula for dividing its tax base among classes of property. In what legislative leaders called a "share of the pie" approach, the new tax system fixed the proportion of total property tax in New York City and Nassau County contributed by four classes—basically, one-, two- and three-family homes; apartment houses and other residential property; utilities; and all other property. The growth of individual residential assessments was also restricted there to 6 percent annually and no more than 20 percent over five years.

This system has definitely redistributed the property tax burden. One-, two-, and three-family homes contribute a portion of total tax collections that represents less than half its share of the market value base; commercial property contributes a portion that is nearly twice its share of the market value base. The assessment ratio for one-, two- and three-family houses in New York City is 6 percent; for other types of residential property it is 45 percent. The effective tax rate on a rental apartment can be many times the rate on a single-family townhouse. Cooperative apartments and condominiums are not assessed according to their market value, but rather as if they were rental apartments. In their case, the higher assessment ratio for apartments is far outweighed by the much lower market values of rental apartments (particularly if subject to rent control) than of condominiums and cooperatives. In 2006 the New York City Independent Budget Office concluded that the post-*Hellerstein* legislation left the city's property tax "even more tilted in favor of one-, two-, and three-family homes than it had been in 1981."[h]

The complications of class shares, fractional assessments, and assessment limits impede the ability of taxpayers to understand the tax process. As former New York City Finance Commissioner Martha Stark said:

> The law is far too complicated. New York City and Nassau County are the only places in the State with fractional assessments, which means people often have to do math just to understand the market value of their property. * * * We are also required to value condos and coops as if they are rental properties. * * * Owners of homes of equal value—whether those homes are horizontal or vertical—should pay the same amount of tax, except where we provide relief for individuals who have fixed incomes. But because of the way we have to treat condos and coops under the law, we cannot achieve this fundamental principle of fairness. State law also caps assessment increases for certain property owners. The caps are incredibly confusing and most taxpayers don't understand that the caps limit the growth of assessments, not taxes or market values.[i]

New York City's preferences for owner-occupied residences give a particularly dramatic example of the troubling equity implications of these widespread and popular provisions. Actual rental properties are greatly disfavored by comparison to more expensive cooperative and condominium properties, which are required to be valued as if they were rental units. Finally, the assessment caps produce "winners" and "losers" even among taxpayers whose values are restricted by that cap. As Commissioner Stark explained:

> If you were to scan the New York Times Real Estate Section on any Sunday, you could probably find an owner of a $1 million brownstone in Park Slope, one of the wealthiest neighborhoods in Brooklyn, paying less tax than the owner of a $1 million home in Bedford–Stuyvesant, one of Brooklyn's less wealthy neighborhoods. Why? The limits on assessment increases tend to provide larger benefits in neighborhoods where sales prices are rising fast and smaller benefits in those neighborhoods where values are rising modestly.[j]

For a city such as New York, with its strong progressive tradition and a preponderance of renters, such disparities evidence the extent to which the workings of the state's complex property tax are not understood by voters.

B. *The Massachusetts Experience.* Like New York, Massachusetts passed a tax limitation measure after the state's highest court reversed its longstanding acceptance of fractional assessment and "extra-legal" classification. Tre-

---

h. New York City Independent Budget Office, "Twenty–Five Years After S7000A: How Property Tax Burdens Have Shifted in New York City" (December 6, 2006), available at //www.ibo.nyc.ny.us/iboreports/propertytax120506.pdf.

i. Testimony of Martha E. Stark, Commissioner, New York City Department of Finance, Before a Hearing of the Assembly Real Property Taxation Committee, April 17, 2007, pp. 2–3, available at www.nyc.gov/html/dof/html/pdf/07pdf/testimony_2007_04_07.pdf.

j. Id.

gor v. Board of Assessors, 377 Mass. 602, 387 N.E.2d 538 (1979), held that taxpayers who were not treated uniformly under fractional assessment systems had the right to have their valuations lowered, not simply to the jurisdiction-wide average assessment ratio, but to the average ratio of the most favored property class. Boston was a particularly egregious example, having had no full city-wide reassessment since the 1920s. Its nominal property tax rate in 1980 was 25 percent—a level that would be completely unsupportable if assessments were anywhere near market levels.

Massachusetts voters responded in 1980 by passing "Proposition 2½," which limited tax rates to 2.5 percent. This simply reflected how long the state's older cities had gone without revaluing their property, for 2.5 percent is an extremely high tax rate if applied to accurate market-value assessments. More significant for all jurisdictions was a 2.5 percent limit on annual growth in property tax collections. However, no attempt was made to alter the market-value basis of assessment. In fact, a city or town's right to impose different tax rates on different classes of property was conditioned on certification of full-value assessment by the Department of Revenue.

Thus Massachusetts joined New York and a number of other states in which a judicial decision overturning unauthorized classification was followed by enactment of an explicit, legal system of classification. This step was disturbing to those who valued uniformity in taxation, but the constitutional requirement of uniformity had long been ignored in favor of de facto classification. The new amendment, which set limits on the degree to which class tax rates could diverge, was far different from the prior regime, in which outdated assessments and the individual assessor's judgment could produce a system in which there were nearly as many classes as taxable properties.

C. *Uniformity and "Base Year Values" in Pennsylvania.* Clifton v. Allegheny County, ___ Pa. ___, 969 A.2d 1197 (2009), dealt with a Pennsylvania statute that explicitly permitted counties to use values established in a given year (the "base year") for future property tax assessments for an indefinite period, disregarding interim changes in market value. The plaintiffs charged that this violated the state's Uniformity Clause, Pa. Const. art. VIII, § 1, which requires that all property in each county be uniformly assessed. The statute did not call for any fixed schedule of reassessments. For example, acting in accord with the statute, Allegheny County enacted an ordinance in 2005 decreeing that assessments in 2006 and subsequent years would be based on property values in 2002. New construction after the base year would generally be valued by reference to base year values of comparable properties, or base year construction costs.

In this way the base year approach closely resembled tax limitation measures, such as California's Proposition 13, that prevent assessed values from increasing in response to changes in market value. In Pennsylvania, however, institution of the base year approach was not accompanied by any amendment to the state's constitutional requirement of uniformity. Allegheny County argued that the stability and predictability of base year assessments benefited the government and taxpayers alike by avoiding the cost and uncertainties of reassessments. It contended that reassessments "cause many taxpayers to suffer from the 'sticker shock' of receiving consecutive notices of substantial increases in the value of their property without any improvements having been made.* * * The County maintains that '[w]hat is pejoratively viewed as the base year's vice is ultimately its saving virtue'—the creation of 'a constant and certain set of property values that do not fluctuate wildly from year to year.' " Clifton, 969 A.2d at 1217–18. The county denied that the base year system produces such pervasive inequities as to render the assessment system unconstitutional.

In rejecting these arguments, the Supreme Court of Pennsylvania emphasized that the base year system produced a disproportionate burden on taxpayers in declining neighborhoods, whose assessment remained unchanged while their property values fell. The court found these variations to bear no rational relationship to a legitimate state purpose. Statistical measures of disparity in the ratio of assessments to market value in Allegheny County were "well outside the standards" (id. at 1225) of the International Association of Assessing Officers (IAAO). For example, the coefficient of dispersion, which measures the variation in the percentage of full value represented by assessments, was more than twice the maximum recommended by the IAAO.

The court found that this situation violated the constitutional requirement of uniformity, but stopped short of holding the base year system necessarily constitutionally deficient in all instances. Although the trial court had found this system unconstitutional on its face, the supreme court only held it unconstitutional as applied in Allegheny County:

> Presumably, inequity will arise in such a system at different rates in different taxing authorities, depending upon the stability of property values in the municipality, the variety of real estate extant, and from other market factors. The point at which an unadjusted base year system becomes constitutionally problematic thus may vary from county to county. We recognize the desirability of the base year system from the county perspective, and it may be that such a system might operate fairly for more tax cycles than the base year in certain counties. Thus, it may be that a county could ensure a constitutional base year method of assessment by requiring periodic reassessment through an ordinance or as a matter of practice. The difficulty—and the risk to an authority employing an unadjusted base year system—is in determining the point at which a base year deviates to an extent where reassessment would be required.

> It is not our charge to determine what may be the best system of assessment. Nor is this Court capable of fixing a point in time at which a base year automatically becomes unconstitutionally non-uniform. As the trial court noted, the General Assembly is the appropriate place in the first instance to fashion a more comprehensive and soundly constitutional scheme.

> Ultimately, our task is decisional, and Allegheny County is currently left with a broken system of property taxation. In its effort to fashion a remedy, the trial court directed the Chief Assessment Officer of Allegheny County to conduct a reassessment no later than March 31, 2009, for use in the 2010 tax year, even if this Court had not yet issued a final order. We agree that reassessment is required. However, recognizing that the passage of time may require adjustment by the trial court, we will

remand this matter to the trial court to determine Allegheny County's progress in executing a countywide reassessment and to set a realistic timeframe for its completion.

Id. at 1229–31.

Allegheny County immediately called for state legislation providing an assessment moratorium while a new uniform statewide system of assessment is developed. It remains to be seen what action, if any, the state will take, and whether the base year approach could be found constitutional as applied in any other county.

How would you explain the application of the IAAO standards to a non-market-value system such as the base year approach? Is it likely that any large diverse county in Pennsylvania could apply the base year approach in a manner the state supreme court would find constitutional?

D. *Political Questions Raised by* Hellerstein. Unlike similar cases overturning fractional assessment systems in many other states, *Hellerstein* dealt with a legislative, not constitutional, requirement of full-value assessment. Why do you think the New York legislature did not simply overrule that decision by statute in the following session? How would the practical and political effects of the *Hellerstein* case have differed if that court had continued the prior interpretation of "full value" as a "uniform percentage of full value"? Was the *Hellerstein* court correct when it wrote that fractional assessment had "time on its side and nothing else"? Was the dissent correct in terming legislative ratification of fractional assessment an empty "ceremony"?

E. *"Extra–Legal" Assessment Approaches.* The *Hellerstein* case helps explain use of the term "extra-legal" to refer to assessment practices, such as de facto classification, that are contrary to statute but sanctioned by long practice. When "for nearly 200 years our statutes have required assessments to be made at full value and for nearly 200 years assessments have been made on a percentage basis," a description of the earlier practice as "illegal" in all but technical contexts may suggest a misleading clarity as to earlier statutory interpretation.

F. *The Situation in Nassau County.* The post-*Hellerstein* legislation made special provision for New York City and for Nassau County on Long Island. Nassau County's astonishing assessment system, based on a combination of 1938 building costs and 1964 land values, was the subject of a 1997 legal action by the New York Civil Liberties Union charging that this imposed unconstitutional discriminatory tax burdens on minority homeowners. The county settled this case by agreeing to reassess all properties by 2003. The resulting shifts in tax values led approximately 97,000 homeowners, one-quarter of the county total, to challenge their 2003 valuations. Bruce Lambert, "Accusations Flying in Nassau Over Reassessments of Property," N.Y. Times, June 11, 2003, at B5.

G. *Discrimination in Favor of Homeowners.* The political impetus to favor homeowners produces greatly reduced tax burdens on owner-occupied property, even within the generally favored residential category, in many states. If Nassau County's outdated assessments could be judged a de facto form of discrimination against minority homeowners, could tax systems favoring homeowners over renters be found similarly discriminatory?

H. *Discrimination Against Time–Share Owners.* The political calculus favoring homeowners operates in the opposite direction with regard to time-share owners, who rarely are voting residents of the jurisdiction in which the time-share is located and who may not even be direct recipients of the unit's tax bills. In Spanish River Resort Corp. v. Walker, 526 So.2d 677 (Fla. 1988), the Florida Supreme Court approved a lower court's holding that tax could be assessed on the value of each "week" in a time-sharing unit, not limited by the comparable value of physically similar units that had not been converted to time-sharing interests. In that case, the assessment of individual "weeks" resulted in valuations ten times as high as those of similar units not subject to time-sharing arrangements. The lower court pointed out that title to the time-share units was transferred by standard warranty deeds protected by title insurance. Sales brochures stated, "[t]he person who buys at Spanish River Resort is an owner with deed, and full rights of ownership. You may lend your property, sell it, rent it, or give it away during the weeks you own it. Or you can keep it forever." Spanish River Resort Corp. v. Walker, 497 So.2d 1299, 1302 (Fla. Dist. Ct. App. 1986).

CSX TRANSPORTATION, INC. v. GEORGIA STATE BOARD OF EQUALIZATION

Supreme Court of the United States, 2007.
552 U.S. 9, 128 S.Ct. 467.

CHIEF JUSTICE ROBERTS delivered the opinion of the Court.

The Railroad Revitalization and Regulatory Reform Act prohibits States from discriminating against railroads by taxing railroad property more heavily than other commercial property in the State. Two decades ago, we held that this statute permits an aggrieved railroad to challenge a State's valuation of its property for tax purposes. Burlington Northern R. Co. v. Oklahoma Tax Comm'n, 481 U.S. 454, 462, 107 S. Ct. 1855 (1987). Because the railroad in that case challenged only the State's application of its valuation methods, we expressly reserved the question whether a railroad may challenge the State's methods themselves. We answer that question today, and hold that railroads may challenge state methods for determining the value of railroad property, as well as how those methods are applied. The statute provides for nothing less.

I

Congress enacted the Railroad Revitalization and Regulatory Reform Act in 1976. 90 Stat. 31. Called the "4–R Act" for brevity, the law aimed to halt the economic decline of the rail industry by, among other means, barring "discriminatory state taxation of railroad property." The 4–R Act prohibits four separate forms of discriminatory state taxation of railroads. Only the first is at issue here: States, the Act provides, may not "[a]ssess rail transportation property at a value that has a higher ratio to the [property's] true market value ... than the ratio" between the assessed and true market values of other commercial and industrial property in the same taxing jurisdiction. 49 U.S.C. § 11501(b)(1). If the railroad ratio exceeds the ratio for other property by at least five percent, the district court may enjoin the tax. § 11501(c).

Petitioner CSX Transportation, Inc., is a freight rail carrier with multiple routes across the State of Georgia. As a consequence, it is subject to Georgia's ad valorem tax on real property. Under Georgia law, most commercial and industrial property is valued locally by county boards. Public utilities such as railroads, however, are initially valued by the State, which then certifies the proposed valuations to the county boards for adoption or alteration. In 2001, Georgia's State Board of Equalization, a respondent here, put CSX's ad valorem tax liability at $4.6 million. A year later, the State's appraiser used a different combination of methodologies to determine the market value of CSX's in-state property.[4] The result was a significantly higher tax levy. The State estimated the railroad's 2002 market value at approximately $7.8 billion, a 47 percent increase over the previous year. That brought the assessed value of CSX's Georgia property to $514.9 million, for a final property tax bill of $6.5 million.

CSX filed suit in the United States District Court for the Northern District of Georgia, contending that the State's 2002 tax assessment violated the 4–R Act. The railroad alleged that Georgia had grossly overestimated the market value of its in-state property while accurately valuing other commercial and industrial property in the State. The result, according to CSX, was that its rail property was taxed at a ratio of assessed-to-market value considerably more than 5 percent greater than the same ratio for the other property in the State.

To make its case, CSX submitted the testimony of its own expert appraiser, who relied on a combination of valuation methods different from those used by the appraiser for Georgia. The CSX appraiser calculated the 2002 market value of the railroad's property to be $6 billion, not the $7.8 billion figure used by the State. CSX maintained that the state appraiser's valuation methodologies were flawed, and urged the District Court to accept the market value estimated by its expert as more accurate.

The District Court refused to do so. Following a bench trial, the court ruled Georgia had not discriminated against CSX in violation of the 4–R Act because the State had used widely accepted valuation methods to arrive at its estimate of true market value. In the judgment of the District Court, the Act "does not generally allow a railroad to challenge the state's chosen methodology," as long as the State's methods are rational and not motivated by discriminatory intent.

---

4. Georgia assesses public utilities using the "unit rule." Under this rule, "an appraiser first determines the value of all assets of an entity, regardless of location," then multiplies "by the percentage of the entity located within [the State] to determine what portion of the value of the company should be allocated to the state." 472 F.3d 1281, 1283 (CA11 2006). The parties agree the unit rule is the appropriate rule for valuing CSX's property. There are, however, numerous methods available to value property under the unit rule, and many of these methods themselves have multiple variations.

A divided panel of the Court of Appeals for the Eleventh Circuit affirmed. The majority reasoned that the "text of the Act does not clearly state that railroads may challenge valuation methodologies," and that such a clear statement was required in light of the intrusion on state taxing prerogatives. Judge Fay dissented. Recognizing the division on this question among the Circuits, compare Consolidated Rail Corp. v. Hyde Park, 47 F.3d 473, 481–482 (CA2 1995) (a railroad may challenge a State's valuation methodology), and Burlington Northern R. Co. v. Department of Revenue of Wash., 23 F.3d 239, 240–241 (CA9 1994) (same), with Chesapeake Western Ry. v. Forst, 938 F.2d 528, 531 (CA4 1991) (a railroad may not challenge a State's valuation methodology), and 472 F.3d at 1289 (decision below), we granted certiorari and now reverse.

II

"[T]he language of § 1150[1] plainly declares the congressional purpose." Burlington Northern, 481 U.S., at 461,107 S. Ct. 1855. States may not tax railroad property at a ratio of assessed-to-true-market value higher than the ratio for other commercial and industrial property in the same jurisdiction. In order to apply the Act, district courts must calculate the true market value of in-state railroad property. A court cannot undertake the comparison of ratios the statute requires without that figure at hand. We said as much in *Burlington Northern*: "It is clear from [the Act's] language that in order to compare the actual assessment ratios, it is necessary to determine what the 'true market values' are." Ibid.

We do not see how a court can go about determining true market value if it may not look behind the State's choice of valuation methods. Georgia insists there is a clear and important distinction between valuation methodologies and their application. As the State would have it, the statute allows courts to question only the latter. We find no distinction between method and application in the language of the Act, and see no passage limiting district court factfinding in the manner the State proposes. The total lack of textual support for Georgia's position is not surprising. The dichotomy the State presses would eviscerate the statute by forcing courts to defer to the valuation estimate of the State, when discriminatory taxation by States was the very evil the Act aimed to ban.

Georgia's position is untenable given the way market value is calculated. Valuation is not a matter of mathematics, as if the district court could prevent discriminatory taxation simply by doublechecking the State's assessment equations. Rather, the calculation of true market value is an applied science, even a craft. Most appraisers estimate market value by employing not one methodology but a combination. These various methods generate a range of possible market values which the appraiser uses to derive what he considers to be an accurate estimate of market value, based on careful scrutiny of all the data available. Appraisal Institute, The Appraisal of Real Estate 49 (12th ed. 2001).

Georgia's appraiser in the instant case, for example, used three different valuation techniques—the discounted cashflow approach, a market multiple approach, and a stock and debt approach. He derived five values from these three methods, ranging from $8.126 billion to $12.346 billion. After selecting a number at the low end of the range and then subtracting another $400 million to account for intangible property not subject to ad valorem taxation, he settled on $7.8 billion as his final estimate of the true market value.

Appraisers typically employ a combination of methods because no one approach is entirely accurate, at least in the absence of an established market for the type of property at issue. The individual methods yield sometimes more, sometimes less reliable results depending on the peculiar features of the property evaluated. As the variation in the state appraiser's market-value range reveals, different methods can produce substantially different estimates.

Given the extent to which the chosen methods can affect the determination of value, preventing courts from scrutinizing state valuation methodologies would render § 11501 a largely empty command. It would force district courts to accept as "true" the market value estimated by the State, one of the parties to the litigation. States, in turn, would be free to employ appraisal techniques that routinely overestimate the market worth of railroad assets. By then levying taxes based on those overestimates, States could implement the very discriminatory taxation Congress sought to eradicate. On Georgia's reading of the statute, courts would be powerless to stop them, and the Act would ultimately guarantee railroads nothing more than mathematically accurate discriminatory taxation. We do not find this interpretation compelling. Instead, we agree with Judge Fay in dissent below: "Since the objective of any methodology is a determination of true market value, a railroad should be allowed to challenge the method[s] used [by the State] in an attempt to prove that the result ... was not the true market value of its property." 472 F.3d at 1294.

The State agrees that it may not be possible to fix true market value with any precision. But it draws a different conclusion from this premise. Because any number of estimates are plausible, Georgia argues, the court is as likely to get an accurate result by verifying the application of the State's methods—so long as they are broadly reasonable—as it is by employing another method altogether. The State warns that allowing railroads to introduce their own valuation estimates based on different methodologies will inevitably lead to a futile clash of experts, which courts will have no reasonable way to settle. At least one of the Courts of Appeals shares this concern. See Chesapeake Western, 938 F.2d at 532 ("There is no absolute way to test the assertions of competing valuations ..." (internal quotation marks and brackets omitted)).

Congress was not similarly troubled. It directed courts to find true market value, however elusive. It made that value the objective benchmark for courts' evaluation of state taxes on railroad property. True market value may well not be a single, precise number, but Congress obviously believed it was susceptible to judicial inquiry and that some approximations were better than others.

Georgia's grim prophecies notwithstanding, the inquiry the statute mandates is not unfamiliar to courts. Valuation of property, though admittedly complex, is at bottom just "an issue of fact about possible market prices," Suitum v. Tahoe Regional Planning Agency, 520 U.S. 725, 741, 117 S. Ct. 1659 (1997), an issue district courts are used to addressing. Railroad property is not frequently sold, but "determinations of market value are routinely made in judicial proceedings without the benefit of a market transaction." Id., at 742, 117 S. Ct. 1659. The District Court in this case made clear that it knew how to find true market value: "In a more typical case, the court would look at both [the railroad expert's] appraisal and [the State's] appraisal to determine the true market value of [the railroad]." 448 F. Supp. 2d, at 1338, n. 8. It refused to do so not because true market value is inherently elusive, but because it believed the Act did not allow it to question the State's methods.

In light of the statute's directive making true market value a factual question to be determined by the district court, what Georgia is really asking for is a limitation on the types of evidence courts may consider as part of their factual inquiry. If Congress had wanted to impose such a limit by reserving to States the prerogative of selecting which valuation methods may be used, it surely could have done so. Out of deference to the States, for example, § 11501(c) provides that "[t]he burden of proof in determining ... true market value [shall be] governed by State law." Congress could easily have included similar language insulating the State's chosen methodologies from judicial scrutiny. It did not. Like Oklahoma's argument in Burlington Northern, Georgia's position in this case ultimately "depends upon the addition of words to a statutory provision which is complete as it stands." 481 U. S., at 463, 107 S. Ct. 1855. We decline to find distinctions in the statute where they do not exist, especially where, as here, those distinctions would thwart the law's operation.

III

Considering the clarity of the statute, we are tempted to leave the discussion at that. "When we find the terms of a statute unambiguous, judicial inquiry is complete...." Rubin v. United States, 449 U.S. 424, 430, 101 S. Ct. 698 (1981). Georgia, however, lodges two objections to our interpretation, each of which merits a reply. First, the State argues that any interpretation of the Act allowing courts to question state valuation methods ignores the background principles of federalism against which the statute was enacted. The majority below expressed a similar concern. "The selection of a valuation methodology," it ruled, "is part of th[e] fundamental power of a state [to tax]," 472 F.3d at 1288, and should not be limited absent a clear statement from Congress. We have long held that the means States adopt to collect their taxes "should be interfered with as little as possible." Dows v. Chicago, 78 U.S. 108, 11 Wall. 108, 110, 20 L.

Ed. 65 (1871). But we are persuaded that allowing railroads to challenge a State's valuation methodologies has been clearly authorized by the terms of the 4–R Act.

As an initial matter, we question Georgia's contention that its selection of valuation methodologies is an important state policy choice intimately connected to its tax power. Georgia does not prescribe any particular methodology as a matter of state law. Its appraisers use different methodologies in different combinations, as they see fit. See 472 F.3d at 1284–1285 (explaining that the state appraiser employed multiple methods and selected a value according to his best judgment). This suit, in fact, is the result of an individual appraiser's decision to employ a different combination of assessment techniques than that used by his immediate predecessors. The methods he selected were his choice, not the dictate of any state statute or regulation. Ibid.

But even if important questions of state policy are, as the Eleventh Circuit believed, "intertwined with the selection of a valuation methodology," id., at 1288, judicial scrutiny of those methodologies is authorized by the 4–R Act's clear command to find true market value. As we explained above, the power to calculate true market value necessarily includes the power to look behind a State's valuation methods. That the statute should vest this authority in the Nation's courts is hardly surprising, given Congress's conclusion that the States were assessing railroad property unfairly.

Our decision in Department of Revenue of Ore. v. ACF Industries, Inc., 510 U.S. 332, 114 S. Ct. 843 (1994), is not to the contrary. That case concerned a different provision of the 4–R Act—namely, the command in § 11501(b)(4) preventing a State from "[i]mpos[ing] another tax that discriminates against a rail carrier providing transportation" in the taxing jurisdiction. This bar on facially discriminatory taxes, we held, did not prevent a State from exempting certain nonrailroad property from otherwise generally applicable ad valorem taxes. ACF Industries, 510 U.S., at 343, 114 S. Ct. 843. At the time the 4–R Act was adopted, a majority of States exempted one or more classes of business property from ad valorem taxation, "including business inventories, raw materials used in textile manufacturing, . . . and mechanics tools," to name just a few. Id., at 344, 114 S. Ct. 843. The States had provided such property tax exemptions for years. In the face of this widespread and historical practice, we declined to read the 4–R Act to prohibit a type of tax exemption the text did not expressly mention. Ibid.

By contrast, we pointedly noted that the Act "prohibit[s] discriminatory tax rates and assessment ratios in no uncertain terms . . . and set[s] forth precise standards for judicial scrutiny of challenged rate and assessment practices." Id., at 343, 114 S. Ct. 843. Georgia's claim that court review of state valuation methodologies is not authorized by a clear statement in the Act ignores the statute's explicit prohibition of discriminatory assessment ratios. A district court cannot accurately calculate or compare those ratios without determining true market value. Congress clearly permitted courts to question state valuation methodologies when it banned discriminatory assessment ratios and made true market value a question to be litigated in federal court.

Georgia also protests that our interpretation will destroy the States' discretion to choose their own valuation methodologies. We disagree. A State may use whatever method or methods it likes, so long as the result is not discriminatory. The Act does not prohibit the use of any valuation methodology. It prohibits discrimination. Far from requiring States to follow a particular method, we hold only that nothing in the statute prevents a railroad from attempting to show that the methods chosen by the State result in a discriminatory determination of true market value.

The judgment of the Court of Appeals for the Eleventh Circuit is reversed.

It is so ordered.

NOTES AND QUESTIONS

A. *Utility Property and the "4R Act."* The 1976 Railroad Revitalization and Regulatory Reform Act, which has since been expanded to motor carriers and air carriers, sought to end the traditional practice of imposing heavier property taxes on railroads than on other businesses. Disproportionate assessment of large multi-state utilities has long been a means of exporting the property tax burden to nonresident shareholders, employees, suppliers, and customers, particularly if regulated utilities could include those taxes in the base for calculating their allowed rate of return. The 4R Act bars the assessment of rail property at a proportion of market value more than 5 percent above the level applied to commercial and industrial property generally. For example, if railroad property is assessed at 60 percent of full market value, relief will be granted if other commercial and industrial property can be shown to be assessed at less than 57 percent of market value. CSX Transportation, Inc. v. Board of Public Works, 312 F. Supp. 2d 839, 842 (S.D. W. Va. 2004). Providing federal court jurisdiction to enforce this mandate constitutes a significant exception to the Tax Injunction Act, 28 U.S.C. 1341 ("The district courts shall not enjoin, suspend or restrain the assessment, levy or collection of any tax under State law where a plain, speedy and efficient remedy may be had in the courts of such State."). That is why almost all state tax cases—even when they involve federal questions—are brought in state rather than federal courts. See generally Ch. 11, pp. 964–72 infra.

B. *Assessment Equity and Assessment Accuracy.* The unanimous opinion in *CSX* can leave the reader puzzled as to the logic of the lower court decisions that took an opposite interpretation of the 4R Act. If the Act was designed to prohibit discriminatory railroad taxation, it can seem immaterial whether that happened through setting railroads' taxable value at a higher percentage of full value than other commercial and industrial properties or by using a valuation method that produces higher market values at the outset. Each approach systematically discriminates against railroad property. In theory, there is a clear distinction between allowing a federal action against use of a discriminatory valuation method and allowing a federal remedy for normal assessment disputes. But this distinction becomes less clear when the dispute centers on the extremely complex calculations that estimate value for an entire railroad system (where, e.g., the purchase price would involve buying all the outstanding stock and debt of the railroad), and when consolidation has left only one corporation holding railroad property in the state. With a unique taxpayer and a unique type of property, a charge of overvaluation could be characterized either as a normal assessment dispute or as a challenge to systematic discrimination. Burlington Northern Railroad v. Department of Revenue, 23 F.3d 239, 241 (9th Cir. 1994), cited congressional reports on earlier versions of the 4R Act which stated that the legislation would not "suggest or require a State to change its assessment standards, assessment practices, or the assessments themselves. It merely provides a single standard against which all affected assessments must be measured. * * *" and that "standards and methods of valuation that any state wishes to use would be totally unaffected by this legislation."

C. *Arbitrary Discrimination and "Mere Errors in Judgment."* This distinction between intentional systematic discrimination and erroneous overvaluation plays an important role in many property tax disputes. In Ram's Head Partners LLC v. Town of Cape Elizabeth, 834 A.2d 916 (Me. 2003) the Maine Supreme Judicial Court held that a property owner who did not claim overassessment but did claim that similar neighboring property was underassessed could have grounds for an abatement. "The undervaluation of one set of similarly situated properties can support a finding of unjust discrimination, even where there is no undervaluation of the general mass of property. * * * On the other hand, 'some specific instances here and there' of undervaluation, '[s]poradic differences in valuations,' or 'mere errors of judgment on the part of the assessors' do not necessarily establish unjust discrimination." Id. at 919. *CSX* suggests that this distinction cannot always be drawn with clarity.

D. *Railroad and Utility Valuation.* The challenge of valuing that portion of the property of a large integrated enterprise that lies within a small taxing jurisdiction has produced a long history of railroad assessment disputes. As in *CSX*, many states today undertake "unit valuations" of the entire enterprise and allocate (e.g., by miles of track) that total among localities containing railroad property, but early railroad assessments were often a local responsibility. An attempt by a New York municipality to value seven miles of track by reference to the earnings of the entire railroad led the Court of Appeals to set replacement cost as a general limit on taxable value: "The cost of reproducing these seven miles of railroad seems to us to be the just and reasonable rule of valuation. There is no reason we can perceive for assessing this property at a greater sum than the cost of replacement." People ex rel. Delaware, Lackawanna & Western R. R. Co. v. Clapp, 152 N.Y. 490, 46 N.E. 842 (1897). Nevertheless, many other state and local jurisdictions embraced the "unit rule" for valuing the property of railroads, telegraph, and express companies, and the U.S. Supreme Court's approval of this basic approach to property valuation led to the "unitary business" principle that now underlies not only ad valorem property taxation of such companies but also the apportionment of state corporate income of unitary multistate businesses. See generally Chapter 7 supra.

C. APPROACHES TO THE VALUATION OF PROPERTY

Assigning an accurate fair market value to all taxable property in a jurisdiction annually is a formidable task. Moreover, the very meaning of fair market value can be ambiguous when property is of a type not frequently bought and sold. Major industrial plants, utility property, and buildings designed for the needs of specific owners often fall into this category. Disputes as to the proper method of measuring their market value may affect hundreds of millions of dollars of a jurisdiction's tax base. Even property without unusual physical features may raise questions as to how legal restrictions, such as zoning, rent control, or lease agreements, should affect the calculation of market value. In such cases a seemingly technical choice among valuation methods in effect determines the base of the property tax.

1. METHODS OF VALUING PROPERTY

There are three basic methods for valuing property: the comparable sales approach, which examines prices for recent sales of similar parcels; the cost approach, which calculates the construction cost new less depreciation; and the income approach, which analyzes the market value of the net income stream produced by the property.

> It is said, for example, that ordinarily the market data approach, guided as it is by actual buyers and sellers of comparable property in the market, is the best guide to market value. Some would say it is the only valid approach. It is also said that the income approach is the most effective approach in determining the value of investment properties and is the "chief approach" to value for large office buildings. Finally, it is generally agreed that the cost approach is the least reflective of market value and is used only as a check of the estimates obtained from the other approaches and usually as an upper limit of market value.

Medical Building Land Co. v. Department of Revenue, 283 Or. 69, 582 P.2d 416, 421 n.10 (1978). In many cases all of these methods are employed and their results adjusted in a process of "correlation" to produce a single value. In *Medical Building Land*, the court referred to this as "the somewhat mystical process appraisers refer to as 'correlation.'" Id., 582 P.2d at 420. The court quoted the following excerpt from the *Encyclopedia of Real Estate Appraising*:

> The term "correlation" implies a reciprocal relation and interdependence of functions—that is, an orderly connection of related elements. In the appraisal process, under the three-approach concept of value, correlation refers to the problem of bringing into focus the varying estimates of value arrived at by two or all of the three approaches—

the Market Approach, the Income Approach, and the Cost Approach. The appraiser makes a thorough study of all pertinent information gathered by him, and analyzes and weighs the strongest and most applicable data under each approach. The final conclusion as to value is based on the approach which is supported by the most convincing data, that is, the primary approach. The accuracy of this estimate is checked by the results reached under the other approaches used, the secondary approaches.* * * Value can never be calculated by adding up the several estimates arrived at in processing various approaches and taking an average of these estimates. Averages do not lead to a sound conclusion as to value; if an error was committed in estimating under any one of the approaches, it would merely be carried forward in a final estimate by average.

Id. at 419 n.2 (quoting Sarles, "Correlation, Analysis, and Conclusion as to Value," in Encyclopedia of Real Estate Appraising 120–121 (E. Friedman, ed., 1968)).

In a perfectly functioning competitive market, with no single buyer or seller able to influence sale price, market value would reflect the factors measured by each of these three methods. The cost of building a replacement structure would act as a ceiling to the price, and buyers would bid an amount reflecting property income and prevailing rates of return, and comparable properties would sell for comparable prices.

The reality of property valuation is often far more complex. The unique location of any parcel of land and inevitable variations among any set of buildings prevent even very similar structures from serving as perfect substitutes for one another. Moreover, buildings that are truly unusual, such as industrial assembly plants or manufacturing structures designed for a specific purpose, may lack comparable sales altogether. Income data for a commercial structure will often combine a return on business carried on there and the rental value of the property itself. Complex lease provisions may leave nominal rent as only a starting point for calculating the return to real property. Many details of business income are proprietary information that the owner will not divulge under ordinary circumstances. Use of the cost approach for older structures presents special difficulties, requiring an estimate of depreciation due to outmoded design, neighborhood deterioration, and physical decay. These factors may be impossible to estimate in the absence of income data.

ROSBROC ASSOCIATES v. ASSESSOR AND BOARD OF REVIEW OF THE CITY OF NEW ROCHELLE

New York Supreme Court, Westchester County.
New York Law Journal, November 3, 1976, pp. 16–17.

SLIFKIN, JUSTICE.

These are proceedings to review real property assessments to the City of New Rochelle pursuant to article 7 of the Real Property Tax Law. The property known as the Sheraton Motor Inn and Office Building is located at 1 Sheraton Plaza and is designated on the Tax and Assessment Map as section 1, Block 247, Lot 1. The assessments under review are those for 1975 and 1976. By virtue of a motion by petitioner at trial, the proceedings were consolidated.

The subject property is improved with a 10 story building which consists of a hotel and related facilities on the first 6 floors and offices on the top four floors. It is located in the major central business district of the City. Further, it is located in the heart of the urban renewal area of the City near the newly constructed "Mall" and near the recently completed Longines Wittnauer building.

During the years under review, the property was assessed as follows:

1975—Land $297,350; Improvement $1,630,000; Total $1,927,350.

1976—Land $300,000; Improvement $1,720,000; Total $2,020,000.

The petitioner's protests and petitions with respect to each year are based on claimed over-valuation and inequality.

With respect to the issue of inequality, a Notice to Admit pursuant to Real Property Tax Law section 716 served on respondents and not denied, established an admission from respondents that for purposes of these proceedings, the following percentages represent the percentages at which other real property in the assessing district were assessed: 1975—45%; 1976—45%.

By reason of the applicable percentages thus established for each of the assessment years under review and the stipulation by the parties as to their use by the court, the issue of inequality will be decided merely by a mathematical computation involved in applying the appropriate percentage to the full market value of the subject property to be found by the court upon the evidence introduced with respect to the issue of valuation.

Petitioner's expert appraiser appraised the fair market value of the property as follows:

1975—Land $523,400; Improvement $1,940,110; Total $2,463,510.

1976—Land $523,400; Improvement $1,976,093; Total $2,499,493.

Respondent's expert appraiser appraised the fair market value of the property as follows:

1975—Land $714,000; Improvement $4,586,000; Total $5,300,000.

[Figures for 1976 are not given. Eds.]

The market value of a piece of real estate is not ordinarily the subject of ready computation. Market value is largely a theoretical construct. Among the factors to be considered are:

1. Physical conditions of premises;

2. Description of the physical characteristics of the property and its situation in relation to points of importance in the area;

3. A consideration of the uses for which the land is adopted and which it is available;

4. The value of the improvements if they are such as to increase the value of the land.

As the court has indicated, the valuation of property is not an exact science. The experts for the respective parties, both of whom are well qualified, considered all the factors enumerated but utilized different approaches in reaching the value attributed to the property.

Land

The court first turns to a discussion of the value to be attributed to the land. The land consists of 118,956 square feet and covers one square city block.

In appraising the land, petitioner's appraiser considered a number of land sales, some of which grew out of the Urban Renewal project in the City. He noted that two large parcels of this project remain unsold. One of these consists of 51,000 square feet and is directly opposite the subject. The other is nearby and contains 108,000 square feet. Petitioner's expert, Mr. William G. Scott, notes that both of these parcels are being offered at less than his conclusion that the subject be valued at $4 a square foot. To this $4 a square foot, he adds a 10 percent factor by reason of frontage on four streets to reach a total value of $523,400.

Petitioner's expert relies on 6 sales. They date from 1967 to 1973 and represent sales prices of $3 to $6 per square foot. Five of the six parcels represent sales by the City and are part of the Urban Renewal project. The parcels range in size from 10,900 square feet to 139,880 square feet. The court notes that no grid or adjustment sheet has been furnished by petitioner's appraiser adjusting the sales to the subject parcel.

Respondent's expert, Mr. Robert W. Jones, relied on 4 sales, including the land sale of the subject in 1972. He notes that urban renewal sales are generally below market value to attract buyers and he adjusts these sales upward. The first sale relied on by respondent was the 1972 sale of the subject parcel and indicated a purchase price of $3 a square foot. The other three sales occurred between 1972 and 1974 and represent unadjusted sales prices of $3.90 to $7 a square foot.

Respondent's expert also fails to include a grid, but indicates adjustments upward of 3 of the sales by reason of their urban renewal character, time of sale, type of property, and plot size. He concludes that the land be valued at $6 per square foot for a total of $714,000. Thus, he finds a 100 percent increase in value of the subject between October, 1972, and the 1975 valuation date.

Based on the foregoing, the court finds that a value of $4.75 per square foot represents the fair market value on the valuation dates in question. Thus, the court concludes that the total fair market value of the land was $565,000.

The court approves of the use of urban renewal sales as comparables (In re Presidential Plaza v. Srogi, 50 A.D.2d 717). Yet, the court agrees that the presence of substantial tracts of unsold urban renewal land tends to depress the land value of the parcels in the area including the subject. In reviewing the testimony, the court notes that there is a ground lease of the premises at $80,000 per year. There was limited testimony with respect thereto as an "in-house" transaction, but were the court to capitalize this lease at 14 percent representing the equalized tax rate and a return of approximately 9 percent, the value obtained would be $571,000, a figure which is extremely close to the value found on a per square foot basis and supports the findings of this court.

Improvement

The court now turns to a discussion of the improvement and its value.

Construction of the subject took place in 1974. As represented by both the description furnished by the appraisers, as well as by the pictures supplied to this court, it is an impressive structure on one square block of land in the heart of the business district of New Rochelle.

In reaching his conclusion as to value, petitioner's expert, Mr. Scott, relied upon an income approach known as the building residual method. His appraisal includes statements of income and expenses for the years in question. Mr. Scott concedes that since the hotel opened in March, 1975, the 1975 year was an incomplete experience. Accordingly, he concludes that the statements of income and expense for the first 6 months of 1976 represent a more realistic financial picture. He has therefore doubled most of these figures to project a full year's operation. It is the income produced by these figures that he utilized in the building residual method for the two years under review.

Petitioner's expert recognizes that hotel income is produced by the combination of real estate together with furnishings, working capital and good will and business ability of the operator. His consideration of the hotel income included a deduction from income of sufficient moneys for a return to and a depreciation of the actual investment in the furnishings. All remaining income was then treated as though developed by the land improvement. This approach would then negate any claim that an income method may not be used to value a hotel property. By making no deduction for the business ability or entrepreneurial skills of the operator, petitioner's expert is able to utilize the income method and further to attempt to establish that the structural improvements are not suitable to the site and constitute, in effect, an overimprovement.

Mr. Scott notes that the office space on the top 4 floors is 75 percent rented, far above the rate of occupancy for the surrounding area, and the hotel rooms are 62.5 percent rented. He points out that the surrounding areas contain a great deal of unrented office space, vacant commercial and retail space, as well as unused vacant land. This leads him to conclude that the Urban Renewal project in New Rochelle has not been a total success and that the subject is an overimprovement albeit the highest and best use.

In view of the above, petitioner's expert concludes that the net annual income before taxes to be capitalized under the building residual method is $462,671. Against this, he applies a capitalization rate of 10 percent on the land, 12 percent on the improvement, together with the equalized tax rate and a recapture rate of 2.5 percent.

Petitioner's expert also deals with the reproduction cost of the building, less economic depreciation and functional obsolescence. Through references to the Dodge Building Cost Calculator, he concludes that the reproduction cost would be $6,351,458. However, he finds a very high degree of functional obsolescence because of his conclusion that the structure is an overimprovement.

Petitioner's expert concludes that because of the high degree of functional obsolescence and the general pattern of prevailing economic conditions in the urban renewal area, the proper means of valuing this improvement is the income method and not the reconstruction cost less the depreciation or summation method.

Respondent's expert notes that for a new building such as the subject, the cost approach is used to assist the appraiser in arriving at a reliable indication of value. He utilizes the Marshall Valuation Service to arrive at a total replacement cost of $6,481,600. He finds a physical and functional depreciation of 5 percent for nominal obsolescence of fixtures and minor design deficiencies. He also points out that the recent economic downturn which he labels "recession/depression" substantially reduced the anticipated return expected from the improvement although properties such as the subject equally suffer a loss of economic rentability for the first several years of operation. The respondent's expert concludes that the normal loss in income due to the nature of this property and the general economic condition was a significant factor in the decline in value of the subject and that the property has not yet reached its economic potential. Therefore, he estimates an economic depreciation of 25 percent.

The total 30 percent depreciation is then applied to obtain a depreciated improvement value by the cost approach of $4,536,800, to which the land value is added and a total value of $5,250,800 is reached by respondent's expert.

As will be discussed at a later point, the key factor in the cost approach is the respondent's recognition of a substantial economic depreciation of the subject.

Respondent's expert also uses an income approach through the imputation of a market rental value for the office space and by estimating the annual hotel revenue. For his purposes, this expert has created and used an economic rent or income rather than the actual income and has applied economic rather than actual costs and expenses. The result reached by respondent's appraiser is a net income before taxes of $764,387. In so doing, he applied estimated expense figures far below the actual experience of the subject. Further, in estimating income, he assumed a 95 percent occupancy rate of the office portion of the building.

Against the net income before taxes, respondent's expert applies a 7.5 percent return to land and improvements, a 1.66 percent recapture rate and the two year equalized tax rate. He then arrives at an improvement value of $4,653,000, which is coincidentally within $100,000 of his depreciated improvements value. Upon the addition of the land value, he found a total value of $5,367,000 through the income method utilizing the building residual method.

Respondent's ultimate conclusion as to value is the sum of $5,300,000 which is a figure lower than that figure which he obtains through the income method and higher than the figure reached through the cost method. Although the mathematical difference is not significant, the ultimate conclusion of a value greater than that obtained under the cost method violates one of the prime rules of valuation for certiorari purposes, to wit, that structural value based on reproduction cost less depreciation fixes the maximum value, even if the capitalized income would indicate a higher valuation. However, since it is clear that respondent relies chiefly on the cost approach, the court will treat his finding of a value of $5,251,000 under the cost method as his ultimate conclusion as to the value of the subject.

Having discussed in detail the approaches set forth in the respective appraisals, the court will now turn to certain legal principles and their application to the case at bar.

While petitioner relies upon an income approach herein, the case law generally indicates that during the early years of income producing property, such a method is not reliable because of the start up time needed to establish the property as a viable income producer. Thus, the cost method should be utilized. On the other hand, unless a building is a specialty or a prestige structure, the income method usually provides the surest guide to value.

While construction and reproduction costs set the maximum value for which property may lawfully be assessed, the theory on which the cost less depreciation method rests is that no investor will pay more for a building than the cost of reproducing it. Moreover, and most significant herein, reproduction cost less depreciation is not relevant to a particular case where the building would normally not be reproduced at the time in question and is not well suited to the site. Where the property is shown to be unable to achieve a stabilized income commensurate with its cost due to overbuilding, the reproduction cost less depreciation must be offset by this factor and reliance placed on use of the income method.

Finally, in the absence of proof that the building is a specialty reliance solely on cost less depreciation is erroneous absent unusual circumstances.

In the case at bar, petitioner's expert's reliance upon the income method is based on his view that the income level utilized represents a realistic one and therefore, in his opinion, is not subject to a successful claim that the subject has not been operated long enough to give a true picture of income. This claim is based on and supported by the rather poor economic picture existing in the urban renewal area of New Rochelle. Thus, while the percentage of room occupancy of the hotel space is lower than that of similar facilities in other areas in the county, it must be considered as having stabilized sufficiently to be relied upon. Further, since the percentage of rental of office space is higher than some of the surrounding properties and since there is a great deal of available office space in the area, it too must be considered to have reached a sufficiently stable use.

In addition, there is no claim that the * * * specialty * * * would have to be reproduced elsewhere if destroyed requiring reproduction cost less depreciation as the test.

While respondent relies on the reproduction cost less depreciation, the fact that their expert finds a 30 percent economic obsolescence is indicative that as claimed by petitioner, the subject is an overimprovement, not well suited to the site and thus, would not be reproduced and therefore, the cost approach may not be used.

Economic or functional obsolescence has been defined as that reduction in the value of an improvement which results from the inability to fully utilize the improvement, not because of the improvement itself, but because of outside factors. Here, because of the downturn in business in general and the lack of success of the New Rochelle Urban Renewal project, the appraisers have agreed that substantial economic or functional obsolescence exists. From this it follows that the building is an overimprovement and would not be reproduced. This requires a conclusion that * * * the cost test may not be relied upon and is not relevant in this case.

The court also notes that the sole proof as to reproduction and replacement cost less depreciation was adduced by reference to certain manuals and not through the testimony of a builder or professional engineer. Such an approach has often been criticized.

Based on the foregoing, the court concludes that the responsible reliance on reproduction cost less depreciation is unwarranted in this case and it finds that the improvement herein is an overimprovement not suited to the site and that it would not be reproduced. Accordingly, the court will deal with the income method and value the property pursuant thereto.

As previously noted, the petitioner's expert relies on actual income and expenses for the first six months of 1976 and doubles these figures to achieve his income and expense figure. Respondent, on the other hand, utilizes economic or projected income and expenses. Where the property is producing its maximum income, the actual income and expenses are extremely relevant. If it is less than the fair rental income, then fair rental income should be considered on the gross rent. However, the alleged fair rental income must be firmly and unequivocally established by comparable market data. If not, it becomes pure speculation.

Further the actual rent received is in ordinary cases an important factor in determining what the fair market rental value is.

In the case at bar, the court finds the use of the actual experience of this property to be a surer guide to the fair market income and expenses than the speculative approach of respondent.

In concluding that the actual experience of the property is a surer guide to fair market income and expenses, the court does not adopt in toto the figures used by petitioner, but finds that the net income before taxes to be capitalized is $500,000. To this the court has applied a basic capitalization rate and an equalized tax rate of 14.3 percent and a recapture rate of 2 percent to obtain an improvement value of $2,571,000 for each of the two years in question. To this is added the land value of $565,000 to obtain a total fair market value of $3,136,000. Thus, the court finds the fair market value of the parcel as follows:

Year	Land	Improvement	Total
1975	$565,000	$2,571,000	$3,136,000
1976	$565,000	$2,571,000	$3,136,000

Accordingly, the court upon the application of the equalization rate of the remaining years, finds the assessed valuation of the subject property to be as follows:

Year	Land	Improvement	Total
1975	$254,250	$1,156,950	$1,411,200
1976	$254,250	$1,156,950	$1,411,200

NOTES AND QUESTIONS

A. *The Land Valuation.* The petitioner's expert relied on offering prices for other parcels at less than $4 per square foot to support his conclusion that the subject parcel should be valued at $4 per square foot. Should the offering price of property be accepted as good evidence of its market value? If not, what does the offering price tend to prove? The respondent's expert opined that "urban renewal sales are generally below market value." Is this statement an oxymoron? How can there be any better evidence of market value (assuming a willing seller and a willing buyer) than the price at which a property changes hands at a recent sale? In Kem v. Department of Revenue, 267 Or. 111, 114, 514 P.2d 1335, 1336 (1973), the court stated, "[a] recent sale of the property in question is important in determining its market value. If the sale is a recent, voluntary, arm's length transaction between a buyer and seller, both of whom are knowledgeable and willing, then the sales price, while certainly not conclusive, is very persuasive of the market value." Why might this price not be conclusive of market value?

By what analytical process does the court arrive at its judgment of the value of the land? What is the significance of the court's statement that if it were to capitalize the ground lease of $80,000 per year at 14 percent, it would obtain a value close to the value it obtained by concluding that the property was worth $4.75 per square foot? For any given income stream, will not the choice of a capitalization rate determine its value? And if one knows the value one is looking for, is it difficult to determine the capitalization rate that will produce that value? In other words, if $I/r = V$, where I is income, r is the capitalization rate, and v is the property's value, and one knows the value of I and V, is there any difficulty in determining r? Do these considerations shed any light on the answer to the second question raised in this paragraph?

B. *Value of the Improvement.* How did the petitioner's expert separate the income produced by the hotel operation from the income produced by the real estate? The petitioner's expert made no deduction for the business ability or entrepreneurial skills of the hotel operator. How did this support his determination of the income stream to be capitalized? Suppose the hotel operator was completely incompetent and grossly mismanaged the hotel. Would this justify an upward adjustment in the income stream used to value the real estate? Why did the petitioner apply a different capitalization rate to the land and to the building? Why did the respondent's expert rely principally on the cost method rather than the income method?

BOARD OF ASSESSMENT APPEALS v. COLORADO ARLBERG CLUB

Supreme Court of Colorado, 1988.
762 P.2d 146.

MULLARKEY, JUSTICE.

* * *

IV

The next question before this court is whether the court of appeals was correct to conclude that the Board could not consider reasonable future use of the Club's property to determine its present fair market value. We have explained that market value is "what a willing buyer would pay a willing seller under normal economic conditions." Our definition is consistent with the basic definition of market value used by appraisers:

> The most probable price in cash, terms equivalent to cash, or in other precisely revealed terms, for which the appraised property will sell in a competitive market under all conditions requisite to fair sale, with the buyer and seller each acting prudently, knowledgeably, and for self-interest, and assuming that neither is under undue duress.

American Institute of Real Estate Appraisers, The Appraisal of Real Estate 33 (8th ed. 1983); see also Comment, "The Road to Uniformity in Real Estate Taxation: Valuation and Appeal," 124 U. Pa. L. Rev. 1418, 1430 (1976) (market value is defined as the price reached "in a fair, arm's length transaction between willing parties") (footnote omitted).

As the court of appeals acknowledged, we have ruled that reasonable future use is relevant to market value in several eminent domain cases. However, the court of appeals reasoned that because the "assessor can periodically reassess the tax on a property, based on changes in the property's use, on new improvements, or on changes in present market value... equity dictates that the principles of the law of eminent domain not be transferred to tax assessment situations." Colorado Arlberg Club, 719 P.2d at 373. For several reasons, we disagree.

First, the one-time nature of an eminent domain payment has nothing to do with our rule that reasonable future use must be considered in calculating just compensation for a government taking. Instead, reasonable future use is considered because it is relevant to the property's present market value. See Board of County Comm'rs v. Vail Assocs., 171 Colo. 381, 388, 468 P.2d 842, 845 (1970) ("It is fundamental that evidence of the highest and best use to which the property may reasonably be applied in the future by [people] of ordinary prudence and judgment is admissible to assist the commission or jury in arriving at the present cash market value of the property being taken."). For example, a tract of undeveloped land with potential for development has a higher present fair market value than the same size tract of undeveloped land with no such potential, i.e., even in its undeveloped state, a willing buyer and a willing seller would agree on a higher price for it.

* * *

A second reason for considering reasonable future use is that it is one element of the technical meaning of market value. It is a well-established rule of statutory construction that "[w]ords and phrases that have acquired a technical or particular meaning, whether by legislative definition or otherwise, shall be construed accordingly." § 2–4–101, 1B C.R.S. (1980). See generally 2A N. Singer, supra, § 47.29 (in absence of contrary evidence, "technical terms or terms of art used in a statute are presumed to have their technical meaning").

"In the market, the current value of a property is not based on historical prices or cost of creation; it is based on what market participants perceive to be the future benefits of acquisition." American Institute of Real Estate Appraisers, supra, at 21; see also Comment, supra, 124 Univ. Pa. Law Rev. at 1431–32 (comparable sales method to determining market value involves "taking into consideration all uses to which the property is adapted and *might be applied*") (footnote omitted and emphasis added). Accordingly, a property's "highest and best use," which is "[t]he use, from among reasonably probable and legal alternative uses, found to be physically possible, appropriately supported, financially feasible, that results in highest land value," is a "crucial determinant of value in the market." American Institute of Real Estate Appraisers, supra, at 28, 243. Further, the Board clearly considered the property's future use to be relevant to its present market value and "[t]he construction of statutes by administrative officials charged with their enforcement should be given deference by a reviewing court." Hewlett–Packard Co. v. State, Dep't of Revenue, 749 P.2d 400, 406 (Colo.1988).

Finally, while we recognize that some courts have been reluctant to allow consideration of future uses in tax assessments, many of the cases on which the Club relies involved assessments based on future uses that were speculative or impossible. See, e.g. People ex rel. Empire Mortgage Co. v. Cantor, 197 A.D. 437, 189 N.Y.S. 646 (1921) (reliance on fanciful "prophetic vision" of development was "even more absurd" in tax case than in eminent domain case); Finch v. Grays Harbor County, 121 Wash. 486, 209 P. 833 (1922) (when cost of clearing land would exceed its value, much of the land could never be drained, and there was no demand for use on which assessor relied, "valuation was grossly excessive").

Other cases cited by the parties prohibit valuing undeveloped property as if it had been improved. See, e.g., City of Newark v. West Milford Township, Passaic County, 9 N.J. 295, 88 A.2d 211, 215 (1952) (value must be based on "actual condition in which the owner holds it" and assessor cannot ignore lack of public utility service or value land as though it already were subdivided); Allied Stores, Inc. v. Finance Adm'r, 76 A.D.2d 835, 428 N.Y.S.2d 316 (1980) (not permissible to determine that property's actual use was no longer viable and to value it as though it had been used more profitably). * * * [T]hese limitations apply to both eminent domain and tax cases in Colorado, and do not preclude consideration of reasonable future uses.

* * *

Other states with statutes more similar to ours, requiring only that the assessment be based on the property's full and fair value, have recognized that "the normal uses to which potential purchasers could put [the property] must be considered" because that is part of the property's market value. Pacific Mut. Life Ins. Co. v. County of Orange, 187 Cal. App. 3d 1141, 1148, 232 Cal. Rptr. 233, 236 (1985); see also Wild Goose Country Club v. Butte County, 60 Cal. App. 339, 212 P. 711, 712 (1922) (in valuing property for tax purposes, "[t]he question is, not what its value is for a particular purpose, but its value in view of all the purposes to which it is naturally adapted."); Division of Tax Appeals v. Township of Ewing, 72 N.J. Super. 238, 178 A.2d 229, 231 (1962) ("assessor must consider the possibility of sale to a buyer who intends a different use, unless such possibility is so remote as to have no real bearing upon current value"). N.J. Stat. Ann. section 54:4–23 (West 1986) provides that the assessor shall "determine the full and fair value" based on the price which the property "would sell for at a fair and bona fide sale." That definition is similar to our definition of market value, and we agree with the distinction stated by the New Jersey Superior Court: "An assessor who values a farm as though actually subdivided into the building lots of a residential development, when in fact that has not yet occurred, would be in error; but he would also err if he refuses to consider that a developer would pay a higher price for the farm than another farmer." Division of Tax Appeals v. Township of Ewing, 178 A.2d at 232.

To summarize, the reasonable future use of real property is an element of its fair market value under its technical definition as well as its common law interpretation in Colorado and elsewhere. Because there is no indication that the legislature intended to reject or distinguish those definitions here, we conclude that reasonable future use is relevant to a property's current market value for tax assessment purposes. The court of appeals' contrary holding was erroneous.

* * *

ERICKSON, J., specifically concurs. ROVIRA and VOLLACK, JJ., did not participate.

NOTES AND QUESTIONS

A. *Choice of Valuation Method as Influenced by the Purpose of Valuation.* What is the proper role of "highest and best use" in determining value for non-tax purposes, such as (1) income taxation; (2) eminent-domain awards; (3) insurance settlements; (4) evaluation of security for bank loans? Should "fair market value" have a different meaning in these contexts than it does for tax purposes?

B. *Current Market Value and Future Value Increments.* Arizona law, Ariz. Rev. Stat. Ann. §§ 42–11054(C), 42–11054(D) (Westlaw 2009), provides: "In applying prescribed standard appraisal methods and techniques: (1) Current usage shall be included in the formula for reaching a determination of full cash value. * * * If the methods and techniques prescribe using market data as an indication of market value, the price paid for future anticipated property value increments shall be excluded." How would you evaluate this provision in light of the analysis of highest and best use in the *Arlberg* case?

2. SPECIAL ISSUES IN LAND VALUATION

a. *Valuation of Contaminated Property*

WESTLING v. COUNTY OF MILLE LACS

Supreme Court of Minnesota, 1996.
543 N.W.2d 91.

COYNE, JUSTICE.

Certiorari on the relation of the County of Mille Lacs to review a decision of the tax court directing reduction of the assessor's estimated market value as at January 2, 1992 of a tract consisting of two contiguous parcels of real estate from $470,100 to $0, and further directing reduction of the assessor's estimated market value as at January 2, 1993 of the same tract of land from $876,800 to $0. We affirm.

This is the third time the estimated market value of this 13.06–acre tract of real estate has come before us. The factual background of this ongoing dispute is set out in detail in our original decision, Westling v. County of Mille Lacs, 512 N.W.2d 863 (Minn. 1994), but for convenience those facts relevant to the present proceeding will be included here.

In 1987 John and Sharolyn Westling purchased from Donald W. Westling, John's father, a 5–acre parcel of land situated in Princeton, Minnesota. In 1988 John and Sharolyn Westling built a 28,000–square–foot office and warehouse which was connected to the manufacturing and warehouse buildings situated on the adjacent land owned by Donald and leased to Westling Manufacturing Company, a remanufacturer of automotive parts.

In 1989 the Westlings purchased Donald's contiguous 8.06–acre parcel on which the 48,500–square–foot manufacturing building and the 15,000–square–foot warehouse building are located. Before the 1989 purchase was completed, an environmental survey disclosed the presence throughout the entire 13.06–acre tract of environmental contamination by tetrachloroethylene, a volatile organic compound used by Westling Manufacturing Company as a degreaser. John Westling concedes that he completed the purchase of the 8.06–acre parcel knowing that it was listed on the Comprehensive Environmental Response Compensation and Liability Information System (CERCLIS). The acquisition of the tract with its improvements was financed by a $1,000,000 mortgage secured by the real estate, the Westling Manufacturing Company lease, and personal and corporate guarantees.

Subsequent to the purchase of the 8.06–acre parcel, the Minnesota Pollution Control Agency listed the 13.06–acre tract on the State Superfund Permanent List of Priorities. The property has since remained on both the CERCLIS and MPCA Superfund lists. The MPCA has also named John Westling as a responsible party because he and his wife owned the property and because he knowingly permitted the Company to use a hazardous substance.

The earlier proceedings concluded with affirmance of the tax court's determination that the assessor's estimated market value of the tract at January 2, 1991 should be reduced from $974,200 to $880,000. When the assessor set the estimated market value of the tract as at January 2, 1992 at $470,100 and at $876,800 as at January 2, 1993, the Westlings objected, contending that the property had no market value on either January 2, 1992 or January 2, 1993.

Shortly after purchasing the 8.06–acre parcel, the Westlings contracted with Wenck Associates for testing to determine the nature and extent of contamination and engineering advice concerning treatment. Although about $560,000 had been expended from January 2, 1992 to November 30, 1994, to investigate, test, monitor, and cure the contamination, an environmental engineer employed by Wenck estimated the present value of the future cost of clean-up at $2,800,000 to $2,900,000: (A) The present value of the cost of a single far-field system of treatment, projected to be performed over a 24–year period, is $2,800,000; or (B) the present value of the cost of a double far-field system, which could be expected to be completed in 12 years, is $2,900,000.

Peter J. Patchin, an appraiser called by the Westlings, testified that if "unimpaired" the tract would have had a market value of $1,350,000 on January 2, 1992 and January 2, 1993. After deducting the loss of value resulting from the stigma attached to polluted properties and the present value of the anticipated costs of clean-up, Mr. Patchin was of the opinion that the market value of the tract was minus $2,835,000 on January 2, 1992 and minus $2,760,000 on January 2, 1993.

Charles R. Glassing, an appraiser called by the County, deducted a stigma discount and an estimated clean-up cost from the value indicated pursuant to the replacement cost, market or sale comparison, and income capitalization methods of evaluation and gave as his final opinions of value: $930,000 at January 2, 1992 and $900,000 on January 2, 1993.

The tax court regarded the modified traditional appraisal methodology adopted by each appraiser acceptable. Remarking that the significant differences in the two opinions with respect to value lay in the facts supporting the stigma discount and cost to cure, not in the methods employed, the tax court concluded that Mr. Patchin's evaluation was the more accurate and reliable.

The Patchin stigma discount was based on a market case study of 14 improved industrial properties sold after clean-up of contamination, while the Glassing stigma discount was based on published studies, including an article written by Mr. Patchin.

Mr. Glassing's cost-to-cure figures were based on an August 1992 letter from the Wenck environmental engineer to John Westling and the engineer's testimony in the proceedings with respect to the market value of the tract on January 2, 1991, when the engineer estimated the cost of clean-up at $910,000 over a 10–year period—an expenditure which then had a present value of $400,000.

The tax court accepted Mr. Patchin's cost-to-cure figures because they were based on the environmental engineer's current cost estimates, and because neither appraiser suggested that the market value of the property, unimpaired by contamination, was greater than the $2,800,000 cost to cure, the tax court directed the reduction of the assessor's estimated market value to $0 as at January 2, 1992 and January 2, 1993.

Although we can understand the frustration of the County over the paradox posed by attaching a zero market value to 13.06 acres of improved real estate which generates $114,000 in annual rent, the evidence before the tax court concerning stigma discount and the cost of cleaning up the contamination amply support its order directing reduction of the assessor's estimated market value to $0 as at January 2, 1992 and January 2, 1993.

Affirmed.

NOTES AND QUESTIONS

A. *Reduction in Value through Neglect or Contamination.* If the market value of property has been diminished through the owner's neglect, should that action be "rewarded" with a lower assessment? Inmar Associates, Inc. v. Borough of Carlstadt, 7 N.J.Tax 482 (1985), aff'd, 214 N.J.Super. 256, 518 A.2d 1110 (App. Div. 1986), aff'd in part and rev'd in part, 112 N.J. 593, 549 A.2d 38 (1988), considered the site of a former industrial solvent recovery plant that had been operated by a tenant of Inmar Associates. The plant had been shut down by the New Jersey Department of Environmental Protection, which took custody of the property and imposed a lien on Inmar's assets to pay for the cost of removing toxic wastes from the site. On the assessment date the land contained approximately 60 storage tanks of oils, methanol, solvents, and paint residues. These cases considered what effect, if any, the presence of toxic waste required by law to be removed before sale should have on a calculation of the property's market value. The Appellate Division found a reduction for this factor contrary to the legislative intent to discourage pollution:

> Basically, where police power is involved, government action is undertaken for the public good. Where the situation involves privately created contamination, remedial action is required because the private party intentionally or unintentionally disregarded the public good. It would indeed be incongruous for the Legislature to enact strict liability provisions for cleanup of hazardous wastes as it has done and at the same time intend that a polluter's tax assessment may be reduced because of the contamination. That would tend to encourage rather than discourage polluting which would be contrary to the legislatively formulated public policy of protecting the environment against toxic pollution. We do not perceive any legislative intent to permit an owner-created exemption to taxation based upon contamination by an owner or its tenant. Polluters can hardly complain of lowered fair market values to a hypothetical buyer because of contamination, which is caused by the business activities of the landowner or its commercial tenant. In the present cases it was the contamination and not the cleanup legislation which lowered the land values in the eyes of hypothetical buyers.

Id., 518 A.2d at 1115. The New Jersey Supreme Court disagreed, finding the constitutional mandate for uniformity in valuation and the legislative provision for assessment at "true value" to require consideration of these effects on market value. "We would be no more able to alter that standard to effectuate environmental policy than is the Legislature able to alter that standard to effectuate economic policy." Id., 549 A.2d at 41.

The *Inmar* case raises many questions that illustrate the conceptual as well as computational problems encountered in the valuation process:

(1) The New Jersey Supreme Court stated that the contaminated property had a "distinct 'value in use' to the owner so long as the owner continued to operate the facility," id., 549 A.2d at 41, even if state law

would not permit a sale in this contaminated condition. If this is so, should the value in use be considered a market value for tax purposes?

(2) If the law requires removal of contamination before any sale, should the market value for tax purposes be based on a hypothetical sale price increased by the cost of this expensive procedure, as a capital improvement?

(3) Does a tax reflecting a lower market value for contaminated property "reward" the taxpayer? Does a tax reflecting a higher market value for a well designed and maintained structure "penalize" its owner?

B. *The Minnesota "Contamination Tax."* After the *Westling* decision, the Minnesota legislature enacted a unique tax on contaminated property, Minn. Stat. §§ 270.91–.98 (Westlaw 2009). The Westlings challenged the tax as an unconstitutional taking under the Minnesota and federal constitutions, a violation of the Minnesota constitutional uniformity clause, and a violation of the federal constitutional guarantee of equal protection. In Westling v. County of Mille Lacs, 581 N.W.2d 815 (Minn. 1998), the Minnesota Supreme Court described the tax in this way:

> In 1993, the Minnesota legislature enacted a new "contamination tax" * * * an annual tax on the "contamination value" of taxable real property in Minnesota. Minn. Stat. sec. 270.91, subd. 1. "Contamination value" is "the amount of the market value reduction, if any, that is granted for general ad valorem property tax purposes for the assessment year because of the presence of contaminants." Minn. Stat. sec. 270.93. The tax applies if the reduction in value was granted by a court, a board of review, or by the county assessor, but is not imposed if the reduction in market value is less than $10,000. Id. In no case may the "contamination value" of a property be greater than the estimated cost of implementing a reasonable response plan. Id.

> The tax is calculated by multiplying the "contamination value" by the property's class rate for ad valorem property tax, multiplied by another factor that varies according to certain characteristics of the property and the property owner. The variable factor depends upon whether the owner or operator of the property was legally responsible for the contamination and whether the MPCA [Minnesota Pollution Control Agency] has approved a response plan for cleanup of the property under Minn. Stat. ch. 18D (1996) or 115B (1996), and work has begun on the response plan. The chart immediately following illustrates the four variable factors imposed under the act. See Minn. Stat. sec. 270.91.

Cleanup Status	Owner or Operator a Responsible Party	Owner or Operator Not a Responsible Party
Approved Response Plan Undertaken	50%	12.5%
No Response Plan or No Cleanup Done	100%	25%

The contamination tax is payable at the same time and in the same manner as the regular ad valorem property tax, and is subject to the same penalty, interest, lien, and forfeiture provisions. Minn. Stat. sec. 270.95. The tax is discontinued when the taxpayer provides the assessor with a written determination by the MPCA stating that all of the requirements of the response plan have been satisfied. Minn. Stat. sec. 270.94.

Because the Westlings are a "responsible party" with an "approved response plan," their property is taxed at 50% of the tax rate for the applicable property class, class 3a, industrial property. Minn. Stat. sec. 273.13, subd. 24 (1996). The Mille Lacs County assessor determined "contamination values" for the subject property of $1,003,400 as of January 2, 1994, and $1,600,000 as of January 2, 1995, and imposed contamination taxes on the property in the amount of $22,278.50 for 1994, payable in 1995, and $36,000 for 1995, payable in 1996.

Id. at 818–19.

The court found the tax constitutional. It held that the classification was reasonable and non-arbitrary, reasoning that the classification could be reasonably related to an (unstated) statutory purpose.

In operation, the contamination tax recaptures revenue lost to counties that continue to provide services to affected properties, even though property taxes have been reduced due to the presence of contamination. It requires property owners who benefit from government services to pay for some of the costs of providing those services. The tax also acts as an incentive to property owners to clean up affected properties. * * *

It is reasonable to assume that the legislature enacted the contamination tax for the purposes of raising revenue, of strengthening the local tax base, of encouraging environmentally responsible behavior by owners and operators of property, and of encouraging cleanup of environmentally contaminated property. These are legitimate public purposes that the legislature may have intended to achieve by enactment of the contamination tax.

Id. at 821–822.

The court also rejected the characterization of the tax as an uncompensated taking:

Relators argue that the subject property has no market value at all; therefore any tax at all imposed on the property is in excess of 100% of the property's value and therefore constitutes a confiscatory tax. * * * In this case, there has been no per se taking of the subject property; the Westlings do not allege that there has been an actual taking of title or permanent physical invasion of the subject property. Nor do the Westlings claim that they have been deprived of all economically beneficial or productive use of their property.

Id. at 822–23.

C. *"Stigma" and Contamination*. In Dealers Manufacturing Co. v. County of Anoka, 615 N.W.2d 76 (Minn. 2000), the Minnesota Supreme Court returned to the question of contamination, this time interpreting Minn. Stat. § 273.11(Subd. 17(a)) (Westlaw 2009), which states:

> In determining the market value of property containing contaminants, the assessor shall reduce the market value of the property by the contamination value of the property. The contamination value is the amount of the market value reduction that results from the presence of the contaminants, but it may not exceed the cost of a reasonable response action plan or asbestos abatement plan or management program for the property.

The taxpayers argued that because stigma can reduce property value even after all contaminants have been removed, it should not be included in "contamination value." The court agreed, finding that

> a stigma factor can attach to property whether contaminants are present, are threatened, or are totally absent. Where, for example, a property has been successfully remediated leaving no contamination, or is in proximity to property that is contaminated, stigma may nonetheless be present as a heavy burden on the value of the property due to the perception of risk of liability, or government imposed restrictions on the use or transferability of the property, among other concerns. * * * Because the term "contamination value" is defined as the reduction in market value resulting from the presence of contaminants, it does not include a stigma factor because stigma may attach to property that is not itself contaminated but nevertheless can have a substantial impact in determining the value of uncontaminated property.

Dealers Manufacturing, 615 N.W.2d at 79–80. The court also found the county's position "inconsistent with Minnesota's property tax scheme that provides that with limited exceptions, all property is to be valued at market value." Id. at 81.

A dissenting opinion by the court's Chief Justice argued that the plain language of the statute

> contemplates reductions resulting from the presence of contaminants, and stigma is such a reduction. * * * Thus while the majority concludes that because stigma is not specifically mentioned in subdivision 17 it must be excluded from that statute, I reach the opposite conclusion. Because the statute does not specifically exclude stigma, it limits the market value reduction—whether it results from stigma or clean-up costs or something else—to the response action plan costs.

Id. at 81–82 (Blatz, C.J., dissenting).

D. *Cases in Other Jurisdictions*. For a comprehensive review of property tax cases dealing with environmental contamination, Thomas A. Jaconetty, ed., Issues Confronting Properties Affected by Contamination or Environmental Problems (International Association of Assessing Officers 2002).

b. *Current Use Valuation of Agricultural Land*

The majority of states provide for preferential assessment of bona fide agricultural property at its value for farming purposes rather than "fair market value." Similar approaches often apply to open space and timberland. Some states simply tax qualifying land at its value for agricultural purposes, with no penalty imposed or repayment required in the event of a later change in use. Some states defer the additional taxes that would be imposed if assessment were upon full market value, requiring repayment, often with interest, in the event of a later change in use. In other states, participating owners contractually agree to retain their property in agricultural use for a specified period of time.

Attempts to limit these preferential provisions to bona-fide agricultural uses face vexing definitional problems. The Florida statute seeks to do this by explicitly providing that "only lands which are used primarily for bona fide agricultural purposes shall be classified agricultural. 'Bona fide agricultural purposes' means good faith commercial agricultural use of the land." Fla. Stat. § 193.461(3)(b) (Westlaw 2009). The statute further provides that a "[s]ale of land for a purchase price which is three or more times the agricultural assessment placed on the land shall create a presumption that such land is not used primarily for bona fide agricultural purposes. Upon a showing of special circumstances by the landowner demonstrating that the land is to be continued in bona fide agriculture, this presumption may be rebutted." Id. § 193.461(4)(c). In Roden v. K & K Land Management, Inc., 368 So.2d 588 (Fla. 1978), the Florida Supreme Court interpreted this statute, observing:

> In this case K & K Land Management purchased approximately 350 acres of producing citrus grove for six times the agricultural assessment. Twenty-five of the acres were developed into an amusement park, but the remainder of the grove was continued to be used for citrus production. The issue was whether the presumption of nonagricultural use in Section 193.461(4)(c) was overcome as to the acreage continued for citrus production. On the record before us, we cannot say the trial court found incorrectly that the presumption had been rebutted and that respondent was entitled to agricultural classification.

Id. at 589.

NOTES AND QUESTIONS

A. *Allocation of Value.* The *Roden* court found that the total sale price of the 350 acres was six times the agricultural assessment, with 25 acres then developed as an amusement park. In order to avoid the presumption of non-agricultural use, the price allocated to the remaining 325 acres could not exceed three times its agricultural assessment. If the agricultural assessment were $1 per acre, so that the price of the entire parcel equaled $2100 ($1 × 350 × 6), and the agricultural assessment of the 325 acres could not exceed three times the non-agricultural assessment (or $975), then the balance of the assessment allocated to the 25 acres dedicated to non-agricultural use would have to equal $1125 ($2100 − $975), or 45 times its agricultural assessment, while the neighboring acres sold at three times their agricultural assessment. What evidence would you require in order to accept this allocation?

B. *Evidence Required to Overcome a Presumption of Non–Agricultural Use.* Note that payment of an amount in excess of three times the agricultural assessment creates only a presumption of non-agricultural use under Florida law. What evidence would you require in order to rebut this presumption? In *Roden*, the dissent argued that "continued use of the land as a grove could not be considered a good faith commercial agricultural use when there is no reasonable expectation of meeting investment costs and realizing a reasonable profit"? Roden, 368 So.2d at 590 (Alderman, J., dissenting). How does the allocation of purchase price discussed in the previous question affect the calculation of "investment costs"?

C. *Reassessment During Construction.* Some states make no effort to limit current-use assessment to bona fide agricultural land. The Illinois "developer's relief" provision, 35 Ill. Comp. Stat. Ann. 200/10–30(a) (Westlaw 2009), provides that platting, subdividing and developing farmland or vacant land of five acres or more cannot lead to a new assessment until completion of construction. Can you suggest a justification for this provision?

D. *The Stakes in Agricultural Classification Cases.* Robbins v. Yusem, 559 So.2d 1185 (Fla. Dist. Ct. App. 1990), helps explain the volume of appeals on this issue in Florida. There, the court agreed that agricultural use actually prohibited by law could not support preferential assessment. Note the magnitude of the valuation reduction at stake in this determination:

> Although the land was zoned for industrial use, the property was actually used for the commercial farming of yucca and calabaza. The property had not been used for farming in 1983, 1984, or 1985. In 1987, the Property Appraiser denied the taxpayer's application for an agricultural classification on the grounds that the agricultural use was illegal under the zoning code and thus could not be considered a "good faith" use of the property within the meaning of the Greenbelt Law, section 193.461, Florida Statutes (1987). * * * The PAAB [Property Appraisal Adjustment Board of Dade County] adopted the special master's recommendation and reduced the property's preliminary assessment from $1,900,584 to $8,730.

Id. at 1186. The court held that land farmed in violation of local zoning ordinances could not satisfy the statutory requirement of "good faith" agricultural use.

E. *Policy Issues Raised by Agricultural Assessment Provisions.* Maryland introduced the first program for use-value assessment of agricultural and recreational land in 1956, and since that time nearly every state had enacted some variation of this approach, sometimes after amendment of the state constitutional uniformity provisions. Proponents see these measures as a means of avoiding development pressure from escalating property taxes; critics see them as a subsidy to developers and speculators holding land for future construction. The economist Henry Aaron has written, "[i]n the absence of evidence supporting artificial deferral, special farmland exemptions are inequitable and should be repealed. They specifically reduce taxes for owners of a rapidly appreciating asset and, hence, rapidly growing wealth." Henry Aaron, Who Pays the Property Tax? 86 (1975). Among the points to consider in evaluating such programs are (1) the ability of farmers to borrow against the value of their property in order to pay taxes; (2) the desirability of preserving farmland in the urban fringe; (3) what assurance, if any, these programs offer that land will be retained in agricultural use in the long term; (4) the criteria for distinguishing between "speculators" and farmers willing to sell their land for a high enough price; (5) the importance of property taxes to a family's decision to continue farming or to sell its land, and (6) fairness to the other property owners in the jurisdiction whose taxes are higher as a result of these preferences.

F. *Agricultural Classification in Other States.* Florida is by no means unique in allowing great latitude in the classification of land for agricultural preferences. Professor Robert Glennon has offered the following commentary on the Arizona system of agricultural assessment:

> Arizona has a tax scheme affectionately dubbed "rent-a-cow" by county assessors and state revenue officials. Trying to protect agricultural interests, the Arizona legislature mandated that agricultural and grazing land be assessed solely by an income approach to value (annual net cash rental), not by market value. Land used for agricultural proposes, even if adjacent to urban areas and a prime target for development, qualifies for this benefit. In a recent Pima County, Arizona case, the Assessor took the position that, when a developer purchased the land for investment, the land no longer qualified as agricultural land. The developer candidly testified that the purchase was for investment and that he had taken initial steps toward developing it. The developer, however, leased grazing rights to a neighboring rancher for five to seven head of cattle for $250 a year. The Arizona Court of Appeals held that the developer was entitled to have the land assessed as agricultural, notwithstanding the owner's intention to develop, and that the paltry annual rental did not provide a reasonable rate of return on the investment. The upshot was that land purchased for $4,500,000 was assessed at $3455. The differential between the assessed and actual value is approximately 1300 times. The beneficiary of this loophole, according to the Pima County Assessor, is "any developer who is big enough to have his own legal staff."

Robert Glennon, "Taxation and Equal Protection," 58 Geo. Wash. L. Rev. 261, 305 (1990) (citations omitted). The case Professor Glennon refers to is Stewart Title & Trust v. Pima County, 156 Ariz. 236, 751 P.2d 552 (App. 1987).

G. *Current Use Value as Affected by Special Value to the Owner.* In Village of Burnsville v. Commissioner of Taxation, 295 Minn. 504, 202 N.W.2d 653 (1972), a power company owned land located in the bottomlands of the Minnesota River, 560 acres of which made up "Black Dog Lake * * * a long, narrow slough with an average normal depth of about 2 feet." Id., 202 N.W.2d at 654. The tract was zoned for heavy industrial use, but low elevation, poor soil, and periodic flooding rendered it inappropriate for most improvements. In prior years, the assessor had treated Black Dog Lake as valueless wasteland. However, the lake offered its owner one advantage, allowing it to discharge water in compliance with the state's thermal pollution control standards, and so avoiding the need for construction of cooling towers. The assessor added to the land value a "use increment" of $3,965,000 (later reduced by him to $1,343,000) to reflect this special value in use. How would you respond to the proposition that land with a negligible market value might nonetheless bear a substantial assessment because of its special utility to a particular owner?

H. *Comparison to Federal "Special Use" Valuation.* Note that special valuation procedures also can apply to family farm and business property under the federal estate tax, substituting present use value for market value at highest and best use. See generally Thomas Zupanc, et al., "The Intricacies of Special–Use Valuation," 35 Tax Adviser 434 (2004).

c. *Valuation of Conservation Land*

VILLAGE OF RIDGEWOOD v. BOLGER FOUNDATION

Supreme Court of New Jersey, 1986.
104 N.J. 337, 517 A.2d 135.

ANTELL, J.

The question presented on this appeal is whether a taxpayer may reduce, for real estate tax assessment purposes, the value of property because of a conservation easement thereon that it granted in perpetuity to a conservation foundation. In an opinion published at 6 N.J. Tax 391 (1984), the Tax Court held that the reduction was not allowable. With one modification the Appellate Division affirmed, 202 N.J. Super. 474 (1985), and we granted certification, 102 N.J. 343 (1985).

Defendant is a private, nonprofit corporation designated as a private foundation under the Internal Revenue Code, 26 U.S.C.A. § 509. The properties in question, Lot 8, Block 7 in Midland Park and Lot 9, Block 1810 in Ridgewood, have been held by defendant since 1969 and make up a tract of approximately 2.8 acres straddling the boundary line between the two municipalities. Pursuant to an agreement dated August 15, 1979, defendant conveyed to the New Jersey Conservation Foundation ("NJCF"), a nonprofit corporation organized to foster and preserve open space, a perpetual conservation easement on the property. The easement, which did not extend to other neighboring lands also owned by defendant, was granted for the benefit of the general public and precludes defendant from removing vegetation, excavating soil, erecting structures, dumping trash, and engaging in any activity that might be detrimental to drainage, flood control, potable water, erosion control, or soil conservation. Except as specifically permitted, it prohibits any act or use "detrimental to the preservation of the Property in its natural state." Access thereto is reserved to defendant, with NJCF being permitted limited entry solely for the purpose of inspecting to insure compliance with the terms and conditions of the easement. The terms of the easement, which are binding on defendant and NJCF, their successors and assigns, further provide that in the event NJCF ceases to function with one of its primary purposes being the preservation of natural resources and open space, the easement shall be transferred and assigned to one of a number of specified conservation organizations and public bodies.

The neighborhood in which the tract is located is zoned for one family dwellings on spacious lots. During the tax years in question, 1980 and 1981, defendant's properties were appraised at their "highest and best use" for single family residences. The Ridgewood property was assessed at $21,200 for each year, and the assessment for the larger tract in Midland Park was $25,400.

On the taxpayer's appeal from both assessments, the Bergen County Tax Board recognized the existence of the easement, the topography of the property, and other restrictions on the property, and reduced the assessments to a nominal value of $1000 each. The municipalities appealed these determinations to the New Jersey Tax Court. After ruling the conservation easements nondeductible, the court restored the Ridgewood Park assessment to $21,200 and increased the Midland Park assessment to $37,600 based on its potential for single family development. With the one modification, which we will describe later, the Appellate Division affirmed substantially for the reasons expressed by the Tax Court.

Easements are of two types: easements appurtenant and easements in gross. "The distinction between the two, of course, is that an easement appurtenant requires a dominant tenement to which it is appurtenant, whereas an easement in gross belongs to its owner independently of his ownership or possession of any specific land." Weber v. Dockray, 2 N.J. Super. 492, 495 (Ch.Div.1949). An easement appurtenant is created when an owner of one parcel of property (the servient estate) gives rights regarding that property to the owner of an adjacent property (the dominant estate). It enhances the value of the dominant estate and cannot exist separate from the land itself. An easement in gross, by contrast, benefits no specific parcel owned by another; it is independent of and unconnected to the ownership or possession of any particular tract. For purposes of real estate tax assessment our courts have held that the fair value of property subject to an easement appurtenant is reduced while the value of the property benefited therefrom is enhanced by the value of the easement. Conservation easements of the kind here considered are easements in gross. While there is no identifiable dominant estate that directly enjoys the benefit thereof, obviously such an easement can enhance the value of other property in the area.

The leading authority on the allowance of a deduction from fair value of an easement in gross is Borough of Englewood Cliffs v. Estate of Allison, 69 N.J. Super. 514 (App.Div.1961). There a tract of land was held by trustees under a will for use as a public park. The trust was irrevocable and the trustees had no beneficial interest in the property. Having in mind the public benefit flowing from the easement and the lack of any private beneficial interest, the Appellate Division held that the value of the easement should be deducted from the fair value of the land. The Tax Court herein interpreted that holding to be limited to cases where the public enjoys free access to the property and not where, as here, the taxpayer retains exclusive access. We give that decision a broader reading. The pertinent language is as follows:

We conclude that it is immaterial for assessment purposes whether the fee owner holds a title subject to a private easement for the benefit of a dominant tenement, a public easement in a dedicated and accepted street, or public rights to use and enjoy a park under a charitable trust. In each case the land has been deprived of an element of value to be subtracted from the value of the fee. Possibility of adding that element in whole or part to other property, as in the case of a dominant tenement, is not the controlling factor. The assessor's duty is to determine true value of the property being assessed; he should not include elements of value transferred to other properties or transferred to the community at large in the form of public rights. [Id. at 529].

Although not specifically enumerated therein, a conservation easement given to insure the preservation of open space is fully comparable to the easements or encroachments there considered and its recognition for tax valuation purposes is consistent with the philosophy of the foregoing statement. The public benefits flowing from such a conservation easement are beyond debate, as shown by the following legislative findings and declaration in N.J.S.A. 54:4–3.63: "The Legislature hereby finds and declares that natural open space areas for public recreation and conservation purposes are rapidly diminishing; that public funds for the acquisition and maintenance of public open space should be supplemented by private individuals and conservation organizations; and that it is therefore in the public interest to encourage the dedication of privately-owned open space to public use and enjoyment as provided for in this act."

New Jersey's policy of granting relief from property tax assessments to encourage the preservation of open space and conserving natural resources finds expression in the Farmland Assessment Act of 1964, N.J.S.A. 54:4–23.1 to–23.24, and the New Jersey Green Acres Land Acquisition Act of 1971, N.J.S.A. 13:8A–19 to–34. Moreover, effective February 5, 1980, the New Jersey Conservation Restriction and Historic Preservation Restriction Act, N.J.S.A. 13:8B–1 to 9, was enacted, which recognizes conservation easements granted to nonprofit organizations and specifically provides that "[t]he existence of any conservation restriction ... acquired pursuant to this act shall be considered by local assessors in establishing the full value of any lands subject to such restriction." N.J.S.A. 13:8B–7. Indeed, had the easement herein been conveyed scarcely six months later than it was, defendant's right to a deduction therefor would be mandated by this enactment. It is clear that elements of value are surrendered by the taxpayer as an incident to transferring this assurance of preserving open space to the community at large. By giving up in perpetuity the right to do anything with the property other than keep it in its natural state, defendant has, as the County Tax Board found, seriously compromised its value as a marketable commodity. *Allison* leaves no doubt that the adverse impact of such an encumbrance on market value must be taken into account in arriving at an assessed valuation.

In construing the holding of *Estate of Allison* the Tax Court relied on In re Appeal of Neptune Township, 86 N.J. Super. 492 (App.Div.1965), where *Estate of Allison* was distinguished. In *Neptune Township* the taxpayer sought a reduction from value by reason of certain deed restrictions limiting a strip of land to use as a bathing area and prohibiting construction of improvements on the premises without the written consent of the grantor. For violation of the conditions the deed provided that title revert to the grantor. In holding that the deed restrictions "may not be considered in fixing the market value of the property as a bathing beach club—the purpose for which it was acquired, and for which it has been used by the taxpayer for purely private purposes," id. at 500, the Appellate Division noted that the case differed from *Estate of Allison* in that the beach property was not dedicated to public purposes, a fact that stands in contrast also to what we have found is the manifest purpose of the easement herein. Moreover, the deed restrictions considered in *Neptune Township* could all be nullified on the "written consent of the grantor." Here, as we have said, the easement was given in perpetuity.

As we noted earlier, effective February 5, 1980, the legislature enacted the New Jersey Conservation Restriction and Historic Preservation Restriction Act, N.J.S.A. 13:8B–1 to–9 (Act). In general, the Act authorizes the assignment of conservation restrictions by landowners to governmental units or charitable conservancies to insure that the land governed by the restrictions will be maintained in its natural integrity. It provides that the existence of such restrictions shall be considered by local assessors in assessing land for tax purposes and directs that no such restrictions may be released without the approval of the Commissioner of Environmental Protection after a public hearing.

We observe that the Tax Court opinion commented that the Act, which became effective almost six months after the granting of the easement, required public hearings as well as the Commissioner's approval before an environmental easement acquired thereunder could be released. Implicit therein is the suggestion that because the easement was granted prior to the effective date of the Act, it had not been given "pursuant to" the Act and was therefore not subject to the requirement of a public hearing and the Commissioner's approval of its being released.

We note first the following provision of N.J.S.A. 13:8B–8: "Nothing in this act shall be construed to imply that any restriction, easement, covenant, or condition which does not have the benefit of this act, on account of any provision hereof, is unenforceable." Moreover, on May 14, 1984, the defendants granted an amended conservation easement to NJCF which was recorded June 13, 1984. It specifically recited that it was a "conservation restriction . . . as defined in N.J.S.A. 13:8B–2(b)" and that it was granted pursuant to the Act. Whatever concerns the Tax Court may have had that the easement might be released without regard to the legislated safeguards seem now to be answered.

In reaching its result, the Tax Court also expressed the belief that the easement was unenforceable because it attempted to restrict the alienability of property. Although affirming the judgment before it, the Appellate Division departed from the reasoning of the Tax Court to conclude that the easement did not violate the rule against restraints on alienation and that the restrictions of the easement were reasonable. We share that view. In other respects the determination under review is reversed and the judgment of the Bergen County Tax Board is reinstated.

NOTES AND QUESTIONS

A. *The* Allison *Case*. Englewood Cliffs v. Estate of Allison, 69 N.J.Super. 514, 174 A.2d 631 (App. Div. 1961), considered the valuation of Allison Park, more than seven thousand landscaped acres on the Hudson River Palisades left to a charitable trust for use of the public by William Allison. The borough of Englewood Cliffs had for many years assessed the park on a nominal valuation of $500, but raised this to over $20,000 in 1958 and to $52,065 in 1959. Interestingly, no argument was raised that Allison Park should be exempt from taxation. It is an indication of the change in public attitudes towards the importance of open space that twenty-five years before the *Bolger* court found "[t]he public benefits flowing from such a conservation easement are beyond debate," *Allison* could accept that the only exempt use of land was as an incident to buildings upon it:

> [T]he statute which confers tax benefits upon non-profit organizations applies by its terms to buildings used for schools, churches, hospitals, and the like, and only exempts land as an incident of the exemption of the buildings upon it. N.J.S.A. 54:4–3.6. There is no provision in that section for parks, playgrounds and the like, where the land itself is of primary importance and any buildings are of minor importance. Allison Park is used by a great many people because of the land itself. The caretaker's house, tools sheds and comfort stations in the park are not buildings which would have any claim to exemption under the statute nor does their existence give the park acreage any claim to exemption.

Id., 174 A.2d at 633.

Instead, *Allison* concerned the appropriate valuation of admittedly taxable land, given its restriction under the terms of the trust to use as a public park. The court had no difficulty in rejecting the borough's position that the effects of these restrictions should be disregarded. Previous efforts by the trustees to sell small amounts of the park property for residential development had been successfully blocked by the state Attorney General and the city of Englewood (although "no willingness by the city to maintain the park had ever been indicated," id. at 635). Therefore the court ordered that the assessment be reduced to one-tenth the unencumbered amount, based upon an admittedly imprecise estimate that the public rights represented nine-tenths of the total value of the property. The State Division of Tax Appeals had argued that reducing the valuation of the property to reflect the influence of the restriction would "permit an owner without the authority of law to create a tax exempt situation which would supersede the exemptions allowed by law and add one more exemption which the Legislature did not allow," id. at 633.

B. *Issues of Public Access*. The *Bolger* court found that the "manifest purpose of the easement" was public, rather than private, as in the beach club at issue in *Neptune Township*. But the land in *Bolger* was not open to the public, and even the New Jersey Conservation Foundation was only "permitted limited entry solely for the purpose of inspecting to insure compliance." In light of the court's reliance on *Allison* and the complete access the public was allowed to Allison Park, how do you think this should affect the outcome? In Wing's Neck Conservation Foundation, Inc. v. Board of Assessors of the Town of Bourne, 2003 WL 21663986 (Mass. App. Tax Bd. July 8, 2003), the Massachusetts Appellate Tax Board refused a property tax exemption for conservation land open only to neighboring landowners who paid an annual assessment to the foundation owning the property. The foundation argued that public access would undermine its goal of preserving wildlife habitat, but the Board found any public benefit merely incidental to the primary purpose of benefiting the neighboring homeowners. Noting that "absence of public access to land has consistently proven fatal to a landowner's claim of charitable exemption," id. at 6, the Board held the land to be taxable.

3. NON–MARKET ADJUSTMENTS TO VALUE

An admittedly accurate estimate of market value, the actual amount that could be realized by the seller in a free exchange between informed parties, often encounters objections from taxpayers who do not consider this to be a fair basis for assessment. Assessment limitations, such as Proposition 13, and agricultural-assessment provisions are examples of successful political efforts to substitute another measure for market value as the statutory or constitutional definition of the tax base. There are also many non-legislative efforts to achieve the same result. For example, taxpayers in a number of states have protested the inclusion of a "view factor" in the calculation of market value, even when the local market demonstrates that buyers will pay a premium for land offering scenic views. This issue ignited particular debate in New Hampshire, although the state Department of Revenue Administration made clear that the state has no "view tax," any more than a "finished basement tax" or "garage tax." A letter to a Concord newspaper asked, "How do you think our forefathers would have felt had Britain tried to tax them for looking at their neighbors' land?," and the Associated Press pondered the plight of a legally blind homeowner paying tax on a view he could not enjoy. See Daphne Kenyon, "Seeing Through the 'View Tax' Myth," State Tax Notes, Sept. 3, 2007, pp. 641–45.

There also are objections to market values that reflect historically high or low points in the market cycle. In the Depression of the 1930s, many homeowners unable to meet their mortgage obligations saw their houses sold in foreclosure for extremely low prices and found themselves liable for the deficiency, the outstanding amount owing after the proceeds were applied against the mortgage debt. This led to a number of legislative attempts to substitute a more acceptable measure of "fair market value" than the amount realized at the foreclosure sale. These efforts encountered many of the same problems of subjectivity illustrated in the cases dealing with current use value. Fair market value is generally interpreted in reference to the fairness of the sale procedure, such as availability of information, lack of duress, and standard terms of sale. If fairness instead refers to the resulting value figure, an entirely different inquiry is required as to what constitutes a fair or just price.

This theoretical line between fair values that are depressed and depressed values that are not "fair and reasonable" can be quite elusive. During the Depression, Professor James Bonbright wrote:

> A friendly critic warns the author to stress more clearly the disagreement among appraisers as to whether the term "value," even when used without any qualifying adjective or adjunct, imports the idea of a *normal* or an *intrinsic* value. In this treatise we ourselves answer this question in the negative. That is to say, we make no distinction between money value and price, preferring to follow those economists who define market price as market value measured in terms of money. To us an abnormal, or evanescent, or extortionate, or dangerously low market price represents just as true a current *value* as does a normal, or permanent, or fair, or reasonably high market price.

1 James Bonbright, The Valuation of Property 29 (1937) (emphasis in original)

In City and County of Honolulu v. Steiner, 73 Haw. 449, 834 P.2d 1302, 1310 (1992), the taxpayer argued that the financial strength of overseas investors and the weakness of the U.S. currency should cause international sales to be excluded from consideration, since these buyers "were paying much higher prices than were 'economically justified' by any measure of value." In rejecting this position, the court cited Bonbright's criticism of the concept of "intrinsic value," and quoted an earlier decision defining market value as "no more than the value in money of any property for which that property would sell on the open market by a willing seller to a willing buyer." In re Puna Sugar Co., Ltd., 56 Haw. 621, 547 P.2d 2, 4 (1976).

Dotson v. Henry County Board of Tax Assessors, 155 Ga.App. 557, 271 S.E.2d 691 (1980), considered the assessment of a dairy farm at $1,425 an acre. The Board of Equalization reduced the value per acre to $1,221, and the Superior Court further lowered it to $1,088. The appellate court found the lower court to have erred "in approving a valuation which tilted market value in favor of an assumed 'highest and best use' ":

> The plaintiff's witnesses, who zeroed in on the value of the land for its existing uses of timber and grazing land, placed values of between $200 and $700 per acre * * *

* * * [A] basing of fair market value primarily on sales for developmental purposes (as the testimony shows was done in the instant case) will in 100 percent of the cases yield a figure having no relation to that obtained by a willing seller/willing buyer contract for the purpose of continuing the existing agricultural or dairy use of the property. * * * "Highest and best use" is thus itself a much more speculative assigned value than existing use. Large tracts of acreage in Henry County, under the evidence here, are not worth more than $200 to $700 for agricultural purposes—in fact one of the defendant's witnesses said he knew of no sales for purely agricultural purposes; yet, this part of the county is admittedly rural and in general the existing uses are agricultural uses. It is true that one of the assessors stated that they took these facts into consideration and in fact assigned values somewhat lower than what they would expect the land to bring on a speculative sale, but the point is that the existing use is agricultural and the assigned value is at least twice the estimated appraisal value for use as woods or dairy farming.

Id., 271 S.E.2d at 692–93.

NOTES AND QUESTIONS

A. *Willing Buyer–Willing Seller.* Ga. Code Ann. § 48–5–2(3) (Westlaw 2009) defines fair market value as "the amount a knowledgeable buyer would pay for the property and a willing seller would accept for the property at an arm's length, bona fide sale." The criterion of "highest and best use" is sometimes considered implicit in any willing buyer-willing seller standard absent an explicit statutory exception, such as a provision valuing agricultural land according to its farming income. The court in *Dotson* took a different view when it described highest and best use as one element that may enter the valuation process under the "catchall phrase allowing the use of 'any other factors deemed pertinent.'" 271 S.E.2d at 692. In a case such as this, how should a court or an assessor choose between the sale price for farming purposes and the sale price for development in determining fair market value? If, as the assessor argued, there were comparable sales of $2,200 an acre, would Dotson be a willing seller at $200 to $700 an acre?

B. *Market Value Implications of Sales for Specific Uses.* The *Dotson* opinion criticized a valuation based on sales for non-agricultural development, pointing out that this "will in 100 percent of the cases yield a figure having no relation to that obtained by a willing seller/willing buyer contract for the purpose of continuing the existing agricultural or dairy use of the property." Is this a criticism of the valuation process, or a criticism of a tax based on market value?

C. *Market Value Implications of Current Income.* The *Dotson* court noted that over 20 years annual taxes on the property had increased from $200 to $4,300, that the farm constituted the owners' sole income apart from Social Security and a small pension, and that "[i]t is uncontroverted that taxes assessed cannot be paid without selling off timber or otherwise going into capital." 271 S.E.2d at 692. How should these factors affect the determination of market value?

D. *"Considering" All Factors.* The Georgia definition of "fair market value," which generally adopts a willing buyer-willing seller standard, Ga. Code Ann. § 48–5–2(3) (Westlaw 2009), also provides (id., § 48–5–2(3)(B)):

> The tax assessor shall consider the following criteria in determining the fair market value of real property:
>
> (i) Existing zoning of property;
>
> (ii) Existing use of property, including any restrictions or limitations on the use of property resulting from state or federal law or rules or regulations adopted pursuant to the authority of state or federal law;
>
> (iii) Existing covenants or restrictions in deed dedicating the property to a particular use;
>
> (iv) Foreclosure sales, bank sales, other financial institution owned sales, or distressed sales, or any combination thereof, of comparable real property;
>
> (v) Decreased value of the property based on limitations and restrictions resulting from the property being in a conservation easement; and
>
> (vi) Any other factors deemed pertinent in arriving at fair market value.

What does it mean to "consider" existing use in valuing property when, as in *Dotson*, property may have one value if limited to its current use and another, radically different, value at its most profitable use? Is the ability to sell the property to a developer in the future part of its current "use"? Is this current value the reason that the Dotsons would not be willing sellers of their land at $200 an acre?

E. *Effect of Price Levels on Fair Market Value.* How should an insurance contract calling for payment of a building's fair market value be interpreted if this structure is destroyed by fire during an economic depression? How should the fact of an economic depression affect the calculation of an award for the taking of property under eminent domain? How would the rationale of the *Dotson* opinion apply in the context of an economic depression? Was *Dotson* an attempt to base the tax on normal values rather than speculative prices? Would its reasoning support taxes based on normal prices in a falling market? How would a court go about calculating normal value in such a situation? If value to the owner is calculated as the amount necessary to compensate for the loss of property, what would be the effect of a general business depression on this measure, considering both the cost of purchasing a comparable replacement and the cost of constructing a new building?

4. THE VALUATION OF SPECIAL-PURPOSE PROPERTY

JOSEPH E. SEAGRAM & SONS, INC. v. TAX COMMISSION OF THE CITY OF NEW YORK

Supreme Court of New York, Appellate Division, First Department, 1963.
18 A.D.2d 109, 238 N.Y.S.2d 228.

STEUER, JUSTICE.

The appeal is from an order confirming the assessments for tax purposes for the tax years 1956–57 to 1961–62, inclusive, on the real estate located at 375 Park Avenue. * * *

The building in question is an unusual one in its nature, though not unique. It has these distinctive features which are the hallmarks of its class: It is generally known by its name (having relationship to the owner) instead of a street address; it is constructed of unusual and striking materials; its architecture is noteworthy; and it is well set back from the streets on which it fronts, the space involved being employed in distinctive decorative effects. The net effect is that this building, and the limited number that resemble it, gives up a substantial fraction of the land that might be built upon, with a consequent diminution of the rentable space, and its construction involves a cost materially in excess of utilitarian standards.

These buildings serve their owners in a fourfold way: 1. They house their activities. 2. They provide income from the rental of the space not used by the owner. 3. They advertise the owner's business. 4. They contribute to the owner's prestige.[1]

Just how a building whose construction is designed to serve these particular purposes is to be appraised presents certain difficulties. The enhancement of the owner's ego is not a factor that can have a market value. In this city at present buildings in this special category, though few, are not unique. The time may come when they are so numerous that they become subject to sale, rent and the other transactions of commerce, so that by trading a market price which reflects the extra-commercial aspect can be ascertained. Meanwhile in this proceeding it must first be determined whether a valuation based on the special character is necessary. It would not be necessary if the building, as a conventional office building, is of a value at least equal to the assessments.

The assessments for the last three years are the only ones in question. There is little material difference in the relevant figures, so a calculation

---

1. In this connection they exemplify a well known economic theory (see T. Veblen, The Theory of the Leisure Class). Though the author did not foresee this particular manifestation of his "Doctrine of Conspicuous Waste," it comes well within the specifications he provides for its successful application: "In order to impress these transient observers * * * the signature of one's pecuniary strength should be written in characters which he who runs may read. It is evident, therefore, that the present trend of the development is in the direction of heightening the utility of conspicuous consumption as compared with leisure." Modern Library Edition, p. 87.

for a single year will suffice to make the determination based on capitalization of net income. For the year ending July 31, 1960, the actual income was $3,005,510. This does not include any income for the space occupied by the owner. Petitioner's expert appraised this space as having a rental value of $927,850, giving a total income of $3,933,360. Petitioner further claims a vacancy allowance of 5%, which would not be unreasonable. The net estimated return would therefore be $3,735,692. Expenses would vary somewhat. Petitioner's average for the three years is $1,401,000. This includes an item of $288,000 in each year for tenant changes. The city has taken the position that this item is not allowable because the improvements are personalty and not a part of the realty, relying on Matter of 666 Fifth Corporation v. Tax Commission, 11 N.Y.2d 915, 228 N.Y.S.2d 670, 183 N.E.2d 76. We find the argument inappropriate. The figure represents a maintenance charge. Whether it has to do with realty or personalty is immaterial. We question the figure on a different ground. Petitioner, having the burden of proof, must justify its calculations. The record is not clear as to how the expert estimated this figure, nor what it includes. It may be gathered that the figure is the total expenditure on behalf of tenants amortized over a period of years—just what period is by no means certain. But the record does show that it includes expenditures of sums which might be considered so far beyond the range of ordinary tenant accommodation in a commercial venture as to be considered fantastic. Expenditures in excess of a million dollars went into the fitting of a restaurant. Some explanation would be required to show that these amounts were proper business charges and that there was a reasonable expectation that rents would be enhanced or made possible through them. In the absence of any attempt at justification, they must be rejected. This reduces the expenses to $1,113,000 annually, with a net income of $2,623,000 (figure rounded out). Using petitioner's capitalization figures for the land and the taxes thereon there is a residual income for the building of $2,186,000. Petitioner claims the proper capitalization rate is 8% (made up of 6% for income and 2% for depreciation) plus taxes. Aside from the claim, this rate is not supported, and the city offered no proof on the subject. These figures represent the conservative view of an investor's expectations and, while they might be subject to revision in the special circumstances here presented, the record is barren of any proof upon which any lesser rate might be adopted. Using these figures, the value of the building would be $17,802,000. While this exceeds the petitioner's estimate by almost $4,000,000, it is still $3,200,000 under the assessment, and only about half the actual cost of construction.

It would seem to follow beyond the hope of successful contradiction that the traditional method of ascertaining value by capitalization is not applicable in this situation. Nowhere in the record is it explained how just two years before the period under review an experienced owner employing a reliable contractor and having the services of outstanding architects put $36,000,000 into a structure that was only worth $17,800,000. Such a startling result requires more than speculation before it can be accepted as fact.

The conclusion, therefore, is that petitioner proceeded upon an untenable theory and failed to show error in the assessments which calls for affirmance of the confirmation by the referee. It would, however, be unfair to leave the impression that a building of this sort presents an insoluble problem and that the owner is never in a position to contest the assessment of the city's appraisers. Nor is it necessary to await the day when the number of buildings of this kind reaches a point where they can be determined to have a market or rental value in consonance with their special features. Naturally, determination will have to await a proper presentation of the issue, but it will not be idle to indicate the lines along which presentation might be made.

Two possible theories occur. The first, and perhaps more obvious, is that advanced by the city here, namely, replacement value—the reasonable cost of construction less depreciation. To date this method of appraisal has been limited to two situations, in both of which the logic of its use is impregnable. The first is where the building is unique and would, if destroyed, have to be replaced (People ex rel. New York Stock Exchange Building Co. v. Cantor, 221 App.Div. 193, 223 N.Y.S. 64, aff'd, 248 N.Y. 533, 162 N.E. 514). The second situation is where the owner claims it as the highest value which can be put on the building. Neither of these categories embraces the issue here. But an approach to that method of valuation may be found through them. Buildings that are unique through their design for a special purpose which not only serves that purpose but renders them unsuitable for any other use are unsalable if the owner is the only one engaged in that enterprise or the number of persons is so few that the practical effect is the same. Likewise, the owner cannot replace the building by purchase. Consequently its value to him is the cost of replacement. Buildings so specialized as to have a restricted use, that is, a use by a limited number of people, are appraised similarly where there is an absence of proof of what such buildings sell or rent for (Matter of City of N.Y. (Kramer Realty), 16 A.D.2d 148, 226 N.Y.S.2d 288). While here the special features do not restrict the use, they do affect the value and the absence of proof of that effect could well lead to a valuation on replacement value as a last resort.

Another approach would be through the rental value of the space occupied by the owner. We have seen that the peculiar feature of this building, and the few that resemble it, is the identification in the public mind of the magnificent structure, and the consequent effect it has on the aesthetic improvement of the neighborhood with the owner. The public does not know or care about the actual ownership of the fee. The same effect could be produced if the building were identified in the public mind by the name of a tenant. In calculating the income of the building the additional increment that a tenant who could afford and would be willing to pay for such a privilege should be included. This increment could be added to the estimated rental of the owner-occupied space. Having determined this figure, capitalization of the result should produce a scientific appraisal.

The order should be affirmed, with costs.

* * *

VALENTE and EAGER, JJ., concur in concurring opinion by BREITEL, J.P.

BREITEL, JUSTICE PRESIDING (concurring).

* * *

Given a profit-minded owner with available experience and resources, and a competent builder, the cost of construction is likely to represent the value of the newly finished product. Consequently, in the absence of credible qualifying explanation, for a new building the cost of construction is, *prima facie,* the true value. Indeed, because it would escape this fact, the taxpayer is in the anomalous position of urging that vast corporate funds were used to construct a building of much less value. This, if so, is never satisfactorily explained and does not do much credit to the sagacity of the corporate managers.

* * * Consequently, in the absence of any satisfactory explanation to show excessive costs, the construction cost establishes value, *prima facie*— a value substantially in excess of the building assessment.

But the discrepancy here between capitalized rental income and cost of construction merits further analysis. The capitalized rental income as computed by taxpayer, using 6% as the rate of capitalization and 2% as the rate of depreciation, but including as an amortized expense the rejected tenant-changes, is $14.5 million. Excluding adjustments for tenant-changes the result would be $17 million—$4 million short of the building assessment, and up to $19 million short of the construction cost. Given a new building, prudently constructed for commercial purposes, the answer must be that the rental value assigned to the owner-tenant is too low, and, perhaps too, that the building as a whole bearing the name of its owner includes a real property value not reflected in commercial rental income. Of course, this would mean that, to begin with, the owner did not build for commercial rental-income purposes alone, and, as a consequence, capitalization of such income without adjustments produces a false result.
* * *

It is self-evident that an owner who builds, as did this taxpayer, a prestige (monumental) building for itself, requires the leasing to other commercial tenants simply as an important way of bearing the heavy costs involved. The prestige building has a rental value not based alone on commercially rented space, but on the building's value in promoting the economic interests of an owner. Thus, such an owner is not wasting assets. Rather, it is investing in a real estate project that will contribute to the production of income in its principal enterprise. Since this practice is becoming a common feature of urban areas, such investment has ceased to be idiosyncratic and is undoubtedly translatable into market value terms.

Typically, such value would be related to owner-occupancy of principal or prestige offices with choice space, the continued power to control its choice of space, and most often, identification by name of the building with that of the owner.[1]

On this view the rental value assigned to the taxpayer's space is understated, if there is merely charged to that space the prorated value assigned to other tenants. And, undoubtedly too, there is value to be assigned to the building as a whole, independent of commercial rental income, since the building, qua building, is also held for business purposes, unrelated to the receipt of commercial rental income.

Worth discarding, although urged, is the argument that because a building does not occupy all of the assembled land, there is an inadequate improvement. This does not follow. The improvement is inadequate to the land only if that is not a sound economic way to construct a building. Indeed, a discernible trend in modern prestige building, for at least a quarter of a century, may make construction to the building line an inadequate improvement—economically. Exclusively utilitarian construction may produce more "rentable" space, but not more valuable space.

VALENTE and EAGER, JJ., concur.

JOSEPH E. SEAGRAM & SONS, INC.
v. TAX COMMISSION OF THE
CITY OF NEW YORK

Court of Appeals of New York, 1964.
14 N.Y.2d 314, 251 N.Y.S.2d 460, 200 N.E.2d 447.

CHIEF JUDGE DESMOND.

* * *

Although we do not concur in everything said in the two Appellate Division opinions, we agree that for an office building like this, well suited to its site, the actual building construction cost of $36,000,000 is some evidence of value, at least as to the tax years soon after construction. Petitioner urges, however, that for a building built to rent and be rentable, capitalization of net income is the only basis for valuation and that the building assessment here can be justified only by assigning an inflated value to the office space occupied by petitioner itself. This, says petitioner, really means that petitioner, having for its own reasons constructed an unusually costly and beautiful building, is being taxed ostensibly for building value but really for the prestige and advertising value accruing to petitioner because the "Seagram Building" has become world-

---

1. Where, as sometimes happens, a major tenant's name is borne by the building, presumably, the rental paid reflects the name-bearing value. Or, in another situation, it may be that the tenant's name is used to enhance the prestige of the building; but in that case the rental income of the other tenants will reflect that value. The permutations are many, and whether the increased value attaches to the real estate or to business good-will may well, in some cases, present problems difficult of solution.

renowned for its striking and imposing beauty. We do not agree with this interpretation of the opinions and order of the Appellate Division.

Usually, the assumed rent for the space occupied by a building owner would for purposes of capitalization of net rent income be computed at about the same rate as the rents actually paid by other tenants. But there can be many reasons why, as both of the Appellate Division opinions state, "the building as a whole bearing the name of its owner includes a real property value not reflected in commercial rental income" since "the owner did not build for commercial rental-income purposes alone, and, as a consequence, capitalization of such income without adjustments produces a false result" and, therefore, "one must not confuse investment for commercial rental income with investment for some other form of rental value unrelated to the receipt of commercial rental income." In other words, the hypothetical rental for owner-occupied space need not be fixed at the same rate as paid by tenants. This does not mean that advertising or prestige or publicity value is erroneously taxed as realty value. It certainly does not mean that a corporate sponsor of esthetics is being penalized for contributing to the metropolis a monumental and magnificent structure.

The order should be affirmed, with costs.

* * *

NOTES AND QUESTIONS

A. *The Seagram Building.* The Seagram Building has been described as "one of New York's, and the country's, great works of modern architecture * * * [designed] by Mies van der Rohe and Philip Johnson, as handsomely proportioned and serene a tower as the twentieth century has conceived." Paul Goldberger, "Three Ways to Get a Sense of Extraordinary New York," N.Y. Times, August 8, 1980, at C9. Its combination of profitability and excellence in design extends to the Four Seasons restaurant located there as well. Recall that the Appellate Division questioned the business justification for the amount spent there: "Expenditures in excess of a million dollars went into the fitting of a restaurant. Some explanation would be required to show that these amounts were proper business charges and that there was a reasonable expectation that rents would be enhanced or made possible through them." Time has diminished both the seeming extravagance of this sum and any suspicion that it was not justified by business considerations. What does the success of the Seagram Building indicate as to the financial benefit of a prestigious address? The Appellate Division opinion suggested, "[t]he public does not know or care about the actual ownership of the fee. The same effect could be produced if the building were identified in the public mind by the name of a tenant." After 1981 the Seagram Company was a tenant in this building. Would association with the building name affect the amount it would be willing to pay to rent space there? Would tenants other than the Seagram Company pay the same premium to rent that space? What benefit from association with the Seagram name could be offered to future purchasers?

B. *"Specialty" Property.* The lower court refers to the *New York Stock Exchange* case, a dispute over tax valuation of the Exchange building. People ex rel. New York Stock Exchange Building Co. v. Cantor, 221 App.Div. 193, 223 N.Y.S. 64 (1st Dep't 1927), aff'd, 248 N.Y. 533, 162 N.E. 514 (1928). There, the Exchange argued that its building was so specialized that it could not be used by another purchaser, even another financial exchange, and so had no market value. In fact, the owners reasoned that the value of the land should be reduced by the demolition costs of the building. This led to the category of "specialty" valuation, a very limited approach whereby unique property that is useful to its owner and would be replaced if destroyed has occasionally been valued by reference to its depreciated cost. What do you see as the arguments for and against such an approach?

C. *Editorial Reaction to the* Seagram *Decision.* The *New York Times* editorial writers made clear their displeasure with the *Seagram* decision. "When it serves society badly, there is something wrong with the law. A clear illustration is in the New York State Court of Appeals decision upholding a lower court judgment that Joseph E. Seagram & Sons is to be penalized in the form of higher taxes for building an extravagantly handsome structure that has become one of the city's chief ornaments. For New York this decision is a catastrophe." The New York Times, June 13, 1974, at 22. In what sense are higher taxes on lavish structures a "penalty"? Would taxes on expensive land have a different economic or political character?

5. THE VALUATION OF PROPERTY SUBJECT TO DIVIDED LEGAL INTERESTS

a. *Property Subject to a Long–Term Lease*

Valuation cases involving property subject to a long-term lease calling for rents that are now below market levels present special issues in defining property for tax purposes. As a factual matter, it is clear that a purchaser will offer less for property subject to such a long-term lease than for identical property available for rent at current market levels. This leaves a legal question as to whether the actual diminished sale price determines the fair market value of the taxable property. If the property subject to tax is deemed to encompass both the landlord's and tenant's interests, the amount by which the landlord's interest is reduced is equal to the amount by which the tenant's interest is enhanced: the present value of the difference between fair market rent (sometimes called economic rent) and the rent required by the lease (sometimes called contract rent) over the remaining term of the rental agreement.[k] The computational question therefore depends upon a prior determination as to the composition of the property to be taxed. If it includes only the landlord's

---

k. This nomenclature is common in valuation decisions, but causes some confusion because it is unrelated to "economic rent" as that term is used in economic literature. For example, The MIT Dictionary of Modern Economics (David Pearce, ed., 4th ed. 1992) defines "economic rent" as "[a] payment to a factor in excess of what is necessary to keep it to its present employment."

interest, fair market value will be affected by the long-term lease, although there may be a question as to whether the lease was an arm's-length or bona fide agreement. If the property to be valued includes both the tenant's and landlord's interests, its fair market value is not affected by the lease.

MERRICK HOLDING CORP. v. BOARD OF ASSESSORS

Court of Appeals of New York, 1978.
45 N.Y.2d 538, 382 N.E.2d 1341, 410 N.Y.S.2d 565.

FUCHSBERG, JUDGE.

Merrick Holding Corp., the owner of land improved by a 29–store shopping center complex in Nassau County, brought this consolidated certiorari proceeding to review the amount at which the property was assessed for the 1968–1975 tax years. The valuation had been arrived at by the income capitalization method. However, instead of accepting actual rental income as a basis for its computations, the county's board of assessors first increased it by amounts, termed "leasehold bonuses," which reflected the difference between the rentals payable to Merrick under long-term leases with three major tenants and the appreciably higher market rental value of the leased spaces. The dispute between the parties focused on the validity of these add-ons.

Special Term, though decreeing some reductions on the basis of other issues not here relevant, upheld the application of the leasehold bonuses and entered judgment accordingly. But the Appellate Division, pointing out that the county's appraiser had conceded that the three leases "were 'not necessarily improvident when they were made'" and taking the view that, without proof of improvidence, it was "improper to apply the leasehold bonus principle to a selected portion of leases in a shopping center in the absence of (undefined) special circumstances," reversed on the law and remanded for a new determination. On remand, Special Term then granted the taxpayer's motion for summary judgment, eliminated the add-ons and entered a new judgment reducing the assessment correspondingly. On the county's appeal to us, we now conclude that the order of the Appellate Division should, in turn, be reversed and the matter remitted for review of the facts. Our reasons follow.

The command of section 306 of the Real Property Tax Law that all property be assessed at full value does not pronounce an inelastic approach to valuation. Nor does the legislative directive specify a particular method for establishing value. And courts, being under no compunction to do so, have not confined assessors to any one course. To ensure that the existence of varied and multifaceted patterns of land use and ownership does not frustrate the design that each contribute equitably to the public fisc, courts have upheld any fair and nondiscriminatory method that appears most likely to achieve that end.

Thus, though commonly the most accurate standard is provided by the sales prices of comparable properties located within the same or similar competitive area in which a parcel being assessed is located, in the absence of sufficiently reliable market data, alternative methods, such as income capitalization or, where necessary, reproduction cost, may be employed. Not surprisingly, as to income producing property, income capitalization has been the preferred mode.

Consequently, the board's employment of income capitalization rather than cost or market in the present case was not exceptional (see, generally, Graham, "Market Valuation of a Regional Shopping Center," 32 Appraisal J. 589). But the appropriateness of this method does not take away from the reality that its application, calling as it does for the exercise of judgment by the appraiser, furnishes, at best, no more than an estimate of the present worth of the benefits to be reaped from the property at issue (1 Bonbright, Valuation of Property, p. 218). The goal at all times remains full value. To that end, assessors may devise reasonable methods that assure that the income they accept as the basis for capitalization is as close a reflection of true value as possible.

Our recent holding in G.R.F., Inc. v. Board of Assessors of County of Nassau, 41 N.Y.2d 512, 393 N.Y.S.2d 965, 362 N.E.2d 597, reflects this flexible approach to problems of valuation. Having found that the circumstances warranted no hard and fast choice between a strict income capitalization approach and one based on cost of reproduction, we there emphasized that "[p]ragmatism * * * requires adjustment when the economic realities prevent placing the properties in neat logical valuation boxes" (G.R.F., Inc. v. Board of Assessors of County of Nassau, 41 N.Y.2d 512, 515, 393 N.Y.S.2d 965, 968, 362 N.E.2d 597, 599, supra).

In short, categorization must yield to more exact means of arriving at value. Since other factors may tend to qualify the reliability of actual income as a sole measure of value, the per se rule articulated by the Appellate Division, which would interdict them, must be rejected. For, though realized income will often turn out to be the surest indicator of full value, when fair market rents exceed rental income the latter may, in whole or in part, be made to defer to more precise means of fixing a base on which to compute capitalization.

So, if examination discloses that rent has been arbitrarily set without regard to the market rental value whether through self-dealing, as, for example, where a landlord and tenant are business affiliates or property is owner-occupied, or, certainly, where there is any indication of collusion, the rent arrangement will be of little, if any guidance to sound appraisal.

On the other hand, in arriving at their valuations, assessors may always consider below market rents that result from arm's length bargaining carried out in good faith. Courts recognize, however, that reliance on contract rents, particularly those involving property subject to below market long-term leases, may yield distorted valuations and that an assessor, therefore, may apply compensatory measures calculated to adjust such income figures to a point at which they become reliable indicators of full value. It was permissible, therefore, for the board of assessors here to try to accomplish that by tempering its use of rental income with leasehold bonuses in amounts representing the differential between the actual rent and the market rent for each of the three stores in question.

In doing so, the board fulfilled its obligation to assess Merrick's shopping center at full value undiminished by the leases by which the property was burdened. Put another way, all the interests in the property save those assessed separately, such as easements, were to be treated conceptually, for real estate tax purposes, as a single "bundle of rights." Presumably, to the extent that any of the center's leases called for below market rents, that fact would be reflected in a lower value of the landlord's interest and a correspondingly higher value of the tenants' interests. The leasehold bonuses added by the county were designed to take into account the value deriving from the tenants' interests a component of full value that it found did not emerge from actual income figures supplied by the landlord. The utilization of a single assessment encompassing both interests, with the tax payable entirely by the landlord, is consonant with this underlying unitary concept of value.

The net result is that a landlord, despite low income occasioned by below market leases, nevertheless remains obligated to pay taxes on the market value of the property taken as a whole. At first blush, this may appear to penalize the unsuccessful entrepreneur for a lack of business acumen. But it must always be remembered that an underlying aim of valuation is to assure that, in providing for public needs, the share reasonably to be borne by a particular property owner is based on an equitable proportioning of the fair value of his property vis-à-vis the fair value of all other taxable properties in the same tax jurisdiction. Otherwise, the landlord who fails to realize the fair potential of his property would, in effect, shift part of his tax burden to the shoulders of his fellow taxpayers.

We recognize that when it developed its shopping area in 1952 and 1953, Merrick may have been required to grant bargain leases to induce nationally known tenants to locate in its center in the expectation that higher rents could be exacted from smaller stores eager to profit from the greater number of patrons the "flagship" stores would draw. Each of the three key tenants—Food Fair, F. W. Woolworth and National Shoes—is a retail chain organization commanding ready recognition from members of the consuming public. Their leases (and that of one other tenant), in the aggregate, embrace fully 45% of the desirable street level shopping center store area. Besides providing for low rents, the leases negotiated between the three tenants and Merrick lacked escalation clauses affording meaningful protection to the landlord against tax increases or other contingencies. It is not surprising then that the proof showed that during the tax periods in question each of these tenants were paying, for other comparable space in the same county, a prevailing price nearly twice as much.

The fact remains that the advantageous leases were yielded to the three tenants with the landlord's eyes open and no doubt directed towards its own short or long-range profit. The county was not a party to these plans; nor was it, or is it, a coentrepreneur who was required to share in Merrick's good or bad fortune. Clearly, the county tax authorities need not depend for valuation purposes on the uncertain results of managerial banes or boons.

For all these reasons it cannot be said that the board's use of leasehold bonuses was inappropriate. Of course, in arriving at the value of the entire property, if Merrick's leases with its lesser tenants were at above market rents these should be offset against the below market rentals received from the three flagship tenants. In that connection, in remitting for review of the facts we note that, though the record contains proof that the rentals paid by Merrick's numerous lesser tenants were not below market, there is no finding as to whether these exceed market and, if so, the extent to which such excess counterbalanced the below market stream of income that flowed from the three major leases to which the bonuses were applied.

Accordingly, the judgment appealed from and the order brought up for review should be reversed and the matter remitted to the Appellate Division for further proceedings as provided by CPLR 5613.

JASEN, GABRIELLI, JONES, WACHTLER and COOKE, JJ., concur with FUCHSBERG, J.

BREITEL, C.J., concurs in result and so much of the opinion as states the rule that the county is entitled to assess the full value of the property regardless of whether the property is burdened by disadvantageous leases.

NOTES AND QUESTIONS

A. *Decisions in Other Jurisdictions.* Many jurisdictions have faced the problem of valuing property subject to an unfavorable long-term lease, and the majority have followed the approach of the New York court in *Merrick.* E.g., Clayton v. County of Los Angeles, 26 Cal.App.3d 390, 102 Cal.Rptr. 687 (2d Dist. 1972); Valencia Center, Inc. v. Bystrom, 543 So.2d 214 (Fla. 1989); Springfield Marine Bank v. Property Tax Appeal Bd., 44 Ill.2d 428, 256 N.E.2d 334 (1970). However, a minority of jurisdictions have rejected this approach with sufficient force to keep the issue continually open to debate. In C.A.F. Investment Co. v. Saginaw Township, 410 Mich. 428, 302 N.W.2d 164 (1981), the Michigan Supreme Court limited the tax assessment to the value of the owner's interest as diminished by an unfavorable lease. One justice wrote, "[a]dding an enhanced value of the lessee's interest to the lessor's interest where the property is bound to a long-term lease and taxing them together is as unjustified as the Internal Revenue Service saying to a taxpayer that he was imprudent to buy long-term Treasury bonds a number of years ago at 5% when he could now buy 90–day Treasury bills at 15% and that his income from those bonds, for tax purposes, will be deemed to be 15%." Id., 302 N.W.2d at 175 (Levin, J., concurring). Do you agree?

B. *Determination of the Property Subject to Assessment.* Does the fact that the new owner obtained all the rights held by the prior owner establish that a sale conveyed "all the 'bundle of rights' that made up the property"? The Wisconsin Supreme Court took this position in Darcel, Inc. v. City of Manitowoc Board of Review, 137 Wis.2d 623, 405 N.W.2d 344 (1987), agreeing with owners who argued "that they did buy all the 'bundle of rights' that comprised the property. They purchased the land the buildings stood on, the physical plant, the right to the rental income through the leases, and the reversions when the leases expired." Id., 405 N.W.2d at 346. How would you respond?

C. *Taxation of a Tenant Holding a Below–Market Lease.* If the New York approach were rejected, should the tenant be taxed on the property right that it holds? How would the market value of this right be calculated? If the tenant were not taxed, would the owner of identical property leased at full market rents be in a position to argue that this disparity violated a requirement of uniformity?

D. *Assessment of Property Subject to an Above–Market Lease.* How should the assessment of property subject to a long-term lease at *above-*market rents proceed in New York? In states that reject the New York approach?

E. *Significance of Business Judgment in Entering the Lease.* How, if at all, should a finding that a long-term lease was not "improvident when made" influence the outcome of a case of this type?

F. *The Effect of a Clear Rule.* Would your view of the merits of the taxpayer's case be affected by the existence of a clear prior legislative or judicial ruling on this issue?

G. *Cash Flow Options.* In Martin v. Liberty Cty. Bd. of Tax Assessors, 152 Ga.App. 340, 262 S.E.2d 609 (1979), following reasoning similar to that in *Merrick*, the court ruled that valuation of the taxpayer's property could not be reduced by reason of an unfavorable 35–year lease.

> Appellant's argument that consideration should be given to the existence of the lease and its adverse effect on the "fair market value" of the property would focus on what *his* remainder interest in the property would bring at a cash sale. Assuming, however, that the lease results in a decreased value of appellant's interest in the property, there would be a proportional increase in the "fair market value" of the leasehold. The "fair market value" of the estates merge to establish the "fair market value" of the fee.

Id., 262 S.E.2d at 611 (emphasis in original). One of the most intriguing aspects of that case concerned the rent schedule, under which the owner "elected to receive cash payments totaling $216,540 during the first four years of the term and an annual rent in the amount of $2.75 per acre thereafter." Id. at 610. If the owner chose to receive the entire present value of the rent due under a long-term lease at the outset of its term, would there be a basis for valuing the property at the nominal value a prospective purchaser would offer for it?

b. Property Subject to Easements and Use Restrictions

TWIN LAKES GOLF AND COUNTRY CLUB v. KING COUNTY

Supreme Court of Washington, 1976.
87 Wash.2d 1, 548 P.2d 538.

FINLEY, ASSOCIATE JUSTICE.

This is an appeal from a decision of the King County Superior Court declaring that the plaintiff-respondent's golf course has no taxable "fair market value" and that certain real property taxes assessed against the golf course and collected under protest by the county must be refunded to the taxpayer.

The dispositive issue is whether the golf course has a "fair market value" for tax assessment purposes. The property is encumbered with both zoning and conveyancing restrictions regarding use and nonalienation of the realty, and has a history of operating at a substantial, apparently unavoidable, financial loss every year.

On January 1, 1972, the King County Assessor made an assessment regarding the 18–hole golf course owned by Twin Lakes Golf and Country Club for the 1973 tax year. He determined that the golf course had a value of $660,600. The King County Treasurer levied taxes on the golf course in the sum of $16,387.10. The Country Club paid the taxes under protest pursuant to RCW 84.68.020, then unsuccessfully appealed the assessment first to the King County Board of Equalization and then to the State Board of Tax Appeals.

The golf course was constructed and essentially has been operated as an integral part of the Twin Lakes Development, a residential community located in the Federal Way area in South King County. The development is composed of 5 subdivisions which contain 1,006 single-family residential lots, 289 of which are adjacent to the golf course. The realty, i.e., the golf course, subject to the assessment involves no buildings or structures. It includes an irrigation system but otherwise consists solely of fairways, greens, and sand traps and is surrounded by homes in the development.

Four of the subdivisions, together with the golf course, were developed and constructed as a planned unit development (PUD) pursuant to the King County zoning code. To obtain PUD zoning, the developer was required to set aside and reserve certain lands for "common open space" as required by the King County zoning code. The King County Council approved the developer's request and zoned four of the subdivisions, including the golf course, as a PUD. The ordinances adopted by the county required the developer to construct a golf course on the realty and to reserve it for common open space and golf course use for the benefit of the lot owners in the development.

The developer, prior to conveying the lots, filed with the King County Auditor a declaration of covenants, conditions and restrictions which provided that each lot owner would have the right to use and enjoy the golf course. The covenants provided that the restrictions were to run with and bind the land for a period of 20 years and automatically were renewed for 10–year periods unless 75 percent of the lot owners terminated the covenants. The deeds given by the developer to lot purchasers referred to the covenants and with each deed purchasers of a lot acquired the right to become a member of the golf club and to use the golf course. The deeds also referenced certain plat maps. The plat maps were recorded by the developer for all five subdivisions and indicated that the property would remain "open space" land free of buildings and other structures.

The Twin Lakes Golf and Country Club was incorporated in 1966 and since then consistently has incurred losses from the operation of the clubhouse, the golf course, and other club facilities. Primarily as a result of the club's lack of income and because of a lack of data on comparable sales of golf courses, the assessor computed and determined the value of the realty by the cost approach, i.e., cost of reproduction, appraisal method. This method is used by the assessor in valuing all other golf courses in King County, Washington. In computing the value of the golf course, the assessor made no reduction in valuation relative to the restrictions upon the use of the realty created by PUD zoning or the protective covenants or by the recorded plat maps. In the assessor's opinion, these restrictions did not affect the value of the realty.

The trial court found and concluded: (1) These restrictions encumbered the property and made the realty a servient estate for the benefit and use of all lots in the development and substantially and adversely affected the value of the golf course. (2) The Country Club cannot alter the present recreational use of the open space. (3) The club consistently has incurred losses from the operation of the golf course, ranging from $22,331 to $44,734 per year. (4) The use of the property as a golf course has been unprofitable and will continue to produce losses. Finally, the trial court concluded that, as of January 1, 1972, the golf course had no "fair market value" for purposes of the assessment of county real-estate taxes.

RCW 84.40.030 establishes the standard of valuation. It provides, in part: "All property shall be valued at . . . its true and fair value in money and assessed on the same basis unless specifically provided otherwise by law."

The words "true and fair value in money" have consistently been interpreted by our courts to mean "fair market value." Bitney v. Morgan, 84 Wash.2d 9, 14, 523 P.2d 929 (1974). "Market value means the amount of money which a purchaser willing, but not obliged, to buy would pay an owner willing, but not obligated, to sell, taking into consideration all uses to which the property is adapted and might in reason be applied." Mason County Overtaxed, Inc. v. Mason County, 62 Wash.2d 677, 683–84, 384 P.2d 352, 356 (1963). The market value of realty is to be measured by considering benefits to be garnered from the use of the property and the burdens placed upon it. Burdens are restrictions which may arise from zoning ordinances or other legal limitations on the use of land. See Pier 67, Inc. v. King County, 78 Wash.2d 48, 57, 469 P.2d 902 (1970).

In Tualatin Dev. Co. v. Department of Revenue, 256 Or. 323, 473 P.2d 660 (1970), the court concluded that a golf course in a planned adult residential community had no market value for tax purposes. The court reached this result because the use of the land as a golf course had been unprofitable and would continue to be so, zoning restrictions required the property to be maintained as open space, and lots were advertised and sold with reference to the inclusion of the golf course in the development plan. Although King County argues otherwise, we find no significant distinction between the instant case and *Tualatin*. When the use of land is so restricted that its ownership is of no benefit or value, the assessment for tax purposes should be nothing.

An assessment may be set aside if the assessor, by failing to take into account the restrictions on the use of the property and its lack of past and potential profitability, so grossly overvalues the property as to result potentially in a constructive fraud upon its owner.

We are persuaded that the trial court properly concluded (1) that the golf course had no fair market value as of January 1, 1972, and (2) that the taxes in question should be refunded.

The judgment of the trial court should be affirmed. It is so ordered.

STAFFORD, C.J., and ROSELLINI, HUNTER, HAMILTON, WRIGHT, UTTER, BRACHTENBACH and HOROWITZ, JJ., concur.

NOTES AND QUESTIONS

A. *Operation at a Loss as a Business Decision.* In Lomas Santa Fe, Inc. v. Commissioner, 74 T.C. 662 (1980), aff'd, 693 F.2d 71 (9th Cir. 1982), cert. denied, 460 U.S. 1083, 103 S.Ct. 1773 (1983), which dealt with federal income taxation, a real-estate developer seeking to depreciate his retained interest in a subdivision golf course for a term of years explained the business reason for this arrangement. He explained that if he relinquished control over the course, it would not be operated "in the style required for promotion of a luxury residential community," and so could not serve as a "marketing tool and sales vehicle in the offer of residential properties." Id., 74 T.C. at 665, 671. Once all subdivision units had been sold he planned to dispose of his interest in the golf course. Is it possible that if members of the homeowners' association in *Twin Lakes* had been willing to assess themselves higher dues, the annual deficit could have been eliminated? How would you investigate this possibility? How, if at all, should it influence the property tax assessment?

B. *The Aftermath of* Twin Lakes. The dramatic finding of zero value in *Twin Lakes* led to many similar cases, particularly in Washington State. A 1986 book by Carol Logan, Slash Property Taxes (subtitled "Born Free— Taxed to Death") explained the *Twin Lakes* ruling in Chapter 3, "Greenspace Turns to Gold":

Nine state Supreme Court justices threw open the door in 1976. Unanimously upholding the Twin Lakes Golf and Country Club, they handed down a landmark decision. The high court thundered that the King County Assessor's $660,000 valuation was wrong. Greens have zero value. Refund those taxes and cease sending bills, the tribunal ordered. * * * PUDs have blossomed in King County, and elsewhere, suggesting that more common areas could gain zero value, if criteria are satisfied.

Indeed, others jumped on the Twin Lakes bandwagon. Holly Hills Association, for one, gained zero value, forever ending its $184,000 greenspace valuation in 1979. The state board also granted zero value to Innis Arden Club Inc. greenspace in 1978. That meant farewell forever to $354,000 per year. They will pay no taxes on $33.5 million for the first 100 years.

"One who focuses narrowly can reach a conclusion of tax avoidance," Twin Lakes' lawyer John Piper said. "But we proved that the whole PUD brought in more taxes than it would have if each home had taken a little more open space: Value migrated to the home. When their value goes up, taxes go up."

Id. at 23–24.

In Sahalee Country Club, Inc. v. State Board of Tax Appeals, 108 Wash.2d 26, 735 P.2d 1320 (1987), the Washington Supreme Court revisited the controversy surrounding taxation of golf courses and open spaces, emphasizing that *Twin Lakes* sought only to ascertain the market value of the taxable property at issue there rather than to establish a new "zero-value" approach to golf course assessment. In *Sahalee*, the court upheld valuation of a similarly restricted golf course at $3.1 million. This decision was based on testimony that comparable golf courses throughout the country had significant market value, that the course had been pledged as security for a $925,000 loan, and that investors could change the operation of the course into a money-making venture if they chose.

C. *Comparing the Effects of Easements and Leases.* The legal issues in the valuation of property encumbered for the benefit of another taxable parcel are more convoluted than those encountered in the context of a long-term lease. A taxing jurisdiction may take the position that the division of interests between landlord and tenant does not affect the valuation of the property for tax purposes. Refusal to value restricted property at its diminished sale price can be inconsistent, however, with valuation of the benefited parcels (such as the residential lots in *Twin Lakes*) at their enhanced sale price. Yet a legal restriction does not "transfer" some quantity of value from one parcel to another. For examples of other approaches to this problem, see Recreation Centers of Sun City, Inc. v. Maricopa County, 162 Ariz. 281, 782 P.2d 1174 (1989); Lake County Board of Review v. Property Tax Appeal Board, 91 Ill.App.3d 117, 46 Ill.Dec. 451, 414 N.E.2d 173 (1980); Locke Lake Colony Ass'n, Inc. v. Town of Barnstead, 126 N.H. 136, 489 A.2d 120 (1985); and Beckett Ridge Ass'n No. I v. Butler County Board of Revision, 1 Ohio St.3d 40, 437 N.E.2d 601 (1982).

c. Federally Subsidized Low–Income Housing

TOWN SQUARE LIMITED PARTNERSHIP v. CLAY COUNTY BOARD OF EQUALIZATION

Supreme Court of South Dakota, 2005.
2005 S.D. 99, 704 N.W.2d 896.

KONENKAMP, JUSTICE.

In this property tax appeal, we address the valuation of an apartment building operating under the Federal Low Income Housing Tax Credit (LIHTC) program. The question is whether the "true and full value" of this low-income housing property must be calculated using market rent rates or whether the actual reduced rents should be used, and if the latter, whether the tax credits should also be included in the valuation. We conclude that both the restricted rents and the tax credits must be considered when assessing the property. Because these components were not accounted for in the assessment, we reverse and remand.

Background

Town Square Limited Partnership owns two apartment buildings in Vermillion, South Dakota. One building has thirty rental units and the other, forty. In this consolidated appeal, the owners challenge the tax assessments imposed by the Clay County Board of Equalization on the thirty-unit building for the years 2001 and 2002. By agreement of the parties, consideration of the forty-unit apartment building was held in abeyance. The thirty-unit apartment complex was designed to house elderly and disabled residents. It was still under construction on November 1, 2001, and at that time, the building was eighty percent complete. On January 29, 2002, the City of Vermillion issued a certificate of occupancy, but the building did not have occupants until July 2002, and was not fully occupied until December 2002.

Congress enacted the Low Income Housing Tax Credit (LIHTC) to address the nationwide undersupply of affordable housing for low-income people. See 26 USC section 42. By creating equity capital through federal tax credits, this program indirectly subsidizes the purchase, construction, and rehabilitation of low income housing. See Sagit Leviner, Affordable Housing and the Role of the Low Income Housing Tax Credit Program: A Contemporary Assessment, 57 Tax Law. 869 (2004) (citation omitted). In allocating federal tax credits to developers of low cost rental housing and thus reducing investor federal tax liability, the LIHTC grants incentives for private construction. Without these incentives, affordable housing for low income individuals might well become increasingly unattainable. David Philip Cohen, Improving the Supply of Affordable Housing: The Role of the Low–Income Housing Tax Credit, 6 JL & Pol'y 537 (1998).

The LIHTC program is administered by the Department of the Treasury through local state agencies. Our state's official "housing credit agency" is the South Dakota Housing Development Authority. It is responsible for the administration and allocation of South Dakota's tax credits. 26 USC section 42(m). The program offers a ten-year reduction in tax liability for owners of low-income rental housing based on the development costs. Credit-financed apartments cannot be rented to anyone whose income exceeds sixty percent of the area's median gross income. "Under the program, nonprofit organizations form partnerships with for-profit entities [to permit] private equity to reach the project while allowing the project's tax credit allocation to pass through to the for-profit limited partner." Jonathan Penna, Fairness in Valuation of Low–Income Housing Tax Credit Properties: An Argument for Tax Exemption, 11 J Affordable Housing & Cmty Dev L 53 (2001).

Town Square qualified under the program to receive total tax credits of $1,592,630, i.e., $159,263 a year for ten years. Each one-bedroom unit has a rent limitation of $375 per month. If the owners comply with the LIHTC restrictions, tax credits are awarded per unit. The project was structured to require that all the units be occupied by low-income tenants. Failure to comply with the restrictions can trigger recapture of tax credits. Even though the tax credits are only available for ten years, the agreement with the South Dakota Housing Development Authority requires a forty-year restrictive covenant on the apartment building encompassing both income restrictions in eligibility for occupancy and in requirements for charging reduced rents.

Clay County's assessment of the thirty-unit Town Square apartment for November 1, 2001 was $1,189,543, and, for November 1, 2002, $1,251,808. When Town Square protested, the county conceded that the assessments were incorrect. Town Square insisted that the assessment should have been $255,000 for November 1, 2001, and $625,000 for November 1, 2002.

To obtain a professional appraisal, Clay County hired Steven Shaykett, a certified real property appraiser. Shaykett used the three required statutory approaches to determine value: cost, market, and income. SDCL 10–6–33. But he concluded that the "greatest weight and reliability [should be] given to the income capitalization approach." Under this approach, he gave alternative appraisals. The first used market rents; the second, restricted rents. In his final opinion, however, he recommended that only market rents should be used. He also concluded that the value of the tax credits should not be considered because they are "intangibles." Using market rents, Shaykett appraised the property at $732,640 as of November 1, 2001, and $910,000 as of November 1, 2002. Town Square's appraiser, Ritch LeGrand, considered the three required approaches to valuation and, like Shaykett, favored the income approach. Unlike Shaykett, however, he used only the reduced rents required to be charged and appraised the property at $255,000 as of November 1, 2001, and $625,000 as of November 1, 2002. LeGrand gave no consideration to the tax credits in his assessment. * * *

Town Square now appeals, questioning (1) whether the county used the proper methodology in assessing the apartment building; and (2) whether the property should be assessed under the discretionary formula in SDCL 10–6–35.2.

Analysis and Decision

Under Article XI, Section 2, of the South Dakota Constitution, "[t]axes shall be uniform on all property of the same class, . . . and the valuation of property for taxation purposes shall never exceed the actual value thereof." Significant to this case, the same constitutional section also states, "[t]axes may be imposed on any and all property. . . . Gross earnings and net incomes may be considered in taxing any and all property. . . ." Id. By statute, "[a]ll property shall be assessed at its true and full value in money." SDCL 10–6–33. In turn, SDCL 10–6–1(6) defines "true and full value" as "the usual cash selling price at the place where the property to which the term is applied shall be at the time of the assessment." The methods required to calculate full and true value are set forth in SDCL 10–6–33:

> The true and full value shall be determined by appropriate consideration of the cost approach, the market approach and the income approach to appraisal. The director of equalization shall consider and document all elements of such approaches that are applicable prior to a determination of true and full value.

Full and true value is "the price in money that property will bring in a competitive and open market under all conditions requisite to a fair sale between a willing buyer and a willing seller. . . ." SDCL 10–6–1.3; Tax Appeal of Brookings Assoc. v. South Dakota State Bd. of Equalization, 482 N.W.2d 873 (SD 1992); Yadco, Inc. v. Yankton County, 89 S.D. 651, 237 N.W.2d 665 (S.D. 1975). In assessing true value, the appraiser has the duty "to use all of those techniques and facts which accurately reflect 'full and true' value and to reject those which do not." Yadco, 237 N.W.2d at 667 (citing Tidball v. Miller, 72 S.D. 243, 32 N.W.2d 683 (SD 1948)).

In this case, both sides agreed that the income capitalization approach was the most reliable method for determining the true value of the Town Square apartment building. The circuit court implicitly accepted that method when it upheld Shaykett's assessment and therefore we concentrate our analysis on the income approach.

Assessment of Property in the Federal "LIHTC" Program

Town Square argues that the actual restricted rents, rather than hypothetical market rents, should be the measure used in the income capitalization approach. The larger question, however, is whether either or both the reduced rents and the tax credits should be used in the assessment of LIHTC properties. Neither side cites a South Dakota statute or regulation dealing with this specific question. Several other states have addressed the issue either through court decisions or legislation. Before we examine out-of-state decisions, we must take caution to note that these cases might have limited value as precedent because they have often been decided on constitutional and statutory provisions incompatible with our own state's provisions.[2]

Generally, our sister states are divided. But a clear majority of courts have ruled that the restricted rents must be taken into account when assessing LIHTC property. Only a few courts have ruled, like the circuit court here, that the use of the reduced rents is improper because a voluntary agreement by a developer to be bound by the restricted rents is not a "government restriction" requiring consideration of the lower rents. In the Matter of Appeal of The Greens of Pine Glen Ltd. Partnership, the court reasoned that "[u]nlike a governmental restriction such as zoning, [LIHTC] restrictions do not diminish the property's value, but instead balance tax credits allowed to the developer against rent restrictions imposed on the developer," and "[b]ecause [LIHTC] restrictions are freely entered contractual covenants, not governmental regulations," the "taxpayer may not artificially alter the value of [the] property below fair market value." 356 N.C. 642, 576 S.E.2d 316, 322 (2003). See also Alliance Towers Ltd. v. Bd. of Revision, 37 Ohio St.3d 16, 523 N.E.2d 826 (Ohio 1988) (market rental rates should be used; artificial effects of government housing assistance programs are not indicative of real estate valuation).

Several courts hold, in line with what Town Square contends, that the restricted rental rates should be used without consideration of the tax credits or other subsidies. Cottonwood Affordable Housing v. Yavapai, 205 Ariz. 427, 72 P.3d 357 (Tax 2003) (tax credits are nontaxable intangibles); Greenfield Village Apartments, L.P. v. Ada County, 130 Idaho 207, 938 P.2d 1245 (Idaho 1997) (property valuation should consider restrictions on rent; concurring opinion argues that valuation should also include benefits of the tax credits); Maryville Properties, L.P. v. Nelson, 83 S.W.3d 608 (Mo.Ct.App. 2002) (restricted rents must be taken into account, but tax credits cannot be considered); Cascade Court, L.P. v. Noble, 105 Wash. App. 563, 20 P.3d 997 (2001) (same); Metro. Holding v. Milwaukee Review Bd., 173 Wis.2d 626, 495 N.W.2d 314 (1993) (property assessment for low-income housing should be based on actual rents and expenses—not addressing tax credits). Town Square insists that tax credits are not taxable under South Dakota law because they are intangibles.

Indeed, some of these out-of-state decisions hinge solely on the question whether tax credits are intangibles. In *Cottonwood Affordable Housing*, for example, the owner of a LIHTC project in Arizona challenged the county assessor's valuation of $2,121,859. Both sides agreed that the

---

2. A number of states have addressed this issue by legislation. By statute Georgia prohibits the consideration of tax credits. Ga. Code Ann. section 48–5–2(3)(B.1) (2003). Illinois amended its tax laws to exclude LIHTCs from the definition of real property. 35 Ill. Comp. Stat. Ann. 200/1–130 (1999) ("Not included therein are low-income housing tax credits authorized by Section 42 of the Internal Revenue Code, 26 U.S.C. 42."). Wisconsin specifically prohibits assessors from considering LIHTCs. Wis. Stat. section 70.32(1g) (2004) ("the assessor may not consider the effect on the value of the property of any federal income tax credit that is extended to the property owner under section 42 of the Internal Revenue Code").

property should be assessed under the income approach, but disagreed on what types of income should be considered. The property owner thought the valuation should be based on the actual project income and expenses, while the county believed that either regular market rent rates should be used or the tax credits should be also considered. Cottonwood Affordable Housing, 72 P.3d at 359. The court rejected use of the tax credits because they were intangibles, "not an integral part of the real estate", and added no "value [to] the property as their use is limited to ten years. . . ." Id. On the restricted rents issue, the *Cottonwood Affordable Housing* court again agreed with the property owner: "A willing buyer, knowing that there is a restriction as to the amount of rent that can be charged, would pay less for a low income housing project than for a regular commercial apartment complex. This property should not be valued as though a buyer would not consider the restrictions." Id. at 360.

On the other hand, by way of diverse rationales, a number of courts have concluded that the restricted rents and the tax credits should both be factored in the assessment either because (1) the state has a broad definition of real property, (2) when only the reduced rents are considered, the value is artificially depressed, or (3) the value of the tax credits are part of the economic reality of the property. For instance, in Rainbow Apartments v. Illinois Property Tax Appeal Bd., 326 Ill.App.3d 1105, 762 N.E.2d 534, 536–37 (2001), the court held that along with considering the restricted rents, "[i]gnoring the effect of the tax credits would distort the earning capacity, and thus the fair cash value, of the property as low-income housing." A willing buyer, the court reasoned, would surely consider the availability of the credits when determining the fair cash value of the property. Id. at 537. Indeed, although valuation of tax credits can be complex, they are nonetheless transferable under the rules governing LIHTCs: "a purchaser of creditworthy property steps into the seller's shoes with respect to unused credits."[3] J. William Callison, The Effect of Tax Credit Restrictions on Valuation for Real Property Tax Purposes, 5 J. Affordable Housing & Cmty. Dev. L. 32 (1995) (citing 26 USC section 42(d)(7)).

Similar decisions can be found in several other states. In Pine Pointe Housing, L.P. v. Lowndes County Bd. of Tax Assessors, 254 Ga.App. 197, 561 S.E.2d 860, 863 (2002), the court examined a tax statute that required zoning, use restrictions, and "[a]ny other factors deemed pertinent," to be used to consider fair market value. LIHTC credits were deemed pertinent because

> [t]he credits have value to a taxpayer with federal income tax liability and can be "passed through" a partnership structure to those taxpay-ers. . . . [A] third party would pay for the value as part of that property's sale price in a bona fide, arm's length transaction. Further-

---

3. If the taxpayer originally qualifying for the tax credits sells the property and the purchaser continues the low income use, the purchaser can assume the tax position of the seller under 26 USC section 42(d)(7)(A). In some instances, appraisers will use the present value of the tax credits in valuing the property.

more, the tax credits go hand in hand with the restrictive covenants that require the property to charge below-market rent.

Id. at 863. Furthermore, included with the tax credits, the restricted rents should be considered because "[i]f viewed in isolation, the rental restrictions would artificially depress the value of the property for tax valuation purposes." Id.

Likewise, the court in Parkside Townhomes Assoc. v. Bd. of Assessment Appeals of York County, decided that LIHTC credits are properly included in a fair market value because the tax credits were "part of the economic reality." 711 A.2d 607, 611 (Pa.Commw.Ct. 1998). "Tax related benefits associated with investment property ownership inherently affect value and the court is not constrained to determine [fair market value] as though the property lacked tax shelter features." Id. (citation omitted). See also In re Ottawa Housing Assoc., L.P., 27 Kan.App.2d 1008, 10 P3d 777 (2000) (both benefits and burdens of LIHTC housing should be considered). Furthermore, in Spring Hill, L.P. v. Tennessee State Bd. of Equalization, 2003 WL 23099679, *15–17 (Tenn.Ct.App.2003), *Pine Pointe*, and *Rainbow Apartments*, supra, the courts specifically concluded that the tax credits are not intangible property.

For several reasons, we think South Dakota law allows for consideration of both the restricted rental rates and the tax credits for LIHTC properties. First, we need not grapple, as other courts have, with the troublesome question whether these tax credits are intangible property. Out-of-state cases holding that intangible property cannot be taxed are of no value here because, for taxation purposes, South Dakota makes no distinction between tangible and intangible property.[4] Ewert v. Taylor, 38 S.D. 124, 160 N.W.797, 801 (1916). Second, South Dakota has a broad definition of real property that would encompass the tax credits: the definition includes the "[l]and and all rights and privileges thereto belonging[.]" SDCL 10–4–2. Third, the LIHTC program is a method for developers and owners to optimize their real estate investment.[5] See Parkside Townhomes, 711 A.2d at 611. To ignore these credits, which enhance value, would be to ignore the realities of the marketplace. Buyers and sellers most certainly consider the benefits and restrictions that come with LIHTCs in determining the market value of real estate. See Pedcor Investments v. State Bd. of Tax Comm'rs, 715 N.E.2d 432, 437 (Ind.Tax 1999) (tax incentives provide financial benefits counteracting the decreased rental income). Surely Town Square would never have agreed to a covenant requiring forty years of restricted rents without the accompanying benefit of the tax credits. As we indicated, to the extent that they have not been used, these tax credits are transferable to new buyers.

---

4. Even if these tax credits could be designated as intangible property, a distinction can be made between taxing intangible property and considering such credits as a value increasing feature.

5. An argument that the tax credits cannot be considered because these benefits ultimately go to one or more of Town Square's partners and not Town Square itself would be of no merit. "The deed restrictions create financial benefits, and these benefits cannot be ignored simply because they pass through to the partners...." Pedcor Investments, 715 N.E.2d at 438.

Despite compelling reasons for valuing both the tax credits as well as the reduced rent restrictions, we must still address this Court's ruling in *Yadco*. That decision rejected a taxpayer's argument that his property should be appraised using the income approach because he had granted an uneconomical long-term lease on the property. The Court declined this position because "the taxpayer's income approach distorted the result by employing actual income from the lease...." Yadco, 237 N.W.2d at 670 (citations omitted). "[T]he county and the state should not be forced to bear the burden of increased taxation merely because a taxpayer, intentionally or through poor business judgment, has consummated a long-term, uneconomical lease." Id. at 658. Thus, the case instructs us that a property owner can reduce a property's value by imprudently agreeing to rental restrictions with consequent economic loss, but the owner should not be allowed to reduce the tax valuation in such a manner.

We find *Yadco* to be distinguishable. Considered in isolation, reduced rental restrictions would negatively affect the income-producing capacity of the apartment complex and thus its value. But here the agreement to maintain the reduced rents under a restrictive covenant allows Town Square to take advantage of substantial federal tax incentives. These incentives provide financial benefits to Town Square's partners, thus offsetting the decreased rental income.[6] With tax credits allocated to the property, its marketable value increases. Unlike in *Yadco*, Town Square's investors have not intentionally or imprudently diminished the value of the property. They have financed and developed a low income apartment complex that may have otherwise not been economically feasible.

Conclusion

The central issue here is whether the restricted rents imposed on Town Square's building and the federal tax credits enjoyed by the owners affect the value of the property. Those tax credits make ownership of the property more desirable. And because the tax credits can be transferred to purchasers, they enhance the value of the property in the marketplace. We conclude that in assessing this property for property tax purposes, both the tax credits and the restricted rental rates must be considered. In endorsing these considerations, we find nothing inconsistent with our relevant constitutional and statutory provisions. Because the ultimate valuation here failed to consider both the restricted rents and the tax credits, we reverse and remand.[7] * * *

Reversed and remanded.

GILBERTSON, CHIEF JUSTICE, and SABERS, ZINTER, and MEIERHENRY, JUSTICES, concur.

---

6. We do not know to what degree the reduced rents and the tax credits offset each other. That is why it would probably be inappropriate to simply ignore both components in an assessment.

7. Because we reverse the circuit court's approval of Shaykett's appraisal, it does not mean that we endorse LeGrand's appraisal. Neither appraiser used both the reduced rents and the tax credits in their computations.

BRANDON BAY, LIMITED PARTNERSHIP
v. PAYETTE COUNTY

Supreme Court of Idaho, 2006.
142 Idaho 681, 132 P.3d 438.

TROUT, JUSTICE.

This dispute centers on the real property valuations of Brandon Bay and Kenmare Trace, two low-income apartment developments located in Payette County, operating under the provisions of the federal Low–Income Housing Tax Credit program (LIHTC). The principal issue in this case is whether the tax credits allocated under the LIHTC should be included in the real property assessment of the apartments for taxation purposes. Appellants Payette County and Robert Mackenzie, the Payette County Assessor, (collectively, Payette) are before this Court on a permissive interlocutory appeal from a district court decision granting partial summary judgment to Brandon Bay, LP and Kenmare Trace, LP (collectively, Partnerships), the owners of the apartment complexes, concluding the tax credits cannot be considered when valuing the real property.

I.

FACTUAL AND PROCEDURAL BACKGROUND

The Partnerships each entered into an agreement with the Idaho Housing and Finance Association (IHFA), pursuant to § 42 of the Internal Revenue Code (26 U.S.C. § 42), to develop low-income apartment complexes in Payette County. Pursuant to the agreements, a designated portion of the apartment complexes may only be rented to low-income persons who pay a reduced rental rate. In exchange for investing in the low-income housing, the Partnerships are allocated an annual tax credit against federal income tax liability for a period of ten years. The Partnerships claim these tax credits on their limited partnership's tax returns and may apply the credits to tax liability unrelated to the low-income housing projects for which the credits were awarded.

In assessing the low-income apartment complexes for ad valorem tax purposes, Payette considered both the reduced rental payments as well as the value of the tax credits allocated to each property. The Partnerships objected, arguing that although the reduced rents should be considered, the tax credits should not be included in the valuation of the real property. The Board of Tax Appeals disagreed with the Partnerships, affirming Payette's decision to utilize the § 42 tax credits in assessing the apartment complexes. The Partnerships then appealed to the district court, this time arguing the tax credits were simply a contract right and, therefore, were specifically excluded by statute from consideration in assessing the low-income housing. The district court granted the Partnerships' motion for partial summary judgment, agreeing the tax credits were a contract right and therefore excluded from consideration in the assessment. Payette was then granted permission to file this interlocutory appeal.

* * *

III.

ANALYSIS

A. Valuation of Real Property

The Partnerships claim, and the district court agreed, that the § 42 tax credits fall under the definition of "contract rights," a type of exempt "intangible personal property," which IDAPA 35.01.03.615.02 expressly excludes from consideration in the valuation of real property. "Contracts and contract rights" are defined by the Idaho Tax Commission as "enforceable agreements, which establish mutual rights and responsibilities, and rights created under such agreements." IDAPA 35.01.03.615.01(a) (emphasis added). Under the plain language of the rule, a contract right by definition must be created under the contract.

The State, however, has no power to create a federal tax credit and, therefore, such a credit cannot be created by a contract between a State agency and the taxpayer. The authority for creating and imposing federal taxes is vested in Congress. The tax credits are created by Congress in § 42 of the Internal Revenue Code. While it is necessary for IHFA and the developer to enter into a written agreement setting forth the low-income housing requirements and the allocation of the tax credits, this agreement does not create the credits. Instead, it is simply the vehicle through which the developer is able to claim the credits on a federal tax return. Section 42 tax credits are not a contract right exempt from consideration in the valuation of real property.

The tax credits are better characterized as "rights and privileges" belonging to the land under the definition of "real property" in I.C. § 63–201(18), as they do not exist separate from an ownership right in the low-income housing. For example, if the developer originally qualifying for the tax credits sells the property, the purchaser assumes the tax position of the seller: "a purchaser of creditworthy property steps into the seller's shoes with respect to the unused credits." 26 U.S.C. § 42(d)(7). Moreover, the tax credits are only received if the owner continues to comply with the requirements for the low-income housing project as set forth in the agreement with the IHFA and governed by 26 U.S.C. § 42. Even after a taxpayer has used all of the tax credits, if the owner fails to comply with the low-income housing restrictions during the remaining duration of the compliance period, the IRS can recapture the credits. 26 U.S.C. § 42(j)(1).

Because the tax credits are rights and privileges that directly relate to the real estate, they are properly considered in assessing the value of low-income housing. The Idaho Code requires that real property is assessed using its market value. Market value is defined as the amount of money that would exchange hands between a willing seller, under no compulsion to sell, and an informed capable buyer with a reasonable time to consummate the sale. I.C. § 63–201(10). Market value, by definition, captures all benefits flowing from the property. Federal low-income housing tax credits are unquestionably part of the stream of benefits that flow from the property. As a practical matter, the tax credits can be considered equivalent to income.

This Court in Greenfield Vill. Apartments, L.P. v. Ada County, 130 Idaho 207, 938 P.2d 1245 [1997], held that when assessing a § 42 low-income housing project, a tax assessor must take into consideration the rent-restricted use of the property as required by former I.C. § 63–202, which requires the "actual and functional use" of property to be taken into consideration when assessing the land. Payette properly valued the property using the reduced rental rates. If only the reduced rents are considered, however, the value of the land will be artificially depressed and its true market value distorted. Just as it would be inequitable to assess the property based upon full market rental value, because the owners are limited in what they can charge for rent, similarly, it would be inequitable to exclude the value derived from the tax credits, which is acquired by the developer in direct exchange for charging below-market rents. We reverse the district court decision granting partial summary judgment to the Partnerships and hold that in order to accurately assess the true market value of low-income housing property, the value of the § 42 tax credits must be considered.

* * *

Notes and Questions

A. *Relationship to Long–Term Lease Cases.* Consider the income limitations on federally subsidized housing as a form of rent restriction similar to a long-term lease. Should a court's position on the long-term lease question control the valuation of subsidized housing in that state? The Arizona court's reasoning in *Cottonwood Affordable Housing,* quoted in *Town Square,* could apply equally to either situation: "A willing buyer, knowing that there is a restriction as to the amount of rent that can be charged, would pay less for a low income housing project than for a regular commercial apartment complex. This property should not be valued as though a buyer would not consider the restrictions." How does the *Town Square* opinion distinguish *Yadco,* which dealt with a long-term lease?

B. *Taxation of Intangible Property.* As these opinions indicate, state courts are divided on the assessment of low-income housing subject to restricted rents but offering investors income tax credits. A majority of these opinions follow the cases here by taking both the rent restrictions and the tax credits into account in the valuation process, but this result has been reversed by legislative action in a number of states. Decisions that reject consideration of the tax credits generally do so on the grounds, alluded to in both these cases, that the credits constitute intangible property and therefore are not subject to the real property tax. In a case such as this, how would you distinguish a tax on intangible property from a tax on real property whose value is affected by intangible elements?

CHAPTER 10

EXEMPTIONS FROM TAXATION

■ ■ ■

In a broad sense, any article or person or transaction not included within the reach of a tax is exempt from the levy. Thus, real property might be regarded as exempt from a personal property tax. However, the term "exemption" is usually given a narrower meaning, as covering all exclusions from the scope of the subject matter of a tax (e.g., property, income, or transactions) which are logically within the tax base. See Department of Revenue v. ACF Industries, Inc., 510 U.S. 332, 347, 114 S.Ct. 843 (1994) ("the term 'exemption' does not mean every exclusion from the reach of a levy, but rather exclusions of 'property, persons, transactions ... which are logically within the tax base'") (quoting Fifth Edition of casebook). Thus, the exemption of property owned and used by charitable and educational organizations under property taxes, the personal exemption under income taxes, and the exemption of food sales under sales taxes illustrate the meaning of the term exemption as it is commonly employed.

Exemptions may be divided into five categories:[a]

(1) *Exemption to protect the minimum of subsistence.* Income taxes, personal property taxes, and death taxes typically exempt minimum amounts of income or property in order to avoid undue burdens. Exemptions of small amounts of income and property are also important from an administrative point of view.

(2) *Exemption of public property, income, and activities.* The broad basis for the exemption of public property, income, and activities is that in substance the government would be paying itself a tax. This problem in practice is complicated by the existence of numerous governmental units within a state, e.g., county, city, town, village, water district, school district. Thus, a state university or hospital established for the benefit of the entire state obtains fire and police protection and other governmental services from the locality in which it operates. Typically, however, the university or hospital is exempt from local levies as well as state taxes. In the area of state taxation of federal properties and activities, the constitutional doctrine of federal

---

a. This classification is based in part on James W. Martin, "General Theory of Tax Exemption," in Tax Policy League, Tax Exemptions 3 (1939).

immunity from state taxation determines the scope of the exemption. See Chapter 5.

(3) *Exemption of private agencies performing public functions.* The limitations and scope of exemptions for charitable, educational, and public welfare organizations, as well as a host of other quasi-public institutions, varying state by state and tax by tax, account for a substantial amount of litigation in the tax field year in and year out. The revenue losses to states and their subdivisions attributable to this type of exemption, particularly with respect to real property taxes, have caused deep concern to students of state and local finance and have resulted in searching questioning as to the validity and scope of the exemptions. In many states, exemption provisions are written into the constitution so that the courts, in approaching the issues in exemption cases, confront constitutional as well as statutory issues.

(4) *Exemptions as a subsidy of desirable enterprise or activity.* Tax exemption has been widely used in this country as a form of subsidy to encourage activities as widely varied as the location of businesses in an area, slum clearance housing projects, and home ownership (through the homestead exemption). Some observers have criticized the use of tax exemption as a form of indirect subsidy on the ground that it is a crude instrument for encouraging activities, since the amount of the subsidy is ordinarily not completely controlled by the state and there is no check on the relationship between the amount of indirect subsidy and the benefits conferred on the community by the exempt activities or property.

(5) *Exemption of Religious Organizations and Activities.* Exemption of religious organizations and activities from property and other taxes has a long tradition in this country. These exemptions raise thorny questions not only as to the general scope of the exemption but also as to whether the exemptions violate First Amendment principles. See, e.g., Texas Monthly, Inc. v. Bullock, 489 U.S. 1, 109 S.Ct. 890 (1989) (invalidating as an establishment of religion a state sales tax exemption for religious periodicals); Walz v. Tax Commission, 397 U.S. 664, 90 S.Ct. 1409 (1970) (sustaining tax exemption for property of religious organizations used exclusively for religious purposes over objection that it violated Establishment Clause of First Amendment).

A. EDUCATIONAL, CHARITABLE, AND RELIGIOUS ORGANIZATION EXEMPTIONS

EXEMPTIONS TO EDUCATIONAL, PHILANTHROPIC AND RELIGIOUS ORGANIZATIONS

Lucy Winsor Killough.
Tax Policy League, Tax Exemptions 23 (1939).b

* * * Let us consider first the reasons for exempting from taxation private organizations which are supplying services which the State would be called upon to supply if it were not for the private organizations. If private schools, colleges, and charitable institutions were taxed, their services and benefactions would be cut down by the amount of their taxes. Then if the State were to take over some of the functions which these institutions have had to give up because of taxation, there would be no net gain to the community. Money would simply have been put into one pocket and taken out of another. There would even be a net loss to the community if it is true, as tax exemption proponents frequently argue, that private institutions are more efficiently managed than public ones.

So far the argument has assumed that taxation would cut down the amount of service rendered by educational and charitable institutions and that, if taxed, they would continue to function but on a somewhat lesser scale. It is frequently implied, however, that private benefactions would cease if it were not for tax exemptions of contributions to and of the property of these private organizations. Tax exemption is cited as a necessary incentive to private giving, and taxation called a menace to philanthropy. For those who believe that taxation would mark the beginning of the end of privately supported education and charity the justification of exemption is complete. If taxation were to make it necessary for government to supply not only those services formerly rendered with funds not collected in taxes, but also to supply many services formerly rendered through private gifts, governmental costs would increase by an amount materially greater than the new tax collections. It follows from this line of reasoning that the community receives a net profit from tax exemption which is the difference between the total value of the services of the tax-exempt organizations and the cost, in foregone taxes, of the exemption.

The second category of exemptions includes those to religious and other organizations which perform services not likely to be thought of as state functions, although commonly held to be socially desirable. The reasons usually given for these exemptions are more general in nature and somewhat less concerned with dollars and cents. Tax exemption of church property is defended on the ground that religious organizations promote

b. This material is reprinted with the consent of the Tax Institute of America, which was formerly known as the Tax Policy League.

morality and thus further the welfare of the state. It is said that without the influence of religion "the whole framework of our civilization would be severely threatened," and that "religion and morality are essential * * * to the very existence of the organic state."

The aspect of the present method which is most in need of modification concerns the problem of control. If an institution falls within a category generally accepted as educational, benevolent, literary, charitable, or whatever fits into a particular legally accepted vocabulary, it is automatically exempted from taxation by constitutional or legislative requirement. There is no way of effectively considering the question as to whether the community or the tax-exempt organization would make best use of the money not paid in taxes at a particular time. The mildest reform would provide for periodic evaluations of the status of even the most deserving recipients of exemption. Similarly no additions should be made to the tax-exempt list without careful evaluation, if, in fact, they should be made at all. These minor changes would require constitutional amendment in many States and the repealing of existing and enactment of new legislation by others and by the federal government. Educational institutions can scarcely uphold their status as bulwarks of democracy if they are unwilling to subject their efforts to this small measure of democratic control.

* * *

This is probably too half-hearted a measure. It might be better if all individuals and institutions paid taxes without exemptions for any contribution to, or expenditure for, however charitable or educational a purpose. When the indirect subsidies had been disposed of in this way the question of direct grants should be considered. In response to a plea for exemptions from a group of hospitals the special California Tax Commission of 1929 stated:

> It is the feeling of the Commission that the exemptions should be curtailed, rather than extended, but it also realizes the extreme difficulty of bringing about such a contraction. With respect to the plea of the hospitals, to which it has given sympathetic study, it has concluded that, while it cannot recommend any expansion of the exemption list, it does desire to record its conviction that recognition should be given to the public importance of the work of certain of these institutions through more liberal public grants and payments where activities of these institutions clearly have the effect of caring for cases which otherwise would be a charge on the public funds.

This recommendation might well be heeded by other States and applied not only to hospitals but also to other organizations.

There are a number of advantages in direct grants. They provide for continuous evaluation of the merits of particular projects. They might be made by more appropriate jurisdictions than frequently happens at present with many communities granting enormous indirect subsidies to institutions largely used by people from other regions. Direct grants would make evident the real financial relationship between the institutions and the community. Direct grants might be a simpler way of distinguishing between functions entitled to public support and those not so entitled than an attempt partially to tax and partially to exempt institutions performing such mixed functions. It seems to the writer that these advantages outweigh the disadvantages many of which have been suggested in the foregoing pages.

There is little reason to believe that any such great change in present practice is probable in the near future. The difficulties involved are emotional as well as legal and financial. The first step should be the prevention of increases in the exemptions, to be followed as far as possible by their gradual elimination.

B. PROPERTY TAXES

In addition to a full exemption for various classes of religious, educational, charitable, and governmental property, most states offer an array of partial property tax exemptions and reductions to benefit taxpayers deemed needy, worthy, or politically powerful, such as widows, veterans, and homeowners. All states offer tax reduction programs for qualifying farmland whose value in agricultural use is less than its market value for development.

Two of the most important other tax relief measures are "circuit breakers" and homestead exemptions. Circuit breakers limit property taxes to a designated percentage of income; as their name implies, they are designed to protect against a tax overload. They generally are administered and financed by the state through an income tax credit, although some are designed as independent programs. As in the case of other programs administered through income tax credits, special efforts are required to reach potential recipients who do not file income tax returns. See generally John H. Bowman, et al., Property Tax Circuit Breakers: Fair and Cost–Effective Relief for Taxpayers (2009).

Homestead exemptions or credits are the most common form of residential property tax relief. They reduce the tax on qualifying residential property, either by exempting a portion of its value or by extending a credit against the tax. These may be limited to certain groups of taxpayers, such as low-income, elderly, or disabled homeowners, or they may apply to all owner-occupied residences. Some states provide tax relief to renters as well, through an income tax deduction. Although the revenue loss from circuit-breaker programs is generally borne by state governments, the cost of homestead allowances usually falls on localities.

An exemption from property taxes generally does not carry with it an equivalent exemption from special assessments, which are imposed to cover the cost of specific public improvements, such as sidewalks or street lighting. Special assessments are often allocated among the benefitted properties according to a physical measure, such as street frontage, rather than valuation.

Taxation of partial interests in exempt property is the rule rather than the exception when an exempt organization leases its property for commercial use. Even when the underlying full ownership interest cannot be taxed, the leasehold may be taxed, and may in fact be assigned a value equivalent to the full value of the property. This situation has arisen frequently with respect to Federal Government property leased to defense contractors. Although the federal interest is immune from state and local tax, City of Detroit v. Murray Corp., 355 U.S. 489, 78 S.Ct. 458 (1958), discussed on pp. 317–18 supra, held that a tax on the non-exempt use could be equivalent to the value of the property itself. Where such a tax is imposed, the taxing jurisdiction has no ability to seize the underlying federal property as a means of enforcing payment of the tax on the leasehold. Nor may leased federal property be taxed if property leased from state or local governments is exempt. The immunity of federal property from state taxation is considered in more detail in Chapter 5.

1. OWNERSHIP AND USE TEST OF THE PROPERTY TAX EXEMPTION

CHRISTIAN HOME FOR THE AGED, INC. v. TENNESSEE ASSESSMENT APPEALS COMMISSION

Court of Appeals of Tennessee, Middle Section, at Nashville, 1990.
790 S.W.2d 288.

CANTRELL, JUDGE.

This is an appeal from a judgment of the Chancery Court of Davidson County which upheld a decision of the Tennessee Assessment Appeals Commission denying the tax exemption of the plaintiff's property except for its chapel which is used for religious purposes and its nursing facility which is a licensed provider of health care.

Facts

The findings of fact made by the commission are uncontroverted and were adopted by the trial court and are hereinafter restated in pertinent part.

The plaintiff, Christian Home for the Aged, Inc., d/b/a Appalachian Christian Village, is a retirement community in Johnson City, Tennessee. It opened in 1966 under the sponsorship of a group of the Christian Churches and Churches of Christ. It is a nonprofit Tennessee corporation that is exempt from federal income taxation under Section 501(c)(3) of the Internal Revenue Code. The corporation is governed by a board of directors whose members are elected by the churches that make financial contributions to the Village. Donations totaled $178,700.00 in 1985 when the total income was $2,637,658.36, excluding entrance fees and donations. Donations in 1987 were three percent of the total income.

All residents must be 62 years of age or over. The Village provides three types of living arrangements depending upon the mental and physical conditions of the resident. Those capable of independent living reside in either the towers, townhouses, or cottages. Persons requiring some assistance in housekeeping, cooking or other necessary daily activities live in the efficiency apartments. And those persons who need nursing care reside in the nursing home.

* * *

In determining whether to accept an applicant for residence in the Village, the board of directors of the Village considers the applicant's moral character, recommendation of the Christian Church or the Church of Christ, his or her physical condition and financial condition.

Residents of the towers, townhouses and cottages make a one time nonrefundable donation to the Village of $62,500 to $67,500, which guarantees lifetime healthcare. As the resident's physical and mental health deteriorates, the resident may move to other units in the Village, without additional charge, except for meals. When the resident vacates a unit, the unit reverts to the Village to be resold.

The residents also pay monthly maintenance fees for townhouses and cottages of $60.00 and $80.00 for the towers. They also pay their pro rata share of the real property taxes.

Residents of the efficiency apartments are not requested to make the "one-time donation," but they pay rent of $485 to $780 per month. If applicable, there is a nursing facility fee of $37.00 per day plus the costs of meals and drugs.

Officials of the Village do not recall refusing an applicant for residence due to inability to pay the fees, yet the ability to pay is a factor in the evaluation of an application. The only example given of subsidization was the recent sale of a cottage for $55,000 when the Village would have asked $65,000 if the applicant could have afforded that much. The Village does not impose any upper limits on financial ability and does accept wealthy persons. The amount of the "donation" or fee for residency is determined by the Village's projection of the costs of operating the facility.

* * *

Dr. O.H. Oliveira, a licensed clinical psychologist, presented testimony as an expert in geriatrics and gerontology on the problems of aging. Dr. Oliveira testified that the Village addresses special needs of the elderly by furnishing residents with opportunities for recreation, social activities and spiritual growth.

In the absence of a community environment, isolation and loneliness can lead to health problems for the elderly including dizziness, chest pains, headaches and loss of memory. Dr. Oliveira testified that these health problems associated with isolation occur far less frequently where elderly people live in a community environment and have ready access to social interaction. Persons living independent of such a community statistically do not live as long, suffer more health problems, and are hospitalized for medical problems longer than persons living in a structured environment such as that provided by Appalachian Christian Village.

Exemption from Property Taxation

Article 2, § 28 of the Constitution of the State of Tennessee provides that "all property real, personal or mixed shall be subject to taxation, but the Legislature may except ... such as may be held and used for purposes purely religious, charitable, scientific, literary or educational, ..."

The legislature exercised their power to grant a tax exemption by enacting Tenn.Code Ann. § 67–5–212 (1989) which states:

> (a)(1) There shall be exempt from property taxation the real and personal property, or any part thereof, owned by any religious, charitable, scientific or nonprofit educational institution which is occupied and used by such institution or its officers purely and exclusively for carrying out thereupon one or more of the purposes for which the institution was created or exists....

We should point out that in this state the exemption in favor of a religious, scientific, literary, or educational institution is liberally construed, Mid–State Baptist Hospital, Inc. v. City of Nashville, 211 Tenn. 599, 366 S.W.2d 769 (1963), whereas there is a presumption against exempting other property from taxation. United Canners, Inc. v. King, 696 S.W.2d 525 (Tenn.1985).

The plaintiff claims that its property is entitled to an exemption as religious and/or charitable property; that is, because the property is used purely and exclusively for those purposes.

Religious Exemption

A religious institution's realty is exempt from property taxation only when it is both occupied and used exclusively by the institution for one of its charter purposes, and the exemption is denied not only to property leased by it to others, but also to property occupied by it but not used exclusively for a charter purpose. City of Nashville v. State Board of Equalization, 210 Tenn. 587, 360 S.W.2d 458 (1962).

Conceding that the plaintiff may be a religious institution, we do not think that the property in question is used purely and exclusively for a religious purpose. "The exclusive use requirement has been interpreted to refer to the direct, physical use of property ..." Book Agents of Methodist Episcopal Church South v. State Board of Equalization, 513 S.W.2d 514, 523 (Tenn.1974). In another case, the receipt of rent disqualified the property from an exemption under Tenn.Code Ann. § 67–5–212. In City of Nashville v. State Board of Equalization, parts of a religious institution's realty used by it for purposes of operating an automobile parking lot, a cafeteria and a snack bar were not "used exclusively" for a religious purpose, within the exemption provisions of the statute.

In Tusculum College v. State Bd. of Equalization, 600 S.W.2d 739 (Tenn.App.1980), the court held that where college-owned residences were occupied for residential purposes and not for purposes of student instruction, and where the college received rent from all occupants other than the president, the property was not exempt from property taxes under Tenn. Code Ann. § 67–5–212 except for one-half of the president's home found to be used for college purposes.

The residents of Appalachian Christian Village pay substantial sums of money to live in the Village. In addition, the towers, townhouses, cottages and efficiency apartments are occupied primarily for residential purposes and not to further any religious purpose within the meaning of the statute.

We agree with the chancellor that the chapel is the only part of the Village which qualifies for the religious exemption.

Charitable Exemption

A charitable institution is defined in Tenn.Code Ann. § 67–5–212(c) as "any nonprofit organization or association devoting its efforts and property, or any portion thereof, exclusively to the improvement of human rights and/or conditions in the community." Again, we would concede, for the purposes of argument, that the plaintiff as an institution fits the statutory definition. That, however, completes only the first step toward a finding that the plaintiff's property is exempt from taxation.

The next step is to determine if the use it makes of its property is purely and exclusively charitable. North Gates Elks Club v. Garner, 496 S.W.2d 887 (Tenn.1973).

While the plaintiff argues that Tenn.Code Ann. § 67–5–212(c) makes the use of its property a charitable one, we think the statute refers only to what constitutes a charitable organization and not to what is a charitable use. If the plaintiff's contention were to be followed then any number of retirement villages could be said to be devoting their property to a charitable use.

* * *

Although Appalachian Christian Village serves the elderly by providing a community in which their special needs can be met, it extends this benefit selectively. The "donations" and rent required are substantial and there has been only one example of subsidization given by the plaintiff. Applications for admission to the Village are scrutinized for financial ability as well as moral character and physical condition. Rarely is a resident directly admitted into the nursing facility. Thus, though the benefits of the Village are significant, only those who are financially and physically well off can receive them. Those less healthy and wealthy are not benefited.

Although it is true that a charitable institution does not lose its charitable character and exemption from taxation because financially able patients are required to pay, Baptist Hospital v. City of Nashville, 156 Tenn. 589, 3 S.W.2d 1059 (1928), in this case financially disabled members of the public are effectively excluded from the benefits provided by the plaintiff.

For these reasons, we do not believe the Village's property is used purely and exclusively for a charitable purpose.

Our review of the record indicates that the chancellor was correct in finding that the decision of the Assessment Appeals Commission denying the exemption of the plaintiff's property, except for the chapel and nursing facility, was supported by substantial and material evidence in the record.

* * *

KOCH, J., and JOE C. LOSER, JR., SPECIAL JUDGE, concur.

NOTES AND QUESTIONS

A. While some states grant a property tax exemption to property owned by religious, charitable, philanthropic, or other exempt organizations, regardless of the use to which the property is put, most ad valorem exemptions, like those at issue in the *Christian Home* case, require not only that the property be owned by an exempt organization, but also that it be used for exempt purposes. See, e.g., Supervisor of Assessments of Montgomery County v. Asbury Methodist Home, Inc., 72 Md.App. 352, 529 A.2d 852, 860 (1987) (sustaining property tax exemption for apartment buildings for elderly that were " 'actually used exclusively for' * * * the charitable purposes of the * * * enterprise"); Full Gospel Apostolic Church v. Limbach, 46 Ohio St.3d 195, 546 N.E.2d 403 (1989) (denying property tax exemption for land used by church during annual revival but farmed for profit at other times). Consequently, the large properties owned by churches, universities, and other philanthropic organizations but held merely for investment and rented for the income produced are typically found on the tax rolls, even though the rental income is devoted to the exempt purposes. See Annot., 54 A.L.R.3d 504. Apart from the question of the wisdom of a policy that exempts property held for investment but whose income is used to carry out the exempt purpose, the ownership-without-use test lends itself to manipulation of "ownership" in order to retain the exemption.

The *Christian Home* court ostensibly denied the exemption to the taxpayer not because it was not a religious or charitable organization, but rather because the use made of the property was not exclusively for religious or charitable purposes. But is the court's opinion faithful to that rationale? The court concedes, "for the purposes of argument, that the plaintiff as an institution fits the statutory definition" of a charitable institution and then declares that "the next step is to determine if the use it makes of its property is purely and exclusively charitable." But how does the court make that determination? Is the court confusing the definition of a charitable organization with the use that such an organization makes of its property?

B. *Property Leased by One Exempt Organization to Another Exempt Organization.* Suppose an educational organization rents a building to another educational organization; does the property lose its exempt status? Is it necessary that the building be used for the owning corporation's own exempt purposes? See Board of Supervisors v. Medical Group Foundation, Inc., 204 Va. 807, 134 S.E.2d 258 (1964) (sustaining exemption for property owned by one charitable corporation and leased to another charitable corporation for exclusively charitable uses); Annot., 55 A.L.R.3d 430; Annot., 54 A.L.R.3d 402. If a charitable organization derives profit from a lease, why should it matter, for purposes of the lessor's exemption, whether the property is leased to another charity or to a private lessee? What is the policy behind denying a charitable organization's use of property for noncharitable purposes, even when the proceeds from such use are dedicated to the organization's charitable purposes?

C. *Partial Exemptions.* In most states, the courts have construed the statutes as providing for partial exemption of property owned by an exempt organization but used only in part of exempt purposes. Chicago Patrolmen's Assoc. v. Department of Revenue, 269 Ill.App.3d 274, 206 Ill.Dec. 544, 645 N.E.2d 549 (1994); Columbus Board of Education v. Tracy, 73 Ohio St.3d 75, 652 N.E.2d 661 (1995). In Defenders of the Christian Faith v. Board of County Commissioners, 219 Kan. 181, 547 P.2d 706 (1976), on the other hand, the court, while acknowledging that the weight of authority was against it, nevertheless held that because one floor of a building was not severable, the entire building lost its tax exemption. The court relied in part on the fact that the state assessment and collection statutes contained no procedure for separately assessing a portion of a building under one ownership.

D. *The Construction of Exemption Provisions.* Courts frequently quote the following statement from Cooley in construing exemptions:

> In other words, since taxation is the rule, and exemption the exception, the intention to make an exemption ought to be expressed in clear and unambiguous terms; it cannot be taken to have been intended when the language of the statute on which it depends is doubtful or uncertain; and the burden of establishing it is upon him who claims it.

2 Thomas Cooley, The Law of Taxation § 672 (4th ed. 1924). Is this rule a proper and helpful tool in deciding exemption issues?

2. THE DELINEATION OF EXEMPT ACTIVITIES

DOVE LEWIS MEMORIAL EMERGENCY VETERINARY CLINIC, INC. v. DEPARTMENT OF REVENUE

Supreme Court of Oregon, 1986.
301 Or. 423, 723 P.2d 320.

GILLETTE, JUSTICE PRO TEM.

Taxpayer, Dove Lewis Memorial Emergency Veterinary Clinic, Inc., appeals from a judgment of the Oregon Tax Court denying its claim to a real property tax exemption for the tax year 1981–82. 10 OTR 33 (1985). The Tax Court ruled that taxpayer was not entitled to the exemption because it did not qualify as a charitable corporation. Pursuant to ORS 305.445, we review anew upon the record to determine whether taxpayer is a charitable corporation and thereby eligible for the tax exemption. We agree that it is not eligible and therefore affirm.

The relevant facts are as follows: In 1965, a group of Portland area veterinarians who were members of the Portland Veterinary Medical Association (PVMA) attempted to provide an emergency service for the treatment of small animals. The service was available after the veterinarians' normal hours of operation; participating veterinarians volunteered their services and agreed to share on-call responsibilities. The system proved to be inefficient due, in large part, to the refusal of some members to respond to calls.

During the ensuing years, one of taxpayer's eventual founders, Dr. Werner, discussed the prospect of forming an emergency clinic with other local veterinarians but could not generate enough interest or financial backing. However, in 1973, a local dog breeder named Lewis contacted Werner and offered to donate a sum of money to start up the clinic as a memorial to his late wife.

Taxpayer was formed under ORS chapter 61 as a nonprofit organization. The Internal Revenue Service granted it nonprofit status on February 26, 1974, exempting it from federal income tax under Section 501(c)(3) of the Internal Revenue Code.

Taxpayer operated its clinic out of a rented building in downtown Portland for approximately seven years, realizing a profit in each year. In 1980, it purchased the subject property and facility with funds derived in part from the net revenues received in the preceding seven years of operation. A small but undetermined amount was made up of donations. Most of the funds, however, came from a loan obtained from a bank.

Taxpayer currently employs a full-time staff consisting of five veterinarians, eight technicians, one secretary and one business administrator. All are paid salaries comparable to persons similarly employed at other veterinary facilities. Taxpayer is open for business from 6 p.m. to 8 a.m. Monday through Thursday, from 6 p.m. Friday through the weekend, and 24 hours on holidays.

In March, 1981, taxpayer submitted an application pursuant to ORS 307.162[1] to Multnomah County for exemption from property tax. On July 7, 1981, Multnomah County informed taxpayer that its application for exemption from property tax was denied. On appeal to the Department of

---

1. ORS 307.162 provides, in pertinent part:

"Before any real property may be exempted from taxation under ORS 307.127, 307.130 to 307.140, 307.150 or 307.160 for any year, the institution or organization claiming the exemption shall file with the county assessor, on or before April 1 in such year, a statement verified by the oath or affirmation of the president or other proper officer of the institution or organization, listing all real property claimed to be exempt and showing the purpose for which such property is used. * * * *"

Revenue, the Department affirmed the Multnomah County Assessor's opinion and denied taxpayer's request for exemption. Taxpayer then filed this case. The Tax Court affirmed the opinion of the Department on February 26, 1985. The present appeal followed.

Taxpayer seeks exemption from payment of ad valorem taxes on its real and personal property pursuant to ORS 307.130, which provides, in pertinent part:

> "Upon compliance with ORS 307.162, the following property owned or being purchased by incorporated literary, benevolent, charitable and scientific institutions shall be exempt from taxation:
>
> (1) * * * only such real or personal property, or proportion thereof, as is actually and exclusively occupied or used in the literary, benevolent, charitable or scientific work carried on by such institutions.
>
> (2) Parking lots used for parking or any other use as long as that parking or other use is permitted without charge."

Taxation is the rule and exemption from taxation is the exception. Corporation of Sisters of Mercy v. Lane County, 123 Or. 144, 152, 261 P. 694 (1927). The burden of establishing entitlement to an exemption is on the taxpayer claiming the exemption. Oregon Methodist Homes, Inc. v. Tax Com., 226 Or. 298, 307, 360 P.2d 293 (1961).

Taxpayer's primary contention is that it is a hospital and that the cases considering the eligibility of hospitals to a charitable exemption are controlling. Of course, the mere fact that an organization is either a hospital or a charity does not establish any inherent right to exemption. Any organization claiming the benefit of the tax exemption statute as a "charitable" institution must have charity as its primary, if not sole, object, and must be performing in a manner that furthers that object.

The articles and bylaws of a corporation are prima facie evidence of the character of the corporation. Foundation of Human Understanding v. Dept. of Rev., 301 Or. 254, 722 P.2d 1 (1986) (articles); Benton County v. Allen, 170 Or. 481, 485, 133 P.2d 991 (1943) (articles); Hamilton v. Corvallis General Hosp. Ass'n., 146 Or. 168, 171–72, 30 P.2d 9 (1934) (articles and bylaws).

Taxpayer's bylaws state:

> "The primary objective of the Clinic shall be to provide emergency veterinary service for small animals directed primarily to those hours when the private clinics would not be operating and on weekends, and in addition thereto, to provide further educational facilities for the dissemination of literature, library and other facilities and any other lawful purpose as set out in the Articles of Incorporation."

Taxpayer is organized to provide "emergency small animal veterinary service." One of the principal founders of taxpayer testified that it was formed "probably out of frustration more than anything else," referring to the failed attempt to provide an all-volunteer after-hours emergency service. Although taxpayer's expressed purpose is beneficial, we cannot say that it is as a matter of law "charitable," as that term is used in ORS 307.130. Neither, however, do the articles and bylaws eliminate taxpayer as a charity. We turn to a consideration of whether taxpayer's activities are sufficiently charitable to entitle it to exemption.

In determining whether an organization is, by its conduct, charitable, the crucial consideration is the element of a gift or giving.

> "This is a sound and salutary rule. It is one reflecting human experience. Unselfish declarations of intended purpose and promises of future worthy endeavor are many times rendered meaningless by inaction and should give the declarer no preferred status unless ultimately resolved into concrete and tangible reality." Oregon Methodist Homes, Inc. v. Tax Com., supra, 226 Or. at 308, 360 P.2d 293.

In Oregon Methodist Homes, Inc. v. Tax Com., supra, this court reviewed the line of "hospital" cases and outlined six factors that are relevant in determining the charitable character of a hospital:

> (1) Whether the receipts are applied to the upkeep, maintenance and equipment of the institution or are otherwise employed;

> (2) Whether patients or patrons receive the same treatment irrespective of their ability to pay;

> (3) Whether the doors are open to rich and poor alike and without discrimination as to race, color or creed;

> (4) Whether charges are made to all patients and, if made, are lesser charges made to the poor or are any charges made to the indigent;

> (5) Whether there is a charitable trust fund created by benevolently and charitably minded persons for the needy or donations made for the use of such persons; and

> (6) Whether the institution operates without profit or private advantages to its founders and the officials in charge. 226 Or. at 309–10, 360 P.2d 293 (Citations omitted).

Even after listing these factors, however, this court issued a precautionary note:

> "We do not hold that all the foregoing factors must be present before a given institution can be declared one of charitable or non-charitable pursuits. Nor do we say that the list includes all items which may assist in a conclusion respecting the charitable or noncharitable status of a given corporation. The itemization represents only those particulars which have been in the past employed by this court in discovering if a given hospital is or is not in fact eleemosynary." 226 Or. at 310, 360 P.2d 293.

In this court's enunciation of the factors to be considered, we noted in *Methodist Homes* that, although all of the factors need not be present, the absence of two factors can negate any claim to exemption. The two factors are the existence of a separate account containing funds and donations committed to charitable use and the absence of profit or private advantage to the organization's founders and officials. 226 Or. at 311, 360 P.2d 293. On our review of the record, we find no testimony or evidence to indicate whether a fund was established for the original donation by Lewis or for any subsequent funds received by taxpayer to be administered for the benefit of any charitable purpose. The only reference to a fund is that of a "building fund," consisting of monies derived from operating revenue and some donations of an undetermined amount.

Concerning profit and private advantage, witnesses for taxpayer testified that the clinic is a nonprofit corporation, that all receipts generated are put back into the clinic to purchase new equipment and property and to cover operating expenses, that no dividends are declared or bonuses paid to directors or members of the organization and that the organization has no capital stock. Taxpayer therefore asserts that no founders or officials of the corporation derive any profit or private advantage from the clinic. However, the gain, profit, or private advantage derived need not be solely pecuniary. For example, in Ackerman v. Phys. & Surgeons Hosp., supra, this court held that a bylaw provision that vested lifetime control in the founders of the corporation and allowed them to designate their successors in a will were "elements of valuable private advantage which a jury might properly consider. * * *" 207 Or. at 664–65, 288 P.2d 1064.

Despite taxpayer's contention to the contrary, we find that here, as in *Ackerman*, the operation of its clinic bestowed certain benefits and private advantages on its founders and officials. Taxpayer's business manager testified on direct examination as follows:

"Q. * * * If an animal comes in and is injured, what happens? What takes place in the Clinic with respect to an animal that comes in that's injured and needs medical care?

"A. First, we examine it and we discuss with the owner the extent of the injuries and the extent of the work that will need to be done and get permission to treat the animal and if we treat it it depends on the time of the night how long the animal stays. If it has to be watched constantly we will keep it until the next morning.

"Q. Then what happens to that animal?

"A. The owner picks up the animal and takes it on to the veterinarian of their choice.

"Q. Okay, so it's just purely emergency until they can get to their—to their own—

"A. Right.

"Q.—veterinarian? *What if they don't have a veterinarian?*

"A. *We provide them with a list of all the veterinarians in the area.*

"Q. *Okay. Do you direct them to any particular veterinarian or just provide a list?*

"A. *No, we just give them a list.*

"Q. *Okay. Now does this list include members of the Portland Veterinary Medical Association? [PVMA]*

"A. *Yes, it does.*

"Q. Does it also include nonmembers?

"A. Yes." (Emphasis supplied.)

Taxpayer's Board of Directors is composed of five members who are elected by members of the PVMA. Of all the veterinarians in the Portland area, half were members of PVMA. It is likely that taxpayer's founders and officials derive a private advantage or benefit from the clinic's client referral process for follow-up treatment or care.

Reviewing the record, we have found other factors which deserve comment. Although the initial donation by Lewis to start up the clinic may have been given in the spirit of charity, taxpayer was formed with the expectation that it would be self-sufficient. As a consequence, its fee schedule was, and is, structured to cover all costs. Unlike most charitable corporations, which depend on the receipt of donations for their survival, taxpayer's reliance on such funding is minimal. Although the fact that a corporation makes a profit or charges a fee for its services does not necessarily vitiate its claimed status as charitable, it is a factor to be considered in the context of the corporation's manner of operation. Ackerman v. Phys. and Surgeons Hosp., supra, 207 Or. at 665–66, 288 P.2d 1064.

We also find from the record that it is only when an individual pet owner says that he or she cannot afford payment that any mention of free or discounted services—the taxpayer's alleged principal charitable activity—occurs. Moreover, taxpayer could not offer any specific examples or documentation that it actually provided free services to indigent pet owners. It appears that, in accordance with taxpayer's business procedures, the rendering of free or discounted services occurs only by happenstance, if at all.

Relief of a government burden is also an indicator of giving. This court stated in Friendsview Manor v. State Tax Com., 247 Or. 94, 105–06, 420 P.2d 77, 427 P.2d 417 (1966), that one reasonable explanation for the government's decision to exempt charitable enterprises from the payment of taxes is that "if such enterprises did not exist the government would be required to use tax dollars to do the job the charitable enterprises are now doing." See also Methodist Book Concern v. Galloway, 186 Or. 585, 597, 208 P.2d 319 (1949). Taxpayer claims that, if relief of a government burden is a factor to be considered, it meets that criterion in that it relieves Multnomah County of a financial and service-related burden by offering small animal examination and treatment services at a rate below its normal fee.

First of all, we are not convinced that, in the absence of taxpayer, the county would feel required to offer similar services. Secondly, the evidence simply does not establish that taxpayer relieves the county of any appreciable burden. Under a contract between taxpayer and the county, taxpayer charges the county $15 for services that other veterinarians, during their hours of operation, provide free of charge. In addition, taxpayer benefits from a service the county provides at no charge, i.e., the removal of dead animals, a service that taxpayer previously paid up to $800 per month to receive. The "relief of a government burden" approach of *Friendsview Manor* is a one-way street: it may help an organization establish it is a charity, but failure to relieve a government burden is not a mark against such an organization. Even as so viewed, however, it is not a street down which this taxpayer can go. It relieves no government burden.

We acknowledge that taxpayer does meet some of the requirements of a charitable organization. However, while taxpayer's activities are worthwhile and commendable, we cannot say that, in view of all the factors we have examined, taxpayer has carried its burden of qualifying as a "charitable" institution under ORS 307.130.

The Tax Court is affirmed.

NOTES AND QUESTIONS

A. *The Establishment of Standards of Public Service to Qualify for Exemption.* The traditional justification for tax exemption of educational institutions, hospitals, parks, libraries, orphanage homes, and other charitable institutions and their properties and income is that the educational or charitable organizations are performing public functions and rendering public services that relieve the state of financial burdens. Should this general, indiscriminate grant of exemption to institutions engaging in educational or charitable functions, limited only by requirements in many states that the property be used exclusively for such general purposes and that no private individual receive any part of the corporation's net earnings, be completely overhauled in the light of modern needs and developments? Exemption of the property of a particular type of institution may or may not be the best way for the community to spend the tax funds thereby lost by the local government. Some have urged that the elected or appointed representatives of the state or locality, not a group of private trustees, should determine the public or charitable uses to which a particular property is put, in order to be relieved of the duty of paying taxes, and that exemption should be subject to state supervision, so as to require the exempt taxpayers to live up to standards which should be set by state law. With government increasingly shouldering the burden of providing much of what used to be in the hands of private institutions—e.g., unemployment insurance, old age pensions, public hospitals, libraries, and social welfare agencies—should the private institutions which seek tax exemption be required to demonstrate the need for dedication of the property to the particular use and to maintain specified standards in providing their services? For an excellent analysis of this problem in the federal income tax context, see Boris I. Bittker & George K. Rahdert, "The

Exemption of Nonprofit Organizations from Federal Income Taxation," 85 Yale L.J. 299 (1976).

B. *Exemptions of Property Dedicated to Future Exempt Uses.* In Weslin Properties, Inc. v. Illinois Department of Revenue, 157 Ill.App.3d 580, 109 Ill.Dec. 696, 510 N.E.2d 564 (1987), the court held that although the taxpayer had not started to build an urgent care center and the attendant roads and parking facilities, it was nevertheless entitled to a charitable exemption for the property it had purchased for the facility. The court based its decision on the fact that significant steps had been made in planning and development of the facility as well as physical adaptation of the property itself. Accord, Norwegian American Hospital, Inc. v. Department of Revenue, 210 Ill.App.3d 318, 155 Ill.Dec. 83, 569 N.E.2d 83 (1991); Des Moines Coalition for the Homeless v. Des Moines City Board of Review, 493 N.W.2d 860 (Iowa 1992).

C. *Narrow and Broad Approaches to the Delineation of the Exemption for Charitable, Educational, and Welfare Organizations.* The California Supreme Court denied a property tax exemption to a hospital's thrift shop, which sold donated clothing and furnishings and whose proceeds were used for the hospital and for contributions to a community chest. Cedars of Lebanon Hospital v. Los Angeles County, 35 Cal.2d 729, 221 P.2d 31 (1950). The court denied the exemption on the ground that the proceeds were not reasonably necessary to the operation of the hospital. Similarly, a hospital that had operated as a nonprofit charitable institution for 50 years and was concededly conducting its operations as a charitable institution failed in its efforts to obtain an exemption, because of its inability to satisfy the requirement that its property be "irrevocably dedicated" to an exempt purpose; the hospital's charter authorized non-exempt activities. Pasadena Hospital Association v. Los Angeles County, 35 Cal.2d 779, 221 P.2d 62 (1950).

The Pennsylvania Supreme Court adopted an equally restrictive definition of charitable function in denying a deduction to a nonprofit corporation that provided residential, educational, and counseling services to troubled teens. Community Service Foundation v. Bucks County Board of Assessment, 672 A.2d 373 (Pa. Commw. 1996). The court held that the foundation had failed to prove that it relieved the government of some of its burden.

The Michigan Court of Appeals, on the other hand, held that the state tax court was too limited in its definition of charity in Edsel & Eleanor Ford House v. Village of Grosse Pointe Shores, 134 Mich.App. 448, 350 N.W.2d 894 (1984). The court's test was whether the institution promotes the general welfare of the public by extending a gift for the benefit of an indefinite number of people, by bringing them under the influence of religion or education, or by erecting or maintaining public buildings or works or otherwise lessening the burdens of the government. The court granted the exemption to a historical property and cultural center.

D. *Housing Incidental to Exempt Activity.* The status of buildings used in part for the housing purposes incidental to exempt uses has caused the courts considerable difficulty. In Ohio, the state supreme court held that, although a residence was not located on the hospital grounds, it was nonetheless tax-exempt because it was sufficiently used in furtherance of or incidental to the hospital's charitable purpose. Warman v. Tracy, 72 Ohio St.3d 217, 648

N.E.2d 833 (1995). The court also held that employees' houses located on tax-exempt land of a nature center were exempt as property used in furtherance of the center's charitable activities. Cincinnati Nature Center Ass'n v. Board of Tax Appeals, 48 Ohio St.2d 122, 357 N.E.2d 381 (1976). A Texas court reached a similar conclusion with respect to the dwelling place of a church's "Minister of Music." City of Amarillo v. Paramount Terrace Christian Church, 530 S.W.2d 323 (Tex. Civ. App. 1975).

In Corporation of the Presiding Bishop of the Church of Jesus Christ of Latter–Day Saints v. Ada County, 123 Idaho 410, 849 P.2d 83 (1993), the court was faced with the definition of "parsonage" for purposes of a religious exemption. The residence in question belonged to the mission president who acts as leader of the church for a tenure of three years. In denying the exemption, the court analyzed the definition of "parsonage" and concluded that

> [a] parsonage is not merely a residence owned by a religious organization in which ordained member of that organization resides. The definition of 'parsonage' as employed in [the statute] is a building owned by a religious organization occupied as a residence by a designated minister who ministers to a specific localized congregation that gathers to worship at frequent and regular intervals.

Id., 849 P.2d at 90.

E. *Parking Lots as Incidental to Exempt Activities.* Parking lots operated by churches and educational institutions have produced exemption controversies. A District of Columbia case held that land adjacent to a church building used by church members to park their automobiles during services was exempt under a statute exempting grounds "reasonably required and actually used for the carrying on the activities and purposes" of the otherwise exempt organization. District of Columbia v. Church of the Pilgrims, 247 F.2d 59, 60 (D.C. Cir. 1957). The Pennsylvania Supreme Court reached the contrary conclusion in denying an exemption to a church parking lot under a statute exempting "churches, meeting houses or other regular places of stated worship, with the ground thereto annexed necessary for the occupancy and enjoyment of the same." Second Church of Christ Scientist of Philadelphia v. City of Philadelphia, 398 Pa. 65, 157 A.2d 54, 55 (1959). The court regarded the exemption provision as limited to land on which religious activities take place.

Can the differences in these cases be explained by the difference in the statutory language granting the exemption? Or do they turn on a more fundamental judicial judgment as to the appropriateness of extending an exemption beyond its clearly intended scope? As a matter of principle, what should be the guiding standard for the taxability of property that is related to (but that does not itself serve) the exempt activity directly, such as housing and parking lots for employees of exempt organizations? If such property is characterized as non-exempt, it will add to the costs of carrying on the exempt activity. On the other hand, if such property is characterized as exempt, it will permit the exemption of property that is functionally indistinguishable from similar non-exempt property. If you were drafting legislation providing for an exemption for property used by religious, charitable, and educational organizations, how would you craft it to achieve its intended purpose and yet to avoid litigation giving rise to the cases described above?

F. *Taxation of Multi–Use Facilities Owned by Charitable and Educational Organizations.* Multi-use facilities owned by charitable or educational institutions are sometimes found to be partially exempt and partially taxable. The public cafeteria or gymnasium in a YMCA could be treated as equivalent to a commercial restaurant or health club rather than part of an exempt institution. Disputes of this sort often focus on space for doctors' offices on hospital premises or in adjacent office buildings owned by the hospital. In Little Falls Hospital v. Board of Assessors, 75 Misc.2d 731, 348 N.Y.S.2d 856 (Sup. Ct. Herkimer Cty. 1973), the court found rental space for private medical practices taxable, as any office building would be. In Barnes Hospital v. Leggett, 589 S.W.2d 241 (Mo. 1979), the court abandoned Missouri's all-or-nothing approach to the exemption, ordering an allocation of taxable value to the portions of a doctors' office building not used solely for nonprofit purposes. A dissenting opinion argued that such an allocation was impractical, pointing to difficulties of imposing a lien for unpaid taxes on only a part of a building. This approach also raises many questions encountered in the valuation and assessment of taxes upon partial interests generally.

G. *Exemption of Property Owned and Used by Religious Organizations.*

(1) *Religious Exemptions and the First Amendment to the United States Constitution.* In Walz v. Tax Commission, 397 U.S. 664, 90 S.Ct. 1409 (1970), the Supreme Court turned aside an attack on the states' traditional tax exemption for the property of religious organizations used exclusively for religious purposes. While conceding that granting tax exemptions to churches necessarily operates to afford them an indirect economic benefit and gives rise to some governmental involvement with religion, the Court, nevertheless, held that the exemption neither amounted to an establishment of religion nor the creation of an excessive governmental entanglement with religion. *Walz* followed the Court's decisions in Board of Education v. Allen, 392 U.S. 236, 88 S.Ct. 1923 (1968), and Everson v. Board of Educ., 330 U.S. 1, 67 S.Ct. 504 (1947), in which it had upheld statutes providing state loans of secular textbooks to children in all schools and transportation of children to parochial schools. Three years after *Walz*, however, the Court struck down a program of state aid to parochial education funded either by tax benefits or direct grants, holding that they constituted an unconstitutional advancement of religion. Committee for Public Educ. and Religious Liberty v. Nyquist, 413 U.S. 756, 93 S.Ct. 2955 (1973); Sloan v. Lemon, 413 U.S. 825, 93 S.Ct. 2982 (1973). The Court distinguished *Walz* on the grounds that the tax exemption for church property was rooted in long-standing historical precedent and that it served as a "neutral" exemption that avoided the "hostility" of the state created by taxation. The dissent argued that *Walz* was indistinguishable.

(2) *Belief in a Divine Ruler as Essential to Religious Exemption.* A case of religious exemption of unusual interest[c] arose under the District of Columbia property tax as a result of the denial of exemption to the Washington Society

---

c. At least for those state and local tax lawyers who attended the Ethical Culture Schools, such as the senior author of this casebook and Judge Joseph Small, the Presiding Judge of the New Jersey Tax Court.

for Ethical Culture, on the ground that its tenets do not "require a belief in and teaching of a Supreme Being who controls the universe." Washington Ethical Society v. District of Columbia, 249 F.2d 127, 128 (D.C. Cir. 1957). The statute exempted church buildings, defined as those "primarily and regularly used for religious worship, study, training and missionary activities." Id. at 127. The Ethical Cultural Society, founded in 1876, holds regular Sunday services with singing, Bible readings, and meditation; conducts a Sunday school; and has leaders who preach and conduct marriage and other services. As described by its followers, "Ethical Culture [is] a way of life," "a deeply religious movement," "a faith attuned to our times," and concerned with "spiritual values" and "spiritual guidelines." Id. at 129. While testimony indicated that many of the Society's leaders believed in a Supreme Being, the Society's followers were not required to accept such a belief. The Court of Appeals reversed the District of Columbia Tax Court, which had held that the Society's building was not used for religious purposes, and rejected the view that belief in a Supreme Being is a prerequisite to the religious exemption. Instead, it included in its conception of "religion" the idea of "devotion to some principle; strict fidelity or faithfulness." Id. at 129. The court noted that there is no doubt about the good faith of the Society and its members that "their beliefs and practices are for them a religion and religious belief." Id. The court also observed:

> To construe exemptions so strictly that unorthodox or minority forms of worship would be denied the exemption benefit granted to those conforming to the majority beliefs might well raise constitutional issues.

Id. See also Strayhorn v. Ethical Society of Austin, 110 S.W.3d 458 (Tex. App.–Austin 2003) (First Amendment requires a broader definition of what constitutes a religion than the "simple Supreme Being litmus test," and Ethical Society qualifies as a religion under the broader definition).

(3) *Challenges to the Legitimacy of Religious Organizations Seeking Property Tax Exemptions.* The exemption of property used for religious purposes raises important First Amendment questions as to the ability of a state to question the legitimacy of any given religious sect. For example, Ideal Life Church of Lake Elmo v. County of Washington, 304 N.W.2d 308 (Minn. 1981), rejected both a religious exemption and a homestead exemption for the residence of a family whose 11 members formed the complete original congregation of the Ideal Life Church. Seven neighbors were added later. The Ideal Life Church had no doctrine, no belief in a supreme being, and no religious ceremonies except a monthly dinner.

In the town of Hardenburgh in upstate New York, more than 200 of the 236 full-time resident taxpayers, including the town assessor, claimed a religious property tax exemption after becoming "ministers" in the Universal Life Church. One resident, a former plumber, obtained a charter from the church for $50. He then ordained the new ministers en masse. This left the property tax burden almost entirely on vacation property owned by nonresidents. After eight years of litigation, the exemptions were denied because the property was owned by individuals and not held in trust for members of a church. Town of Hardenburgh v. State of New York, 52 N.Y.2d 536, 421 N.E.2d 795, 439 N.Y.S.2d 303, appeal dismissed, 454 U.S. 958, 102 S.Ct. 496

(1981). The court found this requirement a reasonable regulation and not an interference with or discrimination against any religious practice or belief. See also Holy Spirit Association for the Unification of World Christianity v. Tax Commission, 55 N.Y.2d 512, 435 N.E.2d 662, 450 N.Y.S.2d 292 (1982) (finding the Reverend Sun Myung Moon's Unification Church to be a religious rather than a political organization).

C. SALES AND USE TAX EXEMPTIONS

COLUMBUS COLONY HOUSING, INC. v. LIMBACH

Supreme Court of Ohio, 1989.
45 Ohio St.3d 253, 544 N.E.2d 235.

Syllabus by the Court

* * *

The taxpayer-appellee, Columbus Colony Housing, Inc., is a nonprofit corporation organized for charitable purposes and exempt from federal taxation under Section 501(c)(3) of the Internal Revenue Code. Its purpose is to provide housing facilities and services to meet the special needs of the deaf, including the deaf multi-handicapped.

The taxpayer operates a four-story, one-hundred-six-unit apartment facility. Thirty-five percent of the residents are deaf and blind. Approximately ten percent of the residents are physically handicapped in that they use either wheelchairs or crutches. Twenty percent are hearing-capable. A majority of the residents are sixty-two years or older.

The apartment facility was built with a direct loan from the Federal Housing and Urban Development ("HUD") Section 202 program as well as with assistance from the taxpayer's parent corporation, the Ohio School for the Deaf Alumni Association. Residents in the apartment facility are tenants with written leases. Thirty-two percent of the annual operating money for the facility comes from the residents and sixty-eight percent comes from the HUD Section 8 program. Residents who satisfy the Section 8 qualifications pay only thirty percent of their average monthly gross adjusted income. Residents who are not qualified to participate in the Section 8 program pay the normal market rent for a one or two bedroom unit.

The rent for a one bedroom apartment is $540, and for a two bedroom apartment, $642. The amount of the rent subsidy (for those who qualify) varies for each tenant. However, the taxpayer receives full rent for each unit whether it comes entirely from the tenant, or in part from the tenant and in part from HUD.

The apartments are equipped with appliances and carpeting. If the resident is deaf, a strobe light communication system is installed. The taxpayer provides a van to take residents to shopping areas and banks. The taxpayer sponsors recreational activities such as crafts, ceramics, and gardening classes. For an additional fee, tenants may obtain meal service four times per week. In its leases, the taxpayer reserves the right to evict residents who fail to pay their rent on time or who otherwise violate the lease.

The Tax Commissioner assessed sales and use tax on purchases by the taxpayer. On appeal, the Board of Tax Appeals held that the taxpayer was a nonprofit organization operated exclusively for charitable purposes within the meaning of R.C. 5739.02(B)(12), that all the requirements for exemption under R.C. 5739.02(B)(12) had been satisfied, and that the commissioner had erroneously assessed sales and use tax.

HERBERT R. BROWN, JUSTICE.

The taxpayer is a nonprofit corporation, exempt from federal taxation under Section 501(c)(3) of the Internal Revenue Code. Further, the taxpayer and the volunteers who participate in the programs at the taxpayer's apartment complex are engaged in a praiseworthy endeavor. However, our task is one of statutory interpretation. The statute which controls our decision is R.C. 5739.02(B)(12).

R.C. 5739.02(B)(12) exempted the following from sales tax:

"Sales of tangible personal property [or services] to churches and to nonprofit organizations operated exclusively for charitable purposes in this state, no part of the net income of which inures to the benefit of any private shareholder or individual and no substantial part of the activities of which consists of carrying on propaganda or otherwise attempting to influence legislation." Am.Sub.H.B. No. 355 (138 Ohio Laws, Part II, 2612, 2614); bracketed material added by Am.Sub.H.B. No. 694 (139 Ohio Laws, Part II, 3460, 4025). (R.C. 5741.02[C][2] provides a concomitant use tax exception.)

"Charitable purposes" is defined in this subsection as:

". . . [T]he relief of poverty, the improvement of health through the alleviation of illness, disease, or injury, . . . [or] the operation of a home for the aged, as defined in section 5701.13 of the Revised Code. . . ."

The taxpayer does not raise "relief of poverty" as a ground for its claim of exemption. Thus our decision turns on the question of whether the taxpayer's apartment complex is operated exclusively for the improvement of health through the alleviation of illness, disease, or injury.

The question must be answered in the negative. The record establishes that the primary function of the taxpayer's apartment complex is to provide residential housing. Indeed, the taxpayer's apartment complex is essentially similar to facilities inhabited by tenants who have no hearing impairment. Admittedly there are social, and perhaps even therapeutic, advantages where those who have a hearing impairment are provided a facility in which they can live together. The services provided by the taxpayer enhance the effectiveness of this community concept. The apartments contain some features which are beneficial to the hearing impaired. But health and alleviation of illness are not the exclusive purposes of the taxpayer's business. The provision of ordinary shelter is also a purpose—clearly the most important. The provision of shelter is a service for which the taxpayer is compensated in full (either by HUD or by the residents).

This court has consistently held that the provision of private housing (even at reduced rates) does not, standing alone, demonstrate the charitable purpose required for exemption under R.C. 5739.02(B)(12).

The General Assembly may choose to expand the exemption granted in R.C. 5739.02(B)(12) to provide relief for nonprofit organizations engaged in such worthwhile projects as the one undertaken by the taxpayer herein. However, our duty is to apply the statutory law as it is written. Accordingly, we find that the taxpayer is not entitled to exemption from sales and use tax on the purchases made by the taxpayer to operate its residential facility. The decision of the Board of Tax Appeals is reversed.

Decision reversed.

MOYER, C.J., and SWEENEY, DOUGLAS and RESNICK, JJ., concur.

HOLMES and WRIGHT, JJ., dissent.

HOLMES, JUSTICE, dissenting.

In view of the facts of this case, where it is clear in the record that the premises have been constructed by a handicapped group for a number of its alumni, and that such facility, and its use, show the special purpose for such handicapped, I must take the position that the exemption per R.C. 5739.02(B)(12) does apply.

I believe, as did the Board of Tax Appeals, that this nonprofit organization was operated exclusively for charitable purposes, and that such charitable purpose, in this instance "the improvement of health," may not technically be in "alleviation of illness, disease, or injury" here, but reasonably may be read to accomplish a similar purpose within the legislative purview.

I would affirm the Board of Tax Appeals.

WRIGHT, J., concurs in the foregoing dissenting opinion.

NOTES AND QUESTIONS

A. *Exempt Purchases Versus Exempt Sales.* Many states exempt sales *to* religious, charitable, and educational organizations for reasons similar to those justifying exemptions for property owned by such organizations and used by them for exempt purposes. What about sales *by* exempt organizations? What is the justification for such an exemption? What are the dangers in granting such an exemption? In general, the states' exemption for sales by exempt organizations are much more limited than their sales to exempt organizations.

B. In Yale Club of Chicago v. Department of Revenue, 214 Ill.App.3d 468, 158 Ill.Dec. 237, 574 N.E.2d 31 (1991), the court analyzed both the educational and charitable sales tax exemption claims of the Yale Club of

Chicago (YCC). The club provided activities and fund raising events for Yale alumni in addition to screening Chicago-area applicants. The court rejected the educational exemption stating "[w]hile the YCC's efforts to encourage top quality students to attend Yale may maintain the educational standards of Yale, they do little to benefit the tax-paying public comprised of Illinois citizens." Id., 574 N.E.2d at 34. It also rejected the charitable exemption on the grounds that "[a]n organization designed to benefit Yale exclusively does not appear to dispense its benefits to an indefinite number of people, or all those who need and apply for it." Id. at 37. If the University of Illinois Alumni Association performed functions similar to those performed by the Yale Club of Chicago, would its purchases qualify for a tax exemption, assuming that the overwhelming majority of students at the University of Illinois are children of "the tax-paying public comprised of Illinois citizens"?

C. *The Incidence of the Sales Tax.* The availability of a sales tax exemption to an exempt organization may turn on the question of whether the incidence of the tax falls on the vendor or the purchaser. In Trustees of Sailors' Snug Harbor of N.Y. v. McGoldrick, 255 App.Div. 64, 5 N.Y.S.2d 322 (1st Dep't 1938), aff'd, 280 N.Y. 537, 20 N.E.2d 7 (1939), the court held that the exemption from sales tax granted to charitable and religious organizations extended not only to a charitable organization's purchases of personal property, but also to its sales of electricity to private tenants in buildings owned by the charity. Since the levy is a consumer's tax, required to be collected by the vendor from the purchaser, does the overall policy underlying exemption to charities warrant such a result? Cf. Sweet Associates, Inc. v. Gallman, 36 A.D.2d 95, 318 N.Y.S.2d 528 (3d Dep't 1971), aff'd, 29 N.Y.2d 902, 279 N.E.2d 602, 328 N.Y.S.2d 857 (1972) (sustaining sales tax exemption for sales of construction materials to a contractor for use in construction for a school district under a time and materials contract). The relation of the incidence of a tax to the question of immunity is considered in greater detail in Chapter 5 supra, dealing with the immunity of federal instrumentalities from state taxation.

D. *Leases of Equipment to Exempt Organizations.* If an exempt organization leases equipment from a non-exempt corporation, is either the lessor or the lessee subject to state sales or use taxes? In Telco Leasing, Inc. v. Allphin, 63 Ill.2d 305, 347 N.E.2d 729 (1976), the court held taxable the profit-making lessor of medical and scientific equipment to exempt hospitals, despite the argument that the hospitals would bear the burden of the tax. The court rejected the contention that the imposition of the tax was a denial of equal protection on the ground that vendors, as contrasted with lessors, would not have been liable for any taxes on sales made to exempt hospitals.

E. *Property and Activities Producing Income Used for Exempt Purposes.* The issue whether an exemption should be limited to the exempt activities themselves, or should cover as well activities and the use of property to earn income which is dedicated to exempt purposes, has been hotly contested in many courts. Should an ordinary business enterprise owned and operated by a nonprofit foundation, which is required to use or pay over its net income solely for the benefit of an exempt educational institution, be exempt from income tax, property tax, and sales tax? In Youth Tennis Foundation v. Tax Commission, 554 P.2d 220 (Utah 1976), the court held that receipts from a tennis tournament sponsored by a charitable organization were exempt from sales tax. In State Tax Commission v. Board of Education, 146 Kan. 722, 73 P.2d 49 (1937), on the other hand, the court held that the sales tax exemption for public, educational, and charitable organizations is limited to purchases and sales directly designed to carry out the organization's exempt functions.

Should such exemptions of this nature be denied because of the resultant possible unfair competition with non-exempt business? Should the result be the same if the educational institution directly owns and operates the business? Is there any basis for distinguishing the ownership and operation by an educational institution (or a foundation all of whose income must be paid over to the educational institution) of a commercial building or apartment house, on the one hand, and a macaroni plant, on the other? In the case of a retail sales tax required to be collected from the consumer, why should the sales of taxable property or services made *by* the exempt organization, as distinguished from sales made *to* the exempt organization, be free of sales tax?

CHAPTER 11

STATE TAX PROCEDURE: ASSESSMENT, COLLECTION, REFUNDS, AND JUDICIAL REMEDIES

■ ■ ■

A. THE ASSESSMENT OF TAXES

The Initial Assessment of Taxes. Of the two general mechanisms for the assessment of state taxes, i.e., self-assessment and assessment by the relevant taxing authority, self-assessment is by far the more common mechanism. An individual taxpayer, for example, prepares a state tax return, reporting her income and deductions, determining her credits, and ultimately computing her tax liability for the taxable period.[a] Corporate income taxes, sales and use taxes, gross receipts taxes, estate taxes, and personal property taxes also are typically self-assessed taxes.

By contrast, real property taxes frequently are assessed in the first instance by the taxing authority. Most states divide the responsibility for assessing real property taxes between state authorities and local authorities, including counties, cities, and school districts. The properties that are most often state-assessed are properties owned or operated by public utilities. The rationale for state-assessment of those properties is two-fold. First, public utilities frequently own and operate properties scattered throughout the state and, because of their integrated or "unitary" nature, it is often difficult to determine their value on a localized basis. See Chapter 9 supra. Second, utility properties often present highly complex and technical valuation questions that local assessors are ill-equipped to address (e.g., determining the impact on the value of a utility's tangible property of the intangible rights or franchises it owns). See Chapter 9, pp. 841–48 supra.

Deficiency Assessments. Following the initial assessment of taxes, whether by the taxpayer or the taxing authority, the taxing authority is ordinarily authorized by statute to audit the taxpayer's return or otherwise to reconsider the taxes that were assessed against the taxpayer.

---

a. To be sure, a portion of her taxes may be withheld by her employer, but the taxes withheld are not "assessed" by the taxing authority. They are simply a prepayment of the taxes that the taxpayer self-assesses on her return.

Thereafter, the taxing authority may adjust the original assessment. An audit generally consists of an examination of books, papers, and other data bearing on the taxpayer's return. If the taxing authority determines that the original assessment was too high, then it may issue a refund, or at least notify the taxpayer that he may be eligible for a refund. On the other hand, if the taxing authority concludes that the original assessment should be increased, it will issue a notice of deficiency or an assessment.

The notice of deficiency typically will trigger a series of remedial options which the taxpayer is entitled to pursue to challenge the deficiency. See Section C infra. Similar options generally are available to taxpayers who file claims for refund of taxes. The nature of these remedies, and, more importantly, the technical requirements for pursuing them, may vary slightly or dramatically depending on the type of tax at issue and the state or locality in which the taxpayer is seeking relief. One feature shared by all these remedial schemes, however, is that they impose strictly enforced statutes of limitations on taxpayers seeking to challenge an assessment.

Due Process Limitations on Assessments. By and large, taxing jurisdictions have extremely broad leeway in establishing limitations on taxpayers' rights to contest assessments. Nevertheless, because taxation often involves an involuntary taking of property, taxing authorities generally must observe due process requirements in making assessments and in affording taxpayers an opportunity to challenge such assessments.[b] The fundamental federal and state due process requirements for tax assessments are adequate notice and an opportunity for a hearing. See Turner v. Wade, 254 U.S. 64, 41 S.Ct. 27 (1920); Londoner v. City & County of Denver, 210 U.S. 373, 28 S.Ct. 708 (1908).

Mullane v. Central Hanover Bank & Trust Co., 339 U.S. 306, 70 S.Ct. 652 (1950), states the prevailing rule concerning the adequacy of notice:

> An elementary and fundamental requirement of due process in any proceeding which is to be accorded finality is notice reasonably calculated, under all the circumstances, to apprise interested parties of the pendency of the action and afford them an opportunity to present their objections. The notice must be of such nature as reasonably to convey the required information, and it must afford a reasonable time for those interested to make their appearance. But if with due regard for the practicalities and peculiarities of the case these conditions are reasonably met, the constitutional requirements are satisfied.

Id., 339 U.S. at 314–15. The requisite notice necessary to commence judicial proceedings clearly is not the same notice required in making tax assessments. For example, personal service of process or notice is not

---

b. If a taxpayer is deemed to have paid a tax "voluntarily," these due process protections may be unavailable. To be deemed to have paid a tax voluntarily, however, a taxpayer must been afforded a reasonable opportunity to challenge the tax before payment—an opportunity the taxpayer forgoes by paying the tax. See McKesson Corp. v. Division of Alcoholic Beverages & Tobacco, 496 U.S. 18, 110 S.Ct. 2238 (1990), pp. 945–54 infra.

essential. Indeed, the Court has approved notice of an assessment by ordinary mail rather than by certified or registered mail. See Mennonite Bd. of Missions v. Adams, 462 U.S. 791, 800, 103 S.Ct. 2706 (1983); Schroeder v. City of New York, 371 U.S. 208, 212–13, 83 S.Ct. 279 (1962).

The due process requirements of notice and review of tax assessments are satisfied by a proceeding before an administrative agency. Judicial review is not necessary to provide due process of law. Thus, in Hodge v. Muscatine County, 196 U.S. 276, 281, 25 S.Ct. 237 (1905), the Court declared:

> If the taxpayer be given an opportunity to test the validity of the tax at any time before it is made final, whether the proceedings for review take place before a board having a quasi-judicial character, or before a tribunal provided by the State for the purpose of determining such questions, due process of law is not denied.

Statutes of Limitations on Assessments and Collections. Statutes of limitations apply not only to taxpayers' appeals of deficiency assessments and claims for refunds, but also to taxing authorities' actions in making assessments and collections. Although statutes of limitations differ widely between types of taxes and between taxing jurisdictions, they typically share a number of common features. For example, statutes of limitations generally do not begin to run unless and until the taxpayer files a return, and they may be extended in the case of alleged impropriety such as fraud on the part of the taxpayer. In the context of personal and corporate income taxes, the statute of limitations for assessing additional taxes may remain automatically open for a certain period (e.g., six months) beyond the close of the federal income tax statute. Moreover, the statute of limitations frequently will be extended or reopened if the Internal Revenue Service ("IRS") makes changes to the taxpayer's federal return. Usually the federal changes do not subject the entire state return to audit. Rather, the federal changes permit only changes by the state taxing authority that relate to the changes made by the IRS, although there is diversity among the states on this issue.

NOTES AND QUESTIONS

A. *Contingent-fee Audits by Independent Third Parties.* Some states authorize third parties to conduct contingent-fee audits. The state contracts with an independent third-party to perform audits of income, sales, or property taxes. Particularly in the area of unclaimed property and escheat laws, the third-party may be hired to perform single-state or multi-state audits. Is there any limitation on a state's right to use contingent-fee audits? Do they safeguard sufficiently taxpayers' due process rights? In light of the fact that the apparent incentive of the examiner is to maximize the amount of tax due, is it possible to achieve a fair and impartial examination?

Contingent-fee personal property tax audits have been challenged in several states with mixed results. In Sears, Roebuck & Co. v. Parsons, 260 Ga.

824, 401 S.E.2d 4 (1991), the taxpayer challenged an agreement between a county board of assessors and Atlantic Resources, Inc. ("Atlantic"), a private auditing company, on the ground that the agreement was illegal and violated public policy. The agreement provided that Atlantic would audit tangible personal property returns and, if the audit resulted in an increased valuation, would receive 35 percent of any additional amount collected, plus 100 percent of all first-year penalties collected.

The Supreme Court of Georgia held the contract void as against public policy because of the contingency scheme of compensation for the services performed. The court reasoned that a taxpayer's entitlement to a "fair and impartial tax assessment[]" was at the heart of the system and indeed "was a basic principle upon which this country was founded." Id., 401 S.E.2d at 5. Such standards were threatened when a private organization had a financial stake in the amount of tax collected as a result of the assessment it recommends. The court, however, approved the concept of using a private firm to perform tax audits so long as the firm was not compensated on a contingent basis. It concluded that the procedure was contemplated in the Georgia statutes. While noting that the power to tax rests exclusively with the government, it recognized that in the exercise of that power the government by necessity acts through its agents.

The North Carolina Supreme Court, on the other hand, sustained a county's use of contingent fee tax auditors. In re Philip Morris U.S.A., 335 N.C. 227, 436 S.E.2d 828 (1993). It declared:

> [C]ourts in other jurisdictions have considered the validity of contingent fee contracts for tax audits. The results reached by those courts are completely mixed and establish no clear line of authority.* * *

> * * *

> Our legislature has specifically prohibited contingent fees in certain settings when it has deemed them to be contrary to the interests of the public. For example, North Carolina law prohibits real estate appraisers giving valuations based on contingent fee arrangements, N.C.G.S. § 93A–80(a)(3), and N.C.G.S. § 120–47.5 outlaws contingent fees for lobbying. Therefore, we conclude that had the General Assembly intended that private tax auditors employed to assist county tax assessors be restricted to an hourly wage or to fixed fee remuneration, it would have expressly said so.

Id., 436 S.E.2d at 830–31.

B. COLLECTION OF TAXES

Overview. Ordinarily, once a taxpayer has exhausted all of its rights to appeal an assessment, the state taxing authority is entitled to begin collection proceedings. If the outstanding deficiency is not paid within a specified time, penalties may attach. Thereafter, states may pursue a variety of collection procedures, generally similar to those available to the IRS to collect federal taxes, e.g., states may be entitled to levy upon bank accounts or garnish wages. States also may be authorized to suspend a delinquent corporation from engaging in business in the state.

Jeopardy Assessments and Other Summary Proceedings. If a taxing authority concludes that collection of a tax will be jeopardized by delay, the taxing authority may make an immediate assessment of the jeopardized tax, including interest and penalties. Jeopardy assessments are immediately due and payable, and collection proceedings may be commenced at once. However, the taxpayer may be permitted to stay collection by filing a bond before the assessment becomes final. Even if collection is not stayed, the taxpayer will be afforded procedures to contest the assessment. A foreign corporation that does business in a state may be required to consent to summary proceedings for fixing tax liabilities without service of process in the state.

Collection of Property Taxes. In light of the crucial importance of property taxation, especially the real property tax, to local revenues, widespread delinquency in property tax payments may become a major problem for local governments. The traditional method of enforcement of property taxes in the United States is by recourse to the property taxed, through the satisfaction of tax liens. Typically, taxes levied on property are made a lien against the property and collection is authorized by warrant. The Supreme Court has observed that the power to collect taxes by distraint and sale is "almost as old as the common law." Springer v. United States, 102 U.S. (12 Otto) 586, 593 (1880).

Although personal liability for property taxes has a long history in American law, the rule developed that, in the absence of an explicit statutory provision, no personal action will lie to recover property taxes. These holdings are grounded on the theory that taxes are not debts, or on the view that because the statute provides only for proceedings in rem, personal liability is not imposed.

Personal Liability of the Taxpayer for Taxes Other Than Property Taxes. The taxpayer is personally liable for the payment of most levies other than ad valorem taxes. Thus, the taxpayer is typically liable for income, sales, gross receipts, franchise, and other state and local taxes. Ordinarily both the vendor and the vendee are liable for sales tax, although the vendor's function is primarily that of a tax collector. The executor or administrator is usually obliged to see to the payment of death taxes, and she may be held personally liable for distributing the property without payment of the tax. Moreover, the taxing authority may independently pursue the property in the hands of the legatees in order to satisfy its claims.

Most jurisdictions recognize personal liability of corporate officers who fail to collect and pay sales and use taxes. Generally, the officer must possess some control over making the returns and paying over taxes to be subject to liability. For example, in State of Missouri v. Longstreet, 536 S.W.2d 185 (Mo. App. 1976), a corporate officer charged with the duty of collecting sales taxes and filing the required returns with the state was found criminally liable after collecting the taxes and failing to file the returns. The court reasoned that to insulate such officers from liability would defeat the intent of the statute, and that liability need only rest on the fact that the officer "receive[d] the payment or consideration involved in the transaction." Id. at 189.

Civil liability may exist even where mere negligence of a responsible corporate officer results in nonpayment of sales tax. In Willis v. Lindley, 61 Ohio St.2d 356, 402 N.E.2d 1185 (1980), the defendant used an account into which he deposited his sales tax collections to secure a small business loan. The Small Business Administration called the loan and subsequently closed the defendant's business, resulting in a tax deficiency owed the state. The court held that, because the defendant supervised the filing of returns and payment of taxes, liability existed, and the loan arrangement in no way altered this liability. Id., 402 N.E.2d at 1186. Similarly, in State v. The Equinox House, Inc., 134 Vt. 59, 350 A.2d 357 (1975), the court indicated that the corporate president-treasurer was personally liable for collecting employee withholding taxes, sales and use taxes, and rooms and meals taxes, in the event the corporation failed to collect such taxes.

NOTES AND QUESTIONS

A. *The Constitutionality of Summary Proceedings.* In Bomher v. Reagan, 522 F.2d 1201 (9th Cir. 1975), the court sustained California's summary tax collection procedure over the objection that it violated the taxpayer's due process rights. The California Franchise Tax Board had sent the taxpayer several requests for payment of delinquent taxes, and, after failing to receive a satisfactory response, issued a warrant for the collection of amounts due. The warrant was executed by levy upon and sale of the taxpayer's automobile. The taxpayer claimed the procedure deprived him of due process because he was given no prior notice or hearing in which the tax debt would have to be proved before his property could be seized. The court held, however, that the taxpayer's right to subsequent judicial review and a tax refund, if necessary, satisfied due process requirements. See also Phillips v. Commissioner, 283 U.S. 589, 51 S.Ct. 608 (1931). See generally Comment, "Procedural Due Process in Tax Collection: An Opportunity for a Prompt Postdeprivation Hearing," 44 U. Chi. L. Rev. 594 (1977).

B. *Requirements of Notice to Mortgagee of Proceeding to Sell Mortgaged Property for Nonpayment of Taxes.* In Mennonite Bd. of Missions v. Adams, 462 U.S. 791, 103 S.Ct. 2706 (1983), the Supreme Court considered whether notice by publication and posting provided a mortgagee of real property with adequate notice under the Due Process Clause of a proceeding to sell the mortgaged property for nonpayment of taxes. Under Indiana law, prior to the sale of real property on which payments of property taxes had been delinquent for a specified period, the county auditor was required to post notice in the county courthouse and publish notice once each week for three consecutive weeks. In addition, the owner of the property was entitled to notice by certified mail to his last known address; however, mortgagees of property that was to be sold were not entitled to notice of any type.

In *Mennonite,* the purchaser of property at a tax sale brought an action to quiet title to the property. The mortgagee of the property opposed the action on the grounds that it had not received constitutionally adequate notice of the pending sale or of the opportunity to redeem the property following the tax sale. The Court sustained the mortgagee's claim, relying on Mullane v. Central Hanover Bank & Trust Co., 339 U.S. 306, 70 S.Ct. 652 (1950), discussed at pp. 933–34 supra, where it had held that published notice of an action to settle the accounts of a common trust fund was not sufficient to inform beneficiaries of a trust whose names and addresses were known sustained.

> This case is controlled by the analysis in *Mullane*. To begin with, a mortgagee possesses a substantial property interest that is significantly affected by a tax sale. Under Indiana law, a mortgagee acquires a lien on the owner's property. * * * A mortgagee's security interest generally has priority over subsequent claims or liens. * * * [T]he tax sale may result in the complete nullification of the mortgagee's interest, since the purchaser acquires title free of all liens and other encumbrances at the conclusion of the redemption period.

> Since a mortgagee has a legally protected property interest, he is entitled to notice reasonably calculated to apprise him of a pending tax sale. When the mortgagee is identified in a mortgage that is publicly recorded, constructive notice by publication must be supplemented by notice mailed to the mortgagee's last known available address, or by personal service. But unless the mortgagee is not reasonably identifiable, constructive notice alone does not satisfy the mandate of *Mullane*.

Id., 462 U.S. at 798.

C. *Collection of Local Taxes*. Local tax ordinances often fail to provide specific procedures for the taxing authority to collect outstanding tax deficiencies. Thus, the taxing authority is required to file a lawsuit under the state's general civil litigation statutes in order to collect the taxes. Under these circumstances, would the local authorities be subject to the general rules regarding notice before litigation may be commenced or to the more limited restrictions applicable to tax proceedings? See also Section D(2), pp. 943–44 infra, regarding burden of proof.

D. *Extra-state Enforcement of Tax Claims*. Historically there was a tradition that the courts of one state would not entertain a suit by another state to enforce a tax claim that had not been reduced to judgment. See, e.g., State v. Karp, 84 Ohio App. 51, 84 N.E.2d 76 (1948). The same rule applies internationally and is known as the "revenue rule." See generally Brenda Mallinak, "The Revenue Rule: A Common Law Doctrine for the Twenty–First Century," 16 Duke J. Comp. & Int'l L. 79 (2006). However, the mobility of business and wealth has made collection of taxes from taxpayers without property in the state increasingly difficult. Because courts were slow to overrule the doctrine against enforcement of revenue laws of another state, and because there was a perception that nonresidents were escaping taxes, legislatures took action. Most states now permit collection of out-of-state taxes.

Typically it is unnecessary to obtain a judgment in the taxing state before filing suit in a foreign jurisdiction. If, however, a judgment has been obtained, the Full Faith and Credit Clause of the United States Constitution requires a state court to enforce the tax judgment of a sister state. A state is not required to give full faith and credit to a sister state's judgment unless there was jurisdiction to enter such a judgment. In 1948, Congress extended the full faith and credit requirements to acts of the legislature, in addition to the judicial judgments of a sister state. 28 U.S.C. § 1738.

In Franchise Tax Board v. Hyatt, 538 U.S. 488, 123 S.Ct. 1683 (2003), however, the Court held that the Full Faith and Credit Clause did not require Nevada to give full faith and credit to California's statutes providing its tax agency with immunity from suit. The Court found that the full faith and credit command "is exacting" with respect to a final judgment rendered by a court with adjudicatory authority over the subject matter and persons governed by the judgment, but is less demanding with respect to choice of laws. Accordingly, the clause does not compel a state to substitute the statutes of other states for its own statutes dealing with a subject matter concerning which it is competent to legislate.

C. CHALLENGING ASSESSMENTS IN ADMINISTRATIVE PROCEEDINGS

The Nature of the Administrative Remedy. Following the receipt of a notice of deficiency or assessment, the taxpayer frequently will be afforded an administrative remedy of some kind prior to paying the assessment. Although the specific features of administrative remedies vary widely, the taxpayer typically will be required to file an administrative appeal within a specified period of time, stating the grounds for disputing the assessment. Usually the taxpayer is afforded an opportunity to protest the assessment informally and, if it does not obtain satisfactory relief, then formally before the administrative body. The informal hearing ordinarily involves a meeting with a representative of the taxing agency who will hear the evidence and legal arguments and decide whether to grant or deny the appeal. The taxpayer thereafter may proceed to present its appeal in a formal or semi-formal hearing before an administrative appeals board. This board is often comprised of tax professionals and lawyers, but may also include laypersons.

In some circumstances, the taxpayer will be required to pay the amount of the assessment before it may pursue any administrative remedies. The remedy under these circumstances usually will be to file a claim for refund with the taxing agency. If the claim is denied, the taxpayer ordinarily will be entitled to sue for a refund in the state's courts.

The Requirement of Exhaustion Of Administrative Remedies. Where statutory procedures exist for obtaining administrative review of the action of a taxing authority, courts typically hold that remedy to be exclusive; failure to exhaust the administrative remedy precludes judicial review. V–1 Oil Co. v. County of Bannock, 97 Idaho 807, 554 P.2d 1304 (1976); Gager v. Kasdon, 234 Md. 7, 197 A.2d 837 (1964); Columbia Developers, Inc. v. Elliott, 269 S.C. 486, 238 S.E.2d 169 (1977).

The minimum exhaustion requirement for taxpayers entitled to de novo review of their tax liability in the state's courts generally consists of paying the tax and filing the claim for refund. The claim must state the specific grounds on which the taxpayer believes it is entitled to relief. The state court's review is normally limited to the grounds stated in the claim.

It is fairly common, however, for the administrative body to adjudicate factual disputes and thereby provide a forum for the parties to develop a factual record that will serve as the basis for judicial review of the dispute. In that case, the judicial review is referred to as "on the record" review. Indeed, the administrative body's jurisdiction may be limited to review of the factual issues, and thus the administrative body may be prohibited from making determinations on purely legal issues. More frequently, however, administrative bodies are authorized to make legal as well as factual determinations, although they often have no authority to rule on constitutional issues. In those instances where the administrative body lacks authority to reach legal issues, courts have held that it is not necessary to raise the legal issue before the administrative body. In addition, if the case does not involve any factual issues, the exhaustion requirement may be waived, i.e., the taxpayer may be entitled to bypass the review by the administrative body altogether and to appeal the matter directly to the state's courts. See e.g., Star–Kist Foods, Inc. v. Quinn, 54 Cal.2d 507, 354 P.2d 1, 6 Cal.Rptr. 545, 547 (1960) (case involved "no dispute as to the facts and no possibility that action by the board might avoid the necessity of deciding the constitutional issue or modify its nature").

Other exceptions to the exhaustion requirement include situations where pursuit of an administrative remedy would be futile or where the case is brought not to challenge specific assessments but rather to correct "wholesale deficiencies" in assessment practices. See, e.g., TRIM, Inc. v. County of Monterey, 86 Cal.App.3d 539, 150 Cal.Rptr. 351, 355 (1st Dist. 1978) (law does not provide administrative remedy "to bring about examination and correction of wholesale deficiencies," and local assessment procedures are designed only to deal with specific assessments); Knoff v. City & County of San Francisco, 1 Cal.App.3d 184, 81 Cal.Rptr. 683, 692 (1st Dist. 1969). However, this exception to the exhaustion requirement apparently would not apply merely because a case is brought as a class action. See, e.g., Schoderbek v. Carlson, 113 Cal.App.3d 1029, 170 Cal. Rptr. 400 (1st Dist. 1980).

D. SUITS TO RECOVER TAXES

While some states have special procedures for bringing a suit for refund of taxes, including courts established for the exclusive purpose of hearing tax disputes, ordinarily taxpayers file tax refund suits in the state's civil courts in the same manner as any other plaintiff would sue to recover a loss. The case generally proceeds much as any other civil litigation would proceed, e.g., with discovery, summary judgment motions, and usually a bench trial. Due to the nature of tax cases, it is frequently possible for the parties to stipulate to most or all of the facts, thereby rendering the trials fairly short.

1. STANDING

NOTES AND QUESTIONS

A. *Standing Principles.* The overwhelming majority of tax cases involve taxpayers attempting to recover their own taxes. There are occasions, however, in which a person has reason to challenge a tax that technically is not her own tax but that nevertheless results in a palpable economic harm to the person. In those cases, because the harm to be remedied is indirectly caused, standing presents a hurdle that the plaintiff must overcome in order for the case to proceed.

In DaimlerChrysler Corp. v. Cuno, 547 U.S. 332, 126 S.Ct. 1854 (2006), for example, the Supreme Court considered a Commerce Clause challenge to Ohio's investment tax credits that were limited to in-state investments. (The decision below is set out in Chapter 3, pp. 153–61 supra). The Court did not reach the merits of the challenge. Instead, it held that the plaintiffs, who were state taxpayers unhappy with the "corporate welfare" that Ohio was bestowing upon DaimlerChrysler, lacked standing in federal court to challenge the tax credits. The Court found that the plaintiffs lacked the essential requisite of standing to sue in federal court, namely that "[a] plaintiff must allege personal injury fairly traceable to the defendant's allegedly unlawful conduct and likely to be redressed by the requested relief." Allen v. Wright, 468 U.S. 737, 751, 104 S.Ct. 3315 (1984) The Court concluded that plaintiffs' principal claim, namely, that the income tax credit depletes state funds to which they contribute through their taxes, and thus diminishes the total funds available for lawful uses and imposes disproportionate burdens on them, was an insufficiently particularized injury that could be redressed by judicial action to establish standing in federal court under Article III of the Constitution.

On occasion courts have found that the standing requirements were met where the injury caused by the tax was only indirect. Thus, in Boston Stock Exchange v. State Tax Comm'n, 429 U.S. 318, 97 S.Ct. 599 (1977), the Court upheld the standing of out-of-state stock exchanges to challenge a tax that was not their own, namely the New York tax preference for purchasers who traded on New York exchanges, because the tax diverted business from the plaintiffs' exchanges to New York exchanges. The taxing scheme caused third parties (stock purchasers) to increase their trades on the New York Stock Exchange and to decrease their purchases on the out-of-state exchanges, thereby causing injury to the plaintiffs. The Supreme Court explicitly characterized the plaintiffs' injury as "indirectly" related to the defendant's conduct. Id., 429 U.S. at 320 n. 3 ("The Exchanges are asserting their right under the Commerce Clause to engage in interstate commerce free of discriminatory taxes on their business and they allege that the transfer tax *indirectly* infringes on that right") (emphasis supplied). Similarly, in Dominion National Bank v. Olsen, 771 F.2d 108 (6th Cir. 1985), the court held that an out-of-state bank had standing to challenge a tax imposed on resident owners of certificates of deposit issued by out-of-state, but not in-state, financial institutions.

The foregoing discussion of standing reflects federal case law on standing under the Constitution and the Internal Revenue Code. States, of course, may have their own rules of standing, although they generally tend to apply the same tests as those utilized by federal courts. Indeed, with respect to federal constitutional challenges to state taxes, a state that adopted a narrower rule of standing than that reflected in federal law arguably would not be providing an adequate remedy, thus permitting the taxpayer to sue in federal court. See Section F infra; Dominion National Bank v. Olsen, 771 F.2d 108 (6th Cir. 1985) (permitting federal court challenge by out-of-state banks against state tax statute allegedly discriminating against out-of-state certificates of deposit because state court denied banks standing on the ground that they were not taxpayers).

In those states (like California) in which the sales tax is technically a tax on the vendor (see Chapter 8, p. 606 supra, distinguishing "vendor" from "consumer" sales taxes), the consumer who is separately charged a sales tax on her bill (and presumably bears the economic burden of the tax) may nevertheless lack standing to challenge the tax. In Loeffler v. Target Corp., 173 Cal.App.4th 1229, 93 Cal.Rptr.3d 515 (2d Dist. 2009), for example, the California Court of Appeal observed:

> There is no statutory or regulatory provision allowing purchasers like plaintiffs to file a claim for a sales tax refund with the [State] Board [of Equalization (SBE)]. Since only taxpayers may file a claim for refund and plaintiffs are not taxpayers, they have no standing to assert a claim with the Board.

Id., 93 Cal.Rptr. 3d at 524. Would the same principle prevent a consumer from seeking a refund of a use tax? The *Target* court also held that the legislature had not provided the consumers with a private cause of action against Target to recover unlawfully collected sales taxes. It indicated, however, that under circumstances not present in the case, e.g., after the SBE has ascertained that consumers have reimbursed the technical taxpayer for an overpayment of sales tax, such an action might be maintained.

B. *Associational or Representational Standing.* Hunt v. Washington State Apple Advertising Commission, 432 U.S. 333, 97 S.Ct. 2434 (1977) established that "associational" or "representational" standing may be established if "(a) [the association's] members would otherwise have standing to sue in their own right; (b) the interests [the association] seeks to protect are germane to the organization's purpose; and (c) neither the claim asserted nor the relief requested requires the participation of individual members in the lawsuit." Id., 432 U.S. at 343. Based upon the foregoing three-part test, would a trade association organized on behalf of companies in a particular industry have standing to challenge a tax that was allegedly imposed in a discriminatory fashion against members of that industry? Would the trade association suffer any harm from the imposition of the discriminatory tax?

C. *Application of Standing Principles.* Suppose a state imposed a tax that favored purchases of a particular natural resource such as coal that was produced within the state. Would an out-of-state coal producer have standing to challenge the tax? Would an adjacent state have standing to challenge the tax? Would a railroad have standing to challenge the tax on the grounds that it resulted in lower demand for the railroad's services due to the fact that purchases of locally produced coal had reduced purchases of coal that required transportation by railroad? See Wyoming v. Oklahoma, 502 U.S. 437, 112 S.Ct. 789 (1992) (upholding Wyoming's standing to challenge Oklahoma law requiring coal-fired utilities to burn a mixture containing at least ten percent Oklahoma-mined coal, causing a reduction in purchases of Wyoming coal and a decrease of one percent in Wyoming's severance tax revenues); Fulani v. Brady, 935 F.2d 1324, 1328 (D.C. Cir. 1991), cert. denied, 502 U.S. 1048, 112 S.Ct. 912 (1992) (recognizing concept of competitor standing but concluding that "where a party is seeking simply to remove a third party's entitlement to a tax exemption, the exemption likely will not bear sufficient links of traceability and redressability to the alleged injury to warrant standing"); Tax Analysts and Advocates v. Blumenthal, 566 F.2d 130 (D.C. Cir. 1977), cert. denied, 434 U.S. 1086, 98 S.Ct. 1280 (1978) (competitor standing denied where plaintiffs challenged competitors' federal income tax deduction of certain payments to foreign governments on the basis of competitive disadvantage in the marketplace).

2. BURDEN OF PROOF

NOTES AND QUESTIONS

A. *Reconciliation of Burden of Proof Principles in Ordinary Civil Litigation and in Tax Cases.* The burden of proof on the ultimate questions of law and fact in tax cases ordinarily is imposed on the taxpayer. This placement of the burden of proof is commonly justified by the fact that taxpayers have better access to the information necessary to prove the correct tax liability. In that regard, it has been said that placing the burden on taxpayers serves to encourage accurate record keeping. Further, taxing authorities' presumption of correctness is premised on the assumptions that taxing authorities are expert in their duties, e.g., analyzing, interpreting and applying tax provisions, and that they have regularly performed their official duties. See, e.g., Simms v. Pope, 218 Cal.App.3d 472, 266 Cal.Rptr. 911, 914 (2d Dist. 1990).

In cases where the taxing authority sues to recover taxes, should the burden of proof remain on the plaintiff as it would in any ordinary civil litigation? Should it be on the taxpayer simply because the substantive dispute is one over taxes? What should happen when the law establishes a presumption in favor of the taxpayer on a case-determinative legal issue? Should the burden of proof for the entire case then shift to the taxing authorities, or should the taxing authorities have the burden only to proffer sufficient evidence to rebut the presumption? As a practical matter, is there a difference between those two alternatives?

B. *Burden of Proof in Bankruptcy Proceedings.* In general, when a debtor enters into bankruptcy, any and all parties with a potential claim against the debtor must file a claim in the bankruptcy court in a timely fashion. Though the debtor is required to rebut the prima facie validity of such claims, the burden of proof shifts to the claimant to present evidence to prove the claim. Thus, the ultimate burden of proof of the validity of the claim and the amount generally is on the creditor. See, e.g., Wright v. Holm (In re Holm), 931 F.2d 620, 623 (9th Cir. 1991).

Where the creditor is a state and the dispute regards the debtor's state tax liability, there is an obvious conflict between the burden of proof imposed in tax cases and the burden of proof in bankruptcy cases. Numerous federal circuit courts, district courts, and bankruptcy courts have been required to resolve this conflict. Although courts have come down on both sides, in the majority of the circuits that have addressed the issue, the state taxing authority bears the ultimate burden of proof of the validity and amount of the claim.

In Franchise Tax Board v. MacFarlane (In re MacFarlane), 83 F.3d 1041 (9th Cir. 1996), cert. denied, 520 U.S. 1115, 117 S.Ct. 1243 (1997), for example, the California Franchise Tax Board ("FTB") filed a claim in bankruptcy court for state taxes allegedly owed by the taxpayer/debtor on the ground that the taxpayer improperly claimed certain bad debt deductions on his 1988 and 1989 tax returns. The bankruptcy court ruled that the claim was prima facie valid. The taxpayer timely objected to the claim and provided the court with evidence that the debts existed in 1988 and 1989 and became worthless in those years. Thereafter, the FTB "submitted no evidence of its own" supporting the denial of the deductions, "but rather sought to rely on alleged inconsistencies in debtor's evidence." Id. at 1046.

The bankruptcy court held that the state failed to meet its burden and entered judgment in favor of the debtor. The district court reversed that determination. The circuit court began its analysis by acknowledging that "[t]here is no question that outside the bankruptcy forum, a taxpayer bears the ultimate burden of proving entitlement to a deduction." Id. at 1044. However, in bankruptcy court, "the ultimate burden * * * is on the creditor." Id. Quoting In re Fidelity Holding Co., Ltd., 837 F.2d 696, 698 (5th Cir. 1988), the court stated, " '[t]he Bankruptcy Code * * * does not differentiate between government and private claimants when proofs of claim are filed.' " Id. at 1045. The court stated further:

> The bankruptcy code is silent on the allocation of the ultimate burden of proof in this case. In the absence of a statutory directive, we consider it appropriate to turn to policy considerations that underlie the bankruptcy code.

Id. The policy concerns involved "balanc[ing] the equities 'between the [FTB] and the other creditors of Debtor's estate.' " Id. The court noted that pursuant to 11 U.S.C. § 607(a)(8)(A), tax claims already receive a statutory priority over other creditor's claims. "[R]elieving the Board of its burden of proof 'would be granting the Board a double benefit not authorized by statute or Ninth Circuit authority.' " Id. On that basis, the court concluded that " '[t]he policy goals of the bankruptcy system are put at risk when one class of creditors is given the benefit of a favorable presumption which has its origins outside of bankruptcy law.' " Id. (quoting In re Wilhelm, 173 B.R. 398, 402 (Bankr. E.D. Wis. 1994)).

3. OTHER ISSUES

NOTES AND QUESTIONS

A. *Class Action Suits Challenging Taxes.* May a representative taxpayer file suit challenging a tax on behalf of a class of similarly situated taxpayers? Courts in some jurisdictions have been receptive to class action tax suits. In Javor v. State Board of Equalization, 12 Cal.3d 790, 527 P.2d 1153, 117 Cal.Rptr. 305 (1974), the plaintiff, individually and purportedly on behalf of some 500,000 purchasers of motor vehicles, sued the retailers and the State Board of Equalization seeking a refund of state sales taxes to the extent they had been measured by the federal excise tax that Congress had retroactively repealed. In holding that the plaintiff had stated a proper cause of action, the California Supreme Court observed:

> It would require a suit by each member of plaintiff class individually to compel defendant retailers to file a claim with defendant Board for a refund of the erroneously collected tax. Such demands would result in a multiplicity of actions. The amount due each member of the class is relatively small and when compared with the costs of suit, would discourage individual legal action. Unless this class action is permitted defendant Board and defendant retailers will be unjustly enriched at the expense of plaintiff class.

Id., 117 Cal.Rptr. at 308.[c]

Courts in other jurisdictions have been less hospitable to taxpayer class actions. For example, in Hagerty v. General Motors Corp., 59 Ill.2d 52, 319 N.E.2d 5 (1974), the Illinois Supreme Court rejected the class action allegations of plaintiff's complaint for a refund of sales taxes paid in connection with automobile repairs. The complaint alleged that the repairs involved the sale of services with an incidental transfer of personal property rather than the sale of tangible personal property at retail. The sales taxes would be substantially higher in the latter case than in the former. The court said:

> In order to determine which tax should have been imposed in a particular transaction, the facts of that transaction must be known. Consequently, a decision in this case sustaining the plaintiff's contention as to her transaction with GM would not establish a right of recovery in any other customer of GM who had work performed on his automobile and replacement parts installed therein. The required common interest of the purported class members in the questions involved is therefore lacking in this case, and the circuit court was correct in striking the class action allegations of the plaintiff's complaint.

Id., 319 N.E.2d at 8. In general, it is fair to say that " 'class actions in tax cases are rare.' " John F. Coverdale, "Remedies for Unconstitutional State Taxes," 32 Conn. L. Rev. 73, 122 (1999) (citation omitted).

---

c. Nevertheless, the California legislature limited the ability of taxpayers to file class action suits by requiring that an administrative claim for refund filed on behalf of a class of taxpayers be accompanied by written authorization by each taxpayer sought to be included in the class, be signed by each taxpayer or the taxpayer's representative, and state the specific grounds on which the claim is based. Cal. Rev. & Tax. Code § 19322 (Westlaw 2009).

B. *Interest on Overpayments of Tax.* Because of the immunity of the sovereign from suit, in the absence of a waiver of immunity, the taxpayer cannot ordinarily recover interest on an unconstitutional levy unless the statute provides for interest. In Public Service Co. of New Hampshire v. State, 102 N.H. 54, 149 A.2d 874 (1959), the taxpayer sought the recovery of interest on a franchise tax paid under protest. In a prior proceeding, the tax was struck down on constitutional grounds. The state, however, had refunded the unconstitutionally collected tax without interest. Repeating its traditional view of sovereign immunity, from which it concluded that "the plaintiff can recover interest only if the Legislature has provided for it by statute," id., 149 A.2d at 876, the New Hampshire court found no basis for the taxpayer's contention that the state statutes, by implication, authorized a refund of interest. Accord Marsh v. Brown, 31 Conn.Sup. 134, 325 A.2d 466 (1974); State ex rel. Cleveland Concession Co. v. Peck, 161 Ohio St. 31, 117 N.E.2d 429 (1954); Petitions of Williams, 166 Vt. 21, 686 A.2d 964 (1996). Some cases have held to the contrary, particularly where suit was brought against the tax collector who, it was held, could not claim sovereign immunity.

In People v. Union Oil Co., 48 Cal.2d 476, 310 P.2d 409 (1957), at the time the taxpayer paid its franchise tax, the relevant statute authorized six percent interest on overpayments if the "overpayment was not made because of an error or mistake on the part of the taxpayer." Id., 310 P.2d at 410 (quoting the statute). Subsequently the statute was amended to allow six percent interest on refunds if the "overpayment was made because of an error or mistake on the part of the commissioner." Id. (quoting the statute). The taxpayer's refund arose out of its election, made on an amended return, to amortize emergency war facilities at an accelerated rate. The state issued a refund without interest on the basis of the amended statute. The court held the statutory amendment providing for interest to be unconstitutional pointing out that it is "the settled law of this state that illegal taxes voluntarily paid may not be recovered by the taxpayer in the absence of a statute permitting a refund thereof." Id. at 412. Because there was no "vested right to the refund of the taxes but rather such action is a matter of legislative grace, it necessarily follows that the right to the payment of interest on such refunds is not vested and the Legislature may enact a statute cutting off such rights theretofore accorded the taxpayer." Id.

At least two courts have held that failure to pay interest on refunds of illegally collected taxes does not constitute the denial of "meaningful backward-looking relief" under McKesson Corp. v. Division of Alcoholic Beverages & Tobacco, 496 U.S. 18, 110 S.Ct. 2238 (1990), pp. 948–57 infra. See Chicago Freight Car Leasing Co. v. Limbach, 62 Ohio St.3d 489, 584 N.E.2d 690 (1992); Pendell v. Department of Revenue, 315 Or. 608, 847 P.2d 846 (1993).

C. *The "Set-off" Remedy.* Ordinarily, when a taxpayer receives a deficiency assessment, the taxpayer is entitled to raise unrelated issues that would result in a refund to offset the deficiency, even if the statute of limitations for claiming a refund has expired. This remedy is referred to as the "set-off" remedy. However, at least one court has denied the set-off remedy to a taxpayer. In Paccar, Inc. v. State, Department of Revenue, 85 Wash.App. 48, 930 P.2d 954 (1997), the taxpayer, after receiving a deficiency notice, paid the deficiency and immediately filed a refund petition for the same period on the theory that the overpayment should be offset against the deficiency. Later the taxpayer filed suit on the same basis. The Washington Court of Appeals held that the date of filing suit was the determinative date in applying the statute of limitations and that, as of that date, the statute of limitations for the taxpayer's refund claim had expired. The taxpayer therefore was not permitted to offset the deficiency by the time-barred overpayment. The court also noted that an equitable remedy was previously available to taxpayers by statute, but the statute had been amended and the offset provision removed by the time that the taxpayer filed suit.

Taxing authorities also generally are entitled to rely on the set-off remedy when taxpayers claim a refund. For example, in Sprint Communications Company L.P. v. State Board of Equalization, 40 Cal.App.4th 1254, 47 Cal.Rptr.2d 399 (1st Dist. 1995), the California Court of Appeal held that the State Board of Equalization was entitled to offset the taxpayer's claim for refund of sales and use taxes by underpayments for the same period that were not timely assessed. The court's holding was based on the fact that suits for refund of taxes are governed by equitable principles, so "a plaintiff who challenges the validity of a tax may recover only if it be shown that more has been exacted than in equity and good conscience should have been paid." Id., 47 Cal.Rptr.2d at 402. The court did not permit the state to offset underpayments for different periods against the taxpayer's claim for refund.

D. *Collateral Estoppel and Res Judicata in Tax Cases.* The doctrine of res judicata gives conclusive effect to a former judgment in a subsequent litigation involving the same controversy. Thus, courts will not entertain a new action on the same cause of action. Generally, res judicata will not apply in a tax case as long as the case involves a different tax year or period than that involved in a prior case between the same parties. However, res judicata will likely preclude litigation by a party in privity to a party in an earlier action for the same tax period.

In Richards v. Jefferson County, Ala., 517 U.S. 793, 116 S.Ct. 1761 (1996), the U.S. Supreme Court rejected a state court's reliance on the res judicata doctrine to preclude a taxpayer from litigating his claim on the merits. The county had attempted to prevent the lawsuit challenging the constitutionality of the county's occupation tax from proceeding on the grounds that the claims had been adjudicated in Bedingfield v. Jefferson County, 527 So.2d 1270 (Ala. 1988). However, the plaintiffs in *Bedingfield* were three individuals who brought suit strictly on their own behalf and did not purport to assert claims on behalf of, or bind, other taxpayers in any way. The Court held that because the taxpayers in *Richards* (two individuals representing a class of all nonfederal employees subject to the county's tax) were not parties in *Bedingfield* and were not adequately represented, the Alabama court's ruling that their claims were barred by *Bedingfield* denied them due process.

The related doctrine of collateral estoppel is more likely to be applicable in tax cases than res judicata. Collateral estoppel precludes litigation of issues that were actually litigated and determined in an earlier action as between parties who were parties, or in privity with a party, to that action. Nevertheless, because collateral estoppel may be defeated by a change of facts, and facts generally do change to some extent between tax periods, even collateral estoppel is extremely rare in tax cases.

For example, in Hooven & Allison Co. v. Evatt, 324 U.S. 652, 65 S.Ct. 870 (1945) (*Hooven I*), the U.S. Supreme Court held, on the basis of the "original package" doctrine, that imported hemp and other fibers were immune from taxation under the Import–Export Clause, while those goods were stored in a warehouse awaiting use in manufacturing. Subsequently, in Michelin Tire Corp. v. Wages, 423 U.S. 276, 96 S.Ct. 535 (1976), the U.S. Supreme Court articulated its contemporary Import–Export Clause doctrine that discarded the "original package" doctrine as a significant factor in Import–Export Clause analysis; it focused instead on whether the tax at issue was nondiscriminatory. See Chapter 3. In Hooven & Allison Co. v. Lindley, 4 Ohio St.3d 169, 447 N.E.2d 1295 (1983) (*Hooven II*), which involved the same issues and same parties as *Hooven I*, the state court held that the state was collaterally estopped from relitigating the issue.

When the case reached the U.S. Supreme Court, as Limbach v. Hooven & Allison Co., 466 U.S. 353, 104 S.Ct. 1837 (1984), the Court overruled *Hooven I*, and decided that the state was not barred by the doctrine of collateral estoppel from assessing the tax against the taxpayer. In reaching its decision, the Court relied on the exception to the collateral estoppel doctrine in situations when a "change or development in the controlling legal principles * * * make that [prior] determination obsolete or erroneous, at least for future purposes." Commissioner v. Sunnen, 333 U.S. 591, 599–600, 68 S.Ct. 715 (1948). Because Hooven had never been provided with an opportunity to demonstrate that the facts of its case were significantly different from those involved in *Michelin*, however, the Court declined to rule on the merits of Hooven's contention that, notwithstanding *Michelin*, the Ohio tax was constitutionally infirm. Instead, the Court remanded the case for further proceedings to permit Hooven to pursue its Import–Export Clause and other constitutional claims.

Under what circumstances can a state successfully assert res judicata against a taxpayer when the earlier litigation involved a different tax year? Under what circumstances, can a state successfully assert collateral estoppel against a taxpayer when the earlier litigation involved a different tax year?

E. PROSPECTIVE OR RETROACTIVE RELIEF AND OTHER LEGAL REMEDIES

McKESSON CORPORATION v. DIVISION OF ALCOHOLIC BEVERAGES AND TOBACCO

Supreme Court of the United States, 1990.
496 U.S. 18, 110 S.Ct. 2238.

JUSTICE BRENNAN delivered the opinion of the Court.

Petitioner McKesson Corporation brought this action in Florida state court, alleging that Florida's liquor excise tax violated the Commerce Clause of the United States Constitution. The Florida Supreme Court agreed with petitioner that the tax scheme unconstitutionally discriminated against interstate commerce because it provided preferences for distributors of certain local products. Although the court enjoined the State from giving effect to those preferences in the future, the court also refused to provide petitioner a refund or any other form of relief for taxes it had already paid.

* * *

III

It is undisputed that the Florida Supreme Court, after holding that the Liquor Tax unconstitutionally discriminated against interstate commerce because of its preferences for liquor made from " 'crops which Florida is adapted to growing,' " 524 So.2d, at 1008, acted correctly in awarding petitioner declaratory and injunctive relief against continued enforcement of the discriminatory provisions. The question before us is whether prospective relief, by itself, exhausts the requirements of federal law. The answer is no: If a State places a taxpayer under duress promptly to pay a tax when due and relegates him to a postpayment refund action in which he can challenge the tax's legality, the Due Process Clause of the Fourteenth Amendment obligates the State to provide meaningful backward-looking relief to rectify any unconstitutional deprivation.

A

We have not had occasion in recent years to explain the scope of a State's obligation to provide retrospective relief as part of its postdeprivation procedure in cases such as this. Our approach today, however, is rooted firmly in precedent dating back to at least early this century. Atchison, T. & S.F.R. Co. v. O'Connor, 223 U.S. 280, 32 S.Ct. 216 (1912), involved a suit by a railroad company to recover taxes it had paid under protest, alleging that the tax scheme violated the Commerce Clause because most of the franchise tax was apportioned to business conducted wholly outside the State. The Court agreed that the franchise tax was unconstitutional and concluded that the railroad company was entitled to a refund of the portion of the tax imposed on out-of-state activity. Justice Holmes explained:

"It is reasonable that a man who denies the legality of a tax should have a clear and certain remedy. The rule being established that apart from special circumstances he cannot interfere by injunction with the State's collection of its revenues, an action at law to recover back what he has paid is the alternative left. Of course we are speaking of those cases where the State is not put to an action if the citizen refuses to pay. In these latter he can interpose his objections by way of defence, but when, as is common, the State has a more summary remedy, such as distress, and the party indicates by protest that he is yielding to what he cannot prevent, courts sometimes perhaps have been a little too slow to recognize the implied duress under which payment is made. But even if the State is driven to an action, if at the same time the citizen is put at a serious disadvantage in the assertion of his legal, in this case of his constitutional, rights, by defence in the suit, justice may require that he should be at liberty to avoid those disadvantages by paying promptly and bringing suit on his side." Id., at 285–286, 32 S.Ct., at 217.

After finding that the railroad company's tax payment "was made under duress," id., at 287, 32 S.Ct., at 217, the Court issued a judgment entitling the company to a "refunding of the tax." Ibid. Thus was the taxpayer provided a "clear and certain remedy" for the State's unlawful extraction of tax moneys under duress.

In Ward v. Love County Board of Comm'rs, 253 U.S. 17, 40 S.Ct. 419 (1920), we reversed the Oklahoma Supreme Court's refusal to award a refund for an unlawful tax. * * * We explained the State's duty to remit the tax as follows:

"To say that the county could collect these unlawful taxes by coercive means and not incur any obligation to pay them back is nothing short of saying that it could take or appropriate the property of these Indian allottees arbitrarily and without due process of law. Of course this would be in contravention of the Fourteenth Amendment, which binds the county as an agency of the State." Id., at 24, 40 S.Ct., at 422.

See also Carpenter v. Shaw, 280 U.S. 363, 369, 50 S.Ct. 121, 123 (1930) (holding, in a case analogous to *Ward,* that "a denial by a state court of a recovery of taxes exacted in violation of the laws or Constitution of the United States by compulsion is itself in contravention of the Fourteenth Amendment").

In Montana National Bank of Billings v. Yellowstone County, 276 U.S. 499, 48 S.Ct. 331 (1928), we applied the same due process analysis to a tax that was unlawful because it was discriminatory, though otherwise within the State's power to impose. Montana officials had imposed a tax on shares of banks incorporated under federal law but not on shares of state-incorporated banks, relying on a Montana Supreme Court decision interpreting state law to preclude such taxation of state bank shares. The Montana National Bank of Billings paid its tax under protest and then brought suit for a refund. The bank contended that the different tax treatment violated § 5219 of the Revised Statutes, a federal statute requiring equal taxation of the shares of state and national banks. On appeal, the Montana Supreme Court overruled its previous interpretation of state law and held that thereafter shares of state banks could also be taxed, thus enabling state officials to comply with § 5219. Montana National Bank of Billings v. Yellowstone County, 78 Mont. 62, 252 P. 876 (1926). The court declined, however, to order a refund of the taxes that the Montana National Bank of Billings had paid during the period when state officials had exempted state banks in reliance on the court's earlier decision. Id., at 86, 252 P., at 883. On writ of error, this Court acknowledged that the Montana Supreme Court's decision to overrule its previous interpretation of state law ensured for the future the equal treatment demanded by federal law. The Court noted, however, that prospective relief alone "d[id] not cure the mischief which had been done under the earlier construction." 276 U.S., at 504, 48 S.Ct., at 333. We held that the Montana National Bank of Billings "c[ould not] be deprived of its legal right to recover the amount of the tax unlawfully exacted of it by the later [Montana Supreme Court] decision which, while repudiating the construction under which the unlawful exaction was made, le[ft] the monies thus exacted in the public treasury," id., at 504–505, 48 S.Ct., at 333, and therefore the bank enjoyed "an undoubted right to recover" the moneys it had paid. Id., at 504, 48 S.Ct. at 333.

The Court in *Montana National Bank* recognized that the federal mandate of equal treatment could have been satisfied by collecting back taxes from state banks rather than by granting a refund to national banks. But as to this possibility, the Court remarked:

> "[I]t is unnecessary to say more than that it nowhere appears that these [taxing] officers, if they possess the power [to assess back taxes], have undertaken to exercise it or that they have any intention of ever doing so. It will be soon enough to invite consideration of this purely speculative suggestion when, if ever, the taxing officials shall have put it into practical effect." Ibid.

Montana National Bank thus held that one forced to pay a discriminatorily high tax in violation of federal law is entitled, in addition to prospective relief, to a refund of the excess tax paid—at least unless the disparity is removed in some other manner.

We again applied this analysis to a discriminatory tax in Iowa–Des Moines National Bank v. Bennett, 284 U.S. 239, 52 S.Ct. 133 (1931). The Court held unanimously that the State of Iowa's taxation of the shares of state and national banks at a higher rate than those of competing domestic corporations violated the Equal Protection Clause. With respect to the banks' claim for a refund of excess taxes paid, Justice Brandeis explained:

> "The [banks'] rights were violated, and the causes of action arose, when taxes at the lower rate were collected from their competitors. It may be assumed that all ground for a claim for refund would have fallen if the State, promptly upon discovery of the discrimination, had removed it by collecting the additional taxes from the favored competitors. By such collection the [banks'] grievances would have been redressed, for these are not primarily overassessment. The right invoked is that to equal treatment; and such treatment will be attained if either their competitors' taxes are increased or their own reduced." Id., at 247, 52 S.Ct., at 136.

But the State did not elect to set matters right by collecting additional taxes from the banks' competitors for the four tax years encompassed by the suit. And the Court found it "well settled" that the banks could not be "remitted to the necessity of awaiting such action by the state officials upon their own initiative." Ibid. The Court held, therefore, that the banks were "entitled to obtain in these suits refund of the excess of taxes exacted from them." Ibid.

B

These cases demonstrate the traditional legal analysis appropriate for determining Florida's constitutional duty to provide relief to petitioner McKesson for its payment of an unlawful tax. Because exaction of a tax constitutes a deprivation of property, the State must provide procedural safeguards against unlawful exactions in order to satisfy the commands of the Due Process Clause. The State may choose to provide a form of "predeprivation process," for example, by authorizing taxpayers to bring suit to enjoin imposition of a tax prior to its payment, or by allowing taxpayers to withhold payment and then interpose their objections as defenses in a tax enforcement proceeding initiated by the State. However, whereas "[w]e have described 'the root requirement' of the Due Process Clause as being 'that an individual be given an opportunity for a hearing *before* he is deprived of any significant property interest,' " Cleveland Bd. of Education v. Loudermill, 470 U.S. 532, 542, 105 S.Ct. 1487, 1493 (1985) (citation omitted), it is well established that a State need not provide predeprivation process for the exaction of taxes. Allowing taxpayers to litigate their tax liabilities prior to payment might threaten a government's financial security, both by creating unpredictable interim revenue shortfalls against which the State cannot easily prepare, and by making the ultimate collection of validly imposed taxes more difficult. To protect government's exceedingly strong interest in financial stability in this context, we have long held that a State may employ various financial sanctions and summary remedies, such as distress sales, in order to encourage taxpayers to make timely payments prior to resolution of any dispute over the validity of the tax assessment.

Florida has availed itself of this approach, establishing various sanctions and summary remedies designed so that liquor distributors tender tax payments *before* their objections are entertained and resolved.[20] As a result, Florida does not purport to provide taxpayers like petitioner with a meaningful opportunity to withhold payment and to obtain a predeprivation determination of the tax assessment's validity;[21] rather, Florida

---

20. If a distributor fails to pay the tax on time, the Division of Alcoholic Beverages and Tobacco may issue a warrant which, when filed in a local circuit court, directs the county sheriff to levy upon and sell the delinquent taxpayer's goods and chattels to recover the amount of the unpaid tax plus a penalty of 50%, along with interest of 1% per month and the costs of executing the warrant. Fla.Stat. § 210.14(1) (1989). In addition, the Division may revoke, § 561.29(1)(a), or decline to renew, § 561.24(5), a distributor's license for failure to abide by Florida law, including the statutory requirement that the Liquor Tax be timely paid.

21. We have long held that, when a tax is paid in order to avoid financial sanctions or a seizure of real or personal property, the tax is paid under "duress" in the sense that the State has not provided a fair and meaningful predeprivation procedure. See, e.g., United States v. Mississippi Tax Comm'n, 412 U.S. 363, 368, 93 S.Ct. 2183, 2187 (1973) (economic sanctions for nonpayment); Ward v. Love County Board of Comm'rs, 253 U.S. 17, 23, 40 S.Ct. 419, 421 (1920) (distress sale of land); Gaar, Scott & Co. v. Shannon, 223 U.S. 468, 471, 32 S.Ct. 236, 237 (1912) (both).

requires taxpayers to raise their objections to the tax in a postdeprivation refund action. To satisfy the requirements of the Due Process Clause, therefore, in this refund action the State must provide taxpayers with, not only a fair opportunity to challenge the accuracy and legal validity of their tax obligation, but also a "clear and certain remedy," O'Connor, 223 U.S., at 285, 32 S.Ct., at 217, for any erroneous or unlawful tax collection to ensure that the opportunity to contest the tax is a meaningful one.

Had the Florida courts declared the Liquor Tax invalid either because (other than its discriminatory nature) it was beyond the State's power to impose, as was the unapportioned tax in *O'Connor*, or because the taxpayers were absolutely immune from the tax, as were the Indian Tribes in *Ward* and *Carpenter*, no corrective action by the State could cure the invalidity of the tax during the contested tax period. The State would have had no choice but to "undo" the unlawful deprivation by refunding the tax previously paid under duress, because allowing the State to "collect these unlawful taxes by coercive means and not incur any obligation to pay them back ... would be in contravention of the Fourteenth Amendment." Ward, 253 U.S., at 24, 40 S.Ct., at 422.

Here, however, the Florida courts did not invalidate the Liquor Tax in its entirety; rather, they declared the tax scheme unconstitutional only insofar as it operated in a manner that discriminated against interstate commerce. The State may, of course, choose to erase the property deprivation itself by providing petitioner with a full refund of its tax payments. But * * * a State found to have imposed an impermissibly discriminatory tax retains flexibility in responding to this determination. Florida may reformulate and enforce the Liquor Tax during the contested tax period in any way that treats petitioner and its competitors in a manner consistent with the dictates of the Commerce Clause. Having done so, the State may retain the tax appropriately levied upon petitioner pursuant to this reformulated scheme because this retention would deprive petitioner of its property pursuant to a tax scheme that is *valid* under the Commerce Clause. In the end, the State's postdeprivation procedure would provide petitioner with all of the process it is due: an opportunity to contest the validity of the tax and a "clear and certain remedy" designed to render the opportunity meaningful by preventing any permanent unlawful deprivation of property.

Justice Holmes suggested in Atchison, T. & S.F.R. Co. v. O'Connor, 223 U.S. 280, 32 S.Ct. 216 (1912), that a taxpayer pays "under duress" when he proffers a timely payment merely to avoid a "serious disadvantage in the assertion of his legal ... rights" should he withhold payment and await a state enforcement proceeding in which he could challenge the tax scheme's validity "by defence in the suit." Id., at 286, 32 S.Ct., at 217.

In contrast, if a State chooses not to secure payments under duress and instead offers a meaningful opportunity for taxpayers to withhold contested tax assessments and to challenge their validity in a predeprivation hearing, payments tendered may be deemed "voluntary." The availability of a predeprivation hearing constitutes a procedural safeguard against unlawful deprivations sufficient by itself to satisfy the Due Process Clause, and taxpayers cannot complain if they fail to avail themselves of this procedure. See Mississippi Tax Comm'n, supra, 412 U.S., at 368, n. 11, 93 S.Ct., at 2187, n. 11 ("[W]here voluntary payment [of a tax] is knowingly made pursuant to an illegal demand, recovery of that payment may be denied").

More specifically, the State may cure the invalidity of the Liquor Tax by refunding to petitioner the difference between the tax it paid and the tax it would have been assessed were it extended the same rate reductions that its competitors actually received. Cf. Montana National Bank and Bennett (curing discrimination through such refunds). Alternatively, to the extent consistent with other constitutional restrictions, the State may assess and collect back taxes from petitioner's competitors who benefited from the rate reductions during the contested tax period, calibrating the retroactive assessment to create in hindsight a nondiscriminatory scheme. Cf. Bennett, 284 U.S., at 247, 52 S.Ct., at 136 (suggesting State could erase the unconstitutional discrimination by "collecting the additional taxes from the favored competitors").[23] Finally, a combination of a partial refund to petitioner and a partial retroactive assessment of tax increases on favored competitors, so long as the resultant tax actually assessed during the contested tax period reflects a scheme that does not discriminate against interstate commerce, would render petitioner's resultant deprivation lawful and therefore satisfy the Due Process Clause's requirement of a fully adequate postdeprivation procedure.

* * *

C

The Florida Supreme Court cites two "equitable considerations" as grounds for providing petitioner only prospective relief, but neither is sufficient to override the constitutional requirement that Florida provide retrospective relief as part of its postdeprivation procedure. The Florida court first mentions that "the tax preference scheme [was] implemented by the [Division of Alcoholic Beverages and Tobacco] in good faith reliance on a presumptively valid statute." * * *

The Florida Supreme Court also speculated that "if given a refund, [petitioner] would in all probability receive a windfall, since the cost of the

---

23. We previously have held that the retroactive assessment of a tax increase does not necessarily deny due process to those whose taxes are increased, though beyond some temporal point the retroactive imposition of a significant tax burden may be "so harsh and oppressive as to transgress the constitutional limitation," depending on "the nature of the tax and the circumstances in which it is laid." Welch v. Henry, 305 U.S. 134, 147, 59 S.Ct. 121, 126 (1938). See United States v. Hemme, 476 U.S. 558, 106 S.Ct. 2071 (1986); United States v. Darusmont, 449 U.S. 292, 101 S.Ct. 549 (1981); cf. United States v. Sperry Corp., 493 U.S. 52, 65, 110 S.Ct. 387, 396 (1989) ("It is surely proper for Congress to legislate retrospectively to ensure that costs of a program are borne by the entire class of persons that Congress rationally believes should bear them"); Usery v. Turner Elkhorn Mining Co., 428 U.S. 1, 16, 96 S.Ct. 2882, 2893 (1976) ("[L]egislation readjusting rights and burdens is not unlawful solely because it upsets otherwise settled expectations. This is true even though the effect of the legislation is to impose a new duty or liability based on past acts") (citations omitted). Because we do not know whether the State will choose in this case to assess and collect back taxes from previously favored distributors, we need not decide whether this choice would violate due process by unduly interfering with settled expectations.

Should the State choose this remedial alternative, the State's effort to collect back taxes from previously favored distributors may not be perfectly successful. Some of these distributors, for example, may no longer be in business. But a good-faith effort to administer and enforce such a retroactive assessment likely would constitute adequate relief, to the same extent that a tax scheme would not violate the Commerce Clause merely because tax collectors inadvertently missed a few in-state taxpayers.

tax has likely been passed on to [its] customers." 524 So.2d, at 1010. The court's premise seems to be that the State, faced with an obligation to cure its discrimination during the contested tax period and choosing to meet that obligation through a refund, could legitimately choose to avoid generating a "windfall" for petitioner by refunding only that portion of the tax payment not "passed on" to customers (or even suppliers). Even were we to accept this premise, the State could not refuse to provide a refund based on sheer speculation that a "pass-on" occurred. We repeatedly have recognized that determining whether a particular business cost has in fact been passed on to customers or suppliers entails a highly sophisticated theoretical and factual inquiry; a court certainly cannot withhold part of a refund otherwise required to rectify an unconstitutional deprivation without first satisfactorily engaging in this inquiry.[31]

In any event, however, we reject respondents' premise that "equitable considerations" justify a State's attempt to avoid bestowing this so-called "windfall" when redressing a tax that is unconstitutional because discriminatory. In United States v. Jefferson Electric Mfg. Co., 291 U.S. 386, 54 S.Ct. 443 (1934), we enforced a statutorily created pass-on defense in a refund action designed to redress a tax overassessment. Comparing such an action to one in assumpsit for "money had and received," we affirmed the Federal Government's power in this equitable action to withhold the amount that the taxpayer had already passed on to others, on the theory that the taxpayer ought not be "unjustly enriched" by his recovery from the Government after he has already "recovered" his losses through the pass-on. We observed that if the taxpayer "has shifted the [economic] burden [of the tax] to the purchasers, they and not he have been the actual sufferers and are the real parties in interest," id., at 402, 54 S.Ct., at 449, and he ought not receive a windfall for their injury.

But petitioner does not challenge here a tax assessment that merely exceeded the amount authorized by statute; petitioner's complaint was that the Florida tax scheme unconstitutionally discriminated against interstate commerce. The tax injured petitioner not only because it left petitioner poorer in an absolute sense than before (a problem that might be rectified to the extent petitioner passed on the economic incidence of the tax to others), but also because it placed petitioner at a relative disadvantage in the marketplace vis-a-vis competitors distributing preferred local products. See n. 25, supra; see also Bacchus Imports, supra, 468 U.S., at 267, 104 S.Ct., at 3053 ("[E]ven if the tax [was] completely

31. We have expressed particular concern about the theoretical, factual, and practical difficulties in engaging in satisfactory "pass-on" analysis in the context of antitrust doctrine. See Illinois Brick Co. v. Illinois, 431 U.S. 720, 741–745, 97 S.Ct. 2061, 2072–2074 (1977); Hanover Shoe, Inc. v. United Shoe Machinery Corp., 392 U.S. 481, 492–493, 88 S.Ct. 2224, 2231 (1968). See generally A. Atkinson & J. Stiglitz, Lectures on Public Economics 160–226 (1980); R. Musgrave & P. Musgrave, Public Finance In Theory and Practice 256–300 (3d ed. 1980); McLure, Incidence Analysis and the Supreme Court: Examination of Four Cases from the 1980 Term, 1 Sup.Ct.Econ. Rev. 69 (1982); D. Phares, Who Pays State and Local Taxes? (1980). For this reason, we have observed that determining whether a particular business cost has been passed on "would often require additional long and complicated proceedings involving massive evidence and complicated theories." Hanover Shoe, supra, at 493, 88 S.Ct., at 2231.

and successfully passed on, it increase[d] the price of [petitioner's] products as compared to the exempted beverages"). To whatever extent petitioner succeeded in passing on the economic incidence of the tax through higher prices to its customers, it most likely lost sales to the favored distributors or else incurred other costs (e.g., for advertising) in an effort to maintain its market share.[32] The State cannot persuasively claim that "equity" entitles it to retain tax moneys taken unlawfully from petitioner due to its pass-on of the tax where the pass-on itself furthers the very competitive disadvantage constituting the Commerce Clause violation that rendered the deprivation unlawful in the first place.[33] We thus reject respondents' reliance on a pass-on defense in this context.[34]

D

Respondents assert that requiring the State to rectify its unconstitutional discrimination during the contested tax period "would plainly cause serious economic and administrative dislocation for the State." Brief for Respondents on Rearg. 20. We agree that, within our due process jurisprudence, state interests traditionally have played, and may play, some role in shaping the contours of the relief that the State must provide to illegally or erroneously deprived taxpayers, just as such interests play a role in shaping the procedural safeguards that the State must provide in order to ensure the accuracy of the initial determination of illegality or error. We have already noted that States have a legitimate interest in sound fiscal planning and that this interest is sufficiently weighty to allow States to withhold predeprivation relief for allegedly unlawful tax assessments,

---

32. Petitioner's relative market share might have stayed constant if the favored distributors reacted by raising their own prices to the same extent as did petitioner when trying to pass on its excess tax burden. If so, however, petitioner still would have suffered a comparative economic injury because the tax pass-on would have enabled the favored distributors alone to derive an increase in total revenue from the discriminatory tax.

33. It is conceivable that a particular distributor's economic injury may be quite severe, for example, if the tax drives it out of the market entirely (though a rational disfavored distributor would not allow itself to incur any greater economic injury through a pass-on than it would have incurred had it simply shouldered the entire burden of the tax deprivation itself). However, the State's obligation under the Due Process Clause to provide a refund (should it choose this avenue of relief) extends only to refunding the excess taxes collected under the Liquor Tax. Petitioner has not sought in this action to recover any actual damages it may have suffered.

34. Respondents suggest that a pass-on defense may nevertheless be invoked as a matter of state law. While they concede that the State waived any sovereign immunity from suit through Fla.Stat. § 215.26's authorization of a state-court refund action, they contend that this waiver extends only to refunds sought where the taxpayer has borne the actual economic burden of the tax, citing State ex rel. Szabo Food Services, Inc. v. Dickinson, 286 So.2d 529 (Fla.1973). We need not consider the import of this contention, however, because respondents misdescribe state law. In this case, the Florida Supreme Court characterized its concern about petitioner receiving a "windfall" due to the alleged pass-on of its tax burden as only an "equitable consideration," not a state-law prohibition on relief. Moreover, no such state-law prohibition was recognized in Szabo Food Service, supra. There, the Florida Supreme Court refused to entertain a refund action brought by a distributor of food products to challenge a sales tax alleged to have been imposed erroneously as a matter of state law. The court noted that the legal incidence of the sales tax was placed not on the distributor but rather on its customers and that state law required the economic burden of the tax to be borne by the customers as well. Id., at 532. The court held that under these unique circumstances the distributor lacked standing to seek a refund, explaining that "[o]ne who does not himself bear the financial burden of a wrongfully extracted tax suffers no loss or injury, and accordingly, would not have standing to demand a refund." Ibid. The court in Szabo did not mention, let alone rely on, a state-law immunity bar to the refund action.

providing postdeprivation relief only. But even if a State chooses to provide partial refunds as a means of curing the unlawful discrimination (as opposed to increasing the tax assessment of those previously favored), the State's interest in financial stability does not justify a refusal to provide relief. As noted earlier, the State here does not and cannot claim that the Florida courts' invalidation of the Liquor Tax was a surprise, and even after the trial court found a Commerce Clause violation the State failed to take reasonable precautions to reduce its ultimate exposure for the unconstitutional tax. And in the future, States may avail themselves of a variety of procedural protections against any disruptive effects of a tax scheme's invalidation, such as providing by statute that refunds will be available to only those taxpayers paying under protest, or enforcing relatively short statutes of limitation applicable to refund actions. Such procedural measures would sufficiently protect States' fiscal security when weighed against their obligation to provide meaningful relief for their unconstitutional taxation.

* * *

IV

When a State penalizes taxpayers for failure to remit their taxes in timely fashion, thus requiring them to pay first before obtaining review of the tax's validity, federal due process principles long recognized by our cases require the State's postdeprivation procedure to provide a "clear and certain remedy," O'Connor, 223 U.S., at 285, 32 S.Ct., at 217, for the deprivation of tax moneys in an unconstitutional manner. In this case, Florida may satisfy this obligation through any form of relief, ranging from a refund of the excess taxes paid by petitioner to an offsetting charge to previously favored distributors, that will cure any unconstitutional discrimination against interstate commerce during the contested tax period. The State is free to choose which form of relief it will provide, so long as that relief satisfies the minimum federal requirements we have outlined.[36] The judgment of the Florida Supreme Court is reversed, and the case is remanded for further proceedings not inconsistent with this opinion.

It is so ordered.

NOTES AND QUESTIONS

A. *McKesson* establishes the fundamental principle that when states impose taxes in violation of clearly established constitutional principles, and taxpayers are compelled to pay such taxes before challenging their validity, states are required to provide the taxpayers with meaningful backward-looking relief. In what circumstances will any relief other than a refund be meaningful? Does it depend on the nature of the constitutional violation? On

---

36. The State is free, of course, to provide broader relief as a matter of state law than is required by the Federal Constitution. See Bacchus Imports, 468 U.S., at 277, n. 14, 104 S.Ct., at 3058, n. 14.

the ability of the state to impose back taxes on the previously favored class of taxpayers? Are there any limitations on states imposing taxes retroactively on a class of taxpayers that has been favored with a tax exemption in the past?

Why did the Court reject Florida's pass-on defense? Is there anything wrong with that defense as a matter of principle? If a taxpayer has not borne the economic burden of a tax, why should it be entitled to a refund? As between the state, which has illegally imposed the exaction, and the taxpayer, who has shifted the burden of the tax to a third party, which party has the stronger claim to the tax dollars? Could the state condition a refund on the taxpayer reimbursing the third parties to whom it passed on the tax?

Other than not enacting unconstitutional tax statutes in the first place, how can a state protect itself against large refund claims from court decisions striking down state statutes as unconstitutional? In *McKesson*, the Court suggested, among other things, that states might enforce relatively short statutes of limitations applicable to refund actions. How far may this suggestion be taken? May a state require a taxpayer to demand a refund within 30 days after payment of taxes assessed by the state? May a state require only certain types of claims, e.g., constitutional claims, for refund to be filed within 90 days after the return was due while allowing other types of claims to be filed within a longer statute of limitation? See American States Insurance Co. v. Michigan Department of Treasury, 220 Mich.App. 586, 560 N.W.2d 644 (1996) (sustaining 90–day statute of limitations for filing refund claims based on constitutional causes of action, even though general statute of limitations for refund claims is four years).

B. American Trucking Associations, Inc. v. Smith. In a companion case to *McKesson*, American Trucking Associations, Inc. v. Smith, 496 U.S. 167, 110 S.Ct. 2323 (1990) (*American Trucking Associations II*), a divided Court held that a Commerce Clause decision establishing a new principle of law may under some circumstances be applied prospectively. *American Trucking Associations II* involved an Arkansas tax, identical for all relevant purposes to Pennsylvania's flat highway use tax that had been struck down as unconstitutionally discriminatory in American Trucking Associations, Inc. v. Scheiner, 483 U.S. 266, 107 S.Ct. 2829 (1987) (*American Trucking Associations I*), p. 146 supra. In striking down the Pennsylvania tax in *American Trucking Associations I*, the Court explicitly overruled its earlier precedents that had rejected Commerce Clause challenges to flat taxes.

The Arkansas Supreme Court held that the challenged highway use tax was unconstitutional in light of *American Trucking Associations I*. Despite its decision on the merits, the Arkansas court refused to order refunds to the taxpayers for all of the taxes paid prior to the decision in *American Trucking Associations I*. The court based its prospectivity holding on the U.S. Supreme Court's decision in Chevron Oil Co. v. Huson, 404 U.S. 97, 92 S.Ct. 349 (1971), which held that, in some circumstances, decisions may be given only prospective effect.

In *American Trucking Associations II*, the U.S. Supreme Court held that its decision in *American Trucking Associations I* should be applied prospectively and that the taxpayers were entitled to meaningful retrospective relief under *McKesson* only with respect to taxes that were imposed for highway use after *American Trucking Associations I*. The rule of law that would appear to emerge from the holdings of *McKesson* and *American Trucking Associations II* is that when a decision striking down a tax is based upon established federal constitutional law, the decision must be given retroactive effect as a matter of federal due process principles, and, if the taxpayer was denied predeprivation remedies, the taxpayer must be afforded meaningful backward-looking relief. When, however, the decision striking down the tax requires reversal of prior precedent, and equitable and other policy concerns favor prospective application of the decision, the decision may be given only prospective effect.

Nevertheless, sharp divisions among the members of the Court in *American Trucking Associations II*—as well as subsequent Court decisions (discussed below)—undermine the force of its judgment permitting prospective application of the decision. Thus, four Justices (O'Connor, Rehnquist, White, and Kennedy) subscribed to Justice O'Connor's plurality opinion which expressed the view that *American Trucking Associations I* should not be given retroactive effect under *Chevron*. On the other hand, four other Justices (Stevens, Brennan, Marshall, and Blackmun) subscribed to Justice Stevens's dissenting opinion, which expressed the view that *American Trucking Associations I* should be applied retroactively and that *Chevron*'s prospectivity doctrine should apply in only the most limited circumstances. The actual decision in the case turned on Justice Scalia's idiosyncratic concurrence in the judgment, which expressed sympathy for the dissenters' views about retroactivity in general but nevertheless joined the plurality for reasons relating to his distaste for the Court's Commerce Clause doctrine.

C. *The Progeny of* McKesson *and* American Trucking Associations II. In James B. Beam Distilling Co. v. Georgia, 501 U.S. 529, 111 S.Ct. 2439 (1991), the Court held that the 1984 decision in Bacchus Imports, Ltd. v. Dias, 468 U.S. 263, 104 S.Ct. 3049 (1984), applied retroactively. The Court reasoned that because *Bacchus* itself had been applied retroactively to the taxpayer in that case, the rule of *Bacchus* likewise had to be applied retroactively to all other taxpayers whose claims were not barred by the statute of limitations, res judicata, or other procedural requirements. The Court rejected a rule of "selective prospectivity" whereby the new rule announced in the case is applied to the litigants, but the old rule is applied to all others whose cause of action arose with respect to facts predating the court's pronouncement. The Court did not reach the question whether *Bacchus* should be applied prospectively under the *Chevron* doctrine because, as Justice Souter stated in announcing the Court's judgment, "it is simply in the nature of precedent, as a necessary component of any system that aspires to fairness and equality, that * * * the applicability of rules of law are not be switched on and off according to individual hardship." James Beam, 501 U.S. at 543. Hence, "[o]nce retroactive application is chosen for any assertedly new rule, it is chosen for all others who might seek its prospective application." Id.

In Harper v. Virginia Dep't of Taxation, 509 U.S. 86, 113 S.Ct. 2510 (1993), the Supreme Court applied the rule in *James Beam* to hold that its decision in Davis v. Michigan Department of Treasury, 489 U.S. 803, 109 S.Ct. 1500 (1989), pp. 323–30 supra, must be applied retroactively. *Davis* held that Michigan violated principles of intergovernmental tax immunity by taxing the retirement benefits paid by the Federal Government while exempting retirement benefits paid by state and local governments. Although the Court's opinion in *Davis* did not clearly indicate whether the Court was applying the rule announced in the case retroactively, the Court in *Harper* concluded that it had in fact applied the rule announced in *Davis* to the parties before the Court.

Does *Harper* indicate that the Court is moving toward the adoption of the view that its decisions should apply retroactively in all instances? In *Harper*, the Court declared that:

> [w]hen this Court does not "reserve the question whether its holding should be applied to the parties before it," an opinion announcing a rule of federal law "is properly understood to have followed the normal rule of retroactive application" and must be "read to hold ... that its rule should apply retroactively to the litigants before the Court."

Id., 489 U.S. at 97. Accordingly, unless the Court explicitly reserves the question of retroactivity in the case under consideration, the decision will be retroactive as to all affected taxpayers under the rule barring "selective prospectivity." See also Landgraf v. USI Film Products, 511 U.S. 244, 279, 114 S.Ct. 1483 (1994) ("While it was accurate in 1974 to say that a new rule announced in a judicial decision was only presumptively applicable to pending cases, we have since established a firm rule of retroactivity") (citing *Harper* and *Griffith*).

In Fulton Corp. v. Faulkner, 516 U.S. 325, 116 S.Ct. 848 (1996), the Court struck down a North Carolina intangible property tax, as applied to corporate stock, on the ground that the tax discriminated against interstate commerce because it varied inversely with the North Carolina presence of the corporation whose stock was subject to tax. In so holding, the Court overruled Darnell v. Indiana, 226 U.S. 390, 33 S.Ct. 120 (1912), which had sustained a similar statute over Commerce Clause objections. In the proceedings below, the North Carolina Court of Appeals, although finding the tax discriminatory, had held that its ruling should apply only prospectively, because to apply the rule retroactively would be "inequitable." Fulton Corp. v. Justus, 110 N.C.App. 493, 430 S.E.2d 494, 501 (1993). It observed that "[b]oth the United States Supreme Court and the North Carolina Supreme Court 'have recognized that in some cases it would be inequitable to apply newly announced rules retroactively if prior to the enunciation of the rules parties had reasonably relied on certain principles in ordering their affairs.' " Id., 430 S.E.2d at 501. The North Carolina Supreme Court did not reach the question of prospectivity, since it sustained the tax.

In light of the fact that the U.S. Supreme Court in *Fulton* overruled *Darnell* for Commerce Clause purposes, *Fulton* would appear to have been a case in which there was at least some room for argument that prospective application of the decision is appropriate, if, in fact, there is anything left to the prospectivity doctrine in civil cases. The Court's treatment—or, more accurately, nontreatment—of the prospectivity issue in *Fulton*, however, raises additional questions (beyond those suggested in *James Beam* and *Harper*) as to whether the Court's decisions may *ever* be applied prospectively.

Without even adverting to the possibility that the decision in *Fulton* might be applied prospectively (as the North Carolina Court of Appeals had held), and thus remanding to the state court to consider the prospectivity question along with others that might arise should the lower courts determine that prospective application was inappropriate, the Court remanded solely to consider questions of *remedy* under *McKesson*. The Court in *Fulton* adverted to the remedial alternatives set forth in *McKesson* (as well as to some related state law issues) in remanding to the state courts to consider these matters "in the first instance." Fulton, 516 U.S. at 347. But in so doing, the Court necessarily pretermitted any consideration of prospectivity, because issues of remedy simply do not arise if the rule of law announced in the case is to be applied on a prospective basis only. In short, the Court, without saying so explicitly, may well have put the final nail in the coffin of the civil prospectivity doctrine by refusing even to entertain the notion that the prospectivity issue was an appropriate matter to be addressed on remand. Indeed, in other cases (not involving state taxation), the Court has cast further doubt about the viability of the civil prospectivity doctrine articulated in *Chevron*. See, e.g., Ryder v. United States, 515 U.S. 177, 184–85, 115 S.Ct. 2031 (1995).

Notwithstanding the Court's strong hints regarding its favoring retroactive application of all of its decisions, the Court has reiterated its position in *McKesson* that a state retains flexibility regarding the appropriate remedy it must afford a taxpayer once it has been determined that the state imposed an unconstitutionally discriminatory tax. See generally John F. Coverdale, "Remedies for Unconstitutional State Taxes," 32 Conn. L. Rev. 73 (1999); Eric M. Rakowski, "*Harper* and its Aftermath," 1 Fla. Tax L. Rev. 445 (1993). If a taxpayer establishes that a tax is unconstitutionally discriminatory, and that it is entitled to a refund, may the state nevertheless limit the refund to the precise amount necessary to eliminate the discrimination or must it grant a refund of the entire discriminatory tax? Over taxpayers' objections that limiting the refund to the amount of the tax discrimination is contrary to sound tax policy because by failing to provide any deterrence to the enactment of unconstitutional taxes, courts have sustained the provision of refunds limited to the amount of the discrimination. Macy's Department Stores, Inc. v. City and County of San Francisco, 143 Cal.App.4th 1444, 50 Cal.Rptr.3d 79 (1st Dist. 2006). See also Ventas Fin. I, LLC v. California Franchise Tax Bd., 165 Cal.App.4th 1207, 81 Cal.Rptr.3d 823 (1st Dist. 2008) (applying same principle to tax that was unfairly apportioned and holding that taxpayer was entitled to refund only on portion of tax in excess of fairly apportioned tax).

D. *State Statutory Limitations on the Availability of Retroactive Relief.* Some state legislatures have severely limited the availability of retroactive relief by imposing strict procedural requirements on taxpayers' right to a refund. For example, in Ragsdale v. Department of Revenue, 312 Or. 529, 823 P.2d 971 (1992), the Oregon Supreme Court relied on state law in determining the relief to which the taxpayer was entitled under Davis v. Michigan Department of Treasury, 489 U.S. 803, 109 S.Ct. 1500 (1989). The taxpayer had challenged an Oregon statute identical to the statute invalidated in *Davis*, claiming a refund for taxes paid under the statute from 1970 through 1988. Oregon law permitted refunds only for taxes due and collected in or after the year in which the claim for refund was made. Because the *Ragsdale* taxpayer had filed her claim in 1989, and had paid her 1988 taxes in 1989, the court determined that she was eligible for a refund for 1988 taxes, but not for the taxes paid during 1970 through 1987. In effect, the Oregon court allowed the state to provide for what amounts to prospective-only relief. The Oregon court also ruled that the Oregon statutes as interpreted by the court satisfied the due process requirements as construed by *McKesson*.

E. *The Right of a Taxpayer to Rely on an Apparently Available Statutory Refund Remedy.* In Reich v. Collins, 513 U.S. 106, 115 S.Ct. 547 (1994), the taxpayer, a federal military retiree, sued Georgia for refunds based on Georgia's failure to exempt the retirement income of former federal employees as it had exempted the retirement of former state employees. Georgia's refund statute provided that "[a] taxpayer shall be refunded any and all taxes or fees which are determined to have been erroneously or illegally assessed and collected from him under the laws of this state, whether paid voluntarily or involuntarily." Id., 513 U.S. at 109 (quoting Ga. Code Ann. § 48–2–35(a)). Moreover, there was no question that the rule of law on which the taxpayer relied—the rule announced in *Davis*—was to be given retroactive effect under *Harper*. Nevertheless, the Georgia Supreme Court held that the taxpayer had no right to a refund under the Georgia statute and had no right to a refund under *McKesson* on the grounds that Georgia allegedly has provided meaningful predeprivation remedies in the form of a declaratory judgment action, injunctive remedies, and administrative predeprivation relief. A unanimous U.S. Supreme Court held that Georgia deprived the taxpayers of due process in attempting to deny them the right to a refund based on the existence of a predeprivation remedy when, by the plain language of its refund statute, it held out to taxpayers the right to a postdeprivation remedy on which they could reasonably rely. In so holding, the Court characterized Georgia's reconfiguration of its scheme in midcourse as "bait and switch." Id. at 111. See also Newsweek, Inc. v. Florida Dep't of Revenue, 522 U.S. 442, 118 S.Ct. 904 (1998) (per curiam) (summarily vacating Florida decision in which state court had denied tax refund relief employing same "bait and switch" technique previously condemned in *Reich*).

F. *The Equitable Nature of Refund Remedies.* In Stone v. White, 301 U.S. 532, 57 S.Ct. 851 (1937), the U.S. Supreme Court stated:

> The action brought to recover a tax erroneously paid, although an action at law, is equitable in its function. It is the lineal successor of the common count in *indebitatus assumpsit* for money had and received.
> * * *
>
> Its use to recover upon rights equitable in nature to avoid unjust enrichment by the defendant at the expense of the plaintiff, and its control in every case by equitable principles, established by Lord Mansfield in Moses v. Macferlan, 2 Burr. 1005 (K.B. 1750), have long been recognized in this Court. It is an appropriate remedy for the recovery of taxes erroneously collected. The statutes authorizing tax refunds and suits for their recovery are predicated upon the same equitable principles that underlie an action in assumpsit for money had and received. Since, in this type of action, the plaintiff must recover by virtue of a right measured by equitable standards, it follows that it is open to the defendant to show any state of facts which, according to those standards, would deny the right * * *.

Id., 301 U.S. at 534–35.

How does the fact that refund actions are equitable in nature affect the determination whether a taxpayer should be entitled to a refund of a tax? Is it relevant to the pass-on defense? Does it affect the amount of a refund to which a taxpayer may be entitled? Suppose, for example, that a taxpayer seeks a refund of taxes imposed under a statute that was invalid because it did not provide for apportionment. Is a taxpayer entitled to a refund of the entire amount of the tax paid or only to that portion of the tax paid in excess of the amount that may be fairly attributed to activities in the taxing state?

G. *Severability Issues.* If a tax has been struck down as unconstitutionally discriminatory, the question arises whether the appropriate remedy is to extend the favored or disfavored treatment to all taxpayers. As the foregoing discussion makes clear, states do enjoy the flexibility as a matter of federal constitutional law to adopt either approach, subject to federal and state constitutional restraints on retroactive lawmaking and subject to the states' ability to provide equal treatment in fact on a retroactive basis. On a prospective basis, of course, the states may freely choose either alternative, because they are not subject to any obligation to provide "meaningful backward-looking relief."

Insofar as the states do enjoy the ability as a matter of federal constitutional law either to extend the favored tax treatment to all potential taxpayers or to remove it altogether, the question of which approach is proper—at least from a judicial standpoint—becomes a state law question of severability. This, in turn, is largely a question of perceived legislative intent: What would the legislature have done had it known that it could not constitutionally provide the beneficial tax treatment only to the favored class—provide it to all or provide it to none?

Courts frequently address these questions in the wake of decisions striking down statutes as unconstitutionally discriminatory. See, e.g., Chapman v. Commissioner of Revenue, 651 N.W.2d 825 (Minn. 2002) (severing discriminatory preference in alternative minimum tax (AMT) for charitable contributions to Minnesota charities, thereby requiring that all charitable contributions be added back to the AMT base); Annenberg v. Commonwealth, 562 Pa. 581, 757 A.2d 338, cert. denied, 531 U.S. 959, 121 S.Ct. 385 (2000) (severing personal property tax exemption that discriminated against interstate commerce thereby extending tax to all taxpayers). Compare Beskind v. Easley, 325 F.3d 506 (4th Cir. 2003) (invalidating state alcoholic beverage laws that discriminated against interstate commerce by forbidding out-of-state wineries to ship directly to in-state consumers, but curing discrimination by extending similar prohibition to in-state wineries rather than eliminating direct shipment ban altogether) with Dickerson v. Bailey, 336 F.3d 388 (5th Cir. 2003) (invalidating state alcoholic beverage laws that discriminated against interstate commerce by forbidding out-of-state wineries to ship directly to in-state consumers, and curing discrimination by striking down restriction on direct shipping by out-of-state wineries). The *Dickerson* case contains an interesting discussion of whether Commerce Clause discrimination should be remedied by extending benefits to the disfavored class or extending burdens to the favored class.

H. *References.* John F. Coverdale, "Remedies for Unconstitutional State Taxes," 32 Conn. L. Rev. 73 (1999); Richard Fallon & Daniel Meltzer, "New Law, Non–Retroactivity, and Constitutional Remedies," 104 Harv. L. Rev. 1731 (1991); Walter Hellerstein, "Preliminary Reflections on *McKesson* and *American Trucking Associations*," Tax Notes, July 16, 1990, p. 325; Eric M. Rakowski, "*Harper* and its Aftermath," 1 Fla. Tax L. Rev. 445 (1993); Amy Silverstein & Andres Vallejo, "When Constitutional Law Clashes with Fairness and Good Policy: Remedies for Unconstitutional State Taxes," State Tax Notes, Jan. 29, 2001, p. 341; Note, "Nonretroactivity in Constitutional Tax Refund Cases," 43 Hastings L.J. 419 (1992).

F. INJUNCTIONS AND OTHER EQUITABLE REMEDIES

NOTES AND QUESTIONS

A. *Injunctions in State Court.* In order successfully to enjoin collection of a tax, the taxpayer must, at a minimum, satisfy the normal prerequisites for equitable relief (probability of success on the merits, risk of irreparable harm if equitable relief is not granted, no adequate remedy at law, etc.). Thus, the availability of an adequate remedy through a refund procedure will ordinarily result in a denial of equitable relief. In addition to common law restrictions, the statutes and case law of many states prohibit suits that would result in interference with tax collection (e.g., injunctive relief).

Indeed, some states (like California) have a strict constitutional prohibition barring injunctions against state taxes. Article XIII, Section 32 of the California Constitution provides:

> No legal or equitable process shall issue in any proceeding in any court against this State or any officer thereof to prevent or enjoin the collection of any tax. After payment of a tax claimed to be illegal, an action may be maintained to recover the tax paid, with interest, in such manner as may be provided by the Legislature

As the California Court of Appeal observed, in explaining the underlying policy behind the constitutional provision:

> "[S]trict legislative control over the manner in which tax refunds may be sought is necessary so that government entities may engage in fiscal planning based on expected tax revenues." The state needs to engage in such planning and revenue collection even during litigation "so that essential public services dependent on the funds are not unnecessarily interrupted. 'Any delay in the proceedings of the officers, upon whom the duty is devolved of collecting the taxes, may derange the operations of government, and thereby cause serious detriment to the public.'"

Loeffler v. Target Corp., 173 Cal.App.4th 1229, 93 Cal.Rptr.3d 515, 524 (2d Dist. 2009) (citations omitted).

B. *Injunction in the Federal Courts to Restrain State Tax Proceedings.* There is a broad prohibition against suits in federal court to enjoin state taxes. As the U.S. Supreme Court explained in Fair Assessment in Real Estate Ass'n, Inc. v. McNary, 454 U.S. 100, 102 S.Ct. 177 (1981), it has long

> recognized the important and sensitive nature of state tax systems and the need for federal-court restraint when deciding cases that affect such systems. As Justice Field wrote for the Court * * *:

> > "It is upon taxation that the several States chiefly rely to obtain the means to carry on their respective governments, and it is of the utmost importance to all of them that the modes adopted to enforce the taxes levied should be interfered with as little as possible. Any delay in the proceedings of the officers, upon whom the duty is devolved of collecting the taxes, may derange the operations of government, and thereby cause serious detriment to the public." Dows v. Chicago, 11 Wall. 108, 110 (1871).

Id., 454 U.S. at 102.

In 1937, Congress codified the principle that federal courts generally must not interfere in the administration of state taxes when it enacted the Tax Injunction Act, 28 U.S.C. § 1341 (also known as the Johnson Act). The Tax Injunction Act provides that "[t]he district courts shall not enjoin, suspend or restrain the assessment, levy or collection of any tax under State law where a plain, speedy and efficient remedy may be had in the courts of such State." In *Fair Assessment*, the Court explained:

> This legislation, and the decisions of this Court which preceded it, reflect the fundamental principle of comity between federal courts and state governments that is essential to "Our Federalism," particularly in the area of state taxation. Even after the enactment of § 1341 it was upon this comity that we relied in holding that federal courts, in exercising the discretion that attends requests for equitable relief, may not even render declaratory judgments as to the constitutionality of state tax laws.

Id. at 103.

The U.S. Supreme Court has construed the Tax Injunction Act liberally to impose a strict bar on federal court jurisdiction to entertain challenges to state taxes, except in the rare situation where the plaintiff can demonstrate that it has no adequate remedy in the state courts. See, e.g., California v. Grace Brethren Church, 457 U.S. 393, 411, 102 S.Ct. 2498 (1982) ("because Congress' intent in enacting the Tax Injunction Act was to prevent federal-court interference with state taxes, we hold the Act prohibits declaratory as well as injunctive relief"); Great Lakes Dredge & Dock Co. v. Huffman, 319 U.S. 293, 63 S.Ct. 1070 (1943) (relying on general equitable principles to extend Tax Injunction Act's prohibition from injunctions to declaratory judgments regarding constitutionality of state taxes).

In Tully v. Griffin, 429 U.S. 68, 97 S.Ct. 219 (1976), the Court considered the application of New York's sales and use tax to sales made by a Vermont furniture store operating six miles from the New York border. Griffin advertised on radio and television and in newspapers that served the Albany–Schenectady–Troy area of New York and made substantial sales at its place of business to New York customers. It regularly delivered furniture to the New York buyers in its own trucks, and its employees also entered New York on occasion to repair furniture it had sold. On that basis, the New York State Tax Commission determined that Griffin was "doing business" in New York and was thus required to collect that state's sales and use tax from its New York customers. When the Commission sought to audit its books, Griffin filed suit in federal court contending that imposition of the tax would be unconstitutional. In order to justify its suit in federal rather than state court, Griffin argued that it had no "plain, speedy and efficient remedy," because a suit in state court would require prepayment of the tax or posting a bond. It argued further that requiring it to bring suit in New York was unfair because it was unfamiliar with that forum and its contacts with New York were so limited. The Commission responded by making an estimated assessment of approximately $218,000, following which a three-judge federal district court granted a preliminary injunction.

The U.S. Supreme Court reversed, without expressly dealing with the issue whether the necessity of prepaying the tax or the unavailability of preliminary relief made the remedy inadequate. The Court found that the taxpayer had means of contesting the levy and obtaining preliminary relief without the prepayment or bond. It declared:

> A federal district court is under an equitable duty to refrain from interfering with a State's collection of its revenue except in cases where an asserted federal right might otherwise be lost. This policy of restraint has long been reflected and confirmed in the congressional command of 28 U.S.C. § 1341 that no injunction may issue against the collection of a state tax where state law provides a "plain, speedy and efficient remedy." As the Court has frequently had occasion to note, the statute has its roots in equity practice, in principles of federalism, and in recognition of the imperative need of a State to administer its own fiscal operations. * * *

> These principles do not lose their force, and a State's remedy does not become "inefficient," merely because a taxpayer must travel across a state line in order to resist or challenge the taxes sought to be imposed. If New York provides an otherwise adequate remedy, the mere fact that Griffin must go to New York to invoke it does not jeopardize its ability to assert its rights. To accept the District Court's holding that it would be "unfair" to make Griffin litigate in New York would undermine much of the force of 28 U.S.C. § 1341.

Id., 429 U.S. at 73–74.

In Rosewell v. LaSalle Nat'l Bank, 450 U.S. 503, 101 S.Ct. 1221 (1981), the U.S. Supreme Court addressed the question whether an Illinois remedy which requires property owners contesting their property taxes to pay under protest and, if successful, to obtain a refund *without interest* is a "plain, speedy and efficient remedy" within the meaning of the Tax Injunction Act when the customary delay from the time of payment until receipt of refund upon successful protest is two years. The taxpayer claimed that the two-year delay between payment and refund was neither "speedy" nor "efficient" and that the failure to provide interest made the state remedy inadequate.

Emphasizing that the Tax Injunction Act requires only that state remedies meet "certain minimal *procedural* criteria," Rosewell, 450 U.S. at 512 (emphasis in original), the Court held that Illinois's refund procedure satisfied the statute. It observed that the Illinois refund procedure provided the taxpayer with a full hearing and judicial determination at which she could raise all constitutional objections to the tax, and it noted that her only claim of procedural defects in the Illinois remedy was delay. Reviewing the lengthy delays that have become commonplace in judicial proceedings throughout the nation, the Court concluded that

> respondent's 2–year wait, regrettably, is not unusual. Nowhere in the Tax Injunction Act did Congress suggest that the remedy must be the speediest. The payment of interest might make the weight more tolerable, but it would not affect the amount of time necessary to adjudicate respondent's federal claims. Limiting ourselves to the circumstances of the instant case, we cannot say that respondent's 2–year delay falls outside the boundary of "speedy remedy."

Id. at 520–21.

With regard to the nonpayment of interest on the refund as an independent ground for the alleged inadequacy of the state court remedy, the Court declared:

> When it passed the [Tax Injunction] Act, Congress knew that state tax systems commonly provided for payment of taxes under protest with subsequent refund as their exclusive remedy. * * *
>
> It is only common sense to presume that Congress was also aware that some of these same States did not pay interest on their refunds to taxpayers, following the then-familiar rule that interest in refund actions was recoverable only when expressly allowed by statute. It would be wholly unreasonable, therefore, to construe a statute passed to limit federal-court interference in state tax matters to mean that Congress nevertheless wanted taxpayers from States not paying interest on refunds to have unimpaired access to the federal courts. If Congress meant to carve out such an expansive exception, one would expect to find some mention of it. The statute's broad prophylactic language is incompatible with such an interpretation.

Id. at 523–24.

Courts occasionally do find that there is no "plain, speedy and efficient" remedy in the state court and on that basis uphold the federal court's jurisdiction to adjudicate the dispute. For example, in Garrett v. Bamford, 538 F.2d 63 (3d Cir.), cert. denied, 429 U.S. 977, 97 S.Ct. 485 (1976), residents of a predominantly minority area brought a class action in federal district court alleging that their properties were assessed at values higher than those established for similar properties in white areas of the county. Alleging that the assessors had engaged in systematic and intentional racial discrimination in making the assessments in question, the plaintiffs sought an injunction requiring the immediate reassessment of all residential property on a nondiscriminatory basis and annual assessments thereafter. The court held that a federal district court had jurisdiction over such a suit when the state procedures provided for neither continuing injunctive relief nor class actions. See also Georgia Railroad & Banking Co. v. Redwine, 342 U.S. 299, 72 S.Ct. 321 (1952).

The Court has held that the broad jurisdictional barrier prohibiting federal court injunctions against state tax proceedings does not apply to suits brought by the United States "to protect itself and its instrumentalities from unconstitutional state exactions." Department of Employment v. United States, 385 U.S. 355, 358, 87 S.Ct. 464 (1966); cf. Moe v. Confederated Salish & Kootenai Tribes, 425 U.S. 463, 96 S.Ct. 1634 (1976) (Indian Tribe not barred by 28 U.S.C. § 1341 from seeking to enjoin enforcement of state tax statute). In Arkansas v. Farm Credit Services of Central Arkansas, 520 U.S. 821, 117 S.Ct. 1776 (1997), however, the Court held that Production Credit Associations (PCAs), even though designated as "federal instrumentalities," do not fall within exception to the Tax Injunction Act for suits brought by the United States or federal agencies. The Court observed:

> The PCAs' business is making commercial loans, and all their stock is owned by private entities. Their interests are not coterminous with those of the Government any more than most commercial interests. Despite their formal and undoubted designation as instrumentalities of the United States * * *, PCA's do not have or exercise power analogous to that of the NLRB or any of the departments or regulatory agencies of the United States. This suffices for us to conclude that instrumentality status does not in and of itself entitle an immunity to the same exemption the United States has under the Tax Injunction Act.

Id., 520 U.S. at 831–32.

The Court has also held that the Tax Injunction Act does not bar federal court actions challenging the validity of tax *credits* on a prospective basis because such actions fall outside the purview of the Act's bar of challenges to tax "assessments"—"the official recording of liability that triggers levy and collection efforts." Hibbs v. Winn, 542 U.S. 88, 101, 124 S.Ct. 2276 (2004). In *Hibbs*, Arizona taxpayers brought an action in federal court challenging the constitutionality under the Establishment Clause of an Arizona statute permitting tax credits for contributions supporting parochial schools. In sustaining federal court jurisdiction over the state's Tax Injunction Act objections, the Court identified the Acts "twin purposes": "It responds to the Government's need to assess and collect taxes expeditiously with a minimum of preenforcement judicial interference; and it requires that the legal right to disputed sums be determined in a refund suit." Id., 542 U.S. at 103. In the Court's view, the taxpayers' challenge in *Hibbs* did not undermine either of these purposes. There was no effort in *Hibbs* to interfere with state tax collection administration by obtaining a federal court order enabling taxpayers to avoid paying taxes. To the contrary, the taxpayers were seeking to *protect* state revenues by attacking an allegedly unconstitutional tax credit and to require the state to collect *additional* taxes on a prospective basis. Moreover, third-party suits not seeking to stop the collection or contest the validity of a tax imposed on the plaintiffs did not in any way undermine the Act's objective of directing taxpayers to pursue refund suits instead of attempting to restrain collection. Four Justices dissented on the ground that the Tax Injunction Act barred federal court interference with all forms of state tax administration.

C. *The Civil Rights Act (42 U.S.C. § 1983)*. Invoking the federal Civil Rights Act, 42 U.S.C. § 1983, taxpayers have attempted to enjoin states in both state and federal court from imposing allegedly unconstitutional taxes. When successful, they have sought attorneys fees under a related federal statute, 42 U.S.C. § 1988. The Civil Rights Act, 42 U.S.C. § 1983, provides:

> Every person who, under color of any statute, ordinance, custom, or usage of any State or Territory or the District of Columbia, subjects or causes to be subjected, any citizen of the United states or other person within the jurisdiction thereof to the deprivation of any rights, privileges, or immunities secured by the Constitution and laws, shall be liable to the party injured in an action at law, suit in equity, or other proper proceeding for redress.

Under 42 U.S.C § 1988(b), the prevailing party in an action to enforce a provision of § 1983 may recover reasonable attorneys' fees.

In Fair Assessment in Real Estate Ass'n, Inc. v. McNary, 454 U.S. 100, 102 S.Ct. 177 (1981), the Court held that an action for damages may not be brought in federal court under 42 U.S.C. § 1983 to redress the allegedly unconstitutional administration of a state's tax system. The case involved the assessment practices of St. Louis County, Missouri, pursuant to which the county assessed properties with new improvements at approximately 33⅓ percent of their current market value, but assessed properties without new improvements at approximately 22 percent of their current market value. The disparity allegedly resulted from the county's failure to reassess old property on a regular basis. Further, the county allegedly targeted properties that were subject to successful valuation appeals in one year for revaluation in the next year. The taxpayers pursued remedies in state court, and their assessment was temporarily reduced to 29 percent of the property's current market value; however, the next year the assessment was increased again to 33⅓ percent. Consequently, the taxpayers brought a § 1983 claim in federal court seeking actual damages in the amount of the overassessments for all years since they first brought their state court action, plus punitive damages.

Justice Rehnquist,[d] writing for himself and four other Justices, held that the action was barred by principles of comity. After describing the well-established bar against interference by a federal court with the administration of state taxes, as codified in the Tax Injunction Act, Justice Rehnquist explained:

> Contrasted with this statute and line of cases are our holdings with respect to 42 U.S.C. § 1983. * * *

> Obviously § 1983 cut a broad swath. By its terms it gave a federal cause of action to prisoners, taxpayers, or anyone else who was able to prove that his constitutional or federal rights had been denied by any State. In addition, the statute made no mention of any requirement that state remedies be exhausted before resort to the federal courts could be had under 28 U.S.C. § 1343. The combined effect of this newly created federal cause of action and the absence of an express exhaustion requirement was not immediately realized. It was not until our decision in

---

d. Then–Justice Rehnquist had not yet been appointed Chief Justice.

Monroe v. Pape, 365 U.S. 167, 81 S.Ct. 473 (1961), that § 1983 was held to authorize immediate resort to federal court whenever state actions allegedly infringed constitutional rights:

> "Although the legislation was enacted because of the conditions that existed in the South at that time, it is cast in general language and is as applicable to Illinois as it is to the States whose names were mentioned over and again in the debates. It is no answer that the State has a law which if enforced would give relief. The federal remedy is supplementary to the state remedy, and the latter need not be first sought and refused before the federal one is invoked." 365 U.S., at 183.

> The immediacy of federal relief under § 1983 was reemphasized in McNeese v. Board of Education, 373 U.S. 668 (1963), where the Court stated "[i]t is immaterial whether [the state official's] conduct is legal or illegal as a matter of state law. Such claims are entitled to be adjudicated in the federal courts." Id., at 674 (citation and footnote omitted). And in the unargued per curiam opinion of Wilwording v. Swenson, 404 U.S. 249 (1971), the Court concluded that "[petitioners] were ... entitled to have their actions treated as claims for relief under the Civil Rights Acts, not subject ... to exhaustion requirements." Id., at 251.

> Thus, we have two divergent lines of authority respecting access to federal courts for adjudication of the constitutionality of state laws. Both cannot govern this case. On one hand, § 1341, with its antecedent basis in the comity principle of Matthews v. Rodgers, supra, and Boise Artesian Water Co. v. Boise City, supra, bars at least federal injunctive challenges to state tax laws. Added to this authority is our decision in Great Lakes Dredge & Dock Co. v. Huffman, supra, holding that declaratory judgments are barred on the basis of comity. On the other hand is the doctrine originating in Monroe v. Pape, supra, that comity does not apply where § 1983 is involved, and that a litigant challenging the constitutionality of any state action may proceed directly to federal court. With this divergence of views in mind, we turn now to the facts of this case, a § 1983 challenge to the administration of state tax laws which implicates both lines of authority. We hold that at least as to such actions, which is all we need decide here, the principle of comity controls.

Id., 454 U.S. at 102–05.

In an opinion joined by Justices Marshall, Stevens, and O'Connor, Justice Brennan protested the conclusion that "sets the 'principle of comity' against the strong policies of 42 U.S.C. § 1983 favoring a federal forum to vindicate deprivation of federal rights, and resolves the issue in favor of comity." Id. at 118 (Brennan, J., concurring). The concurring Justices reached the same decision as the majority, but rested their case on the Tax Injunction Act. It is worth noting that the availability of state remedies was not at issue in the case. As the Court pointed out, the Missouri Supreme Court expressly had held that plaintiffs such as petitioners may assert a 42 U.S.C. § 1983 claim in state court.

This division in *Fair Assessment* reflecting the tension between the principles underlying § 1983 and those underlying the Tax Injunction Act reemerged in Dennis v. Higgins, 498 U.S. 439, 111 S.Ct. 865 (1991). Justices Marshall, Stevens, and O'Connor, as well as Justices Blackmun, Scalia, and Souter, joined Justice White's opinion holding that a taxpayer may rely on § 1983 to bring a Commerce Clause challenge against a state tax in state court. Justice Kennedy, joined by Chief Justice Rehnquist, dissented. The majority opinion declared: "A broad construction of § 1983 is compelled by the statutory language, which speaks of deprivation of 'any rights, privileges, or immunities secured by the Constitution and laws.'" Id., 498 U.S. at 443. The Court reasoned further that "the Commerce Clause confers 'rights, privileges, or immunities' within the meaning of § 1983." Id. at 446. The dissent disagreed with that conclusion and would have held that the taxpayers were not entitled to bring a § 1983 claim. They summarized their criticisms of the majority opinion as follows:

> Today's decision raises far more questions about the proper conduct of challenges to the validity of state taxation than it answers. The Tax Injunction Act, 28 U.S.C. § 1341, prevents any attempt in federal court to "enjoin, suspend or restrain" assessment or collection of a state tax, so long as a "plain, speedy and efficient remedy may be had in the courts of such State." The principle of comity likewise prevents a federal court from entertaining any action for damages under § 1983 to redress allegedly unconstitutional state taxation. Relying upon the "overriding interests of the state in an efficient, expeditious and nondisruptive resolution of ... tax disputes," state courts have refused to permit plaintiffs to proceed under § 1983 where there exists a complete remedy under state law. These questions now become of paramount importance, as we risk destruction of state fiscal integrity in a manner which may require congressional correction.

> Today's opinion gives no hint of § 1983's character as an extraordinary remedy passed during Reconstruction to protect basic civil rights against oppressive state action. Section 1983 now becomes simply one more weapon in the litigant's arsenal, to be considered whenever the defendant is a state actor and its use is advantageous to the plaintiff.

Id. at 464–65 (Kennedy, J., dissenting).

Only four years later a unanimous Court greatly curtailed the ability of taxpayers to obtain any relief under the Civil Rights Act. In accord with its decision in *Fair Assessment*, the Court in National Private Truck Council, Inc. v. Oklahoma Tax Commission, 515 U.S. 582, 115 S.Ct. 2351 (1995), held that state courts are not required to award injunctive or declaratory relief under § 1983 when an adequate legal remedy exists. The Court explained, "[w]hether a suit is brought in federal or state court, Congress simply did not authorize the disruption of state tax administration in this way." Id., 515 U.S. at 590. The Court did, however, acknowledge that there may be extraordinary circumstances under which injunctive or declaratory relief may be available, e.g., when the "'enforcement of the tax would lead to a multiplicity of suits, or produce irreparable injury, [or] throw a cloud upon the title.'" Id. at 591 n.6.

After *National Private Truck Council* is any relief available to taxpayers under 42 U.S.C. § 1983 in either state or federal court? What are the implications of the fact that 42 U.S.C. § 1983 may be brought only against "persons" who deprive others of their constitutional rights? Neither the state nor state officials acting in their official capacities, are "persons" within the meaning of 42 U.S.C. § 1983. See Will v. Michigan Dep't of State Police, 491 U.S. 58, 109 S.Ct. 2304 (1989). Is the typical state tax claim seeking a refund from the state, or from state officials acting in their official capacities, cognizable under § 1983? There are two important exceptions to the general rule that states are not subject to suit under 42 U.S.C. § 1983. First, local governments, and local government officials sued in their official capacities, are persons within the meaning of § 1983. See Monell v. Department of Soc. Servs., 436 U.S. 658, 98 S.Ct. 2018 (1978). Second, even a state official acting in his official capacity, when sued for injunctive or other prospective relief, is a "person" under § 1983 because "official capacity actions for prospective relief are not treated as actions against the State." Kentucky v. Graham, 473 U.S. 159, 167 n. 14, 105 S.Ct. 3099 (1985). Under what circumstances might these exceptions apply to permit an action under 42 U.S.C. § 1983? Is the latter exception meaningful in light of the well-established limitations on taxpayers' ability to sue for injunctive relief?

D. *Original Jurisdiction in U.S. Supreme Court.* The Constitution provides for the U.S. Supreme Court's original jurisdiction over cases in which a "State shall be a Party." U.S. Const. art. II, § 2, cl. 2. Congress has in turn provided that the Supreme Court shall have "original and exclusive jurisdiction of all controversies between two or more States." 28 U.S.C. § 1251(a). In Wyoming v. Oklahoma, 502 U.S. 437, 112 S.Ct. 789 (1992), the Court held that Wyoming had standing to bring an action within the original jurisdiction of the U.S. Supreme Court to challenge an Oklahoma law which allegedly discriminated against interstate business in violation of the Commerce Clause, on the grounds that the discriminatory law would ultimately result in reduced tax collections by Wyoming. Oklahoma's statute required Oklahoma generating plants producing power for sale in Oklahoma to burn a mixture of coal containing at least ten percent Oklahoma-mined coal. Wyoming challenged the law on the grounds that it discriminated against interstate commerce in violation of the Commerce Clause, seeking an injunction permanently enjoining enforcement of the Oklahoma law. The Court held that Oklahoma's claim of indirect harm in the nature of decreased severance tax revenues was sufficient to invoke the Court's original jurisdiction.

Original jurisdiction of the U.S. Supreme Court requires as a preliminary matter establishment of traditional standing. See, e.g., California v. Texas, 437 U.S. 601, 98 S.Ct. 3107 (1978) (holding original jurisdiction to be improper because California had suffered no injury and there was a 'fair probability' that no injury would ever come to pass). However, even if standing exists, it is settled law that the Court has discretion whether to entertain the action. As the Court has declared, "[a] determination that this Court has original jurisdiction over a case, of course, does not require us to exercise that jurisdiction. We have imposed prudential and equitable limitations upon the exercise of our original jurisdiction." California v. Texas, 457 U.S. 164, 168, 102 S.Ct. 2335 (1982). In determining whether to exercise its original jurisdiction, the Court has declared that its original jurisdiction should be exercised "sparingly." Maryland v. Louisiana, 451 U.S. 725, 739,

101 S.Ct. 2114 (1981). It has focused on such factors as the "seriousness and dignity of the claim," California v. Texas, 457 U.S. 164, 168, 102 S.Ct. 2335 (1982), and the availability of another forum where issues may be litigated. Id.

Can the Court's original jurisdiction be invoked in any case where state tax laws allegedly violate the Federal Constitution and can be shown to lead to reduced tax collections in another state? While many states do not allow the deduction of income taxes, most states provide for the deduction of other taxes. Thus, to the extent that a discriminatory tax, other than an income tax, is imposed in one state, the franchise or income taxes collected by other states will decrease as the result of the deduction of the discriminatory tax. Would this provide a sufficient basis for any interested state to challenge the discriminatory tax on the basis that the state can "fairly trace" its loss of tax revenues to the action of the other state? What about tax incentives that one state offers to induce business to move from other states? See Peter D. Enrich, "Saving the States From Themselves: Commerce Clause Constraints on State Tax Incentives for Business," 110 Harv. L. Rev. 377 (1996) (arguing that states have standing to challenge other states' tax incentive programs).

E. *The Scope of Declaratory Relief.* The requirement in some states that taxes be paid before the taxpayer may seek an adjudication of his liability under the usual statutory procedure has been an important factor in the popularity of the declaratory judgment proceeding in tax litigation. Thus, the declaratory judgment has been used to test the constitutionality of a tax, as applied to the plaintiff. See, e.g., Hillsborough v. Cromwell, 326 U.S. 620, 66 S.Ct. 445 (1946). The remedy may be employed to determine the operative date of a levy, Berndson v. Graystone Materials Co., 34 Wash.2d 530, 209 P.2d 326 (1949), or whether a particular person is subject to tax, Tirrell v. Johnston, 86 N.H. 530, 171 A. 641, aff'd, 293 U.S. 533, 55 S.Ct. 238 (1934). A declaratory judgment action also has been used to determine whether a particular type of transaction is taxable as a wholesale or a retail sale under a gross income tax. Department of Treasury v. J.P. Michael Co., 105 Ind.App. 255, 11 N.E.2d 512 (1937).

Declaratory judgment may be denied for a variety of reasons. If the decree will not terminate the controversy, declaratory relief may be denied. City of Pensacola v. Johnson, 159 Fla. 566, 28 So.2d 905 (1947). When the issues of fact are complicated and subject to conflicting inferences which will have to be resolved by the administrative agency, the court will deny a declaratory judgment. Rahoutis v. Unemployment Compensation Comm'n, 171 Or. 93, 136 P.2d 426 (1943). Declaratory judgment may not be used as a device to recover a tax already paid, where the limitations period on refunds has expired. Associated Petroleum Transp., Ltd. v. Shepard, 53 N.M. 52, 201 P.2d 772 (1949). The limitations on injunctions imposed by the Tax Injunction Act have been held to impose comparable limits upon federal courts to grant declaratory relief to taxpayers challenging the propriety of state taxes. Great Lakes Dredge & Dock Co. v. Huffman, 319 U.S. 293, 299, 63 S.Ct. 1070 (1943); Illinois Central R.R. v. Howlett, 525 F.2d 178 (7th Cir. 1975), cert. denied, 424 U.S. 976, 96 S.Ct. 1482 (1976).

F. *Mandamus.* In a proper case, mandamus may be used to force tax officials to act. Like the injunction, mandamus is an extraordinary remedy and will not be granted where other adequate remedies are available. Ordinarily mandamus is restricted to acts that are ministerial in character, requiring no acts of a discretionary or judicial nature. Thus, if the taxpayer is entitled to a refund, and the amount of the refund is not in dispute, mandamus may be used to compel the remittance. Some courts have allowed suits for mandamus to compel acts that require some discretion. See, e.g., Rosen v. Restrepo, 119 R.I. 398, 380 A.2d 960 (1977) (writ of mandamus appropriate to order an assessor to assess a shopping center complex in the same manner in which he has assessed other property in the town).

* * *

INDEX

References are to Pages

UNIFORMITY AND EQUALITY—Cont'd
Equal Protection, this index
Privileges and Immunities Clauses, this index
Property Taxes, this index

UNITARY BUSINESS PRINCIPLE
Corporate Income Taxes, this index

USE TAXES
Generally, 700-714
Base against which rate is applied, 717-722
Catalogs distributed in interstate commerce, 702-708
Collection of tax by vendor
Generally, 722-724
Out-of-state vendor's duty to collect, 726-743
Complementary or compensating nature of, 700, 701
Constitutional limitations on state taxing jurisdiction, 23, 24
Credits for sales or use taxes paid to other states, 712-714
Customer loyalty programs, 720, 721
Discounts, coupons, and rebates, 718, 719
Distributed without charge, application to property, 711, 712
Drop shipments, 740, 741
Equal protection and denial of use tax credit for sales tax paid by nonresidents, 279
Evasion of taxes on out-of-state purchases, 739, 740

USE TAXES—Cont'd
Exemptions
Generally, 927-931
Casual, occasional, or isolated sales, 715, 716
Exempt purchasers vs. exempt sales, 929
Lessees equipment to exempt organization, 930
Merger, reorganization or liquidation, transfers in connection with, 717
News media, 716, 717
Property and activities producing income used for exempt purposes, 930, 931
Imposition of tax long after initial purchase, 710, 711
Multiple taxation, relief from, 712-714
Out-of-state vendor's duty to collect sales and use taxes, 724-726
Produced by taxpayer, use of property, 712
Purchased for use provisions, construction of, 709, 710
Streamlined Sales and Use Tax, this index
Tax payments, 719
Taxable use, storage, and consumption, 708, 709
Temporary use within state, 711
Tips and service charges, 722
Trade-ins, 719, 720
Transportation charges, 721

VALUATION OF PROPERTY
Property Taxes, this index

†